OREGON *Historical Quarterly*

INDEX

VOLUMES 62 THROUGH 81

1961 — 1980

Jean Brownell
COMPILER

WITHDRAWN

REFERENCE BOOK
DO NOT CIRCULATE

OREGON HISTORICAL SOCIETY PRESS

This volume was designed and produced by the Oregon Historical Society Press.

ISBN 0-87595-127-9

Copyright © 1990, Oregon Historical Society
1230 S.W. Park Avenue, Portland, Oregon 97205

All rights reserved. No part of this publication may be reproduced or transmitted in any form or by any means, electronic or mechanical, including photocopying, recording or any information storage or retrieval system, without the permission in writing from the publisher.

The paper used in this publication meets the minimum requirements of American National Standard for Information Sciences—Permanence of Paper for Printed Library Materials. ANSI Z39.48-1984.

Printed in the United States of America.

Preface

THIS THIRD CUMULATIVE INDEX to the *Oregon Historical Quarterly* covers the twenty years from 1961 through 1980. It is also the work of many hands, among them Nancy Hacker, Priscilla Knuth, and Jeanette Stewart, each of whom contributed time and effort to produce the annual indexes during those twenty years. It was their extensive card files that were compiled, correlated, made consistent, and refined in order to produce this volume.

Those familiar with the two earlier *Quarterly* indexes will note that this one essentially follows the style of the earlier ones. As before, volume numbers are in bold-face type, page numbers in standard type. Abbreviations used are listed on the following pages.

Some changes have been made to better reflect contemporary usage. For example, highways are no longer sub-entries to "Roads and trails," but have their own category. Conversely, we have retained the main heading "Negroes," inasmuch as that is the term the articles indexed herein most often use; the transition to "Blacks" occurred during the 1960-80 period.

Purists take note. We have tried to be consistent but have declined to sacrifice clarity in the interest of consistency. Also, we have omitted a clutter of commas that the purist would probably insist upon.

Thanks go to many, including (but not limited to) those already mentioned, but especially to Priscilla Knuth for her guidance and patience, and to Louise Godfrey, Don Leamy, and Don Abbott for long sessions of proofreading.

JEAN BAUER BROWNELL

List of Abbreviations

Besides abbreviations listed, standard abbreviations have been used for states, Canadian provinces, and for months.

Abbreviation	Full Form	Abbreviation	Full Form
AASLH	American Association for State and Local History	KKK	Ku Klux Klan
ABCFM	American Board of Commissioners for Foreign Missions	lieut.	lieutenant
admin.	administration	M.E.	Methodist Episcopal
adv.	advertisement	N	footnote
assn.	association	NW	Northwest
		NWCO.	North West Company
bk.cov.	back cover		
		O & C	Oregon and California
CCC	Civilian Conservation Corps	OHS	Oregon Historical Society
ca.	circa	OMV	Oregon Mounted Volunteers
capt.	captain		
cartog.	cartographer	OR&NCO.	Oregon Railway and Navigation Company
comm.	commission		
DAR	Daughters of the American Revolution	OSNCO.	Oregon Steam Navigation Company
dist.	district	OWR&NCO.	Oregon-Washington Railroad and Navigation Company
ed.	edited, edition, editor	Ore. Prov.	
exped.	expedition	Govt.	Oregon Provisional Government
expl.	exploration, exploring		
expo.	exposition		
		pt.	part
ff	pages following	pub.	published
fr.cov.	front cover		
ft.	fort	REA	Rural Electrification Administration
HBCO.	Hudson's Bay Company	res.	reservation
hwy.	highway		
ILWU	International Longshoreman's and Warehouseman's Union	sen.	senator
		soc.	society
		supt.	superintendent
IOGT	Independent Order of Good Templars	terr.	territorial, territory
IOOF	Independent Order of Odd Fellows	trans.	translated, translator
IWW	Industrial Workers of the World	U., Univ.	University
illus.	illustration	USSR	Union of Soviet Socialist Republics
ins.bk.cov.	inside back cover		
ins.fr.cov.	inside front cover	WW I	World War I
		WW II	World War II

A.F. & A.M., SEE Masons, Ancient, Free and Accepted

A.M. Simpson (steam schooner), photo, **68**/270

ANZUS, SEE Australia-New Zealand-U.S. Security Treaty

"A.R. Wetjen: British Seaman in the Western Sunrise," by Howard M. Corning, **74**/145-78

Aaron, Daniel, *et al:*

The United States: The History of a Republic, 2nd ed. noted, **69**/276

Aaron, Louise, **62**/198,204,300; **63**/91-92,252,363

Abbey, Edward, **80**/408

Abbot, Charles, Lord Colchester, **64**/ 25-26

Abbot, Henry Larcom, **67**/13: Pacific Railroad Survey, **66**/282; **79**/26(map),27-28; topographic sketch The Dalles area, **67**/12

Abbott, Carl:

Colorado: A History of the Centennial State, noted, **77**/303

Abbott, Donald P., **67**/397; **68**/360; **75**/368; **80**/414:

The Hidden Northwest, by Cantwell,

review, **74**/90-91

"Lancaster's Lodge," **75**/277-81

Abbott, George Henry, **79**/39: favors Klamath military post, **69**/225

Abbott, M.H., **64**/179

Abdill, George B., **66**/187,383; **67**/ 80,279,281:

Civil War Railroads, noted, **63**/247

Rails West, review, **62**/294-95

Abe, May, **81**/155,157,163

Abel, Annie Heloise, ed.:

Tabeau's Narrative of Loisel's Expedition..., cited, **66**/331N

Abell, Frank G., **66**/304

Abenaki Indians, **71**/345

Aberdeen, George Gordon Hamilton, Earl of, **70**/296,301,303,311

Aberle, Sophie D., and William A. Brophy:

The Indians, America's Unfinished Business, review, **68**/177-78

Abernethy, Alexander Smith, **63**/231; **72**/354; **77**/299; **80**/335

Abernethy, Camilla, **64**/84,280; **66**/279; **68**/358; **69**/346

Abernethy, George, **62**/143,150; **63**/ 182; **64**/139-40,146; **66**/341; **75**/72:

Gervais law suit, 66/360; historical marker, 66/382; loan for *Oregon American,* 75/184N; Roberts recollections, 63/200; Strong recollections, 62/70

Abernethy, Sarah Fidelia (Mrs. William), 62/239N,244N,246N

Abernethy Cemetery, Cowlitz Co., 66/80

Abert Lake, SEE Lake Abert

Abert Rim, 67/10

Abilene, Kan., 77/370

Abner Coburn (ship), 66/127

Above the Pacific, by Horvat, review, 68/278-79

Abraham, Solomon, 65/401

Abrahamsohn, Abraham: 1856 publication on gold mines, translation noted, 70/366

Abram, David E., 65/414-16; 66/94,190,286,385,389,395; 67/376,379; 68/356,359,360; 69/342,348; 70/374; 71/374; 72/359; 73/362,373; 74/183, 363,365,366; 75/95,366,367-70

Abrams, William S., ed: *Oregon Regional Union List of Serials,* review, 77/382

Academy of Natural Sciences of Philadelphia, 69/150,154,160,163; SEE ALSO Lewis and Clark Herbarium

Academy of Sciences of the U.S.S.R., 73/101,110: *Bulletins,* 73/147; expedition to North America 1839-49, 73/101-70; North American ethnographic collections, 73/101-103,111,136,160,164,170

Accaregui, Angel, photo, 76/166

Accaregui, Floyd, 76/162N: Basque moonshine whiskey recipe, 76/161-62; photo, 76/166

Accaregui, Tony, photo, 76/166

Accolti, Michael, 69/269-70

Acheson, Dean, 62/38-39

Achona Creek, SEE Ochoco Creek

Ackerman, Gale, 63/282

Acme, Ore., 74/273

Acordagoitia, Alfonzo, 76/168N: photo, 76/156

Acordagoitia, Angel, photo, 76/156

Acrobats, 70/8,17

Across the Olympic Mountains: The Press Expedition, 1889-90, by Wood, review, 69/73-74

Active (steamship), 72/132,135,140,143

Activo (sloop-of-war), 79/400

Adair, Bethenia Angeline Owens, 64/228N: photo, 81/258

Adair, John, 63/252; 64/205N; 68/352; 72/77N; 81/190N

Adair, W. Morris, 63/252

Adairville, Ore., 81/190

Adak, Aleutian Islands, 80/35,40,45,48

Adam (Indian), 65/191N

Adam Gray, Stowaway: A Story of the China Trade, by Arntson, review, 64/348

Adams, —, First Ore. Cavalry 1864, 65/93

Adams, Andy, 70/88

Adams, Arthur L., 71/155N

Adams, Charles F., 64/358-59,364; 65/126,222,318,412,414-16; 66/93,189,285,294,386,387,393,394; 67/375,376,379; 68/355,356,359, 360,361; 69/342,348; 70/374; 71/373; 72/359; 73/374; 74/184,208,365

Adams, F., 69/243N

Adams, George R.: diary 1865-67, 64/86

Adams, Grizzly, 68/348

Adams, Herbert Baxter, 79/92

Adams, J.L., 62/217-18,219-20,222; 79/42

Adams, John A., 62/218N

Adams, John Franklin, 80/105

Adams, John Quincy, 70/337,340; 72/5; 76/120,123,124,197,203,205-13, 218: anti-British sentiment, 72/106-107; comments on Floyd, 70/333,341,342; friendship with Boston merchants, 76/205-208,209-13,223-24; New England commercial ties, 72/114-17; noncolonization principle, 72/105-106, 107N,118-20; Oregon Question, 62/8; Pacific Coast strategy, 76/208-13; portrait, 76/196; urges Columbia River post, 70/342-43; views on U.S. expansion, 72/103,105-10,117; SEE ALSO Monroe Doctrine

Adams, John R., 62/218

Adams, Kramer:

Logging Railroads of the West, review, 63/354-55

Adams, Lou, 75/101

Adams, Mary Jane, 73/283

Adams, Ramon F.:

Western Words, A Dictionary of the American West, new ed. noted, 70/78

Adams, Robert, Jr., 71/171

Adams, Steve, 62/106; 65/214

Adams, Thomas (Indian), 64/45-46, 50,51N; 76/361

Adams, W.J.N., 62/203

Adams, W. Lloyd, 70/181

Adams, William Howard:

The Frontier Experience: Readings in the Trans-Mississippi West, ed. by Hine and Bingham, review, 65/307-308

Adams, William Lysander, 62/316; 64/ 128,144; 72/329:

anti-Catholicism, 75/119-20,121; anti-Stark quote, 72/327; quarrel with Mattoon, 64/130-32; supports Dr. Ada Weed, 78/12N,21-22,28,30

Adams, William Lysander:

A Melodrame Entitled "Treason, Stratagems, and Spoils," ed. by Belknap, review, 70/354-55

Adams, Ore., 63/365; 64/90: Finnish pioneers, 72/350; name, 80/105

Adams and Company Express, 63/361; 65/98N

Adams Station, 76/85

Adderly (ship), 66/127

"Address by the Canadian Settlers," trans. by Frein, cited, 66/355N

Addington, Joel, 78/325N

Adelsperger, Augustus Edward, 63/34-35

Adkins, Charles M., 70/147N

Adkins, Edward, 78/130

Adkins, Lucius, 70/147,147N

Adkison, Norman B.:

Nez Perce Indian War and Original

Stories, noted, 68/82

Adler, Jacob:

Claus Spreckels, the Sugar King of Hawaii, noted, 68/82

Adler, Leo, 65/415,416; 66/ 93,189,285,394; 67/379; 68/359,361; 69/348; 70/373

Administrative federalism: Ore. land and water resources, 68/176-77

Admiral (schooner), photo, 68/270

Admiral Benson (steamship): wreck, 81/105

Admiralty Islands, 73/127

Adrian, Anne, SEE Pierre, Anne Adrian

Adrian, Mrs. Pierre (Indian), 71/339,343

Adolphson, John, 62/174

Adrina (ship), 66/122N

Adventure (sloop), 68/110

Adventure at Astoria, 1810-1814, by Gabriel Franchere, trans. and ed. by H.C. Franchere, cited, 71/277,318N

Adventure Cove: bricks, 68/103,105,108,110; Gray's winter camp, 68/110; historic site, 68/110; identification, 68/101-10; map, 68/104; painting, 68/100; photos, 68/107,108-109

"An Adventure in the Surf," by C.B. Watson, 66/171-77

The Adventures of Alexander Barclay, Mountain Man, by Hammond, noted, 78/365

The Adventures of Captain Bonneville, U.S.A., by Irving, ed. by Todd, cited, 66/78; review, 63/343-45

The Adventures of Dr. Huckleberry, by Huckleberry, cited, 71/117N; noted, 71/bk.cov. Sept.

Adventures on the Columbia River, by Cox, cited, 71/318

Advertising: history in Oregon, 70/182

Ady, Abel, 78/363

Aeshbacher, W.D., 63/247

Affleck, Edward L.:

Sternwheelers, Sandbars and Switchbacks, noted, 74/358

Affleck, W.B., 64/38

Afognak Island, 77/184
African Methodist Episcopal Church, Portland, 80/400
Afro-American people, SEE Negroes
"After the Covered Wagons: Recollections of Russell C. and Ellis S. Dement," ed. by E.R. Jackman, 63/5-40
"After Thoughts," by Maria Cable Cutting, 63/237-41
Agar, E.W., 74/13N
Agate, Alfred T.: biographical sources, 65/137
Agee, Jasper: recollections, 67/373
Agency Valley, Malheur Co., 63/312
Ageton, Richard, 74/219
Agnes Oswald (ship), 66/107
Agness, Ore., 76/79
Agogino, George A., 62/203
Agricultural associations, 72/319: cooperatives, 76/239,249; radical organizations, 73/86; SEE ALSO Grange
Agricultural History: An Index, 1927-1976, comp. by Whitehead, noted, 79/337
Agricultural History Center, 79/337
Agricultural History Society, 77/301
Agricultural Literature: Proud Heritage— Future Promise, ed. by Fusonie and Moran, noted, 79/106
Agricultural machinery, 70/72,366; 72/281,283,288; 76/18,19,21: at Lewis & Clark Centennial Expo., 80/60; first combine Yamhill Co., 69/339; 76/18(photo); steam plow, 67/367; Stockton combine, 68/86-87 threshing machines, 75/363— photos, 75/covs. Sept. tractors, 75/69
Agriculture: 18th century British, 70/363; 19th century, 68/86; acreage, 71/57,96; agencies, 69/332-33; Aleutians, 73/160; berries, SEE Berries; bibliography, 70/84,272; 71/290; 73/86; 79/106,339; 81/336; British, 70/ 363; bulk transportation effects, 67/ 158; California, 69/332; 80/209,237- 38; catalogs, 73/ins.bk.cov. Dec.; Civil War impact, 68/86; Clark Co., 63/83;

Clatsop Co. 1872-1920, 64/90; Columbia Co., 62/301; 74/302,317; Cowlitz Farm, 63/104,115-73*passim;* Deschutes area 1920s, 72/94; dry farming, 77/9,157; farming, 62/67-68; federal records, 70/84; Ft. Ross, 68/ 186; 70/178; 73/162,163; 77/186; French Prairie, 66/338,339,344,349N, 351; harvesting, 76/18,19-21; 77/9- 10; Hawaii, 69/83; history, 64/85; 69/83; 77/301-302,304; 81/335-36; history bibliography, 68/86,344; hours, 76/14,18,21; income, 76/14- 15; industrial, 71/365,366; Inland Empire, 71/60,62; irrigation, SEE Irrigation; labor unions, 72/236; Lane Co., 72/87; Lewis & Clark Centennial Expo. display, 80/56; logged-over land, 81/106; market values, 76/248; marketing, 77/253-54,302; mechanization, 77/302; 79/106; 81/336; Mountain States, 74/284; Nebraska, 68/345; Northeast Ore. 1880-90, 67/156 Oregon, 62/203; 71/96,97,98,197— history, 70/182
Pacific NW, 71/60,86,94,97,98— theses, 65/368-71; 72/240-45
Pendleton, 77/192; periodicals, 73/86; Plains, 73/360; plowing, 76/17,18; Polk Co. 1936-74, 81/328; pressure on Eastern Ore. cattlemen, 67/155-58; prices of products, 63/358; publications, 77/260; Puget Sound area, 71/366; railroad effects, 71/28-29; regulations, 69/332-33; root crops, 76/348; "scientific," 63/104-105; Scholls Ferry, 78/91; Siuslaw Valley, 74/273; The West, 74/284; threshing, 76/21,74,75; tools, 81/336; towns encourage, 81/201,202; truck gardening, 76/234,239,248-49; 77/249,250, 251-52(photo),253; U.S. Army, 73/86; Walla Walla-Palouse area, 72/231; Wasco Co. 1858, 68/28-29; Wisconsin cut-over, 64/79-81; Yamhill Co., 76/6- 25*passim;* SEE ALSO Farms; Land; names of crops
Agriculture in the Development of the Far West, ed. by Shideler, noted, 77/301-

302

Ague, 63/193,199,227; 66/351
Aguinaldo, Emilio, 80/182,186
Ahern, George Patrick, 68/346
Aian, Siberia:
  Russian-American Co. post, 73/156-59;
  sketch, 73/158
l'Aigle (ship), SEE *Eagle*
Aiken, Glen, 63/15
Aiken, Henry S., 64/320-21
Aiken, James, 63/15
Aikins, Paul, 64/337
Aima, Mrs. —, Portland Assembly Center, 81/159
Ainsworth, John Commigers, Sr.,
  62/228; 63/238; 64/39,349; 69/198;
  72/332N; 74/139,208,358:
  Applegate correspondence, 71/197;
  house, 71/294; journal, 63/84; railroad interests, 71/39,82,197; Redondo
  Beach promotion, 71/289; Wittenberg
  farm purchase, 64/265
Ainsworth, Thomas H., 65/215
Ainsworth, Wash., 71/22N-23N,61:
  train ferry photo, 71/32
Ainsworth (Liberty ship), 80/47,48
Ainsworth National Bank, Portland,
  62/165
Ainsworth School, Portland:
  history, 63/253-54
Air pollution, 65/384; 67/369; 72/287
Airaku family, 81/159,160
Airfields:
  Clark Co., 69/331; Seward, 80/49;
  Tillamook blimp base, 71/136(photo);
  World War II Aleutians, 80/35-45
  passim; SEE ALSO Airports
Airlie, Ore.:
  history, 72/91
Airlines:
  first U.S. commercial, 68/278; Pacific
  passenger service, 68/89
Airplanes:
  Borah's attitude, 70/180; first Ore.
  builder, 62/204; first in Yamhill Co.,
  67/366; Japanese, 80/37-44*passim;*
  Miller 1892, 73/83; Pacific NW lost
  aircraft, 64/88; spruce wood for,
  72/301; western transportation,

70/367
World War II, 62/32—
  Aleutian Islands 1943, 80/35-48
Airports, 78/360,363; SEE ALSO
  Airfields
Airships, 80/57:
  photo, 80/56
Ai-yel (Indian), SEE Yowaluch, Louis
Akers place, Powder River Valley,
  66/200
Akey, Emma Fausett:
  recollections, 79/408
Akin, Louis:
  biography, 75/88
Akun Island, 77/186
Al Sarena (Buzzard) Mine, 68/90
Alaska, 63/23,24,26,97,106; 68/347;
  69/85; 79/338:
  agricultural history, 70/84,272;
  anthropology, 65/373; bibliography,
  78/358-59; botany, 73/168; boundaries, 72/255,265; 75/85,93; boundary
  dispute, 74/284; centennial, 69/337;
  Civil War incident, 63/254; development, 63/359; earthquake 1964,
  68/347; economy, 67/85; 69/337;
  70/180; fauna, 73/102,163; fur trade,
  70/180; glaciers, 81/135-37; gold
  rush, 70/180; SEE ALSO Gold mines
  and mining; Golovin 1818 report,
  72/108; govt. docs. index, 71/79
  history, 64/347-48; 69/184; 71/365;
  73/72—
  sources, 65/386; 68/347; 69/337;
  74/284
Inside Passage, 67/87; Kauwerak lost
  village, 66/88; land laws 1869, 72/
  135-36; library services, 65/386;
  manuscripts, 65/198
maps—
  1844, 76/128; 1898, 76/ins.fr.cov.
  June
military posts, 70/180; 76/92; native
  claims, 74/284; petition for civil rule,
  72/145; Presbyterians, 63/360; prices,
  76/107; 81/123-47*passim;* purchase,
  65/314; 68/347; 69/337; 71/365;
  72/128-29; 75/318,335; 76/180,200;
  77/85; 78/288; resources, 72/133,147

Russians in, 73/5-70; 78/288—cession, 81/288; claims, 72/109-11,116; exploration, 72/109-11,116; trade, 72/108,109

salmon canning, 63/362; science 1741-1865, 68/186; Seattle trade, 70/217; Seward visit, 72/127-47; statehood movement, 72/227; telephone line, 81/123-24,127; territorial records, 64/277; theses on, 65/362-91; Thornton murder, 65/215; trade, 65/376; travel, 76/103-108; U.S. 14th Infantry in, 74/93; Western Union exped. 1865-67, 64/86; wilderness areas, 73/275

Alaska and Its History, ed. by Sherwood, review, 69/184

Alaska and Japan: Perspectives of Past and Present, ed. by Arai, noted, 74/284

The Alaska Boundary Dispute: A Critical Reappraisal, by Penlington, noted, 74/284; review, 75/85

Alaska Historical Commission, 78/359

Alaska Historical Library and Museum, 64/347

Alaska International Rail and Highway Commission, 63/91

Alaska Meat Company: refrigerator boat photo, 76/114

Alaska Methodist University, 78/358

Alaska, Past and Present, by Hulley, review, 73/72

The Alaska Purchase and Russian-American Relations, by Jensen, noted, 78/288

Alaska Purchase Centennial, 68/184,348

Alaska Steamship Co., 72/230

Alaska Times, Sitka, 72/132,136

Alaska-Yukon-Pacific Exposition, 63/360; 65/365; 72/128; 74/105, 112,135

Alaskan (1943 vessel), 80/49

Alaskan (river steamer), 63/66

Alaskan Eskimos, by Oswalt, review, 69/327-28

The Alaskans (Time-Life Books), noted, 79/338

Alava, Jose Manuel, 79/399,400,401

Albany, Ore., 62/314,315; 79/88: business firms 1885, 67/62-63; early industry, 67/61; Hackleman's Addition, 67/63,65,66,71; history, 68/90; Indian mound sites, 66/90; photo ca. 1925, 74/39; saloon, 68/146,147; street railway, 63/364; woolen mills, 62/175; 67/61-70

Albany Democrat: Oregon writers page, 74/38,43,69; poetry column, 74/46-49; Sunday edition, 74/39-40,69,151; SEE ALSO *Oregon Democrat*

Albany Fort (HBCo. post): 1705-1706 journal printed, 77/84

"The Albany Woolen Mill," by Alfred L. Lomax, 67/61-74

Albany Woolen Mills Co., 67/62-74 *passim*

Albatross (ship), 76/202

Albee, Harry Russell, 74/215

Alberson, —, Harney Co. rancher, 63/322

Alberson, Letha (Leitha), 63/322: photo, 63/313

Albert (Indian), 79/155,317,318

Albert I, King of Belgium: Seattle visit, 78/357

Albert H. Powers Memorial Park, 67/49

"Albert Knowles House in Mapleton, Oregon," by Josephine E. Harpham, 74/271-74

Alberta, Canada: British immigration, 69/337; irrigation, 69/337

Alberta Fruit Market, Portland, 81/170

Albina, Ore., 62/169; 75/127,129,130; 77/300,376; 80/260

Albina Art Center, 68/350

Albina Community Council: records, 73/209

Albina Engine and Machine Works, Portland, photo, 77/108

Albion (schooner), 63/194-95

Albisu, Darlene Etchart, 76/160N,172N

Albrecht, E.F.: Bannock War account cited, 68/232N, 301N,305N,306N

Albricht, Joseph, 80/353; 81/91

Albright, Horace M.: biography, 72/83-84

Alcorn, Gordon D. and Rowena L.,

64/85,87; 65/217; 67/86:
"Evergreen on the Queets," 74/5-33
"Great Sternwheeler, *Bailey Gatzert*,"
63/61-66
Last Trail to Bear Paw, cited, 79/106
Paul Kane, cited, 73/75
"Tacoma Seamen's Rest: Waterfront
Mission, 1897-1903," 66/101-31
"Wreck of the *Peter Iredale*," 64/68-72
Aldecoa, Basilio, photo, 76/166
Aldecoa, Domingo, 76/170
Alden, Bradford Ripley, 63/83; 79/129:
Rogue River War, 66/220N,221N,224
Alden, James, uncle of James Madison
Alden, 70/272
Alden, James Madison, 77/289
Alder Creek, Malheur Co., SEE Bully
Creek
Alder (Badger?) Creek, Wasco Co.,
65/108
Alder Valley, Malheur Co., 63/272
Aldrich, Cyrus W., 72/58
Aldrich, Ed, 77/192
Aldrich, Oliver, 70/23,57
Alemany, Joseph, 70/329
Alert (steamboat), 80/52,62:
photo, 80/50
Aleut Indians:
boats, 73/124,165; Calif. settlement,
73/107,164; carving, 73/126(sketch),
127; clothing, 77/180; costume sketch,
73/126
dwellings, 73/121,124-25,128,165—
sketches, 73/120,122
employed by Russian-American Co.,
77/180-88*passim*; ethnographic collection, 73/101FF,164; food, 77/180,187;
Russian influence, 73/160; Russian
school, 73/124; whale use, 73/165
"Aleutian Experience of the 'Mad M',"
by Lansing S. Laidlaw, 80/31-49
Aleutian Islands, 62/29,30,35; 71/165;
73/119; 80/31,32:
climate, 80/35,42,44,47; gardening
introduced, 73/160; Russian fur posts,
73/122-27; Russian-American Co. in,
72/109; sketches, 73/122,123; SEE
ALSO World War II—Aleutian campaign
Alexander I, Emperor of Russia, 72/

102,109:
negotiations with U.S., 72/110FF
Alexander, Agnes Zook (Mrs. David F.),
66/161
Alexander, Andrew, 68/81
Alexander, Charles, 73/292; 74/156,
161,177:
awards, 74/40; biography, 74/34-70;
death, 74/261; letters quoted,
74/41,47,49,50-51,55,56,69,149,255;
photos, 73/296; 74/42,148; poetry,
74/262; short stories,
74/35,52,70,255,261-62
Alexander, Charles:
"As a Dog Should," cited, 74/40
Bobbie, a Great Collie, comment,
74/54-55,255
Fang in the Forest, comment,
74/40-41,55,255
North Smith, comment, 74/54,55,255
The Splendid Summits, comment, 74/51,
55,255
Alexander, Mrs. Charles, photo, 73/296
Alexander, David Franklin, 66/161
Alexander, Elizabeth Ann Smith, 74/40
Alexander, George, 66/161
Alexander, James H., 78/60,65; 79/7
Alexander, Maud, 63/92
Alexander, Minerva Crabtree, 79/24
Alexander, Robert, 78/52,53,
57,59,121,250,310,328,330-31;
79/23-24:
Free Emigrant Road construction,
78/60-69; trial, 79/5-12,24
Alexander, Thomas:
autobiography, 73/203
Alexander, Tony, 68/81
Alexander (ship), 78/355-56
"Alexander Lattie's Fort George Journal,
1846," 64/197-245
Alexander Mackenzie, Voyages from Montreal, reprint noted, 75/364
"Alexander Piper's Report and Journal,"
ed. by Priscilla Knuth, 69/223-68
Alfalfa, 63/272; 74/317; 81/300
"Alfred Seton's Journal: A Source for Irving's *Tonquin* Disaster Account," by
Wayne R. Kime, 71/309-24
Algoma Lumber Company, 69/77

Algonquin Indians, 79/211
Alice (ship):
wreck, drawing, 77/44
Alice of Leigh (ship), 66/127
Alien Land Law, SEE Land—laws
Alitok (Alitak) Bay, Kodiak Island, 77/183
Alkali, 73/263
Alkali, Ore., 81/270N:
photo 1883, 83/273
Alkali Flat, Wheeler Co., 73/258
Alkali Flats, Gilliam Co., 81/270
Alkali (Mud) Lake, Harney Co., 79/278
All Along the River, Territorial and Pioneer Days on the Payette, by Mills, noted, 64/277
"...all around the town," by Lucile S. McDonald, 64/259-66
"All the Words on the Pages, I: H.L. Davis," by Howard M. Corning, 73/ 293-331; part II, 74/34-70; part III, 74/145-78; part IV, 74/244-67
Allan, George T., 63/179,206-208, 218,227; 66/351N
Allan, Iris:
White Sioux: Major Walsh of the Mounted Police, reprint noted, 72/355
Allegany, Ore., 66/53; 74/92; 80/ 51,52,62N:
photo, 80/50
Allen, A.J.:
Ten Years in Oregon, quoted, 62/123
Allen, Alfred, 70/54
Allen, Alice Benson:
Simon Benson, Northwest Lumber King, review, 72/348
Allen, Andrew, Portland housemover, 69/312N,313,322,323
Allen, Beverly S., 70/259
Allen, E.B., 79/170
Allen, Eleanor, 74/63:
photo, 74/265
Allen, Elisha H., 68/65-66
Allen, Eric W., Jr., 67/361; 70/ 370,373; 71/371; 72/359; 73/373:
America the Raped, by Marine, review, 71/184
"Mountain of the Spirit," 75/49-53
Our National Park Policy, A Critical His-

tory, by Ise, review, 64/73-75
Allen, George W., 70/50
Allen, H.C.:
Conflict and Concord: The Anglo-American Relationship Since 1783, review, 62/407-408
Allen, Harrison, 75/172
Allen, James B.:
The Company Town in the American West, review, 67/357
Allen, James M., 63/84
Allen, John Eliot:
The Bone Hunters, by Lanham, review, 75/78-79
The Magnificent Gateway, review, 80/407
Allen, John Logan:
Passage Through the Garden, review, 77/191-92
Allen, Paul, 64/184
Allen, Scotty, 76/85
Allen, Solomon, 75/353,354
Allen, W.F., 62/219N
Allen, Wiley B., 74/346
Allen, William R., 65/211:
1851 letter, 67/91-92
Allen and Lewis Co., Portland, 71/19
Allen and Roberts, housemovers:
lightship salvage, 69/313-23—
adv., 69/ins.fr.cov. Dec.; photo album, 69/314-21
Allen Creek, Josephine Co., 63/351
Alley, Mrs. James M., 65/412
Alliance (steamer), 80/52,59,61,62
Allison, Ira S., 67/37; 79/403:
Fossil Lake, Oregon, Its Geology and Fossil Faunas, noted, 67/366
Allison, Susan:
recollections noted, 79/337-38
Allopathy, 78/11,12N,24,33
Allsop, Henry, 66/129
Allyn, Henry:
trail diary 1853, 78/140
Allyn, Stan, 63/92
The Almeda Mine, by Libbey, noted, 69/78
Almota, Wash., 71/23
Almota Landing, 71/23N:
photo, 71/24
Aloha, Ore., 62/200

INDEX / 1961—1980 13

Alon-skin (Indian), photo, **68**/236
Alpine, Ore., **69**/183
"Alpine—A School to Remember," by John F. Kilkenny, **75**/270-76
Alpine School, **69**/106-107; **75**/270-76
Alpowa Creek, **79**/181,199
Alprey, Elizabeth, **64**/265
Alsea Bay:
Atalanta wreck, **66**/110,112
Alsea Indians, **81**/411:
head flattening, **69**/171,173; slaves, **81**/413,417
Alsea River, **70**/255
Alt, David D., and Donald W. Hyndeman:
Roadside Geology of Oregon, noted, **79**/338
Alta California, San Francisco, **64**/34; **66**/9N,10N
Altamont, Ore., **78**/363:
name, **66**/282
Althen, Fred, **74**/21
Althouse area, **72**/10,11,33
Atschul, Charles, **72**/93
Aluminum Company of America, **62**/199
Aluminum industry, **62**/199:
Pacific Coast, **63**/361
"Alva E. Stovall and Turn of the Century Education," ed. by Patricia J. Beckham, **72**/281-85
Alvarado, Juan Bautista, **63**/208,235
Alvarado (steamer), **77**/359
Alvarez, Manuel:
biography, **66**/185
Alvord, Benjamin, **65**/6N,7-8,185; **67**/302,305,307; **70**/255; **79**/ 46,130,275N; **81**/423:
Applegate letter to, **66**/81; biography, **65**/327-28N; Columbia River fortifications, **65**/328-29,331; commander Camp Drum, **67**/300; commander Dist. of Oregon, **65**/10,297; death, **65**/328N
First Oregon Cavalry—
approves Drake campaign, **65**/115, 117-18; orders Currey 1864 exped., **65**/25,63-64N; orders Drake 1864 exped., **65**/12,21,25; response to edi-

torial criticism, **65**/77,80,86-87, 97,99N
map 1862-63, **79**/186-87; photo, **65**/64; plans for emigrant escort, **72**/70,72,75; reports on Indian-white relations, **67**/309-10; requests mounted troops, **67**/309,310
Alvord Desert, photo, **67**/24
Alvord Lake, **73**/228,231; **79**/ 274N,275N
Alvord Ranch, **63**/304-24; **69**/276; **71**/99
"Alvord Ranch Interlude: Life on a Celebrated Range," by Evelyn Gilcrest, **63**/304-41
Alvord Valley, **68**/321:
borax operations, **68**/187; **73**/228-29,231-44*passim*; Chinese in, **73**/235,237-39; photo, **79**/274
Amacker, Mary Ann, **71**/370,372; **80**/412:
The Eagle and the Fort, by Morrison, review, **80**/331-32
Ladies Were Not Expected, by Morrison, review, **80**/331-32
Amalgamated Sugar Company, **81**/170
Amato, Frank, **77**/246,247
Amboy, Wash., **67**/373
Ambulances, **64**/256-57
Amchitka Island:
airfield, **80**/40-43; Constantine Harbor, **80**/35,48; photos, **80**/36,47
America (Astor charter 1802), drawing, **76**/319
America (British frigate), **63**/201,218, 220:
described, **70**/295; on NW coast, **70**/295-304
America (Crowninshield ship), **76**/207
America (NW coast 1832), **77**/176
America Moves West, by Riegel and Athearn, 5th ed. noted, **72**/173
America the Raped: The Engineering Mentality and the Devastation of a Continent, by Marine, review, **71**/184
American Academy of Natural Sciences, **80**/207
American Antiquarian Society, **66**/293
American Association for State and Local

History, 67/293N; 71/294,371; 78/369:
convention 1971, 72/359; described, 71/292; publications, 77/291; 79/97; 81/334; services, 81/334

American Association for State and Local History:

Directory of Historical Societies and Agencies in the United States and Canada, noted, 64/277

American Association of Museums, 66/293,385,388:
Smithsonian cooperative program, 66/298

American Association of State Highway Officials, 74/121

American Board missions, 62/240; 77/291; 78/332,338; 79/101-102; SEE ALSO Spalding Mission; Whitman Mission

American Board of Commissioners for Foreign Missions, 62/239; 63/57N: archives, 68/57N; composition, 68/53N; Hawaiian policy, 68/54-74; influence in U.S. govt., 68/55FF; international scope, 68/55-56 missionaries—

Hawaii, 63/358; Polynesia 1820-40, 63/358; Pacific NW, 65/119-20

Pacific operations, 68/72; publications, 68/56; SEE ALSO American Board missions

The American City, A Documentary History, by Glaab, noted, 64/350

American Commonwealth Political Federation, 76/135,136,144

American Expansion: A Book of Maps, by Sale and Karn, review, 64/77

American Falls, 62/379; 65/156; 79/385; 80/87

American Federation of Labor, 75/151; 76/145-49

American Forestry Association, 76/31

American Forts: Architectural Form and Function, by Robinson, review, 79/214

American Forts, Yesterday and Today, by Grant, noted, 66/384

The American Frontier, A Social and Literary Record, by Babcock, noted, 66/188

The American Frontier, Readings and Documents, ed. by Hine and Bingham, noted, 73/360

American Fur Company, 62/250N, 314N; 68/185; 75/77: records, 74/355; 79/339

The American Heritage Book of the Pioneer Spirit, ed. by Ketchum, review, 62/196

American Historical Association, 71/370

The American Historical Association's Guide to Historical Literature, ed. by Howe *et al*, review, 63/342-43

American Indian Historical Society, 69/335

American Indian Medicine, by Vogel, review, 71/179-80

American Indian Policy in the Formative Years, by Prucha, quoted, 70/102-103

American Institute of Interior Designers, Portland Chapter, 70/372

American-Irish Historical Society, 69/102

American Legion, 73/70; 75/151,164; 76/240,243,246-47

American Lumberman, 77/223

The American Mercury, 73/296,298, 300,309,312,321

American Pacific Ocean Trade, Its Impact on Foreign Policy and Continental Expansion, 1784-1860, by Caruthers, noted, 76/182

American Party, SEE Know Nothing Party

American Patriot, 75/134

American Patriotic League, 75/134,186N

American Philosophical Society, 69/17, 163; 70/172,173; 80/207; 81/341N

American Protective Association, 72/81; 75/133-42:
anti-Catholic platform, 75/135,136; demise, 75/138; first Ore. council, 75/185N; in state legislature, 75/185-86N; membership claims, 75/134,135, 136,138-39; official organ, SEE *Portlander*; Ore. state council, 75/139; records, 75/139; regalia, 75/135; Republican membership, 75/135,138; ritual, 75/135,136; school board elections, 75/137,138; South Portland

council, 75/139
American Protective League, 75/149,152
American Public Works Association: *History of Public Works in the United States States*, review, 78/360-61
American Red Cross: canteen photo, 75/268; Ore. influenza epidemic 1917, 64/249-50
American Revolution Bicentennial, 74/349; 75/368,370: awards, 77/385; commissions and committees, 75/86,362,370; 76/91, 386,387; 77/291,385; Oregon participation, 77/289-92,385; Oregon publications, 78/287-88
American River, 65/160; 66/218
American Russian Commercial Co., 75/334N
American Star (vessel), 80/46
The American Story Recorded in Glass, by Marsh, review, 63/353-54
"American Strategy in the Pacific Ocean," by Samuel Eliot Morison, 62/5-56
American studies, 72/178; 73/85; SEE ALSO History—American studies
The American Territorial System, ed. by Bloom, noted, 75/365
The American West, a Reorientation, ed. by Gressley, review, 69/373-74
American Women's Hospital Service, 75/8-9
Americans for Democratic Action: in Pacific NW, 72/233
America's Sunset Coast, by Windsor, review, 80/334
America's Western Frontier: the Exploration and Settlement of the Trans-Mississippi West, by Hawgood, review, 69/69-70
Ames, Francis H.: *Fishing the Oregon Country*, review, 67/363-64
Ames, Frederick L., 69/219N
Ames, J.B., 72/61
Ames, Lucile Perry, 74/63
Amis, James F., 78/322-24
Amish people, 68/90
Amity, Ore., 64/354: Amish settlement, 68/90; history,

65/217
Amity Baptist Church, 68/90
Amity Library Association: history, 64/354
Amlie, Thomas, 76/135-40*passim*, 144,147,148
Amos, Ore., 73/83
Amos Brothers, Calif. freighters, 72/161
Amusement parks: The Oaks, Portland, 80/59
Anaconda Co., Butte, 72/237,238
Anatolii, Archimandrit, 73/153
Anchorage, Alaska, 68/346
Anchustegui, George, photo, 76/166
Ancient, Free and Accepted Masons, SEE Masons, Ancient, Free and Accepted
Ancient Hunters of the Far West, by Rogers *et al*, review, 68/333-35
Ancient Order of Hibernians, 69/112
Ancon (vessel), photo, 77/128
Andelana (bark), 66/119,121: capsized at Tacoma, 66/122
Anderson, Alexander Caulfield, 63/204,219; 68/115: note on Jeffrey death, 68/116
Anderson, Bronco Billy, 78/362
Anderson, George L., 73/275
Anderson, Howard, 81/275
Anderson, Ida (Mrs. Jack), 63/289
Anderson, Irving W.: "J.B. Charbonneau, Son of Sacajawea," 71/247-64
"J.B. Charbonneau, to Date," 72/78-79
Anderson, Jack, Westfall dancehall owner, 63/289,294
Anderson, James R.: book on B.C. plants, 68/115; with Jeffrey, 68/115
Anderson, John, Columbia Co., 74/321-22
Anderson, John (Peter?), *Tonquin* boatswain, 71/278
Anderson, Lawrence, 81/60
Anderson, Lex, 63/283,386
Anderson, Maurice, 75/226
Anderson, Miles, 79/37
Anderson, Mona Wiig, 77/90
Anderson, O.A., Shipbuilding Co., Astoria, 77/101

Anderson, Peter (John?), *Tonquin* boatswain, 71/278
Anderson, Rufus, 68/54,71
Anderson, Samuel, 66/71
Anderson, Thomas McArthur, 74/281; 80/186
Anderson, V.J.:
"Fur Trade on the Umpqua," noted, pt. I, 66/187; pts. II and III, 66/383; pt. IV, 67/80; pt. V, 67/279; pt. VI, 67/281
Anderson, Webb, 63/268
Anderson, William, surgeon on *Resolution*, 80/199
Anderson and Quinn, Malheur. Co. sheepmen, 63/269
Anderson Sundry Co., Portland, 66/306
Anderson Valley, 63/310,324
Anderson Valley Ranch, 63/334
Ando, Kiku (Mrs. Denny M.), 81/154, 168
Andreanof Islands, 77/188
Andreson, John, 73/8,176,181
Andress, Marion, 66/277
Andrews, Alice, 79/203
Andrews, Charles Wesley, 66/327; 73/364:
biography, 66/309; photos, 68/298; postal card photos, 66/307,308
Andrews, Clarence Leroy, 66/160
Andrews, George P., 65/117N; 79/41
Andrews, Gerald S., 62/421:
West on the 49th Parallel: Red River to the Rockies, 1872-1876, by Parsons, review, 66/69-71
Andrews, Peter, 63/333:
stone house photo, 63/332
Andrews, Ralph W., 65/215,314:
Indian Primitive: Northwest Coast Indians of the Former Days, review, 62/184-85
Indians as the Westerners Saw Them, review, 65/199-200
Photographers of the Frontier West, 1875-1910, review, 66/381
Picture Gallery Pioneers, review, 66/381
Andrews, Wesley, SEE Andrews, Charles Wesley
Andrews, William C., 66/148,149N
Andrews, Ore., 73/238N:

post office, 63/333; SEE ALSO Wild Horse, Harney Co.
Andromeda (ship), 66/127
Andrus, Fred, 75/294
Angelo, C. Aubrey, 64/282
Angelus Studio, Portland, 64/352
Anglican Church:
British Columbia, 71/367; Kutenai Indians, 71/336
Angling, SEE Sport fishing
Ankeny, Levi, 64/352
Anliker, G., 72/297
Annakhuts (Annahootz) (Indian), 73/153
Annala, Eino E.:
The Crag Rats, noted, 77/382
Annals of the Thoracic Clinic, by Tuhy, noted, 79/408
Annette Island, 62/57
Annie Faxon (steamer), 71/22: photo, 71/44
Annie Spring, 81/45: photo, 81/44
Annin, R.A., 63/35
Anson, Joseph, family, 70/280
Antelope, Ore., 65/114N; 66/183; 70/69; 72/341,342; 73/260,263, 267,304,306; 75/314-15; 77/161; 81/301,312,313-14:
lost history collection, 66/91; photos, 73/304; 75/314,ins.bk.cov. Dec.; 81/313; sites, 75/311-12,314
Antelope Canyon, 69/301
Antelope Herald, 66/241; 73/307
Antelope Mountain Spring, 79/294,294N
Antelope Springs, 65/19
Antelope Valley, 75/314
Antelopes, 68/354; 69/18,158; 71/8; 75/314; 79/371,373,376,379,380:
description, 69/15-16; discovered by Lewis, 69/23; drawing, 69/fr.cov. March; migration, 69/12
Antevs, Ernst, 79/403
Anthony, Susan Brownell, 68/201; 78/5,6,36
Anthony and Huddleston's store, Eugene, 78/43,64
Anthropology:

American Indian studies, 72/287; areal descriptions in, 64/87; Bering Strait, 77/295-97; Cove rock Indian writings, 65/200; early migrants to Pacific NW, 72/287; Eskimos, 64/347; 69/327-28; Folsom man, 63/89; Fresno scrapers, 72/283,313; Great Basin, 69/333; 72/286; history and, 69/83; Idaho, 63/89; Klamath Basin, 69/333; North Pacific rim, 74/284; Pacific Northwest, 62/203; prehistoric man in Ore., 62/298; 63/254,364; prehistoric man in Yellowstone, 65/373-74; 72/248-52; SEE ALSO Archeology

Anti-Asiatic Association, 76/242-43

Anti-Saloon League, 68/134-35

Antone, Ore., 65/104

Anvils:

museum piece from *Raccoon*, 69/57-59

Aparejos, SEE Pack saddles

Apiary, Ore., 65/308

Apollo Club, Portland, 74/205

Appaloosa, SEE Horses

Appalo, Carlton E.:

Pillar Rock, noted, 72/172

Apperson, John T., 76/299:

First Ore. Cavalry service, 65/14, 26,44,105,394

Applegate, Albert, 81/248

Applegate, Charles:

death, 81/247; finances, 81/248; house, 81/106; photo, 81/232

Applegate, Cynthia Ann Parker (Mrs. Jesse), 81/247

Applegate, Edward Bates, 81/240

Applegate, Fanny, SEE Johnson, Fanny Applegate

Applegate, George, 81/232

Applegate, Gertrude, 81/246

Applegate, Ivan D., 67/55,58,59

Applegate, James, 67/58,59

Applegate, Jesse, 62/118,142N,145,313, 322; 63/230; 65/364; 69/330; 70/260; 71/285; 77/317:

Astoria claim dispute, 81/25N; biography, 72/355; 81/229-59*passim*; character analysis, 81/230,233,235-37,240-42,244,245-53,257-59; death, 81/247; drawing of, 81/232; leadership roles,

81/231,240,243,245; letters, 71/80, 197; opinions of, 81/231; quoted, 62/117,157; railroad interests, 71/71,197; survey 1871, 72/47N; views of pioneers' motives, 81/229-30, 250-51

Applegate, Jesse:

"A Day with the Cow Column," cited, 81/231

Applegate, John Milton, 81/241

Applegate, Lindsey, 66/81; 67/90; 77/317; 79/127; 81/234,240,243: diary, 77/301; photo, 81/232

Applegate, Lisbon, 81/236

Applegate, Lucy, 81/241

Applegate, Luella, 72/93

Applegate, Oliver Cromwell, 62/310N, 322,323; 66/81; 68/258: educational methods, 68/90

Applegate, Peter, 68/70

Applegate, Rachel, SEE Good, Rachel Applegate

Applegate, Robert S., 81/25N

Applegate, Warren, 81/240

Applegate, William Millburn, 81/241

Applegate Creek, 72/42; 73/348

Applegate Cutoff, SEE Southern Immigrant Route

Applegate River, 63/350

The Applegate Trail, by Helfrich and Helfrich, noted, 77/292; review, 72/351-52

The Applegate Trail: Southern Emigrant Route, 1846, by Haines, noted, 77/301

Apples:

French Prairie, 66/339; genesis Pacific NW culture, 64/276; Hood River Valley, 63/365; 70/50,51; 77/377; largest Ore. orchard, 77/378; Olympic Peninsula, 74/9,23; orchard and packing photos, 68/168-72; Sweet Alice origin, 68/170; varieties, 77/377

Appleton, Maggie, 78/370

Appolion (frigate), 72/112,116

Apso-kah-hah (Chief Joe) (Indian), 66/221N,225

Aracan (ship), SEE *Arracan*

Arago (brig), 68/267

Arai, Mrs. —, Portland Assembly Center, 81/156,163

Arai, Tsuguo, ed.:
Alaska and Japan: Perspectives of Past and Present, noted, 74/284
Arapaho Indians, 72/67:
history, 72/172
Arata, Francesco:
photo, 77/259; liquor store photo, 77/259
Arata, G., and Co., Portland wholesale liquor house, photo, 77/259
Arbuthnot, Harriet, 64/20-21
Arcata, Calif., 78/387
Archeology:
bibliography, 69/276; 70/358; 79/404; Big Camas Prairie, 64/282; Birch Creek Valley, 63/89; Bruces Eddy, 63/359; burials, 71/367; Calapooya mounds, 66/90; carved stones, 62/203; Catlow Cave, 72/90; Charcoal Cave, 65/220; 72/90; Clark Co., 63/82; Columbia Plateau, 64/186; 71/367; Columbia River, 62/61N,89-90; 69/333; Cougar Mt. Cave, 64/357; Coyote Flat, 71/367; Deschutes Co., 63/254; Elk Rock Indian drawings, 66/54; Eskimos, 69/327; Far West, 79/403-404; Ft. Okanogan, 63/358; Fort Rock, 67/36,374; 76/89; Ft. Vancouver, 77/292,298; Fraser River stone sculpture, 65/215; Grand Coulee, 69/84; Great Basin, 69/333; 70/352; Henry's Fork site, 71/366; housepits, 62/203
Idaho, 63/89; 67/87,366; 70/87—
Eagle Creek, 69/84; Goldendale site, 64/282
Indian artifacts, 62/198,203; legal rights, 65/220; Long Beach, Wash., 69/84; Mecham site, 62/203; Nevada, 67/86
North America, 70/266—
prehistoric population moves, 67/87
North Bend, 64/355; Northwest Coast, 71/367; obsidian analysis, 70/87; oldest human remains, 69/338; 70/183,365; Pacific NW and Alaska theses, 65/373-74; 72/248-52; Palouse River cave, 68/350; Pence-Duering cave, 63/89; prehistoric dwellings, 63/82; 64/357; Puget Sound survey, 64/277; rhinos, 63/254; rock alignments, 68/333-35; Rogue Valley, 69/340; salmon effigies, 62/198; salt caves, Klamath River, 64/353; San Dieguito culture, 68/333-35; Scappoose Indian village, 64/89; Seward Peninsula, 77/295-96; Snake River, 62/106; 69/84; Spalding Mission, 77/302; state protection, 62/203; stone artifacts, 63/76; The Dalles area, 63/75-77,359; The Dalles mauls, 66/88; Washington, 69/276; Wawawai site, 68/351; Willamette Valley, 76/91; Yakima Valley, 70/273; SEE ALSO Anthropology; Mastadons; Wakemap Mound
Archer, Howard:
Gresham...the Friendly City, noted, 69/329-30
Archer, William S., 81/182-83
Archibald, Dale, 71/370:
Eskimo Artifacts, by Thiry and Thiry, review, 79/407
The Eskimos of Bering Strait, by Ray, review, 77/295-96
The Filming of the West, by Tuska, review, 78/362
Objects of Bright Pride, by Wardwell, review, 81/207-208
Sacred Circles, by Coe, review, 79/213-14
The Spokane Indians, by Ruby and Brown, review, 73/69
Archibald, John, family, 74/358
Architects:
Pacific Northwest 1962, 64/188
Architecture:
Baker Co. 1890s, 66/209; balloon frame, 67/332N; barns, SEE Barns; Canadian chateau style, 70/361; carpenter gothic, 65/315
drawings—
Downing house plans, 67/337,343, 345; Ft. Dalles, 67/334-37,338-42,covs. Dec.; Ft. Simcoe, 67/346
dumb waiter, 67/331; 68/15; Eastern Ore., 65/219; farm houses, 66/383; "filling in," 68/15,16,20N

Fort Dalles, 68/5-6,9— construction details, 68/10-21 French Prairie, 66/338-39,348; house pattern books in Ore., 67/329-30N; Lane Co., 66/383; old building identification, 66/282; "picturesque," 67/326,329; use of wood, 67/330; verandas, 67/332-33N; wall material, 66/283; Willamette Valley, 63/363 *Archives and Manuscript Repositories in the U.S.S.R.: Moscow and Leningrad*, by Grimsted, noted, 74/95 Archives of the Oregon Province of the Society of Jesus, 63/60 Arcouet, Amable, 63/224 Arcouet, Amable, son of Amable, 66/348N Arcouet, Lisette, 66/348N Arcouet, Michel, 66/348N Arctic: Danish shipping, 81/60-74*passim*; Greely 1884 expedition, 69/83; voyages 1830s, 67/371; walruses, 67/368; whaling, 79/106 *Arctic Stream* (ship), 66/129 Arens, Waldo, 70/53 Argillite, SEE Slate *Argonaut* (vessel): seized at Nootka Sound, 79/397 Arica, Chile, 77/118,119-22,124 *Arid Acres: A History of the Kimama-Minidoka Homesteaders, 1912-1932*, comp. by Riedesel, noted, 70/273 Ariel (Merwin) Dam, 68/341 Arima, E.T., 76/240 Arizona: centennial history checklist, 64/282; territorial records, 64/277; territory created, 65/213 Arizona Wool Growers Association, 62/190 Arkansas River, 66/331 Arlington, Ore., 62/201; 70/75; 77/90; 81/270N: history, 75/361-62; map, 81/280; Masonic history 1887-1963, 65/121 Arlington Club, Portland, 77/263 Armitage, George H., 63/83; 79/10 Arms and ammunition:

Civil War field artillery in West, 72/227; Kamchatka 1779, 80/200-204; SEE ALSO Cannon; Firearms; Nuclear weapons Armstrong, Chester H., comp.: *History of Oregon Parks, 1917-1963*, review, 67/184-85 Armstrong, Clarissa Chapman (Mrs. Richard), 68/70-71 Armstrong, Ellis L., ed.: *History of Public Works in the United States*, review, 78/360-61 Armstrong, M.L., 81/272N Armstrong, Pleasant, Yamhill Co., 66/223N Armstrong, Richard, 68/54,69: letters quoted on U.S.-Hawaii relations, 68/61-63,67-68 Armstrong, Samuel C., 68/72 Arneson, James: "Property Concepts of 19th Century Oregon Indians," 81/391-422 Arnold, F.M., 80/138 Arnold, Uriah K., 69/208 Arnold Ice Cave, 73/84 Arnst, Albert: *Logging Railroads of the West*, by Adams, review, 63/354-55 Arntson, Herbert E.: *Adam Gray, Stowaway: A Story of the China Trade*, review, 64/348 Arquet, Amable, SEE Arcouet, Amable *Arracan* (ship), 66/116,127 Arragon, Rex F.: *The American Historical Association's Guide to Historical Literature*, ed. by Howe *et al*, review, 63/342-43 Arrigoni, A., 80/142 Arrigoni, Simon H., 77/245-46: sketch, 77/245 Arrington, Joseph Earl: "Skirving's Moving Panorama: Colonel Fremont's Western Expedition Pictorialized," 65/133-72 Arrington, Leonard J., 63/359; 64/281: *Beet Sugar in the West*, noted, 69/275 *David Eccles, Pioneer Western Industrialist*, review, 77/296 Arrowhead, SEE Wapato

Arrowsmith, Aaron, 69/79
Art and artists, 62/106; 63/88,345-46, 359; 64/349; 65/136-39; 80/209: biographical encyclopedia, 79/106; early Washington, 67/297; Eskimo, 68/347; galleries, 73/285; 79/213-14; Hudson River school, 73/85; Indian, 70/363; 81/341-76; Mounted Rifle Regiment sketches, 67/292; Northwest Coast 18th century, 70/367; Oregon art survey, 68/342; "Out Our Way" cartoons, 71/364; Pacific Northwest, 62/141; 69/332; 73/81; paintings of birds and animals, 74/357-58; paintings of cowboys, 72/180; Rockies excursion 1870, 67/371; Skirving panorama 1849-50, 65/141-46; Spanish on NW coast, 65/215; The West, 68/344; 73/360; 75/94; Western paintings, 71/ 292; SEE ALSO Alfred T. Agate; Louis Akin; J.M. Alden; Charles E. Barber; Eliza R. Barchus; Thomas Hart Benton; Albert Bierstadt; Karl Bodmer; Richard Brooks; Jose Cardero; S.N. Carvalho; William Carey; George Catlin; John G. Chapman; Daniel W. Coit; Cyrus E. Dallin; Nathaniel Dance; George Davidson; Roswell Dosch; Joseph Drayton; Harvey Dunn; Seth Eastman; Peter J. Frankenstein; Georg Geyer; Robert Haswell; Stewart Holbrook; Hewitt Jackson; Francis L. Jaques; B. Martin Justice; Paul Kane; Edward M. Kern; Richard H. Kern; W.H.D. Koerner; Rudolph Kurz; Eugenie Lebrun; Charles Lehr; William R. Leigh; James A. McDougal; Alfred Jacob Miller; Thomas Moran; George T. Morgan; Thomas Nast; Leopold Ostner; Bass Otis; Edgar S. Paxson; Charles Wilson Peale; Nicholas Point; Charles Preuss; C.S. Price; E.B. Quigley; Frederic Remington; Peter Rindisbacher; Cleveland Rockwell; Charles M. Russell; William R. Ryan; Olaf Seltzer; Archibald Skirving; Gustav Sohon; John Mix Stanley; F.D. Stuart; Alfred Sully; Thomas Sully; Mark Tobey; John Trumbull; I.G. Voznesenskii; James Webber; Harry

Wentz; James M. Whistler; Frederick Whymper; John Young
Art of the Thirties, by Kingsbury, noted, 73/285
Artemise (French frigate), 68/57,58
Arthur, J.M., 69/221N
Arthur, Mark, 78/364
Arthur, Peter, 63/205,224
Arthur Middleton (attack transport), 81/333:
Aleutian campaign 1943, 80/31-49; drawings, 80/38; photos, 80/30,33,36
Artillery:
U.S. Army on Pacific Coast 1862, 65/ 331,333; SEE ALSO Cannon
As a City Upon a Hill: The Town in American History, by Smith, review, 70/71-72
As I Remember, Adam: An Autobiography of a Festival, by Bowmer, noted, 76/381
"As It Was...," by Evelyn Sibley Lampman, 76/368-79
"Asa Mead Simpson, Lumberman and Shipbuilder," by Stephen Dow Beckham, 68/259-73
Aschoff, Adolph, 73/84
Ash Butte, 72/341,342; 75/309: photo, 75/310
Ash Hollow, 62/286,287,338,372N; 80/70,71: sketch, 79/374
Ashabranner, Brent, 64/348
Ashbury, —, Calif. 1850s, 66/168,170
Ashford, Wash., 73/345
Ashland, Ore., 62/205,322; 64/323-41*passim*; 66/171; 69/88; 70/280; 77/170:
Chautauqua, 62/180; 64/356; described 1885, 80/235; Fourth of July 1912, 76/354-55; hospital, 64/339-40; hotel project 1922, 64/328-29; Lithia Park, 64/323,325,334; mineral spring project, 64/323,325-27; post office, 71/200; railroad, 80/232; telegraph, 68/223; theater history, 76/ 381; SEE ALSO Ashland Shakespearean Festival; toll gate photo, 80/ins.fr.cov. Fall; water supply, 64/326,329,331-32; Winburn conflict, 64/329,331-35; women's civic clubhouse, 64/338-41

Ashland Chamber of Commerce, 62/ 180,182
Ashland Creek, 64/334
Ashland Development Co., 64/326,328
Ashland Forest Reserve, 76/29
Ashland Hotel, 64/326,328,341
Ashland Normal School, 64/323,325
Ashland Shakespearean Festival, 62/ 180-83
Ashland Tidings, 64/326,335-36
Ashley, James M., 69/336
Ashley, William Henry, 63/364; 68/86: biography, 66/63-65; 70/86; diaries and letters, 66/63-64; fur trade influence, 66/63; report on Oregon, 70/ 365-66
Ashwood, Ore., 62/201; 69/87; 75/ 309; 77/159: history, 72/341-42; mining district, 66/183; photos, 72/340; 75/310; 77/160
Ashwood Prospector, 72/341,342
L'Asino, Portland newspaper, 77/260
Aspinwall, William H., 69/276
The Assiniboines: From the Accounts of the Old Ones Told to First Boy, ed. by Kennedy, review, 63/71-73
Assistance League of Portland, 71/370
Association for Documentary Editing, 80/208
Asthma, 63/51
Astor, John Jacob, 62/199; 66/331, 332; 71/312,313,318N,365; 72/104, 179; 74/285,359; 75/104-105; 76/ 202,208,310,315,319,322-23,325; 77/80: Columbia River mouth interests, 72/ 104; Pacific NW fur trade, 71/309-24
Astor, John Jacob, Baron of Hever, 62/199
Astor, John Jacob, III, 62/305
Astor Library, 70/85
Astoria, Ore., 62/64,68,78,245,314, 421; 63/150, 196,198,205,238; 66/331,333; 69/ 59,88,323; 72/169; 75/84,105,294; 76/323; 77/80,108; 80/62; 81/200: custom house, 63/231,252; early town plan, 81/202; ethnic groups, 74/92;

Finnish people, 70/361; 77/302; fire protection, 77/246
fires— 1883, 73/82; 1922, 66/329
first electric lights, 68/353; first post office, 81/188,194(photo); first postmaster, 81/180; fishing boats, 67/ 175N; fossils, 65/219; founding, 63/ 254; fur trade center, 76/325; government, 69/340; Grace Church centennial, 66/383; guidebooks, 77/292; historic houses, 68/89; 70/184; 71/200; 76/304; history, 63/252; 71/196; hospitals, 71/289; industry, 68/252-53; 77/215-16; Japanese in, 76/238, 239; land claims, 64/227N-29N; log raft photos, 66/180,182; lumber export, 67/175; map, 81/189; mayor, 71/150; newspapers, 71/147; ocean port, 71/93-94,95; old cemetery, 64/ 320N; Olney estate, 64/320-22; "Olney's lottery," 64/319; photographers, 66/329; photos, 66/180,182; 77/ins.fr.cov. June; 81/4; plat, 81/24; port of entry, 77/45; postal history, 81/185,188-89,190N,194; promotion, 64/215,230N,319; 71/177; regatta, 74/215,240; 77/142(photo); salmon canning, 67/111N; sawmill, 68/261; shipping, 71/31; submarine attack WW II, 65/219,314; theater, 74/91-92; town site disputes, 81/24-25,190N, 195N; transcontinental railroad link, 71/68,69,70,93-94; U.S. title restored, 69/59; walking tour, 76/304; waterfront, 74/164; SEE ALSO Fort George
Astoria (steamer), 77/363
Astoria (tug), 68/266
Astoria and Columbia River Railroad, 72/199,301; 74/295,297,325: excursion train, 74/312(photo),313; records, 74/79
Astoria and South Coast Railroad, 67/174; 69/209
Astoria Centennial, 66/329
Astoria enterprise: Irving's account, 71/309-24; overland party, 68/87; 71/316N; Seton's journal, 71/309-24; Thompson River post,

68/87; view of post at Astoria 1813, 69/331; 81/331; review, 63/356
71/314
Astoria Fire Co. No. 1, 64/178
Astoria Iron Works, 69/323
Astoria Marine Iron Works, 80/380
Astoria-Megler Bridge, 63/252
Astoria, or Anecdotes of an Enterprise Beyond the Rocky Mountains, by Irving, ed. by Todd, cited, 71/309FF; editions listed, 66/78; review, 66/77-79
Astoria Pioneer Cemetery, 70/184
Astoria Sesquicentennial, 62/205
Astorian Budget, 75/294
"At the Beach," by William L. Mainwaring, 75/54-55
Atalanta (British ship): described, 66/108; log, 66/112; seamen shanghaied, 66/114; wreck, 66/110-13
Atalanta (German bark), 66/111-12N
Athabaska Pass: fur trade artery, 79/413
Athabaska region, 76/312,321
Athearn, Robert G.: *Union Pacific Country*, review, 73/66
Athearn, Robert G., and Robert E. Riegel: *America Moves West*, 5th ed. noted, 72/173
Athena, Ore., 73/84,285
Atherton, Louis, 67/367: *The Cattle Kings*, cited, 67/141
Atiyeh, Victor, 80/414
Atka Island, 77/188
Atkeson, Ray, 70/76; 76/91; 77/300
Atkha (ship), 73/159
Atkins, Edwin F., 69/219N
Atkinson, A. Monroe, 66/139N
Atkinson, Bob, 80/48
Atkinson, George Henry, 64/209N-10N; 65/211: church schools, 68/350; Oregon City schools, 68/353
Atkinson, Henry, 67/368
Atlantic Springs, 62/353
Atlas of Oregon, by Loy *et al*, noted, 77/291; review, 78/178-79
Atlas of the Pacific Northwest Resources and Development, ed. by Highsmith, noted,

Atlatls (throwing sticks), 63/89: description and use, 81/327
Atlin Lake, 81/142,144-46
Atom bomb, 62/33-34,36,40-41,46-48
Attix, Enid, 66/101N
Attu Island, 80/45,46
Attwell, James: recollections, 73/283
Attwell, James: *Tahmalmaw, the Bridge of the Gods*, noted, 75/88
Attwell, Monty, 73/283
Atwood, Charles A., 74/349
Atwood, Evangeline: *Who's Who in Alaskan Politics*, review, 78/358-59
Atwood, F., 74/21
Atwood, Kay: *Jackson County Conversations*, noted, 77/90,292
Aubichon, Elizabeth, 66/355N
Aubichon, Emilie, SEE Petit, Emilie Aubichon
Aubichon (Obichon), Jean Baptiste, 66/348N
Aubichon, Marie Isabile, 66/348N
Auburn, Calif., 71/250
Auburn, Ore., 62/198; 63/357; 65/209; 66/199,200,202,205; 69/276; 70/280; 72/71; 78/73: Chinese in, 62/236; early justice, 62/ 229-32; gold mining history, 62/213-36; gold rush, 63/254; photo 1861, 62/212; town beginnings, 62/227, 229-30,232-35
Auburn, Wash., 65/381
Auburn canal: built, 62/228
Auburn Canal Co., 62/228,236
Auchampaugh, Philip G., 63/346
AuCoin, Les, 79/411
Audubon, John J., 80/207
Augur, Christopher Colon, 65/ 175N,177,186-88,192,196; 70/233: biography, 65/177N; Ft. Hoskins, 65/178-81; photo, 65/176
Augusta (bark), 63/238
Aumsville, Ore., 64/354

Aune, Harold E., 77/277
Aunt Lize (Indian), 68/353
Aurora, Nev.:
seat of two counties, 72/12
Aurora, Ore., 62/200; 65/218,385; 70/278; 71/200,294; 77/298: church bells, 67/273-76— photos, 67/274,275
first schoolhouse, 79/234; first wagon-making, 63/67; historic houses, 62/299; 68/352; history sources, 79/234; hotel photo, 79/265; music, 79/233-68; museum, 68/357; 69/174; Old Colony Church, 67/273; 79/240, 241(photo)
"Aurora Colony Church Bells," by Clark Moor Will, 67/273-76
Aurora Colony Historical Society, 79/267
Aurora Ox Barn Museum, 68/357; 69/174; 71/200: collections, 79/245-67*passim*
Aurora Pie and Beer Band, 79/238
Aurora Pioneer Band, 79/237,238-45, 250-51,266,267: members, 79/239,243-48*passim*; photos, 79/234,265,ins.fr.cov. Fall; sketch, 79/244
Austin, Boyd, 63/89
Austin, Darrell, 76/267,268
Austin, Josephine (Mrs. Stanley W.), 80/414
Austin, Mary Hunter, 80/408
Austin, Russell D., 64/38; 77/91
Austin, Nev., 63/79
Australia, 62/6,15,29,30,40-41,46-48
Australia-New Zealand-U.S. Security Treaty, 62/39,42
Australian ballot, 68/203
"Authentic Account of the Murder of Dr. Whitman: The History of a Pamphlet," by Belknap, noted, 63/361
Authors:
Pacific Northwest, 71/181-82,286; 72/181; SEE ALSO Authors' names; Literature
"Autobiography, 1874-1945," by William Isaac Gadwa, 80/269-85
"Autobiography of Jacob Kaser," ed. by

John J. Kaser, 81/281-318
Autobiography of Rear Admiral Wilkes, U.S. Navy, 1798-1877, ed. by Morgan *et al*, review, 79/404-406
"Automobile Trip Around Cape Perpetua," by Bess Tompkins Miller, 76/177-79
Automobiles, 71/125,130: accessories catalog 1906, 72/bk.cov. June; Buick, 71/118; 76/352; Chalmers photo, 77/ins.fr.cov. Dec.; Chevrolet 1918 photo, 76/178; Dodge 4-cylinder, 77/355,364; driving, 1909, 69/295-305*passim*; effect on tourism, 74/114-15
firsts—
Bend, 72/94; Pacific NW, 65/219; Portland, 74/108; Tillamook Co., 77/91; Yamhill Co., 67/366
Flanders 1912, 81/327
Ford—
Model T, 71/131; 76/351,352,357, 358; 77/5,63; Model T trip 1919, 72/159-64; roadster, 71/120
Hudson, 71/121—
photo, 75/283; tour by, 75/283-89
impact on road construction, 74/101, 112,134; literature, 74/133; Locomotive, 65/225; 67/366; 81/43-45; motoring 1911, 74/281; no. in Multnomah Co. 1913-14, 74/137; no. in Oregon 1913, 74/111; Oldsmobile, 74/110(photo); 76/350-51; Oregon first gas tax, 66/270; Packard 1911, 74/209; photos, 71/116,122,128, ins.fr.cov. June; 72/162,163,ins.fr.cov. June; 74/110,133,226; 75/280,282, 288; 76/160; 77/ins.bk.cov. June; poor roads, 66/255
racing, 76/355—
New York-Portland 1905, 65/220
repairs, 77/5-6,166-67; replace stagecoach, 76/59; scrap steel industry, 72/287
service stations, 77/358—
first Seattle drive-in, 65/220
social impact, 74/101,112; stage lines, 74/358; Stanley Steamer, 77/153; Studebaker-Garford, 69/293,294

(photo),295,300(photo); The Dalles 1909, **69**/293; tires, **76**/353; **77**/5 travel by, **72**/159-64; **76**/177-79, 352-55— Lakeview-Ukiah, **77**/165,167; overland, **76**/350-51 White Steamer, **77**/77 Avacha Bay, **80**/197,199: map, **80**/ins.fr.cov. Summer Aveling, Eleanor Marx, **74**/280 Averill, D.M., & Co., Portland, **66**/306 Avery, Joseph C., **78**/43,43N Avery, Mary W.: *Government of Washington State*, noted, **68**/341 *History and Government of the State of Washington*, review, **63**/78-79 *John Ledyard's Journey Through Russia and Siberia, 1787-1788*, review, **68**/274-77 *Washington: A History of the Evergreen State*, review, **67**/79-80 Aviation: air transportation, **67**/367; Beaverton amateur aviators, **67**/91; Clark Co. early aviators, **69**/331; early flights, **74**/232,316-17; Hawaii air travel, **68**/278-79 Oregon— pioneer aviators, **62**/197; **71**/198; role in early transportation, **64**/357 Pacific Northwest— air routes, **71**/197; lost aircraft, **64**/88 Tillamook blimp base photo, **71**/136; transpolar flight, **77**/299; SEE ALSO Airfields; Airlines; Airplanes; Airports Avrit, Roy, **78**/345 Awbrey, Thomas N., **78**/43N Axehandle community, Jefferson Co., **66**/183 Axehandle Butte, **75**/310 *Axellius* (ship), **66**/129: wreck, **66**/105 Axtell, Shorty, **74**/13N Ayer, Winslow Bartlett, **69**/208; **71**/225,226N: Hunt dispute, **71**/229FF; Library Assn. of Portland, **71**/225FF

Ayers, S.A., **74**/5 Aylsworth, Larry, **69**/346 Ayre, Robert: *Sketco the Raven*, review, **64**/348 Azalea Garden Club, **67**/47 Azcuenaga, Antone, **76**/155-56

Babb, Andrew Jackson, **78**/44,143: photo, **78**/142 Babb, Mary Mathews, photo, **78**/142 Babbitt, Almon W., **72**/7 Babbitt, Bruce E.: *Color and Light: The Southwest Canvases of Louis Akin*, noted, **75**/88 Babbitt, Edwin B., **65**/397; **70**/257N Babbitt, Lawrence, **70**/18N,19 Babbitt, Rodney, **67**/232 Babcock, C. Merton: *The American Frontier, A Social and Literary Record*, noted, **66**/188 Babcock, Ira L., **62**/116,121,122N, 128,137,139-40,141N,143; **66**/355: Ore. Provisional Govt., **66**/350,352,353 Baber, Ensley, **79**/9,10 Babine Indians, **71**/333,335 Babson, Rea, **70**/52 Babson, S. Gorham, son of Sydney G., **70**/50N Babson, Sydney G.: photos, **70**/51,55 Babson, Sydney G.: "Hood River Valley Wild Night," **70**/50-55 Baby Home, Portland, **80**/59 Bache, Alexander Dallas: biography, **71**/290 Bachelor Butte, **77**/330 Bachelor Flat, Columbia Co., **64**/91 Back, Seid, Jr., **80**/265 Back, Sir George, **64**/284 *Back Roads of Oregon*, by Thollander, noted, **81**/329 Backstos, J.E., **67**/62 "Backstage with Frank Branch Riley, Regional Troubadour," by John Dierdorff, **74**/197-243 Bacon, SEE Prices Badger, Austin, **72**/61 Badger Creek, Wasco Co., **65**/104N,

108N

Badger Flat (Meadows), Nev., **68**/255,315

Baer, Charlotte Quist, **66**/54

Baer, Eleanora A., **63**/358

Baer, Harry, **74**/359

Bagley, Clarence B., **63**/57N,58,59N,207

Bagley, Daniel, **62**/298

Bagley, Eli, **78**/127,325

Bagley, Lillian, **66**/278

Bagley, Samuel, **78**/325

Bagot, Charles, **72**/122,123

Baidarkas (kayaks), **73**/118,124,137, 165; **77**/179,180: sealskin use, **73**/129; sketch, **73**/138

Bailey, B.M., **74**/21,24

Bailey, Edward F., **63**/245

Bailey, Francis Alonzo, **67**/373

Bailey, J.O., **62**/95

Bailey, Joe, **81**/105

Bailey, John, Lane Co. pioneer, **63**/245; **79**/11

Bailey, Margaret Jewett Smith, **63**/184; **65**/220; **74**/286

Bailey, Margery, **62**/182,183

Bailey, William J., **63**/184

Bailey family, overland 1854, **79**/16

Bailey Gatzert (steamer), **63**/61-66,68; **69**/294; **71**/197; **72**/94: photos, **63**/62,63; **74**/320

Bailey Hill, Lane Co., **63**/245

Bailley, Francois, **64**/183

Baillie, T., mate on *Mount Stuart*, **66**/123

Baillie, Thomas, capt. of *Modeste*, **63**/223

Bain, Katherine Waite (Mrs. Walter M.), **65**/401

Bainbridge Island, **73**/309

Baird, George Washington, **75**/142

Baird, Spencer F., **70**/246,246N,251N

Baird Creek: wood trestle, **63**/355

Bakeoven, Ore., **65**/114,115; **69**/298; **73**/260,321

Baker, —, Southern Ore. miner, **76**/69-70

Baker, Abner S., III, **69**/222: "Economic Growth in Portland in the 1880s," **67**/105-23 "Experience, Personality and Memory:

Jesse Applegate and John Minto Recall Pioneer Days," **81**/229-59

Baker, Alice McClay, **80**/52-53

Baker, Dorsey Syng, **70**/168: railroad interests, **71**/61,78N

Baker, Doug, **62**/205

Baker, Ed ("Roaring Ed"), **63**/352

Baker, Edward Dickinson, **69**/73; **70**/179; **73**/51,53,54,58: death, **72**/326; emigrant escort legislation, **72**/56-57; First Ore. Cavalry, **65**/392-93; Mexican War, **71**/365; recommends Crawford, **72**/59,60; U.S. senator, **72**/323-26; volunteer regiment, **72**/324

Baker, Frankie, **66**/89

Baker, Fred, Portland electrician, **66**/59; **76**/264

Baker, Fred S., housemover, **76**/301

Baker, George Luis, **64**/249,252; **66**/46; **74**/208,217,233; **75**/157-58,166, 180; **79**/98: Hunt case opinion, **71**/231; photos, **75**/155; **78**/100, urges victory gardens, **71**/218; Vista House dedication photo, **66**/258

Baker, J.C., **64**/136

Baker, Jack, **80**/53

Baker, John, **67**/227

Baker, Lydell, **74**/205

Baker, Mary Catherine, **64**/110N

Baker, Nat, **75**/127-28

Baker, Newton, **75**/148

Baker, Thomas, **65**/92-93

Baker, W.A., **71**/216

Baker, William A., **79**/106

Baker, W.W., & Co., Portland, **64**/159

Baker, Ore., **62**/234,235; **63**/263-64; **66**/198,203,206,303,309; **68**/228, 235,307; **70**/13: banks, **67**/236,248,250; beef and wool shipping 1892, **67**/131; history, **79**/104; pioneer homes, **71**/199; population 1880-90, **67**/156

Baker-Barkon Co., Portland, **66**/59

Baker Bay, **63**/47-49,196,205,227,232; **69**/310,311,323,340; **72**/89: Johnston claim, **64**/212N-13; photo, **69**/321; *Ruby* anchors, **69**/67

Baker City Academy, 64/175
Baker County, Ore., 62/216,230,231; 66/197,368; 69/274; 70/280: cattle industry, 67/145-58*passim*; Indian raids, 66/203-206; mining laws, 62/224; pioneers, 77/90; population 1880-90, 67/156; postal cards, 66/309; sheep 1880-90, 67/155; wheat production 1880-90, 67/154
Baker County Historical Society: publications, 72/171
Baker County Livestock Assn.: history, 65/216
Baker Library, Howard Univ., 69/219
Baker's Bay, SEE Baker Bay
Bakken, Lavola J.:
The Bullwhacker's Boy, noted, 77/301
Land of the North Umpquas, noted, 74/358
Lone Rock Free State…Oregon's North Umpqua Valley, noted, 71/190
Bakowski, B.B., 66/306: photos by, 69/297,302
Balaena (whaler), 68/54
Balboa, Panama, 77/117,127
Balch, Danford, 63/92; 80/137
Balch, Frederick Homer, 72/92: biography, 71/362
Balch, Frederick Homer:
The Bridge of the Gods, cited, 71/362; 74/37
Balch, James, 72/92
Balch, Lafayette, 64/35
Balch Canyon, Portland, photo, 75/58
Balch Creek, 75/60,64
Bald Mountain: identification, 69/45N; maps, 69/30, 34,35; Port Orford meteorite location, 69/31FF
Baldwin, —, Queets area settler, 74/18
Baldwin, Arabella, 80/299N
Baldwin, David M., 72/341
Baldwin, Elias Jackson, 80/250-51
Baldwin, George: biography, 81/327
Baldwin, Harry, 63/25
Baldwin Hotel, Klamath Falls, 63/253; 69/328; 70/280; 73/81
Balfour, Guthrie & Co., 80/32,48

Ball, Abigail, 81/328
Ball, Ebenezer Burgess, 68/351
Ball, Ethel Townsend, 74/274,277
Ball, H., 65/143
Ball, Isaac, 81/328
Ball, John, 62/122; 66/341; 71/344
Ball, L.W., 67/281
Ball Studio, Corvallis, 66/305
Ballagh, Edison I., 65/309
Ballard, Dr. —, Ft. Henrietta, 66/154
Ballard, D.B., 74/21
Ballard, Frank, 78/353
Ballenden, John, 63/202
Ballentine, A., 67/86
Ballinger, Richard Achilles, 65/314; 74/107
Balloons, passenger: Lewis & Clark Centennial Expo., 80/57
Ballou, Robert:
Early Klickitat Valley Days, cited, 70/ 143N,145N,146N; index noted, 74/281
Ballston, Ore.: history, 81/328
Balmer, Donald Gordon, 63/361; 64/281; 66/89,282
Balsiger, E.R., 64/250
Baltimore Colony, 63/25-26
Bamboo: introduced in Ore., 65/239
Ban, Joseph:
Baptists in Oregon, by Wardin, review, 72/166-67
Ban, Shinzaburo, 76/229-30: portrait, 76/230; shop photo, 76/229
Bancroft, —, capt. of *Loriot*, 63/210
Bancroft, F.A., 67/70
Bancroft, George, 76/213-17*passim*
Bancroft, Hubert Howe, 62/61,323-24,328-31; 63/224; 65/198-99; 66/78; 70/226; 81/233,251: assistants, 75/79,80; authorship of books, 62/325-27,331,334; bibliography, 75/80; biography, 75/79; historical writings, 75/79-80
Bancroft, Hubert Howe:
History of Oregon, corrections, 77/311
Bancroft Company, 62/329,331

Bancroft Library, 62/324-30*passim*: Hammond at, 66/380; manuscripts, 65/198-99; oral history, 68/346

Banditti of the Plains, by Rush, noted, 62/301

Bandon, Ore., 63/34,36; 68/90; 75/339: fires, 75/341-42; harbor project history, 64/355; historical articles, 72/92; photos, 75/341,ins.fr.cov. Dec.; woolen mills, 62/175

"Bandon-by-the-Sea Revisited," by Thomas C. McClintock, 75/339-43

Bands, SEE Music

Banfield, M.C., 62/170,172,177

Bangs, Nathan, 76/366; 78/345-46,347

Bank of California: in Oregon, 70/182

Bank of Italy: in California, 70/179

Bankers and Cattlemen, by Gressley, review, 68/337-38

Banks, Louis Albert: *An Oregon Boyhood*, cited, 74/37

Banks and banking, 77/296,302: Baker, 67/236,248-50; Boise, 68/346; Coquille, 63/34; Eugene, 62/301; history, 62/107; Independence, Ore., 68/90; investments in cattle, 68/337-38; Jacksonville, 66/59,282; SEE ALSO Beekman Bank; Klamath Co., 69/328; Lane Co., 62/107,301; Montana, 65/367; Myrtle Point, 63/34-35 Oregon, 63/361; 64/352; 67/88; 70/177,182; 72/235— capital 1878-90, 67/136; constitutional provisions, 70/177; interest rates, 67/136; pioneer attitude toward, 70/177

panics, 75/28; Portland, 62/165; 66/281; 77/377; SEE ALSO Commercial National Bank, Ladd and Tilton Bank, Metropolitan Savings Bank, Portland Savings Bank; Powers, 77/77; robberies, 72/183; Salem, 65/218; SEE ALSO Ladd and Bush Bank; Siskiyou Co., 71/190; Spokane, 66/283; stocks listed, 69/211; SEE ALSO Bank of Italy; Equitable Savings and Loan; First National Bank; First Security Bank of Idaho;

First State Bank of Milwaukie; Northwestern Bank; Oregon Bank; Oregon National Bank; U.S. National Bank

Bankus, Elmer, 67/42

Bannack Joe (Indian), 70/15

Bannock City, SEE Idaho City

Bannock Indians, 72/69; 81/398: burial customs, 81/412; moved to Yakima Reservation, 70/14N,147N; photos, 68/292,312; treaty, 71/262

Bannock Mountain Road, 65/313

Bannock War, 63/246; 70/125,127, 128,137; 72/351; 73/260,285; 80/335:

Birch Creek battle, 68/232,305; 70/24N,25-26; Brown diary, 68/226-58; casualties, 68/233,234,243N,245N, 301-302,303N,305,306,307,329; cattle killed, 68/322; desertions, 68/243N, 247,248,298N,307; effect on Canyon City, 70/56-59; guides and scouts, 68/237,238N,240,242,301N,305N; 70/18N,23,25N; Indian prisoners, 68/239N,243N,248; Mayer diary, 68/297-316; Murderer's Creek skirmish, 68/303N; sheep killed, 68/305; Silver Creek battle, 68/231N,301-302; 70/21,22,57; sources, 70/5N; volunteers, 70/15N,57,58; Watson recollections, 68/317-29; Wood journal, 70/5-38*passim*

Bannockburn Manufacturing Co., 67/70,71

Bannon, Mrs. Joe, 81/303

Banta, Alice Annie Johnson, 74/26

Banta, John Jackson: birth, 74/5; cabin, 74/4(photo), 11,16,19; death, 74/33; homestead, 74/11,32; Olympic Peninsula exploration, 74/7-16,17,22; photo, 74/4; Queets River colony, 74/5-26

Banvard, John, 65/168

Banzer, John, 62/301

Baptist Academy, Grass Valley, 75/47

Baptist Beacon, Ore. City, 64/136

Baptist Church, 73/263: Amity, 68/90; Auburn, 62/230; Baker Co. 1890s, 66/215; British Columbia, 72/232; Brownsville 114th anniversary,

69/86; Carlton, 76/14(photo),15; first in Pacific NW, 64/124; McMinnville, 69/78

Oregon— history, 69/324-25; 72/166-67; 77/ 300; membership 1856, 64/135N; newspaper efforts 1853-55, 64/124-36 Palestine, Lane Co., 69/276; Peshastin Valley, 79/23 Portland, 69/341; 75/135— Italian mission, 77/256 SEE ALSO Central Baptist Assn.; Columbia Baptist Conference; Corvallis Baptist Assn.; Willamette Baptist Assn.

Baptist Italian Mission, Portland, 77/256

Baptists and the Oregon Frontier, by Miller, review, 69/324-25

Baptists in Oregon, by Wardin, review, 72/166-67

Baranof Island, 72/135; 73/101: called Sitka Island, 73/167; sketch, 73/140

Baranov (Baranof), Alexander, 70/366; 71/311; 73/165; 77/175: Bodega Bay settlement proposed, 73/161; relations with Tlingits, 73/149,152,167

Barbed wire, 71/368: history of manufacture, 63/360; 66/379

Barber, Charles E., 73/276

Barber, Lawrence, 62/197; 63/252,361; 65/217

Barber, William C., 62/300

Barbers: oldest licensed in Oregon, 63/283

Barbershops, 73/204,206

Barbour, John N., 78/248-49

Barchus, Agnes: *Eliza R. Barchus, the Oregon Artist, 1857-1959*, noted, 76/92

Barchus, Eliza R., 76/92

Barclay, A.F., 80/323,324(photo)

Barclay, Alexander: diary, 78/365

Barclay, Catherine (Kate), 76/302

Barclay, Forbes, 63/183; 81/203: house relocation, 76/303—

photo, 76/302

Barclay, Logan, 63/299

Barclay, Maria Pambrun (Mrs. Forbes), 63/181,200-201

Barclay's Fort, 78/365

Bargain Bride, by Lampman, noted, 79/104

Barkdull, John, 78/54,54N,303,304N, 325,325N

Barker, Burt Brown, 62/110,206,302, 421; 63/93,255,371,373-74; 64/93, 189,285,358-59,364; 65/126,222, 318,401,416; 66/93,189, 285,361N, 394; 67/379; 68/357,359,361; 69/ 348; 74/239; 75/6: death, 70/90N; photo, 66/342

Barker, Charles A., 74/30

Barker, F.R., 74/17

Barker, Richard, 65/32,37

Barker, S. Omar, ed.: *Legends and Tales of the Old West*, noted, 65/121

Barker, T.: photo, 72/62

Barkley, Frederick R., and Ray Tucker: *Sons of the Wild Jackass*, reprint noted, 73/282

Barkley, Mrs. William, 62/105

Barkley Springs, 75/235,237

Barklow, James, family, 63/365; 74/94

Barklow, Samuel: diary, 71/290

Barkwill, Minnie McConnell, 71/8N

Barley: Cowlitz Farm, 63/104,144; Ft. Harney, 66/203; French Prairie, 66/339; SEE ALSO Prices

Barlow, A., 80/319N

Barlow, Ben, 65/309

Barlow, Joel: letter on name of Columbia River, 74/269-70

Barlow, Joel: "On the Discoveries of Captain Lewis," quoted, 74/269

Barlow, Mrs. John L., 76/299

Barlow, S.L.M.: papers cited, 71/80N

Barlow, Samuel Kimbrough, 63/30;

77/317; 79/175
Barlow Road, 62/217; 63/10,364; 64/92; 65/212; 68/353; 70/74; 74/282; 76/304; 77/292,317,339; 78/144; 79/42,175: markers, 63/245
The Barlow Road, Bicentennial Edition, 1974-75, noted, 76/304; 77/292
Barnaby (Indian): account of Christian rites among Kutenai, 71/339-42
Barnaby, Joseph, 66/352
Barnes, Frank Grant, 67/366
Barnes, George A., 64/35
Barnes, Jane, 62/105; 63/252; 64/92
Barnett, Homer G.: *Indian Shakers, A Messianic Cult of the Pacific Northwest*, reprint noted, 74/283
Barney, Clinton, 65/31N
Barnhart, Andy, 75/224
Barnhart, Charles, 74/18,19,23
Barnhart, William H., 64/145
Barns, 75/43: Basque stone barn photo, 76/172; Corbett farm, 81/57,59-60; Lane Co., 71/361; Montana, 72/256; Pete French round barn, 63/366; photo, 75/62
Barnum, E.M., 67/312
Barnum (Burnham), Smith, 70/166
Baron, Stanley: *Brewed in America*, noted, 63/248
Barnthouse, Verl G., 77/90
Barr, John, 64/91
Barragy, Terrence J.: "The Trading Age, 1792-1844," 76/197-224
Barrell, Coleman (Colburn?), 64/315
Barrell, Joseph, 67/201; 76/223
Barren Valley, 65/58-59; 72/93
Barrett, John: biography, 71/141-60; 74/359; manuscripts, 71/145NFF; Pacific NW visits, 71/147-52; promotes Pacific NW trade with Orient, 71/141-60; photo, 71/149; railroads support, 71/151
Barrett Spur, 79/206
Barrier, Eugene, 64/33

Barritt, Jackson, 62/314
Barrows, Joe, 81/266,270,273
Barrows, John, 75/346,349
Barrows, William, 62/333
Barry, Bill, family, 76/349
Barry, Bob: *From Shamrocks to Sagebrush*, review, 70/355-56
Barry, Edward, 65/68,297,299
Barry, Iris Lora Thorpe, 74/62
Barry, J. Neilson: *Astoria* notes annotated, 66/79; books and manuscripts, 66/79
Barry, John, 79/170N
Barry, Louise, 63/88; 64/85; 65/214; 66/86; 67/85,367,371; 68/185,345:
The Beginning of the West, Annals of the Kansas Gateway to the American West 1540-1854, review, 74/86-87
The Great Platte River Road, by Mattes, review, 71/182-83
Barry, T.A., 66/10N
Bartel, Walter H., 74/347
Barth, E.K., 64/349
Barth, Gunter, 65/186N,189
Bartholomae, Annette M.: "A Conscientious Objector: Oregon, 1918," 71/213-45
Bartholomew, Anna, 63/245; 65/309
Bartlett, Grace: *Old Chief Joseph and Young Chief Joseph*, noted, 68/184
The Story of Wallowa Lake, noted, 69/330
The Wallowa Country, 1867-1877, noted, 78/91
Wallowa, The Land of Winding Water, noted, 68/184
Barton, Benjamin Smith, 69/27,163, 165,168; 70/171: *Elements of Botany*, cited, 69/168,169
Barton, Jackson, 63/220
Bartram, John, 69/28
Barview, Ore., 71/131; 77/221: photo, 77/221
Baseball, 74/85; 77/358; 81/38: Ashland-Medford, 76/355; Dallas, Ore., 76/379; Japanese team photo, 76/252; mask invented, 76/15; Portland clubs, 74/347; season opening

1910 photo, 77/143
Basi, Wilhelm:
diary, 73/72
Basil, son of Sacajawea, 62/289,290; 71/264N
Basket social:
description, 63/292-93
Basketball, 77/358
Baskets, SEE Indians—basketry
Baskett, George Johnson, 75/363
"Basque Folklore in Southeastern Oregon," by Sarah Baker Munro, 76/153-74
Basque people, 63/268,317; 76/341-43; 81/313:
folklore, 76/155; Idaho, 65/374; 76/173,174; Jordan Valley, 76/153-74; language barriers, 76/170-71; liquor, 76/159-63; medical remedies, 76/164-68; Ontario, Ore., 76/173-74; photos, 76/154-72*passim*; The West, 72/180
Bass, F.W., 74/18
Bassett family, Queets area settlers, 74/18
Batchelder, Charles F., 79/106
Bates, Thomas, 63/157
Battery Elijah O'Flyng, 80/335
Battery Russell, 65/357,359,361
Battien, Pauline:
Joe Moris, noted, 69/79
Battle Rock, Curry Co., 81/106
Bauer, John L., 79/238,255,256
Bauer, Malcolm, 62/110,206,302,422; 63/93,255,372-73; 64/93,189,285, 358,364; 65/126,222,318,414,416; 66/93,189,285,392,393,394; 67/376, 377,379; 68/357,358,359,361; 69/342,343,348; 70/374; 71/373; 72/359; 80/414
Baughman, Clint, 64/331N
Baughman, Elizabeth, 62/249N
Baughman, Samuel, 78/305
Bauman, Albert, 70/315,328,331
Baumgartner, Josephine, 62/421; 63/368
Baumhover, Janet (Mrs. L.A.), 62/110, 206,302,422; 63/93,255,372,374; 64/94,190,286,363; 65/125,221,317, 416; 66/93,189,285; 75/370

Baumont, Elsie, SEE Beaumont, Elsie
Bawdy houses, 69/298,299
Baxter, Farel R.:
Bygone Settlements and Outposts of Northeastern Oregon, noted, 79/104
Baxter, Joseph, 70/166
Baxter, Richard P.:
"Oregon Borax," 73/228-44
Baxter, Robert, 65/284-85,291N
Bay Center, Wash., 71/361:
history, 72/89,171
Bay City, Ore., 71/120; 72/297,311; 77/69,91,222
Bayard, James Asheton, Jr.:
Stark senate seat dispute, 72/333,334-35
Bayfield, —, Nisqually Farm, 63/143
Bayley, James R., photo, 81/258
Baylies, Francis, 72/116
Bayocean, Ore., 65/219; 71/125; 77/221
Beaches, SEE Oregon Coast
Beachey, William C. (Hill), 68/348
Beacon Rock, 78/364
Beacon Rock, by Biddle, reprint noted, 74/282
Bead Lake, 73/349
Beads:
in fur trade, 71/362,369
Beagle, Budd, 70/25
Beagle, Elmer, 64/328N,334N
Beaglehole, John C., 77/290
Beal, Merrill D., 64/282:
"I Will Fight No More Forever": Chief Joseph and the Nez Perce War, review, 64/273-74
Beale, Taverner (Travener), 78/129
Bean, Ellen, 63/253
Bean, Emma, 74/273
Bean, Estelle, 74/271
Bean, Fred, 74/271
Bean, Henry J., 66/363
Bean, Louise, 74/271
Beaner Lumber Company, 77/226
Beaney, William M., SEE Mason, Alpheus T.
Beans, SEE Prices
Bear Creek, Baker Co., 62/228
Bear Creek, Crook Co., 65/78N; 77/332,334; 78/239,241; 79/15,19,40
Bear Creek, Curry Co., 76/43

Bear Creek, Jackson Co.: maps, 69/228,262,263
Bear Creek, Wheeler Co., 73/267
Bear Creek Cemetery, Clackamas Co., 65/216
Bear flag revolt, 77/197
Bear Hunter (Indian), 66/280
Bear Lake, Idaho, 71/196
Bear Paw Mountains, 71/284
Bear River, Calif., 66/169
Bear River, Wyo., 62/366,367,369,370, 372; 72/73; 78/143; 79/20,281: 1852 guide, 80/79-84*passim*; SEE ALSO Smith's Fork, Bear River; Thomas Fork, Bear River
Bear River Mountains, Wyo., 62/372
Bear River Valley, Wyo., 62/372; 79/69,381-82
Bear Valley, Malheur Co., 65/70N,86
Bear Wallow Publishing Co.: *Rendezvous*, noted, 79/340
Beard, Charles Austin, 63/90
Beard, Edward H., 68/342
Beard, Jack, 74/22
Beard, James, 67/261
Bears, 66/81,353; 68/244,295N; 69/ 158; 74/308-309; 75/63,102-103; 76/ 71,75,87; 79/295,381: black, 69/113; grizzly, 67/358; 69/5-6,14,19; 70/354; "Old Clubfoot," 68/91; sheep menaced, 64/112
Beasly's Mill, 70/27
Beatow, Miss —, Coos Valley teacher, 66/56
Beatty, David and Robert O.: *Nevada, Land of Discovery*, noted, 79/337
Beatty, John C., Jr., 74/365; 75/370; 79/413,416
Beatty, Patricia: *Indian Canoe-maker*, review, 62/101 *O the Red Rose Tree*, noted, 73/285
Beatty, Robert O., SEE Beatty, David
Beatys Butte, 77/149; 79/278N
Beaudin, J., 81/165
Beauregard, Pierre G.T., 72/330
Beautiful Oregon, by Atkeson and Lewis, noted, 77/300
"Beautiful Willamette," by Simpson,

cited, 74/150-51
Beaver, Herbert, 63/195-96,208-209,214-15,225; 71/344: church records, 63/216,235; comment on McLoughlin, 81/383; relations with McLoughlin, 63/196
Beaver, Jane (Mrs. Herbert), 62/105; 63/196
Beaver, Wash., 74/7
Beaver (Astor vessel), 71/310
Beaver (Columbia River steamer), 79/394
Beaver (HBCO. steamer), 62/202,299; 63/130,156,194-95,205,224,232,234; 64/199-200; 68/114
Beaver Creek, Crook Co., 65/75,83,107
Beaver Creek, Ida., SEE Deep (Beaver) Creek
Beaver Creek, Jackson Co., 72/41: map, 69/264
Beaver Homes, Ore., 74/358
Beaver money, SEE Money
Beaver River, Canada, 64/238
Beaver Slough, Coos Co., 63/17
Beavercreek, Ore.: Ten O'clock Church, 66/382
Beavers, 69/6; 72/183; 74/77,78, 293,311-13; 75/61-63; 76/324,327; 79/149,150,151; 81/322: dams, 63/17; hats, 69/182; Malade River poison, 63/358; Ogden expedition, 63/350-51; Oregon symbol, 69/86; pelts, 76/319; photo, 76/36; prehistoric, 68/354; skin values 1838, 74/78; trapping, 69/182; traps, 63/350; 68/345; 76/382
Beaverton, Ore., 63/253: diamond jubilee, 69/339; historical articles, 67/89,91
Beck, Dave, 66/74
Beck, Ella (Mrs. William), 64/276
Beck, George, 79/329
Beck, J.C., 74/271
Beck, Sally, 79/203
Beck, William, Aurora band member, 79/239
Beck, William, Cowlitz Co., 64/276
Beck, Ore.: name, 74/271
Becker, Alta (Mrs. Val), 67/239,245

Becker, Cassie, SEE Jones, Cassandra Becker

Becker, Charles, 63/270,284: biography, 67/213-55; children, 67/ 236,239-40,254; collections, 67/213N-14N; death, 67/246; legends, 67/246-51; letter 1900, 72/93; library, 67/ 255,256; marriages, 67/217; photos, 67/249,fr.cov. Sept.

Becker, Charles: "Government Expedition Against the Mormons," cited, 67/219,227N; quoted, 67/220,221,222,225-26 history of Pony Express, cited, 67/218, 228,241; quoted, 67/231-34*passim*

Becker, Charles Parker ("Pink"), 63/290; 67/236,239,240,254

Becker, Ethel Anderson: *Here Come the Polly*, review, 73/70 *Klondike '98*, review, 69/75-76

Becker, Eustace, 67/219

Becker, Ida, 67/249

Becker, James T. (Jim), 67/239,240,254

Becker, John, 68/342

Becker, Mona, 67/239,248: photo, 67/249

Becker, Myra Louise (Mrs. Charles), 63/ 284; 67/213N,217-18,240,255: death, 67/255; described, 67/254; photo, 67/249; quoted, 67/235-36, 244-45,247,250

Becker, Pearl, 62/205,414; 63/85; 64/ 91,357; 65/308,315; 66/83,277, 281,382

Becker, Ray, Centralia pioneer, 70/178; 73/71

Becker, Ray F., 62/421

Becker, Rebecca (Mrs. William), 67/219

Becker, Robert, 66/380

Becker, Val, 67/213N,239,240,245,247, 248,254

Becker, William, 67/219

Becker Ranch (Becker's Range), 67/ 237FF,374: photo, 67/249,251

Beckett, Paul L.: *From Wilderness to Enabling Act: The Evolution of a State of Washington*, noted, 70/77

Beckham, Patricia J., ed.: "Alva E. Stovall and Turn of the Century Education," 72/281-85

Beckham, Stephen Dow: "Asa Mead Simpson, Lumberman and Shipbuilder," 68/259-73 *The Indians of Western Oregon: This Land Was Theirs*, review, 79/334-35 "Lonely Outpost: The Army's Fort Umpqua," 70/233-57 *Requiem For a People: The Rogue Indians and the Frontiersmen*, review, 73/66-67 *The Simpsons of Shore Acres*, noted, 73/74-75 *Tall Tales from Rogue River: The Yarns of Hathaway Jones*, noted, 77/291; review, 75/360-61

Beckley, —, Vice-Admiral, 62/52

Beckwourth, James P., 66/64; 71/250,251

Bedell, A.B., 69/216N

Bedingfield, James, Jr., 69/342,348; 70/374

Bedrock Democrat, Baker, 64/139,175: cited, 67/150,151,157,158; prospectus, 64/179

Bedwell, Stephen F.: *Fort Rock Basin: Prehistory and Environment*, review, 76/89

Beebe, J.J., 64/37

Beebe, Lucius, 62/294

Beebe Company, Portland, 81/49

Beecher, Edward, 75/111

Beecher, Henry Ward, 72/178

Beecher, Lyman, 75/111,114,115

Beef, 68/235,236: Ft. Dalles contracts 1857-58, 68/23N; SEE ALSO Prices

Beehrer, George W., 64/85

Beek, John G., 81/387,389

Beekman, Benjamin B., photo, 74/234

Beekman, Cornelius C., 64/167

Beekman Bank, 62/299; 63/252; 64/137; 66/59; 69/176

Beekman family, 73/363-64

Beekman House, Jacksonville, 63/252,363

Beeman, Caroline McBee, 72/355

Beeman, Thomas, family, 72/355

Beers, Alanson, 62/142N; 66/352,357
Beers, Eliza Hall (Mrs. Robert), 65/234
Beers, Robert, 65/234
Bees, 69/19:
honey bees on frontier, 66/86
Beeson, Lewis, 77/90
Beeswax, 63/51; 67/92:
candles from Ore. Coast shipwreck, 80/60; Carbon 14 test, 63/91; making and use, 63/328-29
Beeswax ship, 74/354
Beet Sugar in the West: A History, 1891-1966, by Arrington, noted, 69/275
Beet sugar industry, 67/368,373; 69/275
Before the Covered Wagon, by Parrish, noted, 73/317
Begbie, Matthew Baillie, 71/367
Begg, Alexander, 72/182
Beggs (Biggs?), William J., Scottsburg printer, 64/139,148
The Beginning of the West, Annals of the Kansas Gateway, 1540-1854, by Barry, review, 74/86-87
The Beginnings of Russian-American Relations, 1775-1815, by Bolkhovitinov, review, 78/359-60
Behm, Magnus Carl von, 80/197-98,200,201,203:
Cook voyage collection, 80/197
Behrens, Dorothy, 79/261
Beinecke, Frederick W., 66/66
Bek, William G., 79/233N,260
Belch, Edward, 74/18
Belcher, E., family, Queets area settlers, 74/21
Belcher, Edward, 63/189,199-200:
Belcher cairn, 63/359
Belford (ship), 66/122
Belieu, James, 69/330
Belknap, George N., 63/361; 64/284:
"American Bibliographical Notes," noted, 78/91
"Authentic Account of the Murder of Dr. Whitman: The History of a Pamphlet," noted, 70/347
The Blue Ribbon University, review, 77/380
Henry Villard and the University of Oregon, review, 77/380

"McMurtrie's Oregon Imprints: A Fourth Supplement," 64/137-82
A Melodrame Entitled "Treason, Stratagems and Spoils," by W.L. Adams, ed. with intro., review, 70/354-55
Oregon Imprints, cited, 73/364; review, 70/62-63—
addenda, cited, 74/286
"Oregon Imprints Revisited," 78/251-79
The University of Oregon Charter, review, 77/380
Belknap, James, 63/12
Belknap, Jeremy, 67/200,205
Belknap, Rollin L., 63/12
Belknap Bridge, McKenzie River, 66/187
Belknap Crater, 66/384
Belknap settlement, 69/183
Belknap's Store, Benton Co., 78/42-43
Bell, J. Frank, Jr., 74/213
Bell, John Colgate:
biography, 80/345N
Bell, Laura, 80/350,355
Bell, O.F., 64/179
Bell, Sarah Ward (Mrs. John C.), 80/345N
Bell, Thomas Cowan, 62/172
Bella (steamer), 76/115
Bella Bella, B.C., 71/184-86
Bella Coola River, 76/315
Bellamy, Edward, 71/289:
Looking Backward, cited, 79/348,355
Bellamy, Ore.:
name, 71/289
Belle Passi, Ore., 66/283
Belleque, Genevieve, 66/348N
Belleque, Pierre, 66/348
Belleque, Pierre, son of Pierre, 66/348N
Belleque, Sophie, 66/348N
Bellinger, Charles B., 62/129; 65/279, 285N,291; 67/263,264,265,267
Bellingham, Wash., 74/5,203:
port history, 74/283; street railway, 80/332
Bellingham and Skagit Railway, 80/332
Bellingham Bay:
coal industry, 66/34N
Bellingham Bay Coal Co., San Francisco, 66/34N

Bellingham Bay Lumber Co., 77/215
Bellingham Securities Syndicate, 79/408
Bells:
Aurora Colony Church, 67/273-76—photo, 67/274,275
in early Oregon, 64/353; St. Helens M.E. Church, 68/187; use in Indian Shaker service, 67/349-54*passim*
Belluschi, Pietro, 64/361; 67/199
Belshaw, Charles, 78/215
Belshaw, George, 78/137
Belton, Howard C.:
memoirs cited, 79/336
Bend, Ore., 66/272; 69/293; 75/289,294; 77/21; 78/179; 79/408:
Clark story, 78/213-19; first auto, 72/94; first white child born, 67/88; lumber mill, 80/104; museum, 69/341; name, 78/219; photos, 77/20; 78/246; platted, 69/341; progress report, 65/218; sawmill, 72/94; street names, 62/201; Wiest home, 68/352; Wychick Ford, 69/87
Bend in Central Oregon, by Hatton, noted, 79/408
Bend Juniper Products Co., 77/89
Bend Woolen Mills, 75/294
Bendire, Charles Emil, 68/232N, 248N,297N,302N:
biography, 66/233-39; death, 66/237,239; Eastern Ore. bird studies, 66/233-39*passim*; fossils collected, 66/237; military service, 66/233; photo, 66/234
Bendire, Charles Emil:
Life Histories of North American Birds, cited, 66/237; page reproduced, 66/238; review, 66/239
"Notes on Some Birds Found in Southeastern Oregon," cited, 66/235N
Bendire Creek, 63/282:
name, 66/239
Bendire Mountain:
name, 66/239
Bendire Range, 78/152
Benedictine Fathers:
Gervais, 70/221-32; Minnesota branch in Ore., 70/312FF; Oregon work, 70/312-32*passim*; Swiss in Oregon, 70/

313FF
Benedictine Sisters, 70/312,322-23:
schools—
Gervais, 70/330,331; Grand Ronde Reservation, 70/312,320-21,327, 329,330,331; Umatilla Reservation, 70/326,330,331
Bengal (vessel), 77/52
Benham Falls, 67/7,10:
photo, 67/fr.cov. March
Benicia, Calif.:
military site, 66/82
Benicia (ship), 66/107
Benjamin, Judah Philip, 73/45
Benjamin, Richard M., 74/359
"Benjamin Stark, the U.S. Senate, and 1862 Membership Issues," by G. Thomas Edwards, 72/315-38; 73/31-59
Bennett, —, capt. of *Augusta*, 63/238
Bennett, Addison, 74/116
Bennett, Alexander, 68/350
Bennett, Charles, 64/275-76:
Ft. Bennett named for, 66/143N; Ore. Mounted Volunteer service, 66/143
Bennett, E., Auburn mines 1861, 62/219N
Bennett, Edward H., 74/212
Bennett, Florence, photo, 74/265
Bennett, James Gordon, 78/6
Bennett, Joseph W.:
Vandals Wild, noted, 70/358
Bennett, Joseph William, 63/34
Bennett, Lawrence E., 71/153
Bennett, Mary Law, 63/259
Bennett, Robert L., 63/246
Bennett, Tom, 71/269
Bennett, William H., 80/15
Benovskii, Mauritius Augustus, Count de, 80/200
Bensell, Royal Augustus, 65/189N
Benson, Amos S., 74/110,116,117,214; 78/357
Benson, Elmer, 76/142,151
Benson, Henry L., 66/363:
letter to West quoted, 66/373; supreme court election contest, 66/365-78*passim*; West accusation, 66/375-76
Benson, Ralph C., 70/50N
Benson, Robert L.:

Oregon Non-Parks, noted, 75/87

Benson, Simon, 63/352; 64/91; 66/ 181,249,251N,269; 78/357: biography, 66/251-52; 72/348; Columbia River Hwy. promotion, 66/ 263,265; 74/109,112,139,214; Multnomah Falls bridge, 66/265; park land donated, 74/138; rafts, SEE Logging industry—rafts; testimonial dinner photo, 66/250; Vista House dedication photo, 66/258

Benson-Evenson Co., San Diego, 66/181,182

Benson Hotel, Portland, 66/250,267,386

Benson Polytechnic High School, Portland, 72/348: army training school 1918, 64/248; emergency hospital, 64/249

Benson Timber Company, 66/181

Bent, A.S., 77/357

Benton, Thomas Hart, 67/371; 70/339, 363; 72/104; 81/185,187,187N,251

Benton County, Ore., 66/365; 77/91; 78/42-43,331: Chinese pheasants in, 65/255; courthouse, 70/184; education ca. 1900, 72/281-85; first military post, 65/173; history, 65/184N; 77/89; 120th anniversary, 69/88; pioneer life, 69/183; settlement, 77/318; settlers, 79/49; tour guide, 77/89

Benton County, Wash., 69/331

Benton County, A Brief History and Tour Guide, by Onstad, noted, 77/89

Benton County Historical Society: officers and directors, 69/80,277; 70/80,274; 71/192; 72/174; 73/76; 74/179; 75/88; 76/93; 77/92; 78/92; 79/108; 80/107; 81/107; publications, 77/89; SEE ALSO Benton County Pioneer-Historical Society

Benton County Pioneer-Historical Society: officers and directors, 62/414; 63/ 85,249; 64/82,278; 65/122,310; 66/ 83,277; 67/81,282; 68/83,281; SEE ALSO Benton County Historical Society

Benton-Lincoln Electric Cooperative,

80/323

Bent's Old Fort, 62/106; 78/365

Berchtold, Frederick, 72/284

Bercier, Marcel, SEE Bernier, Marcel

Berg, Jimmie, 65/308

Bergenhollow ("Patch Hog") School, 64/354

Berger, Henry W., 67/87

Berger, Joe, 66/281

Berger, William Perry, 72/65

Bergerson, Frank, 65/308

Bergerson, Virginia, 65/308

Bergevin, Rosa, photo, 81/254

Bering, Vitus, 71/365; 73/72; 79/212; 80/200

Bering Island, 77/188

Bering Sea, 72/84-85: 1892 settlement, 65/213

Bering Strait, 72/109; 73/103,137; 77/295-96; 80/201: maps, 77/296

Bering's Voyages: Whither and Why, by Fisher, review, 79/212

Berkeley, Calif., 72/159; 78/39,40

Berkhofer, Robert F., Jr., 64/281; 65/213; 78/337: *Salvation and the Savage*, review, 68/336-37

Berland, Edward: influence on Kutenai religious rites, 71/342,347

Berlin (bark), 63/362: photo, 74/196

Bermensolo, Antonio, photo, 76/166

Bermensolo, Petra, photo, 76/166

Bernard, Reuben F., 70/15,17,21,22,57: Bannock War activities, 68/231N, 232N,235,243N,298N,299,302N,306N; photo, 68/300

Bernard and Bartoni, Malheur Co. sheepmen, 63/268

Bernier, Marcel, 63/144N

Berries, 69/149,153,155-58; 76/ 234,239: pioneer varieties, 63/53; SEE ALSO names of varieties

Berry, Alfred Metcalf, 64/39

Berry, Don, 68/279: *Moontrap*, review, 65/406-11

To Build a Ship, review, 65/406-11
Trask, review, 62/192-96
Berry, Mrs. M.P., 80/362
Berryhill, Gene, 77/153:
photo, 77/148
Bersaglieri Columbia Society, 77/257
Bertha (German bark), 66/127
Berthol, Jennie, 74/346
Bertie M. Hanlon (steamer), 77/359-62
Berton, Pierre:
The Klondike Fever: The Life and Death of the Last Great Gold Rush, review, 62/95-96
Bertrand (steamer):
wreck, 71/364
Bessant, —, Cowlitz area settler, 63/162,169
Besser, Luzerne, 80/22,158,295:
biography, 80/22N
Bessey, E.L., 66/53
The Best of True West, ed. by Small, noted, 66/82
Bestor, Norman, 65/138
Bethany, Ore.:
history, 81/104
Bethel, Alaska:
native population, 72/246
Bethel, Mo., 67/276; 73/86; 79/233-38*passim*,256,257
Bethel, Ore.:
school, 79/361
Bethel Mission, Tacoma, 66/115
Bethesda Lutheran Church, 65/212
Betsy (vessel), 78/355-56; 79/339-40
Bettis, Stan:
Market Days, An Informal History of the Eugene Producers Public Market, review, 72/87
Beulah, Ore., 63/286
Beulah Land, by Davis, cited, 66/243,246,247
Bevan, Arthur Dean, 75/20,29
Bewley, Esther Lorinda, SEE Chapman, Esther Lorinda Bewley
Bewley, John, family, 80/207
Bewley, Lorinda, SEE Chapman, Esther Lorinda Bewley
Beyond the Capes: Pacific Exploration from Captain Cook to the Challenger (1776-

1877), by Dodge, review, 73/273-74
Bianco, Joe:
Seeing Portland, a Guide to Points of Interest, noted, 66/82
A Bibliographic Guide to the Archaeology of Oregon and Adjacent Regions, by Johnson and Cole, noted, 70/358
Bibliography:
agricultural history, 68/86,344; 70/84,272; 71/290; 73/86; 74/365; 81/335-36; agricultural literature, 79/106; Alaska, 68/347; 72/225-71; 73/86; 75/94; America in Pacific Basin, 67/280; American history, European sources, 69/83; American legal history, 68/344; American national character, 70/362; American studies, 67/84; 70/84,362; archeology, 69/276; 70/358; 79/404; Arizona, 67/84; atlases, 73/86; Bancroft, Hubert Howe, 75/80; bighorn sheep, 70/360; British Columbia history, 71/191
California, 68/349—
gold rush reminiscences, 71/360; history theses, 67/84,371-72; recent publications, 67/84
Canada history, 67/84; 75/94; China trade, 66/79; Columbia River Highway, 74/141-42; conservation in the West, 73/286; Cook voyages, 63/84; Derby, George H., 71/188; economic geography, 81/325; election 1928, 67/362-63; electric railways, 80/332; Eskimo art, 68/347; Eskimos, 69/327; 77/296; French archives, 72/182; fur trade, 65/79,384; 66/79; 79/99,338; 80/336; geography, 68/347; 73/86; 75/94; geology 1959-65, 67/33,366; Hafen, LeRoy W., 67/371; Hawaii, 69/83; historic preservation, 81/106; historiography, 69/83; history, 73/360; Idaho, 63/91
Indians, 71/388—
American, 62/198; art and culture, 81/375-76; education, 80/208; literature, 79/335-36; Oregon, 70/360; wars and tribes, 81/106
Josephine Co., 78/288; justice courts, 80/330; Klamath Basin anthropology,

69/333; Ku Klux Klan, 81/331; Lewis & Clark Exped., 74/280; 78/285; 80/206; logbooks of U.S. Navy, 81/333; McLoughlin, John, 80/101 manuscripts—

U. of Oregon library, 73/67-68; Wash. State Univ., 75/364

maps, 75/94—

North America 1600-1850, 69/79; Trans-Mississippi West 1540-1861, 66/183-84

military posts, 65/384; Modoc Co., 77/91; Montana, 63/91; 68/349; 72/90; Mormons in mountain West, 69/84; Murray's published works, 79/408; naval history, 72/356; 74/284

Negroes, 75/88—

Oregon, 73/197-211; Pacific NW, 73/197-211; Washington, 69/273

Nevada, 75/93; New Deal in Pacific NW, 71/290; newspapers in Wash., 75/364; Nez Perce Indians, 79/106; oral history, 81/335

Oregon—

geology, 67/33,366; imprints 1845-70, 70/62-63; 73/364; Indians, 70/62-63; mines, 69/333

Pacific Basin exploration 1783-1899, 63/247; Pacific islands, 69/83-84

Pacific Northwest, 62/109; 65/88; 67/368-69,372; 68/349—

biographies, 73/285; books and pamphlets 1968-69, 72/90; cultural history, 77/297; history, 73/67-68; Indian art, 81/208; Indian wars, 68/76; maritime history, 79/408; people and places in books, 81/332; theses, 72/225-79

Paiute War, 74/283; philosophy of history, 69/83; railroads, 70/351; 71/75-96; 80/208-209; Russian archives and manuscripts, 74/95; serials in Ore. libraries, 77/382; social science, 73/360; Spain in Pacific NW, 74/353; state histories, 72/179; technology, 70/84,363; Trans-Mississippi periodicals, 72/349; transportation, 71/75-96*passim*; Tryon Creek State Park, 79/104; U.S. Army in Indian wars,

81/106; U.S. strategy in Pacific, 62/56; utopias, 77/295; Victor, Frances Fuller, 71/291; Wagner, Henry R., 70/179

Washington, 68/186; 72/286—

archeology, 69/276; newspapers, 75/364

Western America—

history, 71/292; 72/179,349; 75/93; literature, 71/291; 73/286

Willamette Valley settlement, 80/309

Bibliography of Klamath Basin

Anthropology, by Swartz, noted, 69/333

A Bibliography of Modoc County and Environs, noted, 77/91

"A Bibliography of Theses and Dissertations Concerning the Pacific Northwest and Alaska: Supplement, 1958-1963," by Erik Bromberg, 65/362-91

"A Bibliography of Theses and Dissertations, Pacific Northwest and Alaska: Supplement, 1964-1970," by Erik Bromberg, 72/225-79

Bicycles:

chainless described, 72/339; police use, 72/339

Biddle, Benjamin R., 65/185N

Biddle, Henry J.:

Beacon Rock, reprint noted, 74/282

Biddle, Nicholas, 64/183; 78/284

Bidlack, Russell E.:

Letters Home: The Story of Ann Arbor's Forty-Niners, review, 62/296

Bidwell, Orlando, 79/178N,180,190

Bidwell Mountains, 72/53

Biedler, John X., 67/215N

Bier, Nick, 79/239

Bierce, Ambrose Gwinett, 62/294; 69/85

Bierstadt, Albert:

western journey dates, 71/292

Bieson, George A., 70/59

Biffel, James, 65/17,19

The Big Blow: The Story of the Pacific Northwest's Columbus Day Storm, by Lucia, noted, 64/186

Big Brother's Indian Programs, by Levitan, noted, 74/96

Big Camas Prairie, 68/239,242,309:

early man site, 64/282
"Big Country: Where Pete French was Shot," by Rankin Crow, 75/67-68
Big Creek, Ida., 68/245,246,313
Big Eddy, 72/151; 75/221,225,226,331
Big Eddy Park, 66/382
Big Marsh Creek, 77/331; 78/61,294; 79/29:
ford, 77/330; 78/295-97; photos, 78/292,296; settlers, 79/48; SEE ALSO West Fork, Deschutes River
Big Meadows:
Drake expedition 1864, 65/53-55
Big Pine Openings, 78/297,310,325
Big Prairie, 77/329
Big Roach (Indian), SEE Grand Queue
Big Saddle, Malheur Co., 63/279
Big Sandy River, Wyo., 62/355; 79/69,379; 80/78,79
Big Springs region, Siskiyou Co., 63/84
Big Timber, Big Men, by Lind, noted, 80/208
Big Tom Hop Wit (Indian), 70/157
Big White (Indian), 65/314
Big Willow Creek, 78/320
Big Wood River, 68/240,241,309
The Big Woods: Logging and Lumbering...in the Pacific Northwest, by Lucia, review, 77/86-87
Bigelow, Daniel R., 66/13
Bigelow, George, 72/92
Bigelow, John P., 65/168
Biggs, Hugh L., 74/240
Biggs, William G., & Co., Jacksonville, 64/139; SEE ALSO Beggs, William J.
Biggs, Ore., 64/90
Bighorn sheep, 69/7:
bibliography, 70/360
Bigler, Henry William, 64/275-76
Bigler, John, 72/12
Bigler's Chronicle of the West: The Conquest of California, by Gudde, review, 64/275-76
"The Bigot Disclosed: 90 Years of Nativism," by Malcolm H. Clark, jr., 75/109-90
Bilbao, Carmen, photo, 76/164
Bilderback, William, 79/411
Bill Hotel, Cannon Beach, 73/80
Billboard legislation, 74/119

Billiard saloons, SEE Saloons
Billiards, 80/17,20
Billings, —, Olympia sheriff, 63/187
Billings, —, Queets area settler, 74/19
Billings, Joseph:
Siberian expedition, 68/276
Billings, Warren K., 72/346-47
Billington, Ray Allen, 65/305; 67/280
Billington, Ray Allen, ed.:
The Frontier Thesis: Valid Interpretation of American History?, noted, 68/82
Billy Gray (vessel), 77/50,51
Bilyeu, Dianna (Mrs. William), 80/377
Bilyeu, Eloise, 80/365-73*passim*,384-85:
photos, 80/366,370
Bilyeu, Jane Reed (Mrs. Peter Lee), 80/377
Bilyeu, Josephine Schulmerick (Mrs. Thomas), 80/376,380,381-90*passim*:
photo, 80/381
Bilyeu, Malinda DeVaney (Mrs. Peter), 80/379-80
Bilyeu, Marion, 80/365-73*passim*,385-86:
photos, 80/366,370
Bilyeu, Peter, 80/377
Bilyeu, Peter Lee, 80/377
Bilyeu, Thomas, 80/377-78,380-82:
photo, 80/381
Bilyeu, William, 80/377
Binford, Peter, SEE Peter Binford Foundation
Bingham, Alfred, 76/139
Bingham, Cyrus James, 68/352
Bingham, Edwin R.:
The Blue Hen's Chick, by Guthrie, review, 69/74-75
"A Convert's Testimonial," 75/336-38
The Eastern Establishment and the Western Experience, by White, review, 70/263-64
The Great Command, by Jones, review, 62/192-96
Kettle of Fire, by Davis, review, 62/192-96
Moontrap, by Berry, review, 65/406-11
"Oregon's Romantic Rebels," cited, 70/5N
To Build a Ship, by Berry, review, 65/406-11

Trask, by Berry, review, 62/192-96

Bingham, Hiram, 62/11; 68/54, 59,60,61; 72/180

Bingham, John A., 66/280

Bingham, John E., witness to Lincoln assassination, 63/91

Bingham, Kate Stevens, 67/366

Bingham Springs, 73/285; 81/344

Binns, Archie, 68/279

Binswanger, Otto S., 75/20

Biogeography Field Guide to Cascade Mountains, by Price, noted, 72/173

Birch, Larry, 80/353

Birch Creek, Baker-Malheur cos., SEE Burch Creek

Birch Creek, Grant Co., 79/303

Birch Creek, near Walla Walla, 66/138

Birch Creek, Umatilla Co., 66/311

Bird, Annie Laurie, 64/282

Birds, 65/214; 75/61,65: Alaska, 73/149; Bendire studies in Ore., 66/233-39*passim*; discoveries by Lewis, 69/23; Fielner trip, 69/229; Malheur refuge, 69/63; method of preparing skin, 69/27; Pacific NW guidebook, 74/282; paintings, 74/358; Vollum collection, 69/237N; SEE ALSO Game birds; names of species

Birdseye, Charles G., 64/146

Birkeland, Torger: *Echoes of Puget Sound: Fifty Years of Logging and Steamboating*, review, 62/98-99

Birkenbeuel, E.B., 67/44

Birks, Grace McClay, 80/51N

Birmingham (vessel), 68/259,260

Birnie, Charlotte Beaulieu (Mrs. James), 63/179; 64/212,296

Birnie, James, 63/83,205,208; 64/201, 211,214,220-45*passim*,296,297; 73/255; 81/25N: death, 63/233; Ft. George house described, 64/222N-23N; HBCO. service, 64/201N-202N; sawmill, 64/201N

Birnie, Robert, 63/205,212; 64/219

Birnie, Rose, SEE Roberts, Rose Birnie

Birth control, 78/26

Bischoff, William Norbert: *Flathead and Kootenay*, by Johnson,

review, 71/279

Bischoff, William Norbert, ed.: *We Were Not Summer Soldiers: The Indian War Diary of Plympton J. Kelly*, review, 78/179-80

Bishop, Mrs. —, Tide Creek area, 72/199-208*passim*

Bishop, Ada, 72/202,203,207

Bishop, Agnes M. (Mrs. George), 66/168

Bishop, Benjamin, 63/42,52-53

Bishop, Bert, 72/202,207

Bishop, Charles: *The Journal and Letters of Captain Charles Bishop on the North-West Coast of America…, 1794-1799*, ed. by Roe, review, 69/67-68

Bishop, Clarence M., Jr., 69/342,348; 70/373; 73/362,373; 74/183,363, 365; 76/383,387; 77/383; 78/366, 370; 79/410,413,415; 80/401-11,414

Bishop, Clarence M., Sr., 62/110,206, 302,423; 63/94,256,373; 64/93,189, 285,363; 65/125,221,317,417; 66/93, 189,285,385,392,395; 67/380; 68/ 361; 69/343,347; 75/6; 77/193: death, 70/370,372; photo, 67/204

Bishop, Mrs. Clarence M., Sr., 62/421

Bishop, Frank, 66/168

Bishop, George Thomas, 66/161,162,167,168

Bishop, Mary Ann Alexander (Mrs. Zebulon), 66/161

Bishop, Maude, 72/202,207,208

Bishop, Mehitable (Hetty) Flint, 63/42,52

Bishop, Rose, 72/202,204,207

Bishop, Temperance, SEE Zook, Temperance Bishop

Bishop, Thomas J., 66/161,167

Bishop, Will, 72/202,205

Bishop, Zebulon C.: biography, 66/161-62; Calif. mines, 66/168-69; Formosa 1855, 66/167; letters 1850-56, 66/161-70; marriage, 66/161; Oregon Territory legislature, 66/161-62,164-65

Bismark Islands, 62/31,32

Bitte, Elizabeth, photo, 81/37

Bitte, Emily, 81/41,42
Bitte, Emma Osolin, 81/32,34,36,41: photo, 81/37
Bitte, Fred: biography and recollections, 81/31-42; drydock invention, 81/31,40 (sketch),41; photos, 81/30,37
Bitte, Georgianna, 81/42
Bitte, John, 81/37(photo),41
Bitterroot (*Lewisia rediviva*), 69/158,167
Bitterroot Valley, 81/331
Bjorkman, Gwen Boyer: *The Descendants of Peter Simmons*, noted, 74/283
The Descendants of Thomas Beekman of Kent, Connecticut, noted, 72/355
Blachly-Lane Co. Cooperative Electric Assn., 80/328
Black, A.H., 63/34
Black, James H., photo, 70/224
Black, Jeremiah Sullivan, 66/33,34N
Black, Samuel, 63/185,190: comment on Indian dress, 81/350
Black, William, capt. of *Raccoon*: biography, 69/59; takes possession of Astoria, 69/59
Black, William, Portland policeman, 80/149N
Black Bart, SEE Bolton, Charles E.
Black Butte, Malheur Co., 65/61
Black Butte, Siskiyou Co., 66/81
Black Elk (Indian), 63/247
Black Hills, Wyo., 62/346; 65/151: name, 66/231N
Black Horse Canyon, 69/124,125
"The Black Laws of Oregon," by Schneider, cited, 73/203-204
Black people, SEE Negroes
Black Rock Desert, 63/309; 64/92; 73/231,233; 76/357
Black Studies, Select Catalog of National Archives and Records Service Microfilm Publications, comp. by Hannestad and Weiher, noted, 75/88
Blackaby, Earl, 70/280
Blackaby, J.R., 70/280
Blackberries: first in Oregon, 68/163
Blackfeet Indians, 62/106; 69/63-65;

75/93; 79/136; 81/341,345,350: adoption of Kutenai Christian-pagan rites, 71/347-48; blacktail deer dance, 71/347-48; Canada, 63/59; folklore, 63/247; horses, 72/81-82; last battle with Kutenai, 71/343; sun dance, 63/73; white allies, 65/314
Blackfoot Lodge Tales, by Grinnell, noted, 63/247
Blacks, SEE Negroes
Blacks in the State of Oregon, 1788-1971, by Davis, cited, 73/211
Blacksmith shops and blacksmithing, 63/17,319; 66/384; 68/25,341; 72/91,92; 73/267; 76/335,352,358; 79/79,105,143,151,161,284; 81/58: Ft. Vancouver, 76/382N; fur trade, 69/182-83; Glencoe, 76/381; Harris anvil, 69/57-59; Heppner, 69/117, 144; horseshoes, 79/283; Klamath Falls, 69/328; McClelland shop, Montague, Calif., 66/81; ornamental ironwork, 76/259-68; overland trail, 72/341,370; 79/375,379; process described, 72/92
Blackwater River, 76/315
Blaine, Catharine V. (Mrs. David E.), 66/82
Blaine, David Edwards: letters and papers, 66/82
Blaine, Wash., 66/101N: 1915 celebration, 74/215
Blair, Abraham, 66/218,226
Blair, Annie, 80/357,359-60,361; 81/75
Blair, Charles: biography, 66/218-32; Klamath mines, 66/218,225-26; letters 1854-62, 66/219-32; Rogue River War, 66/219N, 220-25; Umatilla Co., 66/226-32
Blair, Elenor (Mrs. Prior F.), 81/75N
Blair, Elias, 66/218
Blair, Elizabeth, 66/218
Blair, Harry C., 62/420; 63/368: *The Journals of William Fraser Tolmie, Physician and Fur Trader*, review, 65/207-208
Blair, Joseph, 66/218
Blair, Prior (Prier) F., 67/179; 81/75N
Blair, Rebecca, 66/218

Blair's Bluff, **78**/53,60,61
Blake, W. Earl, **64**/335-36
Blake, W.P., Portland policeman, **80**/149
Blakely, James, **79**/30N
Blakely Hill, **78**/321
Blaker, A.M., **74**/211
Blalock, Nelson G., **81**/269N
Blalock, Ore., **81**/269N,271-78*passim*
Blalock Wheat Growing Co., **81**/269N
Blanc, Mel, **74**/231
Blanchard, Dean, **65**/309; **74**/85
Blanchard, J.A., **80**/295,295N
Blanchard, Richard, **72**/88
Blanchet, Augustine M.A., **75**/115: diary published, **80**/405-406
Blanchet, Francis Norbert, **63**/55-60, 124-25,128,209,214,216; **64**/78; **70**/ 312,314; **71**/344; **74**/89-90; **75**/109- 11,112; **80**/341,350,361,406; **81**/78, 79,87,203: arrival at French Prairie, **66**/344,348; Chinook jargon dictionary editions, **64**/138,157-58,179-80; letter to Bishop of Quebec, **69**/267-71; Ore. Provisional Govt., **66**/350
Blanchet family, **79**/413
Blanco (ship), **68**/266
Bland, Mary Cora, **80**/118,123
Bland, T.A., **80**/118,123
Blanding, Martin, **78**/234,303,304, 305,310,324; **79**/43: photo, **78**/305
Blanket Bill Jarman, by Jeffcott, review, **62**/97-98
Blankets, SEE Prices
Blas, Caroline, SEE Wittenberg, Caroline Blas
Blaschke, Edward, **73**/138,144: plan of New Archangel, **73**/fr.cov. June
Blasdel, S.W., **69**/208
Blaser, Hans, **72**/153
Blessing, Joe, **69**/117
Blethen, Alden J., **72**/263
Bligh, William: Avacha Bay plan, **80**/ins.fr.cov. Summer
Blind Slough, **63**/351; **72**/301; **73**/5N,213
Blitz Weinhard Co., Portland, **64**/267

Blitzen River, SEE Donner und Blitzen River
Blitzen Valley, **69**/63
Blockhouses: Cascades, **62**/314; **67**/321; **68**/41— photo, **62**/316 Deschutes Landing, **68**/41; Empire, Ore., **63**/21; Ft. Simcoe, **68**/41; Klickitat, **67**/322N; **68**/41; Siletz Indian Reservation, **65**/183,191
Blodgett family, Pacific lumber interests, **72**/300
Blomkvist, E.E., **73**/101N: "A Russian Scientific Expedition to California and Alaska, 1839-1849," **73**/100-70
Blonde (British warship), **64**/15,20,26
Blood poisoning, **79**/390,391
Bloom, John Porter, ed.: *The American Territorial System*, noted, **75**/365
Bloom, Will, **71**/269,273: photo, **71**/268
Bloom, Mrs. Will, **71**/268
Blossom, James M., **64**/151
Blow for the Landing: A Hundred Years of Steam Navigation on the Waters of the West, by Timmen, review, **75**/82
Blue, Frederick J.: *The Free Soilers: Third Party Politics, 1848-54*, noted, **74**/284
Blue Bucket Mine, **62**/213-14,216- 17,221; **63**/366; **68**/80; **69**/329; **77**/327; **79**/22,25,27,30,31,42,49
Blue Canyon, **62**/212,223N,224,225, 228,235-36
Blue Canyon Creek, **62**/226
Blue Hen's Chick: A Life in Context, by Guthrie, review, **69**/74-75
Blue Lake, Jefferson Co., photo, **74**/51
"Blue Mountain Eldorados: Auburn, 1861," by Verne Bright, **62**/213-36
Blue Mountain Talewinds, by Weatherford, noted, **79**/339
Blue Mountains, **62**/220,395,397; **63**/10,334; **65**/10,20,24,45,52,68-69; **66**/148,227,235; **67**/243,252; **68**/227N,233,297,302,303,307; **70**/22; **77**/314,333; **78**/102,155,220;

79/32,39,42,391,392; 80/96,98: area reminiscences, 79/339; geological report, 67/21N; gold rush, 62/216-27; wagon routes, 65/95

Blue Mountains National Forest, 63/267

The Blue Ribbon University, by Belknap, review, 77/380

Blue River, Oregon Trail, 62/265; 79/371,372; 80/67

"Blue ruin," 63/191; 64/237-38N: manufacture, 64/237N

Blue Slaughter Spring, 73/260

Blueprint for Modern America: Non-Military Legislation of the First Civil War Congress, by Curry, review, 70/69-71

Blumauer, Mrs. Louis, 75/146

Blumhiter, G., 63/147

Blyze, Cassie, 81/77

Boals, Robert T.: biography, 71/118-19; photo, 71/116

Boarding houses: Cereghino's, Portland, photo, 77/239; Madariaga's, Jordan Valley, photo, 76/166; SEE ALSO Prices

Boardman, Samuel H., 67/44,51,184, 185; 74/130

Boardman, William H., 76/223

Boardman, Ore., 63/365; 64/90

Boardman and Pope Co., 76/208,222

Boatner, Mark M., 65/177N

Boas, Franz, 64/348; 71/339

Boats: building— Columbia River, 81/37-38; Carter Lake, 81/48-49 butterfly boat photo, 75/fr.cov. June Crater Lake, 81/43-56— engines, 81/48,49 fishing skiffs, 78/201— photo, 78/196; sketch, 78/202 gasoline powered, 78/365; junks, 76/226; Klamath Co., 66/382; Klamath Lake landings, 75/362; landing craft photo, 80/36; pilot boat photo, 80/33; sailboats, 76/109-11; SEE ALSO Canoes; Kayaks

Bob Frazier of Oregon, arranged by Duncan, review, 81/321

Bobbie (Silverton collie), 74/54-55

Bobcats: discovered in Ore., 69/23

Bockstoce, John, *et al*: *Steam Whaling in the Western Arctic*, noted, 79/106

Bodega, Calif., 63/205

Bodega Bay, 73/105,115,161

Bodega y Quadra, Juan Francisco de la, 71/197; 74/353; 79/397

Bodie, Calif., 63/79

Bodisco, Alexander, 75/325,326

Bodisco, Waldemar, 75/333,334

Bodmer, Karl, 71/366

Boe, A.L., 70/54

Boegli, William, 66/282

Boelling, Conrad, 70/184

Boer War: effect on U.S. expansionism, 72/212,222,223,224

Bogachiel River, 74/9

Bogart, Garrett, 79/10

Boggs, Lilburn W., 65/406

Bogue, Robert, 62/299

Bogus, Henry, 77/317

Bohan, John, 69/117

Bohan, Pat, 69/117

Bohemia mining district, SEE Gold and gold mining

Bohemian Colonization Club, 72/353

Bohemian John, Linn Co. prospector, 63/92

Boie, Bill, 69/305

Boise, Breyman, 66/5N-12N*passim*

Boise, Mrs. Breyman, 66/5N-12N*passim*

Boise, Elizabeth T., 80/353N

Boise, Ellen F. Lyon, first wife of Reuben P., 66/5N,8-11,19: Ellendale named for, 66/13

Boise, Ellen S., 66/20

Boise, Emily A. Pratt, second wife of Reuben P., 66/20

Boise, Fisher A., 66/19

Boise, Marie (Mae), SEE Latterman, Marie

Boise, Patrick, uncle of Reuben P., Sr., 66/6,7

Boise, Reuben Patrick, father of Reuben P., Sr., 66/6

Boise, Reuben Patrick, son of Reuben P.,

Sr., 66/19
Boise, Reuben Patrick, Sr., 64/316,322N; 75/345,352,359; 80/353: arrival in Oregon, 66/7; biography, 66/6-8,9-10; characterized, 66/5,23; death, 66/24; Ellendale woolen mill, 66/21; Indian commissioner, 66/22; LaCreole Academy, 66/23; land claim, 66/13,16; legislature, 66/14-15; Monmouth Univ., 66/15,23; Oregon Academy, 66/12,23; Oregon Grange, 66/21,22,24; Ore. judicial career, 66/5-24*passim*; Pacific Univ., 66/23; prosecuting attorney, 66/12,14,15; Salem Clique, 66/8; school named for, 66/24; Willamette Univ., 66/23; Williams eulogy, 66/24
Boise, Sallie Putnam, 66/6
Boise, Whitney L., 66/19
Boise, Ida., 63/31; 67/236-37; 68/227N,229; 70/13,15,181; 72/73,183: centennial, 64/282; music 1863-90, 72/270; sketch 1885, 70/14; theater history, 65/382; U.S. assay office, 69/276; SEE ALSO Fort Boise
Boise Basin, 62/216,300
Boise Bridge Company, 68/242N
Boise River, 62/385N; 79/389; 80/95,96: reservoirs, 71/196
Boise School, Portland: name, 66/24
Boisvert, Charles, 74/358
Boit, John, 62/88: *Columbia Rediviva* log quoted, 68/103,105; SEE ALSO Boyd, John
Boki, governor of Oahu, 64/9-10,14-16,18: photo, 64/28
Boki, Madame, SEE Liliha
Bokki, Korean picture bride, 79/60-61
Bolan, A.J., SEE Bolon, Andrew Jackson
Bold Eagle (Indian), SEE Tipyahlahnah Kapskaps
Bolduc, Francois, 63/132-33,150
Bolduc, Jean Baptiste Z., 69/270
Bolin, Major C. (alias David Butler), 68/82

Bolkhovitinov, Nikolai N.: *Doktrina Monro*, cited, 72/102N "Russia and the Declaration of the Non-colonization Principle: New Archival Evidence," trans. by Dmytryshyn, 72/101-26
Bolon, Andrew Jackson, 62/77; 67/313; 80/14
Bolsheretsk, Russia: Cook expedition visit 1779, 80/197-204
Bolton, Charles E. (Black Bart), 72/88-89
Bolton, Herbert Eugene, 70/85,366; 75/93
Bolt's Corner (Rogue Valley store), 80/233
Bomford (Bumford, Brumford), George C., 65/15N; 66/134N,142; 67/303: map of Ft. Dalles military reservation, 67/frontis Dec.
Bonanza, Ore.: history, 75/87
Bond, Allen, 78/124; 79/339: photo, 78/126
Bond, Hettie McClure (Mrs. Isaac William), 78/124,151
Bond, Isaac William, 78/124
Bond, Rachel Robinson (Mrs. Allen), 78/124
Bond, Rowland: *Early Birds in the Northwest*, noted, 74/359 *The Original Northwester, David Thompson, and the Native Tribes of North America*, noted, 74/282
Bond family (Allen and Isaac), SEE McClure-Bond overland party 1853
Bone, Arthur H., ed.: "Walter Pierce Memoirs," 78/101-20
The Bone Hunters, by Lanham, review, 75/78-79
Bonebrake, John Starr: family, 77/285,285N
Bonebrake, P.O., 77/285N
Bones, John W., 64/356
Bones in the Wilderness, by Pratt, noted, 73/285
Bong-Nim, Korean picture bride, 77/61-62
Bonham, Benjamin F., 66/20,21

Bonham, M.N., **64**/91
Bonnell, A.C., **75**/120; **80**/13: photo, **80**/16
Bonner Co., Ida.: place names, **72**/263
Bonneville, Benjamin L.E., **63**/343-44; **64**/86; **65**/177N; **67**/300; **69**/224N; **70**/214; **74**/91; **76**/382; **81**/322: observes Indian Christian rites, **71**/333; Rocky Mountains exped., **71**/310
Bonneville, Ore., **74**/341
Bonneville County, Ida.: history, **66**/121
Bonneville Dam, **73**/213; **74**/131: site photo, **75**/278
Bonneville Power Administration, **70**/181
Bonneville State Park, **74**/130-31,143
Bonneville's Folly (fur trade post), **63**/344
Bonney (Bonny), G.H., **70**/18N
Bonney View Ranch, Prineville, **63**/37
Bonnycastle, John C., **65**/184N; **79**/33
Bonus Expeditionary Force, **65**/295N: Oregon veterans in, **64**/281
Books: progressive movement, **68**/202,204, 206; St. Louis 1808-42, **63**/358; scarcity in early Oregon, **63**/17,23,35; that won West, **68**/348; SEE ALSO Schools—books
Boon, Thomas C.B., **69**/337
Boorstin, Daniel J.: interpretation of American history, **72**/178
Boosterism, **79**/345,348-49: defined, **79**/349; motives, **79**/357
Booth, Amanda Viola, SEE Keyes, Amanda Viola Booth
Booth, Henry, **64**/104N
Booth, Nora Harriet, **63**/253
Booth, Percy T.: *Valley of the Rogues,* noted, **72**/353
Booth, Robert, son of Robert A., **64**/104N
Booth, Robert A., **64**/104N
Booth, William, Salvation Army general, **81**/121
Boothby, —, Wasco Co. 1881, **81**/265,266

Bootlegging, SEE Prohibition
Boots, **77**/303-304; SEE ALSO Prices
Boots and Shoes of the Frontier Soldier, 1865-1893, by Brinckerhoff, noted, **77**/303-304
Bopart, Carl, **63**/301-302
Bopart, Elsie (Mrs. Carl), **63**/301-302
Borah, William Edward, **64**/282; **67**/87; **68**/136,346: biography, **62**/409-10
Borah, by McKenna, review, **62**/409-10
Borax, **68**/187: Alvord Valley, **73**/228,231-42,244; Calif., **73**/228,230,240,241,243-44; Colemanite, **73**/230,240,243; Curry Co., **73**/228-31; Nevada, **73**/231; photos, **73**/234,238,240; price, **73**/242, 243; Priceite, **73**/228-31; processing, **73**/233-35; prospecting, **73**/244; production, **73**/237,241,243; transportation, **73**/237,241-42; Ulexite, **73**/ 233N,243; uses, **73**/229
Bordeaux, James, **67**/370
Bordwell, Constance, **62**/298: *March of the Volunteers: Soldiering with Lewis and Clark,* review, **62**/88-89
Borglum, Gutzon, **63**/364; **70**/178
Born, John F., family, **69**/117
Born To Be a Soldier: The Military Career of William Wing Loring, by Wessels, review, **73**/71
Borneo, **62**/29,33,36
Bornet, Vaughn D.: *Labor Politics in a Democratic Republic...Presidential Election of 1928,* review, **67**/361-63
Borrowe, William: biography, **79**/132N; enlists Warm Springs scouts, **79**/132,137-38, 150N,318,329,330; records, **79**/318-28
Boscana, Fray: *Historical Account...of the Indians of Alta-California,* ed. by Nunis, review, **71**/285
Boston, Ore., **80**/106
Boston (cruiser), **74**/84
Boston Athenaeum, **66**/388; **67**/197,211
Boston Board of Trade, **68**/53

Boston House Hotel, Moscow, Ida., 71/23

"Boston men," 72/108,140,141

Boston traders:

China trade, 76/217; hide and tallow trade, 76/201; role in history, 76/199-202; whaling, 76/201-202

Bostonian (schooner), 70/261

Boswell Springs, Ore., 67/80

Bosworth, R. Josephine, 67/80

Botanists, 80/207:

Oregon, 62/107; 66/233N; Pacific Northwest, 68/111-12,123

Botany:

early texts, 69/168-69; Lewis & Clark Exped., 69/148-70; pressing specimens, 69/159; terms, 69/152

Bothwell, James, 80/158,159,159N

Bottler, George, 64/267

Bottles:

early Jacksonville, 65/218

Boundaries:

Alaska, 75/85,93; California, 76/216-17; Canada, 75/85; Ft. Vancouver, 76/382; Oregon Territory, 75/317; state disputes, 72/9-18*passim*,52N; U.S.-Canada, 62/8,9,119; 66/69-71; U.S.-Mexico, 72/5-6; 76/123-24; U.S., Northwest, 76/212-13,214,215; U.S.-Spain, 72/5; Washington-Idaho, 73/349; SEE ALSO Oregon Question; Surveys and surveying

Boundary Town, by Jones, review, 62/96-97

Bounds, Doris S., 81/341N

Bourke, John Gregory, 75/93

Bourne, Edward Gaylord, 62/310,332,333-34; 70/204

Bourne, Fred L., 71/232

Bourne, G.M., 78/10

Bourne, George, 75/111,112

Bourne, J.B.E., 68/353; 74/293

Bourne, Jonathan, Jr., 78/111,112; 80/205:

biography, 69/204-205; opposes Mitchell, 68/210-13; photos, 68/212; 69/196; stock exchange activities, 69/197,204-22

Bourne, Ore., 62/300; 63/80

Boutwell, Mrs. Burr, 66/388

Bow River:

1800 map cited, 66/280

Bowe, Chuck, 70/53

Bowen, —, Owyhee area guide, 68/237

Bowen, John, 65/301N:

1865 map of Central Oregon, 65/insert March; 79/164,286-87

Bowen, William A.:

Mapping an American Frontier; Oregon in 1850, noted, 77/196

The Willamette Valley: Migration and Settlement on the Oregon Frontier, review, 80/329

Bowerman, Jay, 74/208

Bowers, Henry Francis, 75/131,133,134-35

Bowlby, Henry L., 74/108,135,137,139

Bowles, Samuel:

Our New West, reprint noted, 74/359

Bowling alleys, 79/193,194,195

Bowman, Amos, 62/62; 64/293N

Bowman, Andrew W., 68/38

Bowman, Earl Wayland:

biography, 72/355

Bowman, Henry, 66/311

Bowman, Walter Scott:

biography, 66/311; postal cards, photos, 66/310

Bowmer, Angus L.:

biography, 62/180-82,183; 76/381

Bowmer, Angus L.:

As I Remember, Adam: An Autobiography of a Festival, noted, 76/381

Bowmer, Gertrude Butler (Mrs. Angus L.), 62/183

Bowmer, Lois, 62/180

Bowsfield, Hartwell, ed.:

The Letters of Charles John Brydges, 1879-1882, review, 81/323-24

Boxer Rebellion, 62/14; 72/353; 80/174,191,192-93

Boxing:

commissioners, 77/77; Langford-Wills fight, Panama, 77/127

Boy Life on the Prairie, by Garland, reprint noted, 63/247

Boy Scouts of America:

Garibaldi, Ore., 77/358; Portland

troops photo, 78/100; trace 1853 wagon route, 78/299
Boyakin, William F., 64/134
Boyd, A.J., 79/273-74N
Boyd, Charles, 80/104
Boyd, Hamilton, 80/160
Boyd (Boit?), John, 70/362
Boyd, William, Bend settler 1904, 80/104
Boyer, P.M., 75/45
Boyer, William Herr, 71/219; 74/205
"A Boyhood with Sheep in the Oregon Desert," by Willard (Bill) Leonard, 76/333-58; 77/5-35,149-73
Boyle, James Whitten: daughters, 80/348
Boyle, William Henry, 63/81; 70/22,23,37: biographic sources, 70/22N; Modoc War comments, 70/22N
Boylen, E.N.: *Episode of the West: The Pendleton Roundup, 1910-1951*, noted, 77/90
Boys' and Girls' Aid Society, 80/53-54,61
Bozeman Trial, 71/187
Brackenridge, Henry Marie, 62/289
Brackett, A.H., 81/123
Brackett, G.A., 81/126
Brackett Wagon Road, 81/126,134,139,141
Bradbury, E.A., 80/12
Bradbury, John, 69/16
Braden, L.A., 63/37
Bradford, Daniel F., 69/198
Bradford, T.J., 79/283N
Bradley, Claudia, *et al*, comps.: *List of Logbooks of U.S. Navy Ships, Stations, and Miscellaneous Units, 1801-1947*, noted, 81/333
Bradley, Lewis Rice, 75/93
Brady, Dan, 63/293
Brady, John G., 71/292
Brady, Robert, 75/277-79
Brady families, Morrow Co., 69/117
Bragin, Dmitri: North Pacific voyage, 72/182
Brainard, E.C., 62/224,225
Brainard, Mary Ann, 81/77: photo, 80/363

Brainard, Max S., 64/355
Brainerd, Erastus, 62/106
Branch, E. Douglas: *The Hunting of the Buffalo*, reprint noted, 63/248
Brandeis, Louis Dembitz, 62/94
Brandenburg, George, 75/178
Brandis, John S., 67/376,380; 68/361; 69/343
Brands and branding, 73/74; SEE ALSO Cattle
Brandt, Patricia, and Nancy Guilford: *Oregon Biography Index*, review, 77/297
Branigar, Thomas, 75/363: "The Murder of Cyrenius C. Hooker," 75/345-59
Brannon, A.B., 80/145N,157N,289, 296N,319N: biography, 80/290-91
Branson, B.B., 81/328
Branson, Jay, 63/294
Brant, Sam, 64/121
Brase, Fred, 74/19
Brasfield, James W., 71/19
Bratley, Louis, 81/58: biography, 81/59-60
Brattain, Alfred, 78/325N
Brattain, John (Jonathan?), 78/329
Brattain, Paul, 64/150; 79/11
Bratton, Oscar B., 75/290-91
Bratton, William, 69/156
Brawner, Frank, 74/242
Bray, Charles E., 74/349
Bray, William A., 78/363
Brayman, Mason, 70/14N·15N; 72/183
The Brazen Overlanders of 1845, by Wojcik, review, 78/281
Bread and Roses Too: Studies of the Wobblies, by Conlin, review, 71/358-59
Breaking New Ground, by Pinchot, reprint noted, 74/95
Breakwater (steamer), 66/52; 77/75
Breck, John M., 72/330; 80/137
Breckenridge, John Cabell, 75/121
Breen, John, Crescent City area 1912, 76/53
Breen, Johnny, Morrow Co., 69/117
Breitenstein, Dick: recollections, 66/81

Bremerton, Wash., 80/49
Brenham (tug), 68/266
Brennan, Joseph P., 69/117-19; 80/105
Brennan, Tommy, 69/117
Brent, Thomas L., 62/375N,376,382,384
Brentano, Ron, 62/417:
Sage Brush and Axle Grease, by Hanley and Stanford, review, 80/103-104
Brescher, E.C., 81/167
Breslin, Ed, 69/119
Bretherton, B.J., 74/8
Bretherton, Charles E.:
breaks with Villard, 71/51,63; comments on rate policies, 71/78N; letters, 71/93
Bretherton, Vivien R., 74/54
Brewed in America, by Baron, noted, 63/248
Brewer, Elvira, 78/131
Brewer, Henry Bridgman, 78/347
Brewer, Oliver, 78/131
Brewer, T.M., 66/235N
Brewer, William, immigrant of 1853, 78/131
Brewer vs. Hutchins, 62/148-49
Breweries:
early Pacific NW, 64/267; photos, Portland, 64/269; U.S. history, 63/248
Brewster, William L., 71/232:
Hunt case, 71/226-28; Library Assn. of Portland board, 71/226
Breyman, Miss —, Portland 1860: recital, 64/153
Bribery, 67/272
Brick making, 75/294:
first at The Dalles, 63/365
Bricks, SEE Prices
Bridal Veil, Ore., 63/351
Bridal Veil Falls, 79/203
Bridge, Ore., 72/161,164
Bridge Creek, Wheeler Co., 65/45,71, 92; 73/258-72*passim*; 79/125,169,169N
Bridge of the Gods, 70/278; 75/88; 81/333
The Bridge of the Gods, by Balch, cited, 74/37
Bridge of the Gods, Mountains of Fire, A Return to the Columbia Gorge, by Williams, noted, 81/333

Bridger, James, 62/362N; 66/74; 67/227; 70/364; 71/250,251:
biography, 63/88
Bridges, Grace, photo, 72/208
Bridges, Harry, 76/146-47
Bridges, Rolstyn D.:
obituary, 74/92
Bridges, Ruth, SEE Davis, Ruth Bridges
Bridges:
Astoria, 75/294; Aurora, 79/234; Boise River toll, 68/242N; Butler Creek, 79/178,179; Cannon Beach, 77/283,284(photo); Clear Creek, 73/8,9
Columbia River, 77/87—
interstate, 74/210-12,215-16, 225,226(photo),243; lack of in 1900, 73/334; mouth of, 62/252; 67/372
Columbia River Highway, 74/125,126—
photos, 74/138,142
construction, 73/6,7-9
covered, 78/365—
California, 64/355; Douglas Co., 66/383; Eagle Mills, 64/355; Hoskins, 64/89; Lane Co., 66/187,383; 78/363; Mohawk River railroad, 66/187; Oregon, 65/217; 68/350; 69/87; 78/365; Shimanek, 67/369; Wiley Creek, 66/282; Wimer, 81/106
Cow Creek, photo, 71/253; Crescent Creek, 79/294N
Deschutes River, 77/315; 79/161N,168—
1860s, 65/115; Col. Besson, 78/294N; toll, 65/115N
Gilliam Co., 81/263; Indian, 79/76; John Day River, 79/171; Jordan Creek, 73/284; Kilchis River, 73/6,9; Lane Co., 78/288; Longview, 74/293,296 (photo); McKenzie River, 66/187; Malheur River, 70/280; Middle Fork, Smith River, 76/57; Mill Creek, 62/200; Mosby Creek, 66/187; North American, 78/362-63; North Platte River, 79/77; oldest military west of Mississippi, 64/86; Oregon City, 72/91; Oregon City-West Linn, 74/241; Oregon Coast, 78/363

Oregon Trail, 62/259,341,346,366, 373; 79/76,77,79— number, 79/77N; tolls, 62/259, 341,366,367,373 Owyhee River, photo, 76/158; photography, 78/362-63; pontoons, 73/213 Portland— Burnside, 75/180; Fremont, 78/363; Morrison, photos, 75/30; 79/352; Ross Island, 75/180; St. Johns, 73/80; 77/300 Powder River toll, 68/228N; railroad, 66/187; Rogue River, photo, 76/84; Sacramento River 1885, 80/236; Salem, 64/356; Sam Downes Creek, 73/9; Santiam River, 67/90; Seaside, 77/282,283,284; Siuslaw River, 74/271; Snake River, photo, 71/fr.cov. March; Thomas Creek, 79/290; Tillamook Co., 73/6,8,9,14 toll bridges, 79/76-77,367,375— Boise River, 68/242N; Deschutes River, 65/115N; Oregon Trail, 62/259,341,366,367,373; Powder River, 68/228N trestles, 73/13; 74/296(photo); Tygh, 79/161,168; Umpqua River, 73/72; Walla Walla River, 72/93; West Side Creek, 68/257 Willamette River, 66/90,187— 1885, 80/231; first, 64/356 SEE ALSO Gallon House Bridge; Hayden Bridge; Knight Bridge; Rouse Bridge; Sherar's Bridge Bridles, SEE Prices *The Brieflet*, Portland, 74/205 Briggs, E.D., 64/326,328,332-35 Briggs, Elias M., 77/321,321N; 78/329 Briggs, Elmore E.W., 63/82 Briggs, Isaac, 78/234,235; 79/43N Briggs, J., 78/44 Bright, Jesse David, 72/334,337; 73/35,46: expulsion from senate, 73/31,37,57,58 Bright, Verne, 66/59; 71/361; 74/65,157; 78/73: biography, 74/58-59; diary collection, 73/363; photos, 73/296; 74/265 Bright, Verne:

"Blue Mountain Eldorados: Auburn, 1861," 62/213-36 *Mountain Man*, cited, 74/59 *Pemmican*, by Fisher, review, 62/99-100 *Tale of Valor*, by Fisher, review, 62/99-100 *Western Ghost Towns*, by Florin, review, 63/79-80 Brighton, Ore., 71/130,131; 72/296: photo, 72/298 Brimlow, George Francis, 63/309N; 78/238: *Harney County, Oregon, and Its Range Land*, cited, 67/141 "Two Cavalrymen's Diaries of the Bannock War, 1878," 68/221-58,293-316 Brinckerhoff, Sidney B.: *Boots and Shoes of the Frontier Soldier, 1865-1893*, noted, 77/303-304 *Metal Uniform Insignia of the Frontier U.S. Army, 1846-1902*, noted, 74/283 Brinsmade, Peter A., 68/59 Briody, Thomas, 69/119 Brissenden, Paul, 66/186 Bristol Bay, 77/185 Bristow, Abel, 78/325N Bristow, Elijah, 77/324,328; 78/43,65,71,72,325; 79/10,43N Bristow, Elijah Lafayette, 62/199 Bristow, William Wilshire, 67/197; 78/71,72,147,224,304,306- 307,325N,331; 79/5 Bristow family, Lane Co., 77/69 Bristow's Store, Lane Co., 78/43 British Association for American Studies, 72/178 British Columbia, 62/245; 70/367; 72/88: Anglican Church, 71/367; bibliography, 63/91; 64/86; 72/90; botanical collections, 68/113,114,115,118, 119; Canadian Pacific tunnels, 68/185; Caribou country, 72/168; clothing industry, 65/381; confederation, 77/ 294; depression, 72/232; description and travel, 72/168; Doukhobors, 72/ 254; early historians, 64/86; early settlement, 72/255; economic development, 65/367; 70/179;

education, 65/ 381; first capital, 64/86; government, 72/286; governors, 71/191,281-82; history, 63/362; 71/191,281-82; 73/ 74; 79/337-38,408; Hudson's Bay Co. in, 71/281-82; Indian basketry, 66/88; Indian policy, 77/303; Indians, 67/ 280; 71/333; irrigation, 69/336; Kootenai District, 63/89-90; labor and social reform 1885-1917, 81/333-34; Liberal Party, 65/364; logging, 72/ 287; maritime trade, 72/255-56; mineral industry, 70/366; mining, 65/363, 367; off-shore oil drilling, 70/179; population 1951-61, 72/257; prehistory, 69/337; proposal to join U.S. 1866-70, 63/362; settlement, 77/303; sheep, 65/215; smelt runs, 68/87; Spanish place names, 66/80; steam transportation, 74/358; trapping industry, 72/236; universities, 68/87; urban studies, 72/261-62; Welsh gold miners, 64/86; women pioneers, 79/337-38

British Columbia Dragoons, 72/232

British Columbia Electric Railway Co., 72/232

British Columbia Heritage Series, 62/184

British people:

Alberta, Canada, immigration, 69/337; Oregon population 1860-1910, 80/266,267

Britt, Peter, 66/304,381; 69/86: biography, 78/361 photos by, 80/234,ins.fr.cov. Fall— Ft. Klamath photo, 68/316 photography, 78/361-62

Britton (Brittain?), Daniel, 64/145

Britton and Rey, San Francisco, 66/304

Brix, Mrs. Peter, 78/369

Broadbent, Charles, 63/35

Broadbent, Ore., 63/34

Broadbent Creamery, 63/35

Broadbent School, Myrtle Point, 63/253

Broadwater, C.A., 67/215

Brock, B.F., 63/352

Brock, George, 63/148N

Brock, Jessie, 70/272

Brock, Mahlon, 63/148N; 64/265

Brock, P.W., 70/293N

Brock, Ruth, 63/148N

Brock, Walter Stuart, 67/179

Brockway, Beman B., 73/72

Brockway, Dock, 63/26

Brodie, Edward E., 76/301

Brody, Linda S., and Nancy A. Olsen: *Cedar Mill History*, noted, 80/105-106

Brogan, J.C., 75/309

Brogan, Phil F., 62/198,298-99; 63/254,364,371; 64/87,356-57,359; 65/220,315; 66/91,92,282,284; 67/88; 68/91,351-52,354; 69/347; 70/183,370,372; 75/312(photo); 78/369; 79/412:

"Ashwood, Oregon," 72/241-42

East of the Cascades, review, 66/183

The Great Columbia Plain, by Meinig, review, 70/64

"Oregon Geology: The Century Old Story," 67/5-39

Oregonian column, 67/90,370,374

"The Painted Hills and the Carroll Family," 73/258-68

"Pioneer Trails Dim in Range Country," 75/309-15

The Sandal and the Cave: The Indians of Oregon, by Cressman, review, 64/73

Tough Men, Tough Country, by Lucia, review, 65/209

Broken Hand: The Life of Thomas Fitzpatrick..., by Hafen, new ed. noted, 76/182

Broken Top (mountain), 63/364: photo, 78/246

Bromberg, Erik:

"Bibliography of Theses and Dissertations Concerning the Pacific Northwest and Alaska: Supplement, 1958-1963," 65/362-91

"Bibliography of Theses and Dissertations, Pacific Northwest and Alaska: Supplement, 1964-1970," 72/225-79

Bronaugh, Earl C., Jr., 68/331: photo, 74/234

Bronson, Edgar Beecher: *Reminiscences of a Ranchman*, reprint noted, 63/247

Bronson, George H., photo, 77/264

Brooke, Alan, **62**/5
Brooke (Brooks), Lloyd, **62**/400N; **65**/15N; **66**/134N,142; **67**/303N; **79**/141,141N
Brooke, Bomford and Co., **65**/15N; **67**/303N
Brookfield, Wash., **75**/106
Brookhouse, John, **79**/141N
Brookhouse, Richard, **79**/141N
Brookhouse, Samuel, **79**/141N
Brookhouse area, Wasco Co., **79**/141
Brookings, Ore.: described 1964, **65**/315; early history, **64**/355
Brookings Commercial Co., **68**/349
Brooks, Abraham: Brooks Indian robe described, **81**/345,346(photo)
Brooks, Alfred H., **69**/184
Brooks, Caleb, **63**/365
Brooks, Charles, immigrant of 1853, **78**/129,148
Brooks, Charles, Massachusetts educator, **64**/43
Brooks, Howard C., and Len Ramp: *Gold and Silver in Oregon*, noted, **69**/333
Brooks, James Eugene, ed.: *The Oregon Almanac and Book of Facts, 1961-1962*, review, **62**/296
Brooks, Lloyd, SEE Brooke, Lloyd
Brooks, Richard E., **72**/128
Brooks, Samuel, family, **72**/94
Brooks, Van Wyck, **62**/292,293
Brooks, William (Indian): education, **64**/45,52-53; Lee Mission, **64**/44; Methodist exploitation of, **64**/ 50,53; name, **64**/43,52; obituary, **64**/50
Brooks-Scanlon Lumber Co., **66**/362N; **72**/94
Broomhead, Thomas, **66**/113
Brophy, William A., and Sophie D. Aberle, comps.: *The Indian, America's Unfinished Business*, review, **68**/177-78
Broshears, Joseph S., **63**/108N
Brosnan, Cornelius James, **64**/41N,46N,50

Brosnan, Jeremiah, **69**/103: family, **69**/119; photo, **69**/118
Brosnan, Mary Gaf(f)ney, **69**/119: photo, **69**/118
Brother Jonathan (steamship), **62**/311; **66**/17; **79**/152N; **80**/141: gold lost in wreck, **67**/372; hulk discovered, **73**/81
Brothers, Ore., **79**/337
Brothers of Guernsey (bark), **63**/186,227
Brougher, John C., **62**/107-108; **64**/87
Broughton, William Robert, **63**/205; **74**/278; **75**/88; **79**/397
Broughton (HBCO. sloop), **63**/205
Brouhard, R.A., **66**/60
Brouillet, Jean Baptiste Abraham, **63**/164N,207; **70**/321,322,324; **74**/355; **75**/115,118; **80**/405-406: journal 1848, **72**/286
Brouillet, Jean Baptiste Abraham: *An Authentic Account of the Murder of Dr. Whitman*, cited, **75**/118
Protestantism in Oregon..., quoted, **70**/347
Brounstein, Edward, **76**/387
Brown, Alexander, Portland city attorney, **66**/283
Brown, Bill, SEE Brown, William Walter
Brown, Billie, LaGrande drover, **66**/203
Brown, Chandler P., **62**/110,111,206, 207,302,303,420,421,422; **63**/93,255, 372-73; **64**/93,189,285,358,360-63; **65**/125,221,317,412,414-15,417; **66**/ 94,190,286,385,388,395; **67**/376, 377,379; **68**/359,360; **69**/342,348; **70**/374; **73**/362
Brown, Charles, Auburn miner, **62**/219N
Brown, Charles, Lebanon pioneer, **66**/284
Brown, Clarence, **71**/351,357
Brown, Elias, **69**/86
Brown, F., Auburn miner, **62**/224
Brown, Frank, Jacksonville 1859, **64**/149
Brown, Fred G.: recollections, **69**/329
Brown, George, **68**/62-63
Brown, George H., family, **71**/189
Brown, Gordon, **79**/413-14
Brown, J. Henry:

Political History of Oregon, cited, 66/350N

Brown, James, Jackson Co. 1859, 69/225N

Brown, James ("One-armed"), 80/141; 81/279

Brown, John, Lane Co. pioneer, 79/339

Brown, John A., sea captain: biography, 73/80

Brown, John A.:

"A Businessman's Search: Pacific Northwest, 1881," 71/5-25

The Indians of Western Oregon, by Beckham, review, 79/334-35

Nine Years With the Spokane Indians, by Drury, review, 79/101-102

Brown, John A., and Robert H. Ruby:

The Cayuse Indians, Imperial Tribesmen of Old Oregon, review, 73/277-78

The Chinook Indians, Traders of the Lower Columbia River, review, 79/98-100

Ferryboats on the Columbia River, Including Bridges and Dams, review, 77/86

The Spokane Indians, Children of the Sun, review, 73/69

Brown, Joseph B., 68/6,39

Brown, Martha, 68/187

Brown, Moss K., ed.:

"To Be a Soldier: 1917 Diary," by Martin Luther Kimmel, 75/245-69

Brown, "One-armed," SEE Brown, James

Brown, Richard, professor, 80/414

Brown, S.W., 68/165

Brown, Sagebrush, SEE Long, Charlie

Brown, Samuel H., 70/184

Brown, Silas, 79/11

Brown, Tabitha Moffett, 64/349

Brown, Thomas J., 72/341

Brown, Wilfred H.: letter about sheep, 77/189

Brown, Wilfred H.:

This Was a Man: About the Life and Times of Jesse Applegate..., noted, 72/353

Brown, William C., Polk Co. pioneer, 70/278; 75/363

Brown, William Carey, 68/297, 303N,310N:

Bannock War diary, 68/226-58; biography, 68/221-25; maps cited, 68/223, 244N,311N; papers, 68/221N,225, 301N; photo, 68/222

Brown, William Compton:

The Indian Side of the Story, cited, 70/151N; noted, 63/84

Brown, William Walter (Bill), 67/88; 69/63; 77/12-18: ranch, 77/23

Brown-Shasta Ranch, Siskiyou Co., 66/81

Browne, Carl, 65/271

Browne, J. Ross, 63/79; 64/149; 66/280

Brownell, George Clayton, 68/217; 74/208

Brownell, Jean Bauer:

The American Story Recorded in Glass, by Marsh, review, 63/353-54

A Guide to the Manuscript Collections of the Bancroft Library, Vol. I, ed. by Morgan and Hammond, review, 65/198-99

"Negroes in Oregon Before the Civil War," cited, 73/203

Browning, Harold, 66/91

Browning, Orville H., 73/41

Brownlee, William Craig, 75/111

Brown's Island, SEE Rabbit Island

Brown's Point Light, 66/181

Brownsville, Ore., 64/178; 81/105: history, 66/383; 77/299; Indian mounds, 66/90; Moyer House, 64/88; Presbyterian Church, 66/82; restoration plans, 64/354; Southern Pacific station, 66/91; woolen mills, 62/164, 167,174; 67/65-66

Brownsville Woolen Manufacturing Co., 67/65-66

Brownsville Woolen Mills Co., 67/65

Bruce, Augusta, 74/30

Bruce, James, HBCO. employee, 63/199-200

Bruceport, Wash., 68/340; 72/354: census, 72/89

Brumfield, Kirby:

This Was Wheat Farming, review, 70/72-73

Brumford, George C., SEE Bomford, George C.

Brumley, Joseph L., 78/124,125, 325N,327
Brumley, Margaret Patterson, 78/125
Bruner, Edward M., 63/347
Brunquist, Mrs. Albert J., 67/89
Brunton family, immigration of 1852, 79/365,375,390
Brush, —, capt. of *Poseidon*, 66/113
Brushy Hollow Creek, 63/277
Bruun, C.D., 71/232,233
Bryan, Alan Lyle, 62/203; 64/282: *An Archeological Survey of Northern Puget Sound*, noted, 64/277
Bryan, Enoch A.: *Orient Meets Occident*, cited, 71/75,81
Bryan, William, 71/224
Bryan, William Jennings, 62/190-92; 66/46; 72/213-14,220,223,286; 75/138; 78/171; 80/391
Bryant, Cliff, 71/12
Bryant, Cornelius, 63/359
Bryant, E.S., Columbia Co.: family, 66/382
Bryant, Janet: "The Ku Klux Klan," cited, 75/172
Bryant, John, Boston trader, 72/116N; 76/207
Bryant, John, Columbia Co. pioneer, 65/308
Bryant, Louise Mohon, SEE Reed, Louise Bryant
Bryant, William P., 62/63; 64/293
Bryant and Sturgis, Boston, 76/201,204: investment in Pacific NW trade, 72/115,116; sea otter trade, 72/207
Bryarly, Wakeman: journal, 63/356
Brydges, Charles John, 81/323
Bryer, H., 70/59
"Bubble Skinner," by Giles French and J.F. Morrell, 69/293-305
Bucareli y Ursua, Antonio Maria, 63/88
Buchanan, G. Davidson, 75/144-47
Buchanan, James, 62/185; 66/5,16,32, 33,34; 68/64,66; 69/43; 72/319, 326N; 75/320-21,325-27; 81/187: appraisal of, 63/346-47; spoils system and Utah exped., 64/281
Buchanan, Robert Christie, 65/173N-74N

Bucher, Fred A., family, 72/196-208*passim*
Buchtel, Joseph, 66/304,381
Buchtel and Stolte: photo by, 80/155
Buck, Ben, 64/256-57
Buck, C.J., 76/268
Buck, O.D., 80/300N,319N
Buck, Percy Bradley, 66/121
Buck, Solon J.: *The Granger Movement*, reprint noted, 64/187
Buck Creek, Crook Co., 65/51; 78/240,320; 79/41,296
Buckeye (net tender), 80/39,41: photo, 80/36
Buckeye Bell Foundry, 67/274-75
Buckingham, Elizabeth, family, 78/154
Buckley, Jim, 62/81
Buckley, Wash., 73/338
Buckman, W.P., 62/219N
"Buckskin Bill," Portland 1867, 80/159N
Buckthorn, Robert F., 65/295N
Bucoda, Wash., 74/33
Buddhist Church of Oregon, 81/167
Buddhist churches, 76/233,251
Buehler, Elizabeth Wilson: *The Brazen Overlanders*, by Wojcik, review, 78/281
Ferryboats on the Columbia River, by Ruby and Brown, review, 77/86
Buena Vista, Ore.: map 1882, 72/171
Buena Vista bar, Ida., 63/30
Buena Vista Dam, Calif., 63/311
Buena Vista Ferry, Willamette River, 63/364
Buena Vista Improvement Club, 65/211
Buffalo berries (*Shepherdia argentea*), photo, 69/166
"Buffalo Bill and 101 Ranch Shows," 67/246
Buffalo Bill's Wild West Show, 81/343
Buffalo Horn (Indian), 64/274; 70/22
Buffaloes, 62/338,348; 63/248,360; 65/313; 69/6,12,13-14,16, 18,64,83,158; 74/86; 75/94; 81/29: disappearance, 70/107; hide hunters, 70/364; methods of cooking, 68/77;

Pennsylvania, 70/363; photo, 79/381; sketches, 80/74,fr.cov. Spring; 81/28; western range limits, 69/83

Buggies, photo, 76/84

Building supplies, 79/193: scarcity in mining towns, 79/173,182,188-96*passim*; SEE ALSO Prices

Building the Skagit, by Pitzer, noted, 79/337

Building trades: Italians in, 77/247,254

Bulfinch, Charles, 67/201; 76/210,223

Bulkley, Charles S., 65/216

Bull, —, Grays Harbor 1881, 74/15

Bull, Alpheus, 71/283

Bull Creek, Deschutes Co., 79/145N

Bull Mountain, Lane Co., 78/320

Bull Run Forest Reserve, 76/29

Bullock, George E., 67/270

Bullock, Helen Duprey, 63/371

Bully, Malheur Co., SEE Westfall, Ore.

Bully Creek, 63/264,266,270,282-83,284; 67/252: irrigation dam, 63/272-74; name change proposed, 63/282

Bully Valley, 63/264

Bumble Bee Seafoods Co.: Elmore cannery, 68/70

Bumblebee Packing Co., 73/363

Bumford, George C., SEE Bomford, George C.

Bunby (Burby), Jonathan, SEE Burbee, Jonathan

Bunch, Jennie, 80/59-60

Bunchgrass, 63/265; 67/135; 69/105,107; 80/89

The Bunchgrassers: A History of Lexington, Morrow Co., Oregon, by McMillan, review, 75/360

Bungi dialect, 70/367

Bunker Hill and Sullivan Mine, 66/86; 69/208,213: purchase price, 69/220N

Bunyan, Paul, SEE Myths and legends

Buoy, F., 79/10

Buoy, John, 79/10

Buoy, Laban, 79/21

Burbank, Arthur R.:

diary and journal, 65/212,309; 66/80

Burbank, Luther, 68/173

Burbee, Jonathan, 63/233,245: family, 63/239-40

Burch, Benjamin Franklin, 77/317

Burch, Pauline, 73/201,202

Burch, Samuel Townshend: descendants, 73/202

Burch (Birch) Creek, Baker-Malheur cos., 63/10

Bureau of Catholic Indian Missions, 70/321

Bureau of Municipal Research and Service, University of Oregon: *Selected Characteristics of Oregon Population*, noted, 64/92

Burgess, Thomas, 63/268

Burgess and Kelsay, Malheur Co. sheepmen, 63/268

Burk, C. William (Bill), 73/283: *The Applegate Trail*, by Helfrich, review, 72/351-52

Burk, D.C., 74/18

Burke, Jack, 69/119

Burke, Morris, 72/25,25N

Burke, Robert E., 66/380; 71/189: editor, U. of Wash. *Americana Series*, 73/282

Burke, Thomas, Portland policeman, 80/289,319N: biography, 80/291; photo, 80/286

Burke, Thomas, Seattle judge, 62/405-406

Burke, William P., 80/288,301: biography, 80/290

Burke Canyon: Idaho mine war, 73/86

Burkhart, Calvin P., 67/62

Burkhart, John, Albany pioneer: family, 69/339

Burkhart, John Conner, 62/197

Burley, Wash., 77/295

Burlingame, Anson, 62/10

Burlingame, Henry S., 80/334

Burlington Northern, Inc.: Spokane, Portland and Seattle records given to OHS, 72/358— guide to papers, 74/79-82

Burlington Northern Railroad, 71/197

Burma Shave verses, 67/84
Burnap, James, 67/58
Burnett, —, immigration of 1856, 62/396
Burnett, C. Howard, 80/414: *Rails to the Mid-Columbia Wheatland*, by Due and French, review, 81/101-102
Burnett, C.S., 74/17
Burnett, Peter Hardeman, 62/63,139N, 140,146-48,149,150,297; 67/371; 69/336; 75/116; 78/133-35; 81/16N: quoted, 62/125-26,131-32,238; 81/5
Burnett, Peter Hardeman: *Recollections and Opinions of an Old Pioneer*, reprint reviewed, 71/285
Burnett, Peter R., 64/282
Burney, James, 77/303: *A Chronological History of North-Eastern Voyages of Discovery*, review, 72/84-85
Burnham, Smith, SEE Barnum, Smith
Burns, B.J., 64/148
Burns, E.B., 69/88
Burns, E.V., 74/238
Burns, Hugh, 62/151N; 68/351
Burns, Patrick, 74/358
Burns, Robert, U.S. Lighthouse Service, 69/313N
Burns, Robert Ignatius, S.J.: *The Jesuits and the Indian Wars of the Far Northwest*, review, 68/75-76
Salvation and the Savage, by Berkhofer, review, 68/336-37
Burns, Thomas E., photo, 74/265
Burns, William H., 71/357
Burns, Ore., 63/263,274,286,295,304, 334-39,368; 66/203; 72/93: electric co-op, 80/328; "father" of, 64/356; land office, 64/356
Burnt Creek, Ida., 62/392
Burnt Ranch, Ore., 63/264; 73/260; 79/125,170N-71N: map, 81/282; post office, 81/314; sites, 81/314
Burnt River, 62/215,216,219,395; 63/263,265; 66/198; 68/235N, 298,307N; 72/94; 77/337; 80/97,98
Burnt Wagon Camp, 78/299
Burpee, Isaac, 73/363
Burpee, Lawrence J., 64/283

Burr, George S., 75/163
Burr, William, 65/143
Burrell, O.K., 62/107; 63/361; 64/352: *Gold in the Woodpile, An Informal History of Banking in Oregon*, review, 70/177
Burrell, Walter F., 62/170,177
Burres, John L.: biography, 68/175N; memoirs, 68/175
Burris, Oliver, 68/342
Burris, William, 63/225
Burros, 76/83,102N,348: photo, 76/fr.cov. March
Burroughs, —, Queets area settler, 74/18
Burroughs, John M., SEE Burrows, John M.
Burroughs, Raymond Darwin, ed.: *The Natural History of the Lewis and Clark Expedition*, review, 63/69-70
Burrows, Jack: reminiscences, 72/183
Burrows (Burroughs), John M., 66/137
Burton, Leigh (Lay), 81/270,273,277
Burton, Robert E., 72/352N: *Democrats of Oregon: The Pattern of Minority Politics, 1900-1956*, review, 72/80-81
Burton, William J., 77/73
Burton family, Wasco Co. 1881, 81/266-75*passim*
Burtt, George L., 76/244-45
Bush, Asahel, 64/123,148,150-51; 66/6; 67/264; 68/333; 71/150; 72/321,322,327N; 73/56; 80/358; 81/92: biography, 66/7N; exchange with Ada Weed, 78/7,13-21; photo, 73/42; public printer Ore. Terr., 72/387; Stark opponent, 73/53
Bush, Asahel Nesmith (Nes), 65/219
Bush, Charles J. (Charley), 63/283
Bush, Daniel Webster, 65/120; 68/342; 72/354
Bush, George, Negro pioneer, 64/357; 65/313: bibliography, 73/200; land claim, 73/199

Bush, William Owen, 73/200: photo, 73/198
Bush House, Salem, 69/174
Bushby, Arthur Thomas: journal 1858-59, 64/86
Bushnell, David Ives, Jr., 64/51-53N; 69/37,40-41,42
Bushnell, Elizabeth Adkins (Mrs. James A.), 78/130
Bushnell, James Addison, 78/130
Bushnell, John Corydon, 78/130,247,250N
Bushnell, Ursula, 78/130: photo, 78/326
Business, SEE Trade and commerce
Business administration: Pacific NW theses list, 72/236-39
"A Businessman's Search: Pacific Northwest, 1881," ed. by John A. Brown, 71/5-25
Buskey, Mrs. Frank, photo, 81/254
Buster, Samuel C., 62/219N
Butler, B. Robert, 63/89
Butler, David, SEE Bolin, Major C.
Butler, James, Ontario, Ore. 1918, 67/239
Butler, John, Seward servant, 72/129
Butler, Ovid, 64/59
Butler, Sarah, 75/363
Butler, Thomas, 78/124
Butsch, Mathias, 70/316
Butte, Mont.: labor strike, 72/229; mining history, 65/381; newspapers, 72/264; theater history, 65/382
Butte County, Calif., 66/168-69: post offices, 71/200
Butte Creek, Siskiyou Co., 69/229N
Butte Disappointment, 77/328,329; 78/53-65*passim*,304,313,321,325; 79/29: photo, 78/323; sketch, 78/322
Butte Miners' Union, 65/366,367
Butte Valley, Siskiyou Co., 69/229,230N
Butter: packed to Boise 1889, 67/236-37; SEE ALSO Prices
Butter Creek, 62/401; 63/10,365; 64/ 90; 66/144; 69/103FF;

79/178,200-201
Butterfield Overland Mail Company: mail route, 70/86; stage, 72/168
Butteville, Ore., 63/235N; 65/212
Button, —, mate on *Thos. H. Perkins*, 63/218
Buwalda, John P., 67/26
Byard, Lyman E., 63/146
Byars, Rex, 73/335,342,345
Byars, Will, son of William Henry, 73/335,342,345
Byars, William Henry, 69/338; 73/332,335,345,347,348: biography, 73/332N; photo, 73/350
Bybee-Howell House, 63/252,368-71; 64/353; 66/393; 69/174,346; 70/368,369,372; 71/294
Byers, Charles, 74/21
Byland (Bylan), M.D., 66/154
Byllesby, H.M., 71/351
Byng, Frederick Gerald, 64/9-10,20, 25-26,30
Byot, Monsignor, SEE Jayol, J.F.
Byrne, Elizabeth (Mrs. John), 81/76
Byrne, John, Morrow Co. settler, 69/119
Byrne, L., 80/359,361: biography, 80/349N
Byrne, Mary, SEE Farley, Mary Byrne
Byron, Anson, 64/15,27,29
Byways of the Northwest, by Reynolds, noted, 77/301

C.A. Smith Lumber and Manufacturing Co., 77/75: photo, 77/76
C.C.C., SEE U.S. Civilian Conservation Corps
C.C.C. *Boys Remember*, by Howell, noted, 78/91
C.C. *Funk* (bark): wreck, 66/107,113
The CMR Book, by Willard, noted, 72/172
Cabaniss, T.T., 66/76
Cabbage Hill, 78/103
Cabbages, 74/317: Cowlitz Farm, 63/50,125,137,145,151, 159,161-62; French Prairie, 66/339
Cabell, Mrs. Henry F., 67/47; 73/363
Cabell, Mrs. Henry F., and Mrs. Ben-

jamin M. Reed:
The Portland Garden Club; the First 50 Years, 1924-74, noted, 76/92
"Cabin on the Cowlitz," by Wallace, reprint noted, 80/207
Cable, Martha, SEE Roberts, Martha Cable
Cable railways, SEE Railroads
Cabrillo, Juan Rodriguez, 62/193
Cabul (British ship), 66/123,127N,130: Tacoma-Cape Horn diary excerpts, 66/123,125-26
Cache Valley, Utah, 66/280
Cadboro (schooner), 63/165,168,227, 236; 64/200,213-14,222-41*passim*
Cady, Albemarle, 65/183N,185N
Cady, Thomas, 77/323,323N; 78/44, 52,60-69*passim*,329,330; 79/6,8,9, 11,22:
land claim, 79/21-22
Cail, Robert Edgar:
Land, Law and Man: The Disposal of Crown Lands in British Columbia, 1871-1913, noted, 77/303
Cain, Jim, 69/119
Cain, Josh, 70/272
Cairnsmore (bark):
wreck, 64/72
Calapooia (schooner), 64/221-22,224
Calapooia River (Creek), Linn Co., 63/51N; 67/61:
Indian mounds, 66/90; 80/106
Calapooya, Joseph (Indian), 66/356N, 360N
Calapooya, Pierre (Indian), 66/360N
Calapooya Creek, Douglas Co., 73/72: Rochester grist mill, 66/187
Calapooya (Calapooia) Indians, SEE Kalapuyan Indians
Calapooya mounds, 66/90; 80/106
Calapooya Mountains, 69/232
Calboro, Jean, 66/358N
Calbreath, Evelene, 65/415
Calder, M.D., 64/310N
Calderwood, Stella McDade, 73/233N,360:
photo, 73/242
Caldwell, Catharine (Mrs. Joseph), 66/29

Caldwell, Joseph, 66/29
Caldwell, Margaret, SEE McFadden, Margaret Caldwell
Caldwell, Richard S., 66/61:
First Ore. Cavalry service, 65/63N,75, 88-89,91-109*passim*
Caldwell, Ida., 68/88
Caldwell Brotherhood of Bachelors, 68/88
Calequarter (cedar bark petticoat), 63/193
Calhoun, John Caldwell, 75/319
California, 62/6,8,9,10,66,67,75,118N, 164; 63/202,210,235; 64/283; 69/ 336; 70/33,360,365; 71/365; 72/112: agriculture, 69/332; 75/365; books read by pioneers, 67/84; boundaries, 76/216-17
boundary surveys—
Calif.-Nev. control point, 72/52; disputes, 72/9-14,52N; eastern boundary, 72/12-13,14-17,49-53; Houghton-Ives terminal point photo, 72/16; Nev.-Ore.-Calif. corner, 72/4(photo),9,49,50(photo),51,52-53; Ore.-Calif. boundary, 72/10-53
British—
claim to, 63/202,235-36; consulate established, 68/348; views, 70/298-99
Civil War, 63/88; Civil War governors, 67/84; climate as cure for TB, 80/229; company towns, 67/357; constitution, 71/365; division question, 68/87; Drake name, 73/162; election 1928, 69/85; emigrants, 62/347,348,357; first newspaper, 67/86; fruit industry, 68/162,164; fruit prices, 68/163; fur seals, 70/365; geological survey, 69/273; 70/73,366; 72/180
gold rush, 62/213,214,296—
bibliography of reminiscences, 71/360; camps, 77/197; date of gold discovery, 68/349; journal, 67/370; Siskiyou Co. mining camps, 68/81; world impact of, 65/213
guidebooks, 68/348,349; harbor entry signals, 71/365; hide merchants, 70/179
history, 71/285—

articles on, **68**/328-29; Northern Calif., **81**/328-29; oral interviews, **81**/335; publications, **81**/105,328, 329; references, **74**/93,286; research, **66**/87,280; theses, **67**/371-72 Hudson's Bay Co. in, **74**/353; immigrants, **67**/85; **68**/185 immigration— 1870s, **71**/28; articles of agreement 1849, **65**/213 Indians, **71**/365; **72**/183; irrigation, **70**/365; Japanese in, **70**/178; land development, **70**/179; land office 1858-98, **66**/87; life in, **71**/285,359- 60; lumbering, **64**/283; **75**/365; map 1840, **73**/104; Mexicans in, **71**/285; mining, **72**/182; missionaries, **67**/84; missions, **71**/285,365; Modoc Co. historic geography, **67**/365; moving panorama scenes 1850, **65**/146,160- 62,169; name, **63**/358 Negroes— "black laws," **68**/348; rights activities 1849, **67**/367 oil in 1860s, **69**/273; orange groves, **80**/249,250; Pacific Squadron conquest, **67**/372; pioneer women, **62**/ 202; place names, **70**/178; politics, **70**/178,179; population 1860-1900, **71**/60; ports in diplomatic negotiations, **67**/372; Progressive movement, **68**/86; **70**/84; railroad regulations, **70**/85; ranchos, **69**/332; reapportionment 1965, **72**/181; roads to Oregon, **72**/33 Russia— interest in, **71**/367; settlements, **73**/104-108,114-15,161-64; **77**/186- 87; trade, **77**/175; Voznesenskii expedition, **73**/105-15 salmon canning, **70**/364 settlement, **71**/46— early Americans, **67**/280; first American, **76**/219-20; Russian, **73**/104- 108,114-15,161-64; **77**/186-87; Spanish, **73**/111-12; **76**/199 Seward predictions, **72**/133; shipping, **71**/365; sketches 1840-42, **73**/105-14; Southern Calif. health, **71**/364

Spain— exploration, **74**/353; settlement, **70**/364; **73**/111-12; **76**/199 statehood, **72**/7; **74**/355; trade and commerce, **71**/285,365; travel 1885, **80**/235-55 United States— acquisition, **68**/349; **75**/327N, 328,334; interests in, **76**/199,216-17 utopian colonies, **68**/86; wine industry, **69**/332; woolen mills, **62**/175-76,178 *California* (bar pilot schooner), **77**/45 *California* (steamer), **64**/275 California and Oregon Coast Railroad, **65**/121 California and Oregon Lumber Co., **68**/349; **69**/88 California and Oregon Railroad Co., **71**/283 California and Oregon stage road, **72**/41: map, **72**/ins.fr.cov. March California Geological Survey, **69**/273; **70**/73,366 *California Gold Camps*, by Gudde, noted, **77**/197 California Gulch, **62**/228 *California Heritage: A History of Northern California Lumbering*, by Hutchinson, noted, **75**/365 *California Lumber Merchant*, **77**/217 California-Northeastern Railroad, **80**/104 California-Oregon stage road, SEE California and Oregon stage road California Pacific Eastern Extension Railroad, **71**/51 *California Ranchos and Farms, 1846-1862*, ed. by Gates, noted, **69**/332 California Trail, **77**/318; **79**/105 California Volunteers, **65**/325,392,398; **66**/280: Columbia River service, **65**/350-51; Ft. Hoskins service, **65**/183,185 *California's Utopian Colonies*, by Hine, noted, **68**/82 Calkins, L.V., photo, **80**/324 Calkins, Zena, **62**/218N *Call Bulletin*, San Francisco, **74**/31 Callaghan, Charles W., **71**/351

Callahan Store and Bar, Siskiyou Co., **66**/81
Callender (steamer), **69**/323
Callicum (Indian): portrait, **71**/ins.fr.cov. Dec.
Callison, Rebecca, **63**/83
Callison, William, **63**/83
Calloway, Bragg, **75**/159
Calpo, Madame (Indian), **64**/215
Camanche (monitor), **67**/371
Camas, **63**/18,156; **69**/149,155; **70**/37,87; **76**/339; **81**/399
Camas, Wash., **68**/341; **77**/299
Camas Prairie, Ida., **71**/6
Camas (Drews) Prairie, Lake Co., **79**/290,291,303
Camas Prairie, Umatilla Co., **70**/25,38
Camas (Paulina) Valley, Crook Co., **65**/34N; **77**/189: described 1864, **65**/84-85; road from, **65**/103N
Camas Valley, Douglas Co., **63**/16, 20,24,30,357; **72**/161
Camels, **68**/346: used for packing, **62**/300
Camera Around Portland, by Maddux, noted, **81**/330
Cameron, Simon: emigrant escort established, **72**/58,59
Cammann, Carrie Payne, **63**/263N,303
Cammann, Fred, **63**/263N
Cammann, Mrs. Fred, **63**/263N
Cammann, Phil, **63**/281
Camp, Charles Lewis, **65**/406; **66**/380
Camp Alvord, **65**/68,82N; **68**/254N; **79**/270N,275N
Camp Arbuckle, **62**/106
Camp Baker, **65**/7,397-98: building described, **65**/395; location, **65**/394; name, **65**/394
Camp Bidwell, **68**/248N,254N,256,314, 316,323; **72**/16,46; **79**/132: map, **72**/27— road to Ft. Klamath, **68**/ins.fr.cov. Sept.
photo, **72**/22; roads, **72**/16
Camp C.F. Smith, **68**/254,321; **79**/ 132,163N,255,270N,275,275N: site photos, **68**/252-53, 315

Camp Cedar Springs, **79**/147,149,160
Camp Clikitat, SEE Camp Klickitat
Camp Cornelius, **66**/152N
Camp Creek, Crook Co., **77**/333,335; **78**/24; **79**/33, 274,291
Camp Currey, Silver Creek 1865-66, **68**/301N,302N; **70**/57; **79**/296-97N
Camp Currey, temporary 1864, **65**/75
Camp Curry, **66**/148N
Camp Dahlgran, **65**/95N,104N,106: name, **65**/84
Camp Day, **66**/81; **70**/252: history, **69**/223-68*passim*; location, **69**/233-35,243,246; maps, **69**/265, 266; name, **69**/235; photos 1860, **69**/ 236,238,ins.fr.cov. Sept.; site photos, **69**/233,255
Camp Division, **65**/38N
Camp Drake, **65**/75; **79**/274N
Camp Drum: assists immigrants, **67**/298; buildings described, **67**/298-99; costs, **67**/299; history, **67**/298-304; military reservation, **67**/300,303-305; name changes, **67**/304,305N,307N; sawmill, **67**/298; unfinished, **67**/299; SEE ALSO Fort Dallas
Camp Dubois, **66**/66
Camp Eden, **65**/66
"Camp fever," **63**/102-103,146-47,193, 199,213,228; SEE ALSO Typhoid fever
Camp Gibbs, **65**/91; **79**/296,296N: name, **65**/76
Camp Green, N.C.: described WW I, **75**/247-48,249,50
Camp Harney, **68**/231,248,297,301, 314; **70**/15,21,22,140N,147N; **79**/272N,297,298,301,304N: map, **70**/20; view 1872, **79**/292; SEE ALSO Fort Harney
Camp Henderson: abandoned, **65**/301; location, **65**/301-302; name, **65**/299; site photos, **65**/298,300
"Camp Henderson, 1864," by Preston E. Onstad, **65**/297-302
Camp Klickitat, **66**/143; **67**/322N
Camp Lapwai, SEE Fort Lapwai
Camp Lewis, **69**/85; **71**/219; SEE ALSO

Fort Lewis

Camp Logan, 79/270
Camp Lyon, 65/301; 68/237,238N, 248N,308N,314N; 70/18; 79/132; 81/328
Camp McDermitt (McDermit), 68/ 243N,251,252N,313,314;79/132: map, 68/250— road to Ft. Boise, 68/ins.fr.cov. Sept. name, 68/248
Camp McGarry, 68/255,315; 79/285
Camp Maury, 65/49-50,67; 79/145N, 296: burials at, 66/59; established, 65/37-39
Camp Meriwether, 62/200
Camp Merritt, N.J.: described ww I, 75/256-65*passim*
Camp Mills, Long Island, N.Y.: described ww I, 75/250-56,258
Camp Pleasant Valley, 79/288,293
Camp Polk, 62/203; 77/89; 79/145N
Camp Sa-wa-li-na-is, 69/235N: map, 69/ins.fr.cov. Sept.
Camp Separation, SEE Camp Division
Camp Smith, 65/56,67
Camp Steele, 79/149N,152-53,156,291: location, 79/149N; name, 79/149; site photo, 79/150
Camp Union, 65/48N
Camp Wallen, 65/56N
Camp Warner, 72/28: history, 71/361; road map, 72/27; roads, 72/29N sites, 71/361; 72/29N— new site, 79/280(photo),281N,285, 288; old site, 79/132,279(photo),284 view 1870s, 79/280
Camp Watson (first, Rock Creek), 65/ 85,92,95-96,103-104N,106-107,108
Camp Watson (second, Fort Creek), 65/104N,116; 79/132,170,170N,297
Camp Watson Cemetery: burials, 66/59-62; Watson marker photo, 66/60
Camp White, 72/92
Camp Wilkerson, 64/91
Camp Winfield Scott, 79/132
Camp Winthrop, 79/132
Camp Withycombe, 75/247:

photos, 75/244,246
Camp Wood, 70/178
Camp Woods, 79/284
Camp Wright, 69/341; 70/280; 78/210; 79/25,272N
Campbell, —, The Dalles 1881, 81/271
Campbell, Colin, 79/135
Campbell, Hamilton, 73/250
Campbell, James U., 76/300,301
Campbell, Marjorie Wilkins: *McGillivray, Lord of the Northwest*, noted, 70/272
Campbell, Mary Sophia, 70/60N
Campbell, Michael, 69/119
Campbell, Patrick, 69/119
Campbell, Peter, 69/119
Campbell, Prince Lucien, 67/361; 74/198
Campbell, R.L., 75/44
Campbell, Robert, HBCO.: journal, 65/213
Campbell, Russell, 62/172
Campbell, T.B., 65/184
Campbell, William, 69/119
Campbell Creek, 79/156N
Campi's Hotel, Portland, 77/249
Campment du Sable, SEE Champoeg
Camps and camping, 75/283-89: guide, 74/96
Canada: Alaska earthquake effects, 67/371; archives relating to Pacific NW, 71/368; Arctic exploration, 70/367 boundaries, 70/367— international, 66/69-71; 70/180; Saskatchewan policing, 67/371; waters settlement 1912, 67/360
British competition, 73/360; British control, 76/311; church records, 69/ 85; Columbia River project, 67/66; Columbia River treaty, 68/272-73; contracts, 81/387; dairy industry 1800-1906, 64/283; depression 1930-35, 72/231; English writers, 68/336-37; essays on, 67/84; forts, 70/179; frontier 1534-1760, 71/191; fur trade, 62/ 404; 66/281; 67/86; 70/180; gold rush, 66/88; Hawaiian trade interest, 64/283; historic sites, 71/361-62; his-

tory articles, 68/347; history theses, 63/90; 64/86; 67/84; immigration, 69/85,337; Indian reserve policy, 70/179; 72/227; Indians, 72/253; international boundary survey, 66/69-71; logging railroads, 80/209 maps—

1801, 76/316; early, 67/371 navy, 73/359; northern territories, 72/227; off-shore oil, 70/179; Pacific interests, 76/309-31; Pacific salmon, 67/368; Peace River development, 70/179; photo, 68/332; railroads, 65/377; Saskatchewan steamboats, 70/180; settlements, 81/323; transportation, 70/179; travel guide, 76/77; U.S. relations, 70/180,366,367; 74/215, 284; Western, 70/179,180,367; western manuscripts, 65/198; western provinces, 72/355; writers, 68/336-37; 72/355-56

Canada geese: nests, 69/11

The Canadian Frontier, 1534-1760, by Eccles, noted, 71/191

Canadian Historic Sites: Occasional Papers...No. 1, noted, 71/361-62

Canadian National Railway Company: history, 74/95; records, 67/367

Canadian Northern Railway, 71/366

Canadian Pacific Railroad, 68/87; 72/183:

B.C. tunnels, 68/185; competition with Northern Pacific, 71/143; last spike, 71/366; steamship line, 71/156; winter travel, 71/366

Canadian people:

Oregon population 1860-1910, 80/266-67(tables)

Canals, 73/85; 74/354:

govt. promotion of, 63/355; Lake Washington, 74/354; Ore.Prov.Govt. legislative petition, 66/356; Panama, 73/86; 76/293; South Santiam-Albany, 67/61,62; The Dalles-Celilo, 75/227

Canaman, Catherine, 66/348N

Canavan, Peter, 69/119

Canby, Edward Richard Sprigg, 80/117,259

Canby, James P., 70/140FF,166,169

Canby, Calif., 81/105

Canby, Ore.:

centennial, 72/91; early settlers, 71/285-86; history, 64/353; 70/278; 72/91

Canby Business Mens Club, 74/213

Canby Ferry, 63/364

Canby Historical Society: publications, 71/285

Canby's Cross, 81/328

Cancer, 69/110; 81/89

Candiani, Charles, 77/254,259

Candles, SEE Prices

Cane, Jimmy, 79/150,151, 167,313,316,317,319

Canem (Indian), 62/86

Canemah, Ore., 62/200; 63/252,364

Canemah (steamer), 64/275

Canneries:

Florence, Ore., 78/364; fruit, photo, 78/ins.bk.cov. March; SEE ALSO Fishing and fisheries; Salmon

Cannery towns, 75/106

Canning, George, 64/10,15-16,20-22, 27:

negotiations with Russia, 72/122, 122N,123; Polignac memorandum, 72/101-102; reaction to Monroe Doctrine, 72/101-102

Canning, Patrick, 69/119

Canning, Stratford:

British claims in North America, 72/105-106; conversations with Adams, 72/105-106,107

Canning, William, SEE Cannon, William

Cannon, Joseph, 70/225N

Cannon, Miles, 64/350

Cannon (Canning), William, 66/333, 343; 69/183

Cannon:

Dept. of Oregon requisition 1860s, 65/328,331-35; Ft. Cape Disappointment batteries, 65/333,339,347,349; Ft. Stevens batteries, 65/339-40,347,349, 351,352,357,359; Ft. Vancouver, 81/200; photos, 65/342,346,353,354, 355,356

Cannon Beach, Ore., 66/329; 74/164;

77/283-84: biography, **81**/342-43,374

photos, **77**/68,284

The Canoe and the Saddle, by Winthrop, cited, **74**/91

Canoe Encampment: name, **79**/294N-95N

Canoes, **66**/333; **74**/12-13: B.C. racing, **64**/86; Coquille River, **63**/13-25*passim;* dangers and mishaps, **74**/19,22-23,24,27 Indian, **65**/217; **74**/10,310— burials, **66**/91; Kutenai, **63**/359; ocean-going, **74**/19,22,24; photo, **74**/28; Tlingit, **73**/147-48,168; whaling, **73**/273

Canote, Marie Larkins, **66**/355N

Canton, China, **62**/17; **76**/310,314-29*passim:* painting ca. 1825, **76**/328

Cantonment Loring, **67**/298

Cantwell, "Jumbo," **65**/292

Cantwell, Robert, **68**/279: *The Hidden Northwest,* review, **74**/90-91

Cantwell, Thomas, **69**/119

Canyon City, Ore., **63**/70,264; **66**/309; **68**/231N,303N; **69**/87,274,276; **70**/37; **79**/123,269,270,303: centennial, **63**/366; described 1878, **70**/56-59; election 1878, **70**/59; gold discovery, **63**/366; hotels, **79**/303; photos, **70**/56,58; **77**/fr.cov. June

Canyon City Road, **66**/61: military protection, **65**/11-117*passim*— guards, **65**/63-64N,76,88-89,106 route, **65**/104-105N; Snake Indian depredations, **65**/14N,77-78N; winter camp on, **65**/103; SEE ALSO The Dalles-Canyon City Road

Canyon County, Ida., **64**/282

Canyon Creek, Grant Co., **63**/70; **67**/18

Canyon Creek, Ida., **62**/391

Canyon Road, **68**/89; **71**/69

A Canyon Voyage, by Dellenbaugh, reprint noted, **63**/356

Canyonville, Ore., **81**/105: Hanks house, **64**/89; history, **70**/359; map, **69**/260

Cap' Sumkin (Indian):

Cape Alava: name, **79**/399

Cape Arago: life-saving station, **66**/171

Cape Blanco, **74**/354

Cape Clear (ship), **66**/113

Cape Disappointment, **63**/48,219; **69**/58,78; **71**/11; **77**/278: charts, **69**/bk.cov. Dec. fortifications, **65**/331-52— firepower map, **65**/insert Dec. lightship aground, **69**/309-23; map, **65**/insert Dec.; photos, **65**/340,342, 344; U.S. and HBCO. claims, **64**/335-36N; SEE ALSO Fort Canby

Cape Elizabeth, **74**/17

Cape Flattery, **63**/192; **76**/226,227

"The Cape Forts: Guardians of the Columbia," by Marshall W. Hanft, **65**/325-61

Cape Foulweather, **66**/112

Cape Hancock, SEE Cape Disappointment

Cape Horn, Columbia River, **72**/151

Cape Horn, South America, **69**/269; **77**/175; **78**/91: route to Oregon, **77**/37-60*passim*

Cape Lookout, **63**/45; **74**/278

Cape Meares, **74**/278

Cape Mendocino, **73**/108

Cape Mudge: shipwrecks, **64**/87

Cape Perpetua: first auto trip, **76**/179

Cape Prince of Wales, **65**/365

The Cape Scott Story, by Peterson, noted, **75**/88

Capendale, William, **63**/225

Capendale, Mrs. William, **62**/105; **63**/225

Capital controversy, **66**/165-66; **68**/148; **75**/351

Capital investments: local, **67**/136,162N; outside, **67**/144, 162N; Pacific NW farm land, **71**/62, 76,98; Portland 1880-1890, **71**/64 railroads, **71**/40-45*passim,***78**— foreign capital, **71**/46,47,63,81,89, 90,91

Capital Journal, Salem: opposition to KKK, 75/173; 75th anniversary, 64/354

Capital National Bank, Salem, 65/218

Capital punishment: Montana, 72/246; Oregon 1906-64, 68/350; Pacific Co., Wash., 72/171

Capitol Building, Salem, 74/234

Capitol Business College, Salem, 80/277,281

Caples, Henry, family, 63/82

Caples, John F., 75/127

Capodistrias, Ionnes Antonios, 72/110,113

Cappious, George, 78/125

Capps, S.C., 65/395

Cap's Illahee (mountain), 81/106

Captain Charles M. Weber, Pioneer of the San Joaquin and Founder of Stockton, by Hammond and Morgan, review, 68/339-40

Captain Jack (Indian), 66/76

Captain James Cook: A Bibliography of His Voyages, comp. by Spence, noted, 63/84

Captain Truckee (Indian), SEE Winnemucca I

Captain's Harbor, 73/122

Capwell Horseshoe and Nail Co., 76/352

Carbell, John, 79/11

Carbon Glacier, 73/341

Carbon River, 73/341

Carbonado, Wash., 73/338

Card, W.N., 73/255

Cardero, Jose, 79/398

Cardwell, James R., 68/163

Carey, Ace, 63/283,286,296

Carey, Bessie, 63/290

Carey, Charles Henry, 66/341N,346N, 350N; 70/220; 73/363; 76/361; 78/100(photo): *General History of Oregon*, reprint cited, 72/354

Carey, George, 63/283

Carey, Margaret S., and Patricia Hainline: *Brownsville, Linn County's Oldest Town*, noted, 77/299 *Halsey, Linn County's Centennial City*, noted, 79/104

Shedd, Linn County's Early Dairy Center and Memories of Boston, noted, 80/106 *Sweet Home in the Oregon Cascades*, noted, 81/330

Carey Act, 71/196

Caribbean Sea, 62/18

Cariboo Cowboy, by Marriott, noted, 72/355

Carico, Ore., 74/358

Carl Parcher Russell: An Indexed Register of His...Papers, 1920-1967, noted, 71/191

Carless (Coreless, Coreliss), Joseph, 63/224-25,232

Carless, Mrs. Joseph, 63/224,232

Carley, Maurine, and Virginia Trenholm: *The Shoshonis, Sentinels of the Rockies*, review, 66/74-75

Carlile, John S., 73/33

Carll, W.E., 76/299,301

Carlson, Gordon: *Seventy-Five Years History of Columbia Baptist Conference, 1889-1964*, noted, 65/309

Carlton, Gus, 74/24

Carlson, Jen: *Christmas Every Day in Oregon*, noted, 68/81

Carlson, William H.: *In A Grand and Awful Time*, noted, 68/343

Carlton, Guy, Lord Dorchester, 76/311-12,318-19

Carlton, Ore.: Baptist Church, 76/14(photo),15; history, 65/217; 77/292; Swedish people in, 76/6-25

Carlton Elementary School Bicentennial Club: publications, 77/292,299

Carmack, George ("Siwash George"), 62/95

Carman, George, 63/15

Carman, Henry, 63/15

Carman, James, 63/30

Carman, Julia Ann Grant (Mrs. James), 63/28,30

Carmichael, Lawrence, 62/137; 66/346

Carnarvon Bay (ship), 66/129

Carnedd (ship), **66**/127
Carney, Byron, **76**/143
Carney, Edward, **69**/119
Carney, Michael J., **69**/119
Carney, Samuel J., **69**/119
Carnine family, Cowlitz Co., **74**/93
Caroline Islands, **62**/11,21,29,31: American missionary interests, **68**/72-73
Carp, **74**/298-99
Carpenter, Edwin H., **64**/137N: *GPH: An Informal Record of George P. Hammond and his Era in the Bancroft Library,* review, **66**/380-81
Carpenter, Horace, **69**/88
Carpenters, **67**/294N,326N; **68**/25, 46,47,49,51
Carr, Emily, **63**/359
Carr, Jesse D., **63**/253
Carr, L.S., **74**/16,21
Carr, Mary Jane, **64**/188
Carr, Tom, **81**/270,271,273
Carranco, Lynwood, and John T. Labbe: *Logging the Redwoods,* review, **77**/190-91
Carrier Indians, **71**/333
Carriere, Onizime, **63**/116N, 118-62*passim*
Carriger, Nicholas, **65**/405
Carroll, Caroline, SEE Taylor, Caroline Carroll
Carroll, Charles, **73**/259,263,267
Carroll, Comadore, **73**/263,267
Carroll, George C., **73**/259
Carroll, George W., **73**/260,263-67
Carroll, Joe, **73**/267
Carroll, John W., **73**/258,263,267
Carroll, John Patrick, **65**/379
Carroll, M.D., **81**/89
Carroll, Margaret Scott (Mrs. Samuel), **73**/259
Carroll, Mary, SEE Helms, Mary Carroll
Carroll, Nancy, SEE Wilson, Nancy Carroll
Carroll, Orville W., **79**/107
Carroll, Paul, **73**/258
Carroll, Samuel, **73**/258,259,261,263, 264,266: claim, **73**/259
Carroll, Samuel, Jr., **73**/267

Carroll, Stephen: biography, **73**/258; grave, **73**/258, 266(photo); photo, **73**/259
Carroll, Sylvester (Vess), **73**/263,267
Carroll family, Cowlitz Co., **62**/109
Carroll Rim, photo, **73**/265
Carruthers, Eben H., **70**/374; **72**/359
Carson, Alexander, **66**/333; **77**/81
Carson, Christopher (Kit), **69**/61; **70**/19
Carson, Joseph K., **72**/80; **74**/233
Carson, Virginia (Ginnia G.): "A Pioneer Ice Manufacturer," **63**/67-68
The Swamp Fox of the Willamette, noted, **69**/329
Carson City, Nev., **67**/372
Carson Valley, **69**/230
Carstensen, Vernon, **64**/350; **66**/89: *The Letters of the Lewis and Clark Expedition With Related Documents,* ed. by Jackson, review, **64**/183-84
Carter, Charles H., Jr., **62**/179
Carter, Charles H., Sr., **62**/171- 79*passim;* **67**/71: biography, **62**/170
Carter, Charley, **63**/289,294
Carter, Fred, **62**/169,173,174: biography, **62**/170
Carter, George E.: "The Cattle Industry of Eastern Oregon, 1880-90," **67**/139-59
Carter, Henry A.P., **71**/174
Carter, John L., **73**/190-92
Carter, William David, **64**/169-70
Cartographers, SEE Mapmakers
Cartography, SEE Maps and charts
Cartoons, **63**/362; **68**/343; **71**/364; **72**/131: anti-cartoon bill, **66**/46; political symbols, **66**/39,44-49*passim;* postal cards, **66**/305
Carty, Con, **69**/120
Carty, James, family, Clark Co., **81**/328
Carty, James, family, Morrow Co., **69**/ 119-20
Carty, Patrick, **69**/120
Carty, Willie, **69**/120
Caruthers, J. Wade:

American Pacific Ocean Trade, Its Impact…1784-1860, noted, **76**/182
Carver, Faye, **77**/90
Carver, Jonathan, **76**/312
Carver, Margaret R., *et al*:
Ancestors and Descendants of Michael Troutman Simmons and Andrew Jackson Simmons, noted, **68**/343
Carver, Ore., **74**/357
Cary, Clarence:
American China Development Co., **71**/141
Cary, Isaac, **65**/168
Cary, William de la Montagne, **71**/292
Cascade City, Wash., **74**/281
Cascade College, Portland:
history, **63**/92
Cascade Locks, **77**/257:
history, **81**/333; photo, **63**/62
Cascade Locks, Ore., **74**/131
Cascade Locks Historical Museum, **69**/174
Cascade Range, **62**/399; **63**/10,30,269; **65**/220; **67**/87; **72**/183; **73**/309,311, 314,315; **78**/152,231-34,299-302; **79**/10,12,15,18,19; **80**/258:
Calapooya Divide, **78**/57; description and travel, **74**/44-45,358; first route over, **77**/317; forest reserve, **76**/29; glaciers, **77**/196; Highway 26 natural environment, **72**/173; maps, **74**/358; **78**/68,248,294,ins.fr.cov. Dec.; summit photo, **79**/4; volcanoes, **77**/196; western slopes photo, **75**/ins.bk.cov. March
Cascade Range Forest Reserve, **76**/29
Cascades, Marie Therese, SEE McPhail, Marie Therese
Cascades, Columbia River, **63**/192,203, 234; **68**/158; **73**/68; **77**/315; **79**/202: blockhouses, SEE Blockhouses; military road, **68**/25-26; portage, **79**/176; portage railroad, **71**/22; Skirving panorama view, **65**/157; Upper Cascades photo, **62**/312-13; wagon road, **71**/22
Cascades (sternwheeler), **81**/39:
1910 photo, **66**/180
Cascades Indians, **62**/82; **65**/373
Cascadia, Ore., **74**/44,46
Cascadia deep-sea channel, **72**/90

Cascadia Soda Springs, **69**/339
Cascara, **80**/56
Casco (seaplane tender), **80**/47,48
Case, Paul, **71**/21
Case, Robert Ormond, **74**/54
Case, Samuel, **64**/355:
Modoc War diary, **67**/89
Case, Victoria, **62**/203; **74**/54
The Case of Thomas J. Mooney and Warren K. Billings, by Hunt, review, **72**/346-47
Casey, Charles, Morrow Co., **69**/120
Casey, Charles, Ruby Ranch hand, photo, **71**/252
Casey, James, photo, **81**/254
Casey, Silas, **62**/86
Cashmere, Wash., **62**/201-202
Casinelli, Pietro, photo, **77**/252
Casserly, Eugene, **67**/261
Casserly, James, **69**/120
Cassidy, Butch, SEE Parker, George Leroy
Cassidy, Michael, **69**/120
Casteel, Robert H., **65**/19
Casteel "tunnel," **74**/17,19,27
Castle, Judson, **79**/364,368-71
Castle, Samuel N., **68**/54
Castle, Walter, **79**/360N,361N,362,364
Castle Edel Brau (Twelve-Mile House), **73**/82
Castle Rock, Malheur Co., **68**/237; **79**/299N
Castle Rock, Wash., **67**/366:
history, **64**/91; **67**/279
Castleman, Philip F., **64**/138,163,175
Caston, —, Rainier settler, **63**/238
Caston, Rev. —, overland 1852:
family, **79**/365,380,383,387
Cataldo, Joseph M., **65**/204; **74**/359
Catalog House, Jacksonville, **65**/315
Catalog of Manuscripts in the University of Oregon Library, comp. by Schmitt, review, **73**/67-68
A Catalog of the Everett D. Graff Collection of Western Americana, comp. by Storm, review, **70**/64-66
Catching, Ephraim, **63**/22
Catching Inlet, **66**/52:
school, **66**/55
Catherine II, Empress of Russia,

80/203-204
Catherine Creek, 66/199
Catherine May, An Indexed Register of Her Congressional Papers, 1959-1970, noted, 73/360
Cathlamet, Wash., 62/57,58,59,61; 63/110; 75/105,106: Roberts letters from, 63/179,181, 198,202-36*passim*
Cathlamet Indians, 62/82
Cathlamet on the Columbia, by Strong, cited, 62/57,59; 74/37; quoted, 64/305-306
Catholic Church, 62/197,318,407; 73/270: anti-Catholic attitudes, 75/111-23 *passim*, 131-32,134,140,143,144; archives, 71/368; Benedictines in Ore., 70/312-32; Canadian records, 69/85; Colville, Wash., 64/186; Fillmore-Sublimity services, 70/316-18; French-Hawaiian dispute, 68/57-58; French Prairie, 66/348; fund raising fairs 1868 and 1870, 81/75,82; German colony plans, 70/317N; Gervais, 72/91; Heppner, 69/115-47*passim*; influence on Shakers, 72/148,151,152,157; Jacksonville, 70/314,315,316,318; Jordan Valley (Linn Co.), 64/354; journals 1847-51, 80/405-406; leper colony work, 70/324N; membership, 75/118,141; Mt. Angel, 72/91; number in Ore. 1881, 70/319,320; Oregon, 77/300; Oregon City, 70/327; Pacific NW history, 64/78-79; Pendleton, 70/320
Portland, 77/255-56— All Saints parish, 72/354; novitiate, 81/79; school, 68/146,152 priests in early Ore., 77/244; records, 71/363; 74/89-90; 77/244; 77/291; St. Anthony, 69/117,131; St. James parish burial records, 68/184; St. Paul records, 81/202-203; Salem, 80/342, 343,345,350-51,361; Santa Inez, Calif., 70/317,318,328 schools, 70/319,320,321,325; 75/ 132,162—

Helena, 65/379; Pacific NW, 65/380;

Portland, 65/379; 68/146,152; 72/354; SEE ALSO Sacred Heart Academy, Salem
service described 1905, 80/58-59; The Dalles land claim, 67/303,304N; Utah, 69/336; Vinson, 69/115; SEE ALSO Catholic missions
Catholic Church Records of the Pacific Northwest: St. Paul, Oregon, 1839-1898: Vols. I, II and III, comp. by Munnick and Warner, review, 81/202-203
Catholic Church Records of the Pacific Northwest: Vancouver, Vols. I and II, and Stellamaris Mission, comp. by Munnick and Warner, cited, 74/355; 77/291; review, 74/89-90
Catholic Colonization Society, 75/141
Catholic Ladder, 63/56-60
Catholic missionaries, 71/335,342,343: arrival in Ore. Country, 66/344; French Prairie letter requests, 66/344; Jesuits and fur trade, 67/84; Pacific Northwest, 69/269-71; term "black robe," 69/50-56; to Indians, 62/76; 63/55-60; 64/78; 69/63-65; western, 67/368
Catholic missions, 71/344; 73/69; 75/363: Big Bend, 64/351; Blackfeet, 69/ 64,65; California, 74/286; Coeur d'Alene, 69/64; Cowlitz, 63/131,139, 163; 69/270; Ft. Vancouver, 69/270; French Prairie, St. Paul records, 66/ 348N-61N*passim*; 69/269-71; 74/90; 81/202-203; Lake St. Ignace, 69/271; Montana, St. Peters, 62/106; near Waiilatpu, 81/27N; Pacific NW 1844, 69/270; St. Mary's, 69/64; Stellamaris records, 74/89-90; Vancouver, St. James, 66/348N; 74/90; 75/363; vital records Ore. Country, 74/89-90; Willamette Valley, St. Louis records, 66/ 356N,359-61N; 74/90; Yakima, 63/147
Catholic Sentinel, 64/88; 75/126-27; 77/260: editorial policies, 75/141-42; quoted, 81/87,95; views on labor, 75/ 123-25,141
Catley, Henry, 65/11,102N; 70/180

Catlin, George, 64/349; 65/136,213; 66/65; 75/94: describes prairie dog, 69/21; family letters, 68/77-79; view of Indians, 68/ 78,79

Catlin, Putnam, 68/78

Catlin, Seth, 63/108

Catlow Lake, 72/90

Catlow Valley, 68/321,322,327; 77/149,153: early settlers, 65/219

Catman, Xavier, SEE Katman, Xavier

Cats: early Oregon, 63/18,364; SEE ALSO Bobcats

Cattle, 62/75,297; 67/277; 68/23, 28,230,238,256,321,322; 69/85; 73/114,127,166; 77/10,302: army expeditions, 78/142,144,151, 278; associations, 65/216; Baker Co., 66/199-200,205; Becker letter 1900, 72/93; bibliography, 74/284; branding irons, 65/214; brands, 63/269, 310,323; 72/354; breeders, 63/37-40; 66/183; breeds, 77/7-10,369; buyers, 70/262; Calif. business history, 64/ 283,351; Central Oregon, 72/341; Chicago market, 67/146,148; companies, 78/50; Coos Co., 63/22- 24*passim*; cost of raising one steer, 67/149; Cowlitz Farm, 63/104,115- 73*passim*; dairy, 72/282; depression effects, 81/317 drives, 72/354—

California, 68/151; 80/105; Calif.- Tualatin, 63/305; Canyon City mines, 80/105; Cascades-Mississippi, 63/ 269; Coos Co.-Idaho, 63/26,30-32; east, 68/351; Klamath Co., 69/ 229N,243N,330; McKay Creek-Walla Walla 1855, 66/137-38; Mackenzie-Idaho 1862, 64/90,185; Oakland-Upper Touchet, 74/280; Powder River-Walla Walla 1862, 66/200; Prineville-Coos Bay, 63/37-38; Rogue Valley-Boise 1864, 65/22-23N; Siskiyou Co.-Boise 1864, 65/55; Virginia City mines, 81/105; Willamette Valley-Tillamook, 74/275-76

effect of transcontinental railroad, 67/139-59*passim*; 71/29,62; Elk Co., Nev., 67/85; farm cattle defined, 67/ 140; fences, 77/9; French Prairie, 66/ 337,339; Grande Ronde Valley, 72/94; Grant Co., 63/70-71; Harney Co., 63/ 309-11,319,323; 65/365; 66/67-68; herd law agitation, 68/185; history, 73/360; Idaho rustlers, 64/282; immigrant trade in, 67/313; industry transition 1880-90, 67/146-59; investments in, 68/337-38; 72/229; Johnson County War, 67/359; Kamchatka 1779, 80/203,204; Kittitas Co., 79/ 170; Klamath Co. history, 72/288; Malheur Co., 63/269-70,275; 67/236, 237-38; markets, 67/146-47,151,239; Nisqually, 63/211

Oregon—

business history, 65/216; distribution in, 77/196-97; no. in Eastern Ore. 1880-90, 67/144,145; range cattle industry, 65/216

Oregon Trail, 62/253,254,260,274, 277,283,285,369—

ailments, 79/67,69,365,367,368,388; alkali poisoning, 79/377-86*passim*; 80/76; losses, 79/67-70,80-87 *passim*,377-88*passim*; milk cows, 79/ 370,385; number 1853, 62/241; prices, 79/66N,67N,74N,80,83,85,89, 385; stolen by Indians, 66/134,148, 150-51; 79/170; trade, 79/67N,74N, 86-89*passim*,392; turpentine for sore feet, 62/352

outside capital invested, 67/144; 72/229; Owyhee area, 76/153; Pacific NW range history, 70/262; Pendleton, 77/192; predators, 76/71; prices, SEE Prices; ranching, 81/328; range cattle defined, 67/140; Russian colonies, 77/183,184,187; San Francisco market, 67/146,148; sheep-cattle wars, 69/106; shipped to Montana and Wyoming, 67/149,150; shipping, 72/354; stampedes, 65/215; 69/85; theses index, 72/273; trails, 67/277; Utah 1850-1900, 66/87; Willamette Valley shortage, 76/130; winter feeding, photo, 81/315; SEE ALSO Dairy industry; Grazing; Oxen

Cattle Barons of Early Oregon, pub. by American Media Co., noted, 79/337

Cattle Country of Peter French, by Giles French, review, 66/67-68

"The Cattle Industry of Eastern Oregon, 1880-90," by George F. Carter, 67/139-59

The Cattle King, by Treadwell, cited, 63/309; quoted, 63/311

Cattlemen, 67/141,143-44,151-54,236; 68/337-38; 69/63,119: associations, 68/345; Canyon City meeting 1921, 67/212; Johnson County War, 67/359; Montana vigilantes, 68/346

Cattonair, Michel, SEE Cottonoir, Michel

Caufield, Edwin Gratton, 76/299, 300,301

Caufield, Vara, 62/109: "How McLoughlin House Was Saved," 76/299-300

Caughey, John Walton, 62/325

"Cavalry in the Indian Country, 1864," ed. by Priscilla Knuth, 65/5-118

Cavaness, Wesley W., 63/289; SEE ALSO Wes Cavaness Hall

Caverhill, W.S., 63/366; 68/354

Caves: Arnold Ice Cave, 73/84; Charcoal Cave, 65/220; Cougar Mountain, 64/357; Cow Cave, 64/73; Derrick, Lake Co., 64/87; Gardner, 81/329; Pot Hole Ice Cave, 62/198; Pacific NW types, 65/219-20; SEE ALSO Fort Rock Cave; Oregon Caves

Cayuse, Ore., 68/227,232,297

Cayuse George, SEE Rundell, George

Cayuse Halket (Indian), 69/53-54: at Red River school, 71/330,332,336; death, 71/336

Cayuse Indians, 63/138,181; 65/297N; 66/143; 70/115,121,124; 75/115, 118,122; 78/55; 79/122,136; 81/ 393,399: army scouts, 79/130,275N art—

influence of Plains tribes, 81/341-42,345,347; sketchbook, 81/342-76 burial customs, 81/412; clothing, SEE Indian—clothing; enemies, 81/350, history, 73/277-78 horses, 81/341— horse-stealing, 71/345 Howard council 1878, 70/34-38; iron weapons, 73/64; land ownership, 81/348-49; links to Nez Perce, 81/348-49; maps, 73/278; Molalla encounters, 73/63-65; photo, 81/330; religion, 71/333; slavery, 81/414-15,416; trade, 81/418; Whitman massacre, 81/405-406; Whitman Mission, 71/344

The Cayuse Indians, Imperial Tribesmen of Old Oregon, by Ruby and Brown, review, 73/277-78

"A Cayuse-Nez Perce Sketchbook," by Theodore Stern, Martin Schmitt, and Alfonse F. Halfmoon, 81/341-76

Cayuse War, 1847-48, 66/143N,219, 258; 67/296; 70/347; 81/231,243,244: Oregon militia, 72/229-30; surrender of Whitman murderers, 67/297

Caywood, J.M., 80/317N

Cecil, Kirk P., 64/284; 68/349

Cedar Creek, Wash., 64/276

Cedar Mill History, by Brody and Olsen, noted, 80/105-106

Cedar Springs, 65/22; 79/147

Cedar trees, 73/21,174: Indian use of, 66/80; Port Orford cedar, 68/259,262(photo); western red cedar, 77/353

Cedarville, Calif., 68/256

Celedonia Ranch, Calif., 66/81

Celery, SEE Prices

Celilo Falls, 62/102; 66/201; 72/151; 73/68; 75/94,221,227,230: map, 75/228; photos, 75/229,ins.fr.cov. Sept.

Celilo Indians, 72/345

Celtic Chief (ship), 66/129

Cementville, SEE Knappton, Ore.

Cemeteries, 69/77,78,86,87,341: Allegany, 74/92 Astoria, 70/184— Old Cemetery, 64/320

Baker Co., 72/85-86; Belle Passi, 72/91; Camp Maury, 66/59; Camp Watson, 66/59-62; Canemah, 63/252; Carroll family, 73/260,266(photo),268; Centralia, Mt. View, 74/33; Clackamas Co., 65/216; Clatsop Plains Pioneer, 68/ 350; Coffin Rock, 66/91; Columbia Co., Neer City, 65/308; Coos River, 66/53; Cowlitz Co., Abernethy, 66/80; Cowlitz Farm, 63/203,213, 233; Curry Co., Willow Creek, 66/90; Dallas, 77/269-70; Denmark, Ore., 71/290; Dixie, 77/271; Empire, 74/92; Eugene Masonic, 63/364; Evans, 81/57N; Ft. Klamath, 69/328; Ft. Vancouver National, 66/60; French Prairie, 66/348; Jordan Valley, 62/201; Junction City, Milliorn, 69/86; Kellogg, 81/105; Kelso, Catlin, 62/109; Kings Valley, 64/356; Lewisville, 77/271; Lowell, Highland, 78/322; Maupin family, 81/105; Milwaukie, 65/216; 69/86; Mt. View, 81/57N; Oahu, 70/88; Oregon City records, 73/82; Philomath, Mt. Union, 72/285; photo, child's grave, 77/270; Polk Co., 72/171; Portland, Lone Fir, 63/245; 74/347; Queets River Valley, 74/27 Salem, 71/349—

Lee Mission, 63/248; Pioneer, 72/91; 80/257

Sherman Co., 72/85-86; Shoshone Indian, 62/290; Stayton Old Pioneer (Grier), 64/354; Tacoma Pioneer, 66/129

The Dalles—

Catholic, 70/273; Odd Fellows, 73/305; Pioneer, 78/177

Tichenor, 74/92; Tillamook Co. list, 69/78; Umatilla Co., 72/85-86; Vancouver, Sifton, 81/328; Washington Co., 64/353; Waverly, 65/216

Census:

Alaska 1880, 65/215

Champoeg District—

1845, 66/356; 1849, 66/359

Clackamas Co. 1860, 75/87; Coos Co. 1860, 71/90

Douglas Co.—

1860, 75/363; 1880, 75/87 finding aids and use of, 1790-1890, 72/356; guide to printed records, 70/272; Jackson Co. 1880, 66/80; Josephine Co. 1870, 74/281; Klickitat Co., 74/94; Lane Co. 1860, 71/190 Lewis Co., Wash.—

1850, 72/354; 1860, 72/354; 1880, 75/363

Linn Co., 77/197; Marion Co. 1860, 66/361; Mason Co., Wash. 1880, 74/281; Multnomah Co. 1870, 75/87; Nevada difficulties, 68/87; Niagara, Ore. 1910, 71/352; Oregon 1845, 77/319

Pacific Co., Wash.—

1860, 68/81,184,340,342; 1870, 71/286; 72/89,171; 1880, 74/281

Portland—

1870, 75/87; 1910, 74/112

Seattle 1910, 74/112; Tillamook Co. 1854, 74/357

Washington—

1860, 73/73; 1870, 73/283

Washington Co. 1880, 75/87

Centenary Wilbur Methodist Church, Portland, 64/89

Centennial Anniversary Corvallis Evangelical United Brethren Church, noted, 69/78

Centennial Jubilee History, First Presbyterian Church, Brownsville, by Swanson, noted, 66/82

Centennials:

Alaska, 68/184,348; 69/337

Astoria, 66/329—

Daily Astorian, 75/294; Grace Church, 66/383

Boise, Ida., 64/282; Brownsville First Presbyterian Church, 66/82; Canby, Ore., 72/91; Canyon City, 63/366; Clark Co. fair, 69/330; Clatsop Plains Pioneer Presbyterian Church, 66/91; Columbia River salmon packing, 68/90; Corvallis Evangelical United Brethren Church, 69/78; Eagle Valley, 64/90; Elk City, 70/279; *Enterprise-Courier*, Ore. City, 67/369; Eugene, 64/92; Gervais, 72/91; Great Britain consulate in Ore., 72/357,360-61; Idaho Territory, 64/282,357; Jefferson, Ore., 72/91; 73/82; Klamath souvenir booklet, 69/77; Lewiston, Ida., 63/89; Montana mining, 66/88; Mullan Road, 64/352; Newberg post office, 72/91; Northern Pacific Act, 66/91; Oregon railroads, 63/363; Philadelphia Centennial Exposition, 77/ 196,291; Prineville, 69/87,346; Shoshone Indian Reservation, 68/81; transcontinental railroad, 70/364; Umatilla Co., 63/365; 64/90; Union Pacific Railroad gold spike ceremony, 70/349-51; 71/197; U.S. Army Engineers, 72/287; Utah, 63/358 Vancouver, Wash., 76/382—port, 66/80

Wingville, Ore., 64/90; SEE ALSO American Revolution Bicentennial; Lewis and Clark Centennial Exposition; Oregon Centennial Exposition and Trade Fair; Oregon Centennial of Statehood

Center Ridge, photo, 73/308

Centerville, SEE Athena, Ore.

Central America (ship), 66/33

Central Baptist Association, 64/134N

Central Coal and Coke Co., 77/219

Central Electric Cooperative Inc., 80/328

Central Oregon, SEE Oregon, Central

Central Oregonian, Prineville: 1964 recreation guide, 65/315

Central Pacific Railroad, 67/146,147, 150,168; 72/48,49; 73/231,237: agreement with Union Pacific, 71/55; chartered, 71/41; collier fleet 1880s, 66/171N; construction costs, 71/28; delay in Pacific NW connection, 71/41; finances, 71/80N,88N; history, 73/66; Huntington interests, 71/283-84; opposition, 71/39; rates of return, 72/178; Winnemucca route, 71/54

Central Point, Ore., 70/279

Centralia, Wash.: Armistice Day riot, 69/325; 73/70-71; 75/151; first house, 73/196

The Centralia Case: Three Views of the

Armistice Day Tragedy, by Chaplin *et al*, review, 73/70-71

Century Farms, 67/89-90; 68/352,353; 71/295: Lane Co., 79/339

A Century of News and People in the East Oregonian, 1875-1975, by Macnab, review, 77/192-93

Cereghino, Abramo, 77/246,249,254

Cereghino, Charlie, photo, 77/252

Cereghino, Giuseppi, 77/254: photo, 77/252

Cerny, Alta Savage, 78/160,164

Cervera, Pascual, 76/284-91*passim*

Cervine, Agnes, 67/88

Ceylon, 62/36,44,52

Chadwick, Alta Grete: *Tales of Silver City*, noted, 79/107

Chadwick, Stephen F., Sr., son of Stephen James, 66/89

Chadwick, Stephen Fowler, 67/263,266; 70/27N,34: photo, 81/fr.cov. Fall

Chadwick, Stephen James, 66/89

Chalk Hills, 75/67

Challenger (vessel), 73/274

Chalmers, —, sailor on *Whitlieburn*, 66/107

Chalmers, Alex, 63/37

Chamberlain, George Earle, 65/364; 67/63; 71/215-16,221; 77/267: photo, 81/254; split with Wilson administration, 68/134N

Chamberlain, Levi, 68/56-57

Chamberlain, Virginia Owen, photo, 78/226

Chamberlain, W.R., 77/359

Chamberlin-Ferris Act, 64/55

Chambers, Andrew Jackson, 63/128N

Chambers, David J., 63/128N

Chambers, Frank, 67/181

Chambers, John, son of Thomas M., 63/128N

Chambers, Rowland, 65/185,191N

Chambers, Thomas J., 63/128N

Chambers, Thomas M., 63/128

Chambers, Lane Co., 81/327

Chambers of commerce: Ashland, 62/180,182; Seattle, 63/61;

SEE ALSO Portland Chamber of Commerce; Portland Junior Chamber of Commerce

Chambreau, Edward (Eduard, Ned), 70/147,165; 72/228; 80/297: autobiography quoted, 80/159-60, 298N; biography, 70/131N; comments on Moses, 70/133,134,135; papers, 70/133N; photos, 70/132; 80/314; thesis on, cited, 70/101N; work among Indians, 70/131-35,149,167

Cham-pi (Indian), 79/275N

Champoeg, Ore., 62/138; 63/103,181-82,184,200,203-204,208,214,227,234-35; 66/335,338,358: flood 1861-62, 64/357; 66/358,361; flour mill, 63/83,181-82; settlement, 66/338

Champoeg District, 62/139N,140,144: census 1845, 66/356; land claims, 66/335,357-58

Champoeg meeting, SEE Oregon Provisional Govt.—meeting of May 2, 1843

Champoeg: Place of Transition, by Hussey, cited, 70/259N

Champoeg State Park, 64/361; 69/345: history, 65/415; 66/332N; museum, 69/174

Champoeg State Park, Oregon: A Summary Report of Its History, by Hussey, cited, 66/332N

Chance, David H.: "Archeologists Turn Up Another Fort," noted, 77/298-99 *Exploratory Excavations at Spalding Mission*, noted, 77/302

Chandler, Alfred D., Jr., *et al*: *The Golden Spike, A Centennial Remembrance*, review, 70/349-51

Chandler, Charles H., 66/197N

Chandler, Dan, 76/353; 77/6, 28-35*passim*,168: family photo, 77/28

Chandler, George, Baker rancher, 63/38: arrival in Oregon, 66/198; biography, 66/197-207

Chandler, George Clinton, 64/136

Chandler, Herbert, 66/197N

Chandler, John G., 70/234; 81/199

Chandler, Leah, photo, 76/ins.fr.cov. Dec.

Chandler, Milford G., 66/384

Chandler, Robert: *The United States Forest Service*, by Steen, review, 78/280

Chandler, W.B.: Baker County reminiscences, 66/ 208-17*passim*

Chandler, William, 74/94

Chaney, Ralph Works, 67/26,29

Changing Military Patterns on the Great Plains, by Secoy, review, 62/92-93

Chanticleer Inn, 66/269; 74/110, 113,137

Chapin, Eleanor, photo, 72/208

Chapin, Stan, 77/69

Chaplin, Daniel, 64/181

Chaplin, Ralph, 69/85: *The Centralia Conspiracy*, reprint noted, 73/70

Chapman, Barbara, 78/159

Chapman, C.C., editor *Oregon Voter*, 75/160,169,175

Chapman, Daniel: biography, 65/50N

Chapman, Dorothy and Larry: *The Hills-Neet Story*, noted, 66/383

Chapman, Esther Lorinda Bewley, 80/406

Chapman, Henry H., 65/50N

Chapman, James A., 72/61,66; 80/156: photo, 80/155

Chapman, John Gadsby, 73/276

Chapman, L.G., 72/10

Chapman, Larry, SEE Chapman, Dorothy

Chapman, Lynn, 77/268

Chapman, Reuben A., 68/61-70*passim*

Chapman, William Williams, 71/54; 80/12

The Character and Influence of the Indian Trade in Wisconsin: A Study of the Trading Post as an Institution, by Turner, ed. by Miller and Savage, review, 79/92-97

Charbonneau, Jean Baptiste, 62/288, 289,290; 63/89; 77/91: biography, 66/185; 71/247-64

Danner, Ore., grave, 69/341;

71/254,255,264—
marked, 72/78; photo, 71/246
handwriting facsimile, 71/260; identity, 71/256-64; ledger, 72/79N; signature, 72/78,79; Wind River Reservation grave, 71/256

Charbonneau, Lizette, 62/289

Charbonneau, Toussaint, Jr., 62/288,289

Charbonneau, Toussaint, Sr., 62/288, 289; 65/215; 71/247; 72/179

Charcoal, 67/67

Charcoal Cave, 65/220

Charles, William, 63/179

"Charles Alexander: Youth of the Oregon Mood," by Howard M. Corning, 74/34-70

"Charles Becker, Pony Express Rider and Oregon Pioneer," by Marie Pinney, 67/213-56

"Charles L. McNary and the 1918 Congressional Election," by Howard A. Dewitt, 68/125-40

Charles Nelson (schooner), 66/115,127

Charles W. Wetmore (steamship), 63/92

Charlevon, M., 66/350

Charley (Molalla Indian), SEE Molalla Charley

Charley (Yakima Indian), 64/276

Charley, George A. (Indian), 78/364

Charlie High (Indian), 74/13N

Charlot (Flathead Indian chief), 67/372

Charlotte, N.C.: described WW I, 75/248-49

Charlton, Callie Brown, 75/14,15,18

Charlton, E.P., & Co., Portland, 66/306

Charlton, Richard, 64/25-26,29

Chase, David, 65/212

Chase, Elmore Y., 65/175: biography, 65/189N

Chase, Francis B., 79/151,151N,161,284

Chase, Frank B., 65/212

Chase, Inez Rich, 80/63N

Chase, John W.H., 65/212

Chase, W.C., 80/63N

Chaser, Bob, 81/270

Chatham (brig), 79/339: sketch, 72/fr.cov. June

Chatham Strait, 72/139

Chatillon, Henry, 67/367

Chautauqua, 68/89; 71/196,372; 77/91; 78/115,169-72: Ashland, 64/356; attendance, 80/398; buildings, 80/397; extension education, 80/392,402-403; finances, 80/ 395,402; Gladstone, 80/46; history, 80/391,393; Oregon locations, 80/ 394; photos, 80/394,399,401,fr.cov. Winter; prices, 80/398; principles, 80/ 403; programs, 80/392-403*passim*; recreation, 80/398; Riley lectures, 74/219

Chawa Creek, SEE Ochoco Creek

Cheatham, Julian, 68/356,359,361; 69/348; 70/374

Cheese and cheese industry, 70/182; 74/274-75: factory photo, 71/128; Nestucca Valley, 64/90; prices, 71/120,200; Swiss, Columbia Co., 72/200; Tillamook, 71/120

Chehalem Valley, 65/415; 66/90; 74/345

Chehalem Valley Club, 75/294

Chehalis (horse), 73/285

Chehalis, Wash., 63/192; 73/342: history, 66/32N; Indian warfare, 64/276; McFadden Park, 66/37; oldest house, 66/32

Chehalis Advocate, 66/32N

Chehalis County, Wash.: 1860 census, 70/74,272

Chehalis Indians, 62/109

Chehalis River, 63/193; 68/340; 74/15

Chelapoo (Indian), 79/149,153,158, 313-19*passim*

Chelatchie, Wash., 74/281

Chelmsford (ship), 66/107

Chemawa (Chemaway), Marion Co., 66/335

Chemawa Indian School, 76/10

Chemeketa Falls, 66/338

Chemeketa House, Salem, 71/17

Chemical Industry: early U.S. development, 74/332N

Chenamus (brig), 77/38: log, 77/36; sketches, 75/fr.cov. Dec.; 77/36

Cheney (ship), 66/115

Chenoweth, Francis A., 62/73; 63/ 185,200; 66/32,33,34; 67/306
Chenoweth, Justin, 67/300N,303N, 306N,307N
Chernykh, Alfonsai: Calif. expeditions, 73/113,163
Chernykh, Egor Leontievich (Yegor), 70/178; 73/163-64
Chernykh, Georgii (Egor?) Leontievich, 73/163-64
Cherokee Bob, SEE Talbot, Robert
Cherries: Bing, 68/167,170,199; 71/349; Black Republican, 68/165-67,199; Calif. orchards, 68/162; Lambert, 68/170; Lewelling propagation methods, 68/ 171-72; packing house photo, 68/169; Royal Ann (Napoleon) origin, 68/157N
Cherry, P.L., 64/71
Cherry, Ida., 62/298
Cherry Creek, Jefferson Co., 73/263; 81/300,301,306,307,308,313,314
Cherry Grove: A History From 1852 to the Present, by Nixon and Tupper, noted, 79/336
Chertudi, Igancio, photo, 76/166
Chertudi, Inez, 76/166
Chertudi, Juan, 76/166
Chertudi, Phil, 76/166
Cheshire, C., 78/325N
Chesshire, R.H., 64/276
Chessman, Merle R., 75/294
Chetco, Ore., 75/362
Chetco River, 62/215; 76/49,51,53
Chetco Valley: history, 80/104
Chetleschantunne Indians, 64/90
Chewaucan River, 79/293N
Chewing gum, 80/118,130
Cheyenne, Wyo., 63/242,300; 66/88: prices 1881, 71/8
Cheyenne Indians, 63/356; 81/345, 348,349,350
Cheyne, Andrew: voyages, 72/355
Chiang Kai-shek, 62/15,23,24,27,37, 38-39,43,45
Chicago (U.S. cruiser), 74/84; 75/294
Chicago, Milwaukee, St. Paul and Pacific

Railroad Co.: records, 74/79
Chickens: Chinese introduced in Ore., 65/240, 243; gamecocks, 66/43; prices 1858, 68/28
Chico, Calif., 62/322; 72/159
Chief Joe (Indian), SEE Apso-kah-hah
Chief Joseph: War Chief of the Nez Perce, by Davis and Ashabranner, noted, 64/348
Chief Moses Reservation, SEE Columbia Reservation
Chief Sam (Indian), SEE Ko-ko-ka-wa
Chief Spokan Garry, by Jessett, cited, 71/325-37*passim*
Chiefs Island, 75/227,230,231
Child, Arlene, photo, 74/265
Childbirth, 71/180,270,276; 75/33-34
Children: amusements ca. 1920, 80/367-72*passim*; father's advice, 80/124-33; incubators, 80/55
life— 1870s-80s, 80/270-78; ca. 1920, 80/365-90*passim*
migrant in Oregon, 64/284; Oregon Trail, 81/99,100; work experiences early 1900s, 81/103
Children of the Sun, a History of the Spokane Indians, by Wynecoop, review, 71/187
Chilkat Indians: council with Seward, 72/137-41; solar eclipse, 72/139-40,141
Chilkat (Chilkit) River, 72/139
Chilkoot Pass, 62/96; 66/88: map, 76/ins.fr.cov. June; photo, 76/ins.bk.cov. June
Chilkoot Trail, 81/127-28,147
Chiloquin, Ore., 70/75
Chimney Creek, 68/239,240,242
Chimney Rock, 62/338; 65/151; 72/67; 79/375; 80/71: photo, 65/152; sketch, 79/374
China: American traders' image, 69/83; Bishop visit, 69/68; Communism, 62/ 15,34-46*passim*,54,55; disorganization, 62/14-16,37,38; fur trade, 69/68;

Japan invasion, 62/23-24,25,27,37 market— myth of, 1890-1914, 69/335; Pacific NW, 71/141-60; U.S., 71/170-72, 176-78 missionaries, 62/17; "open door" policy, 62/7,19; 71/153-54,171 trade, 62/6,9,17; 67/200-201; 76/ 198-99,205,206,218,309-31— ginseng, 72/179; Magee family interests, 72/182; products, 72/355 treaties, 62/8-10; U.S. policy, 62/ 7,17,19,25-40*passim* China Baw, 76/81 China Creek, Curry Co., 62/215 China Dam, SEE Niagara Dam China Ditch, 69/330 China Mission Bill 1843, 76/218 *The China or Denny Pheasant in Oregon*, by Shaw, cited, 65/244 China Sam, 69/330 Chinese Academy of Social Sciences, 80/412 "Chinese Brigade," photo, 80/265 "The Chinese in Oregon, c. 1870-1880," by P. Scott and Nancy Parker Corbett, 78/73-85 Chinese people, 70/57,67; 71/9; 72/85; 76/81; 80/237,259,261: Alaska, 66/280; American-born military organization, 80/265; anti-Chinese sentiment, 72/265,353; 75/ 122-31; 78/34,79,85; Astoria, 63/68; 75/294; borax works labor, 73/235, 236(photo),237-38; British Columbia, 72/234; California, 63/331; 68/348; 74/286; 80/244,245; cannery workers, 73/164; 81/322; Columbia Co., 73/ 222; cook at Rock Creek, 81/265N; Curry Co., 80/335; customs, 71/11-12; Dallas, Ore., 76/368-73; discriminatory laws, 80/27,140-41,141N,151, 304-306,311; early Northwest, 64/ 357; exclusions, 75/127; Floyd view of immigration, 70/341; funeral photo, 80/fr.cov. Summer; Heppner 1890s, 80/120; housing photo, 78/ins.fr.cov. March; Idaho, 63/89; Idaho migrants, 72/264; immigration, 75/127; inade-

quacy of American records, 71/349; Inland Empire, 65/365; Jacksonville, 81/328; laborers, 76/18,231; 80/ 307N; Lewelling employs, 68/167,170; miners, 62/224,236; 72/42; 76/77; 80/235; mining train to Helena, 67/ 235-36; Montana nativism, 68/346; North America, 63/361; occupations, 78/73-74,78-79,81 Oregon, 62/175,198— 1860s, 64/325; miners, 62/224,236; place names, 71/349 Pacific exploration, 70/77; photos, 75/ 124; 76/369,370; 78/76,79,fr.&bk. covs. March; 80/fr.cov. Summer population— 1860-1910, 80/267; 1870, 78/78; 1880, 78/80; age brackets, 78/77,81; demographic analysis 1870-80, 78/73-85; marital status, 78/81,84; percent males, 78/77,85 Portland, 74/340; 75/127-30; 81/120— arrests, 80/140N,296,309; crime attributed to, 80/136N; districts, 80/296,305(photo); flood 1894, 67/77; ordinances, 80/151,294,305-306; population 1860-1910, 80/ 136,146,151N,161N,266,268; quarantine, 80/161; tong war, 73/82 queues, 76/372; railroad labor, 67/ 371; 71/9N,284,351,357; 80/162N, 163(photo),234,296; restrictions on, 75/123; riots against, 68/88,167,350; Roseburg, 69/330; Salem, 63/83,314, 331-32; San Francisco, 64/75-76; schooling, 78/79-80,84; Seattle, 62/ 405; ship crews, 73/301; social position, 78/75; Southern Ore., 80/336; stonework, 71/351; Tacoma, 62/305; 75/128 United States, 62/10— armed forces, 80/34 wages, 78/74,79,85; SEE ALSO Gold and gold mining; Labor and laborers "Chinese Pheasants, Oregon Pioneers," by Virginia C. Holmgren, 65/229-62 Chiniak (Chiniat) Bay, 77/183 Chinn, Mark A.:

Ft. Henrietta established, 66/138-39; boat wrecks report, 71/364
OMV service, 66/134-39,142,144; Chittenden, W.L., 62/218,219N
Walla Walla campaign, 66/146-47 Chittim bark, SEE Cascara
Chinook, William (Billy) (Indian), Chitwood, Ore., 66/283
79/330,332: Chokecherries, 69/156,157,158
biography, 79/156-57N; enlistment Cholera, 63/7; 74/86; 75/77,94;
record, 79/320 78/136; 79/364,368-70,374,377,
Chinook, Wash., 75/105; 78/206: 389,392:
1870 census, 72/171 treatment, 79/369
Chinook Indians, 62/57; 63/76; Chopunnish, meaning of, 68/88
64/41-54; 69/68; 71/328; 72/153; Choris, Louis, 62/106
74/340; 75/83: Chouteau, Auguste Pierre, 67/367;
culture, 79/99; epidemic 1830, 64/91; 72/179
extinction, 79/99; food, 69/155; head Chouteau, Pierre, Jr., 65/149
flattening, 69/173; houses, 81/407; Chouteau, Pierre, & Co., 67/370-71
property concepts, 81/399,405,411; Chraighead, E.B., 72/264
religion, 64/351; 71/333; slaves, Christian, Daniel F., 79/11
81/415; Snake brigade, 71/345 *Christian Advocate and Journal*, 76/362
trade, 81/418— Christian Church (Disciples of Christ),
Ft. George, 64/218,222,241 79/338:
The Chinook Indians, Traders of the Lower early Oregon, 77/300; Oregon history,
Columbia River, by Ruby and Brown, 72/166
review, 79/98-100 Christian College, Monmouth, SEE
Chinook jargon, 62/86-87; 63/56; Oregon College of Education
66/223N,341; 73/267; 74/253; Christian Scientists:
79/100: meeting, 80/58; Oregon 1880-1915,
Blanchet dictionary, 64/138,157-58, 72/233
179-80 Christiansen, Richard A., 77/91
Chinook Point, 63/48; 65/347; 67/ Christianson, Arthur, 77/362
366: Christie, Alexander D., 78/286
chart, 69/306; fortifications, 65/ Christie, James H., 69/73
349,351 Christmas, 63/290-91,329-30:
Chinook wind, 66/382; 72/90,183 Aleutians, 80/32; Baker Bay, 72/89;
Chinookville, Wash., 71/361 Dallas, Ore., 76/376-77; Ft. Clatsop
Chipman, Nancy S., 79/412-13 1805, 64/88,356; Fruit Valley 1892,
Chippewa Indians, 63/72-73 72/353; Montana, 65/215; Oregon,
Chirikof (Ukamok) Island, Alaska, 65/121; Swedish, 76/23
77/184 *Christmas Every Day in Oregon*, by Carl-
Chirouse, Eugene Casimir, 66/151N son, noted, 68/81
Chisolm, James, 63/242-43 Christmas Lake Valley, 79/337; SEE
Chisholm Trail, 77/369 ALSO Warner Valley
Chissold, Lotta, 70/7-12*passim*: *A Chronicle of Catholic History of the*
poem, 70/9 *Pacific Northwest, 1743-1960*, by
Chitike Cavalry, 65/46-47,50 Schoenberg, review, 64/78-79
Chittenden, Hiram Martin, 62/310- *Chronicles from Pedee, Oregon*, by Tartar,
11,403,404; 63/90,243-44,344; noted, 75/363
66/64,273; 77/291: "Chronicles of Sacred Heart Academy,
biography, 74/354-55; forestry paper Salem, 1863-1873," ed. by Sara J.
notes, 67/372; Missouri River steam- McLellan, 80/341-64; 81/75-95

Chronicles of Willamette, Volume II, Those Eventful Years of the President Smith Era, by Gregg, review, 72/349-50

A Chronological History of North-Eastern Voyages of Discovery and the Early Eastern Navigations of the Russians, by Burney, review, 72/84-85

Chugach Indians, 77/184,185

Chugach National Forest Reserve, 76/101

Chugach Sound, SEE Prince William Sound

Chuinard, Eldon G., 71/371; 74/183,365; 79/44:

American Indian Medicine, by Vogel, review, 71/179-80

Lewis and Clark, pub. by National Park Service, review, 77/82-83

Men of the Lewis and Clark Expedition, by Clarke, review, 72/82-83

The Natural History of the Lewis and Clark Expedition, by Burroughs, review, 63/69-70

Only One Man Died, award noted, 81/428; review, 80/404-405

Chukchi tribe, Siberia, 77/296

Church, Charles P., 69/213

Church, Joseph, Pacific Co.: family, 71/361

Church of Christ, Scientist, SEE Christian Scientists

Church of the Epiphany, Portland, 81/167

Churches: architecture, 71/186-87; Arlington, 77/90 Astoria, 81/195— Grace Episcopal, 66/383 Aurora Old Colony, 67/273; 79/240,241(photo); Baker Co. 1890s, 66/215; Beavercreek, Ten O'Clock, 66/382; Brownsville First Presbyterian, 66/82; Carver, 71/199; Clackamas Co., Frog Pond Church, 67/273,276; Clatsop Plains First Presbyterian, 62/248; Corvallis Evangelical United Brethren, 69/78; Dallas, Ore., 78/158; Douglas Co. early, 62/205; Drain, 62/205; 70/184; Eugene, 69/77,276;

Garibaldi, 71/129-30; 77/355,358; Gaston, 76/381; Grand Ronde Indian Reservation, 70/322 Hood River, 72/94, 153— Japanese Methodist, 76/252-53 Idaho City, 68/346; Illiuliuk, Alaska, sketch, 73/126; Jacksonville, 63/79; Jordan Valley, St. Bernard's Catholic, photo, 76/166; Kelso Methodist, 66/80; Klamath Falls Methodist, 69/382; Lake Oswego Methodist Episcopal, 73/80; Leslie United Methodist, 70/184; Logan German Methodist, 73/80; Lookingglass, 62/205; McMinnville, St. Barnabas Episcopal, 65/218; Marion Friends, 67/89; Medical Lake, Wash., St. Anne, 64/351; Meridian United Church of Christ, 67/273; Oregon, 77/300; Oregon City, 71/190; Pendleton, 77/298; Pine Grove Community, 70/184; Pleasant Grove Presbyterian, 64/354 Portland, 71/255-56,376— African Methodist Episcopal, 80/400; Centenary Wilbur Methodist, 64/89; East Side Christian, 75/157; Japanese Methodist, 76/233,251-52; oldest, 69/341; 71/199,289,294; Pilgrim Congregational, Albina, 77/376; St. Michael's Catholic, 77/255-56; St. Patrick's, 75/294; St. Philip Neri, 77/ 255-56; Trinity Episcopal, 72/317 records repositories list, 71/363; Russian, 77/182; St. Paul, Ore., 69/270; 71/186-87 Salem, 66/12; 67/369; 80/341N,344,350-51— 1860, 66/17; First Presbyterian, 77/173; St. John the Evangelist, 80/341N,344,351; 81/75,86,88 Seattle, 66/82— Plymouth Congregational, 78/34 Sitka Lutheran, 72/137,140; Tenino, Wash., 72/153 The Dalles, 70/273; 79/162N— Congregational, 64/170; St. Peter's, 79/162N; Shaker, 72/149-58 Union, Sacred Heart Catholic, 65/315; Union Co. oldest building, 65/315;

Vancouver, St. James Catholic, 74/90; Wapato, 72/153; West Union Baptist, 63/79; 71/186; western historic, 71/186-87; Westfall, 63/284,300; Wilderville, 63/246; 81/106; Woodland, Wash., Presbyterian, 64/276; SEE ALSO names of denominations

Churchill, Claire Warner, photo, 74/265

Churchill, Willoughby, 78/215

Churchill, Winston, 62/26,33,38

Churchill, Manitoba, 63/224

Cibola, 75/94

Cider making, 80/274

Cinnabar, 81/312

Cinnabar Springs, 67/90; 69/88

Cioeta, Corinna, 75/368

Circle City, Yukon Terr., 76/115,116

Circuit riders, 72/89

Circuses:

early Pacific NW, 66/92; Eastern Ore. 1890s, 66/214-15; McMahon's, 66/43

Cisterns, 80/26N:

early Jacksonville, 65/218

Cities:

history of American, 64/350; minority groups in, 72/181; plans and plats, 81/201; types, 81/201-202; western, 81/201-202; SEE ALSO Towns

Cities of the American West: A History of Frontier Urban Planning, by Reps, review, 81/201-202

City and Suburban Railway Co., 62/178

City Book Store, Salem, 78/11: lithograph, 78/12

City Club of Portland, 73/210

City of Aberdeen (ship), 66/118

City of Bremerton (steamer), 63/66

City of Florence (ship), 66/122

City of Prineville Railroad, 68/352: history, 70/68-69

City of Rocks, 79/38

City of Seattle (steamer), 74/27

City of Sydney (troop transport), 80/176N

City Stables, Portland, photo, 80/fr.cov. Summer

Civil engineering, 78/360-61

Civil rights:

14th Amendment, 72/181; Mooney and Billings trial, 72/346-47

Civil War, 62/6,10,187,300,301,302; 70/253,254; 72/172; 77/369: Alaska, 63/254; California, 63/88; Columbia River fortifications, 65/325-61*passim*; confiscation legislation, 72/316; disloyalty definitions, 72/315-16; end celebrated at Ft. Canby, 65/352; Far West volunteers, 63/360; Lancaster Light Horse Cavalry muster roll, 66/187; Lane Co. parade 1864, 66/187; Lee surrender parade photo, Portland, 77/133; loyalty disputes, 73/31-59; loyalty oaths, 72/315,316; Montana gold in, 63/360; Nevada volunteers, 64/86; officers in Pacific NW, 62/298 Oregon, 62/197,234; 65/364,384; 72/233—

Indian campaigns 1864, 65/5-118, 392-400; Long Tom Rebellion, 67/54-60; news of in 1864, 65/44-45,84, 88,111-12,115; view of in, 68/152; 72/323-24

Oregon volunteers, 62/203,246,301; Oregonians who served in, 62/298; 63/83; Pacific Coast, 62/298; Pacific NW, 62/203; 63/91,254; partisan violence, 80/141-42; politics, 72/315-38*passim*; railroads, 63/247; secession sentiment, 65/184; The West, 63/360; Washington, 63/82-83; 66/35; Western territories, 80/208; SEE ALSO First Oregon Cavalry

Civil War Chronicle, comp. by Keeler, noted, 68/341

Civil War Dictionary, by Boatner, cited, 65/177N

Civil War Railroads, by Abdill, noted, 63/247

Civil War veterans:

buried in Oregon, 72/85; Oregon, 62/298; Washington, 63/82

Civilian Conservation Corps, SEE U.S. Civilian Conservation Corps

Civilian Conservation Corps, 1933-1942: A New Deal Case Study, by Salmond, review, 69/65-66

Clackamas (dredge), 77/107

Clackamas County, Ore., **62**/140,144,148,150,160; **66**/366; **67**/273; **68**/353; **76**/143,239: annexation question, **74**/207-208; cemeteries, **65**/216; census records 1860, **75**/87; courthouse, **62**/154N; history, **67**/91; **74**/357; irrigation, **66**/381; jails, **65**/211; maps, **74**/357; marriage records, **63**/364; **69**/273; place names, **65**/385; probate records, **69**/341; railroads, **69**/339; records, **74**/208; vital records, **73**/82

Clackamas County Historical, noted, **62**/109; **63**/245; **65**/211; **66**/381

Clackamas County Historical Society: meetings, **69**/227; **70**/274; officers and directors, **62**/103,414; **63**/85,249; **64**/82,278; **65**/122,310; **66**/83,277; **67**/81,282; **68**/63,281; **69**/80,277; **70**/80,274; **71**/192; **72**/174; **73**/76; **74**/179; **75**/89; **76**/93; **77**/92; **78**/ 92; **79**/108; **80**/107; **81**/107; publications, **66**/381; **76**/304; **77**/292,298

Clackamas Indians, **62**/78; **63**/208; **73**/63,64; **75**/109-10

Clackamas Mining Co., **73**/251

Clackamas River, **63**/51N; **66**/162; **76**/38

Clackamas Title Co., **74**/198

Claire (towboat), **63**/361

Clams, **74**/15,18,23: clambakes, **66**/80

Clan Galbraith (ship), **66**/127

Clan McPherson (ship), **66**/127

Clancy, John, **69**/120

Clancy, Mike, **69**/120

Clancy, William, **69**/120

Clanfield, Mary, **78**/364

Clapp, John T.: *Journal of Travels*..., cited, **79**/340

Claquato, Wash.: founding, **66**/382; Fourth of July 1862, **66**/35

Clara Brown (sternwheeler), **63**/64

Clark, —, capt. Yaquina Life-Saving Station, **66**/110N,112

Clark, Arthur H., Co.: history, **65**/213

Clark, Charles, immigrant of 1851,

78/238,323N: biography, **78**/127-28; Central Ore. story, **78**/213-19; Elliott Cutoff advance party, **78**/213,219,224-33*passim*; ignorance of Deschutes, **78**/214,217,219,229; photo, **78**/226; reaches Willamette Valley, **78**/307

Clark, Charles Edgar, **76**/270-95*passim*: photo, **76**/275

Clark, Cleon L., **65**/10

Clark, Mrs. Cleon L., **65**/36

Clark, Daniel, New Hampshire senator, **73**/46,50,51

Clark, Donna M. (Mrs. Keith): *The Beginning of the West*, by Barry, review, **74**/86-87

Remembering—School Days of Old Crook County, by Helm, review, **81**/207

SEE ALSO Clark, Keith and Donna M.

Clark, E.A., **66**/381

Clark, Ella Elizabeth, **63**/362; **64**/353: *Indian Legends from the Northern Rockies*, review, **68**/180-81

Indian Legends of Canada, review, **62**/411-12

Clark, Emanuel, **75**/67

Clark, Frank, **62**/86

Clark, George, immigrant of 1853, **78**/127

Clark, George M.: diary, **80**/105

Clark, George Rogers, **68**/345; **70**/339

Clark, Giles, and Mowry Smith, Jr.: *One Third Crew, One Third Boat, One Third Luck*, noted, **76**/182

Clark, Grace, **78**/214-18*passim*

Clark, Grace Hodgson: killed by Indians, **78**/214-18

Clark, Harry: *A Venture in History*, review, **75**/79-80

Clark, Harvey, **62**/121

Clark, Hodgson, **78**/214-18*passim*

Clark, James, Calif. 1851, **78**/216-18

Clark, James, Lane Co. pioneer, **77**/321,325,327,336,339; **78**/41

Clark, James H. (Jim), **70**/57,58,59; **79**/125,170-71N,272N

Clark, John G., ed.: *The Frontier Challenge: Responses to the*

Trans-Mississippi West, review, 73/274-75

Clark, Keith, 62/199; 63/371; 64/359; 65/10; 77/309,313:

The Indian Heritage of America, by Josephy, review, 70/264-65

Rails to the Ochoco Country, by Due and Juris, review, 70/68-69

"Travelers at the Deschutes, 1813?", 77/79-81

Clark, Keith and Donna M.:

"William McKay's Journal, 1866-67: Indian Scouts," 79/121-71,269-333

Yesterday's Roll Call, comp. by Genealogical Forum of Portland, review, 72/85-86

Clark, Keith, and Lowell Tiller: *Terrible Trail: The Meek Cutoff, 1845*, review, 68/79-81

Clark, Louise M. (Mrs. Robert E.S.), 65/217,308; 66/382: Mounted Rifle Regiment history, 67/366

Clark, Lynwood, 78/217

Clark, Malcolm H., jr.:

"The Bigot Disclosed," 75/109-90

The Blue Ribbon University, by Belknap, review, 77/380

The Case of Thomas J. Mooney, by Hunt, review, 72/346-47

Catholic Church Records of the Pacific Northwest, comp. by Munnick and Warner, review, 81/202-203

The Court-Martial of General George Armstrong Custer, by Frost, review, 70/66-67

Democrats of Oregon, by Burton, review, 72/80-81

The Dry Years, by Clark, review, 67/186-87

The Eugene Register-Guard, by Price, review, 78/286-87

The Hatchet Men: The Story of the Tong Wars..., by Dillon, review, 64/75-76

Henry Villard, by Belknap, review, 77/380

James J. Hill, by Martin, review, 78/358

Joe Lane of Oregon, by Hendrickson, review, 68/333

The Ku Klux Klan, by Jackson, review, 69/179-80

March of the Volunteers, by Bordwell, review, 69/88-89

Mark Twain Burlesque Patterns, by Rogers, 62/292-94

A Melodrame Entitled "Treason, Stratagems and Spoils," by Adams, ed. by Belknap, review, 70/354-55

Pharisee Among Philistines, noted, 77/291

The Public Life of Eugene Sample, by Hynding, review, 75/293-94

Rebel Voices, An IWW Anthology, ed. by Kornbluh, review, 66/186

The Reminiscences of Doctor John Sebastian Helmcken, ed. by Smith, review, 77/294

The Seattle General Strike, by Friedheim, review, 66/73-74

The Shaping of a City, by MacColl, review, 78/89-90

Twain and the Image of History, by Salomon, review, 62/292-94

The University of Oregon Charter, by Belknap, review, 77/380

The Urban West at the End of the Trail, by Larsen, review, 81/103-104

The Vinland Map and the Tartar Relations, by Skelton *et al*, review, 67/182-83

The Voyage of the Columbia; Around the World with John Boit, ed. by Johansen, review, 62/88-89

The Wobblies, by Renshaw, review, 69/179-80

Clark, Maurie D., 71/371; 72/358; 73/ 364; 74/183,365; 75/370; 76/387; 77/199; 78/387; 79/413,415; 80/ 410,414

Clark, Norman H., 64/283; 66/281: *The Dry Years: Prohibition and Social Change in Washington*, review, 67/186-87

Mill Town: A Social History of Everett, Washington, cited, 73/281-82; review, 72/86

Clark, Orange, 67/280

Clark, Robert Carlton, 66/344N,355N,

356N: bibliography, 70/366; biography, 70/366

Clark, Robert D.: "Days at Mercer Lake," 75/301-308

Clark, Robert E.S.: *The Mountain Men and the Fur Trade of the Far West*, ed. by Hafen, review, **66**/185-86

Clark, Robert Fletcher, 78/238,238N: photo, 78/238

Clark, S.D., **63**/357

Clark, Thomas, Davidson son-in-law, 78/207N

Clark, Thomas, Lane Co. pioneer, 70/ 69; 78/127,129,149,213-19,307, 307N,323N: photo, 78/214

Clark, W.B., 80/137N,138,144,144N

Clark, Walter Van Tilburg, **66**/240; 73/286

Clark, William, author, 62/407-408

Clark, William, explorer, 62/288-89, 291; **63**/69-70; **64**/272; **69**/163; 70/87,339; 72/179; 74/269; 75/94: association with Jefferson, 79/100-101; biography, 79/100-101; Charbonneau child, **71**/249,257; field notes discovered, **66**/65-66; Ft. Stevens battery named for, **65**/357; journals 1795 and 1797, 70/363; LePage du Pratz and, **66**/86; plants named for, **69**/161; portraits, 70/367; Supt. of Indian Affairs, **71**/291

Clark, William Andrews, **64**/349

Clark, Willis K., 62/179

Clark and Wilson Lumber Co., Portland, 76/249

Clark County, Wash., **66**/32: aviation, **69**/331; bond issue 1913, 74/211; county fair centennial, **69**/330; first courthouse, **63**/82; history, **63**/82; **64**/82; polo field, **69**/331; post offices, **69**/331

Clark County Historical Museum, **65**/308; **69**/174: dedication, **65**/314

Clark County History: noted, **63**/82-83; **64**/276,351;

65/308; **66**/382; **67**/366; **68**/341; **69**/330-31; 70/358; 72/89,353; 74/93,281; 75/363; 76/382; 77/292,298; 78/364; 80/334; **81**/328; twenty year review, **81**/328

Clark massacre, 78/213-19,216N-17N

Clarke, Charles G.: *Men of the Lewis and Clark Expedition*, review, 72/82-83

Clarke, Edward Young, 75/152-54,175

Clarke, Fred A., **63**/108

Clarke, Gordon W.: *Polk County, Oregon, Place Names*, noted, 78/365 *The Streets We Live On*, noted, 80/105

Clarke, Newman S., **65**/193; 68/8, 23,40; **69**/224N,225

Clarke, Samuel Asahel, 62/212, 230,333; **64**/172

Clarke, T.D., **71**/16

Clarno Basin: fossil beds, **63**/364

A Classified Bibliography of the Periodical Literature of the Trans-Mississippi West, 1811-1957, ed. by Winther, review, **63**/81-82; review of *Supplement, 1957-67*, 72/349

Clatskanie, Ore., **71**/360; 75/105: pioneers, **64**/91; school history, **65**/308

Clatsop, Marguerite, SEE Gervais, Marguerite Clatsop

Clatsop County, Ore., 62/140,246; 72/243; 76/239: Chinese in, 78/75-85; farming methods 1872-1920, **64**/90; first hanging, 73/ 82; history, **63**/252; library service, **63**/252; post offices, **71**/200; postal cards, **66**/329; school superintendent, **81**/9N; sheep, 62/241N; surveyor 1851-54, **81**/194; tidal wave, 77/280-84

Clatsop County Historical Society: Flavel House, **69**/175; Lattie journal, **64**/210; meetings, **69**/277; 70/80, 274; museum, 70/80,274; officers and directors, **64**/82,278; **65**/122,310; **66**/83,277; **67**/81,282; **68**/83,281; **69**/80,277; 70/80,274; **71**/192; 72/ 174; 73/76; 74/179; 75/89; 76/93;

77/92; 78/92; 79/108; 80/107; 81/107; publications, 76/304; 77/292 Clatsop Indians, 63/193,252; 66/349; 75/294; 79/99: houses, 81/407; slaves, 81/413,417; trade skill, 81/419 Clatsop Plains, 62/195,196,240,246; 73/245-57*passim*: pioneer cemetery, 68/350 Clatsop Plains Pioneer Presbyterian Church, 62/248-49: centennial, 66/91; 120th anniversary, 68/90 Clatsop Spit: *Peter Iredale* wreck, 64/68,70-71; 66/129 *Claus Spreckels, the Sugar King of Hawaii*, by Adler, noted, 68/82 Clausen, A.C., photo, 74/265 *Claverdon* (ship), 66/107 Clay, Harry, 81/273 Clay, Sig Fransen, 68/342 Clayoquot Sound, 68/101-103,105: charts, 68/104,bk.cov. June Clayson, Edward, 75/8 Clayton, John Middleton, 75/329,332-33 Clayton, John W., 64/68,70-72N Clayton, Joshua E., 69/214,215,216,221: report on Coeur d'Alene mines, 69/220 Clear Creek, Tillamook Co., 73/8,9 Clear Lake, Linn Co., 64/87; 70/183 Clear Lake, Modoc Co., 62/322; 72/34N Clearwater River, 62/216,222; 79/182, 185,198: log drive, 63/89 Cleaveland, Henry W., 67/329N Cleaver, George L., 75/178 Cleaver, John D., 68/360; 72/358: *The Great Persuader*, by Lavender, review, 71/283-84 *In Pursuit of the Golden Dream*, by Gardiner, review, 71/359-60 *Indian Peace Medals*, by Prucha, review, 73/276-77 *John Phoenix, Esq.*, by Stewart, review, 71/188 Cleeton, T.J., 66/363,365 Clemens, Orion, 63/89; 72/14,15 Clemens, Samuel Langhorne, 62/292-

94; 66/89; 69/337; 73/74,286: and frontier folklore, 68/346 Clergy: World War I views, 71/216-17,220; SEE ALSO Circuit riders; Missionaries Clerke, Charles, 80/197,201,203: death and burial, 80/199,204; monument, 80/202(photo),204N; portrait, 80/202; voyage, 72/84 "Clerke in Kamchatka, 1779: New Information For an Anniversary Note," by E.A.P. Crownhart-Vaughan, 80/197-294 Clery, Mildred, 69/120 Cleveland, George, 74/17,18 Cleveland, Grover, 75/136 Cleveland, Richard Jeffry: *Narrative of Voyages and Commercial Enterprises*, cited, 76/204 *Cleveland Rockwell, Scientist and Artist, 1837-1907*, by Stenzel, noted, 77/289 Cliff, Harry, 64/357 Cliff House, San Francisco, 71/11: photo, 71/10 Climate: Aleutians, 80/35,42,44,47; Arica, Chile, 77/120; Astoria winter 1930, 75/294; blizzards, 72/183; Chinook wind, 66/382; 70/55N; 72/90,183; Columbus Day storm 1962, 63/367, 371-72; 64/88,186; 65/308-309; 75/294; Crater Lake area, 66/92; Dawson, Yukon Terr., 76/115,117 Eastern Oregon— 1862, 79/176,180,199-202; 1866-68, 79/142-67*passim* hail, 73/281; hailstorm, 79/180; Hood River Valley gale, 70/54-55; ice fog, 63/328; Idaho 1862, 79/183-99; ocean storms, 77/47-48 Oregon— rainfall 1867, 76/180; winter, 70/183,318,320,323-24 Pacific NW temperature extremes, 65/220 rain— Ft. Umpqua, 70/245; Southwest Ore., 73/348 rivers frozen over 1886, 66/106;

Skagway, **81**/122,128,130,131,139; snowstorm 1884 photo, **66**/386 storms— 1880, **64**/88; **66**/283; Nov. 1921, **72**/94 Tillamook Bay, **77**/221; Tillamook Co. snow 1919, **72**/314 winter— 1850, **66**/162-63; 1853, **78**/58; 1861-62, **66**/198; 1880-81, **81**/261N, 264,265-69; 1884-85, **80**/274 SEE ALSO Floods; Oregon State Weather Bureau; Williwas Climax, Ore., **67**/374; **71**/200 Cline, Gloria Griffen, **62**/106 Cline, Mildred A., **62**/249N Clingman, Cyrus, **73**/83 Clinkinbeard, Ada, **66**/54 Clinkinbeard, Anna, **66**/54 Clinkinbeard, George, **66**/54 Clinkinbeard, Jay, **66**/54 Clinkinbeard, John J.: family, **66**/54 Clinkinbeard, Karl, **66**/54 Clinkinbeard, Philura (Mrs. John J.), **66**/53 Clinkinbeard, Ralph, **66**/54 Clinton, James, Auburn mines 1861, **62**/217,219; **79**/42 Clocks, marine, **71**/199 Clohessy, Michael J., **71**/155 Clopton, Mrs. Frank B., **68**/227N Closset and Devers, Portland, **62**/165 Cloth: prices Ore. 1840-42, **62**/217 Clothing and dress: bloomers, **78**/19N; B.C. industry, **65**/ 381; children's, **80**/370; frontier soldiers' footwear, **77**/303-304; pioneer children, **64**/263; pioneer men, **63**/ 185; pioneer women, **63**/53N; SEE ALSO Indians—clothing; Prices Cloud Cap Inn, **76**/101; **77**/61-66; **79**/203-209: construction, **75**/101; name, **75**/101; photos, **76**/100; **77**/62; site photo, **75**/100 Clouston, James: journal 1819-20, **65**/309

Clouston, Robert, **68**/113 Cloutrie, A.J., **64**/201N,205N Cloutrie, Helen Lattie (Mrs. A.J.), **64**/201N,205N,206N Clover, **63**/116,139,152 Clover Creek, Malheur Co., **63**/264,272,274,280,301; **67**/236: first water rights, **67**/237 Clover Creek Valley, Union Co., **63**/253 Cluff, Edward, **69**/120; **79**/171N Cluggage, James, **62**/214 Clum, John P., **64**/283 Clutesi, George, **72**/356 Clyman, James, **64**/275,281; **65**/406 Clymer, Elmer, **64**/109 Coaches: hotel coach photo, **77**/ins.fr.cov. Sept.; SEE ALSO Stagecoach transportation Coad, Nola Evelyn, **78**/160,163,164 Coal and coal mining, **75**/331,332,334; **77**/219,296; **81**/327: Bellingham Bay, **66**/34N; Clackamas Co., **74**/357; Coos Bay, **68**/263; Coquille River, **63**/15-16; Cowlitz River, **63**/155,168,171-72; HBCO. operations, **65**/314; Montana, **72**/286; Olympic Peninsula, **74**/9; Painted Hills, **73**/267; Puget Sound 1880s, **66**/171; Renton, Wash., **68**/269; Tillamook Co., **72**/305-308; Vancouver Island, **65**/314; Washington, **72**/181,233 Coalman, Elijah ("Lige"), **63**/363; **73**/81,84: biography, **74**/88-89; Mt. Hood ascents, **74**/88,286 Coalman Glacier, **73**/81 *Coast Country: A History of Southwest Washington*, by McDonald, review, **68**/182-83 "Coast Experiences," by Margaret E. Gammon, **77**/277-84 Coast Fork, Ore.: settlers, **78**/319 Coast Fork, Willamette River: ford, **78**/64 Coast Indian Reservation, **65**/173N-74N,178,364 Coast Range, **63**/30,350; **65**/173; **72**/294,295; **74**/307; **80**/258

Coats, A.F.:
sawmill, 72/301,303,305
Cobb, Irvin S., 69/102
Coboway (Indian), 63/252:
children, 66/349
Coburg, Ore., 67/369; 69/77; 79/23:
history, 72/92
Coburn, Joe, 63/283,286,299
Cochran, Elizabeth, SEE Ware, Elizabeth Cochran
Cochran, James H., immigrant of 1853, 78/124,129
Cochran, John S.:
"Economic Importance of Early Transcontinental Railroads: Pacific Northwest," 71/27-98
The Golden Spike, by Chandler *et al*, review, 70/349-51
"Henry Villard and Oregon's Transportation Development, 1863-1881," cited, 71/75-96*passim*
Cochran, Melville C., 68/227
Cochran, Robert C., 67/66
Cochran, W.T., 67/66
Cochran, William, Rev., 69/54,337
Cochran, Ore., 72/295
Cochrane, Henry C.:
papers, 70/360
Cockburn, Andrew, family, 80/335
Cockburn, Rebecca, 80/335
Cockstock (Indian), 63/214N
Coder, Almeda Helman, 77/90
Codere, Helen, 63/347
Codes, SEE Laws
Cody, William F. ("Buffalo Bill"), 67/213N,227,241,242; 70/86; 72/181:
letter quoted, 67/246; Pony Express rider, 67/228,230
Coe, Ah (Chinese), 76/368-69,373
Coe, David J., 75/347,348,349,353,354
Coe, Elmer A., 66/306,329
Coe, Henry Waldo, 63/363
Coe, Lawrence W., 79/144N
Coe, Nathaniel, 79/144N
Coe, Mrs. Nathaniel, 63/365
Coe, Ralph T.:
Sacred Circles: Two Thousand Years of North American Indian Art, review, 79/213-14

Coe family (Chinese), 76/368-69:
photo, 76/369
Coe Glacier, photo, 77/64
Coeur d'Alene, Ida., 63/90; 64/86:
land rush 1909-10, 64/87; mines and mining, 62/108; 65/214; 66/88
Coeur d'Alene Indian Reservation, 64/86; 69/220
Coeur d'Alene Indians, 63/89; 64/86; 65/364; 69/63-65; 70/115,121
Coeur d'Alene Lake, 70/357
Coeur d'Alene Mine Owners' Assn., 70/180
Coeur d'Alene Mining War of 1892: A Case Study of an Industrial Dispute, by Smith, noted, 62/108
Coffee, SEE Prices
Coffeepot Creek, 78/320
Coffelt family, Coos River Valley, 66/53
Coffey, Mrs. Joel R., 64/359
Coffey, John B., 66/368,371; 75/146
Coffin, G.W., 67/274
Coffin, Laban, 66/10
Coffin, Sarah B. Lyon (Mrs. Laban), 66/9,10
Coffin, Stephen, 75/120
Coffin Mountain, Linn Co., 79/105
Coffin Rock, 74/332:
Indian burials, 66/91
Coffins, 73/264
Cogswell, John, 62/301
Cogswell, Philip, Jr.:
The Growth of a City, by MacColl, review, 81/203-205
Tom McCall, by McCall and Neal,. review, 79/406-407
Cogswell, William F., 64/5
Cogswell Creek, 79/288
Cohn, Philip, 69/115
Coins, SEE Hickeys; Money
Coit, Daniel W.:
letters, 69/276
Colahan, Gertrude, 66/382
Colasuonna, Jerome, photo, 77/248
Colbert, T.J., 69/208
Colchester, Lord, SEE Abbot, Charles
Cold Springs, Ida., 79/184,198
Cold Springs Flat, Southern Ore., 68/91
Cole, —, Tillamook Co. 1919,

72/308-10
Cole, Cornelius, 71/283
Cole, David L., 63/75
Cole, George E., 65/182; 78/43,43N
Cole, L.D., 67/66,67
Coleman (schooner), 66/117
Coles, Blaine B., 74/233
Coleseed, SEE Rape (forage crop)
Colfax, Schuyler, 72/127,144
Colfax, Wash., 71/368
Colleges, SEE Schools
Collier, Barron G., 64/327
Collier Bar, Illinois River, 76/46,48,50
Collier Creek, Curry Co., 76/46,50
Collier Memorial State Park Logging Museum, 69/174
Collingwood (sloop), 63/210,218,235; 70/295,299,307,309N: lithograph, 70/292
Collins, B.P., 80/296N,319N
Collins, Dean, 74/225
Collins, Emma: letters, 72/171
Collins, Everell S., 65/211
Collins, Henry C.: photo, 78/298; residence, 78/295
Collins, Ivan, 73/364: scale model vehicles, 72/358
Collins, Mrs. Ivan, 72/358
Collins, Mary Emily: letters, 72/171
Collins, Patrick, 79/283,283N,284
Collins, Perry McDonough, 65/216
Collins family, Deschutes Co., 79/48
Collins' Overland Telegraph, 72/232
Collinson, Andrew, 76/9
Collingson, Anna, SEE Jernstedt, Anna Collinson
Collinson, Frank, Jr., 76/9
Collinson, Frank, Sr., 76/7-9
Collinson, Matilda (Tillie), SEE Peterson, Matilda Collinson
Collver family, Coos River Valley, 66/53
Colly, Henry, 64/233-34,239
Colman, Edmund, 81/332
Colnett, James, 67/368
Colonel Allan (brig), 76/329
The Colonial Craftsman, by Tunis, cited, 69/182

Colonial Dames of America in the State of Oregon, 62/420,421
Colonial Russian America: Kyrill T. Khlebnikov's Reports, 1817-1832, trans. by Dmytryshyn and Crownhart-Vaughan, noted, 77/290
Color and Light: The Southwest Canvases of Louis Akin, by Babbitt, noted, 75/88
Colorado: first ladies, 63/89; history, 77/303
Colorado (navy vessel), photo, 62/12
Colorado: A History of the Centennial State, by Abbott, noted, 77/303
Colorado Central Railroad, 71/8
The Colour of Canada, by Maclennan, noted, 69/332
Colstrip, Mont., 72/286
Colt, Cornelius Chapman, 74/211,215
Colt, Samuel, gun maker, 70/85
Colter, Grant L., 74/273
Colter, John, 64/281
Columbia (HBCO. bark), 63/119,168, 205; 64/200,224-25,240
Columbia (NWCO. schooner), 76/327-29
Columbia (OWR&NCO. steamer), 69/312; 71/11; 81/35: first electric lights on Columbia River, 71/12; painting, 71/12; schedule 1883, 71/ins.fr.cov. March
Columbia (sidewheel steamer built Astoria 1850), 75/82
Columbia (steamship built N.Y. 1850), 70/245
Columbia (tug), 68/266
The Columbia, America's Great Highway Through the Cascade Mountains to the Sea, by Lancaster, cited, 74/119
Columbia Baptist Conference, Seattle: history, 65/309
Columbia Barracks, SEE Fort Vancouver (military post)
Columbia Basin Electric Cooperative Inc., 80/328
Columbia Basin Project, 64/283; 80/409
Columbia City, Ore., 66/382
Columbia College, Eugene, 73/332N; 79/21,21N
Columbia County, Ore., 62/301,309; 65/383; 66/365; 72/197:

county fair, 74/358—
fairgrounds, 66/382
courthouse, 67/370; creek names, 65/219; early physicians, 65/308; early schools, 65/219; family histories, 73/283; farming, 74/302,317; Finnish settlement, 66/382; fire patrol assn., 73/283; history, 64/91; 65/219,308; 66/382; 70/358; 73/283; 74/358; life in early 1900s, 74/83-85,293-332; Northern Pacific Railroad arrival, 65/309; progress report, 64/90; public health nursing service, 77/89; towns, 73/283

Columbia County Historical Museum, 69/174

Columbia County Historical Society: meetings, 69/277; 70/274; officers and directors, 62/414; 63/85,249; 64/82,279; 65/122,310; 66/83,277; 67/81,282; 68/83,281; 69/80,277; 70/274; 71/192; 72/174; 73/76; 74/179; 75/89; 76/93; 77/92; 78/92; 79/108; 80/107; 81/107; publications, 67/280-81; 68/342; 70/358; 71/360-61; 73/282-83; 74/358; 81/424

Columbia County History, noted, 62/301; 64/91; 65/308-309; 67/280-81; 70/358; 71/360-61; 74/358; 77/89; 81/424

Columbia Gorge, 62/173; 67/296,329; 74/131; 80/407: commercial development, 74/129; described, 74/107; first auto roads, 74/109; geographical limits, 67/370; historic travel route, 74/107-108; history, 74/119,123; 81/333; Lancaster camp photo, 66/252 photos, 66/252; 73/308; 74/100,ins. covs. June; 75/278— Watkins 1884 album given OHS, 66/386 railroads, 74/108; resort, 75/277-81; view from Corbett area, 81/58; SEE ALSO Columbia River Highway

Columbia Indians, SEE Sinkiuse Indians

Columbia Interstate Bridge Commission, 66/252

Columbia Investment Co., Portland, 69/209

Columbia Iron Works, Portland, 64/176

Columbia Lightship (1950), 77/278-79

Columbia Lightship No. 50: excursions to watch salvage, 69/322; history, 69/307-23; photos, 69/314-21,fr.cov. and ins.fr.cov. Dec.; sea location, 69/307,308,323,bk.cov. Dec.

Columbia Lightship No. 88, 69/323

Columbia Lodge, Portland, 77/257

Columbia Plains, 62/399

Columbia Plateau: history of agriculture, 81/336

Columbia Power Cooperative Assn., 80/328

Columbia Preparatory School, 78/285

Columbia Rediviva (ship), 62/8,88; 64/276; 67/200,201; 72/182; 76/199,209,210: cargo, 68/103,105; drawing, 76/198; logs and journals, 68/102,103,105, 106; papers, 67/202; proceeds of first voyage, 67/201; voyages, 68/101; winter harbor 1791-92, 68/101-10

Columbia (Chief Moses) Reservation, 70/137: maps, 70/136,164

Columbia River, 62/8,9,314,399; 63/42-54*passim*,263,348; 66/80,210,317; 69/67; 70/229,295,307; 72/143; 73/317; 75/226; 78/365; 80/258: antecedent stream, 65/316; archeology, 62/61; 63/76; 70/183; bar pilots, 64/198-99N,205-206 bridges, 77/87— Astoria-Megler, 67/372 British claims, 72/105-106,123; 76/210; Broughton exploration, 74/278; called River of the West, 79/211 Canada— dams, 68/350; drainage basin, 63/90; hydroelectric power, 67/86; treaty with U.S., 63/89; 69/272-73; 72/252,253 channel improvement funds, 67/372; commercial importance, 70/341; 76/317; dams, 68/350; 77/87; dangers in early days, 63/227; debarkation points,

77/45; description, 75/87-88,104-107; development, 63/89,90; 75/88; diversion plan, 67/277; Downes' Channel, 75/227; drainage basin, 63/90; excursions, 77/362; exploration, 74/278; 76/317,324; ferries, 67/372; 77/87; fishing, SEE Fishing and fisheries; Five Mile Rapids, 62/89 floods, 77/299— 1894, 72/151; high water, 75/226-27 fortifications, 65/325-61; 70/184; 74/215; 80/335— naval installation, 74/215; shore batteries, 70/184 freight shipments 1880, 71/94; frozen over, 66/106; 67/305N,319; gorge, SEE Columbia Gorge; historic sites, 75/ 107; improvements, 67/113N,166N; 71/79-80; Indian crossing, 72/90; international control, 69/272-73; irrigation, 63/89; lighterage, 71/72 maps and charts, 72/356; 74/358; 75/220— Duflot de Mofras, 64/232; Hudson's Bay Co., 64/197N; lower river, 74/ ins.fr.cov. Dec.; Warre and Vavasour, 64/197N,210N,216-17 mining trade, 71/41; mouth, 75/ 88,104; name change proposed, 74/ 268-70; naval installation, 74/215; navigation, 75/82,105,106; 76/317; 77/ 46,87,108; 79/176,201; ocean shipping route, 71/66,72; photos, 69/331-32; 70/6,8; 74/252,296,305,320; 75/fr.cov. March; pilotage and port charges, 67/163,175; pontoon bridge training site, 73/213; port authority, 70/182; power development, 65/366 railroads, 75/105— routes, 71/30-31,38,39,41-42,47,49, 50,54,55,66-69,71 settlement, 76/317,323,325 shipping, 71/66,72; 72/294-95— freight 1880, 71/94; heaviest ship, to 1849, 64/199; traffic to The Dalles 1858, 68/29 shore batteries, 70/184; sketch 1847, 67/292; Skirving panorama view, 65/ 156-58

steamboats, 67/88— British Columbia, 74/358; first screw propelled, 64/199; navigation head 1856, 68/9,22 transportation, 67/296; 74/163,299-302,321,358; travel 1881, 71/22; tributaries, 75/87-88; Upper Cascades photo, 62/316 United States— claims, 72/104-106,109,117; 76/ 199,210; development treaty with Canada, 63/89; occupation promoted, 70/339-45 Victor Channel, 77/362; Wilkes survey, 63/205 *Columbia River* (schooner), 78/288 Columbia River bar, 69/67,269,307; 77/43,359,360,361,362,364: pilot service, 68/266; 77/44-45,361; threat to navigation, 77/44-45 Columbia River entrance, 63/236, 252,361: charts, 69/306,bk.cov. Dec.; deep sea channel near, 72/90; first defense bill, 65/352N fortification of, 65/325-61; 72/56— Alvord plan, 65/328-29; construction, 65/336-37,339 improvements, 77/361; jetty, 69/ 309N; 77/358; lightships, 69/307, 323; north channel, 69/307N; south channel, 69/269N; SEE ALSO Cape Disappointment Columbia River Fishermen's Protective Council, 76/145 Columbia River Gorge, SEE Columbia Gorge Columbia River Highway, 72/348; 75/289; 81/333: Benson contributions, 66/263,265; bibliography, 74/141-42; bridges, 74/125,126; Chanticleer Inn, 66/269 construction, 66/253-70; 74/115-18,125,138— cost, 66/260; 74/111,116,117-18,137-38; early efforts, 74/108-109; masonry, 74/116,125,142; paving, 66/267,269-70; 74/118,139; tunnels, 74/125,127,138,139 critics, 74/110-11,116-17,118,138; dedication, 74/121-23,137,140-41,215,218; distinguished visitors, 74/126-27,142; economic advantages, 74/113-15,137; ecological considerations, 75/277; extension beyond Multnomah Co., 74/137; first in Ore. with modern engineering, 74/115; Gov. West part in, 66/251N; Hill promotion, 66/253,256; history, 66/249-71; 74/101-44; Highway 30, 74/137; Interstate 80N, 74/103; Lancaster employed, 66/259,261; land acquisition strategy, 66/265,267; maintenance, 74/128,142,144; opening, 66/270; perpetuation as parkway, 74/131,144 photos, 74/100,118,122,132,133, 140,218,292,296— bridges, 66/254,268; 74/138,142; construction, 66/252,253,262,264; Crown Point dedication, 66/256; exhibits, 74/119,141,232; Mitchell Point Tunnel, 66/263; Multnomah Falls dedication, 66/260,268; Rowena Loops, 66/266; Shepperd's Dell, 66/254; Vista House, 66/257,258 political opposition, 66/261; promotion, 74/110,112-15,118,119-21,123; Rhine Valley inspires, 74/106; right-of-way acquisition, 74/116,138; Riley describes, 74/232 scenic route, 74/104,113-14,126-27— *vs.* commercial route, 74/131,139,144 surveys, 74/108,115; waterfalls, 74/ 139; Yeon contributions, 66/262; SEE ALSO Crown Point Columbia River Highway Association, 66/249; 74/111,112 Columbia River jetty, 63/83 "Columbia River Kid," by Harry E. Rice, 74/293-332 Columbia River Maritime Museum: hours, 69/174; officers and directors, 65/310; 66/83,277; 67/81,282; 68/ 83,281; 69/80,277; 70/80,274; 71/ 192; 72/174; 73/76; 74/179; 75/89; 76/93; 77/92; 78/92; 79/108-109; officers and trustees, 80/107-108; 81/

107-108; publications, 75/362; 77/89, 292; 78/90; 80/105,334; 81/105 Columbia River treaty, 69/272-73; 72/252,253 *The Columbia River Treaty: The Economics of an International River Basin Development*, by Krutilla, review, 69/272-73 Columbia Slough, 64/262-64 Columbia Southern Hotel, Shaniko, 69/303 Columbia Southern Railroad, 72/341; 81/101-102 Columbia University, Portland, 78/285 *Columbian*, Olympia: advocates Washington territorial status, 64/36; Dryer control, 64/34; editors, 64/33; established, 64/34-35; name change, 64/37N,39; ownership, 64/39 "The *Columbian*: Washington Territory's First Newspaper," by William A. Katz, 64/33-40 Columbus Day Storm, 1962, SEE Climate Colusa County Historical Society, 73/81 Colvig, William M., 66/220N Colvile, Andrew, 63/233 Colvile, Eden, 63/233 Colville, Wash., 70/139: history of Immaculate Conception parish, 64/186 Colville Indian Reservation, 70/137,161: East, 70/116-17,125; maps, 70/136, 164; photos, 81/330; West, 70/116-18,125 Colville Indians, 70/115,116,118 Colvin, Henry, 63/352; 79/394-96 Colvin, John H., 66/382; 79/394 Colvin, Mable: "The Grip Wheel," 79/394-96 Colvin, Mary McGregor, 64/91; 65/308; 66/382 Colvin, Thomas S., 79/394 Colvin, Weslie, 79/394 Colwell, Lila, 66/59 Combe, George, 63/234 Combes, Jo, 70/57 Combest, Joe, 69/45 Combs, Welcome M., and Sharon C. Ross:

God Made a Valley, noted, 63/357
Combs Flat, 65/27N
Comcan Spring; SEE True Shout Spring
Comcomly (Indian), 63/236
Come to Our Salmon Feast, by McKeown, review, 62/102
Comegys, Henry Clay, 71/14
Comegys, Presley, 78/325N
Comets: Tebbutt 1881, 71/25
Commencement Bay, 66/108
Commerce, SEE Trade and commerce
Commercial Advertiser, Hawaii, 72/131
Commercial National Bank, Portland, 65/395N
Commission on Rights, Liberties, and Responsibilities of the American Indians, 68/177-78
Committee on Public Information, WWI, 71/216
The Commonwealth Review: article on Oregon highways, 74/120
Communications: early Eastern Ore., 66/214; early Ore., 63/245; Pacific NW theses on, 72/263-65; trans-Pacific cable proposed, 71/170-71; Washington 1844-59, 63/204N
Communism, 62/6,7,34,37-43*passim*: Oregon, 75/84-85
Communist Party, 76/139,141
Communistic communities: Missouri, 73/86; SEE ALSO New Odessa; Utopian societies
Community Chest drives, 74/233
Community colleges, 68/186; 69/337; 72/287
Community Hotel Corporation, Ashland, 64/329
Como, Nev., 64/86
The Company Town in the American West, by Allen, review, 67/357
Comparative Cartography, by Stevens and Tree, noted, 69/79
Comparative Notes on the Structure of the Yurok Culture, by Kroeber, noted, 62/108
The Complete Horseshoeing Guide, by Wiseman, noted, 74/359; review,

70/356
Compton, Charles E., 65/287,289
Compulsory school bill, 72/234,258; 75/181: campaign, 75/173-74; Federation of Patriotic Societies and KKK promote, 70/85; 75/162,168,172; Masons sponsor, 75/172; Pierce view, 75/171,172-73,189N
Comstock, Henry Tompkins Paige, 62/226N
Conant, Roger: *Mercer's Belles: The Journal of a Reporter*, ed. by Deutsch, review, 62/186-88
Concomly (Indian), SEE Comcomly
Concord stage, SEE Stagecoach transportation
Condit, Samuel Wilbur, 72/90
Condon, John, 75/78
Condon, T.D., 81/119N
Condon, Thomas, 62/315; 64/182; 65/75,100,105,364; 70/183,217; 72/90; 73/258; 75/78-79; 80/395,400: biography, 67/14FF; Drake sends fossils to, 67/14-16; first Ore. state geologist, 67/5,37; photo, 67/4
Condon Times, Condon, 69/129
Condra, Aaron, 63/246
Condra, Cordelia, 63/246
Condra, Silas R., 62/201; 63/246
Cone, Mrs. Anson, photo, 81/254
Conestoga wagons, 69/336; 70/364
Conflict and Concord: The Anglo-American Relationship Since 1783, by Allen, review, 62/407-408
Conflict and Schism in Nez Perce Acculturation: A Study of Religion and Politics, by Walker, review, 70/68
Conflict on the Northwest Coast: American-Russian Rivalry in the Pacific Northwest, 1790-1867, by Kushner, review, 77/85-86
Congdon, Russell S.: *Wakemap Mound, A Stratified Site on the Columbia River*, by Strong, review, 62/89-90
Conger, James K.: biography, 66/382
Conger, S.F., 69/225N
Congle, John, 80/300

Congregation Beth Israel, Portland, 70/366

Congregational Church, 77/371,375: Albany, 64/165; Beavercreek, 66/382; early Oregon, 77/300; Gaston, 76/381; Portland, 77/376; 78/34; The Dalles, 64/170

Congress of Industrial Organizations, 76/145-51

Conkling, Charles: Steens Mt. photos noted, 69/62

Conlin, Joseph Robert: *Bread and Roses, Too,* review, 71/358-59

Connelen, Bernard, 69/120-21

Connelen, Frank, 69/120-21

Connelen, Patrick, 69/120-21

Connell, Bridget, SEE O'Rourke, Bridget Connell

Connell, John, 69/121

Connell, Patrick, 69/121

Connell, Samuel, 74/208

Connely, Billie, 63/269

Conner, James, 62/140-43

Conner, Stuart W., 63/314

Connerly, W.B., 74/21

Connett, Antoinette, 73/84

Connette, Earle: *Pacific Northwest Quarterly Index,* review, 65/411

Connolly, Anthony J., 69/121

Connolly, James, 81/306,314

Connolly, Pat, 69/121

Connor (Conner?), Michael, 67/88; 71/198

Connor, Patrick Edward, 64/282; 72/73

Conquering the Great American Desert: Nebraska, by Dick, review, 78/282-83

Conrad, Agnes C., 64/6,31

Conrad, Agnes C., ed.: *Don Francisco de Paula Marin: A Biography,* noted, 74/285

Conrad, Anton, 65/270N

Conrad, Frowin, 70/313

Conrad, H.A., 70/146

Conrardy, Lambert, 70/327: letter quoted, 70/323-24; photo, 70/323

"A Conscientious Objector: Oregon,

1918," by Annette M. Bartholomae, 71/213-45

Conservation, 62/188-90,191-92; 67/87; 68/186; 69/332; 74/354; 77/190, 368: Alaska, 76/101; conservationists, 80/407-408; federal policy 1921-33, 65/205-206; forests, 72/83-84,183; San Joaquin watershed, 68/348; stream flow controversy, 70/363; Trans-Mississippi West, 73/286,360; utilitarian *vs.* militant, 74/101-103,134,139-40; wilderness areas, 73/275-76; wilderness concept, 68/345; SEE ALSO U.S. Civilian Conservation Corps

Conservation and the Gospel of Efficiency, by Hays, review, 62/188-92

Constance, Clifford Lord: *Chronology of Oregon Schools, 1834-1958,* noted, 62/108

Constantine Harbor, 80/35,48: photo, 80/36

Constitution (U.S. frigate), photo, 77/fr.cov. March

Constitutional Convention, Oregon, 62/107; 64/316; 66/15-16: slavery issue, 75/121; 81/245

Construction industry: Pacific Northwest, 77/302

Consumers Power Inc., 80/323,328

Continental (steamship), 62/187; 65/216

"A Convert's Testimonial," by Edwin R. Bingham, 75/336-38

Convict labor: road work, 74/109

Conway, Thomas R., 74/286

Cook, Aaron, 64/221N,224

Cook, Albert J., 64/172

Cook, Alfred?, Nisqually area, 63/146

Cook, Amos, 67/92

Cook, James, 62/193,198; 64/187,283; 69/67; 73/273-74; 74/279; 76/312-13; 77/290; 79/99,400; 80/197, 199,201: Alaska, 70/366; Behm collection, 80/197; bibliography, 63/84; cufflinks, 70/372; death, 66/280; 70/88; marine surveys of North America, 69/79

OHS exhibit, 75/363,366,367— catalog, 75/bk.cov. June Russian account of Kamchatka visit 1779, 80/197-204; ship *Resolution* painting, 79/fr.cov. Winter voyages, 72/84-85— bibliography, 63/84; second, 77/303; third, journal, 80/197; third, symposium, 77/300-301

Cook, James W., 62/169

Cook, Lewis Clark, 73/364; 77/386

Cook, Robert E., 77/90

Cook, Truman B.: Merchant Marine diary WW I, 77/107-29; photo, 77/100

Cook, Truman B.: "Crater Lake, 1915," 81/43-56

Cook, Warren L.: *Flood Tide of Empire: Spain and the Pacific Northwest, 1543-1819*, noted, 77/290; review, 74/353-54

Cook family, Tillamook Co., 77/91

Cook Inlet, 77/183,184

Cookbooks, 77/299

Cooke, Amos Starr, 64/318N

Cooke, Edwin N., 66/327: family, 72/353

Cooke, Philip St. George, 71/250

Cooking: dutch ovens, 76/69,348,350; electricity use, 80/121

Cookingham, Edward, 65/412; 71/220; 74/219

Cooksey family, immigrants of 1853, 78/129,148

Cooley, William, 66/393

Coon, Sam, 65/314

Cooney, John C., family, 69/121

Cooney, Mary Ellen Summers, 69/121

Cooper, Alice, 68/186

Cooper, Carl, 74/30

Cooper, David Rose, family, 67/89

Cooper, Elizabeth, 81/76,81N

Cooper, F., Auburn mines 1862, 62/224

Cooper, George M., 81/76N

Cooper, Henry Ernest, 71/175

Cooper, Jacob Calvin, 66/45N

Cooper, Martha W., 81/76N

Cooper, R., 64/22

Cooper Spur, 79/206-207

Cooperatives: cheese-making, 74/276; farmers, 76/136; Washington 1897, 64/353; SEE ALSO Rural electrification

Coopey, Charles, 62/165-77*passim*; 67/70-71,72,73

Coos and Curry Telephone Co., 75/162

Coos Bay, 64/355; 66/171; 70/236, 243; 72/159: coal discovery, 68/263; Dement recollections of area, 63/11-40*passim*; history, 68/350; sawmills, 68/265; school reminiscences 1910, 66/52-57; ships built, list noted, 73/75

Coos Bay, Ore., SEE Marshfield, Ore.

Coos Bay bar: photo, 68/266; pilot boat, 68/266-67

Coos Bay Commercial Club, 68/263

Coos Bay Company, 63/11-12

Coos Bay Lumber Company, 76/60,63; 77/75,216,219

Coos Bay Military Wagon Road, 67/42

Coos Bay Mutual Creamery, 66/52

Coos County, Ore., 66/91; 80/51,55: census 1860, 71/190; Dement recollections, 63/5-40*passim*; history, 68/352; 72/353; 75/363; marriages 1854-65, 68/81; myrtle groves, 67/41-53*passim*; pioneers, 71/289,290; prices 1856, 63/21,23; road photo 1910, 72/162; teachers, 71/290

Coos-Curry Electric Cooperative Inc., 80/328

Coos-Curry Pioneer and Historical Association: meetings, 69/278; 70/275; museum, 69/174; 70/81,275; officers and directors, 64/82,278; 65/122,311; 66/ 84,278; 67/81,282; 68/83,281; 69/ 80,277-78; 70/81,275; 71/193; 72/ 195; 73/76-77; 74/179; 75/89; 76/ 94; 77/93; 78/93; 79/109; 80/108; officers and executive board, 81/108; publications, 72/353; 74/92; 75/363

Coos Genealogical Forum: news letter, 67/279

Coos Indians, 68/90; 70/247

Coos River, 80/51,62N:

first school, 66/53; map, 80/57; SEE ALSO South Fork, Coos River
Coos River Cemetery, 66/53
Coos River Echoes, by Mahaffy, noted, 67/80
Coos River Valley: school history, 66/52-57; water transportation, 66/54-56
Cootie (Cote) (Indian), 63/156,157,159
Cootner, Paul H., 67/160
Coo-wee-min, SEE Coweman
Copalis Rock, 74/13
Cope, Edward Drinker, 67/17; 73/86; 75/78-79
Copious Spring, SEE True Shout Spring
Coppei Creek, 79/180
Copper and copper mining, 69/215; 76/180:
Montana, 64/349; 66/88; Pearl Mine, 72/43; Seven Devils, 72/183
The Copper King's Daughter; from Cape Cod to Crooked River, by McCall, review, 73/278
The Copper Kings of Montana, by Place, noted, 64/349
Copperfield, Ore., 67/90
Copperhat, Capt. —, 74/18
"Copperheads":
Oregon, 65/115-16N,184,296,393
Coquille, Ore., 63/17,34; 72/161: electric cooperative, 80/328
Coquille (steamer), photo, 76/84
Coquille Indians, 63/16-18,20-21; 71/289; 81/404
Coquille River, 62/215; 63/350,357; 70/243:
early settlers, 63/14-40*passim*; lifesaving station, 72/92; navigation, 72/92,353; photo, 76/84
Coquille Valley, 63/16; 74/92
Corbet, Ben, 63/285-86,290,296-97
Corbett, "Boston," 62/199
Corbett, Caroline, SEE Macadam, Caroline Corbett
Corbett, Elijah: biography, 80/317N
Corbett, Elliott R., 62/110,206,302, 423; 63/94,256,373; 64/360-61; 71/236; 75/5

Corbett, Mrs. Elliott R., 64/360; 72/360
Corbett, Henry Ladd, Sr., 71/232; 73/363
Corbett, Henry Winslow, 64/151; 65/392; 73/56:
defeated for senate, 73/55; estate, 71/226N; farm, 81/57; opposition to Stark, 72/329-31,335; photo, 72/328; railroad interests, 71/68
Corbett, P. Scott and Nancy P.: "The Chinese in Oregon, c. 1870-1880," 78/73-85
Corbett, Ore., 81/57
Corcoran, J., 80/300N,319N
Corcoran, R.B., 68/228
Corcoran, R.E., and F.W. Libbey: *The Oregon King Mine, Jefferson County, Oregon*, noted, 63/246,362
Corder, James C., 68/239,242
Cordes, Frederick C., 62/105
Cordon, Guy, 64/59-60
Cordova (ship), 66/127
Cordwood, SEE Fuel
Coreless (Corliss), Joseph, SEE Carless, Joseph
Corey, George H., 74/363; 78/369: *Inferior Courts, Superior Justice*, by Wunder, review, 80/330
Corinne, Utah, 71/8
Corlett, H.W., 69/312N
Cormack, Janet, ed.: "Portland Assembly Center: Diary of Saku Tomita," 81/149-71
Cormorant (British sloop), 64/241; 70/293N,307
Corn: corn laws, 69/73; French Prairie, 66/339; price 1858, 68/28
Cornelison, Lessie Moorhouse, 78/364
Cornelius, Benjamin, Ore. pioneer, 73/80
Cornelius, Nancy Emerine Chastain, 81/327
Cornelius, Thomas R., 65/393-95,398; 70/278:
camp named for, 66/152N; OMV service, 66/143N,149-59; papers, 71/80; photo, 66/136

Cornelius, William Tracy, **81**/327
Cornelius, Ore.:
hotel, **64**/89
Cornell, Bertrand, **79**/361,364,372,374,382-90*passim*
Cornell, Caroline Collier, **79**/363N
Cornell, Edward W., **79**/364:
photo, **79**/362
Cornell, Emily Castle, **79**/360,363N:
photo, **79**/362
Cornell, Gideon, **79**/359
Cornell, Holly, **79**/364,364N:
photo, **79**/362
Cornell, Sylvanus, **79**/359
Cornell, Wilbur Fisk, **79**/363:
photo, **79**/362
Cornell, William:
biography, **79**/359-66; family, **79**/359-64*passim*; journal 1852, **79**/367-93;
photos, **79**/358,362
Cornell, William:
"Guide to Oregon, 1852," **80**/66-100
Cornerstone: The Story of St. Vincent, Oregon's 1st Permanent Hospital, by Lucia, noted, **76**/304
Corning, Alice (Mrs. Dennis), **74**/167
Corning, Dennis, **74**/167
Corning, Glenn Milford, **74**/168,172-73
Corning, Howard McKinley, **73**/292, 315,316,321-22,323-24,331:
biography, **74**/153-54,165-66,168-73,261; birth, **74**/168; literary criticism, **74**/46-50; Ore. literary scene 1920s-30s, **74**/34-70,145-78,244-67;
photos, **73**/296; **74**/42,173,265
poetry, **74**/46,48,153,154,158-59—
best, **74**/263; first published, **74**/35;
process, **74**/264-66
Portland home, **74**/165
Corning, Howard McKinley:
"A.R. Wetjen: British Seaman in the Western Sunrise," **74**/145-78
"All the Words on the Pages, I: H.L. Davis," **73**/293-331
"Charles Alexander: Youth of the Oregon Mood," **74**/34-70
"Crossroads Woman," cited, **73**/322
History of Education in Portland, cited, **73**/324

The Mountain in the Sky, cited, **73**/299,329; **74**/165,174
"The Prose and the Poetry of It," **74**/244-67
These People, cited, **73**/299,329;
74/165; comment, **74**/153-54
This Earth and Another Country: New and Selected Poems, cited, **71**/190
Corning, Leroy Vincent (Roy):
family, **74**/165-72; house photo, **74**/165
Corning, Leta, **74**/167
Corning, Mary Milford (Mrs. Leroy Vincent), **74**/166-68,171
Cornish, Nellie, **79**/103
Cornish people:
in U.S., **70**/356-57
Cornman, Daniel, **68**/224N
Cornoyer, Narcisse A., **66**/142N,144, 145; **68**/305N; **70**/36,38,154; **72**/91:
photo, **70**/167
Cornucopia, Ore., **62**/300; **63**/80;
68/354; **70**/280
Coronado, Francis Vasquez de, **75**/94
Corral Springs, Klamath Co., **78**/239
Corral Valley, Modoc Co., **79**/288
Corregidor, **62**/20,23,30
Corrigal, Lucy, SEE O'Brien, Lucy Corrigal
Corrigal, M.S., **69**/117,143
Corrigal, Malcolm, **63**/269
Corrigan, Pat, **69**/121
Corruccini, Roberto, **77**/254
"Corruption and the Disputed Election Vote of Oregon in the 1876 Election," by Howard C. Dippre, **67**/257-72
Cort, John, **66**/40,41
Corta, Ellen, **76**/155,157N,164, 165N,168N
Corta, Jim, photo, **76**/156
Corta, Mitchell, photo, **76**/156
Corta Ranch, photo, **76**/171
Corvallis, Ore., **62**/312,313; **63**/10-12,200; **65**/185; **66**/15; **67**/88;
69/77,88; **71**/19:
Ft. Hoskins removal protested, **65**/185;
Gird letters, **68**/141-52; high school, **72**/283; hotel prices 1881, **71**/9; pheasant breeding farm, **65**/256; postal

cards, 66/305; state university, 66/165; tour, 77/299

Corvallis and Eastern Railroad, 67/71; 71/349

Corvallis Baptist Association, 64/133-34

Cosmopolis, Wash., 74/15

Cosner, Pat, 70/54

Cospar, Emma E., 81/81N: photo, 80/363

Cospar, Irene, 81/81N

Cospar, Josephine, 81/81N

Cospar, M., 81/81N

Cossack (vessel), 76/219N

Costigan, Howard, 76/143

Costo, Rupert, ed.:

Textbooks and the American Indian, review, 74/87-88

Cotroneo, Ross R., 64/283; 67/87

Cottage Grove, Ore., 63/365; 64/357; 66/187; 72/92: history, 71/361; 73/83,283

Cottle, Royal, 78/43,43N

Cotton, William Wick, 66/249; 74/110

Cottonoir, Edouard, 63/166

Cottonoir (Cotnoir, Cognoir, etc.), Michel, 63/124,162N,173

Cottonwood Canyon, Malheur Co., 63/286

Cottonwood Creek, Crook Co., SEE McKay Creek

Cottonwood Creek, Grant Co., 79/171

Cottonwood Creek, Malheur Co., 63/264,272; 78/155; 79/298

Cottonwood Island, 72/197

Cottonwood trees, 67/85; 69/148,155,157-58,167

Cottrell, Nancy, 64/359; 66/331N

Cottrell, William, 62/180

Couch, Charlie, 77/15-18,24: photo, 77/16

Couch, John H., 64/215N; 66/356; 73/250,256; 74/238; 80/138: fossils found by, 66/92; ship logs, 77/36,60; sketches of *Chenamus*, 75/fr.cov. Dec.; 77/36

Couch, Mary H., 79/203,206: photo, 79/205

Coues, Elliott, 62/334; 69/11,27, 163,167; 70/226; 72/181; 78/284

Coues, Elliott, ed.: *The History of the Expedition Under the Command of Lewis and Clark*, reprint noted, 66/188

Cougar Mountain Cave, 64/357

Cougars, 63/28-29; 66/353; 73/357; 76/333

Coulson, Isaac, 78/129,233

Coulter, C. Brewster, 62/106

Coulter, George H., 74/273

Council Bluffs, Ia., 63/88; 79/66,90

Council Crest: description 1907, 66/281

The Council Fire, Washington, D.C., 80/118,123

Council on Abandoned Military Posts: publications, 76/92

Counties: home rule, 69/86

The Country Boy, by Davenport, cited, 74/38

Country Boys Make Good, by Friend, noted, 71/286-87

County of Caithness (ship), 66/129

Courageous People, by Mallett, noted, 74/94

The Court-Martial of General George Armstrong Custer, by Frost, review, 70/66-67

Courthouse Rock, 62/338; 63/360; 79/375; 80/71: sketch, 79/374

Courts, SEE Judiciary

"Courts, Counselors and Cases: The Judiciary of Oregon's Provisional Government," by Mirth Tufts Kaplan, 62/117-63

Couse (*Lomatium cous*), 69/155,156

The Cousin Jacks: The Cornish in America, by Rowse, review, 70/356-57

Cove, Ore.: Indian rock inscriptions, 65/220

Covena (steamer), 77/363

Coventry, George, 63/84

Covered Bridge Topics: Oregon issue noted, 78/365

Covered bridges, SEE Bridges—covered

"Covered Wagon" (motion picture), 63/9

Covert, James T.:

A Point of Pride: The University of Portland Story, review, 78/285-86
Coville, Frederick V., 62/190
Cow Canyon, Wasco Co., 69/298,301
Cow Cave, Lake Co., 64/73
Cow Creek, Harney Co., 79/301
Cow Creek, Malheur Co., 65/301; 71/250: bridge photo, 71/253; name, 73/284
Cow Creek Canyon, Douglas Co., 72/89
Cow Creek (Spring) Lake, Malheur Co., 68/238N,248N,249N,308
Cow Head Lake: map, 72/27; names, 72/15N-16N
Cow Head Slough, 72/16N
Cow Valley, north Malheur Co., 70/19
Cowan, Edgar, 73/38-39
Cowan, J.L., 67/63
Cowboy Slang, by Potter, noted, 73/74
Cowboys, 63/89,275,324; 65/214,313; 73/286; 74/280; 79/105; 81/331: equipment, 63/325; 72/180; frontier accidents, 63/338; history, 72/180; Lakeview roundup, 70/355; language, 70/78; paintings, 72/180; recollections, 73/279; slang, 73/74
Coweman River, 79/408
Coweman (Coo-wee-min) station, 63/123,137,166,171,173
Cowen, Amanda (Indian), 62/198
Cowichan, B.C., 72/234
Cowley, Malcolm, 66/242
Cowley, Michael M., 66/283
Cowling, Freda, 74/239
Cowlitz (HBCO. bark), 63/217
Cowlitz Convention, 63/107,176; 64/301
Cowlitz County, Wash., 62/301; 66/32; 80/335: census 1860, 73/73; commissioners' journals, 63/83; county seat, 78/364; history, 63/245; 66/80,275,382; 80/335; pioneers, 65/211; 66/382
Cowlitz County Historical Museum, 69/175; 75/87
Cowlitz County Historical Quarterly, noted, 62/109,300-301; 63/83,245; 64/91,185,276; 65/120,211-12,309;

66/80,275,382; 67/279,366; 72/353-54; 74/281; 75/87; 77/90; SEE ALSO *Cowlitz Historical Quarterly*
Cowlitz County Historical Society: publications, 72/353; 73/73,283; 74/ 93,281; 78/90,364; 79/408; 80/ 207; 81/328
Cowlitz Farm, 62/64,72: buildings, 63/114; Catholic mission, 63/131,139; claim jumpers, 63/ 220,229 crops, 63/104— cultivation map, 63/113 employees, 63/106,108-109; established, 63/209; Ft. Cowlitz, 74/90; livestock, 63/104; location, 63/205; measles epidemic, 63/138-41; road from Puget Sound 1848, 63/204; Roberts' tenure, 63/227-28,231
Cowlitz Historical Quarterly, noted, 78/90,364; 79/408; 80/207,335; 81/328; SEE ALSO *Cowlitz County Historical Quarterly*
Cowlitz Indians, 72/153: basketry, 64/185
Cowlitz Landing, 63/55,107,239: settlement, 62/72; 63/55
Cowlitz Prairie, 63/209,239
Cowlitz River, 62/64,68,82; 63/104, 205; 64/297-98; 73/343,344-45: early trails, 63/83; falls of, 63/154, 156,167,170; photo, 74/296; Simpson at, 74/93; steamboats, 66/80
Cowlitz Steamboat Co., 63/108
Cowlitz Valley, 73/342,347
Cows, SEE Cattle
Cox, Anderson, Linn Co., 78/44
Cox, Anderson Miller: recollections, 73/284
Cox, John (Naukane), SEE Coxe, John
Cox, L.B., 62/418; 65/288
Cox, Ross: *Adventures on the Columbia*, cited, 77/79
Cox, Thomas B.: "Lower Columbia Lumber Industry, 1880-93," 67/160-78
Cox family, Deschutes homesteaders, 79/48

Coxe, John (Naukane) (Hawaiian), **66**/280

Coxey, Jacob S., **65**/264,291; **66**/73

Coxey's army, **67**/86; **74**/280,286; **75**/137: composition, **65**/269-70; California, **65**/272; Idaho, **65**/291-93 Oregon— Portland army, **65**/269-91*passim*; discipline, **65**/277,282; Labor Day parade, **65**/290; organization, **65**/ 275-76; train stealing, **65**/278-86; trial, **65**/288-89

Populist support, **65**/265-67,276N, 287; Seattle army, **65**/270,272,274, 292; Stead characterization of, **65**/293-94N; U.S. troops capture, **65**/285-86,289

"Coxey's Army in Oregon, 1894," by Herman C. Voeltz, **65**/263-95

Coyote Butte, Harney Co., **75**/67: photo, **75**/66

Coyote Creek, Jackson Co., **64**/355

Coyote Flat, Malheur Co., **71**/367

Coyote Mountain, Crook Co., **75**/309

Coyote Was Going There: Indian Literature of the Oregon Country, ed. by Ramsey, review, **79**/335-36

Coyotes, **69**/106; **75**/65: threat to sheep, **63**/267; trapping, **69**/138

Cozart, J.J., **79**/269N

Crab Creek, Grant Co., Wash., **70**/ 125,129,131

Crabb, Charles, **74**/18

Crabs, **80**/42

Crabtree, John, **67**/373

Crack-in-the-Ground, Lake Co., **70**/183

Cradlebaugh, John H., **75**/127

Crag Rats (mountain club), **77**/66,382

The Crag Rats, by Annala, noted, **77**/382

Craggies forest camp, **76**/49,82

Craig, John Templeton, **64**/185

Craig, Martha, **70**/22N

Craig, William, frontiersman, **70**/22N: Cayuse War, **66**/358

Craigie, James, **64**/355; **78**/51,60: biography, **78**/51N; photo, **78**/51

Craigmont, Ida., **65**/307

Cram, Thomas Jefferson:

reconnaissance map 1855, **66**/132; Southwest Ore. map no. 9, **69**/30

Cramer, Earnest F., **75**/221-31: fishing platforms, **75**/227-28, 229(photo),230; photo, **75**/231

Cramer, Ernest R., **75**/221,226,227,230

Cramer, Frederick K.: *Fishwheels of the Columbia*, review, **73**/68 "Recollections of a Salmon Dipnetter," **75**/221-31

Cranberries, **70**/272: Oregon industry, **72**/287

Cranbrook, B.C., **71**/339

Crandall, Jennie, **69**/328

Crandall, Lulu Donnell, **67**/299; **70**/280

Crane, L.E., **72**/14

Crane, Ore., **77**/155: photo, **77**/154

Crane and Co., Portland, **62**/170

Crane Creek, Harney Co., **65**/57N

Crane Creek, Malheur Co.: name, **73**/284

Crane Creek Gap, Harney Co., **65**/57N

Crane Lake, Nev., SEE Cow Head Lake

Crane Mountain, SEE Lookout Mountain

Cranston, E.W., Auburn mines 1861, **62**/218N

Cranston, Ephraim, **67**/88

Cranston, James A., **71**/220

Cranston, William, **62**/217; **79**/42

Crater Lake, **62**/322-23; **66**/384; **68**/223N,294; **70**/183,352; **75**/362,363: boating, **66**/382; **81**/46-56— photo, **81**/53 depth, **81**/50; fishing, **81**/55-56; photo, **81**/56; swimming, **81**/54-55; trails to lake, **81**/46-48

Crater Lake Lodge: construction, **81**/45; interior plan sketch, **81**/46

Crater Lake National Park, **62**/417,418; **64**/361; **65**/219; **66**/92,284,388; **71**/293; **81**/43

"Crater Lake, 1915," by Truman B. Cook, **81**/43-56

Crawford, Charles Howard, **62**/229, 233:

Scenes of Earlier Days in Crossing the Plains to Oregon, facsimile ed. noted, 63/357

Crawford, Helen, 62/288,289,290-91

Crawford, James, Pendleton 1903, 80/283

Crawford, John A., 67/63,65

Crawford, LeRoy: diary, 72/61N; emigrant escort service, 72/61,65,74,77; photo, 72/62 Crawford, Mary, SEE Stevens, Mary Crawford

Crawford, Medorum, 62/109; 73/253: biography, 72/59-60,77,229; Baker recommends, 72/59,60; emigrant escort service, 72/55-77; papers, 72/59N,60, 60N,61NFF; photos, 72/54,62; U.S. customs collector, 72/74N

Crawford, Medorum, Jr., 72/77

Crawford, Peter W., 73/82

Crawford, Philomen V., 67/62

Crawford, Samuel G., 72/61,77

Crawford, William C., 62/197,204

Crawfordsville, Ore., 68/187

Creameries, SEE Dairying

Crean family, immigrants of 1853, 78/148

Cree, William, 80/166N

Cree Indians, 65/374; 71/345

Creegan, Hugh, 69/121

Creegan, Michael, 69/121

Creegan, Patrick, 69/121

Creel, George, 71/216,243; 75/148-49

Cregan, Melvin A., SEE Keegan, Melvin A.

Creole people:

Russian in Alaska, 73/112,124,143,164; 77/180,181,182

Cresap, Robert V., 63/82; 65/28

Crescent Bay, 74/6,7

Crescent City, Calif., 62/215; 63/11; 72/11; 76/43: roads, 72/43,44

Crescent Creek, Klamath Co., 78/295: ford, photo, 78/296; map, 78/294

Crescent Lake, Klamath Co., 78/295, 297,299,300

Cressington (ship), 66/107

Cressman, Luther S., 62/90; 67/37; 78/369:

Early Man, noted, 75/87

Prehistory of the Far West: Homes of Vanished Peoples, review, 79/403-404

The Sandal and the Cave: The Indians of Oregon, review, 64/73

Cressman, Luther S., *et al*:

Cultural Sequences at The Dalles, Oregon: A Contribution to Pacific Northwest Prehistory, review, 63/75-77

Cresson, Charles C., 68/236; 70/19

Creswell, Ore.: history, 66/81; 74/281

Creswell Area Historical Society: publications, 74/281

Cricket River (Creek), SEE Silvies River

Crime and criminals, 70/51: bank robberies, 62/199; 66/81; 72/183; convict labor, 74/109; corrections in Ore., 72/287; Cowlitz Co. 1890s, 67/366; early Hawaiian, 67/372; frontier lawlessness, 73/360; fugitives, 77/193; hangings, 62/199,229-30,301; Hickman kidnap-murder, 67/91; horse theft, 81/192,322; Idaho, 62/297; indenture of criminals, 75/353,355; Klamath area 1872, 66/81; mail car dynamiting, 67/374; mail robberies, 72/288; mining camps, 81/191-93; murders, SEE Murders; Oregon 1851, 80/12-13; poisoning, 62/229; prison escape, 62/109; Prov. Govt. cases, 62/160 robberies, 62/66—

banks, 62/199; 66/81; 72/183; gold, Whiskey Gulch, 67/90; mail, 72/288; stage, 66/81; 72/88; train, 80/209

stabbing, 62/231; Tracy-Merrill escape, 73/346; violence, 80/205; 81/191-93; Washington Terr., 72/232; SEE ALSO Portland police

Cristobal Colon (vessel), 76/290,291

Criswell, Elijah H.:

Lewis and Clark: Linguistic Pioneers, cited, 63/69; 69/6N,9N

Crithfield, June:

Of Yesterday and the River, review, 65/306-307

Crittenden, John Jordan, 66/166

Crockett, Ernest L.:

The Murder of Til Taylor…A Great Western Sheriff, review, 72/352
Crocker, Charles, 71/283; 72/130
Crockett, David (Davy), 62/292
Croft, Fred F., 67/65,66
Croft, Mrs. Fred F., 67/67
Croft, Thomas, 74/18
Croft Hotel, Tacoma, 74/18
Crofutt, A. James, family, 64/185
Croisan Canyon, 75/214
Cron, C.P., 68/349
Cronin, Bart, 70/280
Cronin, Charles, 70/280
Cronin, Eugene A.:
described, 67/269; 1876 election dispute, 67/260-71*passim*; votes cast for, as presidential elector, 67/259,267
Cronk family, Columbia Co., 72/200,207
Crook, George, 63/81,83; 64/85; 65/301N; 68/238N,346; 69/84,172,240; 72/29N; 79/27N,50; 81/105:
and Ponca Indians, 70/365; biography, 79/131N
Indian campaign 1866-67, 79/121, 131,138-39,163,168,277-303*passim*, 330,333—
area of operations, 79/132(map),286-87; strategy, 79/292N
kidnapped, 69/84; opinion of Indian scouts, 79/132,298N; photo, 79/268
Crook, Mrs. George, 79/297
Crook County, Ore., 66/368,370; 75/309:
artifacts, 64/87; geology, 66/183; history, 66/183; range war, 66/183; school history and records 1882-1924, 81/207
Crook County Historical Society:
officers and directors, 78/93; 79/109; 80/108; 81/108
Crook Peak, photo, 79/280
Crooked Creek, Lake Co., 79/291N
Crooked Creek (Gibbs Creek), Malheur Co., 65/299; 74/350; 81/328:
described, 65/301; photo, 65/298
Crooked River, 62/213; 63/37; 65/79; 73/278; 77/334,335; 78/211,221,244, 293; 79/15,19,30-47*passim*,146,147, 149,152,295,296,331,332; 80/105:

Big Bend, 65/27; described, 65/27; fords, 79/145; lava flows, 72/90; Meek route, 65/28N; photo, 77/334; Steen route, 65/28N; SEE ALSO North Fork, Crooked River; South Fork, Crooked River
Crooked River Canyon, 64/357
Crooked River Valley:
Drake expedition, 65/12,26-83*passim*; pack train route, 65/22
Crookham, Arthur L., 62/110,206,300, 302,422; 63/93,255,372,374; 64/94, 190,286,363; 65/125,221,317,417; 66/93,189,285,394:
A History of Oregon Methodism, by Yarnes, review, 62/406-407
Crookham, Charles S., 77/385:
The Papers of Ulysses S. Grant, ed. by Simon, review, 69/66-67
Crooks, Joseph Ramsay, 62/205
Crooks, Ramsay, 65/213; 70/339,340; 80/336
Croquet (Croquette), Adrian, 70/324; 80/350-51
Crosby, Alfred, 77/45:
house photo 1855, 81/4
Crosby, Bertha, 63/291,301
Crosby, Charles, 63/277,279,291
Crosby, Magnus, 71/150,150N
Crosby, Nathaniel, Jr., 64/204N,210N; 66/163N; 69/338
Crosby and Smith, Ore. City, 66/163N
Crosby Memorial Library, Gonzaga Univ., 63/60
Crosby Ranch, Malheur Co., 63/291
Cross, Harvey E., 80/397:
biography, 80/296
Cross, Osborne O., 67/298,302; 68/11; 72/58:
recommends military post sites, 67/296-97; view of Ft. Dalles building plans, 68/6-7
Cross and Dimmitt, post card publishers, 66/305
Cross Hollows, Ore., 65/17,20,114N; 73/260; SEE ALSO Shaniko, Ore.
Cross Keys, Ore., 81/303,305:
map, 81/282
Crossen, J.B., 67/267

Crotty, Daniel L:
Electronics in the West, by Morgan, review, 70/267-68
Crouch, Malinda Sutherlin, 80/105
Crouley, Beatrice, SEE Strite, Beatrice Crouley
Crow, David, 75/67
Crow, James, 69/225N
Crow, Martha Landrith, 78/143
Crow, Rankin, 65/57N; 79/272N:
"Big Country: Where Pete French Was Shot," 75/67-68
Rankin Crow and the Oregon Country, review, 73/279
Crow, Ore.:
history, 63/245
Crow Camp, Harney Co., 79/272
Crow Creek, Harney Co.:
Drake expedition, 65/56N,67; name, 65/56-57N; 79/272N
Crow Dog (Indian), 63/75
Crow Indians, 63/247; 72/249,258; 81/350:
cultural influence on Cayuse-Nez Perce, 81/347; hair styles, 81/351,356, 358,360
Crowcamp Hills, 77/335
Crowe, E.H., 66/122
Crowley, Martha Leland, 70/184
Crown Point, 74/123,131-32:
photos, 66/256,257; 74/218
Crownhart-Vaughan, Elizabeth A.P.
(Mrs. Thomas Vaughan), 68/357-58; 69/269N; 71/371; 72/359; 73/101N; 75/369; 79/412; 80/411,414; 81/425:
The Alaska Boundary Dispute, by Penlington, review, 75/85
The Beginnings of Russian-American Relations, by Bolknovitinov, review, 78/359-60
Bering's Voyages, by Fisher, review, 79/212
A Chronological History of North-Eastern Voyages of Discovery, by Burney, review, 72/84-85
"Clerke in Kamchatka, 1779," 80/197-204
Conflict on the Northwest Coast, by Kushner, review, 77/85-86

Explorations of Kamchatka, by Krasheninnikov, trans. noted, 77/290
Feeding the Russian Fur Trade, by Gibson, review, 71/181
Here Comes the Polly, by Becker, review, 73/70
Imperial Russia, by Gibson, review, 77/293
Crownhart-Vaughan, Elizabeth A.P., and Basil Dmytryshyn, trans.:
Colonial Russian America: Kyrill T. Khlebnikov's Reports, 1817-1832, noted, 77/290,bk.cov. Dec.
The End of Russian America: Capt. P.N. Golovin's Last Report, 1862, noted, 80/bk.cov. Winter
"A Russian Scientific Expedition," by Blomkvist, 73/101-70
Crowninshield, Jacob, 76/205:
portrait, 76/206
Croxton, Thomas, 78/90
Crozier, William, 68/237
Crumb, Lawrence N.:
Historic Preservation in the Pacific Northwest: A Bibliography of Sources, 1947-1978, noted, 81/106
Crystal, Ore.:
post office, 69/341
Crystal Spring, Washington Co., Ida., 68/229,242N,298
Crystal Springs Farm, Portland, 62/169
Culbertson, Alexander, 63/73
Cullen, Matthew, 72/358:
Catalogue of Manuscripts, by Schmitt, review, 73/67-68
Market Days, by Bettis, review, 72/87
Culloma (brig), 77/38,39
Culp, Clif, 75/290
Culp, Edwin D., 62/104,415; 63/86,250; 65/123,312; 66/85,279:
"Oregon Postcards," 66/303-30
Stations West, The Story of the Oregon Railroads, review, 75/85-86
Cultural Relations in the Plateau of Northwestern America, by Ray, noted, 71/279
Cultural resources, 80/205
Cultural Sequences at The Dalles, Oregon: A Contribution to Pacific Northwest Prehis-

tory, by Cressman *et al*, review, 63/75-77
Culver, Richard K., photo, 74/ins.fr.cov. Sept.
Culver, Ore., 62/300
Cumberland House, 68/113
Cumberland Presbyterian Church, 79/21
Cummings (Cummins), Chauncy, 78/ 238; 79/48
Cummings, William, 78/127,130,238
Cummings-Moberly Co., 73/10; 77/ 213,214,346:
partner killed, 72/312; sawmill, 72/294,296
Cummins, Frank, 63/269
Cummins, Henry, 64/155
Cumsuuks Island, SEE Lone Pine Island
Cunningham, —, Coquille Valley settler, 63/17-18
Cunningham, Charles, 69/103: family, 69/121
Cunningham, John, killed by Indians 1855, 64/145
Cunningham, Nora B., 64/345
Cunningham Sheep Co., 69/121,135: history, 73/84
Cunnion, Ed, 69/121
Curl, James, 78/43,43N
Curran family, Morrow Co., 69/121-23
Currants, 69/149,153,155,158
Currey, George B., 67/57; 79/47, 130,275N,277:
biography, 65/10N,297N; establishes Camp Henderson, 65/299; depot 1864, 65/68,82N; expedition plans 1864, 65/65N,68-69,82N; First Ore. Cavalry service, 65/10-97*passim*,117, 294-95,298,301; Ft. Hoskins service, 65/186-87; marriage, 65/10N,26N, 105N; name carved on rock, 65/301; photo, 65/18
Currey, James L., 65/70
Currey, Jennie Clarissa Gaines (Mrs. George B.), 65/10N,26,105N
Currey (Smith's, Silver) Springs, Harney Co., 65/51N,83; 79/41,296
Currin, Charlton, 71/275
Currin, George J., 69/107: family, 69/123
Currin, Lottie, 71/275

Currin, Ralph, 69/123
Currinsville, Ore., 69/123
Curry, George Law, 64/140,142,146; 65/173N; 66/5,133-34,149-50; 67/ 301N; 72/319,321,323N,326,332N; 73/55; 75/358-59:
call for volunteers 1854, 67/312; Camp Curry named for, 66/148N; letter to Jeffries quoted, 66/153; OMV messages cited, 66/149-51
Curry, Leonard P.:
Blueprint for Modern America: Non-Military Legislation of the First Civil War Congress, review, 70/69-71
Curry County, Ore., 63/6,37-38; 66/ 365,372,373; 72/47,92; 76/43; 77/382:
borax deposits, 73/228-30; history, 65/315; 67/89; 68/352; 70/279; 80/335; pioneers, 71/289; 74/92; 78/363; recreation guide, 67/89; Sixes precinct, 66/374-75,377
Curry County Echoes, noted, 77/89,292, 382; 78/363; 79/407; 80/104,335
Curry County Historical Society: officers and directors, 79/109; 80/ 108; 81/108; publications, 75/87,362; 77/89,292,382; 78/407; 80/104,335
Curry County Reporter, Gold Beach: golden jubilee edition, 72/315
Curti, Merle, 72/179
Curtin, Catherine M., ed.:
"From Latvia: Fred Bitte," 81/31-42
Curtis, Asahel, 64/352
Curtis, E.J., 78/42
Curtis, Edward D., 62/172
Curtis, Edward S., 65/215,314:
The North American Indian, cited, 71/279,337
Curtis, George Ticknor, 63/346
Curtis, Nathaniel, 69/208
Cushing, Caleb, 62/8; 66/31; 76/197,213,217-18; 78/343; 81/203:
letter from LeBreton cited, 66/354N
Cushman, E.A., 72/197,199,200,202
Cushman, N.A., 74/19
Cushman, Otis, 72/203,207
Cushman, Ore., 74/273
Cusick, John Wickliffe, 67/63

Cusick, William C., **66**/233N
Custer, George Armstrong, **63**/81; **70**/66; **74**/96
Custer, Ida., **63**/89
Custer battle, SEE Indians—wars and hostilities
Custer's Gold: The U.S. Cavalry Expedition of 1874, by Jackson, noted, **68**/82
Customs department: Astoria, **63**/231,252; **81**/190N; Log Cabin, B.C., photo, **81**/144; Oregon and Alaska 1874, **65**/233; Port of Coos Bay, **66**/171N
Cut Creek, **62**/215
Cuthbert, Herbert, **74**/217
Cutlip, Blanche, **66**/54
Cutlip, Guy, **66**/54
Cutlip, Lorenzo, **66**/54
Cutlip, Mark, **66**/54
Cutlip, Nathan (Nate), **66**/54,57
Cutlip, Robert, **66**/54
Cutlip, Sherman, **66**/53,54
"Cutoff Fever," by Leah Menefee and Lowell Tiller, **77**/309-40; **78**/41-72,121-57,207-50,293-331; **79**/5-50
Cutright, Paul Russell, **66**/86; **67**/85: article on Lewis and Clark peace medals noted, **69**/84
Cutright, Paul Russell: *A History of the Lewis and Clark Journals*, review, **78**/284-85
Lewis and Clark: Pioneering Naturalists, cited, **70**/173N; **78**/284,285; review, **70**/348-49
"Meriwether Lewis: Botanist," **69**/148-70
"Meriwether Lewis: Zoologist," **69**/5-28
Thomas Nuttall, Naturalist, by Graustein, review, **70**/171-73
Cutter, Donald D., **63**/358; **65**/215
Cutting, Catherine, **63**/237N
Cutting, Charles, **62**/197
Cutting, Henry, **63**/237N,241
Cutting, Maria Cable: "After Thoughts," **63**/237-41
Cutting Prairie, **63**/237N,241N: name, **63**/239
Cyane (U.S. sloop-of-war), **70**/305

Cyclists: early Washington, **63**/83
Cynthian, Ore., **75**/346,349,352
"Cyrus Olney, Associate Justice of Oregon Territory Supreme Court," by Sidney Teiser, **64**/309-22
Czolgosz, Leon, **75**/140

Dachna (ship), **66**/122
Dacy, Helen Mahoney: recollections, **72**/94
Daggett (Dygett), John C., **63**/238N
Daggett Peak, **66**/82
Daguerreotypes, SEE Photography
Dagwell, Benjamin D., **74**/235
Dahlgren, Ulric, **65**/84
Dahonte, Jacques, **63**/125
Daignault, Simeon, **80**/346
Daily Advertiser, Portland, **64**/139,157
Daily Astorian: centennial, **75**/294; sesquicentennial edition, **63**/252
Daily Journal of Commerce, Portland: 50th anniversary, **63**/363; industry edition, **64**/363; **65**/217
Daily News, Longview, **77**/381
Daily Record, Salem, **80**/359
Daily Reporter, Portland, **72**/264
Daily World, Wenatchee, **65**/381
Dairy Creek, Klamath Co., **76**/353
Dairy Creek, Sauvie Island, **63**/234
Dairying: creameries, **74**/274,276,277—Broadbent, **63**/35; Coos Bay Mutual, **66**/52; Rainier, **64**/91
Hudson's Bay Co., **63**/225,234; Linn Co., **80**/106; Martin's Dairy, **66**/82; milking, **74**/317; separators, **77**/10; Tillamook Co., **71**/117,119(photo), 138-39; transportation, **74**/301 (photo); western Canada 1890-1906, **64**/283; SEE ALSO Cheese
Dairyville, Ore., SEE Hardman, Ore.
Daisy Ainsworth (steamer), **78**/365
Dakin, Susanna Bryant, **66**/380
Dakotas, **73**/286: Indians of, **63**/74-75
Dalgleish, David, **62**/167
Dallas, Alexander Grant, **63**/184

Dallas, Alexander James, 65/143
Dallas, George Mifflin, 65/144
Dallas, Jacob A., 65/141,146: biography, 65/143-45
Dallas, Mary Kyle, 65/145
Dallas, William, 65/143
Dallas, Ore., 63/363; 65/189,191; 66/13,16,385; 70/278; 75/346,363; 76/368-79; 78/158-73; 81/328: bandstand photo, 76/378; businessmen, 77/268; cemetery, 77/369-70; city park, 76/378,379(photo); depot photo, 78/ins.bk.cov. June; description 1871, 68/353; ethnic groups, 76/368; first electricity, 62/200 library, 76/373— photo, 76/ins.bk.cov. Dec. lodges, 76/373,374; map 1882, 72/171; mayors, 72/89; 78/183; memories of, 77/261-76; name, 72/89; pioneer picnic, 76/376; social life, 76/373-79; street photo, 77/ins.fr.cov. Sept.; view, 78/ins.bk.cov. June; woolen mills, 62/169,170
Dallas Manufacturing Co., 62/170
"Dallas Memories," by Evelyn Sibley Lampman, 77/261-76
Dalles, Columbia River, 67/295,296, 297; 81/397,400: Indian slave market, 81/413,414,415-16; Indian trade center, 81/418; map 1852, 67/op. Dec. title page; photos, 81/390,392; Skirving panorama, 65/157
Dalles City (steamer), 80/334
Dallin, Cyrus E., 69/84
Dalton, Ernest C., 68/342
Dalton, Mrs. Ernest C., 68/342
Daly, Arthur, 69/123
Daly, James, 69/123
Daly, John F., 74/219
Daly, Kathryn McDevitt (Mrs. James), 69/123
Daly, Marcus, 64/349; 65/121
Daly, Michael, 69/123
Damascus, Ore.: history, 64/92
Damien, Peter, 70/324N
Damien, Samuel C., 64/207N,208N, 211N
Damon's Point, 74/15,18
Damonte, Jim, photo, 77/252
DaMotta, Phil, 73/206
DaMotta Canyon: name, 73/206
Dams: Ana River, 77/158; Buena Vista, Calif., 63/311; Bully Creek, 63/272-74; Columbia River, 77/87; Detroit, 71/352; Dexter, photo, 78/323; Drew Creek, 77/8,12; Gold Ray, 65/218; Hells Canyon, 65/315; Hills Creek, 78/341; John Day, 62/201; 66/89; Lost River, 72/34N; Merwin, 68/341; Niagara, 71/349-57; North Santiam River, 71/349-57; Skagit Valley, 79/337; Winchester, 70/279; SEE ALSO Bonneville Dam; Lookout Point Dam; The Dalles Dam
Dan Scanlon (vessel), 77/359-62,363
Dana, James Dwight, 63/201; 67/8
Dana, Marshall N., 67/46,47; 75/6
Dana, Martha Ferguson McKeown, 62/198; 63/247; SEE ALSO McKeown, Martha Ferguson
Dana, Richard Henry, 63/192,216,218; 66/86
Dance, Nathaniel, 80/202
Dancehalls: Bandon, 75/340-41,342; Klondike, 63/352; Westfall, 63/283,286,289-90
Dancing: Baker Co. 1890s, 66/214; instructions, 80/287-88
Danebo area, Lane Co., 65/212
Daniels, Mark, 74/231
Daniels, Roger: *The Politics of Prejudice: The Anti-Japanese Movement in California and the Struggle for Japanese Exclusion*, noted, 64/187
Daniels, Sarah A. (Mrs. Beverly R.), 73/82
Daniels Creek, 66/53,55: Simpson logging photos, 68/264; SEE ALSO Lower Daniels Creek
Danish people, 81/268N: Junction City, 72/256; Oregon colony,

65/212; Oregon population 1860-1910, 80/266-67(tables); pre-immigration life, 81/60-74; Rasmussen recollections, 81/57-75

Danker, Donald F., ed.: *Man of the Plains: Recollections of Luther North, 1856-1882*, review, 63/80-81

Danner, Ore.: aerial view, 71/254; name, 71/255N; site of Charbonneau grave, 71/255

Dant, Thomas W., 74/238

Daphne (sloop), 70/305,306,308N,310

Darcy, John, 69/123

D'Arcy, Maria, 80/351: photo, 80/360

D'Arcy, Peter H., 66/363: family, 80/351N; photo, 81/254

Darcy, Virginia, 76/268

Darneille, Anderson, 78/124: photo, 78/126

Darneille, Dorothy, and Elizabeth Hiller, eds.: *Oldtimer Recipes*, noted, 63/357

Darneille, Isaac, 78/244-45

Darneille, Jasper, 78/124-25

Darneille, Mary Lane, 78/124

Darragh, John: biography, 65/116N; 79/133; report, 79/331-32; Snake campaign, 79/133, 139,141,147,161,278,279,281,285, 289,291,294,301,317,318,329-33*passim*

Dart, Anson, 64/277; 78/47: letters, 68/78

Dart, Eliza Catlin (Mrs. Anson), 68/78

d'Artois, Gaston, 65/352; 81/423

Dashing Wave (ship), 66/115

Daugherty, W.P., 63/108N

Daughters of the American Revolution, Oregon Society: Champoeg Memorial Museum, 69/175; Pioneer Mother's Cabin, 69/175; publications, 65/121; 81/105; Tillamook Chapter, 69/78; Young grave marker, 66/90

Davenport, Adda (Alice), 66/42

Davenport, Homer Calvin, 63/364; 64/352; 65/220; 80/400: appraisal of, 66/45-46; Arabian horses, 66/39,47

cartoons, 63/362— anti-cartoon bill, 66/46; lecture circuit, 66/44-46; Lewis & Clark Expo. exhibit, 66/45-46; political gadfly, 66/39,44-46*passim*; symbols, 66/43,49; sketches, 66/48

circus experiences, 66/43; death, 66/50

dog "Duff," 66/40,42— on stage, 66/41; original sketches, 66/42; photo, 66/40

father, 66/43,47,49; gamecocks, 66/43; journalist career, 66/39,41,44, 47; pheasant sketches, 65/255N; photo, 66/38; Roosevelt friendship, 66/44, 47; Silverton tribute, 66/49-50; sketches of artists, 66/47; stage career, 66/41,44-46

Davenport, Homer Calvin: *The Country Boy*, cited, 66/42; 74/38

Davenport, Timothy W. (Tam), 66/47: writings cited, 66/47N

Davey, Frank, 76/238

David (Coquille Indian), 63/16,18

David Douglas Historical Society: officers and directors, 80/108; 81/108

David Eccles: Pioneer Western Industrialist, by Arrington, review, 77/296

Davidson, George, artist, 68/102: painting of Adventure Cove, 68/ 100,103 sketches— Adventure Cove, 68/105; *Columbia Rediviva* in storm, 68/fr.cov. June

Davidson, George, surveyor, 72/139, 139N: Alaska, 63/359

Davidson, John, immigrant of 1853, 78/124,315: family, 78/314

Davidson, Margaret G., SEE Maunder, Elwood R.

Davidson, Nancy Amanda, SEE Hamilton, Nancy Amanda Davidson

Davies, Barbara Elliott (Mrs. David L.), 63/371; 64/359-60; 67/377; 71/101; 73/364

Davies, David Lloyd, 62/110,206,302, 423; 63/94,256,371-73; 64/93,189,

285,359-60,363; 65/125,331,317,415-16; 66/93,285,385-95*passim*; 67/375, 376,377,380; 68/359,361; 69/344, 347; 70/372,373,374; 71/371; 72/ 359; 73/362,373; 74/183,363,366; 75/5; 76/387; 77/385: photos, 66/292; 67/204

Davies, John, ed.:

Douglas of the Forests: The North American Journals of David Douglas, noted, 81/332

Davies, K.G., ed.:

Peter Skene Ogden's Snake Country Journal, 1826-27, review, 63/349-51

Davies, Mary Carolyn, 73/294,295,296, 297; 74/34,62,65: biography, 74/60,244N; described, 74/59

Davies, Mary Carolyn:

The Skyline Trail, cited, 74/49

The Slave With Two Faces, cited, 74/59

Davies, Walter L.J., photo, 74/214

Davis, Anthony L., 66/11

Davis, Arthur P., 70/84

Davis, Benjamin, 78/325N

Davis, C. Gilman:

Historic Western Churches, by Florin, review, 71/186-87

Davis, Carl L., 62/110,206,302,420, 421,422,423; 63/93,94,255,256,372, 373; 64/93,189,285,358,363; 65/125, 221,317,415-16; 66/93,189,285,392, 393,394,395; 67/380; 68/361; 69/ 347; 70/373: logging company, 77/77

Davis, Drury, 79/364,365,382-89*passim*

Davis, E. Carmichael, 64/255

Davis, E.J., 68/214

Davis, Eliot, 66/388

Davis, Everett H.:

"Oregon—First in 'Portable' Irrigation," 78/351-54

"Rural Oregon Lights Up," 80/323-28

Davis, Frank, Jackson Co., 77/90

Davis, Garrett, 73/38

Davis, George W., 81/50

Davis, Hardin, 73/283

Davis, Harold Lenoir, 68/279; 71/182, 368; 72/181; 74/156,159; 80/206:

awards, 66/241,242,243; 73/293,301,305,312,313; biography, 73/293-331; death, 66/240,245; 74/261; education, 73/305,306; evaluation of literary works, 66/245-48; letters, 73/321-24,329; marriage, 73/ 308; Mencken comment, 73/313; painting, 66/244; philosophy, 74/250; photos, 73/301,ins.fr.cov. Dec.; poetry, 66/242; 73/305; 74/247,254; quoted, 74/249-50,253; writings commented on, 74/244-54

Davis, Harold Lenoir:

Beulah Land, cited, 66/243,246,247; 73/322,331; published, 74/245

"By the River," cited, 73/319

The Distant Music, cited, 66/243; 74/248

"Eastern Oregon—The Old-Fashioned Land," cited, 73/319

The Harp of a Thousand Strings, cited, 66/242; 73/331; 74/245; quoted, 74/250

"Homestead Orchard," cited, 73/328

Honey in the Horn, cited, 66/240,242; 73/312-13,317,321,331; 74/248, 254; quoted, 66/246,247

Kettle of Fire, cited, 66/244; 74/248; review, 62/192-96

"Of the Dead of a Forsaken Country," cited, 73/298

"Oregon Autumns," cited, 66/73, 302,310; 74/157

Proud Riders and Other Poems, cited, 66/242; 73/319,331; published, 74/247

Rivers of America series, 73/317

"Running Vines," cited, 73/319

"Sheepherders: The Quiet Westerners," cited, 66/245

Status Rerum, cited, 66/73,302,310; 74/157

Team Bells Woke Me, cited, 66/243; 73/307,309-10

"A Town in Eastern Oregon," cited, 73/310

Winds of Morning, cited, 66/243; 74/ 247; quoted, 66/247; 74/249-50,253

Davis, Hugh H., ed.:

"Three Letters of William Gird, 'Veteran of Turf, Field, and Farm'," **68**/141-52

Davis, Jack ("Diamondfield Jack"), **69**/85

Davis, James Alexander, **66**/240; **73**/304,305,306,307,308

Davis, James S. ("Cashup"), **70**/181

Davis, Jefferson, Confederate States pres., **72**/327,335,337

Davis, Jefferson Columbus, **62**/323: Alaska duty 1869, **72**/135,137,146

Davis, Mrs. Jefferson Columbus, **72**/137

Davis, Joe, Wasco Co. 1881, **81**/277

Davis, John, Coos Bay settler, **63**/12

Davis, John, Yamhill Co., **69**/339

Davis, Joseph, Lane Co., **67**/179; **79**/6

Davis, Josephine Brownlow, ed.: *Yours Sincerely, Ann W. Shepard: Letters From a College Dean*, review, **80**/102

Davis, L.M., **75**/108

Davis, L.S., paleontologist, **67**/18

Davis, Leland, **74**/60,62,174

Davis, Lenwood G.: *Blacks in the State of Oregon, 1788-1971*, cited, **73**/211

"Sources for History of Blacks in Oregon," **73**/197-211

Davis, Levi T., **69**/339

Davis, Lewis Hawkins, **66**/382

Davis, Marguerite N., and C.R. Tully: *The Building of a Community, Multnomah*, noted, **77**/299-300

Davis, Marion Lay (Mrs. Harold L.), **73**/293,325,326: biography, **73**/308; death, **73**/329; letters, **73**/313-15,329

Davis, Mart, **63**/12

Davis, Percy, **73**/305

Davis, Quentin, **73**/305,306,307

Davis, Richard, **73**/305

Davis, Richard Harding, **80**/333

Davis, Rollie, photo, **80**/324

Davis, Russell, and Brent Ashabranner: *Chief Joseph: War Chief of the Nez Perce*, review, **64**/348

Davis, Ruth Bridges (Mrs. James A.), **66**/240

Davis, Samuel, **63**/121,148

Davis, Seth, **74**/6

Davis, Tom, Malheur Co. 1915, **63**/300

Davis, W.N., Jr., **65**/313

Davis, Wilbur A., **63**/75

Davis, William A., **64**/276

Davis, William L., **67**/87

Davis Creek, Lake Co., **76**/336,340,343

Davis Lake, **70**/183

Dawes, Thomas, **70**/305

Dawson, George Mercer, **70**/180: biography, **66**/70; Boundary Commission records, **66**/70

Dawson, Oliver, **76**/382

Dawson, Orion B., **76**/382: photo, **76**/261

Dawson, Orion B.: "The Ironwork of Timberline," **76**/259-68

Dawson, Vernona Cherrington, **70**/279

Dawson, Yukon Terr., **62**/95,96; **76**/115,117: food crisis 1897, **76**/115-16; photo 1899, **76**/114; population 1897, **76**/115

Day, —, Coos Co. settler, **63**/20

Day, Edward Henry, **67**/319N-20N; **69**/223N,235; **70**/252N: biography, **69**/235N

Day, George, Coos Bay settler, **63**/20

Day, John, Astorian, **77**/81

Day, John, OHS director, **62**/110,206,302

Day, Joseph Warren, **65**/309

Day, S.H., **79**/284N

Day, Sherman, **72**/48

Day, W.P., **69**/311,313,322

The Day the Cowboys Quit, by Kelton, review, **74**/280

Days and Ways of Old Damascus, Oregon, by Maybee and Forbes, noted, **64**/92

"Days at Mercer Lake," by Robert O. Clark, **75**/301-308

Dayton, Frank, photo, **70**/206

Dayton, Ore., **62**/73; **65**/173N,177N, 217; **70**/233: early history, **67**/92,373; school, **65**/218

Dayton (steamer), **71**/14,150

Dayton, Sheridan and Grand Ronde

Railway Co., **81**/328
Dead Mans Creek, Ida., **68**/240,309
Dead Man's Hill, Umatilla Co., **78**/103
Deadman Canyon, Lake Co., **68**/319
Deadwood, S.D., **74**/334
Deady, Edward N., **75**/137
Deady, Matthew Paul, **62**/80,294,312, 320,326,328,329,330,333; **64**/302, 309,312-16; **66**/12; **67**/179,294N; **68**/333; **70**/221N; **72**/181,323N, 326N,329,332N; **73**/50; **78**/175; **79**/ 6; 80/147; **81**/250,259: constitutional convention, **66**/15; diary noted, **77**/291; judicial district, **64**/ 312-13; opinion on Stark senate seat, **73**/43N,50; Oregon code, **73**/61; **74**/286; papers, **71**/80N; **73**/43N, 50N,55N; Pennoyer *vs.* Neff decision, **73**/60,62; photo, **73**/42; removal from justiceship, **66**/25,27-28,31; U.S. district judge, **73**/60,62
deAlfonso, Fernando, **76**/341-43
Dealy, David, **68**/233N
Dean, Nathaniel, **72**/93
Dean, Willis J., **63**/31-32
Deardorff, Flemming Byars, **72**/94
Deardorff, Sara Manwaring (Mrs. Flemming B.), **72**/94
DeArmond, Robert N.: *The Founding of Juneau*, noted, **68**/184
DeArmond, Robert N., and Evangeline Atwood: *Who's Who in Alaskan Politics: A Biographical Dictionary of Alaskan Personalities, 1884-1970*, review, **78**/358-59
Death Valley, **63**/311
Debast, Felix, family, **65**/308
Debo, Angie, **67**/186
deBourbourg, Charles E.B., **72**/182
Debs, Eugene Victor, **66**/73; **75**/137
DeChesne, Henry, **81**/382: at McLoughlin deathbed, **81**/382; gives reason McLoughlin entered fur trade, **81**/381,383,386
Deckard, Anderson, **64**/277
Decker, Charles F., **67**/223-24
Decker, Fred W.: "Discovered: A Photo and More Facts About Mary Leonard," **78**/174-76

The Decline of the Progressive Movement in Wisconsin, by Margulies, noted, **70**/79
Decoration Day, **77**/271-72
Decraene (DeCraine), J., **81**/88,88N,90, 91,92: photo, **81**/90
Dedman Ranch, **64**/107
Dee, Ore., **70**/52,53
Deep (Beaver) Creek, Ida., **68**/246, 310,313N
Deep Creek, Malheur Co., **63**/264,266
Deep River, Wash., **75**/106; **81**/106
Deepwater Family, by Duncan, noted, **71**/190-91
Deer, **69**/14,18-19; **73**/261-62; **74**/ 311; **76**/75,80,87; **77**/353,359; **79**/145,147,150-51,153,158,159,376: Champoeg District, **66**/339; discovered by Lewis, **69**/23 hides, **69**/330— tanning, **76**/340; used for moccasins, **73**/262
mule deer named, **69**/10
Deer Creek, Baker Co., **62**/228
Deer Creek, Douglas Co., **63**/24
Deer Creek, Ida., **81**/334
Deer Island area, Columbia Co., **64**/91: history, **66**/382
Deer Lick Crossing, Lane Co., **78**/320
DeFonte, Bartholomew: apocryphal voyage, **63**/88
deForest, Lee, **70**/268
Degarsnnee, Lucien, SEE Garnier, Lucien
Degie, Philippe, **69**/338
DeGraff, Grace, photo, **72**/208
Deguire, Joseph, **66**/361N
Dehlinger, P., **64**/284
DeHorsey, A.T., **63**/200
DeHorsey, F.R., **63**/154N
Del Shaver (steamer), **79**/394
Delafield, Richard, **65**/350
Delaney, Daniel, **70**/278
Delaney, John O'Fallon: diary, **64**/85
Delaney, M., Sacred Heart student, **81**/81N
Delard, Joseph, SEE DeLore, Joseph
DeLashmutt, Inez, **75**/27
DeLashmutt, Van B., **69**/208,211,213;

75/27
Delaunay, Joseph, 77/81
Delavan, W., 66/381
DeLay (Delay), Joseph, 64/261
Delena, Ore., 64/91; 77/89
Delirium tremens, 64/209N
Delisle, William, 73/286
Dell, Floyd:
Oregon visit, 74/64-66; photo, 73/296
Dell, Floyd:
The Golden Spike, cited, 74/65
Moon Calf, cited, 74/64
Dellameter, John, 79/11
Dellenbaugh, Frederick S.:
A Canyon Voyage, facsimile ed. noted, 63/356
Dellerof (vessel), 80/40
Del Norte County, Calif.:
census 1873, 74/93
DeLong, George Dewey:
reminiscences, 73/73
DeLong, Lamand, 73/73
DeLore, Augustin ("Quanna"), 79/
161N,162,166
DeLore (Delard, Delord), Joseph, Sr., 66/341:
biography, 79/155N
DeLore, Joseph, son of Pierre, 79/
168,169N
DeLore, Pierre (Peter), 69/77; 79/
155N,161N,162,165
DeLore (Delard, Delord) family, 69/87-88; 79/155N
DeLorge, Cathy:
An Index of Archived Resources, by Hines, review, 77/297
Delorme, B., 80/350
Deluchi, Louis, 77/259
Delzell, William A., 69/328
deMartini, Antonio, 77/244
deMartini, Raffaele, 77/244,246:
photo, 77/252
Dement, Aileen, 63/39
Dement, Alice (Mrs. Wallace B.), 63/36
Dement, Caroline, daughter of Louisa Lovett Dement, 63/36
Dement, Caroline Spencer (1st wife of Samuel Maxwell), 63/5-27*passim*
Dement, Cecile (Mrs. Ellis S.), 63/39

Dement, Clay, 63/36
Dement, Daniel, 63/40
Dement, Diane, 63/40
Dement, Ellis S., 63/5-40*passim*:
photo, 63/8
Dement, Ellis S.:
"After the Pioneers," 63/36-40
Dement, Faye (Mrs. Russell), 63/40
Dement, Joan, 63/40
Dement, John, Steilacoom 1851, 63/169
Dement, Lester T., 63/32
Dement, Louisa Lovett (2nd wife of Samuel Maxwell), 63/32
Dement, Lucy Ann Norris (Mrs. Russell Cook), 63/33
Dement, Maxwell, 63/36
Dement, Nelly Ann, 63/22-40*passim*
Dement, Raymond B., 63/37
Dement, Roxanne, 63/40
Dement, Russell, son of Ellis S., 63/6, 39-40
Dement, Russell Cook, 63/5-40*passim*
Dement, Samuel, son of Ellis S., 63/6, 39-40
Dement, Samuel Maxwell, 63/5-40*passim*:
family history, 74/94
Dement, Taylor, 63/36
Dement, Wallace B., 63/36
Dement, Winnie, SEE White, Winnie Dement
Dement Creek, 63/15,18,22,33:
name, 63/33
Demers, Modeste, 63/55,209; 64/78;
66/347; 69/54-55,64,270; 71/344;
74/89-90
Demijohn's Tower, Lane Co., 78/55
Demmick, Charles, 77/167
Democrat-Herald, Albany, SEE *Albany Democrat*
Democratic Party:
Breckenridge faction, 72/321-27,337;
73/44,52,53; Catholic support, 75/
133; clubs, 71/148,150; Douglas faction, 72/322,323,327,337; Gold Democrats convention 1896, 68/331-32;
initiative and referendum fight, 68/
209-14; Ku Klux Klan support, 75/
169-72; Long Tom secession activities,
67/54-60*passim*; Marion Co. conven-

tion 1854, **66**/360; Multnomah Co. conventions 1858-60, **70**/321-22; **73**/52,53,55; national convention 1892, **71**/148-49; national officers, **71**/151; New Deal, **76**/135-51*passim*; newspaper support, **71**/147-48; SEE ALSO *Oregon Journal; Oregon Voter* Oregon, **73**/55; **75**/168,178; **76**/137,142—

1858 break, **68**/346; 1876 presidential elector dispute, **67**/257-72*passim* history—

1856-62, **72**/316-38*passim*; 1900-1956, **72**/80-81,227

state officers, **71**/151

Oregon Territory, **75**/119,120, 351,357—

judicial dispute, **66**/27-28,30 Portland, **80**/14-22*passim*,156-68*passim*,298,307; pro-slavery faction, **75**/121-22; senate campaign 1918, **68**/133-35,137; Washington state, **76**/139; SEE ALSO Salem Clique

Democratic Standard, Portland: quoted, **66**/142-43,150-51N

Democrats of Oregon: The Pattern of Minority Politics, 1900-1956, by Burton, review, **72**/80-81,352N

de Mofras, Eugene Duflot, **63**/210; **66**/351N:

Columbia River chart photo, **64**/232 DeMoss family, **72**/85; **77**/285N:

triple octave Shaker chimes, **65**/412 DeMoss Springs, **72**/85; **77**/285 Dempsey, Isaac Iddings, **77**/272 Denby, Charles, **71**/141 Denby, Charles, Jr., **71**/141 *Dendrath Castle* (ship), **66**/129 Denecke, Arno:

The Supreme Court in a Free Society, by Mason and Beaney, review, **62**/93-95 Denlinger, Henry, **65**/29N Denmark, Ore.:

cemeteries, **66**/90; **71**/290 Dennan, James, **69**/123 Denning, Job,

78/125,157,207,213,225,233: photo, **78**/226

Denning, Stephen, **78**/125

Dennis, Bruce, **78**/104 Dennis, Henry, **69**/115,123 Dennis, Margaret Cook, **69**/123 Dennis family, immigrants of 1853, **79**/365,373 Dennison, —, Idaho 1862, **79**/198,199 Dennison, Ami P., **69**/240; **79**/126, 126N,143 Denny, Christian, **65**/231 Denny, David, family, **79**/337 Denny, Eliza Nickerson: land claim, **65**/231-32 Denny, Gertrude Jane Hall White (Mrs. Owen N.), **74**/218: biography, **65**/234; death, **65**/261; marriage, **65**/232-33; pension, **65**/260-61; Whitman massacre, **65**/234,259 Denny, John, brother of Owen N., **65**/243-45,257,259 Denny, Owen Nickerson, **70**/359; **80**/303N,312N: biography, **65**/229-34; death, **65**/259; Gibbs correspondence, **65**/232; Himes memorial to, **65**/246-47; Korean court adviser, **65**/251; marriage, **65**/232-33; Multnomah Co. senator, **65**/257,259; pheasant project, **65**/234-62*passim*; photo, **80**/314; U.S. consul Shanghai, **65**/233-47 Denny, Thomas, family, **62**/205 Dent, Frederick T., **65**/183-84; **68**/6 Dentalium (hiaqua): adornment, **81**/351,352; photo, **81**/396; used as money, **81**/396-97 Dentistry, **67**/280; **77**/357: frontier, **63**/338 Denver, J.W., **64**/149 Denver, Colo.: foreign born population 1870-1910, **80**/263(table) Department of Oregon, SEE U.S. Army Department of the Columbia, SEE U.S. Army Department of the Pacific, SEE U.S. Army de Pourtales, Countess, SEE Holladay, Jennie deQuille, Dan, SEE Wright, William Derby, Florence, **79**/203,210 Derby, George Horatio ("John Phoenix,

Esq."), 62/293: bibliography, 71/188; biography, 71/188; dispute with Thomas Jordan, 68/25-26; sketch by, 81/189

Deroche (Desroches), Charles, 63/157

DeRock, Seraphinus, 65/308

DeRosa, Bonaventura, 77/254: Italian newspaper, 77/259

Derrick Cave, 64/87

DeRussy, Rene: Columbia River fortifications, 65/329-51*passim*

Derval, Denis, SEE Durval, Denis

de Saules, James, SEE Sauls, James D.

Deschutes Canyon, 68/91,184

Deschutes Club: history, 68/184

Deschutes County, Ore., 77/79-81: Charcoal Cave relics, 65/220; creation, 68/91; history, 72/94; pioneers, 62/201; 68/91; prehistoric mounds, 63/254

Deschutes County Farm Bureau, 76/244-45

Deschutes County Historical Society: officers and directors, 77/93; 78/93; 79/109; 80/108; 81/108

Deschutes County Museum, 72/94

DesChutes Historical Center, 81/104

Deschutes Indians, 66/143,146; 79/125

Deschutes Pioneer Association, 67/88; 77/89: members, 73/84; museum, 73/84; publications, 72/94

Deschutes Pioneers' Gazette, noted, 75/294; 77/89; 80/104; 81/104

Deschutes Railroad: canyon roadbed photo, 69/297; construction race to Bend, 69/293

Deschutes River, 62/217,219; 63/10, 147,355; 69/232; 72/342; 73/63,260; 77/331,332; 78/52,221,231,235,241, 245,247; 79/5,10,15,19,27,29,33,40, 48,176,201,294: boating 1963, 65/217; Drake exped. scouts, 65/78-79; early travelers' geographic errors, 78/147,157,207,208, 211,222; fords, 77/315; 78/237,239,

241-42,293,294; 79/127N,145; OMV 1855 march, 66/135; photos, 69/296, 297,304; 73/300; 77/331; 78/250; race to build railroads, 69/293; settlers, 79/49; source, 78/57; toll bridge, 65/115N; Wyeth route, 73/84; SEE ALSO Big Marsh Creek; South Fork, Deschutes River; West Fork, Deschutes River

Deschutes River Basin, 63/91

Deschutes Valley, 76/244

Desdemona Sands Light, 66/181

Deseret, State of: boundaries, 72/6-7; slavery question, 72/7; statehood petition 1849, 72/7; Utah Territory, 72/7

Desert Challenge, An Interpretation of Nevada, by Lillard, review, 67/364-65

Deserts: ancient lakes in western, 66/284; depicted in magazines, 66/86; Great American Desert, 65/313; 67/277; 70/87; 73/66,86; 78/282-83; Nevada, 67/364-65; Oregon, 66/272-73; SEE ALSO Land

des Granges, H., 68/358

DeSmet, Pierre Jean, 62/106; 63/57,59; 64/78,282; 67/87,370; 68/76,347; 69/55-56,64-65,269-70,336; 73/284; 74/354,359; 81/27N: Kutenai mission, 71/342-43; letters, 72/286; papers, 70/77

Desmond, —, Cape Arago lighthouse keeper, 66/174,177

Desmond, Jack, 62/231

Desolation Valley, 68/234

Despain, Charles, 80/285

DeSpain, Jeremiah B. (Jerry), 64/119N

Despard, Marguerite, 66/348N

Despard, Marie Anne, SEE Gervais, Marie Anne Despard

Desroches, Charles, SEE Deroche, Charles

de Stoeck, Edouard, 78/288

Destruction Island, 74/21,24: lighthouse, 66/181

Detroit, Ore., 69/340; 71/349: early history, 64/356

Detroit Dam, 71/352

Detroit Photographic Co., Michigan,

66/304
Deutsch, Herman J., 64/274,283; 70/137N:
The Transportation Frontier: Trans-Mississippi West, 1865-1890, review, 65/304-305
Deutsch, Lenna A., ed.:
Mercer's Belles: The Journal of a Reporter, by Conant, review, 62/186-88
DeVaney, Andrew J.T.J., 80/379
DeVaney, Franklin P., 80/377,379-80
DeVaney, Malinda, SEE Bilyeu, Malinda DeVaney
DeVaney, Robert E., 80/379
DeVaney, Sarepta Missouri, 80/379
Dever, Lem, 75/159,180-82: photo, 75/181
Devereaux, Maryetta, 63/253; 65/217
Deverell, —, Multnomah Co. carpenter, 81/59
Devers, Arthur H., 62/165; 71/155N; 74/234
Devil's Garden, 68/91
Devil's Gate (Gap), 66/198; 80/75
Devil's Woodpile, 66/82
Devine, John S., 63/310-12,333; 68/254,321; 69/63; 72/93
Devlin, Barney, 69/123,138
Devlin, Mike, 69/123
Devlin, Thomas, 62/172
DeVos, Peter, 64/201; 69/270-71
DeVoto, Bernard, 62/292; 63/344; 64/46; 80/408
Dewar, F.N., 74/210
Dewey, George, 76/272,273,283
Dewing, C.E., 65/313
Dewitt, Howard A.:
"Charles L. McNary and the 1918 Congressional Election," 68/125-40
DeWitt, James:
family history and letters, 72/171
DeWitt, O.K., 63/364
DeWitt Museum, Prairie City, 69/175
DeWolfe, C.H., 64/155-56
DeWolfe, Frederick S., 75/294:
Impressions of Portland, 1970, noted, 71/362
Portland West, review, 74/356-57
Dexter, F. Gordon, 69/219N

Dexter Dam, photo, 78/323
Dexter Lake, 78/323
DeYoung, Meichel Harry, 71/146,146N
Diamond, John, 77/321,324,325,328, 336,337N; 78/41; 79/10,23: portrait, 77/326; recollections, 77/328,336-38
Diamond Lake, Douglas Co.: geologic history, 66/282
Diamond Match Company, 72/301
Diamond Peak, 74/323,329,330; 78/ 57,67N,299,308,317; 79/5: immigrant route pass, 78/330; landmark on immigrant route, 78/232,300, 302; name, 77/329,329N-30N; 79/23; on maps, 78/68,248; 79/ins.fr.cov. March,26,34,44; Ore. Central Military Road route, 79/46,47N; Pacific RR Survey party, 79/27-29; photo, 78/308; rail route to Winnemucca, 71/40,45, 50,51,54,55,63,64,68,70,74,81; wagon road route, 79/27,29
Diamond Peak Wilderness Area, 78/308; 79/23
Diamond Ranch, 68/301; 70/21N
Diary of a Student Nurse: The Diary of Ollie Marquiss, 1910-1913, ed. by Hunt, noted, 80/336
Dibblee, Mrs. H.R., 62/200
Dibblee, John, family, 67/89
Dick, Everett:
Conquering the Great American Desert: Nebraska, review, 78/282-83
Dick, Paul S., 74/235
Dicken, Samuel N., 78/369:
Conquering the Great American Desert, by Dick, review, 78/282-83
Pioneer Trails of the Oregon Coast, noted, 72/359; 73/364
The Willamette Valley, by Bowen, review, 80/329
Dickerson, J.H., 74/18
Dickerson Ranch, 67/374
Dickey, Anna, 74/18,21,22
Dickey, Robert L.: cartoon, 74/196
Dickinson, G.W., 65/284
Dickinson & Jurguensery: Albany hosiery mill, 67/61

Dickson, Elizabeth (Elsie), **69**/129
Dictionary of Mapmakers, Part III, by Tooley, noted, **69**/79
Diego Romeriez (ship), **66**/125
Dielman, Leopold, **80**/343,345,346, 350,351,362:
photo, **80**/344
Dierdorff, John, **67**/379; **68**/357,360; **69**/342,343,347,348; **70**/368,370, 373,374; **71**/369,370,371; **72**/357-58; **73**/361,362; **74**/184,210(photo),366; **75**/369:
"Backstage with Frank Branch Riley, Regional Troubadour," **74**/197-243
How Edison's Lamp Helped Light the West, review, **72**/348
Dierdorff, Mrs. John, **73**/372
Digger Indians, **81**/249
Digging for Gold—Without a Shovel: The Letters of Daniel Wadsworth Coit, ed. by Hammond, noted, **69**/276
Diggles, Rebecca Noon, **64**/265
Digregorio, Charles, **81**/172N
Dilke, Charles Wentworth, **62**/297
Dillard, Samuel, **79**/21
Dillard, William Renshaw, family, **72**/170
Dillard, Ore., **63**/36; **68**/353
Dillehunt, R.B., **75**/10
Diller, Joseph Silas, **67**/21,30
Dilley, T.W., **67**/92
Dillon, Charles, **74**/200,201
Dillon, Harry, **69**/123
Dillon, John, Alvord Ranch agent, **63**/329
Dillon, Richard H., **66**/86,280; **70**/22N,87:
The Hatchet Men: The Story of the Tong Wars in San Francisco's Chinatown, review, **64**/75-76
The Siskiyou Trail: The Hudson's Bay Fur Company Route to California, review, **77**/194
Union Pacific Country, by Athearn, review, **73**/66
Wells, Fargo Detective: A Biography of James B. Hume, review, **72**/88-89
Dillon, Richard H., ed.:
William Henry Boyle's Personal Observa-

tions on the Modoc War, review, **63**/81
Dillon, Sidney, **73**/66
Dimsdale, Thomas J., **72**/264
Dindia, Salvatore, photo, **77**/248
Dinwiddie, Robert, **62**/242,251,254, 257-59
Diomedes Islands, **73**/137
Dionne, Jack, **77**/217
Diphtheria, **73**/260,263; **80**/235N; **81**/247:
Oregon 1840, **66**/349
Diplomacy in the Pacific, by Tate, review, **74**/279
"Dipping the Sheep," by William C. O'Connor, **75**/69-71
Dippre, Harold C.:
"Corruption and the Disputed Election Vote of Oregon in the 1876 Election," **67**/257-72
Direct Legislation League, **68**/207-208, 210,215,219
Directories:
Portland professional women, **79**/337
Dirigo (ship), **66**/119
Disappointment Inlet, SEE Lemmen's Inlet
Disaster Log of Ships, by Gibbs, review, **73**/69-70
Disciples of Christ, SEE Christian Church
"Discovered: A Photo and More Facts About Mary Leonard," by Fred W. Decker, **78**/174-76
Discovery (Cook's ship), **76**/312; **80**/197: number of crew members, **80**/201
Discovery (Vancouver's ship), **79**/399
Discovery (magazine), noted, **75**/86,362
Discovery and Exploration of the Oregon Caves, by Walsh and Halliday, noted, **73**/73
Diseases:
blood poisoning, **79**/390,391; "brain fever," **80**/278; catarrh, **81**/130; city control measures, **80**/10,139,161,295; dysentery, **69**/270; epidemic of 1830, Columbia River, **63**/361; grippe, **81**/128; migration effect, **81**/130; Oregon 1881, **70**/320; women's, **78**/7,25-26; SEE ALSO Ague; Asthma; Camp fever; Cancer; Cholera; Delirium

tremens; Diphtheria; Indians—diseases; Influenza; Intermittent fever; Leprosy; Malaria; Measles; Medicine; Meningitis; Mountain fever; Scurvy; Smallpox; Tuberculosis; Typhoid fever; Venereal diseases; Whooping cough; Yellow fever

Dismal Swamp, **72**/7,7N

Disque, Brice P., **65**/197-98

Disston, Ore.: history, **81**/327

Distant Music, by Davis, cited, **66**/243

Distilleries: early Oregon, **64**/327N; Willamette Valley opposition, **66**/346

Ditsworth, Frank, **77**/90

Ditsworth, Maude Harr, **77**/90

Divorce, **72**/181: early Oregon, **62**/128; **63**/51

Dix, Camilla, **62**/242-87*passim*,337-402*passim*

Dix, George, **76**/63

Dix, Mary, SEE Gray, Mary Dix

Dix, Sarah Dunning (Mrs. John), **62**/242-87*passim*,337-402*passim*

Dixie, Ore., SEE Rickreall, Ore.

Dixon, James, Connecticut senator, **73**/35,40,45,51

Dixon, Joseph, **65**/66N: maps— Ft. Dalles military reservation, **68**/fr.cov. March; Steen-Smith exped. 1860, **65**/23N; **79**/34-35

Dixon, Joseph M., **65**/363

Dixon, Tom, **68**/81

Dmytryshyn, Basil, and E.A.P. Crownhart-Vaughan, trans.: *Colonial Russian America: Kyrill T. Khlebnikov's Reports, 1817-1832*, noted, **77**/290,bk.cov. Dec.

"Russia and the Declaration of the Non-Colonization Principle," by Bolkhovitinov, **72**/101-26

"A Russian Scientific Expedition," by Blomkvist, **73**/101-70

Doan, Robert E. (M.?), **73**/233

Doane, G.C.: Yellowstone exped. journal, **71**/365

Doane, Roscoe, **72**/283

Dobbins, Joseph, **71**/360

Dobie, James Frank, **63**/248; **66**/82

Dockstad, Frederick J.: *Great North American Indians: Profiles in Life and Leadership*, noted, **80**/207

Dockstader, Tom, photo, **74**/265

"Dr. Ada M. Weed: Northwest Reformer," by G. Thomas Edwards, **78**/5-40

Documents: editing, **80**/208; govt., relating to Alaska, **71**/79; relating to Meriwether Lewis death, **80**/331

Dodd, Charles H., **71**/155N

Dodds, Gordon Barlow, **63**/90; **73**/286: *America's Western Frontiers*, by Hawgood, review, **69**/69-70

The Frontier Challenge, ed. by Clark, review, **73**/274-75

Hiram Martin Chittenden, His Public Career, noted, **77**/291; review, **74**/354-55

"Man and Nature in the Oregon Country," noted, **77**/291

Oregon: A History, review, **79**/97-98

The Plains Across, by Unruh, review, **81**/96-99,101

The Reader's Encyclopedia of the American West, ed. by Lamar, review, **80**/205-206

The Salmon King of Oregon: R.D. Hume and the Pacific Fisheries, review, **64**/346-47

Wilderness Defender, by Swain, review, **72**/83-84

Women and Men on the Overland Trail, by Faragher, review, **81**/96,99-101

Dodge, Asa, **78**/355

Dodge, Ernest S.: *Beyond the Capes: Pacific Exploration from Captain Cook to the Challenger (1776-1879)*, review, **73**/273-74

Dodge, Frank T., **64**/162-63; **65**/249

Dodge, Grenville M., **63**/88: railroad interests, **71**/54

Dodge, Pardon, **79**/11

Dodge, Richard I., **80**/333

Dodge, Robert E., **62**/110,206,302, 422; **63**/93,255,372,374; **64**/94,190, 286,363; **65**/125,221,317,416; **66**/93,189,285,394

Dodge, William Sumner: Alaska promotion, **72**/132-33,136,145;

meets Seward, 72/129,132; newspaper interests, 72/132; Sitka mayor, 72/129,131; u.s. Customs officer, 72/129

Dodson, Jacob, 73/204

Dodson, Oliver Monroe, 68/354

Dodson, William, 78/325

Dodwell, George B., 71/143

Doehler, Fritz, 72/91

Doesticks, Philander K., see Thomson, Mortimer Neal

Dog River, Hood River Co., 63/365

Dogs, 73/133,148: ancient North American, 70/87; Davenport sketch, 66/40; early Ore., 63/364; hunting, 76/333; Portland control, 80/145,151,162,295; rabies, 63/277; ranches, 63/276-76; 64/109-10; St. Bernards, 76/102n; sheepherding, 76/333,335,337,349(photo),357; training, 76/335; unwanted on immigrant trail, 72/64,66; vaudeville, 66/39-42

Dogtown, see Hardman, Ore.

Doherty, B.P., 69/103,124

Doherty, Bernard P. (Barney), 69/124

Doherty, James G., 69/103,124-25

Doherty, Patrick, 69/103,124

Doherty, Susan, see McDevitt, Susan Doherty

Doherty, Susan (Suzie), see French, Susan Doherty

Dolan, Fannie, see Slevin, Fannie Dolan

Dolan, James, 69/123

Dolan, Pat, 69/123

Dolbeer, John, 73/11; 77/190: locomotive, 63/351

Dole, Hollis M., 66/90; 69/32-33,333; see also Henderson, E.P.

Dole, Philip, 66/383

Dole, Sanford B.: Hawaiian annexation, 71/175

Dole, William P., 75/93

Dolgy (Dolgoi) Island, Alaska, 77/184

Dolidon, E.B., 68/26

Dollar, Robert, 63/352

Dollar, Stanley, 68/271

Dollarhide, Ross, 77/24

Dolph, Cyrus Abda, 72/71; 80/165

Dolph, Joseph Norton, 71/150; 72/71,71n; 73/61,62; 80/151

Dominis, John, 63/193,199; 70/88

Don Francisco de Paula Marin: A Biography, by Conrad, noted, 74/285

Donahue, —, Portland policeman 1862, 80/142

Donald, David, 72/316

Donald, N., 78/44

Donaldson, Ivan J., 78/365: *Fishwheels of the Columbia*, review, 73/68

Donaldson, Isabel, 74/29

Donaldson, James: children, 74/29; homestead on Queets River, 74/27-29

Donan, Pat, 71/196; 73/286

Donation Land Claims, 62/109; 66/135n; 70/111ff,269-71; 74/293; 77/319,323n,324,325; 78/54,127, 234,303,327; 79/21,155n,162n, 168n,339,361: abandoned claims, 74/94; Clatsop Co., 64/204n,205n,227-29n; Coos Co., 63/13,22,26; Cowlitz Co., 65/309; Cowlitz Farm, 63/220; Douglas Co., 66/41; French Prairie, 66/359,361; index to, 74/286; Indian widows of white men, 64/205n; Josephine Co., 78/288; Lane Co., 64/91; 78/325, 326; Lewis Co., 63/107-108,201,214; 66/32; numbering, 64/79; publication, 76/304; rejected claims applications, 69/76-77; sources, 64/79; Wahkiakum Co., 64/296-97n; Walla Walla Co., 66/135n; Willamette Valley, 78/326

Donation Land Law, 71/57,63; 72/255, 319; 73/60-62; 79/13,49,360: abuses, 63/299; amendments for military reservations, 67/304; conflict with Ore. Territory Act, 67/302; women's property rights, 78/23

Donaugh, Viva, 81/168

Donegan, James J., 78/238: "Historical Sketch of Harney County," cited, 68/246n,301n,306n

Donkey engines: sleds, 76/63-64

Donnell, L., 65/14-15; 66/142

Donnelly, Ignatius, 62/294

Donnelly, James ("Mike"), 69/123

Donnelly, John, 66/62
Donnelly, Joseph P., trans.:
Wilderness Kingdom...Journals and Paintings of Nicolas Point, review, 69/63-65
Donnelly, Pete, 71/263
Donner party, 65/405; 74/86
Donner und Blitzen River, 66/67; 68/321,324,327; 75/67; 78/210,224,227, 228,230; 79/274:
Rocky Ford, 78/227,229(photo)
Donnybrook community, Jefferson Co., 72/341
Donohue, Andy, 69/123-24
Donohue, Mike, 69/123-24
Donpierre, David, 66/350
Don't Call it Or-E-Gawn, by Lucia, noted, 65/309
Dooley, Jere J., 69/274
Dooley, John J., 69/274
Doolittle, James R., 73/36,41
Doorways into History, by Harpham, noted, 74/358
Dorby, John, 76/246
Dorchester, Guy Carleton, 76/311-12, 318-19
Dorena, Ore.:
history, 81/327
Dorin, Patrick C.:
The Milwaukee Road East: America's Resourceful Railroad, noted, 80/209
Dorion, Marie L'Aguivoise, 63/254; 73/285:
grave, 72/91
Dorr, Ebenezer, 63/362; 76/222
Dorr & Sons, Boston, 76/208,222
Dorris, Calif., 71/190
Dosch, Roswell, 73/81
Doss, John C., 81/265,265N,266,269, 270,271
Dotta, —, Portland hotel proprietor, 77/246,249
Dotterer, Steven:
Cities of the American West, by Reps, review, 81/201-202
Doty, —, capt. of *Walter H. Wilson*, 66/121
Doty, Mabel E., 68/227N,228N,234N,297N
Doughty, William M., 66/353

Douglas, David, 63/188-89,191,364:
death, 63/190
journals—
1824-27, 81/332; reprinted, 73/285
Pacific NW botanical collections, 68/111-12,115,123,124
Douglas, James, HBCO., 62/91,321; 63/101-38*passim*,182-236*passim*; 64/200; 67/183; 70/293,303; 72/87,88; 77/85,294; 78/89:
biography, 71/281-82,285; Calif.-Mexico cattle operations, 63/205; disciplinarian, 63/191,194,216; McLoughlin land claim, 63/207; opinion of Gordon, 70/303-304
Douglas, James, mining engineer:
Pacific railroads, 70/349-51
Douglas, Jesse Steiwer:
biography, 67/75-76
Douglas, Stephen Arnold, 70/178; 73/274; 75/365:
objection to Pratt nomination, 64/302
Douglas, Walter B., 65/303
Douglas, William Orville, 63/91; 80/408
Douglas County, Ore., 63/23-24,41-42; 67/80; 73/283; 78/42; 79/49:
census 1860 and 1880, 75/87,363;
churches, 62/205; county surveyor, 73/332N; covered bridges, 66/383;
description 1858, 66/383; fiction, 77/301; fur trade expeds., 74/282; history, 66/187,383; 70/74,271; 77/89,301;
homesteading, 73/72; mining camps, 80/105; pioneers, 77/301; post offices, 71/200; postmarks, 71/200;
Rogue River War volunteers, 66/221N;
schools, 74/358
Douglas County Historical Society:
AASLH award, 65/404; Floed-Lane
House dedication, 65/401; officers and
directors, 62/103,414; 63/85,249;
64/82,278; 65/122,311; 66/84,278;
67/82,283; 68/83-84,281-82; 69/80-81,278; 70/81,275; 71/193; 72/175;
73/77; 74/180; 75/90; 76/94; 77/93; 78/93; 79/109; 80/108; 81/109;
publications, 67/80,279,281; 68/81,
280,342; 70/74,271; 72/89,170; 73/72,283; 74/92,280,358; 75/362; 76/

382; 77/89; 78/90,364; 80/105; 81/105

Douglas County Park Dept., 66/282

Douglas County Pioneer Museum, Floed-Lane House, 65/401-404; 69/176; 71/200,286: photo, 65/402

Douglas Electric Cooperative Inc., 80/328

Douglas fir, SEE Fir trees

Douglas of the Forests: The North American Journals of David Douglas, ed. by Davies, noted, 81/332

Douglass and Cone Bros. lumber mill, St. Johns, 62/177

Dowell, Benjamin Franklin, 66/149N; 71/71; 72/231; 81/248,249N,259: papers cited, 71/80

Down the Santa Fe Trail...: Diary of Susan Shelby Magoffin, 1846-1847, ed. by Drumm, noted, 63/356

Downes, John, 76/119

Downey, Dan, 69/125

Downing, Alfred: 1894 Portland flood letter, 67/77; map, 65/104N; 70/164

Downing, Andrew Jackson, 68/6,22N: architectural views, 67/327-33*passim*; books available on Pacific Coast, 67/329-30N; fruit nurseries, 68/162; house patterns used at Fts. Dalles and Simcoe, 67/326,337,343,345

Downing, George S., photo, 81/254

Downing, Susan, SEE Shepard, Susan Downing

Downs, John, 66/71,72

Doyle, Bill, 73/220,221,222

Doyle, James, 69/125

Doyle, John T.: *The Oregon Election*..., quoted, 67/262

Doyle, Michael, 69/125

Doyle, Reuben L. ("Bible-Back"), 64/39

Dozier, Edward P., 63/347

Drain, Ore., 67/374; 80/52,53: normal school, 80/63N

Drain United Methodist Church, 70/184

Drake, Alexander M., 69/341

Drake, Angeline Robb (Mrs. John M.),

65/8-9

Drake, Francis, 64/283; 66/87; 77/290,303: biography, 74/95; off Ore. coast, 80/412; on Pacific Coast, 72/287; Pacific exped. aims, 69/335

Drake, Frank V., 65/288

Drake, J. Francis, 75/146

Drake, John M., 66/59,61: adjutant to Maury, 65/395; biography, 65/7-9 expedition to Indian country 1864, 79/46-47,130,133,146N— campaign summarized, 65/117-18; campsites, 65/10,16N; criticism of, 65/89-90N,102-103; depot site, 65/ 37-38; geographic names, 65/58,61-62; guides, 65/23,38-39N; private journal, 65/13-116

route, 65/5-6N,10,12,16N,28N,38N— maps, 65/insert Dec. Scholl map used, 65/5-6N,58,61-62; scout of Deschutes, 65/78-80

fossils sent to Condon, 65/74-75; 67/14,16; journal versions, 65/5-7,116; photo, 65/18

Drake, June D.: biography, 66/313; photo studio, 66/ 318; postal cards photos, 66/312,314, 315; Silver Falls Park, 66/313

Drake, T.G., 63/200

Drake Peak, 79/285N

Drake's Island of Thieves: Ethnological Sleuthing, by Lessa, noted, 77/303

Drawson, Maynard C.: "'Niagara' and 'China Dam'," 71/349-57

Treasures of the Oregon Country, noted, 76/92; 79/105; 81/329

Drayton, Joseph, 65/137,137N,145,147: sketches in Skirving panorama, 65/137

Drazan, Joseph G.: *The Pacific Northwest: An Index to People and Places in Books*, notes, 81/332

Dredges and dredging, 75/230,362

Drenner, Robert S., 66/383

Dress, SEE Clothing and dress

Drew, Charles S., 64/160-61; 65/ 63N,393; 69/223N; 79/47:

map of Southern Ore. Indian depredations, **69**/226

Drew, Edwin P., **63**/21; **70**/257

Drew, George, **63**/171N

Drew, Harry J.:

Early Transportation on Klamath Waterways, noted, **75**/362

George T. Baldwin, His Life and Achievements, noted, **81**/327

Maud Baldwin—Photographer, noted, **81**/327

Drew, Joseph W., **67**/179; **69**/241N: letter quoted, **67**/294N

Drew, Propst, **66**/382

Drew Creek, **76**/352-53; **77**/8,12,28,29; **79**/289N

Drews Prairie, **79**/290N

Drews Valley, **68**/257,258N,316N,319

"Drifting the Lower Columbia," by John H. McClelland, Jr., **75**/104-108

Driggs, Jeremiah, **78**/234,325N

Drinkwater, Reggy, **76**/333N; **77**/5N

Drips, Andrew, **62**/341; **69**/64: papers, **72**/179

Driscoll, Cornelius, **69**/127

Driscoll, Dennis, **73**/182

Driscoll, Patrick, **69**/127

Drouillard, George, **65**/303-304: Snake River tributary named for, **65**/304

Drouillard, Pierre, **65**/303

Drownings, **78**/64,355; **79**/263

Drugstores, **76**/92

Drum, Barbara, **77**/64-66

Drum, Simon H., **67**/298

Drum, W.F., **68**/232N,243,245,246

Drumm, Stella M., ed.:

Down the Santa Fe Trail and Into Mexico: Diary of Susan Shelby Magoffin, 1846-47, noted, **63**/356

Drummers and Dreamers, by Relander, quoted, **70**/124

Drummon, Willis, **72**/48

Drums and Scalpel: From Native Healers to Physicians on the North Pacific Coast, by Large, review, **71**/184-86

Drury, Clifford Merrill, **62**/193,202; **63**/82; **67**/87; **73**/277,284; **76**/361: bibliography of publications, **71**/368;

Lee "saved Oregon" theory, **78**/332-50; research on Indians at Red River school, **71**/325

Drury, Clifford Merrill:

"Joe Meek Comments on the Whitman Massacre," **75**/72-75

Marcus and Narcissa Whitman and the Opening of Old Oregon, noted, **77**/291; review, **75**/77-78

Nine Years With the Spokane Indians: The Diary, 1838-1848, of Elkanah Walker, noted, **77**/291; review, **79**/101-102

Reminiscences of a Historian, noted, **74**/95

"Sacajawea's Death—1812 or 1884?" **62**/288-91

Drury, Clifford Merrill, ed.:

First White Women Over the Rockies: Diaries, Letters, and Biographical Sketches, review, **65**/119-20

First White Women Over the Rockies: The Six Women of the Oregon Missions, Diaries and Related Documents, 1836-1844, review, **68**/76-77

Drury, Robert, **78**/130,148

Drury, William, **78**/130,148,211,212

Dry Creek, Lake Co., **79**/289N

Dry Creek, Malheur Co., **63**/264

Dry River, **68**/91,351; **69**/87

Dry Sandy River, **62**/354; **79**/379

The Dry Years: Prohibition and Social Change in Washington, by Clark, review, **67**/186-87

Dryad (brig), **63**/193

Dryden, Cecil Pearl:

Give All to Oregon! Missionary Pioneers of the Far West, noted, **69**/332

Dryer, Thomas Jefferson, **64**/33-40; **70**/355; **72**/321; **75**/119; **80**/9,11,12N:

Mt. St. Helens ascent, **71**/197

newspaper career—

Columbian, **64**/33-34; *Oregonian*, **64**/33

Drysdale, John, **70**/234

Dubois, Fred T., **62**/106; **64**/87; **66**/281; **71**/367; **72**/229

Dubrais, Charles, **66**/361

Duby, Will, **78**/103

Ducey, Elizabeth, **74**/365

Duck Lake, SEE Cow Head Lake
Ducks, **68**/238,240,257: Chinese introduced in Oregon, **65**/243
Duckworth, John, **76**/175
Dude ranches, **70**/86
Due, John R., and Giles French: *Rails to the Mid-Columbia Wheatlands: The Columbia Southern and Great Southern Railroads and the Development of Sherman and Wasco Counties, Oregon*, review, **81**/101-102
Due, John F., and Harley K. Halgren: *United Railways of Oregon*, noted, **62**/301
Due, John F., and Frances Juris: *Rails to the Ochoco Country: The City of Prineville Railway*, review, **70**/68-69
Dueling, **62**/140,142-43
"Duff" (Davenport's dog), **66**/39-42: sketches, **66**/40,42
Duffy, John, **69**/127
Duflot de Mofras, Eugene, SEE de Mofras, Eugene Duflot
Dufur, Ore., **69**/295
Duke, William, **63**/12
Duke of York (Indian), **74**/91
Dulles, John Foster, **62**/7,41,50: view of tsarist Russia, **72**/102
Dulley, John B., **63**/18
Dumb waiter, **68**/15
Dumbleton, Charlie, **70**/279
Dumbleton, Harry, **70**/279
Dumbleton, Louis, **70**/279
Dumont, Alexander, **78**/90
Dumreicher, Conrad Carl: court-martial, **63**/103N; Drake clash with, **65**/102-103; First Ore. Cavalry service, **65**/11-48*passim*
Duncan, Alexander, HBCO., **64**/214N, 225,239-40,245
Duncan, Charles T., ed.: *Bob Frazier of Oregon*, review, **81**/321
Duncan, Fred B.: *Deepwater Family*, noted, **71**/190-91
Duncan, George, 1854 immigrant: family, **79**/17
Duncan, George (Indian), **73**/82
Duncan, George, salmon canner, **78**/364
Duncan, Janice K.:

Diplomacy in the Pacific, by Tate, review, **74**/279
Hall J. Kelley on Oregon, ed. by Powell, review, **74**/91
Minority Without a Champion: Kanakas on the Pacific Coast, 1788-1850, noted, **73**/bk.cov. June
Duncan, Kelly, **75**/45
Duncan, Ruth R., photo, **74**/265
Duncan, Warren Malheur, **79**/18
Duncan, William, Metlakahtla mission, **62**/57-58
Duncan Building, Newberg, **65**/218
Duncan Creek, **79**/293N
Duncan's Ferry, Missouri River, **79**/365,367
Dundass, Howard, **69**/127
Dundass, Jack, **69**/127
Dundee, Ore., **69**/181: history, **65**/217
Dunham, —, capt. of *Orbit*, **66**/164
Duniway, Abigail Scott, **62**/198; **64**/ 276,349; **66**/383; **68**/201; **72**/232; **78**/5,25,36,175; **80**/314,331: photo, **81**/258
Duniway, Benjamin C., **80**/331
Duniway, Clyde A., **70**/204
Duniway, David Cushing, **62**/104,109, 415; **63**/86,250; **64**/83,137N,279; **65**/123,312; **66**/85,279,350N; **69**/ 57,76,171N,273
Duniway, David Cushing, and Karen M. Offen, eds.: "William Cornell's Guide to Oregon, 1852," **80**/66-100
"William Cornell's Journal, 1852, with His Overland Guide to Oregon," **79**/359-93
Dunkards: Powers, Ore., **76**/75
Dunn, Edward, **69**/127
Dunn, Francis Berrian, **64**/276-77
Dunn, Harvey, **67**/368
Dunn, Jacob Piatt, **80**/333: *Massacres of the Mountains*, cited, **66**/223N-24N
Dunn, John, **63**/181
Dunn, Richard, **65**/182N
Dunn, S., **69**/79

Dunn, William, 69/127
Dunne, Bill, 72/234
Dunning, George, 65/215
Dunsmuir Museum, Calif., 66/81
Dunstaffnage (ship), 66/127
Duntze, John A., 63/201,218
Dupaty (Dupatti), SEE McKay, Jean Baptiste Desportes
Durant, Thomas Clark, 73/66
Durfee and Peck, fur traders, 70/88
Durgan, Joseph, family, 81/328
Durham, George H., 67/265
Durham (ship), 66/127
Durkee, C.W., 68/228N
Durkee, Laura, 68/203
Durston, John Hurst, 65/382
Duruz, Willis P., 68/171:
"History of Horticulture in the Pacific Northwest," cited, 68/157,205
Principles of Nursery Management, cited, 68/164N
Durval (Derval), Denis, 63/119-20, 126-64*passim*
Dutch Canyon settlement, Columbia Co., 64/91
Dutch Charlie, 79/202
Dutch Harbor, 62/23; 73/127; 80/33,37,47,48: described, 80/34
Dutch ovens, 76/69,348,350
Dutch people:
early American settlements, 81/6-8; Washington Co., 81/332; SEE ALSO The Netherlands
Dutton, —, Heppner sheepman, 81/297
Dutton, Clarence E., 81/50
Dutton, "Doc," 69/295FF
Dutton and Russell, 69/295
Dwight, Theodore, 75/111-12
Dwyer, Mrs. Neil, 64/359
Dwyer, Robert Joseph:
The Gentile Comes to Utah: A Study in Religious and Social Conflict, noted, 73/79
Dwyer, William T., 62/219N
Dyche, William K., 63/89; 71/368
Dye, Charles Henry, 76/299,301; 80/396:
photo, 80/fr.cov. Winter

Dye, Eva Emery, 68/186; 76/299: Chautauqua work, 80/395,396-97,398,402; daughter, photo, 80/ins. fr.cov. Winter; history work, 81/380; photo, 80/fr.cov. Winter
Dyer, —, surveyor, 72/48
Dyer, Moses T., 69/330

Eads, William, 73/72
Eagle (HBCO. ship), 76/227
Eagle (*l'Aigle*, British whaler), 64/7,9
The Eagle and the Fort: The Story of John McLoughlin, by Morrison, review, 80/331-32
Eagle Cliff, Wash., 75/105
Eagle Creek, Hood River Co., 74/129
Eagle Creek, Ore., 62/217: history, 74/282
Eagle Creek mines, Baker Co., 62/234
Eagle-eye (Indian), 70/17
Eagle Gorge, Wash., 73/334,335,336
Eagle Mills Bridge, 64/355
Eagle Point, Ore., 70/279
Eagle Valley, 64/90; 81/300
Eagles, 74/298-99; 79/105
Eakin, Hort C., 77/261-63: photos, 77/262,264
Earhart, Amelia, 74/232
Earl, W.W., 66/306
Earl Creek, 72/308
Earl of Dalhousie (ship), 66/108,109
Early, Ore., 70/280
Early American Industries Assn.:
Tools From Pacific Northwest Collections, noted, 76/181
Early Birds in the Northwest, by Bond, noted, 74/359
"Early Christian Mission of the Kutenai Indians," by Claude E. Schaeffer, 71/325-48
Early Days at the University of Oregon, by Fortt, noted, 77/299
Early Days on the Upper Willamette, by Jensen, noted, 72/171
Early History of Klickitat County, noted, 79/104-105
Early Klickitat Valley Days, by Ballou, cited, 70/143N,145N,146N
Early Portland: Stump-Town Triumphant,

by Snyder, review, 72/169
"Early Sheep Ranching in Eastern Oregon," by Judith Keyes Kenny, 64/101-22
Early Steamboat Navigation on the Missouri River, by Chittenden, noted, 66/273
Early Transportation on Klamath Waterways, by Drew, noted, 75/362
Early Washington Communities in Art, by LeRoy, noted, 67/279
Earp, Wyatt, 69/85
Earthquakes:
Alaska, 67/371; 77/280,283; Amchitka Island, 80/44; Calif.-Ore. boundary 1868, 72/28; Ft. Klamath 1873, 72/28N; measuring devices, 64/87; off-coast, 72/270
Oregon—
1915, 67/370; first recorded major quake, 65/220
Portland, 70/183—
1962, 64/284
San Francisco—
1868, 72/28N; 1906, 72/86
Warner Valley, 70/183
East, E.H., 75/189N
East Cow Creek, 77/335; 78/212
East India Company:
cooperation with HBCO. attempted, 76/314; licenses NWCO., 76/326-27; regulations protect monopoly, 76/311,313, 321,329
East Lake, 70/183
East of the Cascades, by Brogan, ed. by Phillips, review, 66/183
East Oregonian, Pendleton, 77/192-93
East Portland, Ore., 80/260
East Portland Brass Band, 74/346,347, 348(photo)
East Side Christian Church, Portland, 75/157
East Side Railway Co., 71/17N; SEE ALSO Oregon and California Railroad; Oregon Central Railroad
Easterbrook, George T., 69/78
Easterbrook, W.T., 63/357
The Eastern Establishment and the Western Experience..., by White, review, 70/263-64

Eastern Oregon, SEE Oregon, Eastern
Eastern Oregon Land Co., 71/85N
Eastern Oregon Livestock Co., 75/67
Eastern Oregon State Tuberculosis Hospital, 80/269
Eastern Oregon Stock Show, 67/370
Eastern Washington State Historical Society:
manuscripts collection, 77/297
Eastern-Western Lumber Co., 71/226
Eastern-Western Railway, 74/357
Eastman, Charles A., 62/289,290
Eastman, Josiah, 68/145
Eastman, Levi, 62/219N
Eastman, Seth, 73/286
Easton, Mrs. Robert E., 64/310N
Eastside, Ore., 66/55
Eaton, F.B., 75/20,23,24
Eaton, Nathan, 62/143
Ebbert, George Wood, 62/75; 76/381
Eberhardt, Elizabeth, photo, 81/254
Eberhardt, George, photo, 81/254
Eberman, Ninian Elkanah:
donation claim, 64/204N
Ebert, Eloise, 62/110,206,302,422; 63/93,255,373; 64/93,189,285,363; 65/125,221,317,416; 66/93,189,285,394; 68/360; 69/347; 70/373
Ebey, Isaac H., 62/73
Ebey, Jacob, 72/179
Ebey, Winfield Scott, 62/225-26; 72/197:
quoted, 62/226-27
Ebstein, Frederick H.E., 68/228, 229N,249; 70/18
Eccles, David, family, 77/296
Eccles, Henry B.:
quoted, 62/5
Eccles, Julian, 78/369
Eccles, W.J.:
The Canadian Frontier, 1534-1760, noted, 71/191
Echo, Ore., 63/365; 66/141,153; 73/83,285; 81/105:
cannon legend, 66/159-60; Ft. Henrietta site, 66/160; photos, 66/140; Picket Rock episode, 66/141
Echo (steamboat), 81/39:
sketch, 79/244

Echo News, Echo, **66**/141,159-60: McCullough anecdote, **66**/153-54

Echoes of Puget Sound: Fifty Years of Logging and Steamboating, by Birkeland, review, **62**/98-99

Eckerman, Dave, **63**/282

Eckerson, Theodore J., **64**/160

Eckley, Ore., **63**/6

Eclipses of the sun: 1869, **72**/139-41; Feb. 26, 1979, **81**/329

Ecology, **71**/181-82,196; **72**/178

"Economic and Geographical Determinants of Railroad Routes in the Pacific Northwest," by Pierce, cited, **71**/75

Economic conditions, **73**/190: cattle and sheep ranches, **81**/282-83, 317-18; Coolidge prosperity, **73**/219 depression, **73**/85,190,217— 1882-85, **75**/127; 1890s, **71**/169, 177; 1893, **62**/95; Canada, **72**/231, 232; Great Depression, **72**/183; **76**/ 135-36,248; **77**/23,173,353; recollections, **81**/334; Washington, **72**/232 electrification effects, **80**/327; frontier capitalism, **72**/227; geography and, **81**/325-27; Idaho 1948-64, **68**/349; inequality 1790-1860, **73**/85; interurban railway effects, **80**/332-33

Oregon—

"colonial" status, **79**/98; frontier, **80**/329

Oregon Territory 1852, **79**/12

Pacific Northwest, **65**/367; **77**/302— 1966, **68**/186

panaceas, SEE Farmer-labor movement; Townsend Plan

panics—

1893, **65**/263; **66**/181; **75**/136; 1907, **78**/111-12

Portland 1885-1915, **78**/89-90; SEE ALSO Portland—economic conditions; Teapot Dome scandal, **73**/190; transcontinental railroad effects, **71**/27-98; **73**/66; unemployment, **75**/127; urban community costs, **73**/85

"Economic Development of the Pacific Northwest to 1920," by Tattersall, cited, **67**/75N,103-72*passim*

"Economic Growth in Portland in the 1880s," by Abner Baker, **67**/105-23

"Economic Importance of Early Transcontinental Railroads: Pacific Northwest," by John S. Cochran, **71**/27-98

Eddy, Chauncey, **62**/239

Eddy, Israel F., **77**/91

Eddy, Mary Baker: Portland speech 1905, **80**/58

Eddyville, Ore., **77**/91

Edelbrock, Alexius: letters quoted, **70**/318-25*passim*; photo, **70**/315; visit to Oregon, **70**/318-22,332

Edensaw, Charlie (Indian), **71**/367

Edgar, John, **63**/123-25

Edgewood, Calif., **66**/81

Edison Technical School, Seattle, **65**/381

"Editorial Opinion and American Imperialism: Two Northwest Newspapers," by Edward H. Loy, **72**/209-24

Edlefsen, J.N., **62**/179

Edler, Dave, **77**/149-56*passim*: photo, **77**/148

Edmo, Ed (Indian), **72**/157

Edmo, Rachel Cook, (Mrs. Ed), **72**/157

Edmonson (Edmondson), Lloyd, **63**/294

Edson, Lelah J.:

The Fourth Corner: Highlights From the Early Northwest, noted, **70**/359

Edson-Foulke Yreka Ditch, **63**/83

Education:

arts, **68**/342; attitude in Oregon, **73**/ 81; Auburn, Wash., **65**/381; Benton Co. 1890s, **72**/281-85; British Columbia, **65**/381; Columbia Co. 1900, **72**/ 197-208; correspondence courses 1898, **80**/182; Everett, Wash., **65**/378; extension services, **80**/392,402-403; frontier, **63**/320-26; **70**/23; Idaho Terr., **72**/281 Indian, **70**/102—

since 1928, **80**/208

medical in Oregon, **68**/341; Pacific NW theses, **65**/377-80; **72**/258-61; race and, **66**/80; scope and methods, **68**/90; **70**/174; Washington 1861- 1961, **64**/76-77; SEE ALSO Compulsory school bill; Schools

Education and the American Indian: The Road to Self Determination Since 1928, by Szasz, noted, **80**/208

Edward Kern and American Expansion, by Hines, review, **63**/345-46

Edwards, G. Thomas, **70**/364: intro. to Wyeth-Townsend reprint, **72**/170

Edwards, G. Thomas: "Benjamin Stark, the u.s. Senate, and 1862 Membership Issues," **72**/315-38; **73**/31-59

"Dr. Ada M. Weed: Northwest Reformer," **78**/5-40

Fort Stevens..., by Hanft, review, **81**/423

The Jesuits and the Indian Wars of the Far Northwest, by Burns, review, **68**/75-76

Mansfield on the Condition of the Western Forts, 1853-1854, by Frazer, review, **65**/201-202

Military Posts in the Powder River Country of Wyoming, by Murray, review, **71**/187-88

Rebels of the Woods, by Tyler, review, **69**/325-26

The San Juan Water Boundary Question, by McCabe, review, **67**/183-84

We Were Not Summer Soldiers..., ed. by Bischoff, review, **78**/179-80

Edwards, Harold O., **64**/359

Edwards, Herman, **80**/62

Edwards, John, Tillamook pioneer, **72**/297-307,313; **73**/5,179,189,227: biography, **72**/307; death, **73**/224; photos, **72**/306; **73**/225; sawmill, **73**/224,226

Edwards, John Griffith, **72**/341

Edwards, Philip Leget, **74**/73; **79**/122N; **81**/14-15: biography, **81**/142; memorial of 1838, **66**/237,354

Edwards, Thomas D., **79**/17

Edwards, Mrs. Wiley, photo, **81**/258

Edwards Butte: name, **72**/308

Eells, Cushing, **62**/240,242,320; **79**/102

Eells, Myra Fairbanks (Mrs. Cushing), **65**/119; **68**/76

Eells, Myron, **62**/333; **75**/113

"The Effect of O & C Management on the Economy of Oregon," by David T. Mason, **64**/55-67

The Effects of Technological Change on Employment in the Lumber Industry (Ore. State Dept. of Employment), noted, **70**/76

The Effects of the Railroads on Small Town Population Changes: Linn County, Oregon, by Holtgrieve, noted, **80**/209

Effinger, Mrs. John, **79**/203,206,209

Egan (Eagan) (Indian), **68**/301: killed, **68**/233,306; **70**/34; reward offered for, **70**/21; speech, **70**/17

Egan, Clifford L.: "Joel Barlow's Suggestion to Rename the Columbia," **74**/268-70

Egan, Ferol: *Sand in a Whirlwind: The Paiute Indian War of 1860*, noted, **74**/283

Egbert, A.R., **65**/103N

Egbert, Harry C., **68**/309

Eggs, SEE Prices

Ehlen, George Armstrong, **79**/252

Ehlen, Henry Claus, **79**/239,256: compositions, **79**/247

Ehlen, John D., **79**/256

Ehlen, Lawrence, **79**/248

Ehlen, Loren W., **79**/239

Ehlen, William, **79**/266

Ehrenberg, Herman, **65**/213; **68**/348: Klamath map, **65**/214

Ehrman, S. Mason, **63**/372,374; **64**/94, 190,286,363; **65**/125,221,317,416; **66**/93,189,285,394; **67**/376,380; **68**/361; **69**/348; **70**/373; **71**/371

Eide, Ingvard Henry: *Oregon Trail*, noted, **75**/86

Eigner, Judy, photo, **81**/30

Eigner, Ken, photo, **81**/30

Eigner, Nellie Bitte, **81**/31N: photo, **81**/37

Eiguren, Fred, **76**/155N,160,162N,167

Eiguren, Pasco, **76**/158,167

Eisenhower, Dwight David, **62**/7,26, 45,50

Ekland, Roy E.:

"The Diaries and Papers of Eduard Chambreau: First Study," cited, 70/101N

"The 'Indian Problem': Pacific Northwest, 1879," 70/101-37

Eld, Henry, 70/75; 77/194

Elderberries, 69/157

Eldridge, Freeman E.: land claims, 66/359

Eldridge, M.A., 62/219N

Elections: June 1858, 66/17; 1859, 66/361; 1860, 75/121-22; June 1864, 65/ 48N,62,296; 75/122; 1876, 62/197; 67/257-72; 71/196; 1896, 72/286; 75/138; Nov. 1910, 74/208; 1912, 76/255-56; Nov. 1916, 63/88; 1918, 68/125-40; 1920, 76/356; 1922, 75/162,167-68,173-74,188N; 1928, 67/361-63; 1934, 76/137,140; 1936, 76/139; 1966, 68/344; 1970, 75/94; direct primary, 72/80; disputed 1876 electoral vote, 67/257-72; franchise for halfbreed Indians sought, 66/361 general elections— 1912, 76/355; 1936, 76/139 Lake Co., 76/355 Oregon state— 1912, 76/356; 1934, 76/137,140 policing, 80/149,164,297-98,307; presidential 1928, 67/361-63; silver issue 1896, 72/286 U.S. senate campaigns— 1918, 68/125-40; 1920, 76/356 Western States 1966, 68/344

Electoral Commission, SEE U.S. Congress Electoral Commission

The Electric Railway Era in Northwest Washington, 1890-1930, by Turbeville, review, 80/332-33

Electric Steel Foundry Co., Portland: 50th anniversary, 64/352

Electrical West: 75th anniversary, 63/361

Electricity and electric industry, 63/361; 71/351: Bend, 75/294; British Columbia, 72/ 257; Clark Co., 81/328; cooking with, 80/121; Dallas, Ore., 62/200; film, "It

Can Be Done," 80/326,328(photo); Forestry Bldg., 80/55; Los Angeles lighting, 80/247; Pac. NW history, 70/181; 72/348; pioneers in, 62/109; Portland lighting, 80/53; public power proponents, 76/137,138,140,144,146; public utilities, 78/360; Umatilla Co., 63/365; SEE ALSO Hydroelectric power; Power development; Rural electrification

Electronics in the West: The First Fifty Years, by Morgan, review, 70/267-68

Elena (ship), 73/105

"The elephant," SEE "Seeing the elephant"

Elford, W.C., 75/145,147,163,167,179

Elfving, Fritz S., 71/286

Eliakanah (Indian), 63/164

Eliot, G.W., 66/65

Eliot, Thomas Lamb, 62/336; 64/261; 67/217-18N; 72/232; 76/10

Eliot, William Greenleaf, Jr., 80/403: photo, 74/234

Eliot Glacier, 77/61,63,66; 79/206

Eliza (river vessel), 63/49-50

Eliza and the Indian War Pony, by Scott, review, 64/349-50

Eliza R. Barchus, the Oregon Artist, by Barchus, noted, 76/92

Elizabeth (ship 1795), 79/402

Elk City, Ida., 69/108; 79/184N,188

Elk City, Ore., 70/279

Elk Creek, Baker Co.: mining camp, 62/226,227

Elk Creek, Clatsop Co., 77/71,283,284(with photo)

Elk Creek, Klamath Co., SEE Spencer Creek

Elk River, 62/216; 76/80

Elk Rock, Coos Co., 66/55: name, 66/54

Elk Rock Island, Willamette River, 72/90

Elk Rock School ("Quinn College"), 66/54,55

Elk Summit, 79/188

Elkhorn, Nev., 79/77

Elkhorn Valley, 73/83

Elkins, Barbara, 63/368

Elkins, James, Linn Co. pioneer, 67/61

Elks, 63/14,16,21,24,326-27; 69/16, 158; 74/11; 76/80
Elks Club, Medford, 76/246
Elkton, Ore., 62/205; 68/343; 80/52,53: mills, 68/342
Ellenborough, Edward Law, Earl of, 70/307
Ellendale, Polk Co.: name, 66/13
Ellendale Woolen Mills, 66/21
Ellensburg, Wash., 77/301
Ellice (Indian), SEE Ellis
Ellice, Edward, 62/91
Elliott, Arb, 66/205
Elliott, Bill, Baker Co. 1860s, 66/205
Elliott, Dorothy: *Coast Country: A History of Southwest Washington*, by McDonald, review, 68/182-83
Elliott, Elijah, 77/309,311; 78/323N; 79/15: biography, 78/140,146 cutoff train leader, 78/70,121,147-49, 223,236,242,247— lack of knowledge of route, 78/70, 146,147,207,223N,236; leadership questioned, 78/221-22,224,229,327 life threatened, 78/71,223,224,230, 230N; photo, 78/142; portrait, 77/ 308; promotion of Free Emigrant Road, 78/70,143
Elliott, George H., 65/329,331N: Cape Disappointment battery construction, 65/336-51*passim*
Elliott, Grant (Indian), 64/91
Elliott, Henry Wood, 64/281; 73/142,144
Elliott, J.R., 74/139
Elliott, James, 75/138,140
Elliott, Mary McCall, 78/138,140
Elliott, Olivia, photo, 81/194
Elliott, Simon G., 71/283
Elliott, Thompson Coit, 66/148N,343N; 73/363; 77/80
Elliott Creek, Jackson Co., 72/41-42
Elliott Cutoff, 70/358: accidents, 78/151,309,319,319N,325N; advance party, 78/155-57,211-13,219-

20,224-30,231-35,324; advocates, 78/139
campsites— Deschutes River, 79/5; marker photo, 78/296
childbirth, 78/125,128,129,153; connection with Free Emigrant Road, 79/5,12-13; critics, 78/71,139,140; deaths, 78/125,128,151,153,212-13, 247,250,319,324; intersects Oregon Central Military Road, 79/4(photo), 50; leader, SEE Elijah Elliott; leaves Oregon Trail at Malheur, 78/140, 143-44
livestock, 78/299,300,307— losses, 78/151,152,153,233,242,304, 321,324; numbers, 78/124,127,128, 131,147,149; used as food, 78/128, 231,233,234,240,243-44,304,307, 324,328
maps, 78/46,68,156,248-49,294; 79/ 44,45; rediscovered, 77/309N-11N; road commissioners, 77/318
road viewers— attack by Indians, 77/327,334; biographies, 77/324-27; equipment, 77/ 323,336,337,339; geologic specimens lost, 77/334,339; journal lost, 77/ 327; preliminary expeds., 77/323,327; photos, 77/326; report, 77/327, 327N,328; route, 77/309,327-35, 338,339(map)
route, 78/323-24— Cascades crossing, 78/231-34,299- 302; critical decision at lakes, 78/209, 219-23,227,323; desert stretch, 78/ 235,240-41; Deschutes crossing, 78/ 231,293,294; diverges from Meek tracks, 78/213N,219-22,225; geographic confusion, 78/147,155,207- 209,211,222,232; Harney Valley, 78/ 219-31; Malheur ford to Harney Valley, 78/150-57,207-12; Meek tracks, 78/209,219,300; Middle Fork Willamette crossing, 78/311,313-15, 317,319-22; photos, 78/208,212,220, 236; Smyth route unlikely, 78/237- 40; traces, 78/241-42; 79/50(photo) survey authorized, 77/319-20; trail

diaries, 78/123,124,128,132,149,154, 223; SEE ALSO Andrew McClure; James McClure; Benjamin Owen travelers—

Macy train, 79/14,15,16(list),20N,49; prospectors, 79/27,31; rescue, 79/ 48; roster cited, 79/338; vital records, 79/338; Wallen expedition, 79/36, 36N

upper valley sponsorship, 77/318,327, 339; wagons abandoned, 78/325; water, 78/235,239-47; SEE ALSO Free Emigrant Road; Immigration of 1853; Meek Cutoff; Oregon Trail

Elliott R. Corbett Cartographic Memorial Fund, 64/360

Ellis (Ellice) (Indian), 69/53,54: Red River school, 71/330,332,336,347

Ellis, Richard N.:

Conflict and Schism in Nez Perce Acculturation: A Study of Religion and Politics, by Walker, review, 70/68

Ellis, Robert Hale, Jr., 62/110,206,302, 421,422; 63/93,255

Ellison, Joseph W., 64/350

Ellison-White Lecture Bureau, 80/397, 402

Ellmaker, Enos: family, 79/16N; letters quoted, 79/16, 24,89

Ellmaker, Reuben: correspondence, 79/16,24-25

Ellsworth, Harris, 64/358,362

Ellsworth, S. George, 64/281: *The Territories and the United States,* by Pomeroy, review, 71/358

Ellsworth, Stukely, 67/181

Elmendorf, Mary J., 74/63

Elmendorf, William W., 62/203; 63/90: *The Structure of Twana Culture,* noted, 62/108

Elmlund, Frank C., 76/13

Elmlund, Ida Anderson, 76/13

Elmore (steamer), photo, 71/140

Elmore Salmon Canneries, 66/181

Elorriaga, Amalie, photo, 76/164

Elorriaga, Carmen, photo, 76/164

Elorriaga, John A., 76/387

Elorriaga, Marie, photo, 76/164

Elridge, William, 70/235

Elsing, Henry C.: biography, 74/333-34; letters, 74/333-34

Elsing, Mary, SEE Palmer, Mary Elsing

Elwha River, 78/281

Ely, Eugene, 74/316-17

Embick, Stanley D., 62/22,24

Embree, John, 77/264-65

Embree, Thomas Van Buren, 77/264

Embree, William H., 70/147N

"The Emergence of Frances Fuller Victor—Historian," by Hazel Emery Mills, 62/309-36

The Emergence of Plateau Culture, by Swanson, noted, 64/277

Emerson, Charles L., photo, 74/265

Emerson, Pete, 64/139,148

Emigrant Creek, Jackson Co.: map, 69/264

Emigrant Creek, Lane Co., 77/329; 78/309

Emigrant Crossing, Klamath Co.: name, 78/240

Emigrant Hill, Malheur Co., photo, 78/153

Emigrant Springs, Lane Co., 78/54,319

Emigrant Springs, Umatilla Co., 68/233,306N; 78/103; 81/105

Emigrant's Ford, SEE Klamath River

Emigration, SEE Immigration

Emigration and Disenchantment: Portraits of Englishmen Repatriated from the United States, by Shepperson, review, 68/280

Emily Bourne (vessel), 71/365

Emily Farnham (brig), 68/352

Eminent Domain: The Louisiana Purchase and the Making of America, by Keats, review, 75/81

Emma Hayward (steamer), 63/66; 70/139; 71/14N

Emmet, C. Temple, 71/283

Emmet, John P., 65/214

Emmet, John T., 65/214

Emmet, Thomas A., 65/214

Emmet, William J., 65/214

Emmet Guard, 75/128: photo, 80/259

Emmitt, Ivy, **66**/382
Emmitt, Robert A.:
recollections, **66**/81
Emmons, Arthur C., **66**/371,374,377
Emmons, Della Gould:
Leschi of the Nisquallies, noted, **67**/280
Northwest History in Action: A Collection of Twelve Plays..., review, **62**/412-13
Emmons, George Foster, **77**/194:
journal, **67**/281
Emory, Lisa T.E., **69**/330
Emory, William Helmsley, **65**/162,164:
photo, **65**/132; Skirving panorama, **65**/135,138,146-47
Empire, Ore., **63**/13,16,20,25; **68**/265:
early days, **64**/355; Indian agency, **63**/21,38-39
Empire of the Columbia, A History of the Pacific Northwest, by Johansen and Gates, cited, **66**/350N; **77**/291; review, **69**/60-61
Enberg, Anton, **69**/310
Enchanted Prairie, **63**/18
The End of the Trail, by Smith, cited, **77**/301
Endeavor (vessel), **80**/197
Enders, Henry, **64**/323N,329N,335,337; **77**/90
Endicott, William, Jr.:
railroad interests, **71**/89-90
Endicott, Wash., **65**/365
Eneas (Indian):
relations with Moses, **70**/129,157,162
Enegren, Charles, **66**/54
Engelhardt, Zephyrin, **71**/261
Engelman, Jack, **67**/273FF
Engelstad, Kurt, **64**/88
Engeman, Richard H.:
An Historical Atlas, by Farmer, review, **74**/278-79
The Jacksonville Story, noted, **81**/328
Portland West, by DeWolfe, review, **74**/356-57
Engineering, **71**/184:
Pac. NW records, **71**/290
Engineers, **73**/86:
and conservation, **74**/102; earnings, **73**/85; SEE ALSO U.S. Army Engineers
England, SEE Great Britain

Englehart, Mrs. Miles P., **68**/360
English, J.C., **71**/232,233
English, John R.:
Ore.-Calif. boundary survey, **72**/37,38
English people, SEE British people
Enick, George, **67**/352,353
Enoch (Indian), **73**/69
Ensby, Carl, **77**/345
Enterprise, Ore., **65**/382:
history, **79**/104
Enterprise (aircraft carrier CV-6), **79**/213
Enterprise (river steamer built 1862), **67**/58,59
Enterprise-Courier, Ore. City:
100th anniversary, **67**/369
The Enterprising Scot: Investors in the American West, by Jackson, review, **69**/181-82
Entertainment, **69**/83; **70**/9,17:
children's games, **72**/281; early rural, **70**/43; Goldendale 1879, **70**/145-46; Negro minstrels, **70**/262; New Year's, **69**/112-13; opera bouffe, **70**/7FF; sleigh rides, **72**/314; Wild West shows, **70**/86; **81**/343; SEE ALSO Pioneer life; Theater
Environment:
changes, **80**/205; fur trade effects study, **81**/322-23; protection of, **77**/190; SEE ALSO Conservation; Oregon State Dept. of Environmental Quality
Eola, Ore., **64**/125-26,128-29; **69**/340; **73**/82:
map 1882, **72**/171; newspaper 1858, **64**/126
Eola Printing Assn., **64**/125,129
Episcopal Church:
Alberta, Canada, **68**/347
Astoria—
centennial, **66**/383; Grace Church, **81**/195
Canadian archives, **69**/85; Diocese of Olympia history, **68**/342; Emmanuel, **67**/280; Idaho, **63**/89; impact on Pacific NW Indians, **69**/50-56; Portland, Church of the Epiphany, **81**/167; Red River, **69**/50-51; St. John, Milwaukee, **62**/299; term "black robe," **69**/50,54-56

Episcopal missions:
Red River settlement, 71/327-31, 334,335—
Indian students, 71/325-36
Episode of the West: The Pendleton Round-Up, 1910-1951, Facts and Figures, by Boylen, noted, 77/90
Epperson, John C.: biography, 68/226-27N
Epstein, Donald B.: "Gladstone Chautauqua: Education and Entertainment, 1893-1929," 80/391-403
Epstein, Jesse, 79/103
Equality, Wash., 64/353; 70/178
Equality on the Oregon Frontier: Jason Lee and the Methodist Mission, 1834-1843, by Loewenberg, review, 78/86-89
Equator (whaler), 68/54
Equi, Marie D., 75/294
Equitable Savings and Loan, Portland: history, 69/329
Erickson, Martin, 74/32
Ericson, Augustus William, 77/190; 78/287
Erie (U.S. storeship), 70/305
Erlandson, Erland: journals 1832-34, 65/309
Ermatinger, Catherine Sinclair (Mrs. Francis), 63/180
Ermatinger, Francis, 63/180,211,215; 81/27N
Ermenc, Christine, ed.: *Voices of Portland*, noted, 77/300
Ernst, Alice Henson, 62/420: "Homer Davenport on Stage," 66/39-50
Ervine, Richard, 79/21
Erving's store, Marysville, 78/42
"Escape by Land: *Lightship No. 50*," by Ted Stokes, 69/307-23
Escondido, Calif., 73/116
Escort (tug), 69/309,310
Eskimo Adventure, by Keithahn, review, 64/347-48
Eskimo Artifacts Designed for Use, by Thiry and Thiry, review, 79/407
Eskimos, 72/81,181; 73/107; 77/ 295-96:

anthropological studies, 72/249-52; art, 68/347; 70/360; artifacts, 79/ 407; Bering Strait, 77/295-96; burial sites, 73/136,164; dress, 73/135; ethnographic collections, 73/136,164; folk tales, 72/250; fox traps, 67/368; Kodiak, 73/107,164,165; Malemiut, 77/296; north Alaska, 64/134-35; Norton Bay dwellings, 73/134-35; political organization, 72/248; prehistory, 66/281; tribes, 69/327-28; walrus skin boats, 67/86; SEE ALSO Aleut Indians; Unaligmut Eskimos
The Eskimos of Bering Strait, 1650-1898, by Ray, review, 77/295-96
Eskimos of the Nushagak River, by VanStone, review, 69/327-28
Eskridge, Richard Isaac, 79/283N, 301-302N,314
Eslick, Katherine Pinckney, 78/127
Eslick, Samuel, 78/127
Esmeralda County, Nev., 72/12
Espy, Robert Hamilton, 70/272: family, 71/189
Esquimalt, B.C., 65/329; 73/359
Esquimalt and Nanaimo Railway, 68/87
Essex (U.S. frigate): log extracts 1814, 63/84; 64/92
Estacada, Ore., 64/353: history, 67/91
Estes, Hardin W., 66/206
Estes, Levi, 62/219N
Ethnic groups, 66/87; 78/166; 80/205: in cities, 74/285; land rights, 63/247; Wash. and B.C., 1870-1961, 72/232; SEE ALSO Foreign-born
Ethnic Groups in the City: Culture, Institutions and Power, ed. by Feinstein, noted, 74/285
Ethnography: Russian Alaska collections, 73/136,169
Ethnography of the Kutenai, by Turney-High, cited, 71/279
Ethnological Collections in Museums of the United States and Canada, 1967, inventory noted, 68/184
Ethnology, 71/366: Alaskan Eskimos, 64/347; collections

in U.S. and Canada, **68**/184
Etholen, Arvid Adolf, SEE Etolin, Adolf Karlovich
Etna, Calif.:
early pioneers, **63**/357
l'Etoile du Matin (vessel), **64**/208
Etolin, Adolf Karlovich, **73**/119
Etulain, Richard W.:
They Came to a Valley, by Gulick, review, **68**/279-80
This Land Around Us, ed. by Lucia, review, **71**/181-82
Eubanks, Bernard M.:
The Story of the Pump, and Its Relatives, noted, **73**/73
Eugene, Ore., **62**/313; **78**/319; **79**/14,17,19,20,21:
architecture, **65**/315; beginnings, **78**/64; centennial, **64**/92; county clerk's office, **67**/179-81; described, **71**/19,189; early churches, **69**/77,276; electric cooperative, **80**/328
historic buildings, **80**/328—
Peters-Liston-Wintermeier house, **65**/121; Skinner cabin, **72**/89
historic sites, **65**/212; history, **74**/93; Jews, **69**/276; Long Tom rebellion, **67**/55-60; medical history, **66**/187; pageants, **75**/87; photos, **71**/19; **77**/322; public market, **72**/87; railroads, **71**/70-71,94; street names, **68**/353; trade and commerce, **71**/70-71,189; trolley cars, **74**/280; woolen mills, **62**/168,175
Eugene Junior Symphony, **69**/77
Eugene Register-Guard, **81**/321:
history, **78**/286-87; index, **78**/363
The Eugene Register-Guard: A Citizen of Its Community, Vol. I, by Price, review, **78**/286-87
Eugene Skinner (Liberty ship), **74**/281
Eulachon, SEE Smelt
The European Discovery of America: The Northern Voyages, A.D. 500-1600, by Morison, review, **72**/343-44
Euwer, Gene, **70**/53
Eva (steamer), **68**/342
Evacuzette, **81**/169:
staff photo, **81**/ins.fr.cov. Summer

Evangel, San Francisco, **64**/136
Evangelical Church:
Sweet Home, **62**/205
Evans, Alice D., **69**/41
Evans, Baldy, **69**/328
Evans, Dave, Tacoma 1890s, **66**/113-14N
Evans, Elwood, **62**/202,313-33*passim*; **63**/185,221,228-30; **64**/307; **81**/251
Evans, Hiram Wesley, **75**/177,179,180
Evans, Jacob, SEE Evans, W.J.
Evans, Jane Coultas, **66**/281; **78**/218
Evans, Jeremiah, **72**/90
Evans, John, geologist, **64**/357; **67**/13-14:
death, **69**/29,48; explorations in Pacific NW, **69**/38,45N; family, **69**/40-41; journal copy, **69**/37-38,40,44; letters, **69**/31-32,36,37,40,41,48; map of possible route, **69**/46-47; meteorite discovery, **69**/29-49; reports lost, **69**/41N-42,44
Evans, John:
"Geological Survey of Oregon and Washington Territories," cited, **69**/37,39,40,42-44
"Route from Port Orford Across the Rogue River Mountains," cited, **69**/37
Evans, John Stark, **74**/234
Evans, Mr. and Mrs. L.T., **81**/58
Evans, Marian, **67**/379
Evans, Richard X., **69**/41-42
Evans, Robert Mills, **69**/41
Evans, Samuel D., Sr., **69**/330; **81**/105
Evans, Virginia Mills (Mrs. John), **69**/40FF
Evans, W.J., **65**/55N,56; **69**/229N
Evans, Walter H., **74**/216; **75**/154: photo, **75**/155
Evans Creek:
Indian battle, **66**/223N
Evanson, Larry, **77**/345
Evening Telegram, Portland:
Coxey's army reports, **65**/268-93*passim*
Evenson, O.J., **66**/181
Everding, Richard, **72**/172
Everest, Alfred E., **74**/349
Everest, John, **74**/345, 349
Everest, William C., **74**/349

Everett, Wash.:
free speech fight, 69/325; history, 72/86; labor party, 71/363; "massacre," 73/281-82; school history, 65/378

The Everett Massacre: A History of the Class Struggle in the Lumber Industry, by Smith, review, 73/281-82

Evergreen, Wash.:
colony advertised, 74/ins.bk.cov. March; condemned 1940, 74/33; established, 74/16,33; history, 74/5-33; photos, 74/4; postal service, 74/23-31*passim*; school, 74/30; settlers listed, 74/16,17-18,21,22,24

"Evergreen on the Queets," by Rowena L. and Gordon D. Alcorn, 74/5-33

Everman, Hiram, 75/345,347: accessory to murder, 75/349,352; biography, 75/359; bond service, 75/353, 355,358-59

Everman, Return William, 75/345: confession, 75/347,355-56; execution, 75/355; murder of Hooker, 75/346-48; robbery, 75/346; trial, 75/352

Ewell, Elaine, 77/69

Ewers, John Canfield, 64/282; 69/63,64: *The Horse in Blackfoot Indian Culture: With Comparative Material From Other Western Tribes*, review, 72/81-82

"Was There a Northwestern Plains Sub culture? An Ethnographical Appraisal," noted, 68/347

Ewing, James F., 74/213

Ewing, Lyle, 66/385

Ewing Young, Master Trapper, by Holmes, review, 69/61-62

Examiner, San Francisco: Davenport employed, 66/39,44

Exon, John William, 62/109

Expansionism, SEE United States—expansionism

The Expeditions of John Charles Fremont, ed. by Jackson and Spence, Vol. I review, 72/165-66; Vol. II noted, 77/197,290

"Experience, Personality and Memory: Jesse Applegate and John Minto Recall Pioneer Days," by Abner S. Baker, III, 81/229-59

Experiment in Liberty: The Ideal of Freedom in the Experience of the Disciples of Christ, by Osborn, noted, 79/228

Exploration and Empire: The Explorer and the Scientist in the Winning of the American West, by Goetzmann, review, 70/73-74

Explorations of Kamchatka, by Krasheninnikov, trans. noted, 77/290

Explorations of the Northwest Coast, 72/344; 73/273-74: British, 76/312,315; Russian, 62/198; 76/312; Spanish, 62/105; SEE ALSO names of explorers; Voyages

Exploratory Excavations at Spalding Missions, 1973, by Chance, noted, 77/302

Explorers and Settlers: Historic Places Commemorating the Early Exploration and Settlement of the United States, pub. by National Park Service, noted, 69/333

Exploring expeditions: Atlantic Coast, 72/343-44; early U.S., 69/333; journals, 71/309-24*passim*; 73/273; Kamchatka, 77/290; Olympic Peninsula, 78/281-82; Pacific Basin, 70/77; Plains, 72/179; scientific, 80/207; western U.S., 70/73; 71/364; Yellowstone 1870, 71/365; SEE ALSO names of explorers; Voyages

Expositions: Golden Gate, 79/214; SEE ALSO Lewis and Clark Centennial Exposition; Louisiana Purchase Centennial Exposition; Oregon Centennial Exposition and Trade Fair; Panama-Pacific Exposition

Express (magazine), cited, 81/104

Express (motor launch), 66/52

Express companies, 68/88-89: Idaho, 68/88; SEE ALSO Adams and Company Express; Butterfield Overland Mail Co.; Hasty Messenger and Express Co.; Hockaday, John M.; Ish, William K.; Miners' Loon Creek Express; Mossman and Company Express; Pierce and Lewiston Express; Pony Express; Wells, Fargo and Co.

Ezra Meeker, Pioneer, by Green, noted, 70/359

F.S. Redfield (schooner), **66**/127
Fackler, Saint Michael, **63**/89; **65**/308
Fagan, David D., **65**/184N
Fagan, Ed, **81**/301,306: ranch photo, **81**/308
Fagan, Pat, **81**/301,306: ranch photo, **81**/308
Fahl, Ronald J.: "S.C. Lancaster and the Columbia River Highway: Engineer as Conservationist," **74**/101-44
Failing, Edward, **65**/392
Failing, Henry, **73**/56; **80**/146, 149,151,307,316: banking interests, **71**/151; opposition to Stark, **72**/329-31, 335; photo, **72**/328; promotes trade with Orient, **71**/151; railroad interests, **71**/68
Failing, John, **74**/213
Failing, Josiah, photo, **80**/16
Failing, Libby C., **74**/346
Faint the Trumpet Sounds, by Terrell and Walton, noted, **68**/82
Fairchild, Grace: *Frontier Woman on the Dakota Frontier: The Life of a Woman Homesteader*, noted, **74**/284
Fairchild, Lucius, **80**/207
Fairchilds, J.A., **69**/229N
Fairfax, Wash., **73**/338,339,342
Fairfield, Iowa, **64**/311
Fairfield, Ore., **66**/348,359N,360,361
Fairfield (tug), **66**/119,122
Fairhaven, Wash., **74**/5
Fairley, Edward: family journey Ore.-Calif., **80**/229, 231N,233,239,240,243
Fairley, Oliver L. (Ollie), **80**/240
Fairman, Jack D., **63**/286-88,292: photo, **63**/287
Fairman, Selma (Mrs. Jack D.), **63**/292
Fairs: Clark Co. centennial, **69**/330 Columbia Co., **74**/358— fairgrounds, **66**/382 Lane Co., **66**/81; **72**/353 Oregon, **71**/197— first, **63**/345; **64**/89; SEE ALSO Centennials; Oregon State Fair

Siskiyou Co., **66**/82; Umatilla Co. centennial, **64**/90
Fairy Creek, near Coquille, **62**/215
Falcon (British bark), **76**/127
Falkirk (ship), **66**/107
Falkland Islands, **63**/241
Fall Creek, Lane Co., **78**/53
Falls City, Ore.: street names, **80**/105
Falls of Halladale (ship), **66**/122
Falmouth (sloop-of-war), **62**/63; **64**/295
Familiar Birds of the Northwest Shores and Waters, by Nehls, noted, **76**/182
Family life: Oregon Trail, **81**/100-101; Pacific NW, **81**/102-103
Fandango (Lassen) Pass, **72**/33N
Fane, Florence, SEE Victor, Frances Fuller
Fannie Paddock Hospital, Tacoma, **66**/119N,121
Fannie Troup (steamer), **72**/89
Faragher, John Mack: *Women and Men on the Overland Trail*, review, **81**/96,99-101
Farallon Islands, **77**/110
Farb, Peter: *Man's Rise to Civilization, As Shown by the Indians of North America from Primeval Times to the Coming of the Industrial State*, review, **70**/265-66
Fardell, Jan, **69**/331
Fares: electric rail 1889, **80**/398; ferry 1885, **80**/235,237,240 ocean vessel— New York-San Francisco, **71**/58,59; San Francisco-Portland, **71**/11,58,59 railroads— 1900s, **81**/35,59; 1905, **80**/64; Chicago-West Coast, **71**/59; Kansas City-San Francisco, **71**/8,59; New York-West Coast, **71**/59; Omaha-West Coast, **71**/59; Portland-Eugene, **71**/17; Sacramento-Portland, **71**/58; Tacoma-Kalama, **71**/17 river boats— 1904, **81**/35; Portland-Almota, **71**/22; Portland-Kalama, **71**/14,17;

Portland-LaCenter, 71/13; Tacoma-Seattle, 71/16

stagecoach—
1910, 76/54; Albany-Corvallis, 71/19; Chicago-San Francisco, 71/59; Eugene-Corvallis, 71/19; Kansas-Walla Walla, 71/59; Lewiston-Moscow, Ida., 71/23; Omaha-Boise, 71/59; Sacramento-Portland, 71/59; Salt Lake City-Walla Walla, 71/59; Walla Walla-Boise, 71/59

steamboats—
1889, 80/398; 1904, 81/34; 1905, 80/64; St. Louis-Ft. Benton 1862, 66/228; Umatilla-The Dalles 1863, 66/201

streetcars—
1885, 80/255; 1905, 80/64; Portland trolley 1917, 81/204

toll bridge 1852, 80/82; toll road, 1885, 80/235,236; Yellowstone excursion, 74/337

Farewell Bend: confusion, Snake and Deschutes, 78/219

Farewell Bend, Deschutes River, 72/342

Farley, Bridget, SEE Gilleese, Bridget Farley

Farley, James, family, 69/127

Farley, Luke, 69/105

Farley, Mary Byrne, 69/119

Farley, Patrick G., 69/105,127

Farley, Robert, 77/361-62

Farley families, Morrow Co., 69/127

Farm Security Administration, 81/165

Farmer, Judith A., *et al:* *An Historical Atlas of Early Oregon*, review, 74/278-79

Farmer-labor movement: economic panaceas, 76/135,136,138, 141,144; Oregon, 76/135-51; promotion by Commonwealth Federation, 76/140-51

Farmer-Labor Party, 65/363; 68/88

Farmer Labor Political Federation, 76/135

Farmers Alliance, 68/200: Milwaukie, 68/201-203,205,206,207

Farmers Union, 68/132; 76/137,141

Farming, SEE Agriculture

Farmington, Wash., 79/22

Farms, 80/205: average size Ore.— 1870, 71/67; 1870-1900, 71/96 electricity use, 80/324-25; Fraser River first, 63/359; frontier, described, 80/329; home interior photos, 80/326, 327; investment in Willamette Valley, 69/181; machinery photo, 80/328; prices, 71/60,84-85; SEE ALSO prices; production, 71/87; profits, 71/98; value, 71/31; western industrial, 71/365; Wisconsin, 64/79-81; SEE ALSO Agriculture

Farms in the Cutover: Agriculture in Northern Wisconsin, by Helgeson, review, 64/79-81

Farnham, Russell, 70/339,340

Farnham, Thomas Jefferson, 63/185, 195,217; 67/84; 71/250: *Travels in the Great Western Prairies, the Anahuac and Rocky Mountains*..., reprint noted, 79/107

Farnsworth, Philo, 70/268

Farquhar, Francis P., 66/380

Farra, Earl, 77/159,161-62,164

Farrand and French, painted panorama makers, 65/171

Farrar, William H., 66/155N; 80/138

Farrell, Sylvester, 72/172

Farron, Narcisse, SEE Ferron, Narcisse

Farrow, Edward S., 68/223

Farthing, —, mate on *Thos. H. Perkins*, 63/218

Fassill, Henry, 74/7-8

Fastabend, Elizabeth Mische, 66/179

Fastabend, Henry, 66/179

Fastabend, John Antone, 69/312N: biography, 66/179,181-82; ocean-going log rafts, 66/181-82; photo, 66/179; railroad interest, 66/181

Fastabend, Lena, SEE Miller, Lena Fastabend

Fastabend, Sarah A.P. (Mrs. John A.), 66/179

Faught, Bea Graff, 81/58

Fauntleroy, William Hale, 66/155

Fawcett, Nellie, photo, 72/208

Fawcett Creek, 72/308

Fawn (sailing vessel): wreck, **69**/237N; 70/237-38 Fay, Ned, **63**/25 *Fearless* (tug), **68**/266; **69**/307 Feather River, **66**/168 Featherstonhaugh, A., **66**/70 Fechheimer, W.R., **66**/249; **74**/110 *Federal Conservation Policy, 1921-1933,* by Swain, review, **65**/205-206 Federal Records Center, Seattle: Pacific NW public land records, **70**/ 269-71; U.S. Army Engineer files, **71**/290 Federal Reserve Board, **81**/165 Federal Security Agency, **81**/165 Federation of Catholic Societies, **75**/141 Federation of Fraternal Societies, **75**/165 Federation of Patriotic Societies, **72**/81; **75**/144-48,162-63,167,171,179; **76**/247: election ticket, **75**/146; public utility company interests, **75**/162,190N Fee, Chester, **69**/128 Fee, James Albert, **69**/128 Fee, James Alger, **69**/120,128 *Feeding the Russian Fur Trade: Provisionment of the Okhotsk Seaboard and the Kamchatka Peninsula, 1639-1856,* by Gibson, cited, **77**/293; review, **71**/181 Feilner, John, **69**/231; **81**/105: bird collecting trip 1860, **69**/229-30N Feldenheimer, William B., **64**/359 Feldman, Marianne L.: Columbia River historic sites inventory, **75**/87-88 Felix, Bill, **80**/37,45 Felt, Margaret E.: *Gyppo Logger,* noted, **66**/82 Feltskog, E.N., ed.: *The Oregon Trail,* by Parkman, review, **70**/353-54 Fences, **71**/368; **72**/182: cattle range, **67**/151,152 Fendall, A., Sacred Heart student, **81**/81N Fendall, Lonny W.: "Medorem Crawford and the Protective Corps," **72**/55-77 "Medorem Crawford in Old Oregon," thesis cited, **72**/59N Fenn, (Thomas H.?), First Ore. Cavalry,

65/93 Fenton, James D.: residence, **76**/11,12(photo) Fenton, John, **63**/151 Fenton, William D., **62**/94 Fererra, Jimmy, **80**/45-46 Ferguson, J.W., **64**/60 Ferguson, Jack, **67**/227 Ferguson, James, **67**/223,227 Ferguson, (William F.?), **70**/165 Feris, Charles M.: *Hiking the Oregon Skyline,* noted, **74**/358 Fernald, Walter, **67**/236 Ferndale, Wash., **62**/98 Ferns, Archie, **77**/90 Ferrara and Bros. Fish Market, Portland, **66**/260 Ferrell, Mallory Hope: *Rails, Sagebrush and Pine: A Garland of Railroad and Logging Days in Oregon's Sumpter Valley,* noted, **69**/78-79 Ferrera, Albert, **77**/254,259,260 Ferrera, Anthony, **77**/246,260N Ferrera, John, **77**/246,260N Ferriday, Virginia Guest: *Stations West,* by Culp, review, **75**/85-86 Ferriday, Virginia Guest, and Thomas Vaughan, eds.: *Space, Style and Structure: Building in Northwest America,* noted, **75**/368; **77**/291 Ferries, **62**/200; **80**/90: Ainsworth, Wash. train ferry photo, **71**/32; Albina, **77**/376; Almota, **71**/ 23N,24(photo); Astoria, **67**/372; **75**/ 294; auto ferries, **63**/66; **71**/286; Boise River 1852, **80**/96; Calif. gold rush, **62**/105; Clearwater River, **79**/77N Columbia River, **63**/252; **66**/91,235; **71**/286; **77**/87; **79**/202— Condit's, **72**/90; mouth, **67**/372; **75**/294; Portland-Vancouver, **74**/ 210,252(photo); railroad, **73**/334; Westport, **66**/91 Coos Co., **68**/90; Coos River, **66**/57; Coquille River, **70**/243; Cowlitz River, **73**/343; Deschutes River, **67**/313; **77**/ 339; **79**/201; Duncan's, **80**/66; Ft.

Boise, 67/313; Ft. Hall, 72/72,73; Goose Lake, 81/328; Green River, 79/78,380; Humboldt River, 79/77N; Indian, 79/185; Ingram's, 67/59 John Day River, 67/312— Scott's, 81/263N Kalama, 71/14N; Klamath Lake, 75/362 Klamath River, 70/75; 80/105,235— Killibrew's, 72/39N Lane Co., 78/288; Linn Co., 79/104; Lower Applegate River, 80/336 McKenzie River, 78/53,64,65— Seavey, 81/105; Spores, 69/276; 78/64; 79/29 Malheur River, 68/38N; Maxwill's, 67/59; Missouri River, 79/66,365, 367; Mormon, 79/68; 80/74,79 Nestucca River— Woods, photo, 71/122 North Platte River, 79/77N Oregon Trail, 62/257,258,274,283, 341-58*passim*,384,385; 79/76,77— tolls, 62/341,345,356,359,385 Oregon Trunk, photo, 69/304 Owyhee River, 68/249N,299N,314— Duncan's, 76/157 Payette River, 68/229N; Pitt River, 80/237; Platte River, 79/375,376; Ponacles River, 79/384; 80/86; Puget Sound first auto, 63/66; rates 1853, 78/64N; Rinehart, 73/80; Rogue River, 80/233; Sacramento River, 80/ 237; Salem, 64/356; Salmon Falls, 80/ 92; Salmon River, 79/69; Sellwood, 72/90; 77/378; Siuslaw River, 70/ 245; 74/273; Skinner's, 77/324; 78/65; 79/6N Snake River, 66/235— 1852, 69/90,92,96; Ft. Hall, 72/72, 73; Kinney's, 66/235; 68/230; 70/ 18N; Munday's, 68/239,248,308; Olds, 68/229N,298N; Ross Fork, 72/70; Salmon Falls, 80/92; Texas, 71/23N Spores, 69/276; 78/64; 79/29; Sublette's Cutoff, 62/105; Texas Lodge, Wash., 71/23N; toll ferries, 79/76-80*passim*,375,376,384,389;

Umpqua River, 69/330; 73/72; Wallula, 70/167; Westport, 66/91; Wheatland, 63/364; 65/121; 73/82 Willamette River, 63/68; 64/356; 65/121; 80/270— Buena Vista, 63/364; Canby, 63/364; Coast Fork, 78/64; Middle Fork, 78/ 321,322; Wheatland, 63/364; 65/121; 73/82 Yakima River, 70/137 Ferril, Thomas Hornsby, 66/243 Ferris, Mrs. A.H., photo, 80/324 Ferris, Joel E., 62/202 Ferron (Farron), Narcisse, 63/170 Ferry, Elisha P., 70/27N,169 *Ferryboats on the Columbia River, Including the Bridges and Dams*, by Ruby and Brown, review, 77/87 Fessenden, Robert E., 62/421; 70/371: *American Expansion: A Book of Maps*, by Sale, review, 64/77 *A Catalogue of the Everett D. Graff Collection of Western Americana*, comp. by Storm, review, 70/64-66 *Changing Military Patterns on the Great Plains*, by Secoy, review, 62/92-93 *A Guide to Archives and Manuscripts in the United States*, ed. by Hamer, review, 63/244-45 *Letters of Francis Parkman*, ed. by Jacobs, review, 62/403 *Mapping the Trans-Mississippi West*, by Wheat, review, 66/183-85 *The Northwest Gun*, by Hanson, review, 62/92-93 *Pacific Northwest Quarterly Index*, by Connette, review, 65/411 Fessenden, William Pitt: Stark senate seat dispute, 72/333-35; 73/35,38,40,45 Fetterman, William J., 71/188 Feuds: Laws-Callavan, 68/354 Fickert, Charles M., 72/346 Fiction: children's, 73/285; 77/301; frontier, 73/286; western Canada, 73/286; SEE ALSO Literature *Fiddler's Green*, by Wetjen, cited,

74/174,257
Fidelater (steamer), 76/180
Fidler, George, 78/127,323N
Fidler, James, 78/127
Fidler, William W., photo, 78/326
Field, Charles K., 74/201:
Four-Leaved Clover, cited, 74/202
Stanford Stories, cited, 74/201
Field, James:
diary cited, 78/221
Field, Stephen Johnson, 72/181;
73/60,62
Field, Virgil:
Official History of the Washington National Guard, vols. 4 and 5 noted,
63/246
Field, Wright, 74/63
The Field Notes of Captain William Clark, 1803-1805, ed. by Osgood, review,
66/65-67
Fields, Calvin, 64/145
Fields, Ore., 73/231
Fierens, John F., 80/350,352,354;
81/80,81,87,88
Fiero, Conroe, 68/352
Fifteenmile Creek, Lake Co., 72/16N
Fifteenmile Creek, Wasco Co., 65/116N;
79/141N
Fighting Rebels and Redskins: Experiences in Army Life of Col. George B. Sanford, 1861-1892, ed. by Hagemann, noted,
71/287-88
Fights, 69/113,114,147
Figone, Luigi, photo, 77/252
Fiji Islands, 62/29,30,105
Filberts, 66/87:
industry, 81/336
Filipino people:
in California, 68/348
Fillmore, Millard, 64/293; 66/31
Fillmore (Roy Station), Ore., 70/316FF;
72/91:
name change, 70/332
The Filming of the West, by Tuska, review,
78/362
Finch, J.L., 63/220
Finch, Jack, 76/46-49
Finck, Edward J., 79/249:
musical compositions, 79/266

Finck, Henry Conrad, 67/276; 79/
235,236,239,240,248,256,257,266:
photo, 79/236; musical compositions,
79/246,247,252
Finck, Henry T., 79/236,238,239,
249,252,266:
My Adventures in the Golden Age of Music, cited, 79/236,242,251; quoted,
67/276
Findling, Jacob, 79/239
Fine, Joe, 69/63
Fine California Views: The Photography of A. W. Ericson, by Palmquist, review,
78/287
Finerty, John F., 80/333
Finger Rock, Calif., 65/160
Fingvalla (steamship), 66/105
Finlay, Jacques Raphael ("Jaco"),
65/215; 74/359
Finlayson, Duncan, 63/183
Finlayson, Nicol:
journal 1830-33, 65/309
Finlayson, Roderick:
salmon story quoted, 70/303
Finley, J.P., 75/138
Finley, W.B., 69/106
Finn, Benjamin Franklin ("Huckleberry"), 68/350
The Finn Factor in American Labor, Culture and Society, by Ross, noted, 79/340
Finnish-American Historical Society of
the West, 66/388; 70/372:
officers and directors, 65/123,311;
66/84,278; 67/82,283; 68/84,282;
69/81,278; 70/81,275; 71/193; 72/
175; 73/77; 74/180; 75/90; 76/94;
77/93; 78/93; 79/109; 80/108;
81/109; publications, 71/199,361;
72/350; 73/72; 74/91-92,93
Finnish Brotherhood, Portland, 71/372;
73/363
The Finnish Experience in the Western Great Lakes Region, ed. by Karni *et al*, noted,
77/302
Finnish people, 72/350; 73/72:
America, 70/361; 79/341; Astoria,
72/169; 74/91-92; 75/84,294; Blue
Mountains, 80/335; Columbia Co.,
66/382; culture, 74/91-92; economic

conditions, 74/92; first spar tree topped, 73/213; Lewis River, 74/281; 75/83-84,87; Little Kalama River, 75/83-84, 87; loggers, 73/19; 74/93; Michigan, 79/340; Oregon, 66/382; 71/199, 360,361,372; 72/169-70; Pendleton, 72/350-51; population 1860-1910, 80/266-67; Portland, 73/80; theater, 74/91-92; Washington, 71/199; 81/ 106,328; Western Great Lakes, 77/302

Finnish Socialist Club, 74/92

Finns and Finnicans, An Oregon Finntown Novel, by Mattila, review, 72/169-70

The Finns in America: A Students' Guide to Localized History, by Kolehmainen, noted, 70/361

Finseth, Pete, 77/268

Finseth's Mercantile Store, Dallas, Ore., 77/263

Finzer, William E., photo, 71/149

Fir trees:

Douglas fir, 63/364; 69/153; 72/307; 73/7,24,174; 77/351,353; grand fir, 69/153,167; white fir, 73/340; 77/351,353

Fire and Ice: The Cascade Volcanoes, by Harris, noted, 77/196

Fire Control Hill, Ft. Stevens, 65/357-58

Fire departments:

Lebanon, 68/187; Portland, 72/323N; Salem, 64/89; 78/288; 80/340; Sellwood, 62/177

Firearms, 71/369; 72/180,281,283; 74/306,309; 75/61,63,64,101-102; 76/336:

Canadian West, 68/185; Colt dragoon revolver, 66/386; Henry rifle, 64/188; Indian trade guns, 63/77-78; 70/88; Indian warfare use, sketches, 81/354-72 *passim*; Kentucky rifle, 63/15,26; Maynard carbine, 79/138; mountain men, 79/105; Northwest guns, 62/92-93 Parrott rifle, 65/331,333,335,350— photos, 65/330,342,353-55 powder keg, 70/366 Rodman gun, 65/331,333-35, 339,342— photos, 65/330,332,342,346 shooting accidents,

79/189,190,195,196; Spencer carbine photo, 79/120; Springfield musket photo, 79/120; supplied to Indian scouts, 79/138; SEE ALSO Arms and ammunition; Cannon

Firearms, Traps, and Tools of the Mountain Men, by Russell, noted, 79/105; review, 69/182-83

Firebaugh, Calif., 63/274

Fires:

Antelope 1964, 66/91; Astoria, 66/ 329; 73/82; 75/294; Bandon, 75/341-42; fire drills, 78/168-69; fire engines, photo, 75/213; Idaho 1910, 64/283; LaCenter, 76/382; Lakeview 1900, 72/93; Portland, SEE Portland—fires; Portland Woolen Mills, 62/176-77; prairie fires, 62/348; 79/159,198; protection, industrial, 62/171-72; St. Johns 1905, 62/179; school, 75/174; Sellwood 1904, 62/177; shipboard, 81/197-99; Silver Lake, 64/90; 73/83; SEE ALSO Forest fires

Firewood, 76/18; 80/248,281

The First Century at the University of Washington, 1861-1961, by Gates, review, 64/76-77

The First Century of Masonry in Silverton, noted, 70/76

"The First Cheese Factory in Tillamook," by Leland H. Townsend, 74/274-77

First Christian Church, McMinnville, 65/218

First Man West: Alexander Mackenzie's Account of his Expedition..., ed. by Sheppe, review, 64/272-73

First National Bank, Portland, 62/165; 71/151:

centennial, 66/281; museum, 74/362

First National Bank of Baker, 67/236, 248,250

First National Bank of Coquille City, 63/34

First National Bank of Heppner, 69/ 140,141

First Oregon Cavalry, 62/246; 63/263; 73/258; 79/126,130: burial sites, 66/59-62; disbanded, 79/128; first raising of, 65/392-94;

flags, 65/23; history, 65/392-400; journal 1864, 65/13-116; life in, 65/90-91,98; markers, photo, 66/60; mustering broadside photo, 65/4; name, 65/394; officers, 65/10N-12N,393-95; relationship among officers, 65/60-61N,81-82,86-88; training and outfitting, 65/396-98

First Oregon Infantry, 65/10-12N,87N, 97,102,106; 67/55-60*passim*; 79/175: Co. D, 64/169— banner photo, 81/258 projected raising of, 65/87,97,102

First Presbyterian Church, Brownsville: centennial history, 66/82

First Presbyterian Church, Salem, 72/173

First Presbyterian Society of Clatsop Plains, 62/248

First Security Bank of Idaho, 72/183

First State Bank of Milwaukie, 62/204

First Washington Territory Volunteer Infantry, 65/8,98N,102N-103N, 392,398

First White Women over the Rockies..., ed. by Drury, Vols. I and II review, 65/119-20; Vol. III review, 68/76-77

Fischer, Anton Otto, 74/160: *Focs'le Days*, cited, 66/101N; quoted, 66/130-31

Fischer, LeRoy H., ed.: *The Western Territories in the Civil War*, noted, 80/208

Fisgard (British frigate), 63/201,218,220, 224; 64/241N; 70/293N,307,309N: crew employed at Nisqually Farm, 63/224

Fish, 68/244: Alaska, 77/183; Lewis & Clark Centennial Expo. display, 80/56-57; prices, 71/17; 74/271; processing, 71/367; salting and drying, 77/181,183; varieties discovered by Lewis, 69/23; SEE ALSO names of fish

Fish Hawk (Indian), 78/364

Fish Lake, Douglas Co., 75/362

"Fish Trap Art," by Laurence D. Jackson, 78/197-206

Fishburne, Elizabeth M., 63/371; 64/359

Fisher, A.N., 62/177

Fisher, C.L., 64/161

Fisher, Ezra, father of Ezra T.T., 81/4,188

Fisher, Ezra Timothy Taft, 66/154

Fisher, Frederic, 79/16

Fisher, Hiram, 79/16

Fisher, James, immigrant of 1854, 79/16

Fisher, James, Quebec doctor, 81/380

Fisher, John, immigrant of 1854, 79/16

Fisher, Joseph, 76/246

Fisher, Peter, 74/9

Fisher, Raymond H.: *Bering's Voyages: Whither and Why*, review, 79/212

Fisher, Vardis, 72/267: *Pemmican*, review, 62/99-100 *Tale of Valor, A Novel of the Lewis and Clark Expedition*, review, 62/99-101

Fisher, William H.: *The Invisible Empire, A Bibliography of the Ku Klux Klan*, noted, 81/331

Fisher, Wilson, 78/305

Fisher Springs, 68/228N

Fishing and fisheries: Alaska, 63/362; 69/327 boats, 75/105; 78/201— diagram, 78/202; photos, 75/ins.fr. cov. June; 78/196; scows, 78/203 buying, 75/105; 78/201; Canada, 72/182,344-45; canneries, 62/198; 72/354; 75/105-106,294; 78/203; Celilo Falls, 74/309-11 Columbia River, 64/346; 75/37-38,221-31; 78/197-206,365— canneries, 72/354; estuary, 74/164; fleet photo, 75/ins.fr.cov. June Cowlitz Farm, 63/205; Cowlitz River, 63/115-16,118,121,124,126-27,132, 145, 154,197; dipnetting, 72/151, 157N; 75/221-31; dogfish oil industry, 70/178 fishermen— Dalles-Celilo area, 75/224; Finnish, 77/302; life described, 75/221-31; strike 1896, 80/335; unions, 81/322 fishing towns, 72/346 fishwheels, 71/367; 72/151,153,154; 75/37,221,223,224,230; 73/68— photos, 75/36,224; prohibited 1926,

72/157
foreign on Pacific Coast, 69/86; Ft. George 1846, 64/222-45*passim*; gillnetting, 75/294; H & B seining grounds, 67/281; hatcheries, 78/206; hemlock boxes, 77/350; Japanese, 77/297; Japanese glass floats, 77/278-80; ladders, 71/352; legislative history, 81/323; methods, 74/164,297; nets, 72/153,354; NW Coast, 72/109; 76/321-22; Pacific, 64/346-47; Pitt River, 80/237; Queets River, 74/23; Rainier, 74/83,297; Rogue River, 64/346-47; seining, 67/281; 80/207 set nets, 75/105,221,225-26; 78/205—outlawed, 78/205; sketches of, 78/199,205
shellfish, 77/353,359; Siuslaw River, 74/164; theses index, 72/274; traps, 75/105; 78/197-200; tuna industry, 67/85; SEE ALSO Fish; Indians—fishing; names of fish; Sport fishing

Fishing the Oregon Country, by Ames, review, 67/363-64

Fishlow, Albert, 69/83

Fishwheels of the Columbia, by Donaldson and Cramer, review, 73/68

Fisk, HBCO. interpreter, SEE Kipling, Thomas Pisk

Fisk, James Liberty, 64/281-82: Montana immigrant escorts, 72/71-72,72N

Fisk, Robert E., 65/314

Fisk, Wilbur, 74/71,73; 78/344-45

Fist in the Wilderness, by Lavender, noted, 80/336

Fister, Mrs. —, Lincoln Co., 71/268 (photo),269

Fitch, A.D., 80/21

Fitch, Alice, 77/90

Fitch, C.W., Army doctor, 68/241

Fitch, Charles A., 68/205

Fitch, George A., 74/359

Fitch, Thomas, 62/219N

Fitch, Thomas L., 79/125,126,126N

Fitzgerald, Jenkins A., 68/233N,243, 306; 70/16N: letter quoted, 70/23N

Fitzgerald, Mike, 73/267

Fitzgerald, Thomas, Pendleton lawyer, 69/128

Fitzgerald, Tom, Wheeler Co. settler, 73/267

Fitzhugh, Edmund C., 66/34,35: biography, 66/34N

Fitzmaurice, Maurice, family, 69/128-29

Fitzpatrick, Michael J., 69/129-30

Fitzsimmons, Matthew, 66/62

Five-bit Gulch, 62/228

Five Crows (Indian), 80/406

Fivemile Creek, Wasco Co., 65/13; 79/142

Flagg and Standifer Co.: construction camp photo, 66/314; pack train photo, 66/314

Flags, 71/362: Hawaii, 64/27N; 71/365; Russian-American Co., 71/365

Flanagan, James, 63/15,34

Flanagan, Patrick, 63/15

Flanders, Caroline, 79/203: photo, 79/205

Flanders, George H., 69/208

Flanders, J. Couch, 69/208

Flannery, Louis, 78/368: *Melvin Ricks' Alaska Bibliography*, ed. by Haycox, review, 78/359

Who's Who in Alaskan Politics, comp. by Atwood and DeArmond, review, 78/359-59

Flannigan, Frank, 69/130

Flannigan, Patrick, 69/130

Flannigan's Wells, 69/130

Flatbow Indians, 71/332: religion, 71/333

Flathead and Kootenay: The Rivers, the Tribes, and the Region's Traders, by Johnson, review, 71/279

Flathead Indian Reservation, 72/232-33: education, 65/377

Flathead Indians, 62/106; 64/49,51-52,54; 67/372; 69/63-65,270; 71/279,325,332,345; 74/71

Flathead River, 71/379

Flavel, George, 68/266; 70/184; 77/45

Flavel House, Astoria, 69/175,340

Flax: Cowlitz Farm, 63/115-73*passim*; SEE

ALSO Lewis' wild flax
Fleetwood, Ore., **63**/365
Fleetwood (steamer), **71**/12N,19: photo, **71**/21; trial run, **71**/21
Flegel, Al, **69**/342,348; **70**/374; **73**/362; **74**/184,366
Fleischacker, Herbert, **76**/244
Flemery, Felix, **62**/169
Fleming, G.L., **74**/21
Flemming, Hal, **73**/349,358: ranch, **73**/349,351,358(photo)
Flere, —, capt. of *Brothers of Guernsey*, **63**/227
Fletcher, —, Wasco Co. 1881, **81**/266,277
Fletcher, Alice, **65**/214; **67**/278
Fletcher, Crawford, **68**/39
Fletcher, Francis, **67**/92
Fletcher, Lorraine, and Helen O. Halvorson:
"19th Century Midwife: Some Recollections," **70**/39-49
Fletcher, Lorraine, ed.:
"From Denmark: R.P. Rasmussen," **81**/57-74
Fletcher, Robert F., **68**/311: map, **68**/224-25N
Flett, John:
Red River-Pacific Northwest emigration account, **72**/183
Flinn, Cynthis S. (Mrs. L.), **67**/69
Flinn, L., **67**/67,69N
Flinn, Michael A., **75**/20
Flint, A.L., **63**/42
Flint, Asa, **63**/41N,52
Flint, Mrs. Asa, **63**/41N
Flint, Daniel, **64**/269
Flint, Emeline L. Phinney, **63**/41-42
Flint, Eugene, V., **63**/42N
Flint, Isaac A.:
journal of voyage from San Francisco to Oregon, **63**/41-54
Flint, Purdy, J., **63**/42
Flint, Timothy, **70**/180
Flint, Wilson, **64**/269
Floating Marineways, Portland, **81**/41-42
Floed, Emily Lane (Mrs. John Creed), **65**/401

Floed, John Creed, **64**/88; **65**/401
Floed, Mary, **65**/401
"The Floed House," by Josephine Evans Harpham, **65**/401-404
Floed-Lane House, Roseburg, **64**/88, 359; **65**/401-404: photo, **65**/402
Flood, James, **69**/130
Flood Tide of Empire: Spain and the Pacific Northwest, 1543-1819, by Cook, noted, **77**/290; review, **74**/353-54
Floods, **74**/354; **77**/192; **78**/360: Champoeg 1861-62, **64**/357; **66**/ 187,358,361; Columbia Co., **66**/281; Columbia River, **74**/297; **77**/299; control, **69**/272-73; SEE ALSO Reclamation; Douglas Co. 1861, **66**/187; Heppner, **64**/356; **69**/136; **77**/192; Mitchell, **73**/261,267; OK Creek, **67**/ 281; photos, **80**/143,bk.cov. Fall; Portland 1894, **67**/77; Scottsburg 1861, **70**/254-55; Willamette River 1861, **79**/173; winter 1964-65, **66**/89,187, 281; SEE ALSO Tidal waves
Flook, John G., **70**/74
Floras Lake, **71**/290
Florence, Ida.:
gold rush 1862, **63**/359
Florence, Ore., **72**/353; **74**/271; **78**/364:
name, **69**/329
Florin, Lambert, **69**/331:
Ghost Town Album, review, **64**/184-85
Ghost Town Trails, review, **65**/209-10
Ghost Town Treasures, noted, **66**/384
A Guide to Western Ghost Towns, noted, **68**/343
Historic Western Churches: A Photographic Pilgrimage to the Churches of Old, review, **71**/186-87
Western Ghost Town Shadows, review, **66**/77
Western Ghost Towns, review, **63**/79-80
Western Wagon Wheels: A Pictorial Memorial to the Wheels that Won the West, review, **72**/168-69
Florists, **81**/105
Flour:
export to Orient, **71**/100; freighted to

mines 1863, 66/201-202; SEE ALSO Prices

Flour and grist mills, 66/199,201; 71/150; 77/181: Calapooia Creek, 66/187; Cedar Creek, Wash., 64/276; Champoeg, 63/83,182-83; Dallas, Ore., 62/200; 66/385; Deer Creek, 63/24,26; Eagle River Mills, 73/83; early Pacific NW types, 64/357; fanning mills, 63/54; French Prairie, 66/343,344; Kings Valley, 65/182,191N; Kubli, 65/218; Linn Co. oldest, 66/90; McKercher mills, 70/184; Nesmith millstones, 66/292; Oakland, Ore., 79/394; Oregon City 1850, 66/162-63; St. Johns, 62/178; St. Paul, 77/298; Swanson's, Carlton, 76/13; The Dalles, 75/47; Unalaska 1843 sketch, 73/125; Wallowa, 62/201

Flowers, Allen Elmer: family, 73/202(photo),203; manuscripts cited, 73/203

Flowers, Samuel Bowman, 78/125

Flowers: Oregon wild, 68/350; Wallowas, 70/31; SEE ALSO names of flowers

Floyd, Charles, Jr., 70/339

Floyd, John, 62/193; 68/33; 72/104,105; 75/320: biography, 70/335; characterized, 70/333; congressional career, 70/333-46; friend of Wm. Clark, 70/339; labors for Oregon, 70/339-46; meets Astoria personnel, 70/339; painting, 70/334; views on commerce with Orient, 70/340,341,344

Floyd, Letitia, 70/335

Floyd-Jones, DeLancey, 65/175N, 183-184N

Flumgudgeon Gazette and Bumble Bee Budget, 63/254; 81/18N

Fly Lake, 79/144N

Flyer (steamer), 63/66; 66/115

Flying Cloud (clipper ship), 63/359; 66/9; 77/37: 1851 passenger list cited, 66/9N

Flynn, Elizabeth Gurley, 67/372

Flynn, John T., 69/202,208

Fobert, Alex, 72/294,311

Focs'le Days, by Fischer, cited, 66/101N; quoted, 66/130-31

Fogdall, Alberta Brooks: *Royal Family of the Columbia: Dr. John McLoughlin and His Family,* review, 80/101

Fogel, Robert W., 69/83: "A Quantitative Approach to the Study of Railroads in American Economic Growth," cited, 67/106,160,177-78; 71/76-77

Railroads and Economic Growth, cited, 67/102-103,160; 71/75-77

The Union Pacific Railroad, cited, 71/75-76

Fogle, Antone, 81/299,300

Foisy, Medare Godard, 70/62; 72/353

Foley (Folley), A.N., 63/12

Foley (Folley), Euphrates, 63/12

Foley, John, 69/130

Foley (Folley), Robert, 63/12

Folklore, 62/83-84; 75/360-61,362: American Indian, 62/411-14; Basque, 76/153-74; Crescent Lake monster, 69/77; Frankie and Johnny background data, 66/89; frontier, 68/346; Great Basin, 71/196

Oregon— death and funerary beliefs, 66/281; medical beliefs, 66/281; name origin, 69/103; sayings, 70/74; superstitions, 66/281; 67/88

Pacific Northwest, 68/350; pacific NW Indians, 69/84; sea lore, 69/84; Scandinavian in West, 71/196; Swedish, 76/12,25; Western humor, 67/88; Western study, 68/86; SEE ALSO Indians—legends; Myths and legends

Folsom, John L., 75/32: report on U.S. Pacific Coast interests, 75/329,330-32,334N

Folsom, Joseph Libbey, 66/10N

"Fond Recollections," by Virginia B. Holsman, 80/365-90

Fontaine Qui Bouille, 67/367

Food: beaver, 69/17; bread, 80/121; clambakes, 66/80; coffee substitute, 80/369; country fare 1900, 72/199,

200; demonstrations of preparation, 80/120-21; duck, 69/331; hotel 1879, 70/143,145; Lewis and Clark Exped., 69/17,155; logging camp, 72/303; pemmican-making, 66/88; porcupine, 69/17; prairie dog, 69/17; railroad travel 19th century, 70/47; recipes, 78/27; Tillamook Co. 1919, 72/299; travel preparations, 80/230; wild fruits and roots, 69/155; World War II Aleutians, 80/39-43*passim*; SEE ALSO Prices

Food industry: labor unions, 76/146

Foord, John, 71/141

Forager (HBCo. vessel), 63/194-95

Forbes, Forrest D., and Lottie Maybee: *Days and Ways of Old Damascus, Oregon*, noted, 64/92

Forbes, James A., 68/348-49

Force, Harry D., 77/90

Force, John, 62/143; 73/252,253

Forcier, Rose, 66/348N

Ford, J.F.: lightship photos, 69/314-21

Ford, John Thorp, 77/266-67

Ford, Mrs. Kenneth W., 62/423; 63/94, 256,373; 64/93,189,285,363; 65/125, 221,317,416; 66/93,189,285,392,395; 67/380; 68/356,359

Ford, Nathaniel, 62/146N; 64/275; 70/260; 72/89; 75/345: family, 73/202; letter about Hooker murder, 75/356; slavery case, 73/ 201-203

Ford, Walter, 78/163

Foreign-born: 1860-1910, 80/260-68; Central Oregon, 81/313; contributions to western exploration, 70/73; Oriental immigration reappraised, 68/86; SEE ALSO Ethnic groups; Immigration; and under nationalities, i.e. Chinese people, Danish people

Foreman, Thomas C., 80/145N,146N

Forest, Charles, SEE Forrest, Charles

Forest fires, 78/91: 1925, 73/221-22; 1933, 73/182; 1939, 73/182; 1945, 73/182; Bandon, 75/ 341-42; Cave Mountain, 69/235N;

Clark Co., 1902, 74/31; Cowlitz Co. 1902, 67/366; Herman Creek, 75/ 280-81; Idaho 1910, 72/183,230-31; lightning-set, 76/45; man-set, 76/41, 44,73-74; Mt. Baldy, 73/353-54; Oregon 1869, 72/42; Pine Creek, 69/85; pioneer attitude, 73/226; Siskiyou Forest Reserve, 76/45-50,69 Tillamook burn 1933, 66/383; 69/78; 77/86-87,353,365— economic loss, 77/353

Washington Terr. 1869, 72/133; Yacolt burn 1902, 65/308; 78/364

Forest Grove, Ore., 63/31-32,37-38; 70/78,98; 76/381: post office history, 72/288

The Forest History Society, 71/294: officers and directors, 71/288; publications, 71/368

Forest industries, 64/349; 71/198; 77/320: first national colloquium 1966, 69/70; SEE ALSO Logging industry; Lumber and lumber industry

Forest Park, Portland, 62/108; 75/87

Forest rangers, 73/72,355,357; 74/271: fire wardens, 73/190-92; first professional, 76/30

Forest-Soil Relationships in North America, ed. by Youngberg, noted, 67/280

Forester (brig), 71/365

Forestry, 62/107; 67/280: Alaska, 76/101; conservation, 65/205-206; 77/350; forest management, 70/ 182; Mason memoirs, 71/368; Munger memoirs, 64/284; o&c lands, 64/61-67; Pacific NW cooperative, 64/86; 72/ 231; Philippine Bureau, 68/346; reforestation, 73/182; 77/350; 78/115; schools, 76/30-31,39; severance tax, 78/115; sustained yield, 64/62-66; tree farms, 77/350; tree seed certification, 70/182; u. of Washington, 74/358; West, 78/280

Forestry Building, Portland, 62/199; 63/355: described, 80/55; interior photo, 80/54

Forests: Atlantic and Pacific, 72/179; Japanese

bombing of, ww ii, 65/314
Oregon, 72/173—
prehistoric, 62/298; 66/281; resources, 63/91,246
see also names of forests; National forests; Timber; u.s. Forest Service
Forked Tongues and Broken Treaties, ed. by Worcester, noted, 77/303
Forks, Wash., 74/9
Forks of the Willamette, 79/6
Forman, George, 67/371; 69/336
Formosa, 62/6,14,31,32,37,43,51
Formosa Strait, 62/37,45
Forney, P.R., photo, 72/62
Forrest (Forest), Charles, 63/104,211n, 215; 64/202n
Forrest, Linn A., 76/261
Forrest, Nathan B., 69/180
Forrest (brig), 63/48,232
Forrester, J.W., Jr., 70/372,374; 74/363,366; 77/192:
Gold and Cattle Country, by Oliver, ed. by Jackman, review, 63/70-71
Forrester, Michael Aldrich, 77/192,298: *Beyond the Capes*, by Dodge, review, 73/273-74
Forse, A.G., 68/231
Forshaw, Samuel H., 81/105
Forstner, Elizabeth, 79/258
Forsyth, James W., 68/232n,234n,235n, 237,242,243n,306n; 70/168
Forsyth, John, 76/118,124,127,129, 131-32
Forsythe, Benjamin D., 67/313n: Ft. Dalles construction, 67/316
Fort Astoria, see Astoria enterprise; Fort George
Fort Bellingham, 62/98
Fort Bennett, 64/276; 66/139: location, 66/148n; name, 66/143n; stockade built, 66/147-48n
Fort Benton, 62/106; 66/228,229; 70/86; 71/364
Fort Bidwell, see Camp Bidwell
Fort Boise (fur trade post), 62/243,389, 394; 63/89; 67/297n,303,309,311n; 72/55; 77/319,327,334,339; 78/41-53*passim*,63,139; 79/78; 80/90,92,96; 81/20,29:

ferry, 67/313; history, 73/284; name, 63/192; sketch 1849, 81/19; suggested army post near, 67/312n
Fort Boise (military post), 65/55,69,81, 110; 68/36,242,243n,309,313; 72/73; 79/132:
established, 72/75; proposed by Harney, 79/31; road to Camp McDermitt, 68/ins.fr.cov. Sept.
Fort Bridger, 62/289,362n; 67/221, 225,227,246; 70/88; 72/69: photo, 67/226
Fort Canby, 64/70; 68/182; 69/309,322,331:
dedication ceremony, 65/352; photos, 65/338,340,342,346; see also Cape Disappointment
Fort Cape Disappointment, see Fort Canby
Fort Cascades, 70/254
Fort Chimo:
correspondence 1830-33, 65/309
Fort Chipewyan, 70/180
Fort Churchill, Nev., 72/15
Fort Clatsop, 62/314; 64/361; 66/349; 72/83:
replica, 79/100
Fort Clatsop National Monument (Memorial), 62/418; 65/219; 66/388; 69/175,345; 79/411: salt cairn, 80/412
Fort Columbia, 69/331:
Baldwin 0-4-2 engine photo, 65/358; history, 65/349n,358
Fort Columbia State Park, 69/175
Fort Colville (Colvile) (fur trade post), 63/203-204,217,219,233; 68/113, 115,123; 70/115,116; 72/286; 74/90: name, 63/233
Fort Colville (military post), 66/137, 155; 70/118; 79/175
Fort Constantine, 77/184
Fort Creek, 65/104n
Fort Crook, 67/80; 69/229,237n; 81/105
Fort Crook Historical Society, 67/80
Fort Dalles, 64/361; 65/19,49-50,57-116*passim*; 70/21n; 72/85; 79/32, 37,125,126:

abandoned, 68/36
buildings—
architectural plans, 67/331,334-37,338-42; architecture criticized, 68/6-7,9,10; burned, 68/37,38; commanding officer's quarters, 67/332, 340-42; costs, 68/40-41,46-52; described, 68/6-7,9,10-21,30,39-40; guardhouse, 68/18; hospital, 68/10-11,21N; officers' quarters, 67/299; 68/5-6,9,10; opinions on, 67/325, 333N; photos, 67/334,339,342,344; 68/19; stables photo, 68/4; surgeon's quarters, 67/332,343-44; 68/39,46; 69/175
civilian employees, 68/7,22,44; construction costs, 68/36; construction curtailed, 68/36; contracts for supplies, 68/23; expansion, 67/316FF; expenses, 68/7,25,36,40-41,44,46-52; First Ore. Cavalry at, 65/10-11,13,297; furniture, 68/5N,24; garrison 1856, 68/10; ground plan, 68/12-13; history, 67/295-333; 68/5-52; importance, 68/7-8,14,20,22,31,36; Indian scouts at, 79/137-38; inspections, 68/8,21-22N, 31,36,38; maps, 67/308,op. Dec. title pg.; 68/fr.cov. March; military reservation, 67/300-305; names, 67/298,304, 307N; Ninth Infantry at, 67/320,321; Ore. Mounted Volunteers at, 66/142; payroll, 68/7,25,44,47; plan, 67/328; 68/16,17,18,48,50; sawmill, 67/298, 320N; smallpox 1864, 65/26; supply depot, 68/7,8,11,14,20,22; water supply, 68/38; Watson burial orders, 66/61; Wool's conception, 68/8; SEE ALSO Prices
Fort Defiance, 68/103,106,346:
bricks, 68/103,105,108; historic site, 68/110; SEE ALSO Adventure Cove
Fort Deposit, 74/282
Fort Douglas, 70/179
Fort Dunvegan, 70/88
Fort Ellice, 70/179
Fort Garry, 67/368; 71/366:
telegraphic time check 1872, 66/71
Fort George, 63/103,114,252; 66/332,334; 69/269; 76/323,327,329,

330; 81/25N:
blacksmith, 69/183; buildings described, 64/222N-23N,228N; Lattie journal 1846, 64/210-45; named, 69/59; plan, 64/196; trade 1846, 64/210-45*passim*
Fort Gordon, 77/89
Fort Hall (fur trade post), 62/242,276, 361,371,374,375-76,377; 63/192,233; 66/156,198; 67/297N,300; 70/181; 72/55; 76/202; 77/318; 78/136; 79/80,122,383-84;80/85,87;81/18,27,29: abandoned, 62/394N; 79/37; site photo, 80/86
Fort Hall (military post):
ferry, 72/72,73; proposed by Harney, 79/31
Fort Hall Indian Reservation, 81/331
Fort Harney, 63/264; 65/56N,68N; 66/203,233:
bird studies, 66/233,235; established, 79/25
site, 79/272N—
photo, 78/220
SEE ALSO Camp Harney
Fort Henrietta, 66/133; 73/285:
abandoned, 66/154,156-57,159-60; built, 66/137; history, 66/135-60; Indian raids, 66/147,150-51,154; location, 66/135; name, 66/138-39
site—
maps, 66/132,insert 144-45; photos, 66/140; remains, 66/160
troops at, 66/149
Fort Hope, 63/220
Fort Hoskins, 65/105N,121; 66/77; 67/57,92,360; 70/233,234N,253,254; 77/91:
abandoned, 65/186; described, 65/180-83; established, 65/177-81; land leased, 65/180-81, 186N; letterbooks, 65/177N; Mansfield report, 65/189-96; name, 65/178; Ore. Volunteers trained at, 65/185-86; personnel, 65/192-93; plan, 65/175,189,189N; plat, 65/189N,194; removal protested, 65/185; secessionist plot against, 65/184; site dispute, 65/178; supplies, 65/193, 195; troops at, 65/183-84N,192-93

Fort Jones, 63/83; 66/220N
Fort Jones Museum, 69/175
Fort Kaskaskia, 66/331
Fort Kearney (Kearny), 62/241N,274; 63/74; 67/85; 71/182-83,187; 72/67; 78/132,149; 79/365; 80/68,69: forage cost 1850, 67/311N
Fort Klamath, 62/205; 64/356; 65/ 105N; 66/81; 67/374; 68/248N,252, 258,293,316; 72/36N; 79/47,127, 129,132: Bendire bird studies, 66/233,235; cemetery, 69/328; effort to establish, 69/ 224-31*passim*; First Ore. Cavalry at, 65/ 399; history, 65/218; 66/76-77; jail, 69/329; location, 69/231N; photo, 68/317; road to Camp Bidwell, 68/ ins.fr.cov. Sept.; telegraph lines, 68/223
Fort Klamath, Ore.: history, 69/328-29
Fort Klamath, Frontier Post in Oregon, 1863-1890, by Stone, review, 66/76-77
Fort Langley, 62/81; 63/359
Fort Lapwai, 65/398; 68/76; 70/127: Bendire bird studies, 66/233,236
Fort Laramie (fur trade post), 65/151; 70/88; 71/182-83
Fort Laramie (military post), 62/340; 64/86; 67/298,370; 70/178; 71/ 182-83; 72/67; 78/131-32; 79/67, 67N,71,72,365; 80/73: commanders, 67/368; ferry, 62/341- 42; 79/77N; forage costs 1850, 67/ 311N; sketch, 79/72
Fort Leavenworth, 66/82; 67/219,227; 69/276: Ft. Dalles compared to, 67/315; Point sketch, 69/65
Fort Lee, 67/296N
Fort Leland, 81/105
Fort Lemhi, 68/345,346
Fort McDermitt, 76/157
Fort McKinney, 71/187-88
Fort McLeod, 72/355
Fort McLoughlin, 63/181,234
Fort Manuel, 62/289
Fort Miller, 67/324,329N
Fort Naches, 67/322-23
Fort Nez Perce, SEE Fort Walla Walla

Fort Nicholas, 77/184
Fort Nisqually, 62/105; 63/124,193-95, 201,218-19,228,230,234,236; 70/300
Fort Okanogan, 62/202; 63/358; 72/249
"The Fort on the Luckiamute: A Resurvey of Fort Hoskins," by Preston E. Onstad, 65/173-96
Fort Orford, 70/234: buildings, moved, 70/235,236-37, 247,257
Fort Owen, 72/252
Fort Peck, 65/366
Fort Pelly: history, 63/89
Fort Pitt, Nootka Sound, 63/219
Fort Rains, 74/93
Fort Reno, 71/187-88
Fort Rock, Lake Co. landmark, 62/198, 299; 63/365; 66/273,384; 67/374; 70/183,352; 72/90: geology, 63/254; prehistoric site, 64/72
Fort Rock Basin: Prehistory and Environment, by Bedwell, review, 76/89
Fort Rock Cave, 64/72,357; 67/36-37: National Historic Landmark, 64/356; 65/219; photo, 67/36; prehistoric inhabitants, 67/374
Fort Rock Valley, 79/337
Fort Ross, 62/105; 71/365; 72/182; 74/286,352; 76/126,130; 77/186-87: agriculture, 68/186; 70/178; 73/162, 163; description, 73/105-108,162; drawings, 73/104,106,107; established, 73/161; historic marker, 73/108; location, 73/161; map, 73/104; sale, 73/ 107,111,115,164; settlement, 73/105- 107,161,162,163,164; Simpson visit, 73/164
Fort St. James, 76/324
Fort St. John, 63/92
Fort Scott, 66/317
Fort Simcoe (Indian agency), 70/127, 128,131,133,140N,148,280: map, 70/126; photos, 70/152
Fort Simcoe (military post), 63/91; 65/364: commanding officer's quarters, 68/5— color, 67/331; Downing model, 67/

345; photo, 67/346; Scholl plan, 67/ 332N-33N,346; Sword's opinion, 67/333N

construction cost 1856-58, 68/41,52; furniture, 68/5N; officers' quarters plan, 68/50; post site recommended, 67/317N; restoration, 67/326N,332N; road from Ft. Dalles, 67/322N; supplied via Ft. Dalles, 68/7,9,22,31

Fort Simpson, 63/189,204

Fort Spokane (fur trade post), 64/357

Fort Stanwix: History, Historic Furnishings, Historic Structure Report, by Luzader *et al*, noted, 79/107

Fort Steilacoom, 63/106N,169,172-73, 194

Fort Stevens, 64/71; 67/360; 69/331; 72/286; 77/195; 81/423: abandoned, 65/359,361; barracks photo, 65/348; batteries, 65/339-40, 347,349,351-52,357,359; Calif. Volunteers at, 65/350-51; coast survey chart, 65/insert Dec.; firepower map, 65/insert Dec.; history, 65/325-61; 81/423; influenza deaths 1918, 64/248; photos, 65/324,330,332,334,348,360; shelled by Japanese, 68/80

Fort Stevens Military Reservation, 65/359,361

Fort Stevens: Oregon's Defender at the River of the West, by Hanft, review, 81/423

Fort Stevens State Park, 65/359

Fort Stikine, 63/103: Douglas exped., 63/204; McLoughlin murder, 63/183,185; Rae at, 63/184,208-209,212,232,234

Fort Taku, 63/189

Fort Taylor: map, 66/144-45

Fort Thompson, 76/324

Fort Umpqua (fur trade post), 67/279; 81/106: employee lists, 74/282; history, 74/282; marker dedication, 68/342; plan, 67/281

Fort Umpqua (military post), 65/195; 69/223,230,240-41N: history, 70/233-57; inspection report, 70/241; maps, 69/257; 70/248,256;

name, 65/175; photos, 70/240,242, 246,252; post returns, 69/223N,235N; rent claim, 70/253-54; wettest U.S. post 1858, 70/245

Fort Vancouver (fur trade post), 62/ 118,122N,314,406,418; 63/103,119, 123-38*passim*,180-236*passim*; 66/343; 68/341; 69/345; 70/181,297,299, 302; 74/89-90; 75/113,115,319; 76/227; 77/45,194: 1846, 64/197-245*passim*; Agate sketch, 65/137; Blanchet and Demers arrival, 66/347; church records, 77/291; claim jumpers, 63/236; dairy, 63/225; early fort site discovery, 77/292,298-99; first white woman, 63/225N; forge, 69/ 183; Hawaiian laborers, 66/280; 74/ 93; HBCO. letterbooks, 63/184-85; Indian laborers, 63/183; iron works, 69/183; personnel classified, 63/197 relations with French Prairie settlers, 66/333,353— fur trade, 66/333; supply depot for, 66/338,339,353

replica chief factor's house, 80/101; restoration, 68/341; Roberts at, 63/ 228; sawmill, 63/206; school, 63/198, 227; 71/344; Skirving panorama, 65/ 159; trade goods prices, 63/217; warehouse, 63/231

Fort Vancouver (military post), 62/78; 65/109,113,116,118,343; 66/61; 67/54,57,60,294N; 68/35,223,293; 69/66; 71/219; 72/353; 74/281; 79/31,126,175,405; 80/171,334: bids for oats 1857, 68/23; boundaries, 76/382; Columbia Barracks, 69/66; construction costs, 1849-58, 68/41,52; Dept. of Oregon headquarters, 68/33 description—

1856, 81/200; 1870, 65/308 enlisted men 1850s, 74/90; first post commander, 74/93; Fourteenth Infantry, 74/93; Fourth Infantry, 67/300; history, 72/353; military district headquarters, 67/295; Ninth Infantry, 67/ 320; order book 1850-58 to OHS, 66/ 386; restoration, 66/382; Sully visit, 66/87; SEE ALSO Vancouver Barracks

Fort Vancouver Historical Society: officers and directors, 71/193; 72/175; 73/77; 74/180; 75/90; 76/94; 77/93; 78/93; 79/109-10; officers and trustees, 62/103,414; 63/85,249; 64/83,279; 65/123,311; 66/84,278; 67/82,283; 68/84,282; 69/81,278; 70/81,275; publications, 66/382; 67/366; 68/ 341; 69/330-31; 70/358; 72/89,353; 74/93,281; 75/363; 76/382; 77/292, 298; 78/364; 80/334; 81/328

Fort Vancouver National Cemetery, 66/60

Fort Vancouver National Historic Site, 69/175,275; 76/92

Fort Vancouver National Historic Site, Vancouver, Vol. 1, by Hussey, noted, 76/91-92

Fort Vancouver National Monument, 64/276,359; 66/388

Fort Victoria, 63/119,124,151,173,191, 204,220,228; 64/225; 66/219N; 68/ 113,114,115,341; 70/295,297,297N, 303; 71/281-82; 72/87-88; 74/352: Astoria relic, 63/224; described, 73/ 155; HBCO. correspondence, 63/184- 85; 81/208; history, 73/155-56; sketch 1848, 73/155; Voltigeur regiment, 63/90,232

Fort Walla Walla (fur trade post), 65/ 156; 66/132,133-34,227N; 67/321; 77/315; 78/217; 79/134; 80/405; 81/21: army post proposed near, 67/321; buildings described, 66/142; Drayton sketch, 65/137; Indian occupation, 66/143-49*passim;* Jeffries scout to, 66/144-45; Kelly surprise attack, 66/ 147; OMV march 1855, 66/134-35, 137-38; Sinclair in charge, 66/144; vacated, 67/303N

Fort Walla Walla (military post), 68/ 27,30N,33,36,223,226,232,293,294, 297; 69/79; 72/55-56; 79/130, 175,199: Bendire at, 66/233; First Ore. Cavalry, 65/297,397-99; furniture, 68/5N; hospital, 68/22N; importance 1858, 68/ 31,33N; inspections, 68/22N,31,33N;

muster rolls 1856-57, 69/223N,235N; photo, 68/227; post returns 1856-57, 69/223N,235N; Scholl building drawings, 67/331N,333; site suggestions, 67/317N,321,323N,324; sketch 1862, 79/200; smallpox epidemic, 65/44; supplied from Ft. Dalles, 68/7,9,22,31

Fort Wallula, SEE Fort Walla Walla

Fort Walsh, 72/355

Fort Wascopam, 67/296

Fort Washakie, 62/289-90; 70/88

Fort Willapa: 1870 census, 73/283

Fort William, Lake Superior, 66/333; 76/326

Fort William, Ottawa River, 67/368; 70/179

Fort William, Quebec, 81/387

Fort William, Sauvie Island, 63/192, 216,234; 69/276

Fort Yamhill, 62/300; 65/175,178, 185,195; 70/233,253: garrisoned, 65/175N; secessionist plot to seize, 65/184N

Fort Yukon, 76/116

Fort Yuma, 68/114

Fortney, Newton, 65/82

Forts: architecture, 79/214; bibliography, 79/214; Carroll Ranch, 73/260; coastal, 71/279-81; function, 79/214; Hudson's Bay Co., 77/84; Kodiak Island, 73/165; Montana, 65/365; New Archangel, 77/177,179,181; Trans-Mississippi West, 73/284; Wyoming, 71/187-88

Forts of the West, by Frazer, review, 67/359-60

Fortt, Inez Long: *Early Days at the University of Oregon,* noted, 77/299

Fortviot (ship), 66/125

Forty Nine Canyon, 68/256,315

Fortynine Gulch, 62/228

Fossil Flora of the John Day Basin, by Knowleton, cited, 66/237

Fossil Lake: geology and fossil fauna, 67/366

Fossils, 70/90,288:

Astoria search, 65/219; Bendire collection, 66/237; Clarno beds, 63/364; 66/284; Condon discoveries, 70/217; crocodile, 63/364; dinosaur, 64/364; Drake collection sent to Condon, 65/ 74-75; fish, 66/284; Fossil Lake, 67/ 366; gingko, 69/87; Great Plains, 75/ 78; John Day Basin, 66/237; 70/184; 78/87; LaGrande, 66/91; Lewis collects, 69/16-17; mastodons, 63/364; 66/91; "merceri" named, 66/91; Montana, 64/85; new techniques in hunting, 65/220; Ochocos, 70/183; Oregon geology, 67/5,14-18,25-26,29,34,90,92,366,374; Painted Hills, 73/250,264,267; pioneer Pacific Coast studies, 66/92; Rocky Mountains, 75/78; rodents, 69/87; vertebrate, 63/364; Wheeler Co., 69/338; Young farm, 66/92; SEE ALSO Paleobotany; Paleontology

Foster, Chapin D., 68/338

Foster, Henry: family, 80/348N

Foster, Irene, 66/81

Foster, John R., 80/320: biography, 80/320N-21N

Foster, Lloyd, 77/108

Foster, Philip, 62/217,218; 74/282: Eagle Creek farm sold, 68/353; papers given to OHS, 65/412

Foster, William J., 81/265N

Founders and Frontiersmen: Historic Places Commemorating Early Nationhood and the Westward Movement, 1783-1838, pub. by Nat'l Park Service, noted, 69/275-76

"The Founding of Mount Angel Abbey," by Gerard G. Steckler, 70/312-32

Fountains: Ashland, 64/323N Portland, 75/83— drinking fountains, 66/250; 72/348; SEE ALSO Skidmore Fountain

Four-County Corner, 75/87

Four-L, SEE Loyal Legion of Loggers and Lumbermen

The Fourth Corner: Highlights from the Early Northwest, by Edson, noted, 70/359

Fourth of July celebrations, 71/25; 77/196; 78/52: Ashland, 62/234; 76/354-55; Auburn 1860s, 62/234; Bend, 75/294; Canyon City 1867, 79/270; Claquato, Wash. 1862, 66/35; Dallas, Ore., 76/377-78; Douglas Co., 73/283; Ft. Canby 1865, 65/352; Independence Rock, 79/243; Klamath area, 66/81; Lane Co. 1864, 66/187; Linkville, 76/382; Nez Perce, 66/88; Oregon, 77/291; photos, 77/ 130-45*passim,*covs. June; Portland, 64/ 167; 74/346-47; 79/243; Rainier, 74/ 83-85; Roseburg, 74/92; Salem 1869, 64/178; Skagway 1898, 81/139; Washington first, 71/286; Yamhill Co., 76/24,26-27

Fowler, A.C.F., 72/199N

Fowler, Mrs. A.C.F., 72/199

Fowler, Del, family, 67/281

Fowler, Lydia Folger, 78/5,9

Fowler, William W., 66/220N

Fox, Ebenezer D., 71/278

Fox, George L., 70/280

Fox, J.C., 71/278

Fox, Laura, 80/384-85

Fox Creek, Columbia Co., 74/296

Fox Island, 73/122

Fox Rock, 80/256

Fox Valley, Grant Co., 68/303,305N; 70/23,36,57

Fox Valley, Linn Co., 64/354

Foxes, 77/182,183-88*passim*

Frain, Mart, 69/243N

Frain, Wren, 66/219

France: exploring expeds., 73/273-74; Hawaiian relations, 68/57-61,67,69-71; Pacific exploration, 70/77; possessions in America, 73/360

Frances of Assisium, Sister, 80/346

Franchere, Gabriel, 70/226: *Adventure at Astoria, 1810-1814,* cited, 71/277,318N *Journal of a Voyage on the North West Coast of America,* ed. by Lamb, review, 71/277-79 *Relation d'un Voyage a la Cote du Nord-Ouest de l'Amérique Septentrionale,*

cited, 71/318
Franchere, Hoyt C., ed.:
Adventure at Astoria, 1810-1814, by Gabriel Franchere, cited, 71/277,318N
Francis, —, Salem professor, 80/131
Francis, Simeon, 64/357; 72/329,331
Francis Drake, Privateer: Contemporary Narratives and Documents, by Hampden, noted, 74/95
Francis Lee Jaques, Artist of the Wilderness World, by Jaques, review, 74/357-58
Francois (Indian scout), 79/313,314, 315,320
Frank, Aaron M., photo, 74/214
Frank, Gerald W., 62/111,207,303,422; 63/93,255,373; 64/93,189,285,363; 65/125,221,317,414,417; 66/94,190, 287,395; 67/379; 68/360
Frankenstein, Alfred:
"The Royal Visitors," 64/5-32
Frankenstein, Godfrey N., 65/143,147,168
Frankenstein, Peter J., 65/141
Frankfort, Wash., 75/105
Frankfurter, Felix, 62/94-95
Frankiston (ship), 66/122
Franklin, Dorothy:
West Coast Disaster: Columbus Day 1962, noted, 65/309
Franklin, John, 64/284; 77/295
Franklin, William B.:
journal 1845, 81/333
Franklin, William E., 62/297; 64/282-83
Franklin (U.S. Navy frigate), photo, 62/12
Franklin County, Wash.:
post offices, 69/331
Fraser, Alexander, NWCo. clerk, 66/333
Fraser, Alexander, uncle of McLoughlin, 81/377,378,381:
comments on McLoughlin, 81/386
Fraser, George, 66/110-11N,114
Fraser, Joseph, 81/381,383
Fraser, Simon, 76/324; 81/379,380,383-84:
assists McLoughlin, 81/379,380,383-84; portrait, 81/381
Fraser River, 67/86; 72/345; 76/315:
discovery, 65/314; first farm, 63/359;

gold rush, 63/228; profile, 65/215; salmon run decline, 72/346; stone artifacts, 65/215
Frazar, Thomas, 64/160; 80/150
Frazer, Robert W.:
Forts of the West: Military Forts and Presidios and Posts Commonly Called Forts West of the Mississippi River to 1898, review, 67/359-60
Frazer, Robert W., ed.:
Mansfield on the Condition of the Western Forts, 1853-1854, review, 65/201-202
Frazier, Robert B.:
review of collected writings, 81/321
Frazier, Robert B.:
A Century of News and People, by Macnab, review, 77/192-93
Frazier, W. Ronald, 75/279
The Frazier Upland, 81/321
Frederic Remington, by Hassrick, noted, 74/285
Frederiksen, Frederik Ole:
family, 78/364
Free Emigrant Road:
advocates of new cutoff, 78/62,63, 70,143,144; commercial enterprise, 79/12; commissioners, 78/44-45,52,60,64,65,67,250,330; 79/6 construction, 78/60-62,294-309*passim*—bridging downed logs, 78/309,310 (photo); completion, 78/304; 79/7-8; condition in fall 1853, 78/306,307, 327; contractors, SEE Robert Alexander, A. McDowell, A.C. Spencer; costs, 78/61,63,66N,67,329,330N; 79/8,8N; delayed, 78/58,63,66,67, 69; 79/10; equipment, 78/61; road crews, 79/9,10; supplies, 78/62,64-65
litigation, 78/328,330-31; 79/5-12, 22,22N
Middle Fork Willamette crossings—described, 78/317-22; number, 78/313-14,319,322; photos, 78/316, 318
miles saved, 78/136,140; move to improve and extend, 78/328-31; public financing, 78/41-45,329,331
road viewers, 78/41; 79/6,10,22—

report, 78/41,42,232
route, 78/42,53-57,67,294-300,309; 79/6,18,43,48—
maps, 78/45,46,68,156,248-49,294, ins.fr.cov. Dec.; 79/33-34; marking out, 78/53,54,58-59,65,67,69,166, 299; 79/6,10,12,23; Walker route not used, 78/68,310,313-14
terminus, 78/231,293,299,303
traces, 78/295-97,299; 79/48—
photos, 78/298,301; 79/50
travelers, 79/16—
Macy, 79/14,44-45(map); prospectors, 79/25,27,40; railroad survey party, 79/29; SEE ALSO Elliott Cutoff; Immigration of 1853; Oregon Central Military Road
water, 79/19

Free Land For Free Men: A Story of Clackamas County, by Lynch, review, 74/357
Free silver, 63/359; 65/271,273; SEE ALSO Republican Party
The Free Soilers: Third Party Politics, 1848-54, by Blue, noted, 74/284
Free trappers, 63/350; 66/333,340
Freedom Center, 72/246
Freeland Colony, 77/295
Freeman, Constant, 65/357
Freeman, Edward A., 70/204
Freeman, John Finley, 62/297
Freeman, Leigh R., 73/286
Freeman, Olga Samuelson:
A Guide to Early Oregon Churches, noted, 77/300
Freeman's Landing, 65/308
Freemesser, Bernard, 66/40
Freezeout Creek, Baker Co., 62/225,227
Freezeout Gulch, Baker Co., 62/212,228
Frei, Nicholas:
Oregon visit, 70/315-18; photo, 70/315
Freidenberg, John ("Dutch"), 63/282-83
Freight rates, 67/132,148,367; 74/19, 22,24,79-82:
1873, 79/270N; cattle, 67/146,148-49; Coeur d'Alene district, 69/219, 222; dog team, 76/117; lumber, 67/ 161N,168-70; 70/86; 71/35-36,78-79N; Oregon 1860s, 66/227,232N;

Portland-The Dalles 1853-54, 67/299; ship charter, 67/166,175; wool, 67/132-33,134,138
Freight transportation, 63/67,84; 66/277; 67/219,227,230; 73/261; 75/43,86,314,315,363; 76/81:
British Columbia, 72/168; Central Ore., 73/261-62; dog team, 76/117; LaGrande-Ft. Harney 1867, 66/203-205; mule teams, 73/237; photo, 73/fr.cov. Sept.; teams, 72/89; wagon freighting, 68/181-82; Washington coast, 74/29-30,32; whiskey, 73/262; wool, 63/67,84; SEE ALSO Pack trains; Shipping; Trucking; Wagons
Frein, P.J., trans.:
"Address by the Canadian Settlers," cited, 66/355N
Frelinghuysen, Theodore, 68/55
Fremont, Jessie Benton (Mrs. John C.), 65/144,170
Fremont, John Charles, 62/106,201; 63/88,345; 64/281; 67/8,10; 70/33,73; 71/250; 74/86,355; 77/197,290:
accuracy of observations, 72/165; diorama misconceptions, 66/145; exped. accounts read by Ore. immigrants, 68/156; Ft. Vancouver visit, 63/202-203; Klamath battle account, 66/284; Klamath country 1843, 73/203; maps reprinted, 72/165; papers, 72/165; photo, 65/132; quoted, 62/9; second exped. howitzer, 68/345; served dismissal papers, 63/91
Skirving panorama views of expeds., 65/134,136-37,145-46,148-49— photos, 65/152,158,169
Fremont, John Charles:
The Expeditions of John Charles Fremont, ed. by Jackson and Spence, Vol. I review, 72/165-66; Vol. II noted, 77/197,290
Report, cited, 72/6N; indexed, 72/165
Fremont Bridge, Portland, 78/363
Fremont Peak, Wind River Range, 65/154; 79/379
French, Burt, 75/67
French, David, 63/347-49

French, Dillard, family, 69/125
French, Egbert, 70/145N,146
French, Giles, 62/110,206,302,423; 63/94,256,367,373; 64/93,189,285, 363; 65/125,216,221,317,416; 66/93,189,285,392,395; 67/380; 68/361; 69/342,347; 70/373,374; 71/371; 74/183,363,366: "Bubble Skinner," 69/293-305 *Cattle Country of Peter French*, review, 66/67-68 *East of the Cascades*, by Brogan, ed. by Phillips, review, 66/183 "Grass Valley, 1901," 75/43-48 *Newspapering in the Old West*..., by Karolevitz, review, 66/379-80 *The Pioneer Editor in Missouri, 1808-1860*, by Lyon, review, 67/278-79 *Rails to the Mid-Columbia Wheatland*, review, 81/101-102 *Steens Mountain in Oregon's High Desert Country*, by Jackman and Scharff, review, 69/62-63 *They Saddled the West*, by Vernam, review, 76/380-81 *This Was Wheat Farming*, by Brumfield, review, 70/72-73 *The War on Powder River*, by Smith, review, 67/359
French, John William, SEE French, Pete
French, Pete (John William), 64/349, 356; 67/144,152; 69/63,125; 70/21,22N: Bannock War, 68/322; barn, 63/366; biography, 66/67-68 death, 75/67-68— grave, 73/81; site map and photo, 75/66 French-Glenn holdings, 68/321; Great Westerners Hall of Fame, 67/370
French, Susan (Suzie) Doherty (Mrs. Dillard), 69/125
French Camp (Pashya), Umatilla Co., 66/151
French-Canadian people, 68/81; 69/32; 70/74; 74/90: French Prairie— address cited, 66/355N; children, 66/343; church records, 81/203

families listed— 1838-40, 66/344; 1841-42, 66/351 grain, 66/343; HBCO. aid, 66/336-37; Indian wives, 66/334,343; petition to Congress, 66/347; relationship with Methodists, 66/341; schools, 66/ 341,343; settlement, 66/337-39; temperance society, 66/346 Oregon, 62/120; Ore.Prov.Govt. role, 66/352,354-55; Willamette Valley, 66/334-35
French Glenn, Baker Co., 62/226N
French-Glenn Livestock Co., 66/67,68; 67/143,153
French Gulch, Baker Co., 62/227
French Indochina, 62/25,36,41
French Mapping of the Americas: The De l'Isle, Bauche, Dezauche Succession (1700-1832), by Tooley, noted, 69/79
French people: Oregon, 62/298; population 1860-1910 (tables), 80/266-67; relations with Indians, 66/86
French Pete, 81/275
French Prairie, 69/276; 71/349; 72/353: Americans, 66/343,344,347; church records, 81/203; early settlers, 70/74; French-Canadian settlers, 66/331-62; Indian village, 66/338; maps, 66/345; 70/258; Methodist mission, 66/341; Wyeth description, 66/339-40
French Prairie Historical Society: officers and directors, 74/180; 75/90; 76/94; 77/93
Frenchglen, Ore., 63/368; 68/354
Fretwell, Frank M., 74/209
Frey, M.J., 74/238
Fridley, Russell, 68/355,359
Friedheim, Robert L.: *The Seattle General Strike*, review, 66/73-74
Friedman, Ralph, 63/366: *Tracking Down Oregon*, noted, 80/336
Friend, T.E.D.: *Country Boys Make Good*, noted, 71/286-87
The Friend, Honolulu, 64/207N,208N, 209,211N
Friendly Cove:

painting, 74/363
Friends of the Bancroft Library:
GPH: An Informal Record of George P. Hammond and his Era at the Bancroft Library, review, 66/380-81
Friends of Tryon Creek State Park: publications, 79/104
Friendship (vessel), 76/119
Fries, Harvey, 73/175
Friis, Herman R., 63/247:
The Field Notes of Captain William Clark, 1803-1805, ed. by Osgood, review, 66/65-67
Friis, Herman R., ed.:
The Pacific Basin, A History of Its Geographical Exploration, contents listed, 70/76
Fritz, Jacob, 67/332N; 68/36
Frobisher, Martin, 66/88
Frog Pond district, Clackamas Co., 67/273-74:
church, 67/273,276
"From Denmark: R.P. Rasmussen," ed. by Lorraine Fletcher, 81/57-74
"From Ithaca to Clatsop Plains: Miss Ketcham's Journal of Travel," ed. by Leo M. Kaiser and Priscilla Knuth, 62/237-87,337-402
"From Latvia: Fred Bitte," ed. by Catherine M. Curtin, 81/31-42
From Sea to Shining Sea, A Report on the American Environment, noted, 70/360-61
From Shamrocks to Sagebrush, by Barry, review, 70/355-56
From Where the Sun Now Stands, by Henry, review, 62/295-96
From Wilderness to Enabling Act: The Evolution of a State of Washington, by Beckett, noted, 70/77
Fromberg, Mont., 65/380
Frontier:
American frontier fiction, 73/286;
American frontier literature, 70/263;
and teaching of American history, 67/280; army role on, 73/286; Australian frontier fiction, 73/286; capitalism, 72/227; challenge of, 73/274-75; characters in Siskiyou area, 76/70-88; com-

munity development, 73/286,360; family and fertility, 73/85; in American history, 70/86; land speculation, Texas, 72/179; law, 68/344; legal process, 73/245-57; photographers, 81/324; Presbyterianism, 68/344; publicized, 74/90; readings on, 65/307-308; 68/82; 73/360; role of men and women, 81/100-101; Scotch-Irish influence, 74/285; urban planning, 81/201; use of wood, 72/179; women in Dakota, 74/284
The Frontier, Montana, 73/319,321: policy, 73/310-11
Frontier: American Literature and the American West, by Fussell, cited, 70/263
The Frontier Challenge: Responses to the Trans-Mississippi West, ed. by Clark, review, 73/274-75
The Frontier Experience: Readings in the Trans-Mississippi West, ed. by Hine and Bingham, review, 65/307-308
Frontier Index, Nebraska, 73/286
Frontier life, SEE Pioneer life
Frontier theory, 63/358; 65/213:
British forerunners of Turner, 68/344;
comments on Turner thesis, 68/82,86, 345-46
The Frontier Thesis: Valid Interpretation of American History?, ed. by Billington, noted, 68/82
Frontier Woman on the Dakota Frontier: The Life of a Woman Homesteader, by Fairchild, noted, 74/284
Frost, John H., 78/336
Frost, Lawrence A.:
The Court-Martial of General George Armstrong Custer, review, 70/66-67
Fruit:
Boise orchard, Salem, 66/16; Bridge Creek first orchard, 73/262; California, 69/332; depression effects 1893, 68/204,205N; French Prairie, 66/339;
Hood River Valley, 63/365; 70/50FF;
Luelling trees to Ore., 66/87; marketing, 71/85,87; nursery catalogs, 73/bk.cov. Dec.
Oregon, 71/88; 76/180; 81/245,

253—
1870-1900, 71/96; 1880s, 71/31,33-34,35,37,57,62,63-64; pioneer varieties, 66/87

Oregon Trail, 79/376,379,383; packing 1909, 70/279; Pacific Coast industry history, 68/153-74; photos, 68/167-74; pioneer Oregon varieties, 63/53; prices, 68/163; sale of to sailors, 79/361-62; SEE ALSO Berries; names of fruits

Fruit Valley, 72/353
Fruitvale, Calif., 68/164,172
Frum, Sarah Parrish, 68/187
Frush, William H., 64/144
Fry, George, 79/239
Frye, Lewis C., 65/271
Fuel:

cordwood, 75/56-57; sagebrush, 73/234,238-39; wood cutting, 80/274,275; SEE ALSO Firewood

Fukuda, Mrs. —, Portland Assembly Center, 81/160
Fukuda, Roy, 76/234,240
Fulkerson, Ellen Hiatt, 76/382
Fuller, Charles E., 74/61
Fuller, Dennis L., 63/263N
Fuller, Edmund, 66/246
Fuller, Ethel Romig, 74/65:

biography, 74/61; Oregon poet laureate, 74/61; photo, 73/296; poem cited, 73/298

Fuller, Ethel Romig:

White Peaks and Green, cited, 74/66

Fuller, Frank, 70/178
Fuller, Josephine, photo, 80/363
Fuller, R.E., 67/30
Fulton, Arabella:

Tales of the Trail, noted, 66/188

Fulton, Charles W., 62/94:

photo, 81/44

Fulton, James, Wasco Co. pioneer:

army beef contract, 68/23N

Fulton, John M., 68/187:

borax works, 73/231,233,237,239,240

Fun Along the Way, by Leonard, noted, 73/74

Funatake, Mrs. —, Portland Assembly Center, 81/156

Fundy and Wasson sawmill, 68/265
Funerals, 77/269-76:

Chinese, photo, 80/fr.cov. Summer; customs, 80/257; hearse, 77/269, 273(photo); Oregon folklore, 66/281

Funnemark, name origin, 66/103N
Funnemark, Albert Abelseth:

biography, 66/102-105; death, 66/127; memorial to, 66/106

Funnemark, Benjamin, 66/102:

photo, 66/104

Funnemark, Birgitte (Mrs. Albert A.), 64/72:

biography, 66/102-103; characterized, 66/122,130-31; photo, 66/104; Seamen's Rest, Tacoma, 66/101-31*passim*

Funnemark, Christine, SEE Mitchell, Christine F.
Funnemark, Elise, 66/103,106
Funnemark, Jacob, 66/103
Funnemark, Julia, 66/103
Funnemark, William, 66/103
Fur seal industry:

Canada-U.S. dispute, 63/360; Pribilof Islands, 69/79

Fur Seal Industry of the Pribilof Islands, 1786-1956, by Riley, noted, 69/79

Fur trade, 62/90,91,93,99-100,105; 63/358,463; 65/213,214; 68/82,185,274; 69/61,79,83,84; 70/77,88,364; 73/67,70; 75/320,331;79/98-100:

Alaska, 70/180,366; 71/181; American, 62/403-405; 66/63-65,273; 76/314,320,323,325; Ashley influence, 66/64; beaver skin values 1838, 74/78; bibliography, 65/79,284; 66/79; 79/99,338; 80/336

Canada, 63/357; 64/272; 66/281; 67/86; 70/272; 76/309-31—

fur seal dispute with U.S., 63/360; routes before 1825, 64/284; waterway routes, 62/297

China trade, 72/182; 74/77-78—

pelts, 76/315,330; trade products, 72/355

Colorado, 78/365; Columbia Dist. trade items, 65/215; competition, 76/199,200,310,313-14; 77/194; deerskins, 72/179; dialect, 70/367; Douglas Co., 74/282; Floyd reports, 70/ 340,343,344; food, 69/336; fort site photos, 74/282; fur presses, 68/345; fur seal rustlers, 65/215; ginseng, 72/ 179; government relations, 70/86; government trading posts, 73/284; historians, 67/367,370; 68/185; historiography, 70/180; history, 64/348; 67/367,370; 74/355; 80/336; Illinois River, 76/82; Indian religion and, 71/ 326-48*passim*; Jesuits and, 67/84; 68/ 348; Kutenai Indians, 71/343; licenses, 68/345; liquor, 78/364; maps of routes and sites, 66/63; 74/278; 76/308 maritime, 69/67-68; 71/365—

Cape Colony, S. Africa records, 78/355-56; Cape of Good Hope records, 79/99,339-40

Minnesota, 79/339

Missouri country, 67/370-71— upper Missouri, 62/202; 72/179

museum, 67/85; Northwest Coast, 67/200-201; 72/115,116,124; 74/ 285; Ogden expedition, 63/350; Oregon, 77/80-81; Pacific, 74/286; Pacific Coast, 79/99,107; Pacific Northwest, 71/191,277,281-82,291; 72/170, 286,345

posts, 66/384; 76/202,226,324; 77/80; 79/79,89,92-97— Bear River, 68/88; 79/80; Houtama, McKay Creek, 79/135; Thompson River 1812, 68/87; SEE ALSO names of posts

prices 1820, 77/180N; relics, 63/359; 70/180; Rocky Mountains, 74/355 routes, 70/180,366; 76/308— Canada before 1825, 64/284; Hudson's Bay Co., 77/194

Russell journal, 66/384

Russian, 68/276; 71/181; 76/312-13,314-15; 79/107— posts, 62/202; relations with Bostonians, 74/286

Russian-American trade, 73/122,128-29,147; saddles, 69/84; St. Joseph operations, 63/358; seals, 69/79; Siberia, 73/157-59; sites, 68/185; 69/335; Snake River, 77/80-81; social stratification, 70/180; Southwest, 67/280; Spanish to 1822, 66/63; tokens, 70/ 88,179

trade items— beads, 71/362,369; Columbia Dist., 65/215

traders, 81/322— biographical sketches, 66/185; 80/ 206; views of Indians, 68/178-79

trappers, 77/194; 79/105,336— early, 67/367; equipment, 69/182-83,274-75; Illinois River, 76/82; Indian trappers, 71/345; recreation, 65/219; SEE ALSO Free trappers; Mountain men

trapping 1900s, 74/293,311; Umpqua area, 66/187,383; 67/80,279,281; 68/81

voyageurs, 68/346— songs, 70/79

waterway routes, 62/297; 63/90

West, 73/360; 74/86— 1807-1840, 81/322-23

Willamette Valley, 66/332; SEE ALSO names of fur trade companies

The Fur Trade, by Phillips, review, 62/403-405

Fur Trade and Empire: George Simpson's Journal, 1824-25, ed. by Merk, noted, 69/274

The Fur Trade in Canada: An Introduction to Canadian Economic History, by Innis, noted, 63/357

The Fur Trade in Minnesota: An Introductory Guide to Manuscript Sources, by White, noted, 79/339

The Fur Trade of the American West, 1807-1840: A Geographical Synthesis, by Wishart, review, 81/322-23

The Fur Trade on the Upper Missouri, 1840-1865, by Sunder, review, 66/273-74

The Fur Trader and the Indian, by Saum, review, 68/178-79

Furgeson, Franz, 66/54

Furgeson, Harold, 66/54

Furgeson, Oscar, 66/54

Furlong, Henry Patrick, 69/130

Furniss, Norman F.: *The Mormon Conflict, 1850-1859*, review,

62/185-86
Furniture, 62/67; 77/292:
manufacture, 62/200; SEE ALSO Prices
Furnoy, —, Douglas Co. settler, 63/24
Fusonie, Alan, and Leila Moran, eds.:
Agricultural Literature: Proud Heritage—Future Promise, noted, 79/106
Fussell, Edwin:
Frontier: American Literature and the American West, cited, 70/263
Fussner, F. Smith, ed.:
Glimpses of Wheeler County's Past: An Early History of North Central Oregon, noted, 77/195,292

GI Ranch, 65/50N,51N,80N; 68/80; 78/240:
photo, 78/241
GPH: An Informal Record of George P. Hammond and His Era in the Bancroft Library, review, 66/380-81
G.W. Watson (ship), 66/122
Gabelasch, Anton, 77/77
Gadwa, Abraham, family, 80/269, 282,285
Gadwa, Bertha Van Allen, 80/285,285N
Gadwa, Lucy Amelia Swan, 80/269-79
Gadwa, Manch E., 80/269N,285
Gadwa, William Isaac, 80/272,284 (photo):
"Autobiography, 1874-1945," 80/269-85
Gaffney, Joseph W., and Celia Jans:
A History of Sprague, noted, 63/357
Gaf(f)ney, Mary, SEE Brosnan, Mary Gaf(f)ney
Gagnier, Jean Baptiste, 68/81; 70/239
Gaines, Albert P., 65/26N,105N
Gaines, Amanda S., SEE Rinehart, Amanda S. Gaines
Gaines, Anna, 81/81N
Gaines, Jennie Clarissa, SEE Currey, Jennie C. Gaines
Gaines, John Pollard, 62/66; 63/186; 64/145,277; 70/259; 75/120-21, 351,356:
arrival in Oregon, 64/295; pardons Smith, 75/357-58; photo, 75/356

Gaines, Sarah Barlow, 65/26N
Gairdner, Meredith, 63/191,232; 71/333
Gaither, J.K., 71/13,14N
Galbraith, J.G., 68/237,297N
Galbraith, James P., 67/65,66
Galbraith, James W., 65/181N
Galbraith, John S., 65/306
Gale, Charles, 71/355
Gale, J. Marion:
recollections, 78/247
Gale, John:
journal, 71/287
Gale, Joseph, 69/86,337; 78/125,148
Gale, Rebecca Jones, photo, 78/148
Gale, Thomas, 80/296N
Gale, William, immigrant of 1853, 78/125,143:
photo, 78/148
Galena, Ore., 69/107
Gales Creek, 72/309
Gales Creek, Ore., 63/32
Gallagher, Charles, 69/130
Gallagher, J.L.G., 62/219N
Gallagher, Joseph, 69/130
Gallagher, Michael, 66/118
Gallagher, William H.:
journal, 64/282
Gallatin, Albert, 80/206
Gallon House Bridge, 64/356
"Galloping Goose," SEE City of Prineville Railroad
Galloway, James, 63/220
Galpin, Charles, 69/336
Gamage Hotel, Hoquiam, 74/15
Gambling, 70/131N; 80/321; 81/38:
Dawson, Yukon, 76/115; prohibited in Portland 1851, 80/12; slot machines 1905, 80/58; Waldo, Ore., 76/81-82
Game, 80/233,235,237,243,244:
near Alvord Ranch, 63/326-27; protection, 76/80; Queets River Valley, 74/23; Yukon, 76/113
Game birds:
Oregon, 65/235-62; Yamhill Co., 76/22
Gamecock (steamship), 65/211
Games, children's, 75/48
Gammel, W.F., 62/218N
Gammon, Margaret E.:

"Coast Experiences," 77/277-84
Gammon, William, 77/277-79
Ganbani, Batiste, SEE Gobin, Batiste
Ganey, Albert, 66/203
Gannett, Henry, 76/31
Gant, John, 81/20N
Gantenbein, C.U., photo, 71/149
Ganymede (HBCO. bark), 63/102-103, 181,191,232; 64/197,199N; 65/ 207-208: description, 63/227
Garachana, Angel, photo, 76/166
Garber, Hezekiah H., 64/356; 65/184N,187-88,193; 66/77
Garden, James, 65/182N
Gardening: introduced in Aleutians, 73/160; victory gardens, 71/218
Gardening societies, SEE Azalea Garden Club; Italian Gardeners Assn.; Portland Garden Club
Gardiner, Howard C.: *In Pursuit of the Golden Dream: Reminiscences of San Francisco and the Northern and Southern Mines, 1849-1857*, review, 71/359-60
Gardiner, Sarah Louise Crosby, 71/360
Gardiner, Ore., 74/271: "company" town, 68/269; map, 69/ 257; photo, 68/271; SEE ALSO Gardiner City, Ore.
Gardiner City, Ore., 70/255,261; SEE ALSO Gardiner, Ore.
Gardner, Abner Davis, Jr., 65/218
Gardner, Charles, Hoquiam hotel proprietor, 74/15
Gardner, Daniel White, 63/85
Gardner, F.H., 74/17
Gardner, John L., 77/89
Gardner, Mary C. Cornell, 79/363: photo, 79/362
Gardner, Roy, 63/245
Gardner, Thelma Lund, 71/271
Gardner, William, 79/363
Gardner, Wilmer: *Over 100 Years of Old Oregon City*, noted, 77/298
Gardner Cave, 81/329
Gardner family, Cowlitz Co., 65/120

Garfield, Joseph, 67/354,355
Garfielde, Selucius, 63/185,187,230; 66/35
Garibaldi, Ore., 66/181; 71/120,125, 129; 72/296,299,310,312; 73/10,173, 179,221; 77/216-37,341-68: churches, 71/129-30; 77/355,358; economic conditions, 77/365,367-68; high school, 77/358 hotels, 77/213,219,358— photos, 77/218,356 housing, 77/355-57,365— photo, 77/356 library, 77/358; location, 77/220; logging, 71/133; lumber mill, 71/125; museum, 77/367; photos, 71/125; 77/212,348,366; stores, 77/357; theater, 77/357; tourists, 77/367
Garibaldi Beach Hotel, 77/358
Garibaldi Grocery, Portland, 77/248-49
Garibaldi News, 77/357
Garland, Hamlin: *Boy Life on the Prairie*, reprint noted, 63/247
Garnett, Robert S., 67/322N,326; 68/6,30,42
Garnett, Mrs. Robert S.: Ft. Simcoe description, 68/5
Garnier, Lucien, 62/229-30
Garratt and Young, Portland, 62/165
Garretson's Medical Springs, 69/88
Garrett, Christopher, 65/82
Garrett, Melissa Gray, 78/131,148
Garrett, Robert, 78/131,148: Bannock War, 68/323-24,325,326-27
Garrett, Warren, 78/131,148
Garrison, Joseph M., 78/48N: Cascades expedition, 78/48-60,69, 185,313,317
Garrison, Pliny C., 69/77
Garrison, Thomas, 78/323N
Garrison Lake, 68/265
Garry (Indian), SEE Spokane Garry
Garsdale (ship), 66/129
Garvey, Thomas, 68/257
Gary, George, 63/186,200,217,228; 66/341; 73/247: diary, 73/245,250; Methodist-McLoughlin controversy, 63/177;

quoted, 62/151,160
Gary, Mrs. George, 63/186,217
Gary, T.J., 74/208
Gasquet, Calif., 76/53,57,85
Gasquet Mountains, 76/53
Gass, Patrick, 64/183; 81/329
Gaston, Joseph, 64/167; 78/90: Portland history, 70/229; west side railroad promotion, 71/43
Gaston, Mary, 62/204
Gaston, Ore.: church, 76/381
Gaston Valley, 79/336
Gatch, Thomas Milton, 73/346; 80/118
Gatch Falls, 72/91
Gates, Bill ("Swiftwater Bill"), 62/96
Gates, Charles E., 75/164-65,168,169
Gates, Charles Marvin, 62/298; 63/90; 66/350N; 69/60; 70/271; 76/361: *The First Century at the University of Washington, 1861-1961*, review, 64/76-77
Gates, Charles Marvin, and Dorothy Johansen: *Empire of the Columbia, A History of the Pacific Northwest*, cited, 67/106,160, 177-78; review, 69/60-61
Gates, Isabel, 81/151,154,162,165
Gates, John, Portland mayor, 75/128,130
Gates, Paul W., 62/297; 63/358; 64/85, 281,283
Gates, Paul W., ed.: *California Ranchos and Farms, 1846-1862*, noted, 69/332
Gatke, Robert Moulton, 62/107; 72/349; 79/243
Gato, Toyo, 81/157
Gatschet, Albert S.: "Molale tribe raided by the Cayuse," cited, 73/63-65
Gatzert, Bailey: biography, 63/61
Gaunt (Gant), D.B., 70/146
Gavin, John, 81/309-10
Gavin, Matt, 72/311,314; 73/7
Gay, F.N., 79/10
Gay, George, 66/353; 75/363: house dedicated, 64/88
Gay, James Woods:

diary 1850s, 80/104,335
Gay, Martin Baker, family, 80/335
Gaylord, Orange, 78/140
Gaynor, Harry, 76/375
Gazelle (steamer), 62/200; 64/352
Gearhard, William H., 68/258,316
Gearhart, Ore., 74/164
Gearin Hotel, Myrtle Point, 63/363
Geary, Edward Ratchford, 69/225N, 253N-54N; 70/249; 79/39,41: "History of the Presbytery of Oregon," reprinted noted, 62/197
Geddes & Pollman Co., Baker, 67/248
Gee, Samuel, 72/67
Geer, Archie A., 64/353
Geer, George W., 78/58
Geer, Isabelle T. (Mrs. T.T.), photo, 81/254
Geer, L.B., 63/364
Geer, Musa, 63/364
Geer, Ralph C., 64/353; 68/174
Geer, Theodore T., 64/353; 65/254: photo, 81/254
Geese, domestic, 72/201
Geese, wild, 68/240,257,258; 76/339: Pacific NW nesting areas, 65/214; SEE ALSO Canada geese
Geese Creek, 66/205
Geiger, Vincent: overland journey reprint noted, 63/356
Geisendorfer Hotel, Albany, 69/339
Gelb, Barbara S.: *So Short a Time: A Biography of John Reed and Louise Bryant*, review, 75/84-85
Geldemeister, Jerry, 79/340
Genealogical Forum of Portland, 62/301; 64/79; 66/80; 67/88; 68/359; 70/111N,372: bulletin, 68/350; publications, 68/340; 69/76-77; 72/85-86; 74/286; 75/87,363; 77/291
Genealogical Forum of Portland, Oregon, Inc., comp.: *Genealogical Material in Oregon Donation Land Claims*, Vol. III review, 64/79; Vol. IV review, 69/76-77
Yesterday's Roll Call, Statistical Data and Genealogical Facts from Cemeteries in

Baker, Sherman and Umatilla Counties, Oregon, Vol. I, review, 72/85-86

Genealogical Forum of Portland, and Multnomah County Library Staff: *Guide to Genealogical Material in Multnomah County Library*, noted, 68/340

Genealogy, 74/90,93: American guide, 74/283; Clackamas Co. marriage records, 69/273; Coos Co. marriages 1854-65, 68/81; donation land claims, 64/79; 69/76-77 families—

Archibald, 74/358; Barklow, 63/365; 74/92; Beeman, 72/355; Bergerson, 65/308; Boisvert, 74/358; Bryant, 66/382; Burns, 74/358; Caples, 63/82; Carnine, 74/93; Church, 71/361; Colvin, 66/382; Cox, 68/354; Debast, 65/308; Deckard, 73/73; Delore-Delard, 68/350; Dement, 74/94; Derock, 65/308; Dibblee, 68/342; Espy, 71/189; Fluher, 68/342; Gardiner, 71/359-60; Gardner, 65/120; Geisy, 68/342; Gilbreath, 68/342; Gilson, 65/120; Goodell, 74/93; Guild, 64/276; Hamilton, 71/361; Jeaudoin, 66/382; Jones, 68/342; Jordan, 75/363; Kelly, 74/283; Kindred, 71/189; Knight, 64/276; Koch, 64/276; Kulper, 64/276; Lewelling-Luelling, 68/156N; Libel, 68/342; Lieser, 65/308; Linn, 68/82; Love, 73/83; Luhr, 64/276; McFadden, 64/276; MaCoon, 66/382; Malmsten, 71/361; Moore, 73/73; Ostrander, 66/382; Parcher, 65/308; Payne, 65/308; Pearl, 74/358; Peterson, 66/382; Plowman, 71/361; Powell, 66/382; Pringle, 65/308; Pryor, 72/179; Rackleff, 74/92; Reed, 71/360; Rice, 66/382; Robnett, 73/73; Rohrbach, 72/172; Shaver, 65/309; Simmons, 68/343; 74/283; Skinner, 71/252,255; Small, 73/83; Smith, 75/88; Snodgrass, 73/73; Soule, 71/361; Stewart, 66/81; Thwing, 74/358; Veatch, 74/283; Washburn, 66/382; Watkins, 71/360

French-Canadian, 74/90; 81/203;

Irish, 69/101-47*passim*; Multnomah Co. Library guide, 68/340

Oregon—

families, 71/285; settlers 1845, 78/381 sources, 62/109; 63/92,247,364; 64/79; 65/216,308; Washington Co. marriages 1854-56, 69/87; Yamhill Co., 74/286

General II (motorboat), photo, 77/74

General Motors Truck Co., 73/74

Genevra, Calif.: name, 80/239N

Genoa, Nev., 72/180

The Gentile Comes to Utah: A Study in Religious and Social Conflict, by Dwyer, noted, 73/74

Gentry, William T., 65/184N,191N-92, 195

A Geographic Index for Volumes I & II, Genealogical Material in Oregon Donation Land Claims..., noted, 62/109

Geographic names:

Bannock War area, 69/226-58*passim*, 279-316*passim*; Blue Slaughter Spring, 73/260; Bonner Co., Ida., 72/263; California, 70/178; Camp Bidwell, 69/256N; Camp McDermit, 69/248N; Camp McGarry, 69/255N; Carroll Rim, 73/265; Clackamas Co., 65/385; classical town names in U.S., 68/344; Coalman Glacier, 73/81; Corder's Station, 69/239N,242N; Cow Creek Lake, 69/238N,308N; Daily Road, 69/233N; DaMotta Canyon, 73/206; Dead Indian Road, 68/353; Dealy's Station, 69/233N; Lassen's Pass, 69/257N; Logsden, 69/340; Missoula Co., 65/384; Mokst Butte, 68/354; Munday's ferry, 69/239N; Nez Perce Co., Ida., 72/265; Olympic Peninsula, 69/73-74 Oregon, 70/215-16; 75/87,378— publications, 80/105 Owyhee Co., Ida., 72/265; Pacific Coast Spanish, 66/280; Pluvius, Wash., 68/81; Rainier, 68/353; Robisonville, 69/235N; Rodgers Mt., 69/340; Sargent Butte, 73/268; Shafer Creek, 69/244N; True Shout Spring, 69/258N; Upper Willamette area,

72/171; Wonder Rock, 73/83
Geography:
American reactions, 69/83; arid West, 65/313
bibliography, 68/347—
u.s. and Canada, 75/94
Canada, 75/94—
49th parallel 1872-76, 66/69-71
economic, 81/325-27; historical, 73/85; imaginary, 73/286; Modoc Co., 67/363; Oregon unmapped, 64/357; Pacific Basin, 70/76-77; Pacific NW historical, 70/64; Pacific NW theses, 65/376-77; 72/254-61
u.s.—
bibliography, 75/94; 49th parallel 1872-76, 66/69-71
Geologic Setting of the John Day Country, noted, 70/360
Geology:
articles on, 67/90,370,374; 68/91; 73/82; bibliography 1959-65, 67/33, 366; Cape Lookout, 68/350; Cascades, 73/82; Clarno formation, 73/264,268; coastal sediment, 70/183; Columbia Gorge, 80/407; Crook Co., 62/299; Diamond Lake, 66/282; earthquakes, SEE Earthquakes; economic, 72/180; Elkhorn Valley, 73/83; Fort Rock, 63/254; 64/357; Fossil Lake, 67/366; geothermal resources, 72/180; glacial erratics, 63/364; glaciation, 70/183; Harney Co., 62/299; ice caves, 62/198; 73/84; Illinois River, 65/315; John Day country, 68/352; 70/360; 73/264,265; Klamath area, 66/80; 67/22; Lake Co. dunes, 67/370
lava flows, 67/25—
McKenzie, 68/351; Nevada, 69/87; Newberry Crater, 68/354; Oregon, 66/92,284; 69/87; Wallula, 66/275
mapping in Oregon, 67/30; marine minerals, 72/180; meteors, SEE Meteors and meteorites; mineral deposits, 72/180; mineral industry, 67/37,39; Morrow Co., 79/104; Nevada, 69/87; Newberry Crater, 68/354
Oregon, 62/198; 66/92; 75/87; 79/338—

Central Ore., 66/383-84; interpretation, 67/5-39; lava flows, 67/25; 68/351,354; 69/87; mapping, 67/30; "moon" country, 67/39,374; official rock, SEE Thunderegg; prehistoric mounds, 63/254; surveys, 72/180
Owyhee region, 75/87; Painted Hills, 73/264; prehistoric sea, 69/338; St. Johns, 77/300; Smith Rock, 68/354; Snake River Canyon, 69/86; Sutton Mt., 73/264; tertiary lakes theory, 70/366; time chart, 67/27; volcanoes, SEE Volcanoes; Wright Point, 69/341; SEE ALSO Borax; Fossils; Glaciers; Lunar geology
George (Indian, friend of Moses), 70/148
George (Indian, Klamath chief), 69/245-54*passim*:
camp, 69/253,268
George (Indian, Sarah Winnemucca escort), 70/15,16,17
George (Indian), SEE ALSO Indian George
George II, King of England, 64/10-11
George IV, King of England, 64/10-11, 15,18,20-21,25-27,30-31
George, Melvin C., 74/199
George, Otto, 75/279
George, W.A., 62/233
George Drouillard, Hunter and Interpreter for Lewis and Clark, by Skarsten, review, 65/303-304
George Eastman House:
Vollum album photos, 70/240,242
George T. Baldwin, His Life and Achievements, by Drew, noted, 81/327
George W. Elder (steamer), 76/102,102N: photos, 74/305; 76/102
George W. Fenwick (steamer), photo, 74/305
Georgia-Pacific Corporation, 72/293N; 77/75,351:
logging museum, 74/362
Georgiana (steamer built 1914), 74/163,244N
Georgie Burton (steamer), 75/227
Gerard, James W., 64/327
Gerber, Barbara, 81/104
Gerber, Joseph R., 74/357
Gerber, Ulrich, 81/104

Gerlinger, Carl, 78/159
Gerlinger, George T., 64/60; 78/158
Gerlinger, Mrs. George T., 78/158
Gerlinger, Georgiana, 78/160(with photo)
Gerlinger Co., Dallas, Ore., 77/342
German language, 80/200,201,204
German people, 81/196:
anti-German attitudes, 75/149,152;
Aurora colony, 79/233-67; California, 75/93; Catholic immigrants, 75/132;
Cedar Mill area, 80/106; experiences, 80/374-75; gold mines, 81/192;
Inland Empire, 66/89
Oregon, 68/208; 70/312,316,317;
78/158—
population 1860-1910, 80/267
Portland population 1860-1910, 80/136,266; Spokane, 72/246
Germany:
interests in Pacific, 62/7,11,15,18;
World War II, 62/25,26,29,30,35
Gerretsen, William H., Jr., 77/67N
Gertrude, Mother, 70/329,330
Gervais, Adelaide, 66/347,349
Gervais, Celestine, SEE Lucier, Celestine Gervais
Gervais, David, 66/334:
children, 66/351; land claim, 66/357;
marriage, 66/351
Gervais, Francois Xavier, 66/338, 356,360N:
Cayuse War, 66/358
Gervais, Francoise, 66/338,352
Gervais, Isaac, son of Joseph, 66/338, 341,356:
Cayuse War, 66/358,362; land claim, 66/357
Gervais, Isaac, son of Louis, 66/362N
Gervais, Jean Baptiste, 66/335,361:
Cayuse War, 70/347; daughter, 66/360N; land claim, 66/359
Gervais, Joseph, brother of Jean Baptiste, 62/299; 70/347; 71/349; 77/81:
biography, 66/331-62; Cascade wagon route exped., 66/357; children, 66/334,338,341-60*passim*; death, 66/361;
descendants, 66/361; first settler Willamette Valley, 66/334-35

grist mill, 66/343-44—
location, 66/342; value, 66/360
hospitality, 66/339-40,351,358; HBCO. employee, 66/333
house and barn—
description, 66/338-39,340; flood damage 1861, 66/358,361
Hunt overland exped., 66/331-32
land claim—
described, 66/357-58; sold, 66/359;
Wyeth map, 66/345
Lee friendship, 66/340-41,344,346-47;
McKenzie exped., 66/332
McLoughlin relationship, 66/336-37, 353—
estate claim, 66/361
Ore.Prov.Govt. role, 66/350N,352-56;
Parker visit, 66/343; Pudding River named, 66/333-34
relationship with Indians, 66/332—
Cayuse War, 66/358-59
school in home, 66/341; trapping, 66/333; wives, 66/334,338,348, 349,360
Gervais, Joseph, son of David, 66/351N,360N
Gervais, Joseph, son of Louis, 66/362N
Gervais, Julia, SEE Laderoute, Julia Gervais
Gervais, Louis, great-grandson of Joseph, 66/362N
Gervais, Louis, son of Z. Jerome, 66/362N
Gervais, Marguerite Clatsop:
children, 66/338,347,349; marriage, 66/348
Gervais, Marie Angelique Tchinouk, 66/351,359,360:
marriage, 66/349
Gervais, Marie Anne Despard (Mrs. Francois X.), 66/360N
Gervais, Marie Anne Toupin (Mrs. David), 66/351
Gervais, Mary, 66/346
Gervais, Richard, 66/362N
Gervais, Rosalie, 66/351,356
Gervais, Theodore, 81/91,91N
Gervais, Xavier, SEE Gervais, Francois Xavier

Gervais, Z. Jerome, 66/362N

Gervais, Ore., 77/298; 80/279: Benedictines visit, 70/316-18; centennial, 72/91; monastery, 70/331-32; school, 70/331

Getty, Charles, 66/174

Geyer, Georg, 80/368-69

Geyer, Mrs. (Georg?), 80/365-73

Gheen, Ruby Skinner, photo, 71/252

Gholson, Richard Dickerson, 62/84-85

Ghost Town Album, by Florin, review, 64/184-85

Ghost Town Trails, by Florin, review, 65/209-10

Ghost Town Treasures, by Florin, noted, 66/384

Ghost towns, 62/198; 63/79-80,89; 64/91,184-85,282,355; 66/384; 68/343; 77/300: Eastern Oregon, 69/274; Oregon and Washington, 79/105-106; The West, 66/384; SEE ALSO Ashwood; Auburn; Belle Passi; Bodie; Bourne; Chitwood; Cornucopia; Coyote Creek; Custer; Eagle Gorge; Fleetwood; Gold Point; Golden; Granite; Greenhorn; Hardman; Harper; Holden; Idaho City; Izee; Jerome; Kernville; Leesburgh; Leland; Lone Rock; Malheur City; Niagara; Opal City; Pierce; Quartzville; Rock Creek; Rock Point; Rocky Bar; Ruch; Shaniko; Shelburn; Silver City; Susanville; Waldo; Warren; Watson; Yellow Pine

Ghost Towns of Washington and Oregon, by Miller, noted, 79/105-106

Ghost: Cowlitz Co., 65/211

Giannini, Battista, photo, 77/238

Gibbens, Robert, 80/317

Gibbon River, 74/339

Gibbons, Allan S., Jr., 63/368: *Above the Pacific*, by Horvat, review, 68/278-79

Thence Around Cape Horn...U.S. Naval Forces on Pacific Station, by Johnson, review, 66/71-72

West Coast Windjammers, by Gibbs, review, 70/266-67

Gibbs, Addison Crandall, 62/311; 64/167; 65/9,60N,78N,97,185,296,352, 399; 72/322; 75/122; 78/42: and "Copperheads," 65/115-16N,184; creek named for, 65/299; Denny correspondence, 65/232; senate contest 1864, 65/107,109

Gibbs, George, 62/215-16; 64/180, 228N-29N; 67/303N,310N; 70/247: Willamette Valley map 1851, 70/258

Gibbs, James Atwood: *Disaster Log of Ships*, review, 73/69-70 *Sentinels of the North Pacific*, cited, 69/209N,232N *West Coast Lighthouses*, noted, 75/365 *West Coast Windjammers in Story and Pictures*, review, 70/266-67

Gibbs Creek, SEE Crooked Creek, Malheur Co.

"Gibbs-Starling Map, 1851," by Harold Mackey, 70/259-61

Gibney, Patrick, 81/87,88N

Gibson, Frank B., 62/172

Gibson, James R., 77/290: *Feeding the Russian Fur Trade: Provisionnment of the Okhotsk Seaboard and the Kamchatka Peninsula, 1639-1856*, noted, 77/293; review, 71/181

Imperial Russia in Frontier America: the Changing Geography of Supply of Russian America, 1784-1867, noted, 77/290; review, 77/293

"Russian America in 1821: Khlebnikov's Report," 77/174-88

Gibson, John B., 67/300,303N

Gibson, Kenneth: location of Adventure Cove, 68/ 102-103,108,109

Gibson, Mrs. Kenneth, 68/108

Gibson, Walter Murray, 65/313

Gibson, William, The Dalles 1870, 79/ 162N

Giddings, J.L., 77/296

Gidley, Mick: *With One Sky Above Us: Life on an American Indian Reservation at the Turn of the Century*, noted, 81/330

Giesecke, E.W., 62/105; 63/92; 67/88: *Astoria...*, by Washington Irving, ed. by

Todd, review, 66/77-79
Autobiography of Rear Admiral Wilkes, ed. by Moran *et al*, review, 79/404-406
Flood Tide of Empire, by Cook, review, 74/353-54
The Journal and Letters of Captain Charles Bishop, ed. by Roe, review, 69/67-68
Journal of a Voyage on the North West Coast, by Franchere, review, 71/277-79
Giesy, Andrew, father of Andrew H., photo, 79/ins.bk.cov. Fall
Giesy, Andrew H., 79/239,249,250: photo, 79/ins.bk.cov. Fall
Giesy, Andrew Jackson, 72/280; 79/ 235,239
Giesy, Christian, 79/263
Giesy, Christopher, 67/276
Giesy, Elizabeth, photo, 79/ins.bk.cov. Fall
Giesy, Frederick, 79/239,249,250,263
Giesy, Helena, 79/253: photo, 79/ins.bk.cov. Fall
Giesy, Henry, 79/239,262
Giesy, Katherine, photo, 79/ins.bk.cov. Fall
Giesy, Katherine Kimpel, photo, 79/ ins.bk.cov. Fall
Giesy, Lorren, 79/239
Giesy, Martin, 79/235
Giesy, Mary, photo, 79/ins.bk.cov. Fall
Giesy, Matilda, photo, 79/ins.bk.cov. Fall
Giesy, Nicholas, 79/239: photo, 79/ins.bk.cov. Fall
Giesy, Rudi, photo, 79/ins.bk.cov. Fall
Giesy, Samuel, 79/239
Giesy, William, 79/249: photo, 79/ins.bk.cov. Fall
Gifford, B.F., 62/219N
Gifford, Benjamin Arthur, 73/364: biography, 66/317; photo, 66/317; photo studio, 66/317; postal cards, 66/317
Gifford, Frank, 76/261
Gifford, Fred L., 75/187N,188N: finances, 75/175-77,189N-90N; KKK career, 75/154,158-82*passim*; photo, 75/155,181
Gifford, Sanford R., 67/371
Gilbeault, Hilard, 63/118,126,133,142,

145-46,149-50,153,173
Gilbert, A.C., 62/204
Gilbert, E., Auburn miner, 62/219N
Gilbert, Frank T., 66/357N
Gilbert, Grove K., 67/22
Gilbert, Joseph L., 68/81
Gilbert, Kenneth, 74/54
Gilbert, Leland, photo, 74/265
Gilbert, William Ball, 68/330
Gilbert's Station, 72/67
Gilcrest, Evelyn, 63/321(photo): "Alvord Ranch Interlude: Life on a Celebrated Range," 63/304-41
Gilcrest, John, 63/274,304-40*passim*: photo, 63/332
Gilcrest, Mrs. John, 63/304-40*passim*
Gilcrest, John, Jr. (Jack), 63/304-40 *passim*: photos, 63/308,321
Gilcrest, Mary, 63/304-40*passim*: photos, 63/308,321
Gilcrist, Frank, 80/413
Gile, Albion, 62/110,206,302,422; 63/ 93,255,373; 64/93,189,285,363; 65/ 125,221,317,416; 66/93,189,285,394
Gile, Henry S., 69/331
Giles, Daniel, 74/94
Gilfilan, A., 66/55
Gilfillin, Thomas, 69/130
Gill, Frank B., 65/284N
Gill, Harold D., 63/362
Gill, J.K., Company, Portland, 64/158; 66/305
Gill, Ray, 76/146
Gilleese, Bridget Farley (Mrs. James), 69/130
Gilleese, James, 69/130
Gilleese, Joe, 69/130
Gillem, Alvan Cullom, 63/81
Gilles, George, 77/227
Gillespie, Agnes Lenora, 66/81
Gillespie, Jacob, 79/21,21N: family, 77/324
Gillet, Felix, 66/87
Gillette, Preston W., 64/181
Gilliam, Cornelius, 64/276; 65/214; 75/73; 81/188
Gilliam, Homer, 63/269,282
Gilliam, Washington Smith, 75/350,

353-54,355
Gilliam County, Ore., 66/365; 80/195: first settlement, 81/263; history, 75/ 361-62; map 1892, 81/280; ranch experiences 1881, 81/261-79
Gilliam County Historical Society: officers and directors, 77/94; 78/93; 79/110; 80/109; 81/109
Gillihan, Elizabeth, 62/128N
Gillihan, Martin, 62/128N
Gilliss, James, 79/282,283,297
Gilliss, Mrs. James, 79/297
Gilman, Charles A.: biography, 74/7; Olympic exped., 74/7-16
Gilman, Sam: Olympic exped., 74/7-16
Gilmore, Emma M., 62/335
Gilmore, Jesse L.: *H.M. Chittenden: A Western Epic*, ed. by LeRoy, review, 63/243-44 *Westward Vision: The Story of the Oregon Trail*, by Lavender, review, 66/68-69
Gilmore, Samuel Mattison, 80/150
Gilpin, Julia Pratte (Mrs. William), 63/89
Gilpin, William, 62/106; 63/89; 67/85; 70/367
Gilroy, Calif., 80/241
Gilsby, Mrs. —, Tacoma 1890s, 66/125
Gilson, Horace C., 70/180
Gilson family, Cowlitz Co., 65/120
Ginder, William, 81/328
Gingko trees: description, 66/86
Ginseng, 72/179
Ginther, Edward, 70/313,319,322
Giorda, Guiseppe, 67/368
Girasol (vessel), 73/224
Gird, Agnes Stephens, 68/147N
Gird, Edward, 68/146
Gird, Helen A. Edgar, 68/143
Gird, Judson, 68/143,144N,146,150
Gird, Ney, 68/143,144,146,147N,150
Gird, William: biography, 68/141-46; letters, 68/147-52; photo, 68/144
Girl Scouts of America: Garibaldi, 77/358; Portland 1917-1950s, 73/74

Girnwood, J.W., 62/219N
Giusti, Lorenzo, 77/238(photo),254
Give All to Oregon! Missionary Pioneers of the Far West, by Dryden, noted, 69/332
Glaab, Charles N., 63/89: *The American City, A Documentary History*, noted, 64/350
Glacier National Park, 72/237
Glaciers: Alaska, 81/135-37; Cascades, 77/196; erratics in Ore., 66/284; photos, 77/ 64,66; Mt. Washington, 66/282; SEE ALSO Carbon Glacier; Coalman Glacier; Coe Glacier; Eliot Glacier; Newton Clark Glacier; White River Glacier
Glad, Paul W.: *The Trumpet Soundeth: William Jennings Bryan and His Democracy, 1896-1912*, review, 62/188-92
Gladstone, Ore., 66/46; 70/278; 80/391,396,398
"Gladstone Chautauqua: Education and Entertainment, 1893-1928," by Donald E. Epstein, 80/391-403
Gladstone Park, photos, 80/394,399
Glancing Back (Pioneer Lore), noted, 72/353; 74/92
Glass, Gordon, 79/411,416
Glass, Hugh, 67/280
Glass, Sim, photo, 71/252
Glass: American historic, 63/353-54; blowers, 69/77; Coburg factory, 67/369; volcanic, 69/333
Glass fish net floats, 77/278-80
Glauert, Earl T., and Merle H. Kunz, eds.: *Kittitas Frontiersmen*, noted, 79/105
Glavis, Louis Russell: Ballinger-Pinchot controversy, 65/314; Glavis-Ballinger dispute, 76/101
Glazunov, Andrei, 73/131
Gleason, —, Gilliam Co. 1881, 81/274,275
Gleason, M., Portland stonemason, 81/89
Gleason, M.J., photo, 81/254
Glenada, Ore., 74/273
Glenbow Foundation, 70/238

Glencoe, Ore., 76/381
Glendale, Ore., 72/161
Glendale (ship), 66/122
Glenn, Hugh James, 68/321
Glenn, Tolbert T., family, 72/94
Glenn, William S., 68/230N; 70/19N
Glenwood Trolley Park, 67/373
Gleysteen, Jan:
Symphony in Steam, The History of the 4-4-0 or American Type Locomotive, noted, 67/280
Glidden, Joseph Farwell, 70/72
Glidden, Vernon, photo, 74/221
Glimpses of Wheeler County's Past: An Early History of North Central Oregon, noted, 77/195,292
Glisan, Rodney, 62/105
Glover, James N., 74/359
Goats:
angora, 81/328; domestic, 70/54; 80/59; mountain, 81/131,139
Gobin, Antoine, 80/335
Gobin, Jean Baptiste, son of Antoine, 66/351N; 79/142,159,162N,316, 317,320
Goble, Ore., 66/91; 72/197N,199; 73/334; 74/305; 77/89; 81/35
God Made a Valley, by Combs and Ross, noted, 63/357
Goddard, George H.:
Calif.-Utah boundary survey, 72/12-13; Indian difficulties, 72/12-13
Goddard, Joseph H., 80/334: family, 70/358
Goddard, Ormy, 77/90
Godfrey, Louise (Mrs. Richard L.), 76/387; 80/414
Godfrey Park, 65/219
Godley, Calvin C., 62/242-87*passim*, 337-402*passim*
Godley, George W., 62/242,245-46, 250,258,280,343,357,358,379,381, 386-87,388
Godley, Henry D., 62/242-54*passim*, 269,272,276,339,340,356,357,358, 359,377,381
Godley, John W., 62/242-58*passim*,381, 385,386
Godley, Martha Dix (Mrs. Calvin C.),

62/242-87*passim*,337-402*passim*
Goe, Vernon and John T. Labbe:
Railroads in the Woods, review, 63/351-52
Goens, Sebastian, 80/351,352,357,358, 361; 81/79,80,83,87,90-91
Goerig, Laurence H.:
obituary, 64/276
Goethals, George Washington, 72/353
Goetjen, I., 75/44
Goetz, Jacob ("Dutch Jake"), 74/359
Goetzmann, William H., 63/356:
Exploration and Empire: The Explorer and the Scientist in the Winning of the American West, review, 70/73-74
First Man West: Alexander Mackenzie's Account of His Expedition, ed. by Sheppe, review, 64/272-73
"The Grand Reconnaissance," noted, 80/209
When the Eagle Screamed: The Romantic Horizon in American Diplomacy, 1800-1860, noted, 68/343
Goff, David, 75/354; 77/317
Goff, Samuel, 75/345,347,349
Goggin, Daniel T., and H. Stephen Helton, comps.:
General Records of the Department of State, noted, 64/277
Goicoechea, Isidoro, photo, 76/166
Gold and Cattle Country, by Oliver, ed. by Jackman, review, 63/70-71
Gold and gold mining, 62/77,199; 72/33; 73/67; 80/205:
Alaska, 62/95-96; 68/184; 71/365; 72/353; 79/338,364—
1898, 71/121-48; trails to, 81/122-23,127-28,131,143-45,147-48
Almeda mine, 69/78; Althouse, 72/10,11; American rushes, cause, 71/364; Applegate Creek, 72/42; Arizona, 72/13; Armstrong nugget, 68/354; Auburn, 62/213-36; 63/92,254; 72/71; Baker Co., 66/205; 79/123; Benton mine, 73/83; bibliography of reminiscences, 71/360; "Big Ditch," 72/93; Blue Bucket, SEE Blue Bucket Mine; Blue Mountains, 67/21N; bogus dust scandal 1860s, 64/357; Bohemia district, 63/365; 64/355; 72/92; 73/83,

283; Boise Basin 1862, 65/399; 67/371 British Columbia, 63/89; 64/86; 69/ 79; 72/88— Atlin Lake 1898, 81/142,144-46,148 bullion shipped to San Francisco, 69/ 222 California, 62/66,69,151,296; 63/88; 64/87,275; 69/276; 70/365,366; 71/359-60; 72/182; 77/43,91; 79/ 340— 1848, 73/60; Butte Co., 66/168-69; camps, 77/197; date of discovery, 68/ 349; Del Norte Co., 76/53; gold rush journal, 67/370; gold specimens to London, 81/191; Northern Calif., 81/329; sketch 1860, 81/191; Skirving panorama view, 65/164-67; world impact, 65/213 camps, SEE Mining camps; Canyon City, 63/366; 75/314; Chinese, 76/77; 78/73,75,81; 80/336 Coeur d'Alene, 69/85,203,213,217, 219,220— mining war, 62/108 Colville, 67/313; 68/23,29,31; 70/ 113; 79/27,27N; Coos Co., 63/14- 15,19,23; Coquille River, 62/14-15; Curry Co., 78/363; Dawson, 76/116 discoveries— California, 64/87,275; 68/349; Canyon City, 63/366; Colville district, 67/313; Coquille River, 63/14-15; Eastern Ore., 79/42; Idaho, 64/188, 356; 65/198; McQuade Creek, 63/ 92; Orofino Creek, 66/227; Powder River, 66/199; Queen Charlotte Islands, 63/53N; Sixes River, 63/23; Southern Ore., 64/284 Douglas Co., 80/105; dredge, 69/78; Eastern Wash., 62/216; economic effects, 80/22,28,136,138,153,209; Elliott Creek, 72/41-42; flumes, photo, 76/86; Fraser River, 68/23,30; 72/ 345; Gold Hill, 65/218; 72/92; Grant Co., 63/70-71; 79/123; Griffin Creek, 72/86; guidebooks, 68/348; Happy Camp, 72/42 Idaho, 62/106,108,216,297; 63/89; 64/188,356; 66/198; 71/49,55; 72/

58,73; 79/25,49,107,173,190,194, 363— maps listed, 73/284; mine war 1892, 73/86 Indian interference, 79/27N; Jackson Co. quartz mill, 68/90; Jacksonville 1860, 69/233; John Day River, 73/ 258,260; Jordan Creek, Ida., 75/363; Josephine Co., 76/82; journals, 67/ 370; 71/365; 79/340; Juneau area 1880-81, 68/184; Klamath River, 66/ 218,225-26; Klondike, 62/166; 67/ 280; 68/237; 69/75-76,337,338; Kootenai, 62/300; Lane Co., 78/288; Linn Co., 63/92; McQuade Creek, 63/ 92; Malheur Co., 72/93; miners allowed east of Cascades, 67/323N; mining laws, 62/224; 80/207; minting gold, 63/84; SEE ALSO Money; Montana, 66/88; 72/58; Nelson mine, 68/208; Nevada, 72/58; Nome rush, 71/365; Ochoco mine, 73/267 Oregon, 69/333; 71/41-42; 77/ 91,300— beaches, 62/215; coast, 74/94; Eastern Ore., 62/213-14,215-16,221; Southern Ore., 62/107,214-15; 64/284; 66/75-76 Oregon King mine, 72/341; Orofino Creek, 66/227; Owyhee mines, 79/47; Pacific NW rushes 1855-59, 68/23; packers, 75/314; panning instructions, 69/78; Patagonia (Mowry) mine, 72/ 13; pictorial records, 65/165-66,169, 172N; 79/64; Pike's Peak, 72/58; placer mining, 62/107,214; 66/75-76; 73/267; 76/77,82,86; Powder River, 66/199; prospecting described, 71/366 prospectors, 76/67-68— Eastern Ore., 79/25-27,30-31,39- 40,42; photo, 76/fr.cov. March quartz, 69/201-203— mill, Jackson Co., 68/90; mining, 62/214 Quartzville, 70/278; Queen Charlotte Islands, 63/53N; 68/87; Rocky Mts., 72/58,65; Rossland Camp, 63/361; Sailors' Diggings, 72/10,11,42; Salmon River, 79/181N; "salting," 69/335;

Scissors Creek, 73/267; Shively recollections 1848-49, 81/189-93; Siskiyou Mts., 72/41; Sitka 1867, 76/180; Sixes River, 63/23,27-28; Skagit Valley, 79/337; skin-diving for gold, 62/203; Sumpter Valley, 69/78 supply routes to mines, 79/46,47,49— military protection, 79/49 Taku Inlet, 81/141,142,144; Trout Creek district, 72/341; Wenatchee Mts., 72/233; Western States, 64/344-45; Windy Point, 68/348; yield, 62/227 Yukon rush, 64/87; 68/87; 76/101-17; 81/331— Dawson, 76/116 SEE ALSO Mines and mining *Gold and Silver in Oregon*, by Brooks and Ramp, noted, 69/333 Gold Beach, Ore., 69/88: described 1964, 65/315 Gold Democratic party, 68/332 Gold Hill, Ore., 65/218; 72/92 *Gold in the Woodpile, An Informal History of Banking in Oregon*, by Burrell, review, 70/177 *Gold on Sterling Creek: A Century of Placer Mining*, by Haines and Smith, review, 66/75-76 Gold Point, Nev., 63/80 Gold Ray Dam, 65/218 Gold River, B.C., 72/262 *Gold Rush! The Yukon Stampede of 1898*, by Poynter, noted, 81/331 Golden, Frances, 66/55 Golden, William, 64/218: Tansy Point claim, 64/218N Golden, Ida., 63/89 Golden, Ore., 64/355 *The Golden Frontier: The Recollections of Herman Francis Reinhart, 1851-1869*, ed. by Nunis, review, 64/344-46 Golden Hotel, Reno, 77/169 "Golden Gate to Columbia River on the Bark *Keoka*: Isaac A. Flint's Journal," ed. by Ted Van Arsdol, 63/41-54 *The Golden Spike, A Centennial Remembrance*, by Chandler *et al*, review, 70/349-51 *Golden State* (vessel), drawing, 77/54

The Golden Years of Jacksonville: A Pictorial Walking Tour, by Sutton and Pinkham, noted, 62/301 Goldendale, Wash., 70/134: described 1879, 70/140-46; observatory, 81/329; photo, 70/142; railroad completion, 70/221 Goldsmith, Arthur A., 62/179 Goldsmith, Bernard (Barney), 69/208, 213,214,220; 71/19; 80/161,164, 165,166 Goldsmith, Herb, 66/309 Goldsmith, L., and Company, Portland, 81/274N Goldsmith, Max, 71/17 Golf, 77/263 *Goliath* (steamer), 80/10N Golovin, P., 77/86 Golovnin, V.M., 72/109N; 77/86: visit to Russian America, 72/108 Goltra, W.H., 67/63 Goncharov, I.A., 73/158-59 Gonzaga Preparatory School, Spokane, 64/78 Gonzaga University, 65/204-205; 69/124 *Gonzaga University, Seventy-Five Years, 1887-1962*, by Schoenberg, review, 65/204-205 Gooch Falls, 72/91 Good, Rachel Applegate, 66/382 Good Harmony, SEE Harmony Island, Alaska Good Man (Indian), SEE Tats-homi Good Roads movement, 65/305; 66/ 249N,251N; 74/101,104,105,108,109, 120,134,208-13,214,225; 78/110, 357: legislation, 66/251N; Montana, 72/ 231; Oregon, 66/253; 72/230 Good Samaritan Hospital, Portland, 72/280; 80/336 Good Templars, SEE Independent Order of Good Templars *"Good Times Coming?" Black Nevadans in the 19th Century*, by Rusco, noted, 77/303 Goodale, Greenleaf A., 79/165,272,273, 273N: biography, 79/165N

Goodale Ranch, Siskiyou Co., 66/81
Goodall, James P.:
Rogue River War, 66/220N-21N
Goodall, Perry, 78/314
Goodell, J.W., 74/93
Goodell, John, 74/22
Goodhue, Samuel, 77/317
Goodman, Henry:
letter on bicycles, 72/339
Goodman, Mrs. Mark, 79/16
Goodpasture, Alexander, family, 77/324
Goodrich, Alva C., 62/110,206,302,422; 63/93,255
Goodrich, Carter:
Government Promotion of American Canals and Railroads, 1800-1890, review, 63/355-56
Goodsell, David, 69/213
Goodwin, Elmer, 77/352
Goodwin, P.A., 67/69,70
Goodwin, S.P., 70/12N
Goodwin, Sid, 74/231
Goodyear, Zola Cowen, 81/105
Goose Creek, Ida., 62/385
Goose Hollow, SEE Portland
Goose Lake, Lake Co., 65/13; 72/7,29, 33,41; 76/336; 77/7,157; 79/289; 81/328:
described, 72/34; drainage, 72/7N; photo 1908, 76/334
Goose Lake Mountains, 72/41
Goose Lake Valley, 68/257,316,317; 79/23,48,290
Gooseberries, 69/149,155,157,158
Gopher Valley:
history, 67/373
Gordon, Clarence, 67/141
Gordon, John, 63/218; 70/310; 73/359: biography, 70/296,310; commander HMS *America,* 70,293FF; court-martial, 70/309,310,311; takes specie to England, 70/305-306,308; value San Francisco harbor, 70/304; view of Oregon Country, 70/303-304
Gordon, Patrick, 78/303
Gordon, Samuel M., photo, 74/221
Gordon, William, Lord Commissioner of Admiralty, 70/296
Gordon, William, Siskiyou Co. pioneer,

72/44
Gordon Falls, 62/173; SEE ALSO Wahkeena Falls
Gore, Jennie (Mrs. Charles E.), 66/382
Gore, John, 80/199,201,204
Gorman, David, 81/279N
Gosa, Samuel T., 65/308
Goss, John, 71/372
Goss Road, 66/81
Gough, Barry M., 74/364:
"H.M.S. *America* on the North Pacific Coast," 70/293-311
Hudson's Bay Miscellany, ed. by Williams, review, 77/83-85
The Letters of Charles John Brydges, 1879-1882, ed. by Bowsfield, review, 81/ 323-24
London Correspondence Inward from Sir George Simpson, ed. by Williams, review, 74/352
"The North West Company's 'Adventure to China'," 76/309-31
The Royal Navy and the Northwest Coast of America, 1810-1914, review, 73/ 259-60
Gould, Charles:
"Portland Italians, 1880-1920," 77/ 239-60
Gould, Ernest, 69/70
Gould, George, Coos Co. homesteader, 80/63:
family, 80/51,63N
Gould, Harriet McClay, 80/51,63N
Gould, Jay, 71/55; 72/66
Gould, Mildred, photo, 80/65
Gourley, Thomas, 79/408
Government Camp, Ore., 63/30,364
Government Island, 72/353
Government of Washington State, by Avery, noted, 68/341
Government Promotion of American Canals and Railroads, 1800-1890, by Goodrich, review, 63/355-56
Governmental History of Wasco County, Oregon, by Lundell, noted, 71/286
Governor's Committee on Historic Preservation, 78/368
Gowne, E.G., 64/38
Grace Episcopal Church, Astoria, 81/195:

centennial history, 66/383
Grady, H.C., 65/279,281-87,290
Graebner, Norman A., 62/202
Graff, Everett D., 62/291
Graham, Dave, 63/299-300
Graham, E.O., 66/92
Graham, Gladys R., 62/290
Graham, Ina, 71/275
Graham, Loyal M., 66/270N
Graham, Mary, 67/213N
Graham, Samuel, immigrant of 1853, 78/125
Graham, Samuel M., 65/308
Grahame, James A., 63/184
Graham's Landing, 79/394
Grain:
freighting 1905, 73/84; harvesting crew photo, 73/208; shipping, 78/358; SEE ALSO Prices
Grampus (frigate), 70/296N,307,308
Grand Army of the Republic, 75/128
Grand Coulee Dam, 65/366; 72/328
Grand Coulee Reclamation Project, 80/409
Grand Island, Willamette River, 66/283
Grand Prairie, Wash., 63/137-40
Grand Queue (Indian), 71/331-32
Grand Rapids portage, Saskatchewan, 63/90
Grand Ronde Indian Reservation, 69/339; 70/243; 75/363:
Catholic boarding school, 70/312,319, 320,322,327,330,331; church, 70/322
Grand Ronde Valley, 65/173,175
Grand Trunk Railway, 81/323
Grand View, Ida., 62/391N
Grande Ronde River, 62/397,398; 70/27,31:
photo, 70/28
Grande Ronde Valley, 62/222,397; 63/10,30; 65/297; 66/205,227; 70/37, 280; 77/314; 78/139; 79/86,88, 89,391; 80/99,100; 81/418:
history, 72/94; 79/340; schools, 70/360
Grange, 65/375; 68/132,207; 80/395:
Clark Co., 63/83; early Oregon, 62/107; 66/21,22,24; genesis, 68/344; history, 81/336; Lane Co., 72/178;

movement 1870-80, 64/187; number in Ore. 1874-75, 68/200; reaches Oregon, 68/200; Yankton records, 65/219
Granger, William, 70/139
Grangeville, Ida., 69/108
Granite, Ore., 62/201; 63/80; 73/83
The Granite Boulder, by Wiley, noted, 71/362
Granite City Hospital Co., Ashland, 64/339-40
Granite Creek, 70/59
Grant, —, Auburn doctor 1863, 62/233
Grant, —, Coos Co. widow, 63/28-30
Grant, Alice, 78/163
Grant, Allen, 81/300
Grant, Bridget, photo, 81/194
Grant, Bruce:
American Forts, Yesterday and Today, noted, 66/384
Grant, E.W., 74/17,21
Grant, Ed, 74/16
Grant, Fred, Morrow Co., 69/130
Grant, Frederic, ed.:
History of Seattle, cited, 70/220N
Grant, H.M., 67/72,73
Grant, J.E., 74/19
Grant, John Monroe, 77/268
Grant, Julia Ann, SEE Carman, Julia Ann Grant
Grant, Lige, 64/355
Grant, Michael, 69/130
Grant, O.J. (Jay), 63/28,30
Grant, Richard, 62/371,372; 63/212; 81/27N:
Shively comments, 81/27-29
Grant, Roland D., 75/135
Grant, Ulysses Simpson, 62/59; 66/76; 70/67; 75/93,363; 77/299:
administration, 70/105,108; appointments, 72/183; Indian policy, 70/108-109,148N,318N; Pacific NW career, 64/305-306,357; 69/66; papers, 69/66-67; 70/360; 72/172
Grant County, Ore., 62/216; 66/370, 372; 69/274; 78/75:
cattle, 63/70-71; 70/59; gold mining, 63/70-71; Indian war damage, 70/58; mining, 70/59; property evaluation 1877, 70/57; sheep census 1870-80,

64/102
Grant County, Wash.:
post offices, 69/331
Grant County Historical Society
Museum, 69/175
Grants Pass, Ore., 63/350; 67/281;
71/216; 77/382; 80/233
Grapes:
Lewelling, 68/170
Graphic Arts of the Alaskan Eskimo, by
Ray, noted, 70/360
Grasmere, B.C., 71/339
Grass, 63/265,272; 69/335:
seed production, 72/94; Western Ore.,
65/211; SEE ALSO Alfalfa; Bunchgrass
Grass Lake, 66/81
Grass Valley, Ore., 69/303; 75/43-48:
photos, 75/44-46
"Grass Valley, 1901," by Giles French,
75/43-48
Grasslands, SEE Land
Grattan, John Lawrence, 63/74
Graustein, Jeanette E.:
*Thomas Nuttall, Naturalist: Explorations
in America, 1808-1841*, review, 70/
171-73
Grave (Memaloose) Island, 75/221,223,
225,231
Gravelines, Joseph, 79/336
Gravelle, Ambrose (Indian), 71/339
Graves, Lloyd O., 73/363
Graves, Mrs. Lloyd O., 73/363,364
Gray, Agnes Chinneth, 78/130
Gray, Alexander, 62/230
Gray, Alfred O.:
Not by Might, the Story of Whitworth College, 1890-1965, review, 68/183-84
Gray, Andrew Jackson, 67/85
Gray, Blanch, 80/356
Gray, C.L., 66/163N
Gray, Don, 79/340
Gray, George G., 78/144
Gray, George W., 80/356N
Gray, Gertie, 80/356
Gray, Henry, 69/130
Gray, John, fur trader, 69/64
Gray, Mrs. John D., 76/387; 80/413
Gray, Mary Augusta Dix (Mrs. William
H.), 62/239N,240,244,250N,341;

65/119; 68/76
Gray, Otto, 63/37
Gray, Robert, 62/88,198; 63/368; 67/
200-202; 72/182; 73/199; 76/199:
Boston backers, 76/223; china photo,
76/fr.cov. Sept.; financial return 1789
voyage, 68/277; winter camp 1791-92,
68/101-10
Gray, Robert Doke, 78/129,130
Gray, W.P., Canyon City 1878, 70/59
Gray, William, Mass. shipping merchant,
76/208,223-24
Gray, William Henry, 62/121-22,323,
333; 63/181-82,195,209,211,235; 64/
138,170-71,243; 66/352N,353N,355N;
71/285; 75/113,119,122:
Applegate opinion, 81/251; biography,
62/238-42,243-45; California, 64/
206; diaries, 68/76; donation claim,
73/245; leads 1838 missionary party,
68/76-77; Ore. City holdings, 73/
246-47; overland journey 1853, 62/
249-87*passim*,337-402*passim*; photo,
73/249; 75/114; property dispute with
Parrish, 73/245-57
Gray, William Henry:
A History of Oregon, cited, 75/113,122;
reprint noted, 74/359
Gray, William Polk, 62/239N,244N,
248,248N; 73/245
"Gray's Adventure Cove," by Edmund
Hayes, 68/101-10
Grays Harbor, 66/318; 71/145;
73/173; 74/14,18
Grays Harbor City, Wash., 74/15,24
Grays Harbor County, Wash., 72/227
Grays Harbor Lumber Co., 77/219
Grays River, 75/106
Grazing, 76/30,34-35,71:
federal laws, 81/282,316-17; Forest
Service control, 76/32,34,37,71; Historical Records Survey history, 67/142
Greasewood area, Umatilla Co., 72/351
Great American Desert, SEE Deserts
The Great American Desert, Then and Now,
by Hollon, review, 67/277
Great Basin, 67/277; 72/6:
Southeast Ore. geology, 67/21-22;
western boundary, 72/7N

Great Britain:
air force, 62/40; American possessions, 73/360; anti-British attitudes in Ore. Terr., 75/318-19,320; army officers on Santa Fe Trail, 68/86; California policy, 70/298-99,302,306,308; China trade, 74/364; citizens in Pacific NW, 62/145; competition with other powers, 73/360; Hawaii sovereignty, 64/87; historic records gathered for OHS, 71/370,372; impact on Utah mining, 65/214; international boundary survey, 66/69-71; maritime colonies, 72/234 navy, 62/10,17,22,25-26,32,40,44—Esquimalt depot, 65/329; on NW Coast, 70/293-311*passim*; Pacific Station records, 69/84 Oregon claim, 66/336; Ore. Country interest, 69/85; Ore. consulate centennial, 72/357,360-61; Pacific exploration, 70/77; Pacific NW colonies, 75/318-19; Pacific NW interests, 72/57-58, 105-106,123; 74/364; 76/199,312, 319; Portland hospital bed for seamen, 72/280; protection of trade interests, 73/359

Russian relations—
1779, 80/198-99,201,203-204; 1820s, 72/101,107,109-10,112FF; St. Petersburg convention, 72/112-13,119,121-23

sea power, 73/359-60; 75/317,318; treatment of Indians, 66/86; U.S. relations, 74/279,284; 75/317-27; WW II in Pacific, 62/8-45*passim*; SEE ALSO Monroe Doctrine; Nootka Controversy; Oregon Question

The Great Columbia Plain: A Historical Geography of the Inland Empire, by Meinig, review, 70/64

The Great Command: The Story of Marcus and Narcissa Whitman, by Jones, review, 62/192-96

Great Day in the West: Forts, Posts, and Rendezvous Beyond the Mississippi, by Ruth, review, 65/202-203

Great Lakes, 66/333

Great North American Indians: Profiles in Life and Leadership, by Dockstad, noted, 80/207

Great Northern (steamship), 81/105

Great Northern Pacific Steamship Co.: records, 74/79

Great Northern Railway Co., 62/197; 70/181,220; 72/197; 78/358; 80/282: construction, 71/364; merger, 71/197; records, 74/79; steamship co., 71/142, 143,150; trade with Orient sought, 71/142,143

The Great Persuader, by Lavender, review, 71/188

Great Plains, 68/185: settlement, 78/282-83

The Great Platte River Road: The Covered Wagon Mainline via Fort Kearney to Fort Laramie, by Mattes, review, 71/182-83

Great Reinforcement, SEE Methodist missions

Great Republic (clipper ship), 63/359

Great Salt Lake, 62/372; 65/155,160, 168; 78/139; 79/32: Delisle map, 73/286

Great Salt Lake Basin, 62/185

Great Southern Lumber Co., 77/219

Great Southern Railroad, 81/101-102

"Great Sternwheeler, *Bailey Gatzert*," by Rowena L. and Gordon D. Alcorn, 63/61-66

"The Great Train Robbery" (movie), 78/362

Great Western Railway, 81/323

Greathouse family, Illinois 1853, 78/128

Greek people: population Oregon 1860-1910, 80/267; population Portland 1860-1910, 80/266; Utah, 71/292

Greeley, Horace, 64/33; 69/330

Greeley, William B., 65/365; 78/280

Greely, A.W., 69/83

Green, Dan L., 78/132

Green, Edith, 70/371; 72/263

Green, Emma, 80/350

Green, Frank L. *Ezra Meeker, Pioneer*, noted, 70/359

Green, George, Sauvie Island settler, 65/240

Green (Greene), George, scout with

McKay, 79/299,301
Green, Henry Dodge, 74/205; 75/84
Green, John, 68/239N,242,243N,247, 308,309
Green, Jonathan S.: report on Oregon, 70/365-66
Green, Norma Kidd: *Iron Eye's Family: The Children of Joseph La Flesche*, noted, 71/287
Green Basin, Ore.: post office, 71/357
Green Mountain Mining Co., 69/211-12: stock listing form, 69/210
Green River, 62/354N,356,360,361; 67/221; 79/78,380; 80/78,79,80; SEE ALSO Hams Fork, Green River
Green Springs Mountain, 76/353,355
The Green Tie (Whitney Co. newspaper), 73/222,223,224N; 77/345
Green Timber: On the Flood Tide to Fortune in the Great Northwest, by Ripley, review, 70/67-68
Greene, Francis Vincent: journal, 66/70
Greenfield, John S., photos, 70/206,208
Greenhorn, Ore., 63/80; 67/370
Greenhorn Cutoff, SEE Elliott Cutoff
Greens Bridge settlement, Linn Co., 80/380
Greenwood, Frederick, 74/238
Greer, Bert, 64/326,335
Gregg, David L., 68/63
Gregg, Jacob Ray: *Pioneer Days in Malheur County*, cited, 67/150-51N
Gregg, Robert D.: *Chronicles of Willamette, Vol. II*, review, 72/349-50
Gregoire, Etienne, 63/232
Gregoire, Felix, photo, 81/254
Gregoire, Victoire McMillan McLoughlin, 63/232
Gregory, John, 81/388
Greiner, Francis J.: "Voice of the West: Harold L. Davis," 66/240-48
Grekodeliarov, Alaska, SEE Unga, Alaska
Grenada (ship), 66/122
Gresham, Ore., 76/239:

history, 69/329-30; 74/94
Gresham Historical Society, 69/329: officers and directors, 80/109; 81/109
Gressley, Gene M.: *Bankers and Cattlemen*, review, 68/337-38
Gressley, Gene M., ed.: *The American West, A Reorientation*, noted, 69/273
Grey, Zane, 72/181
Greyhound (steamer), 63/61,64
Greyhounds, 69/106
Grier, William N., 65/117N
Grieve, James, trans.: *A History of Kamtschatka and the Kurilski Islands*..., noted, 64/187
Griffin, Henry H., 62/220-21,222,236; 72/85-86
Griffin, John, Gilliam Co. 1881, 81/ 269,272
Griffin, John Smith, 64/123-24; 75/113,116,117,118,119,184N: photos, 75/114; 81/258
Griffin, Lillie, M., 70/279
Griffin, Rachael Smith, 80/389
Griffin Creek, Baker Co., 72/86
Griffins Gulch, 62/221,223,226,227, 236; 69/274; 79/42
Griffith, Anna, 64/276
Griffith, E.J., 76/268
Griffith, Franklin T., 74/235
Griffith, H.E., 75/169
Griffiths, Alexander, 78/148,224,304N, 324
Griggs, Robert, 78/370
Grigsby, B.S. ("Back"): recollections, 66/81
Grigsby's Place (Hotel), Copalis, 74/14,18
Grimes, F.H., 74/22
Grimes Ranch, Jefferson Co., 81/282, 299: house, 81/304; photo, 81/300
Grimsted, Patricia Kennedy: *Archives and Manuscript Repositories in the USSR: Moscow and Leningrad*, noted, 74/95
Grindstone Creek, 65/72N
Grinnell, George Bird, 63/80,247;

74/96:

By Cheyenne Campfires, reprint noted, 63/356

Grinnell, Joseph, 75/324

"The Grip Wheel," by Mable Colvin, 79/394-96

Gritzmacher, Charles Carl, 80/317,319N

The Grizzly Bear: Portraits from Life, ed. by Haynes, review, 67/358

Grizzly Five Hearts (Indian), SEE Hiyum Pakhat Timine

Grizzly Immersed in Charcoal (Indian), SEE Hiyumyatatimuxtuluin

Grizzly Mountain (Butte), Crook Co., 79/149N

Grodinsky, Julius:

Transcontinental Railway Strategy, 1869-1893, cited, 70/351

Grooms, William, 80/19,21,28,137, 137N,138,139,144,315

Grosclose, Jacob, 68/243N,245,311

Grouse, 68/238,240; 69/14

Grover, Lafayette, 66/6,8; 67/179; 72/ 326,326N; 75/123; 80/169,299,319; 81/95:

burned in effigy, 67/263; biography, 67/260-61; photos, 67/258; 80/288; 81/fr.cov. Fall; role in 1876 election dispute, 67/259-70*passim*; U.S. Senate election contested, 67/270

Groves, D., 74/24

Grow, Elizabeth Tyler, 75/152-54,177

The Growth of a City, Power and Politics in Portland, Oregon, 1915 to 1950, by MacColl, review, 81/203-205

Gruening, Ernest, 69/184

Guano Lake, 79/278N

Guardians of Liberty, 75/142-44

Guber, A.A., 72/110

Gudde, Erwin G.:

Bigler's Chronicle of the West: The Conquest of California, review, 77/275-76 *California Gold Camps, noted*, 77/197

Gueffroy, Charles H., 74/238

Guerin, Mrs. Tom, 63/363

Guide to an Urban Wilderness: Tryon Creek State Park, noted, 79/104

A Guide to Archives and Manuscripts in the United States, ed. by Hamer, review,

63/244-45

A Guide to Early Oregon Churches, by Freeman, noted, 77/300

Guide to Genealogical Material in Multnomah County Library, noted, 68/340

Guide to Microfilm in the Oregon State Archives, noted, 70/76

A Guide to the Care and Administration of Manuscripts, by Kane, noted, 63/356

A Guide to the Manuscript Collections of Bancroft Library, Vol. I, ed. by Morgan and Hammond, review, 65/198-99

Guide to the Manuscript Collections of the Oregon Historical Society, Supplement, noted, 74/94

Guide to the Military Posts of the United States, 1789-1895, by Prucha, noted, 66/187-88

Guidebooks:

Astoria, 76/304; 77/292; Benton Co., 77/89; Canada travel, 76/77; Central Ore. tours, 81/329; Corvallis historic houses, 77/299; Lake Oswego, 65/121; Lane Co. historic houses, 67/281; Oregon Coast, 67/281; Oregon historic markers, 67/281; Pacific NW birds, 74/282; Portland, 66/82; 77/291

Guidelines to Acquiring City/County Flags, by Cunningham, noted, 71/362

Guie, Geraldine (Mrs. H. Dean), 81/196N

Guie, H. Dean, 67/326N,332N; 68/ 5N,6N:

The Cayuse Indians, by Ruby and Brown, review, 73/277-78

Children of the Sun, by Wynecoop, review, 71/187

Half-Sun on the Columbia, by Ruby and Brown, review, 67/185-86

How Edison's Lamp Helped Light the West, by Dierdorff, review, 72/348

So This Is Klickitat, by Neils, review, 69/68-69

Guignan, Patrick, 69/130

Guilbeault, Hilard, SEE Gilbeault, Hilard

Guild, Jesse Jacob, 64/276

Guild Lake, 75/129: photo, 70/223

Guilford, Nancy, and Patricia Brandt: *Oregon Biography Index*, review, 77/297

Guinotte, Joseph: papers, 73/86
Guise, Alexander, 69/229,230N
Guistina, Maize O.: recollections, 74/93,281
Gulick, Bill: *They Came to a Valley*, review, 68/279-80
Gulick, Clara Ough (Mrs. Jackson), 72/154
Gulick, Harriet (Subina) (Mrs. Henry), 72/151,152,157
Gulick, Henry, 72/149-50,154,155,157: photo, 72/150
Gulick, Jackson, 72/154
Gulick, Robert J., 68/56
Gummery, —, Cowlitz Farm employee, 63/131
Gundlach, George, 70/59
Gunion, Eddie, 75/224
Gunnison, John W., 63/345
Guns, SEE Firearms
Gunther, Erna, 63/246; 64/284
Gurley, Lottie (Mrs. Wayne), 64/89; 68/359; 71/372
Gurley, Lottie, comp.: *Genealogical Material in Oregon Donation Land Claims, Vol. 1, Supplement*, noted, 76/304
Gustafson, John, 71/189
Gustison, Elizabeth Sutton: *Echoes of Puget Sound*, by Birkeland, review, 62/98-99
Guthrie, Alfred Bertram, Jr., 66/240; 72/264: *The Blue Hen's Chick*, review, 69/74-75
Guthrie, Woody, 70/79
Gutowsky, Albert R., 67/88
Guyer, Philip, 81/341N,353,372
Gvosdev Islands, SEE Diomedes Islands
Gwin, William McKendree, 67/261: pro-immigrant protection, 72/56,57
Gwydyr Castle (ship), 66/129,131N
Gyppo Logger, by Felt, noted, 66/82
Gysin, Elizabeth Grieder, 78/175
Gysin, Johannes, 78/175

H.M. Chittenden: A Western Epic, by LeRoy, review, 63/243-44

"H.M.S. *America* on the North Pacific Coast," by Barry M. Gough, 70/293-311
Ha Ha Mally (Indian), 74/13N
Haakenson, Henrick, 66/105
Hachiya, M., 76/237
Hacker, Isaiah, 63/34
Hacker, Nancy A. (Mrs. Robert L.), 63/368; 69/223N,237N,239N
Hacker, Robert L.: *Fishwheels of the Columbia*, by Donaldson and Cramer, review, 73/68
Hackett, James, 69/130
Hackleman, Abram, 67/63
Hadan Livestock Company, 64/356
Hadley, S.B., 64/146
Haefner, Henry E., 76/52,88(photos): "Reminiscences of an Early Forester," 76/39-88
Hafen, Ann W.: "Jean Baptiste Charbonneau," cited, 71/248N
Hafen, LeRoy R., 71/248FF: bibliography of works, 67/371
Hafen, LeRoy R.: *Broken Hand: The Life of Thomas Fitzpatrick*..., new ed. noted, 76/182 *Western America: The Exploration, Settlement, and Development of the Region Beyond the Mississippi*, noted, 71/363
Hafen, LeRoy R., ed.: *The Mountain Men and the Fur Trade of the Far West*, review, 66/185-86; Vols. II and III noted, 69/274-75
Hagan, Barry J., comp.: *A Preliminary Checklist of U.S. Military Posts*..., noted, 76/92
Hagan, William T.: *The Indian, America's Unfinished Business*, comp. by Brophy and Aberle, review, 68/177-78
Hagelstein Park, 75/234
Hagemann, E.R., ed.: *Fighting Rebels and Redskins: Experiences in Army Life of Col. George B. Sanford, 1861-1892*, noted, 71/287-88
Hagemeister, Leontii Andreianovich, 77/175
Hagemeister Island, 77/185

Hagen, Olaf T.:
index to papers, 70/271
Hager, James, **69**/115
Hager, John S., **67**/261
Haggard, Marco L., **66**/89
Haggeman Pass:
first railroad trestle, **66**/181
Hagny, George, **66**/370
Haida Indians, **68**/347:
carvings, **64**/284; **71**/367
Haidinger, W.H., **69**/49
Hailey, John:
express company, **68**/88
Haine, J.W., **80**/321N
Haines, Abner, **68**/245,246,310N
Haines, Aubrey L., ed.:
Osborne Russell's Journal of a Trapper, 1834-1843, noted, **66**/384
Haines, Charles, **75**/142
Haines, Francis D., Jr., **65**/215; **67**/87:
The Cousin Jacks, by Rowse, review, **70**/356-57
Jacksonville, Biography of a Gold Camp, noted, **69**/330
Haines, Francis D., Jr., and Vern S. Smith:
Gold on Sterling Creek: A Century of Placer Mining, review, **66**/75-76
Haines, Francis D., Sr., **62**/415; **63**/86, 250; **64**/84,280; **65**/124,214,312,313; **67**/367:
The Applegate Trail: Southern Emigrant Route, 1846, noted, **77**/301
The Nez Perce Indians and the Opening of the Northwest, by Josephy, review, **67**/278
Red Eagle and the Absaroka, review, **62**/101-102
Haines, Joseph A., **63**/38
Haines, Madge, and Leslie Morrill:
Lewis and Clark: Explorers to the West, review, **62**/102
Haines, Marie:
Remembering 75 Years of History, noted, **71**/362
Haines, Jordan Valley, **70**/15
Hainline, Patricia H., and Margaret S. Carey:
Brownsville, Linn County's Oldest Town,

noted, **77**/299
Halsey, Linn County's Centennial City, noted, **79**/104
Shedd, Linn County's Early Dairy Center, noted, **80**/106
Sweet Home in the Oregon Cascades, noted, **81**/330
Hair Tied on Top (Indian), SEE Wilewmutkin
Hakluyt, Richard, **73**/86
Hakluyt Society, **69**/67:
publications, **75**/364; reprints, **70**/361
Hale, Andrew, **73**/83
Hale, Calvin T., **79**/339
Hale, Horatio, **64**/179
Hale, J.F., **75**/164
Hale, John Parker:
photo, **73**/32; Stark senate seat dispute, **73**/31,33,37,39,41,51,52,59
Haley, W.G., **72**/329
Halfmoon, Alphonse F., **81**/342,349:
"A Cayuse-Nez Percé Sketchbook," **81**/341-76
Halfmoon, David:
recollections of Nez Perce-Snake skirmish, **81**/373
Halfmoon, Otis, **81**/354:
narration of Nez Perce-Snake skirmish, **81**/373-75
Half-Sun on the Columbia: A Biography of Chief Moses, by Ruby and Brown, cited, **70**/125N-69N*passim*; review, **67**/185-86
Hall, Bob, **70**/57
Hall, Charles, **74**/222:
political campaign 1922, **75**/162-63, 167,169,171
Hall, D.A., **65**/168
Hall, Don Alan:
On Top of Oregon, noted, **76**/382
Hall, George, Auburn sheriff, **62**/ 223,224:
quoted, **62**/231-32
Hall, George, immigrant of 1853, **78**/128
Hall, George A., **75**/138
Hall, Gertrude Jane, SEE Denny, Gertrude Jane Hall White
Hall, Grace E., **74**/38
Hall, Hazel, **74**/34,63

Hall, J. Alfred:
The Pulp and Paper Industry and the Northwest, noted, 71/286

Hall, James, artist:
portrait of William Brooks, 64/42

Hall, James, Queets Valley pioneer, 74/24

Hall, John, founder of Myrtle Creek, 62/205

Hall, John, immigrant of 1853, 78/128

Hall, John H., Ore. governor, 74/149

Hall, Joseph, 63/245; 64/91

Hall, Langley, 78/128,129,149,325,326 (photo)

Hall, Lina Ganty, 64/91,185

Hall, Peter DeSpain, 65/234

Hall, Mrs. Peter DeSpain, SEE Beers, Mrs. Robert

Hall, W.E., 80/137

Hall, Washington, 63/121,123; 68/182

Hall, William Harrison, 77/91

Hall J. Kelley on Oregon, ed. by Powell, review, 74/91

Hallam, Bertha, intro.: "My Medical School," by Lovejoy, 75/7-10

Halleck, Henry Wager, 64/168; 66/76; 67/305N,325N; 68/36: analysis of Indian situation 1866, 79/121-22; Indian scout controversy, 79/129; photo, 79/128

Haller, Granville Owen, 62/78; 66/139N,157N; 68/75; 78/179; 79/245: expeds. against Indians, 67/311-12, 313-14; quoted, 67/295,323N; sends out scouting party, 67/319N-20N; Walla Walla battle report, 67/318N

Haller, Mrs. Granville Owen: Ft. Henrietta named for, 66/139

Hallgren, Harley K., and John F. Due: *United Railways of Oregon*, noted, 62/301

Halliday Bridge, 70/280

Hallock, Absalom B., 80/139,155,166, 166N,168,294,297,313N: biography, 80/289; comment on police system, 80/292-93; influence on Portland police, 80/155N,289; photo, 80/288

Hallock, Ted, 66/59

Hallocula, Annetta, SEE Olney, Annetta

Halloran, James, 65/13

Hallowell, William, 81/387,388,389

Halpin, Lester, 65/251

Halpin, Michael, 69/131

Halsey, John C., 77/81

Halsey, William Frederick, 62/31,32

Halsey, Ore., 73/83: history, 79/104; street names, 79/104

Halsey: Linn County's Centennial City, by Carey and Hainline, noted, 79/104

Halstead, Jacob, 71/17N

Halstead House Hotel, Tacoma, 71/17

Halton, John, 69/131

Halvorson, Alma, 70/47

Halvorson, Clarence, 70/43FF

Halvorson, Halvor, 70/42-49

Halvorson, Helen Olson: biography, 70/39-49

Halvorson, Helen Olson, and Lorraine Fletcher: "19th Century Midwife: Some Recollections," 70/39-49

Halvorson, Henrietta, 70/45,47

Halvorson, Omar, 70/46,47

Halvorson, Walter, 70/46,49

Hamaker, J.O., 76/382

Hamblock, Jane Ann Long, 68/90

Hamblock, John, 68/90

Hamby, Walt, 76/354

Hamelin, Jack, 64/113N

Hamer, Philip M., ed.: *A Guide to Archives and Manuscripts in the United States*, review, 63/244-45

Hamilton, Bruce T.: *Bridges*, by Plowden, review, 78/362-63 *Coyote Was Going There*, ed. by Ramsey, review, 79/335-36 *Fine California Views*, by Palmquist, review, 78/287 *The Fur Trade of the American West*, by Wishart, review, 81/322-23 *McKinley's Bulldog*, by Sternlicht, review, 79/212-13 "Railroad Items," review notes, 80/208-209 *William Clark*, by Steffen, review, 79/100-101

Hamilton, Edward, 64/295; 73/53N
Hamilton, George W., 78/314
Hamilton, Hugh, 66/53
Hamilton, J.L., 80/321N
Hamilton, J.W., Yakima lawyer, 70/163
Hamilton, John D., 78/314
Hamilton, Joseph Layton, 78/124,314
Hamilton, Joseph Layton, Jr., 78/314
Hamilton, L.N., 75/127
Hamilton, M.H., 70/15N
Hamilton, Nancy Amanda Davidson, 78/314
Hamilton, Sarah Watson, 78/236: recollections, 78/300-302,315,317
Hamilton, Ted M., comp.:
Indian Trade Guns, review, 63/77-78
Hamilton, Thomas S., 81/299,301
Hamilton, W.B., Snake River ferryman, 68/229N
Hamilton (ship), 66/79
Hamley, John J., family, 76/381
Hamley and Co., Pendleton, 80/283
Hamlin, Hannibal, 73/41,46
Hamlin, Reason, 79/170N
Hamman, Joseph: stage line, 70/278
Hammer, Seth R., 65/394
Hammitt, Norman P., 71/361
Hammitt, Sarah Francis Zumwalt, 72/353
Hammond, Andrew B.: Ore. railroad construction, 72/301
Hammond, Eleanor, 74/62,157
Hammond, George Peter, 65/198; 78/365: Bancroft Library career, 66/380
Hammond, George Peter, ed.: *Digging For Gold—Without A Shovel; The Letters of Daniel Wadsworth Coit,* noted, 69/276
Hammond, George Peter, and Dale L. Morgan: *Captain Charles M. Weber, Pioneer of the San Joaquin and Founder of Stockton,* review, 68/339-40
Hammond, John Henry, 66/66
Hammond, Vida, photo, 72/208
Hammond, Ore., 65/353
Hammond Life-Saving Station, 64/70

Hammond Lumber Company, 72/301; 74/296; 77/359: Albuquerque, 77/365; Astoria, 77/ 215,216,227; Foss operations, 73/223; Garibaldi, 77/353; Humboldt Bay, 77/ 362; Los Angeles, 77/365 mergers— Georgia-Pacific, 72/293N; Whitney Co., 72/293N; 73/222-23; 77/ 354,362 mill, 73/173; Mill City, 77/215,216; Terminal Island, 77/362
Hammond-Tillamook Lumber Co., 77/354
Hamner, Frank, family, 79/48
Hampden, John, ed.: *Francis Drake, Privateer: Contemporary Narratives and Documents,* noted, 74/95
Hampton, James, 69/229N
Hampton, John Jacob, 66/187
Hampton, Ore., 79/337
Hampton Butte, 66/187
Hams Fork, Green River, 62/364
Hanan (Hannan), Archimedes, 66/145
Hanchett, William H., 63/245
Hancock, Alonzo Wesley (Lon), 67/ 33-34
Hancock, Samuel, 63/116,120
Hancock, Winfield Scott, 64/162; 70/66
Hancock (brig), drawing, 76/198
Hand, William M., 64/173; 66/61: biography, 65/29N,31N; First Ore. Cavalry career, 65/12,14-16,37,60-107 *passim*
Handsaker, Samuel, 78/145
Haney, Bert Emory, 71/224
Hanft, Marshall W., 63/362: "The Cape Forts: Guardians of the Columbia," 65/325-61
Fort Klamath, Frontier Post in Oregon, 1863-1890, by Stone, review, 66/76-77
Fort Stevens: Oregon's Defender at the River of the West, review, 81/423
Seacoast Fortifications of the United States, by Lewis, review, 71/279-81
Hanft, Marshall W., comp.: *Records of Agricultural Agencies in the*

Oregon State Archives, noted, 69/332-33
Hanging Rock, 76/69
Hangings, 75/352,354,355; 79/197; 81/327:
Clatsop Co. first, 73/82; Pacific Co., Wash., 72/171; SEE ALSO Law enforcement; Lynchings
Hanks, J.F., 74/24,29,30: photo, 74/28
Hanks, Jess, 64/89
Hanks, John, 64/89
Hanley, Michael, and Ellis Lucia: *Owyhee Trails, the West's Forgotten Corner*, review, 75/293
Hanley, Michael, and Omer Stanford: *Sage Brush and Axle Grease*, review, 80/103-104
Hanley, William, 69/63,276: quoted, 67/152
Hanlon Drydock and Shipbuilding Co., 77/360
Hanna, Archibald, 64/137N
Hanna, Hiero K., 68/317,319
Hanna, Mark, 66/49: Davenport cartoon, photo, 66/48
Hanna, Stewart, 63/293
Hannah, Dolphes (Adolphus) Brice, 75/128
Hannan, Archimedes, SEE Hanan, Archimedes
Hannestad, Stephen E., and Claudine J. Wieher, comps.: *Black Studies, Select Catalog of National Archives...Publications*, noted, 75/88
Hanrahan, Patrick, 69/131
Hansee, Edgar A., 68/204
Hansell, Stafford, 80/413
Hansen, Julia Butler, 66/382
Hansen, Eleanor, SEE Matthews, Eleanor Hansen
Hansen, Henry P., 79/403
Hansen, T., 62/219N
Hanson, Charles E., Jr., 67/85: *The Northwest Gun*, review, 62/92-93
Hanson (Hansen), Hans, Portland nurseryman, 68/165
Hanson (Hansen), John, Queets Valley settler, 74/19,21,23
Hanson, Ole, 66/73; 75/151

Hanson, Susie Quist, 66/54
Hanson, Theodore, 66/129
Hanzen, Henry, 75/167
Happy Camp, Josephine Co., 72/42
Happy Home Saloon, The Dalles, 70/54
"A Happy Summer on Peacock Spit," by Plumb, reprint noted, 80/207
Happy Valley, Harney Co., 68/321, 322,327
Hard, G.W., 69/229N
Hardeman, Glen O., 69/336
Hardeman, Nicholas Perkins, 66/280: *Wilderness Calling: The Hardeman Family in the American Westward Movement, 1750-1900*, noted, 79/105
Hardeman, Thomas, family, 79/105
Harder, Hans, 69/85
Harder, Jacob, 69/85
Harder, Max, 69/85
Hardesty (Hardisty), Charles, Linn Co. pioneer, 78/234
Hardie, Edward, 63/204
Hardin, Martin D., 70/252,253,254
Harding, Benjamin F., 66/5,8; 72/322,322N 23N; 73/55
Harding, Elisha Jenkins, 66/152N,154, 155,156
Harding, Florence Kling (Mrs. Warren G.), 67/213N,241-42; 78/103-104: photos, 67/244; 78/100
Harding, George Albert, 76/300,301: biography, 79/172-75; drugstore, 79/ 174(photo),175; journal, 79/176-202; photo, 79/173; residence photo, 79/ 202
trip to Idaho mines, 79/172-202— map, 79/186-87
Harding, Henry, 79/175
Harding, J.E., 65/394,398
Harding, James William (Bill), 79/ 172-202*passim*
Harding, Margaret Jane Barlow, 79/175
Harding, Penelope, 79/172
Harding, W.H., 66/22
Harding, Warren Gamaliel: dedication Old Oregon Trail Hwy., 67/ 241,243; 80/105; Oregon visit 1923, 67/241-43; photos, 67/243,244; 78/ 100,102; Pierce recollections, 78/

101-107
80/328

Harding, William (Bill), SEE Harding, James William

Hardisty, Charles, SEE Hardesty, Charles

Hardman, David N., 69/133

Hardman, Nancy E., 69/133

Hardman, Ore., 64/91; 69/133; 73/84

Hardscrabble Point, 78/320

Hare, Ike, 65/296

Hare, W.D., 68/207

Hargreaves, Sheba (Mrs. Fred), 68/203N

Hargrove, J., 69/229N

Harkins, Patrick, 69/131

Harkinson, James, 66/59,62

Harlan, Wilson Barber, 65/314

Harlan, Ore., 64/355

Harlocker, Charles, 63/34

Harlocker, Linton, 63/34

Harlow, Henry, 77/323; 78/44

Harlow, Mahlon, 77/321,324; 78/44, 60,325N; 79/6: residence, 77/320(sketch),325

Harmon, Ray: "Indian Shaker Church," 72/148-58

Harmony Island (Good Harmony), Alaska, 77/185

Harness shops, 80/271,273,274,285: apprenticeship, 80/278-79; photo, 80/284

Harnett, —, British artist, 63/61

Harney, William Selby, 63/184,186N, 187; 67/183; 68/33,35,42,75; 69/ 224-25,326; 70/120; 72/58; 79/31, 32,33,38,125,126

Harney Basin, SEE Harney Valley

Harney County, Ore., 63/286,310-30; 66/368,371; 69/274; 73/279; 77/ 302; 79/38: borax deposits, 73/228,231; history, 64/356; land disputes, 66/67; Peachwood mystery, 63/366; photos, 75/66, 68; range cattle industry, 67/141-59 *passim*; range lands, 63/309; settlers, 78/238

Harney County Historical Society: museum, 69/175; officers and directors, 77/94; 78/94; 79/110; 80/109; 81/109

Harney Electric Cooperative Inc.,

Harney Lake, 63/338,350; 65/40, 50,55,117; 66/59,67; 77/311,332,333; 78/222,223,225,230,235; 79/38,47, 48,282: name, 79/33

Harney Valley, 63/310; 65/25,50-51, 57,66,70; 77/311,315,335,336; 78/ 125,147,220; 79/15,17,18,132: described, 78/207-208,210-11; 79/33; Indians, 65/56,65,81; 78/41,53,139, 149,210,211; photos, 78/230,231; settlement delayed, 79/25

The Harp of a Thousand Strings, by Davis, cited, 66/242

Harper, Ore., 63/279,283-84,303; 67/ 252; 68/91

Harper Ranch, Malheur Co., 63/270, 274,324

Harpham, Everett, 77/285-88

Harpham, Josephine Evans, 63/245; 64/88; 65/121,211,315: "Albert Knowles House," 74/271-74 "County Clerk's Office, Eugene, Ore., 1853-1966," 67/179-81 *Doorways Into History*, noted, 67/281; 74/358 "The Floed House," 65/401-404 "The Night the *Tuscania* Went Down," 77/285-88

Harpooner (HBCO. vessel), 64/208-209

Harrell, James Edwin Ray, 62/244N

Harriet (schooner), 68/263

Harriman, Edward H., 63/355; 69/293

Harriman, Joseph H., 69/310

Harriman Lodge, 68/187

Harris, Albert: biography, 69/57,58

Harris, Bill ("Brass-mouthed Bill"), 63/322,339

Harris, "Black," SEE Harris, Moses

Harris, Carl F., 63/253

Harris, Frankie, 63/313(photo),322

Harris, Gilbert W.: biography, 69/329

Harris, Henry Ellsworth, 63/67-68

Harris, Ira: report on Stark, 72/337; Stark senate seat dispute, 73/31,33,38,40,41,46

Harris, Jack, 63/313(photo),322
Harris, Lawrence T., 66/363,365
Harris, Mary Elizabeth Cooley, 80/104
Harris, Mary Etta Hollister (Mrs. Carl F.), 63/253
Harris, Moses ("Black"), 68/240N,308N; 77/317
Harris, Ralph, 69/57,58
Harris, Simon, 79/253
Harris, Stephen L.:
Fire and Ice: The Cascade Volcanoes, noted, 77/196
Harris, T.S., 65/394
Harris, Truman, 69/58
Harris, William Edwin, 63/67
Harris, William H., Empire City pioneer, 63/11,20:
land claim, 63/13
Harris, William Hamilton, 79/292N,297
"The Harris Anvil," by Clark Moor Will, 69/57-59
Harris Ice Machine Works, Portland, 63/68; 69/329
Harrisburg, Ore., 67/59
Harrison, Benjamin, U.S., president, 64/283
Harriss, —, Beaver, Wash. settler, 74/7
Hart, —, Yreka, Calif., 69/250
Hart, Benjamin H., Yreka, Calif., 69/250N
Hart, Charles, 71/273
Hart, Dan, 63/283
Hart, David C., 69/250N
Hart, Grace, 63/290
Hart, "Grandma," mother of Ivan P., 63/279,285
Hart, Herbert M.:
Old Forts of the Far West, noted, 66/384
Old Forts of the Northwest, review, 65/202-203
Old Forts of the Southwest, noted, 66/384
Hart, Ivan P., 63/269,272,283,286,289, 294,296,300
Hart, James:
Letters of George Catlin and His Family, A Chronicle of the American West, review, 68/77-79
Hart, M.S., 79/163N
Hart, Mart, 63/289,294-95

Hart, Mary (Mrs. Dan), 63/283
Hart, Moses (Mose), Westfall sheepman, 63/268:
stone house, 67/374
Hart, Moses, Yreka, Calif., 69/250N
Hart, Patrick, 69/115,131
Hart, Tom, 63/28
Hart (Warner) Mountain, 72/7,7N,16N; 79/284N:
photo, 79/279; 81/328
Hart and Jones, Westfall saloon, 63/293
Harte, Bret, 62/319
Hartford (vessel), photo, 62/12
Hartin, Michael, 69/131
Hartleib, Francis, 70/316,318
Hartley, Roland Hill, 72/229
Hartman, John P., 74/117
Hartman, Wesley, 77/90
Hartmus, Laurence, 74/63
Hart's Hotel, SEE Westfall Hotel
Hart's Saloon, Westfall, 63/273,286, 294,296:
photo, 63/278
Hartville, Wyo., 73/286
Hartwell, Barbara Bartlett (Mrs. Mortimer H.), 66/189,285,395; 67/380; 68/361; 69/347; 71/372:
Green Timber, by Ripley, review, 70/67-68
Sprigs of Rosemary, noted, 76/381-82
Hartzell, Laura, 74/30
Hartzell, W.S., 74/21
Harvest Queen (steamer), 71/22N
Harvey, Amos, 68/163N
Harvey, Daniel, Jr., 63/232
Harvey, Daniel, Sr., 62/313; 63/212, 232-33; 76/299
Harvey, Eloisa Maria McLoughlin Rae (Mrs. Daniel, Sr.), 63/192,209,212,216: fictionalized biography, 64/349
Harvey, Mrs. Francis Moreland, photo, 81/254
Harvey, James, 63/232
Haskell, Burdette G., 75/128
Haskell, Charles H., 63/12
Haskell, Inez, 71/101
Hassalo (steamer, first of name), 79/176
Hassalo (steamer, second of name), 63/66; 75/82

Hassrick, Peter H.: *Frederic Remington*, noted, 74/285
Hastings, Charles L., 76/301
Hastings, Lansford W., 64/281; 78/88: guide reassessed, 70/85
Hastings, Lucius B., 80/10,10N
Hasty Messenger and Express Co., Portland, 79/346
Haswell, Robert: *Columbia Rediviva* log quoted, 68/105,106; drawing, 76/198
Hatch, F.M., 71/172: Hawaiian annexation, 71/175
Hatch, Peter H., 73/247,253
Hatch, William G., 69/223,241,253
Hatch, Z.J., 63/64-65
The Hatchet Men: The Story of the Tong Wars in San Francisco's Chinatown, by Dillon, review, 64/75-76
Hatfield, Job, 66/383
Hatfield, Mark Odom, 62/110,206,302, 422; 63/93,255,373; 64/93,189,285, 363; 65/125,221,317,416; 66/93,189, 285,392,394; 67/377,378; 74/241; 79/411; 80/412:
Baptists and the Oregon Frontier, by Miller, review, 69/324-25
Hathaway, John Samuel, 64/209, 228N-29N: delirium tremens, 64/209N; suicide, 64/209N
Hathaway *vs.* Walker, 62/152-53
Hatton, R.B. ("Rube"), 68/324
Hatton, Raymond R.: *Bend in Central Oregon*, noted, 79/408 *High Country of Central Oregon*, noted, 81/329 *High Desert of Central Oregon*, noted, 79/336-37
Hats, SEE Prices
Havighurst, Walter, 66/244
Hawaiian Club, Boston, 68/53
The Hawaiian Flag, by Houston, cited, 64/27N
Hawaiian Islands, 62/7,10,23,24,26,29, 69,202,240N; 63/119,182,184,186, 190,199,206,218; 64/7,317-18; 70/ 360; 72/180; 76/119,129; 77/43; 80/197,201:

agriculture 18th century, 69/83; aids U.S. in Spanish-American War, 71/165-66; American missionaries, 62/11; 63/ 358; American missionary policy, SEE Sandwich Islands Mission; articles on, 70/88; artifacts collection, 80/197-99; aviation, 68/278-79; British consul, 64/29; British navy, 70/88,307; Calif. gold report reaches, 72/182; cession to Great Britain, 64/26-27; crime statistics, 67/372
described—
1824-25, 64/25-26; 1852, 71/365 dispute with France 1839, 68/57-58; famine mortality, 72/181; first delegate to Congress, 68/87; flag history, 64/ 27N; history, 69/334; 74/279,285 Hudson's Bay Co. in, 74/352— records, 69/84
Japanese, 71/161-62; manuscripts pertaining to, 65/198; medical school, 69/84; missionaries, 74/279; *Modeste* crew in, 63/182; newspaper microfilm project, 67/372; Niihau history, 65/ 214; photography, 69/84; population characteristics 1778-1850, 66/280; Provisional Govt., 71/161N; revolution of 1893, 68/73; royalty portraits, 64/5-32; Russia declines protection, 72/111; Russians in, 65/213; sheep transported to, 1829, 63/199; ships list 1794-1847, 71/365; shipping, 71/365; 75/76,77; smallpox epidemic 1853, 67/86,372; sovereignty question, 68/186; stepping-stone to Orient, 71/161-78; sugar trust, 71/173,175; trade and commerce, 71/161-78,365; treaty with U.S. 1854, 67/367
U.S. acquisition, 62/11; 76/273— annexation question, 63/358; 65/ 365; arguments for, 71/161-78; commercial reasons, 712/167-78; Japan view of, 71/162-64,175-76
urban society, 69/83; whalers in, 68/54,347; 76/123; SEE ALSO Pearl Harbor
The Hawaiian Kingdom, by Kuykendall, noted, 69/334
Hawaiian Mission Children's Society,

64/318N
Hawaiian people, 70/362; 74/90; 80/140:
California, 74/93; Cowlitz Farm laborers, 63/117,120,129,134,139,142-43, 157; Douglas Co., 73/283; emigration before 1858, 68/348; Ft. George laborers, 64/212,219-22,226-40*passim*; Ft. Vancouver, 68/89; 74/93; Klamath River area 1870s, 68/187; London visit of royalty, 64/5-32; on NW Coast, 70/ 88; Pacific NW pioneers, 65/316; 73/ bk.cov. Sept.
Hawes, Florence Smith, 66/53
Hawgood, John A., 64/283:
America's Western Frontier: The Exploration and Settlement of the Trans-Mississippi West, review, 69/69-70
Hawkins, Gretchen Smith (Mrs. Russell, Jr.), 73/222,223-24
Hawkins, Helen (Mrs. Russell, Sr.), 72/297,305; 73/5,179,189
Hawkins, Margaret, 72/297,305; 73/5,223
Hawkins, Russell, Jr., 72/293-314*passim*; 73/5,8,9,14,182,220,222: biography, 73/223-24
Hawkins, Russell, Sr., 72/293,294,305; 73/5,179; 77/215,216,354: death, 73/223; lumber interests, 72/301
Hawks, Thomas, 64/206N
Hawley, Brooks, and Melvin L. Kathan: *A Brief History of a Town and a Gold Dredge in the Sumpter Valley*, noted, 69/78
Hawley, Ira, 62/299
Hawley, James H., 62/214; 68/186; 70/15N
Hawley, Nirom, 70/358
Hawley, Robert Emmett: *Skqee Mus*, reprint noted, 73/75
Hawley, Willis Chatman, 67/42; 71/221; 80/395
Hawley Pulp and Paper Co., Ore. City, 76/299
Hawthorn, James, 74/24
Hawthorne, Mont, 63/247
Hay, Marion E., 72/227; 74/106,135
Hay, 74/317; 76/19:

hay knife, 76/351-52; photo, 76/20; stacking described, 63/323
Hay Creek, Jefferson Co., 65/21N
Hay Creek Ranch, Jefferson Co., 72/341; 79/147N; 81/297,298,301,311: map, 81/282; photo, 72/342
Hayashi, Francis M., 81/153,167
Haycox, Betty J., SEE Haycox, Stephen W.
Haycox, Ernest, 68/279; 72/229: biography, 65/314; described, 74/52-54; fiction checklist, 65/216; memorial library, 65/216
Haycox, Stephen W. and Betty J., eds.: *Melvin Ricks' Alaska Bibliography*, review, 78/359
Hayden, Benjamin, 66/149; 81/93N: photo, 66/150
Hayden, Estella, 81/93
Hayden, Ferdinand V., 64/281; 70/73; 75/79
Hayden, John H., 80/288,295: biography, 80/290
Hayden Bridge, 66/187
Hayes, —, capt. Ore. Volunteers 1855, 62/78
Hayes, Anna (Mrs. Edmund), 68/102
Hayes, Clara, 74/62
Hayes, Edmund, 62/110,206,302,420, 423; 63/93-94,255-56,370-71,373; 64/93,189,285,363; 65/125,221, 317,416; 66/93,189,285,385,392,395; 67/380; 68/357,361; 69/342,347; 70/368,370,371,372,373,374; 71/ 369,370,371,372; 72/357,358-59,360, 361; 73/362,364; 74/183,363,366; 75/367; 78/369:
The European Discovery of America, by Morison, review, 72/343-44
"Gray's Adventure Cove," 68/101-10
Pacific Crossing, by Luxton, review, 73/273
Hayes, James, Union Pacific press rep., 74/62
Hayes, Jay Orlo: mint industry, 72/182
Hayes, Jeff W.: biography, 79/345-46; boosterism, 79/345-47; photo, 79/347
Hayes, Jeff W.:

Looking Backward at Portland, review, **79**/345-57

Portland, Oregon, cited, **79**/345

Tales of the Sierras, cited, **79**/346

Hayes, Rutherford Birchard: disputed 1876 election, **67**/257-72*passim*; Jacksonville visit, **66**/92; Oregon visit, **72**/171

Hayes, Tom, **76**/46

Hayhurst, Billy, **81**/246

Haymarket riot, **75**/127,133

Haynes, Bessie Doak and Edward, eds.: *The Grizzly Bear: Portraits from Life*, review, **67**/358

Haynes, Joseph T., **75**/137,138

Hays, J., Portland deputy marshal, **80**/28

Hays, John, Grass Valley homesteader, **75**/44

Hays, John, Siam businessman, **71**/155-57

Hays, Samuel P., **66**/89: *Conservation and the Gospel of Efficiency: The Progressive Conservation Movement, 1890-1920*, review, **62**/188-92

Haystack, Sherman Co., **65**/16

Hayter, Carey, **78**/164: family, **77**/268

Hayter, Elizabeth, **78**/159: photo, **78**/160

Hayter, Eugene, **77**/268

Hayter, George, **64**/18

Hayter, John, **64**/12,15: biography, **64**/18; lithograph by, **64**/28

Hayter, Mark, **77**/268

Hayter, Oscar, **77**/268

Haywood, William Dudley, **62**/106; **64**/282; **65**/214,383; **68**/186; **69**/180,337; **74**/280; **75**/93-94

Haywood Quartet (music group), **62**/178

Hazard, Louis H., **63**/34

Hazelia School, Clackamas Co.: history, **66**/382

Hazelnuts, **76**/22

Hazeltine, George Irving, **73**/364

Hazeltine, Martin Mason, **66**/381

Hazeltine, William, **70**/54

Hazen, Henry, **68**/129

Hazen, William Babcock, **69**/84-85,172

He Built Seattle: A Biography of Judge Thomas Burke, by Nesbit, review, **62**/405-406

Head, Bill, **81**/274

Head, Dora, **74**/21,22

Headlight, Tillamook: quoted on compulsory school bill, **75**/174

Healey, John J., **79**/363

Healey, Thomas, **68**/243N,245,311

"A Healing Service in the Shaker Church," by Robert H. Ruby, **67**/347-55

Health: California, **71**/364; public in Oregon, **62**/203

Healy, William, **62**/182

Healy families, Morrow Co., **69**/131

Heaney, Charles, **76**/267-68

Hearne, Samuel, **65**/212

Hearst, George, **71**/146

Hearst, Phoebe Apperson, **71**/146

Hearst, William Randolph, **71**/146

Heart Mountain: The History of an American Concentration Camp, by Nelson, review, **77**/297-98

Heath, William, mate on *Ganymede*, **64**/199N

Heatherly, James R., **71**/189

Heatherton, Frank, **69**/131

Heathfield (ship), **66**/122

Hebard, Grace Raymond, **62**/288,289, 290-91; **68**/186: *Sacajawea*, cited, **71**/255-57

Heceta Beach, **76**/178

Heceta Head, **74**/354

Heck, Silas (Indian), **63**/83

The Hedden's Store Handbook of Proprietary Medicines, by White, noted, **76**/92

Hedges, Ada Hastings, **74**/58,65,157: photo, **73**/296

Hedges, Joseph Eugene, **76**/301

Hedges, William, **74**/58

Hedlund, O., **66**/306

Heesath (Indian), **79**/313,314,316, 317,320

Heffernan, Robert D., Jr., **64**/280; **65**/124,312,416; **66**/85,93,189,279,285, 394; **67**/376,380; **68**/361; **69**/343, 348; **70**/373; **74**/183,365

Heffner, Mrs. Daniel, 67/44
Hegg, E.A., 69/75-76; 73/70
Heifer, Samuel, 62/219N
Heikkala, Jan, trans.:
"Portland Assembly Center: Diary of Saku Tomita," 81/149-63
Heine, William, 65/143
Heinrich, Albert C., 69/328
Heinze, Frederick Augustus, 64/349
Heitfield, Henry, 71/196
Helekomits, Marie, 66/348N
Helen B. Sterling (schooner), 75/362
Helena, Mont., 67/235; 72/231:
stock exchange, 69/204
Helfrich, Devere, 66/80,81,382
Helfrich, Devere and Helen, 78/363; 80/104:
The Applegate Trail, cited, 77/292; review, 72/351-52
Helfrich, Helen, SEE Helfrich, Devere
Helgeson, Arlan:
Farms in the Cutover: Agricultural Settlement in Northern Wisconsin, review, 64/79-81
Heliographs, 73/357; 74/202:
photo, 73/355
Helix, Ore., 63/365; 73/285
Hellman, M.S., 70/241
Hells Canyon, 68/87; 72/233,254:
dam building, 65/315; steamboat run, 63/359
Helm, Boone, 64/357
Helm, Dick, 76/70,79
Helm, Elizabeth Maria Sager, 74/219
Helm, George R., 80/169
Helman, Abel, 69/88
Helmcken, Cecilia Douglas, 77/294
Helmcken, John Sebastian:
biography, 77/294; reminiscences, 77/294
Helmick, Sarah Steeprow, 75/363
Helms, Ad, 76/354
Helms, Irene H.:
Remembering—School Days of Old Crook County, review, 81/207
Helms, Mary Carroll (Mrs. Perry), 73/267
Helms, Perry, 73/267
Helms, William G., 68/352

Helton, H. Stephen, and Daniel T. Goggin, comps.:
General Records of the Department of State, noted, 64/277
Hemanoth (Indian), 79/313,315,316, 321
Hembree, Absalom J.:
death, 66/143N,155; grave monument photo, 66/158
Hembree, Ada, 75/46
Hembree, Al, 75/46
Hembree, James Thomas, photo, 81/258
Hembree, Waman C.:
"Yakima Indian War Diary," cited, 66/148N,149N
Hemenway, Stacy, 69/329
Hemingway, Ezra L., 65/115N
Hemlock trees, 72/303,307,310; 73/17,174; 77/390:
Western hemlock, 77/349,351,353
Henderson, Mrs. —, Chanticleer Inn owner, 66/269
Henderson, Daniel:
The Hidden Coasts: A Biography of Admiral Charles Wilkes, noted, 79/405
Henderson, E.P., and Hollis M. Dole:
"The Port Orford Meteorite," cited, 66/90; 69/32,48,333; map of Evans' route, 69/46-47
Henderson, James H.D.:
military camp named for, 65/299
Henderson, John L., 63/15
Henderson (sternwheeler), 64/352; 66/80; 81/39
"Henderson Luelling, Seth Lewelling and the Birth of the Pacific Coast Fruit Industry," by Thomas C. McClintock, 68/153-74
Henderson's Ranch, 70/18N
Hendrick Hudson (steamer), 77/129
Hendricks, George W., photo, 80/324
Hendricks, H.H., 79/31
Hendricks, James M., 78/325N
Hendricks, Robert J., 67/274; 78/104:
Bethel and Aurora, cited, 79/233N,242
Hendricks, Thomas A., 67/268
Hendrickson, Agness, 66/55
Hendrickson, Gus, 72/301
Hendrickson, J. Hunt, 71/239

Hendrickson, James E.: *Joe Lane of Oregon: Machine Politics and the Sectional Crisis, 1849-1861*, review, **68**/333

"Rupture of the Democratic Party in Oregon, 1858," noted, **68**/346

Hendry, William: journal 1828, **65**/309

Henley, Thomas J., **66**/226N

Henley, Ore., **78**/363

Hennessey, William, photo, **77**/72

Hennessy, Frank D., **62**/172

Hennessy, George, **69**/117,131

Henry, Alexander, the elder, **76**/319

Henry, Alexander, the younger, **63**/203; **77**/81: journal, **63**/84; **64**/92; **66**/332-33; **70**/226

Henry, Andrew, **72**/260

Henry, Anson G., **65**/217

Henry, B. Tyler, **64**/188

Henry, Francis, **65**/217

Henry, Len, **67**/88

Henry, Will: *From Where the Sun Now Stands*, review, **62**/295-96

Henry, William, Willamette post, **77**/81

Henry (brig), **80**/4(photo),15

Henry Davidson Sheldon and the University of Oregon, 1874-1948, by Hitchman, noted, **81**/330

Henry Failing (ship), **66**/119

Henry Villard (steamer), **66**/112N

"Henry Villard and Oregon's Transportation Development, 1863-1881," by Cochran, cited, **71**/75N-96N*passim*

Henry Villard and the University of Oregon, by Belknap, review, **77**/380

Hens, SEE Prices

Hensill, Mary Jane, **62**/300

Hensill, S.M., **62**/300

Hensley, George Newton, **80**/269-71, 280,281

Hensley, J.L., **80**/22

Hepburn, Arthur J., **62**/23

Heppner, Henry, **69**/115; **80**/119

Heppner, Ore., **73**/285; **80**/120: flood, **69**/136; **77**/192; Irish, **69**/103-47*passim*; photos, **69**/126,129; warehouse photo 1880s, **67**/131

Heppner Gazette, **80**/119

Herald (British vessel), **64**/241

Herald, Portland, **80**/290,295N

Herbert, Hilary A., **71**/144-45

Herbs, **69**/157

Hercules (sternwheel towboat), **81**/81

Hercules (tug), photo, **75**/ins.fr.cov. June

Here Comes the Polly, by Becker, review, **73**/70

Herman Creek, **75**/280

Herman Prairie, **63**/18

Hermann, Binger, **63**/26,253; **64**/355; **67**/67; **68**/319-20; **69**/330: letter to Barrett, **71**/154

Hermann, George, **63**/26

Hermann, Henry H., **63**/25-26; **70**/184

Hermann, T.M., **63**/25

Hermes (Coast Guard cutter), **80**/48

Hermiston, Ore., **62**/401N; **73**/285: electric co-op, **80**/328; irrigation district, **63**/365; population growth, **64**/352; pheasant breeding farm, **65**/256

Hermiston Herald: history, **80**/105

Hermits, **77**/184

Herns, Wash., **72**/354

Hero (steamer), **66**/127

Herr, Marian: review of children's books, **62**/101-102

Herren, Effie, **80**/229-57*passim*: photos, **80**/228,256

Herren, Elizabeth Sharp, **80**/229

Herren, Elvira C. (Charlotte), **80**/240N,247,249,251,252

Herren, Frank, **80**/256

Herren, John, son of Theodore, **80**/229-57*passim*: photos, **80**/228,256

Herren, John C., **79**/31: family, **80**/229

Herren, Levi, **80**/256

Herren, Mary E. Lacey (Mrs. Theodore): biography, **80**/229-30,257; journal, **80**/231-57; photo, **80**/228

Herren, Theodore, **80**/229-57*passim*: photos, **80**/228,256

Herren, William J., Marion Co. pioneer, **70**/358; **72**/91

Herren, William J., Heppner area rancher, **81**/262

Herrin Ranch, **76**/352

Herriott, F.L., **62**/129

Heslin, James J., **73**/364: "Historical Societies—Prophets and Profits," **73**/365-72

Heslin, Michael, **69**/131

Heslin, Thomas, **69**/131

Hesse, Margaret Putnam: *Scholls Ferry Tales*, noted, **78**/91

Hessig, John Humboldt, **76**/382

Hester, Wilhelm: photographs, **67**/85

Hetch Hetchy Valley, **74**/134

Heumann, Sebastian F., **66**/382

Hewett, Isabelle, **79**/203,205(photo)

Hewitt, Abraham S., **67**/260,261,269

Hewitt, C.C., **63**/185

Hewitt, Jim, **66**/90

Hewitt, Mary: *Marysville Revisited*, noted, **77**/299

Hewitt, Randall H., **72**/76

Hewot, "Alkali Frank," **73**/260

Heyburn, Weldon B., **67**/371; **72**/ 183,228

Heyter, Augusta, **74**/220

Hiachenee (Hyacheny, Hachinee) (Indian), **70**/34,148,149,161,162: identity, **70**/148N; speech 1878 council, **70**/36-38

Hiaqua, SEE Dentalium

Hiatt, Bill, **70**/59

Hiatt, Isaac, **67**/150: *Thirty-One Years in Baker County*, reprint noted, **72**/171

Hibbard, George, Queets Valley settler, **74**/21

Hibbard, George Allen, **63**/88

Hibbard, George L., **70**/374; **74**/183

Hibbard, Henry, **74**/19,21

Hibbard, L. Eugene, **63**/339

Hibbard, Trenton R.: recollections, **72**/353

Hickey and Clifford, vaudeville team, **66**/41

Hickeys (tokens): Umatilla Co. use, **73**/81

Hickman, Sarah, SEE Read, Sarah

Hickman

Hickman, William A., **67**/225

Hickman, William Edward, **77**/193

Hicks, John D., **63**/359; **66**/89; **72**/179; **74**/350: *My Life With History: An Autobiography*, review, **70**/173-75

Hiday, Mrs. Harry I., comp.: *The U.S. Census of Josephine County, Oregon, 1870*, noted, **74**/281

Hidden, Lowell M., **67**/366

The Hidden Coasts: A Biography of Admiral Charles Wilkes, by Henderson, noted, **79**/405

The Hidden Northwest, by Cantwell, review, **74**/90-91

Higbee, Fred, **74**/5

Higgins, Christopher P., **65**/121

Higgins, Dick, **70**/50

Higgins, Harris, **70**/50

Higgins, Letitia Work, **63**/230N

Higgins, William, Hill *vs.* Higgins, **62**/148N

Higgins, William, Portland marshal, **80**/10,12,13-14,21,24,28: biography, **80**/10N

Higgins families, Morrow Co., **69**/131

Higginson, Ella, **70**/359

High Country of Central Oregon, by Hatton, noted, **81**/329

High Desert of Central Oregon, by Hatton, noted, **79**/336-37

Highland Park Addition, Portland, **64**/265

"The Highroad of the Highlands," by Francis S. Landrum, **75**/233-39

Highsmith, Richard M., Jr., ed.: *Atlas of the Pacific Northwest Resources and Development*, noted, **69**/331; **81**/331; review, **63**/356

Highways, **72**/26: Alaska-South America, **74**/210; Canadian, **70**/179; **77**/303; coast, **77**/219, 222,284(photo); construction, **74**/81; effect of gas tax, **74**/139; engineers, **74**/101,102; first bitulithic paving, **74**/118; first federal in Washington, **66**/284; Hanford, **66**/284; Heppner-Pendleton, **69**/137,145

Interstate 5, **69**/87—completion, **68**/89

Morrow Co., **69**/145; Mt. Hood Loop, **74**/124; national legislation, **74**/101,134,137; national system created, **74**/137; Ocean Beach, **75**/105-106; Ochoco, **73**/267,268; Oregon development, **71**/198; Pacific Hwy., **74**/225; paving, **74**/104,118(photo),139; Redwood Hwy., **76**/59; theses index, **72**/274; U.S. Highway 20, **78**/212 (photo),241-42

U.S. Highway 97, **69**/87—photos, **75**/234,249

Winnemucca-to-the-Sea, **66**/281; SEE ALSO Columbia River Highway; Old Oregon Trail Highway; Roads and trails

Highways Into History, by Fleming, noted, **74**/96

Higley, Alfred V., **74**/30,31: homestead, **74**/31

Higley, Anne, SEE Slater, Anne Higley

Higley, Margaret Donaldson, **74**/28 (photo),29,31,32

Higley, Orte, **74**/30

Higley, Ransom, **74**/31,32: homestead, **74**/33

Higley's Hotel, Lake Quinault, **74**/31,32

Hiking, **74**/358:

Forest Grove-Seaside, **77**/67-71; SEE ALSO Mountaineering

Hilborn, Samuel Greeley, **76**/292-93

Hildebrand, August, photo, **81**/194

Hile, L., **74**/21

Hill, Bennett Hoskin, **63**/194

Hill, Charles, **62**/298

Hill, D.G.:

"The Negro in Oregon, a Survey," cited, **73**/203

Hill, David, immigrant of 1853, **62**/243-83*passim*,338-88*passim*

Hill, Edgar P., photo, **81**/44

Hill, Edna May, comp.: *Josephine County Historical Highlights*, noted, **78**/287-88

Hill, H., Hill *vs.* Higgins, **62**/148N

Hill, Hanks Neville, **78**/131,144,207: recollections, **78**/222-23,224,236,

244-46

Hill, Henry, Wheeler Co. sheepman, **64**/110

Hill, James Jerome, **63**/355; **65**/255; **66**/251; **70**/86; **78**/358:

Deschutes railroad construction, **69**/293FF; nation's longest railroad dream, **71**/197; plan for shipping line to Japan, **71**/143; praised by John Barrett, **71**/159

Hill, Jim, Westfall resident, **63**/273

Hill, John, Coos Co. pioneer, **63**/17,24,26

Hill, John, Lane Co. ferryman, **78**/322

Hill, Laban:

1880 letter, **66**/51; photo, **66**/51

Hill, Lindsey, **78**/144

Hill, Louis, photo, **69**/292

Hill, Louis W., Family Foundation, **70**/371; **71**/295

Hill, Mary Hill (Mrs. Samuel), **66**/251; **78**/110,357

Hill, Minnie, **63**/252

Hill, Reuben Coleman, **64**/134

Hill, Robert M., **78**/224

Hill, Samuel, **62**/298; **66**/249; **78**/107: biography, **66**/251; Columbia River Hwy. project, **66**/253,255,259; family, **78**/357; Good Roads interest, **66**/249N-51N; highway promotion, **74**/105-12*passim*,135-36,137,210,214; marriage, **66**/251; photos, **66**/250; **74**/110; **78**/108; Pierce recollections, **78**/108-11

Hill, Sarah, **72**/181

Hill, Stan, photo, **71**/252

Hill, Tom (Indian), **72**/183

Hill, William G., **70**/74,271

Hill, Mrs. William G.: recollections, **73**/72

Hill, William J., **72**/183

Hill, William Lair, **67**/265; **78**/175: biography, **81**/229N; opinion of pioneers' motives, **81**/229-30

Hillcrest School, Astoria, **62**/199

Hilleary, William Morris, **65**/182N: diary cited, **65**/186N,189N

Hillebrand, Anthony, **76**/301

Hiller, Elizabeth, and Dorothy Darneille, eds.:

Oldtimer Recipes, noted, 63/357
Hillman, Ore., SEE Terrebonne, Ore.
Hillman Creek, 63/264
Hillman Gulch, 63/301
Hills, Cornelius Joel, 64/91-92; 78/325N: family, 66/383
Hills Creek Dam, 78/320
The Hills-Neet Story, by Chapman, noted, 66/383
Hillsboro, Ore., 72/295; 80/11,366,376: hotel, 64/89
Hillsboro Argus, 74/238
Hillside, Washington Co., 80/106
Hillyer, Edwin: gold rush journal 1850, 67/370
Himbert, John, 65/19
Himes, George Henry, 62/417; 64/178,181,342; 66/354N; 70/197N: Denny memorial 1907, 65/246; photos, 70/206,208; 81/254
Himes and Daly, Portland printers, 64/175,177,180-82
Hinchinbrook (Nuchek) Island, 77/184
Hinckley, Theodore C., 63/360; 64/283; 65/215; 66/280; 67/87,280,368: *The Oregon Trail*, by Parkman, ed. by Feltskog, review, 70/353-54
"William H. Seward Visits His Purchase," 72/127-47
Hinds, Richard Brinsley, 70/88
Hindu people, 71/364; 74/306: Astoria, 75/294; Pacific Coast, 70/365
Hine, Robert V.: *California's Utopian Colonies*, noted, 68/82
Edward Kern and American Expansion, review, 63/345-46
Hine, Robert V., and Edwin R. Bingham, eds.: *The American Frontier, Readings and Documents*, noted, 73/360
The Frontier Experience: Readings in the Trans-Mississippi West, review, 65/307-308
Hine, Robert V., and Savoie Lottinville, eds.: *Soldier in the West: Letters of Theodore Talbot..., 1845-53*, review, 74/355-56

Hines, Celinda E., 62/244N
Hines, Donald M., 66/281: *An Index of Archived Resources for...the Inland Pacific Northwest Frontier*, review, 77/297
Hines, Gustavus, 62/121,122N,244, 248N,396,397; 66/347N,350,354N; 78/129,143: comment on Indians, 73/67; quoted, 62/124
Hines, Gustavus: *Oregon*, reprint noted, 74/359
Hines, Harvey Kimball, 62/244N; 78/129,143
Hines, Joseph, 62/244N
Hines Lumber Company, 77/329
Hinkle, John, 68/91
Hinman, Alanson: biography, 71/19N; McConnell partnership, 71/6,13,19,20,21,22; photo, 71/20
Hinsdale, Mrs. G. Spencer, 71/372
Hinshaw, Dwight: *Terrible Trail: The Meek Cutoff, 1845*, by Clark and Tiller, review, 68/79-81
Hinton, Clayton B., 65/121
Hinton, W.J., 62/300-301
Hinton Creek, 69/123,138
Hiram Martin Chittenden: His Public Career, by Dodds, noted, 77/291; review, 74/354-55
Hirata family, 81/156
Hirl, Dan, 69/131
Hirl, Ned, 69/131
Hirohito, Emperor of Japan, 62/27,34
Hirsch, Max S., 62/179; 73/294
Historians: academic, 73/369; amateur, 73/369; and Federal Records Center, 70/363; and National Archives, 71/290; frontier, 70/86; fur trade, 67/369; views on U.S. expansion, 72/209-13,224; Western, 71/292; SEE ALSO names of historians
The Historian's Handbook, a Descriptive Guide to Reference Works, by Pulton, noted, 73/360
Historic American Buildings Survey Catalog of Measured Drawings and Photographs...

in the Library of Congress, noted, 70/77 Historic buildings and houses, 70/261, 273; 71/294,295: Abernethy house, Oak Point, 72/354; Ainsworth house, 67/89; 71/294; Andrews, Peter, house, 63/322-23; Applegate, Charles, house, 81/106 Astoria, 71/200; 76/304— Flavel house, 68/89; 69/175,340; Leonard & Green bldg. 1855 photo, 81/4; Shively house photo, 81/4 Aurora, 62/299; 68/352; 70/184; 71/200,294— Keil house, 62/200,299 Baker, 71/199; Baker cabin, Carver, 71/199; 75/87; Barclay house, Ore. City, 76/302-303; Bellinger house, 68/89; Black, Henry, house, 69/339; Blair house, 67/92; Boelling, Conrad, house, 70/184; Boise, Reuben P., house photo, 66/18; Breyman-Boise house, 69/86-87; Brown, John A., house, 73/80; Brown, Sam, house, 68/352; Brown farmhouse, Lebanon, 66/284; Brownsville railroad station, 66/91; Burkhart house, 69/86,339; Calbert house, Chinookville, 71/361 Calif. mission buildings— San Juan, 80/241,242(photo); San Miguel Archangel, 80/243,243N; Santa Barbara, 80/245; Santa Ynes, 80/244N Caples house, 68/352; 73/80; Case, William M., house, 72/353; century houses, 71/200; Charity Grange Hall, 67/90; Chehalis, 66/32; Cherry house, 68/89; Christian, Daniel, house, 63/245; Coe, H.S., house, 63/363; Cole, David, house, 73/80; Columbia River, 75/88; Colver, Samuel, house, 68/352; Conser house, 68/186; Corbett, Henry W., house photo, 74/ins.fr. cov. March Corvallis, 77/299— Benton Co. courthouse, 68/90; 70/184; 71/294; Gathercoal house, 71/199 Cottage Grove, 70/184; Crook Co. courthouse, 71/294; DeWitt house,

63/364; Dibble, Horace, house, 73/ 80; Diblee family home, 67/89; Drain, 68/89,187; Duncan Bldg., Newberg, 65/218 Eugene, 73/81— Peters-Liston-Wintermeier house, 65/121; Skinner cabin, 72/89 Fenton Bldg., 75/294; Ft. Dalles Surgeon's Quarters, 71/101; SEE ALSO Fort Dalles; Ft. Vancouver chief factor's house replica, 80/101; French Prairie, 66/338-39,348; Gardner, A.D., house, 65/218; 68/89; Gay, George, house replica, 64/88; Geer, R.C. and T.T., house, 64/359; 69/87; Gold Hill City Hall, 63/363; Gold house, Skidgate, 71/367; Graham, Samuel M., house, Marshland, 65/308; Hale, Andrew, house, 73/83; Hall, John, house, 62/ 205; Hanks, John and Jess, house, 64/ 89; Hermann, Henry, house, 63/26; 70/184; Herren house photo, 80/256 Hillsboro— Bluefields photo, 80/366; Geyer house, 80/366-68; Schulmerick house, 80/376 Hines house, Forest Grove, 71/199- 200; Hoskins store, Benton Co., 64/ 89; Houston house, 68/89; Huntington, D.L., house, 66/80; Hustler, J.G., house, 68/352; Idaho assay office, 63/ 89; Irving house, Lake Oswego, 71/ 200; Jackson, C.S., house, 62/204 Jacksonville, 62/299; 67/369; 68/352— Beekman Bank, 63/252; Beekman house, 63/262,363; Bigler house, 71/200; Catalog house, 65/215 Keyes place, Wheeler Co., 64/104; Klosterman house, 62/300; Knight, Adam, house, 68/352; Knowles, Albert, house, Mapleton, 74/271-74; Knox-Steward house, Ontario, 68/352; Kraus house, 71/200 Lane Co., 67/281; 69/340; 74/358— early farm buildings, 66/383 Lewis, L. Allen, house, 68/352; Light House, Medford, 65/218; Lindgren,

Erik, house, 70/184; 73/72; Linn Co., 63/363; 68/186; Long cabin, 69/341; McFadden, O.B., house, 66/32; McGowan house, Kelso, 66/80; Martin, W.M., house, 63/245; Masonic Hall, Dayton, 62/201; Masters, A.J., house, 67/374; 69/86; Mock, John, house, 73/80; Montague, Calif., 66/81-82; Morrow-Sutherland house, 64/353; Moses general store, 70/184; Moyer house, Brownsville, 66/91; 71/200; New Era post office, 65/315; Newell house, 68/89; 69/177; 71/294; Old College Hall, Pacific Univ., 62/200; 69/177; Orth, John, house, 70/184; Palmer house, 66/383; Parrish house, 68/187; Phillips, John, house, 69/86; Philomath College, 73/81; Polk Co. courthouse, 75/346,350; Portland, SEE Portland—buildings; Portland—historic houses

preservation—

Bullock address on, 63/371; landmark ordinances, 66/283; OHS program, 71/101-104,293-95; Skidmore Fountain area, Portland, 62/204

Putnam mill, 68/352; Red Crown Mills, Albany, 66/90; Red House, Sellwood, 72/90; St. Helens, 67/370; St. Johns City Hall, 73/80

Salem, 69/341—

armory, 64/89; Bennett house, 64/275; 66/143N; Bush house, 69/174; Capital National Bank, 65/218; Deepwood house, 71/199; 72/353; Lee house, 66/82,283; Lee mission parsonage, 63/254; 64/353; 65/218; 66/81,283; 67/92; 69/339,341; 71/294,365; Senate Saloon, 62/200

Scott-Gales house, 68/89; Seeck livery stables, 70/184; Shaniko City Hall, 64/91; Silvertooth Bldg., Antelope, 66/91; Six Mile House stage station, 63/253; Slocum house, 66/382; 67/366; 68/352; Smith, Steve, house, 62/200; Steinbach house, 68/352; Stone House, Vale, 68/230N; 70/17,18,19; 73/80; Storybook House, 68/89; 73/83; Sweek, John, house, 64/88; Talbott-Opheim house, 68/89; Thomas Kay Woolen Mill, 69/339; Thompson Flouring Mill, Shedd, 66/90; U.S. survey of, 69/275-76,333; 70/77; Uplands farmhouse, 75/294; Van Vleet house, 63/252; Vaughan, W.H., house, 62/201; Vawter, W.I., house, 69/87; Waldorf, Erik, house, 73/80; Wallace house, 66/358; Waller Hall, Willamette Univ., 68/352; Walton house, 69/77; Wasco Co. courthouse, 62/299; Wood, C.E.S., house, 62/204; Woodcock house, 69/339; Yamhill Co. courthouse, 64/354; 65/217; SEE ALSO Architecture; Barns; Bybee-Howell House; Churches; Floed-Lane House; Hotels; Houses; McLoughlin House; Minthorn House; Theaters

Historic Preservation in the Pacific Northwest: A Bibliography of Sources, 1947-1978, by Crumb, noted, 81/106

Historic sites, 73/284:

Barlow Road, 63/245; 76/304; California, 78/365; Columbia River, 75/87-88; destruction of, 66/300; Eugene, in and near, 65/212; Idaho, 64/277; Marion Co., 63/82; Milwaukie area, 63/245; mining camps, 69/335; national register, 71/287; 80/287; Oregon, 78/365; Oregon City-West Linn area, 63/245; OHS preservation and restoration, 71/101-104,293-95; Polk Co., 69/77; post-1800 fur trade, 69/335; proposed ordinance to protect, 66/283; Trans-Mississippi West, 65/202; United States, 69/275-76, 333; Vancouver, Wash., 67/373; Washington, 64/188; 78/365; Washington Co., 80/106; Willamette Valley, 65/121; SEE ALSO Monuments and markers; National Historic Landmarks

Historic Western Churches: A Photographic Pilgrimage to the Churches of Old, by Florin, review, 71/186-87

Historical Account of the Origin, Customs, and Traditions of the Indians of Alta-California, by Boscana, review, 71/285

Historical Anecdotes Concerning the Lewis and Clark Expedition, noted, 76/92

An Historical Atlas of Early Oregon, by

Farmer, review, 74/278

Historical Missouri: A Pictorial Narrative, noted, 79/106-107

Historical Records Survey: records, 73/85

Historical research, 63/90; 79/107: American frontier, social and literary sources, 66/188; American genealogy guide, 74/283; California graduate research, 66/87; church records guide, 71/363; computer use in, 70/84; 71/290; handbook of reference works, 73/360; oral history catalog, 81/335; records repositories, 77/304; Russian archives, 74/95-96

theses and dissertations— Canada, 63/90; Pacific NW, 65/363-66; 72/227-34; Western America, 71/292

underdeveloped resources, 68/344; Western territories research opportunities, 67/367

Historical societies, 67/197,203; 73/366-67:

directory, U.S. and Canada, 64/277; first American, 73/367-68; functions of, 66/300-301; history and development, 73/365-72; objectives, 73/368, 369,370; Russian, 71/371; Siberia, 71/371; value, 73/366; SEE ALSO Agricultural Historical Assn.; American Historical Assn.; American Indian Historical Soc.; American-Irish Historical Soc.; Aurora Colony Historical Soc.; Baker County Historical Soc.; Benton County Historical Soc.; Canby Historical Soc.; Colusa County Historical Soc.; Creswell Area Historical Soc.; Crook County Historical Soc.; Curry County Historical Soc.; David Douglas Historical Soc.; Deschutes County Historical Soc.; Deschutes Pioneer Assn.; Douglas County Historical Soc.; Eastern Washington State Historical Soc.; Finnish-American Historical Soc. of the West; Forest History Soc.; Fort Crook Historical Soc.; Fort Vancouver Historical Soc.; French Prairie Historical Soc.; Gilliam County Historical Soc.; Gresham Historical Soc.; Harney County Historical Soc.; Jackson County Historical Soc.; Jefferson County Historical Soc.; Jewish Historical Soc. of Oregon; Josephine County Historical Soc.; Klickitat County Historical Soc.; Lane County Historical Soc.; Lincoln County Historical Soc.; Linn County Historical Soc.; Malheur Country Historical Soc.; Malheur County Pioneer Assn.; Marion County Historical Soc.; Massachusetts Historical Soc.; Milwaukie Historical Soc.; Minnesota Historical Soc.; Molalla Area Historical Soc.; Morrow County Historical Soc.; Nevada Historical Soc.; Old Fort Boise Historical Soc.; Old Fort Dalles Historical Soc.; Oregon Historical Soc.; Oregon Pioneer Assn.; Owyhee County Historical Soc.; Pacific County Historical Soc.; Polk County Historical Soc.; Puget Sound Maritime Historical Soc.; Railway and Locomotive Historical Soc.; Sherman County Historical Soc.; Silverton Country Historical Soc.; Siskiyou County Historical Soc.; Skamania County Historical Soc.; South Umpqua Historical Soc.; Southern Oregon Historical Soc.; State Historical Soc. of Missouri; Tigard Area Historical and Preservation Assn.; Tillamook County Pioneer Assn.; Tualatin Plains Historical Soc.; Umatilla County Historical Soc.; Union County Historical Soc.; Upper Willamette Pioneer Assn.; Wasco County Historical Soc.; Washington County Historical Soc.; Washington State Historical Soc.; Yamhill County Historical Soc.

Historically Speaking, noted, 75/363; 81/328

Historiography, 75/93,94: American conservation, 67/87; American frontier, 68/82; American national character, 72/178; American schism, 67/87; bibliography, 69/83; Black revolution in American studies, 72/178; 73/85; Chittenden methods, 63/244; Drake on Pacific Coast, 72/287; "grass roots," 81/233,257; gun culture in

America, 72/180; historical evidence, 71/366; history language, 69/335; image of American woman, 72/178; importance of local history, 79/408; influences on, 81/257,259; Irving's *Astoria*, 71/309-24; Manifest Destiny in America, 64/343-44; Oregon Methodist Mission, 74/72,74N; Oregon pioneers, 81/233FF,250-59; Oregon Trail, 81/96; quantification, 67/367; recent trends in America, 72/178; recent U.S., 67/84; 68/344; role of "new" history, 66/274; Russian-American relations view, 77/85; "safety valve" doctrine, 65/213; "saved Oregon" theory, 78/86-88,332-50; scientific principles applied to, 79/92-96; self-education in, 63/90; theory and history, 63/342

Turner—

frontier theory, 79/92-95; on fur trade, 79/92-97; "safety valve" and Negro migration, 67/85

20th century, 66/274-75; use of European, in America, 72/178; West, 72/182; western, 70/263-64; western criteria, 65/213

History:

agricultural, 69/83; agriculture and farm novel, 67/367; aids to learning, 73/84; American science, 67/367 American studies, 70/84; 73/85— Black revolution, 72/178; trends, 72/178; SEE ALSO Historiography and anthropology, 69/83; and western myths, 68/348; arid West, 65/313; business, 67/367; changing American concepts, 72/179; consciousness and ideology, 72/178; current interest in, 66/296-97,298 economic, 70/362; 72/178— changes in, 72/178; new, 69/83 ethnology and, 71/366 federal programs, 72/178— federal historical office proposed, 73/85 fiction and, 71/366; frontier, 71/291; Harvey Scott view, 70/198,202-10; historical novelists' responsibility, 65/408; immigration and, 65/213; Indian cul-

ture influence, 66/280,282 local history— articles on, 70/85; writing, 70/367 mining frontiers, 65/213; Mormons in western, 69/84; "mug" books, 70/219-21; oral history, 81/172-79,335; organizational synthetics, 72/178; personal factors in writing, 66/89; philosophy, 66/88; political, 79/405; recent American cultural, 69/335; reflections on profession, 67/368 regional history, 70/84,359— archives, 77/297,302; essays, 79/408 relation to anthropology and ethnohistory, 68/348; reorientation of western, 70/363; responsible popularization, 67/372; science, 70/349; teaching, 70/174,178; technological history importance, 66/299; The West, 65/313; 72/182; U.S. 1870s-1890s, 68/341 urban history, 72/181— in America, 73/85

History and Government of the State of Washington, by Avery, review, 63/78-79

History News:

described, 81/334

History of a County Fair, by Nelson, noted, 70/76

A History of Arlington Lodge No. 88, by Weatherford, noted, 64/121

History of Columbia Lodge No. 5, I.O.O.F., by McNeal, noted, 70/76

History of Education in Portland, ed. by Powers and Corning, cited, 73/324

The History of Kamtschatka and the Kurilski Islands with the Countries Adjacent, trans. by Grieve, noted, 64/187

History of Linn County, by Olsen, reprint noted, 71/361

The History of Milwaukie, Oregon, by Olsen, noted, 67/80

History of Oregon, by Bancroft, cited, 77/311

A History of Oregon Methodism, ed. by Yarnes, review, 62/406-407

A History of Pediatrics in the North Pacific, by Babson, noted, 72/173

History of Portland, ed. by Scott: described, 70/219-20; writers, 70/220

History of Portland's Forest-Park, by Munger, noted, **62**/108

History of Public Works in the United States, 1776-1976, ed. by Armstrong, review, **78**/360-61

A History of Sprague, by Gaffney and Jans, noted, **63**/357

History of the Expedition under the Command of Captains Lewis and Clark, 1814 ed.: authorship, **63**/358

The History of the Expedition Under the Command of Lewis and Clark, ed. by Coues, reprint noted, **66**/188

History of the First Methodist Church of Salem, Oregon, noted, **63**/248

The History of the Hudson's Bay Company, 1670-1870, Vol. II, by Rich, review, **62**/90-92

History of the Immaculate Conception Parish in the Colville Valley, by Pash, noted, **64**/186

History of the Indian Tribes of North America, with Biographical Sketches and Anecdotes of the Principal Chiefs, by McKenney and Hall, cited, **64**/51N

A History of the Lewis and Clark Journals, by Cutright, review, **78**/284-85

History of the Oregon Parks, 1917-1963, comp. by Armstrong, review, **67**/184-85

History of the Pacific Northwest, by Evans, quoted, **64**/307

History of the Willamette Valley, Oregon, by Clark, cited, **66**/344N,356N

The History of Union County, Oregon, ed. by Hug, noted, **63**/84

History of Wasco Lodge No. 15, A.F.&A.M. and Allied Orders, by McNeal, noted, **70**/76

Hitchman, James H.: *Henry Davidson Sheldon and the University of Oregon, 1874-1948*, noted, **81**/330 *The Port of Bellingham*, noted, **74**/283

Hite, Bill, **63**/275

Hite, Hiram, **78**/59

Hite, Joseph, **79**/87-88

Hiyum Pakhat Timine (Grizzly Five Hearts) (Indian), **81**/374

Hiyumyatimuxtuluin (Grizzly Immersed in Charcoal) (Indian), **81**/374

H'Kusam, Kwakiutl village, **63**/359

Hobart, Charles, **65**/81,301N,394; **79**/300-301N

Hobart, Okla., **77**/375-76

Hobos, **69**/336; **74**/326-31

Hobsonville, Ore., **75**/294; **77**/69,222: photos, **77**/68,218

Hockaday, John M., **64**/281: express line, **68**/88-89

Hockenbury Systems, Inc., **64**/328-29

Hockersmith, Jackson, **78**/125: photo, **78**/126

Hockersmith, Martha Jane Gale, **78**/125: photo, **78**/126

Hockinson, Wash., **72**/89,353

Hodge, Edwin T., **67**/21,29FF

Hodge, Frederick Webb, **63**/72; **64**/51-53N

Hodge, Ken, **66**/32N

Hodge, Maurice, **73**/101,364

Hodge, Mrs. Maurice, **81**/151,154, 155,165

Hodges, Henry C., **65**/183-84N,193

Hodgkins, Thomas, **67**/281

Hodson, Erma, **66**/55

Hodson, Evan, **66**/54

Hodson, Frank, **66**/54

Hodson, Irene, **66**/57

Hodson, Lena, **66**/54

Hoeck Logging Company, **66**/54

Hoecken, Adrian, **69**/270

Hofer, Ernest, **65**/267N; **73**/302: publications, **74**/159,177

Hoff, Maurice, **63**/82

Hoffman, Abraham, **63**/20,24

Hoffman, Eric, **69**/346

Hoffman, J.J., **80**/156,157

Hoffman, Jessie, **71**/19

Hoffman, Lee, OHS director, **62**/110, 206,302,422; **63**/93,255,373; **64**/93, 189,285

Hoffman, Lee Hawley, photo, **74**/214

Hoffman, William, Jackson Co. pioneer: trail diary 1853, **66**/88

Hoffman Construction Co., Portland, **66**/385

Hoffman Memorial Wayside, **67**/49

Hoffmann, Carl J., **70**/358

Hoffmann, George:

"Political Arithmetic: Charles L. McNary and the 1914 Primary Election," 66/363-78

Hofmann, W.J., 74/215

Hofstadter, Richard: *The Paranoid Style in American Politics*, cited, 72/211

Hofstadter, Richard, *et al*: *The United States: The History of a Republic*, noted, 69/276

Hogan, James, 65/278

Hogan, William, 66/244

Hogg, Thomas Egenton, 67/63: Oregon railroad interests, 71/90,94, 349-51

Hogg Pass, 68/90

Hogg Rock, 71/351

Hoggan, David L.: *The Myth of the New History: The Techniques and Tactics of the New Mythologists of American HIstory*, review, 66/274-75

Hogs, 77/143,155: Baker Co. 1890s, 66/211; cause of disputes, 64/85; Cowlitz Farm, 63/104, 125-26,136,140,142; French Prairie, 66/339,344; prices 1851, 63/53

Hogue, Harry W., 62/177

Hogue, Harvey A.: biography, 66/146N

Hoh Indians: canoes, 74/9,10; food, 74/10; guides, 74/9,10-11; housing, 74/10

Hoh River, 74/9

Hohnstein, Peter, 77/79

Hoke, Carrie (Mrs. Mac), 73/84

Holbrook, Amory, 64/153; 65/232; 75/119,120,121

Holbrook, John, family, 62/109

Holbrook, Philo, 71/233; 74/108,111, 117,118

Holbrook, R.B., 63/66

Holbrook, Sibyl (Mrs. Stewart H.), 64/358,361: *Southwest Indian Crafts*, by Tanner, review, 70/268-69

Holbrook Stewart Hall, 62/111,199, 207,303,422; 63/91,93,255,373; 64/ 93,189,276,285,348,358,361-63; 65/

125,221,317,415; 71/181; 73/189, 213,299,317; 74/239; 75/5; 77/382: painting of Skidmore Fountain, 73/67

Holcomb, Cecil R., 69/208

Holcomb, Samuel B., 80/26,26N,28,134

Holden, Wash., 68/352

Holderness, S.M., 66/355

Holderness, William, 62/142N

Holdredge, Dan, 80/231

Hole-in-the-Wall Park, 75/40-42

Holgate, J.P., 71/19

Holidays, 78/167-68; SEE ALSO Christmas, Fourth of July, etc.

Holladay, Ben, 62/204; 64/262; 68/89; 71/283; 72/132; 75/123; 79/243; 81/82: biography, 80/306N; construction of O&C railroad, 71/46,65; finances, 71/ 45,46,65,80; land grant sought, 71/69; photo, 71/48; purchase of O&C interests, 71/40,46,71; role in elections, 80/306-307; Seaside House, 64/205N

Holladay, Jennie, 81/82

Holladay, proposed city, 62/204

Holladay Addition, Portland: school 1879, 64/264

Holland, Mr. —, The Dalles, 1879, 70/139

Holland, Mrs. —, Burns, Ore. 1905, 63/335

Holland, Gladys, 63/335

Holland, J.J., 63/64

Holland, J.J., Steam Transportation Co., 63/61

Hollenbeck, Bud, 75/226

Hollenbeck, John, 74/17,18,21

Holley, M.W., 79/292-93N

Hollinger, Lot, 66/154,155

Hollingsworth, Elvin, 76/333

Hollon, W. Eugene: *The Great American Desert, Then and Now*, review, 67/277

Holm, Bill: *Indian Primitive*, by Andrews, review, 62/184-85 *Monuments in Cedar: The Authentic Story of the Totem Pole*, by Keithahn, review, 65/210-11

Holm, Frank, 72/284

Holman, Alfred, 70/199
Holman, Charles, 80/320N
Holman, Frederick V., 66/258; 67/366; 74/218
Holman, Hank, 73/264
Holman, James D., family, 68/182
Holman, Rufus C., 66/249; 74/109-10, 118,139,140,215: biography, 66/252; Hunt case opinion, 71/230,233-34; Multnomah Co. commissioner, 66/261; 71/226; photos, 66/250; 74/110
Holman, Mrs. Walter J., photo, 74/236
Holmes, Kenneth L., 62/299; 63/254, 364; 64/87-88,357; 65/211,219,315; 66/92,281,284; 69/171N; 70/368, 371; 71/372:
Ewing Young, Master Trapper, review, 69/61-62
Firearms, Traps and Tools, by Russell, review, 69/182-83
Gold in the Woodpile, An Informal History of Banking in Oregon, by Burrell, review, 70/177
An Historical Atlas, text, 74/278
"Joseph Gervais and Jean Baptiste Gervais," letter to editor, 70/347
Lewis and Clark, Pioneering Naturalists, by Cutright, review, 70/348-49
Requiem for a People, by Beckham, review, 73/66-67
Textbooks and the American Indian, ed. by Costo, review, 74/87-88
"Three Nootka Documents," 79/397-402
Holmes, Leander, 69/330
Holmes, R.J., 62/165
Holmes, Robert D., 65/415,416; 66/93,189,285,394; 67/376,380; 69/348; 70/373; 74/183,365
Holmes, Robin, 73/201-203
Holmes, Thomas J., 80/21,22,24,26, 142,153-56: biography, 80/21N; photo, 80/20
Holmgren, Virginia C., 64/356: "Chinese Pheasants, Oregon Pioneers," 65/229-62
The War Lord, noted, 70/359
Holms, George, 74/24

Holmstrom, Frances, 74/63
Holmstrom, William, 63/252; 66/388
Holsman, Virginia Bilyeu, 80/365-73 *passim*, 385,387-88: photos, 80/370,384
Holsman, Virginia Bilyeu: "Fond Recollections," 80/365-90
Holst, Maren Svendson, 66/103
Holt, Benjamin, 70/366; 79/10: harvesting machinery, 68/87
Holt, Lester, 68/353
Holt, Robert E.L., 64/248
Holton, David S., 65/394
Holtz, Merriam H., 74/231
Home, David, 63/196,205,232
Home Creek, 77/153
Homely (Homily, Homli) (Indian), 68/306N; 70/34,35N,36,150: camp described, 70/167; meeting with Wood, 70/167-69
"Homer Davenport on Stage," by Alice Henson Ernst, 66/39-50
Homestead on the Trask, by Maddux, noted, 77/91
Homesteads and homesteading, 63/247, 275; 67/88,367; 70/273,367; 71/265-69; 74/31,33; 75/241,242,309,312; 76/42,70,72,78,82; 77/13,30,91,157, 158,195; 78/24,48,171N,336,337: act, 63/358; 67/153; 70/273; 73/52—
extended to Alaska, 72/136; extended to Indians, 70/104-105
Alaska law, 72/136; Barren Valley, 72/93; Bend area, 71/286-87; Central Ore., 72/94; claims, 73/259,263,267,268, 334; 74/11,16,17,18,19,27,31,32,33, 271-74,284; Clark Co., 65/308; Columbia Co., 65/308; Coos Co., 63/32-33; Dakota frontier, 74/284; disputes, 81/309-10; Douglas Co., 73/72; Idaho, 70/273; laws, 64/85; 81/282, 316,317; Lincoln Co., 71/265-73; Montana, 65/215; 69/336; Morrow Co., 69/123,130,133,135,143; Nebraska, 68/345; Nehalem Valley, 65/308; Oklahoma, 77/375; Olympic Peninsula, 74/11,32; Portland, 64/262; Sherman Co., 78/174; Skagit Valley,

79/337; Trask River, 77/91; Umatilla Co., 67/90; Wallowa Co., 78/91; Wasco Co., 73/307; women, 74/284

Homsher, Lola M., ed.: *South Pass, 1868; James Chisolm's Journal of the Wyoming Gold Rush*, review, 63/242-43

Honda, Mrs. —, Portland Assembly Center, 81/161

Honduras, 77/373-74

Honey Creek, SEE Sierra Nevada Creek

Honey in the Horn, by Davis, cited, 66/ 240,242; quoted, 66/246,247

Honey Lake, 72/9,14

Honeyman, Jessie Millar (Mrs. Walter J.), 67/42

Honeyman, John, and Co., Portland, 64/176

Honeyman, Nan Wood, 62/198

Honeyman Hardware Co., Portland, 74/347

Honolulu, Cowlitz Farm employee, 63/154,156

Honolulu, Hawaii, 64/5; 67/86; 77/59: 1848-49, 72/182; foreign impact, 68/ 87; foreigners 1847, 72/182; Oahu cemetery, 70/88; puritanism, 70/88; salt trade, 72/317; U.S. Navy visits, 68/ 59,72; urban society in 19th century, 69/83

Hoobler, Dorothy and Thomas: *Photographing the Frontier*, review, 81/324

Hood, Andrew, 73/250

Hood, Brenda, ed.: "'This worry I have': Mary Herren Journal," 80/229-57

Hood, Donald, 75/279

Hood, R.B., 70/139N

Hood, Samuel, 63/234

Hood Canal, 75/11

Hood River, 66/255; 79/203,204,210: ford, 79/201

Hood River, Ore., 68/354; 72/157; 79/203: churches, 72/94,153; Indian settlement, 72/151; railroad, 72/94; stores, 76/242

Hood River Apple Growers Assn., 76/249

Hood River County, Ore., 66/366,372: roads, 74/109,113,137,142

Hood River County Historical Society: meetings, 69/278; 70/275; museum, 69/175; officers, 66/84,278; officers and board members, 62/103,414; 63/85,249; 67/82,283; 68/84,282; 69/81,278; 70/81,275; officers and directors, 64/83,279; 65/123,311; 71/193; 72/175; 73/77; 74/180; 75/90; 76/94; 78/94; 79/110; 81/109; officers and trustees, 80/109

Hood River Valley: described 1908, 70/50-55; early fruit growers, 70/50-54; Japanese, 70/54; 76/234,238,240-44; land prices 1908, 70/52; murders, 70/51; name, 63/ 365; "New Yorkers," 70/53; photo, 70/52-53

Hooker, Cyrenius: biography, 75/345FF; estate, 75/345,350; murder, 75/345-59

Hooker, Joseph, 63/231

Hooker, William Jackson, 63/191; 68/119

Hoolapa, Cowlitz Farm employee, 63/ 149,153

Hoop, Oscar Winslow, 65/182N

Hooper, Beverley, ed.: *With Captain James Cook in the Antarctic and Pacific: The Private Journal of James Burney..., 1772-1773*, noted, 77/303

Hooper, J.A., 68/271

Hooper, Samuel, 76/213,216,217

Hooper, William B., 65/15

Hoostraat, John, 75/169

Hoover, Herbert Clark, 67/90; 68/136; 70/257; 74/233; 80/336: Pierce opinion of, 78/112-13; photo, 78/100

Hope (brig), 72/182

Hope Mining Company, 65/366

Hopewell, Ore., 80/229,256

Hopkins, C.I., 66/33

Hopkins, John W.: First Ore. Cavalry, 65/87,104N,114, 117,394

Hopkins, Lewis H., 68/252

Hopkins, Mark, 71/283

Hopkins, Sarah Winnemucca, 68/243N, 252,299N; 70/31-32; 74/283; 75/93: family, 70/33-34; Bannock War role, 70/15FF; Paiute customs, 70/32-33; photo, 68/fr.cov. Dec.; teacher, 70/162

Hopkins, Sarah Winnemucca: *Life Among the Piutes*, cited, 68/ 229N,235N,299N,302N,306N,307N; 70/16N-34N*passim*

Hopkins and East, Portland, 75/177, 189N

Hopoo, Thomas, 70/88

Hopper, Henry, 77/149(photo),153

Hops, 70/47; 72/283; 76/234,239, 368,373; 77/89,263,268; 80/283: culture, 74/316; dryer photo, 64/270; 74/314; first Pacific Coast, 64/267, 269; first Washington kiln, 64/271; medicinal use, 64/267 pickers, 74/316— photos, 64/270; 74/314; 76/24 Silverton, 64/89; Washington, 64/269,271; Willamette Valley, 64/267-71; Woodland, 66/382

Hoquarten Slough, 72/301,305

Hoquiam, Wash., 66/318; 74/15

Horetzky, Charles, 72/183

Horn, C. Lester:

"Oregon's Columbia River Highway," 66/249-71

Horn, Tom, 65/121

Hornaday, William T., 65/205

Hornby, Geoffrey Phipps, 67/183

Horner, John B., 72/284-85; 73/345; 79/250

Horner Museum, Ore. State Univ., 69/ 176

Horning, Walter G., 64/60-61; 67/48

The Horse in Blackfoot Indian Culture: With Comparative Material from Other Western Tribes, by Ewers, review, 72/81-82

Horse racing, 68/144,145,147N; 73/ 285; 75/43,207; 77/29; 79/282, 283,304: race horses, 68/141,147,147N; race tracks, 68/145; 75/363

A Horseless Carriage Comes to Town, by Wortman, noted, 67/366

Horseradish, SEE Prices

Horses, 63/7-40*passim*,270-72; 67/240, 250,311; 68/144-45,150-51,235; 70/ 57,58,73,74; 74/359; 75/94,205-18, 270; 77/12-13,15: Appaloosa, 62/203; 64/357; 68/88; 72/288; 75/209 army use, 68/226,234,235; 79/146-70 *passim*,275,279-305*passim*,315— forage costs 1850, 67/311N; issued to scouts, 79/132-33,138; losses, 79/ 147,153,313,314 breeds, 75/207,210-11,214; "bunchgrass," 75/208,209; care and handling, 72/82; Civil War shortage, 72/63; corral photos, 67/251; Cowlitz Farm, 63/104,125-26,137-39,156-68*passim*; Davenport Arabian stables, 66/39,47; draft horses, 75/210,214,217-18,279; 76/58,59-60,81; equipment, 63/324-25; farm horses, 76/17-18,21; first in West, 75/94; French Prairie, 66/339, 340,343,350; frontier, 72/168,181; harness, 76/18,21; SEE ALSO Harness shops; history in America, 75/205; horsemeat, 77/17; Klondike, 76/102,103-109; marketing, 77/15,23; Ore.-Calif. journey 1885, 80/230-47*passim*; Oregon Trail 1853, 62/241N,242-87 *passim*,337-402*passim*; 79/81-87; pack horses, 76/46,81; SEE ALSO Pack trains; photos, 75/204-19*passim*,covs. Sept.; 76/18,20,34,84,349; 77/15,16,19,23, 27,74,160,169,248; Pony Express, 67/ 233; prices, SEE Prices; pulling streetcars, 75/207; quarterhorses, 76/314; race horses, SEE Horse racing; ranch owners of, 63/270; replacement by machines, 75/218; riding, 75/215; 76/46,53,55,333,341; role in Ore. history, 64/357; rustling, 66/153; saddles, 64/86; seasickness, 77/75 shoeing— described, 70/356; 74/359; 80/104; prices, 63/23 stagecoach horses, 76/53-57 thefts, 79/182,196— by Indians, 79/40-41,125,126,138, 302N training, 64/148-49,163,175; western, 62/202; wild horses, 67/277; Yakima Indian War use, 66/145,148,150-52,154; SEE ALSO Indians—horses Horsfall, William, 64/355; 66/54 Horsley, Albert, SEE Orchard, Harry Horsley, F.C., 70/59 Horticultural Society of London, 68/ 111,118,119 Horvat, William J.: *Above the Pacific*, review, 68/278-79 Hosfeldt, Mrs. Arthur D., Jr., 62/421 Hosiery mills: first in Oregon, 67/61 Hoskins, Charles, 65/178 Hoskins, John Box, 62/88; 68/105: *Columbia Rediviva* narrative quoted, 68/106 Hoskins, T.J., 69/106 Hoskins, Benton Co., 64/89 Hosmer, J.E., 75/143-44 Hosmer, Paul: orchestra, 77/89 Hospitals: early Ore., 65/220; Marshfield, 76/63; Multnomah Co., 78/177; nurse's diary 1910-13, 80/336; Portland, 76/304; rates 1911, 72/280; Seattle, 78/34 Hot Lake, Harney Co., 73/231: borax works, 73/231,234-42; minerals, 73/241; photos, 73/232 Hot Spring (Lake), Nev., 68/255 Hot Springs, SEE Springs Hotchkiss, John, 74/49 Hotels: Antelope, 77/161; Aschoff's, 73/84; Ashford, Wash., 73/345; Ashland, 64/ 328-29; 68/353; Aurora colony, photo, 79/265; Baker, 73/81; Canada, 70/ 361; Canyon City, 79/303; Cornelius, 64/89; Garibaldi, 77/358; Glenada, 74/273; Grater, Ashwood, photo, 73/ 340; Grays Harbor, 74/15; Guerin, 63/263; Heppner, 69/147; Hillsboro, 64/89; Island House, 65/20; Japanese, 76/232,239,249; Kitsap Co. Log Cabin Inn, 70/272; Madras, photo, 69/302; Medford, 64/338; Ochoco mines, 73/267; Paisley, 77/28; Pataha,

Wash., 79/199; Patrick Creek, 74/18; Portland, SEE Portland—hotels; railway hotels in Canada, 70/361; Rainier, Ore., 74/83; rates, SEE Prices—hotel rates; Shaniko, photo, 77/27; Sherars, photo, 69/297; Waldo, 76/56,83-85; Westfall, 63/283; SEE ALSO Baldwin House, Klamath Falls; Bill, Cannon Beach; Boston House, Moscow, Ida.; Chanticleer Inn; Chemeketa House, Salem; Cliff House, San Francisco; Cloud Cap Inn; Columbia Southern, Shaniko; Crater Lake Lodge; Croft, Tacoma; Gamage, Hoquiam; Gearin, Myrtle Point; Geisendorfer, Albany; Golden, Reno; Grigsby's Place, Copalis; Halstead House, Tacoma; Higley's, Lake Quinault; International, San Francisco; Klondike Kate's, Bend; Langille House, Hood River; Leonard's, Wasco; Mountain House; Neskowin Inn; New Columbia, The Dalles; New England, Seattle; Occidental, Corvallis; Occidental, Seattle; Olympia, Montesano; Oregon, Ashland; Overland, Boise; Packard, Pendleton; Palace, Seaside; Patterson House, Kalama; Perkins House, Drain; Phoenix, Ore. City; Pilot Butte Inn, Bend; Pioneer House, Elk City; St. Charles, Eugene; St. Charles, Seattle; St. George, Victoria; Seaside House; Smeed, Eugene; Sodaville Stage Inn; Stine House, Walla Walla; Tehama (Jones), San Francisco; Timberline Lodge; Town House, Echo; Umatilla House, The Dalles; U.S. Hotel, Jacksonville; Vinton, Grass Valley; Waller's Inn; Weatherby, Burnt River; Whitney Inn, Garibaldi; Wolf Creek Inn Hough, Patrick, 68/341 Houghton, Barney, 69/133 Houghton, J.F., 72/14: Calif.-Nevada boundary survey, 72/14-17,48,52,53 Houghton, Mike, 69/133 Hoult, Alice, photo, 80/363 Hoult, Enoch, 80/357 Hoult, Mary, 80/357 Hounsell, John P., 63/372,374; 64/94,

190,286,363; 65/125,221,317,416; 66/93,189,285,394

Houqua (vessel), 76/221N

Houseboats, 75/362

Houses:

cabins— log, 77/71; photo, 74/4

construction— 1906, 81/37; 19th century, 69/340 cost of, 1902, 62/173; house-moving, 76/300(photo),301,303; house-raising, 74/23

log houses— Chehalis, 66/32; French Prairie, 66/ 338-39; Shrum house, 81/308 (photo),311

pioneer, 62/66-67; 71/199,366; prices 1900, 80/378; sod houses, 71/366; 75/68; SEE ALSO Architecture; Historic buildings and houses

Housing, 67/357: Portland metro area, 67/366; public, 76/144

Houser, Max, 81/204

Houston, Duncan, 66/109,110N,113

Houston, Victor S.K., 64/27N

Houston's Opera House, Klamath Falls, 73/283

How Edison's Lamp Helped Light the West, by Dierdorff, review, 72/348

"How McLoughlin House Was Saved," by Vara Caufield, 76/299-301

How Silently—A History of the Catholic Church of the Big Bend Missions..., by Kowrach, noted, 64/351

Howard, Andy, 64/108

Howard, Guy, 68/248N: photo, 70/100

Howard, Helen Addison: *Northwest Trail Blazers*, noted, 65/121

Howard, Henry, 65/96N

Howard, J.H., Ore. City labor organizer, 62/174-75

Howard, J.S., 69/338

Howard, Jacob M., 73/35-36,40-41, 46,58

Howard, James P., Westfall pioneer, 63/294

Howard, John M., Westfall pioneer,

63/269

Howard, Mrs. Martin, 70/373; 71/371

Howard, Oliver Otis, 64/348; 70/10, 15N,17,22,23N,34,57,124,140,169; 81/345:

Bannock War, 68/221,227N,230N, 231N,235,237,239N,298N,299N, 302N,303,307,322,329; biography, 70/127N; Dept. of Columbia, 70/ 5,101

Indian councils— Priest Rapids, 70/139N,154,155; Sept. 1878, 70/128; Umatilla 1878, 70/34-38; Yakima 1877, 70/127 photos, 68/241,fr.cov. Sept.; 70/100; relations with Moses, 70/119,127-35, 139N,149FF; reports 1878, 68/226N, 297N

Howard, Oliver Otis:

Autobiography, cited, 70/133

My Life and Personal Experiences Among Our Hostile Indians, cited, 70/18NFF, 127NFF; reprint noted, 74/94-95

Nez Perce Joseph, cited, 70/18N; reprint noted, 74/95

Howard, Samuel, 78/127,326(photo)

Howay, Frederic W.:

A List of Trading Vessels, cited, 78/355,356

Voyages of the "Columbia," cited, 68/102,103

Howe, George Frederic, *et al*: *The American Historical Association's Guide to Historical Literature*, review, 63/342-43

Howe, Henry R., 66/123,126-27,130: letter excerpts, 66/123,125-26

Howe, Horace, 63/220,223N

Howe, Horace, Jr., 63/221,223N

Howe, Richard, 65/96N

Howe, Timothy O.: loyalty question, 73/36-37,59

Howe, William Addison, 76/15

Howe Sound, 63/92

Howell, Erle: *Methodism in the Northwest*, review, 68/338-39

Howell, Glenn: C.C.C. *Boys Remember*, noted, 78/91

Howell, John T., **67**/372
Howell, Warren, **66**/380
Howell House, SEE Bybee-Howell House
Howes, James M., **66**/85,279:
Old Yaquina Bay Lighthouse, noted, **70**/75
Howison, Neil M., **63**/188,207:
Peacock testimony, **64**/229N-30N;
report on *Shark*, **64**/243N
Howlish, George (Indian), photo, **68**/236
Howlish Wampo (Indian):
death, **70**/35N; identity, **70**/148N;
speeches at 1878 council, **70**/35-36
Howluck (Howlah) (Indian), **79**/127, 139:
identity, **69**/239-40,253; in Klamath
country, **69**/252-54; name spelling,
69/240; white contacts, **69**/239-40N
Howse, Joseph, **65**/215
Howth (ship), **66**/127
Hoyt, E. Palmer, **74**/54,214(photo)
Hoyt, Henry L., **80**/146,149,150,152, 156,157,157N,158:
photo, **80**/155
Hoyt, Joseph:
biography, **80**/352N
Hoyt, M.L., **69**/215N
Hrdlicka, A., **73**/136
Hubbard, George, SEE Hibbard, George Allen
Hubbard, Thomas Jefferson, **62**/119; **66**/353
Hubbard, Ore., **69**/57-59
Hubbard Lake, **66**/358
Huber and Maxwell, civil engineers, **62**/172
Hucker, Albert, **63**/286
Hucker, Louis, **63**/286
Huckleberries, **76**/87
Huckleberry, Evermont Robbins, **77**/357:
biography, **71**/117-40; photo, **71**/116
Huckleberry, Evermont Robbins:
Adventures of Dr. Huckleberry, cited, **71**/117N
"In Those Days...Tillamook County," **71**/117-40
Hudnutt, J.D.:
Union Pacific railroad survey, **71**/54

Hudson, H.M., **80**/159,159N,296N, 319N
Hudson, William H., lieut. on *Peacock*, **79**/405
Hudson (ship), **75**/94
Hudson Community Park, Columbia Co.:
history, **65**/308-309
Hudson's Bay Company, **62**/64-76
passim,99,105,118-205*passim*,314,318, 371,375-76,394N,400N,407; **63**/101-14*passim*,175,178,237,239,252,350; **64**/197-209*passim*,284,296,349; **65**/ 305-306,309; **66**/336,340,343; **67**/ 279,281,368; **68**/81,88,111,185,340, 341; **69**/59,61; **70**/88; **72**/151; **74**/72; **75**/76,113-22*passim*,318-19, 320; **76**/129,130,314,321; **77**/194, 289,294,315; **78**/86,90,139; **79**/134; **80**/335; **81**/27,27N:
agriculture at fur posts, **72**/183; Alaska operation, **63**/189
archival sources, **66**/332N-33N; **69**/ 346; **71**/368; **79**/339; **81**/341N—
Hawaiian records, **69**/84
Arctic exploration, **68**/237; **70**/367;
arms and motto, **63**/224; articles on, **70**/273; **71**/366
artifacts, **71**/369—
Ft. Vancouver, **77**/298; Ft. Walla Walla, **66**/142
Astoria—
land dispute, **81**/24-25; warehouse photo 1855, **81**/4
attitude toward settlers, **62**/125; **67**/ 303-304; Babine Lake post, **70**/179;
blankets used as Indian clothing, **81**/ 350,352,358(sketch); British naval support, **70**/293,294-95; buildings, **76**/ 92; Cape Disappointment expansion plans, **64**/226N; Cathlamet post, **62**/ 57; cattle in Calif., **63**/205; charter, **76**/311; Columbia River chart, **64**/ 197N; competitors, **76**/310,319; contrast, early and modern company, **65**/ 219; diaries, **63**/225; discipline and control, **63**/101,119,182,186,199, 201,225
employees, **66**/333; **77**/84; **78**/ 51,51N—

Columbia Dept. roster, 66/332; Hawaiian 1856, 67/86; marriages to Indians, 74/90; officers and clerks 1840-42, 63/183; Pacific NW personnel, 70/74,113,131N; remuneration, 63/202,215; servants, 79/107; vital records, 74/90

facilities used by Jeffrey, 68/112FF,117; forts, 73/155-56; gold rush effect, 63/226

history, 62/90-92; 71/366,372—in Pacific NW, 72/87-88,183

Indian children at Red River, 69/50,54; Indian trappers, 71/345; influence on Indians, 76/304; journals, 77/84; Kootenai post, 71/342; land claims in Wash. Terr., 63/221N; land commissioner 1879, 81/323; letterbooks, 63/179-80,184,211; management, 62/81; map, 71/366; marine service problems, 64/200; medals and tokens, 70/88, 179; Ore. City store, 78/134N; Orkney men, 68/87; policy regarding missionary enterprises, 71/327; policy transition, fur trade to settlement, 81/323-24; posts, 81/18,106; Puget Sound Agricultural Co. organized, 63/104; SEE ALSO Puget Sound Agricultural Co.; Red River forts 1821-69, 65/314; relations with Americans, 64/227N-29N; relations with British govt., 73/359; 74/352; relations with Canadian govt., 81/324; relations with Indians, 63/193; Russian-American Co. agreement, 75/331,331N; salmon fishing, 72/345; Sauvie Island dairy, 67/373; sawmills, 63/206; settlement with U.S., 76/382; sheep, 62/240N; shipbuilding, 63/189,204; shipping, 71/366; ships in coastal trade, 68/186; Shortess petition against, 66/353; Simpson policies, 74/352; Stikine territory lease, 68/347; trade routes, 71/291; traders, 78/122; trails in Oregon, 77/194,315, 317; trappers, 78/211; tricentennial, 71/291,366,369; 72/89; Umpqua post, 70/239; SEE ALSO Ft. Umpqua (fur trade post)

Vancouver Island, 71/282—

coal operations, 65/314; headquarters, 63/106N SEE ALSO Cowlitz Farm

Hudson's Bay Miscellany, 1670-1870, ed. by Williams, review, 77/83-85

Hudson's Bay Record Society, 63/350; 65/309: membership, 81/208; publications, 77/83-85; 81/208

Hudspeth, Benoni Morgan, 70/181

Hudspeth Co., Prineville, 73/264

Hudspeth's Cutoff, 64/277; 80/84N

Huffman, Doris A.:

"He Gave Oregon a Heritage of Music," 74/345-49

Oregon's Flamboyant Fourth, 1876, noted, 77/196,291

Hug, Mrs. John, photo, 81/254

Hug Point, 77/71

Huggins, Edward, 63/102,103N,112N, 178N,182,198,230:

Roberts journal presented, 63/112N

Huggins, Letitia Work (Mrs. Edward), 63/230N

Hughes, Charles Evans: 1916 election 64/87; 68/126

Hughes, Edward J., 67/44

Hughes, Jim, Wasco Co. 1881, 81/277

Hughes, John, Heppner resident, 69/133

Hughes, Margaret Powers, 77/75: "A Letter: Albert H. Powers," 77/73-78

Hughes, Matt, 69/133

Hughes, Patrick H., 77/75

Hughes, Riley, 66/243

Hughes, W.E., 69/133

Hughes, William, Heppner pioneer, 69/103,105,111,115,123: biography, 69/133

Hughston, Curtis, 81/265N

Hulbert, Archer Butler, 62/193; 67/367

Hulbert, Dorothy Printup, 62/193

Hulda I (vessel), 78/206

Hulery, John W., 78/124

Hulin, Lester, 78/325N; 79/10

Hull, Alexander, 74/54

Hull, Cordell, 62/26,27,28

Hull, Frank H., 66/306

Hull, Wesley, C., 72/330; 73/40,47

Hulley, Clarence C.:
Alaska, Past and Present, review, 73/72
Hult, Nils B., 69/342,347; 70/374; 72/359; 73/361-62,373; 74/183,360, 361,363,366; 75/368,370; 76/383-86; 77/385; 78/370
Hult, Ruby El, 65/313:
Steamboats in the Timber, review, 70/357
Untamed Olympics, cited, 74/8
Humanities Research Center, Univ. of Texas:
H.L. Davis collection, 66/240
Humason, Orlando, 62/223; 66/149,150-51; 67/307N
Humboldt, Alexander von, 71/367
Humboldt River, 70/33; 77/318; 79/77N,82
Humbug Mountain, 66/282
Hume, Edward E., 70/251N
Hume, James B.:
biography, 72/88-89
Hume, Robert Dennison, 64/346-47; 69/88
Hume, William, 75/105
Humor, 71/188:
Western, 67/88; SEE ALSO Cartoons
Humphrey, Augustus L., 78/43,45N:
biography, 78/43N
Humphrey, Charles F., 68/239
Humphrey, Cynthia (Mrs. George H.), 79/16
Humphrey, George H., 79/16
Humphrey, L., 78/45N:
immigrant guide, 78/45; map of Oregon 1853, 78/46
Humphrey, Leila Carrie, 78/363
Humphrey, V.A., 80/235
Humphreys, Charles, 64/200-201
Humphreys, Lester W., 75/154:
photo, 75/155
Humptulips, Wash., 74/8
Hunderup, August, 77/69
Hungarian people:
Ore. population 1860-1910, 80/267; Portland population 1860-1910, 80/266
Hungry Creek, Southern Ore., 72/41N
Hunsaker, Daniel, 78/325N

Hunsaker, Mary E. Williams (Mrs. Daniel), 78/304
Hunsaker, Thomas H., 78/304-306
Hunt, Aurora, 63/360
Hunt, Charles H., 65/270,273,278,282, 287
Hunt, Henry H., 63/150; 64/218N, 228N
Hunt, Henry T.:
The Case of Thomas J. Mooney and Warren K. Billings, review, 72/346-47
Hunt, Isaac D., 74/213
Hunt, Louise M.:
biography, 71/220-21,245; conscientious objector WW I, 71/213-45; resignation, Library Assn. of Portland, 71/233-34
Hunt, Philip Mulkey, ed.:
Diary of a Student Nurse: The Diary of Ollie Marquiss, 1910-1913, noted, 80/336
Hunt, Theodore, 81/234
Hunt, Thomas Dwight, 66/10
Hunt, Washington, 75/324-25
Hunt, Wilson Price, 66/331,338,362; 68/87; 77/80; 81/234:
letter from McKenzie, 66/333; report on Oregon, 70/365-66
Hunter, Charles, mate on *Atalanta*, 66/110,111,111N,114
Hunter, George:
OMV service, 66/141,142N,149N
Hunter, Gertie (Mrs. Harry), 62/201
Hunter, Louis C.:
Steamboats on the Western Rivers, cited, 66/274
Hunter, Robert M.T., 81/184N
Hunter, V.P., 74/30
Hunter (tug), 68/266
Hunting, 70/251; 75/61,63-64,101-102
The Hunting of the Buffalo, by Branch, reprint noted, 63/248
Huntington, Benjamin, photo, 79/166
Huntington, Collis P.:
biography, 71/283-84; Ore. railroad interests, 71/54,68-69,73,82,93,96; papers cited, 71/82
Huntington, Daniel L., 66/80
Huntington, Edwin, 65/120

Huntington, Gale:
Songs the Whalemen Sang, noted, 65/309
Huntington, J.B., Yakima Co., 70/165N
Huntington, James Webster Perit, 69/239,240N,276; 79/47,125-26,127,130, 144N,163,163N,166,168: biography, 80/363N; family photo, 79/166; list of Indian depredations, 79/169N; McKay escort duty, 79/163N,168N-69N; objections to terms of Indian enlistments, 79/302N,328-29; quoted, 80/364; views on Indian "extermination," 79/130,328-29,330
Huntington, Walter, 74/273
Huntington, William, 63/220
Huntington, Ore., 62/385N,395N: cattle shipping center, 67/142,146; photo ca. 1885-90, 67/124
Hurd, Charles N., 75/159-60,178
Hurd, Clarence, 78/354
Hurd, Edward, 81/265N
Hurlburt, Ralph J., 74/213
Hurlburt, Thomas M., 75/154: photo, 75/155
Hurley, Timothy, 69/133
"Hurrah for Garibaldi!", by Daniel D. Strite, 77/213-37,341-68
Hurst, Stith, 74/22,24
Husbands, Ed, 76/103
Husis Owyeen (Wounded Head) (Indian), 81/351
Hussey, John A., 63/89; 65/306,415; 66/332N:
Champoeg: Place of Tradition, cited, 70/259N
Equality on the Oregon Frontier, by Loewenberg, review, 78/86-89
John McLoughlin's Business Correspondence, ed. by Sampson, review, 75/76-77
Hustler, Jackson G., 64/320-21
Huston, Anna, 72/93
Huston, Henry Clay, 70/74; 78/325N; 79/339
Huston, Robert J., 74/14
Huston, S.B., 68/135
Hutcheson, Austin, 75/279
Hutchins, Isaac, 62/148-49
Hutchins, Nancy, and Alice Meyer:

Portland in Your Pocket, noted, 77/291
Hutchinson, W.H.:
California Heritage: A History of Northern California Lumbering, revised ed. noted, 75/365
Hutchison, Laura Fox, 80/384-85
Hutson family, Hood River Valley, 70/54
Hutterites, 70/180
Hutton, Levi W., 68/346
Hutton, Mary Arkwright, 67/372
Huycke, Harold D., Jr.:
To Santa Rosalia, Further and Back, review, 72/167-68
Hyde, Dayton O.:
Sandy, the True Story of a Rare Sandhill Crane, noted, 69/330
Hyde, George E.:
Spotted Tail's Folk: A History of the Brulé Sioux, review, 63/71-75
Hyde, George Warren: Ore. Territory land survey 1854, 72/14N,47N
Hyde, Henry, Westfall resident, 63/297
Hyde, Henry H., Ore. Terr. constable, 73/247,248
Hyde, Wayne, 63/296
Hyde and Rohrer, cattlemen, 69/229N
Hydroelectric power, 67/86; 78/115: North Santiam projects, 71/349-57
Hydropathy, 78/5-40*passim*: college, 78/5,7-9; publications, 78/10, 11,28
Hyland Cemetery, Lowell, 78/322
Hyman, Harold M.:
Soldiers and Spruce: Origins of the Loyal Legion of Loggers & Lumbermen, review, 65/197-98
Hynding, Alan:
The Public Life of Eugene Semple, review, 75/292-93
Hyndman, Donald W., and David D. Alt: *Roadside Geology of Oregon*, noted, 79/338
Hyskell, Charles, 73/299

I.B. Lunt (brig), 63/238
I.O.G.T., SEE Independent Order of Good Templars
I.O.O.F., SEE Independent Order of Odd

Fellows
I Remember Portland, 1899-1915, by Pratt, noted, 67/80
I.W.W., SEE Industrial Workers of the World
"I Was a Third Generation Pioneer," by W.B. Chandler, 66/208-17
"I Will Fight No More Forever": Chief Joseph and the Nez Perce War, by Beal, review, 64/273-74
Iablochnye Islands, 73/147
Ice manufacturing:
first Pacific NW ice machine, 63/67-68
Iceland:
shipping and life 1880-1900, 81/61-72
Icelandic people, 74/356
Ickes, Harold L., 64/59-60
Idaho, 62/106,202,216,297,409; 63/28,30,263; 66/231-32: archeology, 67/86,366; 70/87; articles on, 68/88,186,346; 70/180,181; assay office, 63/89; Bannock Mt. road, 65/313; beet sugar industry, 67/368 bibliography, 63/91—
1965-66 publications, 68/349
boundaries—
dispute, 68/88; Montana-Idaho, 70/181; Wash.-Idaho, 70/77; 71/196
Chautauqua, 71/196; Coeur d'Alene steamboats, 70/357; constitution and religion, 69/85; Coxey's army in, 65/291-92; depression, 71/196; diamond hunting, 68/88
economic development, 63/359—
growth 1948-64, 68/349; history, 65/215,314; 66/88; outlook, 69/337
elections, 71/196—
1964, 66/282
express companies, 68/88; fire 1910, 64/283; fossils, 68/346; free silver fight, 63/359; geology department, 72/180; gold discoveries, 64/188; 66/198; governors, 64/282; 68/88; 71/196; historic markers, 64/277; history, 63/359; 66/276; 72/183; 73/284; Hoffman view of, in 1853, 66/87; homesteaders, 70/273; Indian wars, 63/89; industry, 77/296
labor disputes, 71/196—

1890s, 68/186
Lewis & Clark campsites, 68/88; local history guide, 66/276; maps, 73/284; 79/ins.bk.cov. Summer; migration, 69/85; military posts, 76/92; mining, 67/87; 70/180; 71/47,55,60,196; 72/58, 73,73N,183; New Deal, 72/228; Nonpartisan League, 66/281; Oregon Trail route, 64/277; panhandle, 67/346; politics, 72/183
population—
1870, 72/73N; characteristics, 68/349 potatoes, 66/284; railroad routes, 71/47,49,50; reclamation, 67/371; salt production 1866-1926, 65/313; statehood movement, 65/364; taxes, 72/90 Territory, 65/364; 72/261; 80/208—
centennial, 64/282,357; created, 63/254; govt. problems, 72/183; governors, 64/282; politics, 72/230 theses on, 72/225-79; trade and commerce 1881, 71/5-6; Wheeler survey, 67/367
Idaho (Columbia River steamer), 70/139
Idaho: A Student's Guide to Localized History, by Wells, noted, 66/276
Idaho City, Ida., 63/30,89
Idaho Department of Highways:
Route of the Oregon Trail in Idaho, noted, 64/277
Idaho Education Association, 72/261
Idaho Power Company, 63/361
Idaho State Federation of Labor, 76/136
Idaville, Ore., 72/297,298,300,308,310, 312; 73/5,7,171; 77/91,213,222
"The Idea of the Railroads: Regional Economic Growth," by Robert L. Peterson, 67/101-104
Igak, Alaska, 77/183
Ike (Indian), 69/229,230N
Illahe, Ore.:
postal service, 71/200
Illige, Ben W. ("Red"):
biography, 73/213-14; photo, 73/214
Illinois River, 62/215; 72/43; 76/46,48,49,50,82-83:
geology, 65/315
Illinois Valley, 62/213,214; 76/81
Illiuliuk (Unalaska), Alaska:

Aleuts removed 1942, 73/127; church sketch, 73/126; mill sketch, 73/125; Russian-American Co. post described, 73/122-27

The Illustrated Biographical Encyclopedia of Artists of the American West, by Samuels, noted, 79/106

Illustrated Historical Atlas Map of Marion and Linn Counties, Oregon, reprint noted, 77/90,292

Illustrated History of Baker, Malheur and Harney Counties, cited, 67/141

Illustrations, SEE Photographs and illustrations

Ilwaco, Wash., 69/310; 70/74,272; 71/189,361; 72/354; 75/105

Ilwaco Beach Lifesaving Crew, 73/73

Imai, Midori, 81/157,170

Imai, Suiyoshi, 81/170

Imai, Taka, 81/170

Imberhorne (British ship), 66/108, 109,112

Imbrie, James J., 70/147N

Immaculate Conception Parish, Colville: history, 64/186

Immigrant Hill, 78/153

Immigration, 67/296; 68/351: 1840s, 75/318; army aids, 67/298, 299,300; Asiatic, 75/105,123; Basque, 76/153-58; broadsides, 72/64,65 California, 67/85; 71/59— effect of gold discovery, 68/349; reasons for, 67/84

Canadian West, 69/85; cattle trade with immigrants, 67/313; Chinese, 78/73-85; Confederate to Montana, 68/346; Czech, 70/278-79; discouragements, 79/25,49; effect of gold discoveries, 68/349; 72/58; 79/25; effect of Indian wars, 68/29; effect of railroads, 67/121-22; 71/28,30,35,36,59; 77/243,246; encouraged by good roads, 74/113

English people, 68/280,345— 1860-1913 to U.S., 73/85; 1865-1900, 65/213

Europeans, 75/93,118,132,133,141— to Washington, 74/281

family groups, 78/123-31; Finnish peo-

ple, 77/302; foreign-born, 80/265-68; Hawaiians, 68/348; Hindus, 70/365; Inland Empire 1870s, 71/60,67; intercountry differences, 73/85; Irish, 69/ 102-47*passim*; Italians, 77/239-60; Japanese, 76/229-36,240; Johansen hypothesis, 68/185; 81/97,101; Korean "picture brides," 79/51-63 maritime journeys, 77/37-60— 1848, 81/61; 1904, 81/33-35; shipboard conditions, 77/37-60

military posts to protect, 67/297-98; Montenegrins, 69/298; Mormons, 67/220; Nevada, 72/180; Norwegians, 70/39-40; numbers, 72/70N,74 Oregon, 62/68,130; 66/86; 67/85; 71/35,59,63—

assembly places, 72/65; character of immigrants, 62/69,75,118N; "Oregon fever," 77/312-13; 79/24-25; promotion, 74/113; reasons for, 72/ 58; 77/312-13; routes, 62/69; study of, to 1850, 80/329

Oriental reappraised, 68/86; Swedes, 76/5-27; Tennessee migrants, 77/196; through Gilliam Co. 1881, 81/275; U.S. 1870-1900, 71/60; west of Rockies, 70/84; western movement history, 72/173; westward trend, 74/227; SEE ALSO Foreign-born; Oregon Trail; Overland journeys

Immigration History Research Center, U. of Minn., 77/302

Immigration of 1836, 66/344

Immigration of 1839: Farnham, 79/107

Immigration of 1840, 62/69,71

Immigration of 1841, 62/75; 72/183: Bartleson, 69/64

Immigration of 1843, 62/75; 63/83; 77/314; 78/101; 81/231,255N: Burnett, 79/105; McKay, 79/134; Olney, 64/311

Immigration of 1844, 81/255

Immigration of 1845, 62/75; 77/311, 317; 78/71,147,221; 79/15: Franklin journal, 81/333; Hampton, John J., 66/187; lost Meek party, 62/ 199,217; Missouri pioneers, 78/281;

wagon tracks photo, 78/208; SEE ALSO Barlow Road; Meek Cutoff

Immigration of 1846, 62/75; 77/318: diaries and letters, 65/405-406

Immigration of 1847, 70/279: through Kansas, 67/85

Immigration of 1848, 75/87; 78/27: Burnett, 79/105; estimated numbers, 67/85

Immigration of 1849, 72/58: Denny family, 62/205

Immigration of 1850, 67/88; 69/84; 70/272,365: Allen, William R., 65/211; Palmer, Peter P., 66/383; starvation, 79/73; through Kansas, 67/367

Immigration of 1851, 70/69; 74/94; 78/127,128: Allen, 65/211; Clark massacre, 78/ 213-19; Crawford memoirs, 63/357; Evans recollections, 66/281; Olney, 64/312; Reinhart, 64/344; through Kansas, 67/371; Zieber journal, 66/81

Immigration of 1852, 70/272,358; 72/ 355; 73/72; 77/337; 78/139: accidents, 79/384; births, 79/381; burials on trail, 79/371,374,386,388, 390; California, 72/180; cholera, 78/ 136; Cornell journal, 79/359-93; deaths, 79/364-74*passim*,385-93*passim*; Dement reminiscences, 63/7-10; Denny, 65/231; disputes, 79/384; food shortage, 79/389,392-93; Gillespie diary, 66/81; illness, 78/136; 79/364,372,374,377,387-92*passim*; insects, 79/372,373; Marsh account, 66/88; number, 68/30,185; 79/367, 370,382; overland parties, 79/365-66; Stout, 64/354; 65/218; through Kansas, 68/185; White, Thomas, 65/212

Immigration of 1853, 68/345; 69/71; 73/83,84; 77/309,311; 78/54,70,71, 121-57,207-50: deaths, 79/20; earliest arrivals in Malheur Co., 78/140; family groups, 78/ 123-31; first ox team to Portland, 78/ 139; first to start on journey, 78/139; Ketcham, Rebecca, diary, 62/249-87, 337-402; Knight, Amelia, diary, 66/

382; lost train, 73/84; mosquitoes, 62/ 281,283,369; Neathamer, 64/89; number crossing plains, 62/241N; 67/306; 68/345; 78/131-32,139,149; oldest man, 78/139; property use, 79/65-90; registers, 78/132,149; roster, 79/338; Smith journal, 79/66-90*passim*; trail diaries, 78/123,124,128,149; wagon tracks photo, 78/208; wedding, 78/ 224; SEE ALSO Elliott Cutoff; Indians— wars and hostilities

Immigration of 1854, 77/311; 78/331; 79/12-13: births, 79/18; deaths, 79/15,16N,19-20,20N; Missouri-Wash. Terr., 72/ 179; number, 68/345; Rinehart-Edwards party, 79/16-19; roster, 79/338; wagon tracks photo, 78/208; Woodhams diary, 81/329

Immigration of 1855, 69/77: Keil party, 79/233,237,257— musical instruments, 79/256

Immigration of 1857, 67/372

Immigration of 1858, 68/345: Beehrer account, 64/85; Watters voyage recollections, 66/90

Immigration of 1859, 67/90; 79/36-38: number, 79/37

Immigration of 1860, 72/55,58: Otter-Vanorman party, 65/117N

Immigration of 1862, 72/64,65-71,74; 74/286; 79/394: Chandler recollections, 66/197-99, 208; Harding diary, 79/172-202; number, 72/70N,74; outlaw attacks, 72/69; Scott, Felix, 64/90; Wittenberg, 64/ 259

Immigration of 1863, 71/292; 72/72-73; 73/72

Immigration of 1864, 69/336: "copperheads," 65/115-16N; Fisk exped., 70/365; Martin, 64/351; overland to Idaho account, 66/188

Immigration of 1865: Gallaher, 64/282

Immigration of 1866, 69/329: Fisk, 65/314; Harland, 65/314

Immigration, post-1870: 1882, 69/274; 1890, 70/78; 1909,

73/85; 1916-17, 73/74

Immigration Rosters of the Elliott Cut-Off: 1853 and 1854, and Immigration Registration at Umatilla Agency, 1853, comp. by Menefee, noted, 79/338

Imnaha River, 70/29

The Impact of the Primary Economy on the Cultural Landscape of Oregon (in German), by Kunnecke, review, 81/325-27

Imperial, Ore., 73/84; 79/337

Imperial Russia in Frontier America: The Changing Geography of Supply of Russian America, 1784-1876, by Gibson, noted, 77/290; review, 77/293

Impressions of Portland, 1970, by DeWolfe, noted, 71/362

Impressive International Trucks, 1907-1947, by Rice, noted, 77/302-303

Improved Order of Red Men, 77/89

Imus family, Kalama, 62/109,300

In Pursuit of the Golden Dream: Reminiscences of San Francisco and the Northern and Southern Mines, 1849-1857, by Gardiner, ed. by Morgan, review, 71/359-60

"In Those Days...Tillamook County," by E.R. Huckleberry, 71/117-40

Independence, Mo., 66/86

Independence, Polk Co., Ore., 72/283; 77/266: map 1882, 72/171; street names, 80/105

Independence Rock, 62/348-49; 65/153; 72/67; 73/286; 79/67,68,377; 80/75

Independent Order of Good Templars: Ore. and Wash. Grand Lodge, 64/176

Independent Order of Odd Fellows: Baker, 64/356; Columbia Lodge No. 5, 70/76; constitution Ore. lodges, 64/168-69,171-72; Dallas, Ore., 76/ 373,374; Haines, 64/356; parade photo 1872, 77/132; photo members, 76/ins.bk.cov. Dec.; pioneer Oregon members, 66/201

Independent Party: Portland election 1873, 80/307

An Index of Archived Resources for a Folklife and Cultural History of the Inland Pacific Northwest Frontier, by Hines,

review, 77/297

Index to Clackamas County, Oregon, Marriage Records, 184?-1900, comp. by Mt. Hood Genealogical Forum, noted, 69/273

Index to the Hagen Papers, ed. by Burk and Book, noted, 70/271

India, 62/25,36,39-40,42: army, 62/39,44

The Indian, America's Unfinished Business, comp. by Brophy and Aberle, review, 68/177-78

Indian Battles Along the Rogue River, by Walsh, noted, 74/95

Indian Battles of the Lower Rogue, by Walsh, noted, 71/361

Indian Canoe-Maker, by Beatty, review, 62/101

Indian Charley, see Charley (Yakima Indian)

Indian Creek, Malheur Co., 63/264, 270,272,281,284

Indian Creek, Morrow Co., 69/106

Indian Festival of Arts, Inc.: publications noted, 63/357; 66/275

Indian George (Columbia River pilot), 64/198N,243N

Indian George (Cowlitz area), see Katel, George

Indian George (Hood River area), 72/94

Indian George (Warm Springs Res.), 65/39N

The Indian Heritage of America, by Josephy, review, 70/264-65

The Indian History of British Columbia, by Duff, noted, 67/280

The Indian History of the Modoc War, by Riddle, reprint noted, 76/181

Indian John, 70/147

Indian Legends from the Northern Rockies, by Clark, review, 68/180-81

Indian Legends of Canada, by Clark, review, 62/211-12

Indian Life: Transforming An American Myth, ed. by Savage, review, 80/333

Indian Mary Park, 67/374

Indian Peace Medals in American History, by Prucha, review, 73/276-77

Indian Primitive: Northwest Coast Indians

of the Former Days, by Andrews, review, 62/184-85

"The 'Indian Problem': Pacific Northwest, 1879," by Roy E. Ekland, 70/101-37

Indian Reservations of the Northwest, Idaho, Oregon, Washington, comp. by Wright *et al*, noted, 62/108

Indian River, Baranof Island, SEE Koloshenka River

Indian scouts, 63/81; 81/342,345: Bannock War, 68/306N; Deschutes, 66/146; enlistment records, 79/318-28; Haller 1855 exped., 67/311; McIntosh biography, 68/88; photos, 66/320; 68/236; 70/26; Sheepeater campaign, 68/223; Umatilla, 70/27; Warm Springs Reservation, 65/11,20, 21N,34-35,37N,42,46-47,50N,51,118; SEE ALSO U.S. Army; Warm Springs Indians

"Indian Shaker Church, The Dalles," by Ray Harmon, 72/148-58

Indian Shakers, A Messianic Cult of the Pacific Northwest, by Barnett, reprint noted, 74/283

The Indian Side of the Story, by Brown, noted, 63/84

Indian Springs, SEE Currey Springs

Indian Territory, 62/105-106

Indian Trade Goods, by Woodward, review, 66/186-87

Indian Trade Guns, comp. by Hamilton, review, 63/77-78

Indian Uses of Native Plants, by Murphey, noted, 62/301

The Indian War of 1864, by Ware, facsimile edition noted, 64/187

Indian Wars of the Rogue River, by Victor, ed. by Sutton, noted, 70/359

Indiana: manuscripts guide, 70/85

Indiana (battleship), 76/271,272; 79/213

Indians, 62/81-83; 67/368; 80/88,205, 206; 81/331: acculturation, 63/78,246,347-49; 64/43,45-54,357; 65/374; 66/74,337; 70/68,87— Cascades to Rockies, 68/347

adornments, 81/352,353 agents, 72/149,179; 74/86; 75/94; 77/317; 78/47,47N— Grande Ronde, 73/63,64 agriculture, 70/106,116,118,365; Alaska, 74/284; allotments to mixed breeds, 81/342 American, 62/59; 63/347-49; 71/365; 74/282— cultures, 70/264-66 American policy towards, 62/82; 65/173N-75N,213; 66/86; 67/367; 68/177-78; and American identity, 70/362; archeology, 67/87; arrowheads, 76/339 art, 63/364; 64/284; 70/352; 71/367; 79/213-14; 81/341-48— bibliography, 81/375-76; coastal, 72/286; cultural records, 81/342,343,348; influences on, 81/345,347-48; landscape sketch, 81/359; naturalistic, 81/345,347,348; NW Coast, 81/207-208; painters and paintings, 70/363; pictographic, 81/342,345,346; prehistoric, 81/329; rock drawings, 66/54; sand drawings, 66/143; slate carving, 68/347; stone sculpture, 62/300; techniques, 81/345,348 artifacts, 62/198; 63/76,89; 65/220; 70/87; artists, 81/345,348; Asiatic origins, 73/283; atlatls, 62/90; 63/89; basketry, 64/185; 66/88; 76/116,339; 79/338; 81/410(photo); bibliographies, 62/198; 68/76; 70/360,363; 71/288; 76/91; 81/375-76; biographies, 80/207; boats, 75/362; boys' interests, 81/343-44 British Columbia, 63/246,359— history, 67/280; reservations, 64/86 burials, 63/359; 71/367; 76/110; 80/237; 81/409,411-12— canoe, 66/91; graves, 77/89; Snake River site, 68/351; South Thompson River, 68/351 California, 63/350-51,365; 64/283; 65/200-201; 72/180,288; 73/283; 74/286; 81/329— 1840, 73/109-10,112-13; Napa Valley, 67/280; sketches, 73/109,112

camps, **81**/357,369,370
Canada, **62**/411-12; **63**/246,359;
65/374,380; **72**/253,345-46,356—
pictographs, **70**/180
cannibalism, **66**/351; **73**/64
canoes, **62**/101,184; **63**/13,359; **65**/
217; **81**/393,396—
photo, **81**/392; races, Skagway, **81**/
139; sea-going, **70**/87; sketch, **79**/398
Catholic missionaries to, **63**/55-60;
64/78; Catholic schools, **70**/320-31
passim; Catlin opinion, **68**/78-79; cattle, **63**/247; cedar bark use, **63**/193;
66/80; Cedar Mill area, **80**/106; ceremonies, **72**/345
chiefs—
Plateau, **70**/123; visit Willamette Valley, **68**/76
childbirth, **71**/180; Christianity, **69**/50-56; **71**/325-48,367; Christmas festivals,
69/335-36; citizenship, **72**/149,179;
claims cases report 1946-78, **81**/332
clothing, **63**/327-28; **72**/265; **73**/64-
65,110; **79**/210—
robes, **81**/345-66*passim*,421
Columbia Gorge, **81**/333; Columbia
River villages, **75**/88; Colville district,
76/304; **81**/330(photos); community,
63/246-47; Coos Bay, **63**/13
councils, Walla Walla—
1855, **67**/84,278,313; 1856, **67**/318N
Cowlitz Farm, **63**/106,155-73*passim*—
measles epidemic, **63**/138,140,183,
194; wages, **63**/115
cradleboards, **63**/359; craft enterprises,
63/246; cultural influence on American
history, **66**/280,282; culture, **70**/264-
66; **72**/356; **76**/91
customs, **63**/350-51—
burials, **76**/110; **81**/409,411-12;
childbirth, **71**/180; marriage, **66**/81
dances, **81**/375,420—
ghost, **67**/368; **70**/123N,266,364;
prophet, **71**/325FF,367; wolf, **72**/258
diseases, **66**/351; **71**/329,343;
76/91,201; **78**/50; **81**/341,342—
measles, **63**/138,140,183,194; mental
illness, **65**/314; smallpox, **67**/309
dwellings, **81**/405,407—

decorations, **81**/342,361,368; earth
lodges, **63**/350; tepees, **76**/339;
Umatilla mat house photo, **81**/406;
Umpqua lodges sketch 1858, **81**/406
economic development, **63**/246-47;
education, **80**/208; election franchise
sought for half-breeds, **66**/361; ethnological studies, **62**/108; **63**/72-73,348;
65/214; face painting, **81**/352,356;
factionalism, **70**/68; farming, **69**/84
fishing and fisheries, **70**/364; **72**/345-
46; **74**/12,13N; **75**/37-38,83,224-
25,227,231; **79**/130,295; **81**/322—
first salmon ceremony, **72**/345; mouth
of Columbia sketch, **81**/402; photos,
75/37,38; rights, **81**/397,403,405;
Selah, **67**/321; Sherars Bridge, **68**/91;
weirs, **81**/404; Willamette Falls, sketch,
81/403
folklore, **69**/84
foods, **63**/18,154,365; **69**/149,155;
72/288; **76**/339,340—
sharing, **81**/395-96,399,405
fur traders' view, **68**/178-79; gambling,
81/412; glove-making, **63**/327-28
government relations, **63**/74-75,186-
87, 201; **65**/202; **66**/86; **67**/356,367;
68/177; **71**/291,292; **72**/179;
73/85,276-77; **74**/94,96,284; **75**/
93—
Pacific NW, **70**/101-37*passim*,149-63
passim
guides, **81**/21,26; SEE ALSO Indian
guides; guns, **62**/92,93; **70**/88; hair
styles, **81**/351,356,363,367; headflattening, **69**/171-73; **81**/418
horses, **65**/214; **67**/310,318,367;
75/205,210; **79**/382,392—
medicine hat pinto, **81**/369,370; numbers owned, **81**/393; Plains, **72**/81-
82; sketches, **81**/34-71*passim*; theft,
78/215,216; trappings, **81**/353-54
Hudson's Bay Co. treatment of, **63**/193
hunting game, **76**/339; **78**/139;
79/107,121,145-59*passim*,285,295—
deer trap, **81**/395; forest fire use,
62/204; **78**/179; movie photo,
79/381; rights, **81**/398,399,404;
routes, **70**/364

Idaho, 62/106—
archeological sites, 67/87; reservations, 64/86
in American literature, 70/362; influence on medicine, 69/336; 71/179,180; inheritance, 81/394,395,400,402,404, 409-12,420
intermarriage with whites, 63/20,193; 74/90—
fur trade wives, 66/90,333,334, 338,349
Jacksonville area, 81/328; Jefferson era thought, 70/85; Josephine Co., 78/288; judicial boundaries, 81/332; Klamath Co. history, 81/327
land—
ownership by individuals, 81/397,400-404; rights, 63/247; 78/45,47,50; sale to whites, 81/403; title, 70/102,112; tribal ownership, 81/397-99,401-402; western cession, 75/85
languages—
Nez Perce dictionary, 66/88; preservation of, 66/92
law, see Indians—property concepts; leather, 63/227-28; legal workshop, 62/108; legends and myths, 62/82, 203,311-13,411-12; 63/80,245,362; 64/348; 67/366; 68/180-81; 72/ 249; 75/83-84,88; 79/335-36,338; Lewis Co., Wash., 73/343-44; life style, 79/334
liquor, 69/252—
sales to, 80/138
Lower Applegate River, 80/336; McLoughlin statement on, 66/337; marriage customs, 66/81; Meacham's work, 80/117,121-23; medicine, 71/ 179-81,184-86; 80/404; medicine men, 79/157N
missionaries to, 62/76-77,406-407; 71/325-48,365; 74/86; 75/10, 93,109-11,115; 76/359-60; 78/91, 335-38,341,343; 79/100-101—
Catholic, 63/55-60; 64/78
money, 81/396-97; Montana, 62/203; Moorhouse photos, 66/319; Mormon policy, 67/231N; movement from East, 68/347; music, 72/157; names owner-

ship, 81/394-95,409; Napa Valley, 67/ 280; native plants uses, 62/301; 66/ 81; North American tribes, 74/282; Northern Calif., 81/329
Northwest Coast, 62/184-85,203; 71/368; 75/364; 76/336—
art, 81/207-208; trade, 72/249
Olympic Peninsula, 74/7
Oregon, 64/73; 66/81,88; 79/ 334-35—
Catholic schools, 70/320-31*passim*; coast tribes, 69/67,172N; prehistoric, 62/89-90; settler relations, 63/20-21; 67/323N; treaties, 67/302
Oregon Trail, 62/255-87*passim*,339-43,362-99*passim*; 70/363; Pacific Coast, 62/57; Pacific NW, 62/98; 65/215; 69/50-56; 70/101-37; peace commissions, 75/72; peace medals, 73/ 276-77
personal property—
acquisition, 81/393-94; effects of environment and mobility, 81/392-93,422; individual ownership, 81/392,393; shared use, 81/395-96
photos, 81/330—
Moorhouse, 66/319
pictographs, 68/87; 70/180; Plateau, 70/121,123; political organization, 63/349; 70/121; Pony Express route, 67/231-32
population, 62/107; 80/207—
1848, 74/95; disease effect, 66/351
Port Orford, 68/81; Portland area, 74/94; 80/258; position in American history, 74/87-88; potlatch, 64/91
prehistoric, 62/89-90; 79/403-404—
archeological sites, 67/87; art, 81/ 329; Asian origins, 73/283; Deschutes village, 67/90; life, 76/89-90; migrations, 70/87,265; mound sites, 66/90; pits, 66/81
property concepts, 19th century, 81/ 391-422—
effect of whites on, 81/391,401-402, 422
Puget Sound, 62/108; 65/379; Quaker view, 75/93; rafts, 75/362
religion, 64/73; 67/187-88; 70/68,

123,167—
Christian influence, 71/352-48,367;
Christianity spread in Pacific NW, 69/50-56; ghost dance, 67/368; 70/123N,266,364; prophet cult, 70/123-24; prophet dance, 71/325FF,367;
Shaker church, 67/347-55; 72/148-58; 74/283; shamans, 81/394,420-21
relocation, 78/50,50N,53; report on rights and responsibilities, 78/177-78
reservations, 62/108; 70/103-106;
78/48; 79/31—
agents, 72/149,179; 73/63,64; 74/86; 75/94; 77/317; 78/47,47N;
79/38,127; SEE ALSO Lindsay Applegate; J.W.P. Huntington; boundaries, 72/18N,19N; British Columbia, 64/86; Idaho, 64/86; land, 63/310;
Oregon superintendent, 79/47,125, 136; transfer to, in 1856, 63/20-21;
65/173,175N; Umatilla Co., 64/90;
Washington superintendent, 79/136;
Willamette Valley, 70/258-61; SEE ALSO names of reservations
rights—
fishing, 81/397,403,405; Ore. Terr.
Act, 67/302N; report on, 78/117-18
scalping, 81/374,375; schools, 74/86;
scouts, SEE Indian scouts; shamans, 81/394,420-21
slavery, 69/173; 73/63,168; 76/226;
79/125,149N,305,328,333,334;
81/412-18—
cremation, 81/409; intertribal, 81/394
Smith River campgrounds, 76/86;
Smithsonian publications, 72/81; social adaptation, 63/246
songs—
ownership, 81/394-95,409; warrior songs, 81/374-75
sources of income, 63/247,347
sources on, 62/297—
Plains, 71/367; theses, 72/274
sports interests, 81/344; status based on wealth, 81/419-21
steam baths, 63/328; 67/371—
sweat lodge, 81/405,407
tanning, 76/340; Texas, 72/82; text-

book descriptions analyzed, 74/87-88;
theses on, 72/274; tobacco curing, 66/81; toll bridge operation, 80/66;
tomahawks, 66/384; tool-making, 70/87; totem poles, 64/284; 65/210-11; 66/88
trade, 72/183; 81/418-19—
beads, 71/362; guns, 63/77-78; 71/362; trade goods, 63/77-78,192-93;
66/186-87,386; with immigrants, 62/343,373,386,397,399; SEE ALSO Fur trade
trade unions, 63/246
trails—
map, 74/278; near Snake River, 81/19-20
Trans-Mississippi West, 73/274,284;
travel, 79/382; travelers' impressions, 81/20-23
treaties, 70/108,114-15; 73/69;
76/91; 77/303; 78/50—
1851, 78/47; 1855, 73/278; 1863, 72/73; Bannock, 71/262; Bruneau 1866, 71/196; Champoeg 1851, 81/398; Confederated Bands, Warm Springs, 79/125N,136; Klamath 1864, 81/414,417; Klamath-Modoc 1869, 79/127; Oregon, 67/302; Paiutes (Snakes), 79/126-27; Shoshone 1868, 71/262; Tenino, 81/398
treatment by whites, 73/66-67,149, 277-78—
English and French compared, 66/86
tribal areas map, 81/408; tribal govt., 63/246
tribes—
index of, 81/332; listed, 80/207;
North America, 74/282; Oregon coast, 69/67,172N
tutelary powers, 81/351; U.S. policy, 65/365; urbanization, 63/247; use of rocks and minerals, 72/180; utensils photo, 81/410; Vancouver Island, 72/88
villages, 79/277N; 80/73; 81/20,21—
Columbia River, 75/88
visit to Washington D.C. 1805-1806, 68/345; vital statistics, 74/86; warbonnets, regional styles, 81/349-50,

356,366
wars and hostilities, 69/71,77,250,252; 72/319; 73/284; 74/86; 79/31,37-38,40-41; 81/22,23,26,27-29—1847-50s, 73/277; 1858, 77/73; Abiqua battle, 77/197; aid to Lincoln Co. growth, 67/373; attacks on South Immigrant Route, 69/223-31,255; 77/318; Bear River, 72/73; 78/143, 144; bibliographies, 68/76; 81/106; Carson Valley, 69/230; Cascades, 74/93; 79/136; Cayuse-Molalla, 73/63; Cockstock affair, 63/215; Coeur d'Alene 1858, 63/89; contributing causes, 79/121-25; counting coup, 81/357,358(sketch); Custer battle, 63/74; discourage immigration, 79/37-38,49; Eastern Ore. battles map 1860s, 71/362; effect on Portland economy, 80/23,136; Evans-Bailey fight 1861, 81/105; fear of at Rock Creek 1878, 81/263; first soldier killed west of Cascades, 67/369; Fisk exped. 1864, 70/365; Ft. Lemhi attack, 68/345; Ft. Rains, 74/93; Fremont-Klamath battle, 66/284; Gilliam Co. 1881, 81/275,278; Harney Valley, 77/327,335-37,339; 78/41, 53,149,211; 79/36,38,41; Howard report, 74/95; Indian view, 63/84; Infernal Caverns, 69/240; 81/105 intertribal, 79/122; 81/394,398, 413—

rules, 79/130; Southern Ore., 79/30,30N; Warm Springs-Paiute, 79/122-23,125-27

Kutenai-Blackfeet, 71/343; Lander Road, 72/69-70; list of depredations 1865-67, 79/169N; McBride party, 79/31; McLoughlin massacre, 69/336; Modoc Co. 1911 massacre, 63/365; Montana 1867, 70/86; Oregon, 62/323,418; Oregon Trail, 70/363; Oregon war bonds, 64/154; Paiute, 73/258,260; 74/283; Port Orford massacre, 81/199; Pyramid Lakes 1860, 69/230; raids on immigrants, 78/47; renegade whites in raiding parties, 78/215; Rogue River, 66/218-

25; 70/359; 71/361; 74/94,95; rumored attack on immigrants 1853, 67/310; scouts, SEE Indian scouts; Sheepeater campaign, 68/223; 70/180; 73/284; Sitka, 73/149,153; sketchbook scenes, 81/340,354-60, 362-72; Snakes, 65/8,10-118*passim*; 69/253N-54N; Snake-Nez Perce skirmish, 81/373-75; Snake River, 72/55,55N; Snake-Warm Springs, 65/12N,34-35,37; Southern Ore., 71/189,361; 78/47,90; 80/105; Steptoe defeat, 71/198-99; Tenino-Molalla, 73/63; Tenmile Prairie, 78/90; theory of concerted attack, 1855-56, 67/314; Umpqua area, 76/382; Walla Walla battle, 66/133,134,137-39,141-44,159; Wallace murder, 63/194,198; war parades, 81/363,fr.cov. Winter; warrior songs and rituals, 81/374-75; white outlaws blamed, 72/69; Wool's charges, 67/315,318-20; Wyoming, 71/187-88; SEE ALSO names of Indian wars

Washington D.C. museum, 70/362; weapons, 77/336; whale claims, 81/408-409; Wheeler-Howard Act, 75/93 whites—

concepts of Indians, 80/333; cultural conflicts, 75/93; Indian aid to, 74/13N; impersonated by Indians, 81/98; interaction with Indians, 81/98

Willamette Valley, 68/76; 72/171; 76/90-91

women—

ownership of slaves, 81/415; property inheritance, 81/409,411

Wright's view of needs, 1856, 67/323N

Indians as the Westerners Saw Them, by Andrews, review, 65/199-200

Indians, Finns, and Their Thunderbirds, by Mattila, review, 75/83-84

Indians of Oregon...A Bibliography of Materials in the Oregon State Library, ed. by Hewlett, noted, 70/360

The Indians of Western Oregon: This Land Was Theirs, by Beckham, review, 79/334-35

Indienne, Robert, 66/360N

Indigo Creek, 77/329; 78/57
Indochina, 62/6,7,19,24,25,27,28,44
Industrial Workers of the World, 64/281,284; 66/73; 67/372; 68/346; 69/86; 71/215,364; 72/301; 73/188,212; 75/93-94,151,174: anthology, 66/186; Becker defense committee, 73/71 books on, 69/179-80,325-26— Centralia case, 73/70-71 characterized, 71/359; effects on labor history, 71/359; Everett massacre, 72/86,264; 73/281-82; formation, 71/363; logging camp improvement, 73/219; Montana, 72/229; songs, 70/79; Spokane, 72/228,231; violence, 70/85; Washington, 68/88; Yakima Valley, 81/336
Industry, 77/296,302; SEE ALSO names of industries
l'Infatigable (vessel), 69/269
Inferior Courts, Superior Justice: A History of the Peace on the Northwest Frontier, by Wunder, review, 80/330
Influence of the Hudson's Bay Company on the Native Cultures of the Colvile District, by Chance, noted, 76/304
Influenza, 76/163,239: 1918 epidemic, 68/138,140— deaths, 64/247-48,250-51,257; Oregon, 64/246-58; Portland, 64/247-55 virus, 64/257-58
Information retrieval systems: Portland, 79/339
Ingalls, David C., 64/228N
Ingalls, Gertrude Balch, photo, 74/265
Ingalls, Rufus, 64/149; 67/303N,331: expenditures for Camp Drum, 67/299
Ingalls, Winfield Scott ("Buz"), 64/355
Ingles, D.C., 73/255
Inglewood Country Club, Seattle, 80/49
Ingossomen Creek, 63/89
Ingraham, Cyrus R., 65/19
Ingraham, Joseph, 72/182
Initiative and referendum, 68/197, 206-207: Oregon, 66/383; 68/207-16,218-19
Ink-making: early Oregon, 63/36

Inland Empire: agriculture, 71/60,62; Chinese in, 65/364; economic conditions, 71/85; growth, 71/85; historical geography, 70/64; immigration, 71/60,87; labor history, 65/363; mining, 71/196; Russian-Germans in, 66/89; trade and commerce, 71/39; transportation, 71/38
Inman, Joel C., 65/120-21; 79/339
Inman, Robert D., 62/165; 65/290N
Inman, William K. (Ken), 64/68N,70
Inman-Poulson Lumber Co., 62/165; 77/225
Innis, Harold A., 62/403,404; 64/273: *The Fur Trade in Canada: An Introduction to Canadian Economic History*, noted, 63/357
Inouye, Isaac, 76/252
Insane asylums: Cowlitz Co., 78/364; Portland, 62/73
Insects: on Oregon Trail, 81/23
Inskip, "Doc," 68/249N
Inskip Station: photos, 71/252,253,263; suggested Nat'l Historic Landmark, 71/264N
In-Sook, Korean picture bride, 79/52-54
Insurance business, 77/296,302: Czech co-op, 70/278-79
International Boundary Commission, 69/231: survey 1872-76, 66/69-71
International Hotel, San Francisco, 80/255
International Longshoremens Union, 75/174
International Woodworkers of America, 76/145
International Working People's Assn., 75/128
Intolerance: anti-Catholicism, 75/111-23*passim*,131-32,134,140,143,144; anti-Chinese sentiment, 66/280; 72/353; 75/122-31; 78/34,79,85; SEE ALSO Chinese people; anti-German attitudes, 75/149,153; anti-Japanese sentiment, 79/51; SEE ALSO Japanese people; anti-Semitism, 75/153,157,165,182,187N; conscien-

tious objectors, WW I, 71/213-45; SEE ALSO Oriental Exclusion Act; Racism Inuzuka, Grant, 81/160 *Invernesshire* (ship), 66/122 *Investing in the Great Northwest*, by Pratt and Ross, noted, 77/302 Investments, 77/302: Eastern capital in West, 69/273; Irish in land and sheep, 69/103-10,133; out-of-state capital, 69/199,207,216-17, 221; Scottish capital in West, 69/181-82; "treasury stock," 69/212; Willamette Valley farms, 69/181; SEE ALSO Portland Stock Exchange and Mining Board *The Invisible Empire, A Bibliography of the Ku Klux Klan*, by Fisher, noted, 81/331 Iolani Palace, Honolulu, 64/5-6 Ione, Ore., 69/120,130; 73/285 *Ione* (steamer), 63/66 Iowa, 64/310-11: laws adopted in Ore., 64/299; newspaper collection, 70/360 *Iowa* (battleship), 76/275 Ipos (edible root), 66/81 *Iralda* (steamer), 74/300-302,304,321: photo, 74/301 *Iranian* (ship), 66/122 Ireland, DeWitt Clinton, 75/294 Ireland, John, 78/358 Ireland, Patty, Wheeler Co. sheepman, 64/109 Ireland, Willard E., 63/90 Irish, Jefferson Henry: biography, 81/327 Irish people, 75/118,123,125,128, 132,133; 76/348; 81/296: Chinese competition, 75/125; Emmet Guard photo, 80/259; geographic names, 69/103; immigrants in U.S., 69/102FF; Lake Co., 70/355-56 Morrow Co., 69/101-47*passim*; 75/270-76— name index, 69/117-47 nomenclature, 69/116-17; Oregon population 1860-1910, 80/136,265, 266; Portland population 1860-1910, 80/267; sheepmen in Central and Southeast Ore., 63/269; songs,

69/112N Irkutsk, Siberia, 80/201,203,204 Irkutsk Archival Research Group, 73/364 *Iron Eye's Family: The Children of Joseph La Flesche*, by Green, noted, 71/287 Iron manufacturing, 63/123: early Pacific NW, 69/183; foundry illus., 69/218; Lake Oswego, 63/92 Iron mining, 63/121,155,168,206 Ironsides, Dr. —, Wash., D.C. lecturer 1863, 62/233 Ironsides, R.B., 72/65,71: diary, 72/67N "The Ironwork of Timberline," by Orion B. Dawson, 76/259-68 Iroquois Indians, 62/105; 63/358: Catholic among Flatheads, 71/325; in Far West, 64/282; trappers, 71/345 Irrigation, 62/106; 63/90,272-74; 70/178,181; 73/258,266; 74/81; 78/360; 80/325; 81/314: Alberta, Canada, 69/337; British Columbia, 69/336; Bully Creek, 63/272-74; Clackamas Co., 66/381-82; Columbia River, 63/89; Drew Creek, 77/8,12; effect on towns, 81/202; Hermiston, 63/365; history, 80/408-409; Idaho, 71/196; laws, 69/274; Ochoco project, 76/245-46; Oregon, 63/362; Owyhee project, 67/214; Pendleton, 77/192 portable systems, 78/351-54— photos, 78/ins.bk.cov. Dec. Powell survey, 69/336; spring water, 77/7; Tule Lake basin, 72/353; Willamette Valley 1911 photo, 78/ins.bk. cov. Dec.; Yakima project, 71/368 Irving, Henry, 74/203-204 Irving, Washington, 70/85,226; 73/286: *Astoria* source material, 71/309-24; house "Sunnyside," 71/309; manuscripts census, 65/213; papers, 71/ 309-10; portrait, 71/308; reliability as historian, 71/317-18,320,321N,323-24 Irving, Washington: *The Adventures of Captain Bonneville, U.S.A*, ed. by Todd, review, 63/343-45 *Astoria*, cited, 75/104; 77/79; editions

listed, 66/78
Astoria, ed. by Todd, review, 66/77-79
Irwin, Charles, 74/211
Irwin, James, 74/24
Irwin, Wallace A., 74/201
Irwin, William Henry, 74/201,204
Isaac Springs, 79/278N
Isaac Todd (ship), 76/327
Isaacs, Henry P., 67/311N
Isabella (brig):
wreck, 63/193,236
Isabile, Marie, SEE Aubichon, Marie Isabile
Ise, John:
Our National Park Policy, A Critical History, review, 64/73-75
Ish, William K.:
express line, 68/88
Island City, Ore., 68/354
Island House, Salem, 66/20
Isle of Bute (bark), 65/243-44
Isom, Mary Frances, 71/221,234:
view of Hunt loyalty case, 71/
222-23,225,234
Ison, L.B., 78/175,177
Istachus, SEE Stickus (Indian)
Isthmus of Panama, 79/361
Italian-American Republican Club, 77/257
Italian Consular Agency, Portland, 77/259,259N,260
Italian Delicatessen, Portland, photo, 77/238
Italian Gardeners Assn., 77/253,256,257: photo, 77/252
Italian Hotel, Portland, 77/249
Italian Information Bureau, Portland, 77/259
Italian people, 74/116,125,142:
agricultural societies, 77/252 (photo), 253,254,256,257; benevolent societies, 77/257-58; building trades, 77/247, 254; farmers, 77/241,252,256; food, 77/259-60; immigration, 77/239-40; laborers, 77/240-44,247,249,250; missionaries in West, 67/368; newspapers, 77/259-60
Oregon—
population 1860-1910, 80/267

Pacific NW, 72/233; pioneers, 77/244
Portland—
businessmen, 77/245-49,254,260N; churches, 77/255-56; housing, 77/ 242(photo),249-50; native origins, 77/246,250-51,253; occupations, 77/ 254; photos, 77/238,242,245,248, 251,252,256,258,259,fr.cov. Sept. population, 77/246—
1860-1910, 80/266
professions, 77/254; social life, 77/256-58; truck gardens, 77/249,250,253
Italian Tribune, Seattle, 77/259,260
L'Italico, Portland, 77/260
Ivashkin, Petr Matveevich, 80/304
Iverna (ship), 66/129
Ives, Butler:
Calif.-Nev. boundary survey, 72/14-17, 48,52,53; field notes, 72/15N; Ore. Terr. public land survey 1854, 72/14N,47N
Ives, Joseph Christmas:
biography, 72/13N; Calif. boundary survey, 72/13,14,49N
Ives, Sherman Brunson, 73/68
Ivory, Perry, 77/11
Iwakoshi, Miyo, SEE McKinnon, Miyo Iwakoshi
Iwao, Kenshi, 76/251
Iwata, Mrs. —, Portland Assembly Center, 81/183
Izee, Ore.:
name, 64/91
Izmailov, Gerassim Gregoriev, 80/ 199,200

"J.B. Charbonneau, Son of Sacajawea," by Irving W. Anderson, 71/247-64
J.M. Chapman (schooner) 80/335
Jack, Joseph L., 79/282
Jack London (steamship), 77/277
Jack rabbits, 68/229; 69/106
Jackass Gulch, 62/227-28
Jackie Butte, 75/66(photo),68
Jack-knife, Clackamas Co., 74/282
Jackman, Edwin Russell, 63/366; 65/216; 69/274:
Desert Challenge, An Interpretation of Nevada, by Lillard, review, 67/364-65
Gold and Cattle Country, by Oliver,

review, 63/70-71
The Great American Desert, by Hollon, review, 67/277
Jackman, Edwin Russell, ed.: "After the Covered Wagons: Recollections of Russell C. and Ellis S. Dement," 63/5-40
Jackman, Edwin Russell, and R.A. Long: *The Oregon Desert*, review, 66/272-73
Jackman, Edwin Russell, and John Scharff: *Steens Mountain in Oregon's High Desert Country*, with photos by Conkling, review, 69/62-63
Jackson (Coos Bay Indian), 70/243
Jackson (Quinault Indian), 74/14
Jackson, Andrew, Coos Bay 1880s, 66/174
Jackson, Andrew, U.S. president, 66/334,344; 70/338; 76/123-25
Jackson, Charles Samuel, 62/204; 66/249; 71/232; 77/192: photo, 66/250; supports Columbia River Highway, 74/110,112,137, 139,208
Jackson, Charles T., 69/29,36FF,45, 48,274: meteorite collection, 69/39
Jackson, Charles T.: "Sketch of the Life and Scientific Services of John Evans, M.D.," cited, 69/29
Jackson, David E., 62/404; 66/64
Jackson, Donald, 62/105,202; 66/86; 78/284,285: article on Lewis & Clark Exped. journals, 68/345; quoted on Lewis, 69/26
Jackson, Donald: *Custer's Gold: The U.S. Cavalry Expedition of 1874*, noted, 68/82 "On Reading Lewis and Clark: A Bibliographical Essay," noted, 70/87
Jackson, Donald, ed.: *The Expeditions of John Charles Fremont, Vol. I, Travels from 1838 to 1844*, noted, 77/197,290; review, 72/165-66 *Journey to the Mandans, 1809*, noted, 65/314 *The Letters of the Lewis and Clark Expedi-*

tion With Related Documents, noted, 77/290; 78/285; reviews, 64/183-84; 80/206-207
Jackson, Mrs. Glenn L., 75/370; 79/413,416
Jackson, Helen Hunt, 80/333
Jackson, Henry (Indian), 81/317
Jackson, Henry M., 72/233
Jackson, Hewitt, 70/371: painting, 79/fr.cov. Winter— "Tide of Empire," 74/362 sketch of *Tonquin*, 71/fr.cov. Dec.
Jackson, Ivy Miller, 78/203
Jackson, J.G., 68/261
Jackson, James, U.S. Army, photo, 71/149
Jackson, Jim (Indian), 72/157
Jackson, John, Garibaldi lumber mill, 77/342
Jackson, John R., Wash. Terr. sheriff, 63/106N,107-108,131,159,171,219,239
Jackson, Kenneth T.: *The Ku Klux Klan in the City*, review, 69/179-80
Jackson, Laurence D.: "Fish Trap Art," 78/197-206
Jackson, Maria Clopton (Mrs. C.S.), 67/44,46; 68/227N
Jackson, R., Tygh Valley miner 1861, 62/218N
Jackson, Roswell, 72/44
Jackson, S.R., 68/260
Jackson, Sara D., 70/233N
Jackson, Sheldon, 63/360; 64/283; 77/296
Jackson, Susie: Indian Shaker service, 67/349-51
Jackson, W. Turrentine, 62/105; 65/214: *The Enterprising Scot: Investors in the American West after 1873*, review, 69/181-82
Jackson, William, fur trader, 81/235
Jackson, William H., artist: Indian photos, 68/292,312
Jackson, William H., Coos Bay settler, 63/11-12
Jackson County, Ore., 66/221N; 78/75: census 1880, 66/80; history, 75/88; interest in Klamath Basin, 69/224-

29,246,249; postal history, **64**/356
Jackson County Conversations, by Atwood, noted, **77**/90,292
Jackson County Historical Society, **69**/176
Jackson County Intermediate Education District: publications, **77**/292
Jackson County Museum, **69**/176
Jackson Creek, Jackson Co., **62**/213
Jackson Hole, **62**/404
Jackson Mountains, **63**/310
Jackson's Creek, Owyhee Co., Ida.: name, **73**/284
Jacksonville, Ore., **62**/214-15,301; **63**/11-12,14,79; **65**/75,76; **66**/21,220, 225,226,383; **69**/176,241,245,246, 247,251,252,254,276,343; **72**/39; **77**/382; **78**/361-62; **81**/105: Beekman Bank, **63**/252; Beekman House, **63**/353; Chinese mining tunnel, **67**/369; citizens killed by Indians, **69**/224-25; convent school, **80**/341; described 1860, **69**/233; gold mining, **69**/330; Halleck reception 1866, **64**/168; historic houses, **63**/353; **65**/315; **67**/369; history, **81**/328; Jewish people, **65**/374; maps, **69**/262,263; smallpox, **81**/84
U.S. Hotel, **63**/252— photo, **66**/58; restoration, **66**/59,92,282
Jacksonville, Biography of a Gold Camp, by Haines, noted, **69**/330
Jacksonville Herald, **64**/148
Jacksonville Historic Preservation and Restoration Projects, noted, **67**/80
The Jacksonville Story, by Engeman, noted, **81**/328
Jacob and Mungass, Corvallis, **71**/19
Jacobi, David, **80**/158,159N,160,167N, 289: biography, **80**/291
Jacobs, Melville, **63**/236; **64**/87; **65**/314
Jacobs, Nancy Ann Osborne (Mrs. William W.), **74**/219
Jacobs, Orange: views on railroad routes, **71**/71

Jacobs, Wilbur R., ed.: *Letters of Francis Parkman*, review, **62**/403
Jacobs Bros.: Oregon City woolen mills, **67**/62,73
Jacobsen, Fred, photo, **74**/265
Jacobsen, Henrik Ferdinand, **66**/109,113: photo, **66**/116
Jacobsen, Parcelia, **66**/113
Jacobson, Victor, **77**/362
Jaeger, E.J., **74**/121,215
Jail Rock, **63**/360
Jails: Auburn, **62**/232; Clackamas Co., **65**/211; first in Oregon, **65**/220; Ft. Klamath, **69**/329; Portland, SEE Portland— jail; Powers, **76**/66; Washington Co. 1851, **80**/11; SEE ALSO Penitentiaries
Jake, Chinese cook, **81**/265
Jamano, Cowlitz Farm employee, **63**/135
James, George: biography, **80**/320N
James, Hiram, **62**/242,243,246,251,254
James, Jimmie, **70**/278
James Douglas: Servant of Two Empires, by Pethick, noted, **72**/87,88; review, **71**/281-82
James J. Hill and the Opening of the Northwest, by Martin, review, **78**/358
James K. Polk, Continentalist, 1843-1846, by Sellers, review, **68**/277-78
James Madison Alden, Yankee Artist of the Pacific Coast, 1854-1860, by Stenzel, noted, **77**/289
James P. Flint (steamer), **72**/94
Jameson, J. Franklin, **62**/334
Jamieson, William, **66**/129
Jamison, Jim, **75**/309
Jamison, S.M., **69**/84
Jane A. Falkenberg (bark), sketch, **77**/54
Jantzen, Blanche, **62**/249N
Jantzen Knitting Mills, **62**/199
Jap Hills, **78**/320
Japan, **62**/6,7,51: army, **62**/39; attacks on U.S., WW II, **77**/195; interests in South Pacific, **62**/11,15,21; navy, **62**/20,21,25-26,29,30, 33,39; Pacific exploration, **70**/77; power in Pacific, **62**/14,15,21,22,24-25;

relations with China, 62/15-17,19,23-24,26,27,36; relations with Russia, 77/290; shelling of Ft. Stevens, WW II, 65/359N; submarines off Ore. coast, WW II, 65/219,314; trade with Pacific NW, 71/141-60; 72/239; U.S. bases in, 62/51; U.S. occupation, 62/34,41; U.S. strategy towards, 62/17,18-30*passim*, 41,43; U.S. trade with, 62/10,25; view of U.S. Hawaii acquisition, 71/161-78 *passim*; World War II military strategy, 62/29-30,33,35; World War II occupation of Aleutians, 80/34

Japanese American Citizens League, 76/253

Japanese Association of Oregon, 76/253: photo, 76/236

Japanese Association of Portland, 76/237

Japanese Island, Alaska, 73/145-47: sketch, 73/146

Japanese Methodist Church: Hood River, 76/252-53; Portland, 76/233,251-52

Japanese Methodist Mission, Tacoma, 76/241

Japanese people, 72/80; 74/81; 76/321: American, 70/85 assembly centers, WW II— conditions compared, 81/165-71*passim*; life in, 81/156-71; list, 81/165N birthrate, 76/237,243; California, 64/187; 70/178; churches, 76/233,251-53; coffee house, 80/62; college opportunities, 81/171N; farmers, 76/234, 239-40,242,248-49,251; fishing in Canada, 72/235; hostility towards, 76/231,234-35,237-38,240,242-48,254, 372; Issei, 76/225,237,253,255N; Kibei Nisei, 81/156,169N; laborers, 70/54; 76/229,230-33,235,239,240 (photo),241; land owners, 76/233-34, 240,241-42; language schools, 76/233, 251; newspapers, 76/233,251; 81/167 (photo),169N; Nikkei, 76/225-57; Nisei, 76/253,255N

Oregon—

1834-1940, 76/225-57; 1880-1920, 67/372; first, 76/226; first permanent resident, 76/228; first wedding,

76/228; population 1860-1910, 80/267

Pacific NW, 65/215; Pacific Univ. students, 76/382

population—

1890, 76/229; 1900, 76/230; 1910, 76/235; 1920, 76/238; 1930, 76/248; 1940, 76/253; 1941, 81/149, 164N,169N; distribution, 76/235,238; Multnomah Co. 1941, 81/164N,165N; NW Oregon counties 1941, 81/169N; per cent Japan-born 1941, 81/149; Portland 1860-1910, 80/267

Portland—

care of in 1918 epidemic, 64/256; population 1860-1910, 80/267; restaurant 1898, 81/119

Portland Assembly Center, WW II— births, 81/161,171N; curfew, 81/161, 171N; deaths, 81/158,162,170N; dental care, 81/158,170N; diary, 81/151-71; facilities, 81/151,154,155,165N, 166N,167N,168N; fire protection, 81/156,169N; food, 81/153-57*passim*, 165N,168N; jobs, 81/153,156,157, 159,166N; newspapers, 81/167 (photo),169N; photos, 81/151,152, 154,163,164; population, 81/165N, 168N,170N; postal service, 81/167 (photo),168N; property disposition, 81/165N; recreation, 81/158-63*passim*,169N,170N,171N; religious services, 81/155,168N; schooling, 81/156,158,159,169N; security, 81/168N; thefts, 81/155,157; transfers to relocation camps, 81/163,171N; typhoid vaccination, 81/156,158,159, 168N; violence, 81/158; visitors, 81/168N; war news, 81/159,170N; whooping cough, 81/153,155,167N; women's role, 81/171N

prejudice in Calif., 64/187; relocation, WW II, 65/375; 72/260; 76/254,255 (photo); 77/195,297-98

relocation camps, WW II, 81/168N— Heart Mt., 81/161,171N,photo ins.fr. cov. Summer; Minidoka, 81/163,171N; Tule Lake, 81/157,158,170N,171N

restaurant 1898, 81/119; seaman, 65/

316; small businesses, 76/229(photo), 232,237-39,242(photo),249,251; societies, 76/233,236(photo),237,250 (photo),251,253; sports photos, 76/ 250,252; United States, 62/18,22; vice, 76/233; West Coast, 70/178

Jaques, Florence Page: *Francis Lee Jaques*, review, 74/357-58

Jaques, Francis Lee: wildlife paintings, 74/357-58

Jared, Grace: *They Met Challenges With Memoirs*, cited, 77/369

Jarman, William R. ("Blanket Bill"), 62/97-98

Jarves, James J., 68/61-69*passim*: Hawaiian govt. printer, 68/64; negotiates Hawaiian trade convention, 68/67

Jason, (Indian), 81/350

Jasper House, 68/113,117

Jayol, J.F., 63/164N

Jeaudoin, Betty J., 66/382

Jeaudoin, Charles, 66/382

Jeaudoin family, Cowlitz Co., 66/382

"Jeff W. Hayes: Reform Boosterism and Urban Utopianism," by Howard P. Segal, 79/345-57

Jeffcott, Percival: *Blanket Bill Jarman*, review, 62/97-98

Jeffers, Robinson, 73/316,318,319,321

Jefferson, Thomas, 64/183,272; 65/214; 66/65,66; 67/367-68; 69/9,16,21, 22,23,25; 70/85; 78/284; 80/206: Barlow letter to, 74/268-70; biology, 69/152; introduces plants to U.S., 69/153; Ledyard plan, 68/274,275; library, 69/25; taxonomy, 69/26-27

Jefferson, Ore., 67/61: centennial, 72/91; 73/82

Jefferson Barracks, 67/368

Jefferson County, Ore., 75/309: history, 72/94

Jefferson County Historical Society: officers and directors, 81/110

Jefferson Guards, Portland, 80/28

Jefferson High School, Portland, 68/340

Jefferson Hosiery Co., Albany, 67/61

Jefferys, Thomas, 69/79: map of Russian discoveries in Pacific

1764, 72/100

Jeffrey, John: conifer named for, 68/119,120,124; disappearance, 68/114-15,116; discovery of new species, 68/124; letter describing journey, 68/113,117; Oregon botanical exped., 68/111-24

Jeffrey, John A., Portland attorney, 75/179

Jeffreys, M., Sacred Heart student, 81/81N

Jeffries (Jeffreys), John T., 80/358N: death, 66/137N; OMV service, 66/137-53*passim*; report on Ft. Henrietta raid, 66/150-51

Jeffries (Jeffreys), Sarah, 80/358

Jenkins, Capt. —, river pilot, 81/39

Jenkins, David P., 74/359

Jenkins, James B., 65/214

Jenkins, Leon V., 75/154: photo, 75/155

Jenkins, Robert E., 65/214

Jenkins, Stephen: donation land claim, 79/339; family, 73/72

Jenks, James B., family, 69/329

Jenks, Leland H., 67/106

Jensen, Ralph, 81/41,43

Jensen, Ronald J.: *The Alaska Purchase and Russian-American Relations*, noted, 78/288

Jensen, Veryl M.: *Early Days on the Upper Willamette: An Informal History*..., noted, 72/171

Jepson, Erick L., 67/280

Jernigan, Thomas, 71/141

Jernstedt, Anna Collins, 76/7-10,17: photos, 76/8,12

Jernstedt, Frank, 76/9-10,11,23: photo, 76/12

Jerome, Ida., 65/209-10

Jesse, Jim, 74/323-25

"Jesse Steiwer Douglas, In Memoriam," by Dorothy O. Johansen, 67/75-76

Jessee, Renic, 63/283

Jessett, Thomas E., 63/89; 64/283: theory of Anglican influence on NW Indians, 71/330-37

Jessett, Thomas E.:

Chief Spokane Garry, cited, 71/325-37 *passim*

"Origin of the Term 'Black Robe'," 69/50-56

Pioneering God's Country, noted, 68/342

Jessup, S.R., 69/88; 79/154N,167

Jesuits:

and fur trade, 68/348; Pacific NW missionaries, 68/75-76

Jesuits and the Indian Wars of the Far Northwest, by Burns, review, 68/75-76

Jessup, Thomas Sidney, 65/188; 68/9,33

Jewel, M.S., 62/219N

Jewell, Charles L., 70/163

Jewell, Marie L. Gulick, 73/148N, 154,155

Jewell, Ore., 80/323

Jewett, William W., 62/110,206,302, 422; 63/93,255,373; 64/93,189,285

Jewish Historical Society of Oregon, Inc.: officers and directors, 77/94; 78/94; 79/110; 80/109-10; 81/110

Jewish people: and development of West, 71/367; anti-Semitism, 75/153,157,165,182,187N; California, 70/179,366; Calif. and Oregon, 68/348; early Oregon, 77/300; Eugene, 69/276; Jacksonville, 63/361; 65/364; Nevada, 70/366; Portland, 70/366; 72/251

Jim Chow Chow (Indian), 74/13N

Jireh Swift (whaler), 68/347

Jobes flour mill, 62/176

Joe Lane of Oregon: Machine Politics and the Sectional Crisis, 1849-1861, by Hendrickson, review, 68/333

"Joe Meek Comments on the Whitman Massacre," by Clifford M. Drury, 75/72-75

Joe Meek, The Merry Mountain Man, by Vestal, noted, 64/187

"Joel Barlow's Suggestion to Rename the Columbia," ed. by Clifford L. Egan, 74/268-70

Joen, —, capt. of *Tillamook*, 77/363-64

Johannsen, Robert W., 63/360; 72/324: *President James Buchanan, A Biography*, by Klein, review, 63/346-47

Johansen, Dorothy O., 62/108,110,206,

320,423; 63/94,243,256,350,373; 64/ 93,189,285,363; 65/125,221,317,416; 66/93,350N,358N; 70/372; 76/361: address on migrations cited, 68/185; migrant theory cited, 81/97,101

Johansen, Dorothy O.:

James K. Polk, Continentalist, 1843-1846, by Sellers, review, 68/277-78

"Jesse Steiwer Douglas: In Memoriam," 67/75-76

Overland in 1846: Diaries and Letters of the California-Oregon Trail, ed. by Morgan, review, 65/404-406

The Pacific Slope, by Pomeroy, review, 67/78-79

The Role of Land Laws in the Settlement of Oregon, cited, 70/111N,113N

Voyage of the Columbia: Around the World with John Boit, 1790-93, review, 62/88-89

Johansen, Dorothy O., and Charles M. Gates:

Empire of the Columbia, A History of the Pacific Northwest, cited, 67/105-106, 140,160,177; 77/291; review 2nd ed., 69/60-61

Johansen, Dorothy O., *et al*:

Libraries and Librarians of the Pacific Northwest, review, 63/243

Johansen, H.E., 66/107

Johansson, C.P., 70/54

John (Rogue River Indian), 63/11,16

John, James, 62/199; 67/372; 68/340

John, Jennie, 67/372

John and James (vessel), 79/339

"John Barrett and Oregon Commercial Expansion 1889-1898," by Salvatore Prisco, III, 71/141-60

John Day Dam, 62/201; 66/89

John Day fossil beds, 70/183; 71/199; 72/288: national monument urged, 70/184,371; OHS resolution, 70/372

John Day Fossil Beds National Monument, 79/411

John Day River, Gilliam and other cos., 62/213,215,216,219; 63/10,362; 65/70,83; 68/235N,237N; 69/107; 70/38,371; 73/260; 75/309; 78/174;

79/32,42,105,125,130N,177: exploration, 66/282; ford, 79/201; geologic history, 70/360; OMV march 1855, 66/135; photos, 81/308,315, ins.fr.cov. Fall; SEE ALSO North Fork, John Day River; South Fork, John Day River

John Day Valley, 63/364; 66/235; 79/126: first pack train, 79/269N; fossils, 66/237

"John Jeffrey and the Oregon Botanical Expedition," by Erwin F. Lange, 68/111-24

John Ledyard's Journey through Russia and Siberia, 1787-1788; the Journal and Selected Letters, ed. by Watrous, review, 68/274-77

"John M. Shively's Memoir," ed. by Howard M. and Edith M. List, 81/5-29, 181-95

"John McLoughlin, Reluctant Fur Trader," by Dorothy Morrison and Jean Morrison, 81/377-89

John McLoughlin's Business Correspondence, 1847-48, ed. by Sampson, review, 75/76-77

John Minto, Man of Courage, 1822-1915, by Lowe, noted, 81/327-28

John Phoenix, Esq., The Veritable Squibob: A Life of Capt. H. Derby, U.S.A., by Stewart, review, 71/188

John W. Cater (bark), 64/207N; 66/219N

Johns, Johnny, 74/18

Johnson, Alexis, 63/120,145,147-49,160-62,166

Johnson, Alice M., 62/90-91; 63/349; 69/346

Johnson, Andrew, Inskip ranch hand, photo, 71/252

Johnson, Andrew, U.S. president, 63/360

Johnson, Archie P., 71/289

Johnson, Bert, 72/314; 73/18

Johnson, C.D., 73/221

Johnson, Charley, Westfall stockman, 63/265

Johnson, Claudius Osborne: *Borah of Idaho,* cited, 62/409; reprint noted, 73/282

Johnson, Clement, 74/24,26: photo, 74/25

Johnson, David, 80/414

Johnson, Dorothy M., 62/106: historical evidence, 71/366; history and fiction, 71/366

Johnson, F.M., Ft. Umpqua 1866, 70/255N

Johnson, Fanny Applegate, 64/91

Johnson, Felix, 69/103,119: family, 69/133

Johnson, Fred E., ed.: "Skagway-Atlin Letters," 81/117-48

Johnson, Gertrude Wiencke: *The Travels of J.H. Wilbur,* noted, 78/91

Johnson, Hester (Mrs. Clement), 74/24, 25(photo),26,32

Johnson, Hiram W., 68/136; 71/214: Progressive Party, 64/87; presidential campaign 1932, 64/283

Johnson, Hjalmar, 64/358,362

Johnson, Ione Townsend, 74/274,277

Johnson, J.A., 66/107

Johnson, J.R., 75/165,178

Johnson, J.W. Fordham, 74/233

Johnson, Jack, Seufert foreman, 75/37-38

Johnson, Jalmar: *Builders of the Northwest,* review, 64/348

Johnson, James, Pacific Co. pioneer: family, 69/78

Johnson, Jehu, 63/283

Johnson, John H., family, 69/133

Johnson, Joseph F., 64/91

Johnson, Kate, 69/119

Johnson, Kirke E.: biography, 81/117,121N,135N,139N; letters, 81/118-48; photo, 81/116

Johnson, Lee C., 62/110,206,302,422; 63/93,255,373; 64/93,189,285: "Trunk Line Railroad Development in Oregon, 1860-87," cited, 71/75

Johnson, LeRoy, Jr., and David Cole: *A Bibliographic Guide to the Archaeology of Oregon and Adjacent Regions,* noted, 70/358

Johnson, M.L., 71/274

Johnson, Martin, 76/15-17: photo, 76/16

Johnson, May, 66/382
Johnson, Nathaniel D., 77/299
Johnson, Olga Weydemeyer:
Flathead and Kootenay: the Rivers, the Tribes and the Region's Traders, review, 71/278
They Settled in Applegate Country, noted, 80/336
Johnson, Overton, and William H. Winter: *Route Across the Rocky Mountains*, reprint noted, 74/282
Johnson, Pet, Westfall cowboy, 63/277
Johnson, Philip, 77/45
Johnson, Que, Westfall rancher, 63/270
Johnson, Robert Erwin:
Thence Around Cape Horn, the Story of United States Naval Forces on Pacific Station, 1818-1923, review, 66/71-72
Johnson, Samuel S., 69/342,348; 70/374; 73/362; 74/184,363,366; 75/370,371; 78/370; 79/413,415; 80/414
Johnson, Mrs. Samuel S., 74/363
Johnson, Thomas, Coos Co. gold miner, 63/15
Johnson, Walter S., 71/286-87
Johnson, William, Coos Co. pioneer, 63/33
Johnson, William, pioneer of 1835, 66/350
Johnson, William, servant to David Douglas, 63/191
Johnson, William Carey, 64/151; 75/127
Johnson County War, 62/297; 67/359; 68/346
Johnson Creek, Clackamas Co., 62/171, 174,176,177; 68/160
Johnson Creek, Coos Co., 62/215; 63/15: mines, 63/19
Johnston, A.J., 80/146N
Johnston, Albert Sidney, 67/221,225
Johnston, Hugh, 70/293N
Johnston, James, 64/212N
Johnston, Robert, Clatsop Co. pioneer, 64/212,213
Johnston, Robert, Wallen exped. lieut., 79/33: map, Warm Springs Agency 1860, 79/124
Johnston, S. Rutherford, 63/253
Jolly, Jack, 76/109
Jolly, William, 79/21
Jonasson, Jonas A., 62/297:
Blanket Bill Jarman, by Jeffcott, review, 62/97-98
Chronicles of Willamette, by Gregg, review, 72/349-50
The First Century at the University of Washington, by Gates, review, 64/76-77
History and Government of the State of Washington, by Avery, review, 63/78-79
100 Years of Witnessing: A History of the First Baptist Church, McMinnville, Ore., 1867-1967, noted, 69/78
A Pioneer's Search for an Ideal Home, by Judson, review, 69/71-72
"Jonathan Bourne, Jr., Capital Market and the Portland Stock Exchange... 1887," by Marian V. Sears, 69/197-222
Jones, —, Auburn miner, 62/235-36
Jones, —, Deschutes homesteader, 79/48
Jones, Mrs. Abe, 74/15
Jones, Aleck, Grant Co. pioneer, 66/199
Jones, Alex, Coos Co. pioneer, 63/18
Jones, B.F., Oregon Nat'l Guard capt., 80/265
Jones, Bill, Westfall sheepman, 63/268
Jones, C.N., 75/156
Jones, Cassandra Becker, 67/213N-14N, 239,248
Jones, Charley, Pacific Livestock Co. supt., 63/274
Jones, D.F., 65/193
Jones, David T., 69/50,53-54: Red River Mission, 71/327,329,334
Jones, Evan, 64/348
Jones, Frank, Westfall saloonkeeper, 63/296
Jones, Gabriel, 63/123N
Jones, Hathaway, 75/360-61; 77/291
Jones, Herman LeRoy, 65/214
Jones, J. Wesley, 65/171
Jones, John, southern route immigrant 1843, 77/317
Jones, John C., Jr., 71/365
Jones, Kate Leonard, 78/247N
Jones, Lewis, Bennington College pres.,

75/279
Jones, Nard, 62/298; 68/279:
The Great Command: The Story of Marcus and Narcissa Whitman and the Oregon Country, review, 62/192-96
Jones, Richard H., 80/414
Jones, Robert, Shaker Church bishop, 67/350,351,353
Jones, Ronald E., 72/81
Jones, Roy Franklin:
Boundary Town, review, 62/96-97
Wappato Indians of the Lower Columbia River Valley, noted, 74/94
Jones, Stephen, Woodland, Wash., 74/93
Jones, Suzi:
Oregon Folklore, noted, 79/336
Jones, Thomas ap Catesby, 62/9; 63/358; 70/306
Jones, Tom, Jefferson Co. rancher, 81/297-98,300:
map of ranch, 81/282
Jones, W.A., Portland Board of Trade, 69/221N
Jones, Walter J., 76/41,43-45,51,52
Jones, Wesley L., 65/364
Jones, William, Portland physician, 75/20,29
Jones, William, Westfall storekeeper, 63/286
Jones, William Lloyd, 66/313:
biography, 66/318; photo studio, 66/318
Jones' Book Store, Portland, 68/202,206
Jones family, Tide Creek area, 72/199, 200,201
Jones Hotel, San Francisco, SEE Tehama Hotel
Jones Lumber Company, 77/225
Jones Mercantile Co., Westfall, 63/ 286,288
Jordan, Arthur, 63/286
Jordan, David Starr, 74/200,202
Jordan, James, Jordan Valley road builder, 71/263
Jordan, Len B., 72/254
Jordan, Michael M., 75/363
Jordan, Thomas, 67/303N; 68/5,25,30, 39,40,42N,43; 79/129-30:
biography, 67/324N

Fort Dalles—
building expense tables, 68/47-51;
building plans, 68/6N; construction, 67/325FF; criticism, 68/8,33; Derby dispute, 68/25-27; improvements criticized, 68/6-7,8,9,40,41; quarters, 68/6; report on buildings, 68/10-21;
requests fire engine, 68/37-38;
Wright defends, 68/8,34
photo, 67/325
Jordan, William Henry, 65/343,345
Jordan Creek, Ore.-Idaho, 63/80; 65/81,84; 71/255; 81/328
Jordan Hill (ship), 66/107
Jordan Valley, Linn Co., 64/89,354
Jordan Valley, Malheur Co., 62/201; 67/370; 68/248N,249,299,308; 70/15; 71/255,263; 72/93; 79/47:
Basque settlement, 76/153-74; photos, 76/154,166-67,174
Joseph, Mother, 65/308
Joseph, the elder (Indian), 71/284
Joseph, the younger (Indian), 62/102, 295-96; 63/78,90; 64/273-74,348; 65/315; 66/383; 67/278; 69/128; 70/5,29; 72/228; 75/93; 78/91,370; 79/106; 81/330,345:
articles on, 70/87; biography, 71/284; 74/95; characterized, 70/162N
"Joseph Gervais, A Familiar Mystery Man," by Thomas Vaughan and Martin Winch, 66/331-62
"Joseph Gervais and Jean Baptiste Gervais," by Kenneth L. Holmes, 70/347
Josephi, Simeon Edward, 72/280; 75/18,33
Josephine County, Ore., 62/215; 78/75:
bibliography, 78/288; census 1870, 74/281; communities, 78/288; history, 67/281; 78/287-88; place names, 78/288; postal townmarks, 71/200
Josephine County Historical Highlights, noted, 78/287-88
Josephine County Historical Society, 63/357; 65/121; 66/80:
meetings, 69/279; 70/276; museum, 69/176; 70/82,276; officers and directors, 67/283; 68/84,282; 69/81,278-79; 70/82,276; 71/194; 72/176; 73/

77-78; 74/180; 75/90; 76/95; 77/94; 78/94; 79/110; 80/110; 81/110; publications, 69/330; 70/359; 72/353; 76/304; 78/287-88

Josephine County Library System: publications, 78/287-88

Josephy, Alvin W., Jr., 62/296; 67/84; 71/345:

The Indian Heritage of America, review, 70/264-65

The Nez Perce Indians and the Opening of the Northwest, review, 67/278

Joset, Joseph, 68/76; 69/270; 71/335; 74/359

Joslyn, Falcon, 74/209

Journal and Letters of Captain Charles Bishop on the North-West Coast of America..., 1794-1799, ed. by Roe, review, 69/67-68

Journal Building, Portland, 66/390,391

"A Journal Kept by George A. Harding," ed. by Steven Tanasoca and Susan Sudduth, 79/172-202

Journal of a Catholic Bishop on the Oregon Trail...Rt. Rev. A.M.A. Blanchet, ed. by Kowrach, review, 80/405-406

Journal of a Voyage on the North West Coast of North America..., by Franchere, ed. by Lamb, review, 71/277-79

Journal of Captain Cook's Last Voyage to the Pacific Ocean, by Ledyard, noted, 64/187

Journal of the Modoc County Historical Society, noted, 81/105,328-29

Journal of Travels To and From California, by Clapp, reprint noted, 79/340

Journalism, 74/294: California, 62/292-93; 75/93; Canada, 75/94; School of Journalism, U. of Ore., 67/360-61; The West, 66/379-80; SEE ALSO Newspapers; names of newspapers

Journalists in the Making, A History of the School of Journalism at the University of Oregon, by Turnbull, review, 67/360-61

The Journals of Captain Meriwether Lewis and Sergeant John Ordway, ed. by Quaife, reprint noted, 66/384

The Journals of William Fraser Tolmie, Physi-

cian and Fur Trader, review, 65/207-208

Joven Teresa (vessel), 76/127

Joyalle (Joyal), Etienne, 63/131

Joyalle, Toussaint, 63/131N

Joyce, John, Wheeler Co. sheepman, 64/109

Jtowis (Indian), 79/150,313-21*passim*

Juan de Fuca Strait, SEE Strait of Juan de Fuca

Judah, Henry Moses, 63/83

Judd, A.E., 66/32N

Judd, Bernice:

Voyages to Hawaii Before 1860, ed. by Lind, noted, 76/182

Judd, Gerrit P., 68/68-69

Judd, Henry B., 69/223N

Judiciary:

Auburn, 62/231

cases—

Ford, 73/201-203; landmark, 73/60-62; Parrish *vs.* Gray, 73/245-57; timber trespass, 69/337; Warren, 75/363

Hudson's Bay Co., 62/119; indenture of criminals, 75/353,355; justices of the peace, 75/349,350; Lane Co., 67/179; Montana Territory, 64/85; Multnomah Co., 73/269-72

Oregon, 62/135-36,153,204—

courts, 69/337—

appellate, 66/28; circuit, 75/352, 353,354; constitutional limits, 73/270-71; county system, 80/18; district, 80/12; first district, 68/317-18,319; justice courts, 80/18,156, 330; reapportionment decisions, 70/363; recorder's courts, 80/17,142, 145,147,156,165,166,169; supreme court, 68/125; 70/182; 73/60-62; 78/176; 80/12,157,303N; supreme court decisions, 70/182

judges—

circuit, 66/19,21-23; 73/60; disqualification for prejudice, 71/197; independence, 73/269-72; judicial council, 69/337; landmark decisions, 73/60-62; police judge, 80/292-93,299N,303N,320; Polk Co., 77/263,266; supreme court judges, 66/12-31*passim*,363-70

trials—
criminal, 78/175; juries, 62/134,139; 73/271
U.S. Supreme Court, 73/271; SEE ALSO Ore.Prov.Govt.—judiciary; Ore. Terr. Govt.—judiciary; Wash. Terr.—judiciary
Judson, Adelia, SEE Leslie, Adelia Judson Olley
Judson, Katherine Berry:
Books on the Pacific Northwest for Small Libraries, noted, 66/78
Subject Index to the History of the Pacific Northwest and of Alaska, cited, 71/79N
Judson, Lewis Edward:
Reflections on the Jason Lee Mission and Opening of Civilization in the Oregon Country, noted, 73/73
"Work Horses in Oregon," 75/205-18
Judson, Lewis Hubbell, Ore. pioneer, 62/142N; 76/365
Judson, Lewis Hubbell, 20th century Marion Co. writer, 63/83; 66/81
Judson, Phoebe Goodell:
A Pioneer's Search for an Ideal Home, review, 69/71-72
Junction City, Ore., 65/121:
Milliorn Cemetery, 69/86; history, 70/272
Juneau, Alaska:
anti-Chinese sentiment, 66/280; history, 68/184
Junger, Aegidius, 70/317
Junior Historians of the Oregon Country:
publications, 77/292
Junior League of Portland, 62/421; 64/359; 65/415; 66/388,390; 70/372; 71/370,371; 76/387
Junior Order of United American Mechanics, 75/134,135,138:
Republican membership, 75/138
Juniper Canyon, 69/105
Juniper Empire: Early Days in Eastern and Central Oregon, noted, 77/300
Juniper Mountain, Malheur Co., 63/ 266,270
Juniper Ranch, 63/317,324,334
Juniper Springs:
shearing plant, 63/267

Juniper Station, 81/269,279
Juniper trees, 66/282; 68/89; 73/267; 77/89; 78/152
Juntura, Ore., 63/267
Juris, Frances:
Old Crook County: The Heart of Oregon, noted, 76/182
Juris, Frances, and John F. Due:
Rails to the Ochoco Country: The City of Prineville Railway, review, 70/68-69
Justice, B. Martin:
drawing, 72/fr.cov. Sept.
Jutstrom, William, 66/55

Kaahumanu (vessel), SEE *Forester*
Kable, George, 78/354
Kageyama, Mariko, 81/157
Kahn, Julius, 71/216N
Kain, Charles E., 65/272-74
Kaiser, Chester C., 69/29N
Kaiser, Leo M., and Priscilla Knuth, eds.:
"From Ithaca to Clatsop Plains: Miss Ketcham's Journal of Travel," 62/237-87,337-402
Kaiser, William, 81/91
Kalakaua, David, 64/5
Kalama (Hawaiian), 63/120,121,127, 131,149,151,160,165,168
Kalama, Wash., 71/14,16,17; 73/73,334:
history, 66/382; 80/334; Northern Pacific Railroad, 64/263; pioneers, 62/109
Kalapuyan Indians, 63/200; 68/353; 73/63; 76/90-91; 77/324,329; 81/ 397,398:
slaves, 81/413,417
The Kalapuyans: A Sourcebook on the Indians of the Willamette Valley, by Mackey, review, 76/90-91
Kalisch, Philip A.:
Poles in American History and Tradition, by Wytrwal, review, 71/281
Kalispel Indians, 70/121; 71/345
Kamaka (Hawaiian), 63/117,144,148, 150,162
Kamamalu (Kamehamehamalu), 64/5-7, 15-16,18-23,31:
appearance described, 64/7,8,9-10,20-23; death, 64/11; name, 64/7

portraits—
Hayter litho. photo, 64/12
Lebrun painting—
described, 64/18-19; photo, 64/8
unknown artists, photos, 64/17,24
Kamchatka, 64/187; 72/110; 73/159; 77/174,175:
cattle, 80/201; defenses, 80/200-201, 203,204; east coast photo, 80/ins.fr. cov. Summer; visit by Cook's third exped., 80/197-204*passim*
Kamehameha I, 64/26-27
Kamehameha II (Liholiho), 64/5-7,9-11,14-16,18-23,25-27,29-31; 66/280: appearance described, 64/7,9-10,18-19,23; death, 64/11,14-15; name, 64/7 portraits—
Hayter litho. photo, 64/12
Lebrun painting—
described, 64/18-19; photo, 64/4
unknown artists, photos, 64/17,24
Kamehameha III, 64/5; 68/57,58
Kamiakin (Indian), 66/133,151,383; 67/310N,314N,322,347; 70/125N
Kamiakin, Tomeo, 67/347
Ka-mi-akin, The Last Hero of the Yakimas, by Splawn, cited, 70/125N,129,131N, 139N,163N
Kamilche, Wash., 74/16
Kamloops, B.C., 68/87
Kamm, Caroline A. Gray (Mrs. Jacob), 62/239N
Kamm, Jacob, 77/91; 81/287
Kanade (Kanode), John, 74/21,24
Kanakas, SEE Hawaiian people
Kanda family, 81/158
Kane, John, 63/274
Kane, Lucile M., 66/66:
A Guide to the Care and Administration of Manuscripts, noted, 63/356
Kane, Patrick, 69/133
Kane, Paul, 63/219; 72/183; 73/75; 75/77; 80/332:
paintings exhibit, 72/358; publication, 72/359
Kane, William John, 63/274
Kane Springs, 63/307
Kanefield Ranch, 63/274
Kaniksu National Forest, 73/357

Kankrin, Egor, 72/125
Kansas:
history, 63/88; 64/85; 65/214; 66/86
Kansas Pacific Railroad, 71/8N
Kansas River, 62/257
Kaplan, Mirth Tufts:
"Courts, Counselors and Cases: The Judiciary of Oregon's Provisional Government," 62/117-63
Kapoos (Indian), 79/313,315,316,321
Kapus, William:
biography, 65/8N
Karle, James H., 69/29N,39
Karluk, Alaska, 77/184
Karmen Island, 73/116,164
Karn, Edwin D., and Randall D. Sale:
American Expansion: A Book of Maps, review, 64/77
Karni, Michael G., *et al*, eds.:
The Finnish Experience in the Western Great Lakes Region: New Perspectives, noted, 77/302
Karok Indians, 68/81; 73/283:
baskets, 69/340
Karolevits, Robert F., 65/313:
Newspapering in the Old West: A Pictorial History of Journalism and Printing on the Frontier, review, 66/379-80
This Was Trucking, A Pictorial History of the First Quarter Century of the Trucking Industry, review, 68/179-80
Karpenstein, Katherine, 65/136N
Karr, Lee W., 74/237
Kasaan National Monument, 76/101
Kaser, Agnes, 81/305
Kaser, Arthur Joshua, 81/305,315 (photo):
foreword and epilog, Jacob Kaser autobiography, 81/281-83,314-18
Kaser, Jacob:
autobiography, 81/283-314; biography, 81/281-83,314-18; death, 81/318; photo, 81/305; ranch buildings, 81/ 299,306,309,310,313,314,317
Kaser, John Jacob, 81/305,318
Kaser, John Jacob, ed.:
"Autobiography of Jacob Kaser," 81/281-318
Kaser, Josua, 81/305,307,309-10,311

Kaser, Julius, **81**/304,310,312
Kaser, Lena Yaisli, **81**/303-305: death, **81**/318; photo, **81**/305
Kaser, Robert Ralph, **81**/313,318
Kaser, Rose Dolores, **81**/313,318
Kaser, Rudolph Theodore, **81**/313,318
Kaser Butte, **81**/283,300(photo)
Kashega (Koshigin), Alaska, **77**/185
Kaslekin (Indian), **79**/313,315,316,321
Kasner, Leone Letson: *Siletz: Survival for an Artifact*, noted, **79**/338
Kathan, Melvin L.: *Panning Gold for Fun and Profit*, reprint noted, **69**/78
Kathan, Melvin L., and Brooks Hawley: *A Brief History of a Town and a Gold Dredge in the Sumpter Valley*, noted, **69**/78
Katmai, Alaska, **77**/184
Katman (Catman, Kateman), Xavier, **63**/132,171
Katz, William Loren: *The Black West: A Documentary and Pictorial History*, review, **73**/279-80
Katz, Willis A., **62**/106; **64**/283: *"The Columbian*: Washington Territory's First Newspaper," **64**/33-40
Kauffman, Paul C., **71**/199
Kautz, August Valentine, **64**/283: biography, **65**/213; Ft. Orford-Rogue River map 1855, **69**/35
Kautzman, Fred G., photo, **74**/265
Kauwerak, Alaska, **66**/88
Kavanaugh, Henry J., **69**/133
Kawabe, Teikichi, **76**/233
Kay, Thomas, **67**/65,73,137
Kay, Thomas, Historical Park, see Thomas Kay Historical Park
Kay, Thomas, Woolen Mill Co., **62**/166,175
Kay, Thomas B., **62**/175
Kayaks, see Baidarkas
Kaye Creek, see Soldier Creek
Kay-li-tau (Indian), **79**/275n
Kayura Indians, **77**/184,185
Keane, Gordon, **67**/52
Kearney, Dennis, **75**/126
Kearny, Stephen Watts, **65**/135; **67**/371:

Franklin journal of exped. 1845, **81**/333
Keating, Michael, **69**/133
Keating, Tom, **69**/133-34
Keats, John: *Eminent Domain: The Louisiana Purchase and the Making of America*, review, **75**/81
Keegan, Charles, **72**/341
Keegan, Mrs. Charles, **72**/341
Keegan, Frank, **69**/135
Keegan, John, **69**/135,139
Keegan (Cregan), Melvin A., **76**/268,382
Keeler, G.W., **69**/225n
Keen, Frederick, **81**/265n
Keene, James R., **69**/204
Keene Creek: map, **69**/264
Keeney, Jonathan, **62**/217; **73**/80; **77**/319,319n,321
Keeney's Ferry, see Kinney's Ferry
Kees, Andrew, **69**/341
Kees, Nancy A. Osborne, **69**/341
Ke-hi-u-keu (Indian), **79**/275n
Keil, Aurora, **79**/262: photos, **79**/262,ins.bk.cov. Fall
Keil, Elias, photo, **79**/ins.bk.cov. Fall
Keil, Emanuel, **79**/239,249,250: photo, **79**/ins.bk.cov. Fall
Keil, Frederick, **67**/276; **79**/245,248
Keil, Glorianda, photo, **79**/ins.bk.cov. Fall
Keil, Hugo, **67**/273,276
Keil, Sarah, photo, **79**/ins.bk.cov. Fall
Keil, William, Jr. (Willie), **63**/83; **70**/74; **79**/237,259-60
Keil, William, Sr., **67**/276; **79**/233,234, 237,239,241,245,248,258,260-67 *passim*: musical compositions, **79**/248,249- 64,267; Willapa settlement, **68**/342
Keil House, Aurora, **62**/299
Keith, Daniel, **78**/148; **79**/30n
Keithahn, Edward L.: *Eskimo Adventure*, review, **64**/347-48 *Monuments in Cedar: The Authentic Story of the Totem Pole*, review, **65**/210-11
Kelleher, Michael, **69**/135
Keller, Clyde, and R.P. Matthews: *Pioneer Landmarks of Washington County*, noted, **80**/106

Kellett, —, capt. of *Starling*, **63**/189,210
Kelley, Hall Jackson, **62**/199; **63**/185, 199,206; **69**/61,62; **70**/71,261; **74**/ 90; **76**/203: description, **63**/185; publications reprinted, **74**/91
Kelley, James Wilson, **80**/289,319N: biography, **80**/291
Kellogg, —, Shasta miner, **63**/51
Kellogg, Charles F., **66**/88
Kellogg, George, Portland physician, **80**/273
Kellogg-Briand Pact, **62**/22
Kelly, —, immigrant of 1853, **78**/303,306
Kelly, "Bunco," **63**/91; **77**/300
Kelly, Charles T., **65**/271,277
Kelly, Clinton, **65**/315; **74**/283
Kelly, George H., Portland resident, **75**/180
Kelly, Hercules Latourette: biography, **68**/330; Gold Democratic convention 1896, **68**/331-32; photo, **68**/331
Kelly, James Kerr, **62**/73; **67**/261,263, 264,265: Ft. Henrietta, **66**/145-47,152-53; legislature, **66**/133-34,152; letter to Layton quoted, **66**/152-53; OMV service, **66**/ 133-38,142,145-48,152-59; photo, **66**/ 136; Snake River exped., **66**/153; Walla Walla battle, **66**/147-48; Yakima War diary quoted, **66**/154,155-56
Kelly, Jane, **80**/351,355,361; **81**/76,79, 80,93N: death, **81**/80N; first Ore. Holy Names nun, **81**/80N; photo, **81**/78
Kelly, John J., **69**/135
Kelly, John W., **75**/173
Kelly, Laura, and Esther K. Watson: *The Kelly Family: Thomas Kelly, His Descendants and Interrelated Families*, noted, **74**/283
Kelly, M.A., Lewiston physician, **79**/184N
Kelly, M. Margaret Jean: *The Career of Joseph Lane, Frontier Politician*, cited, **62**/142N
Kelly, Michael J., **69**/135
Kelly, Milton:

dispute with Idaho governor, **70**/14-15N
Kelly, Penumbra, **65**/280(photo),281-82
Kelly, Plympton J.: Yakima War diary— cited, **77**/291; published, **78**/331-32
Kelly, Roy W. ("Buck"), **68**/331-32
Kelly, Thomas, family, **74**/283
Kelly, William, **65**/394,398; **79**/ 290-91N,297,298,299
Kelsay brothers, Malheur Co. sheepmen, **63**/268
Kelsey, John, **68**/340
Kelsey, Joseph, **68**/163N
Kelso, Wash., **65**/211; **66**/80; **72**/151; **80**/195,207: Coweeman School, **63**/245; described 1900, **64**/276
Kelton, Elmer: *The Day the Cowboys Quit*, review, **74**/280
Kelty, James Monroe, **74**/219
Kelty, Oscar, **75**/363
Kelty, Paul R., **75**/15-17
Kenai Inlet, SEE Cook Inlet
Kenai Moose Range, **76**/101
Kenai Peninsula, **73**/116
Kendall, Benjamin F., **63**/201,207,220- 21,229; **66**/67: photo, **63**/222
Kendrick, John, **62**/198; **74**/285; **79**/399
Kendrick, John, Jr., **71**/365
Kennedy, Arthur Edward, **72**/87
Kennedy, Bennett, **66**/59,62
Kennedy, Melissa Gale, **78**/125
Kennedy, Michael S., ed.: *The Assiniboines: From the Accounts of the Old Ones Told to First Boy*, review, **63**/71-73
Kennedy, P., **78**/125
Kennedy, Warren, **69**/135
Kennedy, William, family, **69**/135
Kennelly, Ardythe, photo, **74**/265
Kennerly, William Clark, **71**/250
Kennet, Calif., **72**/159
Kenny, —, Tacoma port surveyor, **66**/112N,122
Kenny, Judith Keyes (Mrs. James): "Early Sheep Ranching in Eastern Ore-

gon," **64**/101-22
"Stephen Watson Burial Place," **66**/59-62
Kenny, Michael, **69**/103,117,119,121, 123,127,130,131: family, **69**/135; family photo, **69**/135
Kenny families, Morrow Co., **69**/135-36
Kensett, John F., **67**/371
Kentucky Flat, Columbia Co., **74**/323
Keoka (bark), **63**/41-54*passim*
Keppling (Kippling), HBCo. interpreter, SEE Kipling, Thomas Pisk
Kerbyville Museum, **63**/246; **69**/176
Kerfoot, Dan, **63**/297
Kern, Benjamin, **63**/345
Kern, Edward M. (Ned), **63**/345; **65**/136-37
Kern, Richard H., **63**/345; **65**/136-37
Kernan, J.M., family, **69**/136
Kerns, John T., **62**/356N
Kernville, Ore., **66**/282: history, **73**/82
Kerr, David, **74**/22
Kerr, Thomas, **78**/90: diary noted, **77**/90,299
Kersey, Ann Brown, **77**/274-76: photo, **77**/275
Kesey, Ken, **68**/279; **73**/286; **80**/206
Ketcham, Rebecca, **62**/237-38,243,244, 246: biography, **62**/247-49; letter quoted, **62**/246-47; trail diary 1853, **62**/ 249-87,337-402
Ketchum, Richard M., ed.: *The American Heritage Book of the Pioneer Spirit*, review, **62**/296
A Kettle of Fire, by Davis, cited, **74**/248; review, **62**/192-96
Keyes, Amanda Viola (Mrs. Zachary T.), **64**/104
Keyes, Custer, **64**/105N
Keyes, Henry Dick, **64**/101,105N,108, 113-14
Keyes, James, **64**/103
Keyes, Walter E., **64**/104
Keyes, Zachary Taylor, **64**/103-108, 113-22*passim*
Keyes Creek, **64**/104
Keyes Flat, **64**/104

Keys, James (Jim), cousin of James Keyes, **64**/103-104,105N
Keys Ranch, Wheeler Co., **64**/107
Keyser, C. Paul, **62**/108; **67**/51
Khlebnikov, Kirill Timofeyeevich, **77**/86: biography, **77**/174-76; Russian-American Co., **77**/174-75; scientific collection, **77**/176; writings, **77**/174,174N,176
Khlebnikov, Kirill Timofeyeevich: *Colonial Russian America: Kyrill T. Khlebnikov's Reports, 1817-1832*, trans. by Dmytryshyn and Crownhart-Vaughan, noted, **77**/290
"The Colonies of the Russian-American Company," trans. and annotated by James R. Gibson, **77**/177-89
Kickapoo Indians, **72**/18N
Kid on the Comstock, by Waldorf, noted, **70**/361
Kidd, Walter Evans, **74**/63,158
Kidder, Alfred Vincent: *An Introduction to the Study of Southwestern Archaeology*, reprint noted, **63**/356
Kidder, John F.: Calif.-Nev. boundary survey, **72**/14,15-17; field notes, **72**/15-17; Ore.-Calif. boundary monument, **72**/17
Kidder, Leroy L.: diary noted, **81**/329
Kiernan families, Morrow Co., **69**/136
Kiernan Ranch, Siskiyou Co., **66**/81
Kiger, Dick, **77**/164-65
Kiger Canyon, **77**/164
Kiger Creek, **77**/164
Kiger Gorge, photo, **67**/23
Kiger Island: name, **77**/164
Kikawa Maru (steamship), **62**/197
Kilbourn, William (Billy), **66**/206
Kilbride, Patrick, **69**/136
Kilchis (Indian), **62**/196; **72**/300
Kilchis River, **72**/299-300,303; **77**/216,222: coal search, **72**/305-308; logging, **73**/ 11-30,171-92,212-27; name, **72**/300; railroad building, **72**/308-14; **73**/6-9; timber holdings, **72**/300,309(map)
Kilchis Valley, **73**/17,227
Kilham, Edward H., **62**/326

Kilkenny, John F., 69/346; 70/371; 72/360; 78/370:
"Alpine—A School to Remember," 75/270-76
From Shamrocks to Sagebrush, by Barry, review, 70/355-56
The Pendleton Area Finns, by Westersund, review, 72/350-51
"Shamrocks and Shepherds: The Irish of Morrow County," 69/101-47
Kilkenny, John S.: biography, 69/103-11; family, 69/ 105,136; home described, 69/113; photo, 69/100; ranch photo, 69/107
Kilkenny, Lottie Russell, 69/107: children, 69/107
Kilkenny, Mary Ann, 69/103: children, 69/105
Kilkenny, Peter, 69/103: children, 69/105
Kilkenny, Rose Ann Curran, 69/105: children, 69/106; death, 69/107
Kilkenny, Virginia B., 69/117
Killam Creek, 72/308
Killea, Tom, photo, 74/4
Killibrew Ranch, 72/40N
Killibrew's Ferry, 72/39N
Kilmallie (ship), 66/122
Kimball, Francis A., 78/7
Kimball, George, 78/7
Kimball, Gorham Gates, 81/328
Kime, Albert, 63/286
Kime, Billie, 63/279-81,286
Kime, Nancy, 63/284-85
Kime, Wayne R.:
"Alfred Seaton's Journal: A Source for Irving's *Tonquin* Disaster Account," 71/309-24
Kime Ranch, 63/272
Kimerling, A. Jon, and Richard Highsmith:
Atlas of the Pacific Northwest, 6th ed. noted, 81/331
Kimes, James, 78/124
Kimes, Michael, 78/124
Kimmel, Joseph W., 75/241-42
Kimmel, Martin Luther: biography, 75/241-45; photo, 75/240; World War I diary, 75/245-69

Kimmel, Martin Luther: "To Be a Soldier: 1917 Diary," ed. by Moss K. Brown, 75/245-69
Kincaid, Harrison Rittenhouse, 63/83
Kincheloe Point: name, 77/221
Kindred, David, family, 71/189
King, Alexander A., 77/321,325,325N, 336; 79/23: portrait, 77/326
King, Arthur S., 78/353,354
King, Charles, U.S. Army general, 80/184
King, Clarence, 70/73; 75/79
King, Ernest Joseph, 62/5,31
King, F.W., 74/21
King, Harold, 75/279
King, Isaac, 65/185
King, James, Cook exped., 80/201
King, M.G., 72/14,15
King, Merle, 74/21
King, Ralph:
"Pennoyer *v*. Neff: Legal Landmark," 73/60-62
King, Sidney A., 74/240
King Edward (ship), 66/122
King George (Indian): biography, 74/91
King George's Sound Co., 76/313
King, of the Mountains, by Shebl, noted, 76/182
Kings Valley, 64/356; 65/173,178,185, 189; 66/77; 72/281
Kingsbury, Martha:
Art of the Thirties, noted, 73/285
Kinkead, John H., 72/135
Kinney, James, immigrant of 1853, 78/124,148,149
Kinney, Patrick, 78/124,148,149
Kinney, Thomas, immigrant of 1853, 78/124,129,148,149,207
Kinney's (Keeney's) Ferry, Boise River, 66/235; 68/230; 70/18N
Kinnison, "Hy," 66/206,207
Kinsey, Darius, 66/381
Kintner, C.J., 67/367
Kinzer, Donald L.:
The American Protective Association: An Episode in Anti-Catholicism, cited, 75/138-39

Kiowa Indians, 81/345,348,361
Kip, Lawrence:
Ft. Dalles description, 67/325
Kipling, Charles, 63/227
Kipling, Rudyard:
Columbia River fish canneries description, 72/354
Kipling, Rudyard:
"American Salmon," cited, 71/267
Kipling, Thomas Pisk, 64/202N,211-12, 215,220-21,238:
biography, 64/211N
Kippen, W.F., 64/205N
Kirkham, Arthur R., 67/43,44,51
Kirkland Steel Mill, 64/87
Kirkpatrick, Ernest Chalmers, 77/263-64; 78/172-73
Kirkpatrick, J.M., 62/223
Kirkpatrick, Robert:
reminiscences, 65/365
Kirk's Iron Works, The Dalles, 69/293,305
Kirrie, Marjorie:
The Shaping of a Family, A Memoir, by Oliver, review, 81/102-103
Yours Sincerely, Ann W. Shepard, ed. by Davis, review, 80/102
Kiscox, —, HBCO. employee, 63/150,165
Kiser Brothers, Portland photographers, 66/205,206
Kiska Island, 80/35:
Japanese air base, 80/37,40,42,45; Japanese armament, 80/44; submarine base, 80/41
Kissling, Hans W., 77/354
Kistner, Joel P., 78/128
Kitayama, Kuni, 81/154,168N
Kittell, Allen, 81/149N
Kittitas Frontiersmen, ed. by Glauert and Kunz, noted, 79/105
Kittitas Valley, 70/125,133; 79/105: history, 77/301
Kittleman, Laurence R.: geology study, 75/87
Kittredge, William, 70/278
Kitts, Chris, 75/230
Kittson, William, 63/215
Kivkhpak River, SEE Yukon River
Kiwanis Club, 74/242:

Ashland, 64/329
Kiyomura, Roy I., 81/153,166
Kiyomura, Shizue, 81/153,166
Klady, C.L., 74/281
Klakautch (Kloh-Kutz) (Indian):
meets Seward, 72/138-41
Klamath (steamer), 75/239
Klamath Basin, 62/322; 63/350; 77/318; 78/363:
anthropology, 69/333; army exped. reports and journal, 67/223-68; early drovers, 69/225N,229,243-45,249-50; exploration 1855, 66/282; Fremont Indian battle, 66/284; geology, 67/22; history, 65/218; interest in settlement, 69/225-26,231,243,249; maps, 69/228,266-68,ins.bk.cov. Sept.; steamboating, 64/356; travelers 1860, 69/223,229-32
Klamath Centennial Souvenir Booklet, noted, 69/77
Klamath County, Ore., 65/219; 66/365; 72/46,47,353; 73/81; 75/233-39: banks, 69/328
boundaries, 66/80—
survey 1854, 72/10-12
buried treasure, 66/81; cattle industry, 72/288; courthouse, 69/328; early transportation, 66/382; first newspaper, 65/315; geology, 66/80; history, 69/77; map, 75/232; Merrill-Keno history, 70/358; mineral resources, 71/286; postal townmarks, 71/200; railroads, 80/104; recollections 1900s, 70/75; towns, 66/284; transportation history, 75/86,362; ww I armistice celebration, 71/274-76
"Klamath County: False Armistice Day, Nov. 9, 1918," by Claudia Spink Lorenz, 71/274-76
Klamath County Historical Society: history, 66/81; meetings, 69/279; 70/276; museum, 69/176; 70/82,276; officers and directors, 62/103,415; 63/86,250; 64/83,279; 65/123,311; 66/84,278; 67/82,283; 68/84,282; 69/81,279; 70/82,276; 71/194; 72/176; 73/78; 77/292; publications, 66/80-81,382; 69/77,328-29;

70/358; 72/353; 77/195; 78/363
Klamath County Museum: publications, 70/75,271; 73/283; 81/327
Klamath Development Company, 71/275
Klamath Echoes, noted, 66/80-81,382; 69/77,328-29; 72/351,352; 75/86; 76/382; 77/195; 78/383; 80/104
Klamath Falls, Ore., 62/205; 63/365; 66/291N,226,365; 70/75; 76/ 240,353: Baldwin House Hotel, 63/253; 69/ 328; 70/280; 73/81; banks, 69/328; blacksmith shops, 69/328; livery stables, 69/328; Methodist Church history, 64/91; Modoc Line, Southern Pacific, 71/95N; opera house, 73/283; progress report, 65/217,218; theatrical history, 69/328; ww I armistice celebration, 71/274-76
Klamath Hot Springs, 64/351; 78/363
Klamath Indian Agency, 62/322
Klamath Indian Reservation, 63/246; 66/226N; 67/356; 70/75; 79/127: agents, 79/127; physicians, 79/305
Klamath Indians, 62/198; 63/365; 67/ 356; 68/342; 70/75; 73/64; 76/ 71,72; 77/318,323; 78/55; 80/117: Bannock War, 68/319,320-21; crematory, 75/235; economy, 63/246; education, 63/91; fear of Snake Indians, 69/239,252,254; first tribal election 1868, 64/353; fishing rights, 81/405; Fremont battle, 66/284; houses, 81/ 307; inheritance, 81/411; land retention, 65/315; marriage customs, 66/ 81; Mt. Mazama eruption threat, 65/ 315; Ogden exped., 63/350; photo 1860, 69/248; property customs, 81/ 403-404,412,420; relations with whites 1854-60, 69/224-68*passim*; slavery, 81/ 394,413,414,417; sweat baths, 75/235; trade, 81/418; tribal govt., 63/246
Klamath Lake Railroad, 66/284; 69/77; 80/104
Klamath Marsh, 63/355: map, 69/268
Klamath Mountains, 79/291,294
Klamath Reclamation Project, 80/409

Klamath River, 66/284; 68/81; 69/229, 231,243-55*passim*; 70/ 75,251; 72/39,40; 80/235: Big Bend Reservoir photo, 69/234; Emigrants Ford, 69/231,233,235N; falls, photo, 69/77; gold mining, 65/ 214; 66/218,225-26; history, 74/93; maps, 69/226,228,244,265,266,ins.fr. &bk.covs. Sept.; photo, 72/39; salt caves excavation, 64/353
Klamath Short-Line Railroad, 68/350
The Klamath Tribe, a People and Their Reservation, by Stern, review, 67/356
Klapat (Nisqually Farm employee), 63/151,159
Klatskanie, SEE Clatskanie
Klee, S., 74/121
Klein, Philip S.:
President James Buchanan, A Biography, review, 63/346-47
Klein, Roy A., 74/138,142
Klep, Rolf:
Disaster Log of Ships, by Gibbs, review, 73/69-70
Klichka, F.N., 80/203,204
Klickitat, Wash., 63/355; 69/68-69
Klickitat County, Wash.: census records 1860-80, 74/94; history, 79/104-105; post offices, 69/331
Klickitat County Historical Museum, 69/176
Klickitat County Historical Society, 69/331; 79/105
Klickitat Indians, 62/79; 63/183; 66/143; 67/322,323N; 69/68-69; 70/121; 72/153; 79/129; 81/418
Klickitat Log and Lumber Co., 63/92
Kline, John L., 78/128,149,153, 328,328N
Kline, L.J., 71/17
Kline, Mary Holt, 78/128
Klingle, Ruth, 77/90
Klippel, Henry, 67/259,266,268
Kloh-Kutz (Indian), SEE Klakautch
Klondike, Canada, 76/101: dance halls, 63/352; gold rush, 62/95-96; 63/353,359; 67/280; 69/75-76; map, 76/112; theaters, 63/359
The Klondike Fever: The Life and Death of

the Last Great Gold Rush, by Berton, review, 62/95-96

Klondike Kate: The Life and Legend of Kitty Rockwell, The Queen of the Yukon, by Lucia, review, 63/352-53

Klondike Kate's Hotel, Bend, 77/19

Klondike '98, "E.A. Hegg's Gold Rush Album," by Becker, review, 69/75-76

Klondike Saga: The Chronicle of a Minnesota Gold Mining Company, by Lokke, noted, 67/280

Klosterman, August, 62/300

Klosterman, Josephine, 62/300

Klosterman, T.K., family, 69/117

Klytes (Indian), see Morrill, Ozro

Knack, Katie, 74/30

Knapp, Fred C.:

"'Automobiling' on the Pacific Coast," 75/283-89

Knapp, J.C., 64/311n

Knapp, Louis L., 64/359; 75/362

Knapp, Burrell and Co., Portland, 64/168

Knappa, Ore., 63/351

Knappton, Wash., 63/198; 75/105

"Knickerbocker Views of the Oregon Country: Judge William Strong's Narrative," with foreword by W.D. Strong, 62/57-87

Knife-and-Fork Club, Portland, 74/235

Knight, Amelia Stewart: diary 1853, 66/382

Knight, Grace Bowman, ed.: *Memoirs of Earl Wayland Bowman*, noted, 72/355

Knight, J.W., 62/281n

Knight, Joseph, 66/90

Knight, William W., 74/238

Knight family, Cowlitz Co., 64/276

Knighten, Bert, 63/302

Knighten, William Green, 63/270

Knighten Creek, 63/264

Knighton, —, capt. of *Eliza*, 63/50

Knighton, Elizabeth, 62/318

Knighton, Henry M., 62/151,301

Knights of Labor, 68/207

Knights of Pythias, 76/373; 81/49,52,54

Knights of the Golden Circle, 63/254; 67/54

Knives, see Prices

Knollin, A.J., 67/131

Knollin Sheep Company, 81/301

Know Nothing Party, 75/119,131: Oregon, 75/119,120,121; ritual, 75/108,120

Knowles, Albert: children, 74/271; house, 74/272 (photo),273

Knowles, Charles W., 69/208,213; 80/135,158

Knowles, Ebenezer, 74/271

Knowles, Elizabeth (Lizzie), 74/271

Knowles, Ellen, 74/271

Knowles, Frank, 74/271

Knowles, Lillian (Mrs. Albert), 74/271

Knowles, Margie Young, 69/173; 74/271

Knowles, Oren, 74/271

Knowles, William E., 72/163(photo): "To Oregon by Auto, 1915," 72/159-64

Knowles, Mrs. William E., 72/159-64

Knowles Creek, 74/273

Knowlton, Frank Hall, 66/237n; 67/29

Knox Brothers, Paulina sheepmen, 81/302

Knuth, Priscilla, 73/364; 75/368; 79/412:

American Forts, by Robinson, review, 79/214

As a City Upon a Hill, by Smith, review, 70/71-72

Bigler's Chronicle of the West, by Gudde, review, 64/275-76

Born To Be a Soldier, by Wessels, review, 73/71

Cattle Country of Peter French, by Giles French, review, 66/67-68

"Cavalry in the Indian Country, 1864," 65/5-118

A Classified Bibliography of the Periodical Literature of the Trans-Mississippi West, 1811-1957, ed. by Winther, review, 63/81-82; 72/349

Early Portland, by Snyder, review, 72/169

Exploration and Empire, by Goetzmann, review, 70/73-74

From Where the Sun Now Stands, by Henry, review, 62/295-96

Genealogical Material in Oregon Donation Land Claims, by Genealogical Forum of Portland, Vol. III review, **64**/79; Vol. IV review, **69**/76-77

The Golden Frontier, ed. by Nunis, review, **64**/344-46

Great Day in the West, by Ruth, review, **65**/202-203

Heart Mountain, by Nelson, review, **77**/297-98

Indian Life, ed. by Savage, review, **80**/333

Man of the Plains, ed. by Danker, review, **63**/80-81

Modoc County, a Geographic Time Continuum, by Pease, review, **67**/365

Narrative of a Journey, by Townsend, reprint review, **72**/170

Old Forts of the Northwest, by Hart, review, **65**/202-203

"An Oregon Classic: Nellie Pipes McArthur," **79**/91

The Oregon Question, by Merk, review, **69**/72-73

Photographer of a Frontier: The Photographs of Peter Britt, by Miller, review, **78**/361-62

"'Picturesque' Frontier: The Army's Fort Dalles," **67**/293-346; **68**/5-52

Skidmore's Portland, by Snyder, review, **75**/83

Soldier and Brave, by National Park Service, review, **65**/202-203

Soldier in the West, ed. by Hine, review, **74**/355-56

Steamboats in the Timber, by Hult, review, **70**/357

Things I See, by Weatherford, review, **75**/361-62

William Henry Boyle's Personal Observations of the Modoc War, ed. by Dillon, review, **63**/81

Knuth, Priscilla, ed.: "Alexander Piper's Reports and Journal," **69**/223-68

Knuth, Priscilla, jt. ed.: "Alexander Lattie's Fort George Journal, 1846," **64**/197-245 "From Ithaca to Clatsop Plains: Miss

Ketcham's Journal of Travel," **62**/237-87,337-402

"The Round Hand of George B. Roberts," **63**/101-236

Knutson, Charles, **71**/357

Knutson, Chris, **71**/355

Koch, Fred, **67**/273,276

Koch, Henry, **64**/276

Kodachi, Zuigaku, trans.: "Portland Assembly Center: Diary of Saku Tomita," **81**/149-63

Kodiak Island, **62**/23; **73**/102,107; **77**/181-85: described, **73**/116-19; fort, **73**/165; population, **73**/164; Russian settlement 1790s, **73**/116; sketches, **73**/116-18

Koehler, Mark L., **68**/183

Koehler, Richard: railroad interests, **71**/51,78,81,93; reports, **71**/81,89,96; Villard correspondence, **71**/79,88,93

Koenig, Clara Bliss, **77**/89

Koerner, W.H.D., **66**/88; **68**/348

Koger, William Pinckney, **78**/127

Kohrs, C. Conrad, **65**/121

Ko-ko-ka-wa (Chief Sam) (Indian), **66**/221N,225

Kolosh Indians, SEE Tlingit Indians

Koloshenka River, **73**/148,149

Konapee (first white man to cross U.S.): myth *vs.* history, **65**/219-20

Konea (Cowlitz Farm employee), **63**/124

Konno, Mrs. —, Portland Assembly Center, **81**/153

Konoye, Prince of Japan, **62**/26-27,28

Kootenai country, B.C.: described, **63**/90; mines, **63**/89; theaters, **63**/90

Kootenai House, **76**/324

Kootenai Indians, SEE Kutenai Indians

Kootenai Pelly (Indian): Christian training, **69**/51; death, **69**/54; **71**/331,336,344; religious influence, **71**/330,333,334,344; student at Red River Mission, **71**/327-31

Kootenai River, **62**/216; **71**/279: transportation, **74**/358

Kootenay Collins (Indian), **69**/53: death, **71**/344; student at Red River

Mission, 71/330
Kopplien, Mrs. A.R., photo, 80/324
Korea, 62/6,7,15,17,19,36,41,43
Korean National Association, 79/57,59
Korean people:
anti-Japanese attitude, 79/51; cannery workers, 79/56; farmers, 79/51,54,55-56,59,60,61,62; laborers in Hawaii, 79/51; Montana, 79/57; social life, 79/57
women immigrants to Pacific nw— character, 79/63; photos, 79/63; "picture brides," 79/51-63
"Korean Women Pioneers of the Pacific Northwest," by Sonia S. Sunoo, 79/51-63
Korell, Franklin F., 75/172,189N
Kori, A. Ben, 80/403
Kornbluh, Joyce L., ed.:
Rebel Voices: An I.W.W. Anthology, review, 66/186
Korovin Bay, 77/188
Koshigin, SEE Kashega, Alaska
Kotzebue, Otto von, 73/123,125,137
Kotzebue Bay (Sound), 73/119,137
Kotzebue expedition, 62/106
Kowrach, Edward J., 64/351
Kowrach, Edward J., ed.:
Journal of a Catholic Bishop on the Oregon Trail...the Rt. Rev. A.M.A. Blanchet, review, 80/405-406
Kraft, Dave, 72/306(photo),314
Krasheninnikov, Stepan Petrovich, 72/359:
Explorations of Kamchatka, noted, 77/290
Kratt, I.F., 73/162,166
Kraus, Christina Grob, 79/357
Kraus, George, 79/239
Kreiser (frigate), 72/111,112
Krohn, Mrs. John, 68/359
Krohn, Robert, 74/205
Kroner, Ernst, 68/201
Krotske, Charles, 72/197
Kruse, John W., 68/267
Kruse and Banks Shipyard, Coos Bay, 64/255
Krutilla, John W.:
The Columbia River Treaty: The Econom-

ics of an International River Basin Development, review, 69/272-73
Krutz, Adolf (Dolf), 63/293-94
Ku Klux Klan, 67/367; 69/115N,179-80; 72/81; 76/247:
Atlanta headquarters, 75/151,152,158, 159,177,178,179,182; bibliography, 81/331; Black Patrol, 75/166; expose, 75/182; finances, 75/153-54,168,175-77; foreign-born branch, SEE Royal Riders of the Red Robe; hate campaigns, 75/153,157,165; letter regarding robes, 75/183; number of members, 75/152,153,178,180,190; newspapers opposing, 75/189N; official organs, 75/164,181
Oregon, 75/154-82—
Eugene, 75/156; Medford, 75/156, 163-65; Pendleton, 75/157; Portland, 69/180; 75/154,156-61; Salem, 75/ 161,165; Tillamook, 63/359; Umatilla Co., 78/364
photos, 75/108,155,164,167; political efforts, 75/160,161-63,167-75; Protestant support, 75/157,164-66,168-69; regalia, 75/151,154,161,166,183; Seattle, 75/179; vigilantes, 75/157-58; violence, 75/154,163-64,166,167,188N;
SEE ALSO Compulsory School Bill
The Ku Klux Klan in the City, 1915-1930, by Jackson, review, 69/179-80
Kubli, Kasper K., 75/174,180,181
Kubli, Ore.:
grist mill, 65/218
Kuchel & Dresel:
Portland lithographs, 80/29,148
Kukhan-Tan (Indian):
funeral, 73/149-55—
sketch, 73/150
Sitka toion, 73/152
Kullyspell House, 76/324
Kulper, Henry, 64/276
Kumtucky (Indian), 69/245,246:
photo, 69/248; sources on, 69/247N
Kunigk, Willibald A., 66/101N,127,130:
photo, 66/116
Kunigk, Mrs. Willibald A., 66/130
Kunnecke, Bernd:
The Impact of the Primary Economy on the

Cultural Landscape of Oregon, review, **81**/325-27

Kunz, Merle H.: *Kittitas Frontiersmen*, noted, 79/105

Kurihara, Frank H., **81**/153,166

Kurihara, Mary Y., **81**/153,166

Kuril Islands, 72/109; 73/119-20,131; 77/290

Kuril Islands: Russo-Japanese Frontier in the Pacific, by Stephen, noted, 77/290

Kurz, Rudolph Friedrich, **68**/344; 70/364

Kushner, Howard I.: *Conflict on the Northwest Coast: American-Russian Rivalry in the Pacific Northwest*, review, 77/85-86

"'The Oregon Question Is...a Massachusetts Question'," 75/317-35

Kuskokva River, 73/117

Kuskov, Ivan Alexandrovich, 73/161; 77/186

Kussman, Jack, 69/313N

Kutenai Indians, 71/279: calendar, 71/343; ethnography, 71/ 279; female berdache, SEE Qanqon; first white men with, 71/343; legend of Night Runner, 71/331 religion— Barnaby account, 71/339-42; Berland influence, 71/342; Curtis account, 71/337-38; Prophet Dance, 71/325, 333,337,347,367; source of Christian influence, 71/325-48,367; spread of Christian-pagan rites, 71/347 St. Mary's band, 71/339; Tobacco Plains Reserve, 71/331,339; Tunaxa band, 71/343; wars and hostilities, 71/343; SEE ALSO Flatbow Indians

Kutuzov (*Kutusoff*) (Russian vessel), 77/175

Kuykendall, George Benson, 70/149

Kuykendall, Ralph S., 64/27N: *The Hawaiian Kingdom*, Vol. III noted, 69/334

Kwakiutl Indians, 63/347; 65/374; 67/86; 70/367; 71/184-85; **81**/208: H'Kusam village, 63/359

Kyle, Joseph, 65/144-47: biography, 65/141,143; photo, 65/142

Kyle, Mary, SEE Dallas, Mary Kyle

Kyushu Island, Japan, 62/34

Labaree, Henri, 62/231

LaBarge, Joseph, 70/86

Labbe, Antoine G., 74/213

Labbe, John T.: *The Big Woods*, by Lucia, review, 77/86-87 *The Electric Railway Era in Northwest Washington, 1890-1930*, by Turbeville, review, **80**/332-33

Labbe, John T., and Lynwood Carranco: *Logging the Redwoods*, review, 77/190-91

Labbe, John T., and Vernon Goe: *Railroads in the Woods*, review, 63/351-52

LaBonte, Louis, Jr., 62/109; 66/ 334-35,338

LaBonte, Louis, Sr., 66/332,338,339, 349; 67/92; 77/81

LaBonte River, 79/376

Labor and laboring classes: Catholic support, 75/123-25,133; child labor, 77/193; Chinese, 62/175; 69/ 330; 75/123,124(photo),130; convict labor, 74/109; court cases, 62/94; cowboys, 74/280; Deschutes railroad construction, 69/293,298; domestic help, 70/61; Eastern Ore., 69/274; employment of aged, 62/107; employment offices, 77/249; farm organizations, 73/86; history sources, 71/189,196; immigrants, 77/302; Inland Empire, 65/363; Italians, 77/240-44,247,249; Japanese, 70/54; Japanese-Americans, 69/275; Korean in Hawaii, 79/51 labor disputes, 72/353; 78/358— Canada, 74/286,345; Idaho, 68/186; 71/196; mines, 71/196; Oregon, 76/ 137,145,149-50; San Francisco, 74/ 346-47; Washington, 73/70-71,281- 82; 74/86,181

lumber industry, 69/325; 70/76; 77/ 352,353; migrant labor, 69/179; 72/ 251; mine workers, 75/133; numbers at Ft. Dalles, 68/22,44; Oregon coast ww I, 74/356; Pacific islands, 69/83; politics, 67/361-63; 76/135-51; publications, SEE *Oregon Labor Press*; rights,

78/358; road work, 74/115; scarcity 1856, 68/25,26N,27; Seattle 1919-20, 66/73-74,89; shipyard workers, 75/151 strikes, 75/133,151,174—

Anaconda, 72/237,238; Boeing Co. 1948, 72/263; Butte, 72/229; Coeur d'Alene, 63/90; 72/231,233; Fraser River salmon fishermen 1900, 72/ 232; Idaho, 65/365; Portland newspaper, 72/234,263,264; Portland waterfront 1934, 72/227; Vancouver Island 1903, 72/231

theses index, 72/275; unions, SEE Labor unions; violence, 73/70-71,281-82; 75/127,133,151; 76/145; wages, SEE Wages; Washington and B.C. 1885-1917, 81/333-34; wheat harvesters, 70/73; women, 62/94; working conditions in woolen mills, 77/193

Labor Day, 65/290N; 72/354: celebration photo, 77/135

Labor legislation:

Oregon, 62/94; 63/361

Labor Politics in a Democratic Republic: Moderation, Division, and Disruption in the Presidential Election of 1928, by Bornet, review, 67/361-63

Labor unions, 62/106,174-75,176; 72/229,232,233; 74/280; 75/123-25,127,133; 76/136,137,140,145-51; 77/352; 80/208:

agriculture, 72/236; electricians, 75/ 159; fishermen, 81/322; food industry, 76/146; ILWU, Rainier 1905-1906, 81/36; miners', 65/366; textile industry, 77/193; SEE ALSO Trade unions

Labreton, M., 81/25N

LaCenter, Wash., 71/13; 76/382

Lacey, Cora, 80/229-57*passim*

Lacey, Isaac P.:

family, 80/229,235N,239N,243N, 249N,251,252,253

Lacey, Mary E., SEE Herren, Mary E. Lacey

Lacomb, Ore., 72/92

Lacombe, Albert, 63/59

Lacourse, Claude, 66/355N,360N

Lacourse, Joseph, 66/351N

LaCreole:

name debate, 70/260

LaCreole, Ore., 77/317

LaCreole Academy, Rickreall, 66/23

LaCreole Creek, 77/272

LaCrosse, Maeda, 66/54

Ladd, Charles E., 65/412; 75/100: business interests, 71/148,151; Oriental trade interests, 71/151; photo, 75/101

Ladd, Robert J.: biography, 80/288N

Ladd, William Mead, 62/170,177; 68/216; 74/213; 75/101: banking interests, 71/226N; Library Assn. of Portland, 71/226,233,234; Presbyterian Church, 71/226N

Ladd, William Sargent, 62/228; 64/ 159; 69/221N; 72/332N; 73/53N; 74/139; 76/6; 77/61,91; 80/21: estate, 62/169; papers cited, 71/80N; photo, 80/16; railroad interests, 71/68,92N

Ladd and Bush Bank, Salem, 67/264; 71/150

Ladd and Tilton Bank, Portland, 62/ 165; 65/412; 71/148,226N; 73/56; 77/377

Ladd Estate Company, 77/377

Laderoute, Francois Xavier, 66/347,349,350,356,359

Laderoute, Julia Gervais (Mrs. Francois X.), 66/334,357

Ladies of the Invisible Empire, 75/176,180,190N

Ladies Were Not Expected: Abigail Scott Duniway and Women's Rights, by Morrison, review, 80/331-32

Ladoga (ship), 72/112

Lady of the Lake (riverboat), 77/157

Lafayette, Ore., 66/283; 75/353: history, 65/217

Lafayette Academy, 66/11-12

LaFeber, Walter:

The New Empire, cited, 72/210,211

Lafferty, W.P., 75/143

LaFlesche, Joseph, 71/287

LaFleur, Marie, SEE Roy, Marie LaFleur

Lafollett, Charles, 79/145N

LaFollette, Robert Marion, Sr., 66/46;

70/79; 76/137,148,149
Laframboise, Josette, 72/170
Laframboise, Michel, 67/281; 72/170
LaGrande, Ore., 66/203,303: fossils, 66/91; history, 79/104
Lagursa, Louis, photo, 76/166
Lahoamthla (Indian), 79/158,313, 314,322
Laidlaw, Charlotte Stout (Mrs. James), 80/31
Laidlaw, James, 66/113; 72/280,361; 80/31
Laidlaw, John R., 72/361; 80/31: *A Chronicle of Catholic History of the Pacific Northwest, 1743-1960,* by Schoenberg, review, 64/78-79
These Things I Remembered, cited, 78/288
Laidlaw, (William) Lansing Stout: biography, 80/31-32; photo, 80/30; World War II letters, 80/32-49
Laidlaw, (William) Lansing Stout: "Aleutian Experiences of the 'Mad M'," 80/31-49
Laidlaw, Ore., 73/84
Laing, J.K., 64/265
Laing, John A., 74/233
Laird, Hailey, 69/88
Laird's Landing: pioneers, 78/363
LaKamp, Gussie, 74/346
Lake Abert, 77/29: name, 79/291N
Lake Bennett, 76/104,108,109-10; 81/143-44,147
Lake Bigler, 71/200; 72/12,13,17N: name, 72/12N,14
Lake Billy Chinook, 65/220; 67/90; 79/157
Lake Celilo, 72/158
Lake Chelan, 72/233
Lake City, Calif., 68/256,316
Lake Coeur d'Alene, SEE Coeur d'Alene Lake
Lake County, Calif., 71/200
Lake County, Ore., 66/365; 72/46: exploration, 71/361; history, 72/93; 77/90; Irish, 70/355-56; 76/348; land boom, 77/157-59; livestock, 70/ 355; mineral resources, 71/286; roundup

1970, 71/361; sheep, 76/333-58; sheriff, 76/355
Lake Labish, 72/182; 76/234,239
Lake Lahontan, SEE Pyramid Lake
Lake of the Woods, Canada, 66/69,70
Lake Oswego, 64/261; 72/33
Lake Oswego, Ore., 73/80: guidebook 1963, 65/121
Lake Ozette, 64/87
Lake Pend Oreille, SEE Pend Oreille Lake
Lake Quinault, 74/30,31
Lake Saint Ignace, 69/270-71
Lake Shore, Wash., 63/83
Lake Tahoe: Calif. boundary, 72/12,14; name, 72/12N
Lake Timpanogas, 78/57,317
Lake Wallula region, 66/275
Lake Washington Canal, 74/354
Lakeport, Ore., 71/290
Lakeview, Ore., 66/171,272,273; 68/ 257,316; 76/335,351,352: Christmas celebration photo, 77/134; during Bannock War, 68/317-24*passim;* fire 1900, 72/93; history, 73/83; hot springs, 77/149; Irish, 76/349; land fraud cases, 68/317; land office, 68/ 317,318; landmarks, 70/355; newspaper, 66/171N; Overfelt land purchase, 66/87; photos, 68/319; 76/ 334; 77/150; railroad arrives, 77/167; roundup, 70/355; school, 76/335
Lakeview (ferry), 81/328
Lalake (Indian), 69/245-54*passim:* photo, 69/248
LaLande, Jeffrey M.: *Medford Corporation: A History of an Oregon Logging and Lumber Company,* review, 81/205-206
Lamar, Howard R., 63/356
Lamar, Howard R., ed.: *The Reader's Encyclopedia of the American West,* review, 80/205-206
Lamb, —, capt. of *Fingvalla,* 66/105
Lamb, J. & T., Company, 76/208
Lamb, W. Kaye, 73/359; 77/289,294: Hudson's Bay Co. history, 71/372
Lamb, W. Kaye, ed.: *Journal of a Voyage on the North West*

Coast of North America, by Franchere, review, 71/277-79

The Journals and Letters of Sir Alexander Mackenzie, noted, 75/364

Lamb, Wessie Tipping, 71/277-79

Lamberson, Bertha, photo, 63/298

Lamberson, Clara, photo, 63/298

Lamberson, Joseph, 63/269,273, 286,288: photo, 63/298

Lamberson, Mrs. Joseph, photo, 63/298

Lamberson, Lawrence, 63/288: photo, 63/298

Lamberson, May, photo, 63/298

Lamberson, Rosa, SEE McKenzie, Rosa Lamberson

Lambert, A.B., 69/161

Lambert, Albert Weston, 75/137

Lambert, Charles E., 71/289

Lambert, Francis, 62/110,206,302,423; 63/94,256,373; 64/93,189,285,363; 65/125,221,317,412,416; 66/93,189, 285,392,395; 67/380; 68/357,361; 69/347; 70/374; 74/183,363,366

Lambert, James L., 63/234

Lambert, Joseph H., 68/165

Lambert, Rex O., 68/342

Lamely, Job, 67/366

Lamerick, John K., 66/220N

Lamkin, Charles B., 64/335

Lamm Lumber Company, 63/355

Lammarlaw (bark): wreck, 69/331

Lamoose, Ignace, 64/53

Lampman, Ben Hur, 74/159,174,239: *The Centralia Case: Three Views of the Armistice Day Tragedy at Centralia, Washington, Nov. 11, 1919*, review, 73/70-71

The Tramp Printer, cited, 74/177

Lampman, Evelyn Sibley, 76/369(photo): "As It Was...," 76/368-79 *Bargain Bride*, noted, 79/104 "Dallas Memories," 77/261-76 *The Potlatch Family*, noted, 77/301 *Princess of Fort Vancouver*, noted, 64/349 "School Days and Culture," 78/158-73 *Squaw Man's Son*, noted, 80/336 *White Captives*, noted, 76/181

Lampman, Linda, and Julie Sterling: *The Portland Guidebook*, noted, 77/291

Lancaster, Columbia, 62/151; 63/200; 71/361

Lancaster, John L., 74/104

Lancaster, Samuel Christopher, 80/387: biography, 66/251; 74/120-32

Columbia Gorge resort, 75/277-81— photos, 75/278,280

Columbia River Highway, 66/250-65 *passim*; 74/103,106,110-18*passim*,128, 143,214; conservation policies, 74/102-104,105-106,113-14,118-19,120,125-26,131,132,138; engineering achievements, 74/104-106,127,128, 136,139; European travel, 74/106; highway promotion, 74/118-19,120-21,123-25, 141; honored, 74/144; memorial plaque, 74/144; Mt. Rainier park commissioner, 74/106-107; photos, 66/ 254; 74/110; 75/279; publicist, 74/ 119,120-25; resort property, 74/129-30,143; u. of Wash. professor, 74/106; views on motor touring, 74/103

Lancaster, Samuel Christopher:

The Columbia: America's Great Highway Through the Cascade Mountains to the Sea, cited, 74/120

Lancaster, Lane Co., 67/58

Lancaster (Liberty ship), 74/144

Lancaster (U.S. frigate), 72/68

Lancaster Falls, 74/144

Lancaster Light Horse Cavalry: muster roll, 66/187

"Lancaster's Lodge," by Donald P. Abbott, 75/277-81

Land:

accretion ownership, 68/186; 71/197; advertisement, Ore., 69/200,202; B.C. crown lands, 77/303

California—

act, 1851, 74/286; claims, 64/283; land grant colleges, 62/297; range lands, 62/297; state land office 1858-98, 66/87; titles, 68/349; values, 71/60

Cherokee Strip, 77/371

claims, 69/76—

Astoria, 64/227-28N; Baker Bay, 64/

212N; California, 64/283; Camas Valley, 63/357; Cape Disappointment, 64/225-27N; Coquille, 63/17; Douglas Co. history, 63/357; Harney Co. disputes, 66/67; Hawaiian, 68/87; jumping, 77/13; laws, 71/285; marker, 63/16; New Era, 64/265; north Dallas fraud, 66/92; timber, 80/174,180,188,195; under Prov. Govt., 64/204,204N-205N,208N; Washington, 64/296-97; Willamette Valley, 66/334-35,357-58,359; SEE ALSO Donation Land Claims Coeur d'Alene, 64/87; count seat grants, 67/301N development projects, 76/240,244, 246— Klamath Basin, 78/363 disposal of western lands, 70/362 disputes, 67/153,303N— Harney Co., 66/92; Morrow Co., 69/120 eminent domain law, 77/302 fraud, 68/317; 74/282-83; 76/72— north Dallas, 66/92; Oregon trials, 67/368 Free Soil, 73/84; frontier laws and rights, 63/358; 64/85; Gilliam Co., 80/195; grasslands, 81/335 Indian land, 79/121,311— settlement, 73/258; severalty, 72/149 irrigation, SEE Irrigation; Klamath Basin, 78/363; Lake Co. promotion, 77/157 land grant colleges, 72/316— California, 62/297; commissioner's report, 64/147; SEE ALSO Morrill Act laws, 70/181— alien land law, 71/365; 76/237-38, 243-44,245,247; Calif. 1851, 74/286; claim laws, 71/285; eminent domain, 77/302; frontier, 63/358; 64/85; homestead act, 67/153; 70/104-105,273; 81/282,316,317; Ore. Terr. basic law, 74/120; preemption, 67/304N; swamp lands, 67/153-54 lotteries, 71/196; 74/350; military road grants, 71/68,82N,90N; 74/350; 79/43; Montana mineral lands, 67/86;

Morrow Co., 69/120; 79/104; Niagara boom, 71/352 Oregon, 71/285— advertisements, 69/200,202; basic Ore. Terr. law, 75/120; federal lands, 65/382; first survey, 62/301; fraud trials, 67/368; public lands management, 64/55-67; resources management, 68/176-77 o&c lands— politics, 65/376 Pacific NW records, 70/269-71; preemption law extended to Pacific NW, 67/304N; Prov. Govt. land act, 63/211; public domain, 76/29-31,72; 77/149 public lands, 63/247; 67/140; 73/259,263,267,268; 75/93— history, 64/350; Ore. management, 64/55-67; settlement promotion, 74/16,17,ins.bk.cov. March; surveys, 73/334; use, 71/364 railroad grants, 64/55,87; 71/45,46, 51,54,88N; 72/316; 74/166-67 range lands, 63/36— California, 62/297; free, 81/282; history of open range, 81/335; laws, 62/189-90 reclamation, 72/180; SEE ALSO Reclamation; sale of railroad lands, 71/61, 85N,ins.bk.cov. March; Spanish grants in Iowa, 67/368; speculation, 71/88, 364; submerged lands, 71/197; Sumpter Valley, 73/83 surveys— first Oregon, 62/301; public lands, 73/334 swamp lands legislation, 67/153-54; tenure in West, 71/364; timber claims, 80/174,180,188,195 titles, 62/118,124,131— California, 68/349; frauds, 74/282-83; 76/72; in West, 68/340 town sites, 67/304N use policy history— 1862-1935, 64/85; 1921-33, 65/206 values, 73/83— 1870s, 80/270; 1890s, 80/280; 1896, 81/299; 1901, 81/306; 1903, 81/306; 1906, 81/310; building lots,

81/37,273,274,277,279; California, 71/60; Hood River Valley 1908, 70/ 52; Idaho 1862, 79/189; Malheur Co., 75/290-91; Oregon 1880-90, 71/31,33,34,37; Pacific NW, 71/60; Salem 1881, 71/17; Tacoma 1881, 71/15,16; Washington, 71/34; 74/5; Willamette Valley, 71/34,35,37,57, 60,84N-85N; SEE ALSO Prices Washington, 65/366; 72/230; western settlement map, 64/77; Wisconsin frontier, 70/362; wives' holdings, 77/302; SEE ALSO Deserts; Homesteads and homesteading; Oregon and California Railroad lands

Land Laws and Early Settlers of Oregon: Map and Genealogical Data of Pioneer Families, noted, 71/285

Land, Man and the Law: The Disposal of Crown Lands in British Columbia, 1871-1913, by Cail, noted, 77/303

Land of Tuality, noted, 77/292

Land of the North Umpquas, by Bakken, noted, 74/358

Lander, Edwin, 64/302N; 66/31,33,34: Stevens dispute, 66/32

Lander, Frederick West: railroad survey, 71/81-82,292

Lander Cutoff, 63/360; 64/277; 66/198; 70/181; 72/67,69

Landerholm, Carl, 63/57N; 64/276: biography, 63/83

Landes, Abraham, 79/16

Landes, Amanda, 79/16

Landis, Robert L.: *Post Offices of Oregon, Washington, and Idaho*, noted, 70/272

Landrith, Cyrus, 78/129,143

Landrith, Martha Coulson, 78/129,143

Landrith Hill, Coos Co., 66/53

Landrum, Francis S., 69/223N,229N, 235N,247N,248: Camp Day area photos, 69/233,234, 255; photo, 72/16

Landrum, Francis S.: *The Expeditions of John Charles Fremont*, ed. by Jackson and Spence, review, 72/166-67 "The Highroad of the Highlands,"

75/233-39

The Klamath Tribe, a People and Their Reservation, by Stern, review, 67/356

"A Major Monument: Oregon-California Boundary," 72/5-53

The Modoc War, 1872-73, by Thompson, review, 70/175-77

Lane, Amanda Mann (Mrs. Lafayette), 80/352

Lane, Emily, SEE Floed, Emily Lane

Lane, Eva, SEE Waite, Eva Lane

Lane, Frank, 69/136

Lane, Harry, grandson of Joseph, 68/127

Lane, Harry, Indiana senator, 72/334

Lane, Hughie, 69/136-37

Lane, Joseph, 62/63,73-74,329; 63/11, 51,182,194,360; 64/36,207,314; 66/ 5,33; 67/297; 72/230; 73/41,206; 75/118,120,121; 78/47; 79/129: biography, 68/333; Columbia River mouth fortifications, 72/56; Deady-McFadden dispute role, 66/25,27-28; emigrant protection plan, 72/56-57; Floed-Lane House memorial, 65/404; papers, 68/333; relations with Stark, 72/319,321-22,323N,325,327; Rogue River War command, 66/221N,223-24; satirical verse about, 64/154; Stark letter, 73/41-42; Territorial Govt. proclamation, 64/138,140-42; testimony against Stark, 72/336-37; Union Party target, 73/53,54

Lane, Lafayette, 65/401,403

Lane, Polly (Mrs. Joseph), 65/401

Lane, Simon R., 65/401,403

Lane County, Ore., 66/365,366; 78/42N,43,44: architecture early farm bldgs., 66/383; banks, 62/301; barns, 71/361; cemeteries, 71/190,361; census 1860, 71/ 190; Century Farms, 79/339; county clerk's office, 67/179-81; 79/7,7N district courts— 1853-54, 79/5-11; first, 67/179 first courthouse, 79/7N; first fair, 66/ 81; first jury trial, 67/179; first official seal, 79/7N; grave census, 69/77; historic houses, 67/281; history, 66/81,

187,383; history articles, 70/271-72, 358; 72/89,170,353; marriages, 62/ 301; 70/75; military parade 1864, 66/ 187; old houses, 69/340; organization, 77/324; pioneers, 71/189; post offices, 69/329; 72/288; postal townmarks, 71/200; pro-Southern activities, 67/ 54-60; roads, 72/92; SEE ALSO Free Emigrant Road; settlement, 77/318, 324; settlers, 79/13,49; sheriffs, 77/ 325; 79/23; taxable property 1854, 69/77

Lane County Historian, noted, 68/340; 69/77,276,329; 70/74,271,358; 72/ 89,170,353; 73/72,283; 74/93,280; 75/87; 77/193; 80/104,335; 81/105,327

Lane County Historical Society: meetings, 69/279; 70/276; officers and board, 69/81,279; 70/82,276; 81/110; officers and directors, 71/ 194; 72/176; 73/78; 74/181; 75/91; 76/95; 77/94; 78/94; 79/111; 80/ 110; publications, SEE *Lane County Historian*; Skinner cabin replica, 72/89; SEE ALSO Lane County Pioneer-Historical Society

Lane County Pioneer-Historical Society: officers and board members, 64/83, 279; 65/123,311; 66/84,278; 68/84, 282; officers and directors, 62/104, 415; 63/86,250; 67/82,283; publications, 68/340; receives Lane County clerk's office, 67/181; SEE ALSO Lane County Historical Society

Lane County Pioneer Museum, 69/176: commission, 67/181

Lane County Youth and Children's Services: publication, 79/339

Lane Electric Cooperative Inc., 80/328

Lane House, SEE Douglas Co. Pioneer Museum

Lane Pomona Grange: history, 72/87

Lang, Mary Varney, 81/262

Lang, Thomas Stackpole, 81/261,265, 267,280: biography, 81/262-63,264,264N

Lang and Ryan, cattle drovers, 70/262

Lang Syne Society, 74/199

Lange, Erwin F., 62/103,109,414; 63/85,245,249; 64/82,188,278; 66/283; 69/29N,32FF,333: Evans route map, 69/46-47

Lange, Erwin F.: "John Jeffrey and the Oregon Botanical Expedition," 68/111-24 "Major Charles E. Bendire and the Birds of Oregon," 66/233-39

Lange, Robert E.: *A History of the Lewis and Clark Journals*, by Cutright, review, 78/284-85 *Passage Through the Garden*, by Allen, review, 77/191-92

Langell Valley: history, 75/87

Langer, William, 73/57N

Langille, Harold Douglas, 75/102; 76/31-32,103,103N: photo, 76/fr.cov. June

Langille, Herbert B., 76/101N

Langille, James L., 75/101; 79/206: family, 76/101,101N

Langille, Sarah, 76/101N; 79/205

Langille, William Alexander, 75/101,102: correspondence, 76/101-17; prospector, 76/101-17; photos, 76/100,fr.cov. June

Langille House Inn, 79/203

Langille Mountain, 76/101

Langley, B.C., 64/86

Langley, Wash., 63/224

Langlois, Louis Antoine, 63/133,137, 138,139,140,152,163; 66/355; 69/270

Langrische, Jack, 71/366

Langs Canyon, 81/263N

Langsdorff, Georg Heinrich von, 73/125

Lanham, Url: *The Bone Hunters*, review, 75/78-79

Lanning, E.J., 67/63

Laos, 62/41,42,43

LaPerouse, Jean Francis, 73/274

LaPerouse (ship), 74/299-300

Lapham, James, 78/124

Lapham, Maria, 78/212,213,219: grave site photo, 78/220

LaPine, Ore., 67/374; 78/295: electric co-op, 80/328
LaPlace, —, Ft. Ross 1839, 73/162
Laplace, C.P.T., 68/57-60
Lapoitre (Laporte), Jean Baptiste, 63/118,121,127,148,170-71
Lappeus, James H.: biography, 80/134N,290; fight with Semple, 80/306N; photo, 80/135; police career, 80/134-37,160,288,292, 294-98*passim*,307,315,321; saloon, 80/135,157N,158; suit against, 80/312
LaPush, Wash., 62/101; 74/19
Lapwai, Ida., 79/184,199
Lapwai Creek, 79/184
Lapwai Indian Agency, 62/320; 70/154
Lapwai Mission, SEE Spalding Mission
Laramee (Laramie), B., 63/152
Laramie Mountains, 79/72
Laramie River, 62/341-42; 80/73
Larenaga, Pete, 76/169N,173N
Larch trees, 77/353
Large, R. Geddes: *Drums and Scalpel: From Native Healers to Physicians on the North Pacific Coast*, review, 71/184-86
Lariat (magazine), 73/302
Larkin, Thomas Oliver, 70/301; 76/204
Larkin and Green, Blind Slough loggers, 72/301
Larocque, Francois Antoine, 64/92
Larpenteur, Charles, 63/72: biography, 66/185
Larrabee, R.D., 62/177
Larrison, Earl J.: *Owyhee, the Life of a Northern Desert*, cited, 66/272
Larsell, Olof, 65/207
Larsen, Lawrence H.: *The Urban West at the End of the Frontier*, review, 81/103-104
Larsen, Robert A., 80/414
Larson, Herman, 66/91
Larson, Martin, 65/309
Las Cruces, Calif., 80/244
Lasater, J.H., 70/355
Lasenan, Mary, 75/143
Laserson, Max, 72/121
Lassen Pass, 68/257,316N; SEE ALSO

Fandango Pass
Lassen Trail, 81/105
Lassen's Cutoff, 66/87; 73/72; 77/196
Last Chance Gulch, Wheeler Co., 73/267
Last Trail to Bear Paw (Flight of the Nez Perces), 1877, by Alcorn, noted, 79/106
La Stella, Portland, 77/259
Laswell (Lasswell), William B.: electoral dispute activities, 67/266-67; votes cast for, as pres. elector, 67/259
Later Woolen Mills in Oregon; A History of the Woolen Mills Which Followed the Pioneer Mills, by Lomax, review, 77/193-94
Latham, Edward H., 81/330
Latham, Milton S., 65/327
Latona (steamer), 71/137
Latour (Lature), Louis, 63/136
Latourell, Joseph: biography, 72/90-91
Latourell Falls, 79/203
Latourell Falls, Ore.: history, 72/90; post office, 66/90
Latourette, Charles D., 76/301
Latourette, Howard, 72/80
Latourette, Jack, photo, 74/214
Latta, Robert: *Mackerel Skies*, noted, 78/288
Latta's, Seaside, SEE Seaside House
Latter Day Saints, SEE Mormons
Latterman, John, 66/20
Latterman, Marie P. (Mrs. John), 66/20
Lattie, Alexander: biography, 64/197-209,210N; Columbia River bar pilot, 64/199,207; Ft. George journal, 63/252; 64/197-245; Ft. George service, 64/198,201-203; instructions from HBCO., 64/245; land claim, 64/204,208
McClure fracas, 64/202-203— described, 64/235-38; jury verdict, 64/202N-203N,238N-239; Rector version, 64/237N-38N
Ogden claim survey, 64/225-27; relations with American settlers, 64/202, 223,227-28,230; service on HBCO. vessels, 64/199-200
Lattie, Alexander: "Alexander Lattie's Fort George Journal, 1846," ed. by Vaughan and

Knuth, 64/197-245
Lattie, Alexander, Jr., 64/201N
Lattie, Elizabeth E. (Helen), daughter of Alexander, 64/201N
Lattie, Helen (Ellen), SEE Cloutrie, Helen Lattie
Lattie, Helen Clark (Mrs. John), 64/197
Lattie, John, father of Alexander, 64/197
Lattie, John, son of Alexander, 64/201N
Lattie, Mary, daughter of Alexander, 64/201N
Lattie, Mary Catherine Sickas (Elizabeth) (Mrs. Alexander): land claim, 64/205N; marriage, 64/201; name variations, 64/201N; role in Lattie-McClure fracas, 64/234-35
Lattie, William, 64/201,206: land claim, 64/205N
Latvian people: Bitte family, 81/31-42
Laufe, Abe, ed.: *An Army Doctor's Wife on the Frontier*, cited, 70/16N,23N
Laughlin, Bob, 69/137
Laughlin, Davis Washington, 66/283
Laughlin, Ilene Kilkenny, 69/137
Laughlin, Robert, 69/137
Laundries: Chinese, 76/370-73— Salem photo, 78/fr.cov. March
Laurel Hill, 63/30
Laurel Point, 72/196(photo),197
Laurier, Wilfred, 73/359
Lausanne (vessel), 62/70; 63/185; 64/199N,200; 76/359-67; 77/38,39; 78/143,334,345: passenger list, 76/364
"The *Lausanne* Mystery Solved: A Note," by Robert J. Loewenberg, 76/359-67
Lava Beds National Monument, 70/175-76
Lava Butte, 66/384; 70/183; 77/332; 78/294: visitors' center, 66/92; 67/34
Lavadour, Joseph, 78/90
Lavalle (Lavall), Baptiste Vincent, 67/88: journey from Pacific NW to East, 71/198; lost manuscript, 71/291

Lavalleur, Eugene Everett, 66/327
Lavender, David, 65/213; 67/372; 71/291: *Fist in the Wilderness*, noted, 80/336 *The Great Persuader*, review, 71/283-84 *Westward Vision: The Story of the Oregon Trail*, review, 66/68-69
LaVerendrye, Pierre Gaultier de Varennes, 64/283; 72/182
Lavigneur, Francois, 66/348N
Lavigneur, Francois Xavier, 66/348N
Lavigneur, Jean Baptiste, 66/348N
Lavigneur, Joseph, 66/348N
Law, Henry, 72/330; 73/47: 1858 letter, 68/88
Law enforcement, 71/366: British Columbia, 72/86; California, 72/346-47; Clatsop Co. first hanging, 73/82; Columbia Co., 74/323-25; history, 80/5-7; Marion Co. sheriffs, 72/91; Portland, SEE Portland police; preventive patrol concept, 80/147; private forces, 80/7; SEE ALSO Vigilantes; selective enforcement, 80/141; Umatilla Co., 72/352; Wells, Fargo agents, 72/88-89; western, 71/364
Lawford, Henry, 63/17
Lawrence, Abbott, 65/168
Lawrence, Charles, Auburn mines 1861, 62/219N
Lawrence, Charles, Portland deputy marshal 1860, 80/145,145N,162
Lawrence, Elizabeth Heffernan, 69/131
Lawrence, George, 76/381; 80/285
Lawrence, H., capt. of *Peter Iredale*, 64/68,70-72; 66/129
Lawrence, Hattie B., 68/353
Lawrence, Richard C., 69/131
Laws, Amy M. Harris, 69/57
Laws: Alaska homestead, 72/136; Big Blue Books *vs.* Little Blue Book, 64/299; Bingham registration bill, 68/215,216; Carey Act, 71/196; Civil War effects, 70/69-71; common law in West, 70/366; constitutional provisions re evidence, 73/270-71; Dawes Act, 70/105, 107; enforcement in early Ore., 65/220; espionage 1917-18, 71/215; fed-

eral registry, 71/172,172N; frontier variations, 63/101-102,175-78,185-86,194,222-23N,229; Holt judges-of-election bill, 68/215,216; Idaho Territory, 65/365; Indian affairs, 70/85; interest rate 1880, 76/136; land laws, 71/285; Montana Territory, 64/85; Newlands Act, 69/274; 72/180; Ordinance of 1787, 70/85

Oregon, 65/383—

early enforcement, 65/220; school law 1922, 70/85; tort liability, 70/182 prohibition, 68/134; qualifications of judges, 71/197; sedition 1917-18, 71/ 215; Selective Service 1917, 71/214-15; sovereign immunity, 69/86; taxation, 69/86

Washington Territory— code drafted, 64/302-303; reports, 66/35

SEE ALSO Ore.Prov.Govt.—laws; Oregon Territory—laws

Lawson, Dorothy, SEE McCall, Dorothy Lawson

Lawson, James S., 72/14

Lawson, Murray G., 62/404

Lawson, Thomas, 72/351: biography, 73/278

Lawton, Henry Ware, 80/188,190

Lawyer (Indian), 62/106,320,401; 69/51; 71/334; 79/185N: sketch by Sohon, 69/52

Lawyer, Corbett (Indian): Nez Perce dictionary, 66/88

Lawyers, 63/361; 79/5,6,6N: first woman lawyer in Ore., 78/174-77; legal fees, 77/263; 81/279; Portland Italian, 77/254,259,260; The Dalles, 77/261-68*passim*

Lawyer's Canyon, 79/198

Lay, Marion, SEE Davis, Marion Lay

Layton, Davis: OMV service, 66/139N,143-47,154-59 *passim*

Lazarev, M.P., 72/111,112

Leadbetter, Danville, 70/272

Leadbetter Point, 70/272

League for Industrial Democracy, 76/143

League of American Wheelmen, 65/305

League of Women Voters, 80/395: Lake Oswego, publication, 65/121; Portland, publications, 73/210

Leakey, Louis S.B., 70/183

Lean Elk (Indian), 64/274

Leary, David T.: "Slacum in the Pacific, 1832-37: Backgrounds of the Oregon Report," 76/118-34

Leary, John, Morrow Co., 69/137

Leary, John, owner *Bailey Gatzert*, 63/61,64-65

Leary, Patrick, 69/137

Lease, Mary Ellen, 68/201

Leasure, George, 64/271

Leather, 63/24,327-28

Leavenworth, Jesse Henry, 63/360

Leavenworth, Kan., 64/259

Leavitt, A.L., 76/382

Lebanon, Linn Co., Ore., 71/351; 73/267:

Blaine recollections 1850s-60s, 66/82; Brown farmhouse, 66/284; canal, 72/ 92; Denny land claim, 65/231-32; Denny school, 65/232; fever epidemic 1852, 65/231; fire dept., 68/187; history, 67/92

Lebeck, Leander, 69/310N,311N

Leber, Barbel: *The Impact of the Primary Economy on the Cultural Landscape of Oregon*, by Kunnecke, jt. review, 81/325-27

LeBreton, George W., 62/116; 63/215; 66/352,354; 73/246,246N; 81/203: letter to Caleb Cushing, 66/354N

LeBrun, Eugénie, 64/6,15-16,18-20, 24,31: biography, 64/6,19; photos of Hawaiian royalty paintings, 64/4,8

LeBrun, Hercules, 66/359N

LeBrun, Marie Anne Ouvre (Mrs. Hercules), 66/359N

Lechlitner, Ruth, 74/153-54

Leclair (Leclaire), Louis, 63/117,123, 134,139,150,169

LeClaire, William, 63/147N

LeConte, Joseph, 67/25

Ledding, Mrs. Herman, 68/155N,164N: name of Bing cherry, 68/167,170

Ledford, Eli, 69/225N
Ledoux, Louis, 63/168
LeDuc, Thomas, 64/85,350
Ledyard, John, 63/88; 64/187,283: and Meriwether Lewis, 66/86; biography, 68/274-76; Cook voyage journal, 68/274; Russian exped. journal, 68/274-77
Lee, Agnes, 71/275
Lee, Anna Maria Pittman (Mrs. Jason), 63/185; 64/45: biography, 80/335
Lee, Borghild (Peggy) Lundborg, 73/296; 74/65,157,174,244N: biography, 74/58; photo, 73/296
Lee, Charles M., 79/154N,155
Lee, Dan, mate on *Arthur Middleton*, 80/34
Lee, Daniel, nephew of Jason, 63/186, 196; 66/340N; 76/359; 78/339-40; 79/122N; 80/335; 81/14N: described, 74/72-73; letter 1838, 74/74-78; plan for financing Ore. mission, 74/71-78
Lee, Daniel, and J.H. Frost: *Ten Years in Oregon*, reprint noted, 74/359
Lee, E. Trumbull, 75/129
Lee, Edmund, Y., 66/58
Lee, Henry A.G., 64/140; 75/72
Lee, J., painted panorama maker, 65/141
Lee, Jason, 62/69,124,200,299,400N, 406-407; 63/177,185-86,196,200,208, 210,228,234; 64/41-53,353; 65/159, 218; 73/73; 74/71; 76/202,359-60,365; 78/86-89; 79/122N,134; 80/207,335; 81/14N: biography, 77/291; dependence on nephew, 74/73 descriptions of— G.B. Roberts, 63/185; H. Scott, 70/227N,230 difficulties as mission director, 74/72-73; Edwards memorial, 66/347; Gervais friendship, 66/344; historians' views, 74/72; house, 66/82,283; Indian mission school, 64/41,43,45; Indian students exploited, 64/46-50; letters, 78/336,341,343,347-48; mission established, 66/341; mission funds, 64/46-50; Oregon Institute, 66/352; Ore.Prov.Govt. role, 66/350; "saved Oregon" theory, 78/332-50; sermon on Brooks, 64/50; statehood art medal, 68/187; statue, 69/324; Willamette Valley-Salmon River excursion, 66/346-47
Lee, John, 69/137
Lee, Joseph P., 71/274,275
Lee, Lucy Thompson (Mrs. Jason), 64/50; 76/365
Lee, Patrick, 69/137
Lee, Philander, 70/279
Lee, Will, son of Joseph L., 71/275
Lee, Willson, 74/58
Lee, Zerelda B. Smith, 79/154N,161,162
Lee Falls, 75/87
Lee Mission Cemetery, 63/248
Lee Mission parsonage, SEE Methodist Mission parsonage
Leedy, Daniel, 79/16
Leedy, Mary, 79/16
Lees, Robert E., 75/290
Lees, William E., Sr., 75/7: biography, 75/290; letter, 74/350-51
Lees Encampment (Meacham Station), 80/118,130
Leesburg, Ida., 63/89; 67/368
LeFevre, John T., 77/69,70,71
Lefevre, Pierre, 74/359
Legal tender, 72/316: wheat used, 63/181-82,217; SEE ALSO Money
Legend of Indian Mary and Umpqua Joe, by Booth, noted, 76/304
Legends, SEE Myths and legends
Legends and Tales of the Old West, ed. by Barker, noted, 65/121
Leggins (Indian), 68/252N
Leghorn, Ben, 62/201; 70/75
Lehman Springs, 73/285
Lehnherr, Chris, 63/26
Lehr, Charles, 65/145
Leidy, Joseph, 67/17
Leigh, William R., 68/346
Leipzig, Francis Peter, 78/369
Leiter, Wilma, photo, 74/265
Leland, Alonzo, 66/11:

biography, 64/86; map of mining regions Ore. and Wash. Terr. 1863, 79/ins.bk.cov. Summer

Leland, Ore., 69/88

Lelia Byrd (brig), 70/366

Lemade, Eric, 76/268

Lemati, Ore., SEE Cottage Grove, Ore.

Lemhi Indian Reservation, 70/106; 71/366

Lemhi Indians, 81/331

The Lemhi: Sacajawea's People, by Madson, noted, 81/331

Lemieux, —, Ore. writer 1939, 75/265

Lemke, William, 76/138

Lemmens Inlet, 68/102,103,108: chart, 68/104

Lennon, John, 69/137

Lenox, David, 62/156

Lent, D. Geneva, 63/359: *West of the Mountains: James Sinclair and the Hudson's Bay Company*, review, 65/305-306

Lents, Ore., 70/216

Leonard, Alphonse ("Foncy"), 76/333-58*passim*; 77/5-34,150-73*passim*: family photo, 76/338; photo, 77/148

Leonard, Amon: photo, 76/338; ranch, 76/336

Leonard, Andrew, photo, 77/148

Leonard, Daniel G., 78/174,177

Leonard, Helen: *Fun Along the Way*, noted, 73/74

Leonard, James, 78/149

Leonard, Joe, brother of Alphonse, 76/341-43,350,351

Leonard, Joseph, immigrant of 1853, 78/213: family, 78/129

Leonard, Mary G., 78/174-77: photo, 78/176

Leonard, Mary Purdom, 78/129

Leonard, Oral, 76/336,352: photo, 76/338

Leonard, Sarah Elrod, 78/174

Leonard, Spencer, 62/197,298; 63/91

Leonard, Willard ("Bill"), 77/148 (photo):

"A Boyhood with Sheep in the Oregon Desert," 76/333-58; 77/5-35,149-73

Leonard and Green, Astoria: building photo 1855, 81/4

Leonard's Bridge, 81/263

Leonards Hotel, Wasco, 78/174

Leotard, Jules, 70/9

Le Page du Pratz, Antoine Simon, 66/86

Leprosy, 63/198-99: pioneer treatment, 63/198

LeRoi Mine and Smelter, B.C., 64/283

LeRoy, Bruce: *Early Washington Communities in Art*, noted, 67/279

LeRoy, Bruce, ed.: *H.M. Chittenden: A Western Epic*, review, 63/243-44 *Northwest Forts and Trading Posts*, noted, 69/332

LeRoy, Herman Rutgers, 65/214

Leschi (Indian), 62/85-86; 67/280

Leschi of the Nisquallies, by Emmons, noted, 67/280

Leslie, Adelia Judson Olley, 76/365-67

Leslie, David, 62/116,119,121; 63/184; 76/367; 78/338

Leslie, George W., 72/353

Leslie, Leith, 74/262

Leslie Gulch, 74/286

Leslie United Methodist Church, Salem, 70/184

Lesowski, Lynda: *The Magnificent Gateway*, by Allen, review, 80/407 *Salmon Fisheries of the Columbia*, by Smith, review, 81/321-22

Lesquereux, Leo, 67/29; 69/43

Lessa, William A.: *Drake's Island of Thieves: Ethnological Sleuthing*, noted, 77/303

Lessel, O.R., 77/235

Lesueur, Charles A.: drawing of antelope, 69/fr.cov. March

"A Letter: Albert H. Powers," by Margaret Powers Hughes, 77/73-78

Letters and Papers of Rev. David E. Blaine and his Wife Catharine, noted, 66/82

Letters Home: The Story of Ann Arbor's Forty-Niners, by Bidlack, review, 62/296

The Letters of Charles John Brydges, 1879-1882, Hudson's Bay Company Land Com-

missioner, ed. by Bowsfield, review, **81**/323-24

Letters of Francis Parkman, ed. by Jacobs, review, **62**/403

Letters of George Catlin and His Family, by Roehm, review, **68**/77-79

The Letters of the Lewis and Clark Expedition with Related Documents, ed. by Jackson, cited, **77**/290; review, **64**/183-84; 2nd ed. review, **80**/206-207

"Letters of Zebulon C. Bishop, American Traveler," **66**/161-70

"Letters to Mrs. F.F. Victor," by George B. Roberts, **63**/175-236

Leutwyler, Paul, **79**/407

Levant (corvette), **70**/305

Levenbank (ship), **66**/122

Lever, H.A., **66**/109,112

Leverenz, Jon M., cartog.:

Atlas of the Pacific Northwest Resources and Development, noted, **69**/331

Levin, Elena, trans.:

The Beginnings of Russian-American Relations, 1775-1815, by Bolkhovitinov, review, **78**/359-60

Levitan, Sar A., and Barbara Hetrick: *Big Brother's Indian Programs—With Reservations*, noted, **74**/96

LeWarne, Charles Pierce: *Utopias on Puget Sound, 1885-1915*, review, **77**/294-95

Lewell, A., Sacred Heart student, **81**/81N

Lewelling, Clarissa, **68**/201

Lewelling, Henderson, SEE Luelling, Henderson

Lewelling, John, **68**/198: California cherry orchard, **68**/162; fruit nurseries, **68**/155,156,162,164

Lewelling, Meshach, **68**/154-55

Lewelling, Seth: abolitionist, **68**/167,200; Bing cherry, **71**/349; contribution to initiative and referendum, **68**/219; death, **68**/172, 210; depression of 1893, **68**/204,216; describes fruit grafts, **68**/160; estate, **68**/210,216,217; family history, **68**/ 154-55,156N,201; first Italian prune orchard, **68**/164; horticulturist, **68**/ 171,173-74; house photo, **68**/196; Mil-

waukie nursery, **68**/162,164,199; name spelling, **68**/153N; new fruit varieties, **68**/165-74,199; photo, **68**/196; political affiliations, **68**/200

Lewelling, Sophronia Vaughn Olson, **68**/198,205,208,210,219: biography, **68**/201; charges against U'Ren, **68**/197,216-18; photo, **68**/199

Lewelling, William, **68**/201

Lewelling-Luelling family: genealogy, **68**/154-55,156N; in Progressive movement, **68**/197-220*passim*

Lewelyn (ship), **66**/127

Lewes, Adolphus Lee, **63**/173; **64**/211

Lewes, John Lee, **63**/211; **68**/113

Lewes River, **76**/113

Lewis (Indian), **79**/275N

Lewis (Lewes, Fredrick Lee?), **63**/198

Lewis, David C., **80**/292

Lewis, E., Auburn mines 1861, **62**/218N

Lewis, Emanuel Raymond:

Seacoast Fortifications of the United States: An Introductory History, review, **71**/279-81

Lewis, Frank, Portland student 1911, **77**/69

Lewis, James: accounts of death on *Tonquin*, **71**/315,319,320-22

Lewis, Joe (Indian), **75**/74,75

Lewis, John C., **69**/208

Lewis, John L., **76**/148

Lewis, Lucy Meriwether, **69**/168

Lewis, Meriwether, **62**/288,289; **63**/69-70; **64**/183,272; **66**/65,66,384; **68**/86,275,346; **70**/87,348-49; **71**/247; **75**/94; **80**/206: animals discovered, **69**/23; bird hibernation observed, **69**/15; botanist, **69**/148-70; collects fossils, **69**/17 death, **66**/86; **69**/161— documents relating to, **80**/331 descriptions— animals, **69**/5-6; plants, **69**/149-58*passim*; poor-will, **69**/15; quail, **69**/6-7; ragged robin, **69**/149-52

Ft. Stevens battery named for, **65**/357N; herbarium, **69**/159-67; Jefferson comments, **69**/23; Le Page du Pratz and,

66/86; name suggested for Columbia River, 74/269-70; names animals, 69/10; plants discovered, 69/167; plants named for, 69/161; poem about, 74/270; portraits, 69/4; 70/367; zoologist, 69/5-28

Lewis, Oscar, ed.:

The Life and Times of the Virginia City Territorial Enterprise, noted, 73/74

Lewis, Paul M., 77/300

Lewis, Mrs. Richard, 76/387

Lewis and Clark and the Nez Perce Indians, by Ray, noted, 74/94

Lewis and Clark Centennial Exposition, 62/173,335,418; 63/68,335; 67/80; 70/204; 72/166; 74/105; 76/27: buildings, 71/158; 79/356; Davenport exhibit, 66/45-46; entertainment, 80/58; exhibits, 66/45-46; 80/55-57,60; federal appropriation, 70/225; historical function, 70/225N; history, 71/157N,159N; Oriental trade interest, 71/157,158,159N,160; painting, 79/356; photos, 70/223,224,228; 71/158; 77/138-39; 80/54,ins.fr.cov. Spring; postal cards, 66/304-305,307; prices, 80/64, 65; promotion, 71/157,159N,160; Scott's influence, 70/225; site, 70/223; visitor's account, 80/52-65; West Coast celebrities at, 66/45-46

Lewis and Clark College, Portland, 81/174

Lewis and Clark Expedition, 62/88,100-102,105,202,288,290; 66/188,383; 67/85,278; 68/345; 70/73,339; 71/247,337; 72/155; 73/86,199,284; 74/88,94,269; 76/92,325; 77/89-90; 79/100-101; 81/428:

anecdotes, 74/280; animal specimens, 69/22-23; articles on, 70/87; author of publication on, identity, 63/358; bibliography, 74/280; 78/285; 80/206; books carried by members, 69/26,168-69; botanical collections, 68/111; 79/336

camp sites, 67/371; 75/88— Idaho, 68/88; location of Apr. 6, 1806 site, 80/335; lost sites, 70/178; Salmon River, 66/88

Celilo Falls, 75/94; Christmas 1805, 64/88,356; comment on sources, 70/87; correspondence, 77/290; departure point, 69/335; documents and letters, 64/183; 80/331; editing papers of, 68/345; field notes, 66/65-67; food, 69/155; geographic research, 77/191-92; guides, 79/336; handyman, 80/335; herb remedies, 69/156; historic sites associated with, 77/82-83; Indian tales of, 68/181; Jefferson's instructions, 67/367-68

journals, 70/226; 72/82-83; 78/284-85; 79/105; 81/329— editors, 78/284; flora described in, 69/148-70*passim*; head-flattening sketch, 69/171; western animals described in, 69/13

legal aspects, 78/285; manuscript field notes and maps, 66/65-67; maps, 62/105; 66/65-67; 71/362; medical aspects, 72/179; 80/404-405; Montana birds, 71/366; natural history of, 63/69-70; 68/345; 70/348-49; naturalists, 70/171,173; Nez Perce Indians, 74/94; paintings, 72/83; peace medals, 69/84; 73/277; 76/92; physicians, 75/93; Plains Indians reactions to, 67/368; plant specimens, 69/158-68; 79/336; Portland monument, 70/222; public image, 67/368; publications, 81/208,428; roster, 71/249N; 72/82-83; salt cairn, 79/411; 80/335,412; scientific work, 70/348-49; Spanish threat, 74/353

trail—

commemoration, 67/91,368; in Missouri, 68/345; 75/93; photos, 67/371; Salmon River, 66/88

trail markers, 65/315; travels influence on Oregon immigrants, 68/156; Webb comment, 70/348

Lewis and Clark: Explorers to the West, by Haines and Morrill, review, 62/102

Lewis and Clark Herbarium: discovered, 69/163; history, 69/163-68,170; photos of plants, 69/154,160, 162,164,166; specimens to England, 69/161-63,165

Lewis and Clark: Historic Places Associated with Their Transcontinental Exploration, pub. by Nat'l Park Service, review, **77**/82-83

Lewis and Clark: Pioneering Naturalists, by Cutright, review, **70**/348-49

Lewis and Clark Trail Commission, **67**/91,377

Lewis and Clark Trail Heritage Foundation, **79**/411: publications, **79**/336; **80**/335; **81**/329

Lewis County, Wash., **62**/64,240N; **63**/107,237N: census— 1850 and 1860, **72**/354; 1800, **75**/363 Fourth of July 1862, **66**/35; Yacolt burn 1902, **65**/308

Lewis River, Clark-Cowlitz Cos., **74**/281: first area school, **66**/80; settlers, **63**/83; steamboats, **62**/109

Lewis (Snake) River, **79**/383; SEE ALSO Snake River

Lewis's monkey flower (*Mimulus lewisii*), **69**/161

Lewis's syringa (*Philadelphus lewisii*), **69**/160(photo),161

Lewis's wild flax (*Linum lewisii*), **69**/153,154(photo),158,161

Lewis's woodpecker: description, **69**/9; sketch, **69**/8

Lewiston, Ida., **62**/297,320; **63**/359; **65**/382; **70**/21N,27; **71**/23,24,25; **79**/181,181N,199: centennial, **63**/89; view 1862, **79**/182-83

Lewisville, Ore., **77**/271,272

Lewisville, Wash., **70**/358

Lexington, Clatsop Co., Ore., **63**/50

Lexington, Morrow Co., Ore., **73**/285; **75**/360; **79**/104

Libbey, F.W.: *The Almeda Mine*, noted, **69**/78

Libbey, F.W., and R.E. Corcoran: *The Oregon King Mine, Jefferson County, Oregon*, noted, **63**/246,362

Libby, Ore., **69**/88; **72**/353

The Liberal Church at the End of the Oregon Trail, by Bachelder, noted, **71**/190

Liberty, Marion Co., Ore., **73**/346

Liberty, Wheeler Co., Ore., **73**/263

Liberty Brewery, Portland, photo, **64**/267

Liberty loan drives, **68**/138,140; **75**/249: posters, **75**/243,266,ins.bk.cov. Sept.

Liberty loans, **71**/213,216,218-20

Libraries: Alaska, **65**/386; early American, **73**/ 367; early Oregon, **65**/386; Oregon, serial holdings, **77**/382; Oregon Territory, **64**/145-46; Pacific NW, **62**/108; **63**/243; role of historical societies, **73**/367; St. Louis 1808-42, **63**/358; Sitka (New Archangel), **73**/167; Whitman Co., Wash., **65**/386

Libraries and Librarians of the Pacific Northwest, by Johansen *et al*, noted, **62**/108; review, **63**/243

Library Association of Portland, **62**/312; **64**/357; **70**/197; **80**/61,62: board members, **71**/225-26,226N; building photo, **71**/224; Hunt controversy, **71**/213-45

Licenses: passenger boat, **81**/38

Lichter, Harry, **62**/421: *Indian Trade Goods*, by Woodward, review, **66**/186-87

Licking Land Company, Ohio **79**/359,360N

Lieser, Henry Clay, family, **65**/308

Lieuallen, R.E., **66**/394; **68**/360; **69**/347; **70**/373

Life and Letters of George Mercer Dawson, 1849-1901, by Winslow-Sprague, cited, **66**/70

The Life and Times of the Virginia City Territorial Enterprise, ed. by Lewis, noted, **73**/74

Life in California, During a Residence of Several Years, by Robinson, review, **71**/285

Lifesaving, **72**/92; **73**/73: lifeboat drill photos, **66**/176; rescue procedure described, **66**/174-75,177 stations— Cape Arago, **66**/171; Oregon, **64**/70;

SEE ALSO Yaquina Life-Saving Station
Lightfoot, W.J.:
Oregon-Calif. boundary survey, 72/37,38
Lighthouses, 69/311,313,322:
Brown's Point, 66/181; Cape Disappointment, 69/78,307N,309; Destruction Island, 66/181; Fox Rock, 80/256; Heceta Head, 69/77; New Archangel, 73/139; Oregon 1890s, 66/181; Tillamook Rock, 71/11,197; 73/70; Umpqua River, 62/205; West Coast, 75/365
Yaquina Bay, 70/75; 71/294; 73/80; 75/294N—
photo, 75/ins.bk.cov. March
Lightner, William L., 74/110-11,118
Lightships, 69/312N,323:
first on Pacific Coast, 69/307
Liholiho, SEE Kamehameha II
Lilies, 72/92
Liliha (Madame Boki), 64/10,14:
photo, 64/28
Liljeblad, Sven, 62/106:
biography, 68/88
Liljeqvist, L.A., 75/168-69
Lillard, Richard G.:
Desert Challenge, An Interpretation of Nevada, review, 67/364-65
Lily (steamboat), 65/314
Lima, Peru, 77/122-24:
cathedral photo, 77/123
Lina, Ambrose, 66/360N
Lincoln, Abraham (Indian), 70/149
Lincoln, Abraham, U.S. president, 62/199; 64/154; 66/35; 72/60,77, 315,326:
assassination eyewitness account, 63/91; election news reaches Calif., 67/233-34; Mormon view, 64/281; Oregon vote 1860, 72/323; Pacific NW friends, 64/357; quoted, 66/6; western image in 1860 campaign, 66/86
Lincoln, Ore.:
1882 map, 72/171
Lincoln Benton County Co-op:
officers photo, 80/324
Lincoln City, Ore., 67/369
Lincoln County, Ore., 65/385; 66/346:

early school days, 70/279; history, 71/289; homesteading, 71/265-73; pioneer days, 63/253; 64/355; postal cards, 66/330; religious colony, 71/289; source of early growth, 67/373
Lincoln County Historical Society:
meetings, 69/279; 70/276; museum, 69/176; officers and directors, 66/85, 279; 67/82,284; 68/84; 69/81-82, 279; 70/82,276; 71/194; 72/176; 73/78; 74/181; 75/91; 76/95; 77/95; 78/95; 79/111; 80/110; 81/110; publications, 70/75; 74/282; 77/292,298; 81/327
"Lincoln County Homesteader," by Lillian Maki, 71/265-73
Lincoln High School, Portland, 74/347
Lind, Carol J.:
Big Timber, Big Men, noted, 80/208
Lind, Helen Yonge, ed.:
Voyages to Hawaii Before 1860, by Judd, noted, 76/182
Lindberg, Christine, 76/7,8(photo)
Lindberg, John, 76/7,8(photo),9,13
Lindbergh, Charles Augustus:
Vancouver, Wash. visit, 80/334
Linden, Tom, photo, 74/265
Linderman, Frank Bird:
Montana Adventure: The Recollections of Frank Linderman, ed. by Merriam, noted, 71/191
Plenty-Coups, Chief of the Crows, reprint noted, 63/247
Lindgard, Elmer W., 70/269
Lindgren, Erik, 70/184:
cabin, 73/72
Lindgren, Waldemar, 67/18,21
Lindsay, Nathaniel, 78/175
Lindsay, Vachel, 72/267; 73/295
Lindsley, Aaron L., 70/180
Linfield College, McMinnville, 62/200; 64/150; 72/227; 74/128
Link, John, 79/239
Linkville, Ore., 62/322; 66/76; 68/319; 76/382; SEE ALSO Klamath Falls, Ore.
"Linkville Trolley" (Klamath Co. railroad), 80/104
Linkville Weekly Star, Klamath Falls:
history, 65/315

Linman, John (Jack), 66/382
Linn, —, Auburn expressman 1864, 62/234-35
Linn, Lewis Fields, 62/123,124; 66/347; 73/86: Oregon bill, 62/124,129,131
Linn, Philip E., family, 68/82
Linn City, Ore.: history, 72/169
Linn County, Ore., 62/200; 66/19,141, 318; 78/41,42N,43,331; 79/104; 80/209: historic buildings, 63/363; 68/186; history, 65/315; maps, 77/90,197,292; pheasants, 65/247,254; progress report, 65/217; settlement, 77/318; settlers, 79/49
Linn County Historical Society: meetings, 69/279; 70/276; museum, 69/176; officers and directors, 62/104,415; 63/86,250; 64/83,279; 65/123,312; 66/85,279; 67/82,284; 68/85,283; 69/82,279; 70/82,276; 71/194; 72/176; 73/78; 74/181; 75/91; 76/95; 77/95; 78/95; 79/111; 80/110; 81/111
Linnaeus, Carl: books carried by Lewis, 69/26
Linnhaven Orchard Co., Lebanon, 70/279
Linnton, Ore., 62/204
Lino, Joseph, 66/351N
Linsley, N.E., 74/8
Linthicum, Alex W., 62/421
Linthicum, Louise, 62/420
Linum lewisii (Lewis's wild flax), 69/153,154(photo),158,161
Linville, Harrison, 70/19
Lions Club: Garibaldi, 77/367; Tigard, 77/379
Lipman, Wolfe and Co., Portland, 66/305
Liquor, 62/68; 64/200,209N,210N; 70/19,134; 72/75: "blue ruin," 63/191; 64/237N bootlegging, 69/128; 73/84; 76/159-63— photo, 76/160; profits, 76/160 Cowlitz Farm policy, 63/197,214;

drinking, 69/109,113,135,136,144; home brew, 69/108,125; Indian trade, 70/102; 72/73,75; Klamath Falls, 71/139; lumber camps, 73/177; mining camps, 81/190-92; Montana control, 72/172-73; moonshine, 76/161-62; 77/197; Ore.Prov.Govt., 62/140-41; 64/130; Portland, SEE Portland— liquor business; Tillamook Co., 71/139; wholesaling, photo, 77/259; wine industry, 69/332; SEE ALSO Distilleries; Prohibition; Saloons; Temperance
Lisa, Manuel, 62/289; 65/304; 68/346
Lisiansky, Yury, 77/177
List, Edith M. and Howard M., eds.: "John M. Shively's Memoir," 81/5-29,181-95
List of Logbooks of U.S. Navy Ships, Stations and Miscellaneous Units, 1801-1947, comp. by Bradley *et al*, noted, 81/333
List of Officers of the Army of the United States from 1779 to 1900, by Powell, noted, 69/333-34
A List of References for the History of Agriculture, by Rogers, noted, 74/284
A List of References for the History of Agriculture in California, by Orsi, noted, 75/365
Lister, Ernest, 74/211,216
Lister, Queene, 74/64,65,157,174: described, 74/61-62; photo, 73/296
Lister, Thomas, 78/200
Lister, William, 78/123,220
Literature, 71/286: awards, 73/293,301,305,312-13; desert metaphor in Cooper, 72/181; evaluation of Ore. literature, 74/37-38,266; fiction, 74/52-54; history, 74/176; metaphor and North American nationality, 72/178; Methodist influence, 74/150,152; "Oregon" temper, 74/34,35, 37,52,62; Pacific NW anthology, 71/181-82
Pacific NW writers, 73/293-331— 1920s-30s, 74/34-70,145-78,244-67 short stories, 74/176; theses index, 72/275; Western American, 71/291; 72/179,181; 73/286 western novels, 68/87,279-80,348;

69/74-75,336—
1830s, 71/367
SEE ALSO names of authors; Poetry
Lithia Fountain, Ashland, 64/323N
Lithia Mineral Springs, Ashland, 64/323N,325-26; 69/340: photo, 64/324
Lithia Park, Ashland, 62/180; 64/323N,339,340-41: photos, 64/324,331,338
Lithographers, SEE Printers
Littell, Lydia, photo, 74/265
Little Bear Creek, Crook Co., 65/78N
Little Blitzen Gorge, photo, 68/325
Little Blue River, 62/268,269,274; 79/372,373; 80/68
Little Bull Mountain, 77/377
Little Crowbar Point, 78/320
Little Dog (Indian), 65/314
Little High Rock Canyon, 63/365
Little Lookout Mountain, 66/198
Little Meadows, Harney Valley, 65/54
Little Meadows, Jackson Co.: Indian battle, 66/222N
Little Muddy Creek, Jefferson Co., 81/299
Little Sandy River, Ore. Trail, 62/354,355; 80/78
Little Silver Lake, 78/235,240
Little Skookum Bay, 72/148
Little Summit Prairie, 65/106N
Little Tennessee, Wheeler Co.: name, 64/107N
Little White Salmon Valley, 74/281
Little Willow Creek, 78/320
Little Wood River, 68/240,241,309
Littlefield, David, 62/220-21,222,223, 225; 63/92; 69/274; 79/42
Littlefield, Duckworth & Co., 62/236
Litton, Mrs. L.W., 80/59
Littrell, Andrea, 75/68
Liven, C.A., 72/101,104,114N
Livermore, Jonas, 81/270N
Livery stables: Klamath Falls, 69/328
Livestock, 63/269-70; 67/135,142; 68/28: Baker Co. history, 65/216; blooded stock in Ore., 76/6; California,

69/332; distribution in Ore. Terr. 1850, 80/329; Eastern Ore., 73/279; factor in rural disputes, 64/85; industry, 77/296,302; numbers on Ore. Trail 1852, 68/185; Utah law 1848-96, 66/87; SEE ALSO Cattle; Sheep; etc.
Livingston, Anna Pendleton, 69/340
Livingston, Mont., 74/337
Livoniatis (steamer), 71/13
Llama (brig), 63/192,217-18; 76/227
Lloyd, James, 72/115,116,117; 76/205,210,212
Lloyd, Ralph B., 67/50
Local government: county home rule, 65/216
Locke, G.M., 71/222
Lockhart, Ella, 63/12
Lockhart, Esther (Mrs. Freeman G.), 63/12,16-17
Lockhart, Freeman G., 63/12; 68/263
Lockhart, Lilly, 63/12
Lockley, Fred, 64/355; 67/242,366
Lockridge, Jim, 79/156N,157,163,297
Locks: Willamette River, 65/395N; 71/42,46; Yamhill River, 66/181; 76/24-25; SEE ALSO Cascade Locks
Lockwood, Chauncey M., 79/167N: biography, 79/270N
Locomotives: American development, 67/280; displayed in Ore., 68/350; logging use, 73/15-16; 77/72(photo); SEE ALSO Whitney Co.—locomotives photos, 79/265— 1880s, 67/100,103,113,131,137 Puget Sound pioneer, 67/369; steam, 63/351,354-55 types, 63/351-52— Baldwin 0-4-2 photo, 65/358
Locusts, 63/330-31
Loe, Kelley, 76/144
Loeb, Alfred A., 67/42,43,46-47
Loeb State Park, 67/44,47,52
Loewenberg, Robert J.: *The Character and Influence of the Indian Trade in Wisconsin*, by Turner, review, 79/92-97 *Equality on the Oregon Frontier: Jason Lee*

and the Methodist Mission, 1834-43, noted, 77/291; review, 78/86-89 "The *Lausanne* Mystery Solved: A Note," 76/359-67 "'Not...by Feeble Means'," 74/71-78 "Saving Oregon Again," 78/332-50 Log Cabin, B.C., 81/143,144(photo) Log Cabin Inn, 70/272 Log cabins, SEE Houses Logan, David, 79/11; 80/144: biography, 79/6 Logan, Robert, 63/123,137,144-45, 148,150 Logan, Stephen T., 79/6 Logan, William, 65/20,21N,35N,44 Logging industry, 64/354; 65/366; 69/77,78; 71/133-34; 73/73; 74/304; 75/364; 77/73-78,190-91: balloon logging, 70/182; 75/364; British Columbia, 72/287; bucker, 73/19 camps, 72/301,303; 73/5N,173,213; 74/83,93; 75/11-13; 76/41,49,60- 65; 79/394-95— cooks, 73/212-13; 76/65; entertainment, 73/189; food, 73/215-16; photo, 68/264; SEE ALSO Whitney Co. cartoons, 73/28,187,215; chutes, 70/ 358; 71/132(photo); 74/324; Clatsop Co., 75/294; clothing, 73/184-85,188; Columbia Co., 79/294; Coos Co., 77/77; Deep River, Wash., 81/106 donkey engines, 73/10-14,179,182- 83,219-20; 79/395,396— photos, 73/10,180,ins.bk.cov. March, ins.fr.cov. Sept. dynamite, 73/221; felling methods, 66/281; flumes, 75/57,60,365; 78/ 363; grip wheels, 79/395-96; "gyppo" operations, 71/133-34; 77/277; hand cutting, 76/42-43,109; Klamath area, 66/284; labor history, 80/208; loading platforms, 73/5; locomotives, SEE Locomotives; log dumps, 72/310,312; 73/12(photo),13-14,176 loggers, 68/81,348; 72/295; 76/65; 77/263,277— superstitions, 73/213; terms, 73/ 18-30,173-86,215-17

logs— branding, 68/89; decks, 77/229,230; drives, 67/161N; 70/367; handling methods, 77/229,231; photos, 73/ 224; 77/72,212,230,232; prices 1900s, 81/38,39 Middle Fork Willamette, 78/308; Minnesota, 77/73,75; museum, 74/362; Oregon, 71/267-68; oxen, 73/226; 74/93,300; 79/394 Pacific Northwest, 72/348— independent operators, 66/82 photos, 72/298,302,ins.covs. Dec.; 75/215,216; 76/37; Powers, Ore., 77/73-78; Puget Sound, 62/98-99 rafts, 67/176N; 73/173,174,179; 75/105; 77/213,222,229; 79/396— Benson, 66/181; Columbia River to San Diego, 66/181; cradle, 66/181; Fastabend construction, 66/179-82; Ostrander boom, 81/36; photos, 66/178,180,182; 75/106,ins.fr.cov. June; Robertson raft, 66/181 railroads, 63/354-55; 69/77,78; 72/ 94,294,308-14; 73/6,14-16,175-76, 219-20; 74/83,300,357; 76/61-63; 77/190,213,214; 80/104,209— construction, 73/6-7,219; trestles, 77/72,190,222 roads— map, 75/57; photo, 78/310; Portland, 75/56-65 Russian, 77/190; salvage operations, 77/351,367; scaling, 73/173,174-75, 176; 76/ins.bk.cov. March(photo); Skagit log jam, 66/282; slash burning, 73/190-92; soil erosion, 73/185; Spanish, 77/190; spar trees, 73/180 (photo),186,213 techniques, 73/18-30,183-84,185- 86,216; 77/75,190— photos, 73/20,22,fr.cov. March Tillamook Co., 72/293-314; 73/5- 30,171-92,212-27; 77/213-14; trucks, 77/277; unloaders, photo, 73/12; Upper Willamette, 72/171; whistle punk, 73/28-29; SEE ALSO Lumber and lumber industry; Timber *Logging Railroads Chug Down Memory*

Lane, by Schenck, noted, **80**/209
Logging Railroads of the West, by Adams, review, **63**/354-55
Logging the Redwoods, by Carranco and Labbe, review, **77**/190-91
Logie, Isabella, SEE Moar, Isabella Logie
Logie, Robert, **66**/127
Logsden, Ore.: name, **69**/340
Lolo Trail, Ida., **67**/371
Lomax, Alfred L., **62**/104,415; **63**/86, 92,250; **64**/83,90,279; **65**/123,215, 217,311,314; **66**/84,278; **77**/67(photo):
"The Albany Woolen Mill," **67**/61-74
Later Woolen Mills in Oregon: A History of the Woolen Mills Which Followed the Pioneer Mills, review, **77**/193-94
"Letter from a Hiker," **77**/67-71
Pioneer Woolen Mills, cited, **77**/193
Lombard Investment Co., **69**/203
Lonctain, Joseph, **66**/348N
London, Jack, **72**/180
London Correspondence Inward From Sir George Simpson, 1841-42, ed. by Williams, review, **74**/352
Londus, Jim, **69**/135
Lone Cone Mountain, **68**/102,103
Lone Fir Cemetery, SEE Portland—cemeteries
Lone Grave Butte, **79**/278
Lone Pine (Cumsuuks) Island, **72**/149, 151,152: fishing site, **72**/157; photos, **72**/152,156; village, **72**/151
Lone Rock Free State—Oregon's North Umpqua Valley, by Bakken, noted, **71**/190
Lone Tree Valley, **62**/395
"Lonely Outpost: The Army's Fort Umpqua," by Stephen Dow Beckham, **70**/233-57
Lonergan, Frank, **69**/137
Lonergan, Patrick, **69**/137
Lonerock, Ore., **73**/84; **81**/267: post offices, **65**/219; **69**/140
Long, Charlie, **69**/341
Long, James Larpenteur, **63**/71-72
Long, Jane Ann, SEE Hamblock, Jane

Ann Long
Long, Jerry (Indian), **70**/16N,21
Long, Joel M., **62**/172
Long, John E., **62**/146
Long, Marie Gadwa (Mrs. Clifford E.), **80**/285
Long, Reuben A., **66**/272,273
Long, Robert Alexander, **77**/381-82
Long, Stephen Harriman, **64**/281; **70**/87; **71**/364; **72**/179; **73**/66
Long, Terry, **72**/301
Long-Bell Lumber Company, **73**/73; **77**/217,381-82: mills photo, **74**/296
Long Creek, **69**/125; **70**/58; **74**/158
Long Creek Valley, **68**/303
The Long Road Travelled: An Account of Forestry of the University of Washington, by Schmitz, noted, **74**/358
"The Long Tom Rebellion," by James C. Williams, **67**/54-60
Long Tom River, **77**/324
Long Valley, Ida., **66**/88
Long Valley, Ore., SEE Silvies Valley
Longmire, Wash., **73**/345
Longmire family, **65**/365
Longshoremen: West Coast history, **68**/349; **72**/229
Longstaff, F.V., **73**/359
Longtain, Joseph, SEE Lonctain, Joseph
Longview, Wash., **67**/357,366; **74**/293; **77**/217: 50th anniversary, **73**/283; history, **77**/381-82; lumber mills, **73**/73,283
Longview, Portland and Northern Railroad, **62**/299
Looking Glass, the elder (Indian), **62**/274; **81**/369
Looking Glass, the younger (Indian), **81**/351
Lookingglass, Ore., **62**/205; **73**/304
Lookingglass Methodist Church: history, **62**/205
Lookout (Crane) Mountain, **79**/288,289
Lookout Point Dam, **77**/328; **78**/55, 320,321: photo, **78**/323
Loomis, Charles L., **64**/335-36,340
Loomis, Lewis Alfred, **66**/154; **68**/182

Loomis, R.P., 70/50
Loon Lake, 80/51,52
Looney, Charles, 63/303
Looney, Jesse, family, 67/75
Looney, Rachel Rowley (Mrs. Charles), 63/263N,288,303
Loons, 73/349
Loosley, John, 69/328
Loosley, Lucy Walling (Mrs. John), 69/328
Looters of the Public Domain, by Puter, reprint noted, 74/282-83
Lopez, Marcus (Marcos), 73/199
Lopez Island, 79/408
LoPiccolo, Margaret J.: "Some Aspects of the Range Cattle Industry of Harney County, Ore., 1870-1900," cited, 67/142
Lorain, Lorenzo, 69/223,235N,241, 250,251,253,254; 81/324: biography, 69/237N; Camp Day photos, 69/236,237,238,fr.cov. Sept.; describes Camp Day, 69/235-37; Ft. Umpqua photos, 70/240,242,246,252; Ft. Umpqua service, 70/243,247; Indian photos, 70/244 Klamath expedition, 70/252— letters, 69/232FF letters quoted, 70/245,249,251,253; photographer, 69/232,237N; 70/251; portrait, 69/242
Loraine, S.H., 70/251N
Lord, John Keast: Klamath country trip, 69/231-32
Lord, William, Camp Watson soldier, 66/52
Lord Elgin (ship), 66/129
Lorenz, Claudia Spink (Mrs. William), 66/81: "Klamath County: False Alarm Armistice Day, Nov. 9, 1918," 71/274-76 *The Time of My Life*, noted, 70/75
Lorenz, Max, 76/264-65,266
Loretano (vessel), 76/127
Loring, J. Malcolm, 71/372
Loring, Mrs. J. Malcolm, 71/372
Loring, James L., 64/261
Loring, William Wing, 62/64; 67/297,303:

biography, 73/71; 74/93
Loriot (brig), 63/210; 76/129,130
Los Angeles, Calif., 80/254: electric lights, 80/247 population— comparative 1910, 80/260; total and foreign-born 1870-1910, 80/263 (table)
Losiere (Lozier), Ignace, 63/146N,173
Lost Creek, Lane Co., 78/304; 79/13
Lost Lake, Hood River Co., 74/129
"The Lost Port Orford Meteorite," by Ellen C. Sedell, 69/29-49
Lost River, Klamath Co., 63/365; 69/ 249,250,251; 70/176; 72/34,47: dam, 72/34N; natural bridge, 72/35(photo),36N
Lost Valley, Lane Co.: settlers, 78/319
Lost wagon train, SEE Immigration of 1853
Lostine, Ore., 72/93
Lot (Indian), 70/161; 73/69: medal profile, 70/160
Lot Whitcomb (steamer), 63/238; 68/261; 77/91
Lotta Talbot (steamer), photo, 76/141
Lotteries: early Ore., 64/319
Lottinville, Savoie, and R.V. Hine, eds.: *Soldier in the West: Letters of Theodore Talbot...1845-53*, review, 74/355-56
Louden, T.A., 64/311N
Louderback, John, 77/323: biography, 77/323N
Louis (Indian), 73/69
Louis (schooner), 68/267
Louisiana Purchase, 75/81: newspaper reaction, 70/85
Louisiana Purchase Centennial Exposition: Barrett represents, 71/157-59; Orient trade interest, 71/157,158-59
Louisiana Territory, 72/179
Lousignant, Mary Ann, 65/309
Lousy Jack, Wheeler Co. freighter, 73/262
Love, David, 78/123
Love, James, 78/123

Love, John S., 78/123,154: photo, 78/122
Love, Margaret, 78/123
Lovegren, August, 80/106
Lovejoy, Asa Lawrence, 62/140,149, 150,151; 64/243N; 72/317; 73/247
Lovejoy, Esther Clayson Pohl, 69/338: awards, 75/8-10; medical school, 75/7-35; photos, 75/11,35; Portland health officer, 75/8; war service, 75/8-10
Lovejoy, Esther Clayson Pohl: *Certain Samaritans*, cited, 75/8 *House of the Good Neighbor*, cited, 75/8 "My Medical School, 1890-1894," 75/7-35 *Women Doctors*, cited, 75/9 *Women Physicians*, cited, 75/9
Lovejoy, George A., 75/8
Lovelace, Bill, 70/279
Lovelady, Thomas J., 75/349,350
Lovell, Edith Haroldsen, 65/121
Loveridge, Emily Lemoine, 72/280
Lovett, —, Ore. City ice manufacturer, 63/67
Lovett, Louisa, SEE Dement, Louisa Lovett
Lovin, Hugh T.: "Toward a Farmer-Labor Party in Oregon, 1933-38," 76/135-51
Low, Frederick, F., 65/350
Low, Jim, 63/331
Low, Mrs. Jim, 63/330-31
Lowe, Dr. —, pioneer of 1853, 62/242-43,376-86*passim*
Lowe, Mrs. —, pioneer of 1853, 62/242-43,376-84*passim*
Lowe, Beverly Elizabeth: *John Minto, Man of Courage*, noted, 81/327-28
Lowe, Don and Roberta: *Mount Hood, Portrait of a Magnificent Mountain*, review, 77/87-88
Lowe, Herbert, photo, 66/116
Lowe, Jacob, 63/143
Lowe, Joe, Rainier liveryman, 74/84
Lowe, Thomas, HBCo. employee, 63/202,215,218
Lowell, Dan, 64/205N
Lowell, Stephen A., 68/216

Lowell, Ore., 78/54,65,305,319,322, 323(photo),325
Lower Applegate River area: history, 80/336
"Lower Columbia Lumber Industry, 1880-93," by Thomas R. Cox, 67/160-78
Lower Daniels Creek School, 66/53,54,55
Lower Klamath Lake, 69/225,232; 72/7N,37,39N,46: crops, 72/39; drained, 72/38; land reclaimed, 72/46; maps, 69/226,228,266
Lower Lake Creek, 73/283
Lownsdale, Daniel H., 72/317; 80/10N
Lownsdale, Millard Oregon, 77/377; 80/357N
Lowry, Richard S.: *Letters of the Lewis and Clark Expedition*, ed. by Jackson, review, 80/206-207 *Pioneer Conservationists of Western America*, by Wild, review, 80/407-408
Lowthian, Thomas, 69/217
Loy, Edward H.: "Editorial Opinion and American Imperialism: Two Northwest Newspapers," 72/209-24
Loy, William G., and Barbel Leber: *The Impact of the Primary Economy on the Cultural Landscape of Oregon*, by Kunnecke, review, 81/325-27
Loy, William G., *et al*: *Atlas of Oregon*, noted, 77/291; review, 78/178-79
Loyal Legion of Loggers and Lumbermen, 62/106; 65/197-98,365; 72/301; 77/77
Loyal Women of American Liberty, 75/140
Loyalty oaths: Civil War disputes, 73/33,37,43,59
Lozier, Ignace, SEE Losiere, Ignace
Lozier, Jean, 67/88; 71/198
Luark, Michael F., 64/353; 78/90
Lucas, Bill, 79/396
Lucas, Massina M., 80/137N
Luce, David N., 79/269N
Luce, (John? William?), 70/59
Lucia, Ellis, 63/252,363; 64/186:

The Big Woods, review, 77/86-87
Don't Call It Or-E-Gawn, noted, 65/309
Gold on Sterling Creek, by Haines and Smith, review, 66/75-76
Head Rig, Story of the West Coast Lumber Industry, noted, 67/281
The Klondike Fever, by Berton, review, 62/95-96
Klondike Kate: The Life and Legend of Kitty Rockwell, review, 63/352-53
Sea Wall, Adventuring Along the Rugged Oregon Coast, noted, 67/281
Tough Men, Tough Country: Stories of Men Who Met the Rugged Challenge of the Pacific Northwest, review, 65/209
Wild Water: The Story of the Far West's Great Christmas Week Floods, 1964-65, noted, 66/187
"Winnemucca to the Sea," noted, 66/281
Lucia, Ellis, and Mike Hanley: *Owyhee Trails: The West's Forgotten Corner*, review, 75/293
Lucia, Ellis, ed.: *This Land Around Us*, review, 71/181-82
Lucier, Celestine Gervais, 66/360N
Lucier, Etienne, 66/347,354; 77/81: farm, 66/339; Hunt overland exped., 66/333,338; land claim, 66/335-36; Ore.Prov.Govt. 66/350,352,353; quoted, 66/336-37
Lucier, Felicite, SEE Manson, Felicite Lucier
Lucier (Lussier), Joseph, 66/348N
Lucier, Louis, 66/360N
Luckey, James Clinton, 79/154N
Luckiamute Indians, 70/260
Luckiamute River, 63/51N; 65/173,175,177-86*passim*
Lucky Laceys, by Miller, review, 64/349
Lucy (schooner), 71/189
Lucy Lowe (steamer), 74/21-22
Ludlow, Fitzhugh, 62/292
Luelling, Albert, 68/164
Luelling, Alfred, 68/201,204,206,208, 209,217-18N,219: beginning of Oregon nursery, 68/159; describes journey, 68/157,158; Oakland, Calif. nursery, 68/164; photo,

68/159; reasons for move to Oregon, 68/156
Luelling, Eliza, 68/158
Luelling, Henderson, 66/86: abolitionist, 68/156; death, 68/164; family history, 68/154-55,156N; horticulturist, 68/173; Indiana nursery, 68/ 155; Iowa house, 68/155,156; land claim, 68/139; move to Calif., 68/164; name spelling, 68/153N; Oregon nurseries, 68/159-60,162-64; photo, 68/ 154; traveling nursery story, 68/153-54,156-58,198; tribute to, 68/174
Luelling, Levi, 68/164
Luelling, Oregon Columbia, 68/158
Lueling, Seth, SEE Lewelling, Seth
Luelling, W.H., 62/218
Lugenbeel, Pinkney, 65/49N; 67/323-24; 68/6,39: biography, 63/89
Luhr family, Cowlitz Co., 64/276
Luke, Thomas Clifton, 74/231
Lukey (vessel), 79/401
Lull, Roderick, 74/159: *The Outlanders*, cited, 74/177
Lum You (Chinese), 72/171
Lumber and lumber industry, 62/66, 106,198,199; 67/161-62; 69/77,78, 79; 72/86,398; 74/83,297; 77/296: barges, 72/310; Bend, 72/94; British Columbia, 65/364; California, 75/ 365; carriers, 77/342,343(photo); Central Ore., 66/183; Columbia Co., 62/301; company towns, 67/357; Coos Bay, 63/23; Coos Co., 77/75, 76(photo); Cowlitz Farm, 63/173-74 drying— kilns, 77/220,342-44; stacking, 77/348(photo),349
expansion of industry, 71/36-37,62, 77N,88N; exports, 67/114-15,164; 75/76; Ft. George, 64/215,218; grading, 77/341-49*passim*; Grays Harbor, 71/145; Idaho, 63/83; 64/86; inspection, 77/349; Lower Applegate River, 80/336; Lower Columbia 1880-93, 67/162-78; lumberjack legends, 81/329; lumbermen in Idaho, 64/86 markets, 67/163-72*passim*—

Orient, 71/143
Medford area, history, 81/205-206
mills, 73/10,73,75,83,283—
Garibaldi, 73/224; pioneer Tillamook, 73/224,226; Portland, 67/166-71; SEE ALSO Sawmills
Pacific Coast 1850s, 68/260-73*passim*;
Pacific trade to 1900, 72/228; plywood, 77/351,367; Portland, 67/166-71; prices, SEE Prices; production 1880-90, 67/162; publications, 72/293N; 73/364; Puget Sound, 71/368
railroads, 63/82,92,351-53,354-55; 68/350,351; 72/94—
car shortage 1890, 67/170; effect of completion of transcontinental, 67/160-78; 71/28,35,62; rates, 70/86; 71/35-36,78-79N; transcontinental and new markets, 67/115
shingle mill photo, 75/ins.fr.cov. June shipping, 71/368—
photo, 66/124; rail, 67/170-72; 77/346-47; schooner, 78/288; water, 77/347,359-65
shortage ww 1, 77/213; storage, 77/346; strike 1917, 69/325; technological changes, 67/175-77; 70/76; theses index, 72/275; Tillamook Co., 77/213-37,341-68; transportation, 76/34,58; utilization of whole log, 77/350-52; Washington, 65/366; West Coast history, 67/281; wood products diversification, 67/163; SEE ALSO Beaner Lumber Co.; Bellingham Bay Lumber Co.; Benson Timber Co.; Brooks-Scanlon Lumber Co.; C.A. Smith Lumber and Mfg. Co.; Calif. and Ore. Lumber Co.; Clark & Wilson Lumber Co.; Coos Bay Lumber Co.; Douglass & Cone Bros. Lumber Mill; Eastern-Western Lumber Co.; Grays Harbor Lumber Co.; Great Southern Lumber Co.; Hammond Lumber Co.; Hammond-Tillamook Lumber Co.; Hines Lumber Co.; Inman-Poulson Lumber Co.; Jones Lumber Co.; Klickitat Log & Lumber Co.; Lamm Lumber Co.; Logging industry; Long-Bell Lumber Co.; Medford Corporation;

Muckle Bros.; Northwestern Lumber Co.; Oceanside Lumber Co.; Oregon-American Lumber Co.; Owen-Oregon Lumber Co.; Pacific Lumber Co.; Pacific Pine Lumber Co.; Pacific Spruce Corp.; Peterson Bros. Lumber Mill; Plywood industry; Pokegama Sugar Pine Lumber Co.; Pope & Talbot Lumber Co.; Port Blakely Mill Co.; Powers Davis Logging Co.; Powers-Dwyer Logging Co.; Puget Mill Co.; Red River Lumber Co.; St. Paul & Tacoma Lumber Co.; Shevlin-Hixon Mill; Silver Falls Timber Co.; Simpson Lumber Co.; Smith-Powers Logging Co.; West Oregon Lumber Co.; West Shore Mills; Whatcom Falls Mill Co.; Weyerhaeuser Co.; Whitney Co.; Willamette Steam Mills Lumbering & Mfg. Co.; Willamette Valley Lumber Co.
Lumber Code, 64/58
Lummi Indians, 72/173
Lunar Geological Field Conference, 67/39,88,90
Lunar geology:
Oregon field conference guidebook, 66/383-84
Lund, Erik:
biography, 71/265-76; photos, 71/266,268,271
Lund, Fanny Maki, 71/270-71:
photo, 71/271
Lund, Thelma, SEE Gardner, Thelma Lund
Lundell, John:
Governmental History of Wasco County, Oregon, noted, 71/286
Lundgren, Ingeborg, 74/30
Lundy, Herbert, 74/214(photo):
Logging the Redwoods, by Carranco and Labbe, review, 77/190-91
Lupher, Ralph L., 67/26
Lure of the West Lands: With Songs of the Prairie Lands and Other Verses, by Rader, noted, 64/186
Lurline (river steamer), 63/66; 74/321
Luse, H.H., 68/265
Lusk, Hall S.:
"On Judge Henry E. McGinn,"

73/269-72
Lutcher, Mrs. Lawrence, **69**/133
Lutheran Church:
Danebo, **65**/212; German in Ore., **65**/366; Ione, **62**/205; Sitka, **72**/137,140
Luttig, John C., **62**/289
Lux, Charles, **63**/309
Luxton, Norman K.:
Pacific Crossing: Journal of the Mate of the Tilikum, 1901, review, **73**/273
Luzader, John F., *et al*:
Fort Stanwix: History, Historic Furnishing, Historic Structure Report, noted, **79**/107
Luzon, Philippines, **62**/18,23,32,33
Lyle, John Eakin, **70**/260
Lyman, Albert:
journal noted, **79**/407
Lyman, D.H., **74**/21,24
Lyman, Ernest, **77**/90
Lyman, Esther Brakemen (Mrs. Joseph), **78**/124,153,234:
photo, **78**/243; recollections, **78**/242-44,299-300,311,312
Lyman, H.B., **74**/18,24
Lyman, Harriet, **78**/128
Lyman, Horace Sumner, **66**/335N,338, 339N; **70**/220:
History of Oregon, cited, **70**/229
History of Seattle, cited, **70**/220N
Lyman, Joseph, **78**/123,128,153, 242-44,327:
photo, **78**/243
Lyman, Luther, **78**/242,243,311,314
Lyman, Theodore, **76**/208
Lyman, William Denison, **74**/119:
The Columbia River, cited, **70**/229
History of the Yakima Valley, cited, **70**/147N,165N,166N
Lynch, Douglas, **76**/268:
Mark Tobey, by Roberts, review, **62**/410-11
"Lynch, Judge," **66**/89
Lynch, Vera Martin, **65**/211; **66**/277:
Free Land for Free Men: A Story of Clackamas County, noted, **74**/357
Lynchings, **71**/364; **75**/363:
Deer Creek, **68**/342
Lynden, Wash., **69**/71

Lynes family, Deschutes homesteaders, **79**/48
Lyniff, Thomas, **74**/349
Lynn Canal (Channel), **72**/139
Lynton (ship), **66**/122
Lynxes, **66**/353
Lyon, Billy, **66**/114N
Lyon, Caleb, **64**/282; **71**/196; **72**/286
Lyon, Ellen Francis, SEE Boise, Ellen F. Lyon
Lyon, Israel Whitney, **66**/9
Lyon, Lemuel Elisha, **66**/9,10
Lyon, Peter, **62**/296
Lyon, Sarah B., SEE Coffin, Sarah B. Lyon
Lyon, William H., **63**/358:
The Pioneer Editor in Missouri, 1808-1860, review, **67**/278-79
Lyons, Elliott, **81**/327
Lyons, James, **66**/393
Lyons, Letitia Mary, **63**/55N; **66**/350N
The Lyric West, **74**/35,62,63
Lyster, John S., **81**/105
Lytle, Marian Donahue (Mrs. Judd), **72**/94

M.F. Henderson (steamer), **66**/80
Maalo (Hawaiian), **63**/119,144,150
Mabel Church of the Brethren, **62**/107
Macadam, Caroline Corbett, **66**/388
Macadam, Ivison, **66**/388
McAdam, Louise Saste, **66**/359N,360N
McAdams, L., **74**/22
McAdoo, William Gibbs:
photo, **68**/133; urges West candidacy, **68**/133-34
McAfee, J.W., **81**/90N
McAlister, E.A., **79**/363
McAlister, Samantha Cornell, **79**/362 (with photo)
McAlister, Seth, **79**/385N
McAllister, Tom, **75**/41
McArthur, Clifton N., **74**/222; **75**/171-72,174
McArthur, Douglas, **62**/26,30-32,33,34
McArthur, Harriet Nesmith, **66**/9N; **80**/361
McArthur, Lewis Ankeny, **66**/79,334; **70**/215-16; **78**/237,239:
Oregon Geographic Names, cited,

71/357; 78/365
McArthur, Lewis Ankeny and Lewis Linn:
Oregon Geographic Names, 4th ed. noted, 75/368,369,370; 77/292
McArthur, Lewis Linn, father of Lewis Ankeny, **64**/179
McArthur, Lewis Linn, son of Lewis Ankeny, **64**/360:
Across the Olympic Mountains, by Wood, review, **69**/73-74
History of Public Works in the United States, ed. by Armstrong, review, **78**/281-82
The Kalapuyans, by Mackey, review, **76**/90-91
Men, Mules and Mountains, by Wood, review, **78**/281-82
Mount Hood, by Love, review, **77**/87-88
Portland Names and Neighborhoods, by Snyder, review, **81**/206-207
Seattle, by Sale, review, **79**/102-103
The Story of Lige Coalman, by White, review, **74**/88-89
SEE ALSO McArthur, Lewis Ankeny and Lewis Linn
McArthur, Neil, **62**/375N,376,394N
McArthur, Nellie Pipes, **63**/57; **66**/351N; **69**/346; **70**/372; **71**/101: memorial tribute, **79**/91
MacAtee, William, **69**/115
McBean (McBain), John, **66**/135N,137, 146; **70**/27N,35N
McBean, William, **63**/206; **66**/135N; **70**/27N
McBeth, Kate, **72**/183
McBride, Charles, **66**/108-14*passim*
McBride, George Wycliffe, **69**/212
McBride, James, **75**/356; **79**/30-31
McBride, John Rogers, **69**/227N
McBride, Mrs. Quincy, **67**/89
McBride, Thomas Allen, **66**/363,365; **73**/271-72
McCabe, James F., **67**/179
McCabe, James O.:
The San Juan Water Boundary Question, review, **67**/183-84
McCabe family, Morrow Co., **69**/137
McCaffery, Minnie (Mrs. Frank), **72**/94

McCall, Audrey Owen (Mrs. Thomas L.), **72**/360
McCall, Dorothy Lawson:
The Copper King's Daughter: From Cape Cod to Crooked River, review, **73**/278
McCall, Henry, **72**/351
McCall, John Marshall, **62**/323: biography, **65**/32N; First Ore. Cavalry career, **65**/12,14,16,28,31-36,43-118 *passim*,395
McCall, Ruby Hillis, **76**/382
McCall, Thomas Lawson, **62**/111,207, 303,422; **63**/93,255,373; **64**/93,189, 285,363; **65**/125,221,317,414,417; **66**/94,190,286,395; **67**/379; **68**/360; **69**/344,347; **70**/370,373; **72**/351, 357,360; **73**/362; **74**/238,241; **80**/205:
British Consulate centennial toast, **72**/360-61; photo, **67**/204
McCall, Thomas, with Steve Neal:
Tom McCall: Maverick, review, **79**/406-407
McCall, William, **78**/305
McCallon, Bob H., **77**/265-66; **78**/169: family photo, **77**/ins.fr.cov. Sept.
McCallum, Frances T., **66**/379
McCallum, Henry D. and Frances T.:
The Wire That Fenced the West, review, **66**/379
McCallum, Rodney R., ed.:
Travels in the Great Western Prairies, the Anahuac and Rocky Mountains..., by Farnham, reprint noted, **79**/107
McCamant, Wallace, **68**/330-31; **74**/216:
photo, **74**/234
McCann, Don, **63**/277
McCartin, Frank, **69**/137-38
McCartin, Thomas, **69**/137
Macartney, George Macartney, Earl, **76**/314-15
McCarty, David, family, **69**/138
McCarty, Howard, **69**/138
McCarty, Jim, **69**/138
McCarty, L.P., **71**/146
McCarty, William "Brandywine," **64**/214N,220
McCarver, Morton Matthew, **62**/229;

63/182:
Iowa career, 71/368
McCary, Richard, 64/237N
McClane, John Burch, 63/83
McClay, Byron, 80/59N,63N
McClay, David Barton, family, 80/51,52-53,63N
McClay, Elmer, 80/53,59,63N
McClay, James Everett, 75/362
McClay, Melissa Jane Cottle, 80/51
McClay, Oclo:
biography, 80/51; photos, 80/63,65
McClay, Oclo:
"My Trip to the Fair," 80/51-65
McCleary, family, Marion Co., 71/357
McCleave, William, 79/299N
McCleese, William, 76/387
McClellan, Alexander, 81/240
McClellan, George Brinton, 67/309-10; 73/55; 74/91:
conversation with Kamiakin, 67/310N
McClelland, John M., Jr., 62/109; 73/364:
Boundary Town, by Jones, review, 62/96-97
"Drifting the Lower Columbia," 75/104-108,362
Ewing Young, Master Trapper, by Holmes, review, 69/61-62
He Built Seattle: A Biography of Judge Thomas Burke, by Nesbit, review, 62/405-406
Longview, cited, 77/381
Pig War Islands, by Richardson, review, 72/344-45
R.A. Long's Planned City: The Story of Longview, review, 77/381-82
McClelland, John M., Jr., ed.:
A Pioneer's Search for an Ideal Home, review, 69/71-72
McClelland Blacksmith Shop, Siskiyou Co., 66/81
McClintock, Thomas C., 63/359; 80/414:
"Bandon-by-the-Sea Revisited," 75/339-43
"Henderson Luelling, Seth Lewelling and the Birth of the Pacific Coast Fruit Industry," 68/153-74

Oregon: A History, by Dodds, review, 79/97-98
"Seth Lewelling, William S. U'Ren and the Birth of the Oregon Progressive Movement," 68/197-220
McClive, John, 73/247
McCloskey, Maxine E.:
Wilderness, The Edge of Knowledge, review, 73/275-76
McCloskey (Sol J.) grove, Coos Co., 63/34
McCloud, Calif.:
bank robbery, 66/81; history, 72/172
McCloud River Railroad, 66/81
McClung, Donald R., 65/414,415,417; 66/94,190,286,386,388,389,395; 67/377:
photo, 67/200
McClung, Millard H., 70/371; 72/359; 75/370; 76/387; 78/368; 79/412; 80/416:
Emigration and Disenchantment, by Shepperson, review, 68/280
Proceedings of the First National Colloquium on the History of Forest Products, review, 69/70
McClure, Allen, 78/124
McClure, Andrew S., 78/121,140,143, 147,207-13,220,225,232,233,234,329; 79/13,31,68:
photo, 78/226; trail diary 1853, 78/ 124,140,149-57*passim*,220-29*passim*, 246-47; 79/31,67N
McClure, Dudley L.:
Tales of the Golden Beavers, cited, 79/408-409
McClure, Harrison, 78/123
McClure, James F., 78/128,220; 79/11: photo, 78/148; trail diary, 1853, 78/ 124,150-55,212,222,235-37,293-94
McClure, John, 64/198,229N,238; 81/190N:
Astoria claim, 64/227N,229-30N; biography, 64/230N; enmity toward Lattie, 64/202-203,238
fracas with Lattie—
described, 64/234-38; jury verdict, 64/202N-203N,238N-39
McClure, John Archibald Concomlly,

64/230N
McClure, Louisa (Mrs. John), 64/230N
McClure, Nancy Bruce, photo, 78/148
McClure, Rachel Robinson, 78/124
McClure, Robert, photo, 78/148
McClure, Vincent, 78/124,157,207, 211,212,213(photo)
McClure-Bond overland party 1853, 78/ 121,123,124,128,140,143,148-57,207, 211,219-20,224-25,230,235,237,240- 41,293-94; 79/5
MacColl, E. Kimbark: *The Growth of a City*, review, 81/203-205 *The Shaping of a City*, review, 78/89-90
McComas, Evans S., 62/228,232
McComb, Mary, photo, 78/298
McConaha, George N., 64/36
McConkey, Lois: *Sea and Cedar: How the North West Coast Indians Lived*, noted, 75/364
McConnell, Elizabeth (Mrs. Robert), 71/5,8,11,13,20,22
McConnell, James, 71/5,11,13,25N
McConnell, John, 69/215N
McConnell, Kennard J., 71/5
McConnell, Mildred, 71/5
McConnell, Robert: photo, 71/6; search for business site, 71/5-7,12-20; travel 1881, 71/5-25
McConnell, William J., 71/20N
McConville, Edward C., 71/196
MaCoon, Charles, family, 66/382
McCord, David, 67/202,211
McCord, O.H.P., 67/228N
McCord, Serene B., 68/228N
McCorkle, William Andrew Lockbridge, 62/300
McCormack, Bryce, 66/382
McCormack, Frances U'Ren, 68/203N; 77/25
McCormack, Francis, 69/138
McCormack, John, 73/346
McCormack, William K., Jr. (Bill), 77/24-26
McCormack, William K., Sr., 77/25: photo, 77/25; ranch house photo, 77/25
McCormack, William U'Ren, 77/26
McCormick, Alexander H., 76/274,275

McCormick, Hamlin F., 66/382
McCormick, Stephen James, 64/157- 58,179; 80/134
McCormick Shipbuilding Co., SEE St. Helens Shipbuilding Co.
McCormick's Almanac, 74/286
McCornack, Ellen Condon, 67/39
McCosh, James, 74/342
McCourt, Alice, 71/275
McCoy, A.B., 80/28
McCoy, J.M., Portland policeman, 80/158N,289
McCoy, John F., 80/139: biography, 80/144N
McCraken, Ada E. Pambrun (Mrs. John), 63/181,190
McCraken, John, 67/312
McCraken, Merrill and Co., Portland, 64/176
McCready, Lynn S., 62/111,207,303, 422; 63/93,255,373; 64/93,189,285, 363; 65/125,221,317
McCrite, Maggie Lewis Johnson: recollections, 72/93
McCulloch, Perry, 79/31
McCulloch, Walter F., 62/110,206,302, 422; 63/93,255,354: *Federal Conservation Policy, 1921-1933*, by Swain, review, 65/205-206 *Ghost Town Album*, by Florin, review, 65/184-85
McCullough, Rev. Fr. —, 80/357
McCullough, Conde B., 78/363
McCullough, James Mattison, 66/153-54N
McCullough, Mrs. James Mattison, 66/153,160
McCullough family, Morrow Co., 69/138
McCully, David, 79/10
McCully, Violet Geer, photo, 81/254
McCurdy, H.W., 63/82
McCurdy, James G.: recollections, 63/82
McCutcheon (McGutchin), George, 70/15,16
McDade, Stella, SEE Calderwood, Stella McDade
McDaid, family, Morrow Co., 69/138

McDaid Canyon, **69**/138
McDaid Spring, **69**/138
McDaniel, William, Clatsop Co. pioneer, **64**/225N-27N
McDermitt, Ore.-Nev., **63**/307,331; **76**/159,160,170
McDermot, Michael, **69**/138
McDermot, Pat, **69**/138
McDermott, John Francis, **69**/64; **71**/311
McDevitt, Charles, family, **69**/125,138
McDevitt, Susan Doherty, **69**/125
McDonald, —, capt. of *Lucy Lowe*, **74**/21,22
McDonald, —, engineer on *Beaver*, **63**/205,224
McDonald, Alex, Klondike pioneer, **62**/96
McDonald, Angus, **63**/233
McDonald, Archibald, **63**/84,233; **71**/336
McDonald, Finan, **74**/359
McDonald, George, **74**/5
McDonald, James, British consul, **72**/361; **74**/363,366; **77**/384
McDonald, Mrs. James, **72**/361
McDonald, John, of Garth, **64**/92
McDonald, John Alexander, **70**/179
McDonald, Lucile Saunders, **62**/201; **63**/92,362; **64**/353; **65**/212,216; **66**/80:
"...all around the town," **64**/259-66
Coast Country: A History of Southwest Washington, review, **68**/182-83
"Rock Creek Shepherd, 1881," **81**/261-80
McDonald, Nathaniel G., **67**/373
MacDonald, Ranald, **62**/299; **70**/181; **74**/359
Macdonald, William John, **67**/86
McDonald and Vaughn Logging Camp, Coos Co., **66**/53
McDonald's Precinct, SEE Scio, Ore.
McDougal, David, **62**/10
McDougal, Henry, **63**/293
McDougal, James Alexander, artist, **65**/141
McDougall, Charles, **65**/47N
McDougall, Duncan, **66**/333

McDougall, George, **68**/347
McDougall, James Alexander, Calif. senator, **66**/87:
defends Stark, **73**/33-35,36,38; photo, **73**/34
McDowell, Aden (Adin, Alden), G., **67**/179; **78**/43,60,64,325N; **79**/22
McDowell, Irvin:
First Ore. Cavalry, **65**/86,97,104,189, 345,350
McDowell, Lottie Compton, **81**/5N
McDowell, Paddy, **63**/292-93
McEachern Shipbuilding Co., **77**/ 101,103
Macedonian (frigate), **66**/71
McElroy, Cole, **74**/233
McElroy, Sarah (Sally), **64**/34N,37-39N
McElroy, Thornton Fleming, **64**/33-34, 37-38,39N-40:
biography, **64**/34N,283
McEntire families, Morrow Co., **69**/138-39
McEwan, Arthur H., **74**/349
McEwan, George, **62**/398-99
McEwan, Robert S., **62**/241,243,281, 282,285,380,398; **64**/204N
McEwen, Andrew, family, **78**/364
McFadden, Margaret Caldwell (Mrs. Obadiah), **66**/29,36
McFadden, Obadiah B., **62**/81; **64**/304,313-15,322N:
biography, **66**/25-37; characterized, **66**/36-37; judicial career, **66**/25,27-30,31-37; land claim, **66**/32; park named for, **66**/37; photo, **66**/36
McFadden, Theodore F., **64**/276
McFadden Park, Lewis Co., **66**/37
McFarland, C.B., **78**/307,308N
McFarland, James Henderson, **78**/213,225,233
McFatridge, Arthur, **72**/183
Macfeely, R., **65**/192
McGarrell, James, **72**/258
McGarry, Edward, **66**/280
McGarry, J.J., **74**/17
McGhee (McGee), Patrick, **67**/69
McGillicuddy, Dan, **73**/173,182
McGillivray, Duncan, **81**/388
McGillivray, Simon, **76**/323,329

McGillivray, William, 76/324; 81/385,388
McGilvra, John J., 71/368
McGinn, Henry (Harry) E., 66/371; 68/127:
circuit court judge, 73/269-72
McGinnis, Gertrude, SEE O'Rourke, Gertrude McGinnis
McGinnis, Patrick, 69/139
McGinnis, Peter, 69/139
MacGovern, James, 69/137
MacGovern, Michael, 69/137
McGowan, George, 64/356
McGowan, James Douglas: house, 66/80
McGowan, Ned, 64/344
McGowen, —, Westfall merchant, 63/288
McGrath, Joseph F., 69/139
McGraw, Larry, 71/370; 73/364,ins.bk. cov. Dec.
McGregor, D.A.:
They Gave Royal Assent, noted, 71/191
McGregor, Jessie, photo, 72/208
McGregor, Mrs. T.W., 77/356
McGregor, Thomas, 68/231N,248N, 297N,299N,305N,313; 70/25
McGuffey's *Reader*: in Oregon, 65/219
McGuire, Eugene, 74/19,21
McGuire, H.D., 65/254-55
McGuire, M.B.:
The Vancouver Story, noted, 79/107
McHargue, Lulu: recollections, 72/93
Machin, Thomas N., 72/12
McIllvaine, Florence S., 66/25N
McIlwraith, Charles, 75/279
MacInerney, Hugh, 69/137
MacInerney, John, 69/137
McIntosh, —, Ft. Boise, 1853, 62/394
McIntosh, A.E., 77/367
McIntosh, Archie, 79/277,278,279N, 281,284,288-91*passim*: biography, 68/88; 79/277N; leader of Snake scouts, 79/138
McIntosh, Donald, Ft. Dalles clerk, 68/41
McIntosh, Donald, NWCo. employee,

72/183
McIntosh, Peter, 74/275
McIntosh, Robert, 69/311,312,313
McIntyre, Archibald, 67/311N
McIntyre, Charles, 74/13,14N,15
McIntyre, John, 69/139
McIntyre, Joseph P., 76/292
McIsaac, R.J., 70/53
Mackall, W.W., 65/49N,177N,179N; 68/7; 69/227,241,245,247,251,255
McKay, Albert E., 72/280; 75/33
McKay, Alexander, 63/192,208,234; 79/133:
account of death on *Tonquin*, 71/314-15,319-20
McKay, Alexander, son of Thomas, 62/399N-400N; 79/134
McKay, Catherine, 79/136
McKay, Charles:
Oregon Prov. Govt., 66/353
McKay, Donald, shipbuilder: biography, 63/359
McKay, Donald, son of Thomas, 63/ 214; 79/275:
biography, 79/143N; capt. of scouts, 79/275N,305,306; grave, 72/86; medicine show, 79/306,307N; photos, 79/ 120,307
McKay, Douglas, Ore. governor, 72/ 231; 74/131
McKay, Isabelle Montour (Mrs. Thomas), 63/214
McKay, James, HBCo. employee, 63/166N
McKay, Jean Baptiste Desportes, 62/107; 63/234; 66/334,339,340,343,358
McKay, John, son of Thomas, 62/399N-400N; 79/134:
photo, 79/307
McKay, Leila C., 79/151N,311N: photo, 79/310
McKay, Thomas, son of Alexander, 62/ 301,399N-400N; 63/192,208,234-35; 64/46,48; 69/88,338; 72/86; 77/81; 79/134; 81/203:
will, 68/342
McKay, William Cameron, 62/244, 399N-400N; 63/191,208,214,216,234; 64/46; 65/20; 66/148; 67/320; 73/285; 77/298:

biography, 79/121,133-37,151N,305-12; birth date, 79/306N; children, 79/100N,311N; grave, 72/86; marriages, 79/135-36; naturalization, 79/309; photos, 79/307,312,fr.cov. Summer physician, 79/134-35,136,305-308— honorary degree, 79/306 recovery of Paiute children, 79/305; reservation allotment, 79/309,311 Snake War service, 79/139— capt. of Indian scouts, 79/137; Central Ore. operations, 79/142-60, 272N,329-33; journal, 79/134,141-71,269-305; list of Indian scouts, 79/313-18; maps of routes, 79/164, 286-87; pay, 79/137N,305N; qualifications, 79/133-36 Umatilla trading post, 66/137-38,141,152— maps, 66/132,opp.144 Wasson's opinion, 79/312 McKay Creek, Crook Co., 65/25N; 79/146,149: name, 79/146-47N; photo, 79/150 McKay Creek, Umatilla Co., 62/399N; 66/137; 68/232,306N; 70/37; 79/135 McKean, Samuel Terry, 64/230N McKee, E.D., 71/151 McKee, Nelson, 74/21,22 McKee, Paul B., 74/238: photo, 74/214 McKee, Redick, 72/181 McKee, Thomas, 66/381 McKeehan, Donald, 78/284 McKendree, C.H., 68/248N,258N McKenna, Marian C.: *Borah*, review, 62/409-10 McKenna, Michael, 69/139 McKenna, P.J., 69/139 McKenna, Patrick, 69/139 McKenney, Thomas L., 64/47-48,51; 71/292: Indian collection, 70/362; portrait of William Brooks, photo, 64/42 McKennon, Frank, 77/379 McKenny, Thomas Irving, 63/91 McKenny's Cutoff, SEE McKinney's

Cutoff Mackenzie, Alexander, explorer, 62/91, 193; 64/272-73,284; 69/67; 70/180; 77/80-81,289: explorations, 76/312,315; map, 76/316; portrait, 76/320; trade interest, Pacific NW-Canada, 76/315-22; urges China trade regulations, 76/318 Mackenzie, Alexander: *The Journals and Letters of Sir Alexander Mackenzie*, ed. by Lamb, noted, 75/364 *Voyages*, reprint noted, 75/364 McKenzie, Benjamin, 63/216 Mackenzie (McKenzie), Donald, 66/ 333,334; 77/80-81: Snake River expeds., 71/310,345; Willamette exped., 66/332 MacKenzie, Finlay, 68/187 McKenzie, Henry, 72/183 Mackenzie, K.A.J., 75/20,31-32 McKenzie, Roderick, 81/388 McKenzie, Rosa Lamberson, 63/263N,298(photo),301 McKenzie Fork, SEE McKenzie River McKenzie Head, 69/309: chart, 69/306,bk.cov. Dec.; photos, 69/315,318 McKenzie Pass, 79/43,43N Mackenzie River, Canada, 76/315 McKenzie River, Oregon, 62/215; 66/281,332; 74/270,281; 77/317; 78/53,233,307; 79/29,31: Belknap Bridge, 66/187; fords, 78/54,55; photo, 74/45 McKenzie Valley and Deschutes Wagon Road Co., 64/185 McKeown, Archie W., 62/102 McKeown, Martha Ferguson: *Come to Our Salmon Feast*, review, 62/102 *Indians as the Westerners Saw Them*, review, 65/199-200 SEE ALSO Dana, Martha Ferguson McKeown *Mackerel Skies*, by Latta, noted, 78/288 McKervill, Hugh W.: *The Salmon People: The Story of Canada's West Coast Salmon Fishing Industry*,

review, 72/345-46
Mackey, Harold:
"Gibbs-Starling Map, 1851," 70/259-61
The Kalapuyans: A Sourcebook on the Indians of the Willamette Valley, review, 76/90-91
"New Light on the Molalla Indians," 73/63-65
"Siuslaw Head Flattening," 69/171-73
Mackinac (Mackinaw, Michilimackinac), **66**/331
Mackinac Island, **69**/276
McKinley, Charles:
Blueprint for Modern America, by Curry, review, 70/69-71
Conservation and the Gospel of Efficiency, by Hays, review, 62/188-92
The Management of Land and Related Water Resources in Oregon, review, **68**/176-77
The Trumpet Soundeth: William Jennings Bryan, by Glad, review, 62/188-92
McKinley, William, 62/11; 72/214; 75/138,140:
expansionist policy, 72/212,221,223; Philippine insurrection, 72/213,222; photo, 76/280
McKinley, Garrioch and Co., **68**/114
McKinley's Bulldog: The Battleship Oregon, by Sternlicht, review, 79/212-13
McKinnell, Henry, 78/13N
McKinney, Daniel, 62/219N
McKinney's Cutoff, 79/380; 80/79
McKinnon, Andrew, 76/228
McKinnon, Miyo Iwakoshi (Mrs. Andrew), 76/228:
photo, 76/ins.fr.cov. Sept.
McKinstry, George, 65/405
McKnight, William, family, **66**/54
McKusick, Noah, **68**/230N
McLaren, John, **64**/323N
McLaughlan, Daniel M., 72/339
McLaughlin, Ada, photo, 72/208
McLaughlin, Cornelius, family, **69**/139
McLaughlin, Mrs. G.P., 67/89
McLaughlin, James A., **69**/139
McLaughlin, Joseph, Oregon writer: photo, 74/265

McLaughlin, Katie, **69**/139
McLean, Agnes Millican, **64**/185; 77/312N,328,329; 78/304N,306,309,319
McLean, George, 78/319
McLean, John, Canadian fur trader, **69**/53; **71**/334-35
McLean, John, Clatsop Co. settler, **64**/221,228,284
McLean, Mildred Evans:
Recollections of Deep River, noted, **81**/106
McLean, William T.:
Historical Sketch of Coos Bay, noted, **68**/350
McLeary, T.J., **71**/351
Macleay, Donald, **69**/209N
McLellan, Sarah J., ed.:
"Chronicles of Sacred Heart Academy, Salem, 1863-1873," 80/341-64; **81**/75-95
MacLennan, Hugh, 67/84:
The Colour of Canada, noted, **69**/332
McLeod, Alexander Roderick, 63/350; **66**/335N,383:
members of 1826-27 exped., 74/282
McLeod, Donald, HBCo. employee, **64**/224
McLeod, George B., 77/353-54
McLeod, John, Jr., 63/208
McLeod, Kenneth, family, 78/363
McLeod, Murdock (John M.?), 63/143
McLeod Lake post, 67/86
McLoughlin, David, brother of John: portrait, **81**/378
McLoughlin, David, son of John, 63/232; **69**/336
McLoughlin, Eloisa Maria, SEE Harvey, Eloisa Maria McLoughlin Rae
McLoughlin, Honoree, **81**/381-82
McLoughlin, John, 62/76,91,313,314, 406,407; 63/101,202,205,208,211, 220,223; **64**/78,229N,349; 65/215, 407-408; **66**/163,334,362; **69**/61-62,269; 70/301; **71**/285; 72/86,88; 74/90; 76/130,226-27,299,301; 77/85; 78/86; 79/134:
advice to Whitman, 63/181; aid to ex-HBCo. employees, **66**/336-37; authority, 63/186,199; biography, 75/76;

80/101,331-32; business competition with Wyeth, 63/192,206; children, 63/ 232-33,234; controversy with Methodist Mission, 63/177; correspondence, 81/208,378-79,384; death, 81/382; descendants, 78/101; disciplinarian, 63/216 employment by NWCo., 81/377-89— contract, 81/383,387-89; partnership, 81/385 estate, 66/361; family, 68/184; grave, 73/81; leaves HBCo., 63/223; letters, 75/76-77; lumber loan to Methodist Mission, 73/254; McClure opinion of, 81/23-24,25; marriage, 63/208N,216, 235; medical license, 81/380,382; opinion of Americans, 66/337; opinion on Oregon Question, 63/210-11,318; Oregon City claim, 63/176-77,180,207; 64/143; 70/270; 75/120; 78/88; photo, 81/378; piper, 71/372; Quebec incident, 81/380-82; quoted by G.B. Roberts, 63/183,195,196,201,210-11; reason for entering fur trade, 81/377- 86; reburial, 78/288; relationship with Douglas, 63/236; relationship with G.B. Roberts, 63/103,227; relationship with Rev. Beaver, 63/195-96,208,209, 214-15; relationship with Simpson, 63/ 180,182-84,189; 65/306; 74/352; religion, 63/197,207,209,214-15; report on Oregon, 70/302 residences— Ft. Vancouver, 76/382; Ore. City, SEE McLoughlin House revolver, 71/369; Roberts' description of, 63/183,186,191,194,200,207,214; Shortess petition, 66/353; snub of Hall J. Kelley, 63/185,199,206; statue, 69/ 324; 80/101; temperament, 81/386; treatment of Indians, 63/183,186; trip to England, 63/190,199,209,227,233; U.S. citizenship, 63/101,108N McLoughlin, John, Jr., 63/183-85,189, 212,232 McLoughlin, Joseph, 63/232; 66/356 McLoughlin, Marguerite Wadin McKay (Mrs. John): grave, 73/81

McLoughlin, Victoire (Mrs. Joseph), SEE Gregoire, Victoire McMillan McLoughlin McLoughlin House, Ore. City, 62/109; 64/361; 68/352; 69/176; 71/101; 80/101: relocation, 76/299-301— photo, 76/300 restoration, 76/302-303— architect's sketch, 76/301 McLoughlin Memorial Assn., 76/301,302 McMahon, Bernard, 69/159,161,163 McMahon, Francis, 66/110,111,114 McMahon's Circus, 66/43 McMann, W.S., 79/270N MacManus, John F., 69/137 McManus, Margaret, 81/85,95 McManus, P., family, 81/85N McMartin, E., 74/21 McMath, George, 68/358 McMenamin, Frank J., 69/139 McMenamin, Robert W., 69/139 McMillan, A.C., 66/88 McMillan, Eleanor, 73/293 McMillan, Right, 64/265 McMillan, Sam G.: *The Bunchgrassers: A History of Lexington, Morrow County, Oregon*, review, 75/360 McMillan, William H., 80/22 McMillan School, East Portland, 64/261 McMinnville, Ore., 62/203; 66/281: churches, 65/218; history, 65/217; postal cards, 66/305-306 McMinnville College, McMinnville, 64/150 McMonies, Charlotte, 64/259N McMullen, Violet, SEE Mary of Calvary, Sister McMullin, Fayette, 62/86-87 McMurdo, A.D., 69/120 McMurren and Crabill Co., 67/169 McMurray, William, 74/215 McMurry, Donald L.: *Coxey's Army*, cited, 65/164N-94*passim* McMurry, Fielding (Fielden), 78/44; 79/10,21 McMurry, Terence, 79/9,10

McMurtrie, Douglas Crawford, **64**/137,284; **69**/337; **70**/62

"McMurtrie's Oregon Imprints: A Fourth Supplement," by George N. Belknap, **64**/137-82

Macnab, Gordon G.: *A Century of News and People in the East Oregonian, 1875-1975*, review, **77**/192-93 *R.A. Long's Planned City*, by McClelland, review, **77**/381-82

McNabb, —, Ukiah rancher, **76**/335,337

McNally, Frank, **69**/139

McNamee, Sister Mary Dominica, **69**/269N

McNamee family, Morrow Co., **69**/139

McNary, Charles Linza, **72**/228; **74**/ 217,231,233; **75**/162,173,175,180, 181; **77**/63,267: death, **66**/363; first election to public office, **68**/125; O&C land bill, **64**/59; Ore. supreme court contest, **66**/363, 365-76; papers, **68**/126N; photos, **66**/364; **68**/126; political career 1906-18, **68**/125-27; supports Wilson war program, **68**/130; U.S. Senate campaign 1918, **68**/125-40

McNary, John H., **68**/125; **77**/268: 1918 U.S. Senate campaign, **68**/129; photo, **68**/129

MacNaughton, Ernest Boyd, **62**/198; **65**/412; **69**/344; **75**/6,146

McNeal, William H.: *History of Centennial Churches of The Dalles*, noted, **70**/273 *History of Columbia Lodge No. 5, I.O.O.F.*, noted, **70**/76 *History of Wasco Lodge No. 15, A.F. & A.M.*, noted, **70**/76

McNeil Island Penitentiary, **66**/130

McNeill, William Henry, **63**/192,195, 217-18,227; **76**/226-27

McNulty, John, **80**/130

McParlin, Thomas Andrew, **68**/22N

McPhail (Macphail), John, **63**/118N,122

McPhail, Marie Therese (Mrs. John), **63**/122N

McQuade Creek, **63**/92

McRoberts, W.G., **74**/18

McRoy, Charles, SEE McKay, Charles

McTavish, Alexander, **66**/333

McTavish, Donald, **63**/198

McTavish, Dugald, **63**/183-84,198,202, 215; **64**/226N,228N

McTavish, John George, **79**/122

McTavish, Simon, **76**/322; **81**/385,388: portrait, **81**/381

McTavish, William, **76**/322

McTavish, Fraser and Company, **76**/321

McTavish, Frobisher and Company, **76**/315,319,321; **81**/380,383,387-89

McTavish, McGillivrays and Company, **76**/322

McVey, Pat, **69**/139-40

McVennia family, **69**/140

McVey (McVay), James, **63**/12

McVey (McVay), John, **63**/12

McWhorter, Hugh, **80**/46

McWhorter, Lucullus Virgil, **62**/295; **81**/347

Macy, William H., **77**/311,321,323,327, 329,330N; **78**/41-44,52,60-69*passim*, 146,330,331,429; **79**/24: biography, **79**/20N,21-22; land claim, **79**/21; law suit against Alexander, **79**/5-11; leader on Free Emigrant Road, **79**/13-17,19-20,49; promotion of Columbia College, **79**/20-21

Macy's Peak, **77**/330,330N

Macy's River, SEE Salmon Creek

Madarieta, Miguel, photo, **76**/67

Madden, Charles (Charley), **63**/289,294

Madden, E., **63**/286

Madden, George, **69**/140

Madden, John, **69**/140

Maden, John, Jr., **69**/140

Madden, Johnnie, **63**/269,293

Maddux, Harvey: *Camera Around Portland*, noted, **81**/330 *Homestead on the Trask*, noted, **77**/91

Madeira, George, **70**/178

Madigan, John, **79**/288N

Madison, James, **76**/205

Madonna (brig), **77**/48,60

Madras, Ore., **69**/298; **72**/342: photos 1909, **69**/302

Madrugada (vessel), 77/101,102,103, 107-29: mechanical difficulties, 77/109, 111-16— costs, 77/109,118 photos, 77/108,110,113,114,125; structural faults, 77/101-102; torpedoed, 77/129

Madson, Brigham: *The Lemhi: Sacajawea's People*, noted, 81/331

Maeda, Milton, 81/157,169

Magee, Bernard: death, 72/182

Magee, James, 76/207

Magers, Jim, family, 77/263

The Magnificent Gateway, by Allen, review, 80/407

Magnolia (ship), 63/44

Magoffin, Susan Shelby: diary, 63/356

Magone, Joseph, 70/23-25: biography, 70/23N

Magpies, 68/345; 69/18: Bendire notes on, 66/236

Magraw, William Miller Finney, 64/281

Magruder, Grace Kent, 65/308

Magruder, Lloyd, 64/88,283

Magruder, Richard Brooke, 62/301

Maguire, Michael, 69/140

Maguire, Robert F., 69/140

Mahaffy, Charles, 69/140

Mahaffy, Charlotte L.: *Coos River Echoes*, noted, 67/80

Mahan, Alfred Thayer, 62/17; 76/270,284,287: quoted, 62/53

Mahan, Myrabel Bloom, 71/273

Mahar, Franklyn D.: "The Millionaire and the Village: Jesse Winburn Comes to Ashland," 64/323-41

Mahogany Mountain, 68/354; 70/176

Mahon, Jimmie, 67/245

Mahoney, Phil, 69/140

Mahoney, Thomas J., 69/140

Mahoney, William P., 69/140

Maier, Charlie, 81/299

Maier, Ludwig, 81/300,306

Mail service, SEE Postal service

Mails, Thomas E.: *The Mystic Warriors of the Plains*, noted, 74/285

"The Main Reason for Hawaiian Annexation in July, 1898," by Thomas J. Osborne, 71/161-78

Maine (battleship), 76/270,273,295

Mainwaring, William L.: "At the Beach," 75/54-55

Makushkin, Alaska, 77/185

Major, Daniel G.: boundary surveys listed, 72/18-19; Oregon boundary survey, 72/19 Ore.-Calif. boundary surveys— contract, 72/19-21; evaluation of, 72/ 17,45,48,49,51-53; field notes, 72/ 21N,20-44*passim*; initial point, 72/ 24(photo),28,49,51,52; instruments, 72/21-23; lines retraced, 72/36-37,38-39; maps, 72/19N,27,48,covs. March; monuments and memorials, 72/28-33

Major, John J., 72/25N: Ore.-Calif. boundary survey, 72/25

"Major Charles E. Bendire and the Birds of Oregon," by Erwin F. Lange, 66/233-39

"A Major Monument: Oregon-California Boundary," by Francis S. Landrum, 72/5-53

Majors, Harry M.:

Mount Baker: A Chronicle of Its Historic Eruptions and First Ascent, noted, 81/332

Makah Indian Reservation, 63/82

Makah Indians, 64/357; 66/89; 70/87

Maki, Fanny, SEE Lund, Fanny Maki

Maki, Lauri, 71/269

Maki, Lillian: "Lincoln County Homesteader," 71/265-73

Malad River, Utah, 63/358

Malakhov, Vasilii Ivanovich, 73/131

Malaria, 78/125

Malarkey, Herbert, 64/359

Malaspina, Allesandro, 74/353

Malcolm, Philip Schuyler: KKK support, 75/154,156,162,172; photo, 75/155

Malheur and Burnt River Consolidated Ditch and Mining Co., **69**/201

Malheur Butte, SEE Strawberry Mountain

Malheur City, Ore., **63**/282; **67**/236; **68**/354; 70/19; 73/83

Malheur County, Ore., **62**/194,195,216; **63**/264,280,310; **66**/239; **67**/219, 236; 73/80,279: county fair, 70/280; described, **67**/ 252-54; 74/350-51; historical articles, **72**/93; photos, **76**/154,156,158; pioneers, 70/280; sugar beet industry, **81**/120

Malheur Country Historical Society: officers and directors, 73/78; 74/181; 75/91; 76/95; 77/95; 78/95; 79/ 111; 80/110; 81/111; publications, **81**/327

Malheur County Pioneer Assn., **67**/ 221N; 70/280

Malheur County Review, noted, **81**/327

Malheur Indian Agency, **63**/264; **68**/ 230,231,235,236,237,308N; 70/21, 34,57: fraud charged, 70/19,21N; ranch, **63**/310

Malheur Indian Reservation, **66**/206; 70/16N,19N

Malheur Lake, **63**/338,350; **65**/66; **77**/333; 78/210,222,223,225,235; 79/49: pelicans, **66**/235-36

Malheur National Wildlife Refuge, **66**/68; 68/91: described, 75/68; museum, **69**/176; photos, 75/66,68; 78/228

Malheur River, **62**/213,217,219,222, 394; **63**/263-64; **66**/357; **68**/308; 70/18; 77/309,314,315,319,333,335; 78/42,71,125,138,145,150; 79/12,13, 14,15,32,33,36,37,271,275,298,389; 80/96: described, 78/140-41; fords, 77/315; 78/139,140,144,151; Halliday Bridge, 70/280; Indian raids, **66**/203-205; photo, 78/150; SEE ALSO Middle Fork, Malheur River; North Fork, Malheur River; South Fork, Malheur River

Malin, Edward:

"Antler, Bone and Shell," noted, 70/87

Malin, James C., **81**/335

Mallett, Mary Powell: *Courageous People*, noted, 74/94

Malone, Michael P., and Richard D. Roeder, eds.: *The Montana Past, An Anthology*, noted, **71**/287

Maltby, Capt. —, Elk City, **79**/188,192,196,197: biography, 79/188N

"Man and Nature in the Oregon Country," by Dodds, noted, 77/291

Man of the Plains: Recollections of Luther North, 1856-1882, by Danker, review, **63**/80-81

Management of Land and Related Water Resources in Oregon, by McKinley, review, **68**/176-77

Mandan Indians, **63**/347; 70/172

Mandrones, Theodore G., 74/357

Mangan, Lucy, **63**/263N

Mangan, W.H., **63**/66

Manhattan (tanker): NW Passage voyage, **71**/197-98

Manifest Destiny, **64**/343-44; 70/73; 73/66,360; 79/405; SEE ALSO U.S. expansionism

Manifest Destiny and Mission in American History: A Reinterpretation, by Merk, cited, 72/210N,216N; review, **64**/343-44

Manila, P.I., **62**/20,29: during Spanish-American War, 80/177-91*passim*

Manila Bay, **62**/18,20,21

"Manila to Peking: Letters Home, 1898-1901," ed. by Newell, 80/171-86

Mann, Amanda, SEE Lane, Amanda Mann

Mann, Jesse: recollections, 72/151,153

Mann family, 1852 immigrants, 79/392

Mann Lake, **63**/317,324

Mann Lake Ranch, **63**/322,334

Manning, C.C., **65**/104N

Manning, Gordon: *Oregon Biography Index*, ed. by Brandt and Guilford, review, 77/297

Man's Rise to Civilization, As Shown by the Indians of North America, by Farb, review, 70/265-66

Mansell, George, 70/255,257

Mansfield, James M., 73/263

Mansfield, Joseph King Fenno, 65/201-202; 67/76; 68/35: Ft. Dalles— inspection 1854, 67/309; view of, 68/39-40 Ft. Hoskins report, 65/181,189-96; Ft. Umpqua report, 70/247-48; military inspection 1858, 68/30-31

Mansfield, Richard, 70/67

Mansfield on the Condition of the Western Forts, 1853-1854, ed. by Frazer, review, 65/201-202

Manslaughter, SEE Murder

Manson, Donald: marriage, 66/335; quoted, 66/335-36

Manson, Felicite Lucier (Mrs. Donald), 66/335

Manufacturers Association of Portland, 62/164-65,167-68,170; 67/69-70

Manufacturing: effect of interest rates, 67/136; Oregon 1880-90, 71/33-34,35,64; Ore. wood products, 67/162N; Portland 1881-90, 67/113-16; value 1870-1900 (table), 71/96

Manuscripts: Alaska, 65/198; Bancroft Library holdings, 65/198-99; Barry, J. Neilson, papers, 66/79; Burlington Northern papers, 74/79-82; Canada, 65/188; care of, 63/356; catalog, 73/86; Eastern Wash. State Historical Soc. holdings, 77/297; Ft. Vancouver order book, 66/386; guide to collections, 63/244-45; Hawaiian history, 65/198; HBCO. letterbooks, 63/184-85; Indiana guide, 70/85; Irving, Washington, papers, 65/213; lost, of Western travelers, 71/291; Minnesota fur trade, 79/339; Minnesota Historical Soc. holdings, 79/339; music, 79/245,246-47, 251; National Archives, U.S. territorial papers, 75/364; Negro history in U. of Wash. Library, 73/200; Northwest bib-

liography, 65/198-99; Oregon Historical Soc. holdings, 73/ins.bk.cov. June Pacific Northwest— cultural history, 77/297; history, 73/67-68 Russian archives, 74/95; U. of Ore. Library, 73/67-68; Wash. State U. Library, 75/364

Many Stabs (Indian), SEE Wolf Head

Manypenny, George W.: *Our Indian Wards*, reprint noted, 74/94

Manzanita (lighthouse tender), 69/309,323

Manzey, H.G., 68/245

Mao Tse-tung, 62/15,31,37,39,40,41,46

Mapleton, Ore., 76/177: history, 74/271-74; name, 74/271; photo 1915, 74/272

Mapmakers: American commercial, 71/290; bibliography, 75/94; British, 69/79; dictionary, 69/79; French, 69/79; SEE ALSO Arron Arrowsmith; Alfred Downing; S. Dunn; Henry Eld; Thomas Jeffreys; F.M. Johnson; Jon M. Leverenz; Daniel D. Major; Abraham Ortelius; Alexander Piper; Cleveland Rockwell; Thomas W. Symons; David P. Thompson; R.S. Williamson

Mapping an American Frontier: Oregon in 1850, by Brown, noted, 77/196-97

Mapping the Trans-Mississippi West, 1640-1861, by Wheat, review, 66/183-85

Maps and charts, 69/79; 70/182: Abbot, The Dalles area, 67/12; Adventure Cove site, 68/105; Alaska, 77/296; Alaska trails 1898, 76/ins.fr.cov. June; Albany, Ore., 67/68; Alvord 1862-63, 79/186-87; American Board Hawaiian missions, 68/63; American published in Great Britain 1600-1850, 69/79; Antelope-Mitchell area ranches, 81/282; Applegate Trail, 65/121; 72/352; archeological symbols, 68/348; Ashland-Klamath Falls highway, 74/358; 78/68,248,294,ins.fr.cov. Dec.; Cayuse Indians, 73/278; Chinook Point, 69/306; cities and towns on urban frontier, **81**/201-202; city mapping, 70/360; Clackamas Co., **74**/357; Clayoquot Sound, **68**/104,ins.bk.cov. June

Columbia River— dipnet sites, **75**/220,228; Duflot de Mofras, **64**/232; entrance, **69**/306, ins.bk.cov. Dec.; lower river, **74**/ins.fr. cov. Dec.; Hudson's Bay Co., **64**/ 197N; Warre and Vavasour, **64**/ 197N,210N,216-17

compilation and exploration, 70/77; Colville Indian Res., 70/136,164; Coos Co., **80**/57; Cowlitz Farm cultivated land 1845-46, **63**/facing 112 Cram maps, **69**/30—

Western Ore. 1856, **65**/174; Yakima War, **66**/132

Cross Keys, Ore., **71**/282; Dallas, Ore. 1882, **72**/171; Danner, Ore., **71**/254; Delisle, Salt Lake, **73**/286; Dept. of Platte, **69**/85; Deschutes River, **65**/ 217; Dixon maps, **65**/23N; 68/cov. March; **79**/34-35; Downing maps, **65**/ 104N; 70/164; Drake maps, **65**/insert March; **74**/95; Drew, C.S., Southern Ore. Indian depredations, **69**/226; earliest American, **67**/84; Edson-Foulke Yreka Ditch, **63**/83-84; Ehrenburg, Klamath map, **65**/214; Elliott Cutoff, **77**/338; **78**/68,156,248-49,294; **79**/44,45; Eola, Ore. 1882, **72**/171; Evans' route, **69**/46-47; fire insurance, 70/84; first modern system, **72**/182; Fletcher maps, **68**/224-25N; Ft. Boise, **73**/284

Ft. Dalles, **68**/cov. March— 1854, **67**/308; 1856, **62**/308; military reservation 1852, **67**/opp. title pg. Dec.; **68**/ins.fr.cov. March

Ft. Henrietta, **66**/132,144-45; Ft. Hoskins, **65**/190,194; Ft. Ross, **73**/104; Ft. Simcoe, 70/126; Ft. Stevens coast survey chart, **65**/insert Dec.; Ft. Taylor, **66**/144-45; Ft. Umpqua, **69**/257; 70/234,248,256; Ft. Umpqua-Klamath Lake 1860, **69**/257-58; Fremont exped. map evaluation, **65**/134N; French, Pete, murder site, **75**/66; French Prairie

1851, 70/258; fur trade routes and sites 1822-38, **66**/63; **74**/278; **76**/308; Gardiner, Ore., **69**/257; Gibbs 1851, 70/258-61; Great Salt Lake, **73**/286; Habersham's 1878, **71**/362; Hawaiian Islands, **71**/178; Hudson's Bay Co., **71**/366; **72**/183; Humphrey, Ore. 1853, **78**/46 Idaho, **73**/284; **79**/ins.bk.cov. Summer— mines, **73**/284

Independence, Ore. 1882, **72**/171; Indian battles 1860s, **71**/362; Indian trails, **74**/278; Indian tribal areas, **81**/408; Indians, **74**/94,95; Jacksonville, **69**/262,263; Japanese chart Pacific NW Coast, **65**/insert Dec.; Jeffery's 1764, **72**/100; John Day River, **68**/304; Jones Ranch, Jefferson Co., **81**/282; Keene Creek, Jackson Co., **69**/264; Kilchis River, **72**/309 Klamath lakes area—

1855, **69**/228; 1860, **69**/266-67; 1863, **69**/226

Klamath Marsh, **69**/268; Klamath railroad routes, **71**/44; Klamath River 1858, **69**/244; Klickitat Co., **79**/105; Klondike gold region, **66**/88; **76**/112; Leland mines 1863, **79**/ins.fr.cov. Summer; Lemmens Inlet, **68**/104 Lewis and Clark, **66**/65-67; **71**/362—

1804, **62**/105; Drouillard route 1808, **65**/304; maps studied by, **77**/191-92; Missouri route, **68**/345

Lincoln Co. 1882, **72**/171; Linn Co., **77**/90,292; McKenzie Head, **69**/306, ins.bk.cov. Dec.; Malheur Co., **75**/291; **76**/152; Marion Co., **77**/90,292; Mazatlan, Mex., 70/ins.fr.cov. Dec.; Meares' voyages, **74**/278; Meek Cutoff, **78**/156,248-49; **79**/ins.fr.cov. Spring; Melish, U.S.A., **64**/281; military expeds. 1863-65, **71**/362; military in West 1878-80, **65**/insert No. 2, March; Milwaukie, **67**/80; **68**/161; mines in Eastern Ore., **71**/362; mining 1863, **79**/ins.bk.cov. Summer; Minto Pass trail, **71**/357; Modoc Co., Calif., **67**/365; Modoc War, 70/176; Monmouth, Ore. 1882, 72/171; Mullan 1858 military, 66/144-45 National Forests— Pacific NW, 76/28; Siskiyou, 76/41 nautical charts reprints, 74/96; New Archangel, 73/fr.cov. June; Nez Perce Reservation 1864, 66/386; Nicolett, 71/290; Norse voyages to America, 66/88 North America— 1754-61, 68/87; 1848, 64/86; bibliography, 69/79 North Umpqua River, 74/358; Northwest Coast, 72/100,230; o&c lands in Western Ore., 64/56-57; o&c Railroad routes, 71/44; ocean steamship routes, 80/174; Ogden exped., 71/346N; Olympic Mts. exped. routes, 74/8; Olympic Peninsula, 69/73; 74/20; Omaha-West routes 1865, 72/68 Oregon— 1850, 77/196-97; 1855 Pacific Railroad Survey, 71/26; 1860 Steen routes, 79/ins.covs. Spring; 1863 Pengra survey, 79/ins.covs. Spring; 1863 and 1871 surveyor general, 71/ 362; Central Ore., 81/280,282; Eastern Ore. 1879 Army, 79/ins.fr.cov. Summer; gold and gems, 76/181; highways 1921, 71/362; historic markers, 67/173; history atlas, 71/362; 74/278-79; immigrant routes, 78/46, 68,156,248-49,294,ins.fr.cov. Dec.; Indian tribes, 81/408; parks, 67/184; Raisz 1941 travel routes, 79/44; relief, 77/310; Southeast Ore., 67/ 30; Southern Ore., 69/30,34,35,46- 47,257-63; 80/232; U.S. Hwy. 26, 72/173; Western Ore. 1856, 65/174; western o&c lands, 64/56-57 Ore.-Calif. boundary, 72/27,covs. March; Oregon Coast 1856, 70/234; Oregon Historical Soc., 73/363; Ore. Pacific rail routes, 71/52-53; Oregon Territory 1850, 80/329 Oregon Trail, 72/180; 77/316; 78/ 156; 79/34-35; 80/406; 81/186— in Idaho, 64/277; Stansbury 1849, 80/72,77

Pacific Coast 1844, 76/128; Pacific Crest National Scenic Trail, 74/358 Pacific Northwest, 77/301; 81/331— 1855, 67/ins.fr.cov. Dec.; national forests, 76/28; railroads ca. 1885, 67/104; resources atlas, 69/331 Pacific Ocean, 72/100,134,356; Pacific Railroad Survey, 79/26; Pengra 1863 survey, 79/ins.covs. Spring; Perrydale, Ore. 1882, 72/171; Petropavlovsk Harbor, 80/ins.bk.cov. Summer Polk Co.— 1882, 72/171; 75/344; historic sites, 69/77 Pony Express routes, 67/230N; Port Cox (Meares) chart, 68/ins.fr.cov. June; Port Orford meteorite area, 69/30,34,35,46-47 Portland— geologic, 64/284; port, 78/365; rails, 71/66-67; Willamette Heights, 75/57 postal routes, 68/343; Powell Valley, 74/94; Puget Sound, 72/356; 77/295 railroads, 73/284— o&c routes, 71/44; Oregon Pacific routes, 71/52-53; Pacific NW ca. 1885, 67/104; Williamson & Abbot 1855, 79/26 Raisz 1941 travel maps, 78/156,248- 49; 79/44-45; Raymond, Ore. 1930, 78/68; roads and trails, 74/96; Rogue River, 69/30,34,35,262; 71/361; Roseburg 1860, 69/359; Ross, Snake River, 71/366; Russell, Southeast Ore., 67/20 Russian— history atlas, 74/96; Pacific discoveries 1764, 72/100 Russian-American Co.— posts, 73/100,104,145; trade routes, 73/100 Sacramento Canyon, 74/96; Salem 1878, 80/340; Santa Barbara area 1879, 80/248; Scholl map, 65/5- 6N,25N,38,58,61-62; 81/196; Scio, Ore. 1878, 80/378; Scottsburg, 69/ 257; Sheepeater campaign, 68/244N; 73/284; Sherman Co. 1892, 81/280; Shiloh Basin, 72/206; Siletz Reservation linguistic groups, 79/338; Silver City, Ida., 70/273; Siskiyou Nat'l Forest, 76/41; Siskiyou Trail, 77/194; Sitka Bay, 73/145; Skirving 1849-50, 65/168; Snake River, 71/366; 72/68 Stansbury—

1849, 80/72,77; 1852, 62/insert No. 3

Starling, Willamette Valley, 70/258-61; state atlases, 73/86; Steen-Smith exped., 65/6N,23N,66N; Strait of Juan de Fuca, 72/356; T.1S R.1E 1852, 68/161; The Dalles area, 67/12; Thompson journeys 1800, 66/280; Tide Creek, Ore., 72/206; Tillamook Bay, 72/309; Tillamook Co., 74/357 Trans-Mississippi West—

1540-1861, 66/183-85; 1879, 72/68 Tryon Creek State Park, 79/104; Tule Lake area, 72/93; Umpqua massacre site, 66/383; Umpqua River, 69/30, 34,257-60; 70/234

United States—

agencies and cities, 70/360; bibliography, 75/95; Melish, 64/281; U.S. Army, Eastern Ore. 1879, 79/ins.fr. cov. Summer; U.S. Forest Service, 68/ 349; U.S. Geological Survey, 72/45 Vancouver Island 1966, 68/bk.cov. June; Vinland, 67/84,182-83 voyages—

1840s, 77/40; 1850s, 77/42; Norse to America, 66/88; of discovery, 72/343-44; Russian to North Pacific, 73/100 Voznesenskii, 73/100; Warm Springs Reservation 1860, 79/124; Warre and Vavasour, Cape Disappointment, 65/ insert Dec.; Warren 1857, 66/184; Wasco Co. 1892, 81/280

Washington—

coast, 63/92; Eastern Wash. 1879, 70/136; Eastern Wash. 1882, 70/164 Washington Co. historic sites, 68/81; Wash. Terr. 1863 mines, 79/ins.fr.cov. Summer; westward expansion 1790-1900, 64/77; westward movement, 72/ 173; Wilkes Exped., 72/356; 79/405 Willamette Valley—

1851, 70/258; Wyeth sketch, 66/345

Williamson & Abbot Pacific Railroad Survey 1855, 69/34,228; 79/26; world fur trade routes 1783-1840, 76/308; Wyeth, 66/345; Yakima Indian Agency, 70/126; Yaquina Bay, 77/365; Yreka Trail, 69/228; Yukon gold region, 76/112,ins.fr.cov. June Maquinna (Maquilla) (Indian), 79/400: portrait, 71/ins.fr.cov. Dec. Marbel, P.B., SEE Marple, Perry B. Marble, Ansil, 80/334 Marble, Butler, 80/334 *Marblehead* (cruiser), 74/84 *March of the Volunteers: Soldiering with Lewis and Clark*, by Bordwell, review, 62/88-89 *March to South Pass: Lt. William B. Franklin's Journal of the Kearny Expedition of 1845*, ed. by Schubert, noted, 81/333 Marchbank, John, 64/353 *Marcus and Narcissa Whitman and the Opening of Old Oregon*, by Drury, noted, 77/291; review, 75/77-78 Marden, Vic, 76/381 Mardock, Robert W., and Robert W. Richmond, eds.: *A Nation Moving West, Readings in the History of the American Frontier*, noted, 68/82 *Marechal Tucket* (ship), 66/129 Mare's Egg Spring, 69/328 *Margaret* (ship), 72/182; 76/207,221N Margulies, Herbert F.: *Decline of the Progressive Movement in Wisconsin*, noted, 70/79 Mari, —, Portland hotel proprietor, 77/246,249 Maria C. Jackson State Park, 67/46,48,50 Marianas Islands, 62/21,31,32 Marias Pass, 68/224N Marie, Queen of Rumania, 78/357: photo, 78/108; Pierce recollections, 78/107-109 *Marie Dorion and the Trail of the Pioneers*, by Ringhand, noted, 73/285 Marietta, Ohio, 64/310 *Marietta* (gunboat), 76/277-85*passim* Marin, Francisco de Paula y: biography, 74/285; papers, 74/285

Marine, Gene:

America the Raped: The Engineering Mentality and the Devastation of a Continent, review, 71/184

Marine engines, 77/102-107; 81/48-50: photo, 77/104

Marine Gazette, Astoria, 64/171

The Marine Surveys of James Cook in North America 1758-1768, by Skelton and Tooley, noted, 69/79

Maring, Helen, 74/63

Marion (schooner), 66/117

Marion County, Ore., 63/221; 66/19, 21,90,318,370: assessment roll 1855, 66/360; atlas map, 77/90,292; census 1860, 66/361; centennial markers, 63/83; court history, 70/74; courthouse, 66/90; Democratic convention 1854, 66/360; first Ore. sheriffs' meeting, 66/90; history, 72/353; 77/298; sheriff, 72/91

Marion County Historical Society: meetings, 69/279; officers and board members, 68/85,283; 69/82,279; 70/82,276; officers and directors, 62/104, 415; 63/86,250; 64/83,279; 65/123, 312; 66/85,279; 67/83,284; 71/194; 72/176; 73/78-79; 74/181; 75/91; 76/95; 77/95; 78/95; 79/111; 80/110; 80/111; publications, 66/81; 70/74; 72/353; 77/90,292,298; 81/327

Marion County History, noted, 62/107-108; 63/83; 66/81; 70/74; 77/292,298

Marion County Teachers' Institute, 64/154-55

Marion Friends Church, 67/89

Marion Star, Ohio, 78/104,105

Mariposa (steamer), 64/241

Mariposa lily (*Calochortus elegans*), 69/167

Mark Tobey, by Roberts, review, 62/410-11

Mark Twain's Burlesque Patterns, by Rogers, review, 62/292-94

Markers, see Monuments and markers

Market Days, an Informal History of the Eugene Producers Public Market, by Bettis, review, 72/87

Marketing: agricultural, 72/87; fuel wood, 72/178; Oregon fruit, 71/87; theses index, 72/275; wholesale fruit and vegetables, Portland, 74/162-63

Markham, Benjamin C., 66/306

Markham, Edwin, 65/211; 74/37

Markham, Elizabeth, 65/211

Markle, George B., 71/151; 75/60

Markov, S.N., 73/159-60,161,164

Marlette, Seneca H., 72/10,12

Marlitt, Richard, 65/415; 67/332N; 73/364:

Nineteenth Street, noted, 70/371,bk.cov. March

Marmot, Ore., 73/84

Marple, Perry B., 63/11,19

Marquam Grand Theatre, Portland, 66/41,42,317; 74/201,206,346: Davenport lecture, 66/44,45,46

Marquam Gulch photo, 77/242

Marquina, Alexandro, photo, 76/166

Marquina, Joe, photo, 76/166

Marquina, Solero, photo, 76/166

Marquis, James W., 74/219

Marquiss, Ollie: diary, 80/336

Marriages: Clackamas Co. records, 63/364; donation land law effect, 63/51; early Lane Co., 62/301; 70/75; King Co. records, 66/275; Multnomah Co., 74/286; Wasco Co. first recorded, 79/136; Willamette Valley, 66/348N,356N, 359N,360N; Yamhill Co., 68/350

The Marriage Record, Lane County, Oregon, 1852-69, noted, 70/75

Marriage Records of King County, Washington, 1853 to 1884, noted, 66/275

Marro (Marron), Cowlitz Farm employee, 63/126,128,151,165

Marron, Isabella, see Shepard, Margaret L.

Marsden, Walter L., 63/336,338

Marsh, Arthur L., 71/196

Marsh, Mrs. Creat Inman, 68/340

Marsh, Edson: journal 1852, 66/88

Marsh, Eugene E., 62/110,206,302,417-18,420,421,422; 63/93,255,372,374; 64/94,190,286,363; 65/125,221,317, 416; 66/93,189,285,394; 67/376,388; 68/361; 69/348; 70/373; 71/371

Marsh, Josiah: land claim, 68/28,29; The Dalles 1858 description, 68/28-29

Marsh, Othniel Charles, 67/17; 73/86; 75/78-79

Marsh, Sidney Harper, 64/153; 70/200

Marsh, Tracy H.: *The American Story Recorded in Glass*, review, 63/353-54

Marshall, David B.: *Familiar Birds of Northwest Forests, Fields and Gardens*, noted, 74/282

Marshall, George Catlett, 62/5,37,38; 77/299

Marshall, James Wilson, 64/275; 66/218

Marshall, John, 69/140

Marshall, Michael, 69/140

Marshall, W.H., 62/218N

Marshall, William I., 70/230

Marshall Islands, 62/11,21,29,31,32

Marshfield, Ore., 72/164,353; 77/75,77; 80/52,62: city council, 77/77; photo, 77/ins.bk. cov. March; port, 77/77

Marshland, Ore., 67/280-81: Graham house, 65/308

Martin, Albro: *James J. Hill and the Opening of the Northwest*, review, 78/358

Martin, Charles, Klamath Co. homesteader, 69/329

Martin, Charles Henry, 72/81; 74/231, 234; 76/140,142,143,150,151: photo, 76/268

Martin, Charley, Wasco Co. 1881, 81/275

Martin, Christie, 69/329

Martin, Ed, 81/298-99,300,301

Martin, Edward, Morrow Co., 69/140-41

Martin, George A., 74/19,21

Martin, Harry, lumber employee, 72/311; 73/175,222

Martin, Henry Byam, 70/308

Martin, J.M., 62/175

Martin, Lenard, 74/21

Martin, Louisa J. Hughes (Mrs. Charles H.), photo, 76/268

Martin, Lucy N., 73/65

Martin, Mungo, 66/88

Martin, Peter, 80/300N,321N

Martin, R.M., Siskiyou pioneer: cattle drive, 64/351; 65/22-23N

Martin, Richard, Jr., 62/172

Martin, Robert Montgomery, 63/207

Martin, William, immigrant of 1843, 66/353

Martin, William H., 63/245

Martin, William Jennings: Indian war letters, 80/105

Martinez, Esteban Jose, 74/353; 79/397

Martini, "Rosino," photo, 77/238

Martin's Bluff, 66/382

Martin's Dairy, Siskiyou Co., 66/82

Marumoto, Fumi, photo, 76/250

Marvin, Joe, 73/267

Mary (steamer), 62/79; 72/94

Mary Agatha, Sister, 81/81N

Mary Aloysius, Sister, 81/82

Mary Alphonse, Mother, 80/343

Mary Angel Guardian, Sister, 80/346,348,349,352

Mary Angelo, Sister, 81/81N

Mary Cyprian, Mother, 64/88

Mary Dare (bark), 63/194,236

Mary E. (sloop), 74/29

Mary Edwards, Sister, 81/81N

Mary Emerentiana, Sister, 81/76

Mary Emma, Sister, 81/81N

Mary Febronia, Sister, 80/352

Mary Florence (Florentine), Sister, 80/343,347(photo),352

Mary Frances, Sister, 81/81N

Mary Francis of Assisium, Sister, 81/77,83-84

Mary Hedwidge, Sister, 80/356

Mary John the Baptist, Sister, 81/77

Mary Julia, Sister, 81/76

Mary Laurens, Sister, 81/81N

Mary Margaret, Sister, 80/352; 81/81N: photo, 80/347

Mary of Calvary, Sister, 80/342,343, 348,352,357,359,362; 81/92: photo, 80/347

Mary of Seven Dolors, Sister, 80/346

Mary of the Sacred Heart, Sister, 80/343,348,352,359; 81/81N

Mary of the Visitation, Sister, photo, 80/347

Mary Patrick, Sister, 80/359; 81/76,90

Mary Praxede, Sister, 81/90

Mary Procido, Sister, 81/81N

Mary Rose of Lima, Sister, SEE Kelly, Jane

Mary Taylor (pilot schooner), 63/47N

Maryhill Museum of Fine Arts, 62/298; 69/176; 78/107: built, 78/110; dedication, 78/108; name, 66/251; 78/357

Maryland (brig), drawing, 76/218

Mary's Island, 76/103

Mary's Peak, 70/260,261; 72/284

Marysville, Calif., 62/175; 66/169

Marysville, Ore., SEE Corvallis, Ore.

Marysville Revisited, a Tour of Historic Corvallis Houses, by Hewitt, noted, 77/299

Mashampethla (Indian), 79/313,314, 316,317,322,330,332

Mason, A.I., 68/207

Mason, Alpheus T., and William M. Beaney:

The Supreme Court in a Free Society, review, 62/93-94

Mason, Charles H., 62/78

Mason, David C., 63/79

Mason, David Townsend, 62/110,206, 302,420,423; 63/94,256,373; 64/93, 184,285,363; 65/125,221,317,416; 66/93,189,285,392,395; 67/380; 68/ 186,357,358,361; 69/347; 70/374; 73/364; 74/183; 75/6; 78/280: memoirs, 71/368; recollections, 69/70

Mason, David Townsend: "The Effect of O & C Management on the Economy of Oregon," 64/55-67

Mason, Edwin C., 70/19

Mason, N.H.A. ("Hock"), 63/309-11: ranch, 68/255,315

Mason, Ralph S., 62/107,203; 63/362; 66/283

Mason, William S., 71/151

Mason County, Wash.: census 1880, 74/281

Masonry: dry walls, 74/116,125,142— photo, 74/122

Masons, Ancient, Free and Accepted, 72/317; 73/283; 81/263N: Arlington history, 65/121; Corvallis history, 67/88; Dallas, Ore., 76/373; first temple in Ore., 70/184; Lyon Lodge, 81/328; St. Helens, 70/358 Salem hall, 80/345— described, 80/346,348; location, 80/340(map),343; sold, 80/343 Scott orator for, 70/221-22; Scottish Rite, 75/154,168,172; Silverton, 70/76; Wasco lodge, 70/15,76

Massachusetts: influence on U.S. Pacific policy, 76/205,213FF merchants and traders— in Pacific commerce, 76/197FF; in sea otter trade, 76/206-208,221; relations with J.Q. Adams, 76/197,203,204-13, 218,223-24; SEE ALSO Boston traders whaling vessels, 76/202

Massachusetts (battleship), 76/271,272; 79/213; 81/333

Massachusetts (steamship), 64/199,207- 209; 72/288

Massachusetts Historical Society, 66/ 293,388; 67/200,201-202,203,205: publications, 72/182

Massacre Creek, 68/256,315

Massacre Lake, 68/255N,256N

Massacres of the Mountains, by Dunn, cited, 66/223N-24N

Massett, Stephen C., 64/352

Massett Indians, 63/360

Massey, Fred, 63/34

Mast, Reuben H., 67/42-43,50

Masten, Charles C., 63/352

Masten, Edmond C., 62/165

Masterson, George, 79/125

Masterson, Martha Gay, 80/104

Mastodons, 62/298; 63/364

Matheny, Adam, 74/17,27

Mather, James, 65/405

Mather, Kathleen Mahoney, 69/140
Mather, Stephen T., 72/83-84; 74/103: biography 80/408
Mathers, Michael: *Sheepherders: Men Alone*, noted, 77/301
Mathews, Dave C., 78/303,304,306, 325N
Mathews, I.S., 69/229N
Mathews, Philip, 74/7
Mathews, William, 77/81
Mathies, H.G., 75/135,137
Matlock, Edward Lane, family, 78/124,129,148
Matley Flats, Gilliam Co., 69/145,147
Matsen, Kenneth H., and Robert G. Slocum: *Shoto Clay: Figurines and Forms From the Lower Columbia*, noted, 69/333
Matson, Cecil: *Seven Nights—Three Matinees: Seventy Years of Dramatic Stock in Portland, Oregon, 1863-1933*, noted, 81/330
Matson, Fay, 80/52
Mattes, Merrill J.: *The Great Platte River Road: The Covered Wagon Mainline via Ft. Kearny to Ft. Laramie*, review, 71/182-83
Matthews, Courtland, 74/63,176: *Aleutian Interval*, cited, 74/177
Matthews, Eleanor Hansen, 74/63
Matthews, John, 73/206
Matthews, R.P., and Clyde Keller: *Pioneer Landmarks of Washington County*, noted, 80/106
Matthews, Stephen A., 68/81
Matthews, W.W., African M.E. Church pastor, 80/400
Matthews, William J., 65/394,398
Matthews, William Wallace, 66/333
Matthieu, Francis Xavier, 62/417; 66/354N: photos, 81/254,258,fr.cov. Fall; quoted, 66/336
Mattila, Walter, 62/205; 75/86; 73/23,364: *Finns and Finnicans, An Oregon Finntown Novel*, review, 72/169-70 *Indians, Finns, and Their Thunderbirds*, review, 75/83-84

The Theater Finns, review, 74/91-92
Mattison, Ray H., 62/202: historical writings, 70/365
Mattoon, Charles Hiram, 62/218; 64/125: literary quarrel with Adams, 64/130-32; *Religious Expositor*, 64/127-34
Mattson, Sylvia: *Missionary Footpaths: The Story of Anna Maria Pittman*, noted, 80/335
Maud Baldwin—Photographer, by Drew, noted, 81/327
Maulden (Maldenn), —, Snake war 1866, 79/142
Maunder, Elwood R., and Margaret G. Davidson, eds.: *Proceedings of the First National Colloquium on the History of Forest Products Industries, May 17-18, 1966*, review, 69/70
Maupin, Howard, 64/188; 72/341; 75/311-12,272N; 79/171N,272N
Mauris, John, 81/32,34
Maury, Reuben F., 64/282; 79/ 130,145N: biography, 65/13N; Camp Maury named for, 65/39; emigrant protection, 72/70,72-73,75; First Ore. Cavalry, 65/13-14,19,26,38N,97,393,395-98; Gibbs correspondence, 65/115-16N; Mexican War, 65/396
Maury Mountains, 65/42,78N; 77/334: name, 79/145N; photo, 65/30
Maximillian, SEE Wied-Neuwied, Maximillian
Maxwell, Ben, 62/107,197,199,200,299, 300; 63/83,363; 64/89-90,356; 65/ 219,315; 66/81,283,359N; 70/74
Maxwell, Henry, 63/283
Maxwell, Richard, and Evans Walker, comps.: *Records of the Office of Territories*, noted, 64/277
May, Catherine, 72/253: biography, 73/360; Congressional papers, 73/360
May, Ernest R.: *American Imperialism*, cited, 72/211,212-13,221,224

May, F., 65/143
May, Harvey B.:
letters 1889-90, 66/381
May, John, Westfall merchant, 63/282,286
May, Karl:
American western tales, 68/344
May, Samuel E., 81/248
May, Walter W.R., 62/111,207,303,422; 63/93,255,373; 64/93,189,285,363; 65/125,221,317; 73/370; 74/49, 204,238
May Dacre (brig), 63/234
May Day, 78/160(with photo)
May View wheat tram, 67/87
Maybee, Lottie, and Forrest D. Forbes:
Days and Ways of Old Damascus, Oregon, noted, 64/92
Mayer, Frederick:
Bannock War diary, 68/297-316—cited, 68/221,226
biography, 68/293-96; papers, 68/226N,293N,296
Mayer, Ward, 73/5; 74/238
Mayger, Ore., 62/301
Mayhew, H.K., 74/18,21,23
Maynadier, Henry E.:
emigrant escort, 72/59,60,60N,61; photo, 72/62
Maynard, David, 74/90
Mays, Franklin Pierce, 81/266
Mays, Robert, 65/115N
Mays Bridge, SEE Sherar's Bridge
Mayville, Ore., 69/341
Mazama Club, 71/197; 74/232; 75/88; 76/101:
history, 70/359; 71/198; organized, 74/202; publications, 74/88,286; river trips 1963, 65/217
"A Mazama Heads North: Letters of William A. Langille," ed. by Lawrence Rakestraw, 76/101-17
Mazatlan, Mexico:
map, 70/ins.fr.cov. Dec.; specie sent to England, 70/305; U.S. squadron visits, 70/306
Mazzini Society, 77/257
Meacham, Alfred B., 65/365:
biography, 80/117-18,121-23; letter to granddaughter, 80/124-33; photo, 80/116
Meacham, Alfred B.:
The Council Fire, cited, 80/118,123
Wigwam and Warpath, quoted, 80/121-22
Meacham, Nellie, 80/117:
biography, 80/118-21; letter from grandfather, 80/124-33; photos, 80/122,125
Meacham, Walter, 78/102
Meacham, Ore., 67/241; 68/227,228, 233,306; 70/12; 73/285; 78/101,102; 80/105:
Indian raids 1878, 66/206; photo 1880s, 67/103
Meacham Station, 80/117,118,130
Mead, E.C., 64/271
Mead, Edward, 64/352
Mead, Elwood, 67/214
Meade, E.F., 64/87; 67/86
Meador, Joseph, 77/321,324-25, 336,339:
portrait, 77/326
Meadowlark, Western:
discovered by Lewis, 69/23
Meadows, Joseph, SEE Meador, Joseph
Meagher, Thomas Francis, 72/233
Meany, Edmond Stephen, 62/106,406; 63/110N,118N,176N,235N; 66/79:
opinion of H.W. Scott, 70/227
Meany, John:
Vancouver brewery, 64/267
Meares, John, 68/101:
maps of voyages, 74/278
Mears, Fred W., 68/134
Measles, 63/138-42,145,148,194,213; 64/11,14; 65/26; 80/53; 81/342:
deaths, 63/141; epidemic 1848, 63/228
Meat:
Portland 1919, 72/91
Mechanics Pavilion, Portland, 74/347
Medals and tokens:
Chief Lot, 70/160; Chief Moses, 70/fr.cov. June; Chief Seltice, 70/160; designers, 73/276; Hudson's Bay Co., 70/179; Indian peace, 64/85; 73/276-77; North West Co., 70/88
Medford, Ore., 64/338; 80/235:

"Light House," 65/218; Japanese in, 76/246; postal history, 67/374; 71/200 *Medford Clarion*, 75/164 *Medford Corporation: A History of an Oregon Logging and Lumber Company*, by LaLande, review, 81/205-206 Medford Hotel, 64/338 *Medford Mail Tribune*: opposition to KKK, 75/164,173 Medical Lake, Wash.: history, 64/351 Medical Springs, 62/298; 79/104 Medicine, 70/44FF,59,140; 71/22; 77/34,166; 80/64: abortion, 70/48; American, 70/362; Basque remedies, 76/164-68; B.C. Indians, 71/184-85; cure-alls, 79/307; diary of student nurse 1910-13, 80/336; early druggists, 70/279; early 19th century, 80/404; Eugene history, 66/187; frontier neurosurgery, 68/346; frontier practice, 63/336-39; herbs and simples, 69/156,168; 70/365 history— Pacific NW, 72/173; Portland tuberculosis clinic, 79/408 homeopathy, 75/17-18; Hood River doctors and hospitals, 68/354; hops used as, 64/267; Indian influence on, 71/179-80; infant care, 80/55; Japanese doctors, 76/239; maternity care, SEE Midwives; medical education in Ore., 68/341,351; 75/7-34*passim*; medical societies, Wash., 78/34; medicine shows, 79/306,307; military, 65/193; native plant use, 65/219; obstetrics, 75/33-34; optometry college, 72/287; Pacific NW, 72/173; patent medicines, 76/164; 78/25; pediatrics, 72/172 pioneer, 62/300— Pacific NW, 64/87; remedies, 73/73 Portland history, 79/408; preventative, 75/32-33; rabies treatment, 63/277; rhubarb and calomel use, 79/282N; snakebite cure, 79/314; Tillamook Co. 1920s, 71/117-24; toothache, 80/62; turpentine use, 76/339; vaccination of Indians, 63/183; SEE ALSO Allopathy; Diseases; Hydropathy; Physicians

Medlin, Johnnie, 63/269 "Medorem Crawford and the Protective Corps," by Lon W. Fendall, 72/55-77 Mee, Mary Ann, 70/279 Meehan, Thomas, 69/163 Meek, Fred, 62/420 Meek, Helen Mar, 75/73 Meek, Joseph Lafayette, 62/75,142N, 149,299,318,320,321,420; 64/187, 349; 65/407-408; 66/82,383; 67/85; 70/19,226,260; 71/250,285: biography, 66/185; 76/381; carries memorial to Congress, 75/73; letter on Whitman massacre, 75/74-75; Nez Perce wife, 66/90; photo, 81/fr.cov. Fall; rifle, 63/254 Meek, Mary Luelling (Mrs. William), 68/160 Meek, Stephen H.L., 62/199; 68/80; 77/311,315,317; 78/71,146,154,209, 221,222,241 Meek, William: Luelling partner, 68/160; photo, 68/159; sells nursery, 68/164-65 Meek Cutoff, 65/10,47N; 70/358; 77/311,317; 78/323; 79/31: 1845 party, 77/315-16; maps, 78/156,248-49; 79/44,ins.covs. Spring; Peachwood incident, 63/366 route, 65/80N; 68/79-81; 77/315, 332,333,334; 79/33— across Harney Valley, 78/221; map, 77/316; photo, 78/153 tracks, 78/70,147,155,209,219,221, 241,323; 79/6,15,33,271N Meek *vs.* Torney, 62/149-50 Meeker, Ezra, 64/269; 65/207; 68/164; 74/137: Oregon Trail apostle, 71/368; papers, 70/358 Meeker, Jacob Redding, 64/269 Mehama, Ore., 66/90; 73/332,332N, 346; 80/270: history, 72/353 Meier, Henry, 79/239 Meier, Julius L., 66/249; 71/218,220; 74/112,137,139,141,233; 75/165: photos, 66/250; 74/110 Meier, Roger S., 75/370; 79/413,416

Meier and Frank Co., Portland, **66**/305; **75**/165; **80**/413: influenza crisis 1918, **64**/253-54

Meigs, Charles R., **65**/232

Meinig, Donald William: *The Great Columbia Plain: A Historical Geography of the Inland Empire,* review, **70**/64

Melish, John, **64**/281

Mellinger, C.C., Co., Tacoma, **66**/129

A Melodrame Entitled "Treason, Stratagems, and Spoils," by W.L. Adams, ed. by Belknap, review, **70**/354-55

Melons:

French Prairie, **66**/339,340

Melson family:

Ore.-Calif. journey 1885, **80**/229-45 *passim*

Melvin, J., Cowlitz Farm 1848, **63**/146-47N

Melvin Ricks' Alaska Bibliography: An Introductory Guide to Alaskan Historical Literature, ed. by Haycox and Haycox, review, **78**/359

Memaloose Island, SEE Grave Island

Members of the Legislature of Oregon, 1843-1967, noted, **69**/273

Memoirs of an Oregon Moonshiner, by Nelson, noted, **77**/197

Memoirs of Earl Wayland Bowman, ed. by Knight, noted, **72**/355

Memorials, SEE Petitions and memorials

Men Against the Mountains: Jedediah Smith and the Great South West Expedition of 1826-29, by Smith, noted, **66**/275-76

Men and Memories of San Francisco in the Spring of '50, by Barry and Patten, cited, **66**/10N

Men and Milestones in Medicine, 100 Years of Medical Education in Oregon, noted, **68**/341

Men, Mules and Mountains: Lieutenant O'Neil's Olympic Expedition, by Wood, review, **78**/281-82

Men of the Lewis and Clark Expedition: A Bibliographical Roster, by Clarke, review, **72**/82-83

Menard, Pierre, **68**/345

Menasha Wooden Ware Co.: history, **76**/182

Mencken, Henry Louis, **73**/309,310, 312,319

Mendenhall, Don: *The Truth about Cowboys and Indians, and Other Myths about the West,* noted, **81**/331

Menefee, Arthur M., **67**/372

Menefee, Donald, **78**/308: photo, **79**/50

Menefee, Leah Collins, **62**/104,301,415; **63**/86,250; **64**/83,279; **65**/123,311; **66**/81,84,278; **68**/359; **78**/308: photos, **78**/226,298; **79**/4

Menefee, Leah Collins, and Lowell Tiller:

"Cutoff Fever," **77**/309-40; **78**/41-72,121-57,207-50,293-331; **79**/5-50

Menefee, Leah Collins, comp.:

Immigration Rosters of the Elliott Cut-Off: 1853 & 1854, and Immigration Registration at Umatilla Agency, 1853, noted, **79**/338

Menefee Ranch, **77**/330,331

Mengarini, Gregory, **67**/368; **69**/55, 56,64,270; **71**/335

Meningitis, **81**/122,124

Mennonites, **64**/90:

Fraser Valley, **65**/377

Mensch, Fred:

Ore.-Calif. boundary survey, **72**/ 36-37,38

Menzies, Archibald, **68**/111,112,124

Mercer, Asa Shinn, **62**/186-87; **63**/91,360:

Johnson County War reappraisal, **66**/280; photo, **65**/215

Mercer, Asa Shinn:

Banditti of the Plains, **62**/301

Mercer, James K., **80**/309,319N

Mercer, Sam, **66**/91

Mercer Lake, **75**/303-308: photos, **75**/300

Merchandising, **75**/15

Merchant, Warren, **66**/283

Merchant Hotel, Portland, **70**/184; **81**/119N

"Merchant Marine, 1917-1918," by

Truman B. Cook, 77/101-29
Merchants Protective Assn., 71/226N
Mercier, A.T., 74/237
The Mercury, Salem, 81/84
Mercury Publishing Co., 69/208
Merganser, Ore., 78/363
Meridian United Church of Christ, 67/273
"Meriwether Lewis: Botanist," by Paul R. Cutright, 69/148-70
"Meriwether Lewis: Zoologist," by Paul R. Cutright, 69/5-28
Merk, Frederick, 78/333,344:
Fur Trade and Empire: George Simpson's Journal, 1824-25, revised ed. noted, 69/274
Manifest Destiny and Mission in American History; A Reinterpretation, cited, 72/210N,216N; review, 64/343-44
The Oregon Question: Essays in Anglo-American Diplomacy and Politics, review, 69/72-73
Merk, Lois Bannister (Mrs. Frederick), 64/343
Merrell, Lillian, 80/334
Merriam, C. Hart:
Oregon pheasant survey, 65/252-53
Merriam, Harold G., 73/310-11,321
Merriam, Henry C., 80/186
Merriam, John C., 67/25-26,33; 73/258
Merriam, Paul G.:
"The 'Other Portland': A Statistical Note on Foreign-Born, 1860-1910," 80/258-68
Merriam, Willis B.:
History of the Northwest Scientific Association, noted, 62/107
Merrick, Curtis, photo, 74/265
Merrill, Birdine, photo, 72/208
Merrill, David, 62/109; 73/346
Merrill, Fred T., 73/82
Merrill, J.F., 68/247N
Merrill, James Cushing, 66/233N
Merriman, Harold G., ed.:
Montana Adventure: The Recollections of Frank Linderman, noted, 71/191
Merrit, Wesley, 80/179
Merritt, Charley, 63/276
Merritt, Morris L., 64/284; 67/44,51

Mershon, Helen L., 64/353; 65/217
Merwin Dam, 68/341
Meserve, D.W., family, 77/89
Messersmith, William, family, 72/92
Metal Uniform Insignia of the Frontier U.S. Army, by Brinckerhoff, noted, 74/283
Metcalf, Robert B., 65/183,191
Metcalf, Thomas, 70/340
Meteors and meteorites, 79/160:
Hunter's Silver Meteor, 70/183
Oregon, 62/299—
"year of," 69/338
Pacific Northwest, 63/364; 65/220
Port Orford, 66/90,91; 69/29-50, 333—
analysis, 69/31N; specimens, 69/29, 32,33,38-39,49
Sams Valley, 69/333; showers, 70/183; western, 70/375; Willamette, 64/188; 69/333
Methodism in the Northwest, by Howell, ed. by Foster, review, 68/338-39
Methodist Church, 62/293,320,321:
Arlington, 77/90; Astoria 1855 photo, 81/4; Baker Co. 1890s, 66/215; Buena Vista, 69/340; Drain, 62/205; Ft. Klamath, 69/329; Garibaldi, 77/355; Kelso, 66/80; King Co. marriage records, 66/275; Klamath Falls history, 64/91; Lookingglass Church, 62/205; North Bend history, 67/279; Northwest history, 68/338-39; Oregon history, 62/406-407; 75/120,127; records, 71/363; role in Ore.Prov. Govt., 71/368; Salem, 67/369; 80/342, 343N; Seattle conference, 66/82; The Dalles, 67/292,296,298,303,304N; Union, 65/315
Methodist (Lee) Mission Parsonage, Salem, 63/254; 64/353; 65/218; 66/81,283; 67/92; 69/339,341; 71/294,365
Methodist missionaries, 62/119; 73/67; 78/86-89,91,332-50:
French Prairie, 66/340-41,350,351; lay supporters, 78/337-38; objectives, 78/336-37; number in Ore. 1840, 78/338
Methodist Missionary Society, 76/359-60,362,367; 78/333-50*passim*; 80/342:

Oregon committee, 78/348; Oregon politics, 74/71-78

Methodist missions, 62/66,69-70,150, 151,407; 63/176-78,200,217,228; 64/ 41,45-53*passim*; 65/157,159; 66/167, 344,347,353; 71/344,365; 75/109: Clatsop Plains, 73/251-55; 78/336; established, 66/340-41; Gary report, 63/177; governmental role in Ore., 62/119,120,122N,130,137N; 66/350; Indian schools, 64/41,43-45; 72/59; land claims, 63/176-78; Lee fund raising for, 64/45-50; memorial to Congress, 62/119-20; Oregon, 78/335; Ore. expenses, 74/78; plan for Ore. expansion, 74/71-78; reinforcements, 74/75; 78/332,334,341,359-67; St. Louis, 74/73; The Dalles (Wascopam), 67/292,296,298; 74/71; Willamette Valley, 74/71; 77/298; 76/359-60; 78/332-50; William Brooks' service to, 64/45-50,53

Metlakatla, Alaska, photo, 76/103

Metlakatla (Metlakahtla) Mission, 62/57

Metolius River, 79/126,144N

Metropolis (bark), 64/317

Metropolis Hotel, Portland, 68/26

Metropolitan Savings Bank, Portland, 69/208

Metropolitan Steam Railway, 69/209

Metschan, Phil, Jr., 74/208

Metschan, Phil, Sr.: county judge, 70/59N; family photo, 70/58; letter 1878, 70/56-59; photo, 81/44

Metteer, Augusta, 65/219

Metzger, Kenneth, 77/164

Mexican people, 80/62: Spanish-Mexican in early Calif., 71/285

Mexican War, 62/9-10; 66/280; 71/ 292,365; 73/360; 74/95; 75/327N, 329,329N

Mexicana (vessel), 79/398

Mexico: British comment 1845, 70/304; Calif. govt., 76/126,129,131; HBCO. cattle permit, 63/188,205; map 1840-42, 76/128; merchants' money sent to England, 70/305; relations with Russia, 76/126; relations with U.S., 76/122, 125,126-27,129,131; U.S. punitive exped. 1916, 77/167-68

Meyer, Alice, and Nancy Hutchins: *Portland in Your Pocket*, noted, 77/291

Meyer, Christian W., 73/258,260

Meyer, Evelyn Shively, 81/188N

Meyer, H.H., 65/195

Meyer, Wilhelm, 77/288

Meyers, Clem I., 67/377

Meyers, Elmer Leroy (Roy), 65/412,415: reprint of publications noted, 74/282

Meyers, Leonard W., 67/86

Meyers, Mary P. Foster (Mrs. E.L.), 65/412,415

Meyersville, SEE Myrtle Point, Ore.

Miami Cove, 77/220,222

Miami River, 72/296,299; 77/222

Miami River Valley, 77/368

Micelli, Mrs. Victor, 65/401,404

Michigan Mill Company, 67/171,174

Michilimackinac, SEE Mackinac

Michilimackinac Fur Co., 76/322

Microfilm: Hawaiian newspaper project, 67/372; Oregon State Archives, 70/76; Socialist Labor Party papers, 71/363

Mid-Columbia Vegetable Growers' Assn., 76/249

Middle Fork, Malheur River, 78/155, 211; 79/299: ford photos, 78/316,318

Middle Fork, Willamette River, 77/329; 78/54,55,57,65,238,297,307,308,309, 310,317; 79/29,42N,43,47: fords, 77/328; 78/59,65,311,313-15, 316(photo),317,319-23; photos, 78/ 313; source, 78/57; terrain, 77/328

Middleton, Henry: Russian-U.S. convention, 72/113,118,122,124; 76/210

Middleton (transport vessel), SEE *Arthur Middleton*

Midland, Ore., 78/363

Mid-Pacific Railroad, 64/86

Midstate Electric Cooperative Inc., 80/328

Midway Island, 62/11,23,29,35: World War II battle, 62/30
Midwives, 71/99,270,292; 73/84: recollections, 70/39-49*passim*
Migration: effects of, 81/101,103; first from west to east Ore., 67/309; Idaho, 69/85; Negroes westward, 67/85; prehistoric to North America, 72/287; U.S. 1800-1960, 72/178
Miguel, Frank, 80/157N,159N
Mikhailov Redoubt, 73/166: base for exploration, 73/131; description, 73/131-34; sketch, 73/132
Milarkey, Elizabeth, SEE Murphy, Elizabeth Milarkey
Milarkey, Elizabeth Ryan, 69/141
Milarkey, Thomas, 69/141
Milbank Sound, 63/234
Milbury, W.B., 76/41-43
Milbury Mountain, 76/43
Miles, Charles, 64/297N
Miles, Evan, 68/232N,305N; 70/22
Miles, Milton E., 62/36
Miles, Nelson A., 75/142
Miles Canyon, 76/110,111
Miles City, Mont., 74/334
Miley, William, 79/239,243
Milford, Mark Lane: family, 74/165-72; Milford-Corning house photo, 74/165
Milhau, John Jefferson, 69/172; 70/239: reports on Umpqua Indians, 70/247
Military escorts: survey parties, 72/10-11,15,36N; SEE ALSO Protective Corps
Military life, 69/85,223-68; 70/66,233-55
Military organizations: frontier activities, 77/197; Jacksonville volunteers 1859, 69/225; number Pacific NW volunteers 1855-56, 67/315N; Okanogan Valley militia, 67/368; Ore. volunteer call revoked 1854, 67/312; Portland volunteers 1856, 67/321; regular-volunteer disputes, 67/315,318-20,323N; Wasco Co. volunteers 1854, 67/311
Military posts:

bibliographic sources, 66/384; bill to establish at mouth of Columbia, 65/325N; checklist, 76/92; Mansfield reports on western, 65/201-203; Nevada early, 66/87; overland trail, 67/297-98; 72/55-56,67; Pacific NW, 67/217N,321,323N,324; sites recommended 1855-56, 67/317,321,323N, 324; Southwest, 66/82; U.S. 1789-1895, 66/187-88; western, 65/201-203; 67/359-60; Wyoming, 71/187-88; SEE ALSO names of forts and posts
Military Posts in the Powder River Country of Wyoming, 1865-1894, by Murray, review, 71/187-88
Military reservations: 1848 order, 67/303-305; Oregon settlers protest, 67/301,303N-304N; size reduced, 67/304; SEE ALSO Fort Dalles
Military roads, SEE Roads and trails
Mill City, Ore., 71/349,352; 73/173; 77/215,216; 80/270,280: history, 63/253
Mill Creek, Lake Co., 79/289N
Mill Creek, Marion Co., SEE North Mill Creek; South Mill Creek
Mill Creek, Walla Walla Co., 66/152N
Mill Creek, Wasco Co., 67/298: map, 67/308
Mill Town: A Social History of Everett, Washington, by Clark, cited, 73/281-82; review, 72/86
Millar, George P., 66/80
Millar, Justin, 77/337,337N
Miller, —, immigrant of 1853, 78/212,212N
Miller, A.H., 64/138,160-61
Miller, Alan Clark: *Photographer of a Frontier: The Photographs of Peter Britt,* review, 78/361-62
Miller, Alanson, 79/11
Miller, Alexis, 78/325N
Miller, Alfred Jacob, 65/136,138,139
Miller, Andrew, 62/218N
Miller, Axel, 66/103,106
Miller, Bess Tompkins, 76/178(photo): "We Drove the First Automobile

Around Cape Perpetua," 76/177-79 69/63

Miller, Charles W., 75/137

Miller, Cincinnatus Hiner (Joaquin), 65/6,68N,255N; 66/282; 67/236,373; 70/180; 74/37; 80/400: Lewis & Clark Exposition, 66/45-46; on passing of Old West, 66/89; photos, 80/ins.fr.cov. Winter; 81/44; Snake Indian skirmish, 65/14N,20

Miller, Cincinnatus Hiner (Joaquin): *Unwritten History: Life Among the Modocs*, reprint noted, 74/95

Miller, Clifford R.: *Baptists and the Oregon Frontier*, review, 69/324-25 *"The Religious Expositor:* Oregon Pioneer Journal," 64/123-36 *Shining Light, the Story of Moses Williams*, noted, 75/88

Miller, David Harry, ed.: *The Character and Influence of the Indian Trade in Wisconsin*, by Turner, review, 79/92-97

Miller, Donald C.: *Ghost Towns of Washington and Oregon*, noted, 79/105-106

Miller, Emily Giesy, photo, 79/ins.bk. cov. Fall

Miller, Estelle, 76/177: photo, 76/178

Miller, George, Aurora colony, photo, 79/ins.bk.cov. Fall

Miller, George, Garibaldi mill foreman, 77/345,357

Miller, George L., 67/263

Miller, George Masten, 66/81

Miller, George Melvin, 73/83

Miller, Hannah (Mrs. Axel), 66/103, 105,106

Miller, Mrs. Harold A., 65/414,417; 66/94,190,286,395; 67/376,377,379; 68/356,360; 69/342,348; 70/373, 374; 71/371; 72/359; 73/362; 74/184,366

Miller, Helen Markley, 64/349: *Thunder Rolling: The Story of Chief Joseph*, review, 62/102

Miller, Henry, cattleman, 63/274-75, 304,309-12,324,327; 66/87; 67/144;

Miller, Henry, Milwaukie orchardist, 68/165

Miller, Henry, *Oregonian* editor, 62/297

Miller, J.B., logger, 63/352

Miller, J.L., purser on *Republic*, 81/197N

Miller, James Andrew, photo, 79/ins.bk. cov. Fall

Miller, James D., 74/358

Miller, James N.T., 67/268

Miller, Joaquin, SEE Miller, Cincinnatus Hiner

Miller, John:

An Illustration of the Sexual System of Linnaeus, cited, 69/168

An Illustration of the Termini Botanici of Linnaeus, cited, 69/168

Miller, John F., 66/220N

Miller, John R., Wash. Terr. justice, 66/31

Miller, Lena Fastabend: "J.A. Fastabend and Pacific Northwest Log Rafts," 66/179-82

Miller, Lischen M.: *The Haunted Lighthouse*, reprint noted, 74/282

Miller, Loye: journal, 75/87

Miller, Marcus P., 68/237

Miller, May: *Golden Memories of the Paulina Area*, noted, 77/90

Miller, Maynard, 65/360

Miller, Milton Armington, photo, 78/117

Miller, Orlando W.: *Alaska and Its History*, ed. by Sherwood, review, 69/184

Miller, Riley, 63/44

Miller, Robert Aubrey, 80/396

Miller, Robert S., 68/360

Miller, S. Edward, 72/94

Miller, Sarah, Sacred Heart student, 81/81N

Miller, Sarah E. Raffety, 79/162N

Miller, Simon, family, 72/94

Miller, Wesley J., 76/177-78: photo, 76/178

Miller, William, British consul, 67/367

Miller, William P., 79/162N
Miller, William W., 63/109,228,230; 66/36
Miller, William Y., 78/234
Miller and Lux, cattlemen, 63/269-70,275,304-35*passim*
Millers Island, photo, 75/ins.fr.cov. June
Millican, Ada B., 70/272
Millican, George, 64/277; 67/88; 70/74
Millican, Robert, 64/277; 70/74; 79/39
Millican, Ore., 77/18
Millican Memories, by Southworth, noted, 79/336
Millicoma Garden Clubs State Park, 67/50
Millicoma Myrtle Grove State Park, 67/46
Millicoma River, 80/51: map, 80/57
Millie, Faye B., and Helen Pearce: *The 100th Anniversary, First Presbyterian Church, Salem*, noted, 72/173
Milligan, R.W., 76/292
Million, Elmer G.: "Frontier Legal Process: Parrish *vs.* Gray, 1846," 73/245-57
"The Millionaire and the Village: Jesse Winburn Comes to Ashland," by Franklyn D. Mahar, 64/323-41
Milliorn, Thomas A., 79/10
Mills, Abbot Low, 68/216; 74/208
Mills, Andrew J., 63/82
Mills, Finis E., 62/248-49
Mills, Hazel Emery (Mrs. Randall V.), 66/25N; 67/368: "The Emergence of Frances Fuller Victor—Historian," 62/309-36
Mercer's Belles, by Conant, review, 62/186-88
The Negro in the State of Washington, 1788-1967, noted, 69/273
Newspapers on Microfilm in the Libraries of the State of Washington, noted, 75/364
A Venture in History, by Clark, review, 75/79-80
Washington: A History of the Evergreen State, by Avery, review, 67/79-80
Mills, J.H., Montana banker, 62/177

Mills, Mrs. Lewis H., 62/421
Mills, Nellie G., 62/177
Mills, Nellie Ireton, 64/277; 66/88
Mills, Randall Vause, 62/309N
Mills, Tom, photo, 76/166
Mills, Walter Thomas, 68/201
Mills, SEE Flour and grist mills; Sawmills; Woolen mills
Milroy, Robert H., 70/116N,117
Milton, Columbia Co., Ore., 72/169
Milton Academy, Umatilla Co., 78/364
Milton-Freewater, Ore., 64/90,352: history, 63/365-66; 73/285
Milwain, Alexander H., 79/178N
Milwain, Elijah, 79/178N
The Milwaukee Road East: America's Resourceful Railroad, by Dorin, noted, 80/209
Milwaukie, Ore., 62/204; 68/200; 77/46: cemetery, 65/216; 69/86; history, 67/80; 72/169; Lewelling house photo, 68/202; markers, 63/245; plat 1852, 68/161; progressive movement center, 68/207-208; school history, 69/87; Swiss population, 68/219
Milwaukie Historical Society, 67/80
Milwaukie Milling Co., 68/160-62
Mimulus lewisii (Lewis's monkey flower), 69/161
Minear, Leon P., 62/110,206,302,422; 63/93,255,373; 64/93,189,285,363; 65/125,221,317,416; 66/93,189,285, 394; 68/360
Mineral City, Ida., 69/85
Mineral springs, SEE Springs
Minerals and mineral industry: cavansite, 69/87; geology, 72/180; Klamath Co., 71/286; Lake Co., 71/ 286; Oregon, 62/107; 63/362; 67/369; 68/89; slawsonite, 69/87; use in different societies, 68/347; SEE ALSO names of minerals
Miners, S.F., 70/235
Miners: brawls, 1860 sketch, 81/192; Chinese, 74/286; 78/78,81; Coeur d'Alene strike, 63/90; entertainment, 71/366; guidebook, 74/359; language, 70/78;

life of, 77/304; 81/190-93; Montana, 66/88; western frontier 1850s, 64/344-46

Miners' and Travelers' Guide to Oregon, Washington, Idaho, Montana, Wyoming and Colorado, by Mullan, noted, 74/359

Miners' Loon Creek Express, 68/89 Minersville, Ore., 62/236

Mines and mining:

Alaska, 69/327

Baker area, 70/280—

population increase 1880-90 due to, 67/156

blasting, 72/181; Bohemia district, 70/271-72,279; borax, SEE Borax British Columbia, 65/363,367;

69/79—

rail transportation to, 74/358 Calapooia Valley, 68/353; cinnabar, 81/312; Clackamas Co., 74/357 Coeur d'Alene, 65/214; 66/88;

70/180—

Portland investment in, 69/203; railroad from Portland to, 69/217-22 ditch lines, 69/201,330; early Oregon, 65/219; Grant Co., 70/59; guidebook, 74/359; history of western to 1893, 72/347-48

Idaho, 67/87—

rail transportation to, 71/41,49,50,55 Inland Empire, 71/196; Jefferson Co., 63/246,362; 72/340-41; lost Pacific NW mines, 64/357; Manitoba first, 72/182; Marble Mt., 69/88; mining town theaters, 71/366; Montana rail transportation, 71/55; Nevada, 67/ 364-65; Northern Calif. towns, 70/75; Oregon maps, 71/362; promotion of in West, 71/291; Scott River, Siskiyou Co., 72/171

stock exchanges, 69/197-222*passim*—

San Francisco, 70/365

tools and machinery, 77/304; Utah, 65/214; western 1850s, 64/344-45 western frontiers, 67/280; 71/191—

history, 73/360; in history writing, 65/213

Wood River, Ida. rush, 72/183; SEE

ALSO Coal and coal mining; Gold and gold mining; etc.

Mingus, Everett, 72/353

Mining camps, 79/105-106:

Auburn area, 62/226-27; California, 76/197; supply routes to, 79/46,47; trade, 67/87; Waldo area, 76/56; western 1850s, 64/344-46

Mining Frontiers of the West, 1848-1880, by Paul, noted, 71/191

Mink, 74/293

Minnesota Historical Society, 67/203: manuscript holdings, 79/339

Minnick's Ferry, 78/321

Minor, C.A., 69/117

Minority groups, 72/181

Minott, Mrs. Joseph A., 62/110,206,320, 422; 63/93,255,373; 64/93,189,285, 358-59,364; 65/126,222,318,415; 66/ 93,189,285,394; 68/360; 69/347; 70/370

Mint industry, 72/182

Minter, Charles M., 69/330

Minter, Harold Avery:

Umpqua Valley, Oregon, and Its Pioneers, noted, 68/343

Minthorn, Henry John, 78/112; 80/336

Minthorn, William, 81/341N,343

Minthorn House, Newberg, 69/177; 71/294; 80/336

Minthorn House, Boyhood Home of Herbert C. Hoover, by Olsen, noted, 80/336

Minto, Douglas, 81/274N

Minto, Jasper, 81/274N

Minto, John, 64/101,275; 66/331, 357N,362; 67/266; 72/341; 73/65: biography, 81/229-59*passim*—

cited, 81/327-28

character, 81/230,232-33,237-40,242-43,253-57; leadership roles, 81/253, 255,256; marriage, 81/244; opinion of pioneers' motives, 81/229-31,250-51; orchardist, 81/245,253; photos, 81/ 237,259; sheep raising, 81/245,253, 254,256; survey party 1874, 71/349; trail map of North Santiam, 71/357

Minto, John:

"Treaties with Indians: How and Why They were Made by the U.S. Commis-

sion," cited, 70/259N
Minto, Martha Ann Morrison (Mrs. John), 81/244,254,258(photo)
Minto, William, 72/16,16N,48N,53N
Minto Pass, 66/357N; 68/90; 71/349N; 77/298; 81/254
Mintonye, Edna H., comp.: *They Laughed, Too*, review, 69/183
Mints, SEE Money
Miranda (ship), 66/127
Mischief (steamer), 74/24
Mishler, Lyman, 65/357
Mission, John, 79/322,330,332
Mission Bottom, 74/71
Mission Mill, St. Paul, Ore., 77/298
Mission Party, 75/120
Missionaries, 62/106,192-93,250N,320; 66/340; 73/69,73; 79/101-102: Alaska, 69/327; California, 74/286; Catholic, SEE Catholic missionaries; Jesuits; French Prairie settlers' request for, 66/343-44; Hawaii, 72/180; 74/279; Pacific NW, 63/55-60,78,195-96; 65/119-20; 69/50-56,324-25,332; Polynesia, 63/358; Protestant, 62/76, 77; SEE ALSO Methodist missionaries; records in Canadian archives, 69/85; to Indians, 68/336-37; to Nez Perce, 70/68; 72/183; Willamette Valley, 62/119
Missionary Footpaths: The Story of Anna Maria Pittman, by Mattson, noted, 80/335
Missionary Herald, 68/56-57
Missions: Cataldo, 71/186 Protestant, 73/69— Eastern Ore., 79/408
Swan River district 1821-69, 65/314; SEE ALSO American Board missions; Catholic missions; Episcopal missions; Methodist missions
Mississippi Basin: history, 75/81
Missoula (lumber vessel), 77/363
Missoula County, Mont.: place names, 65/384
Missouri, 62/68; 63/43; 79/106-107: pioneers in Oregon, 63/364; 66/208
The Missouri Expedition, 1818-1820: The

Journal of Surgeon John Gale, ed. by Nichols, noted, 71/287
Missouri Fur Company, 62/341N
Missouri Historical Society, 67/368
Missouri Pacific Railroad, 71/7N
Missouri River, 62/337; 66/63,331; 71/292: expeditions 1818-25, 68/185; Greene journal, 66/70; route to Ft. Benton, 66/228 steamboating, 68/185— 1879 boat trip, 66/86; wrecks, 71/364
Mist, Ore., 65/308
Mitcham, Clarence E., 67/88
Mitchel (Mitchell), Israel, 64/151
Mitchell, Bruce, 74/350
Mitchell, Christine Funnemark (Mrs. John Neal): biography, 66/101N-31*passim*; characterized, 66/130-31; photo, 66/104; Seamen's Rest work, 66/101N,102,106
Mitchell, Edward H., 66/304
Mitchell, John, Morrow Co., 69/141
Mitchell, John Hipple, 75/129; 79/98; 80/306N: feud with Scott, 71/92; photo, 68/211; railroad promotion, 71/67-68; senate campaign 1897, 68/210-14
Mitchell, John Neal, 66/130
Mitchell, McKinley, 66/43
Mitchell, Patrick, 69/141
Mitchell, Rose O'Brien, 69/141
Mitchell, Ore., Wheeler Co., 73/258,263; 75/309: business, 73/267; floods, 73/261,267; incorporated, 73/259; name, 73/259; platted, 73/268
Mitchell Point, 72/94: highway tunnel photo, 66/263
Miwok Indians, 71/365; 72/183
Miyo, Rikichi, 76/228
Mizner, Edgar, 62/96
Mizner, Henry R., 70/34
Moar (Moore), Isabella Logie (Mrs. Jonathan), 63/225
Moar, Jonathan, 63/234
Mock's Bottom, 64/261
"Modern Museums and Modern Man," by Charles van Ravenswaay, 66/293-301

Modeste (British vessel), 63/154,181,182, 191,200,214,219-21,223; 64/203N-204N,212; 70/293N,295,299,300,307: lithograph, 70/295

Modjeski, Ralph, 74/211,212

Modoc County, Calif.: bibliography, 77/91; geography, 67/365; Indian massacre 1911, 63/365

Modoc County, A Geographic Time Continuum on the California Volcanic Tableland, by Pease, review, 67/365

Modoc County Historical Society: publications, 81/105,328

Modoc Indians, 62/198; 69/225; 72/16-17,39N; 73/283; 74/95: basket photo, 81/410; battle with Fremont, 66/284; clothing, 81/421; culture, 65/200-201; fear of Snake Indians, 69/252; food, 63/365; hostilities 1860, 69/229-30N,245,247-48,252; 70/251; houses, 81/407; land claim, 72/10; property customs, 81/394,395-96,411,421; slavery, 81/413,414,417; Southern Immigrant route 1846, 77/318; SEE ALSO Modoc War

Modoc National Forest: prehistoric rock art, 81/329

Modoc War, 62/322,323; 63/81,90; 65/200-201; 66/76; 67/89; 69/230; 70/75; 72/172; 73/74; 80/117-18, 122-23,336: Gilliam's camp, 70/176 Indian scouts, 79/120(photo)— tour East, 79/306,307 number of soldiers, 70/175; officers, 70/176; peace commission, 81/245; records, 70/271

The Modoc War, 1872-73: Lava Beds National Monument, by Thompson, review, 70/175-77

Modoc War, Its Military History and Topography, by Thompson, reprint noted, 73/74

Moe, Ella Blanchar, 63/371; 64/359

Moffett, George H., 71/147

Moffett, Walter: biography, 80/315N

Mohawk River: covered railroad bridge, 66/187

Moir, Mrs. Stuart, 62/421

Mokst Butte, 68/354

Molalla, Ore., 62/201; 65/218

Molalla Area Historical Society, 73/80

Molalla Charley, 79/283,320

Molalla Indians, 70/260; 78/55: Cayuse encounters, 73/63-65; clothing, 73/63,65; hunting territory, 73/63; language, 73/63; territory dispute, 81/297-98

Molex (Indian), 74/13

Molinari, Tom, photo, 77/252

Moller, S.J., 69/269N

Moller Barber College, Portland, 80/196

Molleta, Francesco, photo, 77/252

Mollohan family, Morrow Co., 69/141

Molly Maguires, 75/133

Moloy, Mary, 78/224

Molthrop, Elizabeth, SEE Stark, Elizabeth Molthrop

Monadnock (steamship), photo, 62/4

Monaghan, James, 74/359

Monagle, Catherine Doherty, 69/141

Monagle, Charles, 69/141

Monahan, Martin, 62/230

Monahan families, Morrow Co., 69/141

Money, 62/69: barter economy, 62/143; Beaver coins, 63/364; 79/408; Free Silver issue, 75/138; gold coinage in West 1848-61, 63/84; HBCO. money in Pacific NW, 63/181-82; money orders, 80/180; Ore. Terr., 62/109; scarcity in Ore., 63/181-82,184,215,219; 78/65; wheat as legal tender, 63/181-82,217; SEE ALSO Legal tender

Mongrain, David, 66/361

Monk, Maria, 75/111-12

Monker, B.F., 62/219N

Monmouth, Ore., 64/342: map 1882, 72/171; mayors, 72/89; street names, 80/105

Monmouth University, Monmouth, 66/15,23

Monnastes, Henry W., 69/211,213

Monner, Alfred A., 69/331

Monroe, Harriet, 73/294,295,296,305, 314; 74/247:

The New Poetry, cited, 73/316
Monroe, James, 70/342; 72/101,115, 116,117,118,123,125: correspondence, 72/114; on Columbia River occupation, 70/340-41; recommends Pacific squadron, 70/341N,343
Monroe, Victor, 64/302N; 66/31,32
Monroe Doctrine, 76/213: Adams' part in, 72/103,106,118-20; British reaction, 72/121-23,126; influence of Russian ukase, 72/101-103,109, 126; interpretations, 72/101-103,120-21,126; non-colonization principle, 72/ 105-106,107N,118-20; primary aim, 72/121-23,125-26; protection of U.S. commercial interests, 72/114-17,120; Russian views, 72/121,123,126
Montag, Ralph T., 62/179
Montague, Helen Ruth, 67/92
Montague, Richard Ward: Hunt case attorney, 71/223,224; Library Assn. board member, 71/222-26,238; on tolerance, 71/238-39,243
Montague, Calif., 63/365; 66/81-82
Montana: banking, 65/367; 72/228; bibliography, 63/91; 68/349; birds, 71/366; books and pamphlets 1965, 67/368-69; boundary survey 1885, 72/19; business outlook 1968, 69/337; constitution, 72/228; Coxey's army, 67/86; emigrant escorts, 72/71-72; ethnic groups, 75/93; forts, 65/365; free silver issue, 72/230,234 gold— discoveries, 71/251; in Civil War, 63/360; mines, 69/336 historical articles, 68/346; 70/87; homesteading, 65/215,364; 69/336; Indians, 71/325-48; industries, 64/ 349; Jewish people, 72/182; Lewis & Clark Exped. in, 71/366; liquor control, 72/172-73; mineral lands, 67/86 mining, 72/58— camp trade, 67/87; centennial, 66/88; railroad effect on, 71/75 place names, 71/366; population dynamics, 72/246; recollections, 71/191; territorial officers, 62/297;

theses on, 72/225-79; timber depredations, 70/178; Utah & Northern Railway service, 71/55
Montana Adventure: The Recollections of Frank Linderman, ed. by Merriman, noted, 71/191
Montana Council of Defense, 72/229
Montana Improvement Co., 67/167
The Montana Past, an Anthology, ed. by Malone and Roeder, noted, 71/287
Montavilla, Ore., 77/256
Montecarlo, Italo, photo, 77/238
Monteith, John B., 78/91
Monteith, Thomas, 67/62
Monteith, Walter, 78/44
Montenegrin people, 69/298
Monterey, Calif., 62/9: Anglo-American collaboration 1847, 64/283; seizure by Jones, 63/358
Monterey (monitor), 76/274: photo, 62/16
Montesano, Wash., 74/15,16
Montero, Antonio, 63/344
Montgomerie (Montgomery), John E., 63/154
Montgomery, Jack, 70/279
Montgomery, Richard G.: *James Douglas: Servant of Two Empires*, by Pethick, review, 71/281-82 *Victoria: The Fort*, by Pethick, review, 72/87-88
Montgomeryshire (ship), 66/122
Monticello, Wash., 62/72; 63/198,205, 238; 78/90: convention, 63/108; postmasters, 80/335
Monticello & Cowlitz Landing Steamboat Company, 63/108N
Montour, Isabelle, SEE McKay, Isabelle Montour
Montour, Marie Anne Ompherville (Mrs. Nicholas), 66/348N
Montour, Nicholas, 63/204,214; 66/341,348N,353N
Montpelier, Ida., 72/183
Monument, Ore.: electric co-op, 80/328
Monumental Mine, 76/53
Monuments and markers:

Abernethy, Ore. City, 66/382; Applegate, Lindsay, 67/90
Astoria, 75/294—
first generating station, 69/88
Barlow Road, 63/245; Carroll, Stephen, grave, 73/258,266; Crystal School, Klamath Co., 73/81; Ft. Leland, 70/184; Ft. Umpqua, 68/342; Ft. Vancouver, 71/293,294; Glenco smithy, 70/184; Hoover, Herbert, 68/89; houses marked, 69/86,339; Idaho, 64/277; Islay, Scotland disaster, 77/287-88; Japanese shelling site ww ii, 71/199; Lancaster, S.C., 74/144; McKay grave, 69/338; Marion Co., 63/83; Masonic temple, Southern Ore., 70/184; Milwaukie, 63/245; Ore. Central Military Road, 78/308; Oregon City, 63/245; Ore. guidebook, 67/281 Oregon Trail, 74/137—
Big Marsh Creek crossing, photo, 79/28; Emigrant Springs, 67/243; Meacham, photo, 78/102; wagon route 1853, 78/308
Ostrander, Abel, grave, 67/366; Pacific Railway Survey camp site 1855, 78/296 (photo),297; Powers, Grace Wright, 68/89; Tipton, Mace, 68/89; Union Point townsite, 70/184; Waldo, 70/184; Washington, 64/188; 68/343; West Linn, 63/245; Whitman Mission, 71/293
Monuments in Cedar: The Authentic Story of the Totem Pole, by Keithahn, review, 65/210-11
Moods of the Columbia, by Satterfield, noted, 69/331-32
Moody, Audrey:
Oregon Regional Union List of Serials, ed. by Abrams, review, 77/382
Moody, Bill, 77/64-65
Moody, G.W., 62/219N
Moody, Luella, 74/30
Moody, Malcolm A., 76/106,116; 81/274:
bridge, 69/305; photo of material yard, 69/304
Mooney, E. Ray, 64/91; 65/211; 66/80

Mooney, James, 63/72; 72/148,153: "The Tribes of the Columbia Region," noted, 71/279
Mooney, Thomas J., 72/346-47
Moontrap, by Berry, review, 65/406-11
Moore, Adelia Herren, 80/243,245,249
Moore, Albert (Indian), 65/217
Moore, Arline Winchell, 62/103,414
Moore, Augustus C.H., family, 72/171
Moore, Caleb John, 74/281
Moore, Cecil:
recollections, 73/84
Moore, Charles, Grant Co. rancher, 79/269N
Moore, Charley, Grass Valley merchant, 75/45,48
Moore, Eathel Abbey, 66/349N
Moore, George, 68/348
Moore, Henry, 79/31
Moore, Isabella, see Moar, Isabella Logie
Moore, James, immigrant of 1853, 78/128
Moore, John, Idaho sawmill owner, 71/23N
Moore, John H., immigrant of 1853, 78/128
Moore, Jonathan, Sauvie Island settler, see Moar, Jonathan
Moore, Jonathan Limerick, 69/77
Moore, Richard M., 64/277
Moore, Robert, 66/350; 81/105
Moore, S.A.M., 68/141:
letters to, 68/147-52
Moore, Thomas, Camp Warner packmaster, 79/163,165
Moore, Walter E., 69/141
Moore, Willetta:
Oregon Pioneers of 1852 and 1853: The Snodgrass, Deckard and Moore Families, noted, 73/73
Moore brothers, Curry Co., 73/230
Moores, Chester A., 74/238
Moores, Isaac R., 64/180
Moore's Crossing, 79/269N
Moore's Valley, 75/87
Moorhouse, Thomas Leander (Lee), 68/354; 73/278,364:
biography, 66/319; 80/335; Pen-

dleton Round-Up photos, 68/88; photo, 66/321

Moorhouse and Livermore, Pendleton photographers, 66/319

Mora, Francis, 70/329

Moran, Eugene ("Dano"), 69/141

Moran, Patrick, 80/349,352; 81/91

Moran, Thomas, 64/381; 67/86; 70/367

Morekhod (schooner), 73/130-31

Moreland, Julius C., 69/213

Moresby, John, 70/310

Morey, Donald J.:

Population Trends in the Pacific Northwest by Power Supply Area, 1950-1960, noted, 78/341

Morgan, A.H., 65/239-41

Morgan, Agness, 66/54

Morgan, Aubrey Niel, 72/361: *Conflict and Concord*, by Allen, review, 62/407-409

Morgan, Dale L., 62/105,291; 63/344; 64/186,348; 65/198; 66/380; 67/367: death, 72/180

Morgan, Dale L.:

In Pursuit of the Golden Dream, by Gardiner, review, 71/359-60

Wilderness Kingdom, trans. by Donnelly, review, 69/63-65

Morgan, Dale L., and George P. Hammond:

Captain Charles M. Weber: Pioneer of the San Joaquin and Founder of Stockton, review, 68/339-40

Morgan, Dale L., ed.:

A Guide to the Manuscript Collections of the Bancroft Library, Vol. I: Pacific and Western Manuscripts (except California), review, 65/198

Overland in 1846: Diaries and Letters of the California-Oregon Trail, review, 65/405-406

The West of William E. Ashley, review, 66/63-65

Morgan, Elizabeth Darneille, 78/125

Morgan, Esther Skarstedt, 66/382

Morgan, George T., 73/276

Morgan, George Thomas, Jr., 64/86:

Farms in the Cutover: Agricultural Settlement in Northern Wisconsin, by Helgeson, review, 64/79-81

Soldiers and Spruce: Origins of the Loyal Legion of Loggers and Lumbermen, by Hyman, review, 65/197-98

Morgan, Gertrude, 66/54

Morgan, Harry, 73/173,179,182,223; 77/227,354: biography, 73/224; 77/215-16

Morgan, Henry, 78/305

Morgan, Howard, 68/358

Morgan, Ida, 66/54

Morgan, Jane:

Electronics in the West: The First Fifty Years, review, 70/267-68

Morgan, Jock, 70/165

Morgan, John, 78/124

Morgan, Jonathan, 78/305; 79/10

Morgan, Lewis H., 70/265

Morgan, Lucia, 66/54

Morgan, Murray:

Eminent Domain, by Keats, review, 75/81

One Man's Gold Rush, A Klondike Album, review, 69/175-76

Morgan, Paul, 77/354

Morgan, William, Coos Co. pioneer, 66/54

Morgan, William H., 79/9,10

Morgan, William J., *et al*, eds.:

Autobiography of Rear Admiral Wilkes, U.S. Navy, 1798-1877, review, 79/404-406

Moris, Joe, 69/79

Morison, Samuel Eliot, 63/354; 68/102; 73/366; 76/197; 77/290: "American Strategy in the Pacific Ocean," 62/5-56

The European Discovery of America: The Northern Voyages, A.D. 500-1600, review, 72/343-44

The Mormon Conflict, 1850-1859, by Furniss, review, 62/185-86

Mormon ferries, Wyo., 80/74,79

Mormon Station, SEE Genoa, Nev.

Mormon Trail, 72/66-67

Mormon War, SEE Utah War

Mormons, 67/219-27*passim*; 68/345-

46; **69**/84,230; 70/86; **72**/183,255; **73**/74; **81**/201: and Turner thesis, **68**/86; battalion 1847, **71**/250,251,256,259; bibliography, **69**/84; Canada, **69**/337; conflicts 1850-59, **62**/185-86; SEE ALSO Utah War; denounced by immigrants, **72**/75-76; hand cart train, **67**/220; in fiction, **69**/336; in Idaho constitution, **69**/85; Indian relations, **71**/368; Indian view of church, **72**/155; interactions with other immigrants, **81**/99; Pacific Northwest, **62**/197; Pony Express rider, **67**/231N; railroad interests, **71**/55; **73**/66; Salmon River mission, **68**/346; textile arts, **65**/383; view of Lincoln, **64**/281

Morning Democrat, Baker, **66**/309

Morning Star (French bark), SEE *l'Etoile du Matin*

Morning Star (Ore.-built vessel): history of original and 1959 replica, **71**/289

Morrell, James F., photo, **69**/294

Morrell, James F., and Giles French: "Bubble Skinner," **69**/293-305

Morrill, Leslie, and Madge Haines: *Lewis and Clark: Explorers to the West*, review, **62**/102

Morrill, Lot Myrick, **73**/35

Morrill, Ozro (Klytes) (Indian), **64**/43

Morrill Act, **63**/358; **64**/281

Morris, —, Lane Co. 1853, **78**/234

Morris, Alberta Knowles, **74**/271,273-74

Morris, Dorothy L., **75**/370

Morris, Elijah, **63**/19

Morris, Mary (Mrs. Robert), **62**/201

Morris, Robert, Redmond stage stop proprietor, **62**/201

Morris, Thomas D.: *Racism in the United States*, by Reimers, review, **73**/280-81

Morris, William, architect, **81**/84N

Morris, William Alfred, **62**/325-26

Morrisey, Dan ("Peg"), **81**/311-12

Morrison, Archie ("Doc"), **73**/183,184, 219,221,222

Morrison, Dorothy Nafus: *The Eagle and the Fort: The Story of John* *McLoughlin*, review, **80**/331-32

Ladies Were Not Expected: Abigail Scott Duniway and Women's Rights, review, **80**/331

Morrison, Dorothy Nafus, and Jean Morrison:

"John McLoughlin, Reluctant Fur Trader," **81**/377-89

Morrison, Edna, **78**/163

Morrison, Jean, SEE Morrison, Dorothy Nafus

Morrison, Jessie, **76**/374

Morrison, John L., **64**/204; **73**/254

Morrison, Robert Wilson, **81**/242, 243,256

Morrison, Sarah, **78**/161,163: photo, **78**/164

Morrison, William, Whitney Co. employee, **73**/171,175,176,177,221: biography, **73**/8

Morrison (bark), **76**/227

Morrow, Honore Willsie, **64**/350

Morrow County, Ore., **66**/365; **70**/280; **75**/270-76,360; **79**/104: Irish in, **69**/101-47— family names, **69**/117-47 sheep, **69**/105-47*passim*

Morrow County Historical Society: officers and directors, **76**/95; **77**/95; **78**/95; **79**/111; **81**/111

Morrow County Museum, **69**/177; **71**/200

Morrow-Sutherland House, **64**/353

Morse, Roger, photo, **63**/8

Morse, Sidney Edwards, **75**/111

Morse, Wayne Lyman, **72**/253

Morssette, Pat, **74**/63

Mortensen, A.R.: *The Mormon Conflict*, by Furniss, review, **62**/185-86

Morton (Mortzyng), —, showman, **70**/17

Morton, Arthur Silver, **72**/182: *Sir George Simpson*, cited, **74**/352

Morton, Cal, **70**/25

Morton, Oliver H.P.T., **67**/270

Morton, S.C., **74**/113

Mosby, David, **73**/83

Mosby, Isabell, **73**/83

Mosby Creek:
Stewart Bridge, 66/187
Moscow, Ida., 71/5-6,20,23,24
Mose, Eva Charlie:
recollections, 66/81
Moseley, Henry N.:
Oregon: Its Resources, Climate, People and Productions, cited, 71/79N
Moses (Indian), 66/89; 67/185-86; 70/125; 81/330:
account of becoming chief, 70/169-70; characterized, 70/162N; imprisoned, 70/131,137,150; medal photo, 70/fr. cov. June; obtains reservation, 70/137, 169; photo, 70/156; Priest Rapids council, 70/139N; refusal to go on Yakima Reservation, 70/127; relations with Wilbur, 70/128,148-63; relations with Yakima settlers, 70/129-37*passim*, 155-63*passim*; requests reservation, 70/128; Simcoe meeting 1879, 70/148-62; Washington D.C. visit, 70/134-35,169
Moses, Bernard ("Bert"), newspaper columnist, 64/328,331,332,335,338
Moses, Charley (Indian), 67/348
Moses, Henry (Indian), 68/351
Moses, Simpson P., 63/194,195N; 64/35
Mosquitoes, 79/372,373,380,381, 382,384
Moss, Sidney Walter, 62/193; 66/219N; 73/257
Mossman and Co. Express, 79/192
Motanic, Parsons (Indian), 78/364
Moteki, Mr. —, Portland Assembly Center, 81/160
Motion pictures:
armed forces, 80/33,45,48; "Covered Wagon," 63/9; early Springfield, 65/212; gold rush in Calif., 65/172N; "The Great Train Robbery," 78/362; "It Can Be Done," 80/326,328(photo); "Oregon Coast Highway," 74/232; "Singing Waters," 74/232
Westerns, 72/180—
history, 78/362
SEE ALSO Panoramas
Motorcycles, 76/355
Mott, James W., 64/59

Mott, William, SEE Mouatt, William A.
Motte, C., 64/19:
Kamehameha II portrait photo, 64/13
Mouatt, William A., 63/156N,165; 64/242-44
Moulton, W.P., 68/252
Moulton War, 72/183
Mount, Guy, 76/303
Mount Adams, 74/85,202; 79/203
Mount Angel, Ore., 72/91
Mount Angel Abbey, 72/91:
archives, 70/313N; cornerstone laid, 70/332; founding, 70/312-32; name, 70/332; photos, 70/328,331
Mount Angel College:
history, 73/82
Mount Ashland, 64/325
Mount Baker, 81/332:
1902 ascent, 74/202-203
Mount Baker: A Chronicle of Its Historical Eruptions and First Ascent, by Majors, noted, 81/332
Mount Baldy, 73/351,357:
ascent, 79/186-87,198
Mount Bidwell:
map, 72/27
Mount Crawford, Wash., 77/90,299
Mount Currie, 66/88
Mount Edgecumbe, 72/139
Mount Hood, 62/217,261; 63/191,234, 363; 65/159; 67/5-6,11; 70/50,52; 72/124,141; 76/101,260,266; 77/87-88,317; 78/179:
ascents, 74/61,88,202,230,286; 75/100—
first group, 64/315; photo, 74/243
Cooper's Spur, 70/55; crater, 77/65; geologic history, 66/89; glaciers, 73/81; 77/61-66*passim*,64(photo); guide's adventures, 74/89; last eruption, 69/87; name, 63/234; photos, 70/52; 74/243,252,ins.bk.cov. June; 75/100,fr.cov. March; 77/62; 79/344; trip to, 1893, 79/203-10; SEE ALSO Mountaineering
Mount Hood Genealogical Forum:
publications, 73/82; 75/87
Mount Hood, Portrait of a Magnificent Mountain, by Love and Love, review, 77/87-88

Mount Hood Railroad, 70/50
Mount Jefferson, 67/6,11; 70/74,260, 261; 74/202; 75/40-41; 76/382; 77/330
Mount Jefferson Wilderness Area, 73/275
Mt. June Flume Company, 78/363
Mount Lassen: eruption, 72/41N; 77/165-67
Mount McLoughlin, 74/202; 75/235
Mount Mazama, 63/362; 65/315; 67/36; 70/183; 72/90
Mount Newberry, 62/198; 63/364; 70/183; 72/90
Mount Olympus: ascent 1891, 74/22
Mount Pitt, SEE Mount McLoughlin
Mount Rainier, 63/158,234,368; 73/341,345; 74/112,202: eruptions, 64/87,357; name, 63/234; photo, 73/344
Mount Rainier National Park, 65/365; 72/231; 73/106-107,135: history, 68/88; roads, 74/112,139,209
Mount Saint Elias, 66/69; 72/143; 73/117: sketch, 72/fr.cov. June
Mount St. Helens, 63/158; 64/185; 69/337: apes, 66/92; ascent 1853, 71/197; eruptions, 81/333
Mount Scott, 70/216; 73/63
Mount Shasta, 63/350; 66/81; 72/41N,161; 74/202; 80/235: lemurians, 66/87; map, 69/265; Muir visit, 72/173; photo, 80/234
Mount Snelling, SEE Mary's Peak
Mount Stuart (ship), 66/123
Mount Tabor, 74/165; 75/129
Mount Thielsen, 66/92; 77/330,330N
Mount Washington, 76/382: ice age effects, 66/282; photo, 74/51
Mountain, Thomas J., photos, 81/ 254,258
Mountain fever, 65/231
Mountain goats, SEE Goats
Mountain House, Mt. Hood, 62/217,218
Mountain House, Wheeler Co., 65/95,102,103N-104N,106,108-

10,113; 79/170N,185,185N,198
Mountain Man, by Bright, comment on, 74/59
"A Mountain Meadow," by Donald J. Sterling, Jr., 75/39-42
Mountain men, 66/185-86; 69/274-75; 71/365; 79/105: diaries and letters, 66/63-64; diet, 65/214
The Men and the Fur Trade of the Far West, ed. by Hafen, Vol. I review, 66/185-86; Vols. II and III noted, 69/274-75
"Mountain of the Spirit," by Eric W. Allen, Jr., 75/49-53
Mountain Springs, Crook Co., 65/22,23,50N
Mountain States Power Co., 78/354
Mountaineer, The Dalles, 64/162,170, 173,175; 65/29N,35N: editorial criticism First Ore. Cavalry exped., 65/77-78N,80N
Mountaineering, 70/181; 71/197,198; 74/22,202-203,213-14; 75/39-42; 76/382; 79/206-207: accidents, 77/65-66; gear, 77/65; Mt. Baker, 81/332; Mt. Hood, 77/63-66; pack trips, 75/362; rescue teams, 77/66,382; Smith Rock, 64/284,357
Mounted Rifle Regiment, 66/382; 72/58; 74/93,281: chaplain, 65/308; civilian employees, 67/303N; conveys Whitman murderers, 67/297; desertions, 67/298; history, 67/366; leaves Oregon, 67/298; overland journey, 73/71; overland posts established, 67/297,298; sketches, 67/292
Mourelle, Francisco Antonio, 74/353
Movies, SEE Motion pictures
Mowee (Mowie), Cowlitz Farm employee, 63/143,148,150,156,165
Mowry, Sylvester, 65/213; 66/86; 67/295N,301: biography, 72/13N; Calif. boundary survey, 72/13
Moxley, J.Q., 71/21
Moxley, John, 71/23
Moxley, Susan, 71/23

Moxley, Thomas C., 71/5,23
Moxley, Tom, son of Thomas C., 71/20,23
Moyer, E.D., 67/66,67
Moyer, J.M., and Co., 67/66,67-69
Moyer, John M., 67/65,66,67: house, 64/88; 66/91
Muck, A.A., 71/233
Muck, Lee, 64/59-60
Muck Farm, 63/118N
Muckle, James, family, 64/91
Muckle Brothers lumber mill, 67/175
Mud Bay Louis (Indian), SEE Yowaluch, Louis
Mud Creek, Siskiyou Co., 66/81
Mud Hen (steamer), 75/82
Mud Lake, Harney Co., 65/67; 79/278
Mud Springs Canyon, 69/135
Muddy Company, sheepmen, 81/303, 307,309: map, 81/282
Muddy Creek, Jefferson Co., 81/306; SEE ALSO Little Muddy Creek
Muhlenberg, Henry, 69/27
Muir, Andrew Forest, 63/89
Muir, John, 65/214; 74/102,103; 80/408: *Sheep Trails,* reprint noted, 72/173
Muir, Newton, 71/372
Muir, Thomas, 63/362
Muir and McDonald, Dallas tannery, 64/354; 81/328
Mule Creek, Harney Co., 79/298N
Mules, 66/230; 67/221,222,225,227; 68/19,30,226,231N,234,235; 69/250; 70/73,75,147,249; 71/291; 76/102N; 77/8,11; 81/22,193,199: borax freight teams, 73/237,239— photo, 73/fr.cov. Sept. branding, 79/284 drives, 75/237— Calif.-Ore. 1860, 69/231-32 preferred to horses on Ore. Trail, 66/228; races, 79/283; scarcity during Civil War, 72/63; used as mounts, 79/273; SEE ALSO Pack trains
Mulholland, —, Lane Co. 1853, 78/325N
Mulholland, Edward, 79/9,10

Mulkey, George, 73/345
Mulkey, Philip Henry, 81/274,277,278: arrest as secessionist, 67/55-60*passim*
Mulkey, Wesley, 80/15
Mullally, Patrick, 69/141
Mullan, John, 65/121; 67/310; 79/130: biography, 69/79; Ft. Henrietta ruins noted, 66/160; military map 1858, 66/insert June
Mullan, John: *Miners' and Travelers' Guide to Oregon, Washington, Idaho, Montana, Wyoming and Colorado,* reprint noted, 74/359
Mullan, Rebecca W., 69/79
Mullan, Ida., 69/217
Mullan Road, 63/360; 66/228N; 68/294,351: centennial, 64/352
The Mullan Road, comp. and pub. by Payette, noted, 69/79
Mullarkey, Jim, 75/309
Mullen, Addie, SEE Presley, Addie Mullen
Mullen, Joe, 63/293
Mullen, Lee, 63/290
Mullen and Co., Auburn miners, 62/236
Muller, Dr. —, Portland 1873, 81/90
Muller, Curt, 62/94
Muller *vs.* Oregon, 62/94
Mulligan, Charnel, 79/21: land claim, 79/7N,21N
Mulligan, Harry, 69/115
Mulligan, Jack, 69/143
Mulligan, Martha Jane (Mrs. Charnel), 79/21
Mulligan family, Morrow Co., 69/142-43
Mullins, Lynn: railroad bibliography noted, 70/351
Mulroney, Belinda, 62/96
Multnomah, Ore.: history, 72/169; 77/299-300
Multnomah (steamer, launched 1850), 64/295
Multnomah (steamer, launched 1885), 66/117
Multnomah (steamer, launched 1912), 74/358
Multnomah County, Ore., 67/89; 69/

346; 75/168,174; 78/75,77,80,81: annexation question, 74/207-208; bond issue 1913, 74/211; census records 1870, 75/87; Chinese, 78/175-85 commission, 70/369,371; 71/233,294; 74/109-11; 81/204— Bybee-Howell house purchase, 63/368,370; role in Columbia River Hwy. project, 66/249,259,261 courthouse 1867 photo, 80/ins.bk.cov. Summer; created, 80/22; early history, 68/90; election 1872, 80/297; financial condition 1869, 64/177; first sheriff, 80/22; highway engineer, 66/270 hospital, 78/177— influenza cases 1918, 64/249 marriage records, 74/286; roads, 74/109-10; SEE ALSO Columbia River Highway; rural population, 76/239; supreme court election 1914, 66/365-72*passim*; vote for Hayes, 67/257

Multnomah County Bar Assn., 74/237

Multnomah County Library Assn., 77/382: building photo, 71/224; SEE ALSO Library Assn. of Portland

Multnomah County Medical Society: publications, 79/408

Multnomah Engine Co. No. 2, Portland, 64/159

Multnomah Falls, 66/265; 74/115, 123,132,138; 79/203: photos, 66/260; 74/122

Multnomah Hotel, Portland, 75/154,159; 78/109

Multnomah Rod and Gun Club, 65/248-49

Multnomah School District No. 1: Committee on Race and Education report, 1964, 66/80

Mumford, John D., 71/278

Mumford, William P., 71/278

Muncaster, Roy, 77/285-88

Muncaster Mountain, 77/285N

Munday, Perry, 68/239N

Munday, William, 68/243N,245,311

Munday's Ferry, Snake River, 68/239, 248,308

Munger, Thornton Taft, 62/108,199;

64/284; 67/51: *History of the Oregon Parks, 1917-1963*, by Armstrong, review, 67/184-85 "Oregon's Rarest and Most Distinctive Forest Type," cited, 67/44 "Trees in Hazard: Oregon's Myrtle Groves," 67/41-53

Munnick, Harriet Duncan, 62/107,109; 63/83; 66/81,341N,349N,358N,382

Munnick, Harriet Duncan, and Mikell Dolores Warner, comps.: *Catholic Church Records of the Pacific Northwest: St. Paul, Oregon, 1839-1898, Vols. I, II and III*, review, 81/202-203 *Catholic Church Records of the Pacific Northwest: Vancouver, Vols. I and II, and Stellamaris Mission*, noted, 77/291

Munro, Henry, 81/384,385

Munro, Sarah Baker: "Basque Folklore in Southeastern Oregon," 76/153-74

Munson, Mrs. —, Astoria 1895, photo, 81/194

Munson, Lyman B.: OMV service, 66/142N,144,146

Muraviev, Matvei Ivanovich, 72/112; 73/167; 77/181

Murbarger, Nell, 66/82

"The Murder of Cyrenius C. Hooker," by Thomas Branigar, 75/345-59

The Murder of Til Taylor...A Great Western Sheriff, by Crockatt, review, 72/352

Murderers Creek, 68/303N; 70/23

Murders, 62/65-66,197; 67/91; 76/77,82,83; 77/192; 78/174; 80/12,13N; 81/303: Alaska, 65/365; French, 75/66-68; Hooker, 75/345-59; Kennefick, 75/46; Linn Co., 79/104; McGuire, 79/196; Magruder party, 79/188N; manslaughter, 77/17-18,159; Taylor, 69/138

Murphey, Edith Van Allen, 62/301

Murphy, —, capt. of *Henry Villard*, 66/112N

Murphy, Bessie, 77/91

Murphy, D.R., 71/151

Murphy, Daniel, 69/143

Murphy, Edward, 69/143

Murphy, Elizabeth Milarkey (Mrs.

Joseph P.), 69/141,143
Murphy, John, Portland physician 1880s, 75/14,18
Murphy, Joseph, 69/143
Murphy, Leivy A.: letter to G.H. Himes, 64/342
Murphy, Martin, Jr., 75/365
Murphy, Susan D. (Mrs. Daniel H.), 80/359N
Murphy, W.H., 69/143
Murphy, W.J. (Bill), saw filer, 77/226-27
Murray, Alexander Hunter, 69/85
Murray, Andrew, 68/114,118,119, 120,122,123
Murray, Anne Campbell, 69/85
Murray, Charles E., 79/172-202*passim*
Murray, Keith A., 62/202; 67/87: bibliography of publications, 79/408
Murray, Keith A.: *'I Will Fight No More Forever': Chief Joseph and the Nez Perce War*, by Beal, review, 64/273-74 *The Pig War*, review, 69/326
Murray, Robert A.: *Military Posts in the Powder River Country of Wyoming, 1865-1894*, review, 71/187-88
Murray, W., San Francisco 1854, 68/114-15
Murtha, James, family, 69/143
Murtha, Kathleen Cantwell, 69/143
Murths, James, 69/141
Museums, 71/294: Alaska, 64/347; current growth, 66/297; Dunsmuir, Calif., 66/81; ethnological collections in U.S. and Canada, 68/184; First Nat'l Bank, Portland, 74/362; Flavel House, Astoria, 68/89; Ft. Crook, 67/80; Ft. Jones, 69/175; fur trade, 67/85; Garibaldi, 77/367; Georgia-Pacific logging, Portland, 74/362; Goldendale, Wash., 67/373; historical, 66/298; Jacksonville, 70/83; Kerbyville, 63/246; 69/176; Lane Co. clerk's office, 67/181; Lee Mission mill proposed, 66/90; Lewis and Clark Exposition, 80/56; Malheur Co. proposed, 67/213-14N; Oregon, 69/174-78; 71/189; 78/365; Owyhee Co., 70/273; pioneer museum study, 66/383; Portland City Hall, 80/59-60; Skamania Co., 73/283; tax status, 66/298; Tillamook Co., 69/177; training program, 66/297-98; Umatilla-Morrow Co., 71/200; Washington, 64/188; 72/171; Yaquina Bay Lighthouse, 70/75; SEE ALSO American Assn. of Museums; Aurora Ox Barn Museum; Boston Athenaeum; Cascade Locks Historical Museum; Champoeg State Park; Collier State Park Logging Museum; Columbia Co. Historical Museum; Columbia River Maritime Museum; Cowlitz Co. Historical Museum; Deschutes Co. Museum; DeWitt Museum; Douglas Co. Pioneer Museum; Glenwood Trolley Park; Grant Co. Historical Soc. Museum; Harney Co. Historical Society Museum; Horner Museum; Hood River Co. Historical Soc. Museum; Josephine Co. Historical Soc. Museum; Klickitat Co. Historical Museum; Lane Co. Pioneer Museum; Lincoln Co. Historical Soc. Museum; Linn Co. Historical Soc. Museum; Maryhill Museum of Fine Art; Morrow Co. Museum; National Museums Act; Newell House Museum; Old Sturbridge Village; Oregon Historical Society—museum; Oregon Museum of Science and Industry; Peace Pipe Museum; Pioneer Logging Museum; Portland Art Museum; Prineville Historical Museum; Schmink Memorial Museum; Seattle Art Museum; Siskiyou Co. Museum; Wahkiakium Co. Historical Society Museum; Walla Walla Co. Pioneer and Historical Museum; Walter Pierce Museum; Wasco Co.-Dalles City Museum; Winquatt Museum
Museums and Marked Historic Sites in Washington, comp. by Wash. State Library, noted, 64/188
Museums and Sites of Historical Interest in the Oregon Country, noted, 71/189; 78/365
Musgrove, William, 71/13,14N

Music, 62/172,178; 71/8:

Aurora colony, 79/233-67

band music, 79/245-48,251—

dance tunes, 79/245

bands, 77/358—

Bethel, Mo., 79/237-38; military, 68/15,226N; photo, 77/130; Yamhill Co., 74/345

Boise, Ida., 72/270; chamber groups, 79/233,248-50; choral groups, 74/234; 79/233,257; composers, 77/196; 79/233-68*passim*; compositions, 74/346; 77/196; country western, 70/84; dance music, 79/245; early West, 72/182; Edison Gramaphone records, 72/155,158; Elizabethan at Ashland, 62/183; fiddling, 70/359; folk music, 71/364; 79/258-59; instruments, SEE Musical instruments; light opera, 70/7; manuscripts, 79/245,246-47(photos), 251; musicians, 77/196,254; Oregon Trail, 62/260; publishers, 74/346

songs—

folk, 71/364; 79/258-59; hymns, 79/259; Irish, 69/112N; protest songs, 73/84; Russian-American, 71/365; Twana Indians, 65/374; voyageurs', 70/79; western, 70/78-79; whalemen's, 65/309

stores, 74/347

symphony orchestras, 77/89—

Univ. of Oregon, 74/234; SEE ALSO Eugene Junior Symphony; Portland Junior Symphony; Portland Symphony Orchestra

Tacoma 1911-70, 72/271; teachers, SEE Fox, Laura; Vancouver, Wash. early concert, 65/308; vocal music, 79/258-64; Westfall, Ore., 63/285; whistling lessons, 80/386; SEE ALSO Apollo Club; DeMoss Family; Hayward Quartet; Oregon Blues Brigade Fife and Drum Corps; Portland Opera Assn.

Music halls, SEE Theaters

"Musical Heritage of the Aurora Colony," by Deborah M. Olsen and Clark M. Will, 79/238-67

Musical instruments, 79/238,243: back-fire (back-thrust) horns, 79/

252,254(photo)

baritones, B-flat, 79/252,253,255— photos, 79/253,254

clarinets, 79/249(photo),252,256; Columbia Graphanola, 80/389; cornets, 79/252-53,254(photo); DeMoss Family chimes, 65/412; drums, 79/256,257; dulcimers, 79/253; Estey pump organ, 80/371,373; flutes, 79/252,256; forward-thrust horn, 79/252; guitars, 79/253; harmonicas, 79/245,257; instrument makers, 79/238,252,255,256; mandolins, 79/253; ocarinas, 79/255; ophicleides, 79/232(photo),253; Philadelphia valves, 79/252

pianos—

Covington, 68/341; Oregon 1859, 63/25

piccolos, 79/252,256; restoring, 79/267

schnellenbaums, 79/255-56— photo, 79/fr.cov. Fall

trombones, B-flat sackbut, 79/252; tubas, E-flat, 79/252,254(photo)

violins, 79/252—

early Ore., 63/35; photo, 79/249

violincellos, 79/249(photo),252; zithers, 79/256

Muskrats, 74/83,311

Musqueam Indian Reserve, 64/86; 72/247

Musselman, Paul, 69/33,39,40,42

Mustard, Mrs. L.J., 63/269

Mutton:

growth of market for, 67/130-31

Mutton Mountains, 79/126,161: name, 79/143N

"My Darling Red Bird," by Elizabeth Redington Stewart, 80/117-33

My Life With History: An Autobiography, by Hicks, review, 70/173-75

"My Medical School, 1890-1894," by Esther C.P. Lovejoy, 75/7-35

"My Trip to the Fair," by Oelo McClay, 80/51-65

Myer, Henry, 67/92

Myers, Donald, 69/307N

Myers, F.N., 64/352

Myers, H.S., 64/352

Myers, Jefferson D., photo, 70/224
Myers, John, Portland 1886, 75/128
Myers, Joseph D., 63/83
Myers, Leon L., 75/142,143,144
Myers, M.S., 64/352
Myers, Vic, 74/233
Myers, William, Umatilla Indian scout, 70/22
Myong-Soon, Korean picture bride, 79/56-58
Myrick, Josiah, 63/212
Myrick, Maria Louisa (Mrs. Josiah), 62/417; 63/212
Myrtle Bank School, Coos Co., 66/55
Myrtle Creek, 69/330
Myrtle Creek, Ore.: area photo, 68/187
Myrtle Grove School, Coos Co., 63/53,55
Myrtle Point, Ore., 63/5,22,34; 72/164: Guerin Hotel, 63/363; name, 63/365
Myrtle Point Bank, 63/34-35
Myrtle Point Herald, 63/6
Myrtle Point High School, 63/34
Myrtle trees, 63/34; 66/52-53; 67/41-53*passim*: largest, 67/50; names for, 67/41
The Mystic Warriors of the Plains, by Mails, noted, 74/285
Mystrom, A.W., 66/55
The Myth of the New History, by Hoggen, review, 66/274-75
The Mythical State of Jefferson, by Sutton, noted, 66/80
Myths and legends: about The West, 73/66; agrarian, 68/344; American history, 70/84,363; Arcadian, 71/368; Beacon Rock legend, 74/282; Blue Bucket Mine legend, 68/10; Bunyan, Paul, 73/300; Caledonia River, 69/72; egalitarian myth, 73/85; mining camps, 68/344; Oregon tall tales, 79/339; Oregon Trail, 67/371; Rogue River tales, 77/291; Spanish explorers, 70/363; Vinland, 72/182; western history, 70/229-30; Western movies, 72/180; Western writers, 68/348; SEE ALSO Folklore; Indians—legends

Naab, Michael: *Blow for the Landing*, by Timmen, review, 75/82
Naches River, 67/322
Nahcotta (steamer), 69/322; 78/206
Nakajo, Kenneth W., 81/153,158, 161,167
Nakamura family, 81/155
Nakao, Mrs. —, Portland Assembly Center, 81/160
Nakashima, George, 81/158,159
Nakashima, Harry Y., 81/170
Nakashima, Katsuhara, 81/170
Namba, Mr. —, Portland Assembly Center, 81/156
Nanaimo, B.C.: early settlers, 63/359
Nanamkin, Allan, 67/348,352,353,354
Nanamkin, Nancy, 67/348,350: photo, 67/348; Shaker service for, 67/348-55*passim*
Naniwa (Japanese warship), 71/163,164
Nann Smith (vessel), photo, 77/76
Napa, Calif., 73/323,325
Napoothe River, SEE Lewis River
Napton, Percy, 63/282
Narrative of a Journey Across the Rocky Mountains to the Columbia River, by Townsend, reprints reviewed, 72/170; 80/207
Narrative of the Life and Adventures of Major C. Bolin, Alias David Butler, intro. by Dillon, noted, 68/82
Narrows, Ore., 63/338; 75/67: photos, 78/230,231
Narver, Andrew Forrest: biography, 66/281
Narwhal (narwhale), 67/368
Nasatir, A.P., 66/63
Nash, Lee M., 80/414: *Later Woolen Mills in Oregon*, by Lomax, review, 77/193-94
"Portland's First History," cited, 70/219N
"Refining a Frontier: The Cultural Interests and Activities of Harvey W. Scott," cited, 70/202
"Scott of the *Oregonian*: The Editor as Historian," 70/197-232

Nash, Wallis, **64**/355:
Oregon: There and Back in 1877, reprint noted, **77**/300
Naslednik Aleksandr (ship), **73**/116,163
Nass River, **63**/189,204
Nast, Thomas, **66**/43:
Seward cartoon, **72**/131
Natatoriums:
Bandon, **75**/340,342
A Nation Moving West, Readings in the History of the American Frontier, ed. by Richmond and Mardock, noted, **68**/82
National Archives, SEE U.S. National Archives
National Assn. for the Advancement of Colored People:
records, **73**/209
National Consumers' League, **62**/94
National Cowboy Hall of Fame, **70**/278
National Endowment for the Arts, **78**/369
National Endowment for the Humanities, **80**/413
National Forestry Conference, **64**/58
National forests:
area in Oregon, **76**/29-30; listed, **77**/304; lookout points, **76**/34,47-48;
maps, **76**/28,40; ranger stations, **76**/41-53*passim*,77,79; roads, **76**/35,39,41,45; surveys, **76**/31-32,39,50-54;
Transfer Act 1905, **76**/31,32; SEE ALSO U.S. Forest Service
National Historic Landmarks:
Elmore cannery, **68**/90; Fort Rock Cave, **64**/356; **65**/219; program, **68**/86;
Western Juniper Natural Area, **68**/351-52
National Historic Sites:
Benton County Courthouse, **70**/184
National Historic Trails, **78**/370
National Historical Publications and Records Commission, **78**/368
National Lumber Manufacturers Assn., **64**/58
National Memorials:
Fort Clatsop, **65**/219
National Monuments:
John Day fossil beds suggested, **70**/184,371,372

National Museums Act, **66**/298
National Oceanic and Atmospheric Administration:
publications, **74**/96
National Order of the Videttes, **75**/134
National Park Service, SEE U.S. National Park Service
National parks, **68**/88; **78**/91:
beginnings, **73**/84; roads, **74**/128,209;
SEE ALSO names of parks
National Progressives of America, **76**/148
National Security League, **71**/216
National Service Corporation, **75**/177
National Trust for Historic Preservation, **63**/371; **67**/370; **72**/359; **75**/369
National Youth Administration, **76**/264
Nationalism:
American view of England, **73**/286
Nativism, **75**/109-90
The Natural History of the Lewis and Clark Expedition, ed. by Burroughs, review, **63**/69-70
Natural resources, **72**/173
Naturalists:
Beechey exped., **70**/365; early 19th century, **69**/27-28; early U.S. described, **70**/171,348; 49th parallel, **70**/180;
military personnel, **70**/246
Naukane (Hawaiian), SEE Coxe, John
Nautilus (brig), **69**/67
Nauvoo Legion, **67**/222
Navarro, Jose, **76**/155-57
Nave, Pietro, photo, **77**/252
Navigation:
art of, **62**/88-89; Columbia River, **77**/46,87,108; history 1840s-1850s, **77**/37-60; John Day River, **79**/105; Pacific Coast problems, **68**/86; Siuslaw River, **76**/ 177; Willamette River, **77**/45,91,314; Yukon River, **75**/82; **76**/110-15
Naylox Mountain, **75**/234
Neacoxie Creek, **63**/46
Neah Bay, **74**/21
Neahkahnie Mountain, **62**/195; **63**/91; **75**/49-53:
Indian sacred mountain, **75**/49; legends, **75**/51; marked stone photo, **75**/53; photos, **71**/ins.bk.cov. June; **75**/50,52; **77**/70; shipwreck, **73**/198; skel-

etons discovered, 73/198
Neal, John, 80/14
Neal, Steve:
Tom McCall: Maverick, review, 79/406-407
Neathamer, Jacob: journal, 64/89
Neathamer, Sarah Moore (Mrs. Jacob), 64/89
Neawanna Creek, 77/283
Nebraska:
history, 71/182-83; 78/282-83; overland trail, 71/183
Nebraska Territory, 62/312
Necanicum River, 77/282,284
Nedry, H.S., 70/244
Neece, T. Clay, 75/47-48
Neely, William W., 74/271
Neer City, Ore.:
cemetery, 65/308; history, 66/382
Neet, Jake, 63/290
Neet, Joseph, family, 66/383
Neet, Ole J., 69/329
Nee-Wamsh (Indian), 72/151
Neff, J.N., 62/219N
Neff, Marcus:
biography, 73/60,61N; land claim suit, 73/60-62
"The Negro in Oregon, a Survey," by Hill, cited, 73/203
The Negro in the State of Washington, 1788-1967, comp. by Wash. State Library, cited, 73/204; noted, 69/273
Negroes, 70/33,70,362; 76/368:
agencies, 73/209-10; American studies, 73/85; among Indians, 81/365; Baker Co. 1862, 66/199; "buffalo soldiers," 71/292
California, 70/85—
Archy case, 64/282; gold rush, 65/313; in politics, 74/286; rights activities 1849, 67/367
Canada, 70/85,367; cattle drive, 70/262; constitutional restrictions, 80/27; Crater Lake 1915, 81/43,45; history guides, 73/204; in I.W.W., 71/364; Ku Klux Klan, 75/152,157,163-64; labor, 69/199
migration—

1942, 73/207-208; West, 67/85
Nevada 19th century, 77/303
Oregon, 73/203—
attitudes, 73/203; civil rights, 73/209-10; employment, 73/206,207; exclusion laws, 73/199,204,206-207; 75/121; history sources, 73/197-200; pioneers, 64/227N,357; population, 73/207N,209; newspapers, 73/210-11; slavery issue, 72/230
orphanage 1905, 80/55; Pacific NW, 65/313; pictorial history, 73/279; pioneers, 70/178; poll tax, 80/140
Portland, 65/372—
1870, 64/181; Jefferson High School, 72/259; population 1860, 80/136; population 1863, 80/146 racism, 73/280-81; rights in Texas, 73/85; Seattle, 65/372-73; societies, 73/205(photo); suffrage, 70/85; union membership, 73/209; U.S. Colored Troops, 65/313; Washington 1860-80, 72/227; Washington bibliography 1788-1967, 69/273; 73/204; West, 71/291; 73/197-209,279-80; World War I, 71/215; SEE ALSO George Bush; Jacob Dodson; Marcus Lopez; James D. Saules; Slavery; George Washington; York
"Negroes in Oregon Before the Civil War," by Brownell, cited, 73/203
Nehalem, Ore., 65/308; 77/69
Nehalem Bay, 72/296; 73/5N,223
Nehalem Coal Company, 69/208N
Nehalem River, 70/279
Nehalem Valley, 67/373; 74/358:
electric co-op, 80/323; pioneer days, 62/301; pioneer roads, 65/219
Nehls, Harry B.:
Familiar Birds of Northwest Shores and Waters, noted, 76/182
Neihardt, John:
Black Elk Speaks, reprint noted, 63/247
Neilon, John, 71/190
Neils, Allan E.:
"A New Collection: The Burlington Northern," 74/79-82
Neils, Selma M.:
So This is Klickitat, review, 69/68-69

Nellis, N., 74/18
Nelson, Bob, 80/36,37,41,43,49
Nelson, Charles, Oysterville resident, 68/81
Nelson, Charles M., Portland shipbuilder, 81/38-39
Nelson, Douglas W.:
Heart Mountain: The History of an American Concentration Camp, review, 77/297-98
Nelson, E.M.:
History of a County Fair, noted, 70/76
Nelson, Ebner B., 79/171N
Nelson, Elroy, 64/281
Nelson, Herbert B., 65/189N:
"The Vanishing Hop-Driers of the Willamette Valley," 64/267-71
Nelson, L.A., 67/44
Nelson, Ray:
Memoirs of an Oregon Moonshiner, noted, 77/197
Nelson, Roy Paul, 63/362
Nelson, Thomas, 62/72; 64/293,299-302,309; 66/166; 73/201; 75/351
Nemos, William, 62/327; 75/79,80
Neocoxa Creek, SEE Neacoxie Creek
Neptune (tug), 80/41,42,43
Nereide (vessel), 63/232
Nesbit, Robert C.:
He Built Seattle: A Biography of Judge Thomas Burke, review, 62/405-406
Nesika Park, 67/50
Neskowin Inn, 69/88
Nesmith, Hattie, SEE McArthur, Harriet Nesmith
Nesmith, James Willis, 62/75,139N,141, 143-44; 63/254; 64/148,315; 65/192, 220,331; 66/5,8,13,134,221N,223N, 386; 67/312; 68/75; 70/63,253, 254N,260; 72/322,323N,329,333; 75/345,358,359; 81/261,262,280,423: correspondence, 73/43N,45N,50N— letter re Klamath military post, 69/ 224N; Yakima War letter, 67/319
emigrant protection legislation, 72/60, 60N; millstones, 66/292(photo),385; "Nesmith County" proposed, 73/283 opinion of Stark, 73/43,43N,45N,50— vote for Stark, 72/334

OMV service, 66/133-43*passim*; photo, 73/43; senate voting record, 73/52
Nesmith's Mill, SEE Ellendale, Ore.
Nespelem Indians, 70/115: photos, 81/330
Nesselrode, C.V., 72/104: negotiations with U.S., 72/110, 111-13,123-24
Nesselrode, Karl Robert, 63/189
Nessositer Mill, Douglas Co., 63/42
Nestor (tug), 81/36
Nestucca River, photo, 71/122
Nestucca River Valley: cheese industry, 64/90; settlers, 64/90
Netboy, Anthony:
The Salmon: Their Fight for Survival, review, 76/89-90
Neterer, Jeremiah, 67/187
Neuberger, Maurine (Mrs. Richard L.), 62/421
Neuberger, Richard Lewis, 65/211,404; 66/244; 76/138:
Coon debate, 65/314
Neuhausen, Thomas B.:
McNary campaign, 68/128-32,134, 136,138; papers, 68/131N; photo, 68/129
Neustadter, Edwin J., 62/179
Neustadter Bros., Portland, 73/185
Neva (vessel), 77/177
Nevada, 62/51,106,202,297; 63/304, 309-11; 69/85; 71/9,292; 72/173; 79/337; 80/208:
archeology, 67/86; bibliography, 75/93
boundaries—
described, 72/18; disputes, 72/9,13; Nev.-Ore.-Calif. corner, 72/49,50-53; surveys, 72/14-17,19,52
centennial, 63/88; 65/313; cowboy governor, 75/93; early census difficulties, 68/87; early forts, 66/87; emigrant routes, 67/86; first U.S. Senator, 65/313; geology, 72/180; historical articles, 70/366; immigrants, 72/180; interpretation, 67/364-65; livestock, 67/85; mining, 72/58; railroad merger proposed, 64/86; reclamation, 72/ 180; territorial governor, 63/89; white-

Indian relations, 67/371
Nevada-California-Oregon Railroad, 77/157,167: locomotive photo, 77/170
Nevada Historical Society: publications, 72/180; 75/93
Nevada, Land of Discovery, by Beatty and Beatty, noted, 79/337
Neville, James, 69/143
Nevins, Allan, 72/316
New, Harry S., 68/136
The New Age, Portland, 73/210,211
New Albion, 66/87; 73/109,162
New Archangel, 72/112; 73/119,120; 77/175,176-81: described, 73/138-47; established, 73/116; first steamboat built, 73/147; fort, 73/141,142,149; Indian settlement, 73/142,143,144,167-68; Indian attack, 73/149; library, 73/142,167; lighthouse, 73/139; name change to Sitka, 73/167; orphanage, 73/142; plan, 73/fr.cov. June; Russian-American Co. center, 73/101; sketches, 73/139,141; 77/178; SEE ALSO Sitka, Alaska
New Caledonia, Canada, 63/204
New Columbia Hotel, The Dalles, photo, 81/ins.bk.cov. Fall
New Deal, 71/364; 72/286; SEE ALSO Democratic Party
New England Hotel, Seattle, 71/16
New Era, Ore., 64/265-66; 68/201: pioneer post office, 65/315
New Guinea, 62/30,32,37
New Hazard (brig): logbook, 66/79
"New Light on the Molalla Indians," by Harold Mackey, 73/63-65
New Market Theater, Portland, 62/204; 69/209; 74/346; 75/14; 78/370; 79/412
The New Northwest, 78/36
New Odessa colony, Douglas Co., 66/89; 67/80,279
New Orleans, La.: market for buffalo, 66/331
New Orleans (steamship), photo, 62/16
"The New Sounding: Two Maritime Fur Trade Vessels," by Wilfried Schuh-

macher, 78/355-56
New Westminster, B.C., 63/192; 64/86
New Whatcom, SEE Bellingham, Wash.
New World (steamer), 68/351
New Zealand, 62/6,15,29,30,37,42
Newaukum Prairie, 63/239-40: Puget Sound Agricultural Co. farmsite, 63/118,124,228
Newaukum River, 63/108
Newberg, Ore.: gravesite, Ewing Young, 65/415; history, 65/217; 80/336; post office centennial, 72/91
Newberg Graphic: history, 65/217
Newberger, H., 71/20
Newberry, John Strong, 67/11,13: geographic features named for, 67/13
Newberry Crater, 66/92,384: photo, 67/12
Newberry Library, Chicago, 70/64,65
Newell, Charles, Jr. (Charley), 80/171, 173,175-86*passim*
Newell, Charles, Sr.: biography, 80/172
Newell, Edith W., ed.: "Manila to Peking: Letters Home, 1898-1901," 80/171-86
Newell, Ellen Stagg, 80/171-72,195
Newell, George L., Jr., 80/195: photo, 80/196
Newell, George Lemon: biography, 80/171,173-75,195-96; letters, 80/175-86; photos, 80/170, 184,196
Newell, Gordon: *Westward to Alki: The Story of David and Louisa Denny*, noted, 79/337
Newell, Gordon, and Joe Williamson: *Pacific Lumber Ships*, review, 63/80
Newell, Harriet (Indian): name, 64/43
Newell, Laura Hugill, 80/195: photo, 80/196
Newell, Robert, 62/76; 65/407; 66/81,356; 67/87,296N; 71/285; 75/72,73; 78/87; 79/183: Cayuse War commission, 66/358-59; Nez Perce wife, 66/90; Ore.Prov.Govt.

role, 66/353,355N
Newell, William H., 65/80,88,97, 103,105
Newell family, Toutle, Wash., 80/171-73
Newell House Museum, Champoeg, 68/89; 69/177
Newlands, Francis, 62/188
Newlands, Lawrence, 74/233
Newman, —, Ft. Henrietta 1856, 66/154
Newman, Selina, 80/361
Newman, Theodore, 78/125
Newman, Thomas M., 63/75
Newman Canyon, 69/123
Newport, Ore., 74/282; 80/256: early days, 64/355; history, 81/327; photographers, 66/330; postal history, 69/340
Newport, Wash., 73/348: state line location, 73/249
Newport Mines, Coos Co., 63/16
Newport, Oregon, 1866-1936, by Price, noted, 77/292,298
News, Portland, SEE *Portland News*
Newsboy (steamer), 73/230
Newsboys: 1880s, 80/271,273
Newsom, David, 78/74,215; 80/15: letter, 78/216N-17N
Newsome Creek, 79/187,198
Newspaper Collections of the State Historical Society of Iowa, comp. by Cheever, noted, 70/360
Newspapering in the Old West: A Pictorial History, by Karolevitz, review, 66/379-80
Newspapers, 62/142,150; 75/105; 80/271,273: 19th century characteristics, 67/279; and wood pulp 1867-1900, 67/367; Astoria, 75/294; bibliography, 75/364; Chinook, Wash., 75/105; coverage of KKK activities, 75/154-74*passim*; Dallas, Ore. photo, 77/ins.fr.cov. Sept.; Eugene, 78/286-87; frontier, 68/346; 73/286; Hawaiian before 1900 on microfilm, 67/372 history— Eastern Ore., 77/192-93; Eugene, 78/286-87; pictorial, 66/379-80

influence on Ore. Trail emigrants, 81/96-97; Iowa collection, 70/360; lower Columbia River, 75/105; Montana, 65/363
Oregon, 62/107; 63/52,91,362; 64/123-36; 65/29N,212; 71/ 147-48—
directory 1965, 66/90; history, 77/192-93
Pacific Coast first, 77/319; Pacific Co., Wash., 74/93-94; Pacific Northwest, 74/359; Portland, 74/341; Presbyterian 1752-1830, 65/213; prices 1850s, 64/125; St. Louis, Mo. 1808-1842, 63/358; Seattle radical, 72/230; theses index, 72/276; views on U.S. expansion 1900-1903, 72/213-24
Washington, 62/109; 64/33-40; 71/147—
on microfilm, 75/364
Western, 66/379-80; Wyoming, 63/360; SEE ALSO Journalism; names of newspapers
Newspapers on Microfilm in the Libraries of the State of Washington, comp. by Mills and Kloostra, noted, 75/364
Newton Clark Glacier, 77/65
Nez Perce County, Ida.: place names, 72/265
Nez Perce Indian Reservation, 65/214: 1864 map, 66/386
Nez Perce Indian War, 62/202,295-96, 297; 63/246; 64/85,273-74; 65/216; 67/86; 68/75,82,88,251N,346; 70/ 18N,106,124,125,127; 72/356; 81/ 349,351,360-63: Gervais role, 66/358-59; Mayer journal, 68/294; Red Coats, 81/363
Nez Perce Indian War and Original Stories, by Adkison, noted, 68/82
Nez Perce Indians, 62/101-102,106; 63/ 57,90,246; 64/273-74,349-50; 65/ 214,216-17,313-14; 66/88,90,358, 383; 67/86; 68/337; 69/336; 70/ 180,347; 72/183,248,250; 74/95; 75/ 115,209; 78/91,370; 79/106,122, 129,136: acculturation, 67/367; 70/68; allies and enemies, 81/350; and Ore. Trail

travelers 1853, **62**/397,401; and Yellowstone tourists, **67**/371; art, **81**/342-76*passim*; camas use, **70**/87; clothing, **72**/270; **81**/341-76*passim*; factionalism, **70**/68; fishing and hunting rights, **70**/ 364; horse-stealing, **71**/345; horses, **81**/341,393; missions, **68**/336; photos, **81**/330; native food use, **72**/250, 270; property customs, **81**/398,399, 404,407,409,411; Red River school students, **71**/330-31,332,336; religion, **71**/333,347; self-government, **65**/365; slavery, **81**/414,415; Smohalla cult, **70**/124; sorcery, **68**/87,184; trade, **81**/418; treaty negotiations, **70**/115; tribal organization, **70**/121; tribal rolls, **67**/378; utensils, **81**/394; Wallowa camp grounds, **70**/31; willingness to surrender to Cayuse, **67**/297N; with Haller 1854 exped., **67**/311; SEE ALSO Nez Perce Indian War

Nez Perce Indians and the Opening of the Northwest, by Josephy, review, **67**/278

Niagara, Ore.:

history, **71**/349FF

"'Niagara' and 'China Dam'," by Maynard C. Drawson, **71**/349-57

Niagara Dam, **71**/349-57: photos, **71**/350

Nichols, Benjamin F., **72**/89

Nichols, Charlene: recollections, **73**/283

Nichols, Charlie, **62**/198

Nichols, Isabelle Riddle, **72**/89

Nichols, Israel Boyd, **72**/89

Nichols, Roger L., ed.:

The Missouri Expedition, 1818-1820: The Journal of Surgeon John Gale with Related Documents, noted, **71**/287

Nichols family, overland 1852, **79**/365,366,381,388,389

Nicholson, George, **68**/102,110: Adventure Cove site, **68**/109

Nicholson, George:

Vancouver Island's West Coast, 1762-1962, cited, **68**/109

Nicholson, S.C., **68**/240,242

Nickel industry:

Riddle, Ore., **65**/384

Nickum, Joseph M., **62**/174 Nicolai, Harry I., **77**/367 Nicollet, Joseph N., **71**/290 *Nictheroy* (cruiser), **76**/283,284,285 Nielsen, Peder, **66**/107,113: death, **66**/108 "The Night Dr. Barclay's House Was Moved," by Glenn Stanton, **76**/302-303 "The Night the *Tuscania* Went Down," by Josephine Evans Harpham, **77**/285-88 Nightingill Valley, **72**/15 Nighton, H.M., SEE Knighton, H.M. Niihau Island, Hawaii: history, **65**/214 "The Nikkei in Oregon, 1834-1940," by Barbara Yasui, **76**/225-57 Nikolaevsk Redoubt, **73**/116 *Nikolai* (ship), **73**/101,103 Niles, Harry M., photo, **74**/214 *Niles' National Register,* **75**/316 Nimitz, Chester, **62**/31,32 Nimmo, Joseph: *Report on Range and Ranch Cattle Traffic,* cited, **67**/139-40,142,143,148,158 *Nine Years with the Spokane Indians: The Diary, 1838-1845, of Elkanah Walker,* by Drury, noted, **77**/291; review, **79**/ 101-102 Nine-Power Treaty 1922, **62**/19,22,23, 26,27 "The 1916 'Spanish Influenza' Pandemic in Oregon," by Ivan M. Woolley, **64**/246-58 "19th Century Midwife: Some Recollections," by Helen Olson Halvorson and Lorraine Fletcher, **70**/39-49 *98 Years of Change: Island City School,* comp. by Davis, noted, **70**/360 Niondon, M., Sacred Heart student, **81**/81N Niska, Ed: *Indians, Finns, and Their Thunderbirds,* by Mattila, review, **75**/83-84 Nisqually Farm, **62**/65; **63**/102,104, 106,109,119-82*passim*: midshipman school, **63**/224; settlers' hostility, **63**/176; sheep, **63**/211; Tol-

mie at, 63/175-76; u.s. Army trade, 63/106n; Wallace murder, 63/198
Nisqually House, 76/226
Nisqually Indians, 72/148
Nisqually River, 73/345
Nisson, —, capt. of *C.C. Funk,* 66/107
Nitchy, Frederick, 62/170,177
Nitobe, Tama, see Takaki, Tama Nitobe
Nitske, W. Robert, trans.:
Travels in North America, 1822-1824, by Paul Wilhelm, Duke of Wurttemberg, noted, 77/91
Nitz, Carl F., 79/412
Nitz, Carl F., trans.:
"Fire at Sea, 1856," 81/196-200
Nitz, Mrs. Carl F., 79/412
Niver, S.A., 74/24
Nixon, Birgetta, and Mabel Tupper:
Cherry Grove: A History From 1852 to the Present, noted, 79/336
Noah, Beryl, 66/55
Nobili, John, 69/269-70
Noble, Curtis, 63/12-13; 68/263
Noble, Elizabeth, 63/12
Noble, John, son of Curtis, 63/12
Noble, John F., 66/134n,142; 67/303n: biography, 65/15-16n; characterized, 65/60,101; First Ore. Cavalry career, 65/12-106*passim;* journals, 65/16n
Noble, Kate, 63/12
Noble, Lyman, 63/12
Noble, William, 63/12
Noble Knights of Labor, 75/133
Nobles Butte, 79/146
Noble's Trail, 77/196
Nolan, Al, 63/283
Noland, Pleasant Calvin, 78/129,152, 213,225,323n; 79/30n: photo, 78/226
Noland family, overland 1856, 62/ 243n,380,381,384
Nolf, Bruce, 77/79
Nolte, —, Lakeview land promoter, 77/157,158
Nome, Alaska, 76/101: gold rush, 71/365; photos, 71/365
Nonpareil, Ore., 73/304
Nonpareil (brig), 77/38
Non-Partisan Direct Legislation League, 68/215-16
Non-Partisan League, 68/132; 76/149: Idaho 1918, 66/281
Nooksak River, 73/75
Nootka controversy, 71/370; 74/353; 79/397: agreement concluded, 79/400,402; efforts to settle terms, 79/397-402; painting of ships in Friendly Cove, 74/363; Pearce report, 79/399-400
Nootka Indians: chiefs, 79/399,400,401; settlement sketch, 79/398; war canoe sketch, 79/398
Nootka Sound, 67/371; 70/297n,304n; 72/182,250: Spain at, 79/399-400; trade center, 76/322; views 1792, 79/398
Nora (steamer), 81/144
Norblad, Albin Walter, Jr., 65/361
Norcross, Eleanor (Elinor), 73/296; 74/62
Norman, Christian, 78/235
Norman Morison (bark), 63/233
Norris, Basil, 74/333
Norris, Lucy Ann, see Dement, Lucy Ann
Norris, Shubrick, 80/9: biography, 80/320n
Norris, William A., 62/335
Norris, William J., 73/6,7,13,18,173, 179,182
North, Frank, 63/81
North, John W., 72/14
North, Luther, 63/80-81
North America: impact of discovery on Europe, 75/88; national character, 72/178; voyages of discovery, 72/343-44
North American Assn. for State and Local History, 75/369
North American Fur Trade Conference 1978, 79/107
The North American Indians, by Curtis, cited, 71/279
North American Trading Co., Dawson City, 76/115
North Bend, Ore., 63/15; 68/271-72; 72/159,164; 80/62:

Indian fishing site, 64/355; photos, 68/270; 72/163; sawmills, 68/265, 269; shipyard, 68/266,267

North Bend Manufacturing Co., 80/35

North Bentinck Arm, 76/315,324

North Fork, Crooked River, 65/31N

North Fork, John Day River, 68/305N, 307N; 70/57; 79/303

North Fork, Malheur River, 68/237, 307N; 78/154

North Fork, Willamette River, 77/329

North Mill Creek, Marion Co., 66/12

North Pacific (steamer), 71/16

North Pacific Evangelistic Institute, 72/229

North Pacific Exploring Expedition, 63/345

North Pacific Mill Company, 67/166

North Pacific Pediatric Society, 72/173

North Pacific Railroad, 71/39

North Pacific Transportation Company, 72/132

North Platte River, 79/77,374,376; 80/69,70

North Portland School, 64/261

North Santiam River, 72/91: dams, 71/349-71; exploration, 71/349; geology, 71/355; sawmills, 71/351

North Star (launch), 81/38

North Umpqua River, 74/358

North West Company, 62/91,99; 66/ 332; 68/185; 69/59; 74/364; 77/80: American partners, 76/206,217,221-22,329; American shippers, 76/320; Astor recruits men from, 76/323; Babine Lake post, 70/179; Calif. trade, 76/310-31; Columbia River bases, 76/ 321-30*passim*; consolidation with HBCO., 76/329; contract procedures, 81/384, 387; East India Co. license, 76/311, 326-27; employees 1813-14, 63/84; 64/92 employs McLoughlin, 81/379, 380,383-87— contract, 81/387-89 Hawaiian trade, 76/327; historical novel, 70/272; lack of charter, 76/ 325-26; no. furs sold in Canton, 76/ 331; posts, 76/324; records, 70/367;

rivalry, 76/310,311,322,323; Russian trade, 76/314,327,329; salaries, 81/384,385; seal, 81/386; tokens, 70/ 88; 76/330(photo); trade route, 70/ 366; use of American firms to evade trade restrictions, 76/320N,321,329,331

"The North West Company's 'Adventure to China'," by Barry M. Gough, 76/309-31

Northcote, Stafford, 63/226

Northern Islands, Alaska, 77/187-88

Northern Liberties (ship), 76/321

Northern Pacific Railroad, 63/78-79; 65/217,363; 67/86,105,115FF,141, 142,147FF,160,167FF; 69/199,201, 221; 70/77,116; 71/283; 72/286; 73/334,335; 75/127; 81/296: bondholders, 71/69,73,80-81,91; Columbia Co. arrival, 65/309 completion celebration photos— Portland, 67/covs. June; The Dalles, 67/100 construction costs, 71/64,73,74,90,95; Coxey's army conflicts, 65/272,278, 284; economic impact on Pacific NW, 71/27-98; effect as first Pacific NW transcontinental, 71/27-28,38; finances, 71/30,63,64,65,80-81,95; land grants, 70/271; 71/68; land sales, 71/364; map Eastern Wash. grant limits, 70/136; merger 1970, 71/197; Northern Pacific Act centennial, 66/ 91; Orient trade interests, 71/142,143, 150,151; Portland celebration of last spike, 71/26(photo); Portland promotion, 71/66-68; rate policies, 71/86; records, 74/79,334 routes— Ainsworth-Inland Empire, 71/64; Columbia River, pros and cons, 71/40,54,65,66; Puget Sound, 71/49,64,65 Southern Pacific purchase, 71/73 steamship company, 71/46-47,142— schedule, 71/ins.fr.cov. March substitute land list records, 70/271; Tacoma city plan, 67/357; Villard control, 71/65,73; western land marketing, 70/85,367; western terminus, 72/231;

Yellowstone survey 1873, 71/366
Northern Pacific Terminal Co., 67/119
Northern Paiute Indians, 81/350,364
Northern Quebec and Labrador Journals and Correspondence, 1819-35, by Hudson's Bay Record Society, noted, 65/309
Northerner (steamship), 66/17
Northover, "Grandma," daughter of George Katel, 72/354
Northrup, J.C., 71/23N
Northup, —, immigrant of 1853, 78/242,243
Northup, Benson L., 74/30
Northup, Ruth, 74/30
Northwest Area Foundation, 77/383
Northwest Assn. of Private Colleges and Universities, 77/382
Northwest Clarion Defender, Portland, 73/211
Northwest Coast, 68/347; 75/93: British influence 1810-1914, 73/359-60; exploration, 70/77; 72/100(map); fur trade, 70/366; interest in, 72/125 voyages, 69/67-68— ships logs, 67/201
Northwest Cold Storage and Ice Co., 62/165
Northwest Forts and Trading Posts, annotated by LeRoy, noted, 69/332
The Northwest Gun, by Hanson, review, 62/92-93
Northwest History in Action: A Collection of Twelve Plays, by Emmons, review, 62/412-13
Northwest Institute of Ethnic Studies, 72/356
Northwest Literary Review, 74/176
Northwest Ordinance, 62/134-35; 75/365
Northwest Oregon Forest Protective Assn., 73/283
Northwest Passage, 63/88; 65/212; 72/343,344; 76/310,312,317: first commercial voyage, 71/197-98
Northwest Poetry Society, 73/293, 294,295; 74/47,58,66
Northwest Scientific Association: history, 62/107

Northwest Stage Company, 68/229N
Northwest Timber Company, 69/208N
Northwest Trading Company, 69/208
Northwest Trail Blazers, by Howard, noted, 65/121
Northwest Trailblazers: publications, 75/86,362
Northwestern Band, 74/346
Northwestern Bank, Portland, 81/204
Northwestern Electric Co., 75/159,160
Northwestern Fire and Marine Insurance Company, 69/211
Northwestern Lumber Company, 67/175
Northwestern Lumberman, cited, 67/167,168
Northwestern Marriage Insurance Co., 64/352
Norton, Carrie Skinner: recollections, 72/93
Norton, Daniel, 80/289: biography, 80/291
Norton, James, 71/172
Norton Bay, 73/119,131,134
Norville, Catherine, 62/232
Norway, Ore., 63/18,34; 72/353
Norway Myrtle Preserve, 67/51
Norwegian people, 81/59: Lincoln Co. colony, 71/289; loggers, 73/19 Oregon, 62/297— population 1860-1910, 80/267 Portland population 1860-1910, 80/266; Tacoma meetings 1890s, 66/122
Not by Might, the Story of Whitworth College, 1890-1965, by Gray, review, 68/183-84
Nourse (Nurse), George, 68/187
Nova Albion, SEE New Albion
Novo-Arkangelsk, SEE New Archangel
Noyes, Robert H., 64/358,364; 65/126, 222,318,416; 66/93,189,285,294; 67/379; 68/356
Noyes Island: fishing conflicts, 72/231
Nuclear energy: Idaho, 63/359
Nuclear weapons, SEE Atom bomb
Numaga (Indian), 74/283
Numan, Jeremiah, 65/315

Nunis, Doyce Blackman, Jr., 64/282: articles listed, 67/84

Nunis, Doyce Blackman, Jr.: *Past Is Prologue: A Centennial Profile of Pacific Mutual Life Insurance Co.*, noted, 69/334

Nunis, Doyce Blackman, Jr., ed.: *The Golden Frontier: The Recollections of Herman Francis Reinhart*, review, 64/344-46

Nunn, Herbert, 66/249: biography, 66/252-53; Columbia River Hwy., 66/269-70

Nunn, Richard, 72/280; 75/20

Nurseries: Oregon, 66/86,87; West's largest, 64/354

Nus, Wendolen, 69/243N

Nushagak River, 77/185

Nussbaumer family, Columbia Co., 72/202,203

Nuts: Lewelling almond, 68/170; Pacific NW varieties, 66/87; trees brought to Ore., 68/156-57; SEE ALSO names of varieties

Nuttall, Thomas, 63/191-92; 68/123; 69/28; 70/348; 80/207: biography, 70/171-73

Nutter, Donald G., 65/385

Nyden, Evangeline: *Old Sellwood*, noted, 72/354

Nye, James Warren, 63/89

Nye, John W., 81/328

Nye Beach, Lincoln Co., 66/330

Nylund, Ander Victor, family, 64/87

Nyssa, Ore., 81/170

O the Red Rose Tree, by Beatty, noted, 73/285

The OCE Story, by Stebbins, noted, 74/282

OK Produce Co., Portland, 81/166

OMV, SEE Oregon Mounted Volunteers

"OMV's Fort Henrietta: On Winter Duty, 1855-56," by J.W. Reese, 66/133-60

Oak, Henry Labbeus, 62/325,327; 75/79

Oak Grove, Wasco Co., 79/142,143N, 161,161N,166

Oak Island, Sauvie Island, 75/87

Oak Knoll Golf Course, 77/263,264

Oak Point, Wash.: salmon packing, 75/105; sawmill, 75/105

Oakland, Calif., 80/32: total and foreign-born population, 1870-1910, 80/263(table)

Oakland, Ore., 63/364; 70/271; 80/233

Oakley, Obadiah, 67/85

Oakridge, Ore., 62/107; 78/307, 308,320: history, 72/171

Oaks Amusement Park, Portland, 80/59

Oaks Pioneer Park, Portland, 62/299; 66/92

Oatman, Charlie, 67/352

Oatman, Harrison B., 64/145

Oatman, Olive, 64/283

Oats: army needs, 1857, 68/23; Cowlitz Farm, 63/104,115-52*passim*; Oregon, 63/50; SEE ALSO Prices

Oba, Mr. —, Portland Assembly Center, 81/155

"Obadiah B. McFadden, Oregon and Washington Territorial Judge," by Sidney Teiser, 66/25-37

Oberholtzer, Ellis Paxson: *The Referendum in America*, noted, 74/96

Obichon, Emilie, SEE Petit, Emilie Aubichon

Obichon, Jean Baptiste, SEE Aubichon, Jean Baptiste

Obieta, Domingo, 76/168N: photo, 76/156

Objects of Bright Pride: Northwest Coast Indian Art, by Wardwell, review, 81/207-208

O'Brien, Edward J., comp.: *Best Short Stories*, cited, 73/321

O'Brien, Helengray, 64/359

O'Brien, Hugh, 64/212N

O'Brien, Humphrey, 64/212N

O'Brien, J.P., 69/143

O'Brien, Lucy Corrigal, 69/143

O'Brien, Calif., 69/103

O'Brien family, Morrow Co., 69/143

O'Bryant, Hugh D., 64/213N; 66/11N; 80/9,10N: photo, 80/16

O'Bryant, Humphrey, 64/212N-13N

Observation Peak, Jackson Co., 72/47

Obstetrics, 78/11,29; SEE ALSO Midwives

Obukan judo club, Portland, 76/250

O'Cain, Joseph B., 71/365

O'Cain (vessel), 79/406

O'Callaghan, Jerry A., 64/350

Occidental and Oriental Steamship Co., 73/86

Occidental Hotel, Corvallis, 71/19; 80/257

Occidental Hotel, Seattle, 62/187

Ocean Wave (steamer), 63/66

Oceano (ship), 66/129

Oceanography, 68/89: Pacific NW coast, 72/90— atlas noted, 69/331

Oceanside Lumber Company, 77/367

Ocheo (Indian), SEE Ochoco

Ochiai, Tamiyo, 81/156,169

Ochiai, Zenzaburo (Mrs. Tamiyo), 81/169

Ochoco (Ocheo, Ocheco) (Indian), 79/127,146N

Ochoco Creek, 65/26N,28; 79/146,296

Ochoco Farmers' Assn., 76/245

Ochoco Irrigation Project, 76/245-46

Ochoco Mountains, 72/342; 75/310

Ocklahoma (river steamer), photo, 74/305

O'Connell, Con, 63/269

O'Connell, Kenneth J., 69/121

O'Connor, Thomas G., 80/157N,159N

O'Connor, William C.: "Dipping the Sheep," 75/69-71 "Old Ted," 81/319-20

O'Connor family, Morrow Co., 69/ 143-44

Odd Fellows, SEE Independent Order of Odd Fellows

Odell, William Holman, 79/243: activities as presidential elector, 67/ 262,266-68; deputy surveyor-general, 67/267; Electoral Comm. decision, 67/271; Indian commission 1892, 66/ 22; votes cast for (as presidential elector), 67/259,267

Odell Butte, 78/295,296(photo)

Odell Lake, 77/330: history, 81/327

Odermatt, Adelhelm, 70/313: founder Mt. Angel Abbey, 70/331; in Eastern Ore., 70/314-18,319,327,329-30,332; memoirs, 70/314N; photo, 70/331

Odessa, Wash., 72/233

Odessa colony, SEE New Odessa colony

O'Donnell, Harry T., family, 69/144

O'Donnell, Terence, 75/368: *America's Sunset Coast*, by Windsor, review, 80/334 *Garden of the Brave in War*, noted, 81/428-29 *Raised By the Sea*, by Sigurdson, review, 74/356 *Siskiyou Trail*, by Dillon, review, 77/194 *Tall Tales*, ed. by Beckham, review, 75/360-61

O'Donnell, Terence, and Thomas Vaughan: *Portland: A Historical Sketch and Guide*, noted, 77/291

O'Donnell, Thomas, 69/144

Of Yesterday and the River, by Crithfield, review, 65/306-307

O'Fallon, Benjamin, 75/94; 77/91

Offen, Karen M., and David C. Duniway, eds.: "William Cornell's Guide to Oregon, 1852," 80/66-100 "William Cornell's Journal, 1852, with His Overland Guide to Oregon," 79/359-93

Office of Price Administration, 66/362N

Ogden, Gerald, comp.: *The United States Forest Service: A Historical Bibliography, 1876-1972*, noted, 77/304

Ogden, Peter Skene, 62/71-72,81-82, 106; 63/103,138,172; 64/228N,295-96,298; 70/69; 72/89; 74/90; 75/115; 78/139; 79/295-96N; 81/26N: Cape Disappointment land claim, 64/ 225N-26N; correspondence, 81/208; journal 1826-27 exped., 63/349-51;

Roberts recollections, 63/183,202, 204,214,219,223; Snake expeds., 71/ 346; Whitman massacre captives rescue, 63/181

Ogilvie, William, 68/87

Oglala Indians, 63/74,247

Ogle, Hal H., 68/317N

Ogle, Robert, 70/371

Ogle Mountain, Clackamas Co.: mining, 74/357

Oglesby, W.W., 68/305N

O'Halloran, Patrick: letter to *Oregonian* 1918, 71/240

O'Hara, Barnard, 80/289

O'Hara, John P., 75/141

"An Ohioan's Role in Oregon History," by Thomas H. Smith, 66/218-32

Ohrt, Wallace:

The Rogue I Remember, noted, 81/334

Oil and gas industry:

Canada— offshore drilling, 70/179; pipeline, 71/368

drilling, 70/183; exploration in Ore., 68/89; history, 72/181; Mt. David oil well, 69/340; pipelines, 70/179; tanker voyage NW Passage, 71/197

Ojibway Indians, 71/345

Oka, Mr. and Mrs. —, Portland Assembly Center, 81/155

Okajima, Mr. —, Portland Assembly Center, 81/156

Okanagan River, B.C., 62/245

Okanagan Valley, B.C., 69/85; 72/256,257

Okanogan (steamer), 79/182

Okanogan County, Wash.: post offices, 69/331

Okanogan (Okanagan) Indians, 70/115,121,150; 72/153: photos, 81/330

O'Kelly, Nimrod, 66/358N

Okhotsk (brig), 73/119,120,121: sketches, 73/120,130

Okinawa, 62/10,33,51

Ok-Ja, Korean picture bride, 79/54-56

Oklahoma, 77/371,373,375-76

Okun, S.B., 72/121

Olallie Slough, 63/351

Olcott, Ben W., 64/335N; 66/367-72*passim*; 75/162,188N; 76/238: gubernatorial contest 1922, 75/173-74; KKK problem, 75/156,161,163,166, 167,168; photo, 75/170

Old Chief Joseph and Young Chief Joseph, by Bartlett, noted, 68/184

Old Church Preservation Society, Portland, 71/104,199,289,372

Old Crook County: The Heart of Oregon, by Juris, noted, 76/182

Old Fort Boise Historical Society: publications, 73/284

Old Fort Dalles Historical Society, 68/39N

Old Forts of the Far West, by Hart, noted, 66/384

Old Forts of the Northwest, by Hart, review, 65/202-203

Old Forts of the Southwest, by Hart, noted, 66/82

Old John (Indian), 65/191N

Old Jules, by Sandoz, reprint noted, 63/247-48

Old Orchard Road, Portland, 63/362

Old Oregon Trail Highway: dedication, 67/241; 78/101; 80/ 105— photo, 78/102 Emigrant Springs monument photo, 67/243

"Old Peg Leg," Willamette Valley logger, 76/63-65

Old Settlers Association, 62/98

Old Sturbridge Village, 66/385

"The Old Wood Roads," by Ronald T. Strong, 75/56-66

The Old Yaquina Bay Lighthouse, by Howes, noted, 70/75

Olds, P.G., 77/237

Olds, William Parker, 62/169,171,172, 177,179: speech quoted, 62/172-73

Olds Ferry, Snake River, 68/229N,298N

The Oldtimer, noted, 63/246; 65/121; 66/80; 67/281

Oldtimer Recipes, comp. by Hiller and Darneille, noted, 63/357

Oldys, Henry, 65/244N,256

Olequa, Wash., 63/245; 71/289
Oliphant, James Orin, 66/148N; 70/261: cattle works cited, 67/143-58*passim*
Oliphant, James Orin: *Manifest Destiny and Mission in American History*, by Merk, review, 64/343-44 *On the Cattle Ranges of the Oregon Country*, review, 70/262
Oliver, A.V., 77/7,8
Oliver, Charles, Westfall teacher, photo, 63/278
Oliver, Clarence, 81/162,171
Oliver, Mrs. Clarence, 81/160,170
Oliver, Edward L., 66/67,68
Oliver, Egbert S.: "The Columbia County Tarbells," noted, 81/424
The Shaping of a Family, A Memoir, review, 81/102-103
Oliver, Egbert S., ed.: *The Tarbells of Yankton: A Family and a Community, 1891-1932*, review, 80/102-103
Oliver, Harry, 81/102
Oliver, Herman: *Gold and Cattle Country*, ed. by Jackman, review, 63/70-71
Oliver, Iris (Mrs. Harry), 81/102-103
Oliver, J.C., Lakeview rancher, 77/6-12
Olley, Adelia Judson, SEE Leslie, Adelia Judson Olley
Olley, James, 76/362-67*passim*
Ollgard, Christian S.: borax works, 73/233-35,239-43; death, 73/243; photos, 73/242,360
Ollgard, Guy E., 73/231N,239,243: photo, 73/fr.cov. Sept.
Olmstead, Mrs. C.J., 68/226N
Olmstead, Emery, 71/229
Olmstead, Roy, 64/283; 67/187
Olmsted, Frederick Law, 67/357; 74/105
Olmsted, John C., 74/105
Olney, Almedia, 64/321N
Olney, Annetta Hallocula (Mrs. Nathan), 64/317
Olney, Benjamin, 64/321N
Olney, Charlotte Tanner (Mrs. William), 64/310

Olney, Cyrus, 64/302; 66/16,25,31; 73/201; 75/352; 78/216: birthplace, 64/309-10N; Clatsop Co. school supt., 64/319; death, 64/320; grave, 64/320; Hawaiian venture, 64/317-18; judicial district defined, 64/312; "Olney lottery," 64/319; Ore. constitutional convention, 64/316; Ore. legislative service, 64/319-20; Ore. Terr. associate justice, 64/312; 66/5; photo, 64/309; role in Deady-McFadden dispute, 64/313-14; town named for, 64/319; will, 64/320-22; Williams' characterization of, 64/316; Yakima War service, 64/315
Olney, Elizabeth, SEE Stanton, Elizabeth Olney
Olney, Emily, 64/321N
Olney, Marie, 64/321N
Olney, Mary, 64/321N
Olney, Nathan, 64/310N-11,316,321N; 65/63,80,88,91-92,103N,106; 78/216: death, 64/318; expedition 1855, 67/311; Hawaiian venture, 64/317-18; marriage, 64/317; photo, 64/308; Walla Walla campaign aide, 66/145
Olney, Orville, 64/310
Olney, Richard: Coxey's army episode, 65/271N,282-83, 285,290,293
Olney, Sarah (Mrs. Cyrus), 64/319
Olney, Warren, 64/310N
Olney, William, 64/310
Olney, Ore.: name, 64/319
Ol-ole (Indian), 79/275N
Olp, Colleen Connaughy, ed.: *Rankin Crow and the Oregon Country*, by Crow, review, 73/279
Olsen, Charles Oluf, 73/298; 74/64, 65,155-56: described, 74/57; photo, 73/296; stories, 74/57
Olsen, Charles Oluf: *History of Milwaukie, Oregon*, noted, 67/80
Olsen, Deborah M., 79/267: *Minthorn House, Boyhood Home of Herbert C. Hoover*, noted, 80/336

Olsen, Deborah M., and Clark M. Will: "Musical Heritage of the Aurora Colony," 79/233-67

Olsen, Elizabeth, 74/57,64,65: photo, 73/296

Olsen, Nancy A., and Linda S. Brody: *Cedar Mill History*, noted, 80/105-106

Olson, Mrs. Charles: recollections, 66/382

Olson, Culbert, 72/346

Olson, Mrs. Duane R., 62/249N

Olson, Eunice, 66/382

Olson, Florence, 68/208,217,219

Olson, Gene and Joan: *Oregon Times and Trails*, noted, 66/383

Olson, George, 78/204

Olson, Henry, 70/39FF

Olson, John, Queets area settler, 74/24

Olson, Mary, 70/39FF

Olson, Nels, 76/11

Olson, Oliff, 66/382

Olson, Oscar, 62/200

Olson, Randi, 78/204

Olson, Semer, 70/39FF

Olsson, —, capt. of *Samoa*, 77/363,364

Olwell, John, 70/314N

Olwell, Phillip W.: biography, 70/314N; describes Rogue River Valley, 70/314

Olympia, Wash., 62/64,81,86; 63/190, 195,364; 66/35,36,117; 72/148; **81**/202: newspaper history, 1852-85, 72/263; Seward visit, 72/133-35

Olympia (cruiser), 76/272,292; 79/213

Olympia (steamer), 62/321

Olympia Hotel, Montesano, 74/16

Olympia Mill, 66/117

Olympian (steamer), 63/61

Olympic Mountains: exploring expeditions, 74/5N,7-16— map, 74/8; *Press* exped., 69/73-74 Indians, 74/7,9,19; maps, 74/8,20; photo, 74/6

Olympic National Park, 70/182: Queets corridor included, 74/5,33

Olympic Peninsula, 78/281-82: map 1907, 74/20; Olympic loop road opened, 74/32; settlement, 74/5-33;

travel and description 1889, 74/6-23

Omaha, Neb., 72/129: emigrant gathering point, 72/65,66

O'Meara, Arthur E., 68/346

O'Meara, Edward F.: *A Point of Pride: The University of Portland Story*, by Covert, review, 78/285-86 *Continue to Prosper: The Story of All Saints Parish*, noted, 72/354

O'Meara, J.P., 69/144

Omega Mining Company, 70/280

Ompherville, Marie Anne, SEE Montour, Marie Anne

"On Judge Henry E. McGinn," by Hall S. Lusk, 73/269-72

On the Cattle Ranges of the Oregon Country, by Oliphant, review, 70/262

On to Oregon, by Morrow, cited, 64/350

On Top of Oregon, by Hall, noted, 76/382

110 Years with Josephine, the History of Josephine County, Oregon, 1856-1966, by Sutton, noted, 67/281

100 Years of Witnessing: A History of the First Baptist Church, McMinnville, Oregon, 1867-1967, by Jonasson, noted, 69/78

The 100th Anniversary First Presbyterian Church, Salem, 1869-1969, by Pearce, noted, 72/173

One Man's Gold Rush, A Klondike Album, by Moran, review, 69/75-76

One Third Crew, One Third Boat, One Third Luck, by Smith and Clark, noted, 76/182

O'Neal, John, 68/145

O'Neil (O'Neal), Bennett, 64/228N; **81**/24N,25N

O'Neil, Edward, 71/351

O'Neil, Frank, 71/351

O'Neil (O'Neal), James Anderson, 62/128-29,156; 66/353

O'Neil, John, 80/300N

O'Neil, Joseph P.: exploring expeditions, 74/5N,8; 78/281-82

O'Neil Ranch stage station, 63/274,284

O'Neill, Barney, 69/144

O'Neill, James, 80/26

O'Neill, Pete, 69/144
Oneonta (steamboat), 64/162-63: photo, 62/317
Oneonta (tug), 77/109
"One-Room School, 1900," ed. by Ruth Thayer, 72/197-208
Onions, 81/105: Cowlitz Farm, 63/152,156; prices 1858, 68/29; wild, 69/153
Onis, Luis de, 76/199,208
Onishi family, 81/153,155
Only One Man Died: the Medical Aspects of the Lewis and Clark Expedition, by Chuinard, review, 80/404-405
Onstad, Preston E.: *Benton County, a Brief History and Tour Guide*, noted, 77/89
"Camp Henderson, 1864," 65/297-302
"The Fort on the Luckiamute: A Resurvey of Fort Hoskins," 65/173-96
Forts of the West, by Frazer, review, 67/359-60
The Pig War, by Murray, review, 69/326
Retaliation: Japanese Attacks and Allied Countermeasures on the Pacific Coast in World War II, by Webber, review, 77/194-95
Western Ghost Town Shadows, by Florin, review, 66/77
Ontario, Ore., 63/269,275,295,324, 335; 70/280: history, 68/91; 72/93; Knox-Seward house, 68/352; stock shipping center, 67/150; sugar beet harvest, 81/158, 159,160,170
Ontario (U.S. sloop-of-war), 76/210
Opal City, Ore., 73/84
Oppenheimer, D., 70/255
Oppenheimer, E.K., 74/237
Oral History Assn., University of Calif., 71/288
Orandorff, William, 79/9,10
Orange, Adelaide, 62/108
Orange Canyon, SEE Oregon Canyon
Orange groves, 80/247,249: photo, 80/250
Orange lodges, 75/186N: and American Protective Assn., 75/ 134,138,146; and Federations of Patriotic Societies, 75/179
Orbit (brig), 66/164
Orchard, G., 71/15,16
Orchard, Harry, 66/73
Orchard, Jesse, 79/378
Orchard family, overland 1852, 79/365, 366,372,378,381,385,387,389
Orchards: Bridge Creek, 73/262; Hood River Valley, 76/242; Willamette Valley photo, 75/282
Ord, George, 69/22,28
Order of American Freedom, 75/134
Order of the Hoo Hoo, 77/77
Ordway, John, 64/183; 66/384
Oregon: 1830-45, 72/231
agriculture— agencies, 69/332-33; products, 71/ 31,34
air pollution control, 72/287; almanac, 62/296; anniversaries, 70/223; atlas, 74/278-79; 78/178-79; 81/331; attitudes toward, 75/39-42,53,54-55,233-39,301-308,336-38; beaches, SEE Oregon coast—beaches; bibliographies, 63/91; 72/90; biography index, 77/297; borax industry, 73/228-44 boundaries, 63/364— Calif.-Ore.-Nev., 72/5-53; disputes, 72/9-11; Idaho-Ore., 77/314; surveys, 72/10-53*passim*; SEE ALSO Oregon Question
British Army officers in, 68/86; British consulate, 72/360-61; business outlook, 69/337; capital controversy, 62/80; 66/166; centennial firms, 70/182; characterized, 67/202
Civil War period, 67/54-60— reporting of, 65/44-45,62,71,84; Southern sympathizers, 67/54-60 *passim*
climate, 69/200— weather history, 71/198
community colleges, 69/337; compared to Washington, 70/217; composers, 77/196
constitution, 64/316— convention, 79/6

courts, SEE Judiciary; Coxey's army in, **65**/269-95; crime, **80**/13 described— 1864, **68**/151-52; 1964, **65**/309 description and travel, **65**/200 economic development— 1860-90, **71**/27-98; 1880-90, **67**/105-78*passim* economic history, **63**/361; economic structure, **67**/88 economy, **68**/186; **69**/199FF; **78**/178— 1850, **80**/329; statistics 1962, **64**/92 education attitudes, **73**/81 elections— 1864, **65**/48N,62,296; 1962, **64**/ 281; 1965, **66**/282; 1966, **68**/344; Hayes-Tilden dispute, **67**/257-72; presidential primaries, **69**/338 fairs, **71**/197; first hosiery mill, **67**/61; first novelist, **65**/220; first school, **66**/341 folklore, **66**/281; **79**/336— superstitions, **68**/86 gazetteer, **78**/178 geographic names, **75**/368-69— Port Orford area, **63**/364 geologic interpretations, **67**/5- 39*passim*; gold production, **69**/201 governors, **67**/373— provision for absence of, **71**/198 Great Basin character, **67**/21-22; guidebooks, **71**/59,84; high desert, **69**/63; highway program, **74**/138 historic landmarks, **64**/121; **79**/97-98— markers, **67**/281 history, **69**/60-61— economic conditions, **63**/361; in fiction, **66**/242,243; opinions on histories, **81**/251; reprints, **74**/359; settlers, **65**/364 hospitals, **65**/220; human geography, **78**/178; imprints to 1870, **64**/137-82, 284; **70**/62-63; **74**/286; **78**/251-79; industrial development, **72**/287; influenza epidemic 1918, **64**/246-58; insurance, **69**/334; **72**/287; iron and steel, **69**/201; irrigation, **78**/351-54; land

and water resources management, **68**/ 176-77; local government units, **64**/ 185; manufacturing, **71**/33-34,35,64; maps, **71**/362; **77**/196-97,310; military posts list, **76**/92; minerals and metallurgical industry, **69**/86; name, **62**/ 299; **79**/211; national forests, **76**/29- 38; Negroes in, **69**/273; newspapers, **64**/212; SEE ALSO Newspapers; park system, **74**/109; penal philosophy, **80**/27-28; pictorialized in Skirving panorama, **65**/147; pioneer tradition, **72**/227; pioneer women, **69**/77 politics— 1856-62, **72**/316-38; 1900-1956, **72**/80-81 population, **62**/198— 1860-90, **71**/60; 1870, **71**/41; characteristics, **68**/349; foreign-born, **77**/ 246-47; growth in 1880s, **67**/135; maps 1850, **77**/196 post cards, **66**/303-30; printing 1845- 70, **70**/62-63; promotion in 1888, **73**/ 244; public health service, **65**/220; railroads, **70**/181; reclamation projects, **80**/409; resources, **76**/29-38; role in U.S. strategy in Pacific, **62**/9; scenic preservation efforts, **74**/119,139-40; search for business opportunities, **71**/ 17-19 settlement, **73**/360— before 1846, **78**/332-50 sheriffs, **66**/90; state expenditures, **71**/198; state rock, SEE Thunderegg statehood— constitutional convention, **66**/15-16; officers elected, **66**/17; petition for, **66**/347; voting record on, **66**/15 submarine attacks, WW II, **65**/314; taxes, **72**/90; theses on, **72**/225-79; tour guides, **81**/329; touring in 1915, **75**/283-89; water problems, **66**/384; wild flowers, **75**/304-308; wildlife areas, **79**/409; wool industry, **67**/ 125-38 *Oregon* (battleship), **74**/84,132: commissioned, **76**/272; cost, **76**/294 crew, **76**/271,276,292— photo, **72**/ins.fr.cov. Sept.

famous cruise, 76/269-98— distance, 76/272,277; map, 76/282 guns, 76/271,296(photo); history, 79/ 212-13; launching photo, 76/272; logbook, 81/333; photos, 72/ins.covs. Sept.; 76/271,276,278,290,293,ins.bk. cov. Sept.; reactivated, 76/294; scrapped, 76/294; size, 76/295; speed, 76/272, 277,280,285,289,295

Oregon (brig), 67/91

Oregon (OR&NCO. steamer): schedule 1883, 71/ins.fr.cov. March

Oregon (Pacific Coast ss Co. steamer), 81/119,120

Oregon (Pacific Mail steamship), 62/197

Oregon, ed. by Gohs, noted, 70/76

Oregon: A History, by Dodds, review, 79/97-98

Oregon Academy, Lafayette, 66/ 11-12,23

Oregon Advertising Club, 74/240

The Oregon Almanac and Books of Facts, ed. by Brooks, review, 62/296

Oregon Alpine Club, 74/7; 78/282

Oregon American and Evangelical Unionist, 64/123-24; 75/116-18: funds, 75/184N; masthead, 75/108

Oregon American Bicentennial Commission, SEE American Revolution Bicentennial

Oregon-American Lumber Company, 77/219

Oregon and California Advisory Board, 64/55N,60-62

Oregon and California (O&C) lands, SEE Land

Oregon and California Railroad Co., 63/ 78-79; 64/55,87; 67/71,105,172; 69/ 201,221; 70/271; 71/283; 73/83,283; 75/86; 80/229,233; 81/82: absorbs Oregon Central, 71/46 construction, 71/197; 75/123— photos, 75/124; 80/162,163,234 covered bridges, 66/383; first train Portland-Ashland, photo, 67/137; foreign bondholders, 71/47,51,62,63,69, 73,80-81,88-89,90; Grants Pass depot photo, 67/137; history, 71/41-96*passim*; Huntington interest, 71/69,73;

land grants, 64/55-67,87; 71/63,88 maps, 71/44,52; 80/232,238— Portland works, 71/66-67

Oregon Pacific Railroad competition, 71/90; Oregon Steamship Co. absorbed, 71/47,63,81,99

photos—

construction, 75/124; 80/162,163, 234; engineers' camp 1880s, 80/ins. fr.cov. Fall; first train Portland-Ashland, 67/137; Grants Pass depot, 67/ 137; Portland docks and ferry, 80/294 rates, 71/78; reaches Roseburg, 71/46 routes, actual and proposed—

Diamond Peak, 71/74; Portland-Astoria, 71/69; Roseburg-Klamath Lake, 71/51; Siskiyou, 71/51,63,74; Winnemucca, 71/63,64,73

sources, 71/80,95; SEE ALSO Southern Pacific Railroad

Oregon and California Stage station, SEE Twelve Mile House

Oregon and California Wagon Road Co., 62/319

Oregon and Transcontinental Co., 69/208,217N,219N; 71/95

Oregon and Washington Typographical Society, 64/38

Oregon Archaeological Society, 62/89,90

Oregon Argus, Ore. City, 64/128; 65/336; 75/119; 78/12N,21: attacks *Religious Expositor*, 64/130-31; broadside extra 1855, 64/146

Oregon Assn. of Title Men, 74/199

Oregon At Last!, by Van der Loeff, review, 64/350

"Oregon Autumns," by Davis, cited, 66/245

Oregon Bank, Portland, 65/412; 66/386

The Oregon Baptist, 64/134

Oregon (Linn) bill, 62/124,129,131

Oregon Biography Index, ed. by Brandt and Guilford, noted, 77/292; review, 77/297

Oregon Blues Brigade Fife and Drum Corps, 66/385

Oregon boot, 65/316; 80/11N

"Oregon Borax: Twenty Mule Team-Rose Valley History," by Leslie L.D.

Shaffer and Richard P. Baxter, 73/228-44

Oregon Botanical Association: bulletins, 68/116-22; minute book, 68/122

Oregon Botanical Expedition: history, 68/111-24

Oregon Building and Loan Assn., 69/327

Oregon (Orange) Canyon, 68/254,314: map, 68/250

Oregon Cattle and Horse Raisers' Assn., 67/235N

Oregon Cattlemen's Assn., 66/82: 50th anniversary, 65/216

"The Oregon Cavalry," by John M. Drake, 65/392-400

Oregon Caves, 64/361; 66/171N: discovery, 73/73

"Oregon Celebrates!", photos, 77/130-47

Oregon Centennial Exposition and Trade Fair: postal cards, 66/305

Oregon Centennial of Statehood, 66/305: exhibits, 77/289

Oregon, central, 73/258-68,278: geography, 77/195; geology, 77/195; history, 77/195,300; ranching, 81/ 261-80*passim*,281-318*passim*; tour guide, 81/329

Oregon Central Military Wagon Road, 64/91; 74/282; 77/328; 78/58,297, 299,308N,309,310,319; 79/30,43-47: incorporates part of Free Emigrant Road, 79/47; intersects Elliott Cutoff, photo, 79/4; maps, 71/362; 79/44-45; purposes, 79/43,46; route, 79/32,46,47, 50(map); surveys, 65/63N; 77/330; 79/28,46-47

Oregon Central Railroad, 64/172; 67/172; 71/283: Calif. interests, 71/46; Holladay control, 71/46,71; land grant, 71/45,46, 71; reaches Roseburg, 71/46; renamed, 71/46 routes, 71/93— Astoria branch, 71/69,94; East Side *vs.* West, 71/46,71; photo East Side beginning, 71/70; Winnemucca, 71/46

Salem interests, 71/46

Oregon Children's Aid Society, 64/89

Oregon City, Ore., 62/65,79,80,145, 156,159,167,386,399; 63/10,19,58, 103,180-81,190-91,194,207-208,215; 66/166-67,356; 68/187,330,353; 75/119; 77/45; 79/172,173,175: Abernethy marker, 66/382; anti-Chinese violence, 75/129; Blaine recollections 1850s-60s, 66/82; bridges, 72/91; capital controversy, 64/300; Catholic school, 80/341; churches, 71/190; college, 70/199; early Portland rival, 72/169; farmers' market, 74/357; first elevator, 63/245; first telephone, 65/211; foundry, 63/68; Gray property, 73/245-57*passim* history, 69/339— pictorial, 67/369 ice manufacture, 63/67; incorporated, 80/8N; McLoughlin claim, 62/315; 63/176; markers, 63/245; Moss store ledger 1847-48, 66/219N; Mt. View Cemetery, 69/87,341; Ore.Prov.Govt. meeting, 66/353; parks, 76/300,303; population 1843, 66/355; post office, 66/382; prices 1854, 63/19; river boats at, 63/67; Singer Hill, 76/300, 301,303; weather damage 1850, 66/ 162-63; woolen mills, 62/164,167, 175,176,179

Oregon City and Southern Railway, 74/357

Oregon City canal and locks: aid to river navigation, 71/42,46; construction 1873, 71/46

Oregon City Imperial Mills, 63/212

Oregon City Manufacturing Co., 66/381

Oregon City Woolen Manufacturing Co., 65/395N

Oregon City Woolen Mills, 67/71FF

Oregon Civil War Round Table, 63/370

"An Oregon Classic: Nellie Pipes McArthur," by Thomas Vaughan and Priscilla Knuth, 79/91

Oregon coast, 77/67-71: beaches, 75/39,339-43— Road's End, 75/54-55 continental shelf, 63/362; 64/357;

65/220; Lincoln Co., 75/54-55; ocean currents, 77/278; photo mural, 76/91; photos, 75/52,55,ins.bk.cov. March; 77/68,70

Oregon Coast Artillery, 64/90; 67/374

Oregon College of Education, Monmouth, 72/89: history, 72/231; 74/282; publications, 78/365

Oregon Committee for the Humanities, 78/368-69

Oregon Commonwealth Federation, 65/364: convention, 76/142-44; labor union involvement, 76/141,144-46,148-51; lack of agrarian support, 76/141,146-47, 149; third party question, 76/140-44, 147-51

Oregon Construction Co., 65/395N

Oregon, Corvallis and Eastern Railroad, 80/280

Oregon Country, 62/8,9,67-68; 63/84; 64/92: botanical collections in Europe, 68/112, 118-21,123; botanists in, 68/111-12, 123; boundaries, 67/368; 70/343; history of settlement, 70/111FF; map 1840-42, 76/128; record trees, 76/92; Slacum report, 76/118-34; U.S. occupation promoted, 70/339-46; SEE ALSO Oregon Question

The Oregon Country Under the Union Jack, comp. by Payette, cited, 66/332-33N; noted, 63/84; 64/92

Oregon crab apple (*Pyrus fusca*), 69/155

Oregon Creek, 68/251N

Oregon Democrat, Albany, 79/7: broadside extra 1860, 64/152

Oregon Department of Geology and Mineral Industries: publication, 67/33

Oregon Department of Geology and Mineral Resources: history, 72/180

The Oregon Desert, by Jackman and Long, review, 66/272-73

Oregon dunes, 64/284

Oregon, eastern, 73/279: conflict of laws re land claims, 67/302-

305,307; described, 77/314,332-33; early towns, 79/104; history, 77/300; population 1880-90, 67/156; religion, 68/354; settlers excluded, 67/323N

Oregon Electric Railway, 80/209: company records, 74/79

Oregon Electric Railway Historical Society, 67/373

Oregon Equal Suffrage Assn., 68/186

Oregon Exchange Company, 79/408

Oregon Fir (schooner), 75/362

"Oregon—First in 'Portable' Irrigation," by E.H. Davis, 78/351-54

Oregon Folklore, by Jones, noted, 79/336

Oregon Free Press, Ore. City, 64/123,140

Oregon Geographic Names, by L.A. and L.L. McArthur, 4th ed. noted, 75/368,369

Oregon Geographic Names Board, 63/ 370; 69/345; 70/370,372,373; 71/ 295,371-72; 72/359; 78/370; 79/412: Athabaska Pass trip, 79/413

"Oregon Geology: The Century Old Story," by Phil F. Brogan, 67/5-39

Oregon Gold and Gems: Maps, Then and Now, noted, 76/181

Oregon grape, 80/56

"Oregon Grapeshot": letter of John D. Hicks, 74/350-51 letter of Laban Hill, 66/51 letter of Leivy A. Murphy, 64/342 letter of Charles Stevens, 76/180 letter of W.W. Wells, 65/296

"Oregon Grapeshot Ricochet," 75/ 290-91

"An Oregon Heritage: National Forests," by J. Herbert Stone, 76/29-38

Oregon Historic Landmarks: Southern Oregon, by Oregon Society, DAR, noted, 81/105

Oregon Historical Center, Portland, 64/ 358,360; 66/301; 68/355; 69/177: architects, 67/199 cornerstone ceremonies, 66/385— address, 66/293-301; dedication photo, 66/292; time capsule photo, 66/294 dedication address, 67/197-211; finance committee, 66/388; fund drive, 65/412-13,415; 66/295,386,387,389;

opening, 67/377; photos of site, plan, and construction, 67/196,200,206, 208-10,ins.covs. Sept.; planning committee, 66/385-86,388

"Oregon Historical Center Dedication Address," by Walter M. Whitehill, 67/197-211

Oregon Historical Landmarks, by Oregon Society, DAR, noted, 64/121

Oregon Historical Quarterly, 70/197,226, 227; 73/363,365; 75/368; 77/86,290; 80/416; 81/256:

annual publisher's statement, 79/409; 80/409; 81/424; 75th anniversary, 75/4,6

Oregon Historical Society, 62/309-10, 313,335; 63/354,371; 67/198,202, 203-11*passim*,257; 70/204,227,232; 73/371; 74/199:

AASLH awards, 68/359; 69/343; accessions, 72/358; activities, 79/411-12; 81/425-29; affiliated societies, 76/93-96; 77/92-96; 78/92-96; annual meetings, 62/417-21; 63/367-72; 64/358-62; 65/412-15; 66/385-86; 67/375-78; 68/355-59; 69/342-46; 70/368-72; 71/369-72; 72/357-61; 73/361-72; 74/360-64; 75/360-70; 76/383-87; 77/383-86; 78/366-70; 79/410-14; 80/410-17; 81/425-29; annual sponsors, 73/375; 74/184,366; 75/192, 372; 76/184,389; 77/199,389; 78/ 183,373; 79/217,417; 80/212,420; 81/211; awards, 68/358-59; 69/346; 70/372; 71/372; 72/360; 73/364; 76/387; 77/385-86; 79/412-13; 80/ 414; background, 81/255; benefactors, 74/190,372-73; 75/198,379; 76/191, 396; 77/206,396; 78/190-91,382; 79/ 226,426-27; 80/222,430; 81/221; Bicentennial observations, 77/383,384; British manuscripts project, 70/368, 371; building plans, 76/385,386; building site acquisition, 76/385 Bybee-Howell House, 69/174,346; 70/368,369,372—

opening, 67/375; restoration plans, 63/368,370

by-laws, 68/358—

amended, 70/371-72; 73/361; 76/386; changes, 78/370; 81/427; revised, 66/391-92

centennial year, 73/364,372; 74/360, 363—

ball, 74/362

challenge grant, 81/425,426; chief factors, 80/430; 81/221; church records, 71/363

collections—

additions, 81/426; Collins, 74/363; Drake, 66/313; library, 71/370,372; manuscripts guide, 72/358; 74/94; museum, 73/364; photo, 66/309,317, 327; 72/358; program, 78/367; Russian, 75/369; sailing ship models, 74/ 363

committee on performing arts, 71/372; contributing members, 62/111-12,207-208,303-304,423-24; 63/94-95,256-57,374-75; 64/94-95,190-91,286-87, 364-65; 65/126-27,222-23,318-19,417-18; 66/94-95,190-91,286-87,396; 67/ 94-95,190-91,286-87,380-81; 68/93-94,190,286,362; 69/91,187,283,349; 70/91,187,283,375; 71/107,203,299, 375; 72/186,364; 73/89-90,375-76; 74/184-85,366-67; 75/192-93,372-73; 76/184-85,389-90; 77/200-201,389-90; 78/183-84,373-74; 79/217-19,417-19; 80/212-14,421-22; 81/212-13; Cook exhibit, 75/363,366,367; cumulative contributors, 68/366-67; directors reports, 67/377-78; 75/370; 80/ 414-17; documentary films, 77/386; donors, 74/191,373-74; 75/199,379-80; 76/191,396-97; 77/207,397; 78/ 191-92,382-83; 79/227,427-28; 80/ 222-23,431-32; 81/222; Drake collection presented, 66/313; early history, 70/197N,198; education dept., 78/368 exhibits, 74/362; 76/383; 77/289—

Cook, 75/363,366,367; Ratner, 81/426

fellows, 74/190,372; 75/198,378; 76/ 190,395; 77/206,396; 78/190,381; 79/226,426; 80/221-22,430; 81/221; financial history, 74/360; financial statement, 74/360; Foster papers presented, **65**/412; functions, **73**/365; future plans, **71**/103-104,295-96; grants, **77**/383; **80**/413; **81**/425,426; Hatfield letter quoted, **66**/392; Heritage Awards, **66**/393; **76**/387; historical sites, **79**/411; **80**/412; history in school requirements, **81**/427,428; honorary council, **77**/198,387; **78**/181, 369,371; **79**/215,415; **80**/210,418; **81**/209,430; honorary life members, **75**/199-200,380; **76**/192,397; **77**/385, 397-98; **78**/192,383-84; **79**/227-28, 428-29; **80**/223-24,432-33; **81**/223-24; honorary members, **69**/94-96,190-92,286-88,352-54; **70**/94-96,190-92, 286-88,378-80; **71**/110-12,206-208, 302-304,378-80; **72**/190-92,369-71; **73**/94-96,380-82; **74**/192,374; incorporation, **70**/197; **73**/365; Journal Bldg. quarters, **66**/299,390,391; Junior Historians, **75**/86; lecture series, **74**/363; Lee House and Mission Parsonage restoration, **65**/218 library, **63**/60N; **64**/137—

collections, **71**/370,372; holdings, **73**/363-64; use growth, **78**/368

life members, **62**/111,207,303,423; **63**/94,256,374; **64**/94,190,286,364; **65**/126,222,318,417; **66**/94,190,286, 395; **67**/94,190,286,380; **68**/93,189-90,285-86,261-62; **69**/90-91,186-87, 282-83,348; **70**/90,186,282,374; **71**/ 106,202-203,298,374; **72**/185-86,363-64; **73**/88-89,384-85; **74**/184,366; **75**/192,372; **76**/184,389; **77**/199,388; **78**/182,372-73; **79**/216-17,416-17; **80**/211-12,419-20; **81**/210-11; Living Farm project, **70**/368,372

manuscripts—

British, **74**/368,371; Burlington-Northern, **74**/79-82; collections guide, **72**/358; **74**/94; Foster papers, **65**/412; Negro history, **73**/203,204

membership—

largest in U.S., **79**/411; number, **81**/426,427

Minto support, **81**/255-56

museum—

collections, **73**/364; exhibits, **70**/

371,372; **72**/358; gifts to, **66**/386; list, **69**/174N

NEH grant, **80**/413; officers and directors, **62**/111,206,302,422; **63**/93-94, 255-56,373-74; **64**/93-94,189-90,285-86,363-64; **65**/125-26,221-22,317-18, 416-17; **66**/93-94,189-90,285-86,394-95; **67**/93-94,189-90,285-86,379-80; **68**/92-93,188-89,284-85,360-61; **69**/ 89-90,185-86,281-82,347-48; **70**/89-90,185-86,281-82,373-74; **71**/105-106, 201-202,297-98,373-74; **72**/95-96, 184-85,259-60,362-63; **73**/87-88,287-88,373-74; **74**/183,287-88,365-66; **75**/5-6,95-96,191-92,295-96,371-73; **76**/183-84,388-89; **77**/198-99,385, 387-88; **78**/181-82,371-72; **79**/215-16,413,415-16; **80**/210-11,418-19; **81**/209,210,427,428,430-31; patrons, **74**/191,373; **75**/198-99,379; **76**/191, 396; **77**/207,396; **78**/191,382; **79**/ 226,427; **80**/222,430-31; **81**/222; photo collections, **66**/309,317,327; **72**/358

photos—

City Hall quarters, **70**/206; Tourney Bldg. quarters, **70**/208; SEE ALSO Oregon Historical Center

pioneer orchard, **71**/370; preservation and restoration projects, **71**/294-95, 372; presidents' reports, **68**/356-58; **69**/343-46; **70**/370-71; **71**/370-71; **72**/358-59; **73**/362-64; **74**/362-63; **75**/367-70; **76**/383-86; **77**/383-85; **78**/367-69; **79**/411-12; **80**/411-13; **81**/426-27; Public Auditorium quarters, **66**/295,390; **71**/102; **77**/383, 385; questionnaire, **79**/412; Ratner collection, **81**/426; research and museum center, **77**/384; **78**/367; Russian collections, **75**/369; Russian desk, **72**/ 359; sailing ship models, **74**/363; Sauvie Island storage barn, **70**/369,371; service to state gov't, **74**/360; society news, **76**/183-92,388-97; special service certificates, **76**/387; staff, **68**/92, 188,288,360; **69**/89,185,281,347; **70**/ 89,185,281,373; **71**/105,201,297,373; **72**/95,184,362; **73**/87,287,373; **74**/

183,287,365; 75/95,191,295,371; 76/ 183,385,388; 77/198,387; 78/181, 371; 79/215,415; 80/210,415,418; 81/209,430; stewards, 78/370; 79/ 217,417; 80/212,420; 81/211; storage, 78/369; supporting members, 62/ 112,208,304,424; 63/95,257,375; 64/ 95,191,287,365; 65/127,223,319,418; 66/95,191,287,396; 67/95,191,287, 381; 68/94,190,286,362-63; 69/91, 187,283,349; 70/91-92,187-88,283- 84,375-76; 71/107-108,203-204,299- 300,375-76; 72/187,365; 73/90,376; 74/185-86,367-68; 75/93-94,373-74; 76/185-86,390-91; 77/201,390-91; 78/184-85; 79/219-20,419-20; 80/ 214-15,422-23; 81/213-15; sustaining members, 62/112,208,304,424; 63/95- 96,257-58,375-76; 64/95-96,191-92, 287-88,365-66; 65/127-28,223-24, 319-20,418-19; 66/95-96,191-92,287- 88,396-98; 67/95-96,191-92,287-88, 381-82; 68/94-96,190-92,286-88,363- 65; 69/93-94,188-90,284-86,350-52; 70/92-94,188-90,284-86,376-78; 71/ 108-109,204-206,300-302,376-78; 72/ 187-90,365-68; 73/91-94,377-80; 74/ 186-90,368-72; 75/194-98,374-78; 76/186-90,391-95; 77/202-206,391- 96; 78/185-90,376-81; 79/220-26, 420-26; 80/215-21,424-30; 81/215- 21; Sutor bequest, 64/359; technological history research, 66/299; ten-year program, 69/344-46; ten-year statistics, 76/385; treasurers' reports, 67/375; 68/355-56; 69/342; 70/368-70; 71/ 369-70; 72/357-58; 73/361-62; 74/ 360-62; 75/366-67; 76/383; 77/383- 85; 78/366; 79/410; 80/410-11; 25- year review, 80/414-17; volunteers, 69/ 344,346; 70/370,372; 71/370,371-72; 72/358-59; 73/363,373; 76/385; 77/ 385,386; 78/367; 79/412-13; 80/414, 415; 81/427,428,429; will provisions, 71/ins.bk.cov. Dec.; work reviewed, 71/ 100-103,293-95; Young gravesite deed presented, 65/415; 66/90

Oregon Hotel, Ashland, 62/205

Oregon Humane Society, 80/10

Oregon Immigration Commission, 74/113

Oregon Imprints, by Belknap, review, 70/62-63

Oregon Imprints, addenda, by Belknap, noted, 74/286

"*Oregon Imprints* Revisited," by George N. Belknap, 78/251-79

Oregon Improvement Company, 69/211, 217N,219N

Oregon Industrial Commission, 62/94

Oregon Institute, Salem, 62/240; 66/352

Oregon Iron and Steel Company, 69/208,211,219: foundry illus., 69/218

Oregon Iron Works, 62/311; 65/8

Oregon: Its Resources, Climate, People and Productions, by Moseley, noted, 71/79

Oregon Journal, Portland, 67/80; 73/331; 74/110: editorial policies, 75/173; photo collection, 72/358; 73/364; 74/362; supports Columbia River Hwy., 74/112

Oregon Kid (racing boat), 74/304

The Oregon King Mine, Jefferson County, Oregon, by Libbey and Corcoran, noted, 63/246,362

Oregon Knight, 75/135

Oregon Labor Press, 75/154,155; 76/144

Oregon Landmarks Committee, 71/199, 295

Oregon legislature: 1859, 64/354; 1866, 79/128; 1874, 79/363; "holdup" session 1897, 68/ 210-15; members 1843-1967, 69/273; position on Portland police, 80/147; racial restrictions, 80/140; revision of Portland charter, 80/17,20,160-61,168- 69,287-88,300-301,319-20; university act 1876, 77/380

Oregon League for Nursing, 65/383

Oregon Lewis and Clark Heritage Foundation: officers and directors, 74/181; 75/91; 76/96; 77/95; 78/95; 79/111; 80/ 111; 81/111; publications, 75/94; 76/92; 77/89,292; 81/208

Oregon Library Association, 71/370

Oregon Magazine, **74**/145,154
Oregon Midland Railroad, **80**/104
Oregon Mounted Rifles, **67**/369
Oregon Mounted Volunteers, **67**/315, 319,322N:
escort Walla Walla settlers, **66**/159; expiration of enlistment, **66**/155-56,157-59; Ft. Bennett, **66**/139,147 Ft. Henrietta duty, **66**/133-60*passim*— Indian raid, **66**/150-51
Indian skirmishes 1855, **66**/135,137, 141,143; led by Kelly, **66**/133-34,135-38,152-57; loss of horses, **66**/150-51, 153,154-55; Nesmith letter, **67**/319N; The Dalles headquarters, **66**/133-60 *passim*; Walla Walla battle, **66**/147-49; **67**/318; Wright refuses cooperation, **67**/323N
Oregon Museum of Science and Industry, **69**/177
Oregon myrtle, SEE Myrtle trees
Oregon National Bank, **75**/28
Oregon National Guard, **67**/66,67; **74**/346; **80**/265:
Battery A, **75**/252,263-64
Oregon Non-Parks, by Benson, noted, **75**/87
Oregon, northeast: early settlement, **79**/104
Oregon Nursery Company, **64**/354
Oregon: Or a Short History of a Long Journey, by Wyeth, reprint noted, **72**/170
Oregon, Pacific and Eastern Railroad, **72**/288
Oregon Pacific Railroad Company, **67**/63; **69**/201; **71**/94: competition with o&c, **71**/90; former name, **71**/349; Hogg organizes, **71**/90; routes, **71**/52-53; support of Barrett appointment to Asia, **71**/151
Oregon Paving and Contract Co., **69**/208N
Oregon Pioneer Association, **62**/324, 417; **66**/298; **69**/338; **70**/197N,198; **79**/241; **81**/233:
annual meeting 1883, **81**/229; Applegate attitude, **81**/229,230,250,259; Minto participation, **81**/255; 90th anniversary, **64**/358

photos— 1897 meeting, **81**/258; second annual reunion, **81**/cov. Fall
poster 1876 reunion, **81**/228; program 1879 reunion, **81**/252; *Transactions*, **73**/363
Oregon Pioneer Research Bureau, **70**/75
Oregon Pioneers of 1852 and 1853: The Snodgrass, Deckard and Moore Families, by Moore, noted, **73**/73
Oregon Pony, **63**/363
Oregon Portage Railroad, **63**/363
Oregon-Portland Cement Company: history, **66**/281
"Oregon Postcards," by Edwin D. Culp, **66**/303-30
Oregon Provisional Emigration Society, **78**/344,345
Oregon Provisional Government, **62**/ 240; **63**/211; **81**/243:
beginnings, **63**/121-23,136; **66**/353-54; **78**/87-88; bounty on predatory animals, **66**/353; clerk, **66**/352; constitution, **62**/131-32,134-35
elections, **62**/130,132,137,139N,144, 156,158—
May 14, 1844, **66**/355-56; June 3, 1845, **66**/356-57
executive committee, **62**/131; first commander of volunteer forces, **81**/ 188N; French-Canadian support, **66**/353; history, **66**/350N; **69**/60 judiciary, **62**/113,139,140,141,156, 157; **66**/350—
courts—
circuit, **62**/128,134-62*passim*; county, **62**/158-59,161; clerks, **62**/ 140,147; criminal, **62**/146N,147, 157,159,160,161; district, **62**/128, 138; litigation process, **73**/245-57; probate, **62**/137,138,146,155,157, 158; records, **62**/154N; supreme, **62**/137-40,144-45,146-51,152-62 *passim*
judges, **62**/350—
circuit, **62**/139,161; county, **62**/ 160-61; district, **62**/158; justices of the peace, **62**/137-59*passim*; salaries,

62/139,140,143,144,146,159,161, 162; supreme, 62/121-22,128, 137-57*passim*

prosecuting attorneys, 62/153 land claims, 64/204,204N-205N,208N laws—

code, 66/350; land laws, 70/111-13; organic, SEE Organic Law

legislature—

canal and railroad petitions, 66/356; House, 62/133,144-46,147,151,157, 158,161; members, 69/273

meetings, 62/125N—

Feb. 7, 1841, 66/350; Feb. 2, 1843, 66/352; Mar. 6, 1843, 66/352-53; May 2, 1843, 66/353,354

Methodist influence, 71/368; need for, 62/125; 66/350; petition to U.S. Congress, 62/125,129; 75/72-73; postal service, 81/188N; sheriff, 66/350; tax roll 1844, 66/356N; "wolf" meetings, 62/125N; SEE ALSO (above) meetings of Feb. and Mar. 1843

Oregon Question, 62/8,9; 63/311; 65/385; 68/343; 69/59; 70/293-311*passim*,345,346,363; 71/370; 72/230,234; 73/86; 76/204,213,214, 215-16; 78/332,342-43:

Adams' view, 72/103,105-106,117, 119; Anglo-American relations, 69/72-73; 75/317-27*passim*; British claims, 72/105-106,109-10,112,123; Buchanan policies, 75/320-21,325-27; commercial interests, 75/317-35; Congressional view 1820s, 72/104-105,116-17; independence proposed, 81/183-84; joint occupation termination, 75/328N; negotiations, 75/85,317,319,325-28; 76/213,215,216; 81/181-84; periodical literature of Great Britain, 65/213; Polk's "whole Oregon" policy, 75/317-28; Shively role, 81/181-84; U.S. and British naval support, 70/293; U.S.-Russian relations, 72/107-26*passim*; 75/317-18,325-28,331-35; Whigs, 75/317-18,321,328-29

The Oregon Question: Essays in Anglo-American Diplomacy and Politics, by Merk, review, 69/72-73

"'The Oregon Question Is...a Massachusetts Question'," by Howard I. Kushner, 75/317-35

Oregon Railway and Navigation Company, 63/61,64-65,69; 64/304; 65/ 395N; 67/105,123,168FF; 69/201, 208,221; 74/108; 81/266N,269N: acquires Reid interests, 71/63; Albina shops, photo, 67/108; construction costs, 71/64-65,90-91; Coeur d'Alene extension, 69/217,219; documents, 69/198N; engine photos, 67/103, 131; importance to Portland, 71/39-40; route poorly conceived, 71/39; shops and roundhouse, 1886 photo, 81/270; steamboat monopoly opposed, 71/395; stockholders, 71/91; Villard policies, 71/47

Oregon Railway Association, 62/421 Oregon Rangers, 66/139N Oregon Regional Primate Research Center, 77/382

Oregon Regional Union List of Serials, ed. by Abrams, review, 77/382

Oregon Roadside Council, 67/42,44

Oregon Sentinel, Jacksonville, 64/161-62; 65/29N:

broadside extra 1860, 64/152-53

Oregon Shakespearean Festival Assn., 76/381

"The Oregon Shakespearean Festival at Ashland," by Josephine Evans Harpham, 62/180-83

"Oregon Sheep, Wool and Woolen Industries," by Peter A. Shroyer, 67/125-38

Oregon Short Line, 67/105,142,146; 69/145,201; 71/283; 76/229: Baker City branch, 71/39; competition with O&C, 71/90; construction cost, 71/91; Huntington shops photo, 67/ 124; Idaho construction, 71/366; map, 71/52-53; OR&NCO. connection, 71/ 55; Snake River bridge photo, 71/fr.cov. March; subsidiary of Union Pacific, 71/ 55; train photo ca. 1885, 71/fr.cov. March; train seized by Coxey's army, 65/291

Oregon, southern:

landmarks, 81/105-106; maps, 69/30,34,35,46-47,257-63

Oregon Spectator, Ore. City, 62/150; 63/226,238-39N; 64/123,140; 66/357N; 75/116,119,357: first published, 77/319; history, 81/105; political censorship, 63/358

Oregon Stamp Society: officers and directors, 64/83,279

Oregon State Agricultural College, 72/281,283; 73/345,347; 77/91; 80/377-79: cadets, 72/283,284(photo); extension service, 78/353; SEE ALSO Oregon State University

Oregon State Agricultural Society, 65/398; 81/253

Oregon State Archives, 62/109; 63/247; 64/137: agricultural agency records, 69/332; legislature members list, 69/273

Oregon State Bar Association, 74/199, 216,237

Oregon State Board of Health, 62/203

Oregon State Board of Horticulture, 81/253,256,263N

Oregon State Canvassing Board, 66/367,369,372,374,377: letter to Benson quoted, 66/375

Oregon State Dept. of Agriculture, 77/368

Oregon State Dept. of Environmental Quality, 77/368

Oregon State Dept. of Labor, 80/324

Oregon State Fair, 67/373; 81/75,253: first, 63/245; 64/89; 67/373

Oregon State Federation of Garden Clubs, 67/46

Oregon State Federation of Labor, 76/136,137,140,144-45,147

Oregon State Game Commission, 71/352: Chinese pheasant reports, 65/254-56

Oregon State Grange, 76/137,141,146

Oregon State Highway Commission, 67/42,47,48,51,52,184; 78/102; 74/130,234: created, 74/108,136N,212-13; history, 70/182; preliminary work on Columbia River Hwy., 74/111

Oregon State Horticultural Society, 68/163,165

Oregon State Hydroelectric Commission, 71/352

Oregon State Library, 77/382: Barry material, 66/79; librarians, 81/428; 75th anniversary, 81/428

Oregon State Marine Science Center, 69/177

Oregon State Medical Society: officers, 79/308

Oregon State Motor Association, 74/240

Oregon State Normal School, Weston, 73/84

Oregon State Parks Commission, 67/184; 74/130

Oregon State Supreme Court, SEE Judiciary

Oregon State System of Higher Education, 73/324; 77/382

Oregon State Teachers' Institute, 64/154-55

Oregon State University, 65/381; 70/74; 78/351,354; 80/323,324: Benton Hall, 72/92; library, 68/343 School of Agriculture— engineering dept., 78/354; extension service, 78/353,354; soils dept., 78/353

SEE ALSO Oregon State Agricultural College

Oregon State Weather Bureau: history and functions, 71/198

Oregon Statehood Art Medal, 68/187

Oregon Statesman, Salem, 64/123; 75/119, 121,135,357,358; 78/13,104; 79/243: beginnings, 77/319; early broadside extras, 64/139,165-67

Oregon Steam Navigation Company, 62/228; 63/79,108N,212,263; 65/9; 67/161N; 69/198: Ainsworth recollections, 63/84; Portland steamer schedule 1864, 64/162-63; Strong counsel for, 64/304

Oregon Steamship Company: creditors, 71/81; sale to O&C,

71/47,63,81
Oregon Superintendency of Indian Affairs, 70/114,119
Oregon Supreme Court Record, 62/ 138-39,143,160
Oregon Surveyor-General: records, 70/270
Oregon System, 68/206; 72/80
Oregon Technical Institute, 65/218
Oregon Telegraph Company, 64/158-59
Oregon Temperance Society: 1837 petition quoted, 66/346
Oregon Territorial Government: Blue Book battle, 64/299; capital controversy, 64/299-300; established, 75/ 74; 77/314,318-19; 78/47 judiciary, 62/63-64,65-66,72,73,79,80, 135-38,151,152,162; 64/207,293- 300,309-16; 66/5-24,25-37; 79/ 5-11— courts— appellate, 64/299-300,312-13; circuit, 64/296-98,312; county, 79/5-6; supreme, 75/352,365; 79/6; trials, 79/5-11; u.s. district, 79/5-11,14 laws, 62/135-36— 1851-52, 77/319-21; code compiled, 66/13-14; land law, 64/208 legislature, 62/72-73,79-80; 79/6— 1853, 78/41-42; members, 69/273 meeting places, 77/319; naturalization in, 64/207,208N; officers appointed, 75/350-51; papers preserved, 71/101; politics, 75/120-21,365
Oregon Territory, 62/63,65,79,151-52; 66/15: act creating— delay, 81/185,187N; provision for Indian rights, 67/302N Benton letter, 81/185,187,187N; British in, 63/111; Buchanan letter, 81/187 described— 1852, 68/148; 1855, 65/121; 1858, 68/29 immigration in 1850s, 68/29; military force required, 74/95; prices, SEE Prices; settlers excluded east of Cas-

cades, 68/23; wages, 68/25; SEE ALSO Oregon Territorial Government
Oregon Textbook Commission, 70/217
Oregon: There and Back in 1877, by Nash, reprint noted, 77/300
Oregon Times and Trails, by Olson, noted, 66/383
Oregon Trail, 62/312; 63/5,88,264; 64/186,346; 66/383; 71/182- 83,292,365,368; 72/67,207; 73/285; 74/96,281; 78/70,71; 80/206: accidents, 78/135; accounts of travel, 67/88,90,372; SEE ALSO Immigration, Overland journeys; advice and help to travelers, 66/228; 81/97-99; army expeditions, 67/296-97,309,311-12; births, 78/135-36; chronological movements over, 63/88; Columbia River terminus, 77/315,317; Cornell guide, 80/66-100; crossing streams and rivers, 62/254-59*passim*,281,340-41; SEE ALSO Ferries; cutoffs, 64/77; 77/311,315- 18; deaths, 78/135,136,137; described, 62/249-87*passim*,337-402*passim*; 66/ 341; diseases, 78/136; SEE ALSO Cholera; drownings, 81/240; dust, 62/337- 38,349; emigrant escort, 72/55-77; fauna, 62/256,268-70,276,278-79,340, 355,393; flora, 62/255-56,271-87 *passim*,341,344,369,370; fuel supply, 62/255-56,271-87*passim*,346,398,401; fur company routes, 75/77; grass for livestock, 62/345-67*passim*,390,397; 80/66-100; graves, 62/269,270; 72/ 69; guide to 1972 remnants, 74/96; highway dedication 1923, 67/241; hot springs, 78/145
Indian-immigrant conflicts, 72/55,69- 70; 81/98— raids, 68/185; threats, 70/363; SEE ALSO Indians—wars and hostilities influence of, 70/207,210,230; insects, 62/281,283,369; 72/66; journey by carriage, 78/127,128,153,214,215; justice, 79/384-85; landmarks, 66/360; 69/336; 73/286; 78/130,131; SEE ALSO names of landmarks livestock, 78/132-35; 81/16-17— losses, 78/132,137,141,216; num-

bers, 78/132,139; sketch, 78/137 Malheur River ford, 78/139-40,144, 149; markers and monuments, 65/219; 67/243; 74/137; mileage, 78/136; 80/66-100; Meeker memorials, 70/84, 359; military posts on, 72/55-56,67; mineral springs, 80/74,83,84,91,94,97; mirages, 81/18; morale, 66/230; Morrow Co. ranches on, 69/111-12,130; movie scene, 78/ins.fr.cov. June; name, 78/131; National Historic Trail designation, 78/370; need for immigrant protection, 75/72-73; 81/99; newspaper accounts of travel, 78/133 numbers of travelers, 67/85,185,300, 306,345— 1840-60, 81/97; through Kansas 1849-52, 67/85,185,367,371 opinions of journey, 70/230; 81/255; oxen, SEE Oxen; partnerships, 79/71- 72,80-85,365-66,378,382; photos, 75/86; pioneer values, 81/100-101; preaching, 79/373,378; prices, 62/70-72,341,361,371 property, 79/64-90; 81/99— care of and replacement, 79/65,66; food and supplies, 79/73; lease of, 79/83-84,87; legal aspects, 79/65; money, 79/75-80; overloading and discarding, 79/70-74,86,90; types of ownership, 79/65 registers, 78/131-32,139; roles of men and women, 81/100-101; roster of immigrants, 79/338 routes— Idaho, 64/277; maps, 77/316; 78/156; 79/34-35; 80/72,77,406; 81/186; Oregon, 77/309,314-15; Ore. and Calif. routes compared, 79/65,66; Snake River, 78/137-38; 80/89-96; Wyoming, 73/286 Sabbath travel, 79/373,378,379; Salt Lake fork, 80/78,79; scenes, 80/70, 72,74; Sioux Indians, 66/74; Skirving panorama views, 65/133-59; toll bridges, 80/74,75,76,79,93; toll road, 80/82; trading posts, 78/141,141N, 145; travel in 1860s, 72/55FF; travel stereotypes, 72/228; trees, 80/77,80,

81,85,94,99; view in 1955, 78/138; wagons, 78/133,134,138; Walker quoted, 80/90-92 water supply, 62/253-58*passim*,267-84 *passim*,342-65*passim*,381,398,399— alkali, 62/347,348,350,354,366; 79/67-69,82 weather, 62/256,268-70,276,278-79, 340,355,393; Wyoming sites, 70/363; SEE ALSO Barlow Road; Elliott Cutoff; McKenny Cutoff; Meek Cutoff; Sublette Cutoff; Southern Immigrant Route *Oregon Trail*, comp. by Eide, noted, 75/86 *The Oregon Trail*, by Parkman, ed. by Feltskog, review, 70/353-54 Oregon Trail Association, 78/102 Oregon Trail National Historic Sites: program, 73/80 *The Oregon Trail Revisited*, by Franzwa, noted, 74/96 Oregon Transfer Company, 69/211: photo, 80/fr.cov. Summer Oregon Trucking Association, Inc., 77/386 Oregon Trunk Railroad, 70/69; 71/364; 75/364: Columbia ferry photo, 69/304; completion, 75/294 Deschutes Canyon construction, 69/293-305— photos, 69/297,300,302 history 1911-61, 63/92 Oregon Valley Land Company, 64/91 Oregon *vs.* James Connor, 62/140-43 Oregon Volunteers, 70/233; 75/73; 79/49-50,128: Camp Henderson 1864, 65/297-302; Civil War, 62/203,246,301; 72/93; Ft. Hoskins training camp, 65/185-86; Indian skirmishes 1864, 65/63,80,88,91; led by Joaquin Miller, 65/14N,20; Rogue River War, 66/219-20N; Spanish-American War photo, 72/219; Yakima War, 62/78; SEE ALSO First Oregon Cavalry; First Oregon Infantry; Oregon Rifles; Oregon Mounted Volunteers *Oregon Voter*, 68/132; 75/160

Oregon-Washington Plywood Co., 77/367,368

Oregon-Washington Railroad and Navigation Company, 66/305; 74/79,215; 75/272

Oregon Water Power and Railway Company, 62/171

Oregon Weekly Times, Portland, 64/125: opposes vigilantes, 80/11

Oregon, western: described, 77/314

Oregon, Western and Pacific Railroad: construction, 72/301

Oregon Western Railway, 67/281

Oregon Wheat Commission: founded, 72/287

Oregon Wildlife Areas, by Spring and Spring, noted, 79/409

Oregon Worsted Company, 62/171

Oregon Writers' Project, 73/324; 74/177: photo of members, 74/264

Oregonian, Portland, 64/34,37,123,144; 67/276; 74/35,38,49; 75/16,119,135, 156,173,357,358; 77/260: beginnings, 77/319; building, 73/333; carriers' address, 64/138-39,143-44; Coxey's army stand, 65/267-70N,272-92N,295N; editorial comment on U.S. expansion, 72/213-24; educational function, 70/201FF; election 1918 stand, 68/129-30; history, 68/90; opinion on vigilantes, 80/11; photo collection, 73/364; 74/363 photos—

1892 building, 70/fr.cov. Sept.; editor-in-chief's room, 70/214 plagiarism charges, 64/129-30; printing press, 64/34; requests police action, 80/10,19; Scott as editor, 70/197-232*passim*; support of Columbia River Hwy., 74/112

Oregonian (American-Hawaiian ss Co. steamer), photo, 74/258

Oregonian and Indians' Advocate, 67/87: William Brooks interview, 64/49

Oregonian Railroad Company, 63/363

Oregonian Railway Company, 69/181; 70/74

"Oregon's Columbia River Highway," by C. Lester Horn, 66/249-71

Oregon's Flamboyant Fourth, 1876, by Huffman, noted, 77/196,291

Oregon's Golden Years, Bonanza of the West, by Potter, noted, 77/300

Oregon's Historical Markers, by Scofield, noted, 67/281

O'Reilly, Charles R., 75/141

Orenco, Ore., 64/354

Organic Law: 1843, 62/126-28,130,131-32,137,155; 1845, 62/132-35,142N,144-45,147, 157; amended, 62/132; revised 1847, 66/358

Orient Meets Occident, the Advent of the Railway to the Pacific Northwest, by Bryan, cited, 71/75

Oriental Exclusion Act, 76/247; 79/244

Oriflamme (steamship), 79/244; 80/376

"Origin of the Term 'Black Robe'," by Thomas E. Jessett, 69/50-56

Orin family, Pasadena 1885, 80/ 248-53*passim*

Orkney Islands, 63/209,212,225

Orleans, Calif., 74/93

Ormsby, Margaret, ed.: *A Pioneer Woman in British Columbia: The Recollections of Susan Allison*, noted, 79/337-38

Ornithologists, 80/207: early Oregon, 66/233-39*passim*

Oro Fino Hall (Theater), Portland, 74/346; 80/134N: photo, 80/158

Orodell, Ore., 68/297N

Orofino, Ida., 62/106,226; 66/227N: photo, 79/195

O'Rourke, Father —, Heppner, 69/119

O'Rourke, Bridget Connell, 69/121

O'Rourke, Gertrude McGinnis, 69/ 139,144

O'Rourke families, Morrow Co., 69/144-45

Orphanages: Portland 1905, 80/53-55,60

Orr, John, 77/268

Orr, William, 65/214

Orsi, Richard J.:

A List of References for the History of Agriculture in California, noted, 75/365
Ortelius, Abraham: atlas, 72/182; biography, 72/182
Orth, John, 70/184
Orton, Charlie, 69/340
Ortschild, Viola, photo, 72/208
Orwig, Anson J., 64/91
Osborn, Jacob, 74/5
Osborn, Ronald E.: *Experiment in Liberty: The Ideal of Freedom in the Experience of the Disciples of Christ*, noted, 79/338
Osborne, A., Sacred Heart student, 81/81N
Osborne, Ben, Oregon Federation of Labor, 76/140,140N
Osborne, Bennett, 77/317
Osborne, Hy, 66/202
Osborne, R.H., 74/219
Osborne, Thomas J.: "The Main Reason for Hawaiian Annexation in July, 1898," 71/161-78
Osborne (ship), 66/122
Osborne Russell's Journal of a Trapper, 1834-1843, ed. by Haines, noted, 66/384
Osby, Marie, 74/30
Osgood, Ernest Staples, 78/284: *Day of the Cattleman*, cited, 67/141
Osgood, Ernest Staples, ed.: *The Field Notes of Captain William Clark, 1803-1805*, review, 66/65-67
Osolin, Helen, photo, 81/37
Ostergren, Jack, 62/204,205; 63/362
Osterhaus, Joseph, 63/25-26
Ostner, Leopold, 68/88
Ostrander, Abel, 67/366
Ostrander, Nathaniel, family, 66/275,382
Oswalt, Wendell H.: *Alaskan Eskimos*, review, 69/327-28
Oswego, Ore., SEE Lake Oswego, Ore.
Otago (bark), 65/239-40
"The 'Other Portland': A Statistical Note on Foreign-Born, 1860-1910," by Paul G. Merriam, 80/258-68
Otis, Bass, 65/141,144
Otis, Elwell S., 65/283N,285,290; 80/187,190

Otis, H.G., 68/251,253
Otis, Mr., SEE Holbrook, Stewart
Ott, Ore., SEE Myrtle Point, Ore.
Otter (ship), 63/362
Otter-Vanorman party massacre, 65/117N; 66/280; 72/55N
Otter Woman (Indian wife of Charbonneau), 62/288,289
Otters, 72/115,180,182; 74/13,14; 76/76-77: hunting stand photo, 74/14; prices of skins, 74/14; SEE ALSO Sea otters
Our Indian Wards, by Manypenny, reprint noted, 74/94
Our Landed Heritage: The Public Domain, 1776-1936, by Robbins, reprint noted, 63/247
Our National Park Policy, A Critical History, by Ise, review, 64/73-75
Our New West, by Bowles, reprint noted, 74/359
"Our Trip To Mount Hood, 1893," by Marion B. Russell, 79/203-10
Outhouse, John T., 66/11
The Outlander, 74/177
Ouvre, Marie Anne, SEE LeBrun, Marie Anne Ouvre
Over 100 Years of Old Oregon City, by Gardner, noted, 77/298
"Over the Brush and Through the Trees: Surveying, 1900-1909," by Ray L. Stout, 73/332-58
Overbeck, Andrew B., 63/12
Overbeck, Henry, 63/12
Overfelt, Thomas, 63/310-11; 66/87; 67/143
Overholt, David G., 70/59
Overland Hotel, Boise, 70/12N
Overland in 1846: Diaries and Letters of the California-Oregon Trail, ed. by Morgan, review, 65/405-406
Overland journeys, 69/183; 72/170,183; 73/73; 74/359; 80/104,207: 1540-1854, 74/86; Blanchet journal, 80/405-406; Bryarly and Geiger journal, 63/356; cost of, 62/247,263; 66/229; diaries, 77/309N; 81/100; Fisk expeds., 64/281-82; Gay diary, 80/104 guidebooks, 74/359-60; 78/45,

133-34— Cornell, 80/66-100; Hastings' reassessed, 70/85; satire, 70/365; Shively, 81/180(photo) Hills journey 1847-51, 64/91; Johnson and Winter, 74/282; Kidder diary, 81/ 329; Long, 64/281; Mackenzie, 64/ 172,272; Meek, 75/73; migration counts, 74/86; missionary women, 65/ 191-200; Missouri-Colorado 1853, 78/ 131; Mounted Rifle Regiment, 74/93, 281; Nebraska-Oregon 1893, 64/186; paintings, 71/292; Parkman, 70/353- 54; pictorialized 1849-50, 65/149-67, 169-72; provisions for, 66/197,212; 80/230; recollections, 72/93,353,355; wagon trip to Texas and Wash. Terr., 66/188; Young, J.Q.A., 65/308; SEE ALSO Immigration; Oregon Trail; Travel *Overland Monthly*, 74/62,63 *Overland Press*, Olympia, 63/223N Overland Stage Line, 68/229; 70/146N Overstrand, Smith, 72/69 Owen, Benjamin Franklin, 78/157,207- 11*passim*,225,233,234: photo, 78/226; trail diary 1853, 78/128,211,220,222,227-35*passim* Owen, James, O&c Lands board, 64/60 Owen, Jane McClure, 78/128 Owen, John, 65/121; 68/75 Owen, Philip A., 68/5,6N Owen, Robert, 66/86 Owen, Robert Dale, 66/86 Owen-Oregon Lumber Co., 63/92; 81/206 Owens, Elias A., 66/220N Owens, John, 77/317 Owens-Adair, Bethenia, SEE Adair, Bethenia Owens *Owlhyee* (*Owyhee*) (brig), 62/9; 63/193,199 *Owyhee Avalanche*, Silver City, Ida., 68/346; 79/284 Owyhee County, Ida., 71/196; 74/286: history, 79/408; place names, 72/265; 74/281; post offices, 69/341 Owyhee County Historical Society: publications, 70/273; 72/354; 73/284; 74/281-82; 75/363; 79/408

Owyhee Irrigation Project, 67/214 Owyhee Lake, 72/93 *Owyhee Outpost*, noted, 72/354; 79/408 Owyhee River, 63/263; 68/237,238, 249,299,308; 74/281-82; 76/157,161; 79/131; 80/91; 81/328: confusion with Malheur River, 65/57N; photos, 67/253; 76/158; Snake Indian hostilities, 65/81,299; 72/19,55N *Owyhee: The Life of a Northern Desert*, by Larrison, noted, 66/272 Owyhee toll road, 67/371 *Owyhee Trails, the West's Forgotten Corner*, by Hanley and Lucia, review, 75/293 Owyhees, SEE Hawaiian people Oxbow, Baker Co., 67/90 Oxen, 63/7,9-10,38-39; 76/177; 78/216: Baker Co. 1860-70s, 66/199,207*passim*; Cowlitz Farm, 63/142,145,151, 156; Curry Co., 63/38-39 Oregon Trail, 62/262; 66/197— bacon given as medicine, 62/384; shoes, 62/341; turpentine for sore feet, 62/352 use in logging, 73/226; 74/93,300; 79/394 Oxford House (HBCO. post), 63/359 Oxnard, Henry T.: beet sugar industry, 71/175 Oyhut, Wash., 74/14,15 Oyster Loaf Restaurant, Portland, 77/378 Oysterville, Wash., 69/78: census, 71/286; history, 80/335 Ozette, Wash., SEE Lake Ozette Ozyorsk Redoubt, 77/179,181

P Ranch, 68/321,322,328; 69/276; 73/82; 75/67-68: rebuilt, 68/327 *P.B. Weare* (steamer), 76/115 Pa-ay-lay (Indian), 63/165 Pace, LaFay: reminiscences, 77/299 *Pacific* (steamship), 62/319N Pacific Academy, Newberg: history, 80/336 *Pacific Baptist*, 75/136,140

Pacific Basin, 67/280; 70/76-77: bibliography of exploration 1783-1899, 63/247; history problems, 68/87 Pacific Bridge Company, 74/142 Pacific Center for Western Historical Studies: publications, 75/365 *Pacific Christian Advocate*, Portland, 64/124,135: editorial policies, 75/122,126,136 Pacific City, Ore., 64/143; 71/90 Pacific City, Wash.: founding, 63/245; location, 72/89 Pacific Coast, 76/312,313,321: beaches, 74/164,313-15 defense of, 71/279-81,290— 1860s, 65/326-29,336,350 harbor improvements, 71/290; map 1844, 76/128; maritime history, 63/80; navigation problems, 68/86; physiography, 72/90; Seward visit, 72/127-47; surveys, 76/317 Pacific Coast Borax Company, 73/233 Pacific Coast Steamship Company, 81/123: 1883 schedule, 71/ins.fr.cov. March Pacific College, Eugene, 79/21 Pacific County, Wash., 66/32; 72/227: act organizing, 67/366 census records— 1860, 68/81,184,340,342; 69/78,331; 1870, 71/286,361; 72/89,171; 73/283; 1880, 74/281 county seat, 78/91; first and last hanging, 72/171; history, 68/340,342; 70/74,272,358; 73/73; politics, 69/331; postmasters, 69/78; settlers, 69/331; tax roll 1851, 67/366 Pacific County Historical Society: publications, 67/366; 68/81,184,340,342; 69/78,331; 70/74,272,358; 71/189,286,361; 72/89,354; 73/73,283; 74/93; 75/363; 78/91,364; 80/207,335 Pacific Crest National Scenic Trail, 74/358 *Pacific Crossing: Journal of the Mate of the Tilikum*, by Luxton, review, 73/273 Pacific Fur Company, 71/277,309; 76/

322; 77/80: bill of sale, 63/84 personnel, 66/332-33; 77/81— employees list, 63/84 trade— 1810 agreement, 76/323; with China, 76/323 Pacific Gas and Electric Co., 63/361 Pacific Great Eastern Railroad, 63/92 Pacific Highway Association, 74/ 209-10,211,215 Pacific islands, 70/88: articles on, 68/87; bibliography, 69/83-84; history, 69/83; labor trade, 69/83; missionary work, 68/72 *Pacific Journal*, Oysterville, 74/93-94 Pacific Land and Investment Co., 69/202 Pacific Livestock Company, 63/270,274-75,293; 67/144: cattle ranches, 70/280 Pacific Logging Congress, 62/199; 70/182; 77/77,78 Pacific Lumber Company, 77/219 Pacific Lumber Inspection Bureau, 77/347 *Pacific Lumber Ships*, by Newell and Williamson, review, 63/80 Pacific Mail Steamship Company, 62/ 11; 63/312; 65/98N; 69/276; 81/196 *Pacific Monthly*, 65/364,365 Pacific Mutual Life Insurance Co.: history, 69/334 Pacific Northwest: agriculture, 71/60,62,87,88,96; air pollution, 67/369; army importance 1856-60, 67/294FF; army troops 1849-60, 68/45; atomic power, 68/186; aviation, 71/197; bibliography, 66/88; 72/90; biography, 73/285; 74/90-91; business opportunities 1881, 71/5-7,12-23*passim*; change in military status, 68/33; checklist of books, 70/181; circuses, 66/92; cultural development, 70/201FF; description, 71/181-82; early forest reserves, 68/349; early settlement, 76/202; ecology, 74/90; economic growth, 71/27-98; 74/80; ethnohistory, 63/75-77; expansionist views, 72/212-24; first bitulithic paving, 74/118; foreign fishing off coast, 69/86; growth 1880s, 67/122; growth factors, 64/87; Hawaiians in early days, 65/316; historic preservation, 81/106; historical geography, 70/64 history, 63/243; 64/78-79; 69/60-61; 71/181-82,367; 74/90-91— for young readers, 64/348-50; manuscripts, 73/67-68; maritime, 79/405; promotion of regional, 71/79; subject index, 71/79; transportation, 71/ 27-98

income, 63/361; index to people and places in books, 81/332; Indian problems, 70/111-37,148-69; irrigation, 69/61; land, 71/60; literary concepts, 72/227; literature, 71/181-82; maps, 77/301; maritime photographers, 68/ 88; metropolitan problems, 68/86; military posts, 67/294-346*passim*; 76/92; Muir visit, 72/173; natural resources, 71/196; need for mounted troops, 67/ 310,315-16; New Deal in, 71/290; novelists, 68/279; population characteristics, 68/349; power development, 69/61; promotion, 65/365; railroads, 71/27-98; resources and development, 69/331; scientific papers, 71/370; Scottish investment in, 69/181-82; shipping, 69/85; Spanish activities in, 74/ 353-54; taxes, 72/90; theses, 65/362-91; 72/225-79; trade and commerce, 71/27-98; transcontinental railroad completion, 67/101-102,122-23 transportation—

costs, 71/59; history, 71/27-98 travel 1881, 71/5-25; tourist trade, 74/115,119-27,130,134,140-41,217-42*passim*; towns, 81/202; wheat varieties, 81/336

The Pacific Northwest: An Index to People and Places in Books, by Drazan, noted, 81/332

Pacific Northwest Conference of the Methodist Church, Seattle, 66/82

Pacific Northwest Forum, noted, 81/329

Pacific Northwest History Conference, 1964, 66/88

Pacific Northwest Labor History Conference, 71/189,196

Pacific Northwest Political Science Assn., 62/107; 68/86

Pacific Northwest Quarterly Index, comp. by Connette, review, 65/411

Pacific Northwest Regional Planning Commission, 64/58

Pacific Northwest Themes: Historical Essays in Honor of Keith A. Murray, ed. by Scott, review, 79/408

Pacific Northwest Tourist Assn., 74/217

Pacific Ocean, 72/44,45:

British maritime control, 73/359-60; called South Sea, 72/5,5N,6; commerce and opening of, 74/286 currents, 77/43-44,278—

Japanese, 77/279

early pilot, 74/285; exploration, 73/ 273-74; geographic exploration, 70/ 77; maps and charts, 72/100,134,356; military bases, 62/10-11,18-26 *passim*, 51; North Pacific voyage 1772, 72/ 182; rip tides, 77/279; role in history, 76/309; Russian explorations, 72/100; Spain in, 74/353; tidal waves, 77/280-84; trade routes, 76/308; U.S. naval fleet 1818-1923, 66/71-72; U.S. strategy in, 62/5-56; U.S. territories in, 62/7,11; SEE ALSO Shipping

Pacific Photo Company, Salem, 66/327

Pacific Pine Lumber Company, 67/ 163N,174

Pacific Power and Light Company, 63/361; 65/218; 73/322N: history, 72/348

Pacific Railroad Act, 73/52

Pacific Railroad Survey, 62/315; 66/ 282; 70/73; 71/50,81-82; 77/331; 79/27-30; 80/209: campsite marker, photo, 79/296; geographical reports, 69/41; gold discoveries, 67/313; map, 79/26; report, 79/27N

Pacific Railway and Navigation Company: route described, 72/295-97— Nehalem River-Tillamook route, 71/130-31 succeeded by Southern Pacific, 71/130;

Timber station, photo, 72/ins.fr.cov. Dec.; trestle photo, 72/296

Pacific Republic, 72/327,329

Pacific Science Congress, 63/247

The Pacific Slope, A History of California, Oregon, Washington, Idaho, Utah, and Nevada, by Pomeroy, cited, 70/263; review, 67/78-79

Pacific Springs, 62/353,354,355; 77/379; 80/78,79

Pacific Spruce Corporation, 76/248; 77/216,219

Pacific Telegraph Company, 64/147

Pacific Telephone and Telegraph Company, 75/160,162

Pacific University, Forest Grove, 64/153,155,173,353; 66/23-24; 70/199,200,201; 76/382: alumni history, 70/222; College of Optometry founded, 72/287; Old College Hall, 69/177

Pacific Woolen and Clothing Company, 62/165-66,168

Pacific Woolgrowers Credit Corp., 77/24

Pack rats: discovered by Lewis, 69/23

Pack trains, 68/245,246,247; 74/14,16, 96; 75/314; 76/81; 79/176-79,188, 193,201: camel trains, 62/300; Canyon City to Idaho City, 67/235; Crooked River Valley route, 65/22; Eugene to Canyon City, 67/234; John Day Valley, 79/269N; Klondike rush, 76/102,103-109; knots and hitches, 71/291; military supply, 68/230,231N,234,239,243, 244,257; 79/139,143,146,160-67 *passim*,274N,277,282,285; packers and packmasters, 79/156N,160,163N, 274N,277,283N,284; ranches, 79/189N,199-200; rates 1878, 68/252, 253; rigging, 79/303; saddles, 70/84; 79/279N

Packard, Earl LeRoy, 67/26

Packard Hotel, Pendleton, 69/135

Packer John Mountain, 68/244, 247,313N

Packwood, Elisha, 63/148N

Packwood, William, pioneer of 1844, 63/148N

Packwood, William H., pioneer of 1850, 62/224-25,227,228,229

Paddock, George H., 70/26

Paddys Valley, 78/57,310,317

Paden, Irene D.: *The Wake of the Prairie Schooner*, reprint noted, 71/362

Paez, Ramon, 65/143

Pagels, (Peggles), —, Baltimore Colony settler, 63/26

Paget, B. Lee, 74/208

Pa-hu-ick (Indian), 70/155

Pain, Baptiste, 79/143,143N

Paine, Joseph, 74/359

Paine, Lauran, 63/83: *Tom Horn, Man of the West*, noted, 65/121

Paine, Lewis, 72/132

"The Painted Hills and the Carroll Family," by Phil F. Brogan, 73/258-68

Painted Hills State Park, 73/258,264,266: Indian legend, 73/267; photo, 73/265; roadway, 73/268

Painter, Robert M.: journal, 66/148N,152N

Painters and painting, 68/47,49,51; 79/172,188,196,201: painted moving panoramas, 65/133-72; sign painting, 79/183,184,194; with Fremont Exped., 63/345-46; SEE ALSO Art and artists

Paisley, Ore., 77/28,156,157: photo, 77/4

Paiute Indians, 69/253,254; 72/15; 73/258: baskets, photos, 81/410; clothing, 81/421; customs, 70/32-33; fishing cliques, 71/367; hostilities 1860, 70/251; in Bannock War, 70/15FF,22,34; SEE ALSO Bannock War; northern categories, 69/335; SEE ALSO Northern Paiute Indians; on Yakima Reservation, 70/34,106,147N-48N,162; property concepts, 81/398,399,405,411; taken as slaves, 81/413,414; SEE ALSO Snake Indians

Pakenham, Richard, 70/302,303;

75/319; 81/181-84
Palace Hotel, Seaside, 77/71
Paladin, Vivian A., 65/215
Paleontology, 73/86; 75/78-79:
in West, 70/366; Oregon, 62/298-99;
63/364; 67/26; SEE ALSO Fossils
Palette and Tomahawk: The Story of George Catlin, by Plate, review, 64/349
Pallada (frigate), 73/158
Palliser Expedition, 66/70
Palmer, A. Mitchell, 75/150
Palmer, Clarence V. (Pete), 64/354
Palmer, Ephraim, 65/185
Palmer, H. Spencer, 63/90
Palmer, Irma Skinner, photo, 71/252
Palmer, Joel, 62/73; 65/173-74; 66/86,145; 67/294,313; 70/114,115, 233,260; 75/72,294; 79/16N,136: biography, 65/177-78N; Indian policy, 78/48; interest in middle route across Cascades, 78/48-50; letter re Haller expedition, 67/314N-15N; photo, 78/49; visits Klamath Indians, 69/224
Palmer, Mary Elsing, 74/333
Palmer, Peter Parker, 66/383
Palmer, William, Coos Valley pioneer: family, 66/54
Palmer, William, Drake Exped. corporal, 65/28
Palmer House, Scottsburg, 66/383
Palmerston, Henry John Temple, Viscount, 63/189
Palmquist, Peter E.:
Fine California Views: The Photography of A. W. Erickson, review, 78/287
Palouse, Wash., 71/368
Palouse country, 70/77,78: lumbering, 65/366; meaning of name, 70/181; OMV scouts in, 66/153
Palouse Hills, 65/220
Palouse Indians, 66/143; 70/121,170; 71/345; 81/399
Palouse River: name, 65/304
Pambrun, Adele (Ada), 68/342
Pambrun, Andrew D., 70/168: biography, 70/35N
Pambrun, Maria, SEE Barclay, Maria Pambrun

Pambrun, Pierre Chrysologue, 63/201; 71/336: death, 63/232
Pambrun, Mrs. Pierre Chrysologue, 63/190
Pamo (Indian), 79/142,313,315,322
Pan Bread n' Jerky, by Scott, noted, 69/274
Panama, 62/23,24
Panama (steamship), 63/170
Panama Canal, 62/18,20,29; 71/170-71,177; 72/92; 73/86; 77/127: impact on Pacific NW, 72/86; opening, photo, 77/128
Panama Canal Zone, 77/117
Panama-Pacific Exposition, 66/271; 72/161; 74/119
Panama Railroad, 80/209
Panay (U.S. gunboat), 62/24
Pancoast, Charles Edward, 66/161N, 162N
Pandora (survey ship), 64/241
Pangborn, Arden X., 74/54
Panic of 1893, 65/263; 66/181; 75/136
Panning Gold for Fun and Profit, by Kathan, noted, 69/78
Panoramas: description of Skirving panorama, 65/147-67; showings of, 65/167-70
Pantages, Alexander, 63/353; 68/88
Panthers, SEE Cougars
Panton, Andrew C., 72/280
Papea Creek, 79/76
Paper manufacturing, 71/286: O'Neil and Callaghan, 71/351,352,353; western states, 68/89
Paperhanging, 79/190,193,194
Papers of the Socialist Labor Party of America: Guide to a Microfilm Collection, noted, 71/363
The Papers of Ulysses S. Grant, ed. by Simon, Vol. I review, 69/66-67; Vol. II noted, 70/360; Vol. III noted, 72/172
Pappas, Walter, 66/59
Parades, 74/347: Dallas, Ore., 76/378; photos, 77/130-48*passim*,fr.&bk.covs. June; San Francisco 1916, 72/346; Tillamook 1919, 72/304-305

Paradise Park, Mt. Rainier, 73/345
Paramount Theater, Portland, 73/80
Paratunka, Kamchatka, 80/199
Parcher, Ira S., family, 66/382
Parent-Teacher Association: Montana history, 72/260
Paris, Robert, 62/179
Paris, Ida., 65/313
Pariseau, Pierre, 68/81
Park, Helen, 74/63
Parkdale, Ore., 70/50,52
Parke, H.W., 70/300
Parke, John, Royal Marines 1845, 63/201,218
Parke, John S., U.S. Army colonel, 81/328
Parker, A.H., Reno 1881, 71/9
Parker, Allen, 66/90
Parker, Carleton H., 65/198
Parker, Clark, family, 64/91
Parker, Ernest H., 72/280
Parker, George Leroy ("Butch Cassidy"), 72/183
Parker, James H. ("Pink"), 67/236,237
Parker, Mrs. Jamieson, 75/370
Parker, Jess, 77/156-57
Parker, Joe, 78/325N
Parker, John, 67/268
Parker, Samuel, missionary, 63/182,195, 210; 64/85; 66/343; 73/284; 75/77
Parker, Samuel, southern route explorer, 77/317
Parker, William Chinook, SEE Chinook, William (Billy)
Parkers, Jim, 78/325N
Parkhurst, Alfred L.: Crater Lake concessions, 81/43,46-47, 49,52,54,56
Parkhurst, Asa, 81/43,48,52-55
Parkman, Francis, 62/403; 66/82; 67/367: *The Oregon Trail*, ed. by Feltskog, review, 70/353-54
Parkrose, Ore., 77/256
Parks, Azariah, 79/11
Parks, 62/299; 64/323; 65/219; 78/360: California, 78/365; Columbia Gorge, 74/130,131,138,143; damage to,

70/358; Ft. Klamath site, 67/374; Linn Co., 70/184
Oregon, 72/228; 75/40-42; 78/365— first dedicated, 63/253; history, 67/ 184-85
Polk Co., 73/82; Washington, 78/365; Wilhoit Springs proposed, 65/218; SEE ALSO Albert H. Powers Memorial Park; Big Eddy Park; Bonneville State Park; City Park, Dallas; Crater Lake National Park; Forest Park, Portland; Fort Columbia State Park; Fort Stevens State Park; Gladstone Park; Godfrey Park; Hudson Community Park; Indian Mary Park; Kay, Thomas, Historical Park; Lithia Park, Ashland; Loeb State Park; Macleay Park, Portland; Maria C. Jackson State Park; Millicoma Garden Clubs State Park; Millicoma Myrtle Grove State Park; Mt. Rainier National Park; Nesika Park; Oaks Pioneer Park; Olympic National Park; Oregon State Parks Commission; Painted Hills State Park; San Juan National Historical Park; Shore Acres State Park; Silver Creek Falls State Park; Smith Rock Park; Sodaville Springs Park; Tryon Creek State Park; U.S. National Park Service
Parmantier, Alphonse L., 64/351
Parmela family, Lincoln Co., 67/369
Parnell, Dale, 69/347; 70/373
Parnell, William Russell, 68/231N,305N; 79/282; 81/105: biography, 79/282N-83N
Parrett Mountain, 74/345
Parrington, Vernon Louis: appraisal as historian, 63/360
Parrish, George, 64/247-48,251,254
Parrish, Josiah L., 62/240; 63/182; 64/ 238; 66/350; 68/81; 78/66,340: Clatsop Plains property, 73/245-47, 251-55; photo, 73/248; 81/fr.cov. Fall; property dispute with Gray, 73/245-57
Parrish, Phillip H.: *Before the Covered Wagon*, cited, 73/317
Parrish, Samuel Ball, photo, 81/258
Parrish and Atkinson, Portland, 64/174
Parrish *vs.* Gray, 73/245-57

Parrots, SEE Prices
Parrott, Ann Eliza Rhodes, 74/345,347: photo, 74/346
Parrott, Armand Guido, 74/347: photo, 74/346
Parrott, Arthur R., 74/347: photo, 74/346
Parrott, Frances Murray, 74/345N
Parrott, George, 74/347: photo, 74/346
Parrott, Jenny Lind, 74/347: photo, 74/346
Parrott, Maria Everest, 74/345
Parrott, Richard L., 74/347: photo, 74/346
Parrott, Samuel: land claim, 74/345
Parrott, Samuel Henry, 74/347: photo, 74/346
Parrott, Thomas H.: biography, 74/345-49; house, 74/345, 347,349(photo); music compositions, 74/346,347,349; photos, 74/346,348
Parrott, Thomas W., 74/347: photo, 74/346
Parrott, Walter, 74/347: photo, 74/346
Parry, W.F., Lincoln Co. pioneer, 63/253; 64/355
Parry Center, Portland, 68/187
Parson, J.A., Garibaldi lumber mill employee, 77/237
Parson, John E.: *West on the 49th Parallel: Red River to the Rockies, 1872-1876*, review, 66/69-71
Parsons, M.R., 80/149N
Parsons, Mabel Holmes, 74/59
Parsons, Ralph: continental water diversion plan, 67/277
Partlow, James, Portland policeman, 80/159,159N
Parton, James, 69/179
Partridges: Oregon 1881-82, 65/240-41,244
Parvin family, immigrants of 1853, 79/13
Pasadena, Calif., 80/247,248,249,249N
Pascakka (Pashcapam) (Indian), 70/

34,35N
Pasco, Wash.: history, 72/229
Pash, Joseph J.: *History of Immaculate Conception Parish..., Colville Valley*, noted, 64/186
Pashya, SEE French Camp, Umatilla Co.
Pass of Killiecrankie (ship), 66/107
Passage Through the Garden: Lewis and Clark and the Image of the American Northwest, by Allen, review, 77/191-92
Passaya (Indian), 79/142,158,313, 317,323
Passi, Michael: *The Everett Massacre*, by Smith, review, 73/281-82
The Passing of the Great West, Selected Papers of George Bird Grinnell, ed. by Reiger, noted, 74/96
Past Is Prologue: A Centennial Profile of Pacific Mutual Life Insurance Company, by Nunis, noted, 69/334
Pataha House, Pataha, Wash., 79/199
Patch Hog School, SEE Bergenhollow School
Pathfinder, The First Automobile Trip from Newport to Siletz Bay, ed. by Stembridge, noted, 81/327
Patrick, Forrest, 69/331
Patrick, Isaac, 80/105,335
Patrick, J.N.H., 67/263-66,269,270
Patrick Creek, 76/53
Patriotic societies, 75/109-90*passim*
Patrons of Husbandry, SEE Grange
Patt (Indian), 79/142,154,295
Patten, B.A., 66/10N
Patten, Francis J., 68/243,248N
Patterns of Development, by City-County Joint Planning Dept., Washington Co., noted, 66/188
Patterson, Abram S., 78/125
Patterson, Andrew W., 63/245; 67/179
Patterson, Dorothy, 76/387
Patterson, Earle E. (Pat), 71/101
Patterson, Ferd, 64/344; 80/141-42
Patterson, Georgia S. Benson: letter about Mrs. Sam Hill, 78/357
Patterson, Ida: 1843 wagon train account, 80/104

Patterson, Isaac Lee, 75/162; 77/267
Patterson, J.M., 80/357N
Patterson, Joseph, pres. American Assn. of Museums, 66/388
Patterson, Kenneth, 75/279
Patterson, R.M.:
Dangerous River, noted, 72/355
Patterson, Robert, immigrant of 1853, 78/125
Patterson, Robert, Philadelphia surveyor, 69/27
Patterson, Thomas, 64/180
Patterson House Hotel, Kalama, 71/17
Patti, Adelina, 74/205-206
Pattie, James Ohio, 66/86
Patton, Annie:
tree named for, 65/309
Patton, Edwin Cooke:
biography, 66/327
Patton, George, Lord Glenalmond:
founds Oregon Botanical Assn., 68/112
Patton, Thomas McFadden, family, 72/353
Patton, William, Oregon Shakespearean Festival, 62/183
Patton Brothers bookstore, Salem, 66/327
Patton Home for Friendless Men, Portland, 75/145
Patton Post Card Co., Salem, 66/327
Patton Valley, 79/336
Pattullo, T.D., 65/366
Patwonalt (Indian), 79/154,315,317
Paul, Rodman W., 65/213; 67/280:
Mining Frontiers of the West, noted, 71/191
Paul Wilhelm, Duke of Wurttemberg:
J.B. Charbonneau visit, 71/249,257, 258-59
Paul Wilhelm, Duke of Wurttemberg:
Travels in North America: 1822-1824, trans. by Nitske, noted, 77/91
Paulina (Indian), 64/188; 65/9,30, 36,37N,43N,45,50,63N,74N,92,94, 104N; 69/240N; 72/341; 73/258,260; 75/309; 79/123,125-26,127,139,157N:
death, 79/171N,272,272N; held at Ft. Dalles, 65/43N; moves to Klamath Reservation, 79/127; photo, 79/140;

wife and son captured, 79/127,140
Paulina, Ore., 65/84N; 77/90
Paulina Basin, 75/310
Paulina Cove, 75/309
Paulina Lake, 62/198
Paulina Marsh, 76/89
Paulina Valley, 65/84N:
road to Canyon City, 65/95,103N; SEE ALSO Camas Valley, Crook Co.
Pavenstedt, A.F.:
To Santa Rosalia, Further and Back, by Huycke, review, 72/167-68
Pavlovsk Harbor, Kodiak Island, 73/116-19:
sketches, 73/116,117,118
Pawnee Hero Stories and Folk-Tales, by Grinnell, noted, 63/247
Pawnee Indians, 63/74:
folklore, 63/247; U.S. Army scouts, 63/81
Paxson, Edgar S., 65/215
Payette, Bernard Clyde:
Old French Papers, noted, 68/184
The Oregon Country Under the Union Jack, cited, 66/332-33N; noted, 63/84; 64/92
Payette, Francois, 67/87; 81/20N
Payette National Forest:
creek names, 68/313N
Payette River, 68/243N,244,245, 246N,298,310N,311N:
early settlement, 64/277
Payetteville, Ida., 68/229N
Payne, B. Iden, 62/180
Payne, Doris Palmer, 68/257N-58N
Payne, Henry T., frontier photographer, 66/381
Payne, Robert S., family, 65/308
Peace Corps, 66/91
Peace River, 64/284; 76/315
Peace River country, 70/179
Peaches:
Oregon, 63/199—
Chinese species introduced, 65/239
Peachwood, Eliash, 63/366
Peachwood, Elkanah, 63/366
Peachwood, Paulina, 63/366
Peacock, A.L., 66/38,40,48:
Davenport collection, 66/42

Peacock, Samuel E., 72/171
Peacock (pilot schooner), 77/277-79,280: photo, 77/278
Peacock (sloop), 63/218; 64/226N; 76/118,192: launch dispute, 64/229N-30N; wreck, 79/405
Peacock Spit, 80/207; 81/105: shipwrecks, 62/197
Peake, William H., 78/52,52N; 79/6
Peale, Albert Charles, 64/86
Peale, Charles Willson, 70/171: drawings of birds, 69/8,24; museum, 69/9,22
Pearce, Edward D., 69/39N
Pearce, Helen, and Faye B. Millie: *The 100th Anniversary, First Presbyterian Church, Salem*, noted, 72/173
Pearce, Thomas: Falmouth-Nootka voyage 1794-95, 79/400-402; Nootka controversy report, 79/399-400
Pearl, George Leslie, family, 74/358
Pearl (ship), 72/116; 76/208,221N
Pearl (steamboat), 81/39
Pearl Harbor, 62/20,21,22,24,30,105: acquisition, 62/1,11; attack by Japan, 62/28,29,35,36; lease, 71/173,174-75
Pearmine, Lester E., 66/342
Pearne, Thomas Hall, 64/165; 65/109
Pears: early Oregon, 63/53
Pearsall Creek, 76/47,48
Pearsall Peak, 76/47,48
Pearson, Alexander L., 71/19
Pearson, Emil, 76/14-15
Pearson, Flora, 64/349
Pearson, Frances Aiken, 66/282
Pearson, George F., 68/72
Pearson, H.F., 67/279,281
Pearson, Nels, Yamhill Co. farmer, 76/13-15: children, photo, 76/26
Pearson, Nels A., 62/174
Pearson, Thomas, Cowlitz pioneer, 63/220
Peary, Robert Edwin, 63/359
Peas, 72/94: Cowlitz Farm, 63/104,117-73*passim*

Pease, Archie L., 63/64-65
Pease, G. Norman, 74/213
Pease, George A., photo, 81/254
Pease, Robert W.: *Modoc County, A Geographic Continuum on the California Volcanic Tableland*, review, 67/365
Peavy, George W., 64/60
Peck, Lucile Urey: *A Certain Time..., A Special Place*, noted, 79/104
Peck family, Marion Co., 79/104
"Pedagogy in the Wilderness," by Theodore St. Hilaire, 63/55-60
Peddlers: Portland, 77/300
Pedee, Ore.: history, 75/363
Pederson, Hans, 74/217
Pediatrics, 72/172
Pedler (brig), 71/310,311
Peebles, Al, 80/119,128
Peel, Robert, 63/202; 70/301
Peel, William, 63/201-202,218: biography, 70/301; in Pacific NW, 70/300-301; report, 70/301,302
Peers (Pierce), Henry Newsham, 63/108,215,239; 64/240: establishment of Ft. Hope, 63/220
Peffer, Louise, 62/188
Pegford, I.G., 74/19
Peggles, —, Baltimore Colony settler, SEE Pagels
Pekin, Wash., 74/281
Pelicans: Bendire notes, 66/235-36
Pe-li-ni, SEE Paulina (Indian)
Pelly, John Henry, 63/223,225-26
Pelota court, Jordan Valley, 76/166,167
Peltier, Jerome A., 63/90; 66/89: *Warbonnets and Epaulets*, noted, 73/73
Pelton, William T., 67/260,264,270
Peltopera, Elias, 72/350
Pemberton Valley, 66/88
Pement, Juin, 64/359
Pemmican: preparation, 66/88
Pemmican, by Fisher, review, 62/99-100
Pence, A.J. (Jack), 63/12,19

Pence, Lafe, 75/57,58,60
Pend Oreille Lake, 71/49
Pend Oreille Indians, 62/203
Pend Oreille River, 73/349
Pend Oreille Valley, 62/202; 63/90
Pendleton, Ore., 62/399N; 63/31,365; 64/90; 66/319; 69/276; 70/320; 72/153; 73/285; 80/283,285; 81/202: businesses, 80/285,285N; first house, 66/311; history, 77/192-93,298; 80/105; Indian raids 1878, 66/206; photo 1909, 80/284; post office and postmasters, 80/335; woolen mills, 62/164,175
The Pendleton Area Finns, by Swearingen and Westersund, review, 72/350-51
Pendleton Junior High School, 69/130
Pendleton Record: centennial issue, 63/365
Pendleton Round-Up, 66/311; 72/351; 77/90: beginning, 81/343; history, 81/105; photos, 66/300,309,312-15; 68/88
Pendleton Woolen Mills, 77/193,298
Pengra, Byron J., 64/150; 65/63N; 79/30,30N,43: diagram of Ore. surveys, 79/ins.covs. Spring; Ore. Central Military Wagon Road, 71/54,82; 79/46-47; railroad interests, 71/82,94,283
Pengra, Charlotte Emily Stearns, 78/123,146
Penguin (ship), 66/127
Penitentiaries: British Columbia, 65/372; McNeil Island, 66/130; Oregon, 72/323N; Ore. Territory, 64/147-48; 66/165; 75/353
Portland, 62/73— authorized, 80/10N; construction controversy, 80/21N; convict labor, 80/22N views— 1858 litho., 80/ins.bk.cov. Spring; 1867 photo, 80/152,ins.bk.cov. Summer
Penline, George, 78/303,304,306
Penlington, Norman: *The Alaska Boundary Dispute: A Critical Reappraisal*, noted, 74/284; review,

75/85
Pennoyer, Sylvester, 75/130: biography, 73/61; Coxey's army episode, 65/266,274-75,281,286N-87, 290N; photo, 65/266; relationship with Cleveland, 65/288; suit against Neff, 73/60-62
"Pennoyer *vs.* Neff: Legal Landmark," by Ralph King, 73/60-62
Penrose, G. Larry: *Fishing the Oregon Country*, by Ames, review, 67/363-64
Pensions, 72/286
Peo-Peo-Mox-Mox, SEE Peu-Peu-Mox-Mox
Peopeo Tholekt (Swan Alighting) (Indian): drawings, 81/341N,347,361
People's Alliance, 75/125-26
The People's Observer, Portland, 73/211
People's Power League, 76/144,146
Peoria, Ore.: effect of Ore.-Calif. railroad, 73/83; pottery, 73/83; 79/104
Percival, John, 72/180
Perez, Juan, 63/88; 66/215
Perham, E.L., and Co., Albany, 67/61
Perkins, Ed, Wingville pioneer, 66/202
Perkins, Elisha Douglas, 79/70-72
Perkins, Harden, 66/206
Perkins, Henry K.W., 63/184
Perkins, J. and J.N., Canton, China, 76/329
Perkins, J. and T.H., 76/206,217,221-22
Perkins, James, 76/206,207,217,221
Perkins, Lorenzo: murder, 70/128,129,131,139,155,162
Perkins, Mrs. Lorenzo: murder, 70/128,129,131,139,155,162
Perkins, N.G.W., 63/35
Perkins, Richard S., 80/21
Perkins, Thomas Handasyd, 76/88, 210,214: portrait, 76/209; sea otter trade firm, 76/206
Perkins and Co., Boston, 76/329
Perkins House Hotel, Drain, 80/53
Perlman, Mrs. Frank, 68/359,360; 69/346,347; 70/373; 71/371

Pernier, John, 66/86
Perozzi, Domingo, 64/328
Perrine, Fred S., 71/311; 76/302
Perrine, Ira B., 71/196; 72/90
Perry, David, 79/131,279N,281,282, 283,285,291,292,297,301
Perry, Francis C., 70/358
Perry, J.E., 75/146,147,167
Perry, Matthew C., 62/10: photo, 62/13
Perry, Uriah, 69/201
Perrydale, Ore.: history, 75/363; map 1882, 72/171
Perspectives in American Indian Culture Change, ed. by Spicer, review, 63/347-49
Pescadores Islands, 62/37
Peschl, Frank, 77/235
Peshastin Valley, 79/23
Peter Binford Foundation, 69/61
Peter Iredale (bark), 64/68-72; 66/129: wreck photos, 64/69,71
Peter Skene Ogden's Snake Country Journal, 1826-27, ed. by Davis and Johnson, review, 63/349-51
Peters, A.V., 65/121
Petersen, Thomas, 71/368
Peterson, Asa, 65/245-46
Peterson, Axel, 76/10,23-24
Peterson, Charles L., 62/418
Peterson, Frank, family, 66/382
Peterson, Harold L.: *American Indian Tomahawks*, noted, 66/384
Peterson, Heyes: *Rails West*, by Abdill, review, 62/294-95
Peterson, Jack, Queets area settler, 74/24
Peterson, James C., 62/248N
Peterson, Lester R.: *The Cape Scott Story*, noted, 75/88
Peterson, Martin: "The Swedes of Yamhill," 76/5-27
Peterson, Matilda (Tillie) Collinson, 76/7-10: photo, 76/8
Peterson, Nels D., 65/308
Peterson, Norman V., 66/384
Peterson, Norman V., and James R. McIntyre: *Reconnaissance Geology and Mineral*

Resources of Eastern Klamath County and Western Lake County, Oregon, noted, 71/286
Peterson, Ole, 63/83; 65/308
Peterson, Oliver, 71/189
Peterson, Robert L.: *Bankers and Cattlemen*, by Gressley, review, 68/337-38
"The Idea of the Railroads: Regional Economic Growth," 67/101-103
Labor Politics in a Democratic Republic, by Bornet, review, 67/361-63
Peterson Brothers Lumber Mill, 68/350
Peterson Butte, 68/187: pheasants introduced, 65/243,245,252-53; photo, 68/242
Pethick, Derek: *James Douglas, Servant of Two Empires*, noted, 72/88; review, 71/281-82
Victoria: The Fort, review, 72/87-88
Petit, Amable, 66/356N: family, 68/81,184
Petit, Emilie Aubichon, 66/356N
Petitions and memorials: Edwards memorial 1838, 66/347,354; French-Canadian settlers, 66/355; half-breeds' right to vote 1859, 66/361; Linn (Oregon) bill 1841, 62/124,129, 131; Multnomah Co.-Portland consolidation, 64/173; Oregon settlers 1838, 63/211; Oregon Temperance Society 1837, 66/346; Ore.-Wash. Indian war claims, 64/149-50; public schools, 64/ 173; railroad and canal, Ore. City 1845, 66/355; Shortess petition, 66/353
Petosquaicot (Indian), 79/313,315,323
Petree, Mahlon, 79/10
Petrie, Ronald G.: *The Education of Migrant Children in Oregon*, noted, 64/284
Petroff, Ivan, 66/87; 67/368; 69/337: biography, 65/215
Petroleum, SEE Oil and gas industry
Petropavlovsk, Kamchatka: Cook exped. visit 1779, 80/197-204; defenses, 80/201,204; harbor map, 80/ins.fr.cov. Summer; illus., 80/200; monument photo, 80/202
Pettenger, W.E., 62/172

Pettengill, Samuel B., 75/127
Pettis, W.I., 62/174
Petty, Joseph, 78/125,305(photo)
Petty, Mrs. Joseph, 78/319,324,325N
Pettygrove, Francis W., 64/204N; 74/282
Pettyjohn, C., Sacred Heart student, 81/81N
Peu-Peu-Mox-Mox (Yellow Serpent) (Indian), 66/133,137,143,144,160N: death, 66/147,148N; horse stealing, 71/345; seizure of Ft. Walla Walla, 66/134,142,144
Pfeiffer, Phil, 63/283,289
Pharisee Among Philistines: The Diary of Judge Matthew P. Deady, 1871-1892, ed. by Clark, noted, 77/291
Pharmacy: post-1900, 67/89
Pheasant Raising in the United States, by Oldys, cited, 65/244N,256
Pheasants, Chinese: classification and history, 65/235-38; Davenport sketches, 65/255N; Denny project, 65/229,239-48*passim*; Merriam survey 1888, 65/252-53,256
Oregon, 62/300— first official count, 65/254-56; game breeding farms, 65/256; hunting prohibited, 65/246,253-55; legislation to protect, 65/246; Quimby report 1899-1900, 65/255
Pacific Northwest, 70/359— distribution 1884, 65/247-52 ringneck, 65/239-40,244,255
Pheasants of the World, by Delacour, cited, 65/238
Phelan, F.W., 65/276N
Phelan, James, 71/146
Phelps, Lucius W., 78/41,43,43N
Phelps, Orville, 78/363
Philadelphia Centennial Exhibition, 77/196,291
Philadelphus lewisii (Lewis's syringa), 69/160(photo),161
Philippine Islands, 62/6,7,11-14,17-51 *passim*: insurrection, 72/212,213,223; U.S. naval base, 71/168,176; U.S. policy

1900-1903, 72/214-17,220,222
Phillips, Charles, Coos Bay pioneer, 63/15
Phillips, Emma Roberts (Mrs. James T.), 63/107N,110N,203N
Phillips, Mrs. Grady, 72/94
Phillips, Henry B., 77/89
Phillips, John W.: reminiscences, 74/93
Phillips, L.K., ed.: *East of the Cascades*, by Brogan, noted, 66/183
Phillips, Laura, 63/15
Phillips, Paul Chrisler, 66/79,273
Phillips, Paul Chrisler, and J.W. Smurr: *The Fur Trade*, review, 62/403-405
Phillips, Robert Y., 63/15,20,22,24,26
Philomath, Ore., 72/281,285
Philomath College, Philomath, 73/81; 77/91: history, 72/91
Philosophic systems: Enlightenment, 79/100-101
Phinney, Emeline L., SEE Flint, Emmeline L. Phinney
Phipps, Dolph, 77/90
Phipps, William Estill, 75/164
Phkaiosh (Indian), 73/63,65
Phoenix, John, SEE Derby, George Horatio
Phoenix, Ore., 65/7
Phoenix (sailboat), 74/32
Phoenix Hotel, Ore. City, 76/299
Phopina Ranch, Wheeler Co., 64/113
Photographer of a Frontier: The Photographs of Peter Britt, by Miller, review, 78/361-62
Photographers and photography: Astoria, 66/329; Baker, 66/309,381; Buchtel & Stolte, 68/236; California gold rush, 68/348; Canada, 69/332 collections— Boychuck, 81/56; Cronise, 81/94; Gifford, 81/46; Lorain, 69/237N; Vollum, 69/237N; Watkins album, 66/386
Columbia River, 69/331-32— daguerreotypes— Far West 1850s, 64/136,171; Port-

land earliest view, 66/386 frontier, 78/361-62; 81/324; hand painted slide process, 74/220; Hawaiian, 69/84; history salvaged by, 65/ 219; Indian subjects, 65/314; maritime history, 68/88; Newport, 66/330; Oregon, 66/304,309-19*passim*,327; Pendleton, 66/311; Portland, 64/352; 66/309,317,318; postal cards, SEE Postal cards; Salem, 66/327; Seattle, 64/ 352; 66/381; Sedro-Woolley, 66/381; Silverton, 66/313,318; Umatilla Indian Reservation, 66/319; West 1875-1910, 66/381; Yukon 1898, 81/330; SEE ALSO names of photographers

Photographers of the Frontier West, 1875-1910, Their Lives and Their Works, by Andrews, review, 66/381

Photographing the Frontier, by Hoobler and Hoobler, review, 81/324

Photographs and illustrations:

Acarregui, Angel, 76/166; Acarregui, Floyd, 76/166; Acarregui, Tony, 76/ 166; Acordagoitia, Alfonzo, 76/156; Acordagoitia, Angel, 76/156; Adams, John Quincy, 76/196; Adkins, Edward, 78/ins.bk.cov. Sept.

agriculture—

Bristow farm, 78/66; cherry trees, 68/166; Flemming farm, 73/358; Gervais mill site, 66/342; grain harvest crew, 73/208; hop driers, 64/ 270; 77/269; hop fields, 76/24; 80/283; hop pickers, 64/270; 74/ 314; 76/24; irrigation, 78/ins.bk.cov. Dec.; Jernstedt farm, 76/18,20,24; Luelling orchards, 68/168-73; Queets River homestead, 74/4; Rivelli and Montecucco farm, 77/252; threshing grain, 75/fr.cov. Sept.; 76/75; truck farming, 77/252; Wennerberg farm, 76/7

aircraft—

airship at Lewis & Clark Expo., 80/ 56; Curtiss hydro-aeroplane, 66/328; Tillamook blimp base, 71/136

Alaska—

Aleut Indians, 73/126; Eskimos, 73/ 135; Illiuliuk, Unalaska, 73/122,123;

Kodiak Island, 73/116,117,118; Norton Sound, 73/132; Pribilof Islands, 73/128,130; St. Paul harbor, 77/182; Sitka (New Archangel), 72/142; 77/178; Skagway, 81/125,138; Tlingit Indians, 73/147,150; Treadwell stamp mill, 81/120; Unalaska mill, 73/125; Voznesenskii drawings, 73/116-50*passim*

Alberson, Letha, 63/321; Aldecoa, Basilio, 76/166; Aldecoa, Domingo, 76/170; Alexander, Charles, 73/296; 74/42; Allen, Andrew, 69/314; Allen, Eleanor, 74/265; Alvord, Benjamin, 65/64; Anchustegui, George, 76/166; anvil (historic), 69/58; Applegate, Charles, 81/232; Applegate, Jesse, 81/ 232; Applegate, Lindsay, 81/232; Arata, Francisco, 77/259; Arrigoni, Samuel N., 77/245; Augur, C.C., 65/176

automobiles—

1912, 77/141; ca. 1915, 75/288; Chalmers, 77/ins.fr.cov. Sept.; Ford 1915, 72/163,ins.fr.cov. June; Ford Model T, 76/353; Hudson 1915, 75/282; Oldsmobile 1913, 74/110; Studebaker-Garfield, 69/294

Babb, Andrew and Mary, 78/142; Babson, Sydney G., 70/51,55; Baker, George, 75/155; Ban, Shinzaburo, 76/ 230; Banta, J.J., 74/4; Barclay, A.F., 80/324; Barker, Burt Brown, 66/342; Barker, T., 72/62; Barrett, John, 71/ 149; Basque people, 76/166-67; Bayley, J.R., 81/258; Becker, Charles, 67/ 212,fr.cov. Sept.; Beekman, B.B., 74/ 234; bells (Aurora church), 67/274-75; Bendire, Charles, 66/234; Bennett, Florence, 74/265; Benson, Simon R., 66/250; Bergevin, Rosa, 81/254; Bermensolo, Antonio, 76/166; Bermensolo, Petra, 76/166; Bernard, Reuben F., 68/300; Berryhill, Gene, 77/148; Big Pine Openings, 78/313; Bilbao, Carmen, 76/164; Bilyeu, Eloise, 80/370; Bilyeu, Josephine, 80/ 381,384; Bilyeu, Marion, 80/370; Bilyeu, Thomas, 80/381; Bilyeu, Virginia, 80/370,384; Bishop, Clarence, 67/204; Bitte, Elizabeth, 81/37; Bitte, Emma, 81/37; Bitte, Fred, 81/30,37; Bitte, John, 81/37; Bitte, Nellie, 81/ 37; Black, James, 70/224; Blanding, Martin, 78/305; Bloom, Will and Mrs., 71/268; Boals, Robert T., 71/116; Boise, Reuben P., 66/4; Boki (Hawaiian governor), 64/28; Bond, Allen, 78/126; Bond, Isaac W., 78/ins.bk. cov. Sept.; Bonnell, Allison C., 80/16; bootleggers ca. 1920, 76/160; Bourne, Jonathan, 68/212; 69/196; Brainard, Mary A., 80/363; Bridges, Grace, 72/208

bridges—

Interstate dedication, 74/226; Longview, 74/296

Bright, Verne, 73/296; 74/265; Brogan, Phil, 75/312; Bronaugh, Earl C., 74/234; Bronson, George H., 77/264; Brosnan, Jeremiah and Mrs., 69/118; Brown, William C., 68/222

buildings—

Alpine school, 75/271; Aurora Colony Church, 79/240; Aurora Hotel, 79/265; Carlton Baptist Church, 76/ 14; Carnegie Library, Dallas, 76/ins. bk.cov. Dec.; cathedral at Lima, Peru, 77/123; Chautauqua bldg., Gladstone, 80/394,397; cheese factory, Tillamook Co., 71/128; City Book Store, Salem, 78/12; Cliff House, San Francisco, 71/10; Cloud Cap Inn, 75/100; 77/62; 79/205,207,208; Coast Guard station, Garibaldi, 77/ 221; Crater Lake Lodge, 71/46; custom house, Log Cabin, B.C., 81/144; Dallas elementary school, 78/162, 164; Hart Saloon, Westfall, 63/278; Lahainaluna ABCFM seminary, 68/63; Lane Co. Clerk's Office, 67/180; Lane Co. first courthouse, 67/56; Liberty Brewery, Portland, 64/268; "Liberty Temple," Portland, 71/212; Madras Hotel, 69/302; Methodist Mission, The Dalles, 67/292; Mt. Angel Abbey, 70/328; Multnomah Co. Library, 71/224; Odd Fellows

Hall, Dallas, 76/ins.bk.cov. Dec. Oregon Historical Center, 67/210— architectural sketch, 67/196; construction, 67/206,208-209; cornerstone dedication, 66/292; ground breaking, 67/204; model, 67/200; site, 67/ins.fr.cov. Sept.; time capsule, 66/294

Oregon Historical Soc. quarters— City Hall, 70/206; Tourney Bldg., 70/208

Oregon Iron & Steel pipe foundry, 69/218; Oregon Shakespearean Theatre, Ashland, 62/181; *Oregonian* Bldg., Portland, 70/fr.cov. Sept.; Oro Fino Saloon, Portland, 80/158; Palace Hotel, Heppner, 69/129; Pioneer Post Office, Portland, 70/ins.fr. cov. Sept.; police station, Portland 1874, 80/301; Polk Co. Courthouse, 75/351; 77/ins.fr.cov. Sept.; post office, Ashwood, 77/160; Reed's Opera House, Salem, 81/81; Sacred Heart Academy, Salem, 81/ 94,ins.fr.cov. Spring; St. Bernard's Church, Jordan Valley, 76/166; St. Michael's Church, Portland, 77/255; San Juan Mission, 80/242; Seaman's Rest, Tacoma, 66/104; Shaniko Hotel, 77/27; surgeon's quarters, Ft. Dalles, 67/338,339,344; Timberline Lodge, 76/258-68*passim*; U.S. Hotel, Jacksonville, 66/58; U. of O. Medical School 1892-1919, 75/27; Vista House, 74/141,218; Westfall school, 63/278; Whitney Inn, Garibaldi, 77/356

bunkhouse, 66/314; Burke, Thomas, 80/286; Burns, Thomas E., 74/265; Bush, Asahel, 73/42; Bush, William Owen, 73/198; Bushnell, John C., 78/ ins.bk.cov. Sept.; Bushnell, Ursula, 78/ 326; Byars, W.H., 73/350; Calkins, L.V., 80/324; Carey, Charles H., 78/100

cartoons—

by Davenport, 66/4,48; by Dickey, 74/196; by Nast, 72/128; Ku Klux Klan, 75/ins.bk.cov. June; of Seward,

72/131,138; "seeing the elephant," 79/64; Tammany Tiger, 66/48 Carty, James, 69/104; Carty, Maria C., 69/104; Casey, James, 81/254; Casinelli, Pietro, 77/252; Center Ridge, Wasco Co., 73/308; Cereghino, Abramo, 77/238; Cereghino, Charlie, 77/252; Cereghino, Guiseppe, 77/ 252; Cereghino, Guiseppina, 77/238; Chadwick, Stephen F., 81/fr.cov. Fall; Chamberlain, George E., 81/254; Chamberlain, Virginia, 78/226; Chambreau, Edward, 70/132; 80/314; Chandler, Dan, 76/347; 77/28; Chandler, Leah, 76/ins.fr.cov. Dec.; Chapin, Eleanor, 72/208; Chapman, J.A., 80/155; Chertudi, Ignacio, 76/166; Chertudi, Inez, 76/166; Chertudi, Juan, 76/166; Chertudi, Phil, 76/166; Child, Arlene, 74/265; china (Canton ware), 76/fr.cov. Sept. Chinese people, 76/369,370; 78/79,ins.bk.cov. March— Chinatown, Portland, 78/76,ins.fr. cov. March; 80/305; "Chinese Brigade," Portland, 80/265; fish cannery workers, 78/ins.fr.cov. March; 79/ins.bk.cov. March; funeral, 80/fr.cov. Summer; gardens, 75/124; laundry, 78/fr.cov. March; railroad workers, 75/124; 80/163,234 Churchill, Claire, 74/265 city and town views— Albany, Ore., 74/39; 77/140; Alkali, Ore., 81/273; Allegany, Coos Co., 80/50; Almota Landing, 71/24; Annie Spring, 81/44; Antelope, Ore., 73/304; 75/ins.bk.cov. Dec.; 81/313; Arica, Chile, 77/119; Ashland, Ore., 64/324,330; 80/ins.fr.cov. Fall; Ashwood, Ore., 72/340; 75/310; 77/ 160; Astoria, Ore., 71/314; 74/213; 77/14,ins.fr.cov. June; 81/4; Auburn, Ore., 62/212; Aurora, Ore., 79/265; Bandon, Ore., 75/340,341,343,ins.fr. cov. Dec.; Bar View, Ore., 66/307, 327; Bend, Ore., 77/20; 78/246; Boise, Ida., 70/14; Brighton, Ore., 72/298; Canton, China, 76/328;

Canyon City, Ore., 70/56; 77/fr.cov. June; Carlton, Ore., 76/4; Champoeg, Ore., 77/141; Chinook, Wash., 78/ins.fr.cov. Sept.; Dallas, Ore., 76/ 378,379,ins.bk.cov. Dec.; 78/162,164, ins.bk.cov. June; Danner, Ore., 71/254; Dawson, Yukon Terr., 76/114; Detroit, Ore., 66/318; Diamond, Happy Valley, 68/329; Eugene, Ore., 67/60; 71/18; 77/322; Garibaldi, Ore., 77/ 212,214,215,218,221,234,348,356, 359,366; Gladstone, Ore., 80/399,fr. cov. Winter; Goldendale, Wash., 70/ 142; Grants Pass, Ore., 67/178; Grass Valley, Ore., 75/44-45,46; Halsingborg, Sweden, 76/4; Heppner, Ore., 67/131; 69/126,129; Hobsonville, Ore., 77/68; Huntington, Ore., 67/ 124; 68/298; Jordan Valley, Ore., 76/174; Kaluaaha, Hawaii, 68/67; Lakeview, Ore., 68/319; 76/334; 77/ 134; Madras, Ore., 69/302; Mapleton, Ore., 74/272; Meacham, Ore., 67/103; Metlakahtla, Alaska, 76/103; Moro, Ore., 77/136,137; Newport, Ore., 66/326; North Bend, Ore., 68/ 270; 72/163; Orofino, Ida., 79/195; Paisley, Ore., 77/4; Pendleton, Ore., 66/310,319,322-25,330; 80/284; Pilot Rock, Ore., 70/25 Portland, Ore., 64/268; 70/fr.cov. Sept.; 71/212,224; 73/298; 75/27, 268,ins.bk.cov. Sept.; 80/58,143, 158,259,264,ins.bk.cov. Spring; 81/ 152,154— 1852, 80/4; 1854, 80/23; 1858, 72/320; 1865, 80/148; 1867, 80/ 152,ins.bk.cov. Summer; 1873 fire, 80/308; 1876 flood, 80/fr.cov. Fall; 1877-78, 80/318; 1884, 75/12; 1892, 70/fr.cov. Sept.; 1895, 75/30; 1905, 79/353; 1910, 74/260,ins.fr. cov. June; 1913, 79/344; 1915, 79/ ins.fr.cov. Dec.; 1920s, 77/242; 1935, 74/265; 1955, 74/267; bands, 74/348; 77/130; Chinatown, 78/ins.fr.cov. March; 80/305; Chinese Brigade, 80/265; Chinese funeral, 80/fr.cov. Summer; Fulton Park

Addition, 69/202; harbor, 66/120, 128,307; 79/ins.fr.cov. Dec.; 80/29, 294; Italian people, 77/256,fr.cov. Sept.; Ladd's Addition, 77/251; parades, 71/212; 73/205; 77/130, 132,133,135,143,144; police, 80/ 322; police bldg. 1874, 80/301; police badge, 80/ins.bk.cov. Fall Powers, Ore., 76/60; Rainier, Ore., 74/292,296,326-27,ins.bk.cov. Dec.; Rockaway, Ore., 71/ins.fr.cov. June; Salem, Ore., 78/4,12,fr.cov. March; 81/81,86; Santa Barbara, Calif., 80/ 246; Seaside, Ore., 77/68,281; Seattle, Wash., 71/14-15; Shaniko, Ore., 77/20,27; Silverton, Ore., 66/315; Sitka (New Archangel), Alaska, 72/ 142; 73/139,140,141,146,148; 77/ 178; Skagway, Alaska, 81/125,138; Sumpter, Ore., 77/134; The Dalles, Ore., 67/12; 68/34-35; 73/300, 303,320; 81/270,278,ins.bk.cov. Fall; Timber, Ore., 72/ins.fr.cov. Dec.; Tofino, B.C., 68/103; Umpqua City site, 70/ins.bk.cov. Sept.; Walla Walla, Wash., 79/200; Wasco, Ore., 74/ 246-47; Westfall, Ore., 63/271,278; 67/242; Yakima City, Wash., 70/131 Clark, Charles, 78/226; Clark, Charles E., 76/275; Clark, Robert, 78/238; Clark, Thomas, 78/213; Clausen, A.C., 74/265; Clerke, Charles, 80/202 coastal views—

Adventure Cove site, 68/107,108-109; Aian Bay, 73/158; Bar View jetty, 77/ins.fr.cov. Dec.; Bar View life-saving crew, 71/131; beach view, 75/ins.bk.cov. March; Cannon Beach, 77/68; Cape Espenberg, Kotzebue Sound, 73/138; Neahkahnie Beach, 66/309; Nootka Sound, 79/398; ocean waves, 75/55; Tillamook Bay bar, 77/68; Umpqua life-saving station, 66/176; Yaquina Head lighthouse, 75/ins.bk.cov. March

Coe, Frankie, 76/369; Coe, Margaret, 76/369; Colasuonna, Jerome, 77/248; Collinson, Anna, 76/8; Collinson, Matilda, 76/8; Condon, Thomas, 67/

4; Cone, Mrs. Anson, 81/254; Conrardy, Lambert, 70/323; Cook, Truman B., 77/100,113; Corbett, Henry W., 72/328; Cornelius, T.R., 66/136; Cornell, William, family, 79/358,362; Corning, Howard M., 73/296; 74/42, 173,265; Cornoyer, Narcisse, 70/167; Corta, Jim, 76/156; Corta, Mitchell, 76/156; Cosper, Emma E., 80/363; Couch, Charlie, 77/16; Craigie, James, 78/51; Crawford, LeRoy, 72/62; Crawford, Medorum, 72/54,62; Crook, George, 79/268; Crowninshield, Jacob, 76/206; Culver, Richard K., 74/ins.fr.cov. Sept.; Currey, George B., 65/18; Currin, George, family, 69/ 142; Curry, George L., 66/136; dairying, Tillamook Co., 71/119; Damonte, Jim, 77/252; D'Arcy, Maria, 80/360; D'Arcy, Peter, 81/254; Darneille, Anderson, 78/126; Darneille, Isaac, 78/ 245; Davenport, Homer, 66/38; Davies, David L., 66/292; Davies, Walter L.J., 74/214; Davis, Harold L., 73/301,ins.fr.cov. Dec.; Davis, Rollie, 80/324; Dawson, O.B., 76/261; Dayton, Frank, 70/206; Deady, Matthew P., 73/42; 76/fr.cov. Dec.; Deer Creek Station, Wyo., 67/235; Decraene, J., 81/90; DeGraff, Grace, 72/208; Dell, Floyd, 73/296; DeMartini, Raffaele, 77/252; Dement, Ellis, 63/8; Denning, Job, 78/226; Denny, Gertrude Hall, 65/258; Denny, Owen N., 65/230,258; 80/314; Dever, Lem, 75/181; Devers, Arthur, 74/234; Diamond, John, 77/326; Dielman, Leopold, 80/344; Dierdorff, John, 74/ 210; Dindia, Salvatore, 77/248; Dockstader, Tom, 74/265; Donaldson, Jane, 74/28; Donaldson, Maggie, 74/28; Downing, George, 81/254; Drake, John M., 65/18; Drake, June D., 66/313 drawings and paintings—

Couch drawings of *Chenamus*, 75/ fr.cov. Dec.; 77/36; Davidson, *Columbia Rediviva* voyage, 68/100,105,fr.cov. June; Hawaiian royalty, 64/5-32*passim*; Nez Perce Indian sketches, 81/340-

72*passim*; Voznesenskii, Alaska and Calif. 1840, 73/109-14*passim* Drury, William, 78/ins.bk.cov. Sept.; Duncan, Rush R., 74/265; dunes east of The Dalles, 74/251; Duniway, Abigail S., 81/258; Dye, Eva Emery, 80/ 297,fr.cov. Winter; Eakin, Hort C., 77/ 262,264; Eberhardt, George and Elizabeth, 81/254; Edelbrock, Alexius, 70/ 315; Edler, Dave, 77/148; Edwards, John, 72/306; 73/225; Edwards, Mrs. Wiley, 81/258; Eigner, Judy, 81/30; Eigner, Ken, 81/30; electricity use, 80/326-28; Eliot, William G., 74/234; Elliott, Elijah, 77/308; 78/142; Elliott, Olivia, 81/194; Elorriaga, Amalia, 76/164; Elorriaga, Carmen, 76/164; Elorriaga, Marie, 76/164; Emerson, Charles L., 74/265; Emory, William H., 65/132; Evans, D.A., 75/155; Failing, Henry, 72/328; Failing, Josiah, 80/16; Fairman, J.D., 63/287; Fastabend, J.A., 66/179; Fawcett, Nellie, 72/208; Ferris, Mrs. A.H., 80/324; Fidler, William W., 78/326; Figone, Luigi, 77/252; Finck, Henry Conrad, 79/236; Finzer, William E., 71/149 fishing—

butterfly boats, 75/ins.fr.cov. June; canneries, 74/298; 78/ins.fr.cov. March; Celilo Falls, 75/ins.fr.cov. Sept.; dipnetting, 75/222; fishwheel, 75/224; scaffolds, 75/229; sites on Columbia River (map), 75/220,228; traps, 78/196,198,199,fr.cov. Sept., ins.fr.cov. Sept.

flora—

buffalo berry, 69/166; clarkia, 69/ 150; flax (wild), 69/154; gum plant, 69/162; rice root, 69/164; syringa, 69/160

Flowers, Allan E., family, 73/202; Floyd, John, 70/334 forests—

fire trail construction, 76/36; lookout house construction, 76/34; myrtle trees, 67/40,45; pine forest, 65/158; Port Orford cedar, 68/262; Siskiyou National Forest, 76/40

Forney, P.R., 72/62; Fort Rock Cave, 67/36

forts and military sites—

Camp Bidwell, 72/22; Camp C.F. Smith area, 68/252-53,315; Camp Day site, 69/233,234,236,238,255,fr. &bk.covs. Sept.; Camp Harney, 79/ 292; Camp Henderson site, 65/298, 300; Camp Steele site, 79/150; Camp Warner sites, 79/279,280; Camp Withycombe, 75/244,246; Ft. Canby, 65/338,340,342,344,346; Ft. Dalles, 67/292-346*passim*,fr.&bk.covs. Dec.; 68/4,16,17,18,19,24; Ft. Harney site, 78/220; Ft. Henrietta site, 66/140; Ft. Klamath, 68/316; Ft. Ross, 73/ 106,107; 77/186; Ft. Simcoe, 70/ 152; Ft. Stevens, 65/324-60*passim*; Ft. Umpqua, 70/240,242,246,252,ins.bk. cov. Sept.; Ft. Victoria, 73/155; Ft. Walla Walla, 68/227; San Francisco Presidio, 80/176; Vancouver Barracks, 75/246

fossil beds—

Crook Co., 67/15; John Day, 67/28 Frank, Aaron M., 74/214; Fraser, Simon, 81/381; Frei, Nicholas, 70/ 315; Fremont, John C., 65/132; Fuller, Josephine, 80/363; Fulton, Charles W., 81/44; funeral (Chinese), 80/fr.cov. Summer; Funnemark, Birgitte, 66/104; Funnemark, Christine, 66/104; Gadwa, William I., 80/272; Gaines, John P., 75/356; Gale, William and Rebecca, 78/148; Gantenbein, C.U., 71/149; Garachana, Angel, 76/166; Geer, T.T. and Isabelle, 81/254; geologic time chart, 67/27; Giannini, Battista, 77/ 238; Giesy, Andrew, 79/249,ins.bk.cov. Sept.; Giesy, Elizabeth, 79/ins.bk.cov. Sept.; Giesy, Fred, 79/249; Giesy, Helen, 79/ins.bk.cov. Sept.; Giesy, Henry, 79/249; Giesy, Katherine, 79/ ins.bk.cov. Sept.; Giesy, Katherine K., 79/ins.bk.cov. Sept.; Giesy, Mary, 79/ ins.bk.cov. Sept.; Giesy, Matilda, 79/ ins.bk.cov. Sept.; Giesy, Nicholas, 79/ ins.bk.cov. Sept.; Giesy, Rudi, 79/ins. bk.cov. Sept.; Giesy, William, 79/ins.bk.

cov. Sept.; Gifford, Benjamin A., 66/317; 75/ins.fr.cov. March; Gifford, Fred L., 75/155,181; Gilbert, Leland, 74/265; Gilcrest, Evelyn, 63/321; Gilcrest, John, Jr., 63/308,321; Gilcrest, Mary, 63/308,321; Gird, William, 68/144; Giusti, Lorenzo, 77/238; Gleason, M.J., 81/254; Glidden, Vernon, 74/221; Goicoechea, Isidoro, 76/166; Gordon, Samuel M., 74/221; Grant, Bridget, 81/194

graves—

Charbonneau, J.B., 71/246; grave marker for baby, 77/270; Hembree, A.J., grave marker, 66/158; Watson, Steven, marker and monument, 66/60

Gray, William H., 73/249; 75/114; Greenfield, John S., 70/206,208; Gregoire, Felix, 81/254; Griffin, John S., 75/114; 81/258; Grover, Lafayette, 67/258; 80/288; 81/fr.cov. Fall; Gulick, Henry, 72/150; Haefner, Henry E., 76/52,88; Hale, John P., 73/32; Hall, Langley, 78/326; Halleck, H.W., 79/128; Hallock, Absolom B., 80/288; Hammond, Vida, 72/208; Hanks, J.F., 74/28; Harding, Florence K., 67/244; Harding, George S., 79/173,174; Harding, Warren G., 67/243,244; 78/100,102; Harney Co. view, 78/231; Harris, Mrs. Francis M., 81/254; Harris, Frankie, 63/321; Harris, Jack, 63/321; Hayden, Benjamin, 66/150; Hayes, Jeff W., 79/347; Hayter, Elizabeth, 78/160; Hedges, Ada, 73/296; Hembree, James T., 81/258; Hendricks, George W., 80/324; Herren, Effie, 80/228,256; Herren, Johnie, 80/228,256; Herren, Mary, 80/228; Herren, Theodore, 80/228,256; Hewett, Isabel, 79/205; Hildebrand, August, 81/194; Hill, Edgar P., 81/44; Hill, Hanks Neville, 78/245; Hill, Laban, 66/51; Hill, Louis, 69/292; Hill, Samuel, 66/250; 74/110; 78/108; Himes, George H., 70/206,208; 81/254; Hinman, Alanson, 71/20; Hockersmith, Jackson and Martha, 78/126; Hoffman, L.H., 74/214; Hole-in-the-Wall Park, 75/40; Holladay, Ben, 71/48; Holman, Rufus, 66/250; 74/110; Holman, Mrs. Walter J., 74/236; Holmes, Thomas J., 80/20; Hoover, Herbert, 78/100; Hopper, Henry, 77/148; horses, work, 75/204-19*passim*,fr. &cbk.covs. Sept.; Hoult, Alice, 80/363

houses—

Pete Andrews stone house, 63/332; Barclay House, Ore. City, 76/301,302; Bluefields, Hillsboro, 80/366; Boise house, Ellendale, 66/18; Robert D. Clark cabin, 75/304; Curry Co. homestead cabin, 76/79; James D. Fenton house, 76/12; Floed-Lane House, Roseburg, 65/402; George A. Harding house, 79/202; Mahlon Harlow house, 77/320; Herren house, 80/256; Kaser house, Switzerland, 81/286; Albert Knowles house, 74/272; log cabin 1910, 63/8; Luelling house, Iowa, 68/155; Luelling house, Milwaukee, 68/202; Erik Lund house, 71/271; B.H. McCallon house, 77/ins.fr.cov. Sept.; McCormack ranch house, 77/25; McLoughlin House, Ore. City, 76/300,301; Phil Metschan house, 70/58; Milford-Corning house, 74/165; Thomas H. Parrott house, 74/349; Piggott's "castle," 74/260; Albert H. Powers house, 77/ins.bk.cov. March; Seven Gables, Tigard, 77/378; Shively house, Astoria, 81/194; Simpson estate, Shore Acres, 68/273; Dan Strite house, 77/356; Charles G. Thayer house, 72/197; Winburn house, Ashland, 64/330; Wittenberg house, Cloverdale, 64/260

Howard, Guy, 70/100; Howard, Oliver Otis, 68/241,fr.cov. Sept.; 70/100; Howard, Samuel, 78/326; Hoyt, E. Palmer, 74/214; Hoyt, Henry L., 80/155; Huckleberry, E.R., 70/116; Hug, Mrs. John, 81/254; Humphreys, Lester, 75/155

hunting—

sagehen hunt, 77/148; sea otter hunting stand, 74/14; sea otters, 80/47

Huntington, J.W.P. and family, 79/166; Hurlburt, Tom, 75/155; Illige, Ben W., 73/214 Indians—

Aleut carving of sailor, 72/147; Aleut Indians, 73/126; Alon-skin, 68/236; Bannock family, 68/312; Bannocks at Snake River Agency, 68/292; baskets, 81/410,ins.fr.cov. Winter; bowl, 81/ 410; Brooks, William, 64/42; Brooks robe, 81/346; Callicum, 71/ins.fr.cov. Dec.; canoes, 81/392; Cayuse-Nez Perce drawings, 81/340-72*passim*,fr. cov. Winter; chasing buffalo (movie scene), 79/381; dentalia, 81/396; Eskimos, 73/135; fishing, 74/12; 75/38; 81/402,403; Garry, Spokane, 69/52; head-flattening, 69/171,172; Howlish, George, 68/236; Indian chiefs, Southern Ore., 69/248; Indian scout, 70/26; Indian scouts in Bannock War, 68/236; Indian "war whoop," 68/ins.fr.cov. Dec.; Indians near Ft. Umpqua, 70/244; Indians with teepee, 70/ins.bk.cov. June; Lawyer, 69/52; lodges, 70/244; 81/406; Lone Pine village, 72/152,154,156; Lot medal, 70/160; Maquilla, 71/ins. fr.cov. Dec.; Moses and wife, 70/156; Moses medal, 70/fr.cov. June; Nanamkin, Nancy, 67/348; Paulina, 79/ 140; Paulina battle site, 65/36; Pinouse, 79/120; Schooly, 79/120; Seltice medal, 70/160; Shaker church building, 72/154,158; Shaker church interior, 67/348; Sidwaller, Frank, 79/120; Siletz Indians, 81/420; Smohalla and his priests, 70/122; stone sculpture of owl, 78/fr.cov. Dec.; sweat lodge, 81/390; Ta-home, 79/ 120; Tats-homi, 66/320; Thomas, Jake, 79/120; Tlingit Indians, 73/ 147,150; Umapine, 68/236; Winapsnoot, 68/236; Winnemucca, Sarah, 68/fr.cov. Dec.; Warm Springs scouts, 79/120

Ingalls, Gertrude, 74/265; Irving, Washington, 71/308; Jackson, C.S., 66/250; Jackson, James, 71/149;

Jacobsen, Fred, 74/265 Japanese people—

ancestral society, Portland, 76/236; internees, ww II, 76/254; 81/151-67 *passim*,ins.fr.cov. Summer; Rose Festival float, 76/250; sports, 76/250,252 Jenkins, Leon, 75/155; Jernstedt, Frank, family, 76/12; Jernstedt, Fred, 76/18; Johnson, Mr. and Mrs. Clement, 74/25; Johnson, Kirke E., 81/ 116,136; Johnson, Martin, family, 76/ 16; Jordan, Thomas, 67/325; Kamamalu (Hawaiian), 64/8,12,13,17,24 Kamchatka, 80/200—

Clerke monument, 80/202 Kaser, Jacob and Lena, 81/305; Kautzman, Fred G., 74/265; Keil, Aurora, 79/262,ins.bk.cov. Sept.; Keil, Emanuel, 79/249,ins.bk.cov. Sept.; Keil, Elias, 79/ins.bk.cov. Sept.; Keil, Glorianda, 79/ins.bk.cov. Sept.; Keil, Sarah, 79/ins.bk.cov. Sept.; Keil, William, 79/262,ins.bk.cov. Sept.; Kelly, Hercules, 68/331; Kelly, James K., 66/136; Kelly, Jane, 81/78; Kelly, Penumbra, 65/280; Kendall, Benjamin F., 63/222; Kennelly, Ardythe, 74/ 265; Kenny, Michael, family, 69/134; Kersey, Violet, 77/275; Kiger Gorge, 67/23; Kilkenny, John S., 69/100; Killea, Tom, 74/4; Kimmel, Martin Luther, 75/240; King, Alexander, 77/ 326; Kopplien, Mrs. A.R., 80/324; Korean picture brides, 79/63; Kraft, Dave, 72/306; Kramer, Earnest F., 75/231; Kunigk, W.A., 66/116; Kyle, Joseph, 65/142; Lagursa, Louis, 76/ 166; Laidlaw, Lansing S., 79/30 lakes—

Blue Lake, 74/51; Crater Lake, 67/35; 81/44,53,56; Harney Lake, 78/230; Klamath Lake, 75/239; Mercer Lake, 75/301

Lamberson family, 63/298; Ladd, Charlie, 75/100; Ladd, W.S., 80/16; Lampman, Evelyn Sibley, 76/369; Lancaster, Samuel, 66/250,252,254; 74/ 100; 75/278; Langille, Doug, 76/fr. cov. June; Langille, Will, 76/100,ins.fr.

cov. June; Lappeus, James H., 80/135; Latourette, Jack, 74/214; Laurel Point near Rainier, Ore., 72/196; lava beds, McKenzie Pass, 67/28; Lee, Borghild (Peggy), 73/296; Leiter, Wilma, 74/265; Leonard, Alfonse (Foncy), 76/338,353; 77/148; Leonard, Amon, family, 76/338; Leonard, Andrew, 77/148; Leonard, Bill, 76/353; Leonard, Catherine, 78/ins.bk.cov. Sept.; Leonard, Ella, 76/353; Leonard, Joseph and Mary, 78/ins.bk.cov. Sept.; Leonard, Mary, 78/176; Leonard, Willard, 77/148; Lewelling, Seth, 68/196; Lewelling, Sophronia, 68/199; Lewis, Meriwether, 69/4

Lewis and Clark Centennial Exposition— site, 70/223; 79/355; views, 70/224,228; 71/156,158; 77/138,139; 79/356; 80/54,56,ins.fr.cov. Sept. Liholiho (Hawaiian), 64/4,12,13,17, 24; Liliha (Hawaiian), 64/28; Lindberg, John and Christine, 76/8; Linden, Tom, 74/265; Lister, Queene, 73/296; Littell, Lydia, 74/265

logging and lumbering, 68/264; 71/266,fr.cov. June; 72/302,fr.&ins.bk. cov. Dec.; 76/ins.fr.cov. March— cartoons, 73/28,187,215; log rafts, 66/178,180,182; 75/ins.fr.cov. June; mills, 68/271; 73/ins.fr.cov. June; 74/ins.bk.cov. Dec.; 76/109; 77/76,212,214,215,218,226,234,348; operations, 71/132; 73/10,12,20,22, 172,178,180,181,213,217,225,covs. March,ins.fr.cov. Sept.; 74/178,324, fr.cov. Dec.; 76/65,ins.bk.cov. March; 77/224-36*passim*,343,348; railroads and trains, 72/296,298; 73/14,15, 218,220,221; 76/62; 77/72,346

Lomax, Alfred L., 77/67; Lorain, Lorenzo, 69/242; Love, John S., 78/122; Lovejoy, Esther Pohl, 75/11,35; Lowe, Herbert, 66/116; Luelling, Alfred, 68/159; Luelling, Henderson, 68/154; Lund, Erick, 71/266,268,271; Lundy, Herbert, 74/214; McAdoo, William G., 68/133; McCall, Thomas

L., 67/204; McCallon, B.H., family, 77/ins.fr.cov. Sept.; McCamant, Wallace, 74/234; McClay, Oclo, 80/63, 65; McClung, Donald, 67/200; McClure, A.S., 78/226; McClure, James and Nancy, 78/148; McClure, Robert, 78/148; McClure, Vincent, 78/214; McConnell, Robert, 71/6; McCormack, William K., 77/25; McDade, Stella, 73/242; McDougall, James A., 73/34; McFadden, Obadiah, 66/26; McGinn, Henry E., 75/270; McGregor, Jessie, 72/208; McKay, Donald, 79/120,307; McKay, John, 79/307; McKay, Leila, 79/310; McKay, Margaret C., 79/135; McKay, William Cameron, 79/307,312,fr.cov. June; McKee, Paul B., 74/214; Mackenzie, Alexander, 76/320; McKinley, William, 76/280; McKinnon, Miyo Iwakoshi, 76/ins.fr. cov. Sept.; McLaughlin, Joseph, 74/265; McLoughlin, Ada, 72/208; McLoughlin, David, 81/378; McLoughlin, John, 81/378; Macmichael, C., 72/62; McNary, Charles, 66/364; 68/126; McNary, John H., 68/129; McTavish, Simon, 81/381; Madarieta, Miguel, family, 76/167; Malcolm, Philip S., 75/155

manuscripts—

Charles Becker letter, 67/216; J.B. Charbonneau letter, 72/78; Lee Mission account of William Brooks, 64/44; *Madonna* log, 77/60; Alexander Piper journal, 69/256; Louis Scholl requisition for fire engine, 68/37

maps—

Astoria plat, 81/24; Astoria to Salem, 81/189; Avacha Bay, 80/ins.fr.cov. Summer; Bowles 1865, 72/68

California—

auto route to Ore. 1915, 72/160; Northern Calif. 1840, 73/104; Southern Calif. 1879, 80/248

Camp Day, 69/233,ins.covs. Sept.; Camp Harney 1877, 70/20; Camp McDermit 1874, 68/250; Camp Warner, 72/27

Cape Disappointment—

Japanese submarine route, 65/insert; U.S. Coast Survey, 65/insert; Warre and Vavasour plan, 65/insert Cape Horn sailing routes, 77/40,42; Columbia lightship location 1903, 69/308; Columbia River, 75/220, 228; Columbia River mouth, 64/214-15,232; 69/bk.cov., both sides, Dec.; 74/ins.fr.cov. Dec.; Coos Co.-Portland travel, 80/57; Cram map of Oregon, 65/174; deMofras, 64/232; 76/128; Dept. of Columbia 1892, 81/280; Diamond Lake area, 79/145; Drew, whites killed in Southern Ore., 69/226; Elliott Cutoff route, 78/150,153,208-50*passim*,292-323*passim*; 79/4,14,28,47,50; Evans route, Port Orford area, 69/46-47; Ft. Dalles, 67/328; 68/12-13; Ft. Dalles Military Reservation, 68/32,covs. March; Ft. George plan, 64/196; Ft. Hoskins plan, 65/190,194; Ft. Umpqua, 70/248,256; Free Emigrant Road 1853, 77/338; 78/46; French, Pete, murder site, 75/66; fur export routes, N. Pacific, 76/308; Gibbs-Starling map 1851, 70/258; Goddard 1855, 67/ins.fr.cov. Dec.; Hawaiian Islands 1846, 68/63; Idaho 1879, 72/68; Indian tribes in Ore., 81/408; Kaser Ranch area, 81/282; Kautz 1855, 69/35; Klamath area, proposed fort site, 69/226; Klamath Co. 1905, 75/233; McKenzie route 1793, 76/316; Major's survey, 72/covs. March; Malheur Co., 76/152; Mansfield, Ft. Dalles, 67/308; Mazatlan, Mex., 70/ins.fr.cov. Dec.; Meares' chart 1787, 68/ins.fr.cov. June; Meek route 1845, 78/248-49; Milwaukie area 1852, 68/161; mining regions Ore. and Wash. Terr., 79/bk.cov. June; Mullan, Ft. Dalles-Ft. Walla Walla, 66/insert; national forests in Pacific NW, 76/28; o&c lands in western Ore., 64/56-57; Odell and Crescent lakes area 1940, 78/294; Olympic Peninsula, 74/8,20 Oregon—

Central Ore. 1855, 79/26; Cram map, 65/174; Eastern Ore., 67/20; 79/34-35,164,286-87,ins.fr.cov. June; landforms 1941, 78/156,248-49; 79/44; Pengra 1863, 79/ins.fr. &bk.covs. March; physiographic 1930, 78/68; Southern Ore., 69/30, 34,35,257-68; Southeastern Ore., 79/276

Oregon (battleship), Cape Horn route, 76/282; Ore. and Wash. 1855, 67/ins.fr.cov. Dec.; Ore.-Calif. boundary survey, 72/fr.cov. March; Oregon Trail (Stansbury), 80/72,77; Oregon Trail in Ore. and Idaho, 77/316 Pacific Ocean—

1844, 76/128; 1868, 72/134; steamship routes, 80/174

Piper route 1860, 69/257-58; Polk Co. 1882, 75/344; Portland townsite, 80/8,24,168; Portland wood roads, 75/57

railroads—

Harrisburg-Ashland, 80/232; logging, Tillamook Co., 72/309; Northern Calif. 1885, 80/238; Oregon, 71/52-53; Ore.-Calif., 71/44; transcontinental in Ore., 67/104

Russian discoveries in Pacific 1764, 72/100; Russell, Eastern Ore., 67/20; Salem plat 1878, 80/340; Scio plat 1878, 80/378; Shively overland travel, 81/186; Siskiyou National Forest, 76/40; Sitka, Alaska, 73/145, fr.cov. June; Southern Immigrant Route, 69/228; Summit Lake area 1902, 78/ins.fr.cov. Dec.; Tide Creek area, 72/206; Umpqua City plat, 70/256; Vancouver Island, 68/bk.cov. June; Voznesenskii voyages, 73/100; Warm Springs Indian Agency, 79/124; Warre and Vavasour, 64/215-16; Wasco Co. 1892, 81/280; Willamette Valley, 66/345; Williamson 1851, 69/34; Wyeth, 66/345; Yakima Indian Agency 1862, 70/126; Yakima Indian Reservation 1879, 70/136; Yakima War 1855, 66/132; Yukon gold rush routes, 76/112,ins.fr.cov.

June
Marie, Queen of Rumania, 78/108; Marquina, Alexandro, 76/166; Marquina, Joe, 76/166; Marquina, Solero, 76/166; Martin, Charles H. and Mrs., 76/268; Martini, Rosino, 77/238; Murumoto, Fumi, 76/250; Mary Florence, Sister, 80/347; Mary Margaret, Sister, 80/347; Mary of Calvary, Sister, 80/347; Mary of the Visitation, Sister, 80/347; Matthieu, F.X., 81/254,258, fr.cov. Fall; Maynadier, H.E., 72/62; Meacham, Alfred B., 80/116; Meador, Joseph, 77/326; Meek, Joseph L., 81/ fr.cov. Fall; Meek, William, 68/159; Meier, Julius, 66/250; 74/110; Menefee, Don, 79/50; Menefee, Leah, 78/ 208,226,229; Merrick, Curtis, 74/265; Merrill, Birdine, 72/208; Metschan, Phil, 70/58; 81/44; Miller, Bess, 76/178; Miller, Emily Geisy, 79/ins. bk.cov. Sept.; Miller, Estelle, 76/178; Miller, George, 79/ins.bk.cov. Sept.; Miller, James Andrew, 79/ins.bk.cov. Sept.; Miller, Joaquin, 80/ins.fr.cov. Winter; 81/44; Miller, Milton A., 78/117; Miller, Wesley J., 76/178; Mills, Tom, 76/166

mining—

gold miners, 81/191,192; Green Mountain Mining Co. document, 69/210; prospector and mule, 76/ fr.cov. March

Minto, John, 81/237,258; Minto, Martha, 81/258; Mitchell, John H., 68/ 211; Molinari, Tom, 77/252; Molleta, Francisco, 77/252; Montecarlo, Italo, 77/238; Moorhouse, Thomas L. (Lee), 66/321; Morgan, Harry, 77/216; Morrell, James F., 69/294; Morrison, Sarah, 78/164; Morse, Roger, 63/8; Mountain, Thomas, 81/254,258

mountain views—

Ash Butte, 75/310; Broken Top crater, 67/31; Butte Disappointment, 78/322,323; Carroll Rim, 73/265; Diamond Peak, 77/fr.cov. Dec.; 78/ 292,308; Emigrant Hill, 78/153; Mt. Hood, 67/35; 74/252,ins.bk.cov.

June; 75/100,fr.cov. March; Mt. Hood glaciers, 77/64,66; Mt. Lassen eruption, 77/166; Mt. Rainier, 73/ 344; Mt. Shasta, 80/234; Mt. Washington, 74/51; Neahkahnie Mt., 71/ ins.bk.cov. June; 75/50,52; 77/70; Newberry Crater, 67/12; Olympic Mts., 74/6; Painted Hills, 73/265; Peterson's Butte, 65/242; Saddle Mt., Clatsop Co., 67/38; Shell Rock Mt., 74/100; Steens Mt., 63/308; 67/24; 77/152; Sutton Mt., 64/106; Wallowa Mts. meadow, 70/30; Whitehorse Butte, 68/252-53; Wind River Mts., Wyoming, 65/152

music—

bands, 74/348; 77/130; 79/234,244, 265,ins.fr.cov. Sept.; instruments, 79/ 253,254,fr.cov. Sept.; Music scores, 79/246,247; orchestra, 79/249; sheet music, 80/386

Myers, Jefferson D., 70/224; Navarro, Joe, 76/158,167; Nave, Pietro, 77/ 252; Negro people, 73/196,198,202, 205,208; Nesmith, James W., 73/42; Neuhausen, Thomas B., 68/129; Newell, George L., 80/170,184,196; Newell, George L., Jr., 80/196; Newell, Laura, 80/196; Niagara Dam, 71/350, 353,354,356; Niles, Harry M., 74/214; Noland, Pleasant, 78/226; Obieta, Domingo, 76/156; O'Bryant, Hugh D., 80/16; Odermatt, Adelhelm, 70/311

offices—

lawyers' office, 77/264; *Oregonian* editor-in-chief's office, 70/214

Olcott, Ben W., 75/170; Ollgard, Christian, 73/242; Olney, Cyrus, 64/308; Olney, Nathan, 64/308; Olsen, Charles Oluf, 73/296; Olsen, Elizabeth, 73/296

orchards—

cherry, 68/166; Luelling, 68/168-73; orange groves, 80/250; Willamette Valley, 75/282

Oregon Pioneer Assn. group photos— 1874, 81/fr.&bk.covs. Fall; 1897, 81/258; 1905, 81/254

Oregon writers, group photo, 73/296;

Oregon Writers Project 1939 group photo, 74/265; Ortschild, Viola, 72/208; Osolin, Helen, 81/37 overland trail views, 78/134,137,138; 79/68,371; 80/70,72,74,86— Ash Hollow, 79/374; Big Marsh Creek ford, 78/296; Chimney Rock, 65/152; 78/130; 79/374; Courthouse Rock, 79/374; Crescent Creek ford, 78/296; Ft. Boise, 81/19; Ft. Bridger, 67/226; Ft. Hall area, 80/ 86; Ft. Laramie, 79/72; movie scene, 78/ins.fr.cov. June; 79/76; Protective Corps officers, 72/62; Snake River immigrant route 1859, 79/384 Owen, Benjamin F., 78/226; Owens-Adair, Bethenia, 81/258; Pacific Photo Co., 66/326 packing and freighting, 67/229— pack train, 66/314; Pony Express saddle, 67/234; wagons, 70/ins.fr. cov. June; 77/19 Palmer, Joel, 78/49 parades— Albany 1912, 77/140; Eugene 1912, 77/141; Moro 1902, 77/136; Portland, 71/212; 73/205; 77/132,133, 135,143,144,258; 80/259,265 Parrish, Josiah L., 73/248; 81/fr.cov. Fall; Parrish, S.B., 81/258; Parrott, Thomas H., family, 74/346; Pearson, Emil, 76/20; Pearson, Erwin, 76/20; Pearson, Greta, 76/20; Pearson, Nels, 76/20; Pease, George A., 81/254; Pennoyer, Sylvester, 65/266; Perkins, Thomas Handasyd, 76/209; Petty, Joseph, 78/305; pheasant basket, 65/ 245; pheasants, Chinese, 65/228; Pierce, Ernest, 74/265; Pierce, Walter, 75/170; 78/100,102,fr.cov. June; Pierre, Anne Adrian, 71/338; Pilot Rock east of Echo, 66/140; Pinchot, Gifford, 78/114; Piper, Alexander, 69/242; Piper, Edgar, 74/110; Pittock, Henry L., 74/110; Plecas, Mary R., 74/265; Pohl, Emil, 75/35; Pohl, Frederick, 75/35 police— Portland, 80/322; Portland first

badge, 80/ins.bk.cov. Fall Pomeroy, Calvin, 81/258; Powell, Luther I., 75/155; Porter, Bill, 69/ 300; Porter, J.D., 69/300; Portland Grade Teachers' Assn. group photo, 72/208; Portland Italian people 1911, 77/256; post cards, 66/290,306,307, 309; Powers, Albert H., 77/74,78,ins. covs. March; Powers, Margaret, 77/ins. bk.cov. March; Pratt, Orville C., 75/356 printed materials— advertisements— Allen, Andrew, 69/ins.fr.cov. Dec.; Chautauqua, 80/392; Oregon Steam Navigation Co., 70/ins.bk.cov. March; Oro Fino saloon, Portland, 80/135; Pierce Mfg. Co., 78/352; Queets River land, 74/ins.bk.cov. March books— Bendire, 66/238; Trall, 78/8,16,20 documents— Know Nothing Party, 75/108; Ku Klux Klan, 75/108,155,157,164,167, 183; postmaster appointment, 81/180 newspapers and magazines— *Saturday Evening Post* cover 1900, 72/fr.cov. Sept.; *West Shore* "Ho for Oregon!", 69/200; ww 1, Portland newspaper notices, 64/252; 71/217 Oregon imprints— first document, 62/116; Fourth of July 1850, 77/131; Grand Emancipation Celebration 1869, 73/ins.bk. cov. Sept.; Lane proclamation 1849, 64/141; O.S.N. Co.'s Notice, 64/ 163; pamphlet cover, 64/163; Read and Reflect!, 64/156; To Arms!, 65/5 posters— Ku Klux Klan lecture 1921, 75/fr.cov. June; Liberty Loan drive, 68/139; 71/fr.cov. Sept.; 75/243,266; Ore. Pioneer Assn. 1876, 81/228; Simpson campaign, 68/272; Skirving Panorama, 65/130; ww 1, 71/244; 75/261 programs— Chautauqua, 80/392; *Lausanne* farewell exercises, 76/364; Ore. Pioneer Assn. 1879 meeting, 81/252 quail, 69/8; Quilici, John, 77/238 railroads—

bridges, 71/fr.cov. March; 81/132; construction, 69/300; 71/70; 80/ 162,163,234,ins.fr.cov. Fall; depots and shops, 67/108,178; 71/66-67, ins.fr.cov. June; 78/ins.bk.cov. June; 81/270; ferries, 69/304; 71/32; Northern Pacific schedule 1883, 71/ ins.fr.cov. March; survey crew, 81/ 116,fr.cov. Summer; trains and locomotives, 62/312-13; 65/358; 66/ 312; 67/100,103,108,113,131,137; 71/4,32,74; 74/312; 77/170; transcontinental completion celebration, 67/100,covs. June; 71/26; 77/133; trestle, 76/84

ranches—

Alvord, 63/313,332; Becker, 67/249, 251; Chernykh, 70/114; Cherry Creek, 81/308,311,315; Coos Co. view, 63/4; Corta, 76/171; Elkhorn, 80/52; Grimes, 81/300; Hay Creek, 72/342; Hyland, 78/322; Inskip, 71/252,253,263; John Day, 81/ins.fr. cov. Fall; Rock Creek, 81/263,265; Rogue River, 76/77; Urlezaga, 76/ 177; Urquiaga, 76/172; Whitehorse, 63/313; 68/322,323

ranching—

cattle, 63/8; 67/238,254; 77/8; horse herds, 77/15; rabbit drives, 69/ 114; 75/273; sheep, 64/100,106,118; 67/bk.cov. Sept.; 68/248; 69/122, 132,305,covs. June; 73/306; 74/252; 75/70; 76/154,156,171,332,344, 348,351,ins.fr.cov. Dec.; 77/20,152, 169; 81/268,300,320

Ransdell, Olive, 74/265; Ratto, Giombattista, 77/252; Raver, Paul J., 80/ 324; Read, Anna, 72/208; Read, W.C., 74/26; Recio, Emily, 80/170; Recio, Josie, 80/170; Redington, J.W., 80/ 121; Redington, Nellie M., 80/122,125; Redon, Juan and Nellie, 71/99; Reed, Simeon G., 72/328; Rementeria, Janero, 76/166; Rigdon, Steven, family, 79/

48; Riley, Frank Branch, 74/206,210, 214,218,221,234,236,243,fr.cov. Sept.; Riley, Lotte, 74/206; Riley, Pat, 77/ 25; Rinehart, W.V., 65/18; Rippey, Irene, 72/208

rivers and streams—

Big Nestucca, 71/122; Blitzen, 78/ 229; Columbia and Columbia Gorge, 63/62; 70/6; 74/100; 75/36,104, 278; 81/58; Crooked, 67/ins.fr.cov. March; 77/334; Deschutes, 67/9, bk.cov. March; 69/296-97,304; Elk Creek, Cannon Beach, 77/284; Klamath River Canyon, 72/39; Little Blitzen Gorge, 68/325; Lost River natural bridge, 72/33; Malheur, 78/ 150; Owyhee, 67/19,253; Pine Creek drainage, 78/208; Queets, 74/28; Rogue, 76/84; Silvies, 78/210; Snake, 70/28; South Fork, Crooked River, 78/241; South Fork, John Day, 68/ 304; Trout Creek near Ashwood, 75/ 313; Umpqua, 70/ins.bk.cov. Sept.

roads and trails—

Camp Warner military road, 72/27; Chilkoot Pass, 76/ins.bk.cov. June; Columbia River Highway and construction, 66/253-66*passim*; 74/118, 122,126,133,140,fr.cov. June; Coos Co. road, 72/162; Cornell Road, 75/ 58; forest fire trail, 76/36; Highway 20, 78/212,236; immigrant road near Big Marsh Creek, 78/298; McKenzie River road, 74/45; Rogue River trail bridge, 76/84; Ruby City-Winnemucca road tracks, 71/263; Thompson Road, 75/59; White Pass trail, 76/104,107; Winnemucca-Alvord Ranch road, 63/ 313

Roberts, George B., 63/100; Roberts, J.H., 69/314; rock inscription, pioneers, 65/300; 68/311; 77/80; Rogers, H.W., 71/116; Roosevelt, Eleanor, 76/268; Roosevelt, Franklin D., 76/ 268; Roosevelt, Theodore, 78/110; Rose Valley Borax Co. views, 73/232, 234,236,238,240,fr.cov. Sept.; Royal Riders of the Red Robe, 75/176; Russell, Marion, 79/205; Sandburg, Carl,

74/155; Saunders, Frank M., 81/260; Saylor, Sydner, 78/305; Scharff, John, 73/236; Schinner, A.F., 70/331; Scholl, Louis, 67/325; Schoppe, Charles F., 80/316; Schrunk, Terry, 67/204; Schumann-Heink, Ernestine, 70/331; 78/173; Scott, Ella, 70/242,250; Scott, Harvey W., 70/196,224,232; Scott, Mr. and Mrs. John B., 70/242, 250; Scott, Leslie M., 74/234; Seghers, Charles J., 70/325; Semenza, Lorenzo, 77/252; Semenza, William, 77/252; Settlemeier, Bob, 63/321; Seward, William H. (cartoons and statue), 72/128, 131,138; Seymour, George F., 70/fr. cov. Dec.; Shafer, Julie Holman, 74/ 236; Shea, Thomas E., 74/214; Sherars Bridge, Deschutes River, 73/330; Sherbet, Andrew L., 74/265; Sheridan, John, 69/146; Sheridan, Philip H., 65/ 176; Sheriff, Ralph, 74/265; Sherwood, Vern, 76/178; Shively, John M., 81/fr. cov. Spring; Short, Robert V., 81/254; Sibley, Joseph E., 77/262; Simonatti, Sam, 77/248; Simpson, Asa Mead, 68/ 260; Sinclair, Archie, 74/265; Sinclair, James, 66/144; Skinner, W.S., family, 71/252; Sladen, J.A., 70/100; Slater, James H., 75/126; Smith, Earl R., 63/ 262; Smith, Elphie, 72/208; Smith, Ferdinand C., 70/60; Smith, John, 79/ 148; Smith, Lucinda, 70/60; Smith, Mary A., 80/363; Smith Rocks, 67/ 32; Smythe, George C., 78/238; Snow, Zera, 68/331; Spada, Frank, 77/252; Spalding, Henry H., 75/114; Spanish-American War scenes, 72/219,224, 284; 80/176,181,196; Spencer, Asahel C., 78/63; Spooner, Julia, 72/208 sports— baseball, 76/252; 80/401; football, 80/401; judo club, 76/250; pelota, 76/166,167; physical culture class, 80/399 springs— Ashland mineral, 64/324; Sod House Springs, 78/228; Upper Watson Springs, 65/30; Vale hot springs, 78/145; Yellowstone, 74/337

Stafford, William, 81/178 stage transportation views— Huntington stage station site, 68/298; stage coaches, 67/229; 77/27; stage wagon, 76/55; Yellowstone Express coach, 74/336 Stark, Benjamin, 72/318; Stearns, David S., 74/234; Steel, Will G., 81/ 44; Sterling, Donald J., Sr., 74/214; Stevens, Mrs. E.T.C., 79/205; Stevens, James, 74/155; Stewart, John, 78/122; Stoll, Marie, 74/265 stores and shops— Arata Co., Portland, 77/259; Ashwood store and post office, 77/160; Harding drug store, 79/174; harness shop, 80/284; Italian grocery, 77/ 238; Japanese store, 76/299; Yasui Bros., Hood River, 76/242 Stout, Ray L., 73/fr.cov. Dec.; Stovall, Alva and family, 72/282,285; Strite, Dan, 72/292; Strong, Thomas N., family, 75/62; Strong, William, 62/60; 64/292; Sturgis, William, 76/204; Sumner, Charles, 73/32; Sunday, Billy, 78/171 surveying, 72/covs. March; 73/fr.cov. Dec.— crews, 73/352,354; markers and monuments, 72/4,16,24,30,32,40, 44,50 Takaki, Tama Nitobe, 76/ins.fr.cov. Sept.; tanager, 69/24; Tandy, Robert, 78/226; Tandy, Will, 77/326; Taylor, Margaret, 74/265; Teeple, L.R., 74/ 214; Teutch, William, 63/8; Thayer, Harriet, 72/208; Thayer's Landing, Columbia Co., 72/197; Thielsen, Mrs. Horace, 81/254; Thompson, Agnes, 74/25; Thompson, Harry, 74/25; Thompson, L.S., 72/62 tokens and medals— Lot (Indian) medal, 70/160; Moses (Indian) medal, 70/fr.cov. June; North West Co. trade token, 76/330; Seltice (Indian) medal, 70/160 Townsend, T.S., 74/276; Trumbull, Lyman, 73/32; Turn Verein members, Portland, 80/264; Twelve Mile Canyon, 72/ins.bk.cov. March; Uberuaga, Margarita, 76/164; U.S. cavalryman, 70/4; Upshaw, Francis Marion, 77/370; Upshaw, Frank, 77/372; Upshaw, Ora Estelle, 77/372; Upshaw, Walter, 77/372; Upshaw, William L., 77/372; U'ren, William S., 68/198; Urlezaga, John, 76/166,167

valley views—

Alvord Valley, 79/274; Hood River Valley, 70/52-53; 79/204; Willamette Valley, 74/257; 75/282; 78/ins.bk.cov. Dec.

van Ravenswaay, Charles, 66/292; Vaughan, Thomas, 67/200,204; Vaughn, George W., 80/16

vessels—

A.M. Simpson, 68/270; *Admiral* (schooner), 68/270; *Alice*, shipwreck, 77/44; *Altona* (river boat), 77/141; *America* (ship), 76/207; *Ancon*, 77/128; *Annie Faxon*, 71/24; *Arthur Middleton*, 80/30,33,36,38; Astoria regatta, 74/214; *Bailey Gatzert*, 63/62-63; 74/320; *Berlin* (bark), 74/146; *Bonita* (river boat), 77/141; *California* (schooner), 77/45; *Chatham*, 72/fr.cov. June; *Chenamus*, 75/fr.cov. Dec.; 77/36; *Collingwood*, 70/292; *Columbia* (OR&NCO. vessel), 71/12; *Columbia Lightship No. 50*, 69/315-21*passim*,fr.cov. Dec.; *Columbia Rediviva*, 68/100,fr.cov. June; 76/198; *Constitution* (U.S. frigate), 77/fr.cov. March; *Coquille* (river steamer), 76/84; diesel engine for ship, 77/104; *Echo* (river steamer), 79/244; *Elmore* (steamship), 71/140; fishing vessels, 75/ins.fr.cov. June; *Fleetwood* (steamer), 71/21; "floating marine way" drawing, 81/40; *George W. Elder*, 74/305; 76/102; *George W. Fenwick*, 74/300; grain fleet at Portland, 66/120, 128; *Hancock*, 76/198; *Iralda*, 74/301; *Jane A. Falkenberg*, 77/54; *Lausanne*, 76/360; lumber schooner at Coos Bay, 68/266; lumber vessels at Tacoma, 66/124; *Madonna* log, 77/60; *Madrugada*, 77/108,110,113,

114,125; marine motor, 81/50; *Maryland* (brig), 76/218; *Mexicana*, 79/398; *Modeste*, 70/295; *Monadnock* (U.S. steamship), 62/4; *Nann Smith*, 77/76; *Nikolai I* (steamer), 73/146; *Ocklahama*, 74/305; *Oneonta* (river steamer), 62/312-13; *Oregon* (battleship), 72/ins.covs. Sept.; 76/272,276,278, 290,296; *Oregonian* (steamer), 74/258; Panama Canal opening, 77/128; *Peacock* (pilot schooner), 77/278; *Peter Iredale*, 64/69,71; *Pamona* (river boat), 77/141; *Republic* (steamship), 81/199; *Resolution*, 79/fr.cov. Dec.; *S.I. Allard*, 77/103; *Samoa*, 77/364,366,ins.fr.cov. Dec.; school "bus" on Coos Bay, 66/53; shipyard at Astoria, 77/ins.fr.cov. June; *Spokane* (steamer), 70/138; *Struan* (ship), 66/100; *Sutil*, 79/398; *T.J. Potter*, 74/164; *Telegraph*, 74/323; *Tillamook* (steamship), 77/364; *Tonquin*, 71/fr. cov. Dec.; *Tuscania*, 77/286; U.S. naval vessels, 62/12,13,49; *Western Shore* (ship), 68/268; *Wide West* cabin, 70/ins.fr.cov. March; *Wisconsin* (ship), 74/fr.cov. March

Victor, Frances Fuller, 62/308; Viganego, Mateo, 77/252; Villard, Henry, 71/48; Vollum, Dr. and Mrs. Edward P., 70/242; Walker, Robert F., 77/326; Wagner, Agnes Stewart, 78/122; Warner, Fred and Elizabeth, 78/122; Washington, George (Negro pioneer), 73/196

waterfalls—

Benham Falls, 67/fr.cov. March; Multnomah Falls, 66/268; 74/122; Niagara Falls, 80/372; Pringle Falls, 77/331; Silver Creek Falls, 66/302; Wahkeena Falls, 74/126; Yellowstone Falls, 74/335

Watson, Chandler B., 66/172; 68/318; Watson, James, 76/126; Wattles, Willard and Mrs., 74/155; Weed, Ada M., 78/35; Weed, Gideon A., 78/35; West, Oswald, 66/250,328,342; 68/133; Westfall, Jasper, 63/287; Wetjen, Albert R., 74/148,155; Wetjen, Mrs.

Albert R., 74/155; Wetjen, Charles A., 74/148

whaling—

whale fishery figures, 75/316; whales, 75/323; whaling scene, 75/330

White, Daniel, 78/126; White, Mrs. Lennox, 78/102; Whiteaker, John, 72/328; Wilbur, James H., 70/148; Wilcox, T.B., 74/110

wild animals—

antelope, 69/fr.cov. Jan.; beaver, 76/36; buffalo, 80/fr.cov. Spring; coyotes, 76/337; prairie dogs, 69/20; 80/70

Will, Fred, 79/249; Williams, George H., 70/224; Williams, Thomas, 78/126; Wilmot, Robert, 74/265; Wilson, Bruce, 79/205; Wilson, Holt, 75/100; Wilson, Julia, 80/360; Wilson, Tina, 79/205; Winters, George W., 80/324; Wittenberg, Caroline, 64/260; Wittenberg, David, 64/260; Wittenberg, Minnie, 64/260; Wolfer, George J., 79/232; Wood, Charles Erskine Scott, 70/100,fr.cov. March; 75/100; Wood, E.R., 80/324; Wood, Erskine, 75/100; Woodfield, William, 66/329; woodpecker, 69/8; Woods, George L., 79/128; Wool, John E., 67/317

woolen mills—

Albany, 67/64,68; blanket from Albany mill, 67/64

Wrenn, Sarah B., 74/265; Wright, Donald T., 77/61,64; Wright, Joe, 73/350; Yellowstone Park geyser, 74/338; Yeon, John B., 66/350; 74/110; Yturraspe, Jesse, 76/166; Yturri, Anthony, 76/164; Yturri, Dolores, 76/164; Yturri, Domingo, 76/166; Yturri, George, 76/166; Yturri, Lewis J., 76/164; Yturri, Maria, 76/164; Yzaguirre, Sabina, 76/164; Zolezzo, Mike, 77/252

Physicians, 69/88,117,133,223N,237, 241,253,329; 77/298,337:

British Columbia, 71/184-86; Burns, 63/336,338; Columbia Co., 64/357; 65/308; Coos Bay, 64/355; Dallas, Ore., 77/264-66; Douglas Co., 66/

187; early Oregon, 65/220; Eugene, 63/245; Ft. George, 66/334; Ft. Henrietta, 66/154; Ft. Hoskins, 65/189N, 192-93; 66/77; Ft. Vancouver, 80/207; French Prairie 1850, 81/382; Hudson's Bay Co., 65/207-208; Jordan Valley, 76/164; Klamath Indian Reservation, 79/305; Portland Italian, 77/254,259; Salem, 65/189N; Southwest Ore., 71/290; Tillamook Co., 71/117-40; 77/357

women—

early Oregon, 69/338; 75/7-35*passim*; first with medical degree, 78/12

Pi-ach-nut (Indian), 70/38

Picard, Basile, 66/348N

Picard, Regis, 66/348N

Pichet, Louis, 66/361

Pickens, John S., 70/235

Pickering, Abner, 70/140,141,143

Pickering, Timothy, 76/208

Picket Rock, Umatilla Co.:

described, 66/141; photo, 66/140

Pickett, Charles E., 66/355; 68/340; 81/18-20:

biography, 81/18N

Pickett, James T., 70/359

Pico, Jose Antonio, 71/260; 72/78-79

Picture Gallery Pioneers, by Andrews, review, 66/381

"'Picturesque' Frontier: The Army's Fort Dalles," by Priscilla Knuth, 67/293-346; 68/5-52

Piegan Indians, 66/70

Piepsa (Indian), 79/153,156,157,313, 314,315,316,318,322

Pierce, Barbara L.:

"Economic and Geographical Determinants of Railroad Routes in the Pacific Northwest," cited, 71/75

Pierce, Cornelia Marvin (Mrs. Walter), 67/218,248

Pierce, Elias Davidson, 62/106; 64/356

Pierce, Ernest, photo, 74/265

Pierce, Frank Richardson, 74/54

Pierce, Franklin, 64/302,312-13; 66/25,30

Pierce, Joe E., 66/92

Pierce, Lloyd, 78/102-103

Pierce, R.H., Co., Eugene, 78/351,353
Pierce, Walter M., 67/241; 72/80,232; 76/247; 78/357:
campaign fund 1922, 64/334-35; Ore. school law 1922, 70/85; photo, 78/ 100,fr.cov. June
Pierce (Pierce City), Ida., 63/89
Pierce and Lewiston Express, 68/88
Pierce County, Wash., 63/230; 66/32: school history, 65/381
Pierre, Anne Adrian (Indian), 71/ 339,343:
photo, 71/338
Pierson, —, Yakima War scout, 62/79
Piette, Aloysius, 80/344,345,346,352
Pig War, SEE San Juan boundary dispute
The Pig War, by Murray, review, 69/326
Pig War Islands, by Richardson, review, 72/344-45
Pigeons, passenger, 69/12
Piggott's Castle, Portland, 63/363
Pigs, SEE Hogs
Pike, —, Harney Co. hermit, 63/333-34
Pike, Albert:
Journeys in the Prairie, 1831-1832, reprint noted, 70/86
Pike, Zebulon Montgomery, 68/345; 80/206,331:
1805-1806 exped., 69/335
Pilbean, Benjamin, 65/184N
Pilcher, Joshua, 72/179; 77/91
Pilgrim Congregational Church, Albina, 77/376
Pile drivers, 73/8-9,14
Pillar Rock, Wahkiakum Co., 62/82; 72/172
Pilling, William, 64/180
Pillow, Charles B., 66/145N
Pillow, Gideon J., 73/35
Pilot Butte:
history, 64/87
Pilot Butte Inn, 75/294
Pilot Rock, Jackson Co. landmark, 66/82; 72/47
Pilot Rock, Ore., 63/365; 64/90; 70/25,26:
photo 1880s, 70/25
Pilot Rock News:
centennial issue, 64/90

Pilots and piloting:
boats, 77/45,278; Columbia River, 77/44-45,45N,278
Pinchot, Gifford, 62/188,190; 64/75; 65/314; 76/30-32; 78/280; 80/408:
photo, 78/115; Pierce recollections, 78/113-15
Pinchot, Gifford:
Breaking New Ground, reprint noted, 74/95
The Fight for Conservation, reprint noted, 73/282
Pine, Ore., 66/199
Pine Creek, Baker Co., 66/205
Pine Creek, Calif., 76/351
Pine Creek, Harney Co., 78/207,211,320
Pine Creek, Umatilla-Walla Walla cos., 79/200
Pine Forest Range, 63/309
Pine Hollow, 79/142,162
Pine Openings, 79/48; SEE ALSO Big Pine Openings
Pine trees:
lodgepole, 69/167; logs photo, 76/ins.bk.cov. March; yellow pine, photo, 75/288
Pinkney, David H., 81/428
Pinkney, William, 72/107
Pinney, George Miller, 67/215N
Pinney, Marie, 67/216:
"Charles Becker, Pony Express Rider and Oregon Pioneer," 67/213-56
Pinnick, Ralph E., 81/5N
Pinouse (Indian), photo, 79/120
Pinxton (Pinkston?), —, The Dalles 1879, 70/139N
Pioneer and Democrat, Olympia, 64/39
Pioneer and historical societies, SEE Historical societies
Pioneer Conservationists of Western America, by Wild, review, 80/407-408
Pioneer Days in Canyonville, Vols. 1 and 2 noted, 70/359
The Pioneer Editor in Missouri, 1808-1860, by Lyon, review, 67/278-79
Pioneer Families of the Oregon Territory, 1850, noted, 63/247
The Pioneer Finnish Home, noted, 73/72
Pioneer Fruit Co., 77/248

Pioneer Gulch, 78/309,310: photos, 78/308,310

Pioneer History of Coos and Curry Counties, Oregon, by Dodge, index noted, 75/363

Pioneer Hotel, Portland, 77/249

Pioneer House, Elk City, Ida., 79/194

"A Pioneer Ice Manufacturer," by Virginia Carson, 63/67-68

Pioneer Landmarks of Washington County, by Keller and Matthews, noted, 80/106

Pioneer Landmarks of Washington County, Oregon, by Benson, noted, 68/81

Pioneer life, 62/64-66,71,109,246-47; 69/71,183; 70/40-49,60-61,67-68; 72/91; 75/83,88,360,363; 76/92,381; 80/207,270-71,273-79,335,336: Alvord Ranch, 63/304-41*passim*

Baker Co.— 1860s, 66/200-207*passim*; 1890s, 66/209-17*passim*

beeswax making and use, 63/328-29; bread-making, 64/267; childbirth, 71/270; children's pastimes, 63/326-28; 64/262-63; Coos Co., 63/6-40*passim*; 66/52-57; Douglas Co., 77/301; entertainment, 63/292-93; early western Canada, 72/355; group reading, 65/120; hazards, 63/9-10; hospitality, 62/72; humor, 62/80-81; kitchen tools, 64/263; Kittitas Valley, 77/301; Lane Co. 1852, 80/335; laundry facilities, 63/316; legal process, 73/245-57; Lower Applegate area, 80/336; mining camps, 64/344-46; Monmouth, 64/343; Nooksak River, 73/75; Northern Calif., 80/207

Oregon Trail— camp life, 62/268,367-68; Sabbath observance, 62/250,252,255,261, 276,346; work schedule, 62/251,254, 262,282; SEE ALSO Oregon Trail

picnics, 72/172; Portland, 64/259-66 *passim*; recipes, 63/357; 73/73; recollections, 76/382; refrigeration methods, 64/351; remedies, 73/73; sad irons, 68/351; Shishmaref, Alaska, 64/ 347; soap-making, 63/328; social life, 63/326-35; spinning thread, 69/338; storage cellars, 63/316; survival, 68/

88; teaching, 72/94; turn-of-century, 75/270-76; view of in Pacific NW, 70/ 205; Washington, 65/120,211-12; weddings, 65/217; Westfall, 63/263-303 *passim*; Wheeler Co., 73/261-67; Willamette Valley, 80/270-71,273-79; SEE ALSO Homesteads and homesteading

Pioneer Logging Museum, Portland, 63/355

Pioneer Trails, noted, 77/292,298; 78/364; 80/105,335; 81/105

"Pioneer Trails Dim in Range Country," by Phil F. Brogan, 75/309-15

A Pioneer Woman in British Columbia: The Recollections of Susan Allison, ed. by Ormsby, noted, 79/337-38

Pioneer Woolen Mills, Dallas, Ore., 62/169

Pioneer Woolen Mills, by Lomax, cited, 77/193

The Pioneering Price Family, by Price, noted, 66/383

"Pioneering Spirit," by Walter E. Upshaw, 77/369-79

Pioneers: Anglophobia, 81/230,231; depicted in Davis novels, 66/242,243,244; memoirs, 67/71-72; motives for emigration, 81/229-30,242,250; opinions of, 81/ 229-59*passim*; painting by Holbrook, 73/67; recollections, 70/78; Scott's view of, 70/210,213,218,229; Wood's comments on, 70/13,15,18,23

Pioneers!, noted, 77/91

Pioneers and Incidents of the Upper Coquille Valley, by Wooldridge, noted, 74/94

A Pioneer's Search for an Ideal Home, a Book of Personal Memoirs, by Judson, review, 69/71-72

Pio-Pio-Mox-Mox, SEE Peu-Peu-Mox-Mox

Piper, Alexander: biography, 69/223N,235N,240N; Ft. Umpqua duty, 70/240,243,244,247 Klamath expedition, 70/251-52— instructions, 69/245-46,249,251; reports, 69/241-55; route maps, 69/ 257-68; value, 69/241 photo, 69/242; suggestions re perma-

nent post, 69/246,249
Piper, E.E., Hubbard councilman 1961, 69/57
Piper, Edgar B., 74/110(photo),211
Piper, Martin Luther, 65/288
Piper, William W., 81/84N
Pipes, Nellie, SEE McArthur, Nellie Pipes
Pisgah Home, Portland, 68/342,352
Pisk, Thomas, SEE Kipling, Thomas Pisk
Pistol River, 62/215
Pit River, 69/251; 72/7,26N; 81/105,328:
name, 63/350
Pit River Indians, 69/230,245,255; 72/16N; 81/394,413,414,417:
burial customs, 81/411; clothing, 81/421
Pitcher, John, 70/15
Pitt (Indian), 69/53:
death, 69/54; 71/336; student at Red River Mission, 71/330,332
Pittman, Anna Maria, SEE Lee, Anna Maria Pittman
Pittock, Henry Lewis, 64/37,162; 74/112,139N,208,218; 78/123:
newspaper interests, 71/147,147N; photos, 66/250,258; 74/110
Pittock, Robert, 78/123
Pittock Block, Portland, 75/159
Pittock House, Portland, 69/177
Pitts, Rodney, 72/288
Pittsburg, Calif., 72/159
Pitzer, Paul C.:
Building the Skagit, noted, 79/337
Piute Indians, SEE Paiute Indians
Place, Marian T., 64/186,349:
Retreat to the Bear Paw: The Story of the Nez Perce, review, 71/284
Place, Marian T. and Howard:
Story of Crater Lake National Park, noted, 75/363
Place names, SEE Geographic names
Placerville, Ida., 68/244N,310
Plaindealer, Roseburg, 73/332N
The Plains Across: The Overland Emigrants and the Trans-Mississippi West, 1848-1860, by Unruh, review, 81/96-99,101
Plains Indians, 71/291; 72/231; 81/350:
art, 81/341-42,344-45,347; history,

71/367; religion, 71/367
Plamondon, —, died 1872, 81/87
Plamondon, Simon, 63/102N,107, 116-74*passim*,239:
Cowlitz Farm sawmill, 63/173-74; family, 72/354
Plamondon's (Plomondon's) Landing, 63/117-41*passim*
Planning Council on the Arts and Humanities, 68/342
Planta, Joseph, Jr., 64/16,18
Plants:
and glaciation, 69/338; ecological range in U.S., 69/149; Lewis describes, 69/148-70*passim*; northern edible, 72/183
Plate, Robert:
Palette and Tomahawk: The Story of George Catlin, noted, 64/349
Plateau Indians, 81/341,349,351,364
Platt, Emma (Mrs. John A.), 81/334
Platt, John A., 81/334
Platt, Kenneth:
Salmon River Saga, noted, 81/334
Platte River, 62/272,274,280,281,285, 337,346N,347; 65/153-54; 66/231; 72/67; 79/373,375,376; 80/68,69, 73,74; SEE ALSO North Platte River; South Platte River
Playing cards, SEE Prices
Plays:
gold rush, 70/365; light opera, 70/7; Pacific NW history, 62/412-13; SEE ALSO Theater
Pleasant Grove Presbyterian Church, 64/354
Pleasant Hill, Ore., 77/324,328; 78/59,63,64,65; 79/13:
settlers, 78/319
Pleasant Valley, Calif., 65/160
Pleasanton, Alfred, 73/284
Plecas, Mary R., photo, 74/265
Plenty-Coups (Indian), 63/247; 65/215
Plowden, David:
Bridges: The Spans of North America, review, 78/362-63
Plumas County, Calif., 66/87
Plumb, Harland:
"A Happy Summer on Peacock Spit,"

reprint noted, 80/207
Pluvius, Wash., 68/81
Plymouth, Ore., 72/281
Plymouth Congregational Church, Seattle, 78/34
Plywood industry, 77/351,367
Pocahontas, Ore., 66/199,200,202
Poe, Alonzo M., 64/34
"A Poet Responds," by William E. Stafford, 81/172-79
Poetry magazine, 73/293-97*passim*,305; 74/35,57,58,62,63
Poets and poetry, 68/340; 81/172-79: awards, 73/293; evaluation, 74/56-57,63,262-63; "golden age," 74/48 Oregon, 73/295-98,331; 74/37,38, 57-66,150,153-56,262— photo, 73/296
Ore. and Wash., 62/298; periodicals, 74/35,57,58,62,63; societies, SEE Northwest Poetry Society; Stafford comments, 81/172-79; status, 74/152-53; Washington, 74/63
Pohl, Emil, 75/8,34: photo, 75/35
Pohl, Frederick, 75/8: photo, 75/35
Poindexter, Miles, 63/360
Poindexter, Philip, 65/214
Poindexter, T.W., 70/59
Poinsett (steamer), 76/132
Point, Nicolas, 69/55,270; 70/77; 80/406: biography, 69/64; Indian missions, 69/63-65; journals and paintings published, 69/63-65
Point Adams, 69/310: battery site problems, 65/336-37,339, 341; fortification proposed, 65/331 life-saving station, 64/70— photo, 65/354 map, 65/insert Dec.; tour of fort, 65/345
Point Arena (steamer), 74/6
Point Chinook, Wash., 74/90
Point Grenville, 63/192; 79/408
A Point of Pride: The University of Portland Story, by Covert, review, 78/285-86
Point of Rocks (Cape Elizabeth), Wash.,

74/17
Point of Rocks, Klamath Co., 75/233-34
Point Prominent, 79/303
Point Rose, 63/189,204
Point Warrior, 63/234
Poison Spider Creek, 62/347N
Poisons: strychnine, 74/318
Pokegama, Ore., 69/77,340
Pokegama Sugar Pine Lumber Co., 80/104
Poker Joe (Indian), 64/274
Pokibro, Ted (Indian), 68/301N
Poles in American History and Tradition, by Wytrwal, review, 71/281
Poletika, P.I.: reports on U.S. expansion, 72/103-105,111,112,114,124,125; Russia-U.S. convention, 72/124,125
Polhemus, James Henry, 74/238
Police: municipal function history, 80/5-7,11,321-22; SEE ALSO Portland police
"Police Function in Portland, 1851-1874," by Charles Abbot Tracy, III, 80/5-29,134-69,287-322
Polines (Alkali?) Butte, 79/145,146
Polish people, 71/281
"Political Arithmetic: Charles L. McNary and the 1914 Primary Election," by George Hoffmann, 66/363-78
Political parties, 80/13: cartoons, 66/43; formation in Ore., 75/356-58; influence on Portland police appointments, 80/290,291,292, 297-99; Oregon, 65/314; 66/8; radical elements, 76/136,144; Tammany Tiger, 66/48; territorial structure, 75/365; third party movements, 76/135-51; SEE ALSO names of parties
Politicians in Business: A History of the Liquor Control System in Montana, by Quinn, noted, 72/172-73
Politics: 1856-62, 72/319-32; 1900-1956, 72/ 80-81; Alaska, 78/358-59; American states, 69/335; American voting, 68/ 86; and Montana liquor business, 72/ 172-73

California—
campaign funds, 64/283; racial prejudice, 64/187
conservation issue 1897-1913, 64/187; conservatism, 79/98; Coon-Neuberger debate on public power, 65/314; Hayes-Tilden electoral vote dispute, 67/257-72; Idaho, 62/409; influence on Portland police dept., 80/290,291, 292,297-99; Lane biography, 68/333; McCall in, 79/406; McNary in, 66/363-78; Montana 1928, 65/215-16; New Deal, 69/65-66,335
Oregon, 62/199—
1914 primary, 66/363-78; 1949-75, 72/171; 75/344; name, 72/89; parks, 79/406; 1960, 62/297; censorship, 73/82; population 1852, 75/345
63/358; change in, 65/314; county home rule, 65/216; extremism, 66/281; Indian organization, 63/349; June 1864, 65/107; lobbyists, 66/89; political appointments, 66/89; progressive movement, 68/197-200; 69/60; reminiscences, 79/336; role of Davenport, 66/39,44,45; senate election 1918, 68/125-40; territorial, 75/365; women in, 62/198
Pacific Northwest, 63/360—
theses on, 65/374-76; 72/252-54
Polk nomination, 68/185; Portland 1885-1915, 78/89-90; public power issue, 65/314; radical, 76/136,144; role of James Buchanan, 63/346-47; third party movements, 76/135-51; u.s. 1828-48, 69/83; Washington, 65/366; 66/32; 72/286
West—
1960, 62/297; 1962, 64/281; 1966, 68/344
The Politics of Conservation: Crusades and Controversies, 1897-1913, by Richardson, noted, 64/187
The Politics of Prejudice: The Anti-Japanese Movement in California..., by Daniels, noted, 64/187
Politkovskii, Vladimir Gavrilovich, 73/70
Politkovsky (gunboat), 73/70
Polk, James Knox, 62/9; 68/185; 72/6; 75/73-74:
against 1829 Oregon bill, 70/343;

biography, 68/277-78; Ore. boundary, 75/317-28; Ore. judicial appointments, 64/293; position on Oregon Question, 70/299,305,307,311; 81/181-85,187; role in postal service expansion, 81/184
Polk County, Ore., 63/41; 66/19; 75/345,352,354; 78/11:
agriculture, 76/234,239-40—
1936-74, 81/328
courthouse, 75/346,350—
photo, 77/ins.fr.cov. Dec.
first journalistic effort, 64/125; geographic names, 80/105; historic sites, 69/77; history, 72/98; map 1882, 72/171; 75/344; name, 72/89; parks, 73/82; population 1852, 75/345
Polk County Historical Society:
meetings, 69/280; officers and board, 68/85,283; 69/82,279-80; 70/83,277; 72/177; officers and directors, 63/250; 64/84,280; 65/124,312; 67/83,284; 71/195; 72/177; 73/79; 74/181; 75/92; 76/96; 77/95; 78/195-96; 79/112; 80/111; 81/111; officers and executive comm., 66/85,279; publications, 69/77; 72/89; 73/202; 75/363; 80/105; 81/328
Polk County Observer, Dallas, 77/268:
office photo, 77/ins.fr.cov. Sept.
Polk County, Oregon, Place Names, by Clarke, noted, 78/365
Polk County Pioneer Sketches, cited, 66/13N; reprint noted, 78/364
Pollard, Lancaster, 62/198,299; 63/254,364; 64/88,357; 65/220,415; 71/101:
Libraries and Librarians of the Pacific Northwest, by Johansen *et al*, review, 63/243
Pollman, William, 67/248
Polynesia:
American missionaries, 63/358
Pome, John, 74/22
Pomeroy, Calvin S., photo, 81/258
Pomeroy, Earl Spencer, 64/186; 65/213:
The Company Town in the American West, by Allen, review, 67/357
The Fur Trade on the Upper Missouri, 1840-1865, by Sunder, review,

66/273-74

The Pacific Slope, A History of California, Oregon, Washington, Idaho, Utah, and Nevada, cited, 70/263; review, 67/78-79

"The Significance of Continuity," noted, 68/82

The Territories and the United States, 1861-1890, Studies in Colonial Administration, review, 71/358

Ponacles River, 79/384,385

Pony Express, 62/106: carries Lincoln election news, 67/228, 233; Deer Creek station sketch, 67/ 235; horses, 67/233; last surviving riders, 67/228,246N; map, 67/230N; Oregon riders, 64/90; riders' wages, 67/ 229; saddle photo, 67/234; station keepers, 67/233,233N; stations, 67/ 230,232,233

Pony Slough, 63/32

Poole, Harry, Klamath Falls 1918, 71/275

Poole, John R., 62/214

Poole, Rose Torrey, 71/275

Poole, Rufus, 64/59

Poole Slough, Benton Co.: religious colony, 71/289

Poor, D.E., 69/207N,214

Poor, Henry V.: biography, 70/349; on transcontinental railroad, 70/350

Poor, John R., 81/263,265

Poor Farm of Siskiyou County, Calif., 76/68

Poorwill: bird hibernation, 69/15

Pope, Seth Luen, 69/88

Pope, William Henry, 69/88

Pope and Talbot Lumber Co., 77/225

Pope Manufacturing Co., 72/239

Population, 62/67: 1850-1910, 80/262; cities compared 1870-1910, 80/260,263; frontier families, 73/85; north of Columbia River 1850, 62/65

Oregon Territory— 1840-50, 62/130; distribution 1850, 80/329; nature of, 62/68

Pacific NW trends 1950-60, 68/341;

Pacific slope movements, 74/286; prehistoric migrations, Siberia-Alaska, 75/ 87; railroad effect on towns, 80/209; rural pattern changes 1790-1960, 64/ 85; Willamette Valley, 66/344,351,356; SEE ALSO Census; Ethnic groups; Foreign-born; Oregon—population; Portland—population; and under nationalities, i.e., Chinese people, Danish people, etc.

Population Trends in the Pacific Northwest by Power Supply Area, 1950-1960, by Morey, noted, 68/341

Populism, 70/79: Idaho, 65/364; Montana, 72/228; Washington, 72/227,232

Populist Party, 65/263; 68/200,201, 218,220; 71/367; 72/179: Coxey's army support, 65/265-67, 276N,287; Idaho, 68/186; initiative and referendum campaign, 68/209-16; Ore. City convention 1892, 68/204

Porcupines, 69/17

Porier, Xavier, 63/198

Port, Luke A., 72/353; 73/82

Port Angeles, Wash., 63/254; 74/6,354

Port Blakely Mill Company, 68/88

Port Cox (Cox's Harbor), 68/101, 102,106: chart, 68/ins.fr.cov. June; photo, 68/103

Port Discovery, 70/300

Port Elgin (ship), 66/122

Port Essington, B.C., 72/346

The Port of Bellingham, by Hitchman, noted, 74/283

Port of Portland, 62/300; 74/302; 77/107

Port of Umatilla, 63/365

Port Orford, Ore., 63/15,25,36; 68/261,263; 70/243,255; 77/87; 79/407; 81/198: described— 1879, 63/361; 1964, 65/315 founding, 63/253; history, 72/92; Indian agency, 68/81; sawmill, 68/265

Port Orford cedar, SEE Cedar trees

Port Orford meteorite, 66/90,91,284; 67/13; 69/29-50,274

Port Orford Post, **69**/340
Port Townsend, Wash., **62**/73; **63**/246; **74**/6
Portages:
Yukon River, **76**/111
Porter, Art, **69**/300
Porter, Chester O., **72**/227
Porter, Clyde H.:
"Jean Baptiste Charbonneau," cited, **71**/248
Porter, David W.:
First Ore. Cavalry service, **65**/11-22 *passim*,26,28,37,41,56,71-72,76,82, 91-111*passim*,394
Porter, James D., **76**/387
Porter, Johnson D., Jr., **69**/ 294-305*passim*:
photo, **69**/300
Porter, Johnson D., Sr., **69**/294,305
Porter, Kenneth Wiggins, **62**/106; **67**/103N:
Peter Skene Ogden's Snake Country Journal, 1826-27, ed. by Davies, review, **63**/349-51
Porter, William, railroad contractor, photo, **69**/300
Porter and Clarkson, contractors: camp photos, **69**/300; Madras No. 1 construction camp, **69**/295,298
Porter Brothers:
Deschutes Canyon railroad construction, **69**/293FF
Portland, Ore., **62**/65,95,204,217,222, 228,245,311; **63**/31,34,37-38,190, 263,277,335; **65**/326; **66**/45,46,368; **70**/278; **74**/316; **76**/27; **77**/358; **78**/89-90:
1867, **70**/60-61; 1860s-70s, **64**/261- 66; 1880s, **62**/164,168
additions, **81**/206—
Fulton Park, **69**/202; Highland Park, **64**/265; Holladay, **64**/264; Ladd's, **77**/250,251(photo),253
ambulances, **64**/356-57; animal control, **80**/145,151,162,295; annexations 1854-1910, **80**/260; archives, **79**/239; area 1851-1910, **80**/260; assessor, **80**/ 10,18; banks, SEE Banks—Portland; baseball, **71**/289; boarding houses,

77/249; boosterism, **79**/345-57; bridges, SEE Bridges—Portland; British consulate, **72**/280,360-61; building activity, **67**/120,167
buildings, **69**/341—
armory, **70**/184; **78**/357; **80**/259 (photo); Chamber of Commerce, **62**/ 165; City Hall, **73**/80; **80**/59,60; Civic Auditorium, **74**/216,217; **77**/ 383; Forestry Building, **62**/199; **63**/ 355; **80**/54-55; Italian Hall, **77**/258; Ladd carriage house, **69**/346; Liberty Temple, **71**/212(photo),219; oldest, **70**/184; oldest federal, **70**/184; Pioneer Post Office, **70**/370-71; **71**/199, 294; Skidmore Fountain area, **62**/ 204; Studio Building, **80**/398; Town Hall, **73**/80; Turn Halle photo, **80**/ 265; Union Depot, **66**/92; **73**/333; U.S. Courthouse photo, **74**/ins.fr.cov. March; West Hall, U. of Portland, **73**/ 80; White Temple, **78**/100(photo),357
business district photos—
ca. 1913, **79**/344; ca. 1915, **79**/ins.fr. cov. Winter
business firms, **63**/253; **72**/339,346; capital rank 1888, **69**/203
cemeteries—
Lone Fir, **63**/245; **74**/347
census records—
1870, **75**/87; 1954, **75**/5
charters, **64**/146; **80**/17,20—
1864, **80**/146-47; 1868 amendments, **80**/160,161; 1870, **80**/168-69; 1874, **80**/320
Chinatown, **74**/162; **78**/77—
photo, **78**/ins.fr.cov. March
Chinese people, **78**/75
churches, **77**/255-56,376—
oldest building, **69**/341; SEE ALSO Churches—Portland
City Council—
first meeting, **80**/10; meeting places, **65**/217; powers defined, **80**/8
city dump, **77**/242(photo),250; City Park, **80**/61; city planning, **74**/212; Coeur d'Alene district interest, **69**/ 203,221N; commercial patterns, **67**/ 366; convention center, **74**/124,125,

233; corruption, 80/321-22; Council Crest, 66/281; 74/165; Coxey's army, 65/269-90*passim*; crime 1851-74, 80/ 10,15,19,25,136-54*passim*,294,296, 302-11*passim*

described—

1856, 80/25; 1900, 73/333; 1905, 80/53-62

drinking fountains, 66/250; 72/348 earthquakes—

1962, 64/284; 1968, 70/183

economic development 1880s, 67/105-24; 71/27,31,33; economy 1850-74, 80/13,15,22-23,28,136,137,153,160, 294,309; elections 1851-74, 80/9,13, 134,137,306,317; ethnic groups, 71/ 289; expansion 1875-85, 71/66 exports, 71/27—

tables 1881-90, 67/109-12

finances—

fees, 80/138,144,151; fines, 80/142,150,294,296N,302N,306; revenue, 80/9,149

fire department, 72/323N

fires, 75/125-26,174—

1854, 80/21; 1872, 80/301-302; 1873, 80/308(photo),309

first architect, 80/289; first officials, 80/9,10; first ordinances, 80/10,10N, 20N

flood photos—

1862, 80/143; 1876, 80/fr.cov. Fall foreign-born impact, 80/268; fountains, 75/83; SEE ALSO Skidmore Fountain; gambling, 80/12,15,17,20,159-60,321; geologic map, 64/284; Goose Hollow district, 73/82; growth 1880s, 69/203-204; guidebooks, 66/82; 77/291; harbor, 76/293 health—

conditions, 80/160; department, 75/ 8; inspection, 80/306; officer, 80/10 historic houses—

Brown house, 71/200; Crosby house, 69/86; 81/4(photo); first log house, 66/92; Kelly house, 65/315; Piggott's castle, 63/363; 74/260(photo); Pittock house, 67/89; 68/350; 69/177; 81/294

historic sites, 71/119; 73/80 history, 77/291—

1885-1915, 78/89-90; 1915-1950, 81/203-205; neighborhoods, 77/ 292,300; 81/206; review of first, 70/219N; to 1854, 72/169

hospitals, 76/304; 80/139

hotels, 72/294; 76/232—

Benson, 66/250,267,386; 72/348; Campi's, 77/249; Columbia photo, 80/143; Esmond, 80/53; Golden Rule, 75/13; Italian, 77/249; Merchant, 70/184; 81/119N; Metropolis, 68/26; Multnomah, 75/154,159; 78/ 109; New Perkins, 77/262; Perkins, 74/199; Pioneer, 77/245; 80/141; Portland, 73/333; 74/photo ins.fr.cov. March; 80/272; St. Charles, 69/207; 71/12,17; 80/308(photo); Thompson's Two Bit House, 70/144-45; Washington, photo, 80/ins.fr.cov. Summer

housing, 67/366; impressions of in 1898, 81/119-21; incorporated, 80/8,260; Indians feared, 80/23; influenza epidemic 1918, 64/247-57; Italian people, 77/239-60

jail—

built, 80/10N,11; burned, 80/21; conditions, 80/135-36,137,139; locations, 80/11,167,299N; prisoner labor, 80/161; second building, 80/28,29; used as hospital, 80/139N

Japanese assembly center WW II, 81/ 149-71; Japanese people, 76/241,250 landmarks, 71/199; 73/80—

ordinance, 66/283

law enforcement, 70/183; SEE ALSO Portland police; library, SEE Library Assn. of Portland; licenses, 80/29, 144-45,162

life in—

1881, 80/271-73; 1900-10, 75/56-65 liquor business—

crusade against, 80/314-17; domination of city govt., 80/160,321; licensing, 80/152,159,162,316N; regulation, 80/17,20,25-26,29,29N,146,313 lower Columbia impact, 66/283;

lumber mills, 67/163,165; manufacturing 1881-90, 67/113-16
maps—
land claims, 80/8; police beats 1870, 80/168; townsite 1856, 80/24
markets, 68/350; 77/253-54—
Front St., 74/165; wholesale, 74/162-63; Yamhill, 74/161
Marquam Gulch photo, 77/242
mayors, 63/362—
authority, 80/9,17,20,165,287-88, 300,319-20; photo of first, 80/16
militia, 75/129; Mt. Tabor district, 74/165; music, 67/80; Negro people, 73/209; neighborhood history, 77/292,300; 81/206; North Peninsula impact, 66/283; ordinances, 80/10, 20N,138N,139,144; Palatine Hill pumping station, 69/338
panoramas—
1858 litho., 80/29; 1865 litho., 80/148; 1867, 80/152
Park Blocks origin, 81/202; penitentiary, 66/165; photographers, 66/209,317,318
photos, 71/362; 74/260,356; 80/4, 23,143,152,158,264,294,301,305, 306,308,318; 81/330—
1884, 75/12; 1895, 75/20; 1920s, 74/36,ins.fr.cov. March; 1925-62, 81/330; 1930s, 73/298; 74/178,264; clocks, 74/162,178; harbor, 74/fr. cov. March; houses, 74/165,260,349; Lownsdale Square, 74/267; streets, 74/36,265,ins.fr.covs. March and June
physicians, 75/14-35*passim*; plats and plans to 1890, 81/202; police department, SEE Portland police
population, 71/35—
1850-1910, 80/262; 1860, 80/136; 1863, 80/146; 1864, 80/149; 1868, 80/161; 1880-90, 67/121; 1910, 74/112; compared to other cities, 80/263; foreign-born 1850-1910 (tables), 80/262,266; Negroes, 73/209
port, SEE Port of Portland; Portland Heights, 65/217; postal cards,

66/305,306
prices—
1881, 71/12,16; 1898, 81/12
prostitution, 80/17,136,153,294,294N; public transportation, 63/253; quality of life, 80/322; racial discrimination, 80/298; racial justice, 70/183
railroads, 71/39-40,50,63-73*passim*,93, 95—
opinions on routes, 71/68-72,73,92; rates, 67/170
transcontinental—
celebration photo, 67/cov. June; depots and workshops, 71/66-67, 197; economic importance, 71/29, 65,73,95
real estate transactions 1880-90, 67/112,118-19; recital hall, 71/289; recollections, 68/340; recorder, 80/8,17, 160,165; reduction works, 69/221; restaurants, 76/228,232; 77/245,249,378 rivals, 71/43-45,94; 72/169,214; 74/105,112,113,135,340—
Astoria, 71/68,93-94; Puget Sound, 71/31,45,69; San Francisco, 71/69, 74,92; Seattle, 79/355-57
saloons, 77/249; SEE ALSO Saloons; schools, SEE Schools—Portland; Scott's view, 70/220; Seward visit, 72/144; shantytown, 81/41; shipping terminal, 77/45; site described, 80/258; stock companies, 81/330; stock exchanges, 69/197-222; stores, 76/229(photo), 230,232; 77/249; streetcars, 72/228; 80/52,58(photo),271
streets—
Ankeny, 72/317; cobblestone, 62/199; Cornell Rd., 75/58(photo),64 Front St.—
1858, 77/30; ca. 1905 photo, 79/352 grading, 75/58; Green, 75/84; Mt. View, 75/58; names, 63/363; 70/216; 81/206; photos, 74/ins.fr.covs. March and June; 77/242,ins.bk.cov. June; plank road, 77/300; Skyline, 75/61; Stark, 72/317; Thompson (Ridge) Rd., 75/57(map),59(photo); Thurman, 75/58
suburban drain, 68/351; taxes, 80/9,

10,18,147,151,295,303; theaters, SEE Theaters; theses index, 72/277; Third St. Plaza, 65/276; town hall, 71/369, 372; townsite claim dispute, 72/317, 319,331-32

trade and commerce, 71/27-97*passim*,159,198— position, 67/170; with China 1851, 80/13

transportation, 70/183; 81/289; trolley fare 1917, 81/204; Tualatin Valley impact, 66/283; typhoid epidemic, 75/321; urban development publications, 67/366; 81/103-104; utopian prediction, 79/345-57; vice, 76/233; view 1858, 72/320; vote for Hayes, 67/257; wall construction materials, 66/283

waterfront, 74/37,161—

"firsts," 65/217; photo 1905, 79/ins.fr.cov. Winter

wholesale trade 1883-90, 67/116-18,123; Willamette Heights, 75/56-65; wool receipts 1882-92, 67/132; wool trade, 62/164,168,172-73; woolen mills, 62/164-79; World War II, 71/213-45; zoo, 64/89; 80/61; SEE ALSO Albina; East Portland; Mock's Bottom; Montavilla; Sellwood

Portland (North American Transp. Co. steamer), 62/95

Portland (sternwheeler), 75/82

Portland, A Historical Sketch and Guide, by O'Donnell and Vaughan, noted, 77/291

Portland Academy, Portland, 63/31; 74/200,213: history, 63/253

Portland Academy and Female Seminary, Portland, 64/146; 74/347: commencement 1860, 64/153; first graduate, 79/362; roll of honor 1868, 64/174

Portland Advertising Club, 74/120, 212,232

Portland and Valley Plank Road, SEE Canyon Road

Portland and Valley Plank Road Co., 80/13

Portland and Willamette Valley Railway,

74/357

Portland Art Museum, 73/285: board members, 71/226N; children's classes, 80/389

"Portland Assembly Center: Diary of Saku Tomita," trans. by Kodachi and Heikkala, ed. by Janet Cormack, 81/149-71

Portland Automobile Club, 74/213

Portland Board of Trade, 65/9; 67/135, 163; 69/203,208,209,220-21; 71/ 68,72: building statistics, 67/167

Portland Cable Railway Co., 64/353

Portland Chamber of Commerce, 67/44; 71/155N; 74/120,212,224; 76/237: building photo, 74/ins.fr.cov. March; Recreational and Natural Resources committee, 67/43

Portland Children's Home, 80/53

Portland Civic Auditorium: OHS quarters, 66/295,390,391; use as hospital, 64/249-50,255-56

Portland Commercial Club, 74/199

Portland Cordage Company, 69/208

Portland Cracker Company, 81/280

Portland-Deschutes Land Co., 76/244

Portland Electric Company, 62/167

Portland, Eugene and Eastern Railway, 74/357

Portland Executives Club, 74/242

Portland Federated Trades, 68/207

Portland Federation of Women's Organizations, 71/232

Portland Fish Company, 75/226

Portland Flouring Mills Company, 71/148,150: Ladd interests, 71/148

Portland Forest Park, 62/108

Portland Garden Club, 67/46-47; 76/92

The Portland Garden Club; the First 50 Years, 1924-74, by Cabell and Reed, noted, 76/92

Portland General Electric Company, 63/361:

"It Can Be Done" (film), 80/326,328

Portland Gladiators, 74/347

Portland Grade Teachers' Assn., photo,

72/208
The Portland Guide Book, by Lampman and Sterling, noted, 77/291
Portland Historic Landmarks Comm., 71/199
Portland Home Builders Assn., 66/393
Portland in Your Pocket, by Hutchins and Meyer, noted, 77/291
"Portland Italians, 1880-1920," by Charles Gould, 77/239-60
Portland Junior Chamber of Commerce, 74/231
Portland Junior League, SEE Junior League of Portland
Portland Junior Symphony Orchestra, 74/205
Portland Knitting Company, 62/199
Portland Library Association, SEE Library Association of Portland
Portland Macadam and Paving Company, 69/211
Portland Metropolitan Planning Commission: publications, 67/366
Portland Mortgage Company, 69/329
Portland, My City, by Pratt, noted, 68/340
Portland Names and Neighborhoods: Their Historic Origins, by Snyder, review, 81/206-207
Portland Neighborhood History Project: publications, 77/292,300
Portland News, 75/127,128
Portland Observer, 73/211
Portland Opera Association, 77/254
"Portland, Oregon, A.D. 1999," by Jeff Hayes, 79/346FF
Portland police, 72/339; 75/154, 156,157: arrest statistics, 80/138,142,161,163, 294,295N,296,302,309,311; beats, 80/ 168(map),293,296N,302,318-19; bicycles used, 72/339; Board of Commissioners, 80/134N,146,159N,167N, 168,287,288,293,318,320; building, 80/167,297,299,299N,301(photo); casualties, 80/157,317; Committee on Health and Police, 80/19,149,150, 153,164,167,313; conflict with private watchmen, 80/296; corruption, 80/

159-60,321-22; council authority, 80/ 8,10,17,144,150-55,303,310,312-13, 320; crime prevention, 80/147-49, 312,318; finances, 80/140,296N,297, 298,302,309,312-13
first badge, 80/139—
photo, 80/ins.bk.cov. Fall
first chief, 80/149N,167; 81/261; first full-time officers, 80/149; first permanent day and night force, 80/166; first police judge, 80/292; first salaried force, 80/155; first uniform, 80/286 (photo),297; functions defined, 80/8-9,17-18,29,165,287; history 1851-74, 80/5-29,134-69,287-322; influence of business, 80/311,321-22; legislature reorganizes, 80/17-19,20,147,160,287; letterbooks, 72/339N; marshal, 80/8-9,10,14,18,19,20,26,29,134,137,139, 144-45,146-60*passim*,165-66; mounted division photo, 80/322; number on force, 80/9N,23-24,28,140,146,154, 155,164,167,289,310,318-19; ordinance establishing 1870, 80/165; policies, 80/293; political influence, 80/ 156-57,158,167N,168-69,292; racial legislation effects, 80/27-28,140-41; salaries, 80/149,287,289,300; state *vs.* city control, 80/147,155,168-69,287-88,299,300-301; vice investigation 1867, 80/159-60
Portland-Port Angeles and Victoria Railroad, 74/17
Portland Post Card Company, 66/306
Portland Press Club, 73/299; 74/120
Portland Railway, Light and Power Company, 72/81; 75/172
Portland Reduction Works, 69/208N, 221-22
Portland Rose Festival, 68/350; 74/121,215,233: photos— 1908, 77/146; 1917, 77/258; Japanese float, 76/250
Royal Rosarians, 74/216,219
Portland Savings Bank, 65/257,395N; 75/28
Portland Shipping Company, 69/208
Portland State University (College),

63/75; 81/102
Portland Stock Board, 69/198
Portland Stock Exchange and Mining Board:
charter members, 69/208-209; companies listed, 69/211; history, 69/197-222; stock listing form, 69/210-12; "treasury stock," 69/212
Portland Symphony Orchestra, 74/230, 232-33
Portland Turn Verein, 79/241,251
Portland Typographical Union, 64/160
Portland West, by DeWolfe, review, 74/356-57
Portland Woman's Club, 67/91
Portland Women's Yellow Pages, noted, 79/337
Portland Woolen Mills, 62/169; 67/71
"The Portland Woolen Mills, Inc.," by Alfred L. Lomax, 62/164-79
Portland Youth Council, 76/252
Portland Zoological Gardens: history, 64/89
Portlander:
anti-Catholicism, 75/137,138
Portneuf River, 62/372-74,378; 80/85: ferry 1852, 80/86
Portraits, SEE Photographs and illustrations
Portrum, Sarah Alice, SEE Fastabend, Sarah A.P.
Portsmouth (U.S. naval sloop), 70/305
Portugal:
Pacific exploration, 70/77
Poseidon (ship), 66/113
Post offices:
Agness, 76/79; Amos, 73/83; Andrews, 63/333; Antelope, 75/311,314; Ashland, 71/200; Ashwood, 77/159,161(photo)
Astoria—
history, 81/188-89,190N; photo, 81/4
Auburn, 62/235; Benton Co., Wash., 69/331; Bridge Creek, 73/264; 79/169; Burnt Ranch, 81/314; Butte Co., Calif., 71/200; California, 70/280; Camp Polk, 68/91; Carico, 74/358; Chetco, 75/362; Chetco Valley, 69/341; Clark Co., 64/351; 69/331;

Clatsop Co., 71/200; Cottage Grove, 64/357; Crystal, 69/341; Curry Co., 80/335; Eugene (Skinner's), 77/324; first west of Rockies, 81/188N; Forest Grove, 72/288; Forks, Wash., 74/9; Franklin Co., Wash., 69/331; Glenada, 74/273; Grant Co., Wash., 69/331; Green Basin, 71/357; Greenleaf, 68/353; Harney Co., 63/333; Idaville, 73/7; Jackson Co., 64/356; Klamath Co., 71/200; Klickitat Co., 69/331; Lake Co., 69/341; Lane Co., 63/246; 70/272; 72/288; Latourell Falls, 66/90; Liberty, 73/263; Lincoln Co., 62/201; Lonerock, 65/219; Lower Applegate area, 80/336; lower Rogue region, 69/338; Millican, 77/18; Mitchell, 73/259; Morrow Co., 70/280; Multnomah Co., 72/288; New Era, 65/315; Newberg centennial, 72/91; Newport history, 69/340; Northern Calif., 80/207
Oregon—
19th century, 71/200; townmark scarcity, 71/200
Oregon City, 66/382; Owyhee Co., 69/341; Pacific Northwest, 70/272; Pendleton, 80/335; Pleasant Hill, 77/324; Rainier, 62/301; records, 68/343; Rickreall, 62/200; Rural, 76/74; Seaton, 74/271; Sisters, 68/91; Skamania Co., 64/351; 69/331; Skinner's (Eugene), 77/324; South Bend, Wash., 78/91; Springfield, 69/338; Swastika, 71/200; 72/93; Tiernan, 72/92; Tillamook, 67/369; Trail, 69/88; Umatilla Co., 78/364; Umpqua City, 70/236N; Union Co., 72/288; upper Willamette Valley, 72/171; Vancouver, Wash., 63/83; Waldo, 76/81; Washington, 69/331; West Side, 77/8; Wheeler Co. first, 73/264; Wilderville, 76/56; Wonder, 76/56; Yamhill Co., 72/288
Postal cards:
catalog, 66/204; dating, 66/304; laws regarding use, 66/303-304
Oregon—
caption errors, 66/304; comic cards,

66/305; exhibits, 66/304-305; first printers, 66/304; photos, 66/303-30*passim*; sales outlets, 66/304-305; scenes, 66/304

popularity, 66/303,304; prices, 66/305; railroad promotion, 66/305

Postal service, 76/53-59*passim*,74,79, 81,393:

airmail, 67/246; Alaska 1898, 81/124, 127; British Columbia express, 71/200; Camas Valley-Bridge, Ore., 72/161, 164; cost of postage 1849, 81/180; Deer Lodge-Philipsburg, Mont., 67/ 235; early Oregon, 77/319; Evergreen-Clearwater, Wash., 74/24,26,27; Evergreen-Lake Quinault, Wash., 74/30,31; Evergreen-Tahola, Wash., 74/23; Ft. Kearney 1853, 62/271; Ft. Klamath, 69/329; Ft. Laramie 1853, 62/342; Ft. Yamhill, 62/300; history, 71/200; Idaho routes, 73/284; Illahe, Ore., 71/ 200; Jacksonville-Salt Lake City, 69/ 224N; Josephine Co., 71/200; Klamath Falls, 69/257; Klamath River, 74/93; Lakeview, 68/257; Lane Co., 69/329; Lincoln Co., 69/340; mail contracts, 74/86; mail stage, 69/88; Medford, 67/374; 71/200; Missouri-Oregon contract 1847, 81/188; Myrtle Point-Rural, 71/200; New York-Calif. 1858, 68/88; Oakland, Ore.-Yreka, 73/332N; Ohio-Oregon 1862, 66/229N; Okanogan Co., Wash., 69/331; Oregon-Calif. express, 70/280; Oregon-Missouri, 68/351; 81/188; Oregon-Salt Lake City, 68/144,151; Ore.Prov.Govt., 81/ 188N; overland service 1861, 72/57; Pacific Coast service 1846, 81/184; postal cards legalized, 66/303; Puget Sound 1856, 62/98

railroads, 70/272—

mail cars, 68/351

rates 1849, 81/180; Rogue River, 70/280; 75/360; Rogue River-Chetco, 71/200; rural, 72/288; Sacramento-Portland 1860, 72/170; Siuslaw Valley, 74/271; Smith River-Chetco, 69/338; steamship, 69/276; transcontinental airmail, 67/246; U.S. records, 68/343;

SEE ALSO Express companies Post-a-min-e (Poustaminie) (Indian), 79/150N,330 Postcards, SEE Postal cards Postlethwaite, John, 71/367 *Postmarked Washington: Benton, Franklin and Klickitat Counties*, by Ramsey, noted, 69/331 Postmarks: scarcity in Oregon, 69/341 Pot Hole Ice Cave, 62/198 Potato Hills, Deschutes Co. landmark, 65/114N Potatoes, 74/302,317; 76/239,244-45; 77/9: Cowlitz Farm, 63/104,115-73*passim*; French Prairie, 66/339; Idaho, 66/ 284; prices 1858, 68/29; Sitka, 73/ 147; The Dalles 1862, 66/200 *The Potlatch Family*, by Lampman, noted, 77/301 *Potomac* (lumber brig), 68/261,265 *Potomac* (U.S. Navy frigate), 76/118,119 Potter, Albert, 62/190 Potter, David M., ed.: *Trail to California: The Overland Journal of Vincent Geiger and Wakeman Bryarly*, reprint noted, 63/356 Potter, E.L., 63/37 Potter, Edgar R.: *Cowboy Slang*, noted, 73/74 Potter, Louisa, SEE Riley, Louisa Potter Potter, Miles F.: *Oregon's Golden Years, Bonanza of the West*, noted, 77/300 Pottery: Peoria, 79/104; Ramsay, 79/6N Potts, John, 69/156 Pottsmith, Marie Holst: *They Laughed, Too*, comp. by Mintonye, review, 69/183 Poulin, Andre Z., 80/358 Poulton, Helen Jean: *The Historian's Handbook, a Descriptive Guide to Reference Works*, noted, 73/360 Poultry, 77/377,378; SEE ALSO Chickens; Ducks; Geese Powastomany Creek, 79/169 Powder River, Baker Co., 62/222-28

passim; 66/198,199; 79/42,340,391; 80/98,99:
mines, 63/357
Powder River, Mont., 74/336
Powder River, Wyo.:
military forts, 71/187-88
Powder River Valley, Baker Co., 66/197-202,227
Powderly, Terence, 75/133
Powel, John, family, Queets area settlers, 74/21
Powell, Adaline Duvall, 74/94
Powell, Alva H., family, 66/382
Powell, Edith McLaughlin: recollections, 78/364
Powell, Fred Wilbur, ed.:
Hall J. Kelley on Oregon, review, 74/91
Powell, Henry Clay, 73/83
Powell, Jackson, 69/329
Powell, Joab, 64/354; 70/279; 72/92
Powell, John A., 73/83
Powell, John P., 74/94
Powell, John Wesley, 67/21; 70/73, 362,364,367; 75/79; 80/408
Powell, Lazarus W., 73/58-59
Powell, Leonard J.:
biography, 80/353N
Powell, Luther L., 75/155-57,159,160, 161,164,178-80,190N:
photos, 75/155,158
Powell, William H.:
List of Officers of the Army of the United States from 1779 to 1900, reprint noted, 69/333-34
Powell, William S., 64/138,169
Powell Butte Cooperative Assn., 76/246
Powell Buttes, 65/78N
Powell Valley:
history, 74/94
Power development, 62/167:
atomic, 68/186; Columbia River, 63/361; Coon-Neuberger debate, 65/314; Oregon public power movement, 72/233; Pacific Northwest, 63/359,361; public ownership controversy, 65/364; 76/137,138,140,144,146; public utility districts in Ore., 68/146; steam, 62/176; water, 62/167,171,172; SEE ALSO Electricity and electric industry

Powers, —, Protection Island farmer, 65/249-50
Powers, Albert Henry, Jr., 77/77:
photo, 77/ins.bk.cov. March
Powers, Mrs. Albert Henry, Jr., 62/110, 206,302,422; 63/93,255,372-73; 64/93,189,285,358-60,363; 65/121,125-26,221-22,317-18,415-16; 66/93,189, 285,294,393,394; 67/379; 68/359, 361; 69/348; 70/372,373,374; 72/360; 73/373; 74/184,365; SEE ALSO Powers, Ruth McBride
Powers, Albert Henry, Sr., 76/59-61,66:
biography, 77/73-77; family, 77/73, 75; memorial park, 67/49; photos, 77/74,78,ins.covs. March; residence, 77/77
Powers, Alfred, 73/324:
History of Oregon Literature, cited, 74/176
Powers, Amos, 77/73
Powers, Dinah Burton, 77/73
Powers, Edward, 79/10
Powers, Frederick W., 77/75,77
Powers, Grace Wright, 62/298
Powers, Ike, 63/269
Powers, Johannah Elizabeth, 77/75:
photo, 77/76
Powers, Nathaniel, 73/77
Powers, Ruth McBride (Mrs. Albert H., Jr.):
"Oregon's Early Furniture," noted, 77/292,298
Royal Family of the Columbia, by Fogdall, review, 80/101
Powers, Squire, 78/325N
Powers, Truman P., 62/249N
Powers, W.L., 78/353
Powers, Minn., 77/77
Powers, Ore., 76/46,59,61,65,74; 77/77:
jail, 76/66; name, 77/77; platted, 77/77; South Carolina settlement, 76/74-75
Powers Davis Logging Co., 77/77
Powers-Dwyer Logging Co., 77/73
Powhatan (navy vessel), photo, 62/12
Poynter, Margaret:
Gold Rush! The Yukon Stampede of 1898, noted, 81/331

Prairie: described, 62/252-53,260-61; fires, 62/348 Prairie Creek, Lane Co., 78/320 Prairie dogs, 68/345; 69/17; 80/ 69,73; 81/16-17: drawings, 69/20; 80/70; Lewis describes, 69/19-21; towns, 79/374,376 *Prairie Schooner*, noted, 73/322 Prairie Springs, Wasco Co., 65/114 Prater Creek, 79/297N Prather, Mart, 63/268 Prather, Theodore, 75/359 Prather Warehouse, Siskiyou Co., 66/81 Pratt, Emily A., SEE Boise, Emily A. Pratt Pratt, James, 65/347 Pratt, John Francis, 63/92 Pratt, Julius W.: *Expansionists of 1898*, cited, 72/209FF Pratt, L.E., 66/20 Pratt, Laurence, 74/63: *Bones in the Wilderness*, noted, 73/285 *Fragments of Now*, noted, 70/78 *I Remember Portland*, noted, 67/80 *An Oregon Boyhood*, noted, 70/78 *Portland, My City*, noted, 68/340 *A Saga of a Paper Mill*, noted, 74/177 Pratt, Orville C., 62/63,145N,299,329; 64/293; 66/11,12,166; 73/201; 75/ 351,352,354,357,358-59; 81/194: capital controversy, 64/299-300; photo, 75/356 Pratt, Shannon, and Lawrence R. Ross: *Investing in the Great Northwest*, noted, 77/302 Pratt, William C., 71/196 Preachers: Baptist in mining camps, 81/191,192, 193; circuit riders, 72/89; SEE ALSO Missionaries *Prehistory of the Far West: Homes of Vanished Peoples*, by Cressman, review, 79/403-404 *Preliminary Bibliography of Washington Archaeology*, by Sprague, noted, 69/276 *A Preliminary Checklist of U.S. Military Posts*..., comp. by Hagan, noted, 76/92 *A Preliminary Guide to Church Records Repositories*, by Suelflow, noted, 71/363

Prentiss, Edward, 75/72 Prentiss, Jonas Galusha, 75/72,73,74 Prentiss, Stephen, 75/73 Prentiss, Warren, 75/72,75 Presbyterian Church, 62/197,293; 70/180: Alaska, 64/283; anti-Catholicism, 75/ 138; Brownsville, 66/82; Clatsop Plains, 62/240,248-49; 66/91; influence on Shakers, 72/148; newspapers and periodicals 1752-1830, 65/213; Oakville, 62/200; Oregon oldest, 64/354 Portland, 70/199— First, 73/333; oldest building, 69/341 Salem, 72/173; Southern Ore., 75/88; Woodland, Wash. 75th anniversary, 64/276; SEE ALSO Cumberland Presbyterian Church Prescott, C.H., 69/208,220 Prescott, Ore., 81/36 *President* (Boston vessel 1807), 78/356 *President James Buchanan, A Biography*, by Klein, review, 63/346-47 Presidio, San Francisco, SEE San Francisco—Presidio Presley, Addie Mullen, 63/263N,301-302 Presley, Oscar, 63/270 *Press* Expedition, 78/281 Preston, James P., 70/340N Preston, John, Virginia state treasurer, 70/340 Preston, Mary White, 78/125 Preston, William, 1853 immigrant, 78/125 Preston, William P., 78/125 Preston's Peak, photo, 76/28 Pretot (Prestor), Jean Baptiste, 63/140,144-46,154 Prettyman, Henry W., 68/165 Prettyman, Perry E., 62/300 Preuss, Charles, 65/136; 67/8,10 Prevost, Alice Marie Fraser, 81/378 Prevost, John Bartow, 69/59 Priaulx, Arthur W., 64/358,362; 67/281: *Railroads in the Woods*, by Labbe and Goe, review, 63/351-52 Pribilof Islands, 69/79; 73/119,122,

128-31
Price, A.J., 79/37-38,38N
Price, Clayton S., 66/383; 73/81
Price, F.E., 78/354
Price, George W., 65/181
Price, Gladys Bibee:
Te-yok-keen, noted, 63/357
Price, Hazen, 66/55
Price, Jay:
Wasco Co. recollections, 68/91
Price, Larry W.:
Biogeography Field Guide to Cascade Mountains, noted, 72/173
Price, Lewis Richard, 62/105
Price, Maurice A., family, 66/383
Price, Pearle M., 68/81
Price, Richard L.:
Newport, Oregon, 1866-1936, noted, 77/298
Price, Thomas:
borax discovery, 73/229
Price, Warren C.:
The Eugene Register-Guard: A Citizen of Its Community, Vol. 1, review, 78/286-87
Priceite, SEE Borax
Prices:
1896, 72/89; Alaska, 76/107; Alaska gold rush, 81/123-47*passim;* alfalfa 1896, 81/300
Auburn mines—
1862, 62/227; 1868, 62/236
bacon—
1853, 79/73N,74N,76N; 1858, 68/28; 1862, 66/227
barley—
1858, 68/28; 1878, 68/242N,257
beans—
1852, 79/393; 1862, 79/184
beaver skins 1838, 74/77-78
beef—
1852, 79/393; 1858, 68/28
blankets—
1850s, 66/164; 1867, 79/318; Ft. Vancouver, 63/217
board—
1905, 80/65; Cheyenne 1881, 71/8; Winnemucca 1881, 71/9
board and room—

1887, 74/344; 1889, 74/7,14-15; 1915, 74/138N
boarding house 1881, 70/319; boat, 76/109; bootleg liquor, 76/159,163; boots 1851, 63/53; bricks, 63/53; bridles 1867, 79/318; building materials 1856-58, 68/46,48-51
butter, 77/378—
1851, 63/53; 1858, 68/28; 1881, 71/13
California, 68/163; candles 1862, 79/184
cattle, 63/16; 67/147-49—
1858, 68/28; 1917, 67/239
celery 1881, 71/9; Chautauqua 1902, 80/398
cheese—
1900, 72/200; 1923, 71/120
Cheyenne 1881, 71/8; chickens 1858, 68/28; clay pipes, 62/72
clothing, 62/166—
1880s, 80/279; 1885, 80/251,252, 255; 1905, 80/64-65
coffee—
1850s, 66/164; 1852, 79/393; 1862, 66/227; 1863, 63/31
Coos Co. 1856, 63/21,23; corduroy and moleskin 1840-42, 63/217; corn 1858, 68/28; correspondence course 1898, 80/182; cotton shirts 1840-42, 63/217; Corvallis hotel 1881, 71/9; cows, 63/16,19; dishes 1885, 80/251; Eastern Ore.-Idaho 1863, 63/31
eggs, 66/232—
1858, 68/28; 1881, 71/13
elk meat 1856, 63/21; entertainment 1905, 80/64; Eugene hotel 1881, 71/ 19; express envelope 1852, 79/393; fanning mills, 63/54
firewood—
1885, 80/248; 1890s, 80/281
fish, 74/271—
1881, 71/17
fishhooks 1852, 79/393; fishing gear 1915, 81/56
flour, 63/182—
1850s, 66/163; 1852, 79/393; 1853, 79/73-74N,76N,90; 1862, 79/184, 191; 1863, 63/31

food—
1885, 80/248; 1890s, 80/281
Fort Dalles—
1851, 67/301; 1853-55, 67/295N;
1858, 68/28-29
Ft. Hoskins 1850s, 65/195; Ft. Vancouver 1840-42, 63/181,217; freight teams, 66/277; fruit, 68/163; fruit trees 1856, 68/28; furniture 1881, 71/17; furs 1820, 77/180N; grain, 68/28,29; hats 1851, 63/54
hay, 67/240-41—
1858, 68/28; 1878, 68/226N, 228N,229N,230N,243N,244N,247;
1885, 80/236,239,242
hens, 66/232; hogs 1851, 63/53; horseradish 1881, 71/9
horses, 77/23—
1858, 68/28; near Ft. Laramie, 62/341
horse-shoeing—
1856, 63/23; Alaska, 76/107;
Oregon Trail, 62/371
hospital rates 1911, 72/280
hotel rates—
1881, 71/8-19*passim*; 1885, 80/255;
1905, 80/53,59,64
houses 1900, 80/378
Idaho—
1861, 66/231-32; 1863, 63/31
Kalama hotel 1881, 71/17
knives—
1862, 79/184; 1867, 79/317,318
land, SEE Land—values; legal fees, 77/263; 81/279; Lewis & Clark Exposition, 80/64,65; livestock 1858, 68/28; lodging and meals 1887, 74/334,342, 344; logs 1900s, 81/38,39
lumber—
1840s, 66/349; 1851, 63/53; 1910, 76/15; 1930s, 77/353; 81/39
meals—
1887, 74/334,342,344; 1911, 77/67,69,71,378
medical services 1881, 71/22; medication 1905, 80/64; mirrors 1862, 79/184; money order 1898, 80/180; nails 1851, 63/53; needles 1862, 79/184; newspapers 1850s, 64/125
oats—
1858, 68/28; 1878, 68/226N, 228N,244N,247N,257
onions 1858, 68/29; Oregon City 1854, 63/19; Oregon Territory, 63/52-54; 64/121N,298; 66/163-64;
Oregon Trail, 62/70-72,341,361,371; otter skins, 74/14; oxen, 78/216; ox-shoeing, 62/341; parrots 1905, 80/62; playing cards, 62/71; Portland, SEE Portland—prices; postage 1849, 81/180; potatoes 1858, 68/29; poultry, 77/377; produce 1858, 68/28,29; real estate, SEE Land—values; rents, SEE Rents
saddles—
1851, 63/54; Oregon Trail, 62/70-71
salmon 1866-71, 81/322; San Francisco hotel 1881, 71/11; Seattle hotel 1881, 71/16
sheep, 76/158,346; 77/23,173—
1870, 64/113N; 1881, 67/130;
1897, 81/301
shingles 1851, 63/53; shoes, 63/53; South American ports 1840s-50s, 77/58; spoons 1862, 79/184; staples, Yukon Terr. 1897, 76/115,116; steam engine 1849, 81/190; stirrups 1851, 63/54
sugar—
1850s, 66/164; 1863, 63/31;
Oregon Trail, 62/72
sundries, 80/64; Tacoma hotel 1881, 71/17
tallow—
1853, 79/79; 1862, 79/184
tents, 62/361
tobacco—
1840-42, 63/217; 1867, 70/317
toys 1885, 80/351; tuition 1894, 80/281; Umatilla Co. 1862, 66/227; venison 1885, 80/233; vessels 1838, 74/77; wagons, 79/81; wallpaper 1862, 79/184; Wasco Co. land, 68/28,29
wheat, 63/182-83,184—
1838, 74/77; 1840-42, 63/181,217;
1850s, 66/183; 1863-81, 71/97;
1872, 71/61; 1880s, 71/61; 1881, 71/19,86,87; 1911-15, 71/98
Willamette Valley—
1840s, 66/349; 1851, 63/51,53-54

wine, 62/371; Winnemucca 1881, 71/9; wood 1881, 71/13; wool, 64/212N; 76/158; wool pelts 1881, 81/276,279; woolen pants 1840-42, 63/217; World War I, 77/173; yeast 1862, 79/184; Yukon Territory 1897, 76/115,116; SEE ALSO Fares

Prichard, Charles C., family, 67/281

Prichard, Louise, 62/249N

Pridewell, William, 67/228

Priest, Loring B.:

Uncle Sam's Stepchildren: The Reformation of U.S. Indian Policy, 1865-1887, cited, 70/105NFF

Priest Rapids, 70/124,150,154,155,169

Priest River, 73/351

Prigg, Frederick, 73/247,248,250, 256,257

Prim, Paine Page, 66/19; 68/317,319

Primitive Pragmatists: The Modoc Indians of Northern California, by Ray, review, 65/200-201

Prince, John T., family, 77/382

Prince of Wales (HBCO. vessel), 63/171; 68/113

Prince of Wales Fort, 77/84

Prince Robert (ship), 66/107

Prince William (Chugach) Sound, 77/183,184

Princess Charlotte (Indian), 63/236

Princess of Fort Vancouver, by Lampman, review, 64/349

Princess Royal (vessel), 79/397

Princeton (aircraft carrier), 62/52

Princeton College, 74/333,342N,343

"Princetonian Out West," by Henry C. Elsing, 74/333-44

Prine, Barney, 69/87

Prineville, Ore., 63/37-38; 66/183; 72/341; 77/27: centennial, 69/87; city railroad, 70/68-69

Prineville and Eastern Railway, 77/27

Prineville Centennial Commission, 69/346

Prineville Historical Museum, 69/177

Pringle, John, family, 65/308

Pringle, Virgil K., 65/405

Pringle Falls, photo, 77/331

Printers and printing, 72/287,353; 78/91: early Oregon, 64/139; 65/29N; 70/62-63— bibliography, 64/137-38; imprints, 78/251-79 lithographic techniques, 66/304; Newberry Library, 70/65; postal cards, 66/304,305; The Dalles 1862, 66/199; West, 66/379-80

Printing presses, 64/33: *Alta California*, 64/34; *Oregon Free Press* fonts, 64/140; Ramage, 64/34; western, 66/379-80

Prisco, Salvatore, III:

"John Barrett and Oregon Commercial Expansion, 1889-1898," 71/141-60

"John Barrett, Exponent of Commercial Expansion," cited, 71/144N

John Barrett, Progressive Era Diplomat, noted, 74/359

Prisons, SEE Jails; Penitentiaries

"Private Journal," by Charles Erskine Scott Wood, 70/5-38,139-70

The Private Letters and Diaries of Captain Hall, ed. by Schneirsohn, noted, 77/91

Probing the American West: Papers From the Santa Fe Conference, ed. by Toole *et al*, noted, 64/186-87

Probst, Samuel, 69/225N

Proceedings of the First National Colloquium on the History of the Forest Products Industries..., 1966, ed. by Maunder and Davidson, review, 69/70

Proctor, A. Phimester, 65/215

Proctor, Redfield, 71/152

Produce, SEE Prices

Produce business: Portland, 77/247,248,253-54

Progressive movement, 69/60; 70/79,84,178,179,362; 72/178

Progressive party, 62/106; 63/360; 71/368; 78/114: California, 64/87; Oregon, 65/366; 72/227,230; Pacific NW, 63/359; Washington, 65/216; 66/89; 72/232

Prohibition, 62/204; 67/186-87; 74/ 216; 75/119; 77/90,197: bootlegging, 76/159-63; British Columbia, 72/230; enforcement, 76/159, 162-63; "home brew," 69/108,125; local option laws, 73/349; moonshine liquor, 76/161-62; Morrow Co., 69/ 108,109,125,128; Ore. 1918 election, 68/130,134-35; Pendleton, 69/128; Washington, 66/281; 72/228,230

Prohibition Party, 78/34,39

Promontory Point, 71/9

Promysel (brig), 73/116,131,164: sketch, 73/118

"Property Concepts of 19th Century Oregon Indians," by James Arneson, 81/391-422

The Prophet Dance of the Northwest and Its Derivatives, by Spier, cited, 70/123N; 71/325,333,334,335

Prospector, Cowhand and Sodbuster: Historic Places Associated...in the Trans-Mississippi West, by National Park Service, noted, 69/275-76

Prosser, W.H., 62/219N

Prostitution: Indians, 81/414; Portland, 80/17,136, 153,294,294N

Protection Island: pheasant haven, 65/249,252

Protective Corps: advertising, 72/64,65,65N; appropriations for, 72/57,61N,63; difficulties, 72/66,74,75; discipline, 72/75; distance traveled 1862, 72/71; escort of emigrants 1861-64, 72/55-77; functions, 72/61,75,76; opinions on, 72/ 76; physicians, 72/61,61N,62(photo), 66; recruits, 72/63,71,72N; salaries, 72/61,61N; staff, 72/61,62(photo); strength, 72/63,72N,74; supplies, 72/63,71; title, 72/61

Protestant Ladder, 63/57,59

Protestant Vindicator, 75/111

Proud Riders and Other Poems, by Davis, cited, 66/242

Proudfoot, William, 71/19

Providence Academy, Vancouver, Wash., 67/373

Providence Hospital, Portland: nursing school history, 65/382

Providence Hospital, Seattle, 78/34

Provost, Etienne, 69/335

Provost Brothers Hardware Store, Ashland, 64/333

Prucha, Francis Paul, 64/85; 65/214: *American Indian Policy in the Formative Years*, quoted, 70/103-104 *Guide to the Military Posts of the United States, 1789-1895*, noted, 66/187-88 *Indian Peace Medals in American History*, review, 73/276-77

Pruett, J. Hugh, 69/29-30,37,49

Prunes: first Italian orchard, 68/164; Golden origin, 68/170; Olympic Peninsula, 74/23

Pryor, Nathaniel, 72/179

Pshairsh (Indian), 73/64

Public buildings, 78/360

The Public Lands: Studies in the History of the Public Domain, ed. by Carstensen, noted, 64/350

The Public Life of Eugene Semple: Promoter and Politician, by Hynding, review, 75/292-93

Public ownership: public power controversy, 65/364; 76/137,138,140,144,146

Public utilities: districts in Ore., 76/146; regulation in Calif., 72/178

Public works, 78/360-61: private capital, 78/361

Publishers and publishing: postal cards, 66/304-30*passim*; SEE ALSO Printers and printing

Pudding River, 63/51N:

name, 66/333-34; train wreck, 63/67

Pueblo, Colo., 78/131

Pueblo (Puebla) City, Harney Co., 79/277N

Pueblo Mountains, 79/277,278

Pueblo Valley, 81/328

Puget, Peter, 63/254,364; 70/181: grave, 63/362

Puget Island, 74/311

Puget Mill Company, 77/225

Puget Sound, 62/9,64,73,96,98-99, 194,321,406; 63/41; 70/295,297,300; 72/173,344-45; 78/334:

archeological survey, 64/277; business directory, 66/80; charts, 72/356; described 1869, 72/133; funds disbursed by army, 67/294N; harbor, 71/47-48; Indian population, 62/86; lumber ships, 67/85; name, 63/234; navigation, 75/82; navy yard, 71/197; pioneers, 62/97; population 1858, 67/294N; Portland rivalry, 71/31,69; railroad terminus, 71/47-48,69; Seward visit, 72/133; shipbuilding, 71/197; shipping, 71/199; steamboat racing, 63/64-65; trade and commerce, 71/31

Puget Sound Agricultural Company, 62/64,65,240N; 71/366: American attitude toward, 63/111,175-76,221-22N,229; Cowlitz Farm, 63/209; SEE ALSO Cowlitz Farm; establishment, 63/190,209; officers and salaries, 63/215; organization, 63/194; possessory rights, 63/221N-23N; prospectus, 63/184-85; share dividend, 63/190; squatters on claims, 63/220; tax payment, 63/230

Puget Sound Cooperative, 77/295

Puget Sound Homestead Assn., 64/177, 180-81

Puget Sound Light and Power Company, 63/361

Puget Sound Maritime Historical Society: publications, 71/197,199,368

Pugh, John W., 72/12

Pullman, Wash., 71/368: history, 72/227

The Pulp and Paper Industry and the Northwest, by Hall, noted, 71/286

Pumphrey, William, 63/245

Pumpkins, 66/339

Pumps: history, 73/73; made in Oregon, 73/73

Punebaka (Cowlitz Farm employee), 63/139,150,156

Pup Mountains, 79/152,152N

"Pure Gold—1896," by Berkeley Snow, 68/330-32

Purington, —, 1890s sea captain, 66/114N

Purkhiser, Grace Pierce, 81/5N

Pursh, Frederick, 69/152; 70/171: death, 69/161; Lewis plant specimens, 69/159-63; ragged robin drawing, 69/150

Pursh, Frederick: *Flora Americae Septentrionalis,* cited, 69/161

Puter, Stephen A. Douglas: *Looters of the Public Domain,* reprint noted, 74/282-83

Putnam, Charles F., 65/406

Putnam, George Palmer, 72/263; 74/239: opposes KKK, 75/173

Putnam, Jacob, 66/6

Putnam, Rozelle Applegate, 81/236,246

Puyallup Indians, 72/148

Pyle, James M., 72/61

Pyramid Lake, 65/160; 69/230,232,254; 71/291

Pysht Bay, 74/6,7

Qangon (Indian), 71/342,343,343N

Quakenasp Gulch, 62/236

Quadra, Juan Francisco de la Bodega y, SEE Bodega y Quadra, Juan Francisco de la

Quadra Island: shipwrecks, 64/87

Quadratus (brig), 68/265

Quaempts, Bessie, 78/365

Quaid family, Morrow Co., 69/145

Quaife, Milo Milton, 66/384; 78/284

Quails: described, 69/6-7; sketch, 69/8

Quaker Church: history, 71/362; Marion Friends Church, 67/89; 75th anniversary state organization, 69/86

A Quaker Forty-Niner: The Adventures of Charles Edward Pancoast..., ed. by Hannum, cited, 66/161N

Quakers, 80/336

Quanna, SEE DeLore, Augustin

Quarterdeck Review, noted, 75/362; 77/89, 292; 78/90; 80/105; 81/105

Quartz Mountain, 76/353; 79/290N

Quartzville, Ore., 63/92; 70/278; 73/83

Queen Ann Cottages, Bandon, 75/339-43*passim*: photo, 75/343
Queen Margaret (bark), 66/127
Queen of the Pacific (steamer): 1883 schedule, 71/ins.fr.cov. March
Queen Sally (Indian), 62/57
Queets River, 74/9,10,19,22: photos, 74/28; ships enter, 74/24,29
Queets River Valley: game, 74/23; included in Olympic National Park, 74/5,33; settlement, 74/16-33
Quemoy Islands, 62/37,45
Que-pe-ma (Kwi-uh-pum-ma) (Indian), 79/144N
Quicklime, 81/197
Quicksand, 67/372
Quigley, Edward Burns, 70/371
Quileute Indians, 62/101; 66/382
Quilici, John, 77/238(photo),254
Quillayute, Wash., 74/19,24
Quillayute River, 74/19
Quimby, L.P.W., 65/255
Quinault Indian Reservation: federal land policy, 72/270
Quinault Indians: aid to whites, 74/13N; canoe freighting, 74/22,24
Quinault River, 74/10-11,13,13N; 78/282: sketch, 74/12; spelling, 74/11N
Quincy, Josiah, 71/151
Quincy, Ore., 71/361; 72/198
Quinlan, Frank, 76/387
Quinn, —, Coos River pioneer, 66/54
Quinn, Frank, 69/145
Quinn, John: "The Trough at Rockwall Springs," 76/175
Quinn, Larry D.: *Politicians in Business: A History of the Liquor Control System in Montana*, noted, 72/172-73
Quinn, Patrick, 69/145
Quinn, W.D., 75/159-60,178
Quinn, William E., 63/269
Quinn College, SEE Elk Rock School
Quinn River Crossing Ranch, Nev.,

63/309
Quinn's, Wasco Co., 81/271,272,277
Quinton, Ore., 81/266N
Quist, Charlotte, SEE Baer, Charlotte Quist
Quist, Susie, SEE Hanson, Susie Quist
Quivira, 75/94: site, 70/363
Quoth the Raven, A Little Journey into the Primitive, by Salisbury, noted, 64/92

R.A. Long's Planned City: The Story of Longview, by McClelland, review, 77/381-82
R.C. Young (steamboat), 68/187
R.R. Thompson (steamer), 63/66
Raabe, J.T., 66/393
Rabaul, Bismark Islands, 62/31,32
Rabbeson, Antonio B., 63/116N
Rabbit (Brown's) Island, 75/221
Rabbit Valley, 65/84N
Rabbits, 69/106; 75/270,273: eradication in Ore. 1900s, 65/220; leap measured, 69/14; rabbit drive photos, 69/114; 75/273; snaring, 69/138; SEE ALSO Jack rabbits
Raccoon (British sloop), 66/280; 76/327: forge, 69/57-59
Race and Equal Educational Opportunity in Portland's Public Schools, noted, 66/80
"The Race of the *Oregon*," by Ralph E. Schaffer, 76/269-98
Racism, 72/230; 73/280-81; 77/244; 79/98; SEE ALSO Intolerance; Nativism
Racism in the United States: An American Dilemma?, by Reimers, review, 73/280-81
Rackleff, William, family, 74/92
Rackleff, William E., son of William: diary, 80/105
Radar, 80/49
Rader, J., 81/83
Rader, Mabel Madison: *Lure of the West Lands: With Songs of the Prairie Lands and Other Verses*, noted, 64/186
Radford, Arthur William, 62/41
Radford, William, 71/17
Radical Heritage: Labor, Socialism and

Reform in Washington and British Columbia, by Schantes, noted, **81**/333-34

Radicalism: in Pacific NW, **73**/70-71,281-82; in West, **74**/280

Radio broadcasting: Oregon, **74**/230-31,232-33,234; Seattle, **73**/309; World War II, **80**/32, 34,43,44,45,48

Rae, Eloisa Maria McLoughlin, **76**/299; SEE ALSO Harvey, Eloisa Maria McLoughlin Rae

Rae, John, brother of William Glen, **63**/212; **68**/347

Rae, John, son of William Glen, **63**/212

Rae, Margaret Glen, SEE Wygant, Margaret Glen Rae

Rae, Maria Louise, SEE Myrick, Maria Louise Rae

Rae, William Glen, **63**/180,184, 208-209,212

Rafinesque, Constantine S., **69**/22,28

Raft River, **66**/198,230N; **78**/214, 215,218; **79**/385; **80**/87

Rafton Foreshore park, **75**/87

Rafts, SEE Logging industry—rafts

Ragan, William, **79**/171N

Ragged robin (*Clarkia pulchella*), **69**/149,167: drawing, **69**/150; Lewis describes, **69**/151-52

Ragsdale, Daniel, **78**/129

Ragsdale, Lucy, **78**/129

Rahm, Stanley, **77**/18

Rail (Reille?), Baptiste, **63**/166N

Rail Canyon, Malheur Co., **63**/279,291

Railroads, **62**/164; **68**/181; **70**/70; **72**/317; **75**/364; **77**/296: accidents, **74**/93; agricultural effects, **80**/209; Alaska construction 1898, **81**/ 133,134; army transportation, **71**/366; Ashland, **80**/232; Bend completion photo 1911, **77**/140; bibliography, **70**/217; boxcar shortage, **67**/370; cable railway, Portland, **64**/353; caboose rides, **77**/28,155,170,171; Canada, **65**/377; **70**/179; **74**/95,359; capital investments in, **71**/40-45*pas-*

sim,78; Central Ore., **66**/183; **72**/94 Chinese laborers, **71**/349,351,357— photos, **80**/163,164

Clackamas Co., **69**/339; Coeur d'Alene connection, **69**/217-21; Columbia River portage, **71**/22; commodity rates, **74**/81-82

construction, **73**/6; **75**/127; **77**/214— Alaska, **81**/133,134; Chinese labor, **71**/349,351,357; costs, **71**/51,64-65, 73,82; Deschutes Canyon, **69**/293- 306; foreign labor, **77**/241,243,244, 247,350; **78**/74; immigrant labor, **75**/123

contradictory local interests, **71**/40- 45,80; Corbett interests, **71**/68 costs, **71**/51,64-65,73,82— variable and fixed, **71**/78-79

Coxey's army conflicts with, **65**/278- 86,291,293-94; Deschutes Canyon, **69**/ 293-306; dinky trains, **72**/312,313,314; Eastern Ore., **77**/300; effect on Ore. towns, **80**/209; effect on Pacific NW, **71**/27-98,142; **74**/80,80N; electric, **72**/90; **80**/332-33; elevated railways, **73**/6; engineering, **66**/181; expansion 1880s, **69**/199-201; Failing interests, **71**/68; finances, **71**/45,46,47,51,63, 65,69,80,81; **73**/66; foreign bondholders, **71**/46-47,62-63,80-81,89,90,91, 93; freight, **77**/75,346-47; freight rates, **71**/61,78-79,86,92; gauges and geography, **68**/349; Golden Spike Centennial, **70**/349-51; government control WW I, **71**/214; government ownership, **74**/81; government promotion, **63**/355-56

grading, **71**/358— photo 1886, **80**/209

guidebooks, **71**/84; handcars, **80**/209 history, **73**/360; **80**/208—

Pacific NW, **71**/27-98,283-84 Hood River, **72**/94; Idaho history, **72**/ 227; Idaho mines, **71**/49,50,55; immigration promotion, **67**/122,130,135N, 155; **71**/29,35,58,59,60,61; in development of West, **70**/86; Indian lands needed for, **70**/105; interurban, **65**/ 377; **80**/209; Jenks' impact theory,

67/106,122; Klamath area, 80/104 land grants, 64/55-67; 70/351N,362; 71/45,46,51,54,63,82,88,90— rates of return, 72/178 land sales, 80/269-70 logging railroads, 63/92,351-53,354-55; 67/173-76; 69/77,78-79,339; 72/94,294; 73/5-18*passim*; 80/ 140,209— construction, 72/308-14; photo, 72/309 longest system, 71/197; mail cars, 68/351 maps, 73/284— Pacific NW, 71/44,52-53 Montana mines, 71/55; Mormon interests, 71/55; 73/66; narrow gauge lines, 63/92; 71/54,55,61,63,73; 73/347; 77/157,167,168; Nevada, 64/86 Oregon, 62/301; 75/85-86— 1887, 69/201; centennial, 63/363; effect on towns, 80/209; Prov. Govt. petition, 66/356 Pacific Northwest, 62/297-98,405— effect on, 71/27-98,142; 74/80,80N; history, 71/27-98,283-84 passenger fares 1898, 80/282-83 photos, 66/318; 69/292,296,297,300, 302; 72/309— collections, 73/364 politics, 71/40,197; portage, 65/211; 71/22; postal card advertisements, 66/ 305; profits, 71/78; promotion of trade, 71/142,143; railway hotels, 70/ 361; rates, 72/179; regional networks, 67/106-23*passim*,130; regional *vs.* transcontinental, 71/30-31,38,41-43,50,57 regulations, 70/85— California, 72/178; Oregon, 72/233; Washington, 65/366 robberies, 80/209 routes, 71/38-40— Ainsworth-Lake Pend Oreille, 71/61; Astoria-Portland, 66/181; Blackfoot, Wyo.-Portland, 71/54; Cascade Line (Natron Cutoff), 71/95-96; Columbia River, 71/30-31,38,41-42,47,48,49, 69,71; Crescent Bay-Humptulips, Wash., 74/8; Deschutes River-Bend,

63/92; Drain-Portland, 80/52; Grainger, Wyo.-Huntington, Ore., 71/55; Horton-Junction City, 68/ 351; Howe Sound-Ft. St. John, 63/92; Idaho, 71/47,49,50; Klamath Lake-Nevada, 71/44,51,95-96; Lakeview-Reno, 77/168; Macleay-Portland, 75/86; Marshfield-Myrtle Point, 66/52; Modoc Line, 71/95; Nahcotta-Megler, 78/206; Newport-Detroit, Ore., 80/280; Oregon-Calif., 71/46,50,51; Port Angeles-Aberdeen, 74/341; Portland-Rainier 1904, 81/35; Portland-Weston, 74/341; Puget Sound, 71/47,49,64; Snake River, 71/50,65,82; Weed-Klamath Falls, 62/205; Winnemucca via Diamond Peak, 71/40-74*passim*,81; Yaquina-Corvallis, 80/257 Scottish capital invested, 69/182; Scott, Harvey, interest, 70/217; Sherman Co., 81/101-102; Snake River, 67/87; snow sheds, 71/9,54; sources, 71/75-96; stations, 75/85-86; steamship subsidies, 71/39,46-47,52,63, 81,142,143 street railways— Albany, 63/360; Bellingham, 80/ 332; Helena, 72/231; Seattle, 63/61 strikes, 75/133,136-37; Sumpter Valley, 69/78-79 surveys, 80/209— Doane, 71/365; Hudnutt, 71/54; Lander, 71/81-82, 292; Stevens, 71/49,81; Yellowstone, 71/365,366; SEE ALSO Pacific Railroad Survey Sweet Home, 81/330; tariffs, 74/80-81; towns, 80/52 transcontinental, 67/280; 71/8-9,27-79; 73/66; 76/177— alternate routes, 71/30; benefits to Oregon, 71/29,77; best route, 71/65-74; celebration of completion, photo, 77/133; centennial, 70/364; changes in range cattle industry 1880-90, 67/ 139-59; completion, 68/185; effect on lumber industry 1880-93, 67/160-78; effect on Ore. sheep and wool industry, 67/125-38; first, 72/127;

impact, 71/27-31,75-78; in economic growth of Portland, 67/105-23; in regional development, 67/101-78; myths, 67/101-102; *vs.* regional railroads, 71/30-31,38,41-43,50,57; views on, 70/86,349-51

Trans-Mississippi 1865-90, 65/305; travel promotion 1880, 80/229 trestles, 63/355; 66/181; 77/72, 190,222—

photos, 72/296; 77/242

trip recollections, 69/329; troop trains, 80/175; Vancouver, Wash., 63/82; *vs.* canals, 73/85; Wasco Co., 81/101-102; western, 62/294-95; Willamette Valley, 73/283; Winnemucca, Nev., 71/40-68 *passim;* work camp, 80/235,236; wrecks, 63/67; 64/357; Wyoming, 71/54; Yacolt, 65/308; SEE ALSO Astoria and Columbia River Railroad; Astoria and South Coast Railroad; Bellingham and Skagit Railway Co.; Burlington Northern Railroad; California and Oregon Coast Railroad; California and Oregon Railroad Co.; California-Northeastern Railroad; California Pacific Eastern Extension Railroad; Canadian National Railway Co.; Canadian Northern Railway; Canadian Pacific Railroad; Central Pacific Railroad; Chicago, Milwaukee, St. Paul and Pacific Railroad Co.; City and Suburban Railway Co.; City of Prineville Railroad; Colorado Central Railroad; Columbia Southern Railroad; Corvallis and Eastern Railroad; Dayton, Sheridan and Grand Ronde Railway; East Side Railway Co.; Eastern-Western Railway; Esquimalt and Nanaimo Railway; Grand Trunk Railway; Great Northern Railway Co.; Great Southern Railroad; Great Western Railway; Kansas Pacific Railroad; Klamath Lake Railroad; Klamath Short-Line Railroad; Longview, Portland and Northern Railroad; McCloud River Railroad; Metropolitan Steam Railway; Mid-Pacific Railroad; Milwaukee Road; Missouri Pacific Railroad; Mt. Hood Railroad; Nevada-California-Oregon Railroad; North Pacific Railroad; Northern Pacific Railroad; Oregon and California Railroad Co.; Oregon Central Railroad Co.; Oregon City and Southern Railway; Oregon, Corvallis and Eastern Railroad; Oregon Electric Railway; Oregon Midland Railroad; Oregon, Pacific and Eastern Railroad; Oregon Pacific Railroad; Oregon Portage Railroad; Oregon Railway and Navigation Co.; Oregon Short Line; Oregon Trunk Railroad; Oregon-Washington Railroad and Navigation Co.; Oregon Water Power and Railway Co.; Oregon Western and Pacific Railroad; Oregon Western Railway; Oregon Railroad Co.; Oregonian Railway Co.; Pacific Great Eastern Railroad; Pacific Railway and Navigation Co.; Panama Railroad; Portland and Willamette Valley Railway; Portland Cable Railway; Portland, Eugene and Eastern Railway; Portland-Port Angeles and Victoria Railroad; Portland Railway, Light and Power Co.; Prineville and Eastern Railway; Santa Fe Railroad; Seattle-Walla Walla Railway Co.; Siuslaw Railroad; Southern Pacific Co.; Spokane, Portland and Seattle Railway; Sumpter Valley Railroad; Tanana Valley Railroad; Texas and Pacific Railroad; Transcontinental Steam Railway; Union Pacific Railroad; Union Railroad; Utah and Northern Railway; Vancouver, Klickitat and Yakima Railroad; Vernonia, South Park and Sunset Steam Railroad; Walla Walla and Columbia River Railroad; Western Pacific Railroad; White Pass and Yukon Railway; Willamette Valley and Coast Railroad; Willamette Valley and Eastern Railroad; Willamette Valley Railroad Co.; Willamette Valley Southern Railway; Yakima and Pacific Coast Railroad

Railroads and Economic Growth, by Fogel, cited, 71/75

Railroads in the Woods, by Labbe and Goe, review, 63/351-52

Rails, Sagebrush and Pine: A Garland of

Railroad and Logging Days in Oregon's Sumpter Valley, by Ferrell, noted, 69/78-79

Rails to the Mid-Columbia Wheatlands, by Due and French, review, 81/101-102

Rails to the Ochoco Country: The City of Prineville Railway, by Due and Juris, review, 70/68-69

Rails West, by Abdill, review, 62/294-95

Railway and Locomotive Historical Society:

Bulletin, index noted, 73/86

The Railway Hotels and the Development of the Chateau Style in Canada, by Kalman, noted, 70/361

Rainbow (Coos River steamer), 66/54,57

Rainbow (Spoop) Falls, 65/211

Rainey, Sam, 66/44

Rainier, Ore., 62/200,301; 63/238; 66/91; 72/197; 73/283; 74/ 293,300,302; 81/32,34,35: described, 74/83,295; early 1900s, 81/36-38; Fourth of July, 74/83-85; history, 68/90; 74/358; hoboes, 74/ 326-31; name, 68/353; photos, 72/ 196; 74/292,296,326-27,ins.bk.cov. Dec.; pioneers, 77/299; population, 74/322,323; railroads, 74/83,295, 297,312(photo),313,325-26; school history, 65/308; shipping, 74/299-302, 304,321,326-27(sketch)

Rainier Creamery, 64/91

Rainier National Park Committee, 74/106-107

"Rainier, Oregon: A Day to Remember," by Harry E. Rice, 74/83-85

Rains, Gabriel James, 62/78; 66/133,142; 67/320N: asks for volunteers, 67/314; need for mounted troops, 67/310; report on Indian situation 1854, 67/307; winter campaign view, 67/312; Yakima War, 67/314,315,316-17

Raised by the Sea, by Sigurdson, review, 74/356

Raisz, Erwin: Oregon 1941 landform map, 78/248- 49; 79/44-45

Rajotte, Frank, 72/294

Rajotte, Fobert and Winters, 72/294; 73/173: railroad construction camp, 72/311,313

Rakestraw, Lawrence: "A Mazama Heads North," 76/101-17

Ralls, M., SEE Rhawl, M.

Ralston, —, Gilliam Co. 1881, 81/ 274,279

Ralston, Mrs. William, 65/243

Ralston, William Elliott: *Photographers of the Frontier West, 1875- 1910*, by Andrews, review, 66/381 *Picture Gallery Pioneers*, by Andrews, review, 66/381

Ramp, Len, 62/107; 65/315

Ramp, Len, and Howard C. Brooks: *Gold and Silver in Oregon*, noted, 64/333

Ramsay (Ramsey), Barnett, 67/179; 73/83; 79/6,6N

Ramsay, George D., 65/341

Ramselius, J., 77/359

Ramsey, Guy Reed, 64/351; 65/211: *Postmarked Washington: Benton, Franklin and Klickitat Counties*, noted, 69/331

Ramsey, Jarold, ed.: *Coyote Was Going There: Indian Literature of the Oregon Country*, review, 79/335-36

Ranches, 71/366; 73/258,279; 77/150,195,300: Agency, 69/276; Anawalt, 68/238, 308N; Anderson Valley, 63/334; Anderson's, 76/48-49; Antelope-Mitchell area map, 81/282; Bernard's, 72/43; Bidwell's, 79/190; Blaisdell, 76/350; Bonney View, 63/37; Bravo, 76/51; Brogan, 75/309; Brown-Shasta, 66/ 81; Brown's, 77/13; burned during Indian wars, 70/57; Calif. ranchos 1846- 62, 69/332; Carroll, 72/260-62; cattle ranches, 79/337; Celedonia, 66/81; Central Ore., 79/336; Century, 72/94; Chandler's, 77/29; Chernyk, 73/114- 15,163; Cluff's, 79/171N; Cole's, 72/ 40,41N; Cook, 76/51-52; Coos Co., 63/5-40; Cove, 77/7; Crosby, 63/ 291; D H S, 71/366; Daily (Dealy), 68/

233,306; Dalton, 72/47; Davis, 78/295; Dedman, 64/107; Diamond, 68/301; 70/21N; Dickerson, 67/374; Dodson's, 68/324; Double o, 69/276; Elkhorn, 80/51,52(photo),63; Express, 68/228,298; Fagan, photo, 81/308; Fahy, 68/265; Flemming, 73/349,351,358(photo); food, 77/16-17, 22; Geddes, 68/228; Gilliam Co. experiences 1881, 81/261-79; Good, 81/282(map),313,314; Goodale, 66/81; Harney Co., 63/304-41; Harper, 63/270,274,324; Harris, 69/329; Hawkins, 72/297-99; Helms, 76/354; Henderson's, 70/18N; Hinton Creek, photo, 69/107; Huffman's, 77/11; Inskip's, 74/282; Jack London, 73/323,328; Jackson's, 79/189; Jones, 81/282; Juniper, 63/317,324,334; Kanefield, 63/274; Kaser, 81/282 (map),299-318*passim*; Keys, 64/107; Khlebnikov, 73/115,163,164; Kiernan, 66/81; Kilkenny, 69/105,107-108; Killibrew, 72/40N; Kime, 63/272; King, 68/226N; Klamath Lake, 64/356; Kostromitinov, 73/163; Lake Co., 72/93; Lawson, 72/351; Leonard's, 76/336; Lone, 73/230; McCall, 72/351; 73/278; McClure, 68/228; McCormack, 77/24,25(photo),26; McDermot's, 68/230N; McNabb's, 76/335; Mann Lake, 63/322,334; Marial, photo, 76/166; Mason, 68/255,315; Maupin, 75/312; Maxon, 68/230N; Mays, 81/282(map); Menefee, 77/330, 331; 78/239,295; Meyer, 73/260; Milk, 68/256; Miller, 68/229; Morrow Co., 69/105-47*passim*; Mountain House (Stone and Allen), 79/170,170N; Muddy Creek, 73/263; 75/309; Nelson's, 79/171N; Olmsteads, 68/226; Owyhee, photo, 76/166; Point, 77/7; Popina, 64/113; Priday, 77/159; Quinn River Crossing, 63/309; Railroad, 71/366 ranch houses, 77/14-15— Alvord, 63/312-16; Grimes, 81/304; Hawley, 62/299; McCormack, 77/25 Red River, 79/194; Reeves, 63/274;

Rigdon, 78/58; Ringneck, 74/40; River, 81/282(map),311(photo),314, 315,318; Roaring Springs, 68/321, 322,326; Robinson, 79/339; Ruby, 68/249N,299N; 71/254-55; Russian in Calif., 73/114-15,163-64; s s Bar, 68/353; Scott, 63/274; sheep ranches, 69/105-47*passim*; 76/79-81; Shirk Bros., 68/321; 77/153; Shrum, photos, 81/208; Siskiyou area, 76/48-52; Small, photo, 81/ins.fr.cov. Fall; Smith, A.M., 68/258N,316N; Smith's, 77/18-19; Star, 68/247,313; Stephens, 68/297; Stewart's, 68/303N; Stovall, 72/282 (photo),283,284; Summit, 68/233, 306; Sutton, 73/263-64; 79/169N; U C M, 70/52; Urlezaga, photo, 76/166; Urquiaga, photo, 76/172; Van Arsdale, 76/333; Wagner, 77/77; Ward's, 72/40; wheat ranches, 70/75; Wheeler Co., 64/103-22*passim*; White's, 68/243,247,313N; Whitney Co., 73/5,13,223,224; Willow, 68/237; Winn, 78/364; Wither's, 77/25; Wyman, 81/300(photo),306; X L, 77/7,8; Z X, 77/25,158,159,173; 81/426; SEE ALSO Alvord Ranch; Becker Ranch; Burnt Ranch; Carr, Jesse D.; Dude ranches; G I Ranch; Gearhart, William H.; Grimes Ranch; Haines, Joseph A.; Hay Creek Ranch; Mason, N.H.A.; Miller and Lux; P Ranch; Pacific Livestock Co.; Scriver, F.G.; Sheep Ranch; Whitehorse Ranch

Rand, Ernest P., 64/60

Randall, —, Queets area land claimant, 74/18

Randall, Frank, 68/301N

Randall, J.H.: labor army, 65/269

Randall, James G., 72/337

Randolph, Ore., 63/14,15

Randolph (vessel), 78/363

Range management, 67/369: overgrazing, 67/135

Range wars, 67/152

Ranger (tug), 68/266

Rank, Tom, 66/169

Rankin, John, 75/174,180

Rankin, Joseph, **65**/291-92N

Rankin Crow and the Oregon Country, by Crow, review, **73**/279

Ransdell, Olive, photo, **74**/265

Rape (forage crop): Cowlitz Farm, **63**/115

Raphael Tuck and Sons, London, **66**/304

Rarey, John Solomon, **64**/138,148-49

Rasmussen, —, corporal 1879, **70**/146

Rasmussen, Alice, **81**/57,58

Rasmussen, Ane Christine, **81**/58

Rasmussen, Lilly Marie Catherine, **81**/58

Rasmussen, Rasmus P.: recollections, **81**/57-74*passim*

Rasmussen, Ruby Clara, **81**/58

Rattlesnake Camp: name, **65**/68N; SEE ALSO Fort Harney

Rattlesnake Creek, Ida., **68**/239N,309

Rattlesnake Creek, Malheur Co., **65**/56N, **68**N,70N; **68**/251N,314N; **79**/272N

Rattlesnake Point, Klamath Co., **75**/233: map, **75**/232

Rattlesnake Station, Jefferson Co., **68**/251

Rattlesnakes, **69**/15,23,24-25; **73**/348; **76**/336; **77**/161; **79**/378

Ratto, Giombattista, photo, **77**/252

Rauch, George L., **67**/44,52

Ravalli, Anthony, **67**/368; **69**/269-70

Raver, Paul J., photo, **80**/324

Raw Dog, SEE Hardman, Ore.

Rawling, Gerald, **63**/58

Ray, C.R., **65**/218

Ray, Dorothy Jean (Mrs. Verne F.), **66**/88:

Alaskan Eskimos, by Oswalt, review, **69**/327-28

Eskimo Adventure, by Keithahn, review, **64**/347-48

Eskimos of the Nushagak River, by Van Stone, review, **69**/327-28

Graphic Arts of the Alaskan Eskimo, noted, **70**/360

Ray, Frank H., **65**/218

Ray, Verne F., **64**/52N:

Ancient Hunters of the Far West, by Rogers, review, **68**/333-35

Cultural Relations in the Plateau of

Northwestern America, cited, **70**/121,122; **71**/279

Cultural Sequences at The Dalles, by Cressman *et al*, review, **63**/75-77

Fort Rock Basin, by Bedwell, review, **76**/89

The Horse in Blackfoot Indian Culture, by Ewers, review, **72**/81-82

Lewis and Clark and the Nez Perce Indians, noted, **74**/94

Perspectives in American Indian Cultural Change, by Spicer, review, **63**/347-49

Primitive Pragmatists: The Modoc Indians of Northern California, review, **65**/200-201

Red Man's Religion, by Underhill, review, **67**/187-88

Ray, William, Linn Co. blacksmith, **72**/92

Raymond, Ephraim: reminiscences, **66**/87

Raymond, Louis C.: Ore. physical map 1930, **78**/68

Raymond, Narcisse, **66**/134,135,137

Read, Anna, photo, **72**/208

Read, George C., **68**/59

Read, Sarah Hickman, **74**/32

Read, William Clarence, **74**/25,27,32,33: birth, **74**/26; death, **74**/32N; photo, **74**/26

The Reader's Encyclopedia of the American West, ed. by Lamar, review, **80**/205-206

Real estate: Portland transactions 1880-90, **67**/112,118,120; SEE ALSO Land

Real estate dealers, **69**/200,208,209

Rebel Voices: An I.W.W. Anthology, ed. by Kornbluh, cited, **69**/180; review, **66**/186

Rebels of the Woods: the I.W.W. in the Pacific Northwest, by Tyler, review, **69**/325-26

Recio, Emily Newell: biography, **80**/171,172-74; photo, **80**/170

Recio, Josie, **80**/173,174: mentioned in letters, **80**/175-86*passim*; photo, **80**/170

Reclamation, **67**/371; **70**/84:

Churchill Co., Nev., 72/180; Grand Coulee project, 80/409; idea of, 72/181; Klamath project, 80/409; legislation, 74/354; Newlands project, 69/336; Oregon projects, 72/409; western, 74/354; 80/408-409

Recollections and Opinions of an Old Pioneer, by Burnett, reprint review, 71/285

"Recollections of a Salmon Dipnetter," by Frederick K. Cramer, 75/221-31

"Recollections of Cloud Cap Inn," by Donald T. Wright, 77/61-66

Recollections of Deep River, by McLean, noted, 81/106

"Recollections of Salem," by Boise, quoted, 66/12

"Recollections of the Bannock War," by Chandler B. Watson, 68/317-29

Reconnaissance Geology and Mineral Resources of Eastern Klamath County and Western Lake County, Oregon, by Peterson, noted, 71/286

The Record (Wash. State Univ.), noted, 70/77

Records of Agricultural Agencies in the Oregon State Archives, comp. by Hanft, noted, 69/332-33

Records of the Office of Territories, comp. by Maxwell and Walker, noted, 64/277

Recreation:

Pacific Northwest, 72/277

Rector, William Henry, 64/237N-38; 72/329

Red Bluff, Calif.: described 1885, 80/237

Red Buttes, Ore. Trail landmark, 62/347-48

Red Cross, SEE American Red Cross

Red Crown Flour Mills, Albany, 66/90; 67/65

Red Deer River: Thompson route map, 66/280

Red Eagle and the Absaroka, by Haines, review, 62/101-102

Red House, Sellwood, 72/90

Red Man's Religion, by Underhill, review, 67/187-88

Red Moccasin Tops (Indian), SEE Sarpsis Ilpilp

Red River, 66/69-70: carts, 70/88,179 Episcopal mission school, 69/50-54; 71/327— Pacific NW Indians at, 71/327-31 farming, 70/367; fur trade dialect, 70/ 367; law, 70/179; settlement, 62/92; 63/180,210,215,217-19; 64/87; 69/ 84,337; 70/88,179; 71/290,366

Red River Lumber Company, Calif., 77/219

Reddick, —, Sauvie Island pioneer, 64/149

Redding, John, 81/42

Redding, Calif., 72/159

Redick, S.S., Ft. Umpqua carpenter, 70/235

Redington, Elizabeth, SEE Stewart, Elizabeth Redington

Redington, John W.: biography, 80/119-20; family photo, 80/121

Redman, Christopher C., 75/127

Redmond, Ore., 63/37-38; 75/294; 80/328

Redon, Juan, 63/317,340; 71/99: photo, 71/99

Redon, Maggie, 63/317,340

Redon, Nellie Snow, 71/99: photo, 71/99

Redondo Beach, Calif., 71/289

Redwolf, Josiah (Indian), 67/86

Redwood Highway, 66/87

Redwood trees, 66/87; 76/50,51,54,59; 80/376: lumbering, 77/190-91,354; photos, 76/52,ins.fr.cov. March; preservation, 77/190

Reed, Augustine, 70/235

Reed, Mrs. Benjamin, 75/369

Reed, Mrs. Benjamin, and Mrs. Henry F. Cabell:

The Portland Garden Club; the First 50 Years 1924-74, noted, 76/92

Reed, C.J., 75/84

Reed, D.B., 81/265N

Reed, F.D., 81/138

Reed, Henry E., 70/225N

Reed, John, Malheur traveler 1813,

77/79,81
Reed, John H., 69/225:
biography, 69/225N-26N; letters re Klamath military post, 69/227-29
Reed, John Silas, 62/198,204; 70/5N; 72/180:
biography, 75/84-85
Reed, Juliet Buchanan, 77/369
Reed, Louise Mohan Bryant (Mrs. John S.), 75/84-85
Reed, Pauline B., 75/369
Reed, Reason, family, 78/90
Reed, Simeon G., 69/198,217N; 73/56:
Coeur d'Alene mines investment, 69/203,220N; farm, 76/6; opposes Stark, 72/329-31,332N; papers cited, 71/80,86; photo, 72/328; railroad interests, 71/39,68,84-85; stock exchanges, 69/197,208
Reed, Simon, family, 71/360
Reed College, Portland, 68/176,340; 80/102:
50th anniversary, 63/363; site photo, 77/252
Reeder, U.E., 66/382
Reed's Opera House, Portland, 77/298
Reed's Opera House, Salem, 73/80; 80/131; 81/80:
photo, 81/81; site map, 80/340
Reedsport, Ore., 70/279
Rees, Willard H., 63/214; 66/332N; 81/242
Reese, J.W.:
"OMV's Fort Henrietta: On Winter Duty, 1855-56," 66/133-60
Reese, R.E., 69/216,217
Reeves, C.S., 77/45
Reeves, Selah C., 64/199N,206N
Reeves Ranch, Clover Creek, 63/274
The Referendum in America, by Oberholtzer, noted, 74/96
Reflections of Carlton, From Pioneer to Present, noted, 77/292,299
Reflections on the Jason Lee Mission and Opening of Civilization in the Oregon Country, by Judson, noted, 73/73
Regan, Tim, 70/18N
Regionalism, 75/94; SEE ALSO Nativism
Register Guard, Eugene, SEE *Eugene Regis-*

ter Guard
Reid, Bernard J.:
gold rush letter, 63/88
Reid, John Phillip:
"Replenishing the Elephant: Property and Survival on the Overland Trail," 79/64-90
Reid, Russell, 71/257
Reid, William:
dictations cited, 71/89; railroad interests, 69/181; 71/89,92-93,94
Reiger, John F., ed.:
The Passing of the Great West, noted, 74/96
Reiistakka, Donald, 66/388
Reiley, Charles Joseph, 69/144
Reiley, Michael, 69/144
Reiley, Pat (Shan), 69/144
Reille, John B., 63/166N
Reilly, Pat, 81/302,303
Reilly, Tom, 81/303
Reimers, David M.:
Racism in the United States: An American Dilemma?, review, 73/280-81
Reindeer, 77/295:
Alaska industry, 64/347; native management, 72/238
Reinganum, Paul, 71/51
Reinhart, Charley, brother of Herman Francis, 64/344
Reinhart, Herman Francis, 64/344-46
Reinikin, Franz, 80/203,204
Reiter, John, 73/82
Relander, Click, 63/90; 64/351:
Drummers and Dreamers, quoted, 70/124
Indian Legends from the Northern Rockies, by Clark, review, 68/180-81
Indian Legends of Canada, by Clark, review, 62/411-12
Strangers on the Land, noted, 64/351
Reliable (steamship), 72/354
Relics of the Road: GMC Gems, 1900-1950, by Rice, noted, 73/74
Religion:
frontier, 73/360; mid-19th century Protestantism, 72/178; occult in Oregon, 65/366; religious intolerance, SEE Intolerance

Religious Expositor, Eola: editors, **64**/134; first issue, **64**/126; transfer to Corvallis, **64**/128

"*The Religious Expositor*: Oregon Pioneer Journal," by Clifford Miller, **64**/123-36

Remembering—School Days of Old Crook County, by Helms, review, **81**/207

Remembering 75 Years of History, by Haines, noted, **71**/362

Rememteria, Janero, photo, **76**/166

Remington, DeLafayette: steam traction engine, **64**/353-54; **67**/92

Remington, Elmer, **75**/45

Remington, Frederic, **63**/88; **64**/186; **70**/263-64: biography, **74**/285; cavalryman sketch, **70**/4; *Oregon Trail* illustrations, 70/353

Remington, William P., **73**/222

Reminiscences of a Pioneer, by Thompson, cited, **66**/338N

Reminiscences of a Ranchman, by Bronson, reprint noted, **63**/247

"Reminiscences of an Early Forester," by Henry E. Haefner, **76**/39-88

Reminiscences of an Old Timer, by Hunter, cited, **66**/149N; quoted, **66**/142

The Reminiscences of Doctor John Sebastian Helmcken, ed. by Smith, review, **77**/294

Reminiscences of Fort Crook Historical Society, comp. by Bosworth, noted, **67**/80

Remme, Louis, **63**/361

Remote, Ore.: history, **74**/94

Renay, Francis, **66**/355

Renfrew, Alexander, **79**/10

Reno, Marcus A., **68**/82

Reno, Nev., **77**/169-70

Renshaw, Patrick: *The Wobblies: The Story of Syndicalism in the United States*, cited, **69**/325; review, **69**/179-80

Rents: room 1905, **80**/53 room and board— 1887, **74**/344; 1889, **74**/14-15; 1915, **74**/138N Washington 1889, **74**/5; SEE ALSO

Prices—hotel rates

"Replenishing the Elephant: Property and Survival on the Overland Trail," by John Phillip Reid, **79**/64-90

A Report: Master Carvers of the Lummi and their Apprentices, noted, **72**/173

A Report on Oregon Schools, 1832-1960, noted, **62**/108

"Rep. John Floyd, 1817-1829: Harbinger of Oregon Territory," by John H. Schroeder, **70**/333-46

Reps, John W.: *Cities of the American West, a History of Frontier Urban Planning*, review, **81**/201-202

Republic (steamboat): 1856 fire, **81**/196-200; photo, **81**/199

Republican Party, **62**/106; **68**/209; **72**/181; **75**/133,135,138,161-62,173; **76**/355,356; **77**/257; **80**/22,167N, 298,307,321: free silver issue split, **68**/210-14; initiative and referendum fight, **68**/209-14; Ku Klux Klan support, **75**/167,168,173; Marion Co. ticket 1870, **64**/181; Montana, **72**/234; Multnomah Co., **75**/ 168,174; newspapers, **72**/327 Oregon, **75**/160,162,167-68— 1876 presidential elector dispute, **67**/257-72*passim*; 1914 primary, **66**/363,365,374,375,377 Portland convention 1859, **64**/151; position in Portland police matters, **80**/158,167N,168,300; radical senate opposition to Stark, **72**/333-38; **73**/ 31-59*passim*; senate campaign 1918, **68**/125-40; variety 1862, **72**/316; Washington, **72**/254; Wash. Territory, **66**/35-36; **72**/231

Requiem for a People: The Rogue Indians and the Frontiersmen, by Beckham, review, **73**/66-67

Resolution (Cook's vessel), **76**/312: at Kamchatka, **80**/199; number in crew, **80**/201; painting, **79**/fr.cov. Winter

Resorts: Warm Springs Indian Reservation, **65**/315; SEE ALSO Summer resorts

Resource management, 69/332: federal and state, 68/176-77

Restaurants: Columbia River Hwy., 66/269; first drive-in Pacific NW, 64/85; Oregon State Fair, photo, 79/ins.fr.cov. Fall; Japanese, 76/232,238,239

Retaliation: Japanese Attacks and Allied Countermeasures on the Pacific Coast in World War II, by Webber, review, 77/194-95

Retreat to the Bear Paw: The Story of the Nez Perce, by Place, review, 71/284

"Reuben P. Boise, Last Associate Justice of the Oregon Territory Supreme Court," by Sidney Teiser, 66/5-24

Revais (Revey), Antoine, SEE Rivet, Antoine

Revival meetings, 80/63

Rey, Agapito, 66/380

Reynolds, —, 1862 immigrant, 66/197,199

Reynolds, Mrs. Carl, 76/387

Reynolds, Herbert, 77/64

Reynolds, Jeremiah N., 64/16

Reynolds, John F., 65/175N; 81/199

Reynolds, R. Moland: *Byways of the Northwest*, noted, 77/301

Reynolds Creek, 68/239N,248,314: name, 73/284

Rhawl, M., 81/92

Rhea, Elijah, 81/270N

Rhett Lake, 72/34N,35,37N,41; SEE ALSO Tule Lake

Rhinoceros: Oregon fossils, 63/254

Rhoades, Jacob, 66/219N,220-21N

Rhoads, James B., 76/387

Rhodes, Alphonso, 74/345

Rhodes, Ann Eliza, SEE Parrott, Ann E.

Rhodes, Mrs. E.L., 66/161

Rhodes, Eugene Manlove, 68/344

Rhodes, Henry, 67/86

Rhododendron Festival, Florence, 72/353

Rice, Mr. and Mrs. —, 1845 Oregon divorce petitioners, 62/128N

Rice, Annie Lovelace, 74/293-332*passim*

Rice, Elias, 74/315

Rice, George W., family, 66/382

Rice, Gini: *Impressive International Trucks, 1907-1947*, noted, 77/302 *Relics of the Road: GMC Gems, 1900-1950*, noted, 73/74

Rice, Harrison, 71/189

Rice, Harry E.: biography, 74/83-85,293-332

Rice, Harry E.: "Columbia River Kid," 74/293-332 "Rainier, Oregon: A Day to Remember," 74/83-85

Rice, James N., family, 66/382

Rice, Lee M., and Glenn R. Vernam: *They Saddled the West*, review, 76/380-81

Rice, Milton B., 67/44,52

Rice, Sherred M., 74/293-332*passim*: farm, 74/293,296(photo)

Rice, W.F., 79/272N

Rice root (mission bells) (*Fritillaria lanceolata*), 69/165: photo, 69/164

Rich, B.B., 66/305,307

Rich, Charles Coulson, 65/214

Rich, E.E., 77/289: *The History of the Hudson's Bay Company, 1670-1870*, Vol. II, review, 62/90-92

Rich Flat, 62/228

Richard, Marcus, 81/91

Richard Hoe (Liberty ship), 80/42

Richards, John, 81/321

Richards, John Keil, 79/252,267

Richards, William, 68/54

Richardson, David: *Pig War Islands*, review, 72/344-45

Richardson, Elmo R.: *The Politics of Conservation: Crusades and Controversies, 1897-1913*, noted, 64/187

Richardson, John, died 1843 Ft. Hall, 81/18

Richardson, John, novelist, 71/367

Richardson, John Champion, 69/276

Richardson, Samuel T., 66/363

Richardson Gap, 70/278

Richmond, Robert W., and R.W. Mardock, eds.: *A Nation Moving West, Readings in the History of the American Frontier*, noted,

68/82
Richter, Sara Jane, 80/208
Rickard, Aileen Barker, 80/51N,52
Rickard, Casper, 78/124
Richard, John, 78/124
Ricketts, Arthur, 63/296
Ricketts, Vincent, 78/234
Rickreall (Dixie), Ore., 62/200; 68/90; 76/376; 77/266,271-72; 81/261, 262,280:
George Gay house replica, 64/88; name dispute, 70/260
Rickreall Creek, 63/51N
Ricks, Melvin, 78/359
Ricord, John, 70/88
Ricord, Pascal, 63/164
Riddle, Mrs. Frank, SEE Winema
Riddle, George W.:
History of Early Days in Oregon, reprint noted, 74/94
Riddle, Glenn N., 67/369
Riddle, Jeff C.:
The Indian History of the Modoc War, reprint noted, 76/181
Riddle, Toby (Mrs. Frank), SEE Winema
Riddle, Ore.:
nickel industry, 65/384
Ridenour, Glenn, 62/249N
Ridgeway, Les, 63/293,296-97
"Riding the Wind: Cape Horn Passage to Oregon, 1840s-1850s," by Paul G. Merriam, 77/37-60
Riedesel, Gerhard, comp.:
Arid Acres: A History of the Kimama-Minidoka Homesteaders, 1912-1932, noted, 70/273
Riegel, Robert E., and Robert G. Athearn:
America Moves West, 5th ed. noted, 72/173
Rifles, SEE Firearms
Rigby, George F., 72/43N
Rigdon, Stephen, 67/55; 78/58; 79/43N,48:
photo, 79/48; residence photo, 79/48
Rigdon, Zilphia, 79/48(with photo)
Riggs, Neil R., 66/350N
Riggs, Samuel, 69/339
Riggs, Solomon, 69/339

Rignard, Peter, 65/28
Rilea, Thomas E., 76/79
Riley, Dave, 77/268
Riley, Earl, SEE Riley, Robert Earl
Riley, Edward Francis, 74/218: obituary, 74/198-99
Riley, Elaine Strowbridge (Mrs. Frank B.), 74/204
Riley, Frank Branch, 69/346; 71/372: actor, 74/200-201,204; awards, 74/ 234,237,239,241,242; biography, 74/ 197-243; Chautauqua lectures, 74/219; Good Roads promotion, 74/208-13, 214,225; interstate bridge promotion, 74/210-12,215-16; lecture tours, 74/ 197,217-32,237-38,239,240; mountaineering, 74/202-203,213-14,232; narrator for motion pictures, 74/232; photos, 66/258; 74/206,210,214,218, 221,234,236,243,fr.cov. Sept.; radio speeches, 74/205,229,230,233-34
Riley, Frank Branch:
"Lure of the Great Northwest," 74/217,222,223,229— photo, 74/fr.cov. Sept.
Riley, George P., 64/181
Riley, Lotte von Strombeck: biography, 74/204; photo, 74/206
Riley, Louisa Potter, 74/198
Riley, Margaret: biography, 74/204
Riley, Martha Smith, 74/199
Riley, Pat, photo, 77/25
Riley, Robert Earl, 62/421
Riley, Stephen L., 67/69
Riley, Stephen T., 66/388; 67/201
Riley, Thomas F., 68/239,243; 70/15
Riley, William: biography, 74/204
Riley and Hardin, 1885 cattlemen, 67/143
Rimrock, 75/312,315: photo, 75/314
Rindisbacher, Peter, 71/290
Rinearson, —, govt. valuer in PSA case, 63/230
Rinearson, Jacob S., 62/241N; 65/393
Rinearson Slough, photo, 74/324
Rinehart, Amanda Gaines (Mrs. William

V.), 65/26N,105N
Rinehart, James H., 79/17
Rinehart, L.B.:
ferry, 68/230N; 70/18N
Rinehart, Lewis, 73/80; 79/17:
family overland journey, 79/16-19
Rinehart, William Vance, 65/87N-88,108-15*passim*,299N; 67/55-60*passim*; 70/16N,21N; 79/127:
biography, 65/85N; comment on
Indian dept., 67/356; First Ore.
Cavalry service, 65/68N,70N,85N; marriage, 65/26N,105N; Mulkey suit,
67/60; name carved on rock,
65/200,301; photo, 65/18
Ringgold, Cadwalader, 63/345
Ringhand, Harry E.:
Marie Dorion and the Trail of the Pioneers, noted, 73/285
Rio de Janiero, 77/56-57
Rio Grande Pueblo Indians, 63/347
Riots:
Centralia, 69/325; Seattle, 75/128;
Vancouver, B.C. anti-Oriental, 68/88;
SEE ALSO Haymarket riot
Ripley, James W., 65/328,331,335,341
Ripley, Thomas E.:
Green Timber: On the Flood Tide to Fortune in the Great Northwest, review,
70/67-68
Rippey, Irene, photo, 72/208
Risley, Orville, 80/138,299,299N
Ritchie, Carl, 62/183
Riurik (ship), 73/123
Rival (steamer), 66/117; 79/176
Rivelli and Montecucco farm, 77/252
"River Evening," by Francis Seufert,
75/37-38
River of the West, SEE Columbia River
River traffic, 72/89:
Coos River, 66/52-55; Coquille, 72/
92,353; effect of Ore. City locks, 71/
42; Klamath Co., 66/382; names of vessels in, 72/89; navigation companies,
71/13N,22N; St. Louis-Ft. Benton, 66/
229N; Salem-Astoria, 63/67; Southwest
Ore. 1905, 80/50,52,63; tonnage,
71/94
Rivers:

appropriations to improve, 71/38,79-80,290; Pacific Northwest, 62/299;
Western Ore. dependence for transportation, 71/41; SEE ALSO names of rivers
Rivers of America Series:
proposed authors, Columbia River
volume, 73/317
Riverside, Ore., 80/52,63
Riverside Community Church, Hood
River, 72/94
Rives, Jean Baptiste (John), 64/9,14,16,
19-20,25,29-31:
biography, 64/31N; characterized,
64/20
Rives, Wright, 70/254,255
Rivet, Antoine, 66/156N
Rivet, Francois, 63/203-204; 69/338
Rivet, Joseph, 66/356
Riviere au Boudin, SEE Pudding River
Roads, Vincent, 62/218N
Roads and trails, 62/69,319; 65/86N;
67/91; 71/198; 72/40,41N; 73/73,
360; 79/32N,47:
Antelope-Trout Creek, 75/311-12; Ash
Butte, photo, 75/310; Ashland-
Klamath Falls, 69/340; Astoria-Salem,
71/188; Astoria-Willamette Valley survey 1851-54, 81/194; Baker-Bridgeport
toll road, 69/274; Bannock Mt. road,
65/313; Bartle-Weed, 72/161;
Berkeley-North Bend 1915, 72/159-64;
Boise Road, 79/399; Boise-Silver City-
Winnemucca, 65/301N; Bonnycastle
1859, 65/38N; Bowen toll road, 68/
228N; Brewery grade, photo, 69/305;
Calif.-Oregon trail, 78/123; 79/105,
293N; Camas Valley-Bridge, 72/161;
Camp Bidwell area, 72/16; Camp C.F.
Smith to Ft. Klamath, 68/254N; Camp
McDermit to Camp Bidwell, 68/254-
56; Camp Warner, 72/27,29N; Canyon
City, 75/311; Canyon City-Yreka, 65/
28,72; Cascades-The Dalles, 71/22;
Cascadia-Deschutes, 74/46; cattle
trails, 68/344; Champoeg-Salem trail,
66/358; Chico road, 79/278,278N;
Columbia Gorge, 74/101-44; SEE ALSO
Columbia River Highway; Columbia
River north side, 79/202

conditions—
1885, 80/231,236,240,241,243;
1916-17, 73/74
construction, 74/284; 78/91—
described 1919, 72/311-12,313-14;
equipment, 72/283,292(photo),313
Coos Bay-Coquille River, 63/15; Coos
Co., 72/162(photo),164; Coos River
Valley, 66/54,55; Corvallis-Yaquina
Bay, 71/90; Coweeman Valley-Kelso,
65/211; Cowlitz-Puget Sound 1848,
63/204; Cowlitz River, 63/83; Crescent City-Ellensburg, 72/44; Crescent
City-Jacksonville, 72/43; Daily Road,
68/233N; Dallas-Drain, 69/329; Daniels Creek and Coos River, 66/57; early
road builders, 62/299; east side territorial road, 78/52,64,319; 81/105;
ecology, 73/276; Edson trail, 67/87;
Elk City, 79/185; Ellensburg-Salem,
66/16; emigrant road around Mt.
Hood, 67/289; SEE ALSO Barlow Road;
Empire-Coquille trail, 63/22; Eugene-Canyon City, 65/116N; Eugene-Diamond Peak-Eastern Ore. wagon route,
65/63N; first auto roads, 74/101,108;
Florence-Waldport, 76/177-79; Forks
of Willamette-Ft. Boise, 65/212; Ft. Bidwell-Camp Warner, 72/16,27,28; Ft.
Boise-Eugene, 72/56; Ft. Dalles-Canyon City, 66/61; Ft. Dalles to Ft. Simcoe, 67/322N; Ft. Hall to Ft. Boise,
72/70; Ft. Hall-Salmon River mines,
72/70; Ft. Hoskins-Siletz, 65/180; Ft.
Kearney, South Pass and Honey Lake,
73/284; Ft. Klamath, 75/238; Ft.
Klamath-Union Creek, 73/206; Ft.
Pierre to Ft. Laramie, 67/85; Ft.
Vancouver-Steilacoom, 71/188; Ft.
Vancouver-The Dalles, 71/85,188;
Fremont route, 79/32,38; Gordon
range trail, 74/44; Grants Pass-Crescent City, 76/54,57,59; historic,
74/96; Hudson's Bay Co. trails, 77/
194,314,317; Idaho-Calif., 73/284;
Idaho pioneer, 64/277
immigrant routes, 77/195-96,309-40;
78/50-51—
photo, 78/ins.fr.cov. Dec.

Indian trails, 72/34; 75/315—
Calapooia, 77/329; Cascades, 71/
349; 78/57,232; 79/27; Deschutes,
77/329; Klamath, 77/323; Malheur
Valley-Harney Valley, 78/139; Malheur Valley-Grande Ronde Valley, 78/
139; maps, 74/278; Snake River,
77/314; southern Nez Perce, 68/87
Jacksonville-Scottsburg, 63/12; Jacksonville-Yreka, 69/233,241; Jefferson-Stayton, 73/236; Klamath wagon road,
79/288,289,290,294; Lake Quinault-Queets, 74/26; Lakeview-Ashland,
76/352-55; land grants for, 70/69,70
Lane Co., 68/340; 72/92—
Route F, 62/299
Lassen trail, 81/105; Lewis and Clark
trails on Salmon River, 66/88; SEE
ALSO Lewis and Clark Trail Commission; Lincton Mt. road, 73/83; Logie
trail, 75/87; Lolo trail, 67/371;
Longmire-Paradise Park, 73/345;
McKenney's Cutoff, 80/79; McKenzie
Pass, 74/46; 79/43,43N; McKenzie
River, photo, 74/45; memorials proposed, 74/137
military roads, 77/328,330—
Coos Bay, 67/42; Corvallis-Yaquina
Bay, 71/90; Ft. Klamath-Union Creek,
73/206; Ft. Vancouver-Steilacoom,
71/188; Ft. Vancouver-The Dalles,
71/85,188; maps, 71/362; Sheepeater
campaign, 73/284; Surprise Valley-Ft.
Wagner, 72/27(map),28,29N; The
Dalles, 73/261; 75/311; SEE ALSO
Oregon Central Military Wagon
Road; Southern Oregon Military
Wagon Road; The Dalles Military
Wagon Road
Minto Pass trail map, 71/357; Modoc
Co., 67/365; Mt. Hood loop, 74/124;
Mt. Hood-Maupin, 74/46; Mt. Rainier
National Park, 74/112,139,209; Myrtle Creek, photo, 76/84; Narrows-Buena Vista, 75/67; Narrows-Diamond, 75/67; national historic,
78/370; Nehalem Valley, 65/219;
75/283; Nevada emigrant routes,
67/86; Newport-Siletz Bay 1912,

81/327; Noble's trail, 77/196; North Umpqua-Deschutes exploration, 67/80,279; northern Cascades, 67/87; Oakridge-Westfir, 77/329; Okanagan trail, 76/324

Olympic Peninsula, 78/281-82— loop road opened, 74/32

Oregon—

Central Ore., 72/59; 75/309-15; crossing southern border, 72/33-45N*passim*,161; early motor roads, 66/259; HBCO. trails, 77/194,315, 317; Northeast Ore., 68/227-28; Southern Ore., 70/359

Oregon-California, 70/236,252; 72/33,43; 77/196— 1885, 80/230; 1915, 72/159-64; stage road, 73/83; wagon road, 62/319

Oro Fino, 79/185; Pacific Crest Trail, 74/358; Paulina Valley-Canyon City, 65/95,103N; Plains, 72/68(map),180; plank roads, 73/85

Portland—

Canyon Road, 68/89; 71/69; Macadam, 72/90; Old Orchard, 63/363; woods roads map, 75/57; SEE ALSO Portland—streets

Portland-Astoria, 66/270; Portland-Hood River, 66/253,255,259; Portland-Rainier 1904, 81/35; Portland-Sacramento Valley, 72/40,41N; Portland-Tillamook wagon road, 72/ 294-95; Portland-Tualatin Plains, 80/13; puncheon, 76/57,59; road signs, 74/209; Rocky Mts. route, 65/215; Rockyford Lane, 75/67; Ruby City-Winnemucca, 71/263; Santiam, 73/263; 74/46; SEE ALSO Santiam Pass; Siskiyou Mts., 69/87; 77/194; 80/235

Skinner toll road, 71/263; 72/93— Inskip Station photos, 71/252-53; wagon tracks photo, 71/263

Skyline trail, 74/358; southern Nez Perce trail, 68/87

stage roads—

Idaho-Calif., 73/83; Oregon-Calif., 72/41; 73/83; stage stops, 73/

260,261

Steens road, 79/34-35(map),245; stock trails, 75/3N; Stockton-The Dalles, 65/ 22-23; Susanville-Bartle, 72/159,161; Sweet Home 1880s, 81/330; Sweet Spring road, 69/329; Tacoma-Mt. Rainier, 74/112; The Dalles-Calif. trail, 67/80,279; The Dalles-Canyon City, SEE The Dalles-Canyon City Road; The Dalles-Ft. Henrietta, 66/139; The Dalles-Klamath Reservation, 69/87; The Dalles-Madras 1909, 69/295-305*passim*; The Dalles-Snake route, 79/32; The Dalles-Yreka, 69/225; Tilkenny toll road, 69/295

toll roads,

68/228N,242N,244N,247N— Ashland, photo, 80/ins.fr.cov. Fall; Baker-Bridgeport, 69/274; Bowen, 68/228N; Gasquet, 76/85; northern Calif., 80/236; Owyhee, 67/371; Siskiyou Summit, 80/235; Skinner, 71/ 263; 72/93; Tilkenny, 69/295; The Dalles-Canyon City, 73/258,261-62; 79/123

trans-Canadian, 76/317,319,324; Tryon Creek State Park trails, 79/104; upper Willamette Valley, 72/171 wagon roads, 75/309; 76/39,50—

Blue Mts., 65/95; Brackett, 81/126, 134,139,141; Central Ore., 72/59; Eugene-Eastern Ore., 65/63N; Ft. Kearney, South Pass and Honey Lake, 73/284; Klamath, 79/288,289,290, 294; McKenzie Valley-Deschutes, 64/ 185; Portland-Tillamook, 72/294-95; Santiam, 73/273; Scott's wagon trail, 77/319N; Wilson, 68/228N; SEE ALSO Siskiyou Mountain Wagon Road; Willamette Valley and Cascades Mountain Wagon Road Co.

Walla Walla-Steilacoom, 67/309,310N; Wallen exploration 1859, 65/6N,28N, 38N,53N,72N; Wasco Co., photo, 74/252; Washington 1911, 74/281; Washington Co., 66/281; water as route determinant, 73/260; west side territorial road, 68/351; Westfield-Springfield, 66/16; Willamette Valley-

Lincoln Co. 1837, 66/346-47; Willamette Valley territorial road, 73/83; Wilson wagon road, 68/228N; Yellowstone 1870-1915, 68/346; Yellowstone Park, 74/354; Yreka trail, 65/28; SEE ALSO Bozeman Trail; California Trail; Canyon City Road; Chilkoot Trail; Chisholm Trail; Elliott Cutoff; Free Emigrant Road; Good Roads movement; Highways; Hudspeth's Cutoff; Lander Cutoff; Lassen's Cutoff; Logging industry—roads; Meek Cutoff; Mormon Trail; Mullan Road; Oregon Trail; Salt Lake Cutoff; Santa Fe Trail; Southern Immigrant Route; The Dalles-Canyon City Road; White Pass Road's End, Lincoln Co., 75/54-55

Roadside Geology of Oregon, by Alt and Hyndman, noted, 79/338

Roaring River, 79/387

Roaring Springs, 68/325,327: described, 68/326

Roaring Springs Ranch, 68/321, 322,326

Robb, Angeline, SEE Drake, Angeline Robb

Robb, James R., 65/8

Robberies, SEE Crime and criminals

Robbins, George Collier, 80/137

Robbins, Orlando (Rube), 68/298N, 301; 70/25N

Robbins, Roy M.:

Our Landed Heritage: The Public Domain 1776-1936, reprint noted, 63/247

Robbison, James C., 79/10

Robe, Robert, 78/44; 79/10

Roberg, David N., 64/248

Roberge, Earl:

Timber Country, noted, 75/364

Robert, Henry Martyn, 72/287

Robert, Willis, 81/306

Robert Newell's Memoranda, ed. by Johansen, cited, 66/358N

Roberts, Alvin B., 68/341

Roberts, Arthur K., 67/51

Roberts, Colette:

Mark Tobey, review, 62/410-11

Roberts, E.C., 67/52

Roberts, Emma, SEE Phillips, Emma

Roberts

Roberts, Frances, 63/110,203N

Roberts, George, son of George B., 63/110N

Roberts, George Barber, 62/65N; 64/197,200N,206N,208N; 74/72: and Puget Sound Agricultural Co., 63/ 178N,190,230; at Ft. Vancouver, 63/ 227; autobiography, 63/226-28; biography, 63/101-10; citizenship, 63/107; Cowlitz Farm journal, 63/112-72; grievances, 63/185,187-88,207,229; letters to Frances Fuller Victor, 63/175-236; photo, 63/100; views on British rights in Pacific NW, 63/209-10

Roberts, John, Episcopal missionary, 62/288,291; 71/257N: quoted, 62/290

Roberts, John H., 69/312N,313,322,323

Roberts, Martha Cable, 63/102-103, 107,212,227,233,237

Roberts, Miriam: bibliography of Ore. geology theses, 1959-65, noted, 67/366

Roberts, Rose Birnie, 63/109-10,151, 195N,228,233: obituary, 63/233-34N

Roberts, William E., 70/372,374; 72/360; 74/184,365

Roberts Mountain, 80/233

Robertson, James Rood, 62/417

Robertson, Oran B., 80/413

Robertson, William H., 65/11,47N,49,95

Robertson rafts, SEE Logging industry—rafts

Robertsonville, Ore., SEE Robisonville, Ore.

Robidoux, Antoine, 63/358

Robidoux Fort: sketch noted, 66/86

Robie, Albert H.: biography, 70/21N-22N

Robins, E.A., 67/332N

Robinson, A.B., Lewis Co. pioneer, 63/239N

Robinson, Alfred:

Life in California during a Residence of Several Years in That Territory,..., with preface by Nunis, cited, 76/204;

review, 71/285
Robinson, George W., 81/265N
Robinson, Horace W.:
Northwest History in Action: A Collection of Twelve Plays, by Emmons, review, 62/412-13
Robinson, Jesse:
biography, 65/26N; First Ore. Cavalry service, 65/13-15,17,97,394,396-97
Robinson, John, Ft. Bridger 1858, 67/227
Robinson, L.R., Ranch, 79/339
Robinson, Lucretia, SEE Strong, Lucretia Robinson
Robinson, Michael C.:
Water for the West: The Bureau of Reclamation, 1902-1977, noted, 80/408-409
Robinson, S.S., 78/117-18
Robinson, Thaddeus P.:
Ore.-Calif. boundary survey, 72/10-21,43N
Robinson, Willard B.:
American Forts: Architectural Form and Function, review, 79/214
Robinson Hill, Portland:
panoramic view from, 71/13
Robison, —, The Dalles 1881, 81/280
Robison, E. Jesse, 79/10
Robisonville (Robinsonville, Robertson-ville), Ore., 68/35
Robnett, Ralph, 68/187
The Robnett Family Record, by Turnbow, noted, 73/73
Rocchia, Andy, 66/283
Rochester Grist Mill, 66/187
Rochon, Augustin (August), 66/81
Rock collecting, 81/104
Rock Creek, Gilliam Co., 66/135; 79/177,201; 81/262,263N:
area photos, 81/263,265
Rock Creek, Harney Co., 65/57, 58,62,66; 79/290
Rock Creek, on Ore. Trail in Idaho, 62/381,382; 79/385
Rock Creek, Wheeler Co., 65/103N-104N,105,108
Rock Creek (town), Ida., 63/89
"Rock Creek Shepherd, 1881," by Lucile McDonald, 81/261-80

Rock inscriptions:
Astor party in Deschutes Co., 77/79-81—
photo, 77/80
pioneers, 65/300; 68/311
Rock mounds, 73/82
Rock Point, Ore., 72/92
Rock quarries:
St. Helens, 65/309
Rockaway, Ore.:
beach photo, 71/ins.fr.cov. June
Rockey, A.E., 74/208
Rockville, Ore., 68/354; 81/263N,264N
Rockville Wool Stock Raising and Trading Co., 81/263,264,264N,271
Rockwell, Cleveland, 69/306; 70/371; 77/289:
paintings, 74/362
Rockwell, Eleanor Ruth, 71/101,221
Rockwell, John A., 75/323-24
Rockwell, Kitty ("Klondike Kate"), 63/352-53
Rocky Bar, Ida., 63/89
Rocky Mountain Fur Company, 65/407; 66/64
Rocky Mountains, 62/346-74*passim*; 66/63; 76/315; 79/107,375,377,378:
eastern boundary, 66/69-71; Haggeman Pass rail trestle, 66/181; routes across, 65/215; 74/288; Skirving panorama scenes, 65/151-54
Rocque, John:
map of North America, 68/87
Rodeos, 73/74:
Ashland, 76/354
Rodgers, Eli C., 69/340
Rodgers, R., 62/219N
Rodgers, Mrs. S., pioneer of 1853, 78/324
Rodgers Mountain, 69/340
Rodney, G.B., 63/200
Rodney, T.M., 63/200
Rodnick, David, 63/73
Rodolph, Fred, 72/40
Roe, Frank Gilbert, 62/105
Roe, Michael, ed.:
The Journal and Letters of Capt. Charles Bishop on the North-West Coast, 1794-1799, review, 69/67-68

Roeder, Richard B., and Michael P. Malone, eds.:

The Montana Past, An Anthology, noted, **71**/287

Roehm, Marjorie Catlin:

Letters of George Catlin and His Family, a Chronicle of the American West, review, **68**/77-79

Rogers, Alex, **62**/217,218; **79**/42

Rogers, Amos E.:

Umpqua City speculation, **70**/236, 243,247,253

Rogers, Anson, **66**/54

Rogers, Cornelius, **62**/121,137,240

Rogers, Cynthia, **66**/54

Rogers, Earl M.:

A List of References for the History of Agriculture in the Mountain States, noted, **74**/284

Rogers, Frank, **66**/54

Rogers, Franklin R.:

Mark Twain's Burlesque Patterns, review, **62**/292-94

Rogers, H.W., Garibaldi dentist, **77**/357

Rogers, Harry, labor organizer 1903, **62**/174

Rogers, Herbert, **66**/53

Rogers, Mrs. Herbert, **66**/53

Rogers, John P.:

letters cited, **80**/105

Rogers, John Rankin, **71**/367

Rogers, Joseph, Baker banker, **67**/236N,248

Rogers, Leah, **66**/54

Rogers, Malcolm J., *et al*:

Ancient Hunters of the Far West, review, **68**/333-35

Rogers, Robert, **73**/86; **79**/211

Rogers family, Coos Co., **66**/53,54

Rogness, Mrs. Earl, **69**/347

Rogue Ridge, Malheur Co., **63**/276,282

Rogue River, **62**/215,216; **63**/350; **66**/220,225; **68**/350; **75**/360-61; **77**/291:

early days, **64**/284; ferry, **76**/304; **80**/233; first white man, **79**/407; guide to Gold Beach-Agness stretch, **71**/361; maps, **69**/30,34,35,262; **71**/361; photos, **76**/84; reminiscences,

81/334; salmon fishery, **64**/347

The Rogue I Remember, by Ohrt, noted, **81**/334

Rogue River Indians, **62**/418; **63**/11,20; **65**/191-92; **66**/221; **70**/234; **72**/353; **80**/23; **81**/404:

history, **73**/66-67; reservation described 1856, **65**/173-75N

Rogue River National Forest:

history, **72**/354

Rogue River Valley, **62**/214; **63**/11,51; **64**/325,327,337; **66**/225N; **70**/236, 252,270; **77**/317:

history, **81**/334; population 1870, **71**/41; postal service, **70**/280; **71**/200; regarded as Eden, **70**/314; riverboats, **71**/41; settlers, **79**/129; trade and commerce, **71**/41

Rogue River wars, **62**/79; **63**/11,19-20; **66**/218-25; **70**/359; **71**/361; **72**/89; **81**/105

Rohrbaugh, Lewis Bunker:

The Rohrbach Genealogy, noted, **72**/172

Rohrman, Alma:

reminiscences, **77**/298

Roi (Roy), Marie LaFleur, **66**/348N

Roi (Roy), Thomas, **66**/348N

Roland Prairie, Coos Co., **63**/20,22,26

Rolland, Siegfried B.:

Gonzaga University...,1887-1962, by Schoenberg, review, **65**/204-205

Rollins, C.R., **75**/44

Rollins, Philip Ashton, **67**/18

Rolyat, Ore., **79**/337

Romanes, Billy, **63**/12

Romano, Raphael E., **77**/254,260

Romantic Revolutionary: A Biography of John Reed, by Rosenstone, review, **77**/88-89

Romanticism:

American and European, **70**/84

Romine, Pete, **66**/204

Ronan, Peter, **65**/121

Rondeau, Charles, **66**/341

Roop War, **72**/9,13

Roork, J.H.:

biography, **80**/343N

Roosevelt, Anna Eleanor, photo, **76**/268

Roosevelt, Franklin Delano, **62**/32-37

passim,298:
Timberline Lodge dedication, **76**/264,266,268(photo)
Roosevelt, Theodore, **62**/20-21; **63**/244; **65**/383; **66**/44,47; **69**/102; **70**/222,225,263-64,363; **71**/216; **72**/180; **76**/273; **80**/205:
forest conservation, **76**/31-32,101; influence of West on philosophy, **63**/358; Japanese immigration, **76**/235; letter to Erskine Wood, **75**/103; Pacific NW visit 1903, **65**/316; photo, **78**/110; Pierce recollections, **78**/111-12,113,114; quoted, **62**/18
Rooster Rock, **66**/181
Roote, Col. (Edwin A. Root?), **80**/183
Rose, Maurice, **75**/176,179
Rose City (steamship), **80**/105
Rose Lodge, Ore.:
Grange hall, **71**/268,272-73; history, **71**/267-73
Rose Manning Opera Bouffe, **70**/7N: players, **70**/7FF
Rose Valley Borax Company:
history, **73**/231-45; name, **73**/233-34; photos, **73**/232,234,236,238,240,fr. cov. Sept.
Roseborough, Alex, **78**/363
Roseburg, Ore., **62**/74,205; **63**/24,32, 36,38,365; **65**/383; **70**/247; **72**/232; **75**/137; **80**/233:
electric co-op, **80**/328
Floed-Lane house (museum), **64**/88; **65**/401-402—
photo, **65**/402
history, **72**/181; map 1860, **69**/259
Rosecrans, Gertrude, **77**/90
Rosenberg, Mrs. Richard, **68**/358-59
Rosenbluth, Robert:
autobiography, **66**/89
Rosenfeld, Mrs. James, **64**/359
Rosenheim, A., **80**/156,157
Rosenstone, Robert A.:
Romantic Revolutionary, a Biography of John Reed, review, **77**/88-89
Roseville, Calif., **77**/170
Rosland, Ore., **67**/374; **78**/297N
Ross, Alexander, **66**/332N; **72**/182: finds Indian boys for Red River school,

71/328; Snake country brigade, **71**/345-46,366(map); Sunday observance, **71**/336
Ross, C. Ben, **68**/88; **72**/231
Ross, Carl:
The Finn Factor in American Labor, Culture and Society, noted, **79**/340
Ross, Carrie, **74**/346
Ross, Mr. and Mrs. Ed, Astoria post office site donors, **81**/188N
Ross, Edwin C., pioneer of 1847, **62**/333
Ross, Gertrude Robinson, **74**/156
Ross, John, Arctic explorer, **67**/371
Ross, John E.:
Rogue River war, **66**/221N,224
Ross, Lawrence R., and Shannon Pratt: *Investing in the Great Northwest*, noted, **77**/302
Ross, Sharon C., and Welcome M. Combs:
God Made a Valley, noted, **63**/357
Ross, W.W., Waldo pioneer, **64**/158
Ross Fork, Ida., **72**/70
Rossland Camp mining area, **63**/361
Rotary Club, **74**/242
Rotchev, Alexander Gavrilovich, **62**/105; **71**/365; **73**/105,107
Rothermel, James A., **79**/304N,305N
Rotten Belly (Indian), **69**/54
"The Round Hand of George B. Roberts," **63**/101-236
Rourke, Sam, **63**/68
Rouse, Irving, **63**/356
Rouse, Joshua B., **73**/83
Rouse Bridge, **66**/187
Rover, Ruth, SEE Bailey, Margaret Jewett
Rowand, John:
biography, **63**/359; letter to George Simpson, **64**/284
Rowe Creek, **69**/128-29
Rowena Loops, photo, **66**/266
Rowinski, Ludwig J.:
Klondike '98, by Becker, review, **69**/75-76
One Man's Gold Rush, by Morgan, review, **69**/75-76
Rowland, Catherine M., comp.:
Index to Appropriation Ledgers in the

Records of the Office of the Secretary of the Interior, noted, 64/277

Rowland, Jeremiah, 62/148N: biography, 66/283

Rowley, John, Westfall pioneer, 63/288

Rowley, Lydia (Mrs. John), 63/288

Rowley, Rachel, SEE Looney, Rachel Rowley

Rowse, A.L.: *The Cousin Jacks: The Cornish in America*, review, 70/356-57

Roy, John R., 70/59

Roy, Thomas, SEE Roi, Thomas

Roy, Wash.: history, 70/259

Roy Station, SEE Fillmore, Ore.

Royal, —, capt. of *Otago*, 65/239

Royal, Emma Julia Cornell, 79/362: photo, 79/363

Royal, James Henry Bascom, 79/363: journal 1854-55, 81/105

Royal Botanic Garden, Edinburgh, 68/112,116,118,122: plants sent by Jeffrey, 68/123

Royal Canadian Mounted Police, 63/59; 71/364; 72/355-56; 81/123,141

Royal Family of the Columbia: Dr. John McLoughlin and His Family, by Fogdall, review, 80/101

Royal Horticultural Society, 63/188

Royal Marines, 63/201,218

The Royal Navy and the Northwest Coast, 1810-1914, by Gough, noted, 77/290; review, 73/359-60

Royal Riders of the Red Robe, 75/176: photos, 75/167,176

"The Royal Visitors," by Alfred Frankenstein, 64/5-32

Royce family, Deschutes homesteaders, 79/48

Royston, Ore.: mail robbery 1908, 72/288

Ruby, Robert H.: *Drums and Scalpel*, by Large, review, 71/184-86 "A Healing Service in the Shaker Church," 67/347-55

Ruby, Robert H., and John A. Brown: *The Cayuse Indians, Imperial Tribesmen of*

Oregon, review, 73/277-78

The Chinook Indians, Traders of the Lower Columbia River, review, 79/98-100

Ferryboats on the Columbia River, Including Bridges and Dams, review, 77/86

Half-Sun on the Columbia: A Biography of Chief Moses, cited, 70/125N-69Npassim; review, 67/185-86

The Spokane Indians, Children of the Sun, review, 73/69

Ruby (vessel): NW Coast journal, 69/67-68

Ruby Beach, Jefferson Co., Wash., 74/10

Ruby City, Ida., 71/255N

Ruby Ranch, 68/249N,299N; 71/254-55

Ruch, Ore., 73/347,348

Ruckel, Joseph S., 64/146-47

Rudeen, Charles S., 75/180

Ruegger, Albert, 80/335

Ruegger, Emma, 81/105

Rufus, Ore., 70/280

Ruge, Karl, 79/234,260

Ruggles, Samuel, 64/318

Ruhl, Robert, 75/164

Rujada forest, 62/299

Rumiantsev, Nikolai Petrovich, 73/105,161

Rummelin, G.P., and Sons, Portland, 75/102

Rundell, George, 65/23-25,38-39N, 44,65,67,107: name spelling variations, 65/23N

Ruperts Land, 63/224; 64/87

Rural, Ore., 76/74

Rural electrification: attitudes, 80/324,325; film on, cited, 80/326,328; first REA financed line, 80/323; history, 80/323-28; Oregon co-ops listed, 80/323,328; Washington, 72/229

Rural Electrification Administration: Oregon co-ops financed, 80/328

"Rural Oregon Lights Up," by Everett H. David, 80/323-28

Rusco, Elmer R.: *"Good Time Coming?" Black Nevadans in the 19th Century*, noted, 77/303

Rush, Benjamin, 64/183; 69/27; 80/206

Rush, N. Orwin: *Banditti of the Plains: The Story of the First Book Giving an Account of the Cattlemen's Invasion of Wyoming in 1892*, noted, 62/301

Rush, Richard, 72/118,122,123

Rush to Idaho, by Wells, noted, 64/187-88

Rusk, John P., 68/136

Russel, Abel, 78/325N

Russel, John, 78/325N

Russell, A.J., 66/381

Russell, Carl Parcher: bibliography, 71/191; biography, 71/191

Russell, Carl Parcher: *Firearms, Traps and Tools of the Mountain Men*, noted, 79/105; review, 69/182-83

The Fur Trade, by Phillips and Smurr, review, 62/403-405

George Drouillard, Hunter and Interpreter..., review, 65/303-304

The Grizzly Bear, ed. by Haynes and Haynes, review, 67/358

Indian Trade Guns, comp. by Hamilton, review, 63/77-78

The West of William H. Ashley, ed. by Morgan, review, 66/63-65

Russell, Charles Marion, 66/88; 72/83,172

Russell, David Allen, 65/195N,357N

Russell, Francis, 62/296

Russell, Mrs. G.F., 79/203

Russell, Israel C., 67/13,21-22: map of Southeast Ore., 67/20

Russell, Jonathan, 70/342

Russell, Kate Summers, 69/145

Russell, Lewis, 62/165; 74/108

Russell, Marion B., 79/205(photo): "Our Trip to Mount Hood, 1893," 79/203-10

Russell, Osborne, 62/138,142N,195; 66/384

Russell, William J., 69/145-46

Russell and Blyth, Portland, 62/165

Russell Creek, SEE Dement Creek

Russell, Majors and Waddell, 67/219,228

Russell Slough, 76/336,339

Russellville, Ore., 76/234,239

Russia, 62/8,10,15,34-54*passim*: Academy of Science, 80/197,203 Alaska, 72/101-26; 73/101-70*passim*— fur trade, 70/180; sale of, 71/365; science in, 68/186; trade, 69/327 California, 73/101-70*passim*; 75/126; convention of 1824, 72/112-13,119, 122,123-26; declines to protect Hawaiian Islands, 72/111; expansion policy in Pacific, 72/108-11; fur trade, 70/ 180; 71/181; historical societies, 71/ 371; history archives, NW Coast, 69/ 346; history atlas, 74/96; history collections at OHS, 75/369; influence in North America, 73/160,165,168; Kamchatka Peninsula, 71/181; Museum of Ethnology (Kunstkamer), 80/197; navy, 62/52

North American possessions and colonies, 73/101-70; 77/174-88,290,293; 78/360— boundary settlement, 72/107,124; 75/85,317,325-26; U.S. annexation, 75/335; 78/288

NW Coast claims, 76/200,212,213; NW Coast history archives, 69/346

Pacific exploration, 70/77; 72/84-85,182; 73/101FF,131,273— Bering Strait, 77/295; map, 72/100

Pacific NW interests, 79/212; relations with Great Britain, 73/107,112,114N, 119,122; relations with HBCO., 75/331; relations with Japan, 77/290; relations with U.S. 1820s, 72/101-26; 75/317-27*passim*; 78/288,359-60; scientific expedition to North America, 73/101-70; territorial claims, 72/105N,108-109,114,115-16,118

trade— Alaska, 69/327; efforts to exclude U.S. traders, 75/317-18,322N,325-27N; San Francisco, 75/331

trans-polar flight, 77/299; Ukase of 1821, 68/186; 72/103,107-17,125-26; 76/200,211,213,220; vessels on NW Coast, 76/200,220; World War II lend-lease, 71/198; SEE ALSO Union of

Soviet Socialist Republics
"Russia and the Declaration of the Non-Colonization Principle: New Archival Evidence," by N.N. Bolkhovitinov, trans. by Basil Dmytryshyn, 72/101-26
"Russian America in 1821," by James R. Gibson, 77/174-88
Russian-American Company, 62/105; 63/105-106; 65/363,385; 70/361; 71/365; 72/105N,121,269; 73/70; 74/286; 76/126,200: agriculture, 73/108,115,122,123,162, 163; American suppliers, 75/331N, 332N,334; building materials, 73/124, 129,133,141; cannon, 73/124,142, 143,165,166,167; complaints about Boston merchants, 72/108; craftsmen, 77/181; criticism, 72/108; employees, 77/180-81; flag described, 73/117, 146(sketch),167; forts, 77/177,184, 185; fur trade, 77/178,182-87*passim*; influence on Indian dwellings, 73/144, 160,168-69; Japanese settlement plan, 73/145-47; library at Sitka, 73/167; livestock, 73/114,122,127,162,166; magnetic observatory, 73/147 North American colonies and posts, 73/105-70*passim*; 77/177-88— administrative center, 73/101,139; construction, 73/107,121,123-24, 125,129,139-41; departments, 73/ 117,122; described, 73/105-56; fort construction, 73/106,132(sketch), 133,166; gardens, 73/165; maps, 73/100,104,145; oldest, 73/122; sketches, 73/104-41*passim*
North American explorations, 73/131; North American trade territory, 72/ 105N,121; opposition to Russia-U.S. convention, 72/124; pacific voyage routes, 73/100(map),101,103,105; position on Ukase of 1821, 72/108-109,125; properties and buildings, 77/ 179-85; reorganization, 77/175; schools, 73/143; sea otter hunting, 77/179-80,183; ship building, 73/ 70,119,147,164; Siberian posts, 73/ 157-59,170; Sitka property 1869, 72/ 135; supplies, 77/175,176,178,293;

trade agreements with British, 75/331, 332N; trade goods, 73/143,147; trade monopoly, 72/109; trade with Alta California, 77/175; trading posts, 77/175; vessels, 77/178(sketch),199; wheat contract, 63/184
Russian Geographical Society, 75/369
Russian History Atlas, by Gilbert, noted, 74/96
Russian Orthodox Church, 73/119,122, 123,125,130,139
Russian people, 63/205,209; 72/136: Alaska, 63/189; California, 71/ 365,367; Columbia River ports, 71/ 198; creoles, 73/112,143,164; Hawaii 1815-17, 65/213; Marion Co., 72/ 250,353; music in America, 71/365; North America, 73/101-70; Oregon population 1860-1910, 80/267; Portland population 1860-1910, 80/266; relations with Cook in Kamchatka 1779, 80/198-204; Vancouver, B.C., 65/372; 72/251; SEE ALSO New Odessa colony
Russian River, 73/163
"A Russian Scientific Expedition to California and Alaska, 1839-1849," by E.E. Blomkvist, 73/101-70
Ruth, Kent: *Great Day in the West: Forts, Posts, and Rendezvous Beyond the Mississippi*, review, 65/202-203
Ruth Realty Company: records, 74/79
Rutherford, J.A., 64/85
Rutherford, Laud R., 68/342
Rutledge, Blasingim, family, 79/13
Rutledge, Marion, 76/361
Ruxton, George Frederick, 65/306
Ryan, —, capt. of *Isabella*, 63/193,236
Ryan, Thomas, 66/16N
Ryan, William Redmond, 65/146: Skirving panorama sketches, 65/139
Rye, 75/43-44
Rynerson, C.M., 75/154-55,156
Ryo Yei Maru (ship), 64/87

"S.C. Lancaster and the Columbia River Highway: Engineer as Conservationist,"

by Ronald J. Fahl, 74/101-44
S.G. Reed (steamer), 63/66
S.I. Allard (vessel), 77/101-106*passim*: photo, 77/103
Sabin, Robert L., 71/226,227
Sacajawea (Indian), 62/100; 65/220; 74/88: biography, 65/215; conflicting death dates, 62/288-91; 71/257N; identity, 71/257; myth, 68/186; son born, 71/247-48,249
"Sacajawea's Death—1812 or 1884?" by Clifford M. Drury, 62/288-91
Sacramento, Calif., 68/261; 72/159; 78/32: Seward visit, 72/130
Sacramento River: canyon described 1841, 70/75
Sacramento Union, 79/284
Sacred Circles: Two Thousand Years of North American Indian Art, by Coe, review, 79/213-14
Sacred Heart Academy, Salem, 64/354: boys' school closed, 80/349; buildings, 80/348,354-55; chronicles 1863-73, 80/341-64; 81/75-95; church fairs, 81/75,82,85; community attitude toward, 80/350,356,359-60,363-64; cornerstone ceremonies 1872, 81/87-89; curriculum, 80/352,358; end-of-term exercises, 80/351-52,355,357, 362-64; enrollment, 80/341N,346,352, 356,357,358,364; 81/79,81,85,90,95; faculty 1870, 81/81N; fund-raising, 81/85,92; graduates photos, 80/363; 81/78; new building, 81/84,87,89,90, 93-94; newspaper comments, 81/84,87-89,95; photos, 81/86,94,ins.fr.cov. Spring; property, 80/343,353; Protestant students 1869, 81/77; sisters, photo, 80/347; sites, 80/340(map), 341N; students listed 1870, 81/81N; uniforms, 81/90
Sacred Heart Catholic Church, Union, 65/315
Saddle Back Rock, Ariz., 65/164
Saddle Mountain, Clatsop Co., 63/45; 67/38
Saddlemakers, 76/381

Saddles, 62/70-71; 63/54: described, 76/380-81; makes of, 64/86; Western, 67/368
Sage, Rufus B., 71/258
Sage, Walter N., 64/86: *The History of the Hudson's Bay Company, 1670-1870*, Vol. II, by Rich, review, 62/90-92
Sage Brush and Axle Grease, by Hanley and Stanford, review, 80/103-104
Sage Brush Tonic Company, 62/297
Sage Creek, Wyo., 62/348
Sage Hen Spring, 68/302N; 70/22; 79/297
Sage hens, 68/238,240: photo, 77/148
Sagebrush, 69/157,158; 78/207; 80/89,94,99: fuel, 73/234,238-39; photos, 78/208; 79/47
Sagebrush Ranch, by Miller, noted, 64/349
Sagebrush Springs, Jefferson Co., 65/80N
Sagema (Indian), 79/158,295,313-24 *passim*
Sahale stick, SEE Catholic Ladder
Sahaptin Indians, SEE Shahaptian Indians
Sailors: Pacific Northwest, 66/101-32; shanghaiing, 66/114; 77/300; SEE ALSO Seafaring
Sailors' Diggings, 62/215; 72/10,11,42
Sails, Paddlewheels, and Whalebacks, by Lomas, noted, 70/76
St. Amant, Joseph, 66/333
St. Anne Church, Medical Lake, Wash., 64/351
St. Barnabas Episcopal Church, McMinnville, 65/218
St. Bernard's Catholic Church, Jordan Valley, photo, 76/166
St. Charles Hotel, Eugene, 71/19
St. Charles Hotel, Seattle, 78/357
St. Denis, Joe, 70/168
St. George Hotel, Victoria, 72/132
St. George Island, Alaska, 77/187: Russian-American post described, 73/129-31; sketches, 73/130,131

St. Georgii (vessel), 80/204
St. Germain, —, d. 1848 Lewis Co., 63/143
St. Germain, Joseph, 63/143N
St. Germain, Pierre, 63/143N
St. Helens, Ore., 62/64,199,205,301, 314,319; 63/171,208,234; 64/90; 66/161; 71/69; 72/198; 77/46; 81/202: history, 65/219; 72/169; lodges, 71/361; rock quarries, 65/309; schools, 65/386
St. Helens (McCormick) Shipbuilding Co., 77/101,104
St. Hilaire, Theodore J.: "Pedagogy in the Wilderness," 63/55-60
St. James Catholic Church, Vancouver, 74/90
St. James Mission, SEE Catholic missions
St. Joe National Forest, 65/365
St. John the Evangelist Church, Salem, 80/341N,344,351
St. Johns, Ore., 62/167,177-78,199; 66/283: band, 62/178; fire, 62/179
St. John's Church, Salem, 81/75,88: panorama view 1877, 81/86
St. Johns History, noted, 77/292,300
St. Johns Mission school, Clark Co., 66/382
St. Joseph, Mo., 63/358: 1847 immigration, 66/86
St. Joseph Academy, Sprague, Wash., 63/357
St. Lawrence Island, Alaska, 73/119,131
St. Louis, Mo.: books, libraries, newspapers, 63/358; Hunt party, 66/331; in 1850s, 68/345; merchant influence on society, 64/282; military headquarters, 68/86
St. Louis Mission, SEE Catholic missions
St. Martine, Andrew, 63/131,169
St. Mary's Academy, Portland, 80/341,343; 81/77
St. Mary's School, Eugene, 79/21
Saint-Memin, Charles: Lewis portrait, 69/4
St. Michael's Catholic Church, Portland, 77/255-56(with photo)
St. Michael's Island, Alaska, 73/131
Saint Mihel (transport ship), 80/42,49
St. Onge, Joe, 77/237
St. Patrick's Catholic Church, Portland, 75/294
St. Paul, Ore., 67/373; 77/298: church and school described, 69/270; church records, 81/203; mission school, 80/341
St. Paul and Tacoma Lumber Co., 77/219: Tacoma docks, 66/119
St. Paul Island, Alaska, 73/120,128-29,131; 77/187: sketch, 73/128
St. Paul Mission, SEE Catholic missions
St. Paul's Harbor, Kodiak Island, 77/182(with sketch)
St. Peter and St. Paul, SEE Petropavlovsk
St. Peter's Mission, 62/106
St. Peter's Mission Church, The Dalles, 79/162N
St. Philip Neri Catholic Church, Portland, 77/255-56
St. Regis Paper Company, 63/355
St. Vincent Hospital, Portland, 75/29
Saito, Fukuhira, 81/158
Saito, Hideko, 81/154,155,167
Saito, Norio, 81/154,155,167
Saito, Sachiko (Yukiko), 81/159
Saito, Toyomaru, 81/153,155,158
Saito, Mrs. Toyomaru, 81/153,155,158
Sakata, Harry, 81/155
Saldern, Louis, 63/352
Sale, Randall D., and Edwin D. Karn: *American Expansion: A Book of Maps*, review, 64/77
Sale, Roger: *Seattle, Past to Present*, review, 79/102-103
Salem, Ore., 62/80,312,322; 63/41,182; 66/15,357,358,365; 68/353; 70/71; 77/298; 78/5,11; 80/274: armory, 64/89; Bennett house, 64/275; Boise recollections, 66/12; bridges, 64/356; capital controversy, 64/300-301; capitol, 66/21; Chinese laundry photo, 78/fr.cov. March; churches 1860, 66/17; citizens' resolu-

tion 1861, 64/155-56; city hall, 70/278; Civil War era, 70/74; courthouse, 62/107; Deepwood estate, 73/82; described, 66/17; 71/17; ferries, 64/356 fire department—

fire fighting history, 64/89; station, 80/340; volunteer dept., 78/288

first Catholic church, 80/341N,344, 350-51; first city govt., 62/200; first hospital, 69/88; first political meeting, 63/182; first streetcar, 62/107; history, 73/73; Indian pits, 66/81; Lee house, 66/283; Lee Mission parsonage, 63/259; map 1878, 80/340; Marion Square history, 64/89; Mission Mill museum proposed, 66/90; opera house, 73/80; photographers, 66/327; plats and plans, 81/202; schools, 69/88; Seward visit, 72/143-44; smallpox 1870, 81/82-83

streets, 75/207—

guide 1880, 63/83; names, 73/73 Thomas Kay Historical Park, 66/90,283 views—

1858 litho., 78/4; 1877, 81/86 water rights, 71/352; woolen mills, 62/164,166-67,175

Salem Brass Band, 81/88

Salem Clique, 68/333:

leaders, 66/8

Salem Iron Works, 72/91

Salem Thespian Society, 64/139,164

Salespeople:

drummers, 76/352

Salisbury, O.M.:

Quoth the Raven, A Little Journey into the Primitive, noted, 64/92

Salish Indians, 65/374; 68/347; 72/173:

intervillage ties, 65/214; legends, 63/90; loom, 67/368; Montana, 66/89

The Salishan Tribes of the Western Plateau, by Teit, cited, 71/279

Sally (Indian, wife of Chenamus), 64/233

Sally, Queen (Indian), SEE Queen Sally

Salmon, 62/89; 67/175; 69/88,327; 72/180; 74/11,164,271,297; 75/37-38,221-31; 77/353,358; 79/79,387;

81/19:

canneries, 62/198; 73/275; 74/32,100,163-64; 81/322— Alaska, 63/362; British Columbia, 72/345-46; Columbia River, 72/354; Elmore, 66/181; Pacific Coast, 70/364; photo, 74/298; Washington, 72/172,354

Columbia River, 64/346; 78/197-206—

fisheries history, 81/322

Cowlitz River, 63/115-35*passim*,154,197,205; 73/345; curing, 73/121,125,129,134,141; Ft. George, 64/222-45*passim*; Fraser River runs, 72/346; impact of sport fishing, 76/90 Indians—

British Columbia, 72/345-46; trade, 81/418

industry, 76/89-90—

Canadian West Coast, 67/368; 72/345-46; Cowlitz Farm, 63/205; Hume fisheries history, 64/346-47; Pacific NW, 65/376

Japanese fishermen, 72/345; Kipling report, 71/198; new run, 71/198; Noyes Island conflict, 70/366; Ore. species, 63/191,232; Pacific discovery, 70/365; packing centennial, 68/90; Portland report 1881-90, 67/110-11; protection of, 76/80; Rogue River, 64/346-47

shipping, 71/62—

first to Boston, 62/9

statistics, 81/322; survival, 76/89-90; traps in Alaska, 72/355; Umpqua River, 67/279,281; Willamette Falls ladder, 68/350; SEE ALSO Fishing and fisheries

Salmon Creek (Macy's River), Lane Co., 77/329; 78/320-21

Salmon Falls, Snake River, 62/386; 72/55,70; 79/387; 80/92:

Indian massacre 1860, 65/117N

Salmon Fisheries of the Columbia, by Smith, review, 81/321-22

The Salmon King of Oregon: R.D. Hume and the Pacific Fisheries, by Dodds, review, 64/346-47

Salmon Mountains, 80/98
The Salmon People: The Story of Canada's West Coast Salmon Fishing Industry, by McKervill, review, 72/345-46
Salmon River, Ida., 62/216,222; 65/217; 68/243N,244N,311; 69/337; 79/37:
gold discoveries, 66/198; Lewis and Clark sites, 66/88; Skirving panorama view, 65/156
Salmon River, Lincoln Co., 66/346; 71/267; 73/84
Salmon River Canyon, Ida.: history, 81/334
Salmon River Saga, by Platt, noted, 81/334
The Salmon: Their Fight for Survival, by Netboy, review, 76/89-90
Salmonberry River, 72/295-96
Salmond, John A.:
The Civilian Conservation Corps, 1933-1942; A New Deal Case Study, review, 69/65-66
Salomon, Roger B.:
Twain and the Image of History, review, 62/292-94
Saloons, 68/152; 70/131N-33N; 74/83; 76/115:
Albany, 68/146,147; Antelope, Silvertooth's, photo, 75/ins.bk.cov. Dec.; "blind pigs," 69/299; Eagle City, Ida., 69/85; Heppner, 69/139; Pendleton, 77/298
Portland—
Cozy, 80/317; Eureka, litho., 80/ins.bk.cov. Spring; Gem, photo, 80/158; Jones', 80/195; Oro Fino, 80/134N,135,137N,157N,158; Webfoot, 80/315
Salem, Senate, 62/200; The Dalles, Happy Home, 70/54; Westfall, Hart's, 63/273,286,294,296,298(photo); SEE ALSO Anti-Saloon League
Salt and salt mining:
California, 73/116,164; Idaho, 64/86; 65/313; trade, 72/317
Salt Creek, Polk and Yamhill cos., 81/243,244
Salt Lake, Utah, SEE Great Salt Lake

Salt Lake City, Utah, 67/221,224:
Lion House, 67/225; Steptoe's Barracks, 67/224
Salt Lake Cutoff, 67/85
Saltis (Indian), SEE Seltice
Saltmarsh, Arthur V., 70/279
Saltmarsh, Dean, 77/90
Saltmarsh Trail, 67/90
Salushkin (Saluskin) (Indian), 70/139N, 154,155N
Salvation and the Savage: An Analysis of Protestant Missions and American Indian Response, 1787-1862, by Berkhofer, review, 68/336-37
Salvation Army, 80/61; 81/121
Sam Downes Creek, 72/306-307; 73/9,171,227
Sammons, Edward C., 62/110,206,302, 422; 63/93,255,373; 64/93,189,285, 358,364; 65/126,222,318,412,416; 66/93,189,285,394; 67/379; 68/359, 361; 69/348; 70/374; 72/360; 74/184,238,365; 79/413,415
Sammons, Florence Knapp (Mrs. Edward C.), 75/283-86
Samoa, 62/7,11,29,30
Samoa (steamer), 77/363,364,366: photos, 77/364,366
Sampson, William R., 62/103,414; 63/83,85,249; 64/83,276:
John McLoughlin's Business Correspondence, review, 75/76-77
West of the Mountains: James Sinclair and the Hudson's Bay Company, by Lent, review, 65/305-306
Sampson, William Thomas, 76/286,289
Samuel Roberts (vessel), 68/261; 79/407
Samuels, Harold and Peggy:
The Illustrated Biographical Encyclopedia of Artists, noted, 79/106
San Antonio, Calif.:
described 1885, 80/242-43
San Blas, Mexico, 70/298,304,305,306
San Carlo (ship), 79/400
San Diego, Calif., 62/10
San Diego (cruiser), 77/129
San Francisco, Calif., 62/10,18,164, 174,187,292-93,311,324; 63/25,43, 309,331; 68/114,122,259,263,266,

272,348; 71/359-60; 72/21,49,159, 161,317; 77/37,43,59; 80/255: Chinese tong wars, 64/75-76; described 1850, 72/182; earthquake, 63/339-40; 78/387; 80/195 harbor— development, 69/274; value, 70/298N,304 Hudson's Bay Co. in, 63/180,184,238; newspapers, 71/147; Preparedness Day parade 1916, 72/346-47; Presidio, 80/175-76; Seward visit, 72/130,131-32,133; Skirving panorama view, 65/161; World's Fair 1915, 72/161 *San Francisco* (steamer): wreck, 71/365 San Francisco Bay, 65/160-61: Wilkes sketch, 65/138 San Francisco Mining Exchange, 70/365 San Francisco Stock and Exchange Board, 69/204 *San Francisco Xavier* (vessel), 74/354 San Joaquin Valley, 63/309,311 San Juan boundary dispute, 63/112,186, 203,228,236; 65/216; 67/183-84; 68/87; 70/178,359; 72/344-45 San Juan Island, 65/326: U.S. troops 1861, 65/325 San Juan Islands, 69/326; 74/354: history, 72/344-45; religious colony, 79/408 San Juan Mission, 80/241: photo, 80/242 San Juan National Historical Park, 69/326 *The San Juan Water Boundary Question*, by McCabe, review, 67/183-84 San Luis Obispo, Calif.: described 1885, 80/244 San Miguel Arcangel Mission, 80/ 243,243N *San Pedro* (steamer), 77/363 San Souci (Sanssoucil), —, Champoeg settler, 63/182 Sanak Island, 77/185 Sanborn, Ruth, 67/26 Sanborn, W.R., 72/25N Sanborn, Washington Irving, 65/118

Sand and gravel industry: Oregon, 71/198 Sand Hollow, Morrow Co., 69/105, 106,113,124,130,136,137,143; 75/270 Sand Prairie crossing, Middle Fork, Willamette River, photos, 78/316 Sand Ridge School District, Linn Co., 64/354 Sand Springs Butte, 81/308 *The Sandal and the Cave: The Indians of Oregon*, by Cressman, review, 64/73 Sandburg, Carl: Oregon visit, 74/154-56; photo, 74/155 Sanders, Henry, 63/18 Sanders, James, 78/234 Sanders, Wilbur F., 65/121 Sanderson, Jeremiah, 70/85 Sanderson, William: *The Acid Test*, noted, 68/343 Sandhill cranes, 69/330 Sandmeyer, E.T., 81/303 Sandoe, James, 62/182 Sandoz, Mari, 63/247-48 Sandoz, Thomas F.: *The Salmon King of Oregon: R.D. Hume and the Pacific Fisheries*, by Dodds, review, 64/346-47 Sandwich Islands, SEE Hawaiian Islands Sandwich Islands Mission: education of missionaries, 68/56; Hawaiian influence appraised, 68/64-65; influence on U.S. govt., 68/53-74; objection to French influence, 68/59-61,67-71 Sandy, George H., 79/183 Sandy, Ore., 68/353; 74/89; 79/203: history, 73/84 Sandy River, 66/281 *Sandy: The True Story of a Rare Sandhill Crane Who Joined Our Family*, by Hyde, noted, 69/330 Sanford, George B., 68/232N,233N, 235,307N: biography, 71/287-88 Sanford, Henry, 63/17 Sanger, Ore., 79/104 Sangster, —, capt. of *Lord Elgin*, 66/129

Sangster, James, 63/165; 64/243-44
Sanitary aid societies, 62/203
Sanpoil Indians, 70/115,116,121,150
Santa Barbara, Calif.:
described 1885, 80/245; photo ca. 1905, 80/246
Santa Fe Railroad, 62/197
Santa Fe Trail, 63/356; 78/131; 72/58,92:
campsites 1848, 66/280
Santa Rosa (vessel), 80/254
Santa Rosalia, Mexico, 72/167-68
Santiam Canal Company, 67/63
Santiam Canyon, 66/318
Santiam Indians, 70/260
Santiam Pass:
early search for, 78/50-51; route, 64/352
Santiam River, 62/215; 63/51N; 66/357; 77/317; 80/270; SEE ALSO North Santiam River
Sara, Wash., 63/82
Sargent, Aaron, 72/57
Sargent, Isaac N., 73/268
Sargent Butte, 73/268
Sargent house, Jacksonville, 65/315
Sarpsis Ilpilp (Red Moccasin Tops) (Indian), 81/363
Sarpy, Peter, 71/287
Sasaki, Mrs. —, Portland Assembly Center, 81/155
Sasame (Indian), 79/157,313,314, 316,323
Saskatchewan:
place names, 67/86; policing boundary 1890-1910, 67/371; river system, 72/234; steamboating, 67/87
Saskatchewan Journals and Correspondence, ed. by Johnson, noted, 70/273
Saskatchewan River:
steamboats, 65/314; 66/88
Sato, Mrs. Kinjo, 81/156-57,162,163
Satterfield, Archie:
Moods of the Columbia, noted, 69/331-32
Satus Creek:
Indian battle 1856, 66/158
Sauls, James D., 64/225N-26,239:
biography, 64/226N-27N; *Shark* misadventure, 64/243
Saulteaux Indians, 71/345
Saum, Lewis O., 66/86:
The Fur Trader and the Indian, review, 68/178-79
Saunders, Frank M., 81/265:
biography, 81/261,262,264,280; diary, 81/265-79; photo, 81/260
Saunders, George, 81/261,276
Saunders, Philip, 80/149,149N,159, 161,164,167; 81/261:
biography, 80/267N; letters, 81/266,267,268,269,276
Saunders, Schuyler S., 66/32
Saunders, Thomas M., 70/241
Saundersville, Wash., SEE Chehalis, Wash.
Sause, Henry, 73/173:
biography, 72/310,312
Sause Brothers Towing Co., 72/310
Sauve, Laurent, 63/225; 67/373
Sauvie Island, 63/192,205,227,234; 64/353; 66/393; 67/373; 71/13,13N-14N,289; 77/257; 80/12:
archeology, 65/373; cotilion 1858, 64/149; Green farm, 65/240-41,253; HBCO. dairy, 63/225,234; name, 63/225,234; pheasants introduced, 65/240-41,252-53
Savage, Alta, 78/163
Savage, L., Sacred Heart student, 81/81N
Savage, Steven, 73/63-65
Savage, William, pioneer of 1845, 75/363
Savage, William N., 63/172N
Savage, William W., Jr.:
The Character and Influence of the Indian Trade in Wisconsin, by Turner, review, 79/92-97
Savage, William W., Jr., ed.:
Indian Life: Transforming an American Myth, review, 80/333
Savannah (frigate), 70/305
Save the Myrtle Woods, Inc., 67/41-53*passim*
"Saving Oregon Again: A Western Perennial?" by R.J. Loewenberg, 78/332-50
Sawmills, 62/167,176,179; 64/215,218-

19; 67/61-76*passim*; 68/269; 69/330; 73/226; 75/105,106; 76/86,382; 77/216; 80/281: Astoria, 67/164,165,174,175N; 68/261; Auburn, 62/277; Baker, 67/169; Benton Co., 76/177; Camp Drum, 67/298; capacities, 77/217, 219; Central Ore., 77/216; Clark Co., 67/165,173,174; Clatsop Co., 77/ 215-16; Columbia City, 67/164; Coos Bay, 68/263; Cowlitz Co., 77/381; 79/408; Cowlitz Farm, 63/114-74*passim*,206; Cushram, 74/273; Eastern Ore., 77/216; edgers, 77/220,236 (photo); Empire, 68/265; Florence, 78/364; Ft. Dalles, 67/298,320; 68/ 14,17; Ft. Vancouver production figures, 63/206; Fundy and Wasson mill, 68/265; Gardiner, 68/269,271; Gresham, 76/228; history, 77/222-23; Hoquiam, 68/267; Idaho, 65/385; Ilwaco, 72/354; Knappton, 67/164, 175; 68/267; knives, 77/345; Lane Co., 72/256; lath mills, 77/351; Lee Mission, 62/200; lower Coquille, 68/ 265; Marion Co., 77/215,216; Meadow Lake, 76/15; Moscow, Ida. area, 71/23; Niagara, 71/351; North Bend, 68/265,270; numbers in Ore. and Wash. 1880-89, 67/162; Oak Point, 75/105; Olympic Peninsula, 74/9 Oregon—

1840s, 64/201N,218N,228N; 1860s, 65/182,191N

Ore. City 1850, 66/162-63; photos, 77/68,214,218,348,366; planing mills, 77/344-45,348; Port Orford, 68/265; Portland, value of products 1882-87, 67/163; sawing methods, 77/231-35; sawyers, 77/223-27,231-33; shingle mills, 77/224(photo),229,351,367; Siskiyou Co., 76/86; South Bend, Wash., 68/267; Tillamook Co., 72/ 295-312*passim*; 73/224,226; Tule Lake, 72/353; Tumwater, 63/206; Whatcom Co., 77/215

Saws:

band saws, 77/225; circular saws, 77/ 217,224-25,236; edgers, 77/235; fil-

ing, 77/226-29; gang saws, 77/233, 235-36; head rig, 77/225,229,231,233; photos, 77/224,226,228,230,234,236, ins.bk.cov. Sept.; resaws, 77/237; sash saw, 77/223,235; trimmers, 77/236-37

Sawtelle, Charles G., 70/34

Sawtooth City, Ida., 67/87

Sawyer, A.P., 69/208

Sawyer, Reuben H., 75/165,176,180-81: KKK lecture, 75/157— adv. poster, 75/fr.cov. June

Sawyer, Robert W., 79/43

Sawyers, Hilda, 80/62

Sawyers, Jake, 80/53N

Sawyer's Inc., Portland, 66/306,317

Saxer, Henry, 64/267

Say, Harold Bradley, 74/54

Say, Thomas, 69/28

Saylor, Sidner, 78/129,250: photo, 78/305

Saylor, William H., 75/31

Sayre, Florence: recollections, 66/88

Scammon, Charles M., 70/365

Scandinavian people, 75/294; 77/101; 81/329:

Columbia Co., 66/382; Junction City festival, 70/272; Klondike mining, 67/ 280; Mormon immigrants, 67/220; Oregon, 71/265-73; Pacific Northwest, 63/351; 65/309; Trans-Mississippi West, 71/196; Washington, 71/368; 72/228; SEE ALSO Danish people; Finnish people; Norwegian people; Swedish people

Scanlon, Hugh F., 70/75

Scappoose, Ore., 63/208,234,351; 64/89,91; 67/280; 71/360; 81/35: history, 66/382

Scappoose Poultry Project, 69/338

Scarborough, James Allen, 63/235N-36; 64/200N,213N,224

Scarborough, Polly (Mrs. James A.), 63/236

Scarborough Hill, 63/235-36; 65/347

Scarborough Point, SEE Chinook Point

Scarsfield, Martin, 81/265N

Scaylea, Josef, 69/331

Scenes of Earlier Days in Crossing the Plains

to Oregon, by Crawford, facsimile ed. noted, **63**/357

Scenic Preservation Association, **74**/140

Schaefer, Michael, **67**/273,276

Schaeffer, Claude Everett: bibliography, **71**/367; biography, **71**/333N,367; interviews with Kootenai, **71**/331,339

Schaeffer, Claude Everett: *The Assiniboines: From the Accounts of the Old Ones Told to First Boy*, ed. by Kennedy, review, **63**/71-73

Blackfoot Shaking Tent, noted, **71**/191

"Early Christian Mission of the Kutenai Indians," **71**/325-48

The Fur Trader and the Indian, by Saum, review, **68**/178-79

"The Kutenai Female Berdache: Courier, Guide, Prophetess and Warrior," noted, **68**/348

Primitive Pragmatists: The Modoc Indians of Northern California, by Ray, review, **65**/200-201

Spotted Tail's Folk: A History of the Brule Sioux, by Hyde, review, **63**/74-75

"William Brooks, Chinook Publicist," **64**/41-54

Schafer, Joseph, **68**/344; **70**/229: on Harvey Scott, **70**/209,227; opinion of Jesse Applegate, **81**/231,257 Pacific Northwest history— published, **70**/225N; textbook use, **70**/227

Schaffer, Georg Anton, **65**/213

Schaffer Creek, SEE Shafer Creek

Scharff, John, and Edwin R. Jackman: *Steens Mountain in Oregon's High Desert Country*, review, **69**/62-63

Schaupp, Frank, **74**/18,18N,33N

Scheans, Daniel J., **63**/75

Scheld, W.T. (Pete): recollections, **72**/172

Schenk, Henry, **63**/277,279-80,286,297

Scherer, J.A.B., **65**/198

Schieffelin, Ed, **62**/95; **70**/359

Schier, J.M., **65**/276-78N

Schiller, Rudolph, **66**/381

The Schillers, Portland baseball team, **74**/347

Schinner, A.F., photo, **70**/331

Schiwek, Joseph A., Jr.: *Catholic Church Records*, trans. by Warner, review, **74**/89-90

Schlebecker, John T.: *The Wagonmasters: High Plains Freighting*, by Walker, review, **68**/181-82 *The Wire That Fenced the West*, by McCallum, review, **66**/379

Schlesser, Norman D.: *Fort Umpqua, Bastion of Empire*, noted, **74**/282

Schley, Winfield S., **76**/278

Schlickeiser, C. Fritz, **78**/175

Schlickeiser, Rosa, **78**/175

Schmidt, Henry D., **73**/223

Schmidt, John C., **65**/183-84,185N-86

Schmidt, Margaret Hawkins (Mrs. Henry D.), **73**/223

Schmidt, Marie, **62**/108

Schmidt, Martha, **79**/261

Schmink Memorial Museum, Lakeview, **69**/177

Schmitt, Martin, **64**/137N; **69**/204N: *Catalogue of Manuscripts in the University of Oregon Library*, review, **73**/67-68

"A Cayuse-Nez Percé Sketchbook," **81**/341-76

Schmitz, Henry: *The Long Road Travelled: An Account of Forestry of the University of Washington*, noted, **74**/358

Schneider, Frank M.: "The Black Laws of Oregon," cited, **73**/203-204

Schneider, Philip J.: *Alaska, Past and Present*, by Hulley, review, **73**/72

Schneirsohn, Eric, ed.: *The Private Letters and Diaries of Captain Hall*, noted, **77**/91

Schnell, J. Homer, **63**/263N

Schnere, Joe, **69**/299,301

Schoenberg, Wilfred P., **62**/106; **63**/125N,147N,164N: *A Chronicle of Catholic History of the Pacific Northwest, 1743-1960*, review, **64**/78-79 *Gonzaga University, Seventy-Five Years*,

review, 65/204-205
Scholastica, Mother, 70/312,322,327
Schole (Indian), 79/150,313,315, 316,324
Scholes, France V., 66/380
Scholl, Elizabeth Fulton, 68/23N
Scholl, Louis, 68/25,26,38,43; 79/32,33:
army explorations guide, 65/5N-6N, 23N,38-39N; biography, 67/326N, 329N,332N; 68/23N; 81/196; description of Ft. Dalles, 68/5-6; duties at Ft. Dalles, 68/5N; Ft. Dalles sketches, 68/12-13,16,17,18,32,37,43,48,50; grave, 72/85
maps—
Drake 1864, 65/5,38N,58,61-62; Fletcher-Scholl 1878, 68/225,ins.bk. cov. Dec.; Wallen expedition, 65/50N partnership with Noble, 65/15N; penmanship, 68/42N; photo, 67/325
supervising architect Ft. Dalles, 65/5; 67/326N—
architectural drawings, 67/331, 332N,334-36,338,340-43,345,fr.&bk. covs. Dec.; cost of surgeon's quarters, 68/41,46; use of Downing architectural patterns, 67/326,328-29,330-33
voyage S.F. to Portland 1856, 81/196-99
Scholl, Peter, 78/91
Scholls Ferry Tales, by Hesse, noted, 78/91
Scholz, Richard F., 75/277
Schonchin, Peter, SEE Sconchin, Peter
"School Days and Culture," by Evelyn Sibley Lampman, 78/158-73
Schoolbooks:
American Indian image in, 74/87-88; early Ore. scarcity, 63/17; McGuffy reader, 65/219; Sanders speller, 63/22
Schooling, Henry R., 79/21
Schools:
Alaska—
New Archangel, 77/181; Shishmaref, 64/347
Alpine, 64/106; 75/270-76; Alvord Ranch, 63/320-23; Amboy, 67/373; Ashland normal, 64/323,325; Auburn, 62/230,233; Aurora first, 79/234; Baker Co., 66/212; Bend, 68/91; 81/

104; Benton Co., 72/281-85; Bergenhollow (Patch Hog), 64/354; Bethel, Ore., 79/361; Bridge Creek, 73/262-63; British Columbia, 65/366; Calapooia, 73/283; California, 80/207; Camas Centre, 80/335; Cedar, 70/278; Cheney, 67/368; church schools evaluated, 80/382; Clackamas Co., 66/382; Clatskanie, 65/308
Clatsop Co.—
1863, 64/319; superintendent, 81/9
Clatsop Plains, 62/248; Columbia City, 67/280
Columbia Co., 65/219,308; 66/382—
1900, 72/197-208
community centers, 81/207; community colleges, 68/186; 69/337; 72/287; Coos Bay 1910, 66/52-57
Coos Co., 63/26,28; 66/52-57—
first, 63/16-17; teachers, 63/17; 71/290
Coos River Dist. No. 1, 66/53-55; Cottage Grove, 70/279; Cowlitz Co., 63/245; 80/207; Crook Co. history and records 1882-1924, 81/207; Crystal, 73/81; Dallas, Ore., 78/158-59; Dayton grade school, 65/218; Deep River, Wash., 81/106
Douglas Co., 74/358—
1895, 80/105; superintendent, 73/332
Drain normal, 80/63; Eagle Point, 70/279; Elk Rock, 66/54,55; Eugene, 79/21; financial history, 73/81; fires, 75/174; Ft. Stevens, 81/423; Ft. Vancouver, 63/198,227; 66/341; French Prairie, 66/341,343; frontier, 73/360; Gales Creek, 63/32; Garibaldi, 77/358; Gervais, 70/331; Goble, 67/281; Grand Ronde Indian Reservation, 70/312,319,320,322,327,330,331; Grande Ronde Valley, 70/360; Grass Valley, 75/36-37; High Heaven, 70/278; high schools history, 81/330; Hopewell, 70/278; Island City, 70/361; Jacksonville convent school, 80/341; Japanese Assembly Center, Portland, 81/156, 157,169; Japanese language, 76/233, 251; Josephine Co., 67/281; Junction City, 67/369; junior high schools in

Ore., 65/378; Kelso, 63/245; Lakeview, 76/335
land grant colleges, 72/179,316—
California, 62/232
Lebanon, 65/232; Lee Mission, 64/41,43,45; legislation, SEE Compulsory school bill; Lewis River area first, 66/80; Lickskillet, 68/91; Lincoln Co., 70/279
Linn Co., 62/200,201—
1878, 80/271; Sand Ridge District, 64/354
Little Kalama, 75/84; Lone Rock, 67/279; McBride, 68/342; Madras, 77/89; medical, 78/9; Mehama, 73/332; Methodist, 78/285; Millicoma River, 80/51; Milwaukie, 69/87; Montana history, 72/261; Myrtle Point, 63/34,253; Neer City, 67/281; New Archangel, 77/181; Oakdale, 81/328; oldest building still in use, 62/200 Oregon, 68/350—
chronology 1832-1960, 62/108; early teachers, 65/308; first, 66/341; junior high schools, 65/378
Oregon City, 68/353; Oysterville, 80/335; Pendleton, 77/298; Pierce Co. history, 65/381; Polk Co., Liberty Dist. No. 58, 81/328
Portland, 63/31,92,253-54; 64/261-62; 68/350; 80/271-72—
before 1852, 77/319; Catholic, 78/285-86; east side log school, 64/261; first free school, 66/11,23; first schoolhouse, 72/319; high schools, 71/219; 74/119; Holladay Addition, 64/264; Methodist, 78/285; North Portland, 64/262; race and opportunity, 66/80
public, 62/203; 66/11,23—
vs. private, 72/219,331
Queets River, 74/30; racism, 72/230; Rainier history, 65/308; religious instruction issue, 75/132,140; Russian school for Aleut Indians, 73/124; St. Helens, 62/301; 65/386; St. Paul, Ore., 69/270-71; 80/341; Salem, 64/354; 69/88,339; 80/274,277; Scio, 64/354; school board elections,

75/137,138,146,179; Siuslaw Valley, 74/273,274; Skamania Co., 74/281; Soap Creek, 68/352; South Bend, Wash., 67/366; 68/81; Spokane, 65/304,377; subscription, 63/22; Sutherlin, 73/72
teachers—
certification, 63/362; Coos Co., 63/17; 71/290; Coos Valley, 66/56; early Oregon, 65/308; first, public school, 63/26; Holladay School first, 64/264; Queets River, 74/30; Westfall, 63/278
The Dalles convent school, 80/341; Tide Creek, 72/197-208; Tillamook Co., 71/127-29; Umpqua Co., 68/81; Uniontown, 75/84; Vancouver, Wash., 76/382; Vancouver Barracks, 74/333, 340,341,344; Wasco Co. second, 79/162; Washington Co., 63/253; 64/353; 66/281; 68/342; weaving and dying school, 62/169; West Union log school 1878, 63/253
Westfall, 63/283—
photo of first, 63/278
Weston, 74/340,341,342-44; Wilbur, 73/332N; Yamhill Co., 67/369; SEE ALSO Ainsworth School; Alaska Methodist University; Baker City Academy; Benedictine Sisters—schools; Benson Polytechnic School; Boise School; Capitol Business College; Cascade College; Catlin-Gable School; Chemawa Indian School; Columbia College; Columbia Preparatory School; Columbia University; Corvallis High School; Glencoe School; Gonzaga Preparatory School; Gonzaga University; Hillcrest School; Holy Names Academy; Jefferson High School; LaCreole Academy; Lafayette Academy; Lewis and Clark College; Lincoln High School; Linfield College; Milton Academy; Moller Barber College; Monmouth University; Mount Angel College; Oregon Academy; Oregon College of Education; Oregon Institute; Oregon State Normal School; Oregon Technical Institute; Pacific Academy; Pacific Col-

lege; Pacific University; Philomath College; Portland Academy; Portland Academy and Female Seminary; Portland State University; Providence Academy; Red River Episcopal Mission; Reed College; Sacred Heart Academy; St. Johns Mission; St. Joseph's Academy; St. Mary's Academy; Simon Fraser University; Southern Oregon College; Stanford University; Trinity School for Boys; Tualatin Academy; Umpqua Academy; Umpqua College; University of Oregon; University of Oregon Medical School; University of Portland; University of Washington; Washington High School; Washington State School for the Deaf; Willamette University; Woodlawn School

Schooner Creek, 63/253

Schoppe, Charles F., 80/296N,317: photo, 80/316

Schott, Hugh, 62/290

Schrader, Otto, 73/8,13,176

Schriver, W.E., 63/93

Schroder, Bob, photo, 73/220

Schroder, Harvey, 69/307N

Schroeder (Schroder), Henry, Coos Co., 63/25-26

Schroeder, John H.:

"Rep. John Floyd, 1817-1829: Harbinger of Oregon Territory," 70/333-46

Schroeder, William, 63/25

Schrunk, Terry D., 70/371; 74/242: photo, 67/204

Schubert, Frank N., ed.: *March to South Pass: Lt. William B. Franklin's Expedition of 1845*, noted, 81/333

Schuebel, Christian, 76/238

Schumacher, W. Wilfried: "A New Sounding," 78/355-56— additions to, 79/339-40

Schulmerich, Conrad, 80/374-76: family, 80/382,388

Schulmerich, Margaret von Schnetzer, 80/374-76

Schultz, George, 1853 immigrant, 78/124

Schultz, James Willard, 71/342; 80/333

Schulze, Paul, 69/208

Schumann-Heink, Ernestine, 74/206: photos, 70/331; 78/173; visit to Dallas, Ore., 78/172-73

Schunesen, John Andrew, 64/91

Schuster, A., 70/146N

Schutz, Charles, 81/261N

Schuyler, Alfred E., 69/163

Schuyler, Lucy Dix, 62/242

Schuyler, Philip Church, Jr., 80/151, 151N,320: biography, 80/320N; overland journey 1853, 62/242-87*passim*,337-402*passim*

Schwabauer, George, 79/253

Schwader, William, 79/239,248

Schwagerman, Adolph, 70/74

Schwald, Charles, 72/94

Schwald, Margaret (Mrs. Charles), 72/94

Schwantes, Carlos: *Radical Heritage: Labor, Socialism and Reform in Washington and British Columbia*, noted, 81/333-34

Schwartz, Walter A., 64/351

Schwatka, Frederick, 64/277; 68/88; 69/76

Science: American 1780-1820, 70/84

Scientists: early Oregon, 64/357; 66/233

Scio, Ore., 63/364; 64/354; 67/373; 80/377,380: history, 72/92; map, 80/378; pioneers, 68/353; reminiscences, 67/92

Scio Flouring Mill, 67/373

Scion, F.G., 62/218N

Sconchin (Indian), 69/247: photo, 69/248

Sconchin (Schonchin), Peter (Indian), 66/81

Sco-pa-num (Indian), 63/127

Scotch Bob's, Idaho landmark, 68/239

Scotch-Irish people: in West, 74/285

Scott, Aaron W., 64/276

Scott, Alexander, 75/47-48

Scott, Bernard Orme, 65/233

Scott, Beryl, SEE Scott, Paul

Scott, Clem, 76/13

Scott, Ella, 70/249: photos, 70/242,250
Scott, Evelyn Bloom, 71/268
Scott, Felix, Jr., 63/83; 64/90,185; 77/319,319N,320: wagon trail, 77/319N
Scott, Felix, Sr., 63/83; 78/325
Scott, Fonetta White, 65/233,244,261-62
Scott, Harvey Whitefield, 62/172,314, 407,418; 64/277,353; 65/255,365; 67/70; 68/210,214,216; 71/101,147, 159N; 74/199; 75/16; 78/139; 79/243; 80/331: biography, 70/197-232*passim*; editorial on Coxey's army, 65/267; feud with Mitchell, 71/92; first president OHS, 70/197; historical views, 70/202FF; Lewis and Clark Expo. work, 70/225; library, 70/218; on F.F. Victor's work, 62/320; on Oregon, 70/201-11; photos, 70/196,224,232; place names, 70/215-16; regional history, 70/203-204,212-31; *Telegram* reorganized, 71/147; view of transcontinental railroads, 67/106,122,127
Scott, Harvey Whitefield: *History of the Oregon Country*, ed. by Leslie Scott, described, 70/231 *History of Portland*, described, 70/219-21 *National Cyclopaedia of American Biography*, contributions, 70/221 "The Unity of History," cited, 70/ 204-205
Scott, Hiram, 62/339-40; 72/182: biography, 66/185
Scott, Howard, Portland marine engineer, 77/106
Scott, J.W., 70/21N
Scott, John, son of Levi, 77/317
Scott, John B., 69/223,240-41: death, 70/252; Ft. Umpqua service, 70/245,247; photos, 70/242,250
Scott, Mrs. John B., 70/249: photos, 70/242,250
Scott, John D.: *We Climb High: A Chronology of the Mazamas, 1894-1964*, noted, 70/359
Scott, John H., Umpqua pioneer:

recollections, 73/72
Scott, Leslie M., 62/110,206,302,422; 63/93,255,373; 64/93,189,285,363; 65/125,221,317,412,416; 66/93,189, 285,356N,394; 68/360; 69/347; 70/231,370; 74/208: letters cited, 70/198NFF; photo, 74/234
Scott, Levi, 69/223; 77/317; 78/42
Scott, Lyman S., 65/185-86
Scott, Marian Herr: "Recent Books About the Pacific Northwest for Children and Young People," 64/348-50
Scott, Marion, 64/90; 78/325N
Scott, Paul and Beryl: *Eliza and the Indian Pony*, review, 64/349-50
Scott, Robert C., 67/375
Scott, Robert Nicholson, 70/257N
Scott, Samuel: article on Warm Springs Reservation noted, 62/108
Scott, Thomas Fielding, 64/174; 72/336
Scott, U.B., 63/65-66; 71/12,14,17,19
Scott, Walter L.: *Pan Bread 'n Jerky*, noted, 69/274
Scott, William B., 67/18
Scott, William Richard, 63/89
Scott, Winfield, 63/186,203; 65/117N,189,326
Scott Bar, Calif., 80/207
"Scott of the Oregonian: The Editor as Historian," by Lee M. Nash, 70/197-232
Scott Ranch, 63/274
Scott Valley, Calif.: history, 72/172; 81/328
Scottish-American Investment Co., 69/181
Scottish Glen (ship), 66/127
Scottish Locke (ship), 66/129
Scottish people, 69/181-82: among Mormons, 70/86; sheepmen, 68/187
Scotts, Ore., 81/263N
Scotts Bay, 70/280
Scott's Bluff, 62/339-41:

name, 72/182
Scotts Mills, Ore., 62/107
Scotts Valley, Douglas Co., 73/304
Scottsburg, Ore., 63/11-12; 66/383; 68/263,343; 69/232; 70/236,241, 254-55,261; 76/92; 80/51,53: map, 69/257
Scouler, John: quoted, 66/334
Scouts, Indian, SEE Indian scouts
Scoville, Sylvester, 76/107
Scows, 76/177
Scriven, Margaret, 62/249N
Scriver, F.G., 68/244,247,310N,313N
Scudder, H.C.:
The Alaska Salmon Trap: Its Evolution, Conflicts, and Consequences, noted, 72/355
Scurvy, 67/305; 80/197
Sea and Cedar: How the North West Coast Indians Lived, by McConkey, noted, 75/364
Sea Bees, 80/35
Sea Home, Wash., SEE Sehome, Wash.
Sea lions, 65/220; 77/180,187
Sea Otter (schooner), 67/88: wreck, 71/198; 77/79
Sea otters, 69/18,68; 70/366; 72/115,180,182; 80/46: catch, 77/180; depletion, 76/200,201; extermination on Wash. coast, 74/14N historical importance— California, 76/198-200; Hawaii, 76/ 201; Indians, 76/201; NW coast, 76/198-200
hunting, 77/179-88*passim*— photo, 74/14
Oregon coast 1970, 73/81; pelts, 76/ 197-201,205; photo, 80/47; return to Pacific Coast, 72/287
trade— Boston merchants, 76/197-98,203-208,221N; exporting, 77/183; Great Britain, 76/313; largest firms, 76/ 219-23; skin values, 74/14N
vessels, 76/198,200
Seabeck, Wash., 75/8,13: history, 72/229
Seacoast Fortifications of the United States:

An Introductory History, by Lewis, review, 71/279-81
Seafaring: recollections— Arctic and North Atlantic, 81/60-74; North Atlantic, India and Cuba, 81/31-34
Seale, Richard W.: 1784 North America map, 64/86
Seals, 69/79,83; 70/343; 73/130-31,166; 77/187,188; 79/76: Alaska, 64/281; 65/215; California, 70/365; hides, 73/128-29; sketch, 73/130
Sealy Dresser Co., Portland, 77/377
Seamen's Rest, Tacoma: described, 66/106-107,130-31; diary quoted, 66/114,115,117-18; established, 66/101N,102,106; financing, 66/129; history, 66/101-31*passim*; photo, 66/104; records, 66/101N, 108,114,123; relocation, 66/123
Searcey, Mildred: *Way Back When*, noted, 73/285
Searcy, B.K. (F.?), 64/121
Sears, Marian V.: "Jonathan Bourne, Jr., Capital Market and the Portland Stock Exchange... 1887," 69/197-222
Seaside, Ore., 66/330; 67/89; 74/164,313: photos, 77/68,281; tidal wave, 77/280-84
Seaside House (Hotel), 64/205N
Seaton, Alfred, 77/81
Seaton, Ore., 74/271
Seattle (Indian), 63/364; 68/351
Seattle, Wash., 62/95,97,187,197,405, 406; 70/220; 74/339; 75/93,292; 78/33; 80/49,205: Alaska trade, 70/180; art museum, 62/410; Blaine letters and papers, 66/82; Brooklyn area, 72/245; Century 21 Exposition, 63/91; city planning, 74/105,112,117; conventions, 74/121; cost of hotel room 1881, 71/16; Coxey's army in, 65/270,272, 274,292; defense 1856, 66/89; economic development, 65/365; first

drive-in gas station, 65/220; foreign-born 1870-1910, 80/263(table),264; founding, 74/90; 79/103; history, 72/256; 79/102-103,337; hospital, 78/34; intercity rivalry, 74/340; labor strike 1919, 63/90; 66/73-74; 75/151; lithograph, 71/14-15; newspapers, 71/147; 72/230,263-65 population— 1880-1960, 72/333; 1910, 74/112; 80/260,263; foreign-born, 80/ 263,264 port development, 74/354; promotion, 71/147; reform politics, 70/178; riots, 75/128; Seward visit, 72/133; street railway, 63/61; theses index, 72/278; trade and commerce, 70/180; 71/16; urban development, 81/103-104 Seattle Art Museum, 62/410 Seattle City Light, 72/228 Seattle Coal and Transportation Co., 67/369 Seattle Drydock and Shipbuilding Co., 63/61 Seattle Genealogical Society, 66/275 *The Seattle General Strike*, by Friedheim, review, 66/73-74 Seattle Hospital, 78/34 Seattle Pacific College, 65/378 *Seattle, Past to Present*, by Sale, review, 79/102-103 Seattle Port Commission, 74/354 Seattle Seminary, 65/378 Seattle Steam and Navigation Co., 63/61 *Seattle Times*: editorial comment on U.S. expansion, 72/213-14 Seattle-Walla Walla Railway Co., 63/61 Seavey, Alexander, 79/21 Seaview, Wash., 66/20; 68/182 Seawall, Henry, 64/182 Seawall, James H., 64/182 Sebree, U., 69/311 Secoy, Frank R.: *Changing Military Patterns on the Great Plains*, review, 62/92-93 Secret Ravine, Placer Co., 71/250 Secret societies, 75/133-82*passim* Security Bank, Myrtle Point, 63/35

Sedell, Ellen C.: "The Lost Port Orford Meteorite," 69/29-50 Seeck livery stable, Lebanon, 70/184 *Seeing Portland, A Guide to Points of Interest*, by Bianco, noted, 66/82 "Seeing the elephant," 63/50; 79/65-90: cartoon, 79/64; meaning, 70/365; 79/89N Seekseequa (Seekseekwa) Creek, 67/13; 79/144N Seeley, Lyman, 66/389 Seely, A.C., 64/248 Segal, Howard P.: "Jeff W. Hayes: Reform Boosterism and Urban Utopianism," 79/345-57 Seghers, Charles John, 70/178; 72/232: asks Benedictines to Ore., 70/312-32 *passim*; biography cited, 70/312N; photo, 70/325 Schome, Wash., 74/5 Selah fisheries, Yakima River, 67/321 *Selected Characteristics of Oregon Population*, comp. by U. of Ore. Bureau of Municipal Research Services, noted, 64/92 Seller, M., and Co., Portland: history, 62/204 Sellers, Charles: *James K. Polk, Continentalist, 1843-1846*, review, 68/277-78 Sells, John, 63/293 Sellwood, Frank C., 62/172 Sellwood, Ore., 77/300: fire department, 62/177; history, 72/ 90,354; woolen mill, 62/171-73,177-78 Sellwood Board of Trade, 70/171-72 Sels, H.R., 70/59 Seltice (Saltice, Saltis) (Indian), 70/151,161: medal profile, 70/160 Seltzer, Olaf, 72/83 Semenza, Lorenzo, photo, 77/252 Semenza, William, photo, 77/252 Semple, Eugene, 67/162N,169; 70/ 178; 72/230; 80/295,295N: biography, 75/292-93; fight with Lappeus, 80/306N Semple, Robert, 64/283

Semple, W.A., 67/69
Senator (British ship), 66/107,122N
Sengstacken, Agnes Ruth, 63/17N
Sen-jago Indians, sketches, 73/109
Senorita (steamer), 68/25,26
Sentinel (steamship), 66/115
Sequin (brig), 77/46
Sequoia tress, SEE Redwood trees
Service, Robert W., 63/264
Service (launch), 77/108,109
Serviceberries, 69/149,155,167; 81/19
Sessions, Edward P.:
reminiscences, 81/328
"Seth Lewelling, William S. U'Ren and the Birth of the Oregon Progressive Movement," by Thomas S. McClintock, 68/197-220
Seton, Alfred:
anonymous article attributed to, 71/311,311N; arrival at Astoria, 71/310; financial backing for Bonneville, 71/310; journal, 71/309-24*passim*; insurance business, 71/310,311N; Snake expedition, 71/310; Willamette expedition, 71/310
Seton, William, 76/320
Seton, William Magee, 76/320
Seton, Maitland and Co., New York, 76/320
Settle, John and James, families, 72/91
Settle, John H., 66/154N,156
Settlemeier, Bob, 63/318:
photo, 63/313
Settlemeier, Jesse Holland:
nursery business, 68/204N-205N
Seufert, Francis A., 72/148N,151; 73/364:
photos, 72/152,154,156
Seufert, Francis A.:
"River Evening," 75/37-38
The Salmon People, by McKervill, review, 72/345-46
Seufert Brothers, 75/230,231
Seufert family, 73/68
Seven Mile Creek, near Walla Walla, 79/180,199
Seven Nights—Three Matinees: Seventy Years of Dramatic Stock in Portland, Oregon, 1863-1933, by Matson, noted,

81/330
Seventh Day Adventist Church, 80/402
Seventy-Five Years History of Columbia Baptist Conference, 1889-1964, by Carlson, noted, 65/309
Severance, Bert, 77/341
Severance, Luther, 68/66,69
Sevey, Bill, 63/283
Sewage, 78/360
Seward, Frederick, 72/129
Seward, Smith, SEE Suard, Smith
Seward, William Henry, 62/10; 72/329,330; 73/48; 75/318; 78/288: Alaska mementos, 72/146-47; Alaska purchase, 72/124-28,146; attempted assassination, 72/129,132; cartoon, 72/131; Chilkat council, 72/139-41; journey to Alaska, 72/127-47; newspaper notices, 72/130,131-32,143-44; Oregon visit, 72/143-44; Sitka address, 74/284; speeches, 72/130,137,141, 143,143N; statue, 72/128; views on U.S. expansion, 72/130,132-33,135
Seward, Alaska, 80/49
Sewell, Howard, 76/267
Sex, 78/26-27
Seyl, Susan:
Photographing the Frontier, by Hoobler and Hoobler, review, 81/324
Seymour, George F., 63/218:
commands Pacific Station, 70/293-308*passim*; portrait, 70/fr.cov. Dec.
Seymour, Samuel, 65/135
Sgibnev, A.:
history of Kamchatka translated, 80/199-204
Shackelford, Mrs. William, 68/39N
Shackleford, Charlotte (Mrs. R.S.), 64/297N; 66/135N
Shafer, Julie Holman, photo, 74/236
Shafer (Schaffer) Creek, 68/243,244N, 310,313
Shaffer, Leslie L.D., and Richard P. Baxter:
"Oregon Borax: Twenty Mule Team-Rose Valley History," 73/228-44
Shaffer, Ralph E.:
"The Race of the *Oregon*," 76/269-88
Shafter, William R., 80/193

Shahaptian Indians, 63/76; 71/333,337; SEE ALSO Nez Perce Indians
Shaker Church (Indian), 74/283: altar, 67/348,352; Bible, 67/347,352, 353,354; Christian influence, 72/148-49,152,153N,157 church building, The Dalles, 72/149,155,157-58— 1971 site, 72/158N; photos, 72/154,158 Colville Reservation, 68/348; history, 67/347; mesmerism, 72/149; origin, 72/148-49,151,153; rituals, 72/149, 152,153,155-57; service described, 67/347-55; Siletz, 72/153N; Yakima curing ritual, 72/249; White Swan, 72/155,157
Shakespearean Festival, Ashland, 76/381
Shallow Lake, B.C., 76/108
Shambaugh, Benjamin F., 70/204
Shamrock (steamship), 72/354
"Shamrocks and Shepherds: the Irish of Morrow County," by John F. Kilkenny, 69/101-47
Shaniko, Ore., 64/90-91; 65/17N,20, 118N; 66/183; 67/374; 69/301,303; 70/69; 72/341; 73/84,261,262,321; 75/315; 77/27: photos, 77/20,27,162; rail center, 77/27,161; wool industry, 77/161; SEE ALSO Cross Hollows
Shaniko Flat, 73/261,319,320
Shanks, John P.C., 70/116N,117
Shannon, Fred A.: *The Centennial Years, A Political and Economic History of America*..., ed. by Jones, noted, 68/341
Shannon, Lee, 69/145
Shannon (ship), 63/202
Shantytowns: Portland, 81/41
The Shaping of a City: Business and Politics in Portland, Oregon, 1885 to 1915, by MacColl, review, 78/89-90
The Shaping of a Family, A Memoir, by Oliver, review, 81/102-103
Shark (U.S. schooner), 63/207; 64/ 199N,203,209,227N,243-44; 70/305: survivors' building, photo, 81/4

Sharp, S. Price: Olympic expedition, 74/6-16; Queets River settlement promotion, 74/5-24, 32,33
Sharples, Abram, 63/245
Sharp's Peak, Harney Co., 73/231
Shasta Indians, 63/350; 66/220; 73/283; 81/415
Shasta Valley: described 1885, 80/235
Shattuck, Erasmus D., 64/151
Shaug, Charles W., 68/29
Shaver, Delmer, 81/39
Shaver, George M., 81/39
Shaver, George W., family, 65/309
Shaver, Homer T., 62/111,207,303,422; 63/93,255,371,373; 64/93,189,285, 359,363; 65/125,221,317,414,417; 66/94,190,286,395; 67/378,379; 68/360; 69/343,347; 70/373
Shaver, James W., 81/39
Shaver, Lincoln, 81/39
Shaver, U.R., 71/13
Shaver (sternwheeler), 81/39: photo, 66/181
Shaver Transportation Co., 81/39,41,41N,42
Shaw, Alfred W., 67/270
Shaw, Alva C.R., 62/241N; 64/125; 65/199
Shaw, Frank, Wash. Terr. volunteer, 62/85
Shaw, Jean, 77/298
Shaw, Joshua, 62/241N
Shaw, Laurence L., 67/376,380; 68/361; 69/348; 70/373; 71/371
Shaw, William, immigrant of 1853, 79/17
Shaw, William B.: *The China or Denny Pheasant in Oregon*, cited, 65/244
Shaw Milling Company, 80/280
Shawe, Victor, 74/54
Shay locomotive, 63/92,351,355
Shea, Con, 72/354
Shea, John G., 70/85
Shea, Tom E., photo, 74/214
Sheahan, George, 74/238
Sheahan, William, 76/301

Shearer, Edward, 63/123
Shebl, James M.:
King, of the Mountains, noted, 76/182
Shedd, Ore., 66/90; 80/106
Shedd, Linn County's Early Dairy Center, by Carey and Hainline, noted, 80/106
Sheehan, M.F., 80/289
Sheep, 67/135,277; 75/270; 77/12,187,195:
bellwhether anecdotes, 81/319-20;
bighorn, 69/7; 70/360; branding, 64/121
breeds, 76/333,344—
Merinos, 72/341; 81/353; Rambouillet, 77/151
bummer lambs, 76/344-46,356; buying, 76/355-58; 77/18,22-23,26,165;
care of in early Ore., 63/134-35; castrating and docking, 77/32-34
Central Oregon, 66/183; 72/341—
numbers, 81/297,299,301
Clatsop Co., 62/241N; companies, 73/84; Cowlitz Farm, 63/104,115-208*passim*; dipping, 75/69-71; 76/340; 81/300,301
drives, 75/286; 76/341,343,357—
Northern Calif.-Boise 1865, 81/328;
photo, 73/306; to East, 67/130-31
Eastern Oregon—
1870s, 64/102-22*passim*; flock movement to, 67/129; numbers 1880-90, 67/155
federal range law effect, 81/282,316-17; feed, 76/346,356; 77/171; grazing, 77/149,157,173; 81/254;
gummers, 77/26-27,189
herding, 76/155,157,158,339,340—
"ark," 76/350; equipment, 76/348, 350,357-58; photos, 76/156,158, 171,349
Hudson's Bay Co. purchase in Calif., 63/205,208; Judas goats, 77/154-55;
Lake Co., 76/333-58; lambing, 76/343,344,345,352,355,356; 77/6,30-32,156,173; markets, 77/21; medication, 77/34; Minto activities, 81/245;
Minto report 1892, 81/256; Morrow Co., 69/105-47*passim*; Nevada, 67/85;
Nisqually Farm numbers, 63/211

Oregon—
1880-90 numbers, 67/129; 1900, 62/164
Oregon Trail 1853, 62/240-87*passim*, 337-402*passim*; parasites, 76/338,340;
pelts, 81/261N,269,272,276,279; pens and fences, 64/116; 76/332(photo), 333,347; photos, 69/122,132; 74/252;
75/70; 76/ins.fr.cov.Dec.;77/152,301;
81/268,300,320; pioneer dip formula, 63/127; Polk Co., 72/89; predators, 76/333,336,347-48; pressure on Eastern Ore. cattle industry, 67/155-56, 157; prices, SEE Prices; ranch experiences 1881, 81/261-80,297-314; rustling, 77/21; sales, 76/355-58; 77/21, 22,23,157; shearing, 64/117-21; 76/336,340; 81/300,301; sheep-cattle wars, 69/106; sheepdogs, 77/151, 152,154
sheepherders and sheepmen, 65/313; 68/187—
Basques, SEE Basque people; cooking, 76/341,348,350; Eastern Ore., 73/82; Irish, 69/105-47*passim*; Malheur Co., 63/265-69; nationalities, 81/312-13; photos, 64/100,106,118;
Wheeler Co., 64/103-22*passim*
shipping,
77/26,27,154-56,168,170-71—
to Hawaii 1829, 63/199
trails, 75/311; U.S. numbers 1880-90, 67/129; wagons, 76/154(photo),350;
Wasco Co., 73/306; Wheeler Co., 73/262,264; Willamette Valley, 77/164;
winter losses, 81/261N,266; wintering, 77/18,19,21; 81/315(photo)
Sheep Mountain, Kenai Peninsula, 76/101
Sheep Ranch, Malheur Co., 67/91; 68/246,251,298N,299N; 70/15,16N,17:
photo, 68/249
Sheep Rock, Crook Co., 65/80N:
Drake scout to, 65/78-79; location, 65/42
Sheepeater Indians, 70/180
Sheepherders: Men Alone, by Mathers, noted, 77/301
"Sheepherders: The Quiet Westerners,"

by H.L. Davis, cited, 66/245
Sheepy Ridge, Siskiyou Co., 72/7N
She-He-Ke (Indian), SEE Big White
Shekewayanin (Indian), 79/313,315, 317,325
Shelburn, Ore., 62/200; 65/210; 68/353
Shelby, Eugene, 65/273
Sheldon, Henry Davidson: biography and letters, 81/330
Shelikhov, Grigorii Ivanovich, 77/181
Sheller, Roscoe, 64/310N
Shellrock Mountain, Hood River Co., 66/251N; 74/109: photo, 74/100
Shelton, E.H., 68/226N,238: death, 68/297N
Shelton Cooperative Sustained Yield Unit, 64/62
Shenandoah (Confederate vessel), 63/254; 67/85: raids on whaling fleet, 68/347
Shepard, Ann W.: letters, 80/102
Shepard, Cyrus, 62/299; 64/43N,45,49; 66/346-47; 71/344; 76/227; 78/347; 79/122N; 81/14N
Shepard, Margaret Lisle, 75/140-41
Shepard, Susan Downing (Mrs. Cyrus), 64/49
Shepard, Ward, 64/59
Shepherd, George, member of Jesse James gang, 67/220
Shepherd, J., mate on *Alexander*, 78/355,356
Shepherd, Mac, 67/220
Sheppe, Walter, ed.: *First Man West: Alexander Mackenzie's Account of his Expedition...to the Pacific in 1792*, review, 64/272-73
Shepperd, George, 66/267; 74/138
Shepperds Dell: land donated for park, 66/267; photo, 66/254
Shepperson, Wilbur S.: *Emigration and Disenchantment: Portraits of Englishmen Repatriated from the United States*, review, 68/280
Sherar, John, 73/260

Sherar, Joseph H., 65/115N; 69/295; 75/314
Sherar's Bridge, Deschutes River, 65/ 115N; 73/260; 77/315: photo, 69/297
Sherbet, Andrew L., photo, 74/265
Sheridan, Bridget Brady, 69/105
Sheridan, James, family, 69/105,146
Sheridan, John, 69/105,117,119,120: family, 69/146; photo, 69/146
Sheridan, Philip Henry, 65/195N; 66/77; 67/92,317N; 68/221N; 70/66-67; 79/27N: biography, 65/177N; Ft. Hoskins service, 65/177-80,183,186; photo, 65/176
Sheridan, Terence, 79/300N,301
Sheridan, Ore., 65/217
Sheriff, Ralph, photo, 74/265
Sheriffs, 72/91,308,352: Oregon, 66/90,350; Umatilla Co. 1902-20, 66/282; Washington Terr., 63/219, western, 63/91
Sherman, Joe, 74/231
Sherman, John, 73/39,41,51
Sherman, William Tecumseh, 68/294
Sherman County, Ore., 72/85-86: influence of railroads, 81/101-102; map 1892, 81/280
Sherman County Historical Society, 70/72
Sherwood, Andrew Jackson, 63/34
Sherwood, Morgan B., 63/359-60; 65/215
Sherwood, Morgan B., ed.: *Alaska and Its History*, review, 69/184
Sherwood, S.F., 70/139
Sherwood (Smockville), Ore., 69/88; 76/381
Shevlin-Hixon Mill, Bend: history, 80/104
Shideler, James H., ed.: *Agriculture in the Development of the Far West*, noted, 77/301-302
Shiel, George K., 69/41N; 72/353; 81/75N: biography, 69/40N; Evans file, 69/40
Shield, J., Idaho 1881, 71/25
Shields, John, 80/335

Shields, Michael, 69/146
Shiloh Baptist Church, 64/125
Shiloh Basin, 72/197,197N; 74/358
Shima, George, 76/244
Shimizu, Kikuno, 81/153,155,166
Shimizu, T., lumber company cook, 81/153,155,166
Shimizu, Mrs. Toshi, 81/155,156
Shimkin, Demitri B.:
The Shoshonis, Sentinels of the Rockies, by Trenholm and Carley, review, 66/74-75
Shimura, Akira, 81/162
Shine, Robert E., 63/34
Shineberg, Dorothy, ed.:
The Trading Voyages of Andrew Cheyne, 1841-1844, noted, 72/355
Shingles, SEE Prices
Shining Light, The Story of Moses Williams..., by Miller, noted, 75/88
Shinn, Oliver, 66/198-99
Shiomi, Robert, 81/158,167
Ship provisioning, 80/199,201,203
Shipbuilding and repair, 69/86,331; 77/101-104; 80/38:
Astoria WW I, 80/38; Bremerton naval dry dock, 80/49; Celilo Falls 1862-63, 66/201; clipper ships, 63/35; Coos Bay list, 73/75
dry docks, 71/197; 80/49—diagrams of, 81/40; floating, 81/31,41-42
first Pacific Coast lightship, 69/307; Ft. Vancouver, 63/189,204-205; history, 71/368; North Bend, 68/266, 267; Portland, 81/38-39; Raymond WW I, 70/272; St. Helens shipyards, 74/358; steamboats, 63/61; World War II, 73/207-208; SEE ALSO Marine engines
Shipley, Adam Randolph, 80/21
Shipman, —, Cowlitz Farm 1848, 63/146
Shipp, Oriel, photo, 71/276
Shipping, 62/164,299; 65/366; 71/167-68:
Arctic and North Sea 1880-1900, 81/60-74; Astoria, 71/31,95; Bellingham, 74/283; California, 75/76,77; charter rates, 67/166,175; Columbia River,

74/79,299-300; federal registry law, 71/172,172N; Germany-Pacific Coast, 72/167-68; Hawaiian Islands, 71/365; 75/76,77; Hudson's Bay Co., 63/193; Lewis River, 62/109; livestock, 80/254 lumber, 71/368; 77/129,347, 359-65—
from lower Columbia, 67/165,166, 171-72; schooner voyage, 78/288
Puget Sound, 62/98-99; 71/199; Tahiti, 75/76; trans-Atlantic, 72/167-68 trans-Pacific, 76/309-31—
costs, 76/319,320; map, 76/308
U.S. maritime supremacy, 76/200,202, 314,314N; West Coast maritime history conference, 81/335; World War II lend-lease, 71/198; SEE ALSO Holland, J.J., Steam Transportation Co.; Monticello and Cowlitz Landing Steamboat Co.; Occidental and Oriental Steamship Co.; Oregon Steam Navigation Co.; Oregon Steamship Co.; Pacific Mail Steamship Co.; Portland Shipping Co.; River traffic; Seattle Steam Navigation Co.; White Collar Line
Shipstead, Henrik, 73/282
Shipwrecks, 75/227; 77/45,48:
beeswax ship, 80/60; Cape Mudge, 64/87; Clatsop Spit, 64/68,70-71; 66/129; Columbia Bar, 63/193; Columbia River, 70/184; junk at Cape Flattery 1834, 63/192; life-saving equipment, 80/60; Missouri River, 71/364; Oregon coast, 68/86; Peacock Spit, 63/197; Rogue River 1850, 81/190; West Coast history, 73/69-70; SEE ALSO *Admiral Benson; Alexander; Alice; Andelana; Atalanta; Axellius; Bertrand; Birmingham; Bostonian; Brother Jonathan; C.C. Funk; Cairnsmore; Columbia Lightship No. 50; Daisy Ainsworth; Farallon; Fawn; George W. Elder; Isabella; Lammarlaw; Peacock; Peter Iredale; Randolph; San Francisco; San Francisco Xavier; Sea Otter; Struan; Swan; T.J. Potter; Tacoma; Tonquin; Tuscania; Vancouver* (HBCO. bark); *Vancouver* (HBCO. schooner); *Vandalia; William and Ann*

Shirk, David Lawson, 67/152; 68/321
Shirk, William, 68/321:
Bannock War, 68/327-29
Shishmaref, Alaska:
1920s, 64/347
Shitike Creek:
name, 79/159N
Shively, Charles W., 81/8,9N
Shively, John M., 64/206N; 65/405;
66/86:
Astoria claim, 64/227N-30N; biography, 81/6-9,181-85,187-89,194-95;
Burnett description, 81/5; compares
Easterners and Westerners, 81/193;
death, 81/195; documents photo, 81/
180; house photo, 81/4; marriages,
81/9,187; papers, 70/85; photo,
81/fr.cov. Spring; recollections, 81/10-
29,181-95; role in 1846 Oregon Treaty,
81/5,181-84
Shively, Martha Ann Johnson (1st wife
of John M.), 81/8
Shively, Nancy, 81/5N
Shively, Susan Elliott (2nd wife of John
M.), 81/9,187,195
Shively's Gulch, Jackson Co., 81/195
Shmalev, Vasilii, 80/201,203,204
Shoalwater Bay, 62/59; 69/78:
Indians, 71/189,286; 78/364
Shockley, William, 70/268
Shoemaker, John H., family, 64/91
Shoes and shoemaking, 74/345,346,347;
SEE ALSO Clothing; Prices
Shogren sisters, Portland, 76/385
Shonquest, Fred A., 79/294N
Shonquest Meadows, Deschutes Co.,
79/294-95N
Shook, Lloyd Dean:
pioneer grave, 63/253
Shorb, J.C., 70/253
Shore Acres State Park, 68/272:
L.J. Simpson estate, 68/272-73—
house photo, 68/273
Shore Crossing (Indian), SEE Wahlitits
Shore family, 1853 immigration, 78/148
Short, Jack, 65/274
Short, Luke, 65/216
Short, Robert Valentine, 63/236:
photo, 81/254

Shortess, Robert, 62/66,121; 64/
207N,218; 66/353; 81/236-37,240
Shortie's Riffle, Quinault River:
name, 74/13N
Shoshone (steamer), 62/297; 63/359
Shoshone County, Ida.:
history, 64/282
Shoshone Falls, 80/89
Shoshone Indian Cemetery, 62/290
Shoshoni (Shoshone) Indians, 63/365;
66/74-75; 70/251; 72/67; 77/167;
81/341,350,398:
history and social organization,
67/368; religion, 71/333; trade,
81/418; treaty 1868, 71/262
The Shoshonis, Sentinels of the Rockies, by
Trenholm and Carley, review,
66/74-75
Shoto Clay: Figurines and Forms from the Lower Columbia, by Slocum and Matsen,
noted, 69/333
Shoultz, Mr. and Mrs. Larkin, 81/57
Shreffler, S.L., 65/277,282,288-89N,
291-92N
Shriver, G.W., 62/220
Shroyer, Peter A.:
"Oregon Sheep, Wool and Woolen
Industries," 67/125-38
Shrum, Andrew Jackson, 81/306,
307,309:
log house described, 81/311—
photo, 81/308
Shrum, Day P., 81/306,307,310
Shrum, Roy, 81/307,309
Shrum, Volney, 81/301,306-307:
house, barn and ranch photos, 81/308
Shrum, Wade, 81/306,307
Shull, Marjorie A.:
letter-to-the-editor, "Vaquero Foreman," 71/99
Shultz-Wilson gang, 80/164N
Shumagin Island, 73/117-22
Shumard, Benjamin F., 69/44
Shuswap, B.C., 72/227
Siam:
Bangkok Tramways Co., 71/155; Siam-
American Trading Co., 71/155; trade
with U.S., 71/153,155; U.S. minister to,
71/152-53

Siberia:
historical societies, 71/371; travel, 71/181,365
Sibley, Joseph E., 77/261-68*passim*: photo, 77/262
Sibley and Eakin Law and Abstract Office, Dallas, 77/261: photo, 77/ins.fr.cov. Sept.
Sibson, William S., 69/209
Sick, Emil, 70/64
Sickles, Dan, 75/142
Siddall, Daniel, 76/102,103,103N,105
Sidwaller, Frank, photo, 79/120
Siegmund, Nairne, 77/354,358
Sierra (motor vessel), 67/86
Sierra Club, 73/275; 74/102
Sierra Nevada:
Skirving panorama view, 65/160-61
Sierra Nevada Consolidated Mining Co., 69/208,213FF
Sierra Nevada (Honey) Creek, 79/285
Sieta (Indian), SEE Howluk
Signay, Joseph, 63/55
Signpainting, SEE Painting
Sigurdson, Clarence:
Raised by the Sea, review, 74/356
Siletz Indian Agency, 65/183,191N
Siletz Indian Reservation, 65/178N,191; 70/251,257; 79/338:
blockhouse, 65/183,191; boundaries, 70/233; linguistic groups map, 79/338; number Indians, 70/243; troops at, 65/183N
Siletz Indians, 77/91; 79/338: costume photo, 81/420
Siletz River, 65/173,178,180
Siletz: Survival for an Artifact, by Kasner, noted, 79/338
Sill, Jesse, 77/386
Siltcoos Lake, 70/235
Silver, Emanuel, 67/88; 71/198
Silver and silver mining:
Nevada, 78/33; Oregon, 69/333; Utah, 69/274; Washoe, 68/348
Silver City, Ida., 63/80,89; 68/239N, 308; 70/15,17,273; 72/183; 79/ 105,107
Silver Creek, Harney Co., 65/51N,53, 54,83; 68/301,302N; 77/333;

79/38,40,387
Silver Creek Falls, Marion Co., 66/313: photo, 66/302
Silver Creek Falls State Park, 66/313
Silver Falls Timber Company, 66/314
Silver issue, 1896, 64/87
Silver Lake, Lake Co., 65/55; 67/17,22; 76/89; 77/157; 78/239; 79/294N
Silver Lake, Ore., 73/83:
1894 fire, 64/90; 66/183
Silver Purchase Act of 1934, 62/51
Silver Springs, Harney Co., SEE Currey Springs
Silverton, Ore., 64/353; 66/39,41,42, 45,49; 70/47,76; 74/38; 80/171: hop-growing center, 64/89; photographers, 66/313,318
Silverton Country Historical Society: officers and directors, 77/96; 78/96; 79/112; 80/111; 81/111
Silvertooth Building, Antelope, 66/91
Silvies (Cricket) River, 65/53N,54-56, 66,67,70; 77/333-34,335; 78/149, 209,210,221,222,225; 79/33,40, 270,297:
Drake expedition, 65/69; Indian fishery, 79/271; name, 65/56; 77/315; photo, 78/210
Silvies (Long) Valley, 63/312,324; 65/69N; 79/270,271
Simcoe, John Graves, 76/318,319
Simcoe Mountains, 66/138N
Simcoe Valley, 66/155
Similkameen River, 62/245
Sim-Ki-Ki (Indian), 79/146N
Sim-ki-ki Spring, 79/146
Simmons, Andrew Jackson, 68/343
Simmons, Jasper, 74/283
Simmons, Lonzo, 79/182
Simmons, Michael Troutman, 62/64; 63/107,123,194,206; 64/35,37,39; 68/343; 74/90
Simmons, Milton, 74/283
Simmons, Peter, genealogy, 74/283
Simmons, William Joseph, 75/151-52, 154,177,179
Simms, John A., 70/118,154: biography, 70/118N
"Simmy," survey crew cook:

photos, 73/350,352,355
Simnasho, Ore., 64/353
Simon, John Y., ed.:
The Papers of Ulysses S. Grant, Vol. I, 1837-1861, review, 69/66-67; Vol. II noted, 70/360; Vol. III noted, 72/172
Simon, Joseph, 68/210: "holdup" legislature, 68/213-14
Simon Benson: Northwest Lumber King, by Allen, review, 72/348
Simon Fraser University, 77/300-301
Simonatti, Sam, 77/247,254: photo, 77/248
Simplot, J.R., 69/85
Simpson, A.W., 68/261
Simpson, Aemilius, 63/189
Simpson, Asa Mead, 67/164; 71/368: biography, 68/259-72; family, 68/269; photo, 68/260; ships lost, 68/269
Simpson, Ben, Ft. Yamhill storekeeper, 62/300
Simpson, Gene M., 65/256
Simpson, George, HBCO. governor, 62/91; 63/111,210,218-19,223,235; 64/284; 65/215; 69/50,337; 71/366; 74/93; 78/89; 81/323: Cape Disappointment claim, 64/225N-26N; Indian boys sent to Red River, 71/327-29; relations with McLoughlin, 63/180,182-83,189; 65/306; Roberts' characterization of, 63/183-84; Sitka visit, 73/144,147; visit to Pelly family, 71/331-32
Simpson, George: "Character Book," cited, 77/84 *Journal, 1824-25*, noted, 69/274 *London Correspondence Inward from Sir George Simpson, 1841-42*, ed. by Williams, review, 74/352
Simpson, Isaiah, 68/265
Simpson, James H., 65/137
Simpson, Jerry: *Victorian Port Townsend*, noted, 63/246
Simpson, Louis Jerome, 77/75: biography, 68/271-72; photo, 68/272
Simpson, Louis P., 68/261-62
Simpson, Louisa, 80/355
Simpson, Robert W., 68/267
Simpson, Samuel Leonidas, 70/218:

"Beautiful Willamette," opinions of, 74/50-52
Simpson, Thomas H., 64/339
Simpson Lumber Company, 70/358
Simpson's Hardware Store, Ashland, 64/333,339
The Simpsons of Shore Acres, by Beckham, noted, 73/74-75
Simtustus (Indian), 79/127
Since 1890: A History of Equitable Savings and Loan Association, by Rosson, noted, 69/329
Sinclair, Archie, photo, 74/265
Sinclair, Catherine, Scottish author, 63/225
Sinclair, James, HBCO. trader, 63/180; 65/215,305-306; 66/134N,135N,137, 156; 79/136: family, 63/359; photo, 66/144
Sinclair, Mrs. James, 66/156
Sinclair, William, HBCO. clerk, 63/124,132,215
Single tax, SEE Taxes and taxation
Singleton, Ralph H.:
The Tarbells of Yankton, ed. by Oliver, review, 80/102-103
Sings for Herself (Indian), SEE Adrian, Mrs. Pierre
Sinkiuse (Columbia) Indians, 67/185; 70/34,120,121,125-27,128
Sinnott, Nicholas John, 75/171
Sinnott Memorial, Crater Lake, 62/323
Sioux Indians, 63/71,74-75,247; 71/188; 72/183: art style, 81/346; cultural influence on Cayuse-Nez Perce, 81/342
Sir Robert Fernie (ship), 66/115
Siskiyou County, Calif., 72/7,47: boundary survey 1854, 72/10-12,39N; dumpground, 72/7,7N; history, 69/79; 70/75; 72/171; 74/93; mining camps, 68/81
Siskiyou County Historical Society, 65/219: publications, 66/81-82; 72/171; 73/283; 74/93; 78/365; 80/207; 81/329
Siskiyou County Museum, 69/177
Siskiyou Indians, 63/351; 69/231,232

Siskiyou Mountain Wagon Road, 64/ 355; 68/353; 69/87

Siskiyou Mountains, 62/213,214; 66/ 220,284; 68/353; 69/233,241: botanical collection, 68/114,121; brush, 72/42; view from summit, 72/ 11,41,41N

Siskiyou National Forest Reserve, 76/39-88

Siskiyou Pioneer, noted, 63/357; 64/351; 66/81-82; 68/81; 69/79; 70/75; 73/ 283; 74/93; 78/365; 80/207; 81/329

Siskiyou Pioneer and Yearbook, noted, 71/190

Siskiyou Pioneer Sites Foundation: officers and directors, 62/415; 63/86,250; 64/84,280

Siskiyou Trail: The Hudson's Bay Fur Company Route to California, by Dillon, review, 77/194

Sisters, Ore.: early settlement, 68/91

Sisters of Mercy of Philadelphia, 70/331

Sisters of Notre Dame de Namur: arrival in Oregon, 69/269; school at St. Paul described, 69/270-71

Sisters of Providence: archives, 76/304

Sisters of St. Ann, 65/378

Sisters of the Holy Names of Jesus and Mary, 64/354; 70/312,321: schools established, 80/341; SEE ALSO Sacred Heart Academy, Salem

Sitka, Alaska, 63/105,182; 64/225,245; 71/196; 73/105,167; 76/200: Americanization, 66/280; capital of Alaska, 73/135; churches, 72/137; city council, 72/135,137,145; described 1869, 72/135-37; land title confusion, 72/135-36; mayor, 72/129,145; military control, 72/135,136,146; Seward visit, 72/127-47; view 1867-68, 72/142; SEE ALSO New Archangel

Sitka Bay: map, 73/145; sketch, 73/147

Sitka Island, 73/105,138-49: first Russian settlement, 73/152; SEE ALSO Baranof Island

Sitka National Monument, 76/101

Sitwella, Joe, 79/159,278,317,324

"Siuslaw Head Flattening," by Harold Mackey, 69/171-73

Siuslaw National Forest, 68/349; 70/257

Siuslaw Railroad, 62/168

Siuslaw River, 63/350; 69/77; 70/235, 239,245; 74/271: ferry, 74/273; navigation, Mapleton to Florence, 76/177; transportation on, 74/273

Siuslaw Valley, 72/353: history, 74/271-74

Six Mile Creek, Idaho, 62/369

Sixes Precinct, SEE Curry County

Sixes River, 62/215; 63/6; 69/32, 45,48; 73/322: mines, 63/23,27-28

Sixteen Mile House, Union Co. stage station, 63/253

16 Mule Wheat Team, Arlington, Oregon, noted, 70/75

Skagit River, 66/282; 79/105

Skagit Valley, 79/337: history, 72/232

Skagway, Alaska: description 1898, 81/121-48*passim*— crime, 81/129,138-39; health conditions, 81/121-22,124; photo, 81/125

Skagway and Yukon Transportation and Improvement Co., 81/127N

"Skagway-Atlin Letters: Kirke E. Johnson," ed. by Fred E. Johnson, 81/117-48

Skamania County, Wash., 66/32; 81/333: post offices, 69/331

Skamania County Heritage, noted, 73/ 283; 78/364-65

Skamania County Historical Society: museum, 73/283; officers and directors, 73/283; publications, 73/283; 74/281; 78/364-65

Skamokawa, Wash., 63/79,351; 75/105

Skanewa (Indian), 79/153,153N,315, 317,324

Skarsten, M.O.: *George Drouillard, Hunter and Interpreter for Lewis and Clark*..., review, 65/ 303-304

Skavlan, Margaret, 74/63
Skedaddle (steamer), 75/82
Skeen, William, 78/363
Skelly, Luke, 69/146
Skelton, Jack, 63/282
Skelton, R.A., and R.V. Tooley: *The Marine Surveys of James Cook in North America, 1758-1768*, noted, 69/79
Skelton, R.A., *et al*: *The Vinland Map and the Tartar Relations*, review, 67/182-83
Sketco the Raven, by Ayre, review, 64/348
Skidmore, Arthur E.: recollections, 74/93
Skidmore, John N., 74/93; 80/145N, 146N
Skidmore, Stephen G.: biography, 75/83
Skidmore Fountain, 62/204; 63/363; 73/67; 75/83
Skidmore's Portland: His Fountain and Its Sculptor, by Snyder, review, 75/83
Skiff, Nolan, 62/204
Skilloot Indians, 81/393
Skinner, Alonzo A., 62/161; 70/259
Skinner, Emory J., 63/263N
Skinner, Eugene F., 63/364; 67/179; 69/77; 77/324; 78/62,64,325; 79/ 6N,7N,11,42,43: cabin replica, 72/89; 73/80; correspondence, 78/363; land claim, 79/7N; watch, 71/361
Skinner, Hugh, photo, 71/252
Skinner, Mona, photo, 71/252
Skinner, Phoebe, 80/348
Skinner, Ray, photo, 71/252
Skinner, S.K., grandson of Silas, 71/248N: photos, 71/263; preserves Charbonneau grave, 71/255
Skinner, Silas: Inskip Station house photo, 71/252; toll road, SEE Skinner Toll Road
Skinner, Tom, Jordan Valley 1930s, 68/248N
Skinner, W.S., son of Silas, 71/255: photo, 71/252
Skinner, William, Lane Co. pioneer, 79/11

Skinner, William, Jr., Jordan Valley pioneer, photo, 71/252
Skinner Toll Road, 67/370,371; 71/ 263; 72/93
Skinner's Ferry, 78/64
Skipanon River: land claims, 64/204
Skirving, Archibald, 65/139
Skirving, John: art work, 65/140-41; biography, 65/139-40
Fremont panorama, 65/134,136, 140,145— composition details, 65/149-67; first showing, 65/167-68; guidebooks, 65/169-70; London exhibit, 65/168-70; Paris exhibit, 65/171; play-bill photo, 65/opp. contents pg. June
"Skirving's Moving Panorama: Colonel Fremont's Western Expeditions Pictorialized," by Joseph Earl Arrington, 65/133-72
Skokomish Indians, 62/203: legends, 63/90
Skokomish River, 78/282
Skomoquis Indians, 62/82
Skoog, Larry: *The Americana Series*, University of Washington, review, 73/282
Bread and Roses, Too, by Conlin, review, 71/358-59
The Centralia Case, by Chaplin *et al*, review, 73/70-71
The Day the Cowboys Quit, by Kelton, review, 74/280
Finns and Finnicans, by Mattila, review, 72/169-70
Mill Town, by Clark, review, 72/86-87
The Murder of Til Taylor, by Crockatt, review, 72/351
Owyhee Trails, by Hanley, review, 75/293
The Theater Finns, by Mattila, review, 74/91-92
Wells, Fargo Detective, by Dillon, review, 72/88-89
Skookum Charlie (Indian), 73/267
Skquee Mus, Or Pioneer Days on the Nooksak, by Hawley, reprint noted, 73/75
Skull (Prater) Creek, 79/297

Skulps (Indian), SEE Tawahitt
Skwalth (Squalth) (Indian), 79/157,273, 273N,285N,313:
killed, 79/273,274,325
Skyline Corporation, 75/176
Slabtown, SEE Cottage Grove, Ore.
"Slabtown," Portland, 77/300
Slacum, William A., 63/210; 64/48; 66/334,335; 78/332-50*passim*: biography, 76/118-34; Mexican interests, 76/121-23,125-27,132-33 Oregon expedition, 76/124-25, 129-30— report, 76/118,130,131
"Slacum in the Pacific, 1832-37: Backgrounds of the Oregon Report," by David T. Leary, 76/118-34
Slade, Joseph A. (Jake), 67/230-31
Sladen, J.A., 74/340: photo, 70/100
Slate: Haida Indian carvings, 68/347
Slate Creek, Josephine Co., 76/53
Slater, Anne Higley, 74/31N,32
Slater, G. Hollis, 63/196N
Slater, J.O., 68/242
Slater, James H., 62/298; 67/134; 70/330; 75/126: photo, 75/126
Slater, Ralph, 74/31N,32
Slavery, 63/358; 71/291; 75/119; 80/27; 81/236,245: abolition, 72/316; Brazil, 77/57; congressional debates 1849, 72/7; Ford case, 72/89; 73/201-203; frontier attitudes, 73/205
Oregon, 64/357— issue, 73/201; 75/119,121; 81/185, 187; slaves brought to, 73/201, 204,206
Oregon Indians, 81/412-18; United States, 77/57; Utah, 72/180; Whiteaker attitude, 64/357
Slavianka River, 73/113; SEE ALSO Russian River
Sleepy Hollow Restorations, Inc., 71/313N: Seton's journal discovery, 71/309
Sleighing, 79/209

Slevin, Fannie Dolan, 69/123,146
Slevin, Peter, 69/123,146
Sliunin, N.V., 73/157-58
Sloan, Joseph, 64/148; 80/159, 159N,160,321N
Sloat, John D., 63/210; 70/306
Slocum, John (Squ-sacht-un) (Indian), 67/347; 72/148,153,157
Slocum, Robert G., and Kenneth H. Matsen:
Shoto Clay: Figurines and Forms from the Lower Columbia, noted, 69/333
Slocum House, Clark Co., 66/382
Sloths, 66/91
Small, Dana, 62/88-89
Small, Earl: recollections, 73/83
Small, H.C.: First Ore. Cavalry service, 65/12,14, 21,28,31-33,37-109*passim*,399; 66/59
Small, James, John Day rancher, 70/57: biography, 79/167N
Small, Jimmie, Bully Creek rancher, 63/270
Small, Joe Austell: *The Best of True West*, noted, 66/82
Smalley (Smallery), —, Gilliam Co. 1881, 81/275,276,279
Smalley, Eugene V., 70/77
Smallpox, 75/32,245; 80/197,204; 81/76,82-83,84,341: Hawaii 1853, 67/86,372; Oregon 1864, 65/26,44; vaccination of Indians, 63/183; Wishram Indians 1854, 67/309
Smeed Hotel, Eugene, 73/81; 74/93
Smelt (eulachon), 68/87; 69/9
Smeltzer, Jean A.: *Census of Klickitat County*, noted, 74/94
Smith, —, capt. of *Cape Clear*, 66/113
Smith, A.E., "Iron Chink" inventor, 62/198
Smith, Alice E.: *The History of Wisconsin, Vol. I, From Exploration to Statehood*, noted, 74/359
My Life With History: An Autobiography, by Hicks, review, 70/173-75
Smith, Alvin Thompson, 62/142N
Smith, Andrew Jackson, 64/276; 65/6N,175N; 68/41; 69/252N:

Harney expedition, 65/53N,56-57; 79/38-42— route map, 79/34-35 Snake Indian hostilities, 65/57,59, 117N; 72/55 Smith, Annie Laurie, 66/54 Smith, Asa Bowen, 62/240,242; 69/51; 81/341: character, 68/77; letters, 68/76 Smith, Avery A., 78/44 Smith, C.A., SEE C.A. Smith Lumber and Manufacturing Co. Smith, C.H., Salem carpenter 1872, 81/89N Smith, C. Hamilton: drawing of prairie dog, 69/20 Smith, C.L., panorama artist, 65/171 Smith, Celiast (Mrs. Solomon), 63/193 Smith, Charles, Olympia pioneer, 62/64-65 Smith, Charles E., brother of Ferdinand, 70/61N Smith, Charles Ferguson, 79/163 Smith, Charles W., Douglas Co. pioneer, 81/105 Smith, Charles Wesley: *Pacific Northwest Americana*, cited, 66/78 Smith, Clara, 70/61N Smith, Courtland L.: *Salmon Fisheries of the Columbia*, review, 81/321-22 Smith, Delazon, 72/323N; 75/120; 79/6,8: "Oberlin unmasked," cited, 75/93 Smith, Dorothy Blakey, ed.: *The Reminiscences of Doctor John Sebastian Helmcken*, review, 77/294 Smith, Earl R., 63/262(photo),286,298-99; 64/351: "The Westfall Country: Limning in the Open Spaces," 63/263-303 Smith, Edyth G.: recollections, 64/357 Smith, Elijah, 69/217N,219N Smith, Elizabeth Ann, SEE Alexander, Elizabeth Ann Smith Smith, Elmo, 66/273 Smith, Elphie, photo, 72/208

Smith, Enoch, 75/347-50,353-58 Smith, Ernest, 66/54 Smith, Etta (Mrs. Earl R.), 63/301 Smith, Fabritus R., 62/107 Smith, Ferdinand C.: family, 70/61-62; photo, 70/60 Smith, Flora, Westfall resident, 63/284,301 Smith, Florence A. Mason, 77/91: reminiscences, 66/52-57 Smith, Frank, Coos Co. settler, 66/54 Smith, Frank, Morrow Co., 69/147 Smith, Fred M.: diary 1865-67, 64/86 Smith, Frederick W. (M?), 71/155N Smith, G. Herbert, 72/349-50 Smith, George, Coos Valley settler, 66/54 Smith, Greenberry, family, 75/88 Smith, Gretchen E., SEE Hawkins, Gretchen Smith Smith, Gypsy, 74/212 Smith, Helena Huntington, 65/215: *The War on Powder River: The History of an Insurrection*, review, 67/359 Smith, Henry Nash: *Virgin Land*, cited, 70/263 Smith, Honey Lake, 62/297 Smith, Ira, 68/348 Smith, J.B., Portland deputy marshal, 80/28 Smith, J.B., Portland labor organizer, 65/275-77 Smith, J.S., Portland 1851, 80/9 Smith, Mrs. Jack, photo, 81/254 Smith, James Allen, 63/359: *The Growth and Decadence of Constitutional Government*, reprint noted, 74/95 Smith, James F., 80/299,299N Smith, James W., Arlington 1882, 81/270N Smith, James W., Ore. Civil War veteran, 62/298 Smith, Jane Ruggles, 79/155N Smith, Jedediah Strong, 64/281,349; 66/64,88,275-76,335; 67/371; 68/ 86,87,348; 70/178; 71/346; 81/235: bibliography, 65/313; Umpqua massa-

cre site map, 66/187
Smith, Jefferson Randolph ("Soapy"), 70/278; 81/126: gang roundup, photo, 81/138; shooting of, 81/137-38
Smith, Jeremiah, family, 75/88
Smith, Jess, Coos Valley settler, 66/54,57
Smith, John: 1853 overland journey, 79/66-90— diary, 78/124
Smith, John, Morrow Co., 69/147
Smith, John, Warm Springs Indian agent, 79/148,154: biography, 79/148N; photo, 79/148
Smith, John Rowson, 65/143
Smith, Jonathan Bayard: papers cited, 74/269
Smith, Joseph, Auburn miner 1861, 62/219N
Smith, Joseph, Salem 1854, 79/15N
Smith, Joseph Shoewalter, 64/181
Smith, Kenneth, 76/387; 80/413
Smith, Less, 66/54
Smith, Leta May: *The End of the Trail*, noted, 77/301
Smith, Lucinda (Mrs. Ferdinand C.): letter to sister 1867, 70/60-61; photo, 70/60
Smith, Margaret J., SEE Bailey, Margaret Jewett
Smith, Margery Hoffman, 76/263
Smith, Maria, daughter of Ferdinand, 70/61N
Smith, Mary A., photo, 80/363
Smith, Mary Jane, family, 75/88
Smith, Matt K., 64/38
Smith, Milton, Rainier tugboat owner, 64/91; 81/36,39
Smith, Milton W., 75/137
Smith, Mowry, Jr., and Giles Clark: *One Third Crew, One Third Boat, One Third Luck*, noted, 76/182
Smith, N.R., 63/51
Smith, Nathan, Coos Valley settler, 66/53
Smith, Page: *As a City Upon a Hill: The Town in American History*, review, 70/71-72
Smith, Pat, 81/269,277

Smith, "Peg-Leg," SEE Smith, Thomas L.
Smith, Persifor (Persifer) M., 63/231
Smith, Pete, Yakima Co. herder 1879, 70/166
Smith, Richard, Bannock War soldier: Army funeral described, 70/26-27
Smith, Richard, immigrant of 1853, 78/129
Smith, Robert, Gresham sawmill owner, 76/228
Smith, Robert, southern route explorer, 77/317
Smith, Robert Wayne, 80/414
Smith, Rollin, 63/301
Smith, Royal Converse, 63/245; 64/276
Smith, Rufus, Auburn miner 1861, 62/291N
Smith, S. Stephenson, 76/143
Smith, Sarah (Mrs. Asa B.), 65/119-20: diary, 68/76,77
Smith, Sarah Avis, 64/91
Smith, Seba, 62/292
Smith, Si (Indian), 75/224
Smith, Sidney, 66/353,355
Smith, "Soapy," SEE Smith, Jefferson Randolph
Smith, Solomon Howard, 63/193,198-99,227; 64/202,205N,207,218,220; 66/249N; 71/344: Ft. George trade, 64/213N-15; French Prairie teacher, 66/340,341; marriage, 66/349
Smith, Susie Aubrey, 68/358
Smith, Tamar, 62/234
Smith, Thomas G., Echo settler, 66/141
Smith, Thomas H.: "An Ohioan's Role in Oregon History," 66/218-32
Smith, Thomas H., Ore. City 1850s, 66/163N
Smith, Thomas L. ("Peg-Leg"), 67/227, 280; 68/68
Smith, Tom, Coos Co. 1900s, 66/54
Smith, Victor B., 68/88
Smith, W.D.L.F., family, 66/53
Smith, Walker C., 73/71: *The Everett Massacre: A History of the Class Struggle in the Lumber Industry*, review, 73/281-82

Smith, Warren D., 67/30
Smith, William (Bill), Coos Valley 1911, 66/54-55
Smith, William J., Linn Co. pioneer, 66/141
Smith, William S., Brigadier General, 72/92
Smith, Wilmer Cauthorn: *The Smith Chronicle, Two Centuries of an American Farm Family*, noted, 75/88
Smith Act: Seattle trial 1953, 72/230
Smith and Watson Iron Works, Portland, 69/209
Smith Camp, SEE Camp Smith
Smith family, Cowlitz Farm area settlers, 63/221
Smith-Hughes Act: Oregon, 66/55
Smith Iron Works, Portland: photo after 1873 fire, 80/308
Smith-Powers Logging Company, 66/54; 76/60-65; 77/75: railroad photo, 77/72
Smith Rock, 64/284,357; 67/6; 68/354; 69/337-38
Smith Rock Park, 62/198
Smith *vs.* Cunningham, 62/144
Smith *vs.* Ford, 62/139N
Smithfield, Lane Co.: history, 81/327
Smith's Fork, Bear River, 62/366
Smith's Road, Harney Valley, 65/53-54, 56-57
Smith's Spring, Harney Co., SEE Currey Springs
Smithsonian Institution, 66/298,319; 69/237N; 70/246; 81/341N: Evans material, 69/40,42; Feilner ornithological exped., 69/229; Port Orford meteorite specimen, 69/32N,33; publications, 72/81-82
Smockville, SEE Sherwood, Ore.
Smohalla (Indian): cult, 70/123,124,125N,127,131; drawing, 70/122
Smoot, Reed, 71/196
Smullin, Joe, 70/53
Smur, Elias, 65/357

Smurr, John Welling, 62/403,404
Smyth, Darius Hynson, Sr., 78/238, 239: photo, 78/229; recollections, 78/237-40
Smyth, George A., 78/238
Smyth, George A., Jr., 71/99
Smyth, George C., 78/130,237,238; 79/48: photo, 78/238
Smyth, Howard, 75/279
Smyth, John T., 71/99; 78/238
Smyth, Margaret Dent, 78/130
Smyth, Prestley, 78/238
Smythe, William E.: *The Conquest of Arid America*, reprint noted, 73/282
Snake (Paiute) Indians, 65/8,10; 70/16,36,37,38; 72/19,67,69; 73/64,65; 78/217,219; 79/39,121; 81/373-75: attacks 1860, 69/253N-54N; camp on Upper Watson Springs destroyed, 65/37N; campaigns against, 65/297; 67/311-12; 79/41-42,125-27,130,131, 132,137,139-71,269-333; SEE ALSO Snake War; capture of snake women, 65/46,47-48,51-52; Central Ore. camps, 79/127,149,152,330,331-32; claim to Warm Springs Reservation area, 65/43N; difficulty in locating, 65/46,82N; Drake-Currey expeds. 1864, 65/31-118*passim*; feared by Klamaths, 69/239,252,254; fortifications, 79/288,289; horses captured from, 65/37,44
hostilities, 79/122-23,125-26— causes, 79/121FF; harassment of Camp Maury, 65/39,40-42,49; harassment of Canyon City Road, 65/12N,37N,71,74N; number horses captured, 79/126; proposed war against whites, 69/225; raid on Warm Springs Reservation, 65/12N,43N, 117N; Snake-Wasco battle site 1863, 65/27; Ward party massacre, 67/311
leaders captured, 79/125
McCall-Watson battle, 65/31-37— location, 65/34N,57N; site photo, 65/36

Oregon bands, 79/139—
Paulina band location, 79/127N
prominent chiefs, 69/240N; recovery of captured children, 79/305; scouts for army, 79/277,278,281,291; skirmish on South Fork John Day, 65/72-74; smoke signals, 79/145,171; Warm Springs scouts hostility toward, 65/45, 46; women and children killed, 79/ 149,152,329,330,333; SEE ALSO Paiute Indians

Snake Plains, 62/374

Snake River, 62/106,378,383,385N,395; 63/264; 66/153,198,231,235; 68/ 299; 72/55; 75/82; 77/314; 78/ 78,80,82,181,387,389; 80/85,91,92, 96,97; 81/19:
artifacts, 71/366; ferries, SEE Ferries fords—

Ft. Boise, 80/96; Three Island, 80/90 Hells Canyon Dam, 68/350; Indian burial ground, 68/351; lower Snake lore, 63/89; map, 72/68; north and south side immigrant routes, 72/73; photo, 70/28
railroads, 67/87—

ferry landing photo, 71/32; routes, 71/49,55,67,82

rapids, 68/298N; sketch, 79/381
steamboats, 67/88—

navigation 1870, 63/359

travel 1881, 71/23; wheat train, 67/87

Snake River country:
geology, 64/282; Ogden expedition 1826-27, 63/349-51

Snake River Valley, 79/383,384

Snake War of 1866-68:
captured stock, 79/132-33,270,279, 302N,328,331,333; causes, 79/121-26; Crook campaign 1866-67, 79/121-71, 269-333; Darragh's scouts, 79/133, 139,279,281,291,294,318-33*passim*; extermination issue, 79/129-30,139N, 305N,328-33; Indian leaders, 79/139 livestock—

cattle, 79/142,144,151,170,278; horses, 79/132-33,138,146-70*passim*, 275,279-305*passim*,313,314,315

maps, 79/164,276,286-87,ins.fr.cov.

Summer; McKay journal, 79/141-71, 269-305; McKay's scouts, 79/121-70 *passim*,269-333*passim*; prisoners, 79/ 149,270N,272,275,278,279,282,283, 284,299,301,329-30,332; rations, 79/ 144-47*passim*,153,163,165,165N,169, 270,271,274,282-85*passim*,301,303, 314-15

Snakes:
Klamath area, 66/81; on Oregon Trail, 81/17

Snell, Earl, 74/159

Snelling, David, 78/234

Snelling, George L., 70/261

Snelling, Vincent, 70/261

Snelling, William Joseph, 70/261

Snider, John W., 63/372,374; 64/94, 190,286,363; 65/125,221,317,414; 66/386,389

Snipes, George, 68/29

Snodgrass, Lynn, family, 64/277

Snohomish, Wash., 73/213

Snow, Berkeley:
The History of the Deschutes Club, noted, 68/184
"Pure Gold—1896," 68/330-32

Snow, Eliza, SEE Young, Eliza Snow

Snow, MacCormac, 68/330

Snow, Spencer, 66/386

Snow, Warren S., 67/222

Snow, Zera, 68/330:
biography, 68/330-31; Gold Democratic convention 1896, 68/331-32; photo, 68/330-31

Snow Mountains, SEE Steens Mountain

Snowden, Clinton A., 64/302

Snyder, Mrs. Cecil, 76/387

Snyder, Charles, 79/239

Snyder, Eugene E.:
Early Portland: Stump-Town Triumphant, review, 72/169
Portland Names and Neighborhoods: Their Historic Origins, review, 81/206-207
Skidmore's Portland: His Fountain and Its Sculptor, review, 75/83

Snyder, Hi, 63/279-81,286

Snyder, James W.:
"A Bibliography of the Early American China Trade, 1784-1815," cited,

66/79
So Short a Time: A Biography of John Reed and Louise Bryant, by Gelb, review, 75/84-85
So This Is Klickitat, by Neils, review, 69/68-69
Soap Creek, Benton Co., 65/255
Soap-making, 63/328
Soapstone carving, 68/347
Social Darwinism, 72/209,213,224
Social life, SEE Entertainment; Pioneer life
Social Science Research Council, 63/347
Social work:
Pacific Northwest theses, 72/247-48
Socialist Labor Party of America: papers 1877-1907, 71/363
Socialist Party, 71/215:
Astoria, 74/92; Oregon, 76/137, 140,143,151
Society of Jesus, Northwest Province, 64/78; SEE ALSO Jesuits
Sociology:
Pacific Northwest theses, 72/245-46
Sod House Springs, 78/227: photo, 78/228
Soda Springs, Bear River, 62/370-71; 73/286; 80/83
Sodaville, Ore., 63/363; 73/83: history, 66/91
Sodaville Spring, Linn Co., 66/91; 72/92
Sodaville Spring Park, Linn Co., 63/253
Sodaville Stage Inn, 63/363
Soderini, Tiberius, 69/270
Sofia (ship), 66/127
Sohns, Louis, 77/299
Sohon, Gustavus, 73/278; 80/209: Indian sketches, 69/52
Soil conservation: federal policy 1921-33, 65/205-206
Soldier and Brave: Indian and Military Affairs in the Trans-Mississippi West..., by National Park Service, review, 65/202-203
Soldier (Kaye) Creek, Harney Co., 68/249N
Soldier in the West: Letters of Theodore Talbot, 1845-53, ed. by Hine and Lottin-

ville, review, 74/355-56
Soldiers and Spruce: Origins of the Loyal Legion of Loggers and Lumbermen, by Hyman, review, 65/197-98
Soldiers Who Served in the Oregon Volunteers, Civil War Period, comp. by DAR, Oregon Society, noted, 62/301
Solduck River, 74/19
Sollace, Henry N., 67/359
Solomon, Gus, 70/370
Solomon Islands, 62/30-32
"Some Pioneer Experiences of George Chandler," ed. by W.B. Chandler, 66/197-207
Somekawa family, 81/153
Somerville, Thomas, 63/191
Son of the Lakes, A Story of the Klamath Indians, by Stone, noted, 68/342
Songs, SEE Music
Songs of American West, ed. by Lingenfeltes and Dwyer, noted, 70/78
Songs of the Great American West, comp. by Silver, noted, 70/78
Songs the Whalemen Sang, by Huntington, noted, 65/309
Sonoma County, Calif., 63/325
Sonora (schooner), 71/197
Sons of Freedom, 72/247-48
Sons of Temperance, 64/155-56
Sons of the Union Veterans of the Civil War, 63/91; 66/385
Sons of the Wild Jackass, by Tucker and Barkley, reprint noted, 73/282
Soon-Hi, Korean picture bride, 79/58-60
Sopah (Indian), 79/154,313,314,315, 316,317,324
Sosoly (Indian), 79/313,315
Soule, Cornelius, 71/312
"Sources for History of Blacks in Oregon," by Lenwood G. Davis, 73/197-211
Sousa, John Philip, 78/171
South America: prices at ports 1840s-50s, 77/58
South Bend, Wash., 78/91
South Fork, Coos River, 66/54,56,57
South Fork, Crooked River, 65/23N, 32N,57N; 78/240:

photo, 78/241
South Fork, Deschutes River, 77/330
South Fork, John Day River, 65/22N,41, 72,74N,85,107; 68/231N,303N; 70/23,57: Drake scouts, 65/83; Indian skirmish 1864, 65/73; map, 68/304; military camp, 65/75-76; Snake Indians, 65/ 40,71
South Fork, Malheur River, 65/57N,58N; 68/299N
South Mill Creek, 66/12
South Pass, 62/353N,354; 72/67: described, 65/154; 80/77-78; map, 80/77
South Pass City, Wyo., 72/67
South Pass, 1868: James Chisholm's Journal of the Wyoming Gold Rush, ed. by Homsher, review, 63/242-43
South Platte River, 79/373; 80/69
South Sea, SEE Pacific Ocean
South Sea Company, 76/311,321
South Umpqua Historical Society: publications, 76/92
South Umpqua River, 62/215
South Umpqua Valley: history, 76/92
South Vietnam, 62/41-43
Southeast Asia Treaty Organization, 62/42-45,51
Southern Immigrant Route (Applegate Cutoff), 63/253; 68/255N,257N,340; 69/77,223; 72/7N,33,34,37; 75/238; 77/195-96,292,301,317-18; 79/49, 105; 81/105: casualties, 69/223N,226; hazards, 77/318; Indian attacks, 69/223FF; maps, 65/121; 69/226,228,244,264-65; 72/fr.cov. March; military post, SEE Camp Day; not a cutoff, 77/318; photos, 72/352; travel 1860, 69/241, 250,251,255
Southern Oregon, SEE Oregon, Southern
Southern Oregon College, Ashland, 62/180,182,183: Winburn Hall, 64/340
Southern Oregon Historical Society, 66/388; 73/79: meetings, 70/277; museum, 69/176;

officers and board, 70/83,277; officers and directors, 62/104,415; 63/86, 250; 64/84,280; 65/124,312; 66/85, 279; 67/83,284; 68/85,283; 69/82, 280; 71/195; 72/177; publications, 77/301; 81/328
Southern Oregon Military Wagon Road Company, 74/350
Southern Oregon State Normal School, SEE Southern Oregon College, Ashland
Southern Pacific Company, 64/171,197, 205; 63/304; 64/55; 66/42; 67/ 105,117; 70/181,280; 71/15,197; 72/ 301,310; 73/223; 74/93; 76/235; 77/346-47; 80/209: acquires O&C, 71/73; acquires P R & N, 72/295; Brownsville station, 66/91; Buck Rock tunnel, 67/374; Idaville siding, 72/310-11,312; 73/5; Modoc Line, 71/95,96; photo 5-engine train, 71/74; policy towards Coxey's army, 65/272; postal cards, 66/305; records, 74/79; red electrics, 74/357 routes—
Cascade (Natron) and Siskiyou routes, 71/74,95-96; 80/104; Salem-Medford, 73/347; Tillamook Bay, 77/222
Shasta Daylight, 74/235; wreck, 71/189
Southern Publicity Assn., 75/152,153
Southwell, Mary, 78/218
Southwest Indian Crafts, by Tanner, review, 70/268-69
Southwest Portland Real Estate Co., 69/202,208N
Southworth, Jo Smith: *Millican Memories*, noted, 79/336
Southworth, M.M., 80/145N
Sou'Wester, noted, 67/366; 68/81,184, 340,342; 69/78,331; 70/74,272,358; 72/89,171; 73/73,283; 74/93; 75/ 363; 78/91,364; 80/207,335
Space, Style and Structure: Buildings in Northwest America, ed. by Vaughan and Ferriday, noted, 75/368; 77/291
Spada, Frank, 77/254: photo, 77/252
Spaid, Stanley S., 65/178N
Spain:

American merchants in Calif., 76/199; 62/231-32 American possessions, 73/360; archives opened, 74/353 efforts against Lewis & Clark exped., 81/208— plot to intercept, 74/353 fleet 1898, 76/273-91*passim* in Pacific, 74/285— control, 74/353; exploration, 63/88; 70/77; 73/273; 74/353; landing on Washington coast, 79/408; Nootka Sound, 79/398-400; SEE ALSO Nootka Controversy; Northwest Coast, 76/ 207,213; Pacific NW, 74/353-54; source materials, 65/386; South Pacific interests, 62/11

Spalding, Eliza, daughter of Henry H., SEE Warren, Eliza Spalding

Spalding, Eliza Hart (Mrs. Henry H.), 62/76-77,239; 68/76; 75/77,114

Spalding, Henry Harmon, 62/76,77,192-93,239,240N,332,333; 63/57; 64/243N,274; 69/54; 70/170,347; 71/344; 75/77; 78/338,339; 80/406: anti-Catholicism, 75/113,114,116-17; letter to Blanchet, 75/115,116,117; letter to Waller, 75/116-17; portrait, 75/114

Spalding (Lapwai) Mission, 63/57; 71/ 344; 75/115: excavations, 77/302

Spangle, Wash., 66/51

Spanish-American people: Calif. costume sketches, 73/110,111; Southwest U.S., 73/274

Spanish-American War, 62/11; 72/218, 353; 76/269-98; 79/213; 80/174; 81/131,135,139: action near Manila, 80/177-91; battle of Santiago, 76/289,290(photo),292; capture of Manila, 80/179; effect on Hawaii annexation, 71/164-66,177, 178; fatalities, 80/178,179,183N, 185,187,188; guns, 80/177-78N; Hawaiian assistance, 71/165-66; Miller letters, 66/80 photos, 80/176,180,181,196— veterans, 71/149

Spanish Tom, Auburn outlaw 1862,

Sparks, Bill, 62/205

Sparta, Ore., 79/104

Spaulding, Mrs. —, Westfall resident, 63/301

Spaulding, Josiah, 63/185-86

Spears, F.M., 62/230

Speck, Gordon: *Samuel Hearne and the Northwest Passage,* noted, 65/212

Spelling: pioneer errors, 62/299

Spence, C.E., 74/208

Spence, Mary Lee, and Donald Jackson, eds.:

The Expeditions of John Charles Fremont, Vol. I, Travels from 1838 to 1844, review, 72/165-66

Spence, S.A., comp.: *Captain James Cook: A Bibliography of His Voyages,* noted, 63/84

Spencer, Arthur C., Sr., 71/232

Spencer, Arthur C., III: *David Eccles,* by Arrington, review, 77/296 *Life in California,* by Robinson, review, 71/285 *Recollections and Opinions of an Old Pioneer,* by Burnett, review, 71/285 *Romantic Revolutionary,* by Rosenstone, review, 77/88-89 *So Short a Time,* by Gelb, review, 75/84-85

Spencer, Asahel C., 78/225; 79/8,9,11: biography, 79/22 Free Emigrant Road contractor, 78/62, 64,231,250,294,297,299,303,304, 307,330— money paid to, 78/329; reports road completed to Deschutes, 78/72; 79/5; route, 78/308-309 photo, 78/63

Spencer, Edward, 80/335

Spencer, Hiram, 79/84-85

Spencer, Israel, 74/358

Spencer, Joseph, 63/7,9

Spencer, Omar C., 62/110,206,301, 302,422; 63/93,255,373; 64/93, 189,285,363; 65/125; 68/342;

73/363; 75/6
Spencer, Mrs. Omar C., 73/363
Spencer, Salina, 79/22
Spencer, William V., 65/87N: biography, 65/102N
Spencer Butte, 78/364
Spencer-Clark Import Co., Portland, 71/155N
Spencer Creek, Klamath Co., 69/235: called Elk Creek, 69/265N; map, 69/ins.fr.cov. Sept.; photo, 69/234
Speranskii, Mikhail Mikhailovich, 72/111,113,125
Sperlin, Ottis Bedney, 64/297N
Sperry, Corpus, 78/218N
Sperry, Mary Simpson, 68/269-70
Sperry, William, 78/218N
Spicer, Edward H., ed.: *Perspectives in American Indian Culture Change*, review, 63/347-49
Spicer, Frank, 81/301
Spier, Leslie, 65/200; 69/51; 70/123N: first to identify Christian-pagan Indian customs, 71/325; Prophet Dance theory, 71/325,333-35,337-39
Spier, Robert F.G.: *Man's Rise to Civilization*, by Farb, review, 70/265-66
Spike, Pamela, 66/160N
Spillane, Dennis, 69/147
Spillane, Patrick, 69/147
Spirit of a Cow Bison (Nupika Lukpu) (Indian): Christian neophyte among Kutenai, 71/339-47
Spiritualism, 68/201,203
Spittle, Frank, 81/195
Splawn, Andrew Jackson: *Kamiakin, Last Hero of the Yakimas*, cited, 67/139; 70/125,129,313; quoted, 70/129,163
Splawn, William, 70/133
Spokane, Wash., 63/35; 64/283; 71/196; 72/286; 80/209: early culture, 70/180; economic history, 65/364; free speech fight, 69/325; history, 72/183; lumber industry, 70/180; oldest bank, 66/283
Spokane (steamer), 70/139:

photo, 70/138
Spokane Berens (Indian), 69/53-54: death, 71/336; Red River student, 71/330
Spokane County, Wash.: courthouse, 68/346
Spokane Garry (Indian), 64/283; 69/65; 70/125,161; 73/69: Christian practices, 69/51FF; Jessett biography, 71/325-37*passim*; journey to Red River, 71/329; Red River student, 71/327-31,336; religious influence, 71/332,333-35,336-37; sketch by Sohon, 69/52
Spokane House, 63/90; 71/366; 76/324
Spokane Indians, 65/379; 66/89; 70/115,121,124,150; 72/246; 73/69; 79/101-102: history, 71/187; missions, 71/325-48
The Spokane Indians, Children of the Sun, by Ruby and Brown, review, 73/69
Spokane Oil Speculation Fund, 72/233
Spokane, Portland and Seattle Railway, 71/197; 74/83; 75/364: records, 72/358— traffic dept. 1898-1970, 74/79-82 SEE ALSO Astoria and Columbia River Railroad
Spokesman Review, Spokane, 72/230
Spoon Springs, 78/242
Spooner, Julia, photo, 72/208
Spoop Falls, SEE Rainbow Falls
Spores, Jacob, 67/179; 77/323,324; 78/42,43,53,60,65,69,325N,329,330; 79/7,9,10
Spores Ferry, McKenzie River, 69/276; 78/64; 79/29: rates, 78/64N
Sport fishing, 67/363-64
Sports: baseball in Portland, 71/289; football, 69/137; hunting, 69/106; photos ca. 1920, 80/399,401; wrestling, 69/135
Sportsman, William, 77/317
Spotted Tail's Folk: A History of the Brule Sioux, by Hyde, review, 63/71,74-75
Sprague, Miss —, Coos Valley teacher, 66/55

Sprague, Charles A., 62/110,206,302, 422; 63/71,93,255,362,373; 64/93, 189,285,358,364; 65/126,222,318, 416; 66/93,189,285,394; 67/376,379; 68/356,359,360,361; 69/342,343, 347,348; 70/89,370; 72/264; 74/239; 81/170: Heritage Award, 66/393; rating among Oregon governors, 65/220 Sprague, Franklin B., 73/206 Sprague, Roderick: *Preliminary Bibliography of Washington Archaeology*, noted, 69/276 Sprague, Wash., 63/357 Sprague River, 79/47,290 Spreckels, Claus, 62/202: biography, 68/82 Spreckels, J.D., 71/175 *Sprigs of Rosemary*, by Hartwell, noted, 76/381-82 Spring, Bob and Ira, 69/331-32: *Oregon Wildlife Areas*, noted, 79/409 Spring River, Deschutes Co., 77/331 Spring Valley, Crook Co., 65/50 *Springbank* (ship), 66/122 Springdale, Ore., 81/57 Springer, Frank K., 72/339N Springer, Jake, 79/184 Springfield, Ore., 63/355; 65/212; 77/321; 78/235,319: airport, 78/363 Springs, 68/246,255,256,314; 77/7; 79/376,387,388: Baranov Island, 77/181; California, 80/236,243,245; Cascade Range, 71/189; Clackamas Co., 65/218 hot springs, 65/315; 77/181; 79/278N— Indian myth, 63/362; Oregon, 72/ 287; Vale, 78/139,140,145(photo) Klamath area, 64/351; 78/363; mineral, 76/11; Oregon Trail, 62/346, 347; 80/66-100*passim*; soda, 79/271, 271N,382; Sodaville discovery, 66/91; Warm Springs resort opened, 65/351; western geothermal resources, 72/180; SEE ALSO Annie Spring; Antelope Mt. Spring; Antelope Springs; Atlantic Springs; Barkley Springs; Bingham

Springs; Blue Slaughter Springs; Boswell Springs; Cascadia Soda Springs; Cedar Springs; Cinnabar Springs; Cold Springs; Crystal Spring; Currey Springs; DeMoss Springs; Emigrant Springs; Fisher Springs; Garretson's Medical Springs; Indian Springs; Isaac Spring; Kane Springs; Lehman Springs; Lithia Mineral Springs; McDaid Spring; Mare's Egg Spring; Medical Springs; Mountain Springs; Pacific Springs; Prairie Springs; Roaring Springs; Sage Hen Spring; Sagebrush Springs; Sim-ki-ki Springs; Sod House Springs; Soda Springs; Spoon Springs; Steamboat Springs; Thousand Springs; True Shout Spring; Tub Springs; Well Spring; Wilhoit Springs Sprouse, Mrs. John A., 69/346; 72/ 360; 74/184,365; 75/369; 80/413 Spruance, Raymond A., 62/30 Spruce Production Division, SEE U.S. Spruce Production Corporation Spruce trees, 73/17,24: airplane stock, 72/301,308; Engelmann's, 69/167; largest, 73/172-74, 225; photos, 72/302,303,ins.bk.cov. Dec.; 73/172,225; Sitka spruce described, 69/152; timber, 72/301,306, 308,310 Spry, Irene M., 65/215; 66/70 Spry, William, 79/9,10 Squalth (Indian), SEE Skwalth Squamish Indians, 72/245,250 Squatters, 63/11,175-76,185,220; 73/341,344 *Squaw Man's Son*, by Lampman, noted, 80/336 Squaw Rock, Siskiyou Co., 66/82 Squaxin Indians, 72/148 Squirrels: migrations, 69/11-12 Staats, Stephen, 64/275 Stack, P.J., 69/147 Staconey (Indian), 79/150,158,313, 315,317,323 Stadelman, George, 70/374; 72/360; 74/184,365 Stafford, Mrs. —, Auburn teacher,

62/233
Stafford, Jim, 81/177,178
Stafford, Lang, 71/357
Stafford, William E.:
biography, 81/174; photo, 81/178
Stafford, William E.:
"A Poet Responds," 81/172-79
Stafford, William M., 62/218N,222
Stafford, Ore., 67/273
Stafrin, Conrad, 77/266,268
Stafrin, Mildred, 78/159
Stafrin, Ruby, 78/159
Stag Hound (clipper ship), 63/359
Stagecoach to Linkville, noted, 75/86
Stagecoach transportation, 66/52,228; 70/278; 73/260,261; 76/39; 79/ 169N,170,269:
Bannock War attacks, 70/15; Central Ore. photo, 77/25
coaches—
Concord, 76/54,55-56; described, 66/281-82; mail, 69/88; Shaniko, photo, 69/302; Yellowstone, photo, 74/336
described, 70/12-13; Douglas Co., 68/342; drivers, 76/55; express, 79/ 154,155; fares, 71/19,23,59; Klamath country, 75/86; mail coaches Coos Co., 69/88; memories of, 70/279; overland 1860s, 66/81; photos, 72/168; 77/ 25; robberies, 66/81; 71/189,286
routes, 66/299—
Albany-Corvallis, 71/19; Ashland-Klamath Falls, 69/338; Ashland-Lakeview, 77/155; Atchison-Walla Walla, 71/59; Boise-Kelton, Utah, 68/229N,239; Caldwell-Jordan Valley, 76/158; Chicago-San Francisco, 71/59; Crescent City-Waldo, 76/53, 54; Deadwood-Miles City, Mont., 74/ 334-36; Eugene-Mapleton, 69/329; Grants Pass-Crescent City, 76/39,50-51,53-59; Heppner-Pendleton, 69/ 135; Hood River-Mt. Hood, 75/101; 79/203-204,209-10; Idaho-Sacramento Valley, 64/86; Kelton, Utah-Umatilla, 68/298; Monticello-Olympia, 62/321; Nevada-California-Idaho, 68/348; Omaha-Boise, 71/59; Ore-

gon-California, 63/92,357; Ore. City-Salem, 68/90; Pendleton-Ukiah, 69/ 119; Roseburg-Redding, 72/88; Sacramento-Portland, 71/59; 72/91,107; Salem-Chico, 62/322; Salt Lake-Walla Walla, 71/59; Scottsburg-Drain, 80/51-52; Shaniko-Lakeview, 77/28; Shaniko-Prineville, 66/183; Southern Ore.-Portland, 80/13; The Dalles-Canyon City, 64/90; Walla Walla-Boise, 71/59; Wallula Landing-Walla Walla, 66/229; Willamette Valley-Coos River, 66/52; Winnemucca-Boise, 68/238N; Winnemucca-Burns, 68/304-307,309; Yreka-Jacksonville, 72/41N,ins.fr.cov. March (map) stations, 62/201; 63/274,282; 76/ 56-59,85—
Burnt River, 72/94; Bute's, 68/229; Cayuse, 69/227,232,297; 70/12,27; Cole Ranch, 68/353; Corder's, 68/ 239,242N,309N; Dixie Creek, 68/ 239N,242,309N; Inskip, 71/264N; Meacham, 69/227,228,233,306; 70/ 12; Mountain House, 68/352; Parrish home, 68/187; Skinner's, 68/ 248; Snake River site photo, 68/298; Starveout, 66/81; Summit, 68/251N; Twelve Mile House, 68/145; Weston, 70/12,27; Wilson's, 68/229N
The Dalles, 69/133; Tillamook Co., 77/91; travel time, 76/39,59; SEE ALSO Butterfield Overland Mail Co.; Hamman Stage Lines; Northwest Stage Co.; Overland Stage Line
Stagg, John, family, 80/171-72
Staiger, William, 79/243
Staley, W.I., 80/281
Staling, G.W., 66/119,121,122
Stallcop, Fred, 64/276
Stampede Lake, SEE Mud Lake
Stamper, Jack, railroad brakeman, 73/175
Stampfl, Peter, 70/316
Stanbery, Margaret Hart, 68/149,152
Standard, Portland, 75/127,128
Standard Theatre, Portland, 66/40,41
Standing Bear (Indian), 63/247
Standing Rock, 65/154

Standish, Philander H., 67/367
Stanfield, Robert Nelson, 69/107; 74/224; 75/173,175; 76/355-56; 77/12,21,24,168; 78/280: 1918 election campaign, 68/130-37; photo, 68/131
Stanfield, Ore., 63/365; 64/90; 73/ 285; 77/22,27,28,171: name, 69/138
Stanford, James, 69/331
Stanford, Leland, 71/283; 72/130; 73/86
Stanford, Omer: *Sage Brush and Axle Grease*, review, 80/103-104
Stanford University, 74/200
Stangland, Carl, 69/311N,322N
Stanley, G.F.G., 72/182
Stanley, John Mix, 64/5; 65/138,138N; 80/209
Stansbury, Howard, 65/168,313: maps— 1852, 62/insert Sept.; Oregon Trail 1849, 80/72,77
Stanton, Alexander Hamilton, 79/ 281N,292
Stanton, Alfred, 68/163N
Stanton, Charles E., 74/222
Stanton, Edwin McMasters, 79/129
Stanton, Elizabeth Olney, 64/321N
Stanton, Glenn: "The Night Dr. Barclay's House Was Moved," 76/302-303
Stanton, H.C.: recollections, 71/189,286
Staples, George W., 80/141-42
Stapleton, James P., 74/211
Star of Oregon (schooner), 69/337
Star Point, Benton Co., 65/121
Starbuck, Valentine, 64/7,9,29-30
Stark, Asa, 62/197
Stark, Benjamin, 65/217; 80/142: accused of disloyalty, 72/327-28,332; appointed U.S. Senator, 72/326; biography, 72/317-38; 73/31-59; borrows money from Bush, 72/327N; Breckenridge Democrat, 73/52; building, 72/ 320(photo),331; business interests, 72/ 317; 73/56; Democratic convention,

73/55; letters, 73/31N,42N-56Npassim; move to Connecticut, 73/56; nicknames, 72/319; obituary, 73/56; Ore. constitutional convention, 72/321, 323N; photo, 72/318; political career, 72/316-58passim; Portland land claim, 72/317-18,319,322,331-32,332N; relations with Lane, 72/319,321-27passim; senate voting record, 73/52 U.S. Senate seat dispute, 72/315-38: loyalty debate, 73/31-40,43,44-50; newspaper comments, 73/43-44,54, 55N; investigation committee, 73/ 46-51
views on public schools, 72/319,331, 331N; views on secession, 72/323-24, 329-30,332,336
Stark, Bob, 76/387
Stark, Elizabeth Molthrop (Mrs. Benjamin), 72/319; 73/53N,56,61N
Stark, Richard, 72/325,326N
Starkey, John, 68/234N
Starkweather, Harvey G., 74/208
Starkweather, William A., 64/152
Starling, Edmund A.: biography, 70/259; Willamette Valley map, 70/258-61
Starling (schooner), 63/189,199
Starr, Addison M., 72/331-32; 80/21,142,142N,150N,156N
Starr, Ina Draper Hart, 72/93
Starr, Lewis M., 80/142
Starr, Lint, 66/142
Starr, N.A., Springfield 1881, 71/17
Starveout stage station, 66/81
State Historical Society of Missouri: publications, 79/106-107
State Line Herald, Lakeview, 66/171N
State of California (steamer), 71/21: 1883 schedule, 71/ins.fr.cov. March
Stations West, The Story of the Oregon Railways, by Culp, review, 75/85-86
Statues: elk, Portland, 80/59; Lewis and Clark, 81/329; McLoughlin, John, 80/101; Roosevelt, Theodore, 66/385; Sacajawea, 81/329
Status Rerum, by H.L. Davis *et al*, 71/182,368:

cited, 73/302,310
Stauff, George, family, 63/26
Stauffer, John, Sr., 79/250
Stauffer, Ore., 79/337
Staver, LeRoy, 80/413
Stayton, Ore., 67/62; 68/187:
Gardner house, 65/218; pioneer
(Grier) cemetery, 64/354
Stead, William T., 63/360; 65/264-
65N,271,293-94N
Steadman, Robert, 62/180
Steam donkeys, SEE Locomotives
Steam engines, 75/69; 81/190
Steam shovels, 72/311,312,313;
73/8,17:
photo, 72/292
Steam Whaling in the Western Arctic, by
Bockstoce *et al*, noted, 79/106
Steamboat Creek, Jackson and Josephine
cos., 62/215
Steamboat Slough, 75/106
Steamboat Springs, 62/371-72; 79/382;
80/83
Steamboats, 75/82-83,332,335:
Coeur d'Alene Lake, 70/357; Columbia River, 63/31,65,84,361; 65/120;
66/52,229; 74/163-64,358
companies, 63/61,65—
Cowlitz River, 63/108; rivalry,
63/64-66,68,84,108N
Cowlitz River, 66/80; "dog and
broom" symbol, 63/64-65; Flathead
Lake, 75/286; Klamath Basin, 64/356;
Klamath Co., 66/88; Klamath Lakes,
66/382; list of references, 72/89; Missouri River, 74/354; Pacific Northwest,
63/61-66; 65/305; Portland-Rainier
1904, 81/35; racing, 63/61,64-65,68;
river steamers, 67/88; Saskatchewan
River, 65/314; 66/88; Snake River,
63/359; western, 66/274
Steamboats in the Timber, by Hult, 2nd ed.
review, 70/357
Steamboats on the Western Rivers, by Hunter, cited, 66/274
Steamships, SEE Vessels
Stearns, Daniel W., 69/330
Stearns, David Lloyd:
Of Yesterday and the River, by Crithfield,

review, 65/306-307
Stearns, David S., photo, 74/234
Stearns, Orson Avery, 64/356; 78/363
Stearns, Samuel Eastman, 64/169
Stebbins, Ellis A.:
The OCE Story, noted, 74/282
Steckler, Gerard G., 70/178:
"Charles John Seghers, Missionary
Bishop," cited, 70/312N
"The Founding of Mount Angel
Abbey," 70/312-32
Steeb, —, U.S. Shipping Commissioner,
66/113
Steel, George A., 69/208N,209
Steel, James, 69/208N,221N
Steel, William Gladstone:
Crater Lake excursion 1903, 81/53;
map of Olympic Mts., 74/8; photo,
81/44; superintendent Crater Lake
National Park, 81/43
Steel industry:
Oregon scrap, 72/287
Steel manufacturing:
Washington, 64/87
Steele, Alden H., 68/38N
Steele, Frederick F., 79/141:
biography, 79/141N; camp named for,
79/149; "extermination" order, 79/
149N,329; Indian scout controversy,
79/128-29; opinion of Indian scouts,
79/304N,330; reviews Indian scouts,
79/142
Steele, J.S., 65/395
Steen, Enoch, 65/66N; 68/41; 69/
252N,253N-54N:
biography, 79/274-75; road exploration, 65/6N,28N,38N,48N,59N,61;
79/38-41
Southeast Ore. exploration, 72/55—
Harney Valley, 79/38-42; routes,
79/34-35(map),149N
Snake campaigns, 65/117N; 72/55;
79/41-42,130
Steen, Harold K.:
The U.S. Forest Service: A History, review,
78/280
Steens Mountain, 63/304,307,310; 65/
55,58,63,68; 67/22; 68/230N,237,
249,299N,320,329; 69/62-63; 70/

21N,57; 78/210,220; 79/274: Indian land, 81/399; name, 79/42, 274N; photos, 63/308; 67/24; 77/152; survey efforts, 68/321-27

Steens Mountain in Oregon's High Desert Country, by Jackman and Scharff, review, 69/62-63

Steens-Pueblo Mountains, 73/228, 231,241

Steep Trails, by Muir, reprint noted, 72/173

Steffen, Jerome O.: *William Clark: Jeffersonian Man on the Frontier*, review, 79/100-101

Steffens, Lincoln, 72/180

Stegner, Wallace, 72/181

Steilacoom, Wash., 62/85; 72/133

Steinbach, Hanna Stauffer, 79/250

Steinbach, John, 79/250

Steinbeck, John, 65/313

Steinberger, Justus, 65/98,392,398: asks Ft. Umpqua abandonment, 70/255; biography, 65/98N-99N

Stein's Ridge, Crook Co., 77/335: inscription on rock, 77/333; photos, 77/332

Steiwer, Frederick, 74/233: family, 67/75

Steiwer, Jack P., Jr., 68/356,359,361; 69/347; 70/371,372,374; 72/359; 73/362,373; 74/363,365,366; 75/ 370; 76/388; 77/387; 78/369; 79/411,416

Steiwer, William H., 64/101N

Stella, Wash., 66/181; 81/38: photos, 66/178; 75/ins.fr.cov. June

Steller jay, 65/220

Steller sea lion, 65/220

Stem Winder Mining Co., 69/208,212, 213,220N,222

Stemalth (Indian), 79/313,314,315, 317,318,324

Stembridge, J.E., ed.: *Pathfinder, The First Automobile Trip from Newport to Siletz Bay, Oregon, July, 1912*, noted, 81/327

Stenzel, Franz R., 65/215; 77/289: *Cleveland Rockwell*, noted, 77/289 *James Madison Alden, Yankee Artist of the*

Pacific Coast, 1854-1860, noted, 77/289

Stenzel, Katheryne, 77/289

Stephan, John J.: *Kuril Islands: Russo-Japanese Frontier in the Pacific*, noted, 77/290

Stephens, E.A., 69/213N

Stephens, James B., 62/147; 64/144

Stephens, John H., 68/297N

Stephens, Oren M., 62/202

Stephenson, Clarence Bruce (Bill), 62/ 110,206,302,419-22; 63/93,255,367-69,373; 64/93,189,285,358,364; 65/ 126,222,318,412,416; 66/93,189, 285,394; 67/379; 68/359,361; 69/348; 70/372,374; 72/360

Stephenson, Wendell Holmes: memorial fund, 72/172

Steptoe, Edward Jenner, 63/89; 67/ 224N; 68/42,75; 69/79; 70/170,367; 71/198; 73/73; 79/131: reinforces Wright, 67/322; Utah expedition, 67/326N

Steptoe Butte, 70/181

Stereopticon, 80/371: photo, 80/372

Sterling, Donald J., Jr., 62/205; 63/ 363; 69/342,348; 70/372,374; 73/ 362; 74/184; 76/387; 77/388; 78/ 369-70; 79/410-14,415; 80/410-14: *Journalists in the Making*, by Turnbull, reviews, 67/360-61 "A Mountain Meadow," 75/39-42

Sterling, Donald J., Sr., photo, 74/214

Sterling, Mrs. Donald J., Sr., 65/415

Sterling, James, Jacksonville miner, 66/75

Sterling, James, Major survey guide, 72/25N,41,41N

Sterling, Julie, and Linda Lampman: *A Portland Guide Book*, noted, 77/291

Sterling Creek, 66/75-76

Stern, Theodore, 63/246,362: *The Klamath Tribe, A People and Their Reservation*, review, 67/356

Stern, Theodore, *et al*: "A Cayuse-Nez Percé Sketchbook," 81/341-76

Sternberg, Charles Hazelius, 67/17

Sternlicht, Sanford: *McKinley's Bulldog: The Battleship Oregon*, review, 79/212-13

Sternwheelers, Sandbars and Switchbacks..., by Affleck, noted, 74/358

Stettler *vs.* O'Hara, 62/94-95

Steunenberg, A.K., 68/88

Stevens, —, capt. of *Whitlieburn*, 66/107

Stevens, —, The Dalles 1879, 70/139,140

Stevens, Benjamin D., 69/88

Stevens, Charles: 1867 letters, 76/180

Stevens, Edward T.C., 79/203

Stevens, Harley C., 72/71,71N

Stevens, Harriet F.: journal, 65/216

Stevens, Hazard, 62/310N

Stevens, Henry, and Roland Tree: *Comparative Cartography*, reprint noted, 69/79

Stevens, Henry C.C., 79/203N: album photos, 79/205,207,208

Stevens, Isaac Ingalls, 62/73,85,315,330; 63/82,84,176N,181,187,221,228; 64/302-303; 65/215,345; 66/33,34N; 67/311; 68/75; 69/41; 70/21N,114, 115,119; 71/49,81; 79/129,136; 80/209: Lander dispute, 66/32; Walla Walla councils, 67/313,318N; Wool criticizes, 67/313,318N

Stevens, J.D., 68/201,205,208,210,216, 217,218,219

Stevens, James, 74/155-56,173-74: recollections, 71/368

Stevens, James: *Brawnyman*, cited, 73/300; 74/155 *Paul Bunyan*, cited, 73/189,300 *Status Rerum*, cited, 73/302,310; 74/157

Stevens, John Frank, 67/87; 71/364; 73/86

Stevens, Mary (Mrs. Edward T.C.), 79/203,205(photo)

Stevens, Mary Crawford (Mrs. Harley C.), 72/71

Stevens, William M., 63/83; 77/324;

79/9,10

Stevens Pass, 71/364

Stevenson, Cassie, 63/290

Stevenson, George, 66/382

Stevenson family, overland 1853, 78/154

Steveston, B.C., 72/286

Steward, Irene, 74/63

Stewart, —, Queets area settler, 74/19

Stewart, Agnes, SEE Warner, Agnes Stewart

Stewart, Billy, Grant Co. stockman, 70/57,58

Stewart, C.B., 64/70

Stewart, Charles S., 64/16

Stewart, D.E., 62/179

Stewart, Elinore Pruitt: *Letters of a Woman Homesteader*, facsimile ed. noted, 63/247

Stewart, Elizabeth Redington, 80/121(photo): "My Darling Red Bird," 80/117-33

Stewart, Frank A.: Curry Co. history, 68/352; 70/279

Stewart, George R.: *John Phoenix, Esq., The Veritable Squibob: A Life of Capt. H. Derby, U.S.A.*, review, 71/188

Stewart, Helen: trail diary 1853, 78/123,132,149

Stewart, Hugh, 79/15,16N,49

Stewart, Janet, 78/123

Stewart, John, immigrant of 1853, 78/123,154,325-26: genealogy, 66/81; photo, 78/122

Stewart, Joseph, 70/18N,19: Ft. Umpqua duty, 69/223N; 70/ 235-45*passim*

Stewart, Loren, 62/111,207,303,421, 422; 63/93,255,373; 64/93,189,285, 363; 65/125,221,317

Stewart, Maurice B., 69/29N

Stewart, Omer C., 63/356

Stewart, Peter G., 73/255

Stewart, William Drummond, 65/136, 138-39,146-47,153

Stewart, William Morris: biography, 65/313

Stewart Bridge, Lane Co., 66/187

Stewarts (Bear?) Creek, Jackson Co.: maps, **69**/228,262,263

Stickus (Stickas) (Indian), **73**/285; **81**/403

Stikine River, **63**/189,227

Stimmel, Tom, **75**/41

Stine House Hotel, Walla Walla, **70**/10

Stingle, Jim, **63**/268

Stinkingwater Creek (Slough), **78**/211; **79**/298N

Stipp, H.S., **64**/38

Stirrups, SEE Prices

Stirton, R.A., **67**/34

Stinson, Ashby Logan, **64**/172,176,181; **67**/61

Stitzel, Jacob, **80**/140N,157

Stock (Indian), **70**/36

Stock, Chester, **67**/26

Stock exchanges, **69**/197-222*passim*: callers, **69**/204

Stock Whitley (Stock-ote-ly) (Indian), **65**/37; **66**/318N: characterized, **65**/49N; death, **65**/48-49; Indian scout leader, **65**/11,21; Snake battle, **65**/31,32,34-35

Stockton, Robert F., **66**/87; **70**/307

Stockton, Calif., **68**/260,339,348

Stockwell, Samuel B., **65**/167

Stoddard, Lothrop: "Into the Darkness," cited, **78**/115; Pierce recollections, **78**/115-17

Stoeckl, Edward de, **75**/332,333

Stokes, Ted: "Escape by Land: *Lightship No. 50*," **69**/307-23

Stoll, Marie, photo, **74**/265

Stone, Buena Cobb, **69**/223N: *Fort Klamath, Frontier Post in Oregon, 1863-1890*, review, **66**/76-77 *Son of the Lakes, A Story of the Klamath Indians*, noted, **68**/342

Stone, Charles P., **73**/58

Stone, Charley: log chute near Garibaldi, **71**/133

Stone, Ebenezer W., **68**/228,229N

Stone, J. Herbert, **78**/280: "An Oregon Heritage," **76**/29-38 *Civilian Conservation Corps*, by Salmond, review, **69**/65-66

Stone Age in the Great Basin, by Strong, review, **70**/352

Stone House, Vale, **68**/230N; **70**/ 17,18,19

Stone Ledge ford, Williamson River, **68**/358

Stoneberg, Frank, **79**/339

Stoner, Don, **68**/349

Stoops, John, family, **79**/13

Stoops, William, **64**/91

Storer, Samuel, **72**/135

Stores: Agness, **76**/79; Ashland hardware, **64**/ 333,339; Ashwood, **77**/160(photo), 161; Brown Ranch, **77**/23; drygoods, **75**/15; Eugene, **79**/6N; Ft. Laramie area, **79**/375; Grass Valley, **75**/45-47; grocery, **75**/48; Hockinson, Wash., **72**/89; Hood River, **76**/242; Italian, **77**/254; Japanese, **76**/229(photo),230, 232,249; Lake Quinault, **74**/31; Lane Co., **78**/43,58; mercantile in early Ore., **62**/66; Millican, **77**/18; Oregon City, **74**/282; Portland ca. 1895, **75**/15-16; prices 1896, **72**/89; Queets River, **74**/ 25,32; Waldo, **76**/81-82; Westfall, **63**/ 286,288; Wilderville, **76**/56; Wonder, **76**/56; SEE ALSO Anthony and Huddleston's store; Belknap's store; Bolt's Corner; Calahan Store and Bar; City Book Store; Crosby and Smith; Drug stores; Erving's store; Finseth's Mercantile Store; Garibaldi Grocery; Hedden's Store; Italian Delicatessen; Jones' Book Store; Oro Fino Store; Patton Bros. bookstore; Turner's store

Storm, Colton, comp.: *A Catalogue of the Everett D. Graff Collection of Western Americana*, review, **70**/64-66

Story, Irving, **65**/211

Story Creek, **78**/320

Story of Crater Lake National Park, by Place, noted, **75**/363

The Story of Lige Coalman, by White, review, **74**/88-89

The Story of the Pump, and Its Relatives, by Eubanks, noted, **73**/73

The Story of Wallowa Lake, by Bartlett,

noted, 69/330
Stott, Raleigh, 62/169
Stout, Elizabeth, 73/332N
Stout, Ephraim, 73/332N
Stout, Jonathan, 68/182
Stout, Lansing, 80/168
Stout, Lewis, 64/354; 65/218; 73/332N: family, 70/272
Stout, Ray L., 65/415: "Over the Brush and Through the Trees: Surveying, 1900-1909," 73/332-58
Stovall, Alva E.: biography, 72/281-85; photos, 72/282,285
Stovall, Charles, photo, 72/282
Stovall, Dennis, 72/283,284: *Suzanne of Kerbyville*, cited, 72/283
Stovall, Frank, photo, 72/282
Stovall, George, family, 72/281-85
Stovall, William, photo, 72/282
Stoves, photo, 74/25
Stoy, William H., 64/174
Strahan, Philip, 77/90
Strahorn, Robert E., 69/337
Strait of Anian, 76/312
Strait of Georgia, 66/69
Strait of Juan de Fuca, 62/9; 74/354: charts, 72/356
Strait of Magellan, 76/279; 77/41
Strand, A.L., 74/235: *Management of Land and Related Water Resources in Oregon*, by McKinley, review, 68/176-77
Strangers on the Land, by Relander, noted, 64/351
Strasser, Conrad, 81/310
Stratton, Riley Evans, 66/17; 70/254
Stratton, Thomas, 81/332
Stratton, Winfield S., 69/204
Straub, John, 69/77
Strawberries, 76/234,242: plants brought to Oregon, 68/ 162,163N
Strawberry Mountain, 65/70N
Strawn, John: *The Black West: A Documentary and Pictorial History*, by Katz, review,

73/279-80
Streater, Charles, 74/29
Streater, Jane Donaldson, 74/29,29N,30: photo, 74/28
Street cars, 74/281; 80/61,241: 1905 fare, 80/64; photo, 80/58; Portland, 75/20,28,57-58; SEE ALSO Railroads—street railways
The Streets We Live On, by Clarke, noted, 80/105
Strikes, 74/81: Coeur d'Alene mines, 63/90; cowboys, 74/280; Seattle 1919, 63/90; 66/73-74; 75/151; waterfront 1934, 74/233
Strimp, Henry, 62/219N
Strite, Beatrice Crouley, 73/227-28; 77/354,357
Strite, Daniel D., 72/293N; 73/227: photos, 72/292; 73/4
Strite, Daniel D.: *How to Become a Logger*, cited, 73/28,187 "Hurrah for Garibaldi!" 77/213-37, 341-68 *Medford Corporation*, by LaLande, review, 81/205-206 "Up the Kilchis," 72/293-314; 73/5-30,171-92,212-27
Strite, Richard, 73/17
Strohecker, Armand, 63/363
Stromberg, William, 73/23,222
Strong, Caroline, 64/305N
Strong, Curtis C., 64/305N; 75/33
Strong, Dexter K., 67/158
Strong, Ellen, 64/305N
Strong, Emory: *The Chinook Indians*, by Ruby and Brown, review, 79/98-100 *Stone Age in the Great Basin*, review, 70/352 *Wakemap Mound, A Stratified Site on the Columbia River*, review, 62/89-90
Strong, Fred B., 64/305N
Strong, Henry Pierce, 64/293,294
Strong, J.E., 64/158
Strong, James Clark, 62/58-59; 64/295: biography, 64/294N
Strong, Laura (Mrs. Henry Pierce), 64/293
Strong, Lucretia Robinson (Mrs. Wil-

liam), 62/58,62; 64/294,296-97N, 305N

Strong, Mary Elizabeth Stone, photo, 75/62

Strong, Robert H., 71/226

Strong, Ronald T.: "The Old Wood Roads," 75/56-66

Strong, Thomas Nelson, 62/57-58; 64/297,305N; 65/273,275; 75/57: family and residence photos, 75/62

Strong, Thomas Nelson: *Cathlamet on the Columbia*, cited, 62/58; 74/37

Strong, William, 63/186,188,196,245; 66/34,35,166; 67/269; 75/351: appointment, 64/293; appraisal of, 64/306-307; arrival in Ore., 64/295; assoc. justice Wash. Terr., 64/304; biography, 64/293-307; capital controversy role, 64/300; capt. in Indian wars, 64/303; cases, 64/299; disputes with Pratt, 64/299-301,309; OSNCO. counsel, 64/304; photo, 62/60; Wash. Terr. code, 64/302-303

Strong, William: "Knickerbocker Views of the Oregon Country: Judge William Strong's Narrative," 62/57-87

Strong, William Duncan, son of Thomas Nelson, 64/293N: biography, 62/57-61

Strong, William J., son of William, 64/305N; 75/61,63

Stroughton, Alex R., 62/143

Strowbridge, Joseph Allen, 75/137

Struan (ship), 62/200: photo, 66/100

Strugle, A., 74/18

Stuart, Frederick D.: map, 65/137

Stuart, Grace D., 62/197,202,298; 63/91

Stuart, Granville, 71/366

Stuart, James, capt. Ore. Mounted Rifles, 67/369; 68/351

Stuart, James C., 67/70

Stuart, Reginald R., 62/197,202,298; 63/91

Stuart, Robert, 71/316N; 75/86; 77/81

Stubbs, —, Tacoma chaplain, 66/115

Stuck, Hudson, 72/180

Studebaker, Peter, 71/152

A Study of the Pioneer Museum and Historic Tradition of Brownsville, Oregon, noted, 66/383

Stummanu (Indian), SEE Brooks, William

Stump, Mortimer, 63/92

Sturgeon, 75/223,226; 79/176: photo, 74/299

Sturgis, Russell, 76/208,223

Sturgis, William, 75/321; 76/ 83,210,213-16: commercial interests on NW Coast, 72/ 115,116; portrait, 76/204; protests Russian territorial claims, 72/114,116

Sturtevant, Andrew Jackson, 79/303N

Suard (Seward?), Smith, 66/147N

Subject Index to the History of the Pacific Northwest and of Alaska as Found in U.S. Government Documents, 1789-1881, by Judson, noted, 71/79

Sublette, Milton G., 64/282

Sublette, Solomon P.: biography, 66/185

Sublette, William Lewis, 66/64; 81/235

Sublette Cutoff, 62/105,354N,362N; 63/88; 80/78,79,80

Sublimity, Ore., 70/316

Submarines, 80/32,35,49: Japanese off Ore. coast, WW II, 65/219,314— chart of course, 65/insert Dec. Kiska base, 80/41

Succor Creek, 68/299N: area history, 68/354

Suda, Mrs. —, Portland Assembly Center, 81/157,158

Sudduth, Susan, and Steven Tanasoca, eds.:

"A Journal Kept By George A. Harding," 79/172-202

Sue H. Elmore (steamer), 73/8

Suffrage, SEE Woman suffrage

Sugar: cane, 73/261; Hawaiian reciprocity treaty, 71/173,175; Sugar Trust, 71/ 173,175; SEE ALSO Prices; Sugar beets

Sugar beets, 69/275:

industry, 77/296—
Japanese workers 1942, **81**/158,170
Union Co., **63**/253
Sugimoto, Rev. —, Portland Assembly Center, **81**/153
Suicide, **75**/358
Sulktashkosha, SEE Moses (Indian)
Sullivan, Gabrielle:
Martin Murphy, Jr., California Pioneer, 1844-1884, noted, **75**/365
Sullivan, J.W.:
Direct Legislation by the Citizenship Through the Initiative and Referendum—
distributed, **68**/208; used by Progressives, **68**/206-207
Sullivan, Patrick, **69**/147
Sullivan Gulch, **64**/264; **74**/286
Sully, Alfred, **66**/87
Sully, Thomas, **65**/141; **66**/87
Sulphur (British vessel), **63**/189,199
Sumas, Wash., **62**/96-97; **74**/203
Sumerlin, Grade, 80/63N
Summer Creek, **79**/293
Summer Lake, **67**/22,37; **77**/25, 157,158; **79**/293N
Summer resorts, **74**/129-30; **75**/339
Summer Valley, **79**/293
Summers, George, **64**/226N:
Ft. George described, **64**/222N-23N
Summers, Jake, **63**/23
Summers, Mary Ellen, SEE Cooney, Mary Ellen
Summers, Michael, family, **69**/147
Summersville, Curry Co., **63**/23
Summerville (Somerville), Ore., **70**/31; **79**/17
Summit Creek, **78**/58
Summit Lake, **76**/104; **78**/57,299
Summit Valley, Malheur Co., SEE Bear Valley
Sumner, Charles:
photo, **73**/32; Stark senate seat dispute, **72**/333-38; **73**/33,37-38,41,44-45, 50-51
Sumner, Edwin Vose, **68**/235,237, 248N,249N,308; **70**/254N
Sumner, Walter Taylor, **74**/217
Sumner, Ore., **66**/52

Sumpter, Ore., **73**/83:
history, **69**/78
Sumpter Valley:
land prices, **73**/83
Sumpter Valley Dredging Company, **69**/78
Sumpter Valley Railroad, **69**/78; **73**/83
Sunday, Billy, photo, **78**/171
Sunder, John E., **64**/85:
The Fur Trade on the Upper Missouri, 1840-1865, review, **66**/273-74
Sunoo, Sonia S.:
"Korean Women Pioneers of the Pacific Northwest," **79**/51-63
Sunriver Properties, **79**/294-95N
Suplee, Ore., **77**/90
Supplee, L.M., **63**/35
Supply (U.S. storeship), **62**/63; **64**/295,297N,298
The Supreme Court in a Free Society, by Mason and Beaney, review, **62**/93-95
Supreme Order of the Star Spangled Banner, **75**/118-19
Surf Duck (sailboat), **74**/29,30:
photo, **74**/28
Surprise Valley, **72**/28; **79**/127; **81**/328:
boundary survey, **72**/15; name, **72**/15
Survey of the Arts in Oregon, Report of the Governor's Planning Council, noted, **68**/342
Surveyors, **81**/25N,194:
contract form, **72**/19-21; deputy surveyors, **73**/334; instructions, **72**/25N;
U.S. Surveyor General, **73**/334; wages, **72**/19,19N
Surveys and surveying, **73**/360; **77**/221:
boundary surveys—
California, **72**/12-53*passim*; Indian lands, **72**/18; Houghton-Ives, **72**/14-17,48,52,53; international boundary 1872-76, **66**/69-71; Major, SEE
Major, Daniel; Mason-Dixon, **72**/45N; Nevada, **72**/10-53*passim*
Oregon-California—
1854, **72**/10-12,43N; 1868-73, **72**/18-53; 1913, **72**/38; 1916, **72**/36-37; 1919, **72**/37; 1921, **72**/38; 1952, **72**/38

Oregon-Idaho 1867, 72/19; Oregon-Washington 1854, 72/19; reconciliation, 72/47N; townships and subdivisions, 73/334,336,339,345,348,354; 74/24; Utah 1871, 72/19; Washington-Montana 1885, 72/19 British Columbia, 77/303; catchall sections, 75/233; chains described, 72/29N; contracts, 73/334,335; Cook marine survey, North Pacific, 69/79; costs and appropriations, 72/10,11N, 13,14N,19,20N; camps, 73/335, 349-51,352-56 crews, 73/334,338,351— Alaska 1898 photo, 81/116,fr.cov. Summer cooks, 73/335,349-51,352-56; Curry Co., 78/363 difficulties, 72/26N,36N— brush, 72/42N,44; earthquakes, 72/28; Indians, 72/12-13,15,16-17,18N, 19N; legislative confusion, 72/7-9 Douglas Co., 78/364; federal in West, 75/365; first in Ore. Terr., 62/301; immigrant road, 77/318; Indian reservations, 74/24 instruments, 72/10,21-23,26— 1872-76, 66/71; solar compass, 63/51; 73/334,335,336 maps, 72/covs. March meridians, 72/11N— Greenwich, 72/8,9,18,53; London, 72/8; 120th, 72/12,17,49,49N; U.S. ambiguities, 72/7-9; Washington, 72/8-9; Willamette, 72/14,42,47 military roads, 77/330; SEE ALSO Oregon Central Military Road monuments and memorials, 72/17,28, 48,51,52-53— Ore.-Calif.-Nev. corner, 72/17,28, 48,51,52-53— photos, 72/4,16,24,50 photos, 72/30,32,40,44; types used by Major, 72/31-33 national forests, 76/31 Oregon, 73/347-48— first, 62/301; map 1863, 79/ins.fr. cov. Spring Owyhee expedition, 79/47; procedures,

73/334; public lands, 72/14N,47N,53N; railroads, 72/308-309, 313-14; 74/7-16; SEE ALSO Pacific Railroad Survey; road viewers, SEE Elliott Cutoff; roads, 74/108 supplies, 73/342,351— packing, 73/349,351,352,356— photo, 73/350 techniques, 72/10-53*passim*— astronomic, 72/45N; astronomical stations, 72/23,25,25N,34,36,42,49N; geodetic, 72/45N; lunar culminations, 72/26-28; tangents, 72/11; telegraph use, 72/13,20N,48,49,49N trail-breaking, 73/349,351,352,354; Washington, 73/334-35,349-58; Wash. coast, 63/92; Wheeler survey records, 65/313; White Pass, 81/113-34; "witness tree" use, 69/339; "witnesses," 72/31,32(photo) *Susan G. Owens* (ship), 65/7 *Susan Sturges* (schooner), 63/360 Susanville, Calif., 72/9 Susanville, Ore., 64/91; 69/110; 79/303 Sutherland, James, 68/87 Sutherland, John, Amos postmaster, 73/83 Sutherland, John, Cowlitz Farm shepherd, 63/119,124,127,130,132,134, 145-49*passim* Sutherlin, John Franklin: 1858 letter, 66/383 Sutherlin, Owen, 66/383 Sutherlin, Ore., 73/72 Sutherlind, Annie, 81/85 Sutherlind, Frances, 81/85 *Sutil* (schooner), 79/398 Sutor, Jennings F., 62/420; 64/359 Sutter, John Augustus, 63/205,212; 64/275; 65/160; 72/179; 73/164 Sutter's Fort, 62/75; 63/41,345; 65/160; 66/355 Sutter's Mill, 62/213 Sutterville, Coos Co., 63/33 Sutton, Al, 73/263-64 Sutton, Dorothy and Jack, eds.: *Indian Wars of the Rogue River*, by Victor, noted, 70/359

Sutton, Jack, 62/301; 63/246,357; 65/121; 66/80; 67/281; SEE ALSO Sutton, Dorothy
Sutton Mountain, 64/105; 73/264: photo, 64/106
Sutton Ranch, Wheeler Co., 64/105,108-22*passim*
Suzuki, George M., 81/153,166
Suzuki, Kinzo, 76/227-28
Suzzallo, Henry, 65/198
Svendson, Birgitte M., SEE Funnemark, Birgitte Svendson
Svendson, Christine, 66/103
Svendson, Hannah, SEE Miller, Hannah (Mrs. Axel)
Svendson, Maren, SEE Holst, Maren Svendson
Svensen, Ore., 63/351
Swain, Donald C.: *Federal Conservation Policy, 1921-1933*, review, 65/205-206 *Wilderness Defender: Horace M. Albright and Conservation*, review, 72/83-84
The Swamp Fox of the Willamette, by Carson, noted, 69/329
Swan, James G., 62/324,330; 72/286; 78/91
Swan (dance barge), 70/279
Swan (excursion steamer), 77/257
Swan Alighting (Indian), SEE Peopeo Tholekt
Swan Island Ship Repair Yard, 62/300
Swan Necklace (Indian), SEE Wetyetmas Wyakaikt
Swan River Mission, 65/314
Swans, whistling, 69/10
Swanson, Earl Herbert, Jr., 62/203; 63/89,358-59; 64/277; 67/87: *Utaztekan Prehistory*, noted, 69/333
Swanson, Fred L., 66/82
Swanson, Hulda Anderson, 76/13,15
Swartz, —, immigrant of 1853, 78/311
Swartz, B.K., Jr.: *Bibliography of Klamath Basin Anthropology*, 2nd ed. noted, 69/333
Swastika, Ore.: post office, 71/200; 72/93
Swaze, J.T., 68/228N
Swearingen, Mrs. Mervin, 72/350

Swearingen, Thomas W., 70/340
Swedenburg, F.G., 64/332
"The Swedes of Yamhill," by Martin Peterson, 76/5-27
Swedish people: British Columbia, 75/88; Columbia Co., 74/323; food, 76/25 laborers— Deschutes railroad workers, 69/298; loggers, 73/19; rock blasters, 73/6 population— Oregon 1860-1910, 80/267; Portland 1860-1910, 80/266 Yamhill Co., 76/5-27
Sweek, John: house, 64/88
Sweek, Maria: diary, 76/381
Sweeny Camp Bluffs, Lane Co., 78/321
Sweet, William A., 73/362; 74/184,366; 76/387; 78/369,370; 79/413,415; 80/413,414
Sweet, Zara, 63/148N
Sweet Home, Ore., 62/205; 69/339: history, 81/330
Sweet Home in the Oregon Cascades, by Carey and Hainline, noted, 81/331
Sweetland, Monroe, 76/143,148: Oregon Farmer-Labor Party correspondence, cited, 76/137N-51N*passim*
Sweetwater River, 62/348,350,351, 353,354; 72/67; 79/81,82,377: Oregon Trail route, 80/75-77
Sweetwater Valley: Skirving panorama view, 63/153-54
Sweetzer Bros., cattlemen, 67/143-44
Swenson, C.J., 73/177
Swift, Earle, Jr., 64/323N
Swift and Company, 63/268; 67/131; 81/39
Swigert, Charles F., 64/352
Swigert, Ernest, 68/102
Swim, Ore.: name, 63/364
Swindells, William, Jr., 75/370; 79/413,416
Swing, William, 62/197,199,203,204; 63/92,362,363; 64/353; 66/281
Swinnerton, H.M., 62/218N-19N

Swiss people, **81**/104:

Cedar Mill area, **80**/106; cheesemaking, **72**/200; Columbia Co., **72**/197-208; Lane Co., **80**/335 Oregon, **68**/208,219; **81**/296-318— population 1860-1910, **80**/267 Portland population 1860-1910, **80**/266; pre-immigration life, **81**/281,283-96

Switzler, Cynthia, **81**/328

Switzler, Jehu, **74**/93

Switzler, John, **64**/262

Switzler, John D., **81**/328

Swords, Thomas, **67**/333N; **68**/9

Sydney Inlet, **62**/105

Sykes, Jacob B., **70**/251

Sykes, Lorin, **79**/84

Sylvester, Edmund, **64**/35

Sylvia de Grasse (vessel), **64**/207N

Symons, Thomas William, **65**/104N; **70**/164:

Dept. of Columbia map 1892 ed., **68**/ins.bk.cov. Sept.— cited, **68**/224N,234N,248N,254N, 255N,298N,301N,306N,307N,310N, 311N,313N

Symphony in Steam, The History and Development of the 4-4-0 or American Type Locomotive, by Gleysteen, noted, **67**/280

Szasz, Margaret Connell:

Education and the American Indian: The Road to Self-Determination Since 1928, noted, **80**/208

T.J. Potter (steamer), **63**/61,64-66,68,92; **68**/81; **69**/331: photo, **74**/164

Tababoo (Indian), **66**/146

Tabeau, Pierre Antoine, **64**/92; **66**/331N

Table Lake, Jefferson Co., **75**/41

Table Rock, Jackson Co., **81**/106: area history, **70**/279; Indian council 1853, **66**/225N

Table Rock Sentinel, Jacksonville, **64**/139,144: carriers address 1856, **64**/147

Tabor, Horace A.W., **69**/204

Tabor, S.J., **62**/219N

Tackensuatis (Indian), SEE Rotten Belly

Tacoma, Wash., **62**/86,405; **71**/14; **72**/153,255; **74**/5,16,17,339; **75**/127: described 1881, **71**/15; history, **65**/ 217; intercity rivalry, **74**/340; music, **72**/271; newspapers, **71**/147; "old town," **66**/113-14; recollections, **70**/ 67-68; Seamen's Rest, **66**/101-31*passim;* shanghaied sailors, **66**/14; ships at, 1898-1901, **66**/107-108,122,124,127; trade and commerce, **71**/16,144

Tacoma (steamer):

1883 shipwreck, **66**/171N; **73**/283; rescue of crew, **66**/173-75,177

Tacoma Rescue Mission, **66**/130

"Tacoma Seamen's Rest: Waterfront Mission, 1897-1903," by Rowena L. and Gordon D. Alcorn, **66**/101-31

Tacoma Water Utilities Division, **66**/127

Tacoma Woolen Mill, **62**/170

Taft, William Howard, **74**/107

Taft, Ore.:

history, **64**/355

Tagish Lake, **76**/110

Tahiti, **70**/299,307

Tahmalnaw, The Bridge of the Gods, by Attwell, noted, **75**/88

Taholah, Wash., **74**/13,23

Ta-home (Indian):

photo, **79**/120; SEE ALSO Tawhom

Taiwan, SEE Formosa

Takaki, Robert, **76**/237

Takaki, Shintaro, **76**/228

Takaki, Tama Nitobe, **76**/228: photo, **76**/ins.fr.cov. Sept.

Takelma Indians, **81**/394,395,408,411, 414,421

Takeoka, Daiichi, **76**/253

Takeoka, George, **81**/160

Takliks (Indian), **81**/375

Talbot, Guy W., **71**/219,220,231; **74**/138,140,215: Portland utilities, **71**/219N

Talbot, John Brooke, **74**/355

Talbot, Robert ("Cherokee Bob"), **64**/344

Talbot, Theodore, **65**/150: journal cited, **74**/355; letters 1845-53,

74/355-56
Talbot (corvette), 70/307,308N
Tale of Valor: A Novel of the Lewis and Clark Expedition, by Fisher, review, 62/100-101
Tales of Silver City, Idaho, by Chadwick, noted, 79/107
Tales of the Golden Beavers, by McClure, noted, 79/408-409
Tales of the Trail, by Fulton, noted, 66/188
Tall Tales from Rogue River: The Yarns of Hathaway Jones, by Beckham, noted, 77/291; review, 75/360-61
Tallman, Ore., 68/353
Tallow, SEE Prices
Tally Ho! (brig), 63/189
Tamana (schooner), 70/362
Tamar (ship), 66/129
Tamehamalu, SEE Kamamalu
"Tammany Tiger": Davenport cartoon, 66/48
Tamowhamit (Indian), 79/313,315, 316,317,326
Tam-ow-ins (Indian), 79/157N
Tanabe, Mr. and Mrs. —, Portland Assembly Center, 81/156
Tanager, "Louisiana" (western): drawing, 69/24; Lewis describes, 69/24
Tanana Valley Railroad, 69/184
Tanasoca, Steven: *Utopias on Puget Sound, 1885-1915*, by LeWarne, review, 77/294-95
Tanasoca, Steven, and Susan Sudduth, eds.: "A Journal Kept By George A. Harding," 79/172-202
Tanbara, Mr. —, Portland Assembly Center, 81/156
Tandy, Robert, 77/324; 78/143,207, 211,220,225,231,232,233,234,323N; 79/22-23
Tandy, Sarah Snelling, 77/327
Tandy, William Snelling, 77/321,324, 327,336; 78/207,234,325N; 79/22-23: portrait, 77/326; stone inscribed, 77/ 332(photo),333
Tandy Creek, 79/23
Tandy family, immigrants of 1851,

63/246
Tangent, Ore., 69/329
Tanger, Carl A., 69/331
Tanida, Mrs. —, Portland Assembly Center, 81/160,161
Tanner, —, Lane Co. 1853, 78/234
Tanner, Clara Lee: *Southwest Indian Crafts*, review, 70/268-69
Tanner, Edward A., 70/201
Tanner Creek, 74/129
Tanneries: American to 1850, 66/86; Dallas, Ore., 81/328; Rickreall Creek, 64/354
Tanning bark, 72/283
Tapal (Indian), SEE Newell, Harriet
The Tarbells of Yankton, ed. by Oliver, review, 80/102-103
Tariff, 62/166; 63/182: Cleveland promise to lower, 71/149; on HBCO. imports, 63/220,226; Wilson-Gorman, 71/149
Tarshis, Rebecca, 62/400
Tartar, Lena Belle: *Chronicles from Pedee, Oregon*, noted, 75/363
Tate, James: HBCO. journal 1809-12, 77/84
Tate, Merze, 62/105; 63/358; 64/87,283: *Diplomacy in the Pacific, A Collection of Twenty-Seven Articles*..., review, 74/279
"U.S. Diplomacy: Influence of Sandwich Island Missionaries and the ABCFM," 68/53-74
Tatnall, Josiah, 62/10
Tats-homi (Indian), photo, 66/320
Tattersall, James N., 63/361: "The Economic Development of the Pacific Northwest to 1920," cited, 67/103-70*passim*; 71/75
The Importance of International Trade to Oregon, cited, 67/170N
Taube, Edward: "Turn Again: The Name Oregon and Linguistics," 79/211
Tawahitt, Skulps (Indian), 79/313,314, 315,316,317,325-26
Tawas (Indian), 79/313,315,326

Tawhom (Indian), 79/149,158,313,314, 315,316,318,325; SEE ALSO Ta-home Taxes and taxation, 62/159: early state, 69/86; first gas tax, 66/ 270; 74/139; Ft. Vancouver, 63/219, 223N; frontier assessments, 72/179; HBCO. suits and U.S. indemnity, 63/230; Kansas Territory, 70/363; Klamath River, 72/9; Lake Co. land auction 1909, 64/91; Montana, 65/367; mortgage tax law, 67/119 Oregon— 1844 tax roll, 66/356; federal income returns 1862, 64/160; highest in nation 1922, 64/334; property, 72/ 235; tax law, 70/217 Pacific NW states compared, 72/90; property tax, 69/86; Puget Sound Agricultural Co., 63/230; single tax, 68/204,206,207; timber tax, 69/337; U.S. excise tax, 70/70; Washington, 65/235; 69/86; SEE ALSO Tariff Taxicabs: horse-drawn, 73/333 Taxidermy: Forestry Bldg. display, 80/55; Portland City Hall exhibit, 80/60 Taylor, Ben, Sutton Ranch owner, 73/264 Taylor, Calvin, 72/180 Taylor, Caroline Carroll (Mrs. E.W.), 73/267 Taylor, Charles L., 68/187: borax works, 73/231,233,237,239,240 Taylor, E.W., Wheeler Co. 1900s, 73/267 Taylor, Elbert, 78/131,323N Taylor, F.A., Ore. City 1846, 73/250,256 Taylor, F.E., Real Estate Board, 74/223 Taylor, Fred, ed. *Wall Street Journal*, 75/294 Taylor, George R.: *The Transportation Revolution, 1815- 1860*, cited, 70/351 Taylor, Glen H., 71/196,368; 72/232 Taylor, Hobart, 72/93 Taylor, James, Clatsop Plains settler, 62/241N,243-44,298-99,400: house photo 1855, 81/4 Taylor, James B., 63/365 Taylor, Lewis, 65/192-93

Taylor, M.B., 75/47 Taylor, Margaret, Ore. writer: photo, 74/265 Taylor, Sarah C. Gray, 78/131 Taylor, Scott, 80/279 Taylor, Tilman D., 66/282; 69/138; 72/352; 73/285; 77/192 Taylor, William E., 65/405 Taylor, Zachary, 64/293; 75/329,333; 81/301 Taylor family, immigrants of 1853, 78/148 Taylor Street Methodist Church, photo, 80/308 Teabo, Joseph, 63/122N Teachers: Columbia Co. 1900, 72/197-208; early Douglas Co., 68/81; unions, 72/231; Wash. certification, 65/377; SEE ALSO Schools Teal, John B., 77/266 Teal, Joseph, 79/167N,270N-71N Teal, Joseph Nathan, 78/114 Teal, Will, 77/266 *Team Bells Woke Me and Other Stories*, by Davis, cited, 66/243 Teapot Dome scandal, 78/105,106 Teasdale (Teesdale), Edward G., 65/288 Tebault, C.W., 62/199 Technology: and science in 19th century, 73/85; history, 66/299; philosophy, 67/370; social interdependencies, 73/85; wood use, 72/179 Teeple, L.R., photo, 74/214 Teeter, Charles Nelson: Boise Basin letters, 64/86 Teeter, Darius: Boise Basin letters, 64/86 Teeter's Landing, Klamath Co., 78/363 Tehailact (Indian), 79/313 Tehama County, Calif., 81/328 Tehama (Jones) Hotel, San Francisco, 66/10N Tehoutinse Creek (McKay Creek?), 66/137 Teio, Alex (Indian), 72/151,153 Teiser, Sidney: "Cyrus Olney, Associate Justice of

Oregon Territory Supreme Court," **64**/309-22

"Obadiah B. McFadden, Oregon and Washington Territorial Judge," **66**/25-37

"Reuben P. Boise, Last Associate Justice of the Oregon Territory Supreme Court," **66**/5-24

"William Strong, Associate Justice of the Territorial Courts," **64**/293-307

Teit, James A.:

The Salishan Tribes of the Western Plateaus, cited, **71**/279

Telegram, Portland, **75**/173,189N: origins, **71**/147-48

Telegraph, **65**/216; **70**/27,88,199: Ashland-Ft. Klamath, **68**/223; construction 1862, **72**/57; Ft. Garry time check 1872, **66**/71; North America-Europe, **72**/232; Portland, **79**/345-46 stations—

Anawaldt Ranch, **68**/238N; Boise, **68**/227N; **70**/14; Malheur Agency, **68**/230; Sheep Ranch, **68**/246

transcontinental line, **67**/233-34; use in Bannock War, **70**/10FF; use in surveying, **72**/13,20N,48,49,49N; Walla Walla office, **70**/10

Telegraph (steamer), **63**/66; **74**/321: photo, **74**/323

Telephone (steamer), **63**/65-66,68; **64**/91: photo, **74**/332

Telephones, **69**/108: first farm line, **72**/171; first in Ore. City, **65**/211; first in Westfall, **63**/284; first to Bridge Creek, **73**/267; Jordan Valley, **72**/93; Klamath Co., **76**/382; Siskiyou Co., Calif., **72**/171; Skagway 1898, **81**/123,129; Tillamook Co., **71**/121

Telford, Ray: reminiscences, **69**/328

Telokaikt (Telokite) (Indian), **81**/342

Temerario (torpedo boat), **76**/274, 280-95*passim*

Temperance, **74**/76,76N; **78**/9,27,34,35,36; **80**/314-17: crusade, **65**/313

early Oregon— newspapers, **64**/130-31; petition, **66**/346

Eugene, **77**/380; Portland, **70**/131N-33N; Salem resolution, **64**/155-56

Temperley, Harold, **72**/101

Temple, Christopher, **65**/214

Temple, Mr. and Mrs. Roy, **78**/308

Templeton, Herbert A., **62**/421

Ten Eyck, Anthony: attacks missionaries, **68**/64-65; criticism of, **68**/61,62,66

Ten O'Clock Church, Beavercreek, **66**/382

Tenafly, N.J.: description ww I, **75**/261-62

Tendoy (Indian), **72**/258

Tengwald, C.Y., **76**/247

Tenino, Wash.: churches, **72**/153

Tenino (steamer, 1st of name), **79**/184

Tenino Indians, **73**/63; **79**/126; **81**/397,398,413,414

Tenmile, Ore., **73**/304

Tenmile Creek, Malheur Co., **68**/ 251N,254

Tenmile Creek, Wasco Co., **66**/135

Tennant, W.J., **80**/160

Tents, SEE Prices

Terakawa, Tansal, **81**/153,160,167

Terrebonne, Ore.: history, **72**/94

Terrell, Charles E., **75**/169

Terrell, John U., and George Walton: *Faint the Trumpet Sounds,* noted, **68**/82

The Terrible Trail: The Meek Cutoff, 1845, by Clark and Tiller, cited, **78**/221; review, **68**/79-81

The Territories and the United States, 1861-1890, Studies in Colonial Administration, by Pomeroy, review, **71**/358

Terry, David S., **72**/181

Terry, Ellen, **74**/203-204

Teruzuki, Mr. and Mrs. —, Portland Assembly Center, **81**/156

Tetherow, Solomon, **77**/319,319N,320

Tetherow Butte, **79**/295N

Teton Range, **62**/373

Teutch, William, photo, **63**/8

Tex, Della, 77/90
Texas (battleship), 76/270
Texas and Pacific Railroad, 71/54
Texas Ferry, Snake River, 71/23N
Textbooks and the American Indian, ed. by Costo, review, 74/87-88
Textile industry:
Oregon, 62/164-79—
wages, 62/174-75
SEE ALSO Woolen mills
Textile Workers Union, 62/174
Teyayas (Indian), 79/313,315,326
Te-Yo-Keen (Hear Ye), ed. by Price, noted, 63/357; 66/275
Thailand, 62/19,25,29; SEE ALSO Siam
Thalia (British warship), 70/294N,301
Thayer, Charles G., 72/197:
residence photo, 72/196
Thayer, Eli, 64/151-52; 70/219
Thayer, Harriet:
biography, 72/197-98; letters, 72/198-208; photo, 72/208
Thayer, James, 79/413,416; 80/413
Thayer, Ruth, 63/249; 64/359; 68/359
Thayer, Ruth, ed.:
"One-Room School, 1900,"
72/197-208
Thayer, Susan G., 72/197
Thayer's Landing, Columbia Co., 72/
197,198(photo)
The Dalles, Ore., 62/78,79,89,222-24, 244-45,382,394,400,402N; 63/31,191, 203,234,263,301,335,350; 64/170, 173,311-12,317; 66/59,61,88,200, 201,244,317; 68/36; 69/231,232,245, 254,293; 70/7,69,139; 73/307,318; 74/253; 75/226; 77/311,315,317; 78/174,175; 79/32,33,87,88,142, 168,176,201; 81/202:
anthropology, 63/75-77; board of trustees, 67/313; building stone, 68/
20,30; church history, 70/273;
churches, 79/162N; Congregational Church, 64/170; convent school, 80/
341; Crandall memories, 70/280; described 1858, 68/28-29,30; electric co-op, 80/328; fire, Apr. 1881, 81/271; first brickyard, 63/265; fossils near, 70/183

growth, 67/301,312-13—
1856-58, 68/23-25,27-30
head of navigation, 68/9,23; history, 73/84; library, 73/314; lodge history, 70/76; mounted volunteers headquarters 1855-56, 66/133-60*passim*
photos, 73/300,303—
1879, 81/ins.bk.cov. Fall; Second St. 1884, 81/278
protest against military reservation, 67/301; Shaker Church, 72/149-58; steamboat excursions to, 63/68
town site—
1852 provisions, 67/301N; included in military reservation, 67/303; litigation, 67/304N
U.S. mint, 68/354; woolen mills, 62/164; SEE ALSO Fort Dalles
The Dalles-California trail, 67/80,279
The Dalles-Canyon City Road, 65/103N; 73/258,260-61; 79/123,139:
map, 79/164,286-87; SEE ALSO Canyon City Road
The Dalles-Celilo Canal, 75/230
The Dalles Chronicle, 65/315; 73/307
The Dalles City (steamboat), 63/88
The Dalles City Fire Co., 68/38N
The Dalles Dam, 62/102; 63/75; 72/157N,158; 75/221
The Dalles Military Wagon Road, 69/87; 72/261; 75/311:
route 1864, 65/95,103-104N
The Dalles Optimist, 73/307
The Netherlands:
navy, 62/25; Pacific exploration, 70/77
The Nook (Quinton, Ore.), 81/266, 269-78*passim*
The West, SEE West
The Theater Finns, ed. by Mattila, review, 74/91-92
Theaters, 74/91-92:
actors and actresses, 74/204,205,207; Ashland Shakespearean history, 62/
181-83; Baker Co. 1890s, 66/124;
Boise, Ida., 65/382; Butte, Mont., 65/
382; Klamath Falls, 69/328; 73/283; Kootenai, 63/90; light opera tour 1878, 70/7N; mining towns, 71/366;

Oregon, 76/381; Pacific NW history plays, 62/412-13; plays 1904-1905, 74/205,207 Portland, 74/205-207,346; 81/330— 1866, 64/170; 1890s, 66/41; history, 71/289 Salem, 66/81; Spokane, 72/265; stage stars 1850s, 70/366; Victoria, B.C., 72/263; Yukon Territory, 63/352-53,359; SEE ALSO Marquam Grand; New Market Theater; Oro Fino Hall; Paramount Theater; Reed's Opera House; Standard Theater; Tivoli Theater; Willamette Theatre

Them Was the Days, by McKeown, noted, 63/247

Thence Around Cape Horn, the Story of U.S. Naval Forces on Pacific Station, 1818-1923, by Johnson, review, 66/71-72

Theresa of Jesus, Mother, 80/342

These Things I Remembered and Poured Out My Soul, by Laidlaw, noted, 78/288

Theses:

British Columbia history, 71/191; 73/74

Pacific NW and Alaska— 1958-63, 65/362-91; 1964-70, 72/225-79

Western history bibliography, 75/93

Thexton, Myrtle, 77/90

They Came to a Valley, by Gulick, review, 68/279-80

They Gave Royal Assent, by McGregor, noted, 71/191

They Laughed, Too, comp. by Mintonye, review, 69/183

They Saddled the West, by Rice and Vernam, review, 76/380-81

They Settled in Applegate Country, by Johnson, noted, 80/336

Thibault (Thibeault), —, PSA employee, 63/121-22N,171,198

Thibault, Jean, 63/122N

Thibeault, —, Lewis Co. pioneer, 63/ 121-23N,138,171,173

Thibeault, Louis, 63/122N

Thibaw (Thibault?), Rev. —, 81/87,88N

Thiel, Daniel, 66/388

Thiel, William: diary, 78/364

Thielsen, Mrs. Horace, photo, 81/254

Thing, Joseph, 67/85; 74/74,76N

Things I See, by Weatherford, review, 75/361-62

Thirty-One Years in Baker County, by Hiatt, reprint noted, 72/171

Thiry, Paul and Mary: *Eskimo Artifacts Designed for Use*, review, 79/407

This Earth and Another Country: New and Selected Poems, by Corning, cited, 71/190

This Land Around Us: A Treasury of Pacific Northwest Writing, ed. by Lucia, review, 71/181-82

This Was Trucking, A Pictorial History, by Karolevitz, review, 68/179-80

This Was Wheat Farming, A Pictorial History, by Brumfield, review, 70/72-73

"'This Worry I Have': Mary Herren Journal," ed. by Brenda Hood, 80/229-57

Thmiothy (Indian), SEE Timothy

Thollander, Earl: *Back Roads of Oregon*, noted, 81/329

Thom, James W., 72/93

Thomas, Dr. —, author of 1809 fur trade narrative, 65/314

Thomas, Albert Lewis: biography, 66/330

Thomas, Benjamin, Portland policeman 1864, 80/149N

Thomas, Eleazer, 80/117

Thomas, Florence, 76/268

Thomas, George D., Protective Corpsman, 72/61

Thomas, J.L., Queets area settler, 74/19

Thomas, Jake, photo, 79/120

Thomas, John, Gilliam Co. ranch hand 1881, 81/276,277

Thomas, John, Vancouver robber 1852, 80/14

Thomas, Lee: biography, 74/281

Thomas, Lorenzo, 65/335

Thomas, Susie, SEE Williams, Susie Thomas

Thomas Creek, Modoc Co., 79/290N; 81/105

Thomas Fork, Bear River, 79/69,73,80

Thomas H. Perkins (brig), 63/217-18

Thomas Kay Historical Park, Salem, 66/90,283; 67/91

Thomas Nuttall, Naturalist: Explorations in America, 1808-1841, by Graustein, review, 70/171-73

Thomasen, Ethel, 78/213

Thomason, Capt., SEE Thompson, Francis A.

Thomason, Josephine, 65/307

Thomason, William P., 70/359

Thompson, —, Auburn miner, 62/235-36

Thompson, —, capt. of *Chelmsford*, 66/107

Thompson, A.W., civil engineer, 72/10

Thompson, Agnes, photo, 74/25

Thompson, Alfred, 74/210

Thompson, C., Sacred Heart student, 81/81N

Thompson, D.M., 67/62

Thompson, Daid T., 70/279

Thompson, David., capt. of *Earl of Dalhousie*, 66/109,112

Thompson, David, explorer, 62/202, 421; 63/90; 65/215; 66/69,70,280; 67/86; 68/87; 71/343; 76/310,324: biographical references, 74/90,282; geology of Canada, 68/348

Thompson, David P., 62/243,244; 65/395: biography, 65/395N; township survey, 69/244

Thompson, Dennis L., 77/89

Thompson, E.L., 62/170-71,174,176, 177-78

Thompson, Erwin N.: *Journal of a Catholic Bishop on the Oregon Trail*, ed. by Kowrach, review, 80/405-406 *The Modoc War, 1872-73: Lava Beds National Monument*, review, 70/175-77

Thompson (Thomason), Francis A., 63/192

Thompson, H.Y., 67/262,265

Thompson, Harry, 74/32: photo, 74/25

Thompson, Henry (Indian), 69/338; 75/224

Thompson, "High Pockets," 73/182, 188,190,191

Thompson, J.G. ("Whispering"), 63/ 365; 64/90

Thompson, L.S., photo, 72/62

Thompson, L.T.: narrative of Evans-Bailey Indian fight, 81/105

Thompson, Lair, 62/94-95

Thompson, Levant F., 64/271

Thompson, Lucy, SEE Lee, Lucy Thompson

Thompson, Michel, 81/343

Thompson, Missouri Ann Wright: recollections, 69/330

Thompson, Peter: *The Enterprising Scot*, by Jackson, review, 69/181-82

Thompson, R.H., Seattle city engineer, 74/106,117

Thompson, Robert R., 62/243,244N, 380,389,390,392,393,394,395; 66/151; 67/312; 69/198; 79/141: biography, 79/141N; Redondo Beach promotion, 71/289

Thompson, Theodore, 80/279

Thompson, "Whispering," SEE Thompson, J.G.

Thompson, William, immigrant of 1852, 66/338N; 68/237N

Thompson, William Green, 62/177

Thompson Flouring Mill, Scio, 66/90

Thomson, James, 66/388

Thomson, Mortimer Neal, 62/292

Thoracic Clinic, Portland: history, 79/408

Thorn, E.D., 62/218N

Thorn, Jonathan: biography, 66/79; death, 71/315,319; relations with Indians, 71/314,318; *Tonquin* voyage, 71/313-15

Thornbrough, Gayle, and O.O. Winther, eds.: *To Oregon in 1852: Letters of Dr. Thomas White*, noted, 65/212

Thornburg, —, killed by Hubbard, **62**/119

Thorne, James, **63**/123N

Thornton, Harrison: murder, **65**/215

Thornton, Jesse Quinn, **62**/148-51, 313,321,329; **63**/194; **65**/220; **66**/350N,352N; **79**/7,8: *Oregon and California in 1848*, reprint noted, **74**/359

Thornton, S., Queets area settler, **74**/18

Thorpe, Iris Lora, SEE Barry, Iris Lora

Thor's Crown, SEE Crown Point

Thoughts Through the Years, by Drenner, noted, **66**/383

Thousand Springs, **62**/385N

Three Fingered Jack, **76**/382

"Three Letters of William Gird, 'Veteran of Turf, Field and Farm'," ed. by Hugh H. Davis, **68**/141-52

"Three Nootka Documents," by Kenneth L. Holmes, **79**/397-402

Three Sisters (mountains), **67**/6,11; **73**/82,84; **74**/202; **76**/382; **77**/330; **78**/231,247,307: photo, **78**/246

Throckmorton, Arthur L., **63**/371: *South Pass, 1868: James Chisolm's Journal of the Wyoming Gold Rush*, ed. by Homsher, review, **63**/242-43

Throckmorton, Charles B., **68**/231N, 305N; **70**/26,34

Thumb, Tom, **63**/125

Thunder River, SEE Donner und Blitzen River

Thunder Robe (Indian), **71**/343

Thunder Rolling: The Story of Chief Joseph, by Miller, review, **62**/102

Thundereggs, **64**/357; **66**/282; **67**/34,88,370; **75**/311

Thurman, —, Auburn mines 1861, **62**/219N

Thurston, Elizabeth (Mrs. Samuel R.), **66**/12

Thurston, Lorrin A., **71**/175

Thurston, Samuel Royal, **62**/70,74; **63**/182; **64**/298; **65**/408; **66**/7,12; **75**/120,332

Thurston, Ore., **78**/234

Thwaites, Reuben Gold, **70**/204; **78**/284: biography, **65**/213

Thwaites, Reuben Gold: *Original Journals of the Lewis and Clark Expedition*, cited, **69**/5FF,149FF

Thwing, Charles Hugh, family, **74**/358

Tibbetts, Calvin, **64**/224

Tibbetts, Jonathan S., **73**/72

Tibout, Jochain, **63**/121N

Tichenor, H.B., **68**/265

Tichenor, William, **68**/352; **70**/237,245

Tichey, Joe, **77**/236

Tichtooly (Indian), **79**/313,314,316, 317,325

Ticks, **76**/338-39,340

Tidal waves, **77**/280-84

Tide Creek area, Columbia Co., **72**/197-208: map, **72**/206; name, **72**/197N; school, **72**/197-208

Tiernan, Ore.: post office, **72**/92

Tigard, Rosa (Mrs. Charles), **80**/106: recollections, **72**/91

Tigard, Ore., **77**/377,378: history, **72**/91

Tigard Area Historical and Preservation Association: officers and directors, **81**/111-12

Tilden, Sam (Indian), **64**/85

Tilden, Samuel J.: disputed 1876 election, **67**/257-72 *passim*

Tilikum (schooner), **73**/273

Tillamook, Ore., **72**/294,299,303; **74**/357; **77**/69,91,358: doctors, **71**/117-18; electric co-op, **80**/328; first cheese factory, **74**/274-77; location, **77**/222; pioneer community, **65**/409-10; population 1923, **71**/117; post office, **67**/369

Tillamook (steamer), **77**/363: photo, **77**/364

Tillamook Bay, **62**/195; **72**/294,305; **77**/220-22: history, **71**/289; jetty, **77**/221; map, **72**/309; photos, **77**/68,221; rivers flowing into, **72**/299-300; sawmills,

72/294,296-97
Tillamook burn, SEE Forest fires
Tillamook County, Ore., 66/19,372; 72/294,295:
cemeteries listed, 69/78; census records 1854, 74/357; doctors in 1920s, 71/117-20; early days, 62/196; early sawmills, 72/308; 73/224,226; history, 73/82; 74/357; Huckleberry recollections, 71/117-40; logging, 71/133-34; 72/296-314; 73/5-30,171-92,212-27; maps, 74/357; photos, 71/119,122,129,131,136,140,covs. June; roads 1920s, 71/117,118,119; schools, 71/127-29; sheriff, 72/308; timber, 72/300,309; 73/17,174; World War II years, 71/134-40
Tillamook County Pioneer Association, 69/78:
publications, 74/357
Tillamook County Pioneer Museum, 69/177
Tillamook Head, 74/313
Tillamook Indians, 62/82,195; 66/347; 81/405,407,413,415:
prehistory, 65/374
Tillamook Memories, noted, 74/357
Tillamook People's Utility District, 80/328
Tillamook River, 72/300,305
Tiller, Lowell E., 62/199; 63/366,371; 64/359; 65/10
Tiller, Lowell E., and Keith Clark: *The Terrible Trail: The Meek Cutoff, 1845*, cited, 78/221; review, 68/79-81
Tiller, Lowell E., and Leah C. Menefee: "Cutoff Fever," 77/309-40; 78/41-72,121-57,207-50,293-331; 79/5-50
Tillman, Thomas A., 72/5N,25N: Ore.-Calif. boundary survey, 72/19N, 38-39,39N
Tilton, A.E. and C.E., New York, 65/199
Tilton, Alfred E., 65/199
Tilton, Charles E., 63/363; 65/199: railroad interests, 71/68,92
Tilton, James, 62/84-85
Tilton, McLane W.: papers, 70/360

Tilton, Warren, 64/60
Timber:
B.C. legislation, 77/303; cruising, 72/303-304; Eastern Ore., 79/47; Olympic Peninsula, 74/7,9,11; Oregon, 62/67,68; 76/38; Pacific Northwest, 77/101; policies, 71/368; Puget Sound, 71/368; railroad lands, 72/300; redwood, 76/50,51,54,59; sales, 78/280,308; sustained yield, 64/61-67; Tillamook Co., 72/300-301; 73/17,174; Washington 1905, 72/300; SEE ALSO Forests
Timber, Ore., 72/295: photo, 72/ins.fr.cov. Dec.
Timber Conservation Board, 64/58
Timber Country, by Roberge, noted, 75/364
Timberline Lodge, 68/351: art work, 76/267-68; dedication, 76/266-68; drawing, 76/262; history, 76/259-68; ironwork, 76/259-68; photos, 76/258-68*passim*
Timberman (Forest Industries Yearbook), 77/217
The Time of My Life, by Lorenz, noted, 70/75
Times, London, 64/6-10,14-15,18
Times, Seattle, 73/308
Times-Herald, Burns: diamond jubilee edition, 64/356
Times Mountaineer, The Dalles, 81/264
Timmen, Fritz:
Blow for the Landing: A Hundred Years of Steam Navigation on the Waters of the West, review, 75/82
Timothy (grass): Cowlitz Farm, 63/116
Timothy (Indian), 69/336; 71/198; 79/285,326
Tincup Creek, 76/47-48
Tinners, 68/47,49,51
Tippie, Mrs. Alda, 63/42N
Tipyahlahnah Kapskaps (Bold Eagle) (Indian), 81/363
Tire Creek, 78/316(photo),321
Tisdale, J.G., 74/17
Title companies, 77/261
Tivoli Theater, Portland, 66/41

Tlingit (Kolosh) Indians, **64**/92; **71**/ 292; **72**/137; **73**/167-68; **77**/177,180; **81**/208:

armor, **73**/144; barter, **73**/141,143, 147; battles, **73**/144,152; blockhouse, **73**/149

boats, **73**/142,147,168— sketch, **73**/146

burials, **73**/143,144; Catholic church, **73**/142-43,144; clans, **73**/152-53,169; clothing, **73**/146-51*passim*; cremation, **73**/154; culture, **79**/99; funerals, **73**/149-55; games, **73**/169

houses, **73**/142,144,149-50— Russian influence, **73**/168-69; sketch, **73**/150

jewelry, **73**/148,150(sketch),151; leaders, **73**/149,152,153,169; Russian influence, **73**/160; Sitka Island settlement, **73**/142-44,167; slaves, **73**/168

"To Be a Soldier: 1917 Diary," by Martin L. Kimmel, **75**/241-69

To Build a Ship, by Berry, review, **65**/406-11

"To Oregon by Auto, 1915," by William E. Knowles, **72**/159-64

To Oregon in 1852: Letter of Dr. Thomas White, ed. by Winther and Thornbrough, noted, **65**/212

To Santa Rosalia, Further and Back, by Huycke, review, **72**/167-68

"To see the elephant," SEE "Seeing the elephant"

Toatman, Dr. —, Coos Co. settler, **63**/15

Tobacco:

Arikara, **69**/152,158; Indian curing, **66**/81; SEE ALSO Prices

Tobacco Plains Reserve, **71**/331,338

Tobey, Mark, **62**/410-11; **79**/103

Tobie, Harvey Elmer:

The Adventures of Captain Bonneville, ed. by Todd, review, **63**/343-45

Methodism in the Northwest, by Howell, review, **68**/338-39

Not by Might, The Story of Whitworth College, by Gray, review, **68**/183-84

Tobie, Harvey Elmer, ed.:

A History of Oregon Methodism, by

Yarnes, review, **62**/406-407

Tobin, Thomas J., **72**/354

Tod, John, **63**/211

Todd, —, The Dalles 1863, **66**/201

Todd, A.E., **74**/209

Todd, Abbott Levi James: biography, **71**/286; **72**/89

Todd, Edgeley W., ed.:

The Adventures of Captain Bonneville, U.S.A., in the Rocky Mountains and the Far West, review, **63**/343-45

Astoria, or Anecdotes of an Enterprise Beyond the Rocky Mountains, by Irving, review, **66**/77-79

Todd, John, Clackamas Co. 1862, **79**/176,176N,198

Todd, John Young, **65**/115N; **73**/260; **79**/302N:

army beef contract, **68**/23N; biography, **68**/23N

Todds Bay, SEE Knappton, Wash.

Todds Bay (ship), **63**/198

Todhunter, W.B., **63**/310; **67**/144; **68**/321

Todhunter and Devine, stockmen, **67**/143,144; SEE ALSO Whitehorse Ranch

Tofino, B.C., **68**/102,106: chart, **68**/104; photo, **68**/103

Tojo, Hideki, **62**/26,28,35

Tokens, SEE Medals and tokens

Tokyo, Japan, **62**/29

Toledo, Ore., **66**/283; **70**/279; **76**/248; **77**/216

Toledo, Wash., **64**/298; **71**/14,15N; **72**/151

Toledo (steamer), **67**/366; **71**/15N

Toll roads, SEE Roads and trails

Tolman, James C., **63**/12

Tolmie, William Fraser, **63**/109,111N, 115-16N,149,163,169,178N,182-83, 204,209,228:

arrival in Pacific NW, **63**/191,232; journals 1830-43, **65**/207,208; Nisqually Farm, **63**/108N,175,198,215, 219; PSA claims, **63**/178N

Tolowa Indians, **81**/395: clothing, **81**/421; inheritance, **81**/ 411,412; property customs, **81**/392,

396,402-403,404,407,419; slavery, 81/ 412,413,414; whale claims, 81/408-409

Tom Hall Fork (Green River?), 62/362

Tom Horn, Man of the West, by Paine, noted, 65/121

Tom McCall: Maverick, by McCall and Neal, review, 79/406-407

Tomahaw Fork (Green River?), 62/362

Tomahawks, 66/384

Tombstone, Ariz., 62/95

Tomita, Hideto, 81/158,162,163,170

Tomita, Hisako, 81/163

Tomita, Nanako, 81/153,155,156,162

Tomita, Saku: diary, World War II assembly center, 81/151-71

Tomo Cachi (Indian), 64/9

Tongue Point, 69/323; 74/215: buoy station, 66/181; photo, 75/ins.fr. cov. June

Tonkon, Moe M., 67/376,380; 68/361; 69/342,347,348; 70/371-72,373; 71/ 371; 72/359; 73/361,362-64,373; 74/ 183,360,362,365; 75/367,368,370; 79/413,416

Tonningson Bros., Westfall sheepmen, 63/265,269

Tonopah, Nev., 73/239

Tonquin (vessel), 62/105; 63/92; 64/348; 66/79; 76/323; 79/133: accounts of sinking, 71/314-23; crew, 71/278; drawing by Jackson, 71/fr.cov. Dec.; engraving, 71/314; model, 78/90

Toole, K. Ross, *et al,* eds.: *Probing the American West: Papers From the Santa Fe Conference,* noted, 64/186

Tooley, R.V.: *Dictionary of Mapmakers,* noted, 69/79 *French Mapping of the Americas: The De L'Isle, Bauche, Dezauche Succession (1700-1830),* noted, 69/79

Tooley, R.V., and R.A. Skelton: *The Marine Surveys of James Cook in North America, 1758-1768,* noted, 69/79

Tools: frontier, 69/182-83; of mountain men, 79/105; Pacific NW, 76/181

Tools From Pacific Northwest Collections, by

Early American Industries Assn., noted, 76/181

Toombs, Robert Augustus, 73/39,45

Toonk, J.M., 71/17

Topp, Charles, 63/285

Toppenish Creek, 70/147,165N

Topping, George, 63/34

Torney, R.D., 62/149

Torp, Frederick H., 76/387; 80/413

Totem poles, SEE Indians—totem poles

Totten, Joseph G., 65/329,331N, 335,350

Touchet River, 66/147; 79/181,199

Tough Men, Tough Country: Stories of Men Who Met the Rugged Challenge of the Pacific Northwest, by Lucia, review, 65/209

Toulon (bark), 64/210,242; 72/317

Toupin, Marie L'Aguivoise Dorion, SEE Dorion, Marie L'Aguivoise

Toupin, Marie Anne, SEE Gervais, Marie Anne Toupin

Tourism, 73/360; 74/138,141: artists in Rockies, 67/371; Ashland baths, 70/280; booster clubs, 74/232; motion pictures, 74/232; national, 74/114-15

Oregon, 74/134— automobiling 1915, 75/283-89; first auto camp, 64/323N; Hill role in promotion, 66/255,259; postal cards, 66/303-305,330; promotion, 74/ 115,119-27,130,140-41,217-42*passim*

Santiam Highway, 67/374; Yellowstone, 67/371

Toutle, Wash., 80/171

Toutle River, 80/174,195

"Toward a Farm Labor Party in Oregon, 1933-38," by Hugh T. Lovin, 76/135-51

Town House, Echo, 69/131

Town planning, 81/201-202

Towns, 69/83: central Missouri, 70/362; company towns, 67/357; early Eastern Ore., 79/104; effects on society, 70/71-72; future, 70/363; kinds in U.S. history, 70/71; Pacific Northwest, 70/71; railroads and territorial towns, 71/364

Townsend, Edward D., 67/317N

Townsend, George, 80/145N,156
Townsend, James W., 62/218N
Townsend, John Kirk, 63/184,191,198; 71/333:
Narrative of a Journey Across the Rocky Mountains to the Columbia River, 1978 ed. noted, 80/207; reprint noted, 72/170
Townsend, Leland H., 74/274,277: "The First Cheese Factory in Tillamook," 74/274-77
Townsend, Lulu McClay, 80/51N
Townsend, Millard, 65/248
Townsend, Thaddeus S.: creameries, 74/274,276; photo, 74/276; pioneer butter-maker award, 74/276,277
Townsend Plan, 76/141
Toye, William A., 80/62
Toys, SEE Prices
Tracing Your Ancestors, by Turner, noted, 74/283
Tracking Down Oregon, by Friedman, noted, 80/336
Tractors, 77/9-10
Tracy, Benjamin, 76/270
Tracy, Charles Abbot, III: "Police Function in Portland, 1851-1874," 80/5-29,134-69,287-322
Tracy, F.P., 74/73
Tracy, Harry, 62/109; 73/346
Tracy, Paul, 74/63
Tracy, Roy Palmer, 74/54
Tracy and Company, Portland: 1861 broadside adv., 64/157
Trade and commerce, 62/69,70-72; 73/66: aided by Columbia River Hwy., 74/113,136-37; barter system, 73/246,257; 78/65
British, 74/352; 76/314—London market, 76/321; monopoly regulations, 76/311,319,326; with Pacific NW, 72/167; SEE ALSO East India Co.; Hudson's Bay Co.
B.C. Indians and trade unions, 63/246; business ethics, 78/89
California, 76/199,327—hides, 70/179

China, 62/6,9,17; 67/200-201; 74/364; 75/325N; 76/198-99,205,206, 218,309-31; 78/355-56; 80/13—first with Pacific NW, 76/319; Portland-China 1851, 80/13; trader's view of, 1785-1840, 69/83; via Russia, 76/314-15; volume, 76/330-31
Columbia River—decline in beef exports, 67/177; lumber exports, 67/164,177 competition, 76/200,311,322; East India, 62/9; Ft. George, 64/222-45 *passim*
Hawaiian Islands, 71/161-78; 74/285; 76/123,202,327—with France, 68/58; with U.S., 68/60, 67; 71/173
history, 79/92-97
Indian trade, 79/77-79,86,92-97, 98-100,385,387,392—regulation of, 70/102
influence on Alaska boundary, 75/93; influence on Pacific coast, 76/197,224; international, 76/309; Japan, 62/10, 25,28; 68/186; Kamchatka-Russian America, 72/110; lend-lease to U.S.S.R., 71/198; Maine-San Francisco, 68/348; Mexico, 76/121; Montana mining camps, 67/87; Northeastern Whig views, 75/320FF
Northwest Coast, 75/317-35—costs, 72/115-16; value, 72/115-17 opening of Pacific trade, 74/286; opium, 76/206,217,218
Oregon, 62/168; 76/125—business enterprises, 66/304-306; centennial business firms, 70/182; importance of international, 63/361; importers, 71/155N; imports 1840s, 77/319; reason for occupation of, 70/343-44
Oregon missionary finance plan, 74/76-78; Orient, 70/86; 71/141-60; Pacific Basin, 76/125; Pacific Island labor trade, 69/83; Pacific Ocean, 62/6,8,10,11
Pacific Northwest, 74/79,364—exports, 71/77,170; Orient, 71/141-60; trading schooners, 70/266-67;

United Kingdom, 72/167 poaching, 76/199 Portland, 62/168; 78/89-90— China 1851, 80/13; export tables 1881-91, 67/109-12,133; imports 1883-90, 67/117; transcontinental railroad effects, 67/107-23; wholesale trade 1880s, 67/116-17 publicity on West Coast, 74/359; railroad effect on Pacific NW trade patterns, 71/36,56-57; relation to Monroe Doctrine, 72/108,114-17,120; Russia-U.S. rivalry, 77/85-86; Russian colonies, 76/327; Russian markets, 71/144; sandalwood, 68/87 smuggling— firearms, 76/199,200; furs, 76/315; liquor, 76/200 South Africa, 78/355-56; South America, 76/120; theses on, 72/227-45*passim*; trade agreements, 75/332,334; trade centers, 76/321-25*passim*; trade coins, 73/81; Ukase of 1821, 70/200, 208,211 U.S.-Orient— Barrett influence, 71/147-60 growth— 1893-98, 71/177; 1894-1903, 71/159 Hawaiian Islands as step towards, 71/ 161-78; Open Door policy, 71/153-54,157,171; promotion, 71/141-60, 170-72 U.S. trade expansion, 76/209,218; West Coast publicity, 74/359; western, 67/84; SEE ALSO Fur trade; Indians— trade; Shipping Trade goods: beads, 66/187; coins, 73/81; Ft. George, 64/222-45*passim*; Ft. Vancouver, 63/217; 64/298; Indian, 63/193; 66/186-87; 81/350,352,353; toys, 63/192; wheat and flour, 63/181-82,184,217 Trade unions, 72/178; 78/358; SEE ALSO Labor unions "The Trading Age, 1792-1844," by Terrence J. Barragy, 76/197-224 *The Trading Voyages of Andrew Cheyne,*

1841-1844, ed. by Shineberg, noted, 72/355 *Trail to California: The Overland Journal of Vincent Geiger and Wakeman Bryarly*, ed. by Potter, noted, 63/356 Trails, SEE Roads and trails Train, George Francis, 72/144 Train, Samuel S., 65/189N *Train Robbery: The Birth, Flowering, and Decline of a Notorious Western Enterprise*, by Patterson, noted, 80/209 Trainor, —, capt. of *Coleman*, 66/117 Trall, Russell T., 78/5,7-9,22,32: publications, 78/8,16,20,27; theories, 78/24-27 Transcontinental Steam Railway, 69/209 Trans-Mississippi Commercial Congress, 71/158: photo of delegates, 71/156 Trans-Mississippi West: bibliography, 63/81-82; economic history, 73/275; effect of railroad expansion, 73/66; ethnic groups, 73/274, 279-80; frontier economic opportunities, 66/86 maps— 1540-1861, 66/183-85; 1879, 72/68 readings in, 65/307-308; transportation 1865-90, 65/304-305 Traschel, Frank, 66/382 Transportation, 64/90; 77/302: army supply trains, 68/7; articles on, 67/367; Ashland to Linkville, 62/322; bibliography references, 71/75-96; bulk methods, 67/158; Canyon City-Salem 1876, 67/267; Columbia River, 62/63,244; 65/385; Coos Co., 66/52 costs— competitive, 71/58; regional and world-wide, 74/79 early Canada, 70/179 history— early coastal, 66/87; Klamath Co., 75/86,362; Pacific NW, 71/27-98 horse-drawn vehicle photos, 75/ins.fr. cov. March; 77/ins.fr.cov. Sept.; Klamath Co., 66/382; 75/86,362; mining demands, 68/23; Modoc Co., 67/365; Ore. Territory, 62/66,72; Oregon-

California, 62/322
Pacific Northwest, 63/91—
articles on, 70/181; handicaps, 71/41; history, 71/27-98
Portland metropolitan, 70/183; public, 78/360; Puget Sound to Olympia, 62/64; rail *vs.* ships, 67/112-13,171-72; regional rail network effects, 67/106-23*passim*; San Francisco-Oregon 1850s, 66/163; San Francisco-Portland packet line, 68/266; South Bend, Wash., 78/91; stage lines, SEE Stage transportation; transcontinental railroad completion effects in Ore., 67/101-78*passim*; Vancouver-Cowlitz Farm, 62/64; West, 70/86; western development 1865-90, 65/304-305
The Transportation Frontier: Trans-Mississippi West, 1865-1890, by Winther, review, 65/304-305
Trappers, SEE Free trappers; Fur trade; Mountain men
Trappers and Mountain Men, by Jones and Morgan, review, 64/348
Trapping industry:
British Columbia, 72/236
Trask, Elbridge, 62/195-96; 64/202, 214,218-19,235; 65/407,410
Trask, Mrs. Elbridge, 64/234-35
Trask, by Berry, review, 62/192-96
Trask River, 72/300,303,305:
history, 77/91; photo, 72/fr.cov. Dec.
Travel:
1870s, 80/269-70; accommodations in Siskiyous, 76/85-87; automobile, 71/366; SEE ALSO Automobiles; Columbia River Hwy., 66/249-71*passim*; Coos Co.-Portland 1905, 80/51-52; Deschutes 1813, 77/79-81; historic American accounts, 70/353; Idaho boxcar 1917, 72/183; journals, 71/291,312-13,365; LaGrande-Baker 1898, 66/303; lost manuscripts of western travels, 71/291; Marysville-Jacksonville 1853, 63/11; North American 1822-24, 77/91; ocean, 71/190-91,312-13,365; Oregon, 71/286-87,292; Oregon-California 1885, 80/231-57; Oregon-China-California 1850s, 66/161-

70*passim*; Pacific Northwest, 71/5-25; provisions for, 71/181; railroad immigrant car, 70/47; ship immigrants, 70/40; ship travel 1885, 80/254-56 stagecoach, 71/365; 72/168—
accommodations, 81/105; Cheyenne-Deadwood, 72/168; Sacramento-Portland 1860, 72/170
Trans-Mississippi West 1865-90, 65/304-305; trans-Pacific, 76/229; upper Willamette Valley, 72/17; west of Mississippi, 70/86; western waters, 70/86; Willamette Valley to Coos Valley 1910, 66/52; Willamette Valley to Lincoln Co. 1837, 66/346-47; Winnemucca-Burns, 63/304-307,309; Yale Factory-Norway House, 70/367
"Travelers at the Deschutes, 1813?" by Keith Clark, 77/79-81
Travels in North America: 1822-1824, by Paul Wilhelm, trans. by Nitske, noted, 77/91
Travels in the Great Western Prairies, the Anahuac and Rocky Mountains and in the Oregon Territory, by Thomas J. Farnham, reprint noted, 79/107
The Travels of J.H. Wilbur, ed. by Johnson, noted, 78/91
Traynor, William J.H., 75/134,135
Treadwell, Edward F.:
The Cattle King, cited, 63/309N,311N
Treadwell stamp mill, Alaska, 81/121: photo, 81/120
Treasures of the Oregon Country, by Drawson, noted, 76/92; 79/105; 81/329
Treaties and conventions:
Adams-Onis 1818, 76/208; Amity and Commerce 1831, 76/122; Burlington, 75/123; Columbia River, 63/89; 69/272-73; Convention of 1818, 70/339; 76/212-13; Florida 1819, 72/5; "Gentlemen's Agreement," 1907, 76/235, 247; Guadalupe-Hidalgo 1848, 72/6; Hawaiian Islands-France 1839, 68/58; Monticello Convention, 63/108; Nine-Power Treaty 1922, 62/19-27*passim*; Nootka Sound 1790, 76/212; 79/397-402; Oregon Treaty 1846, 63/185,201-202,229-30; 76/213,216; 81/184;

Paris 1763, **76**/311
Russia-U.S., **75**/333-34—
1824, **72**/113,118,118N,123-26; **76**/201-13*passim*; St. Petersburg 1810, **76**/212; Treaty of Commerce 1832, **75**/332; Ukase of 1821, **68**/186; **72**/103,107·17,125-26; **76**/200,211, 213,220
Treaty of Ghent, **70**/342; **72**/113N; **76**/212; U.S.-Hawaii Reciprocity 1875, **69**/334; Wanghai 1844, **76**/218; Webster-Ashburton, **70**/294; SEE ALSO Indians—treaties
Tree, Roland, and Henry Stevens: *Comparative Cartography*, reprint noted, **69**/79
Trees:
Annie Patton tree, Cowlitz Co., **65**/309; Condra tree, Salem, **63**/246; Cowlitz Co., **67**/366; fossils, **67**/29; "Hangman's Tree," **72**/93; largest, SEE Spruce trees; Oregon Trail, **80**/77,80, 81,85,94,95,99; Pow-wow tree, Gladstone, **68**/187; records, **79**/105; species in U.S., **72**/179; Stuart oak, **67**/369; varieties in early Oregon, **63**/52N; SEE ALSO Forestry; names of trees; Timber
"Trees in Hazard: Oregon's Myrtle Groves," by Thornton T. Munger, **67**/41-53
Trenholm, Virginia Cole: *The Arapahoes, Our People*, noted, **72**/172
Trenholm, Virginia Cole, and Maurine Carley: *The Shoshonis, Sentinels of the Rockies*, review, **66**/74-75
Trent (steamship), **72**/315; **79**/406
Tressen, Fred, **74**/24
Trevett, Emily, **79**/203
Trevillian, Buckner W., **68**/353
Triar, H.H., **62**/149
Trilliums, **73**/179
Trilobites: first found in Oregon, **68**/352
Trimble, Joel Graham, **68**/294
Trinity Episcopal Church, Portland, **72**/317

Trinity School for Boys, **72**/317,331
Tripier-Lefranc, Madame, SEE Lebrun, Eugénie
Tripler, Charles S., **66**/119N
Tripp, Frank A., **78**/234,311,311N,314, 315,325N
Tripple, R.A., **74**/22
Trogen, Stanley, **78**/370
Trolley Park, Glenwood, **69**/177
Trombley, "Chick," **77**/237
Trommald, Mrs. John P., **64**/363; **65**/125,221,317,416; **66**/93,189,285,392, 395; **67**/380; **68**/361; **69**/347; **70**/374; **74**/183,363,366
Tronsen, Oscar, **66**/127
Trotter, Bill, **67**/228
"The Trough at Rockwall Springs," by John Quinn, **76**/175-76
Troup, Charley, **80**/119
Troup, Claude, **63**/61,64
Troup, James W., **63**/61,64,65; **74**/358
Trout, **68**/240; **74**/50; **79**/182,190, 381,382,383,384
Trout Creek, Harney Co., **68**/234,314N; **77**/153
Trout Creek, Jefferson Co., **65**/19N,20, 114; **72**/340,341,342; **75**/309,310, 311; **79**/163,165-69*passim*,277,290; **81**/297,299,303: photo, **75**/313
Trout Creek, Malheur Co., **68**/249N, 314N
Trout Creek Canyon, Jefferson Co., **75**/312
Trout Creek Valley, Jefferson Co., **79**/169
Troutdale, Ore.:
Coxey's army, **65**/279,281-83
Truax, Sewell, **63**/33; **65**/394: survey 1858, **72**/43N
Truckee River, **72**/12
Trucking industry, **74**/79: franchises, **74**/81; photos 1940, **76**/154,171
Trucks:
Dodge photo 1936, **76**/36; International, **77**/302; logging photo 1940, **76**/ins.bk.cov. March; pictorial history, **68**/179-80; **73**/74; photos, **77**/238,248; varieties, **68**/180

True, Will, Westfall storekeeper, 63/282,286

True Shout Spring, 68/258,316

Truitt, Warren, 65/246

Truk, Caroline Islands, 62/21,31

Trullinger, John C., 67/174

Trullinger, Paul A., 75/85

Truman, Harry S., 62/7,37,38,40,50

Trumbull, John, artist, 73/276

Trumbull, Lyman: photo, 73/32; Powell loyalty dispute, 73/58-59; Stark senate seat dispute, 72/333-38; 73/33,37,40,41,46,59

The Trumpet Soundeth: William Jennings Bryan and His Democracy, 1896-1912, by Glad, review, 62/188-92

"Trunk Line Railroad Development in Oregon, 1860-87," by Johnson, cited, 71/75

Trutch, Joseph William, 63/90

The Truth about Cowboys and Indians, and Other Myths about the West, by Mendenhall, noted, 81/331

Tryon Creek State Park, 79/104

Tshimakain Mission, 79/102

Tsimshian Indians, 62/57,184

Tsuji, Mrs. —, Portland Assembly Center, 81/160

Tsunamis, SEE Tidal waves

Tsusumi family, 81/153,155

Tualatin, Ore.: Sweek house, 64/88

Tualatin Academy, Forest Grove, 70/199

Tualatin (Tuality, Twality) County, Ore., 62/140,144,149,156,158: bibliography, 76/381; history, 76/381

Tualatin Indians, 70/260: head flattening, 69/171

Tualatin Plains, 62/138; 63/205,234; 71/69

Tualatin Plains Historical Society: officers and board members, 62/104, 415; 63/86,251; officers and directors, 64/84,280; 65/124,312; 66/85,279; 67/83,284; 68/85,283; 69/82,280; 70/83,277; 71/195; 72/177; 73/79; 74/181; 75/92; 76/96; 77/96; 78/96; 79/112; 80/111; 81/112

Tualatin River, 63/51N

Tualatin Valley, 66/283: electric railways, 72/90; history, 80/106

Tualatin Valley Heritage Club, 75/294

Tuality (Tualatin): name, 66/281

Tub Springs, 69/105,120

Tuberculosis, 78/23N: contagion, 80/243N,272-73,277; Portland clinic history, 79/408; prevalence in 19th century, 80/229,249N; symptoms, 80/231-57*passim;* treatment, 78/24-25; women, 78/24-25

Tucannon River, 79/181,199

Tuck, Raphael, and Sons, London, 66/304

Tucker, David Grant, 62/199

Tucker, Ernest Fanning, architect, 62/61

Tucker, Ray, and Frederick R. Barkley: *Sons of the Wild Jackass,* reprint noted, 73/282

Tuckerman, Edward, 69/161-62

Tuckers, Ira, 69/36,49N

"Tugboat Annie," 71/199

Tugboats, 69/309-23*passim;* 77/107, 109,117

Tuhy, John E.: *The Annals of the Thoracic Clinic,* noted, 79/408

Tuisku, Jennie, 68/341

Tule Lake, Klamath Co., 72/7N,36,37, 38,93: boating, 66/382; draining, 72/36-37; land reclaimed, 72/46; map, 72/bk. cov. March; name, 72/34N; settlers, 72/353

Tule Lakes, Harney Co., 78/221

Tulelake, Calif., 72/93

Tully, Cecil R., and Marguerite N. Davis: *The Building of a Community, Multnomah,* noted, 77/299-300

Tumalo Creek, 79/145N,295N

Tumwater, Wash., 62/64; 63/206

Tuna industry, 67/85

Tunis, Edward: *The Colonial Craftsman,* cited, 69/182

Tunnels: Columbia River Hwy., 74/125,138—

Mitchell Point, 74/127,139— photo, 74/133

Tupper, Mabel, and Birgetta Nixon: *Cherry Grove: A History from 1852 to the Present*, noted, 79/336

Turbeville, Daniel E., III: *The Electric Railway Era in Northwest Washington, 1890-1930*, review, 80/332-33

Turkington, Adelia Judson, SEE Leslie, Adelia Judson Olley

"Turn Again: The Name Oregon and Linguistics," by Edward Taube, 79/211

Turn Verein, Portland: building photo, 80/265; members photo, 80/264

Turnbow, Alva S.: *The Robnett Family Record*, noted, 73/73-74

Turnbull, George S., 62/107; 63/91; 64/148-49; 66/171N; 74/239: *Journalists in the Making, A History of the School of Journalism at the University of Oregon*, review, 67/360-61

Turnbull, James, 80/21

Turnbull, William, capt. of *Fannie Troup*: biography, 72/89

Turner, "Auctioneer," 78/13-14

Turner, Creed, 80/12

Turner, Frederick Jackson, 63/358; 70/179,210,363; 71/291; 72/179: comment on Columbia River Hwy., 74/117; history of agriculture, 69/335; methodology, 69/335

Turner, Frederick Jackson: *The Character and Influence of the Indian Trade in Wisconsin*, ed. by Miller and Savage, review, 79/92-97

Turner, George L., 79/13-14: biography, 78/141,142N; promotes cutoff route, 78/141-43,144; trading posts, 78/141

Turner, Harold J., 62/421,422; 63/ 93,255,372,374; 64/94,190,286,363

Turner, Joyce D., 62/249N

Turner, Stephen W.: *Tracing Your Ancestors: A Guide to Research in American Genealogy*, noted, 74/283

Turner, T.D., 74/22

Turner, Tim, 76/265

Turner, W.I., 76/259-65*passim*

Turner, Ore., 63/364

Turner's store, Malheur River, 78/143

Turney-High, Harry H.: *Ethnography of the Kutenai*, cited, 71/279

Turnips: Cowlitz Farm, 63/115,137,145,148, 151,162,164; French Prairie, 66/339

Turrill, Joel: praises missionaries, 68/65; U.S. consul in Hawaii, 68/63

Turtles, 64/261

Tuscania (steamship), 71/214: photo, 77/286; survivors' association, 77/288; torpedoed, 77/285-88

Tusk, Tony, 63/288

Tuska, Jon: *The Filming of the West*, review, 78/362

Tussing, Amor A., 67/69

Tutherly, Herbert E., 70/146,147

Tuttle, Daniel Sylvester, 63/254; 70/181

Tuyll, F.V., 72/111,113,118

TVault, William Green, 62/149-50,151; 64/148; 77/319N; 81/188N

Twain, Mark, SEE Clemens, Samuel Langhorne

Twain and the Image of History, by Salomon, review, 62/292-94

Twana Indians, SEE Skokomish Indians

Twelve Mile Creek, Ore.-Calif., 72/16N

Twelve Mile Creek, Ore.-Calif. border: boundary survey difficulties, 72/16N,52; name, 72/16N; photo of canyon, 72/ ins.bk.cov. March

Twelve-Mile House (Castle Edel Brau), 73/82

Twelve Mile House, Corvallis, 68/145

Twenty Mule Team Borax Co., 68/187; 73/233

"Two Cavalrymen's Diaries of the Bannock War, 1878," ed. by George F. Brimlow, 68/221-58,293-316

Two Years Before the Mast, by Dana, 63/192,218: Kemble essay, 66/86

Twohy Brothers, contractors, 69/293
Twomile Creek, Coos Co., 62/215
Tyee (tug), 66/109,111
Tygh Indians, 79/144N:
railroad construction workers, 79/150N
Tygh Ridge, 67/6
Tygh Valley, 62/217,218,219; 65/17;
79/126,161,163,165
Tyler, John, 62/9; 76/217
Tyler, Robert Lawrence, 62/106;
64/281:
Rebels of the Woods: The I.W.W. in the Pacific Northwest, review, 69/325-26
Typhoid fever, 75/32; 79/190:
Cowlitz Farm, 63/146,194,203,228;
SEE ALSO "Camp fever"
Typographical unions:
first in Pacific NW, 64/38; Portland
parade entry 1865, 64/166

U and I Sugar Company, 67/372:
history, 69/275
U.S. Hotel, Jacksonville, 63/252;
69/252:
photo, 66/58; restoration, 66/
59,92,282
Ubbelohde, Carl:
Edward Kern and American Expansion,
by Hine, review, 63/345-46
Uberuaga, Margarita, photo, 76/164
Udall, Stewart:
biography, 80/408
Ukamok Island, 77/184
Ukivok Island, 73/137
Ullman, Al, 79/411
Uma-how-lits (Umahowlish) (Indian),
79/130
Umapine (Indian), 68/233N; 70/36:
photo, 68/236
Umatilla, Ore., 62/300; 63/206,365;
64/90; 70/8,169; 73/285
Umatilla (steamboat), 66/80
Umatilla Advertiser, 64/175
Umatilla County, Ore., 66/141,227,319;
72/85-86,350,352; 73/81:
centennial, 63/365; 64/90; courthouse, 77/298; described 1862,
66/226-27; first electric lights,
63/365; second oldest town, 73/83;

sheriff, 66/282
Umatilla County Historical Society:
officers and directors, 76/96; 77/96;
78/96; 79/112; 80/111; 81/112;
Peace Pipe Museum, 69/178; publications, 77/292,298; 78/364; 80/105,
335; 81/105
Umatilla Electric Cooperative Assn.,
80/328
Umatilla House, The Dalles, 62/316:
photo, 81/ins.bk.cov. Fall
Umatilla Indian Agency, 62/243,389N;
63/81; 70/34,154; 78/139,141N,364;
79/392:
cost, 66/135; house described, 66/
135; OMV fort, 66/137
Umatilla Indian Reservation, 79/365;
80/105; 81/341N,342:
Catholic school, 70/322-24,330; history, 64/90; land severalty act, 70/
322,324,330; physicians, 79/306,308
Umatilla Indians, 70/115; 79/136;
81/398:
Bannock War, 68/233,306; Haller
1854 expedition, 67/311; Howard
council 1878, 70/34-38; mat lodge
photo, 81/406; schools, 70/326,330,
331; severalty lands, 70/322,330;
Smohalla cult, 70/124; trade with
settlers, 73/262; tribal organization,
70/121
Umatilla Landing, 62/228; 63/31,263
Umatilla-Morrow County History
Museum, 71/200
Umatilla Reclamation Project, 80/409
Umatilla River, 62/399; 66/132,153,
156,201; 79/200,392:
ford, 79/179,200; OMV scouts 1855-
56, 66/141,152; photo, 66/140
Umatilla Sun, Umatilla:
century fair edition, 64/90
Umatilla Valley, 79/392
Umnak Island, 77/185
Umpqua:
meaning, 64/355
Umpqua Academy, Wilbur, 81/105
Umpqua Canyon, 63/52
Umpqua City, Ore., 68/261,343;
70/255:

location, 70/234,235; origin, 70/236; plat, 70/256; post office, 70/236N; speculation, 70/253-54

Umpqua College, 68/186

Umpqua County, Ore., 73/72; 76/382; 78/42

Umpqua Gazette, Scottsburg, 64/148

Umpqua Indians, 63/20,193; 68/89; 69/173; 70/243,247,249-51; 74/358: agency closed, 70/249; hostilities, 62/ 197; house sketch 1858, 81/406; moved to reservation, 71/189; photos, 70/244

Umpqua Mountains, 63/52

Umpqua National Forest, 66/282

Umpqua River, 62/216; 63/11-13, 37,350; 68/261,263,342; 69/232; 70/233,252,257,261; 73/72; 74/93; 80/51: aerial photo, 70/ins.bk.cov. Sept.; ferries, 69/330; flood 1861, 70/254-55; French Canadian settlers, 68/81; fur trade, 66/187,383; 68/81; maps, 69/30,34; 70/234; pioneers, 66/383; *Tacoma* wrecked, 66/171-75,177; transportation, 63/13; 74/280,358; SEE ALSO North Umpqua River; South Umpqua River

Umpqua Trapper, noted, 66/187,387; 67/80,279,281; 68/81,280,342; 69/330; 70/74,271; 73/72,283; 74/92,280,358; 75/362; 77/89; 78/90,364; 80/105; 81/105

Umpqua Valley, 63/16,19-20,42N; 77/317; 79/27: botanical collection, 68/114,121; history, 68/343; 71/190; 80/105; population 1870, 71/41; river traffic, 71/41

Umpqua Valley, Oregon, and Its Pioneers, by Minter, noted, 68/343

Unalaska Island, 73/122-27; 77/184, 185-86: sketches, 73/122,123,125,126; SEE ALSO Illiuliuk Alaska

Unaligmut Eskimos: customs, 73/134-36; sketches, 73/ 134-35

Unander, Sig, 74/238

Under Eleven Governors, by Belton, noted,

79/336

Underhill, J.E.: *Wild Berries of the Pacific Northwest,* noted, 76/181-82

Underhill, Ruth M.: *Red Man's Religion,* review, 67/187-88

Underwood, Ben, 80/130

Underwood, D.B., 65/394-95

Underwood, J.B., 67/55,57

Underwood, Rex, 74/234

Unga (Grekodeliarov), Alaska: described, 73/121-22; sketch, 73/120

Unga Island, 73/120; 77/185

Ungar, Frank, 81/41

Unimak Island, 77/186

Unimak Pass, 80/49

Union, Union Co., Ore., 66/199: oldest church building, 65/315; woolen mills, 62/166,175

Union County, Ore.: history, 63/84; resources, 65/385

Union County Historical Society, 63/84,253; 68/354

Union Depot, Portland, 66/92

Union Flat: mining camp, 62/228

Union Gap, Wash., 70/147N

Union Iron Works, San Francisco, 69/307; 76/272,292: photos, 76/271,272

Union Meat Company, Troutdale: Coxey's army episode, 65/279,281,284

Union of Soviet Socialist Republics: archives, 74/95; SEE ALSO Russia

Union Oil Company of California: Heritage Award, 66/393

Union Pacific Country, by Athearn, review, 73/66

Union Pacific Railroad, 63/78; 67/87, 105,146FF,150; 69/217,220,222,274; 70/79,86,181,364,371; 73/306; 74/62,109,128; 75/272: construction costs, 71/28,39,64-65; Coxey's army conflict, 65/272,278- 79,283-86,291N; finances, 71/54,80; Golden Spike centennial, 71/197; Gould control, 71/55; history, 73/66; illustration 1870, 71/4; land grant opposed, 71/54; postal cards, 66/305;

records, 74/79; rivalry, 71/51,54-55 routes—

Cheyenne-Ogden, 71/8; Grass Valley-Shaniko, 81/102; OR&N connection, 71/39,55; Portland-Hood River, 79/ 203,210; proposed, 71/29,39,49-50, 54-55; survey by Hudnutt 1867, 71/54

Seward journey 1869, 72/129-30

The Union Pacific Railroad: A Case in Premature Enterprise, by Fogel, cited, 71/75

Union Party, 67/54; 76/138; 80/157N; 81/245:

Oregon convention 1864, 64/165; Oregon victory, 73/55; organized, 73/53; platform, 73/54

Union Point, 69/339

Union Railroad, 72/288

Unione Dei Rivenditori Di Frutta Ed Erbaggi, 77/254

Unitarian Church:

early Oregon, 77/300

United Air Lines, 67/91

United Brethren Church:

Corvallis, 69/78; early Oregon, 77/300

United Nations, 62/41,54

United Railways of Oregon, by Hallgren and Due, noted, 62/301

United States:

Alaska purchase, 72/127-29; boundary waters commission 1912, 67/368; Calif. ports and diplomacy, 67/372; Civil War effects, 70/69-71; colonial system, 70/85; environment, 70/360 expansionism, 64/343-44; 75/319, 327N,329,334-35—

1820s, 72/101-26; 1860s, 72/130, 132,145; 1900-1903, 72/209-24; changes, 72/218-23; commercial, 74/359; Idaho press, 65/368; opinion leaders, 72/212-13,224; opposition, 72/132,222-24; westward, 76/125,199,208,212,213,218

foreign policy since 1920, 62/410; forest divisions, 72/179

Hawaiian relations—

missionaries and, 68/53-74; treaties, 67/367; 68/67

history of science, 67/367

Indian policy, 67/367; 70/101-37*passim*,149-63*passim*; 72/234— war debt, 67/319N

international boundary survey 1872-76, 66/69-71; laws extended to Oregon, 80/134N; loyalty disputes, 73/31-59; maritime rights, 75/327,328; Northwest Coast exploration, 70/77; Orient trade interests, 71/141-78*passim*

Pacific Northwest, 72/229—

federal funds used in, 67/294N,372; 68/186; maritime supremacy, 72/127-29

presidents, 78/118-20; 80/334— first ten, 68/341

relations with Great Britain, 62/407-409; 75/317-27—

1820s, 72/101-26; U.S. view of England, 73/286

relations with Russia, 75/317-18, 325-35—

1820s, 72/101-26

services to emigrants, 81/98; states' regional expenditures, 69/83; stock exchanges, 69/197N

strategy in Pacific—

1818-1923, 66/71-72; bibliography, 62/56; since 1792, 62/5-55

technology, 71/290

territories, 75/365—

administration, 71/358; governors, 71/196; officers 1861-90, 71/358; system, 73/86

urban transition, 70/174; war and conflict, 70/179; water resources development, 68/86

United States Air Force, 62/45,46,47; SEE ALSO U.S. Army Air Force

United States Army, 62/20,22,46,50-51; 66/155,156; 74/90,95; 80/14:

air force, SEE U.S. Army Air Force Alaska, 72/135—

posts, 70/180

and National Parks, 68/88; artillery, 63/194; 65/331,333; 71/279-81; artists with, 65/136,145; Astoria bldgs., 1855 photo, 81/4; brevet rank usage, 68/225N; business dealings 1850s, 74/356; California, 63/83; SEE

ALSO Calif. Volunteers; "camp" and "fort" usage, 67/304N-305N; camps, 79/132; SEE ALSO names of camps; cavalry, 63/86; 66/62; 70/4; civilian employees, 67/294FF,313N; civilian opinion 1898, 80/178; Coast Reservation protection plan, 64/174-75; Colored Troops, 65/87N; Columbia River and Puget Sound Dist., 68/33; Columbia River mouth defense, 64/ 325-61*passim*; Crater Lake 1886, 81/50; credit system, 68/8; crime and punishment, 70/178 Department of California— jurisdiction, 69/224N; number troops 1849-60, 68/45 Department of Oregon, 63/112— created, 68/33; 79/31; jurisdiction, 69/224N; number troops 1849-60, 68/33,45; strength 1860, 65/325 Department of the Columbia, 64/178; 70/101,111; 79/129 Department of the Pacific, 65/173,327- 61*passim*; 70/364; 79/31— bldg. expenses 1849-58, 68/41,52; number troops 1849-60, 68/33,45 deployment of troops 1789-1895, 66/ 188; disputes with volunteers, 67/315, 318-20,323N; District of Oregon, 65/ 10-118*passim*; District of Owyhee, 79/ 132; District of the Lakes, 79/132; dragoon equipment, 68/348; Eighth Infantry, Cos. A and B, 65/350-51; enlistment, 80/171; exped. against Mormons, 67/219,221FF; First Artillery, 67/298,299,300; First Dragoons, 71/291; footwear, 77/303-304; forage costs 1850, 67/311N Fourteenth Infantry, 66/61,62; 74/93; 80/176N,183N,186,190,191— history, 72/353 Fourth Infantry, 66/220N; 80/188; **81**/199— reaches Oregon, 67/300 Grays Harbor garrison, 68/340; in West, 67/76,293-94; Indian campaigns, SEE Indians—wars and hostilities Indian policy, 70/104,110,

151-54,367— extermination issue, 79/129, 149N,328-30 Indian scouts with, SEE Indian scouts; Indian wars bibliography, 81/106; Indian wars logistics, 72/230; influence of politics 1861-65, 65/48,97 Japanese relocation WW II— assembly center conditions, 81/165- 71; authority, 81/149-50; Multnomah Co., 81/164-65; Oregon, 81/150FF; procedures, 81/164,165; relocation camps, 81/150,163,168-71 Jefferson Barracks, 68/86; Klamath exped., 69/223,232-68; 70/251-52; lieutenant commission, 72/224; liquor problems, 70/367 maps— Cram 1855, 66/132; Mullan 1858, 66/opp.pg.144 military reservations, 63/111; Modoc War numbers, 70/175-76; mounted forces, 64/85; 65/87 Ninth Infantry, 67/320,321,323— Co. A, 65/343,345,350 officers— listed, 69/333-34; pay scale Vancouver Barracks, 64/276; sketch 1900, 72/fr.cov. Sept.; staff *vs.* field, 65/94,99 Oregon— first troops, 64/207; Oregon Artillery, 64/352; Oregon Coast Artillery, 64/90 Oregon Territory 1849-52, 74/355-56 Oregon Trail— patrol, 67/311,312; relief to travelers, 68/185 Pacific Division— number troops 1849-60, 68/45 Pacific Northwest— 1850-56, 67/293-333*passim*; importance to, 67/292-95; money disbursed, 67/294; post inspections, 68/30-31,39-40; SEE ALSO Fort Dalles pay 1898, 80/175,191; payroll at Ft. Dalles 1856-58, 68/25,44; post-Civil War, 73/286 posts—

1849-58, 68/52; Alaska, 70/180; construction expenditures, 67/305N; construction policy, 68/6,8,13-15,16 quartermaster purchases, 68/226-58 *passim*; railroad survey, 80/209; Reports of Persons and Articles Hired, 67/294N; road exploration, 67/309, 310N; scientists with, 66/233; Seventh Cavalry, 70/66; Spruce Production Division, 64/250; 72/301; 77/213; supply contracts, 63/106N; 68/23,345 Third Artillery, 81/199—

Co. L, Klamath exped., 69/223, 232-68—

photos, 69/236,238

in Oregon 1850s, 69/223N Trans-Mississippi West, 73/284,286 transportation, 71/366—

troop transport 1942, 80/35 Twenty-fifth Infantry, 80/177; Twenty-third Infantry, 80/179

uniforms—

Indian wars, 81/360-62; insignia, 74/283

volunteers 1898, 80/175,176,177; weapons, 81/361; western army women, 67/367; winter campaign views, 67/312,317N,318

World War I—

camps, 75/247,250,253,255,257-58; diary, 75/245-69; equipment, 75/259; morale, 75/251-52,258-59,265-69; servicemen photos, 75/244,246,268; training, 75/245-48,254,259-60,264

World War II, 62/30,32,33; Yakima War policy, 68/31-32,42; SEE ALSO First Oregon Cavalry; First Oregon Infantry; Military life; Mounted Rifle Regiment; Second Oregon Volunteer Infantry; Washington Territory Volunteers

United States Army Air Force:

Aleutians 1943, 80/35-45*passim*; Morrow Co. air base, WW II, 69/120

The U.S. Army and the Indian Wars in the Trans-Mississippi West, 1860-1898, comp. by Reber *et al*, noted, 81/106

United States Army Engineers, 71/188, 279-81; 77/285,286,361; 79/27:

map of Oregon 1879, 79/276,ins.fr. cov. Summer; Pacific NW civil files, 71/ 290; Portland Dist. centennial, 72/287

United States Army Military History Institute:

publication, 81/106

United States Army Signal Corps, 70/88

United States Bureau of Indian Affairs: criticized, 67/356; difficulties, 70/108-10; education policy, 80/208; funds disbursed at Grand Ronde, 67/294N; Indian collection, 70/362; Oregon country, 62/123-24; textbooks used in schools, 74/67

United States Bureau of Land management, 67/48:

history resources, 70/182; mineral prospecting permits, 73/244

United States Bureau of Reclamation, 69/336; 72/286:

history, 80/408-409

United States Census, SEE Census

The United States Census of Jackson County, Oregon, 1880, by Genealogical Forum of Portland, noted, 66/80

United States Civilian Conservation Corps, 64/75; 69/65-66,85; 76/35; 77/90; 78/91:

photo, 76/36

United States Coast and Geodetic Survey, 71/364:

Crescent City station, 72/11; Davidson exped. to Alaska, 72/139-40

United States Coast Artillery Corps: history, 71/279-81

United States Coast Guard, 69/310, 312N,323; 77/91:

Aleutians, 80/31-49; Barview station, 77/221(with photo),358,361-62,367; Pacific Northwest, 72/232; Point Adams station, 77/361; Yaquina station, 71/91

United States Congress:

Civil War legislation effects, 70/69-71; Confiscation Act, 73/52; election 1918, 68/125-40; exclusion and expulsion policies, 73/56-57; Indian policy difficulties, 70/105-14*passim*; land grants, 72/316; laws passed 1862, 72/

316; lobbying 1846, 81/185; opposition to Ukase of 1821, 72/116-17; senate Civil War membership disputes, 72/315-38; Thirty-seventh Congress acts, 73/52; views on emigrant escorts, 72/56-58; Webb-Kenyon Act, 68/134; Wilderness Act of 1964, 68/86

United States Congress Electoral Commission 1876: decision for Republican electors, 67/271,272; investigates 1876 electoral vote, 67/257,268-72; records, 67/269

United States Department of the Interior, 71/368: transfer of Indian affairs issue, 70/110

United States Department of State, 62/ 9,15,34; 68/60-74*passim*; 72/101-26*passim*

United States Department of the Treasury, 62/9

"U.S. Diplomacy: Influence of Sandwich Island Missionaries and the ABCFM," by Merze Tate, 68/53-74

United States Exploring Expedition, SEE Wilkes Expedition

United States Forest Service, 70/279; 72/183,287; 76/259,268; 77/350: bibliography, 77/304; biographical sketches, 70/182; development, 68/ 349; foresters recruited WW I, 77/285; history, 76/29-38; 78/280; land exchanges, 78/308; location disputes, 68/186; mapping, 70/182

multiple use management— fire control, 76/34,35,37(photo),44-50; grazing, 76/32,34,37,71; Pinchot directives, 76/33,37; recreation, 76/ 35,37; timber harvest, 76/35,37-38

personnel, 76/30,33,41-45; 78/280; publications, 77/304; recollections, 68/349; 69/274; records, 71/368; regional offices, 76/33,34; SEE ALSO National Forests

The United States Forest Service: A Historical Bibliography, 1876-1972, comp. by Ogden, noted, 77/304

The U.S. Forest Service: A History, by Steen, review, 78/280

United States General Land Office, 73/334

United States Geological Survey: first Oregon field studies, 67/21; log 1969, 72/46-47; maps, 72/45

U.S. Government Mapping Agencies: Recent Activities and Changes...City Mapping, noted, 70/360

The United States: The History of a Republic, by Hofstadter *et al*, noted, 69/276

The U.S. Indian Claims Commission, Final Report, Aug. 13, 1946-Sept. 30, 1978, noted, 81/332

United States Life Saving Service, 69/309N: Bandon station, 72/92; Oregon photos, 66/176; rescue of crew of *Lightship No. 50*, 69/310

United States Lighthouse Service, 69/78,311,313,322

United States Marshal, SEE Portland police

United States Military Academy, West Point, 65/136; 72/77,77N

United States National Archives, 67/ 293N; 70/259; 71/262,358: history profession and, 71/290; international boundary records, 70/273; military records, 67/294N; regional history, 71/368; Solicitor of the Treasury records, 70/273; U.S. territorial records, 75/365

United States National Bank, Jacksonville, 62/59,92,282: photo, 66/58

United States National Bank, Portland, 71/148

United States National Park Service, 70/ 175,177; 71/191; 72/83-84; 79/411; 80/101:

1916 act, 68/185; founding, 70/364; publications, 65/202-203; 71/287; restoration research, 79/107; salt cairn conveyed to, 80/335,412; survey of historic sites and bldgs., 69/275-76,333

United States National Park Service: *Soldier and Brave: Indian and Military Affairs in the Trans-Mississippi West*, review, 65/202-203

United States Naval History: A Bibliog-

raphy, noted, 74/283-84
United States Navy:
admiral visits Portland, 78/117-18; aircraft photo, 80/36; Asiatic fleet, 62/10,20
bases—
Aleutian, 71/165; 80/34,35,48; Hawaii, 71/173,174-75; Philippines, 71/168,176; Tillamook blimp base photo, 71/136
Battle Fleet, 62/17,20,21,24,29; California, 70/305,306,311; East India Squadron at Honolulu, 68/59; Eighth Fleet, 62/52; Great White Fleet, 67/91; history, 74/283-84; logbooks 1801-1947, 81/333; naval construction, 76/270-72,294; need for two-ocean navy, 76/293-94
Pacific Fleet, 62/28,29,33—
1818-1923, 66/71-72
Pacific Squadron, 67/372; 70/360—
at Honolulu, 68/72
photos, 74/fr.cov. March; 75/268; Seventh Fleet, 62/33,45
ships—
influential warships, 79/212-13; named *Oregon*, 67/91; visit to Portland, 74/84
Sixth Fleet, 62/52
World War II, 62/28-29,32-33—
strategy, 62/31-32,33,35
yards—
drydock, 80/49; Puget Sound, 71/197
United States Plywood Corporation, 67/50
United States Post Office Department: records, 68/343
United States Rural Electrification Administration, 80/323-28
United States Sanitary Commission: Oregon branch, 64/159
United States Secret Service, 78/338,340
United States Spruce Production Corporation, 72/301; 77/213: Portland division, 64/250
United States War Department: transfer of Indian affairs issue, 70/110
Unity, Wash.:

1870 census, 71/361
University Club, Portland, 74/234
University of British Columbia, 72/233
University of Idaho Library: special collections, 77/297
University of Oklahoma Press: history, 70/179
University of Oregon, Eugene, 62/94; 63/75; 81/341N:
charter, 77/380; fine arts group, 74/64; Gerlinger Hall, 78/158; history, 77/299,380; 81/330; library, 64/137; 66/319
manuscripts—
guide, 73/67-68; re Blacks, 73/203,204
medical school, SEE University of Oregon Medical School; press, 67/361; regents, 71/216; Reserve Officer Training Corps, 72/258; School of Journalism, 67/360-61; School of Music, 74/234
University of Oregon Centennial Cookbook, noted, 77/299
The University of Oregon Charter, by Belknap, review, 77/380
University of Oregon Medical School, Portland, 68/351; 78/177: buildings, 75/19,26; faculty, 75/18, 20,29; history, 75/18-35; seventy-fifth anniversary, 63/363; sketch, 75/27
University of Oregon Mothers' Club: history, 80/104; publication, 77/299
University of Oregon Museum of Natural History: publications, 75/87
University of Portland, 69/124; 73/80; 78/285-86
University of Washington, Seattle, 62/298,406; 65/365; 78/34; 81/103: centennial history, 64/76-77; College of Forest Resources history, 74/358; early athletics, 63/90; first president, 62/186; manuscripts pertaining to Blacks, 73/200; School of Forestry, 73/171
Unruh, John D., Jr.:
The Plains Across: The Overland Emigrants and the Trans-Mississippi West,

1840-1860, review, **81**/96-99,101
Untamed Olympics, by Hult, cited, **74**/8
Untermeyer, Louis, comp.:
Modern American Poetry, cited, **73**/316
"Up the Kilchis," by Daniel D. Strite, **72**/293-314; **73**/5-30,171-92,212-27
Up-To-The-Times-Magazine, **65**/364
Uplands Farm, Washington Co.: house, **75**/294
Upper Dairy area, Washington Co., **75**/87
Upper Klamath Lake: described, **75**/233; map, **75**/232; photos, **75**/235,239; tourist resort, **68**/187
Upper Musselshell Valley, **72**/232
Upper Ostrander community, Cowlitz Co.: recollections, **66**/80
Upper Watson Springs: Snake Indian skirmish, **65**/32N, 34N,84N; photo, **65**/30
Upper Willamette Pioneer Association, **72**/171
Upshaw, Edah Helen Lenz, **77**/378
Upshaw, Francis Marion, **77**/369-70: family history, **77**/369,375; portrait, **77**/370
Upshaw, Ora Estelle, **77**/373: photo, **77**/372
Upshaw, Walter E., **77**/372(photo): "Pioneering Spirit," **77**/369-79
Upshaw, William L., **77**/370-79: photo, **77**/372
Urban planning, **67**/357: Portland metropolitan area publications, **67**/366
Urban renewal, **65**/375; **72**/262-63: Washington Co., **66**/188
Urban studies, **68**/88; **72**/181; **81**/103-104: articles on, **70**/84,362,363; cities in American life, **70**/71-72; fringe problems, **69**/86; history of frontier development to 1890, **81**/201-202; Oregon settlement interpretation, **70**/182; Pacific NW theses, **72**/261-63
The Urban West at the End of the Frontier, by Larsen, review, **81**/103-104

U'Ren, Charles, **81**/297
U'Ren, Frances, SEE McCormack, Frances U'Ren
U'Ren, William Simon, **62**/106; **65**/211; **66**/383; **70**/79,356; **74**/308; **77**/25; **80**/205: association with Lewellings, **68**/197-98,203-10,216-20; charges against, **68**/197,216-18; Oregon Progressive movement, **68**/197-220*passim*; photo, **68**/198
Urlezaga, Eloisa, photo, **76**/167
Urlezaga, Gloria, photos, **76**/166,167
Urlezaga, John: family photos, **76**/166,167; ranch photo, **76**/177
Urlezaga, John, Jr., photo, **76**/167
Urquiaga Ranch, Arock, photo, **76**/172
Urrutia, Virginia, **78**/364
Usuda, Mrs. —, Portland Assembly Center, **81**/160
Usugi, Edward, **81**/162
Utah, **62**/185-86; **63**/358: boundaries 1850, **72**/7-8
boundary surveys— Goddard 1855, **72**/12-13; Major 1871, **72**/19
cattle industry history, **66**/87; centennial, **63**/358; churches, **69**/336; **73**/74; early exploration, **69**/336; government, **71**/292; history, **68**/345-46; industry, **77**/296
mining, **65**/214— 1863-1963, **64**/281; economic impact, **72**/180
statehood, **64**/281; women, **71**/292; SEE ALSO Deseret, State of
Utah and Northern Railway, **70**/87; **71**/55
Utah-Idaho Sugar Company, SEE U and I Sugar Company
Utah (Mormon) War, **62**/185-86; **68**/33,345; **79**/32N: army expedition, **67**/219,221-27; Mountain Meadow massacre, **67**/221
Utaztekan Prehistory, ed. by Swanson, noted, **69**/333
Ute Indians, **63**/246; **70**/86: religion, **71**/333

Utilities industry:
Pacific NW investments in, 77/302
Utley, —, Lakeview land promoter, 77/157,158
Utopian communities:
bibliography, 77/295; California, 68/82; Puget Sound, 77/294-95; SEE ALSO Aurora, Ore.; Bethel, Mo.; Equality, Wash.; Freeland Colony
Utopianism:
Boston, 79/347; means of transformation envisioned, 79/348; Portland, 79/349-57; writers on, 79/347-49,355
Utopias on Puget Sound, 1855-1915, by LeWarne, review, 77/294-95

Vail, —, First Ore. Cavalry, 65/301
Vail, John, 73/283
Vale, Ore., 63/264,269,275,277,284-86,295,297; 73/80; 78/145:
hot springs photo, 78/145
Valentine's Day, 78/166-67
Valley Manufacturing Company, Woodburn, 72/91
Valparaiso, Chile, 77/57-58
Valsetz, Ore., 63/351
Van Arnam, Mrs. Philip, 68/359; 71/371
Van Arsdol, Ted, 65/308:
history of Vancouver Barracks, 67/366
Van Arsdol, Ted, ed.:
"Golden Gate to Columbia River on the Bark *Keoka*: Isaac A. Flint's Journal," 63/41-54
Van Brimmer fort, Siskiyou Co.: described, 66/81
Van Cleft, G.H., 72/10
Vancouver, George, 63/205,234; 71/365; 77/290:
biography, 79/107,397,399; exploring expedition, 71/370
Vancouver, B.C., 70/180:
anti-Oriental riot, 68/88; 72/233; first European vessels at, 65/314; Indians, 72/247,248; population 1880-1960, 72/181; skid road, 72/247,248
Vancouver, Wash., 62/64,65; 72/301,346; 80/14:
early concerts, 65/308; first railroad, 63/82; Gay Nineties, 63/82-83; historic sites, 67/373; history, 80/334; port centennial, 66/80; post office, 63/83; race track, 75/363; World War I, 77/299; SEE ALSO Fort Vancouver
Vancouver (HBCO. bark), 63/156; 64/206N,210,242:
construction, 63/189N,204; wreck, 63/193,204,231; 77/45N
Vancouver (HBCO. schooner):
wreck, 63/164,189,204
Vancouver (sternwheeler), 69/331; 71/13N
Vancouver Barracks, 65/308; 72/353; 74/333,340,341,349:
history, 67/366; officers' pay scale 1861, 64/276; photo, 75/246; World War I, 75/245-47; SEE ALSO Fort Vancouver (military post)
Vancouver Island, 62/92,105; 63/106, 210; 64/276; 69/67; 71/281-82; 73/155,169; 77/44,294:
history, 72/87-88; HBCO. coal operations, 65/314
Vancouver, Klickitat and Yakima Railroad, 67/173-74
The Vancouver Story, by McGuire, noted, 79/107
Vandalia (brig), 68/342
Vandals Wild, by Bennett, noted, 70/358
Vandehey, John, family, 81/332
Vandehey, Scott:
Wooden Shoes West: A Saga of John Vandehey, noted, 81/332
Vanderburg, W.S., 68/207
Van der Loeff, Anna Rutgers, 64/350
Vandervert, J.J., 78/325N
Vandervert, William P., 78/293N-94N
Vandevert, Claude, 72/94
Van Dusen, Adam, 63/252
Van Dusen Insurance Agency, Astoria, 63/252
VanDyke, James, 72/10
"The Vanishing Hop-Driers of the Willamette Valley," by Herbert B. Nelson, 64/267-71
Vannoy family, Southern Ore. pioneers, 66/282

Van Orman, Reuban, **66**/280
Van Orman, Richard A., and O.O. Winther:
A Classified Bibliography of the Periodical Literature of the Trans-Mississippi West: A Supplement (1957-67), review, **72**/349
Vanorman (Van Orman) party massacre, SEE Otter-Vanorman party massacre
Van Pearse, Celia F., **62**/336
VanPeer, Henry, **65**/180-81N,191N
Vanport, Ore., **81**/204
Van Ravenswaay, Charles, **66**/292, 385,393:
"Modern Museums and Modern Man," **66**/293-301
Van Renssalaer, James, **62**/242-87 *passim*,337-86*passim*
VanStone, James W., **62**/106:
Eskimos of the Nushagak River, review, **69**/327-28
Van Vleet, Louis, **63**/252
"Vaquero Foreman," by Marjorie A. Shull, **71**/99
Varness, Mrs. Marvin, **66**/101N
Varney, —, capt. of *Thos. H. Perkins*, **63**/217-18
Varney, Albert N., **81**/264N,268N,272, 273,279
Varney, James A.:
biography, **81**/263,263N,264N,265
Vaudeville, SEE Theaters
Vaughan, Elizabeth A.P. Crownhart (Mrs. Thomas), SEE Crownhart-Vaughan, Elizabeth A.P.
Vaughan, Thomas, **62**/110,206,302, 421,422; **63**/93,115N,255,367,369, 372-73; **64**/93,189,285,358-61,363; **65**/125,221,317,413,414,415,416; **66**/93,189,285,296,365,386,389,390, 392,393,394; **67**/198,376,379; **68**/ 357,358,359,360; **69**/342,344,345, 346,347; **70**/368,369,371,372,373; **71**/369,371,372; **72**/357,359,360,361; **73**/292,364,373; **74**/183,363,364,365; **75**/369,370; **76**/386; **77**/384,385; **78**/368-69,370; **79**/412,415; **80**/197, 411; **81**/425,427,428:
AASLH president, **79**/411; Athabaska Pass trip, **79**/413; awards, **76**/385;

photos, **67**/200,204; reports, **67**/377-78; **71**/100-104,293-96; **80**/414-17
Vaughan, Thomas:
"A Bicentennial Overview: Publications," **77**/289-92
Bob Frazier of Oregon: A Collection of Columns, Editorials and Informal Essays, review, **81**/321
Empire of the Columbia, a History of the Pacific Northwest, by Johansen and Gates, review, **69**/60-61
Oregon Imprints, 1845-1870, by Belknap, review, **70**/62-63
Prehistory of the Far West: Homes of Vanished People, by Cressman, review, **79**/403-404
The Royal Navy and the Northwest Coast of North America, 1810-1914, by Gough, review, **73**/359-60
"Scorekeeping," **75**/5-6
Vaughan, Thomas, and Virginia G. Ferriday, eds.:
Space, Style and Structure: Building in the Northwest America, noted, **75**/368; **77**/291
Vaughan, Thomas, and Priscilla Knuth: "An Oregon Classic," **79**/91
Vaughan, Thomas, and Terence O'Donnell:
Portland: A Historical Sketch and Guide, noted, **77**/291
Vaughan, Thomas, and Martin Winch: "Joseph Gervais, A Familiar Mystery Man," **66**/331-62
Vaughan, Thomas, ed.:
Paul Kane, the Columbia Wanderer, noted, **72**/359
The Western Shore: Oregon Country Essays Honoring the American Revolution, noted, **77**/292
Vaughan, Thomas, *et al*:
Captain Cook, R.N., the Resolute Mariner: An International Record of Oceanic Discovery, noted, **75**/bk.cov. June
Vaughan, Walter, **77**/354
Vaughan, William H., **62**/201
Vaughan, William T., **78**/146-47
Vaughn, Frank E., **69**/209

Vaughn, George W., photo, 80/16
Vaughn, Hank, 69/341; 73/285
Vaughn, John, family, 78/127
Vaughn, Warren Nichols, 65/409-10
Vavasour, Merwin, 63/109N,219,235; 66/356N; 70/302; 79/413: Columbia River survey, 64/210— chart, 64/216-17
Vazlov Vorovsky (ship), 62/197
Veal, R., and Son Chair Factory, Albany, 62/200
Veatch, John C., Jr., 62/100,206,302, 422; 63/93,255,373; 64/93,189,285, 363; 65/125,221,317,416; 66/93,189, 285,394; 68/360; 69/347; 70/373; 75/6
Veatch, Sylvia, 80/104
Veatch family, Lane Co.: genealogy, 74/283
Vedder, O.F., 70/220
Vegetables: French Prairie, 66/339; Oregon pioneer varieties, 63/51N,53; scarcity 1862, 66/200; SEE ALSO names of vegetables
Venable, Janie (Mrs. Tom), 63/301
Venable, Tom, 63/269,301
Venereal diseases, 66/351
Veniaminov, Ioann, 69/184; 73/ 121,123,124,128,129; 74/286
Venison, SEE Prices
Venter, Ida Sparks: reminiscences, 71/361
Ventura, Calif., 80/246
Venture (steamer), 72/94
A Venture in History: The Production, Publication, and Sale of the Works of Hubert Howe Bancroft, by Clark, review, 75/79-80
Verboort, Ore., 62/200
Vercruysse, Louis, 69/269-70
Verdi, Nev., 72/49,49N
Verendrye, Pierre Gautier de Varennes, Sieur de la, 68/184; 71/366
Verhaag, L., 81/92
Verhaegen, Peter, 67/370
Vermilion Creek, 62/259
Vernam, Glenn R., and Lee M. Rice: *They Saddled the West*, review, 76/380-81

Vernon, Buffalo, 63/294
Vernon, Dick, 63/269
Vernonia, Ore., 62/301; 65/308; 67/280; 71/360,361: electric co-op, 80/323; name, 70/279
Vernonia, South Park and Sunset Steam Railroad, 69/87
Veronica, Mother, 80/352; 81/77,80, 82,83
Vershel (Verstille), Peter, 71/278
Versteeg, Nicholas, 75/127,128
Vert, John, 68/354
Vessels: battleships, 76/270-72,275; 79/ 212-13
Boston trading, 76/198,202,203,206, 221N— armed, 76/200; drawing, 76/207; list of, in sea otter trade, 76/221
capital ships, 76/270; Columbia River, 75/76-77; cost of, 1838, 74/76-78; cruisers, 76/283,284,286; fire at sea, 81/197-99; fur trade, 79/339; Liberty ships, 69/331; 72/286; lightships, 77/111,278
lumber, 63/80; 77/222,359-65— Puget Sound, 67/84; schooner photo, 64/124; voyage, 78/288
Manila galleons, 70/77; Merchant Marine, WW II, 77/101-29,363; monitors, 76/274; named *Oregon*, 67/91; ocean routes map, 80/174; Pacific Northwest, 70/266-67; Puget Sound, 67/84
repair— Portland, 62/300; Puget Sound drydock, 71/197
Russian, 73/101-70*passim*; 76/200,220 sailing, 72/115,167-68; 77/37-60; 78/288— photo, 79/ins.fr.cov. Winter; sail mending, photo, 77/114; shipboard life, 71/190-91
sea otter trade, 76/221
steamships, 80/13,15— coastal, 80/52,61
torpedo boats, 76/274,283; towing, 72/30; U.S. Naval, 62/10-52*passim*; whalers, 76/202; SEE ALSO Boats;

Canoes; names of vessels; Navigation; Shipbuilding; Steamboats; Tugboats

Vestal, Samuel, 71/14

Vestal, Stanley, 64/187

Veyret, F., 63/164N

Viazemskii, Aleksandr Alekseevich, 80/203

Vice, SEE Crime and criminals

Victor, Frances Fuller, 62/63N,65; 63/102,110,112,344; 66/148; 74/90; 75/79,80; 76/361; 81/251: bibliography, 71/291; biography, 62/309-36 opinion of the Lees, 74/72— views on Jason Lee, 78/332-50*passim* Roberts letters to, 63/175-236; Rogue River Indian War material republished, 70/359; Scott's opinion of, 70/226-27

Victor, Henry Clay, 62/311,318-19

Victor, Orville J., 62/312N

Victor Rock, 62/323

Victoria, B.C., 62/321,324; 73/155-56: history, 72/87; Seward visit, 72/132, 133,143; theater history, 72/263; SEE ALSO Fort Victoria

Victoria (steamship), 74/27

Victoria Daily Times: centennial edition, 63/362

Victoria: The Fort, by Pethick, review, 72/87-88

Victoria Voltigeurs, 63/90,232N

Victorian Port Townsend, by Simpson, noted, 63/246

Vida, Ore., 62/201; 79/43

Vienna, Ida., 67/87

Viereck, Harry, 77/69

The View from Wenas: A Study in Plateau Prehistory, by Warren, noted, 70/273

Viganego, Matteo, photo, 77/252

Vigée-Lebrun, Elizabeth-Louise, 64/6,19

Vigilantes: Boise, 70/181; California, 71/364; Crook Co., 66/183; Montana, 66/89 Portland, 75/157-58— newspaper opinion, 80/11 San Francisco, 80/11,11N,25

Villa, Pancho, 77/167-68

Villard, Henry, 62/405; 67/119,122; 69/199,217N-19N; 77/380:

papers, 71/40,78FF; photo, 71/48; rail and shipping interests, 71/30,38-39,47, 50,51,61-90*passim*,95

Villiger, Anselm, 70/313,317N,318,329

Vincennes (steamship), 63/345

Vincent, Dean, 74/216

Vincent, Frederick W., 77/298

Vinette, Arthur, 65/271

Vining, Irving E., 64/325-26,329

Vinland, 67/182-83; 72/182

The Vinland Map and the Tartar Relations, by Skelton *et al,* review, 67/182-83

Vinson, Ore., 69/115

Virgin Land, by Smith, cited, 70/263

Virginia City, Mont., 63/79

Virginia City, Nev., 63/79

Visetti, Carlo, 77/254,260

Vista House, 74/123,132,144: construction photo, 66/257 dedication, 74/218— photo, 66/258 photos, 74/100,141; pioneer memorial, 74/141

Vitti, Vita, 77/249,254

Vitus, Louis, 81/105

Viva voce law, 75/120,121

Vocational education, 66/55

Voeltz, Herman C., 63/359: "Coxey's Army in Oregon, 1894," 65/263-95

Vogel, Virgil J.: *American Indian Medicine,* review, 71/179-80

Voget, Fred W., 63/246; 66/75

Vogt, Evon Z., 63/347

"Voice of the West: Harold L. Davis," by Francis J. Greiner, 66/240-48

Voices of Portland, ed. by Ermenc, noted, 77/300

Volcano Mountain, 75/362

Volcanoes, 62/299; 66/283; 67/33, 34,370; 72/90; 75/309: Cascade Range, 73/83; 77/196; Clarno, 73/268; Mt. Baker, 81/332; Mt. Hood, 77/65; Mt. St. Helens, 81/333

Voltigeur regiment, Canada, 63/232

Volz, Leonard, 66/388

Von Schmidt, Allexey W., 72/15N: map, 72/29N; Ore.-Calif. boundary survey, 72/49-53 Ore.-Calif.-Nev. corner monument, 72/53— inscriptions, 72/51; photos, 72/4,50; sketch, 72/4 von Stotzingen, R.F.: German religious colony plan, 70/317N Voorhies, Gordon, 62/170,174,177 Voorhies, Mrs. Peter, 70/5N Voss, J.C.: voyage around the world, 73/273 Voss, Ralph J., 67/376,380; 68/357,361; 69/348; 70/373; 74/183,365 *The Voyage of the HMS Blonde*, by Byron, cited, 64/15 *Voyage of the Columbia: Around the World with John Boit, 1790-1793*, ed. by Johansen, review, 62/88-89 *Voyage of the U.S. Frigate Potomac*, by Reynolds, cited, 64/16 Voyages: commercial wintering 1850-1910, 79/ 106; England-Nootka Sound, 79/400- 402; entertainment, 77/52-55; food and water, 77/49-51; maps, 77/40, 42,44; "Mercer's Belles," 62/186-88; Norse to North America, 66/88; perils, 77/48,59; ports of call, 77/56-59 routes— Cape Horn 1840-50s, 77/37-60; Oregon-Africa, 78/288 supplies, 77/49; weather, 77/41,43,46- 48; Wilbur journal, 78/91; Wilkes, 79/406; SEE ALSO Exploring expeditions; Shipping; Travel *Voyages to Hawaii Before 1860*, by Judd, ed. by Lind, noted, 76/182 Voyageurs, 63/90,203; 66/86: fur trade routes, 63/90; songs, 70/79 *The Voyageurs and Their Songs*, by Blegen, noted, 70/79 Voye, Mrs. James, 71/275,276 Voznesenskii, Ilia Gavrilovich: collections, 73/102,105,138,147,157, 160; expeditions 1839-49, 73/100

(map),101-70 sketches, 73/101-70— Alaska and Aleutians, 73/116-55; California, 73/105-16; list, 73/105; Siberia, 73/156-59 Vreeland, Chess, 81/122N,123,127,128, 133,141,143,148

Wachimtott (Indian), 79/313,315,316, 317,327 Wachter, Bernardine, 70/330 Waconda, Ore., 67/89 Wade, Benjamin Franklin, 73/58 Wade, Murray, 66/305; 74/145 Wadhams, William, 80/320: biography, 80/321N Wadsworth, Elisha, 78/124,128,153 Wadsworth, Harriet Brakeman, 78/124,153 Wages and salaries: Alaska— 1800s, 77/175,180; 1898, 81/ 123,133,134,140,141,142,146 California 1885, 80/249 carpenters— 1856, 70/235; 1890s, 80/280 civil engineers, 73/85; clergy 1881, 70/319; construction, 69/270; deck hand 1905, 81/36; domestic help 1867, 70/61; farm labor, 76/13 Fort Dalles— 1856, 68/25; 1857, 68/47-51 harness-making, 80/274,278,279,282; herding, 76/158; highway construction, 74/138; Idaho 1861, 66/231-32; immigrants, 73/85 laborers, 78/79— farm, 76/13; Japanese 1908, 70/54; Willamette Valley 1851, 63/54 land clearing, 76/231; minimum wage laws, 62/91; mining, 76/116; North West Company 1803, 81/384-85; Oregon textile industry, 62/174-75; Pony Express riders, 67/229; portage military road, 68/26N; Portland 1878, 64/265 ranch hand— 1878, 81/262; 1880, 81/264; 1890s, 80/281

St. Paul 1844, **69**/270; seaman 1830s, **74**/77; teachers, **74**/339,340,341; The Dalles 1858, **68**/29; Umatilla Co. 1862, **66**/226,232

Wagner, Clinton, **79**/289N,292

Wagner, Henry, U.S. Army capt., **68**/ 247N,248,252,257,309N

Wagner, Henry Raup: bibliography, **70**/179

Wagner, Joe, **81**/300,313

Wagner, Norman S.: *Western Mining…on the American Frontier from Spanish Times to 1893,* by Young, review, **72**/347-48

Wagner, Robert: Jackson Co. recollections, **77**/90

Wagnon, Dan, **62**/168

Wagon Creek Valley, Harney Co., **79**/298,301

Wagonmasters: High Plains Freighting…to 1880, by Walker, review, **68**/181-82

Wagons, **72**/94; **74**/79; **76**/177; **79**/37,65,70,81,83: abandoned, **79**/81,82,84,86,89; described 1885, **80**/230 freighting, **68**/181-82; **72**/161, 168-69— 1867, **66**/203; 1885, **80**/236 kinds, **72**/168-69— Conestoga, **69**/336; **70**/364; Studebaker, **72**/161 lore, **80**/104 manufacture, **72**/91— first in Pacific NW, **63**/67 organization of trains, **63**/88 photos, **72**/168; **76**/154— covered (movie view), **79**/76 pioneer, **72**/168-69; replaced, **79**/87,89 travel— Crater Lake 1909, **65**/219; Santiam-Malheur 1846, **66**/357; Texas-Wash. Terr., **66**/219

Wagontire Mountain, **68**/80; **77**/13, 315; **78**/210,221,237,239; **79**/15,145N

Wahenakee (Indian), **79**/150,313,315, 316,328

Wahkeena Falls: photo, **74**/126; SEE ALSO Gordon Falls

Wah-Kee-Nah (Indian), **62**/59

Wahkiakum County, Wash., **64**/297N; **66**/32

Wahkiakum County Historical Society Museum, **69**/178

Wahl, Eva L. (Mrs. Henry L.), **80**/269N

Wahlitits (Shore Crossing) (Indian), **81**/349: sketch, **81**/363

Wah-pass Creek, SEE Wickiup Creek

Wahtum Lake, **74**/129

Waiilatpu, **73**/285; **75**/73,74

Waiilatpu mission, SEE Whitman Mission

Wainwright, Robert Page, **68**/247

Wait, Aaron Emmons, **66**/17,27N

Waite, Davis H., **71**/367

Waite, E.M., **64**/38

Waite, Eva Lane, **65**/401

Waite, Katherine, SEE Bain, Katherine Waite

Waite and Denlinger, Salem printers, **64**/174

Wakabayashi, Shozui, **76**/233

Wakarusa River, **62**/256

The Wake of the Prairie Schooner, by Paden, reprint noted, **71**/362

Wakemap Mound, A Stratified Site on the Columbia River, by Strong, review, **62**/89-90

Wakila (Indian), **62**/196

Waldo, Daniel, **62**/150; **73**/206

Waldo, Peter, **73**/206

Waldo, William, **72**/10

Waldo, Ore., **69**/276; **70**/184; **76**/58,59,81

Waldo Hills, **64**/353; **66**/330; **74**/38

Waldorf, John T.: *Kid on the Comstock,* ed. by Bryant, noted, **70**/361

Waldport, Ore., **68**/352

Walker, Courtney Meade, **69**/76,275; **74**/73; **79**/122,122N

Walker, Deward E., Jr.: *Conflict and Schism in Nez Perce Acculturation: A Study of Religion and Politics,* review, **70**/68

Walker, Dow, **75**/174,180

Walker, Elkanah, **62**/193,240,242; **77**/291: diary, **68**/76; **79**/101-102

Walker, Evans, and Richard Maxwell, comps.:

Records of the Office of Territories, noted, 64/277

Walker, Franklin:

San Francisco's Literary Frontier, cited, 73/282

Walker, Henry P.:

The Wagonmasters: High Plains Freighting from the Earliest Days of the Santa Fe Trail to 1880, review, 68/181-82

Walker, Joseph Reddeford, 65/313

Walker, Leverett H., 65/357

Walker, Mary Richardson (Mrs. Elkanah), 65/119-20:

journal, 68/77

Walker, Nellie M.:

Marcus and Narcissa Whitman, by Drury, review, 75/77-78

Walker, Robert Fletcher, 77/325,325N; 78/52-53,57,58-59,66,67,69,310,317, 330; 79/6,10,12,23:

portrait, 77/326

Walker, W.R., 77/321,336,339:

identity, 77/325

Walker, William, Dallas woolen mill owner, 62/169

Walker, William, Roseburg pioneer, 75/349

Walker, William T., 77/325,325N

Walker Island, 74/85

Walker Range (Rim), 77/331

Walker River, 63/309

Walking Tour of Astoria, by Gault, noted, 76/304; 77/292

Wall, Enos Andrew, 72/183

Wall Street, New York:

bombing, 75/151

Walla Walla, Wash., 62/220-26 *passim*,300,320,389; 63/92,138,232; 64/ 356; 65/364; 70/10,27,168; 72/73, 94; 75/115; 79/180,199,304; 81/202: cattle trade, 70/262; railroad, 71/61, 78; sketch, 79/200; wheat shipments, 71/85,86

Walla Walla and Columbia River Railroad, 70/168

Walla Walla County, Wash., 62/78; 66/32,200:

census index 1880, 71/361; donation land claims, 66/135N; Indian hostilities 1855-56, 66/136-60*passim*

Walla Walla County Pioneer and Historical Society Museum, 69/178

Walla Walla Indians, 66/133; 70/115; 79/130,136; 81/374,400,405,418: councils—

1855, 67/84,278,313; 72/264; 1856, 67/318N; Howard 1878, 70/34-38

horse stealing, 71/345; religion, 71/ 333; Smohalla cult, 70/124; war-bonnets, 81/350

Walla Walla River, 66/142

Walla Walla Valley, 66/148; 67/297, 319; 68/341; 78/101:

cattle ranch 1853, 67/302,303N; Ft. Bennett, 66/143N,147,148N; massacre of settlers 1855, 66/134; OMV winter duty 1855-56, 66/149; proposed military post, 67/323N; settler escort, 66/159; 67/318N-19N

Wallace, Leander C., 63/194,198

Wallace, Margaret:

"Cabin on the Cowlitz," reprint noted, 80/207

Wallace, Robert F., 79/413,416; 80/413

Wallace, Victor M., 62/109; 80/207

Wallace, William, Astorian, 77/81: house, 66/358

Wallace, William Henson, 68/88

Wallace Island, 75/105

Wallace Slough, 66/181

Wallawith (Indian), 79/313,315,317,327

Wallen, Henry D., 65/6N,68; 68/41:

The Dalles-Salt Lake Valley wagon route exploration, 65/25N,28N,38N, 53N; 72/58-59; 79/32-38,271N— immigrant escort, 72/59; 79/36-37; Indian encounters, 79/36; route, 79/36N,40,149N

Waller, Alvin F., 63/224; 75/109-11

Waller's Inn, 68/187

Walling, Albert G., 64/148,170-72,175,177; 66/39; 80/139

Walling, G.W., and Co., 68/165

Wallintanon (Indian), 79/158,313,315, 316,317,326

Wallis, James, **78**/234
The Wallowa Country, 1867-1877, by Bartlett, noted, **78**/91
Wallowa County, Ore., **68**/294; **78**/91: guide, **68**/184
Wallowa County Chieftain, Enterprise: anniversary editions, **63**/365; **65**/315
Wallowa Lake, **69**/330
Wallowa Milling and Mercantile Co., **62**/201
Wallowa Mountains, **65**/219: description, **70**/29-31; photo, **70**/30
Wallowa, the Land of Winding Water, by Bartlett, noted, **68**/184
Wallowa Valley, **79**/340
Wallpaper, SEE Prices
Wallula, Wash., **62**/320; **66**/229N,275; **70**/8,10,27,167,168; **71**/22,61; **79**/200: Hudson's Bay Co. fort, **66**/139,142
Wallula (tug), **69**/309,310,311
Wallula Landing, **66**/229N; SEE ALSO Wallula, Wash.
Wallula region: articles on, **66**/275
Walnut Creek, Calif., **72**/159
Walnuts: Willamette Valley orchards, **66**/87
Walpole (U.S. Army storeship), **64**/208
Walsach (Wall-sack) (Indian), **70**/34, 35N,36
Walsh, Frank K.: *Indian Battles Along the Rogue River*, noted, **74**/95 *Indian Battles of the Lower Rogue*, noted, **71**/361
Walsh, Frank K., and William R. Halliday: *Discovery and Exploration of the Oregon Caves*, noted, **73**/73
Walsh, James Marrow, **72**/355
Walsh, John, **69**/147
Walsh, Thomas J., **65**/215; **67**/87
Walter, Charles, **70**/184
Walter H. Wilson (ship), **66**/121
"Walter Pierce Memoirs: Presidents and Visitors," ed. by Arthur H. Bone, **78**/101-20
Walter Pierce Museum, **69**/178
Walterville, Ore., **64**/277

Walton, Daniel, **80**/295,295N,296N
Walton, Elisabeth, **66**/81
Walton, George, and John U. Terrell: *Faint the Trumpet Sounds*, noted, **68**/82
Walton, Morry, **70**/53
Walton, Pauline, **69**/77
Walton family, Long Creek area, **69**/125
Waltzir (Indian), **63**/173
Walworth, Reuben H., **68**/54,64,65,68
Wampole, Elias, **66**/135N
Wanapum Indians, **70**/123
Wanless, Chick, **80**/41,43
Wann, Harry, **77**/355
Wapato (*Sagittaria latifolia*) (wild potato), **63**/52N; **69**/149,152,155; **81**/391,419
Wapato, Ore.: churches, **72**/153
Wapato Indians, **74**/94
Wapinitia, Ore., **79**/143N
Wappato Indians of the Lower Columbia River Valley, by Jones, noted, **74**/94
The War Lord, by Holmgren, noted, **70**/359
War of 1812: veterans in Oregon, **62**/197
The War on Powder River: The History of an Insurrection, by Smith, review, **67**/359
Warbass, Edward D., **63**/170,172
Warbonnets and Epaulets, by Peltier, noted, **73**/73
Ward, Alexander, **67**/311
Ward, Bernard (Barney), **69**/147
Ward, Frank, **66**/54
Ward, Frederick K., **68**/235,237,243; **70**/15
Ward, Jim, **69**/147
Ward, John P., **80**/145N,146N
Ward, Newton, **67**/311N
Ward, Pat, **69**/147
Ward, Roy A., **64**/250
Ward, Sarah E., SEE Bell, Sarah Ward
Ward, Terrill, **71**/23
Ward, Tom, Coos Valley settler, **66**/54
Ward, W.M., Portland policeman, **80**/289: biography, **80**/291
Ward, William Morrow Co., **69**/147

Ward, William, Ward massacre survivor, 67/311N

Ward massacre, 66/89; 67/310; 79/15,49,129:

Haller expeditions, 67/311-12; sources on, 67/311N,312N

Wardin, Albert W., Jr.: *Baptists in Oregon*, review, 72/166-67

Wardner, James F., 66/86; 72/183

Wardner, Ida., 69/217: mining, 69/213,215

Wardwell, Allen: *Objects of Bright Pride: Northwest Coast Indian Art from the American Museum of Natural History*, review, 81/207-208

Ware, Elizabeth Cochran (Mrs. Joel T.), 78/124,129

Ware, Eugene F.: *The Indian War of 1864*, reprint noted, 64/187

Warm Spring George (Indian), 79/275N

Warm Springs, Ore., 69/298; 72/153

Warm Springs Creek, 79/33

Warm Springs Indian Agency, 65/20: agents, 79/38,126,148N; map, 79/124

Warm Springs Indians, 65/11,21,31-52 *passim*,72,118; 70/37,38,124; 81/413: agriculture, 79/160N-61N; attitude toward Snakes, 79/125,330; ceremonial dances, 79/142N,143,151,290; "Chitike Cavalry," 65/46-47,50; hunting, 79/150-51,271,275 scouts for army 1866-67— army policy, 79/128-31,328-33; captured stock, 79/302N,328; clothing account, 79/315-16; commendations, 79/304N; deaths, 79/285,285N,288, 321,324,326; enlistment, 79/132-33, 137-38,142N,302N,318-29; firearms, 79/138,288; furloughs, 79/132,150, 153,157,160N,295,302N; guidons, 79/142; horses, 79/132-33,138,143, 270,313-14; lists, 79/318-28; name spelling variations, 79/140N; number, 79/137,138,318; outfitted, 79/138, 141,315-18; pay, 79/132-33,302,328-29; provisions, 79/314-15; scalps, 79/151,153,157,330,332; sickness, 79/285,285N,296,301; slaves, 79/

329,333; tobacco account, 79/317; value, 79/129,132,330

trade with settlers, 73/262; tribal divisions, 79/138

Warm Springs Reservation, 62/108,217; 64/353; 65/12,20-21N,44,50,84-85; 69/232; 79/30,39,42,121,125,147, 303-304:

blacksmiths, 79/143N,151N,154N; economic development, 71/365; employees, 79/154N,156N-57N; established, 79/125,136; geographic area, 79/126; geology, 65/315; history, 80/104; out-buildings, 79/143N; physicians, 79/125,136,137N,154; raid by Snake Indians, 79/125-26; resort opened, 65/315; schoolhouse, 79/143N

Warner, Elizabeth Stewart, 78/123,124: photo, 78/122

Warner, Fred, 78/123: photo, 78/122

Warner, John, 78/123,250

Warner, Mary Stewart, 78/123

Warner, Mason Y., 78/223,236

Warner, Mikell Delores Wormell, trans.: *Catholic Church Records of the Pacific Northwest*..., reviews, 74/89-90; 77/291; 81/202-203

Warner, Olin L., 75/83: Indian medals, photos, 70/160,fr.cov. June

Warner, Thomas, 1853 immigrant, 78/123

Warner, William Horace, 65/138; 79/279N

Warner Lakes, 72/16N

Warner Mountains, SEE Hart Mountain

Warner Valley, 66/273; 68/319, 321,324: earthquake, 70/183

Warner Valley Stock Co., 72/268

Warners (Hart, Crump) Lake, 79/277,281: name, 79/279N

Warre, Henry J., 63/109N,219,235; 64/197N,210-11,225; 66/356N; 70/320; 79/413: Columbia River survey, 64/210N— chart, 64/216-17

Warren, Billy (Indian), 75/363
Warren, Claude N., 62/203; 64/282; 68/334,335:
The View from Wenas: A Study in Plateau Prehistory, noted, 70/273
Warren, Daniel Knight, 70/279
Warren, Eliza Spalding, 64/349-50; 65/119
Warren, Ellen S. Case, 75/294
Warren, Frank F., 68/183
Warren, John A., 65/414,417; 66/94,190,286,395; 67/379; 68/360
Warren, John Quincy Adams: letters published, 69/332
Warren, Columbia Co., Ore.: history, 65/308
Warren, Ida., 63/89
Warren and Son, publishers, 69/332
Warrenton, Ore.: history, 74/356
Warrior Point, 63/234
Warrior Rock, 71/360
Wasco, Ore.: 1915 photo, 74/246-47
Wasco (steamer, first of name), 62/79
Wasco County, Ore., 62/229; 66/365, 368,370; 75/314; 81/261: assessor's office, 73/305,306,307,308; bills to organize, 67/301N-302N,306; Chinese, 78/75-85; county fair history, 70/76; courthouses, 71/286; created, 67/306-307; first election, 67/309; first recorded marriage, 79/136; growth 1855-59, 68/27-30; history, 71/286; homesteaders, 73/307; "Indian country," 67/307; influence of railroads, 81/101-102; Japanese, 76/239; land prices, 68/28,29; map 1892, 81/280; photos, 73/308,320; population 1854, 67/307,309; second schoolhouse, 79/162; sheep census 1860-80s, 64/102; stock raising, 68/23N,29
Wasco County Historical Society: officers and board members, 81/112; officers and directors, 62/416; 63/87,251; 64/84,280; 65/124,312; 66/85,279; 67/83,284; 68/85,283; 69/82,280; 70/83,277; 71/195; 72/177; 73/79; 74/182; 75/92;

76/96; 77/96; 78/96; 79/112; 80/111; publications, 76/304; 77/292
Wasco County-Dalles City Museum Commission, 67/370; 68/39
Wasco Electric Cooperative Inc., 80/328
Wasco Indians, 63/347-49; 65/27; 70/124; 72/151; 79/126,130; 81/397: army scouts, 79/130N,157,278,281; ceremonial dances, 79/160; political organization, 63/349
Wasco Sun, The Dalles, 81/264
Wascoite (mineral), 67/370
Wascopam (Indian village), 67/296
Wascopum (Wascopam) County, SEE Wasco County
Washakie (Indian), 66/74; 69/84
Washburn, Catherine A.S., 78/145N: 1853 journal quoted, 78/145
Washburn, Charles Wesley, 78/145
Washburn, Columbus S.R., family, 66/382
Washington, George, Negro pioneer, 65/313; 73/200: photo, 73/196
Washington: agriculture, 71/86,98; atlas, 81/331; beet sugar, 67/372
bibliography, 62/109; 63/91—1963-64, 67/84; 1965, 67/368-69; 1966, 68/186
boundaries, 71/196—Idaho dispute, 68/88; politics, 70/77
business—opportunities 1881, 71/13-17; outlook, 69/337
company towns, 67/357; constitution, 70/77; early sawmills, 63/206; eastern, 77/301; economy, 68/186; election 1964, 66/282; first Fourth of July, 71/286; fruit trees, 68/164; geological survey, 72/180
government, 63/78-79—history, 68/341
guide, 72/286; harbor charts, 72/356; Hindu people, 71/364; historic buildings, 71/361; historical markers, 68/343
history, 62/405-406; 63/78-79; 67/79-80—

articles on, 70/78; publications, 81/106,328,329,330,333,335,336; southwest region, 68/182; references, 74/89-90,93,94,281 I.W.W. in, 68/88; industry, 77/296; labor, socialism and reform 1885-1917, 81/333-34; land lotteries, 71/196; logging, 69/68; migration and market growth, 68/349; military posts, 76/92; museums, 64/188; pension politics, 72/286; pioneer memoirs, 69/71-72; place names, 65/220; politics 1919-20, 68/88 population— 1860-1900, 71/60; characteristics, 68/349 prohibition, 66/281; 67/186-87; Seward visit, 72/133-34; taxes, 69/86; 72/90; theses, 72/225-79,286; wheat, 71/60,98; woolen mills, 62/175; SEE ALSO Washington Territory *Washington* (ship), 76/319 *Washington: A History of the Evergreen State*, by Avery, review, 67/79-81 Washington Commonwealth Federation, 72/264; 76/136,139,142 Washington County, Ore., 66/161, 165,366,367,372: annexation question, 74/207-208; bibliography, 76/381; census 1880, 75/87; early hotels, 64/89; election 1852, 80/14-15; environmental preservation, 66/283; executions, 80/12; first marriages, 68/350; historic sites map, 68/81; history, 62/200; 66/281; 76/381; 80/106; jail described 1851, 80/11; land claims, 64/89; probate records, 74/286; roads, 66/281; schools, 63/253; 66/281 Washington County City-County Joint Planning Department, 66/281: *Patterns of Development*, noted, 66/188 Washington County Historical Society: meetings, 69/280; 70/277; museum, 69/178; 70/83,277; officers and directors, 68/283; 69/82,280; 70/83,277; 71/195; 72/177; 73/79; 74/182; 75/ 92; 76/96; 77/96; 78/96; 79/112; 80/112; 81/112; publications, 68/81;

76/381; 77/292; 80/106; 81/104 Washington Education Association, 71/196 Washington Good Roads Association, 74/109 Washington Guard, photo, 80/259 Washington High School, Portland, 71/219: fire, 75/174,189N *Washington Historical Quarterly*: first issue, 70/227 Washington Iron Works, Seattle, 73/219 Washington National Guard: official history, 63/246 Washington Peak, Del Norte Co., Calif., 76/75 *Washington Pioneer*, Olympia, 64/37N,39 *Washington Standard*, Olympia, 63/236 Washington State Historical Society: publications, 69/71; 74/354; 77/291 Washington State Labor Council, AFL-CIO, 72/230 Washington State Library: publications, 75/364 Washington State School for the Deaf: history, 67/366 Washington State University Library: McWhorter Collection, 81/341N,347; manuscripts, 75/364; 77/297 Washington Superintendency of Indian Affairs: history, 70/119; 72/229 Washington Territory, 62/61,63-64: 1879, 72/286; act to establish, 70/77; Civil War, 80/208; creation of, 62/72-73; donation land claims, 70/113; Indian problems 1870s, 70/103-37,148-70 judiciary, 62/85; 66/25,28,31-37— courts, 63/176,178,185,208-209, 223N,229; 64/297-304*passim*; 66/33, 387; 80/330; politics, 66/32; salaries, 66/33 law code 1854, 64/302-303; petition to form territory, 63/107-108; 64/301; printers, 62/106 Washington Territory Volunteers, 65/8,68,98N,102N-103N,392,398 Washington Water Power Company, 63/361; 65/364

Washougal, Wash., 64/276; 77/299
Wasniah (Cowlitz Farm employee), 63/129
Wasserman, Philip, 80/299,305,305N
Wasson, Joe, 65/301N; 81/105
Wasson, Warren: letters, 70/366
Wasson family, Coos Co., 68/90
Water: alkali, 73/263; power for woolen mills, 62/167,171-72 resources— development, 68/86; international control, 69/272-73; multiple use, 69/332; Oregon problems and needs, 66/384; Portland, 69/338; public, 78/360; transfers in West, 69/83 rights, 67/237— controversy, 76/343; establishment, 77/13; Westfall country, 63/272, 274-75 shipboard supplies, 77/49,51; tank wagon photo, 77/19; wells, 77/9; SEE ALSO Irrigation; Reclamation
Water cure, SEE Hydropathy
Water for the West: The Bureau of Reclamation, 1902-1977, by Robinson, noted, 80/408-409
Waterbury, Edwin, 72/66
Waterman, John Orvis, 80/11,12N
Waters, Aaron C., 64/87; 67/30
Waters, Abner, 65/185: biography, 79/168N
Waters, James, 62/197; 67/66
Waters, Walter Kenneth, Jr.: *Klondike Kate: The Life and Legend of Kitty Rockwell*, by Lucia, review, 63/352-53
Waters, Walter W., 64/281; 65/295N
Waters-kow-kow (Indian), 79/275N
Watkinds, William H., 80/295N; 81/89N
Watkins, Carleton Emmons, 66/381,386: photos by, 80/152,ins.bk.cov. Summer— The Dalles photo, 68/34-35
Watkins, Elton, 75/172,174
Watkins, Erwin C., 70/127,153
Watkins, Font, 64/109

Watkins, Fred: family, 71/360; notes on Columbia River vessels, 73/283
Watkins, George, 81/271,271N,276
Watkins, William H., 65/78N,80,84N, 91,95,97; 66/61; 80/131: opinion of Gibbs' senate defeat, 65/107,109; physician First Ore. Cavalry, 65/393; political and military service views, 65/88-89
Watrous, Stephen D., ed.: *John Ledyard's Journey through Russia and Siberia, 1787-88; the Journal and Selected Letters*, review, 68/274-77
Watson, Chandler B.: biography, 66/171N; 68/317N; Coos Bay reminiscences, 66/173-75; photos, 66/172; 68/318
Watson, Chandler B.: "An Adventure in the Surf," 66/171-77 "Indians and Indian Wars of Southern Oregon," cited, 68/317N "Recollections of the Bannock War," 68/317-29
Watson, Edward B., 78/238
Watson, Grove, 70/254,255
Watson, J. Frank, 69/209
Watson, James, 78/127,149,238: photo, 78/126
Watson, James Finley, 78/238
Watson, John P., 69/209
Watson, Loren, 78/238
Watson, Sarah, SEE Hamilton, Sarah Watson
Watson, Stephen, 62/323; 73/258: biography, 65/32N; burial sites, 66/59,61; death, 65/5,32,35; First Ore. Cavalry service, 65/12,19,21,23, 27,31,49N,87N; funeral described, 65/39N; photo of monument, 66/60
Watson, Thomas E., 69/180; 75/ 153,187N
Watson, Ore., 72/93
Watson Springs, SEE Upper Watson Springs
Watt, Joseph, 67/125,128; 72/228
Watters, Mary Ellen: recollections, 66/90
Watterson, Henry, 66/46

Wattles, Mr. and Mrs. Willard, photo, **74**/155

Watts, John W.: disputed elector, **67**/259-68*passim*

Watts, Lyle F., **78**/280

Watts, Mildred Boyle, **65**/308

Watts, Nellie Shutt: recollections, **72**/94

Watts, Rose, **70**/358

Watts family, Columbia Co., **66**/281

Watzek, Aubrey R., **63**/372,374; **64**/94, 190,286,363; **65**/125,221,317,416; **66**/93,189,285,386,394; **67**/376,380; **68**/357,358,361; **69**/348; **70**/373

Watzek, Charles H., **64**/359

Wauna, Ore., **75**/106

Wauna (sternwheeler), **81**/39

Waverly Cemetery, **65**/216

Wawawai, Ida., **65**/307; **71**/23,24

Wa-will-pin (Indian), **70**/36

Way Back When, by Searcey, noted, **73**/285

Wayland, Dick, **70**/54

Waymire, James A., **62**/323; **65**/21,22,24,40: biography, **65**/14N-15N; First Ore. Cavalry service, **65**/43-71*passim*; scout, **65**/118; Snake skirmish, **65**/14,19

Waymire, John, **62**/200

We Climb High: A Chronology of the Mazamas, 1894-1964, by Scott, noted, **70**/359

We Proceeded On, ed. by Lange, noted, **77**/89; **79**/336; **80**/335; **81**/329

We Were Not Summer Soldiers: The Indian War Diary of Plympton J. Kelly, 1855-1856, ed. by Bischoff, noted, **77**/291; review, **78**/179-80

We-a-we-wah (Weyouwewah) (Indian), **65**/74N; **69**/240N; **79**/123,125-26, 127,139,273N,281N,285N

Weather, SEE Climate

Weatherby, John, **81**/266,267,277

Weatherby, Ore., **68**/229N

Weatherby Hotel, Burnt River, **72**/94

Weathered, —, Elk City 1862, **79**/194

Weatherford, James K.P., **67**/73

Weatherford, Marion T., **64**/358,364; **65**/121,126,222,416; **66**/93,189,285,

394; **67**/379; **68**/359,361; **69**/348; **70**/374; **71**/372; **72**/360; **74**/184, 365; **80**/413:

The Bunchgrassers, by McMillan, review, **75**/360

The Complete Horseshoeing Guide, by Wiseman, review, **70**/356

Rankin Crow, by Crow, review, **73**/279

16 Mule Wheat Team, Arlington, Oregon, noted, **70**/75

Things I See, review, **75**/361-62

Weatherford, Mark V.: *Bannock-Piute War*, cited, **70**/5N,15N,19N

Weatherford, W.W.: *Blue Mountain Talewinds*, noted, **79**/339

Weaver, George W., **65**/171

Weaver, Hans, Jr., family, **68**/81

Weaver, James Baird, **65**/267

Weaver, Pauline (Powell), **66**/280

Webb, Charles Henry, **62**/292-93

Webb, Walter Prescott, **65**/213,313; **66**/82,379

Webb-Kenyon Act, **68**/134

Webber, Bert: *Retaliation: Japanese Attacks and Allied Countermeasures on the Pacific Coast in World War II*, review, **77**/194-95

Webber, Harold A., **62**/172

Webber, James, **80**/201

Webber, John, *Atalanta* seaman, **66**/ 110,111,114

Weber, Charles M.: papers, **68**/339-40

Webster, Daniel, **63**/207; **69**/84,324; **75**/321-22,328-29,333-34; **76**/ 212-17*passim*

Webster, John McAdam, **65**/363

Wedderburn, Ore.: described 1964, **65**/315; salmon cannery, **69**/88

Weddle, Ferris: *Western Wagon Wheels*, by Florin, review, **72**/168-69

Wedemeyer, Albert C.: quoted, **62**/5,37,39

"A Wee Dash of Heliotrope," by Erskine Wood, **75**/101-103

Weed, Abner E., **69**/79
Weed, Adaline Melinda Willis: financial problems, 78/30; lectures, 78/13-14,22-28; opposition, 78/12-21,29,31; photo, 78/35
Weed, Benjamin, 78/34
Weed, Gideon Allen, 78/5-39*passim*: contributions to medicine, 78/34; photo, 78/35; Seattle mayor, 78/34
Weed, Mabel, 78/34,40
Weed, R.M., **65**/271
Weed, Calif., **69**/79; 72/161
Weeks, George, railroad fireman: photo, 77/72
Weeks, George W., 63/12
Weeks, Henry, **71**/278
Weeks, John, **71**/278
Weidle, Clara Bremmer, **66**/275
Weidler, George W., **67**/166,169,171
Weigand, W.F., 75/46
Weiher, Claudine J., and Stephen E. Hannestad, comps.: *Black Studies, Select Catalog of National Archives...Publications*, noted, 75/88
Weikel, Ann, 80/414
Weinhard, Henry, **64**/267
Weiser Indians, 70/14N
Weissenfel, Louis, 72/91
Weister, George M., Company, Portland photographers, **66**/306
Welborn, Mrs. G.W., 62/290
Welch, D.P., 73/252,253,254
Welch, Jack, **63**/283
Welch, James, **64**/223N; **81**/194N: Astoria land claim, **64**/228N-30N,236
Welch, Nancy Dickerson, **64**/228N
Welch, Sarah, **63**/283,286
Welcome, Portland, 80/273
Well (Wells) Spring, Morrow Co., **62**/401; **66**/135; 79/201
Welles, Gideon, **65**/328
Wellington, John H., **65**/309
Wellington, B.C., **64**/88; 72/286
Wellington (ship), **66**/107
Wells, Daniel H., **67**/223,224,225
Wells, Giles: cattle drive 1864, **65**/50,55
Wells, John: Buena Vista recollections, **67**/92

Wells, Merle W., **62**/106; **64**/187; **65**/216; **66**/276,281: *Hiram Martin Chittenden*, by Dodds, review, 74/354-55 *Only One Man Died*, by Chuinard, review, 80/404-405 *The Oregon Desert*, by Jackman and Long, review, **66**/272-73 *Stone Age in the Great Basin*, by Strong, review, 70/352
Wells, Nathaniel Augustus, family, 77/91
Wells, W.B., capt. of *Senorita*, **68**/27
Wells, William W.: letter to Gibbs, **65**/296
Wells, Fargo and Company, **71**/365; 72/88-89; 73/72,258
Wells, Fargo Detective: A Biography of James B. Hume, by Dillon, review, 72/88-89
Wells Spring, SEE Well Spring
Welsh people, **81**/298: in Dakota Territory, **67**/87
Welty, Raymond L.: quoted, 62/226
Wemme, E. Henry, 74/108,208
Wemme, Ore., **66**/362N
Wenatchee, Wash., **67**/87
Wenatchee Indians, 70/121,161
Wenatchee Mountains: mining 1853-99, 72/233
Wendling, Ore., 76/382
Wengenroth, Daniel, 72/91
Wengenroth, William A., 72/91
Weninger, F.H., **81**/80
Wennerberg, Daniel, 76/6
Wennerberg, John, 76/5-27: farm, 76/9-10,17— photo, 76/16
Wentworth, Lloyd J., **67**/51
Wentworth, Lydia M., **67**/366
Wentz, Harry, 73/81
Wergen, Gerhard, 70/53
Werschkul, Leslie J., **66**/342
Wes Cavaness Hall, Westfall, **63**/283, 286,289
Weskamatamthla (Indian), 79/157, 313,315,328
Wessels, William L.:

Born To Be a Soldier: The Military Career of William Wing Loring, review, 73/71

Wessinger, Frederic G., 71/371; 73/364; 74/183,363,365; 75/370; 76/387; 77/383-85; 78/366,367-69; 79/413,416; 80/413

Wessinger, Henry W., 62/110,206,302, 422; 63/93,255

Wessinger, Nancy, 68/359

West, Calvin B., 62/197,202,298; 63/91

West, George R., 65/143

West, Jessamyn, 63/247

West, John, Red River 1821-23, 69/50

West, Josiah, 64/90

West, Lamira, 64/90

West, Leoti, 64/357

West, Oswald, 62/198; 63/297; 65/220; 66/331N,359N,363,374; 74/109,208; 75/162,188N; 77/267; 80/205:

and public beaches, 68/351; appoints McNary to Supreme Court, 68/125; Benson-McNary contest quotes, 66/373,375-76; Columbia River Hwy. recollections, 66/249N,251N; judicial appointee, 66/363,373,375; photos, 66/250; 68/133; rated as governor, 65/220; U.S. Senate campaign, 68/133-35,138-40

West, Oswald:

"Oregon's First White Settlers on French Prairie," cited, 66/331N,343

West, Robert W., 70/66

West, Victor C.:

Pacific Lumber Ships, by Newell and Williamson, review, 63/80

West, William, Gilliam Co. farmer 1880, 81/268N

West, William M., family, 74/358

West:

agricultural development, 74/284; air transportation, 70/367; American concepts of, 70/73,363; Americana collections, 75/93; army and Indian wars, 81/106; articles on, 69/273-74; barbed wire, 66/379

bibliography, 71/291; 75/93—

history and literature, 72/179; interpretations, 63/88; Trans-Mississippi West, 63/81-82

cartoons, 71/364; city growth theory, 63/89; civil service, 75/93; Civil War impact, 80/208; company towns, 67/357; cultural identity, 71/292; cultural patterns, 69/337; description and travel, 72/127,170; 81/96-97; desert concepts, 71/364; desert country, 67/277; development, 71/363; 73/66,360; dictionary, 70/78; early man, 75/87; effect on common law, 70/366; elections 1970, 75/94; electronics, 70/267-68; encyclopedia, 80/205; English migration 1865-1900, 65/213; expansion atlas 1790-1900, 64/77 exploration, 69/69,70; 80/206—

study of, 67/86

foreign-born percentages, 80/261,263; frontier image, 62/202; Grinnell travels, 74/96; growth influences, 65/213; historiography, 70/263-64; 72/182 history, 64/186-87; 75/93—

field in American West, 65/313; marine animal influence, 65/220; oral, 81/335

image—

Davis novels, 66/240,242-45; frontier, 62/202; German novels, 67/344; Steinbeck, 65/213; Twain, 66/89

impact on nation, 71/292; in paperback books, 64/283; interpretation bibliography, 63/88; irrigation history, 80/408-409; journalism, 66/379-80; land tenure, 71/364

law and order, 71/364—

gunmen, 72/181

legendary heroes, 73/360; Lincoln and Douglas views, 70/178

literature, 73/286—

frontier books reprints, 74/359

medieval legacy, 67/86; military posts, 66/384

mining frontiers, 64/344-45—

history, 67/86

myths, 81/331—

in movies, 72/364

Negroes in, 71/291; 73/279-80; New Deal, 71/364; newspapers, 66/279-80;

oral history, **81**/335; ornithology, **80**/207; paleontology, **73**/86; photographers, **81**/324; pictorial record, **65**/135-36; radical movements, **74**/280; railroad influence, **78**/358; ranching, **81**/336; reclamation, **70**/84; remains of, **68**/168; science in, **70**/73 settlement, **69**/69-70— railroad influence, **78**/358 Skirving panorama views, **65**/148-49; songs, **70**/78; state expenditures, **71**/ 198; territories described, **80**/208; towns, **81**/201-202; travel to and from 1540-1854, **74**/86; urban development, **81**/103-104; urban frontier, **73**/274; *vs.* East, **81**/331; water transfers, **69**/83; watershed resources, **72**/181; women, **81**/334

West and Gilliam, Malheur Co. sheepmen, **63**/269

West Coast: description, **80**/334; SEE ALSO Pacific Coast

West Coast Disaster: Columbus Day 1962, by Franklin, noted, **65**/309

West Coast Lighthouses, by Gibbs, noted, **75**/365

West Coast Lumbermen's Association, **64**/58; **77**/347,349,351

West Coast Telephone Company, **68**/341

West Coast Windjammers in Story and Pictures, by Gibbs, review, **70**/266-67

West Fork, Deschutes River, **77**/330, 331; **79**/48; SEE ALSO Big Marsh Creek

West Fork, Douglas Co.: covered bridge, **66**/383

West of the Mountains: James Sinclair and the Hudson's Bay Company, by Lent, review, **65**/305-306

The West of William H. Ashley, ed. by Morgan, review, **66**/63-65

West on the 49th Parallel: Red River to the Rockies, 1872-1876, by Parsons, review, **66**/69-71

West Oregon Electric Cooperative Inc., **80**/323

West Oregon Lumber Company, Portland, **76**/249

West Shore, **69**/203:

cited, **67**/131,135,143,144,151,157, 158,163FF; editorials on mining stocks, **69**/199N,211N; Oregon promotional ads, **69**/200

West Shore Mills, Astoria, **67**/174, 176-77

West Side, Ore., **77**/8

West Union, Ore.: Baptist church, **64**/87,124; log school 1878, **63**/253

Westering Women, by Miller, review, **64**/349

Western (steamboat): Missouri River 1879, **66**/86

Western America: The Exploration, Settlement, and Development of the Region Beyond the Mississippi, by Hafen *et al,* 3rd ed. noted, **71**/363

Western American, Astoria, **75**/181

Western Americana, **70**/68: Da Capo, **74**/94-95,282-83; Far West Frontier series, **74**/359; Graff Collection, **70**/64-66; Shorey, **74**/94; Yale paperback facsimiles, **63**/356; Ye Galleon Press, **74**/95

Western Cover Society: publications, **71**/200

Western Forests for All, Proceedings of the 58th Western Forest Conference, noted, **69**/332

Western Ghost Town Shadows, by Florin, review, **66**/77

Western Ghost Towns, by Florin, review, **63**/79-80

Western Mining: An Informal Account... from Spanish Times to 1893, by Young, review, **72**/347-48

Western movement, **67**/280: Canada-U.S. experiences, **80**/106

Western Pacific Railroad, **62**/197; **63**/66

Western Political Science Association: 1964 proceedings, **66**/89

Western Shore (ship), **68**/267-69: watercolor, **68**/268

The Western Shore: Oregon Country Essays Honoring the American Revolution, ed. by Vaughan, noted, **76**/387; **77**/291,292

Western Star, Milwaukie, **64**/123

The Western Territories in the Civil War, ed. by Fischer, noted, 80/208

Western Union Telegraph Expedition, 64/86; 65/216; 77/296

Western Wagon Wheels: A Pictorial Memorial to the Wheels that Won the West, by Florin, review, 72/168-69

Western Words, A Dictionary of the American West, by Adams, noted, 70/78

Westersund, Mrs. Swen, and Mrs. Mervin Swearingen:

The Pendleton Area Finns, review, 72/350-51

Westfall, Bill, 63/280,290

Westfall, Blackie, 63/273

Westfall, Daisy (Mrs. Jasper), 63/290,297

Westfall, Henry, 63/301-302

Westfall, Jasper, 63/296-97: photo, 63/287

Westfall, Johnnie, 63/297,301

Westfall, Levi, 63/264-65,272,281

Westfall (Bully), Ore., 64/351; 67/219,237,252; 72/93: early days in, 63/263-303*passim*; historic sites near, 67/374; name, 63/282; photos, 63/271; 67/242; settlement, 63/281-83

Westfall Commercial Co., 63/282,286

"The Westfall Country: Limning in the Open Spaces," by Earl R. Smith, 63/263-303

The Westfall Country: The Story of an Eastern Oregon Community, by Smith, noted, 64/351

Westfall (Hart's) Hotel, 63/273,279, 281,283

Westfir, Ore., 77/329

Weston, Ore., 70/12,27; 74/340,341: schools 1887, 74/342-44

Weston (brig), 76/121-24*passim*

Weston Normal School, see Oregon State Normal School, Weston

Westport, Wash.: ferry, 66/91; settlers, 69/331

The Westward Movement and Historical Development of the Americas in the Pacific Basin, ed. by Hinckley, noted, 67/280

Westward on the Oregon Trail, by Place, noted, 64/186

Westward to Alki: The Story of David and Louisa Denny, by Newell, noted, 79/337

Westward Vision: The Story of the Oregon Trail, by Lavender, review, 66/68-69

Wetjen, Albert Richard, 73/292,299,301; 74/35: awards, 74/147,158,161; biography, 74/148-78*passim*; death, 74/261; Hollywood experience, 74/175,177; homes, 74/150,157,159; letter quoted, 74/174; photos, 74/148,155; poetry, 74/152,160,262; relations with Charles Alexander, 74/149,151-52; short stories, 74/147,157,161,175; views on literature and writing, 74/150-52,157,158,159-60; writings commented on, 74/259-62

Wetjen, Albert Richard: "Blessed Isle," cited, 74/261 *Captains All*, cited, 74/147 *Fiddlers Green*, published, 74/174,257 "For My Lady," cited, 74/261 "Fortitude," cited, 74/259 "Pound For Pound," cited, 74/257,259 "Strain," cited, 74/158,259 *Way For a Sailor*, cited, 74/147,174 *Youth Walks on the Highway*, described, 74/174-75

Wetjen, Edythe, 74/147-48,150,156, 157,174,177: photo, 74/155

Wetmore, Clarence, 63/341

Wetyetmas (Swan Necklace) (Indian), 81/349

Weyerhaeuser Company, 63/79,355; 64/355; 72/237; 73/221,283; 77/217,219; 80/174: Longview mill, 73/224

Whales and whaling industry, 67/86; 70/184; 74/286,352; 76/123,197, 199,201-202,205: American-Russian relations, 75/317-35*passim*; British Columbia, 63/360; Confederate raids, 68/347; described, 75/315; fleet at Hawaiian ports, 68/54; Floyd's view, 70/343; history 19th century, 70/365; Indian claims,

81/408-409
journals, 73/86—
Williams 1858-61, 65/313
Massachusetts, 75/316,322-23; New England tonnage, 75/316,323,324
North Pacific Coast, 72/109; 75/316-35—
number vessels in trade, 76/202
Olympic Peninsula, 64/357; Pacific Ocean, 70/77,179; Pacific records, 72/181-82; political aspects, 75/317-35*passim*; sketches, 75/323,330; statistics, 76/220; steam whalers, 79/106; value, 75/324; vessels, 76/202; whalebone survey marker, 72/33
Whalley, John W., 69/207,209; 80/169
Wharton, Herbert:
reminiscences, 66/382
Wharton, Wallace, John Day rancher, **81**/314
Whatcom County, Wash., 69/71:
history, 70/359; 80/332
Whatcom Falls Mill Company, 77/215
Whealdon, Isaac, 69/78
Wheat, Carl I.:
Mapping the Trans-Mississippi West, 1540-1861, cited, 70/259N; review, 66/183-85
Wheat, 68/23N,28; 69/332; 72/279, 283; 76/239; 77/8; **81**/335,336:
amount shipped Columbia River—1880, **71**/94; 1885, 71/87
cattle damage, 63/139; Cowlitz Farm, 63/115-73*passim*,205,234; Durum controversy, 70/84; Eastern Ore. 1880-90, **67**/154-55
exports, 75/76—
Pacific Northwest, **71**/28,31
farm investment 1890-1915, **71**/98;
French Prairie, 66/337,339,343,344, 351; hauling, 70/75; HBCO. legal tender, 63/181-82,217; investment returns Pacific NW 1911-15, **71**/98; May View tramway, 67/87; Ore. production 1870-1900, **71**/96; Pacific Coast shipping 1890s, 66/101-102,109,119,122; Portland export center, 67/107-10; prices, SEE Prices; production, 63/211 railroad effects—

Mid-Columbia ranching, **81**/101-102; Oregon industry, **71**/29,31
shipping rates, **71**/61—
1867-81, **71**/97
Washington, **71**/60,98; wheat ship photo, 66/120; Willamette Valley, **71**/31,87; WW I restrictions, **71**/218
Wheatland Ferry, 63/364; 65/121
Wheaton, Frank, 68/231N,233N,302N; 70/10,12,34
Wheaton, VanRenssler Roswell, family, 69/331; 70/74
Wheeler, A., Brownsville merchant 1869, 64/178
Wheeler, Burton K., 65/366,375
Wheeler, Coleman H., 65/125,221,317, 416; 66/93,189,285,394; 67/376,380; 68/361; 69/348; 70/373; 74/183
Wheeler, George Montague, 70/73; 75/79:
survey—
records, 65/313; Utah and Idaho, 67/367
Wheeler, Gervase, 67/331N
Wheeler, Henry H., 73/260
Wheeler, James, Jr., 65/6N
Wheeler, Keith:
The Alaskans, noted, 79/338
Wheeler (Nelson P.?) family, 72/300
Wheeler, Newton, 64/225N,227N,234
Wheeler, Olin Dunbar, 77/90
Wheeler, William Almon, 67/268, 271,272
Wheeler, William L., family, 63/245
Wheeler, Ore., 72/296; 73/5N
Wheeler County, Ore., 66/365; 73/258; 75/309:
family histories, 73/258-68; first post office, 73/264; history, 77/195; name, 73/260; prehistoric sea, 69/338; sheep ranching, 64/101-22*passim*
Wheeler County Historical Commission: publications, 77/195,292
Wheeler-Voegelin, Erminie:
"The Northern Paiute of Central Oregon," cited, 69/240N
Whelatit (Indian), 79/313,316,317, 318,327
When the Eagle Screamed: The Romantic

Horizon in American Diplomacy, 1800-1860, by Goetzmann, noted, **68**/343
Whidby Island, **62**/73; **63**/190,201
Whig Party, **72**/10,12,319; **80**/14, 15,21; **81**/245:
Oregon Territory, **66**/28,31
Whipple, Jean Webster:
Retreat to the Bear Paw, by Place, review, **71**/284
Whipple, Stephen G., **68**/226N, 297,299N
Whiskey, SEE Liquor
Whiskey Creek, Jackson Co., **73**/83
Whiskey Flat, Grant Co., **69**/107
Whiskey Run, Coos Co., **62**/215
Whistler, James McNeill, **71**/364
Whitcomb, James H., **74**/93
Whitcomb, Lot, **74**/93:
journey to Oregon, **66**/86
White, Miss —, Alvord Ranch teacher, **63**/304-305,320,322-23,328,334-35, 337,340
White, A.J., Portland 1894, **65**/271N
White, Al, **75**/129
White, Bruce M., comp.:
The Fur Trade in Minnesota: An Introductory Guide to Manuscript Sources, noted, **79**/339
White, Clarence H., **81**/106N: biography, **80**/397-98
White, Cornelius, **63**/47N
White, Daniel, **78**/125: photo, **78**/126
White, Dave, **66**/142
White, Elijah, **62**/123-25,140-41, 142N,143; **63**/245; **64**/143; **66**/353; **72**/59; **74**/75N; **77**/317; **81**/195N: quoted, **62**/141
White, Eugene D., **69**/200
White, F.M., **63**/34
White, Fonetta (Nettie), SEE Scott, Fonetta White
White, G. Edward:
The Eastern Establishment and the Western Experience: The West of Frederic Remington, Theodore Roosevelt, and Owen Wister, review, **70**/263-64
White, G.W., **63**/34
White, George Ared, **72**/92

White, Gertrude Jane Hall, SEE Denny, Gertrude Jane Hall
White, Helen McCann, **63**/360; **64**/281
White, Isam, **71**/17
White, J.S., McMinnville pastor, **70**/319
White, James Seeley:
The Hedden's Store Handbook of Proprietary Medicines, noted, **76**/92
White, John, Portland 1862, **72**/332N
White, Judd, **65**/233
White, Mrs. Lennox, photo, **78**/102
White, Leonard, **65**/233; **70**/259
White, Leslie, **70**/265
White, Levi, **71**/17
White, Luther, **77**/319,319N,320; **79**/21
White, Martin, **67**/280
White, Richard, **63**/108
White, Samuel F., **75**/279
White, Thomas:
1853 Butteville letter, **65**/212
White, Victor H.:
The Story of Lige Coalman, review, **74**/88-89
White, W.J., Sellwood 1902, **62**/172
White, Wilson, **81**/289
White, Winnie Dement, **63**/34
White Bird (Indian), **64**/274
White Bluffs, Wash., **70**/128
White Captives, by Lampman, noted, **76**/181
White Collar Line, **63**/65
White Horse Ranch, SEE Whitehorse Ranch
White Lake City, Ore., **78**/363
White Pass, Yukon Terr., **76**/103: Canadian customs post, **81**/122,123; description 1898, **81**/122-23,128; photos, **76**/104,107; telephone line, **81**/123-24; wagon road, **81**/123,126
White Pass and Yukon Railway: bridge photo, **81**/132; construction, **81**/139; survey, **81**/132,133-34,140; survey crew photos, **81**/116,fr.cov. Summer
White River, Hood River and Wasco cos., **79**/142,161
White River Glacier, Mt. Hood, photo, **77**/66

White Salmon, Wash., **66**/255: Shaker church, **72**/153,155 White Shield Home, Portland, **64**/249 *White Sioux: Major Walsh of the Mounted Police*, by Allan, reprint noted, **72**/355 White Sulphur Springs Hotel, Ashland, **68**/353 White Swan, Wash., **72**/155,157 Whiteaker, John W., **64**/165; **66**/17,19; **67**/17; **69**/225; **70**/254; **73**/52N,53; **75**/122; **79**/41: appoints Stark, **72**/324-26,329,331, 332; asks emigrant protection, **72**/55; grave, **63**/364; Nesmith's opinion of, **73**/45N; photo, **72**/328; slavery advocate, **64**/357; **65**/392-93 Whitehead, Vivian B., comp.: *Agricultural History: An Index, 1927-1976*, noted, **79**/337 Whitehill, Walter Muir, **66**/388; **67**/377; **70**/371: "Oregon Historical Center Dedication Address," **67**/197-211 Whitehorse Creek, Harney Co., **81**/328 Whitehorse Ranch, **63**/307,310,317,324; **68**/254N,314,321,329; **70**/21; **71**/99; **76**/160: centennial, **72**/93; map, **68**/250; photos, **63**/313; **68**/252-53,322,323 Whitehorse Rapids, Yukon Terr., **76**/111 Whiteley, Opal Stanley: biography, **71**/198 Whiting, William L., **68**/223N Whitley, Stock (Indian), SEE Stock Whitley *Whitlieburn* (ship), **66**/107 Whitman, Marcus, **62**/192-93,213,238, 239,245N,309,310,334; **63**/138,181, 207,209; **64**/85; **70**/69; **71**/368; **73**/277,285,365; **75**/73,74,77,114; **77**/291; **78**/101,338,339; **79**/134; **81**/20,240,342: meets Luelling party, **68**/158; relations with Indians, **62**/77; "saved Oregon" theory, **62**/75-76,331-34; **70**/230-31; **78**/332; sheep raising, **62**/240N; SEE ALSO Whitman massacre Whitman, Narcissa Prentiss, **62**/77,192- 93,238,239,245N; **63**/364; **64**/349; **65**/119-20,315; **68**/76; **73**/277,285;

75/72,74-75; **77**/291 Whitman, Perrin Beza, **62**/320; **75**/73 Whitman massacre, **62**/76,77,193,318; **63**/78,138,207; **64**/346,349; **65**/234; **68**/336-37; **72**/286; **74**/219; **75**/78, 115-22*passim*; **77**/314; **78**/288; **80**/405-406; **81**/26N: causes, **75**/74-75,116-17; Meek letter, **75**/74-75 Whitman Mission, **62**/320,331-32; **63**/ 181; **64**/349; **66**/358; **68**/76,77; **69**/128; **71**/344; **72**/91; **75**/113; **78**/332; **81**/20,26: Skirving panorama view, **65**/156 Whitman Mission National Historic Site, **69**/178 Whitmore, Thomas, **78**/64,64N Whitney, Anna, **79**/162N Whitney, H.P., **63**/32-33,38 Whitney, James, **69**/147 Whitney, Jones, **79**/162N Whitney, Josiah Dwight, **69**/273 Whitney, Michael, **69**/147 Whitney, William, **69**/147 Whitney Company: background, **72**/300-301 camps, **77**/219,222— Blue Star, **73**/219-21,222; Idaville, **73**/5,7,11,13,175,177; photos, **73**/4, 217,ins.fr.cov. Sept.; Red Star, **73**/216- 17,219,221,222; White Star, **73**/17- 18,171,173,175-76,182,186-92,313 commissary, **73**/188; cookhouse crew, **73**/177,179,181(photo),214,217; first log, **73**/172(photo),173-74,225 (photo),227; food, **73**/215-16; headquarters, **73**/5; Hammond merger, **72**/293N; **73**/222-23; **77**/354,362; history, **73**/179 locomotives— Andy Gump, **73**/7,8,18; Big Jack, **73**/ 14(photo),15,175,176,178(photo), 179,217; Galloping Goose, **73**/6,171; Molly 'O, **73**/15(photo),16,171N,173, 178,200,221(photo) log rafts, **73**/173; logging operations, **73**/5-30,171-92,212-27 logging railroads, **73**/5,6-7,175-76; **77**/213,214,222—

construction, 72/308-14; contractors, 72/311,313; incline railroad, 73/ 218(photo),219,220-21(photos); map, 72/309; survey crew photo, 72/306 mills at Garibaldi, 73/173,179; 77/213-17,341-68— capacity, 77/216,217; construction, 77/212(photo),213-14; number employees, 73/224; photos, 73/ins.fr. cov. June; 77/212,214-15,218,234, 348,366; production, 73/224; 77/359 payrolls, 73/187-88; shops, 73/5; spruce production, 72/301,308; Tillamook Co. holdings, 72/294,299-300, 309(map); Tillamook Co. operations, 72/294-314*passim*; timber cruising, 72/303-304; women employees, 73/217

Whitney (E.C.?) family, 72/300

Whitney Inn, Garibaldi, 77/213,219: photos, 77/218,356

Whitredge, Worthington, 67/371

Whitsett, Jackson J., 69/330

Whittaker, Vern, 74/274

Whitten, —, The Dalles lawyer 1881, 81/267,271,276,279

Whittle Transfer Co., Ashland, 64/338

Whittlesey, Charles, 65/415

Whitworth, George A., 68/183

Whitworth Creek, Lake Co., 79/290N

Whooping cough, 63/194; 81/153,155

Who's Who Among Pacific Northwest Authors, ed. by Wright, noted, 71/286

Who's Who in Alaskan Politics, a Biographical Dictionary of Alaskan Political Personalities, 1884-1974, comp. by Atwood and DeArmond, review, 78/358-59

Whymper, Frederick, 64/86: map, 72/134; view of Sitka, 72/142

Wick, Grace, 62/198

Wickaninnish Bay:

Tonquin disaster, 71/314-15

Wickiup (Indian dwelling): description, 63/328; 65/299

Wickiup Creek: name, 65/27N

Wide West (steamer), 70/5; 71/22: photo, 70/ins.fr.cov. March

Wied-Neuwied, Maximilian A.P., 63/73

Wiescher, —, Portland, 1881, 71/12

Wiesner, Adam, 64/271

Wiest, Levi D., 69/341

Wight, E.L., *et al*, eds.: *Indian Reservations of the Northwest, Idaho, Oregon, Washington*, noted, 62/108

Wilbur, George C., 76/237,243

Wilbur, Hiram, 80/10,10N

Wilbur, James H., 70/148N: Chief Moses meeting 1879, 70/148- 62; journal cited, 78/91; Indian agent, 70/128N; receives Paiutes, 70/ 140N,147N; relations with Moses, 70/119,128FF,163

Wilbur, John P., 76/234

Wilbur, Ralph William, 62/177; 67/70

Wilbur, Ore.: academy, 73/332N

Wilbur Methodist Church, SEE Centenary Wilbur Methodist Church

Wilcox, Deb, 75/45

Wilcox, Hollis, 75/45

Wilcox, Ralph, 62/149

Wilcox, Robert W., 68/87

Wilcox, Theodore Burney, Jr., 74/237

Wilcox, Theodore Burney, Sr., 74/ 139,208: business interests, 71/148; letters, 71/150N; photo, 74/110; supports Barrett appointment in Asia, 71/148

Wild, Peter: *Pioneer Conservationists of Western America*, review, 80/407-408

Wild Berries of the Pacific Northwest, by Underhill, noted, 76/181-82

Wild Goose Bill, SEE Condit, Samuel W.

Wild Horse, Harney Co., 63/317, 333,340: Andrews stone house photo, 63/332

Wild Horse Prairie, Curry Co., 76/70

Wild Water: The Story of the Far West's Great Christmas Week Floods, 1964-65, by Lucia, noted, 66/187

Wild west shows, 72/181; 79/306,307: Buffalo Bill's, 81/343

Wilderness: American metaphor, 70/182; Parkman's comment, 70/353; psychological effects, 70/181

Wilderness Calling: The Hardeman Family in the American Westward Movement, 1750-1900, by Hardeman, noted, **79**/105

Wilderness Defender: Horace M. Albright and Conservation, by Swain, review, **72**/83-84

Wilderness Kingdom: Indian Life in the Rocky Mountains, 1840-1847, The Journals and Paintings of Nicholas Point, S.J., trans. by Donnelly, review, **69**/63-65

Wilderness, The Edge of Knowledge, by McCloskey, review, **73**/275-76

Wilderville, Ore., **76**/56: church, **63**/246

Wildhorse Creek, Umatilla Co., **68**/226, 233,294,306

Wildlife: federal conservation, **65**/205-206; first description Columbia River, **63**/69-70; first reclamation site, **80**/409; guidebook, **79**/408

Wilewmutkin (Hair Tied on Top) (Indian), **81**/351

Wiley, Andrew, **64**/352

Wiley, James W.: Olympia newspaper career, **64**/33-40*passim*

Wiley, Joseph R., **80**/289,319N,321N: biography, **80**/290

Wiley Creek: covered bridge, **66**/282

Wiley Trail, SEE Santiam Pass

Wilhelm, Rudie, Jr., **62**/111,207,303, 422; **63**/93,255,373; **64**/93,189, 285,363; **65**/125,221,317,414,417; **66**/94,190,286,395; **67**/379; **68**/360; **69**/342,348; **70**/374; **73**/362; **74**/184,366

Wilhelm, Mrs. Walter E., **67**/46

Wilhoit Springs, **65**/218; **66**/39

Wilkerson, John L.: *History of the Salem Oregon Fire Department,* noted, **78**/288

Wilkes, Charles, **63**/203,218-19; **64**/ 229N; **65**/161,165; **70**/73,259: autobiography, **79**/404-406; biography, **79**/405; courts-martial, **79**/406; Skirving panorama contributions,

65/134-35,138,145,147,157,159

Wilkes Expedition, **62**/8; **63**/199,201- 205,210,217,358,369; **70**/75; **72**/147; **77**/194; **79**/404-405: artists with, **65**/137— drawings and sketches, **63**/369; **65**/158 Columbia River survey, **63**/205; extent of exploration, **79**/405 maps and charts, **79**/408— charts reprinted, **72**/356 scientific report, **79**/405

Wilkins, Caleb, **66**/90

Wilkins, Mitchell, **63**/245; **79**/9,10

Wilkinson, J.A., overland 1859, **79**/84

Wilkinson, James, **64**/183; **68**/345; **70**/86

Wilkinson, Melville C., **70**/8,18,19, 21,127

Wilkinson, Morton S., **73**/58-59

Wilkinson, W.D., **67**/30,32

Will, Clark Moor, **62**/104,415; **69**/346; **79**/234,238,245,258,266: "Aurora Colony Church Bells," **67**/273-76 "The Harris Anvil," **69**/57-59 "Musical Heritage of the Aurora Colony," **79**/238-67

Will, George, **79**/239,243

Will, Jonas M., **65**/218

Will, S.W., **79**/257

Will, Urban, **79**/239

Willamette (steam locomotive), **63**/351

Willamette (steamer), **76**/106,106N

Willamette Baptist Association, **75**/142: religious publications supported, **64**/124-25,127,136

Willamette Basin Project Committee Conference 1965, **66**/384

Willamette Cattle Company, **76**/130

Willamette Falls, **63**/224,234-35; **66**/338,339,381; **77**/45; **78**/88: Indian fishing, sketch, **81**/403; water power, **63**/67

Willamette Falls Canal and Locks Company, **65**/395N

Willamette Falls Canal Company: prospectus, **64**/167

Willamette Falls Electric Company:

portage railroad, 65/211
Willamette Farmer, 81/253
Willamette Forks, Ore., 77/324,327,339; 78/42,44,319; 79/6: view, 77/322
Willamette Gold and Silver Mining Company, 62/246
Willamette Gorge, 75/87
Willamette Iron Works, 65/9; 81/41,42
Willamette Medical School, 75/14,17, 18,20-21
The Willamette Meteorite, 1902-1962, by Lange, noted, 64/188
Willamette River, 63/147-48; 66/162, 343,357,358; 74/281; 75/87,338; 78/65:
Albany canal, 67/61,62 channels— changes, 71/197; Salem channel, 65/315
Drayton sketch, 65/137 exploration, 77/80— McKenzie, 66/332
ferries, 67/59
floods— 1861, 66/358,361; 1894, 67/77
freight shipments 1875, 71/94; frozen over 1886, 66/106; fur trade 1821, 66/333; Grand Island, 66/283; history, 67/92; landings, 67/276 navigation, 75/82; 77/45,91,314— 1830s, 66/339; difficulties, 71/41; lights, 72/90
pioneer trading point, 65/315; railroad routes, 71/45,50,51; rival towns, 72/169; river traffic, 63/67; Rouse Bridge, 66/187; sailing vessels photo, 66/120; shipping, 72/294-95; transportation, 74/163,202; Wyeth trip, 66/339-40; SEE ALSO Coast Fork, Willamette River; Middle Fork, Willamette River; North Fork, Willamette River
Willamette Steam Mills Lumbering and Manufacturing Co., 67/166-67,169, 171-72,173,176
Willamette Theatre, Portland, 64/170
Willamette University, Salem, 62/407; 70/200N; 73/332N; 81/103: catalogs, 64/154,157,160,165,174,

312; commencements 1860s, 64/154, 160,165; first Pacific NW law school, 70/182; history, 72/349-50; reminiscences, 80/117-18; site map, 80/340; trustees, 72/353
Willamette Valley, 63/16,24,30,41-42, 55,82,201-18*passim*,263; 75/283-84, 336; 77/311; 78/11,30,31,341: agriculture, 71/31,87; air pollution, 78/179; Americans in, 66/343,344, 347; botanical collection, 68/114,119; diphtheria epidemic 1840, 66/349; early settlement, 80/329 exploration, 77/309,317,323-24, 328-29— McKenzie, 66/332
first nut orchard, 66/97; first school, 66/341
French Canadians in— first settler, 66/334-35; McLoughlin aid to, 66/336-37
fur trapping, 66/332; geographic names, 72/71; grain and wheat exchange, 66/343; history of upper valley, 72/171; immigrant destination, 77/315,318
Indians, 73/65— camp grounds, 66/81
land claims, 66/334-35; land value, 71/37,57,63; landmarks, 65/121 map, 78/68— 1851, 70/258-61
photo 1915, 74/256
population— 1838-40, 66/344; 1841-42, 66/351; 1845, 66/356; 1870, 71/41
postal cards, 66/327; prices, SEE Prices; railroads, 71/38,71; river traffic, 71/41; Scott's view, 70/210-11; settlement, 73/73; Skirving panorama view, 65/159; trade and commerce, 71/19,41,72; travel described 1885, 80/231
Willamette Valley and Cascade Mountain Wagon Road Company, 64/356: land grant, 70/69
Willamette Valley and Coast Railroad, 71/94
Willamette Valley and Eastern Railroad,

77/91
Willamette Valley Chautauqua Association, 80/391,393-403
Willamette Valley Lumber Company, 78/158
The Willamette Valley: Migration and Settlement on the Oregon Frontier, by Bowen, review, 80/329
Willamette Valley Railroad Company, 78/90
Willamette Valley Southern Railway, 74/357
Willamette Woolen Manufacturing Company, Salem, 66/20; 67/62,125,128; 80/351-52,353: location map, 80/340
Willamina, Ore., 71/269: history, 65/217
Willapa, Wash., 79/262: pioneers, 68/81
Willapa Bay, 79/263
Willapa Transportation Company, 72/354
Willard, Alexander Hamilton: photo, 72/83
Willard, Mrs. Alexander Hamilton: photo, 72/83
Willard, Frances E., 78/36
Willard, John: *The CMR Book*, noted, 72/172
Willey, Waitman T., 73/46,48,50
William and Ann (HBCO. vessel): wreck, 63/193
"William Brooks, Chinook Publicist," by Claude E. Schaeffer, 64/41-54
William Clark: Jeffersonian Man on the Frontier, by Steffan, review, 79/100-101
"William Cornell's Guide to Oregon, 1852," ed. by Karen M. Offen and David C. Duniway, 80/66-100
"William Cornell's Journal, 1852, with His Overland Guide to Oregon," ed. by Karen M. Offen and David C. Duniway, 79/359-93
"William H. Seward Visits His Purchase," by Ted C. Hinckley, 72/127-47
William Henry Boyle's Personal Observations on the Modoc War, ed. by Dillon, review,

63/81
"William McKay's Journal, 1866-67: Indian Scouts," by Keith and Donna Clark, 79/121-71,269-333
William Renton (ship), 66/122
"William Strong, Associate Justice of the Territorial Courts," by Sidney Teiser, 64/293-307
Williams, Charles, family, 78/321
Williams, Chuck: *Bridge of the Gods, Mountains of Fire, A Return to the Columbia Gorge*, noted, 81/333
Williams, Dickse, 64/104N
Williams, Eliza Azelia: whaling voyage journal, 65/313
Williams, Evva: *First White Women Over the Rockies: Diaries and Letters*..., ed. by Drury, reviews of Vols. I and III, 65/119-20; 68/76-77
Williams, George, logger, 73/222
Williams, George Henry, 63/91; 64/302,309,312,315-16; 65/107,109; 66/24,25; 72/323N; 73/201; 79/10,98: photo, 70/224
Williams, Glyndwr, ed.: *Hudson's Bay Miscellany, 1670-1870*, review, 77/83-85
London Correspondence Inward From Sir George Simpson, 1841-42, review, 74/352
Williams, Griffith E., family, 73/84
Williams, Hannah Levering Wegner, 78/125
Williams, Howel, 79/403
Williams, J.R.: cartoons, 71/364
Williams, James C.: "The Long Tom Rebellion," 67/54-60
Williams, Joseph: *Narrative of a Tour to Oregon Territory, 1841-42*, quoted, 66/351
Williams, L.L., 65/63: road exploration diary 1863, 67/80, 279,281; 68/81
Williams, Lou, artist, 71/372
Williams, Mary E., SEE Hunsaker, Mary

E. Williams
Williams, Mary E. Prettyman, 62/300
Williams, Moses:
biography, 75/88
Williams, Ralph E., Jr., 74/238
Williams, Richard W.:
recollections, 63/91
Williams, Robert, Civil War veteran, 63/82
Williams, Robert L., 66/220N
Williams, Sam (Indian), 72/354:
biography, 72/151-55
Williams, Susie Thomas (Mrs. Sam), 72/151
Williams, T. Harry, 72/315
Williams, Thomas, pioneer of 1853, 78/125,325:
photo, 78/126
Williams, Thomas K., 62/243N,389N; 78/139
Williams "Island," Columbia River, 72/151,152
Williams Station, Nev., 62/297
Williamson, Brook, 66/110N
Williamson, Henry, 66/362
Williamson, Joe, 63/80
Williamson, Robert Stockton, 67/11; 72/49N; 75/237:
maps, 69/34,228; 79/26; railroad survey, 66/282; 79/27-30
Williamson River, 63/365; 79/47:
map, 69/267
Willis, Louis A.:
The Oregon Veatch Family, noted, 74/283
Willis, Nathaniel Parker, 62/292
Willis, Park Weed, 78/40
Williwas, 80/35,36,45
Willner, Don S.:
Wilderness, The Edge of Knowledge, ed. by McCloskey, review, 73/275-76
Willow Creek, Baker Co., 62/228
Willow Creek, Calif., 66/81
Willow Creek, Jefferson Co., 79/147, 149,156,177,178,201
Willow Creek, Malheur Co., 68/230N
Willow Creek, Morrow and Gilliam cos., 62/401; 63/10; 66/136,155; 69/137,138,141

Willow Creek Cemetery, Curry Co., 66/90
Willow Spring, Wyo., 62/346,347
Willow Springs Camp, SEE Well Spring
Willow trees, 69/148,155
Wills, George W., 69/78
Wills, Jacob, 69/78
Wills, William C., 62/223
Willson, William H., 62/142N; 63/224; 66/352; 70/183; 73/253
Wilmot, David, 73/39,40
Wilmot, R.B., GAR veteran, 74/219
Wilmot, Robert, photo, 74/265
Wilson, Albert E., 62/137; 64/ 201N,213N,215,218-19; 81/190N:
lumbering enterprise, 64/201N, 215N,218N,224
Wilson, Alexander, 69/22,28
Wilson, Alfred V.:
Ore. Mounted Volunteer service, 66/142N,144,145,149
Wilson, Andy, Westfall sheepman, 63/279-80
Wilson, Bushrod Washington, Sr., 67/88
Wilson, C.C., 77/227
Wilson, Carrie Ladd:
recollections, 73/72
Wilson, Charles L., 71/222,225,228
Wilson, Clementine, 79/203,206:
photo, 79/205
Wilson, Emerson J., 75/363
Wilson, George, Coos Bay seaman, 66/174
Wilson, George F., 72/280; 75/20,29
Wilson, Henry, U.S. vice-pres., 73/59
Wilson, Holt C., 72/280; 75/20:
photo, 75/100
Wilson, Isaac, 79/281N
Wilson, James B., 62/336
Wilson, John L., 62/106
Wilson, John Q., 62/230
Wilson, Joseph, Iowa judge, 64/311
Wilson, Joseph Rogers, 63/253; 74/213
Wilson, Joseph S., 72/18,19,45,48
Wilson, Josephine, 67/353-54
Wilson, Judith B., 62/421
Wilson, Julia, 80/361:
photo, 80/360

Wilson, Nancy Carroll, 73/261
Wilson, Robert B., OHS director, 62/110,206,302,422; 63/93,255,372,374; 64/94,190,286,363; 65/125,221,317
Wilson, Robert Bruce, Jr., 79/203,206: photo, 79/205
Wilson, Virginia, 79/203
Wilson, William: Umpqua area recollections, 73/283
Wilson, William M.: 1878 letter to, 70/56N
Wilson, Willie, family, Morrow Co., 69/147
Wilson, Woodrow, 62/80; 68/125,128, 133,134N,137,138; 72/229; 75/148: portrait, 75/243
Wilson Brothers Shipbuilding Company, Astoria, 77/101: photo, 77/ins.fr.cov. June
Wilson G. Hunt (steamer), 64/162-63; 72/133
Wilson River, 72/300,305
Wilson's Creek, Baker Co., 62/228
Wimer, William J., 69/207N
Wimer Bridge, Jackson Co., 81/106
Winans, William Park, 70/115FF: Colville Reservation opinion, 70/116
Winapsnoot (Winimpsunt) (Indian), 70/34,35N: 1878 council speech, 70/35; photo, 68/236
Winburn, Jesse, 69/88; 70/280: Ashland development project, 64/325-29,331-35; biography, 64/325,340N; characterized, 64/336-38; estate, 64/331; gift of civic clubhouse, 64/338-39; politics, 64/334-36
Winch, Martin Tobin, and Thomas Vaughan: "Joseph Gervais, A Familiar Mystery Man," 66/331-62
Winch, Mrs. Simeon R., 69/347; 70/373; 71/372,373
Winchester, Alice, 70/372
Winchester, Ore.: Floed-Lane trading post, 65/401; map, 69/359
Winchester Bay, 70/233
Winchester Dam, 70/279

Winchester Exploring Expedition, 68/261; 70/236
Winchuck River, 72/11,44; 76/43
Wind River, Skamania Co., 79/202
Wind River Mountains, Wyo., 62/352,355: Skirving panorama view, 65/154—photo, 65/152
Wind River Reservation, 62/288
Wind River Valley, Wyo., 63/242
Windem, Martin, 76/111
Winder, Charles S., 67/321: biography, 72/182; diary, 71/365
Windmills, 71/364
Windows: glazing, 79/196
The Winds of Morning, by Davis, cited, 66/243; quoted, 66/247
Windsor, Florence Bowman: reminiscences, 77/298
Windsor, Merrill: *America's Sunset Coast*, review, 80/334
Wine, SEE Prices
Wine industry, SEE Liquor
Winema (Indian), 66/81
Winema (steamer), 75/238
Wingate, Gabriel, 69/209
Wingfield, George, 77/168-70
Wingville, Ore., 66/202,206: centennial, 64/90
Winkleman, George, 77/157-58
Winkler, Fred H.: *Borah*, by McKenna, review, 62/409-10
The Myth of the New History, by Hoggan, review, 66/274-75
Winn, George Robert, 78/364
Winnemucca (Capt. Truckee) (Indian), 70/33
Winnemucca (son of Capt. Truckee) (Indian), 68/251N,252N,299N; 69/253; 70/16-17,33; 79/127: identity, 69/239-40,254; photo, 68/fr.cov. Dec.; son, 68/252N
Winnemucca, Lee (Indian), 70/15,16,21
Winnemucca, Mattie (Indian), 70/15, 17,31
Winnemucca, Natchez (Indian), 70/21
Winnemucca, Sarah (Indian), SEE Hopkins, Sarah Winnemucca

Winnemucca, Nev., 63/269,275,304-305,307,324,327; 70/262; 71/9; 73/235,237: cattle shipping center, 67/142,146; highway to Calif. coast, 66/281 railroad routes, 71/40,45,50,51,54,63, 64,68,96— maps, 71/44,52-53 Winnemucca Mountains, 63/305 Winquatt Museum, The Dalles, 69/178; 72/155 Winship, Nathan, 74/285; 76/202 Winship settlement, 62/301 Winslow-Spragge, Lois: *Life and Letters of George Mercer Dawson, 1849-1901*, cited, 66/70 Winsor, Eunice Huntington, 75/87 Winston, Patrick Henry, 71/368 Winter, William H., 66/355N Winter, William H., and Overton Johnson: *Route Across the Rocky Mountains*, reprint noted, 74/282 Winter Ridge, 67/10 Wintermeier, C.A.: house, 65/121 Winters, Judge —: 1913, photo, 74/110 Winters, George W., photo, 80/324 Winters, John, 79/339 Winters, Tom, 70/149 Winters, V.W., 72/294 Winters, William Henry, 68/231N,243, 305N; 70/140,147,149,158, 159,162,163 Winther, Oscar Osburn, 64/186; 65/212,213; 71/291-92: *Great Northwest, A History*, cited, 67/140-41 *The Transportation Frontier: Trans-Mississippi West, 1865-1890*, review, 65/304-305 "Transcontinental Railroads: Gateways to the Orient," cited, 67/280 Winther, Oscar Osburn, ed.: *A Classified Bibliography of the Periodical Literature of the Trans-Mississippi West, 1811-1957*, review, 63/81-82 Winther, Oscar Osburn, and Gayle

Thornbrough, eds.: *To Oregon in 1852: Letters of Dr. Thomas White*, noted, 65/212 Winther, Oscar Osburn, and Richard A. Van Orman: *A Classified Bibliography of the Periodical Literature of the Trans-Mississippi West: A Supplement (1957-67)*, review, 72/349 Winthrop, Robert Charles, 75/322-23 Winthrop, Theodore: *The Canoe and the Saddle*, cited, 74/91 Wintler, Ella, 74/281 Wire, Frank, 65/255 Wire, barbed, SEE Barbed wire *The Wire That Fenced the West*, by McCallum and McCallum, review, 66/379 Wisconsin: farming, 64/79-81; history, 74/359; life in 19th century, 70/39-42; logging, 70/42; Progressive movement, 70/79 *Wisconsin* (battleship), 74/84: photo, 74/fr.cov. March Wisdom place, Baker Co., 66/199 Wise, Jonah B., 71/219,225N,226N; 74/213,216,219: Library Association board, 71/225, 226,227 Wise, Stephen S., 80/400: biography, 70/366 Wiseman, Robert F.: *The Complete Horseshoeing Guide*, review, 70/356; 2nd ed. noted, 74/359 Wishart, David J.: *The Fur Trade of the American West, 1807-1840: A Geographical Synthesis*, review, 81/322-23 Wishram Indians, 63/347-48; 70/124: smallpox deaths, 67/309 Wislizenus, Friedrich Adolph, 69/335 Wistar, Caspar, 63/70; 69/27 Wister, Owen, 70/263-64; 73/286 Wiswiyalwit (Indian), 81/374 *With Captain James Cook in the Antarctic and Pacific: The Private Journal of James Burney*..., ed. by Hooper, noted, 77/303 *With One Sky Above Us: Life on an American Indian Reservation at the Turn of the*

Century, by Gidley, noted, **81**/330
Withycombe, James, **65**/220; **68**/127; **74**/215,216
Wittenberg, Caroline Blas (Mrs. David), **64**/259-66: photo, **64**/260
Wittenberg, Charlotte, **64**/261-63
Wittenberg, David, **64**/259-66: homestead, **64**/263-65; photo, **64**/260
Wittenberg, Edward, **64**/265
Wittenberg, Herman, **64**/259,261,265-66; **81**/280
Wittenberg, Mary, daughter of David, **64**/259,266
Wittenberg, Minnie, photo, **64**/260
Wittenberg, Samuel, **64**/261
Wittenberg, Sarah, **64**/259
Wiyot Indians: described, **62**/184
Wizard Island, Crater Lake: Knights of Pythias excursion 1915, **81**/52,54; photo, **81**/56
Wiznant, Archie, **62**/199
Wobblies, SEE Industrial Workers of the World
The Wobblies: The Story of Syndicalism in the United States, by Renshaw, cited, **69**/325; review, **69**/179-80
Wocamtos (Indian), **79**/314
Wocus: Indian use of seeds, **66**/81
Wodaege, August, **66**/275
Wojcik, Donna M.: *The Brazen Overlanders of 1845*, review, **78**/281
Wolf Coming Up (Kiwakumkaken) (Indian): children, **71**/343; Christian contacts, **71**/339-47; horse-stealing, **71**/345; Ogden expedition, **71**/346-47
Wolf Creek, Harney Co., SEE Stinking-water Creek
Wolf Creek Inn, **66**/282
Wolf Head (Many Stabs) (Indian), **71**/343
Wolf meetings, SEE Oregon Provisional Government—meetings of Feb. 2 and Mar. 6, 1843
Wolfe, Kenneth, **67**/51

Wolfer, Christina Stauffer, **79**/250
Wolfer, George J., **67**/273,276; **79**/238,239,243,250,253,266: photo, **79**/232
Wolfer, Martin, **79**/253
Wolfer, Otillia Will, **79**/258
Wolfer, William, **79**/250
Wolff, Christoff W., **79**/235,243
Wolff and Zimmer, architects, **64**/353,361
Wolff and Zwicker Iron Works, Portland, **69**/312,313; **71**/155N
Wolff, Zimmer, Gunsel and Frasca, architects, **67**/199
Wolverton, Charles E., **67**/63
Wolves, **66**/339-40,353; **69**/18,113; **75**/73,75; **79**/378: Pacific Northwest, **65**/220; **72**/228
Woman suffrage, **67**/87; **68**/186; **71**/292; **74**/208: Montana, **65**/216; Oregon anniversary, **64**/88; Washington Territory, **78**/35-36,37-39,364; Wyoming, **67**/87
Woman's Party, **68**/138
Women: changes in image of, **72**/178; donation land claimants, **76**/304; emigration guidebook, **72**/181; first white women over Rockies, **65**/119-20; frontier experiences, **74**/284; hair styles 1885, **80**/235,235N overland travel, **66**/230—bravery, **81**/22 pioneer homemaker, **66**/213; pioneers in B.C., **79**/337-38; professional, **79**/ 337; rights movement, **78**/5-7,28,175; roles defined in mid-1800s, **81**/100; western, **64**/349; White Pass Trail, **81**/128; SEE ALSO Indians—women
Women and Men on the Overland Trail, by Faragher, review, **81**/96,99-101
Women of the Klan, **75**/181
The Women Who Made the West, ed. by Yost, noted, **81**/334
Women's Christian Temperance Union, **68**/134; **78**/34,36,38; **80**/395
Women's Civic Clubhouse, Ashland, **64**/338-41
Women's Club, Dallas, Ore., **78**/158

Women's Temperance Prayer League, **80**/314
Wonder, Ore.: name, **76**/81
Wonder Rock (King Tut's Tomb), Marion Co., **73**/83
Wood, Charles, Olympia brewer, **64**/269
Wood, Charles and Dorothy: *Spokane, Portland and Seattle Railway, the Northwest's Own Railway*, noted, **75**/364
Wood, Charles Erskine Scott, **62**/102, 204; **65**/288; **68**/221N,239N,302N; **70**/128N; **74**/216; **75**/83,103; **77**/61; **78**/90: Bannock War experiences, **70**/7-38; biography, **70**/5; Moses meeting, **70**/135,148-62; photos, **70**/100,fr.cov. March; **75**/100; Umatilla council, **70**/34-38
Wood, Charles Erskine Scott: "Famous Indians," quoted, **70**/162N "The Pansy," cited, **70**/10-11 *Poet in the Desert*, cited, **74**/34 "Private Journal, 1878, 1879," **70**/5-38,130-70
Wood, Dorothy, SEE Wood, Charles
Wood, Erskine, **62**/102; **70**/5N; **72**/360; **78**/369: photo, **75**/100; recollections of Chief Joseph, **78**/370
Wood, Erskine: "A Wee Dash of Heliotrope," **75**/ 101-103
Wood, H.E., Portland accountant, **66**/367-68
Wood, James, Ashwood pioneer, **72**/341
Wood, Joseph, overland to Calif. 1849, **67**/85
Wood, Lovett, **71**/155N
Wood, Nanny Smith (Mrs. C.E.S.), **70**/146N
Wood, Robert L.: *Across the Olympic Mountains: The Press Expedition, 1889-1890*, cited, **78**/281; review, **69**/73-74 *Men, Mules and Mountains: Lieutenant O'Neil's Olympic Expeditions*, review, **78**/281-82

Wood, Tallmadge Benjamin, **64**/206N
Wood, W. (L.?,S.?), Portland doctor, **62**/177
Wood, William G., **62**/219N
Wood, William L., **72**/280
Wood: frontier uses, **72**/179; marketing, **72**/178; tools and technology, **72**/179,282(photo); SEE ALSO Prices
Wood River Valley, Klamath Co., **69**/328
Woodard, Steve, **63**/269
Woodburn, Ore., **66**/327; **72**/91; **76**/235
Woodburn Iron Works, **64**/353
Woodcarving, **80**/57
Woodcock, Ed: Malheur City recollections, **73**/83
Woodcock, Eldon, **76**/335,352,355
Woodcock, William C., **71**/19
Wooden Shoes West: A Saga of John Vandehey, by Vandehey, noted, **81**/332
Woodfield, Francis William (Frank): Astoria photos, **66**/328; **71**/289; biography, **66**/329
Woodhams, William H.: diary 1854, **81**/329
Woodland, Wash., **65**/120: hops, **66**/382; Presbyterian church, **64**/276
Woodlawn School, Portland: history, **66**/188
Woodmen of the World, **63**/289; **76**/373
Woodruff, Billie, **63**/290,294
Woodruff, Tell, **63**/290
Woods, Ernest R., photo, **80**/324
Woods, Eugene, photo, **74**/265
Woods, George Lemuel, **62**/319-20; **64**/167,172; **79**/128-29; **80**/363: portrait, **79**/128
Woods, Joseph Jackson, **67**/300N: describes Camp Drum buildings, **67**/298-99
Woods, Louisa A. McBride (Mrs. George L.), **80**/362
Woods, Rufus, **63**/90
Woods Creek, Benton Co., **72**/281, 283,284

Woodson, Ore., 62/301
Woodward, A.B.:
photo of O.O. Howard, 68/241
Woodward, Arthur:
Indian Trade Goods, review, 66/186-87
Woodward, Buell, 62/219N
Woodward, Frances:
Theses on British Columbia History and Related Subjects, noted, 71/191; 73/74
Woodward, Lillie, 63/290
Woodward, Samuel L., 74/211
Woodward, Steve:
Westfall residence, 63/303
Woodward, Tyler, 69/209
Woodward, Walter C., 66/218N
Woodward, William F.:
Hunt case view, 71/233-34,240;
Library Association board, 71/226, 233-34
Woodworth, G.D.:
Hood River Valley land sales, 70/50-52
Woody (Lesney) Island, 77/184
Wool, John Ellis, 63/84,186,188,203; 64/303; 65/173,178,192; 67/305N, 315; 68/8,14,23; 70/114,234; 77/91; 79/136:
asks for more troops, 67/320; attitude towards Indians, 67/315N; criticizes volunteers, 67/315N,318-320; Ft. Vancouver stay, 67/319-20; orders volunteers arrested, 67/318N,323N; photo, 67/317; settlers excluded east of Cascades, 67/323N; Yakima War policy, 68/42
Wool and wool industry, 62/164-79; 67/61-74,125-38; 75/315; 77/21:
carding machines, 67/61,62; clothing, 67/66; effects of transcontinental railroad, 67/125-38
exports—
1859-80, 67/128; 1882-90, 67/ 111,133
marketing, 70/84—
photo, 77/20
Ore. markets, 67/136; Portland wool receipts 1873-1918, 67/132
prices, 67/134—
Eastern Ore., 64/121N; SEE ALSO Prices

rail shipments, 67/131; tariff effects 1873-1913, 67/133-34; wool train photos, 77/23,169; SEE ALSO Woolen mills
Wooldridge, Alice H.:
Pioneers and Incidents of the Upper Coquille Valley, noted, 74/94
Woolen mills, 66/20; 67/137:
Albany, 67/61-70; Ashland, 67/128, 137; Brownsville, 67/65,69,73,137; difficulty raising capital for, 67/137; LaGrande, 76/234-35; number in Ore. 1856-80, 67/137; number on Pacific Coast 1903, 62/175; Oregon City, 67/62,73,128,138; Pendleton, 77/193; Salem, 67/62,67,73,125,137; Salt Lake City, 77/167; Stayton, 77/193; stock listed, 69/211; Waterloo, 67/67,73; SEE ALSO Portland Woolen Mills, Inc.
Wooley, Jacob, 63/148,150
Wooley, John F., 67/179; 79/11
Woolley, Ivan M., 73/84:
"The 1918 'Spanish Influenza' Pandemic in Oregon," 64/246-58
Worcester, Donald E., ed.:
Forked Tongues and Broken Treaties, noted, 77/303
Worden, Frank L., 65/121
Worden (destroyer), 80/32,34:
sinking, 80/36,42
Work, Hubert, 67/214
Work, John, 63/132,135-36,233N,360
Work, Josette Legace (Mrs. John), 63/204
Work, Letitia, SEE Huggins, Letitia Work
"Work Horses in Oregon," by Lewis E. Judson, 75/205-18
Workman, B., 74/17
Works Progress Administration, 70/62; 76/259,268:
adult education project, 73/324; history of *Washington Guide*, 72/286
World War I, 62/7,18,19,24; 67/239; 72/293; 74/215; 75/242FF; 77/ 173,299:
aliens, 71/214,215; American attitudes, 75/251,265-69; anti-German senti-

ment, 75/149,152; anti-war movement, 75/85

Armistice Day— false celebration, 71/275-76; photo, 71/276

clergy, 71/216,220; Committee on Information, 75/148-49; conscientious objectors, 71/213-45; diary, 75/245-69; draftees, 75/265; effect on Ore. politics, 68/127-40; effect on street names, 81/207; enlistment, 71/214-15; espionage and sedition laws, 71/215; fund-raising, 68/138,140; 71/213,216, 218-20; 75/249; government controls, 71/213,214; government news bureau, 71/216; I.W.W., 71/215; Liberty ships, 69/331; Liberty Temple, Portland, 71/212(photo),219; memorial, 74/233; Office of War Information, 71/216, 243; Ore. participation, 71/213-45; parades, 71/212(photo),219; peace organizations, 71/222; Portland participation, 71/213-45; posters, 71/221, 244,fr.cov. Sept.; 75/149,243,261,266; Selective Service Act, 71/214-15; 75/148,265; shipping, 72/167; songs, 71/218,219,ins.bk.cov. Sept.; spruce wood use, 72/301,302(photo),303, 308; training, 75/245-69; troops transport, 81/105; troops assigned to logging and lumber mills, 77/213; U.S. air force, 75/255; U.S. camps, 75/247-69 *passim*; vessels torpedoed, 77/129, 285-88

World War II, 62/6,7,21,25,28-35,36; 73/69,224; 77/294-95,300:

Aleutian campaign—

air war, 80/35-45*passim*; Canadian navy, 80/48; casualties, 80/39,42,43; food, 80/37,39,41; gear, 80/32; guns, 80/35,37,41,44,46; Japanese base, SEE Kiska Island; Japanese broadcasts, 80/34,43,44,48; morale, 80/32-42*passim*,46; naval battle, 80/46; recreation, 80/33,45,48; ship damage, 80/36,46; U.S. bases, 80/40-49 *passim*

bond sales, 71/137-40; Columbia River training site, 73/213; draft, 71/368;

enemy prisoners in Idaho and Utah, 72/180; Ft. Stevens shelling, 68/90; 71/199

Japanese—

plan to bomb Southern Ore., 65/314; submarine off Ore. Coast, 65/219,314

Japanese relocation, 81/149-50— centers, 72/80; diary of internee, 81/151-71

Pacific air operation, 68/278; ship torpedoed, 81/170; South Pacific, 80/31

Tillamook Co., 71/134-40—

naval air station photo, 71/136 troop landing photo, 80/36; troop transport, 81/105; Vancouver, Wash., 80/334; weather effects, 80/46

Wormington, H.M.: archeology in North America, 68/335

Worthington, —, Weston settler, 74/342

Wortman, Ralph:

A Horseless Carriage Comes to Town, noted, 67/366

Wounded Head (Indian), SEE Husis Owyeen

Wovoka (Indian), 70/178

Wrangel, Ferdinand Petrovich von, 63/189; 71/367; 76/126; 77/176

"Wreck of the *Peter Iredale*," by Rowena L. and Gordon D. Alcorn, 64/68-72

Wren, Charles, 63/129

Wrenn, George P., 71/19

Wrenn, Sara B., photo, 74/265

Wright, —, Coos Co. pioneer, 63/33

Wright, Ben, 63/83

Wright, Dean, 76/261,265

Wright, Donald T., photos, 77/61,64

Wright, Donald T.:

"Recollections of Cloud Cap Inn," 77/61-66

Wright, Dunham, 62/298: view of Indians, 68/91

Wright, Edgar W., ed.:

Lewis and Dryden's Marine History of the Pacific Northwest, cited, 63/42N,238N; 69/307N,309N

Wright, Frances, ed.:

Who's Who Among Pacific Northwest Authors, noted, 71/286

Wright, George, 62/79; 66/160N; 67/

325; 68/5,39,42; 69/223N,227,253; 72/70; 73/73; 78/210; 79/130; 81/423: biography, 71/196 campaigns— 1856, 67/321-24; 1858, 68/ 30-31,75-76 commander Dept. of Oregon, 65/117N-18N,393-94; 67/320N; death, 65/ 297N; defends Ft. Dalles expenditures, 68/7-8,9N,22; Ft. Dalles quarters, 68/ 6,9,21; issues flour to Indians, 67/323; Pacific Coast defense advocated, 65/ 326-28; plan for Snake campaign, 65/ 117N-18N; report on Indian subsistence, 67/323N; Wool instructions re Stevens, 67/318N; Yakima War orders, 67/321

Wright, George, Jackson Co., 68/91

Wright, Joe, survey crew member: photo, 73/350

Wright, Joseph Albert, 73/46,51

Wright, Louis, Clark Co. doctor, 80/334

Wright, Richard: *Yellowhead Mileposts*, noted, 77/303

Wright, William ("Dan de Quille"), 73/74

Wright, William ("Uncle Billy Horseradish"), 70/279

Wright, Z.T.: Special Advance Thresher Train, photo, 67/113

Wright Lake, SEE Clear Lake, Modoc Co.

Wright Point, 78/210,229; 79/40: name, 78/210; view, 78/228

Writers: Oregon, 73/293-311; 74/34-70,145-78,244-67; SEE ALSO Literature; names of writers

Wunder, John H.: *Inferior Courts, Superior Justice: A History of the Justices of the Peace on the Northwest Frontier, 1859-1889*, review, 80/330

Wurm, Ross: *Ghost Town Trails*, by Florin, review, 65/209-10

On the Cattle Ranges of the Oregon Country, by Oliphant, review, 70/262

Wyam Indians, 62/102,198; 63/348-49

Wyatt, Thomas, 66/229

Wyatt, Wendell: *The Columbia River Treaty*, by Krutilla, review, 69/272-73

Wyeth, John B.: *Oregon: or a Short History of a Long Journey*, reprint noted, 72/170

Wyeth, Nathaniel Jarvis, 63/192,198, 206-207,234; 64/214; 66/341; 69/62; 71/250,333; 72/170,259; 75/76-77; 76/3,202-203; 79/122; 80/207; 81/14N,16N,322: expedition, 62/119N,122N,128; exploration Deschutes River, 73/84; journal quoted, 66/239-40; Willamette Valley map, 66/345

Wyeth, Nathaniel Jarvis: *Correspondence and Journals*, ed. by Young, reprint noted, 74/359

Wygant, Margaret Rae (Mrs. Theodore), 63/212,232,234

Wygant, Theodore, 63/212

Wynecoop, David C.: *Children of the Sun: A History of the Spokane Indians*, review, 71/187

Wynnstag (ship), 66/129

Wyoming: forts, 71/187-88; Johnson County war, 66/280; 67/359; New Deal, 71/364; political history, 70/79; railroads, 71/54; woman suffrage, 67/87

Wyoming (battleship), 74/84

Wyoming (steamship), 62/10

Wyoming, A Political History, 1868-1896, by Gould, noted, 70/79

Wyoming Stock Growers Association, 67/359

Wytrwal, Joseph A.: *Poles in American History and Tradition*, review, 71/281

x y Company, 76/322: records, 79/339

Xenia, Ill., 71/5,7

Xulno (Indian), 71/343

Yacolt, Wash.:
businesses, 66/382; early train, 65/308; Yacolt burn, SEE Forest fires
Yaden, John: recollections, 66/382
Yaeger, Mrs. Paul, 68/359
Yager, James P.: journal, 71/292
Yainax, Ore., 62/322; 68/258,316; 70/75; 79/127
Yaisli, Lena, SEE Kaser, Lena Yaisli
Yaisli family, Cross Keys, Ore., 81/303-304
Yakima, Wash., 70/147N; 72/153: agricultural history, 81/335-36; newspaper history, 65/383; sketch of North Yakima, 70/131
Yakima and Pacific Coast Railroad, 68/81
Yakima City, Wash., 70/147N: settler relations with Moses, 70/129-37*passim*,158-65*passim*; volunteers, 70/129-30,134-35
Yakima Indian Reservation, 70/115,125: agency map, 70/126; Moses at, 70/128,135,148FF; Paiutes sent to, 70/34,140
Yakima Indians, 63/348; 64/351; 66/143,155; 67/314N,323N; 70/115; 72/148,229,231,261; 80/23: police, 70/129; political organization, 70/121; Shaker church services, 67/347-55; 72/249; Smohalla cult, 70/124
Yakima River, 63/147; 67/324: Selah Indian fisheries, 67/321
Yakima Valley, 63/42; 66/138N; 71/368: grazing lands, 66/89
Yakima Wars, 62/59, 77-79; 69/223N; 70/115,198-99; 73/73; 79/27N,105: battle of Walla Walla, 66/147-49; 68/341; Cram map 1855, 66/132; diary cited, 66/148N,149N; end of 1858 campaign, 68/30-31,75-76; flour issued to Indians, 67/323; Haller defeat, 67/313-14; history 1856, 67/313-24*passim*; hostile tribes, 66/133, 144; Indians killed or hanged 1858,

68/30; Jesuit peace efforts, 68/75-76; McKay post burned, 66/137
Ore. Mounted Volunteer campaign 1855-56—
battle of Walla Walla, 66/147-49; Chinn expedition, 66/134-39; Kelly expedition, 66/145-49; Kelly report, 66/157-59
Rains-Nesmith joint expedition, 66/133; relation to Ft. Dalles, 67/295-96, 315; Steptoe defeat, 68/31,34; Townsend recommendations, 67/317N; treaties, 68/35; Umatilla agency burned, 66/134; war debt, 67/319N; Wool's policy, 68/42
Yakona Indians, SEE Yaquina Indians
Yale, Louis, 74/359
Yale University Library, 65/5N
Yamamoto, Isoroku, 62/29-30
Yamhill, Ore., 63/232; 65/217
Yamhill County, Ore., 62/140,144,156; 66/19,365,366,368,370; 74/345; 75/345,352:
county seat, 75/353,354; early marriages, 68/350; first airplane, 67/366; first auto, 67/366; first motorcycle, 67/366; history, 64/354; 67/369,373; 70/278; pioneers, 66/382; 74/286
Yamhill County Courthouse, 64/354; 65/217
Yamhill County Fair: history, 70/278
Yamhill County Historical Society, 66/388:
meetings, 69/280; 70/277; officers and directors, 62/104,416; 63/87,251; 64/84,280; 65/124,312; 66/85,279; 67/83,284; 68/85,283; 69/82,280; 70/83,277; 71/195; 72/177; 73/79; 74/182; 75/92; 76/96; 77/96; 78/96; 79/112; 80/112; 81/112
Yamhill Indians, 70/260
Yamhill River, 63/51N; 66/347: locks, 66/181
Yamhill Valley: Swedish people, 76/5-27
Yankee (bark), 64/317-18N
Yankton, Ore., 64/91; 81/424: history, 80/102-103

Yankton Grange: records, 65/219

Yaqui Indians, 63/347

Yaquina, Ore., 80/356

Yaquina (vessel 1880s), 80/255

Yaquina Bay, 66/110; 71/71: Indian agency, 70/351

Yaquina Bay Lighthouse, 70/75; 71/294; 73/80; 75/294N: photo, 75/ins.bk.cov. March

Yaquina (Yakona) Indians, 69/171-73

Yaquina Life-Saving Station, 66/110N,112

Yarnes, Thomas D.: *A History of Oregon Methodism*, ed. by Tobie, review, 62/406-407

Yasui, Barbara: "The Nikkei in Oregon, 1834-1940," 76/225-57

Yasui, Masuo, 70/54; 76/241,243,249: Hood River store, photo, 76/242

Yasui, Renichi, 76/241

Yasui, Shidzuyo Miyake, 76/241

Yellin, Samuel, 76/259

Yellow fever, 77/59-60

Yellow Hawk (Indian), 79/275N

Yellow Pine, Ida., 63/89

Yellow Serpent (Indian), SEE Peu-Peu-Mox-Mox

Yellowhead Highway, 77/303

Yellowhead Mileposts, by Wright, noted, 77/303

Yellowstone Expedition, 71/365,366

Yellowstone Falls, photo, 74/335

Yellowstone National Park, 62/310: archeology, 65/374; description 1887, 74/337-39; excursion fare, 74/337; photos 1880s, 74/335-39*passim*; road system, 72/256; 74/354; travel, 71/366

Yeon, John Baptiste, 63/351-52; 66/ 249,269; 71/198; 77/386: biography, 66/351; Columbia River Hwy. efforts, 66/263; 74/116,118, 125,139,140,214,215; photos, 66/ 250,258; 74/110

Yeon Building, Portland, 66/251

Yerba Buena, Calif., SEE San Francisco

Yesler, Henry L., 64/349

Yesterday's Roll Call, Statistical Data and Genealogical Facts from Cemeteries in Baker, Sherman and Umatilla Counties, Oregon, Vol. I, comp. by Genealogical Forum of Portland, review, 72/85-86

Yi-a-must, SEE Gervais, Marguerite Clatsop

Yoakam, Drusilla, 63/15

Yoakam, George W., 63/15,23

Yoakam, Jasper A., 63/15,23

Yoakam, John, 63/15-16,23-25

Yoakam, Martha, 63/23

Yoakam, Susan, 63/15

Yocum, Oliver C., 74/89

Yola (ship), 66/127

Yoncalla, Ore., 62/315; 66/240

York, Clark's Negro servant, 73/199

York boats: description, 70/179

York Factory, 63/218,224; 70/88

Yost, Conrad, 79/247

Yost, Nellie Snyder, ed.: *The Women Who Made the West*, noted, 81/334

Youell, John, 62/111,207,303,420,421, 422; 63/93,255,369-70,372-73; 64/ 93,189,358-60,363; 65/125,221,317, 412,414,415,416,417; 66/93,94,189, 190,285,287,386,387,389,393,394, 395; 67/375,376,379; 68/355,356, 358,360; 69/342,343,346,348; 70/374; 73/362,364; 74/184,366: *Simon Benson: Northwest Lumber King*, by Allen, review, 72/348 *This Was Trucking, A Pictorial History*, by Karolevitz, review, 68/179-80

Youell, Mrs. John, 76/387; 78/369

Young, Brigham, 62/185; 64/349; 69/84: family, 67/224

Young, Carl, 74/271

Young, Eliza Snow (Mrs. Brigham), 64/349

Young, Ewing, 63/215; 64/214N; 65/364; 66/92,280; 67/280; 69/275; 70/278: biography, 69/61-62; birthplace, 65/ 220; death, 66/350; distillery, 65/346; estate, 62/116,120-21,136,137,150,

160; 66/349-50,352; gravesite, 65/415; 66/90; monument, 66/90
Young, Fred, Bridge Creek rancher, 73/263
Young, Frederic George, 62/309,310, 313,325,335; 66/218N,349N; 70/ 210,222; 73/365; 74/120,199: editor *Oregon Historical Quarterly*, 70/197; on Harvey Scott, 70/202,227; Oregon Historical Society organization, 70/197
Young, Hal, 74/234
Young, J.W., Auburn miner 1861, 62/219N
Young, Janette Lewis (Mrs. William Stewart): diary, 63/82
Young, Joaquin, 62/137N
Young, John, Abbot survey artist, 67/13
Young, John C., 68/216-17
Young, John Even, 62/165
Young, John Philip, 71/146
Young, John Quincy Adams: biography, 65/308
Young, Margerie, SEE Knowles, Margerie Young
Young, Nellie May, 63/82: *William Stewart Young, 1859-1937, Builder of California Institutions*, noted, 68/341
Young, Otis E., Jr.: *Black Powder and Hand Steel: Miners and Machines on the Old Western Frontier*, noted, 77/304 *Western Mining: An Informal Account... from Spanish Times to 1893*, review, 72/347-48
Young, Samuel Ewing, 67/62,63,70
Young, Samuel Hall, 70/180
Young, Walker, 78/325N
Young, William, 1853 immigrant, 78/129
Young, William Stewart, 63/82; 68/341
Young Chief (Indian), 70/34
Young Mens Christian Association, 64/182: at Oregon Agricultural College, 73/347; Spirit Lake camp, 74/89
Youngberg, Nels, 76/10-11,15

Youngquist, Walter: *Over the Hill and Down the Creek*, noted, 68/82
Youngs Bay, 62/244; 63/235
Young's Creek, Lane Co., 78/319
Youngs River, Clatsop Co., 74/278; 77/109
Yount, George C.: memoirs, 67/280
Yours Sincerely, Ann W. Shepard: Letters from a College Dean, ed. by Davis, review, 80/102
Yowaluch, Louis (Ai-Yal) (Indian), 72/148,149,151,153,155
Yreka, Calif., 69/229,230N,247,249, 250,251,255; 71/190; 72/33,171: history, 78/365; 81/328
Yreka trail (road), 65/28; SEE ALSO Southern Immigrant Route
Yturraspe, Jesse, photo, 76/166
Yturri, Anthony, photo, 76/164
Yturri, Dolores, photo, 76/164
Yturri, Domingo, photo, 76/166
Yturri, George, photo, 76/166
Yturri, Lewis L., photo, 76/164
Yturri, Maria, photo, 76/164
Yugoslavian people, 72/313
Yukon (steamship), 80/48
Yukon Field Force: 1898 expedition, 64/87
Yukon Relief Expedition, 73/72-73
Yukon River, 62/96; 73/131,133: frozen over, 76/117; navigation, 75/82; 76/110-15; portages, 76/111; rapids, 76/110-11
"Yukon shoes," 81/122,123
Yukon Territory, 62/95; 68/87: customs service, 76/110 gold rush, 64/87; 66/280; 81/331— letters, 76/101-17 map, 76/112; photos, 76/103,104, 107,109,114,ins.bk.cov. June; prices 1897, 76/115,116
Yumsumkin, Johnson (Indian), 81/342
Yurok Indians, 62/108
Yzaguirre, Sabina, photo, 76/164

z x Ranch, Paisley, 81/426
Zabala, Telisporo, 63/317,330

INDEX / 1961—1980

Zagoskin, Lavrentii, 73/131
Zakoji, Hiroto:
Termination and the Klamath Indian Education Program, noted, 63/91
Zamora, Joe, 63/285
Zatica, Joe, 76/157-58
Zehner, Art, 69/57
Zennanatti, Louis, 67/245
Zenner, Ambrose:
"Pages from Mount Angel's Early History," cited, 70/313N,314N, 317N,332N
Zerbinatti, Pietro, 69/270
Zieber, Eugenia:
journal, 66/81
Zieber, John S., 66/5
Ziegler, Amelia, 75/15

Ziegler, Henry, 79/238
Zimmer, Norman, 64/361
Zimmerman, Frank L., 71/155N
Zimmerman, Julian, 65/302
Zimmerman, Peter, 76/137-39,146
Ziniker, Edward, 81/105
Ziniker, John, 80/335
Zion's Herald, 64/49
Zolezzo, Mike, photo, 77/252
Zook, Henry, 66/161
Zook, Temperance (Mrs. Henry), 66/161
Zoos:
Portland 1905, 80/61
Zorn, Henry, 63/83; 66/81
Zubcova, Z.N., 73/160
Zumwalt, Andrew J., 70/272

Colophon

TYPEFACE: Galliard

TYPESETTING: Betty Sessions, Lincoln City, Oregon

PROOFREADING AND PASTE-UP: Heather Alexis Morrison, Portland, Oregon

PRINTING AND BINDING: BookCrafters, Chelsea, Michigan

PAPER: 60 lb. Booktext natural